PHILIP'S

C000242311

STREET

Lincolnshire

Boston, Grantham, Grimsby, Lincoln, Peterborough, Scunthorpe

First published in 2003 by

Philip's, a division of
Octopus Publishing Group Ltd
2-4 Heron Quays, London E14 4JP

Second edition 2007
First impression 2007
LINBA

ISBN-10   0-540-09082-4 (spiral)
ISBN-13   978-0-540-09082-2 (spiral)

© Philip's 2007

Ordnance Survey®

This product includes mapping data licensed
from Ordnance Survey® with the permission of
the Controller of Her Majesty's Stationery Office.
© Crown copyright 2007. All rights reserved.
Licence number 100011710.

Data for the speed cameras provided by
PocketGPSWorld.com Ltd.

Ordnance Survey and the OS Symbol are
registered trademarks of Ordnance Survey, the
national mapping agency of Great Britain.

Post Office is a trade mark of Post Office Ltd
in the UK and other countries.

Printed by Toppan, China

Contents

Digital Data

The exceptionally high-quality mapping found in this atlas is available as digital data in TIFF format, which is easily convertible to other bitmapped (raster) image formats.

The index is also available in digital form as a standard database table. It contains all the details found in the printed index together with the National Grid reference for the map square in which each entry is named.

For further information and to discuss your requirements, please contact james.mann@philips-maps.co.uk

Mobile speed cameras

The vast majority of speed cameras used on Britain's roads are operated by safety camera partnerships. These comprise local authorities, the police, Her Majesty's Court Service (HMCS) and the Highways Agency.

This table lists the sites where each safety camera partnership may enforce speed limits through the use of mobile cameras or detectors. 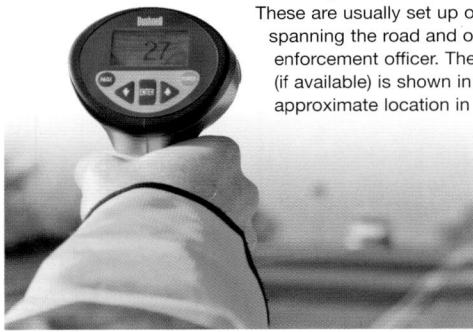 These are usually set up on the roadside or a bridge spanning the road and operated by a police or civilian enforcement officer. The speed limit at each site (if available) is shown in red type, followed by the approximate location in black type.

A15
60 Ashby de la Launde & Bloxholm, Ashby Lodge
60 Aswarby S/B

A15-B1191
60 Dunsby Hollow

A16
40 Burwell
50/60 Deeping Bypass
60 Ludborough, North Thoresby
60 Stickney Fenside
60 Wyberton, Boston Tytton Lane

A17
60 Fleet Hargate
60 Moulton Common
60 Wigtoft, Hoffleet Stow

A52
60 Horbling and Swaton
60 Horbling, Bridge End
60 Ropsley

A153
40 Billinghay
50 Tattershall

A158
40/50 Scremby to Candlesby

A631
60 Dale Bridge
50/60 Hemswell

B1188
30 Branston
60 Canwick (Highfield House)
60 Potterhanworth

B1191
60 Martin Dales

Key to map symbols

III

Symbol	Description
(22a)	**Motorway** with junction number
	Primary route – dual/single carriageway
	A road – dual/single carriageway
	B road – dual/single carriageway
	Minor road – dual/single carriageway
	Other minor road – dual/single carriageway
	Road under construction
	Tunnel, covered road
(30) (30)	**Speed cameras** - single, multiple
	Rural track, private road or narrow road in urban area
	Gate or obstruction to traffic (restrictions may not apply at all times or to all vehicles)
	Path, bridleway, byway open to all traffic, road used as a public path
	Pedestrianised area
DY7	**Postcode boundaries**
	County and unitary authority boundaries
	Railway, tunnel, railway under construction
	Tramway, tramway under construction
	Miniature railway
Walsall	**Railway station**
	Private railway station
South Shields	**Metro station**
	Tram stop, tram stop under construction
	Bus, coach station

Acad	**Academy**	Inst	**Institute**	Recn Gd	**Recreation Ground**
Allot Gdns	**Allotments**	Ct	**Law Court**		
Cemy	**Cemetery**	L Ctr	**Leisure Centre**	Resr	**Reservoir**
C Ctr	**Civic Centre**	LC	**Level Crossing**	Ret Pk	**Retail Park**
CH	**Club House**	Liby	**Library**	Sch	**School**
Coll	**College**	Mkt	**Market**	Sh Ctr	**Shopping Centre**
Crem	**Crematorium**	Meml	**Memorial**	TH	**Town Hall/House**
Ent	**Enterprise**	Mon	**Monument**	Trad Est	**Trading Estate**
Ex H	**Exhibition Hall**	Mus	**Museum**	Univ	**University**
Ind Est	**Industrial Estate**	Obsy	**Observatory**	W Twr	**Water Tower**
IRB Sta	**Inshore Rescue Boat Station**	Pal	**Royal Palace**	Wks	**Works**
		PH	**Public House**	YH	**Youth Hostel**

Symbol	Description
◆	**Ambulance station**
◆	**Coastguard station**
◆	**Fire station**
◆	**Police station**
✚	**Accident and Emergency entrance to hospital**
H	**Hospital**
+	**Place of worship**
i	**Information Centre** (open all year)
	Shopping Centre
P P&R	**Parking, Park and Ride**
PO	**Post Office**
	Camping site, caravan site
	Golf course, picnic site
Prim Sch	**Important buildings, schools, colleges, universities and hospitals**
	Built up area
	Woods
River Ouse	**Tidal water, water name**
	Non-tidal water – lake, river, canal or stream
	Lock, weir, tunnel
Church	**Non-Roman antiquity**
ROMAN FORT	**Roman antiquity**
87 / 237	**Adjoining page indicators and overlap bands** The colour of the arrow and the band indicates the scale of the adjoining or overlapping page (see scales below)

Enlarged mapping only

	Railway or bus station building
	Place of interest
	Parkland

■ The small numbers around the edges of the maps identify the 1 kilometre National Grid lines ■ The dark grey border on the inside edge of some pages indicates that the mapping does not continue onto the adjacent page

The scale of the maps on the pages numbered in blue is 5.52 cm to 1 km • 3½ inches to 1 mile • 1: 18103

The scale of the maps on pages numbered in green is 2.76 cm to 1 km • 1¾ inches to 1 mile • 1: 36206

The scale of the maps on pages numbered in red is 11.04 cm to 1 km • 7 inches to 1 mile • 1: 9051

IV

Key to map pages

Map pages at 1¾ inches to 1 mile
138

Map pages at 7 inches to 1 mile
234

Map pages at 3½ inches to 1 mile
180

Map pages at 3½ inches to 1 mile
180

East Yorkshire and Northern Lincolnshire STREET ATLAS

North Yorkshire STREET ATLAS

South Yorkshire STREET ATLAS

Nottinghamshire STREET ATLAS

Kingston upon Hull

Hedon
Marfleet
East Ella 179 180 181
Northfield 178
North Ferriby
Barton-upon-Humber
New Holland
Goxhill
East Halton 12 13
Ulceby
A160
Immingham 186 187
Habrough
Kirmington 22
Keelby
Great Limber
Laceby
Healing 23
Great Coates 24 25
Cleethorpes
190 191 192 193
Grimsby 188 189

Donna Nook 38

Grainthorpe
North Somercotes 51
Saltfleet 50
North Cockerington
South Cockerington
Manby 62
North Reston
Strubby
A1031

Mablethorpe 64
Trusthorpe
Sandilands 77
Huttoft
Mumby
Chapel St Leonards 90
Ingoldmells
Orby
Skegness 206
103
Burgh le Marsh 102
Old Bolingbroke 101

Beesby 76
Bilsby
Aby 75
Alford
Willoughby 88
Partney
Spilsby 100

Burwell 74
Swaby
Tetford 87
Asgarby

Scamblesby 73
Hemingby
West Ashby
Horncastle 85
Haltham 97

Louth 198
Legbourne 61
Fulletby 86
Hagworthington
Horsington 84
Woodhall Spa 96
Martin
Mareham le Fen 98
East Kirkby 99
Revesby

Fulstow
Ludborough 49
Utterby
Fotherby
South Elkington 60
Hatton 199

North Thoresby
Marshchapel 37
Holton le Clay 36
New Waltham 195
Humberston

Waltham 194
Ashby cum Fenby 35
Rothwell
Caistor 33
North Kelsey
Grasby
North Owersby 44
Walesby 45
Osgodby
Bishopbridge
Tealby
Sixhills 58
Hainton
Donington on Bain 59
Market Rasen 56 57
Faldingworth
Lissington
East Barkwith 71
Rand 70
Wragby

Brookenby 47
Binbrook
Ludford
Washingborough 82
Southrey 83
Bardney
Fiskerton

Nettleham 81
Branston
Nocton 95
Metheringham

Lincoln 80
200 201 202 203
234
204 205

Waddington 93
Coleby
Harmston 94

Scampton 67
Saxilby 66
Burton
North Carlton
Sturton by Stow 67

Dunholme 69
Welton 68
Langworth
Nettleham

Glentham 55
Hackthorn
Ingham
Fillingham 54
Owmby-by-Spital
A15

Waddingham 43
Willoughton 42

Scawby 31
Hibaldstow 30
Redbourne
Kirton in Lindsey 32

Brigg 196
Wrawby 21
Barnetby le Wold 20
North Kelsey

Scunthorpe 184 185
182 183
Broughton 19
Santon
Appleby

Barrow upon Humber 11
Burnham 10
Bonby
Wootton
New Holland 5
A15

Barton-upon-Humber
Alkborough
Winterton 9
Burton upon Stather 8
Whitton
Broomfleet 1
Elloughton 2
North Ferriby 3

South Cave
North Cave

Adlingfleet 7
Luddington
Eastoft
Burringham 17
Messingham 28
West Butterwick 29
Scotter
Owston Ferry

Ealand 16
Crowle
Beltoft
M180

Epworth 27
Upperthorpe
Misterton 39
Walkeringham
Wroot 26

Blyton 41
Pilham
Gainsborough 197
Lea
Sturton le Steeple
Upton 53
Kexby
Fillingham

West Stockwith 40
Torksey 65
North Clifton
Harby 79
North Scale
Eagle
Swinderby 92
Collingham 91
Besthorpe
Newton on Trent
North Scarle 78
Saxilby

Stainforth 14
Hatfield 15
Stainforth
Thorne
Carcroft
Armthorpe
Bessacarr
Doncaster
Adwick le Street
New Rossington
Tickhill
Harworth
Bawtry
New Edlington
Maltby
Dinnington
Blyth
Carlton in Lindrick
Worksop
Whitwell
Creswell
Shireoaks
Shirebrook
Woodhouse
Mansfield Woodhouse
Mansfield
Market Warsop
Edwinstowe
Boughton
East Markham
Retford
Tuxford
Sutton on Trent
Bilsthorpe
Carlton
Selby
Barlby
Howden
Goole
Snaith
Gilberdyke
South Cave
North Cave

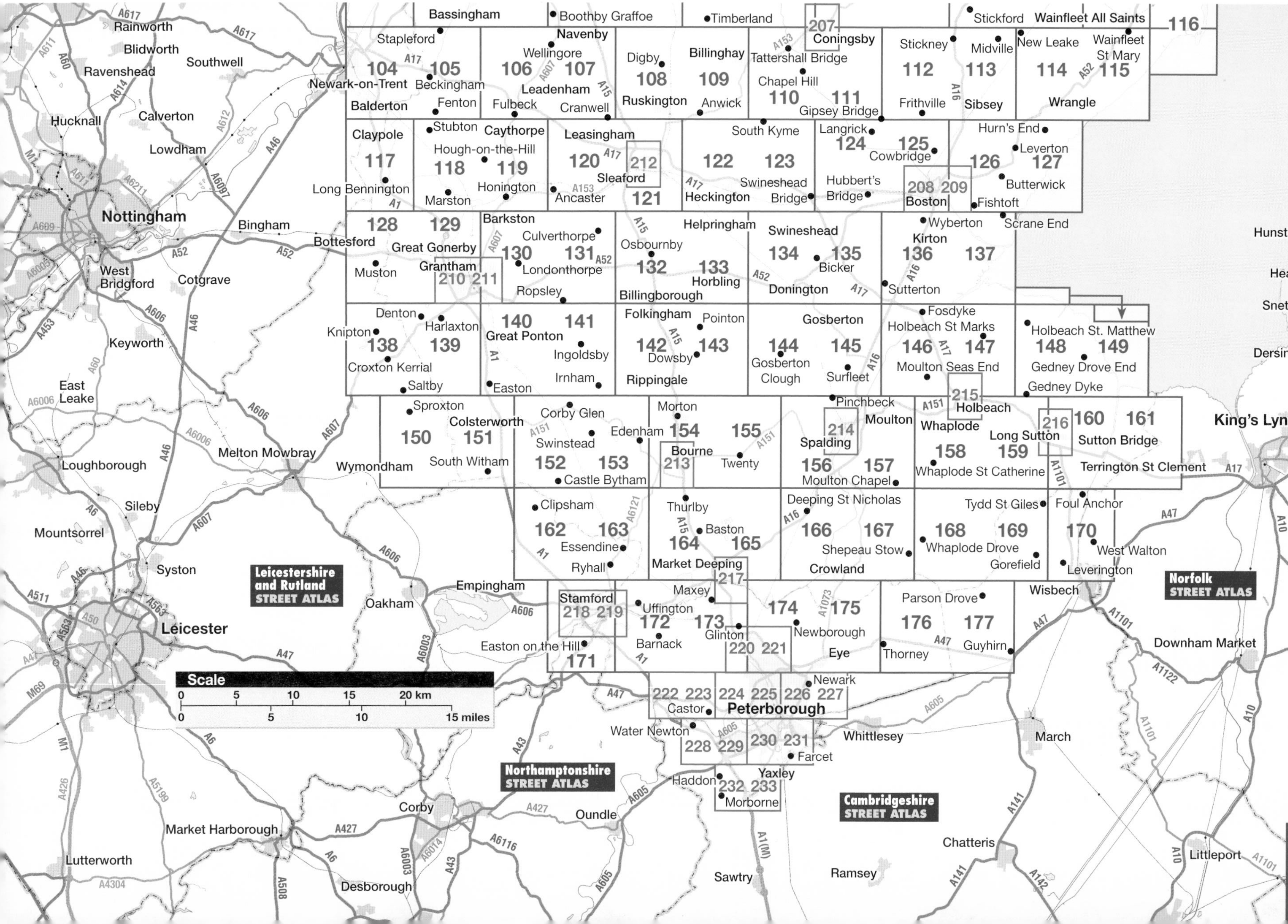

Norfolk STREET ATLAS

Cambridgeshire STREET ATLAS

Northamptonshire STREET ATLAS

Leicestershire and Rutland STREET ATLAS

Scale — 15 miles / 20 km

Key map grid references and place names:

116

Wainfleet All Saints 115 · Wainfleet St Mary 115
New Leake 114 · Wrangle 114
Stickford · Midville · Sibsey 113 · Leverton 127 · Butterwick 127
Hurn's End · Scrane End
Stickney 112 · Frithville · Cowbridge 125 · Boston 126 · Fishtoft · Wyberton 136 · Kirton 136 · Sutterton · Fosdyke · Holbeach St Marks 146 · Moulton Seas End 147 · Holbeach 159
Coningsby · Chapel Hill 110 · Gipsey Bridge · Langrick 124 · Hubbert's Bridge · Swineshead · Heckington · Helpringham · Swineshead 134 · Donington 135 · Gosberton 145 · Surfleet · Pinchbeck · Moulton 157 · Whaplode 158
Tattershall Bridge · Billinghay 109 · Anwick · South Kyme 122 · Horbling 133 · Bicker · Billingborough 132 · Folkingham 142 · Pointon · Dowsby 143 · Rippingale · Gosberton Clough 144 · Twenty · Spalding 156 · Moulton Chapel 166 · Deeping St Nicholas · Shepeau Stow 167 · Crowland
Timberland · Digby · Ruskington 108 · Leasingham · Sleaford 120 · Ancaster 121 · Osbournby · Culverthorpe 130 · Londonthorpe 131 · Ropsley · Ingoldsby 141 · Irnham · Corby Glen 153 · Swinstead · Castle Bytham · Clipsham · Essendine 163 · Ryhall · Bourne 154 · Morton · Edenham · Thurlby 164 · Baston 165 · Market Deeping · Maxey 217 · Uffington 172 · Barnack 173 · Stamford 171 · Easton on the Hill
Boothby Graffoe · Navenby · Leadenham 107 · Cranwell · Caythorpe · Hough-on-the-Hill 119 · Honington · Barkston 129 · Grantham 210 211 · Harlaxton · Great Ponton 140 · Colsterworth 151 · South Witham 150 · Sproxton · Saltby · Croxton Kerrial 139 · Denton · Knipton 138
Bassingham · Wellingore 106 · Beckingham 105 · Fenton · Fulbeck · Stubton · Marston · Great Gonerby 129 · Bottesford · Muston · Wymondham
Stapleford · Newark-on-Trent 104 · Balderton · Claypole 117 · Long Bennington 128

Lincolnshire grid: 104–233

King's Lynn · Hunstanton · Heacham · Snettisham · Dersingham · Downham Market · Littleport · Chatteris · Ramsey · March · Whittlesey · Guyhirn · Thorney · Eye · Newborough · Peterborough · Glinton · Castor · Water Newton · Yaxley · Morborne · Haddon · Farcet · Sawtry · Oundle · Corby · Desborough · Market Harborough · Oakham · Empingham · Melton Mowbray · Leicester · Syston · Sileby · Loughborough · Mountsorrel · Keyworth · Cotgrave · Bingham · Nottingham · West Bridgford · East Leake · Lutterworth · Hucknall · Calverton · Lowdham · Southwell · Blidworth · Ravenshead · Rainworth

Grid squares include: 148 149 · 160 161 · 216 · 158 159 · 168 169 · 170 · 176 177 · 215 · 214 · 174 175 · 217 · 218 219 · 220 221 · 222 223 224 225 226 227 · 228 229 230 231 · 232 233 · 207 · 212 · 213

Route planning

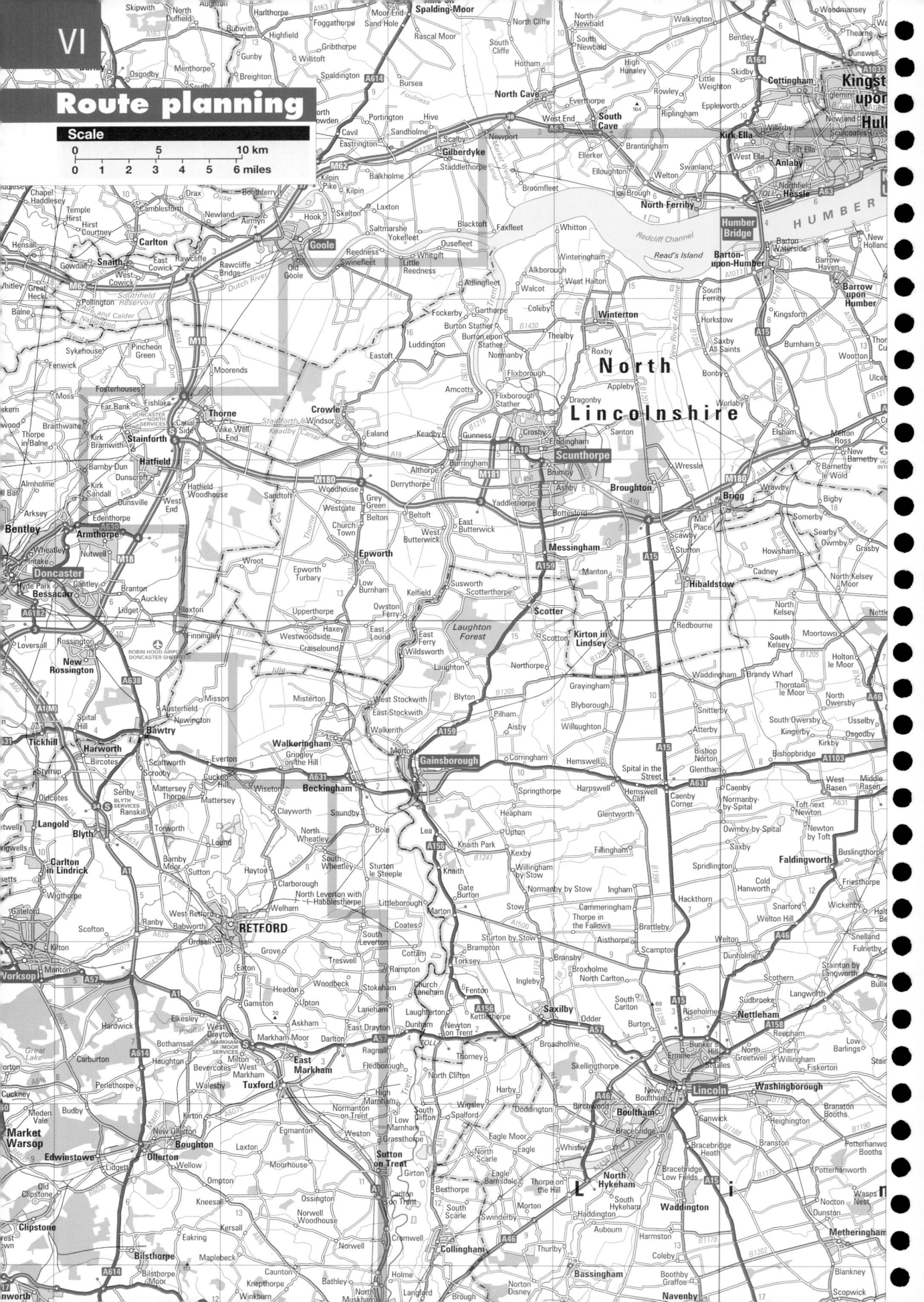
Scale
0 5 10 km
0 1 2 3 4 5 6 miles
North Lincolnshire
HUMBER
Humber Bridge
Kingston upon Hull
Cottingham
Hessle
Anlaby
Goole
Snaith
Carlton
Thorne
Stainforth
Hatfield
Doncaster
Bentley
Armthorpe
Bessacarr
New Rossington
Bawtry
Harworth
Tickhill
Blyth
Langold
Carlton in Lindrick
Worksop
RETFORD
Tuxford
East Markham
Ollerton
Boughton
Market Warsop
Edwinstowe
Clipstone
Bilsthorpe
Crowle
Epworth
Haxey
Misterton
Walkeringham
Beckingham
Gainsborough
Scunthorpe
Broughton
Brigg
Barton-upon-Humber
Barrow upon Humber
Winterton
Messingham
Scotter
Kirton in Lindsey
Hibaldstow
Saxilby
Lincoln
North Hykeham
Boultham
Waddington
Washingborough
Nettleham
Welton
Faldingworth
Collingham
Sutton on Trent
Bassingham
Navenby
North Cave
South Cave
Gilberdyke
North Ferriby
Brough
Kirk Ella
Laughton Forest
Robin Hood Airport Doncaster Sheffield
M62
M18
M180
M181
A1(M)
A1
A15
A18
A57
A63
A614
A631
A46
A159
A156
A158
A638

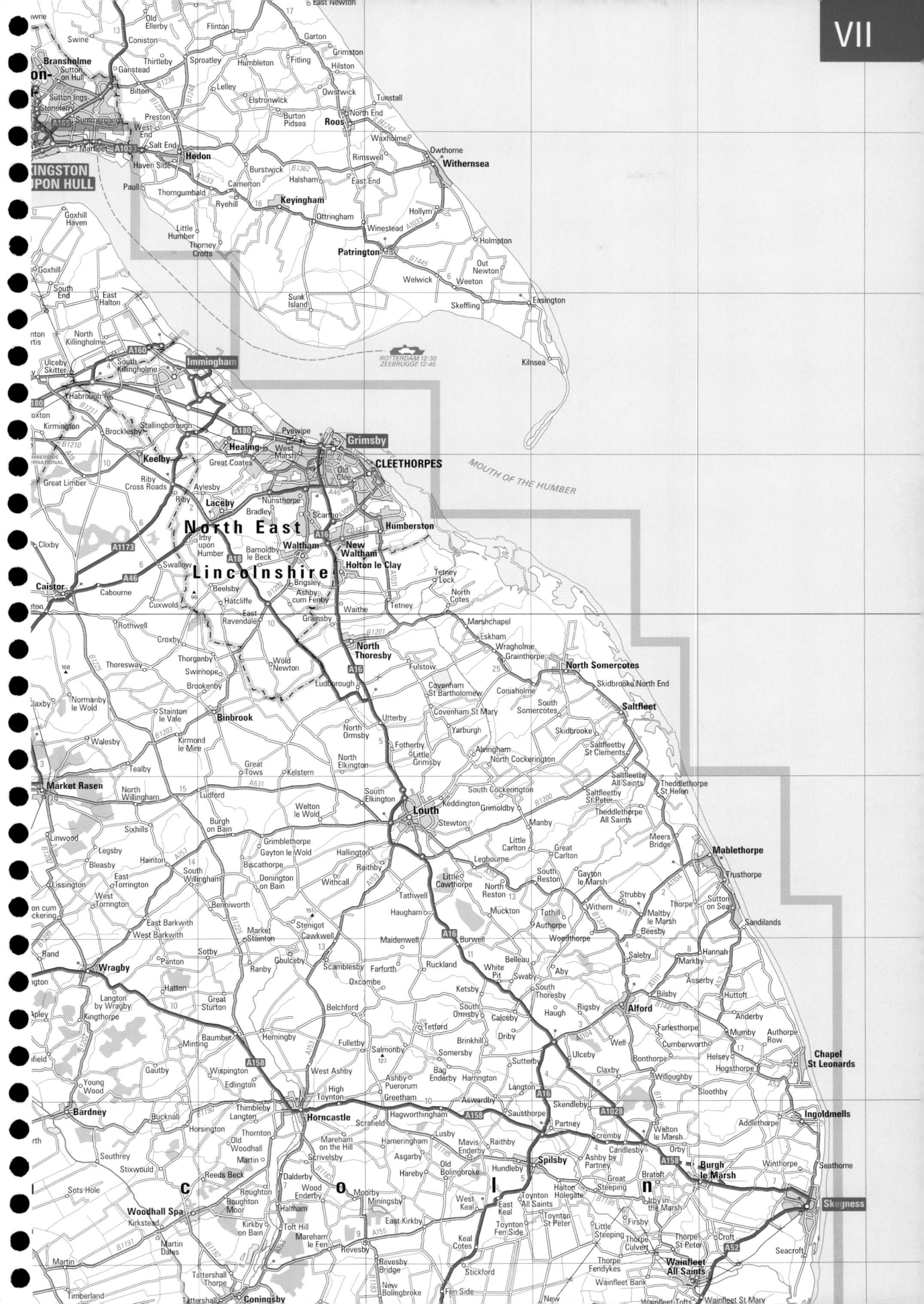
East Newton
Old Ellerby
Flinton
Garton
Grimston
Hilston
Swine
Coniston
Bransholme
Sutton on Hull
Ganstead
Thirtleby
Sproatley
Humbleton
Fitling
Bilton
Lelley
Owstwick
Tunstall
Sutton Ings
Stoneferry
Summergangs
Elstronwick
Burton Pidsea
Roos
North End
Preston
West End
Waxholme
Marfleet
Salt End
Hedon
Rimswell
Owthorne
Withernsea
KINGSTON UPON HULL
Haven Side
Burstwick
Halsham
East End
Paull
Camerton
Thorngumbald
Ryehill
Keyingham
Hollym
Ottringham
Goxhill Haven
Winestead
Little Humber
Thorney Crofts
Holmpton
Patrington
Out Newton
Goxhill
Welwick
Weeton
South End
East Halton
Easington
Sunk Island
Skeffling
North Killingholme
Ulceby Skitter
South Killingholme
Immingham
ROTTERDAM 12:30
ZEEBRUGGE 12:45
Kilnsea
Habrough
Kirmington
Brocklesby
Stallingborough
Pyewipe
Grimsby
Healing
West Marsh
Keelby
Great Coates
CLEETHORPES
MOUTH OF THE HUMBER
Old Clee
Great Limber
Riby Cross Roads
Aylesby
Riby
Laceby
Nunsthorpe
Bradley
Scartho
Humberston
North East Lincolnshire
Clixby
Irby upon Humber
Waltham
New Waltham
Barnoldby le Beck
Holton le Clay
Swallow
Tetney Lock
Caistor
Cabourne
Beelsby
Brigsley
Ashby cum Fenby
North Cotes
Cuxwold
Hatcliffe
Waithe
Tetney
East Ravendale
Grainsby
Marshchapel
Rothwell
Eskham
Croxby
North Thoresby
Wragholme
Grainthorpe
Thorganby
Thoresway
Swinhope
Wold Newton
Fulstow
North Somercotes
Brookenby
Ludborough
Covenham St Bartholomew
Conisholme
Skidbrooke North End
Normanby le Wold
Stainton le Vale
Binbrook
Utterby
Covenham St Mary
South Somercotes
Saltfleet
Yarburgh
Skidbrooke
Walesby
Kirmond le Mire
North Ormsby
Fotherby
Little Grimsby
Alvingham
Saltfleetby St Clements
North Cockerington
Tealby
Great Tows
North Elkington
Kelstern
Saltfleetby All Saints
Theddlethorpe St Helen
Market Rasen
North Willingham
Ludford
South Elkington
South Cockerington
Saltfleetby St Peter
Welton le Wold
Louth
Keddington
Grimoldby
Theddlethorpe All Saints
Burgh on Bain
Sixhills
Stewton
Manby
Linwood
Grimblethorpe
Gayton le Wold
Hallington
Little Carlton
Great Carlton
Meers Bridge
Mablethorpe
Legsby
Hainton
Biscathorpe
Raithby
Legbourne
Bleasby
South Willingham
Donington on Bain
Withcall
Little Cawthorpe
South Reston
Gayton le Marsh
Trusthorpe
East Torrington
Lissington
North Reston
Strubby
West Torrington
Tathwell
Thorpe
Sutton on Sea
Benniworth
Haugham
Muckton
Tothill
Withern
Maltby le Marsh
Authorpe
East Barkwith
Stenigot
Sandilands
West Barkwith
Market Stainton
Cawkwell
Beesby
Maidenwell
Burwell
Woodthorpe
Rand
Hannah
Sotby
Saleby
Markby
Panton
Goulceby
Scamblesby
Farforth
Ruckland
Belleau
White Pit
Aby
Wragby
Ranby
Oxcombe
Swaby
Asserby
Langton by Wragby
Hatton
South Thoresby
Bilsby
Huttoft
Ketsby
Great Sturton
Belchford
South Ormsby
Calceby
Rigsby
Alford
Kingthorpe
Haugh
Anderby
Farlesthorpe
Mumby
Authorpe Row
Baumber
Tetford
Brinkhill
Well
Minting
Hemingby
Fulletby
Salmonby
Driby
Ulceby
Bonthorpe
Cumberworth
Chapel St Leonards
Somersby
Helsey
Hogsthorpe
Gautby
Wispington
West Ashby
Bag Enderby
Harrington
Sutterby
Claxby
Willoughby
Young Wood
Edlington
Ashby Puerorum
Langton
Sloothby
High Toynton
Greetham
Aswardby
Skendleby
Thimbleby
Bardney
Bucknall
Langton
Horncastle
Hagworthingham
Sausthorpe
Ingoldmells
Partney
Horsington
Thornton
Scrafield
Addlethorpe
Scremby
Welton le Marsh
Old Woodhall
Mareham on the Hill
Lusby
Hameringham
Mavis Enderby
Raithby
Candlesby
Orby
Southrey
Martin
Scrivelsby
Asgarby
Ashby by Partney
Winthorpe
Stixwould
Hundleby
Spilsby
Burgh le Marsh
Seathorne
Reeds Beck
Old Bolingbroke
Hareby
Dalderby
Great Steeping
Bratoft
Sots Hole
Roughton
Wood Enderby
Moorby
Halton Holegate
Toynton All Saints
Irby in the Marsh
Skegness
Woodhall Spa
Roughton Moor
Miningsby
West Keal
East Keal
Haltham
Toynton St Peter
Kirkstead
Kirkby on Bain
Toft Hill
East Kirkby
Toynton Fen Side
Little Steeping
Firsby
Martin Dales
Mareham le Fen
Revesby
Keal Cotes
Thorpe Culvert
Thorpe St Peter
Croft
Seacroft
Martin
Revesby Bridge
Thorpe Fendykes
Wainfleet All Saints
Tattershall Thorpe
Stickford
Wainfleet Bank
Timberland
New Bolingbroke
Fen Side
Tattershall
Coningsby
New
Wainfleet Tofts
Wainfleet St Mary
Lincoln
A165
A1033
A160
A180
A18
A1173
A46
A16
A1098
A1031
A631
A157
A153
A158
A1104
A1111
A52
A1028
A155
B1238
B1240
B1362
B1242
B1445
B1211
B1210
B1219
B1203
B1225
B1200
B1373
B1449
B1202
B1190
B1195
B1183
B1191
B1192
B1196

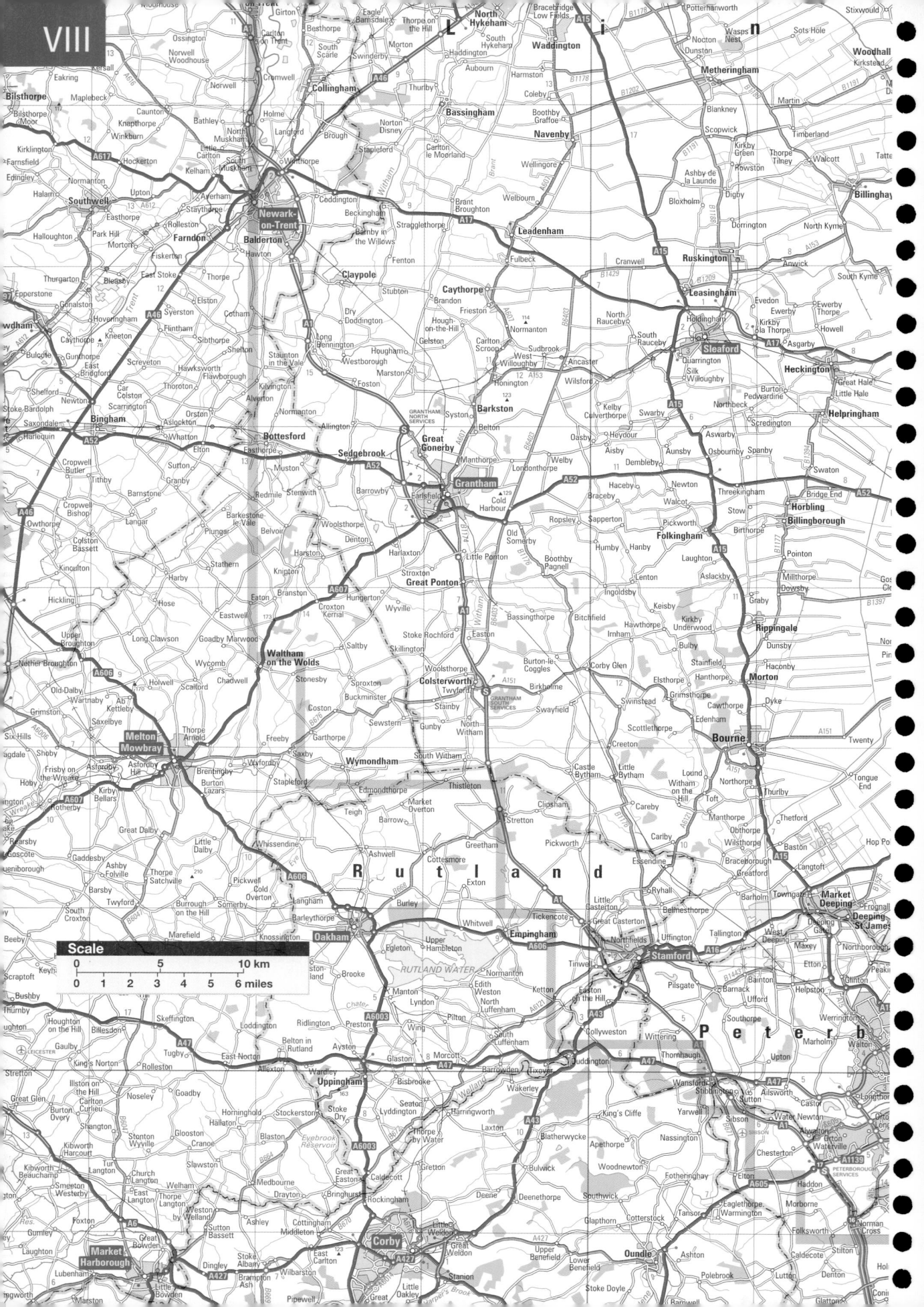
Scale
0 5 10 km
0 1 2 3 4 5 6 miles
L i n
Rutland
Peterb
North Hykeham
Waddington
Metheringham
Woodhall
Collingham
Bassingham
Navenby
Billinghay
Newark-on-Trent
Balderton
Farndon
Southwell
Leadenham
Ruskington
Leasingham
Claypole
Caythorpe
Sleaford
Heckington
Helpringham
Barkston
Bingham
Bottesford
Sedgebrook
Great Gonerby
Grantham
Horbling
Billingborough
Folkingham
Great Ponton
Rippingale
Waltham on the Wolds
Colsterworth
Morton
Melton Mowbray
Bourne
Wymondham
Stretton
Oakham
Empingham
Market Deeping
Deeping St James
Stamford
Uppingham
Corby
Market Harborough
Oundle
Rutland Water
Eyebrook Reservoir
Wansford
Duddington
Ancaster
Cranwell
Cold Harbour
Castle Bytham
Little Bytham
Essendine
Ketton
Tinwell
Grantham North Services
Grantham South Services
Peterborough Services
Welland
Witham
Trent
Chater
Eye
Leicester
Sibson
A1
A15
A17
A46
A52
A606
A607
A6003
A47
A43
A16
A605
A427
A6
A151
A153
A617
A612
B1178
B6403
B1174
B1176

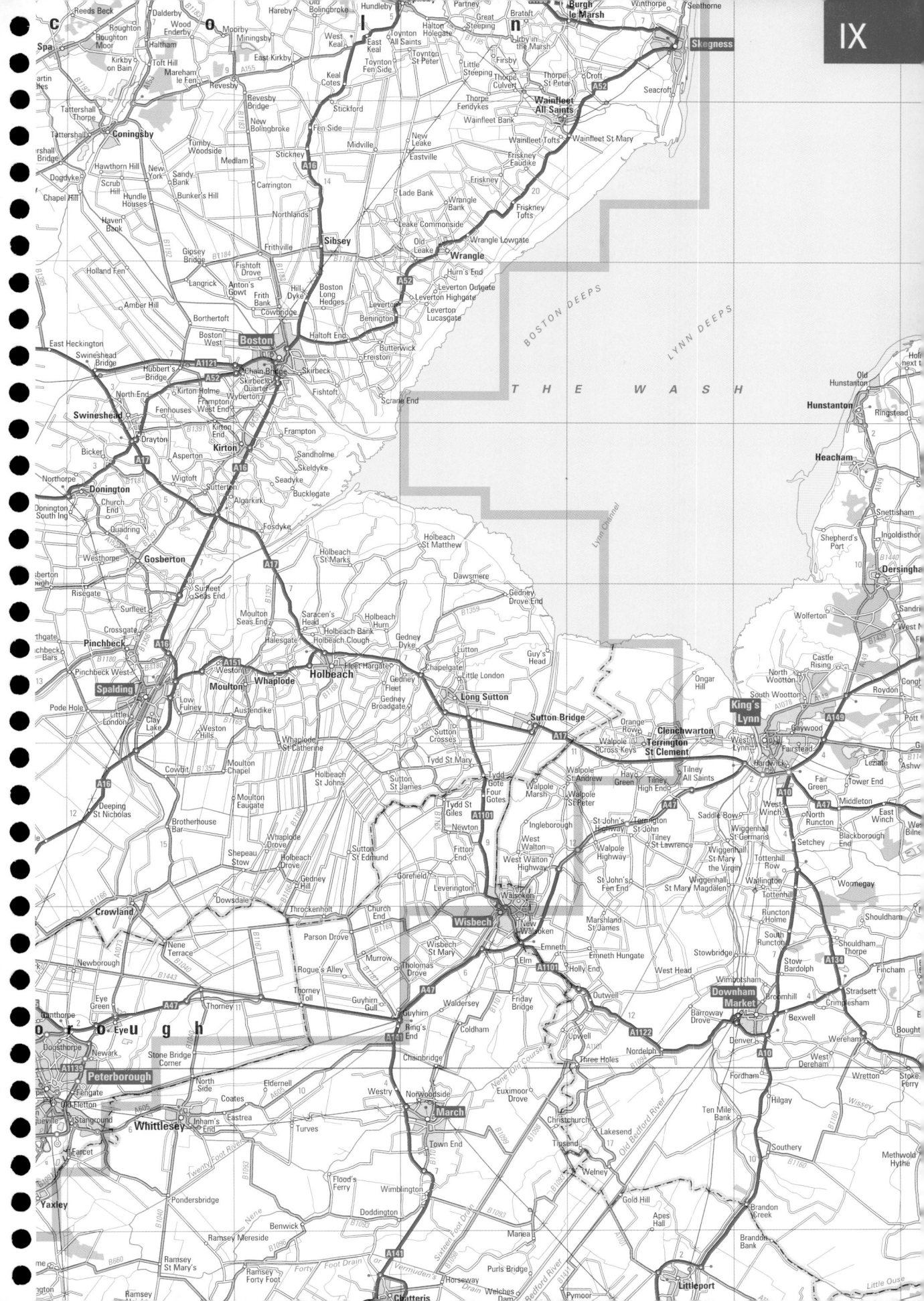
Reeds Beck
Dalderby
Hareby
Old Bolingbroke
Hundleby
Partney
Great Steeping
Bratoft
Burgh le Marsh
Winthorpe
Seathorne
Skegness
Roughton
Roughton Moor
Wood Enderby
Moorby
Miningsby
West Keal
East Keal
Toynton All Saints
Halton Holegate
Irby in the Marsh
Spa
Haltham
Kirkby on Bain
Toft Hill
Mareham le Fen
Revesby
East Kirkby
Toynton Fen Side
Toynton St Peter
Firsby
Little Steeping
Thorpe Culvert
Thorpe St Peter
Croft
Seacroft
Keal Cotes
Tattershall Thorpe
Tattershall
Coningsby
Revesby Bridge
New Bolingbroke
Stickford
Thorpe Fendykes
Wainfleet All Saints
Wainfleet Bank
Fen Side
Midville
New Leake
Eastville
Wainfleet Tofts
Wainfleet St Mary
Tumby Woodside
Medlam
Stickney
Friskney Eaudike
Dogdyke
Hawthorn Hill
New York
Sandy Bank
Carrington
Friskney
Scrub Hill
Chapel Hill
Hundle Houses
Bunker's Hill
Lade Bank
Wrangle Bank
Friskney Tofts
Haven Bank
Northlands
Leake Commonside
Old Leake
Wrangle Lowgate
Wrangle
Frithville
Sibsey
Gipsey Bridge
Holland Fen
Fishtoft Drove
Langrick
Anton's Gowt
Frith Bank
Hill Dyke
Boston Long Hedges
Hurn's End
Leverton Outgate
Leverton Highgate
Leverton
Leverton Lucasgate
Amber Hill
Cowbridge
Benington
Borthertoft
Boston West
Boston
Haltoft End
East Heckington
Swineshead Bridge
Hubbert's Bridge
Chain Bridge
Skirbeck
Skirbeck Quarter
Wyberton
Butterwick
Freiston
Fishtoft
Scrane End
North End
Kirton Holme
Frampton West End
Fenhouses
Swineshead
Drayton
Kirton End
Kirton
Frampton
Bicker
Asperton
Sandholme
Skeldyke
Seadyke
Bucklegate
Northorpe
Wigtoft
Sutterton
Algarkirk
Donington
Donington South Ing
Church End
Quadring
Fosdyke
Westhorpe
Gosberton
Holbeach St Marks
Holbeach St Matthew
Dawsmere
Gedney Drove End
Risegate
Surfleet
Surfleet Seas End
Moulton Seas End
Saracen's Head
Holbeach Bank
Holbeach Hurn
Holbeach Clough
Halesgate
Crossgate
Pinchbeck
Pinchbeck Bars
Pinchbeck West
Gedney Dyke
Lutton
Guy's Head
Weston
Moulton
Whaplode
Holbeach
Fleet Hargate
Gedney
Fleet
Chapelgate
Little London
Long Sutton
Spalding
Gedney Broadgate
Pode Hole
Low Fulney
Austendike
Little London
Clay Lake
Weston Hills
Whaplode St Catherine
Sutton Crosses
Sutton Bridge
Orange Row
Clenchwarton
Walpole Cross Keys
Terrington St Clement
Tydd St Mary
Cowbit
Moulton Chapel
Holbeach St Johns
Sutton St James
Tydd Gote
Four Gotes
Walpole St Andrew
Hay Green
Tilney High End
Tilney All Saints
Walpole Marsh
Walpole St Peter
Deeping St Nicholas
Moulton Eaugate
Tydd St Giles
Newton
Ingleborough
St John's Highway
Terrington St John
Tilney St Lawrence
Brotherhouse Bar
Whaplode Drove
Sutton St Edmund
Fitton End
West Walton
West Walton Highway
Walpole Highway
Shepeau Stow
Holbeach Drove
Gedney Hill
Gorefield
Leverington
Walsoken
St John's Fen End
St Mary Magdalen
Dowsdale
Crowland
Throckenholt
Church End
Wisbech
New Walsoken
Marshland St James
Parson Drove
Nene Terrace
Wisbech St Mary
Emneth
Emneth Hungate
Newborough
Murrow
Rogue's Alley
Tholomas Drove
Elm
Holly End
West Head
Eye Green
Thorney
Thorney Toll
Guyhirn Gull
Guyhirn
Waldersey
Friday Bridge
Outwell
Gunthorpe
Eye
Ring's End
Coldham
Upwell
Dogsthorpe
Newark
Stone Bridge Corner
Peterborough
Chainbridge
Three Holes
Nordelph
North Side
Eldernell
Fengate
Old Fletton
Coates
Westry
Norwoodside
Euximoor Drove
Stanground
Whittlesey
Eastrea
Inham's End
Turves
March
Christchurch
Lakesend
Farcet
Town End
Tipsend
Welney
Flood's Ferry
Wimblington
Pondersbridge
Doddington
Gold Hill
Yaxley
Benwick
Apes Hall
Ramsey Mereside
Manea
Ramsey St Mary's
Ramsey Forty Foot
Purls Bridge
Horseway
Welches Dam
Pymoor
Littleport
Chatteris
Ramsey
Brandon Creek
Brandon Bank
Old Hunstanton
Hunstanton
Ringstead
Heacham
Snettisham
Shepherd's Port
Ingoldisthorpe
Dersingham
Sandringham
Wolferton
Castle Rising
North Wootton
South Wootton
Roydon
King's Lynn
Gaywood
West Lynn
Fairstead
Hardwick
Leziate
Ongar Hill
Fair Green
Tower End
Middleton
Saddle Bow
North Runcton
East Winch
West Winch
Wiggenhall St Germans
Wiggenhall St Mary the Virgin
Setchey
Blackborough End
Tottenhill Row
Wiggenhall St Mary Magdalen
Watlington
Wormegay
Tottenhill
Runcton Holme
Shouldham
South Runcton
Shouldham Thorpe
Stowbridge
Stow Bardolph
Fincham
Wimbotsham
Downham Market
Stradsett
Crimplesham
Broomhill
Barroway Drove
Bexwell
Denver
Wereham
West Dereham
Fordham
Wretton
Stoke Ferry
Hilgay
Ten Mile Bank
Southery
Methwold Hythe
Boughton
BOSTON DEEPS
LYNN DEEPS
THE WASH
Lynn Channel
Old Bedford River
Sixteen Foot Drain
Twenty Foot River
Forty Foot Drain
Vermuden's Drain
Nene (Old Course)
Nene
Wissey
Little Ouse
Bedford River
A16
A52
A17
A1121
A151
A47
A1101
A10
A149
A148
A1078
A134
A1122
A141
A1139
A605
A1073
A155
A153
B1183
B1195
B1192
B1184
B1183
B1395
B1181
B1391
B1397
B1357
B1359
B1180
B1165
B1168
B1166
B1167
B1169
B1187
B1040
B1443
B1093
B1098
B1099
B1101
B1160
B1440
B1439
B660
B1096
B1095

Administrative and Postcode boundaries

East Riding of Yorkshire

SE | TA

SE | SK

TA | TF

North Lincolnshire

West Lindsey

East Lindsey

Lincolnshire

North Kesteven

Nottinghamshire

South Kesteven

Leicestershire

Boston

South Holland

NE Lincs

Norfolk

Cambridgeshire

SP | TL

TF | TL

Scale
| 0 | 10 | 20 | 30 km |
| 0 | 5 | 10 | 15 | 20 miles |

Legend:
- County and unitary authority boundaries
- District boundaries
- Postcode boundaries
- Area covered by this atlas

Place names and postcode districts:
Stainforth, Thorne, Crowle, Broomfleet, Brough, Anlaby, Kingston upon Hull, North Ferriby, Alkborough, Garthorpe, Winterton, Barton-upon-Humber, Barrow-upon-Humber, Appleby, Ulceby, Immingham, Healing, Grimsby, Cleethorpes, Humberston, Hatfield, Edenthorpe, Wroot, Belton, Epworth, Scunthorpe, Broughton, Barnetby le Wold, Keelby, Laceby, Grasby, Waltham, Holton le Clay, Messingham, Hibaldstow, Brigg, Caistor, Haxey, Scotter, North Kelsey, South Kelsey, North Thoresby, North Somercotes, Walkeringham, Beckingham, Hemswell, Osgodby, Tealby, Utterby, Gainsborough, Market Rasen, Ludford, Louth, Manby, Mablethorpe, Marton, Ingham, Faldingworth, Lissington, Hainton, Legbourne, Burwell, Sutton on Sea, Rampton, Saxilby, Nettleham, Welton, Wragby, Goulceby, Belchford, Tetford, Alford, Hogsthorpe, Chapel St Leonards, Harby, Lincoln, Washingborough, Cherry Willingham, Bardney, Horncastle, Hagworthingham, Spilsby, Ingoldmells, Skegness, Besthorpe, North Scarle, Swinderby, Waddington, Branston, Woodhall Spa, Burgh le Marsh, Collingham, Bassingham, Metheringham, Ravesby, Wainfleet All Saints, Navenby, Timberland, Coningsby, Stickney, Newark-on-Trent, Leadenham, Billinghay, Ruskington, South Kyme, Sibsey, Wrangle, Balderton, Claypole, Caythorpe, Sleaford, Heckington, Boston, Butterwick, Long Bennington, Marston, Helpringham, Swineshead, Kirton, Bottesford, Great Gonerby, Barkston, Donington, Fosdyke, Holbeach St Matthew, Sedgebrook, Grantham, Horbling, Gosberton, Harlaxton, Ropsley, Folkingham, Billingborough, Pinchbeck, Whaplode, Holbeach, Long Sutton, Sutton Bridge, Knipton, Great Ponton, Rippingdale, Corby Glen, Spalding, Moulton, Terrington St Clement, Sproxton, Colsterworth, Bourne, Cowbit, Tydd St Giles, West Walton, Wymondham, Thurlby, Hop Pole, Gedney Hill, Gorefield, Wisbech, Clipsham, Market Deeping, Crowland, Church End, Ryhall, Deeping St James, Thorney, Guyhirn, Stamford, Helpston, Eye, Wittering, Castor, Peterborough, Yaxley

Postcode districts shown: HU1–HU15, DN3, DN7–DN10, DN14–DN22, DN31–DN41, LN1–LN13, NG23, NG24, NG31–NG34, LE14, LE15, PE1–PE14, PE20–PE25, PE34, SE, SK, TA, TF, TL, SP

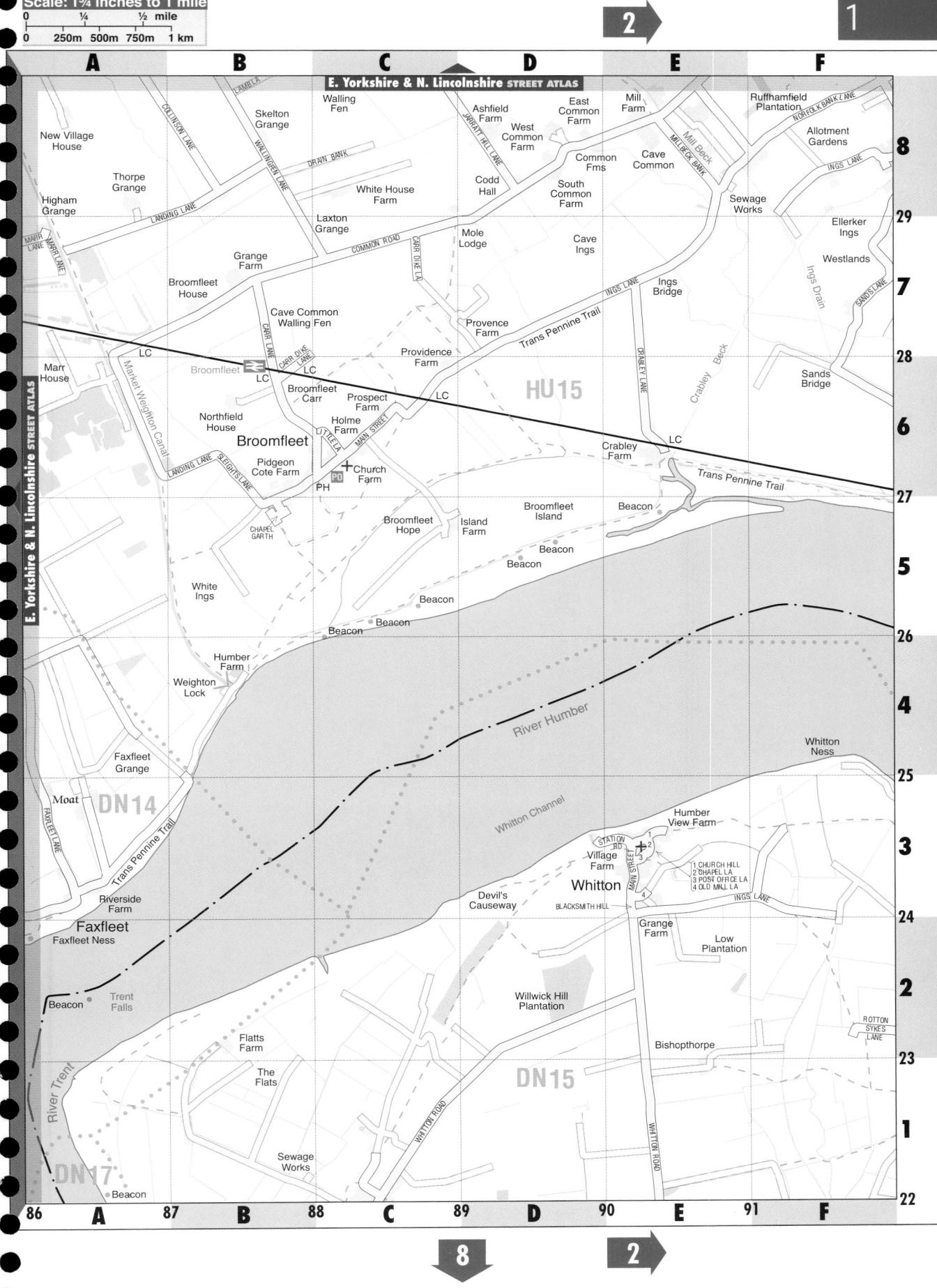

Scale: 1¾ inches to 1 mile

1

2

8

2

E. Yorkshire & N. Lincolnshire STREET ATLAS

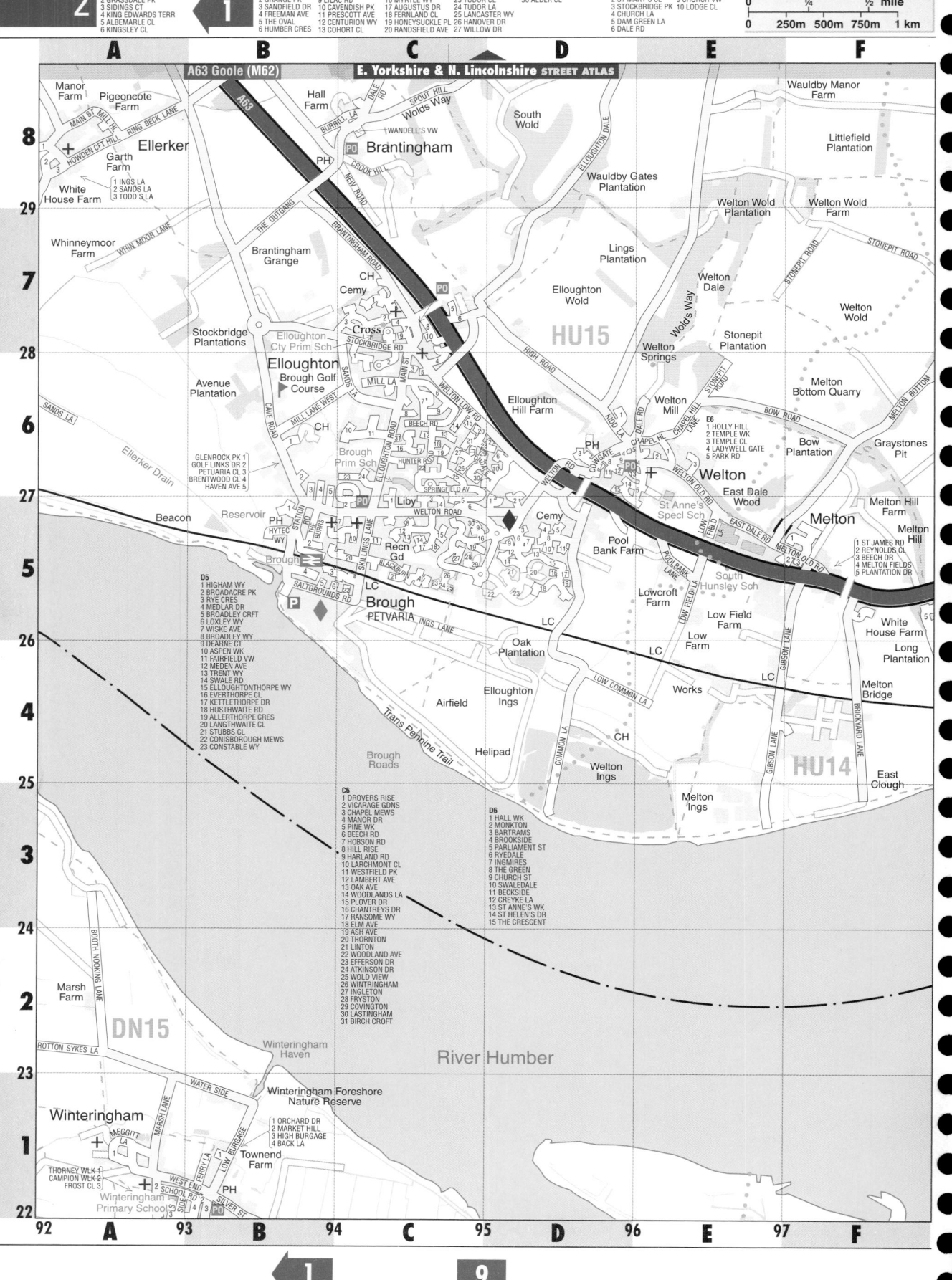

B5
1 HAVEN GARTH
2 GRASSDALE PK
3 SIDINGS CT
4 KING EDWARDS TERR
5 ALBEMARLE CL
6 KINGSLEY CL

C5
1 TREMAYNE AVE
2 GRANGE PK
3 SANDFIELD DR
4 FREEMAN AVE
5 THE OVAL
6 HUMBER CRES

7 WRYGARTH AVE
8 LEGION CL
9 LILAC RD
10 CAVENDISH PK
11 PRESCOTT AVE
12 CENTURION WY
13 COHORT CL

14 FRESH FIELDS
15 NURSERY CT
16 MYRTLE WY
17 AUGUSTUS DR
18 FERNLAND CL
19 HONEYSUCKLE PL
20 RANDSFIELD AVE

21 BUCCANEER WY
22 ARKLEY CL
23 TUDOR CL
24 TUDOR LA
25 LANCASTER WY
26 HANOVER DR
27 WILLOW DR

28 BIRCH CL
29 HAZEL CT
30 ALDER CL

C7
1 SPINDLEWOOD
2 ST MARY'S CL
3 STOCKBRIDGE PK
4 CHURCH LA
5 DAM GREEN LA
6 DALE RD

7 CHURCH ST
8 THORNHAM'S WY
9 CHURCH VW
10 LODGE CL

E. Yorkshire & N. Lincolnshire STREET ATLAS

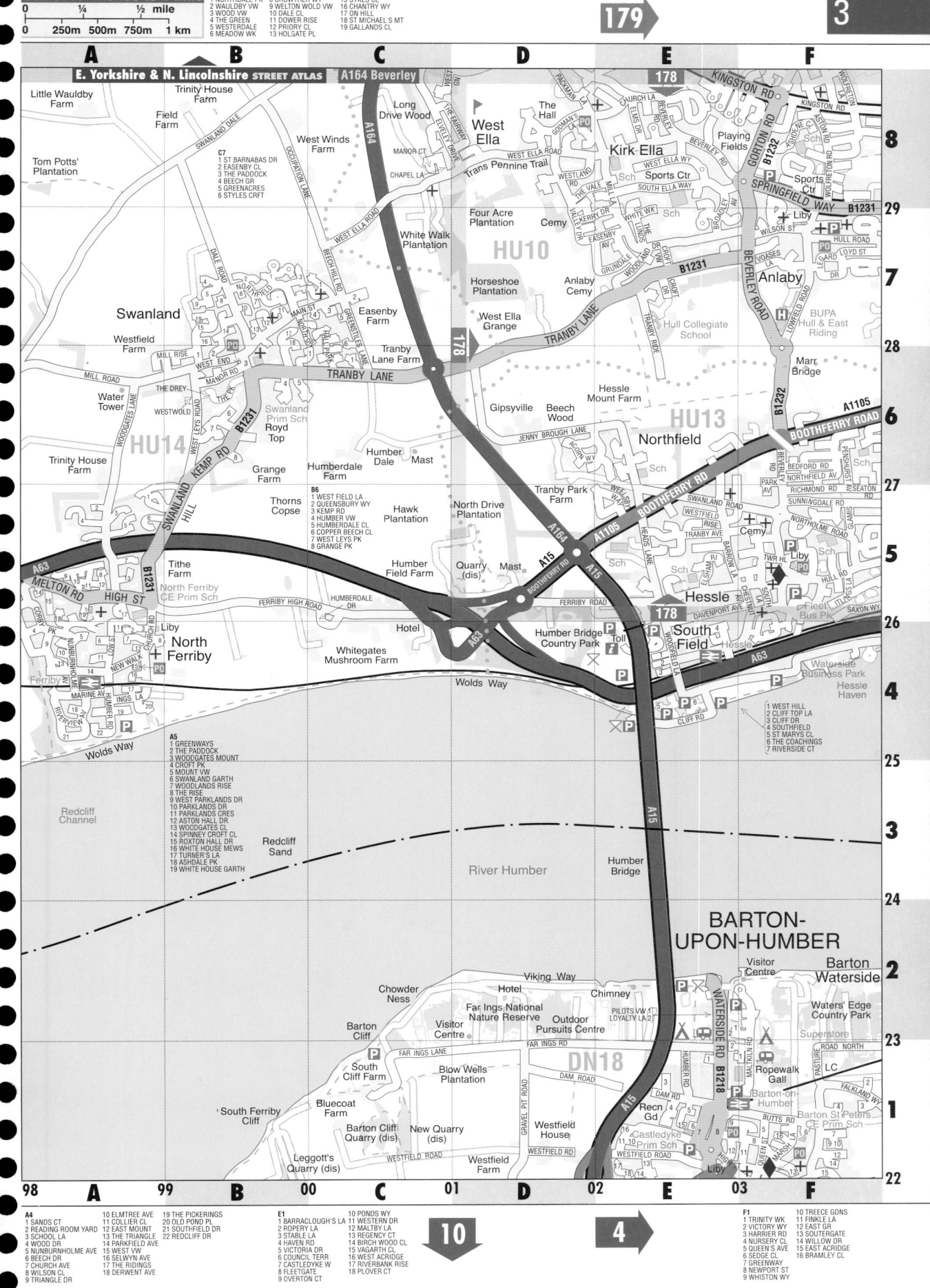

Scale: 1¾ inches to 1 mile
0   ¼   ½   mile
0   250m 500m 750m 1 km

E. Yorkshire & N. Lincolnshire STREET ATLAS

B7
1 NORTHDALE PK
2 WAULDBY VW
3 WOOD VW
4 THE GREEN
5 WESTERDALE
6 MEADOW WK

7 THE SPINNEY
8 CROWTHER WY
9 WELTON WOLD VW
10 DALE VW
11 DOWER RISE
12 PRIORY CL
13 HOLGATE PL

14 CHANTRY WAY E
15 SYKES CL
16 CHANTRY WY
17 ON HILL
18 ST MICHAEL'S MT
19 GALLANDS CL

A164 Beverley

C7
1 ST BARNABAS DR
2 EASENBY CL
3 THE PADDOCK
4 BEECH GR
5 GREENACRES
6 STYLES CRFT

B6
1 WEST FIELD LA
2 QUEENSBURY WY
3 KEMP RD
4 HUMBER VW
5 HUMBERDALE CL
6 COPPER BEECH CL
7 WEST LEYS PK
8 GRANGE PK

A5
1 GREENWAYS
2 THE PADDOCK
3 WOODGATES MOUNT
4 CROFT PK
5 MOUNT VW
6 SWANLAND GARTH
7 WOODLANDS RISE
8 THE RISE
9 WEST PARKLANDS DR
10 PARKLANDS DR
11 PARKLANDS CRES
12 ASTON HALL DR
13 WOODGATES CL
14 SPINNEY CROFT CL
15 ROXTON HALL DR
16 WHITE HOUSE MEWS
17 TURNER'S LA
18 ASHDALE PK
19 WHITE HOUSE GARTH

E1
1 BARRACLOUGH'S LA
2 ROPERY LA
3 STABLE LA
4 HAVEN RD
5 VICTORIA DR
6 COUNCIL TERR
7 CASTLEDYKE W
8 FLEETGATE
9 OVERTON CT

10 PONDS WY
11 WESTERN DR
12 MALTBY LA
13 REGENCY CT
14 BIRCH WOOD CL
15 VAGARTH CL
16 WEST ACRIDGE
17 RIVERBANK RISE
18 PLOVER CT

F1
1 TRINITY WK
2 VICTORY WY
3 HARRIER RD
4 NURSERY CL
5 QUEEN'S AVE
6 SEDGE CL
7 GREENWAY
8 NEWPORT ST
9 WHISTON WY

10 TREECE GDNS
11 FINKLE LA
12 EAST GR
13 SOUTERGATE
14 WILLOW DR
15 EAST ACRIDGE
16 BRAMLEY CL

A4
1 SANDS CT
2 READING ROOM YARD
3 SCHOOL LA
4 WOOD DR
5 NUNBURNHOLME AVE
6 BEECH GR
7 CHURCH AVE
8 WILSON CL
9 TRIANGLE DR

10 ELMTREE AVE
11 COLLIER CL
12 EAST MOUNT
13 THE TRIANGLE
14 PARKFIELD AVE
15 WEST VW
16 SELWYN AVE
17 THE RIDINGS
18 DERWENT AVE

19 THE PICKERINGS
20 OLD POND PL
21 SOUTHFIELD DR
22 REDCLIFF DR

Scale: 1¾ inches to 1 mile

0   ¼   ½   mile
0   250m   500m   750m   1 km

E. Yorkshire & N. Lincolnshire STREET ATLAS

179 · **180** A1079 Beverley (A1174)

Grid columns: A B C D E F
Grid rows: 8 29 7 28 6 27 5 26 4 25 3 24 2 23 1 22
Bottom grid: 04 A 05 B 06 C 07 D 08 E 09 F

HU5 · HU2 · HU10 · HU3 · HU1 · HU4 · DN18 · DN19

Key places and labels:
East Ella, West Park, Anlaby Park, Pickering Park, Gipsyville, Priory Park, Waterside Business Park, St Andrews Quay, Albert Dock, Hotel Dock, Victoria Pier, Hull Arena, Victoria Dock, Mus, St Stephen's, Theatre

New Holland Pier, New Holland Mere, New Holland, Summercroft Farm, Fairfield Pit Nature Reserve, New Holland CE Methodist Prim Sch, Barrow Haven Reedbed Nature Reserve, Pasture Wharf Nature Reserve, Sailing Club, Oxford Grange Farm, Barrow Haven, Windmill, The Castles (Motte & Baileys), Mill Farm, Castle Farm, West Marsh Farm, Spring Farm, Barrow Blow Wells Nature Reserve, West Hann Farm, Coulbeck Farm, Barrow Hann, Hann Farm, Field Farm, Leys Farm, Mill Farm

Roads:
Springfield Wy, Hull Rd, Boothferry Road, Askew Avenue, Anlaby Road, Hessle Road, Castle St, Clive Sullivan Way, Trans Pennine Trail, A1105, A1106, A63, A165, A1079, Beverley Rd, Ferensway, Lincoln Castle Way, New Holland Rd, Barrow Rd, Marsh Lane, West Hann Lane, East Hann Lane, Oxmarsh Lane, Ferry Road, B1206, B1231, West Marsh La, West Marsh Lane, Summergroves Way, Priory Way, Falkland Way

179 · **180**

For full street detail of the highlighted area see pages 179 & 180.

← **3**

↓ **11**

E2
1 SCHOOL LA
2 WENTWORTH CR
3 FULFORD CRES
4 WESTBURN AVE
5 MORGAN WY
6 GLENEAGLES CRES
7 ALBERT ST
8 MOUNT PL
9 PEPLOE LA
10 PEPLOE CRES
11 DANESGATE

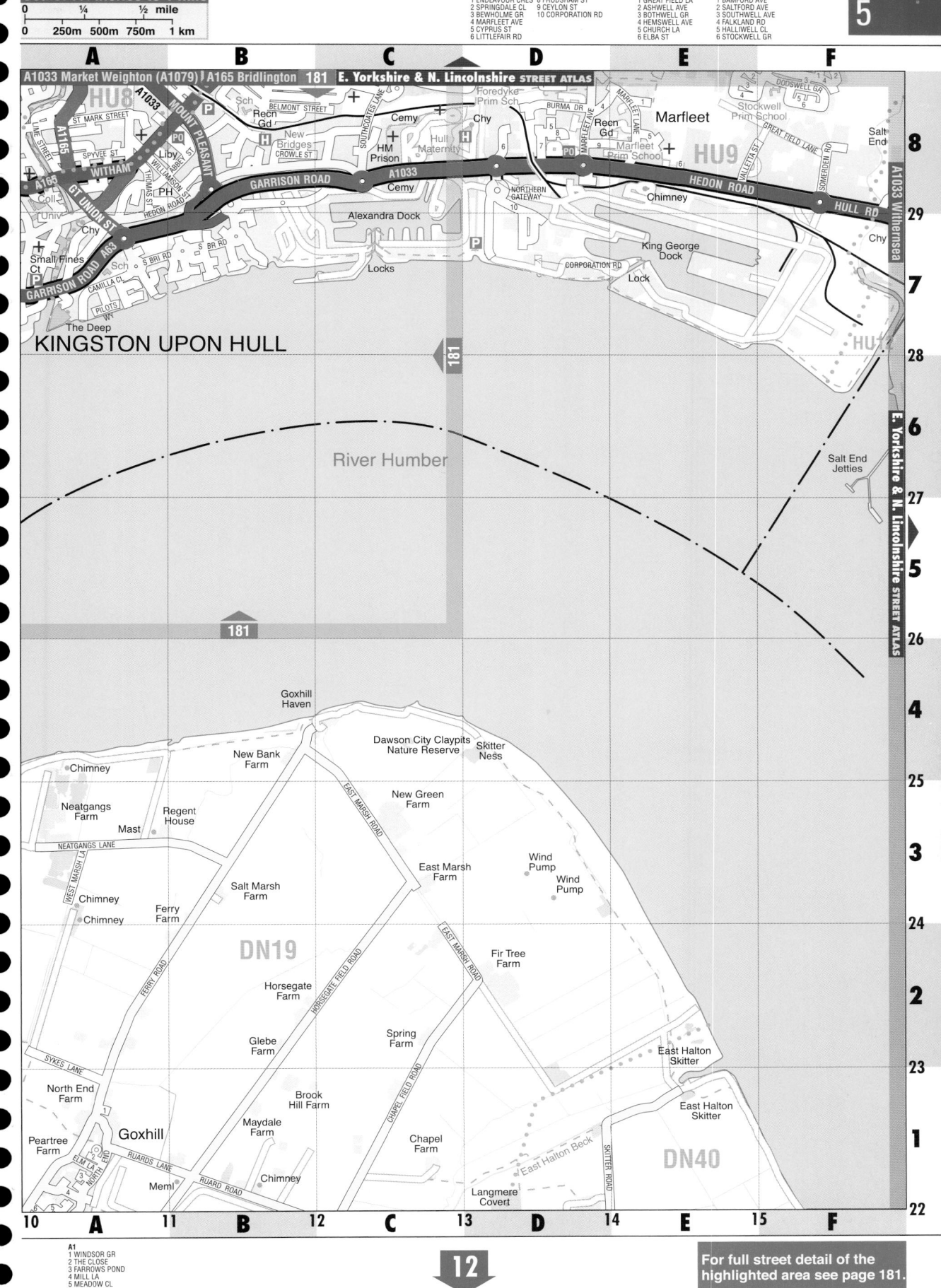

Scale: 1¾ inches to 1 mile

0   ¼   ½   mile
0   250m 500m 750m 1 km

5

A1033 Market Weighton (A1079) A165 Bridlington 181

HU8

Marfleet

Stockwell Prim School

HU9

Salt End

KINGSTON UPON HULL

The Deep

GARRISON ROAD   A1033

Alexandra Dock

Northern Gateway

Chimney

King George Dock

Lock

HEDON ROAD

HULL RD

A1033 Withernsea

Corporation Rd

Locks

River Humber

Salt End Jetties

181

E. Yorkshire & N. Lincolnshire STREET ATLAS

Goxhill Haven

New Bank Farm

Dawson City Claypits Nature Reserve

Skitter Ness

Chimney

Neatgangs Farm

Mast

Regent House

New Green Farm

Neatgangs Lane

DN19

Chimney

Ferry Farm

Salt Marsh Farm

East Marsh Farm

Wind Pump

Wind Pump

Chimney

Fir Tree Farm

Horsegate Farm

Glebe Farm

Spring Farm

East Halton Skitter

North End Farm

East Halton Skitter

Peartree Farm

Goxhill

Maydale Farm

Brook Hill Farm

Chapel Farm

DN40

Sykes Lane

Elm La

Ruards Lane

Ruard Road

Meml

Chimney

East Halton Beck

Skitter Road

Langmere Covert

8
29
7
28
6
27
5
26
4
25
3
24
2
23
1
22

10   A   11   B   12   C   13   D   14   E   15   F

12

For full street detail of the highlighted area see page 181.

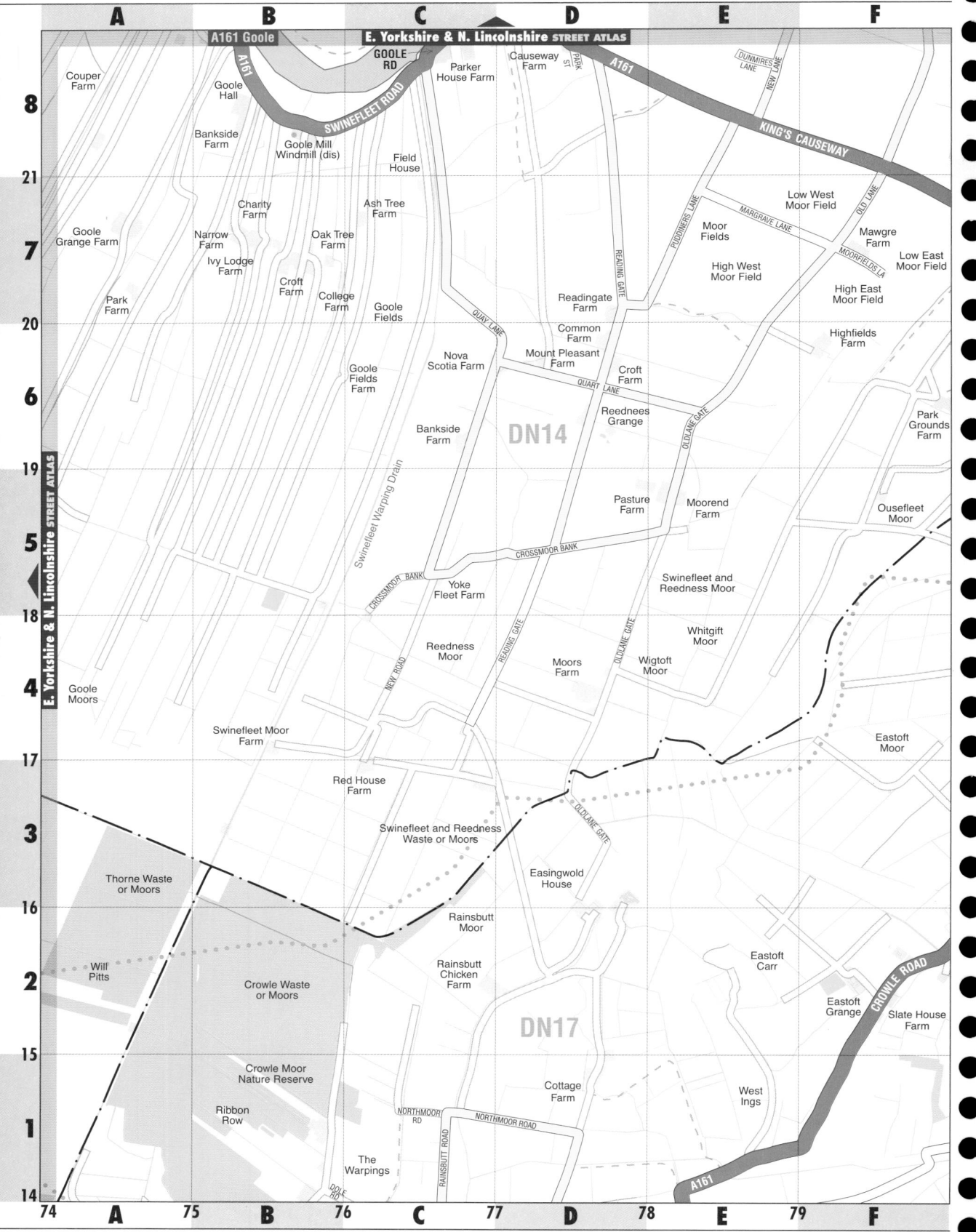

A161 Goole

A161

GOOLE RD

SWINEFLEET ROAD

KING'S CAUSEWAY

E. Yorkshire & N. Lincolnshire STREET ATLAS

Couper Farm

Goole Hall

Bankside Farm

Goole Mill Windmill (dis)

Parker House Farm

Causeway Farm

Field House

Low West Moor Field

Mawgre Farm

Low East Moor Field

Charity Farm

Ash Tree Farm

Goole Grange Farm

Narrow Farm

Oak Tree Farm

Moor Fields

High West Moor Field

Ivy Lodge Farm

Croft Farm

College Farm

Goole Fields

Readingate Farm

High East Moor Field

Park Farm

Goole Fields Farm

Nova Scotia Farm

Common Farm

Mount Pleasant Farm

Croft Farm

Highfields Farm

Bankside Farm

Reednees Grange

Park Grounds Farm

Swinefleet Warping Drain

DN14

QUAY LANE

QUART LANE

READING GATE

OLDLANE GATE

Pasture Farm

Moorend Farm

Ousefleet Moor

CROSSMOOR BANK

Swinefleet and Reedness Moor

CROSSMOOR BANK

Yoke Fleet Farm

Whitgift Moor

Goole Moors

Reedness Moor

NEW ROAD

READING GATE

Moors Farm

OLDLANE GATE

Wigtoft Moor

Eastoft Moor

Swinefleet Moor Farm

Red House Farm

Swinefleet and Reedness Waste or Moors

OLDLANE GATE

Easingwold House

Eastoft Carr

Eastoft Grange

CROWLE ROAD

Slate House Farm

Will Pitts

Thorne Waste or Moors

Rainsbutt Moor

Rainsbutt Chicken Farm

DN17

Crowle Waste or Moors

Crowle Moor Nature Reserve

Ribbon Row

Cottage Farm

West Ings

NORTHMOOR RD

NORTHMOOR ROAD

RAINSBUTT ROAD

The Warpings

DOLE RD

A161

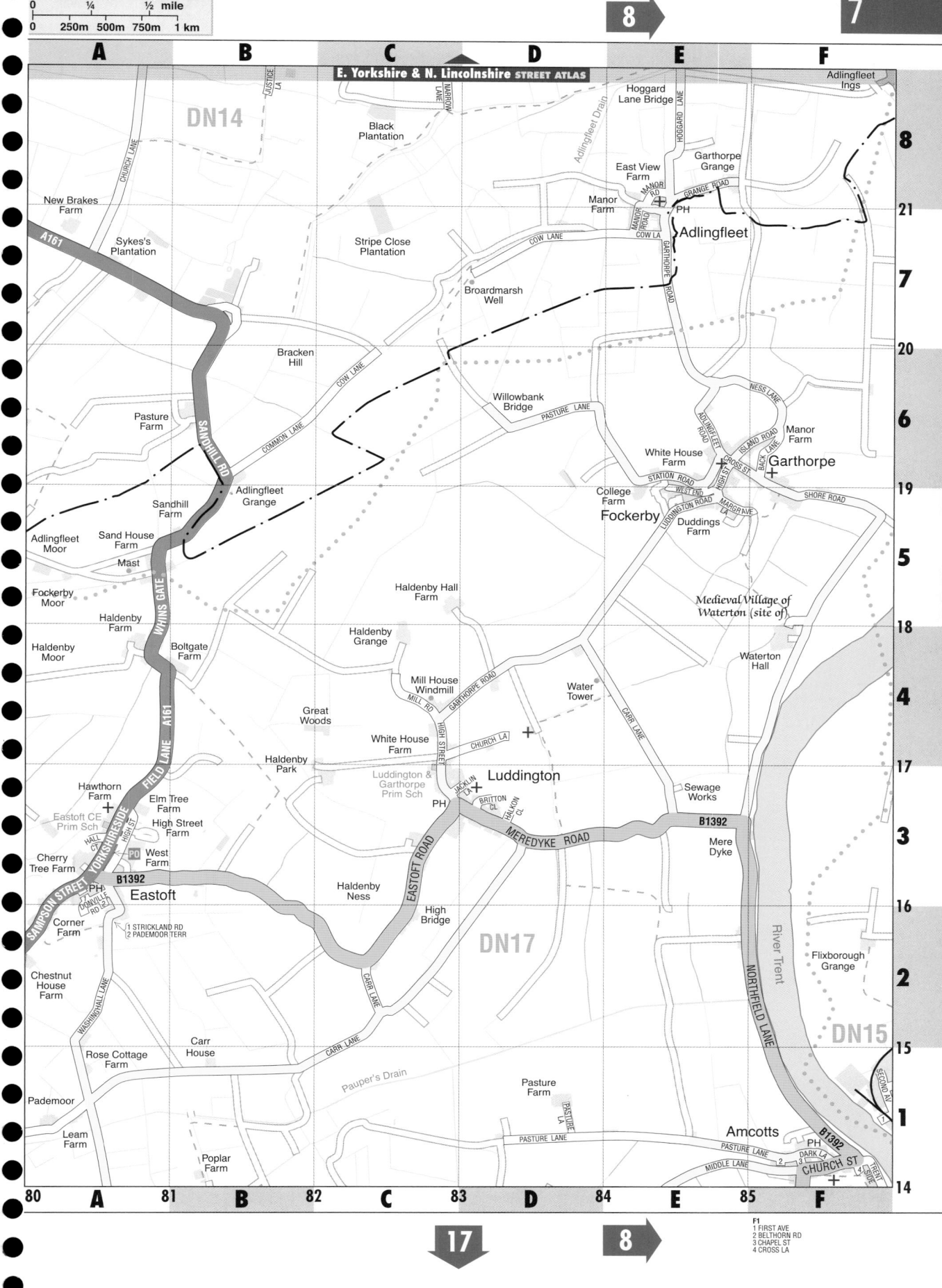

E. Yorkshire & N. Lincolnshire STREET ATLAS

DN14

Adlingfleet Ings

Hoggard Lane Bridge

Black Plantation

East View Farm

Garthorpe Grange

Manor Farm

New Brakes Farm

Sykes's Plantation

Adlingfleet

21

Stripe Close Plantation

Cow Lane

7

Broadmarsh Well

Bracken Hill

20

Willowbank Bridge

Pasture Lane

Ness Lane

6

Pasture Farm

Common Lane

Cow Lane

White House Farm

Manor Farm

Garthorpe

Island Road

Back Lane

Station Road

Cross St

West End

College Farm

19

Adlingfleet Grange

Sandhill Farm

Sand House Farm

Fockerby

Duddings Farm

Adlingfleet Moor

Mast

Margr Ave

Haldenby Hall Farm

Medieval Village of Waterton (site of)

5

Fockerby Moor

Haldenby Farm

Haldenby Grange

Waterton Hall

18

Haldenby Moor

Boltgate Farm

Mill House Windmill

Water Tower

4

Great Woods

Garthorpe Road

Mill Rd

Carr Lane

Haldenby Park

White House Farm

High Street

Church La

17

Hawthorn Farm

Elm Tree Farm

Luddington & Garthorpe Prim Sch

Luddington

Jacklin La

Sewage Works

Eastoft CE Prim Sch

High Street Farm

PH

Britton Cl

Halkon Cl

B1392

Mere Dyke

3

Cherry Tree Farm

West Farm

PO

Eastoft Road

Meredyke Road

Eastoft

B1392

Haldenby Ness

16

Corner Farm

1 STRICKLAND RD
2 PADEMOOR TERR

High Bridge

DN17

Chestnut House Farm

Flixborough Grange

2

Carr House

Carr Lane

DN15

Rose Cottage Farm

Carr Lane

Pauper's Drain

15

Pademoor

Pasture Farm

Pasture La

River Trent

Leam Farm

Northfield Lane

Amcotts

PH

B1392

1

Poplar Farm

Pasture Lane

Middle Lane

CHURCH ST

Dark La

14

F1
1 FIRST AVE
2 BELTHORN RD
3 CHAPEL ST
4 CROSS LA

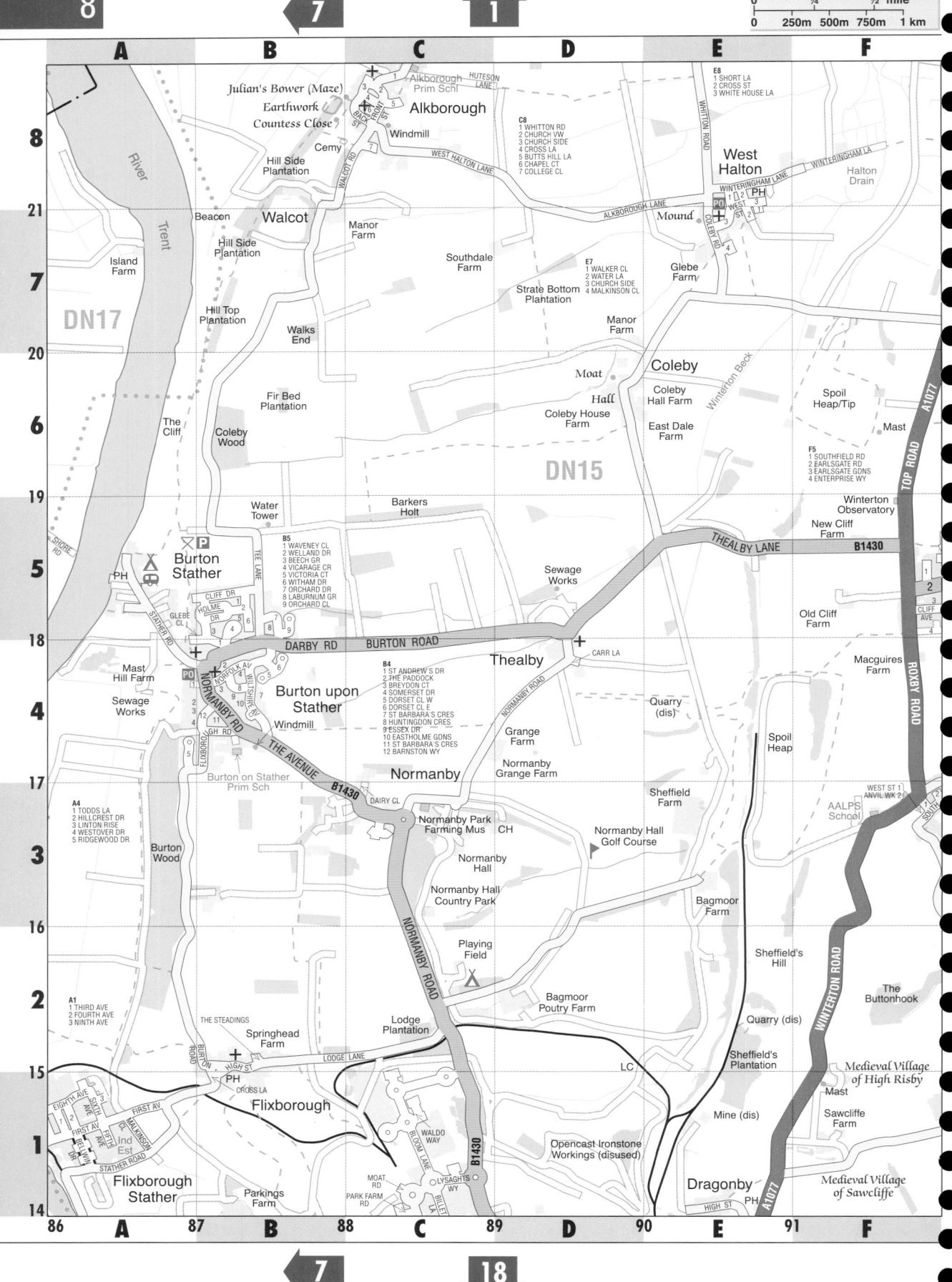

Scale: 1¾ inches to 1 mile

0   ¼   ½   mile
0   250m 500m 750m 1 km

A   B   C   D   E   F

Julian's Bower (Maze)
Earthwork
Countess Close

Alkborough Prim Schl

HUTESON LANE

Alkborough

E8
1 SHORT LA
2 CROSS ST
3 WHITE HOUSE LA

C8
1 WHITTON RD
2 CHURCH VW
3 CHURCH SIDE
4 CROSS LA
5 BUTTS HILL LA
6 CHAPEL CT
7 COLLEGE CL

Windmill

WEST HALTON LANE

West Halton

WINTERINGHAM LA

Halton Drain

8

Cemy

Hill Side Plantation

River Trent

WALCOT RD

BACK ST

TRENT ST

WINTERINGHAM LANE

PO

PH

WEST ST

21

Beacon

Walcot

Hill Side Plantation

Manor Farm

Southdale Farm

ALKBOROUGH LANE

Mound

WHITTON ROAD

COLEBY RD

Glebe Farm

7

Island Farm

DN17

Hill Top Plantation

Walks End

Strate Bottom Plantation

E7
1 WALKER CL
2 WATER LA
3 CHURCH SIDE
4 MALKINSON CL

Manor Farm

20

The Cliff

Fir Bed Plantation

Moat Hall

Coleby

6

Coleby Wood

Coleby House Farm

Coleby Hall Farm

East Dale Farm

Winterton Beck

Spoil Heap/Tip

Mast

TOP ROAD

A1077

19

SHORE RD

Water Tower

Barkers Holt

DN15

F5
1 SOUTHFIELD RD
2 EARLSGATE RD
3 EARLSGATE GDNS
4 ENTERPRISE WY

Winterton Observatory

New Cliff Farm

THEALBY LANE

B1430

5

PH

Burton Stather

P

TEE LANE

B5
1 WAVENEY CL
2 WELLAND DR
3 BEECH GR
4 VICARAGE CR
5 VICTORIA CT
6 WITHAM DR
7 ORCHARD DR
8 LABURNUM GR
9 ORCHARD CL

Sewage Works

Old Cliff Farm

CLIFF AVE

ROXBY ROAD

18

CLIFF DR

HOLME DR

GLEBE CL

STATHER RD

DARBY RD

BURTON ROAD

Thealby

CARR LA

Macguires Farm

Mast Hill Farm

PO

NORFOLK AV

WILSTHORPE

Burton upon Stather

B4
1 ST ANDREW'S DR
2 THE PADDOCK
3 BREYDON CT
4 SOMERSET DR
5 DORSET CL W
6 DORSET CL E
7 ST BARBARA'S CRES
8 HUNTINGDON CRES
9 ESSEX DR
10 EASTHOLME GDNS
11 ST BARBARA'S CRES
12 BARNSTON WY

NORMANBY RD

Quarry (dis)

Spoil Heap

WEST ST
ANVIL WK

AALPS School

4

Sewage Works

Windmill

THE AVENUE

Normanby

NORMANBY ROAD

Grange Farm

Normanby Grange Farm

Sheffield Farm

17

A4
1 TODDS LA
2 HILLCREST DR
3 LINTON RISE
4 WESTOVER DR
5 RIDGEWOOD DR

Burton on Stather Prim Schl

B1430

DAIRY CL

Normanby Park Farming Mus

CH

Normanby Hall Golf Course

3

Burton Wood

Normanby Hall

Normanby Hall Country Park

Bagmoor Farm

Sheffield's Hill

WINTERTON ROAD

The Buttonhook

2

A1
1 THIRD AVE
2 FOURTH AVE
3 NINTH AVE

THE STEADINGS

Springhead Farm

Playing Field

Bagmoor Poultry Farm

Quarry (dis)

Sheffield's Plantation

Medieval Village of High Risby

BURTON RD

HIGH ST

Lodge Plantation

LODGE LANE

LC

Mast

Mine (dis)

Sawcliffe Farm

1

EIGHTH AVE

SIXTH AVE

FIRST AV

FIRST AV

MALKINSON CL

Ind Est

STATHER ROAD

PH

CROSS LA

Flixborough

WALDO WAY

BLOOM LANE

B1430

MOAT RD

LYSAGHTS WY

Opencast Ironstone Workings (disused)

Dragonby

HIGH ST

PH

A1077

Medieval Village of Sawcliffe

Flixborough Stather

Parkings Farm

PARK FARM RD

BILLET LA

14

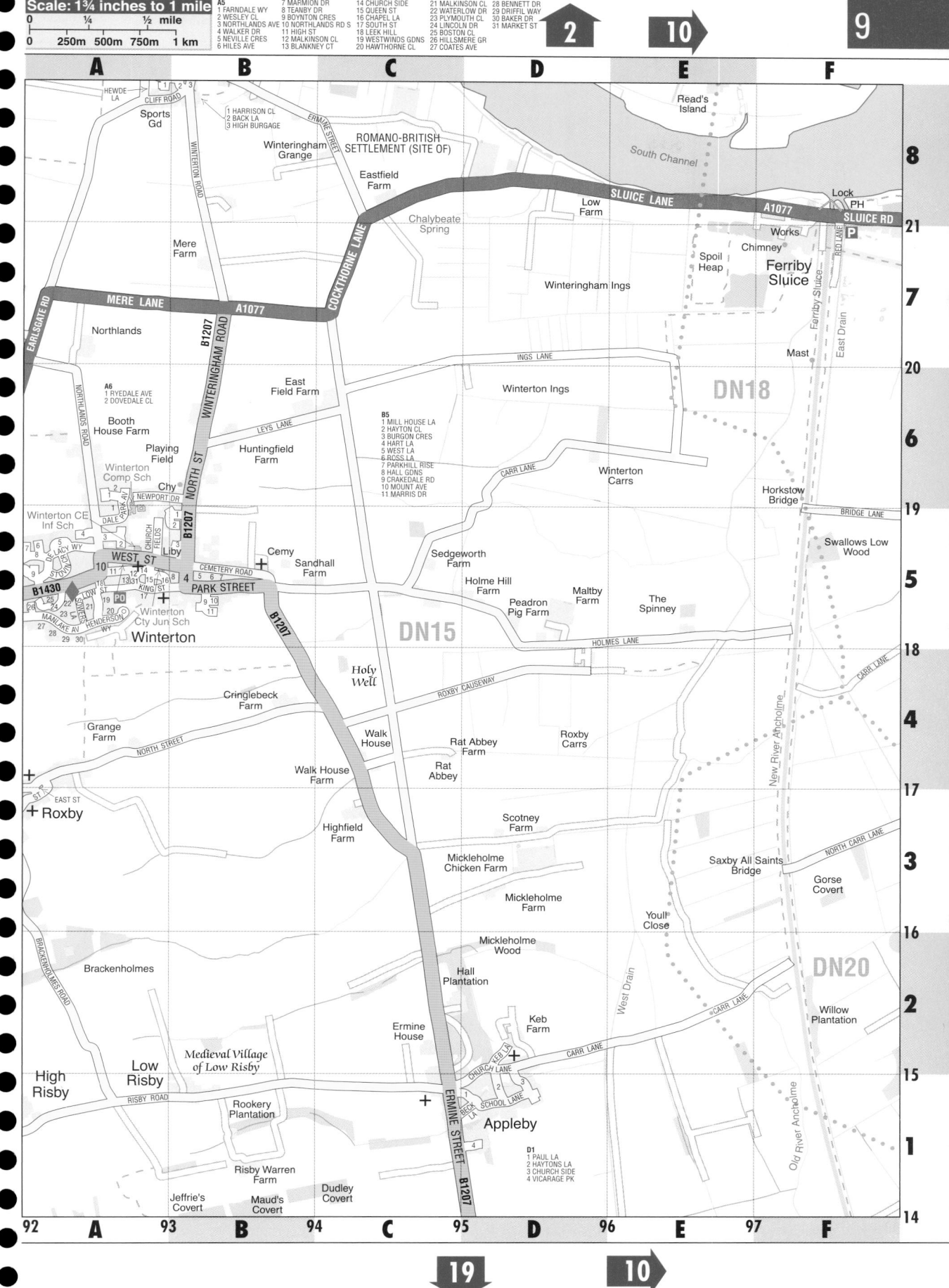

Scale: 1¾ inches to 1 mile

0 ¼ ½ mile
0 250m 500m 750m 1 km

A5
1 FARNDALE WY
2 WESLEY CL
3 NORTHLANDS AVE
4 WALKER DR
5 NEVILLE CRES
6 HILES AVE

7 MARMION DR
8 TEANBY DR
9 BOYNTON CRES
10 NORTHLANDS RD S
11 HIGH ST
12 MALKINSON CL
13 BLANKNEY CT

14 CHURCH SIDE
15 QUEEN ST
16 CHAPEL LA
17 SOUTH ST
18 LEEK HILL
19 WESTWINDS GDNS
20 HAWTHORNE CL

21 MALKINSON CL
22 WATERLOW DR
23 PLYMOUTH CL
24 LINCOLN DR
25 BOSTON CL
26 HILLSMERE GR
27 COATES AVE

28 BENNETT DR
29 DRIFFIL WAY
30 BAKER DR
31 MARKET ST

A   B   C   D   E   F

HEWDE LA
CLIFF ROAD
1 HARRISON CL
2 BACK LA
3 HIGH BURGAGE

Sports Gd

Winteringham Grange

ROMANO-BRITISH SETTLEMENT (SITE OF)

Read's Island

South Channel

8

Eastfield Farm

SLUICE LANE

Low Farm

A1077

Lock
PH
SLUICE RD

21

WINTERTON ROAD

Mere Farm

Chalybeate Spring

Winteringham Ings

Spoil Heap

Chimney

Works

P

Ferriby Sluice

7

EARLSGATE RD

MERE LANE   A1077

COCKTHORNE LANE

Northlands

B1207

WINTERINGHAM ROAD

NORTH ST

East Field Farm

LEYS LANE

INGS LANE

Winterton Ings

Mast

20

DN18

A6
1 RYEDALE AVE
2 DOVEDALE CL

Booth House Farm

Playing Field

Huntingfield Farm

B5
1 MILL HOUSE LA
2 HAYTON CL
3 BURGON CRES
4 HART LA
5 WEST LA
6 ROSS LA
7 PARKHILL RISE
8 HALL GDNS
9 CRAKEDALE RD
10 MOUNT AVE
11 MARRIS DR

CARR LANE

Winterton Carrs

Horkstow Bridge

BRIDGE LANE

19

Winterton Comp Sch

Chy

NEWPORT

Winterton CE Inf Sch

DALE

PARK CL

CHURCH FIELDS

B1207

Liby

WEST ST

Cemy

Sandhall Farm

Sedgeworth Farm

Holme Hill Farm

Maltby Farm

The Spinney

Swallows Low Wood

5

B1430

LOW STREET

HENDERSON WY

DELACY WY

KINGSTON

KING ST

PO

CEMETERY ROAD

PARK STREET

Peadron Pig Farm

CARR LANE

18

Winterton Cty Jun Sch

Winterton

MANLAKE AV

B1207

DN15

HOLMES LANE

New River Ancholme

4

Grange Farm

Cringlebeck Farm

Holy Well

ROXBY CAUSEWAY

Roxby Carrs

17

EAST ST

ST

Roxby

NORTH STREET

Walk House

Walk House Farm

Rat Abbey Farm

Rat Abbey

Scotney Farm

Saxby All Saints Bridge

NORTH CARR LANE

Gorse Covert

3

Highfield Farm

Mickleholme Chicken Farm

Youll Close

16

Brackenholmes

BRACKENHOLMES ROAD

Mickleholme Farm

Mickleholme Wood

DN20

Willow Plantation

2

Medieval Village of Low Risby

Low Risby

Hall Plantation

Ermine House

Keb Farm

KEB LA

WEST DRAIN

CARR LANE

CARR LANE

15

High Risby

RISBY ROAD

Rookery Plantation

ERMINE STREET

BECK

CHURCH LANE

SCHOOL LANE

Appleby

Old River Ancholme

Jeffrie's Covert

Maud's Covert

Dudley Covert

Risby Warren Farm

B1207

1
2
3

D1
1 PAUL LA
2 HAYTONS LA
3 CHURCH SIDE
4 VICARAGE PK

4

1

A7
1 ANDREWS RD
2 SANDS LA
3 QUEEN ELIZABETH AVE
4 OLD POST OFFICE LA
5 LOW ST
6 SKINNERS LA
7 SCHOOL LA
8 BEAULAHLAND
9 BEAULAH VILLAS
10 MILL LA
11 OLD WARP LA
9
3
F8
1 CHAPEL LA
2 GEORGE ST
3 PRIESTGATE
4 ST MARY'S LA
5 BURGATE
6 BECK HILL
7 SAXON CL
8 EAST ACRIDGE
9 NORMAN CL
10 GREEN LA
11 CHURCH VW
12 WHITECROSS ST
13 CASTLEDYKE ST
14 CASTLE CT
15 PRESTON LA
16 STEPHEN CRES
17 HIGHFIELD CRES
18 NICOLSON DR
19 DANSON CL
20 KINGSTON VW
21 RIVER VW
22 LODGE AVE
23 ORCHARD CL
24 THE BRIDGES
25 PARK VW
26 HAWTHORN GATE
27 LINCOLN DR
28 BLYTH CT
29 FAIRFIELD DR
30 MILLBROOK WY
31 RAVENDALE
32 PRINCE CHARLES DR
33 QUEEN ELIZABETH WY
34 PRINCESS DR
Scale: 1¾ inches to 1 mile
0 ¼ ½ mile
0 250m 500m 750m 1 km
A B C D E F
8
21
7
20
6
19
5
18
4
17
3
16
2
15
1
14
Greengate Farm
Leggott's Quarry (dis)
Viking Way
Fox Covert
Green Gate
GRAVEL PIT ROAD
FERRIBY RD
HOLYDYKE
A1077
St Peter's
Recn Gd
B1218
BOWMANDALE
Baysgarth House Mus
Baysgarth School
CAISTOR ROAD
MEADOW DR
FORKEDALE
TOFTS ROAD
Swimming Pool
Baysgarth L Ctr
Bowmandale Prim Sch
HORKSTOW ROAD
BAYSGARTH VW
PRINCE PHILIP DR
EASTFIELD ROAD
Eastfield Farm
NORTH END 1
THE RISE 2
FARRISHES LA 3
Elm Farm
PO
HIGH ST
FERRIBY ROAD
A1077
SLUICE ROAD
South Ferriby
A15
E8
1 REGENCY CT
2 FURNISS CT
3 HUMBER VW
4 HESSLE VW
5 HILLSIDE DR
6 HARROWDYKE
7 BERETUN GN
8 RAMSDEN AVE
9 CLIFF GR
10 TOFTS RD
11 SUNNYBANK
12 WARRENDALE
13 GRANGE AVE
14 MOUNT AVE
15 PARK AVE
16 BEACON AVE
17 PROVIDENCE CRES
18 MILSON CL
19 BRADWELL CL
20 PELHAM CL
21 LUNN'S CR
22 MILLFIELDS
23 PITMAN AVE
24 WARWICK DR
25 MASONS CT
26 NICHOLAS CT
27 GEORGINA CT
28 SUMMERDALE
29 ELMDALE
30 BOWMANDALE
31 BIRCHDALE
32 WELTON CL
33 STEVENSON'S WY
34 HARVEST AVE
35 SHARPE CL
36 WEBB CL
37 GODDARD CL
38 APPLEYARD DR
39 VARAH CL
40 FEYZIN DR
41 RIVERBANK RISE
42 EIDER CL
43 HERON WAY
Grange Farm
South Ferriby Prim Sch
HIGH STREET
B1204
The Grange
Chalk Pit
MIDDLEGATE LANE
Beacon Hill
BARTON-UPON-HUMBER
Barton Hill Farm
BRIGG ROAD
HORKSTOW ROAD
Pit (disused)
North Wold Farm
Field House Farm
Barton Field Farm
Kingsforth
Chapel Farm
Kingsforth Farm
BRIDGE LANE
Manor Wold Farm
Horkstow Wolds
Turton's Covert
Pit (dis)
BRIGG ROAD
CHAPEL LA
B1204
OSTLER'S LA
Hall Top Farm
Viking Way
Horkstow
DN18
CARR LANE
A15
Quarry (dis)
MAIN STREET
The Oaks
Fox Covert Plantation
Old Belt Plantation
Beaumontcote Farm
Horkstow Grange
Field House Farm
Quarry (dis)
Bennett's New Covert
Pit (Dis)
SAXBY HILL
Saxby Wolds
B1218
B1206
NORTH CARR LANE
Hill Side Plantation
Pikendale Plantation
Grange Farm
Saxby All Saints
CHURCH LA
Bonby Lodge
Crow Wood Plantation
PARK LA
PARK LANE
MIDDLEGATE LANE
SAXBY ROAD
Forth Carr Plantation
CHURCH LANE
Tinsley Farm
Bonby Top Farm
South Plantation
Bonby
North Wold Farm
Bonby Ings
Sports Ground
PO
PH
MAIN STREET
DN20
South Wold Farm
Eleven Acre Plantation
CARR LANE
FUSSEY GD
WOLD ROAD
B1204
MIDDLE BARN HILL
Turnpike Top Farm
Land Drain
Bonby Carrs
BONBY ROAD
NEW RD
Worlaby
TOP RD
THE HILL
B1206
Bonby Ings
98 A 99 B 00 C 01 D 02 E 03 F

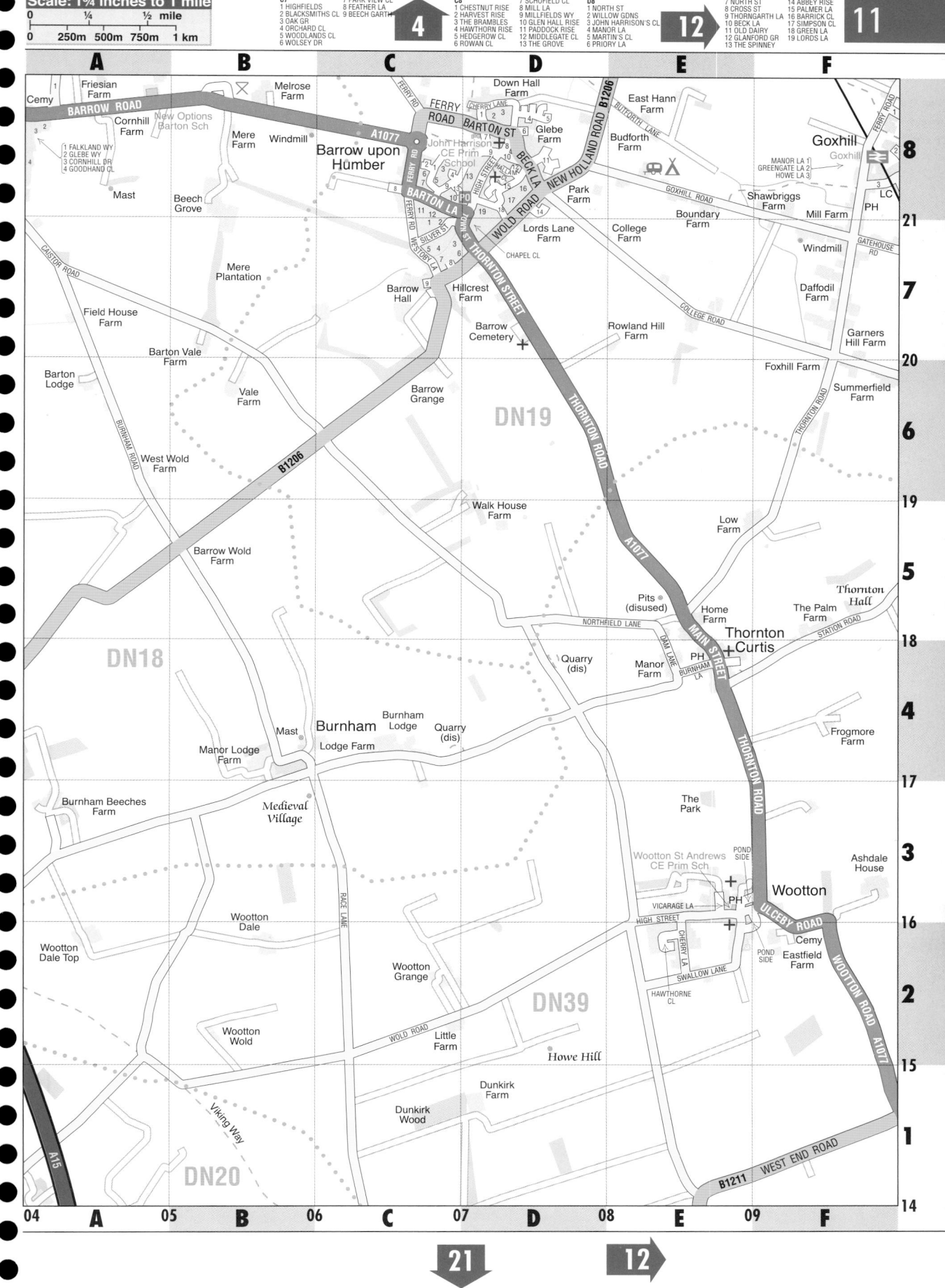
Scale: 1¾ inches to 1 mile
0 ¼ ½ mile
0 250m 500m 750m 1 km
C7
1 HIGHFIELDS
2 BLACKSMITHS CL
3 OAK GR
4 ORCHARD CL
5 WOODLANDS CL
6 WOLSEY DR
7 PARK VIEW CL
8 FEATHER LA
9 BEECH GARTH
4
C8
1 CHESTNUT RISE
2 HARVEST RISE
3 THE BRAMBLES
4 HAWTHORN RISE
5 HEDGEROW CL
6 ROWAN CL
7 SCHOFIELD CL
8 MILL LA
9 MILLFIELDS WY
10 GLEN HALL RISE
11 PADDOCK RISE
12 MIDDLEGATE CL
13 THE GROVE
D8
1 NORTH ST
2 WILLOW GDNS
3 JOHN HARRISON'S CL
4 MANOR LA
5 MARTIN'S CL
6 PRIORY LA
12
7 NORTH ST
8 CROSS ST
9 THORNGARTH LA
10 BECK LA
11 OLD DAIRY
12 GLANFORD GR
13 THE SPINNEY
14 ABBEY RISE
15 PALMER LA
16 BARRICK CL
17 SIMPSON CL
18 GREEN LA
19 LORDS LA
A B C D E F
Cemy
Friesian Farm
BARROW ROAD
Cornhill Farm
New Options Barton Sch
Melrose Farm
1 FALKLAND WY
2 GLEBE WY
3 CORNHILL DR
4 GOODHAND CL
Mere Farm
Windmill
A1077
Barrow upon Humber
FERRY RD
FERRY ROAD
BARTON ST
CHERRY LANE
Down Hall Farm
John Harrison CE Prim School
Glebe Farm
HIGH STREET
BECK LA
B1206
NEW HOLLAND ROAD
BUTFORTH LANE
East Hann Farm
Budforth Farm
Goxhill
FERRY ROAD
MANOR LA 1
GREENGATE LA 2
HOWE LA 3
Mast
Beech Grove
BARTON LA
PO
WOLD ROAD
Park Farm
GOXHILL ROAD
Shawbriggs Farm
LC
PH
Mill Farm
Boundary Farm
College Farm
Lords Lane Farm
CHAPEL CL
SILVER ST
WESTOBY LA
TOWN ST
THORNTON STREET
GATEHOUSE RD
Windmill
CAISTOR ROAD
Mere Plantation
Barrow Hall
Hillcrest Farm
Daffodil Farm
COLLEGE ROAD
Field House Farm
Barrow Cemetery
Rowland Hill Farm
Garners Hill Farm
Barton Vale Farm
Barton Lodge
Foxhill Farm
Vale Farm
Barrow Grange
DN19
THORNTON ROAD
Summerfield Farm
BURNHAM ROAD
West Wold Farm
B1206
Walk House Farm
Low Farm
Barrow Wold Farm
A1077
Thornton Hall
Pits (disused)
Home Farm
The Palm Farm
NORTHFIELD LANE
STATION ROAD
Thornton Curtis
MAIN STREET
DN18
Quarry (dis)
DAM LANE
Manor Farm
PH
BURNHAM LA
Burnham Lodge
Mast
Burnham
Quarry (dis)
Lodge Farm
Manor Lodge Farm
Frogmore Farm
THORNTON ROAD
Burnham Beeches Farm
Medieval Village
The Park
Wootton St Andrews CE Prim Sch
POND SIDE
Ashdale House
Wootton
PH
VICARAGE LA
RACE LANE
Wootton Dale
HIGH STREET
ULCEBY ROAD
Cemy
Wootton Dale Top
CHERRY LA
POND SIDE
Eastfield Farm
Wootton Grange
SWALLOW LANE
HAWTHORNE CL
WOOTTON ROAD
DN39
Wootton Wold
WOLD ROAD
Little Farm
Howe Hill
A1077
Dunkirk Farm
Dunkirk Wood
Viking Way
WEST END ROAD
A15
DN20
B1211
8 21 7 20 6 19 5 18 4 17 3 16 2 15 1 14
04 05 06 07 08 09
21
12

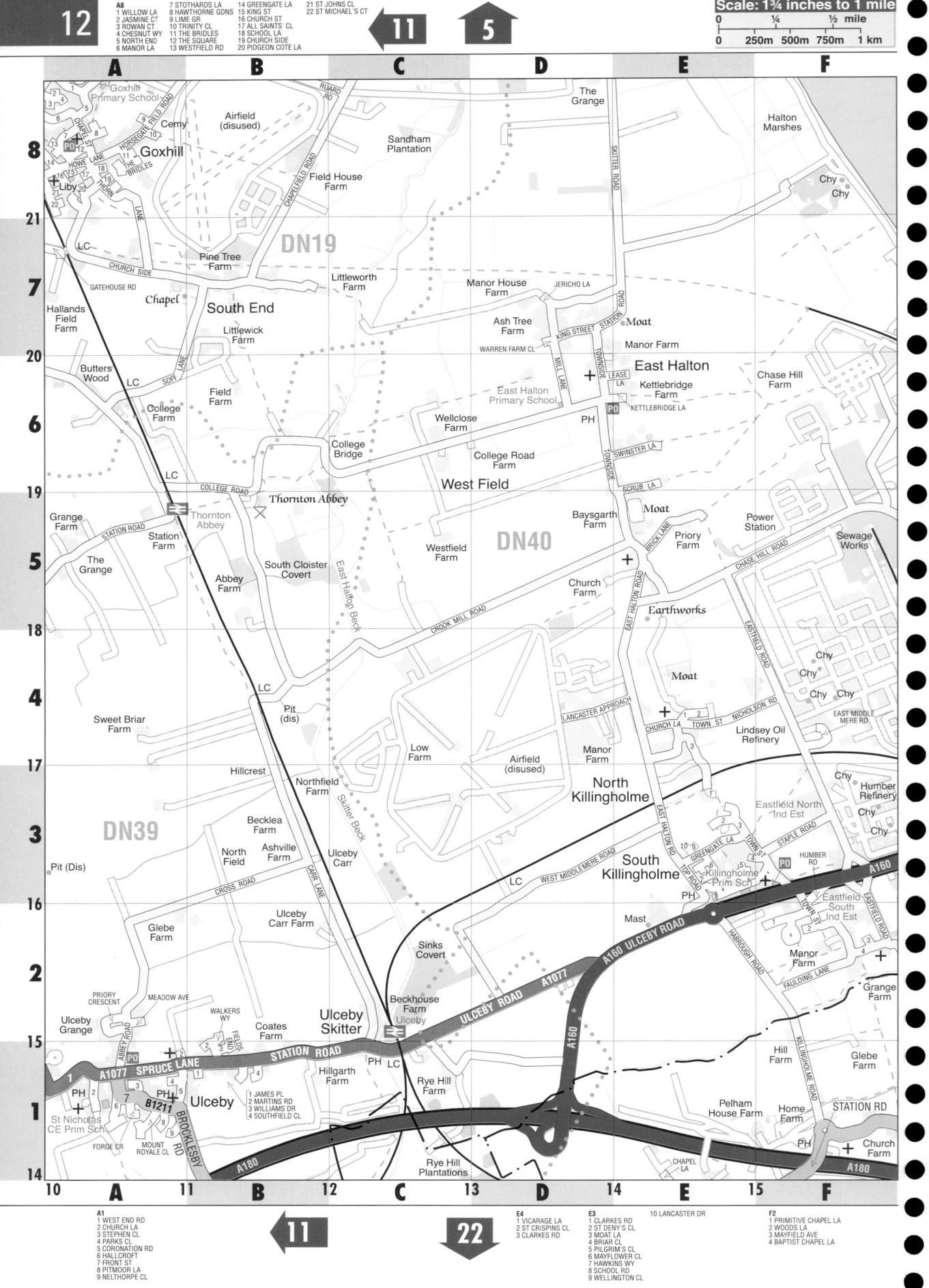

12

A8
1 WILLOW LA
2 JASMINE CT
3 ROWAN CT
4 CHESNUT WY
5 NORTH END
6 MANOR LA

7 STOTHARDS LA
8 HAWTHORNE GDNS
9 LIME GR
10 TRINITY CL
11 THE BRIDLES
12 THE SQUARE
13 WESTFIELD RD

14 GREENGATE LA
15 KING ST
16 CHURCH ST
17 ALL SAINTS' CL
18 SCHOOL LA
19 CHURCH SIDE
20 PIDGEON COTE LA

21 ST JOHNS CL
22 ST MICHAEL'S CT

Scale: 1¾ inches to 1 mile

0   ¼   ½ mile
0 250m 500m 750m 1 km

A1
1 WEST END RD
2 CHURCH LA
3 STEPHEN CL
4 PARKS CL
5 CORONATION RD
6 HALLCROFT
7 FRONT ST
8 PITMOOR LA
9 NELTHORPE CL

E4
1 VICARAGE LA
2 ST CRISPINS CL
3 CLARKES RD

E3
1 CLARKES RD
2 ST DENY'S CL
3 MOAT LA
4 BRIAR CL
5 PILGRIM'S CL
6 MAYFLOWER CL
7 HAWKINS WY
8 SCHOOL RD
9 WELLINGTON CL

10 LANCASTER DR

F2
1 PRIMITIVE CHAPEL LA
2 WOODS LA
3 MAYFIELD AVE
4 BAPTIST CHAPEL LA

A   B   C   D   E   F

8

21

7

20

6

19

5

18

4

17

3

16

2

15

1

14

Foulholme Sands

CHERRY COBB SANDS RD

Cherry Cobb Sands

Oil Terminal

HAVEN RD

LC

HAVEN ROAD

Killingholme Haven Pits Nature Reserve

Killingholme Marshes

STATION ROAD

LC

Mast

Sewage Works

Killingholme High Lighthouse

Burkinshaw's Covert

EAST MIDDLE MERE ROAD

ROSPER ROAD

LC

MARSH LANE

Oil Refineries

MARSH LANE

LC

DN40

HUMBER RD

South Killingholme Haven

186

LC

A160

Chy

HUMBER ROAD

A1173

WEST HAVEN

Water Tower

LC

LC

WEST RIVERSIDE

187

Immingham Dock

Houlton's Covert

MANBY ROAD

SOUTHERN WY

SOUTHERN ROAD

SEVEN QUAY RD

ROBINSON ROAD

LC

East End Farm

186

Immingham Golf Course

MANBY ROAD BY PASS

GRESLEY WAY

LC

Cemy

MILL LANE

CH

STANSFIELD GDNS

CHURCH LANE

WASHDYKE LANE

WOODLANDS AV

Football Gd

MANBY RD

P

BATTERY ST

P

Sports Ground

Chimney

LAPORTE ROAD

Chimney

Humber Bank Factories

PILGRIMS WY

Recn Gd

BLUESTONE LANE

CLIFTON DR

SONIA CREST

PARK

WINSLOW DR

P

Liby

Sch

SPRING ST

WORSLEY RD

P

KINGS RD

KINGS RD

A1173

QUEENS RD

DN41

ROYAL DR

Sch

PH

P

PRINCESS ST

PELHAM ROAD

MARGARET ST

PILGRIM AVENUE

TALBOT RD

Immingham

A1173

Spoil Heap

EUROPA WAY

Luxmore Farm

B1210

PO

P

Sch

HADLEIGH RD

CORFE WALK

NETHERLANDS WY

Kiln Lane Ind Est

KILN LANE

LC

HORSON WAY

HABROUGH RD

HUME BRAE

Sch

For full street detail of the highlighted area see pages 186 & 187.

186   23   187   187

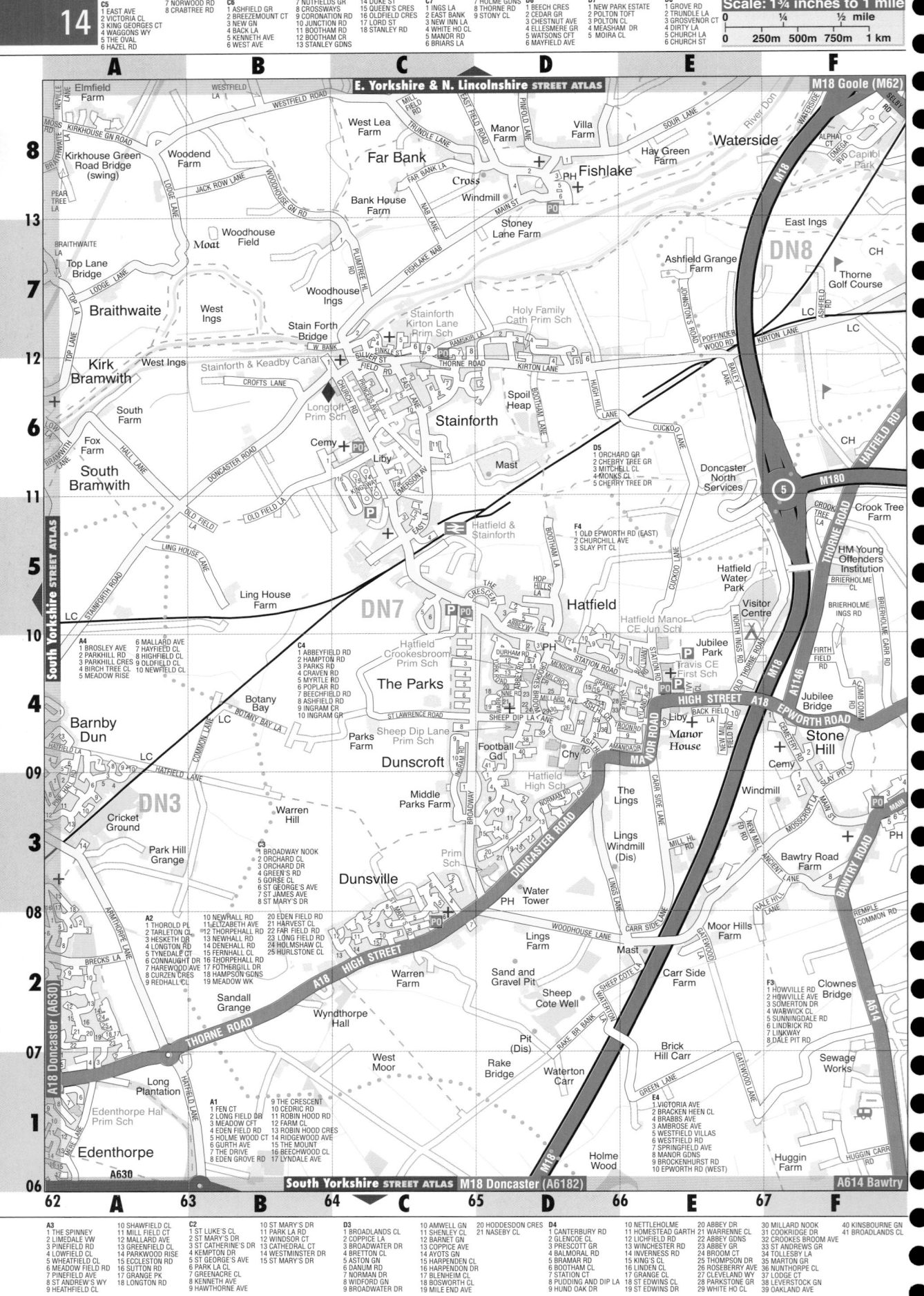

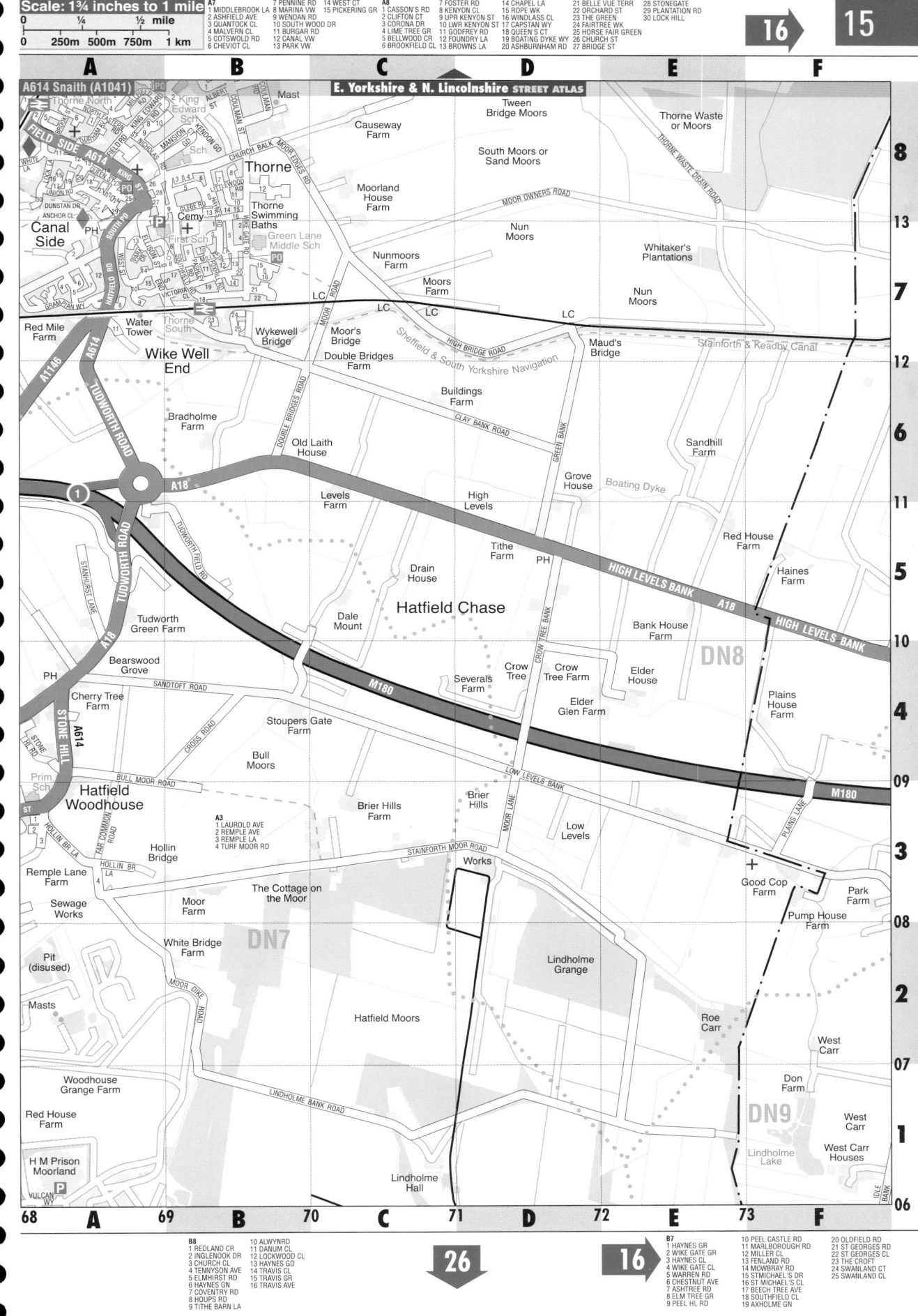

A7
1 MIDDLEBROOK LA
2 ASHFIELD AVE
3 QUANTOCK CL
4 MALVERN CL
5 COTSWOLD RD
6 CHEVIOT CL

7 PENNINE RD
8 MARINA VW
9 WENDAN RD
10 SOUTH WOOD DR
11 BURGAR RD
12 CANAL VW
13 PARK VW

14 WEST CT
15 PICKERING GR

A8
1 CASSON'S RD
2 CLIFTON CT
3 CORONA DR
4 LIME TREE GR
5 BELLWOOD CR
6 BROOKFIELD CL

7 FOSTER RD
8 KENYON CL
9 UPR KENYON ST
10 LWR KENYON ST
11 GODFREY RD
12 FOUNDRY LA
13 BROWNS LA

14 CHAPEL LA
15 ROPE WK
16 WINDLASS CL
17 CAPSTAN WY
18 QUEEN'S CT
19 BOATING DYKE WY
20 ASHBURNHAM RD

21 BELLE VUE TERR
22 ORCHARD ST
23 THE GREEN
24 FAIRTREE WK
25 HORSE FAIR GREEN
26 CHURCH ST
27 BRIDGE ST

28 STONEGATE
29 PLANTATION RD
30 LOCK HILL

A   B   C   D   E   F

A614 Snaith (A1041)

E. Yorkshire & N. Lincolnshire STREET ATLAS

Thorne North
King Edward Sch
King Edward St
Mast
Thorne

Causeway Farm

Tween Bridge Moors

Thorne Waste or Moors

8

FIELD SIDE   A614

South Moors or Sand Moors

13

Canal Side
Thorne Swimming Baths
Moorland House Farm

Nun Moors

Whitaker's Plantations

Cemy
First Sch
Green Lane Middle Sch
PO

Nunmoors Farm

7

Nun Moors

Water Tower
Wike Well End
Thorne South
Wykewell Bridge
Moor's Bridge
Double Bridges Farm

Moors Farm

LC   LC   LC

HIGH BRIDGE ROAD

Maud's Bridge

LC

Stainforth & Keadby Canal

Red Mile Farm

Sheffield & South Yorkshire Navigation

12

A1146   A614

Bradholme Farm

Buildings Farm

CLAY BANK ROAD

GREEN BANK

Sandhill Farm

6

TUDWORTH ROAD

Old Laith House

Grove House

Boating Dyke

Levels Farm

High Levels

Red House Farm

11

A18

Tithe Farm
PH

HIGH LEVELS BANK   A18

Haines Farm

5

STANHURST LANE

TUDWORTH-FIELD RD

Drain House

Hatfield Chase

Bank House Farm

HIGH LEVELS BANK

A18

Dale Mount

CROW TREE BANK

DN8

10

Tudworth Green Farm

Crow Tree
Crow Tree Farm
Elder House

Plains House Farm

4

Bearswood Grove

SANDTOFT ROAD

Severals Farm

Elder Glen Farm

M180

PH

CROSS ROAD

Stoupers Gate Farm

Low Levels Bank

09

STONE HILL   A614

Cherry Tree Farm

Bull Moors

M180

Prim Sch

Brier Hills Farm

Brier Hills

Hatfield Woodhouse

MOOR LANE

A3
1 LAUROLD AVE
2 REMPLE AVE
3 REMPLE LA
4 TURF MOOR RD

Low Levels

Good Cop Farm

Park Farm

3

HOLLIN BR LA

Hollin Bridge

HOLLIN BR LA

STAINFORTH MOOR ROAD

Works

PLAINS LANE

Pump House Farm

Remple Lane Farm

Sewage Works

Moor Farm

The Cottage on the Moor

Lindholme Grange

08

TAR COMMON ROAD

White Bridge Farm

DN7

Roe Carr

West Carr

2

Pit (disused)

MOOR DIKE ROAD

Hatfield Moors

07

Masts

Don Farm

Woodhouse Grange Farm

LINDHOLME BANK ROAD

DN9

West Carr

Red House Farm

Lindholme Lake

West Carr Houses

1

H M Prison Moorland
P
VULCAN WY

Lindholme Hall

IDLE BANK

06

68   A   69   B   70   C   71   D   72   E   73   F

B8
1 REDLAND CR
2 INGLENOOK DR
3 CHURCH CL
4 TENNYSON AVE
5 ELMHIRST RD
6 HAYNES GN
7 COVENTRY RD
8 HOUPS RD
9 TITHE BARN LA

10 ALWYNRD
11 DANUM CL
12 LOCKWOOD CL
13 HAYNES GD
14 TRAVIS CL
15 TRAVIS AVE
16 TRAVIS AVE

26

16

B7
1 HAYNES GR
2 WIKE GATE GR
3 HAYNES CL
4 WIKE GATE CL
5 WARREN RD
6 CHESTNUT AVE
7 ASHTREE RD
8 ELM TREE GR
9 PEEL HL RD

10 PEEL CASTLE RD
11 MARLBOROUGH RD
12 MILLER CL
13 FENLAND RD
14 MOWBRAY RD
15 STMICHAEL'S DR
16 ST MICHAEL'S CL
17 BEECH TREE AVE
18 SOUTHFIELD CL
19 AXHOLME GN

20 OLDFIELD CL
21 ST GEORGES RD
22 ST GEORGES CL
23 THE CROFT
24 SWANLAND CT
25 SWANLAND CL

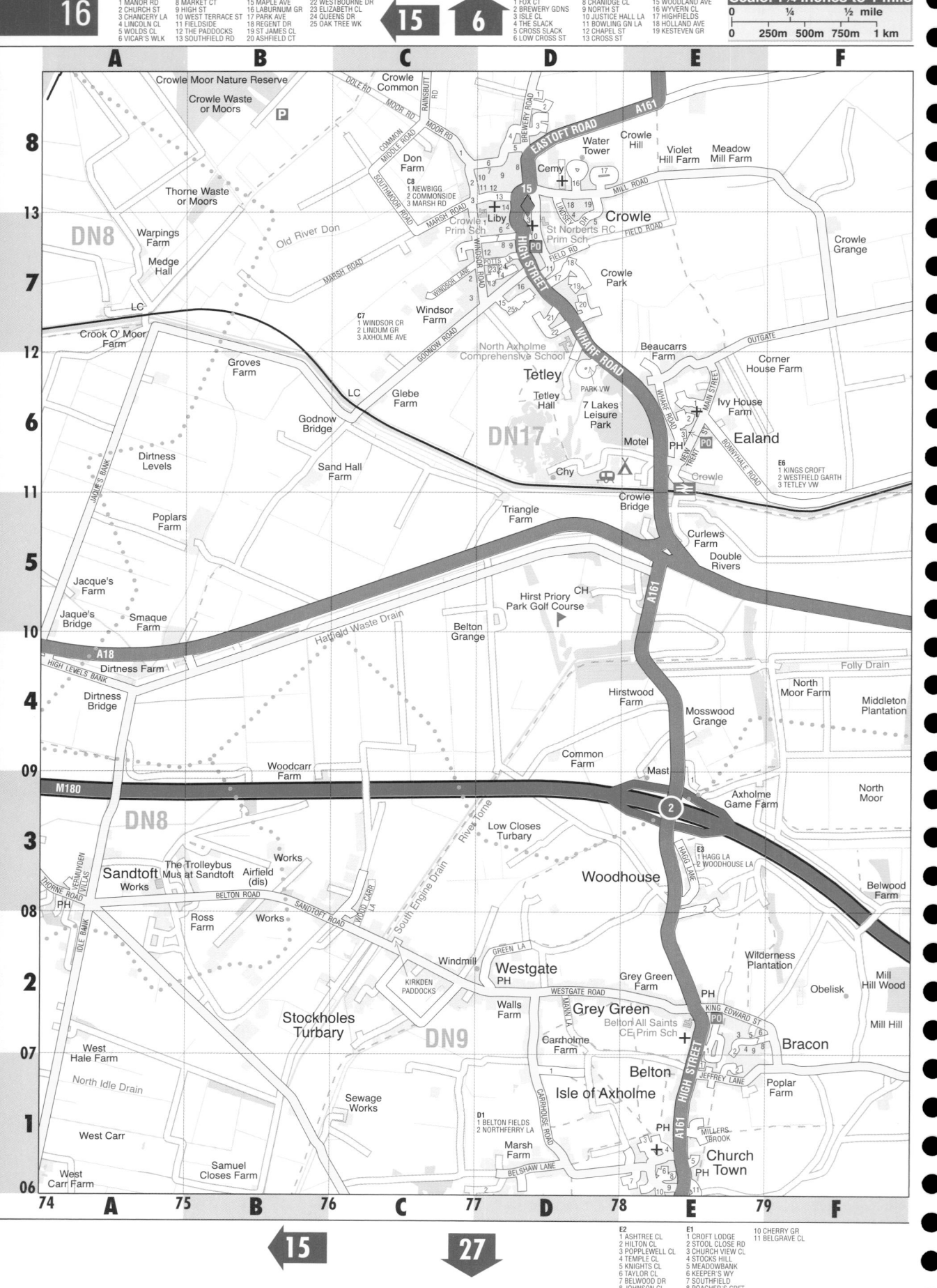

D7
1 MANOR RD
2 CHURCH ST
3 CHANCERY LA
4 LINCOLN CL
5 WOLDS CL
6 VICAR'S WLK
7 JOHNSON'S LA
8 MARKET CT
9 HIGH ST
10 WEST TERRACE ST
11 FIELDSIDE
12 THE PADDOCKS
13 SOUTHFIELD RD
14 CROWLAND RD
15 MAPLE AVE
16 LABURNUM GR
17 PARK AVE
18 REGENT DR
19 ST JAMES CL
20 ASHFIELD CT
21 MULBERRY DR
22 WESTBOURNE DR
23 ELIZABETH CL
24 QUEENS DR
25 OAK TREE WK

D8
1 FOX CT
2 BREWERY GDNS
3 ISLE CL
4 THE SLACK
5 CROSS SLACK
6 LOW CROSS ST
7 COX LA
8 CRANIDGE CL
9 NORTH ST
10 JUSTICE HALL LA
11 BOWLING GN LA
12 CHAPEL ST
13 CROSS ST
14 PRINTING OFFICE LA
15 WOODLAND AVE
16 WYVERN CL
17 HIGHFIELDS
18 HOLLAND AVE
19 KESTEVEN GR

15 6

A   B   C   D   E   F

8

Crowle Moor Nature Reserve
Crowle Waste
or Moors
P

Crowle
Common

D8
1 FOX CT
2 BREWERY GDNS
3 ISLE CL
4 THE SLACK
5 CROSS SLACK
6 LOW CROSS ST

EASTOFT ROAD
A161
BREWERY ROAD
Water
Tower
Crowle
Hill
Violet
Hill Farm
Meadow
Mill Farm

Thorne Waste
or Moors

COMMON MIDDLE ROAD
SOUTHMOOR ROAD
DOLE RD
MOOR RD
Don
Farm
RAINSBUTT RD

C8
1 NEWBIGG
2 COMMONSIDE
3 MARSH RD

Cemy
MILL ROAD
Crowle

13

DN8

Warpings
Farm
Medge
Hall

Old River Don
MARSH ROAD

Crowle
Prim Sch
Libry
PO
St Norberts RC
Prim Sch
FIELD ROAD
Crowle
Grange

15

7

MARSH ROAD
WINDSOR ROAD
POTTS
HIGH STREET
Crowle
Park

Crowle
Grange

LC

C7
1 WINDSOR CR
2 LINDUM GR
3 AXHOLME AVE

Windsor
Farm
GODNOW ROAD
North Axholme
Comprehensive School
Tetley

WHARF ROAD
Beaucarrs
Farm
OUTGATE
MAIN STREET
Corner
House Farm

12

Crook O' Moor
Farm

Groves
Farm

LC
Glebe
Farm

Tetley
Hall
7 Lakes
Leisure Park
PARK VW

Ivy House
Farm
Ealand

6

JACQUE'S BANK

Dirtness
Levels

Godnow
Bridge
Sand Hall
Farm

DN17

Motel
Chy
PH
NEW TREN
PO
Crowle

E6
1 KINGS CROFT
2 WESTFIELD GARTH
3 TETLEY VW

BONWHALE ROAD

11

Poplars
Farm

Triangle
Farm
Crowle
Bridge
Crowle

5

Jacque's
Farm

Jacque's
Bridge
Smaque
Farm

Hirst Priory
Park Golf Course
CH
A161

Curlews
Farm
Double
Rivers

10

A18
Dirtness Farm
Hatfield Waste Drain
Belton
Grange

Folly Drain

09

HIGH LEVELS BANK

Dirtness
Bridge

Woodcarr
Farm
Hirstwood
Farm
Mosswood
Grange
North
Moor Farm
Middleton
Plantation

4

M180
DN8

River Torne
Common
Farm
Mast
Axholme
Game Farm
North
Moor

3

THORNE ROAD
VERMUYDEN VILLAS
IDLE BANK

Sandtoft
The Trolleybus
Mus at Sandtoft
Works
Airfield
(dis)
Works
Low Closes
Turbary
2
HAGG LANE
E3
1 HAGG LA
2 WOODHOUSE LA
Woodhouse
Belwood
Farm

08

PH
Ross
Farm
BELTON ROAD
Works
SANDTOFT ROAD
WOODCARR LA
South Engine Drain
Windmill

GREEN LA
Westgate
PH
Grey Green
Farm
Wilderness
Plantation
Mill
Hill Wood

2

Stockholes
Turbary
KIRKDEN
PADDOCKS
Walls
Farm
WESTGATE ROAD
MAIN LA
Grey Green
PH
KING EDWARD ST
PO
Obelisk
Mill Hill

07

West
Hale Farm
DN9
Cartholme
Farm
Belton All Saints
CE Prim Sch
Bracon
Poplar
Farm

North Idle Drain
HIGH STREET
JEFFREY LANE

1

West
Carr
Sewage
Works
D1
1 BELTON FIELDS
2 NORTHFERRY LA
Belton
Isle of Axholme
MILLERS BROOK
A161
PH

06

West
Carr Farm
Samuel
Closes Farm
Marsh
Farm
BELSHAW LANE
CARHOLME ROAD
PH
Church
Town

74   A   75   B   76   C   77   D   78   E   79   F

15 27

E2
1 ASHTREE CL
2 HILTON CL
3 POPPLEWELL CL
4 TEMPLE CL
5 KNIGHTS CL
6 TAYLOR CL
7 BELWOOD DR
8 JOHNSON CL
9 BRACON CL

E1
1 CROFT LODGE
2 STOOL CLOSE RD
3 CHURCH VIEW CL
4 STOCKS HILL
5 MEADOWBANK
6 KEEPER'S WY
7 SOUTHFIELD
8 POACHER'S CRFT
9 CHURCHTOWN

10 CHERRY GR
11 BELGRAVE CL

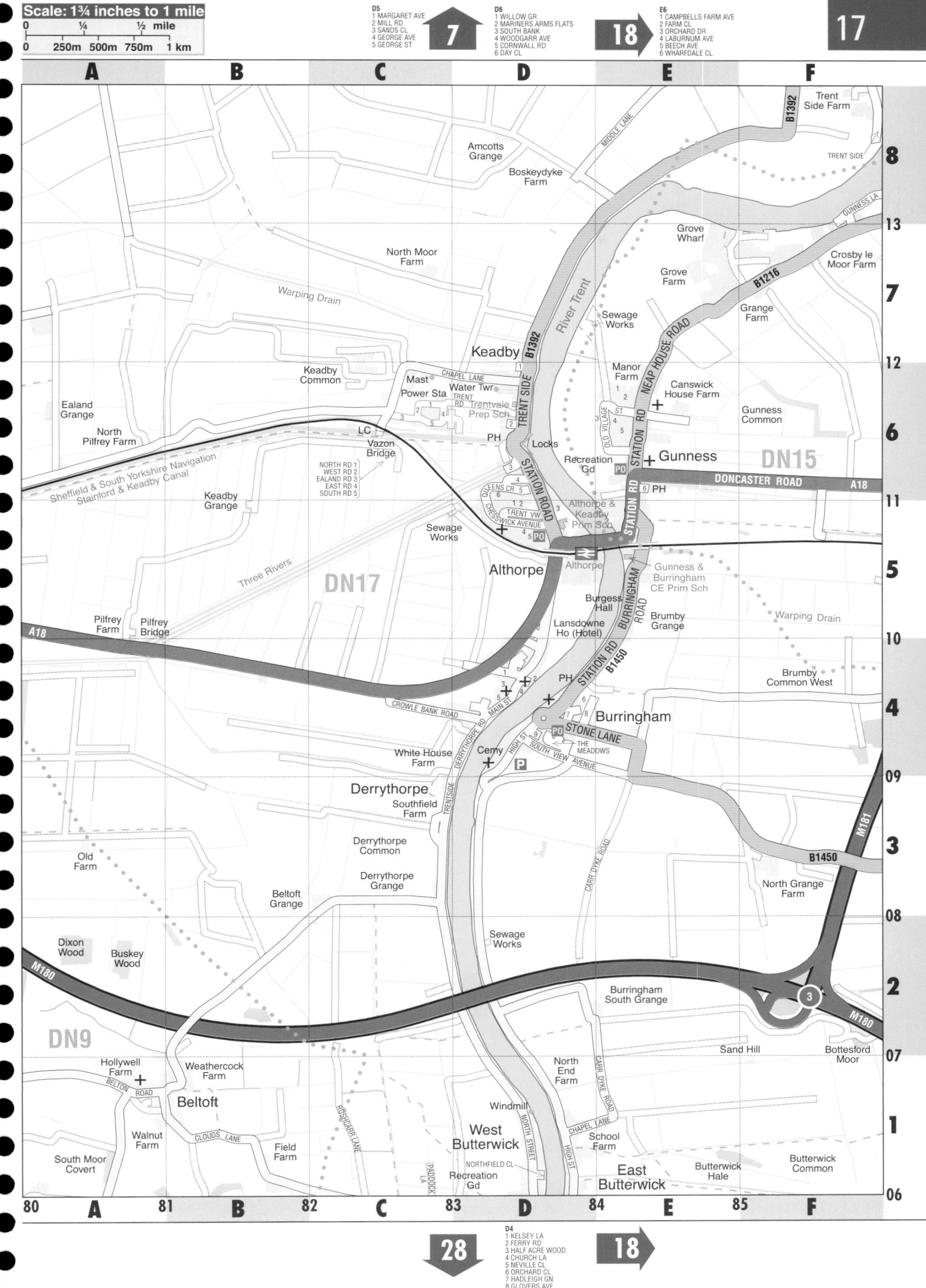

Scale: 1¾ inches to 1 mile

0 | ¼ | ½ mile
0 | 250m | 500m | 750m | 1 km

D5
1 MARGARET AVE
2 MILL RD
3 SANDS CL
4 GEORGE AVE
5 GEORGE ST

7

D6
1 WILLOW GR
2 MARINERS ARMS FLATS
3 SOUTH BANK
4 WOODGARR AVE
5 CORNWALL RD
6 DAY CL

18

E6
1 CAMPBELLS FARM AVE
2 FARM CL
3 ORCHARD DR
4 LABURNUM AVE
5 BEECH AVE
6 WHARFDALE CL

17

28

D4
1 KELSEY LA
2 FERRY RD
3 HALF ACRE WOOD
4 CHURCH LA
5 NEVILLE CL
6 ORCHARD CL
7 HADLEIGH GN
8 GLOVERS AVE
9 PASTURE AVE

18

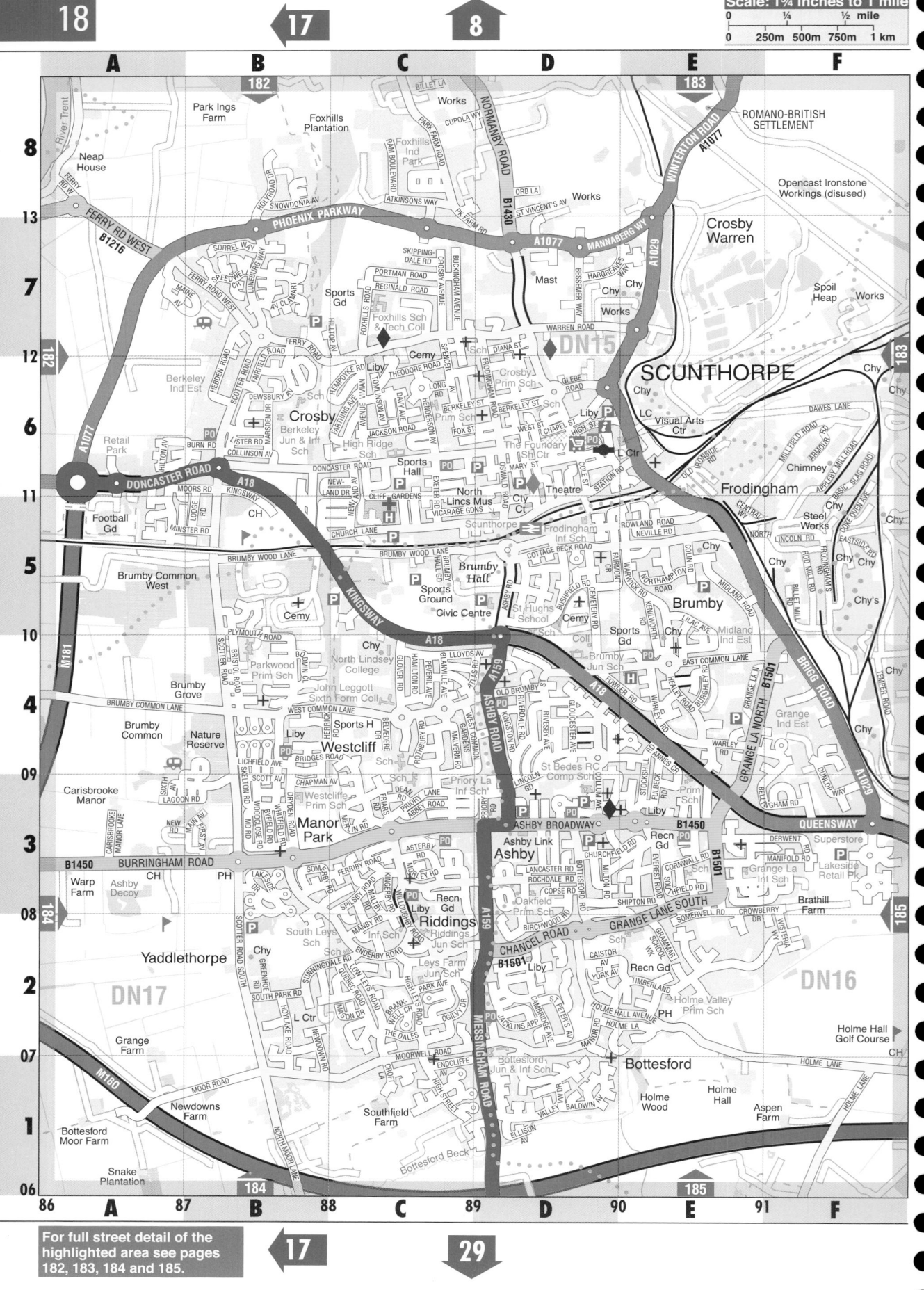

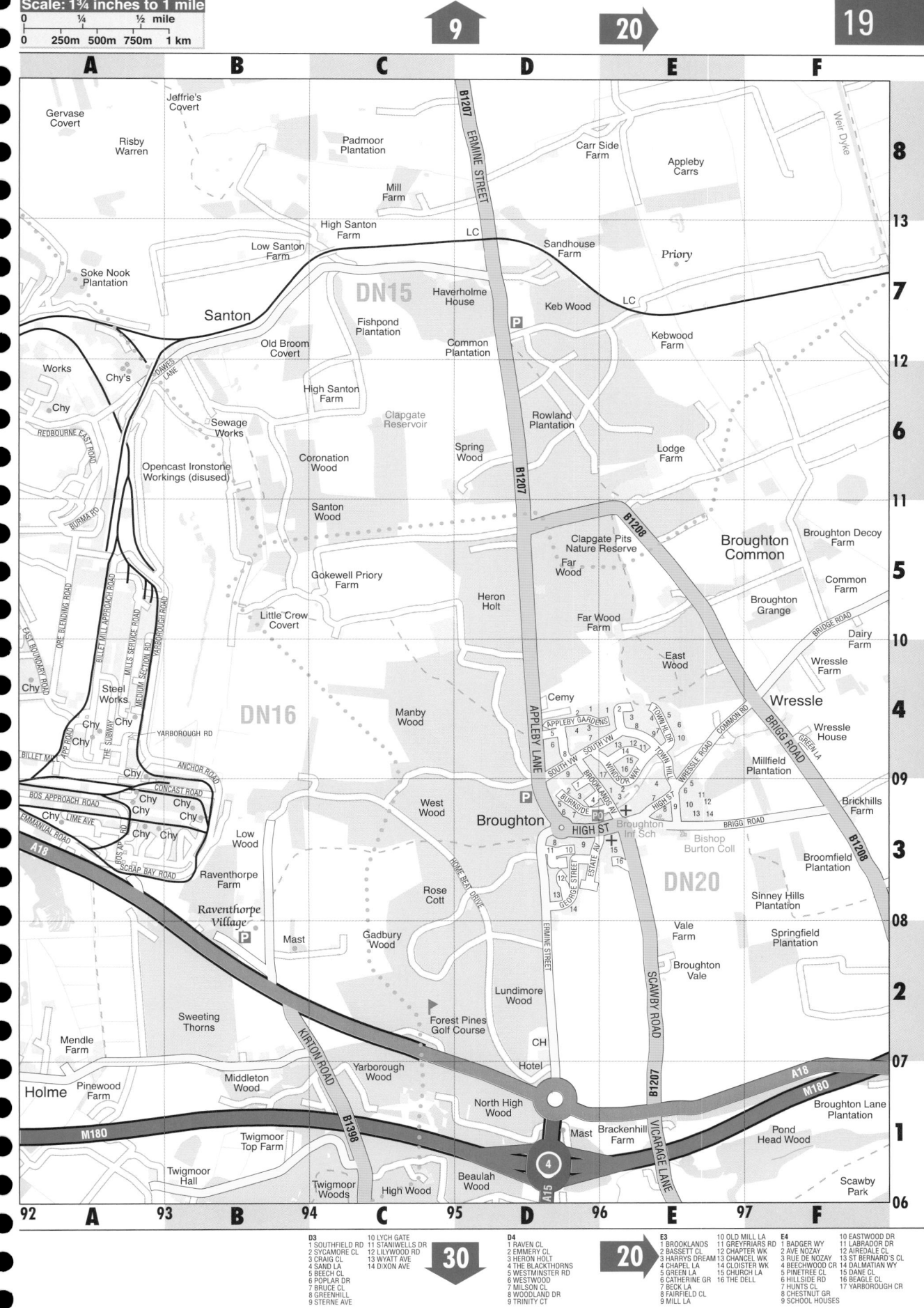

Gervase Covert

Jeffrie's Covert

Padmoor Plantation

Risby Warren

Carr Side Farm

Appleby Carrs

Weir Dyke

Mill Farm

High Santon Farm

Low Santon Farm

LC

Sandhouse Farm

Priory

Soke Nook Plantation

Santon

DN15

Haverholme House

Keb Wood

LC

Kebwood Farm

Works

Chy's

Old Broom Covert

Fishpond Plantation

Common Plantation

Rowland Plantation

Chy

Chy

REDBOURNE EAST ROAD

DAWES LANE

Sewage Works

High Santon Farm

Clapgate Reservoir

Spring Wood

B1207

Lodge Farm

BURMA RD

Opencast Ironstone Workings (disused)

Coronation Wood

B1208

Broughton Common

Broughton Decoy Farm

Santon Wood

Clapgate Pits Nature Reserve

Far Wood

Common Farm

ORE BLENDING ROAD

BILLET MILL APPROACH ROAD

MILLS SERVICE ROAD

YARBOROUGH ROAD

Gokewell Priory Farm

Heron Holt

Far Wood Farm

Broughton Grange

BRIDGE ROAD

Dairy Farm

EAST BOUNDARY ROAD

Little Crow Covert

Wressle Farm

Steel Works

DN16

Manby Wood

East Wood

Cemy

Wressle

Wressle House

Chy

Chy

THE SUBWAY

YARBOROUGH RD

Appleby Gardens

TOWN DR

Millfield Plantation

GREEN LA

BRIGG ROAD

BILLET MILL

APP RD

ANCHOR ROAD

APPLEY LANE

SOUTH VW

SOUTH VW

WINDSOR WAY

TOWN HILL

WRESSLE ROAD

COMMON RD

Brickhills Farm

B1208

CONCAST ROAD

Chy Chy Chy

BROOKLANDS

HIGH ST

BRIGG ROAD

BOS APPROACH ROAD

Chy Chy Chy

Low Wood

West Wood

BURNSIDE

Broughton

HIGH ST

Broughton Inf Sch

Broomfield Plantation

LIME AVE

EMMANUAL ROAD

SCRAP BAY ROAD

Raventhorpe Farm

HOME BEAT DRIVE

GEORGE STREET

ESTATE AV

Bishop Burton Coll

DN20

Sinney Hills Plantation

A18

Raventhorpe Village

Mast

Gadbury Wood

Rose Cott

Vale Farm

Springfield Plantation

Mendle Farm

Sweeting Thorns

ERMINE STREET

Lundimore Wood

Broughton Vale

SCAWBY ROAD

Holme

Pinewood Farm

Middleton Wood

KIRTON ROAD

Yarborough Wood

Forest Pines Golf Course

CH

Hotel

B1207

A18

M180

Broughton Lane Plantation

M180

B1398

Twigmoor Top Farm

North High Wood

Mast

Brackenhill Farm

VICARAGE LANE

Pond Head Wood

Twigmoor Hall

Twigmoor Woods

High Wood

Beaulah Wood

A15

4

Scawby Park

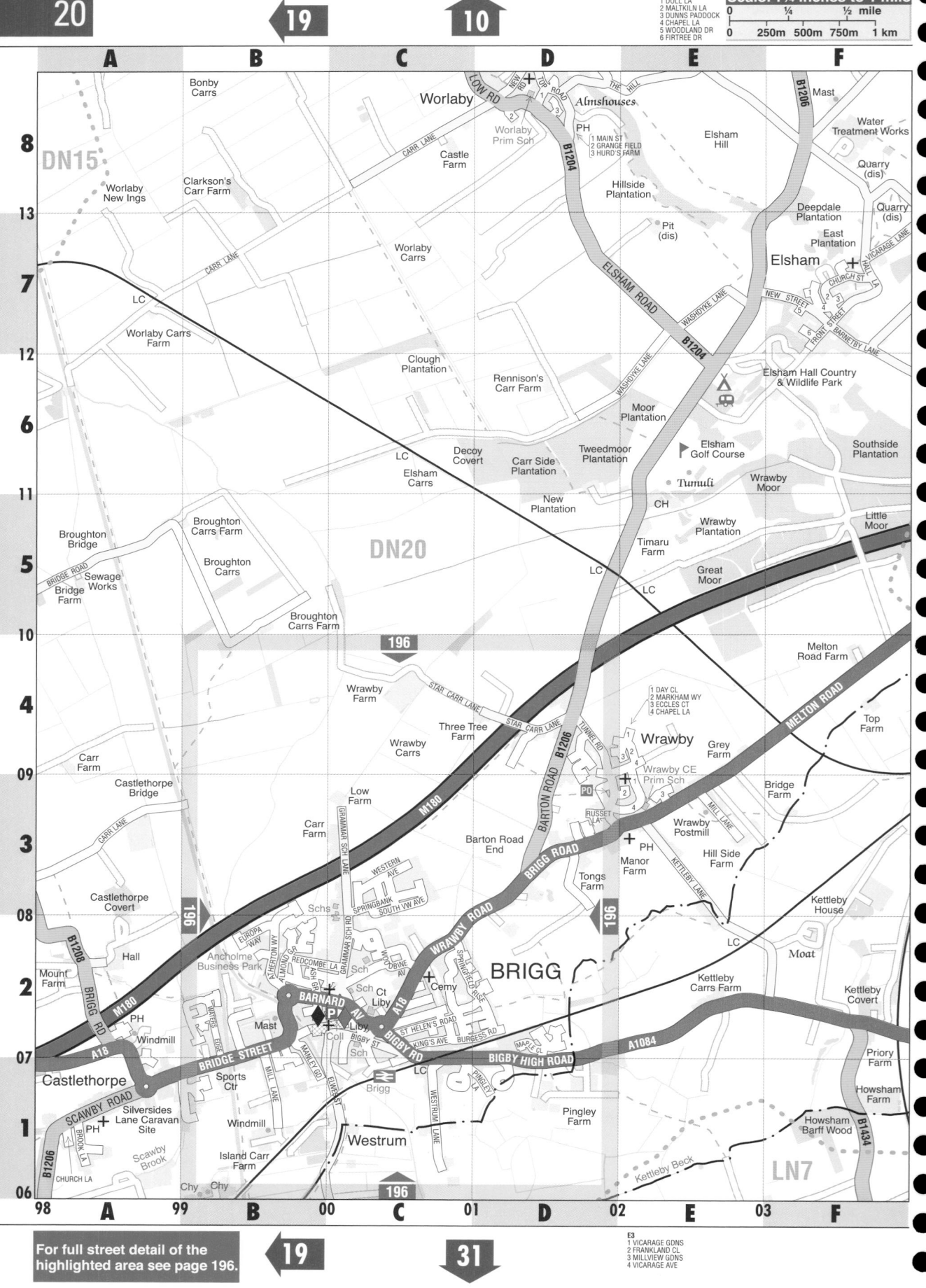

19
10

F7
1 DOLL LA
2 MALTKILN LA
3 DUNNS PADDOCK
4 CHAPEL LA
5 WOODLAND DR
6 FIRTREE DR

Scale: 1¾ inches to 1 mile
0   ¼   ½ mile
0   250m 500m 750m 1 km

DN15

Bonby Carrs

Worlaby

Almshouses

Elsham Hill

B1206
Mast

Water Treatment Works

Worlaby New Ings

Clarkson's Carr Farm

Carr Lane

Castle Farm

Worlaby Prim Sch

1 MAIN ST
2 GRANGE FIELD
3 HURD'S FARM

PH

Hillside Plantation

Deepdale Plantation

Quarry (dis)

Elsham

Quarry (dis)

LC

Worlaby Carrs Farm

Carr Lane

Worlaby Carrs

Clough Plantation

Pit (dis)

ELSHAM ROAD

East Plantation

CHURCH ST

NEW STREET

FRONT STREET

BARNETBY LANE

VICARAGE LANE

Rennison's Carr Farm

B1204

Moor Plantation

Elsham Hall Country & Wildlife Park

Broughton Bridge

Broughton Carrs Farm

LC

Decoy Covert

Elsham Carrs

Carr Side Plantation

Tweedmoor Plantation

Elsham Golf Course

Tumuli

Wrawby Moor

Southside Plantation

DN20

New Plantation

CH

Wrawby Plantation

Bridge Road

Sewage Works

Broughton Carrs

Broughton Carrs Farm

LC

LC

Timaru Farm

Great Moor

Little Moor

Bridge Farm

Carr Farm

Castlethorpe Bridge

196

Wrawby Farm

STAR CARR LANE

STAR CARR LANE

TUNNEL RD

B1206

1 DAY CL
2 MARKHAM WY
3 ECCLES CT
4 CHAPEL LA

Wrawby

Grey Farm

MELTON ROAD

Melton Road Farm

Top Farm

Carr Lane

Three Tree Farm

Wrawby Carrs

Low Farm

M180

Carr Farm

Wrawby CE Prim Sch

PO

Bridge Farm

Castlethorpe Covert

BARTON ROAD

Barton Road End

RUSSET LA

Wrawby Postmill

Kettleby House

Hall

196

GRAMMAR SCH LANE

WESTERN AVE

BRIGG ROAD

Tongs Farm

Manor Farm

PH

Wrawby Hill Side Farm

196

LC

Moat

Mount Farm

M180

PH

EUROPA WAY

ATHERTON WY

ALMOND DR

REDCOMBE LA

GRAMMAR

ASH

SOUTH VW AVE

SPRINGBANK

WOODBINE AV

Sch

BRIGG

Kettleby Carrs Farm

Kettleby Covert

B1208

BRIGG RD

A18

Windmill

Anholme Business Park

WAYS GR

Schs

Sch

Ct Liby

BARNARD PL

Liby

Cemy

SPRINGFIELD RD

A1084

A18

Castlethorpe

BRIDGE STREET

Sports Ctr

Mast

Coll

BIGBY RD

St HELEN'S ROAD

KING'S AVE

BURGESS RD

BIGBY HIGH ROAD

Priory Farm

SCAWBY ROAD

MILL LANE

ELMWEST

Bigby St

Sch

MARLEY GR

WESTRUM LANE

PINGLEY LA

MASTLE CL

LC

Howsham Farm

PH

Windmill

Brigg

Pingley Farm

B1434

B1206

BROOK LA

CHURCH LA

Scawby Brook

Silversides Lane Caravan Site

Island Carr Farm

Westrum

Kettleby Beck

Howsham Barff Wood

LN7

Chy

Chy

196

196

E3
1 VICARAGE GDNS
2 FRANKLAND CL
3 MILLVIEW GDNS
4 VICARAGE AVE

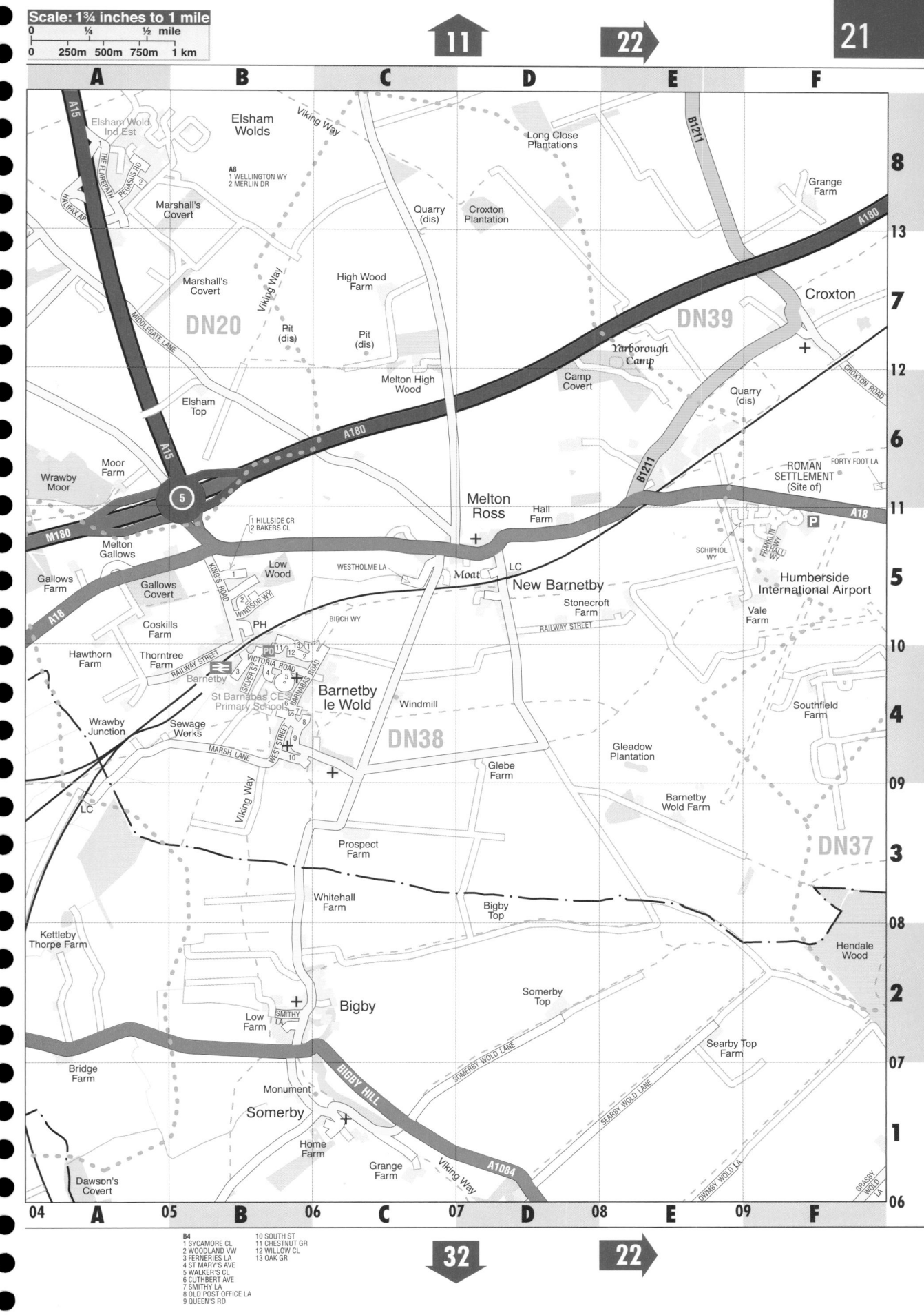

Scale: 1¾ inches to 1 mile

0 ¼ ½ mile
0 250m 500m 750m 1 km

Elsham Wold Ind Est
Elsham Wolds

A8
1 WELLINGTON WY
2 MERLIN DR

Marshall's Covert

Long Close Plantations

Quarry (dis)

Croxton Plantation

Grange Farm

Marshall's Covert

High Wood Farm

DN20

Croxton

DN39

Pit (dis)

Pit (dis)

Melton High Wood

Yarborough Camp

Camp Covert

Quarry (dis)

Elsham Top

CROXTON ROAD

MIDDLEGATE LANE

Moor Farm

Wrawby Moor

ROMAN SETTLEMENT (Site of)

FORTY FOOT LA

B1211

5

Melton Ross

Hall Farm

A18

Melton Gallows

M180

P

FRANKLIN HALL WY

SCHIPHOL WY

1 HILLSIDE CR
2 BAKERS CL

Gallows Farm

Gallows Covert

KING'S ROAD

Low Wood

WESTHOLME LA

Moat

LC

New Barnetby

Humberside International Airport

WINDSOR WY

Coskills Farm

PH

BIRCH WY

Stonecroft Farm

Vale Farm

RAILWAY STREET

Hawthorn Farm

Thorntree Farm

RAILWAY STREET

Barnetby

VICTORIA ROAD

PO

SILVER LA

St Barnabas CE Primary School

Barnetby le Wold

Windmill

DN38

Southfield Farm

Wrawby Junction

Sewage Works

WEST STREET

SANDERS ROAD

Gleadow Plantation

LC

MARSH LANE

Viking Way

Glebe Farm

Barnetby Wold Farm

DN37

Prospect Farm

Kettleby Thorpe Farm

Whitehall Farm

Bigby Top

Hendale Wood

SOMERBY WOLD LANE

Somerby Top

Searby Top Farm

Bridge Farm

Low Farm

SMITHY LA

Bigby

BIGBY HILL

Monument

Somerby

Home Farm

Grange Farm

Viking Way

A1084

SEARBY WOLD LANE

OWMBY WOLD LA

GRASBY WOLD LA

Dawson's Covert

B4
1 SYCAMORE CL
2 WOODLAND VW
3 FERNERIES LA
4 ST MARY'S AVE
5 WALKER'S CL
6 CUTHBERT AVE
7 SMITHY LA
8 OLD POST OFFICE LA
9 QUEEN'S RD
10 SOUTH ST
11 CHESTNUT GR
12 WILLOW CL
13 OAK GR

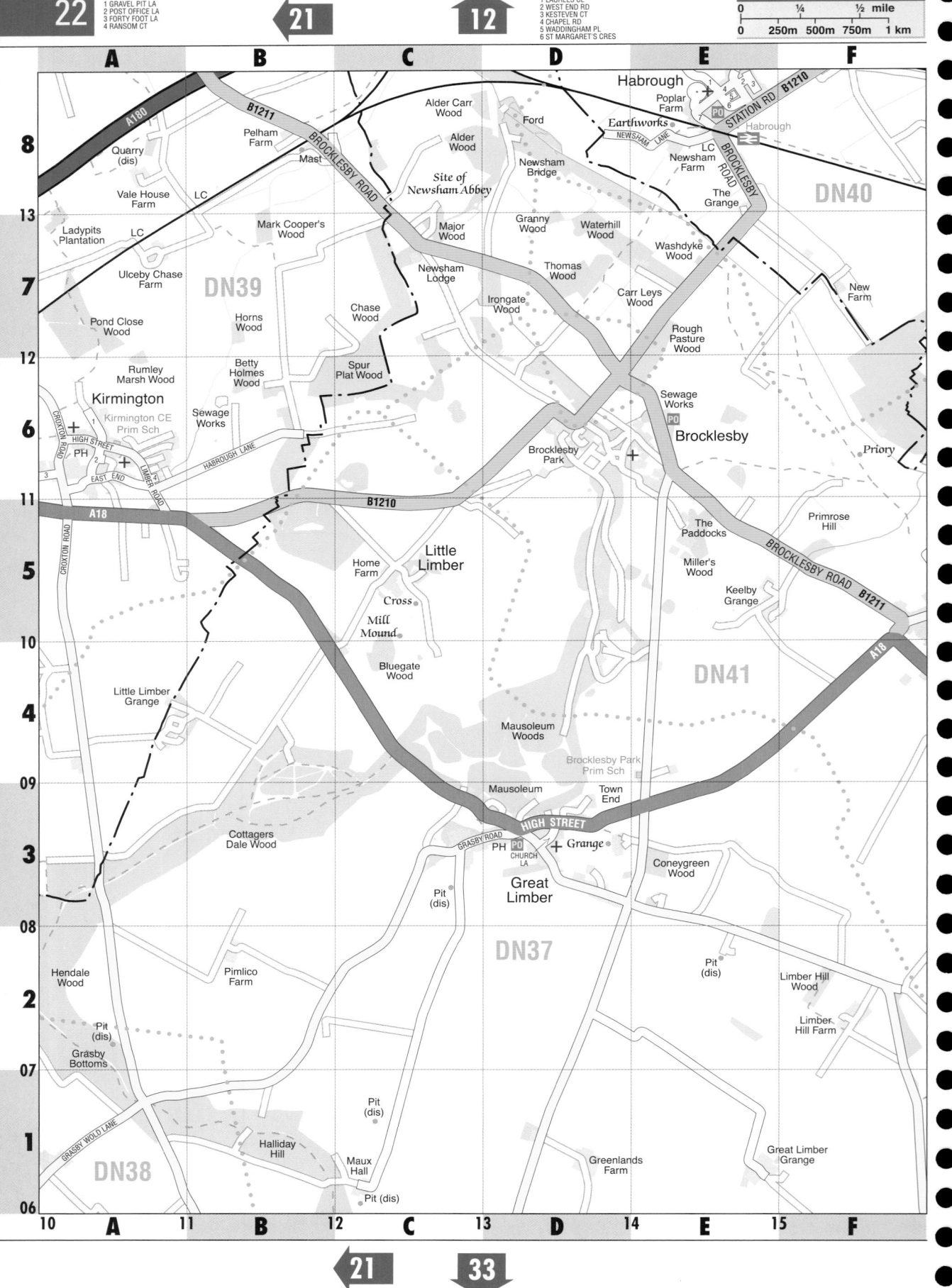

E8
1 LAURELS CL
2 WEST END RD
3 KESTEVEN CT
4 CHAPEL RD
5 WADDINGHAM PL
6 ST MARGARET'S CRES

7 WEST END RD

Scale: 1¾ inches to 1 mile

0   ¼   ½ mile

0   250m   500m   750m   1 km

Map labels

- A180
- B1211
- Quarry (dis)
- Pelham Farm
- Mast
- Alder Carr Wood
- Alder Wood
- Ford
- Habrough
- Poplar Farm
- STATION RD
- B1210
- PO
- Earthworks
- Newsham Bridge
- NEWSHAM LANE
- Habrough
- Newsham Farm
- LC
- BROCKLESBY ROAD
- DN40
- Vale House Farm
- LC
- BROCKLESBY ROAD
- Site of Newsham Abbey
- The Grange
- Ladypits Plantation
- LC
- Mark Cooper's Wood
- Major Wood
- Granny Wood
- Waterhill Wood
- Washdyke Wood
- Ulceby Chase Farm
- DN39
- Newsham Lodge
- Thomas Wood
- Carr Leys Wood
- New Farm
- Pond Close Wood
- Horns Wood
- Chase Wood
- Irongate Wood
- Rough Pasture Wood
- Rumley Marsh Wood
- Betty Holmes Wood
- Spur Plat Wood
- Kirmington
- Kirmington CE Prim Sch
- Sewage Works
- Sewage Works
- PO
- Brocklesby
- Priory
- HIGH STREET
- PH
- LIMBER ROAD
- EAST END
- HABROUGH LANE
- Brocklesby Park
- CROXTON ROAD
- B1210
- A18
- B1210
- The Paddocks
- Primrose Hill
- BROCKLESBY ROAD B1211
- Home Farm
- Little Limber
- Miller's Wood
- Keelby Grange
- Cross
- Mill Mound
- DN41
- Bluegate Wood
- A18
- Little Limber Grange
- Mausoleum Woods
- Brocklesby Park Prim Sch
- Cottagers Dale Wood
- Mausoleum
- Town End
- GRASBY ROAD
- Grange
- Coneygreen Wood
- PH PO
- CHURCH LA
- Pit (dis)
- Great Limber
- DN37
- Hendale Wood
- Pimlico Farm
- Pit (dis)
- Limber Hill Wood
- Pit (dis)
- Limber Hill Farm
- Grasby Bottoms
- Pit (dis)
- GRASBY WOLD LANE
- Halliday Hill
- Maux Hall
- Greenlands Farm
- Great Limber Grange
- DN38
- Pit (dis)

21
12
21
33

Scale: 1¾ inches to 1 mile
0 ¼ ½ mile
0 250m 500m 750m 1 km

A5
1 WIVELL DR
2 BROADWAY
3 EASTFIELD RD
4 CHURCHILL AVE
5 TOMLINE RD
6 WINDSOR CL
7 MANOR ST
8 WEST VIEW CL
9 ST ANNE'S RD
10 VICTORIA RD
11 MANOR CL

186 13

F5
1 WESTWOOD RD
2 POPLAR RD
3 ASHLEIGH CT
4 LUCAS CT
5 ROWAN DR
6 LARKSPUR AVE
7 CLEMATIS AVE
8 PRIMROSE CL
9 CARLTON RD
10 SNOWDROP CL
11 WREN CL
12 BEVERLEY CT
13 MCVEIGH CT
14 APPLE TREE CT
15 SWALLOW DR
16 ROOKERY RD
17 FORD'S AVE
18 CORNFLOWER CL
19 MALLARD CL
20 IVY FARM CT
21 PINNEY'S CT
22 MAPLE GR
23 BLUEBELL CT
24 SALADINE CT
25 FORSYTHIA AVE

187 24

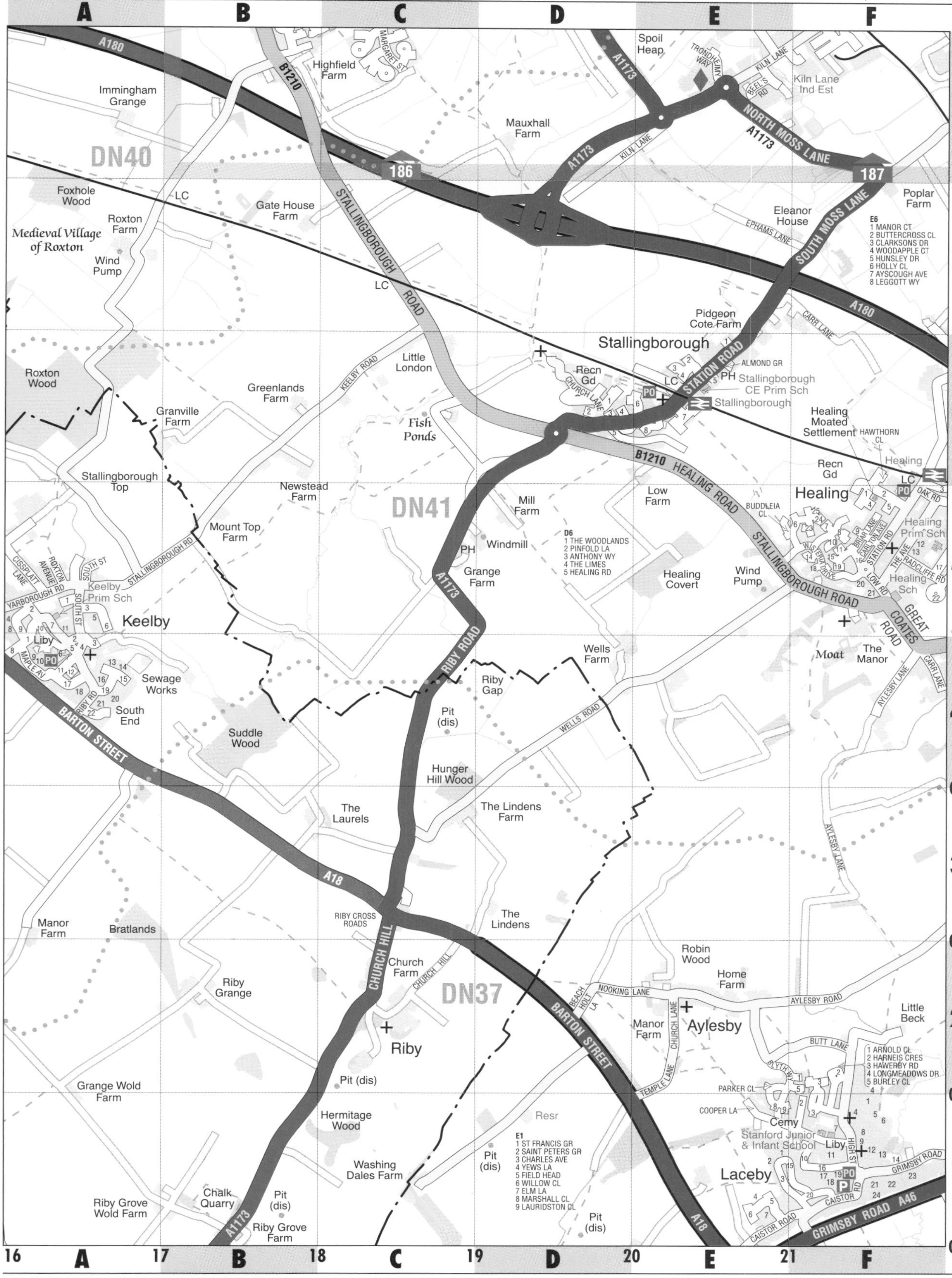

For full street detail of the highlighted area see pages 186 & 187.

A4
1 PELHAM CRES
2 KING ST
3 CHURCH LA
4 ST BARTHOLOMEW'S CL
5 ST MARTIN'S PL
6 HALLS LA
7 WEST LA
8 MILL LA
9 MAPLE CL
10 HULBERRY CL
11 CADDLE RD
12 KAREN AVE
13 BECK CL
14 MIDFIELD WY
15 WOODLANDS AVE
16 ROWAN CL
17 MILSON RD
18 LONGMEADOW RISE
19 SUDDLE WY
20 RAITHBY AVE
21 THORNTON GDNS
22 COTHAM GDNS

34 24

F1
1 STANFORD CL
2 GIBRALTAR LA
3 HAWERBY RD
4 SEED CL LA
5 AUSTIN GARTH
6 PHILLIPS LA
7 BUTTERFIELD CL
8 NEW CHAPEL LA
9 OLD CHAPEL LA
10 CEMETERY CRES
11 THE MEAD
12 CHURCH LA
13 FIELD CL
14 SPRING LA
15 KEITH CRES
16 CEMETERY RD
17 ST MARGARET'S CL
18 KNIGHTS CL
19 ALTOFT CL
20 KENMAR RD
21 WHITGIFT CL
22 TREVOR CL
23 GEORGE BUTLER CL
24 GRANGE AVE

A5
1 OAK RD
2 MEADOW DR
3 NICHOLSON RD
4 PINE WK
5 CHESTNUT WK
6 LINDSEY DR
7 RADCLIFFE RD
8 ELM GR

23

Scale: 1¾ inches to 1 mile

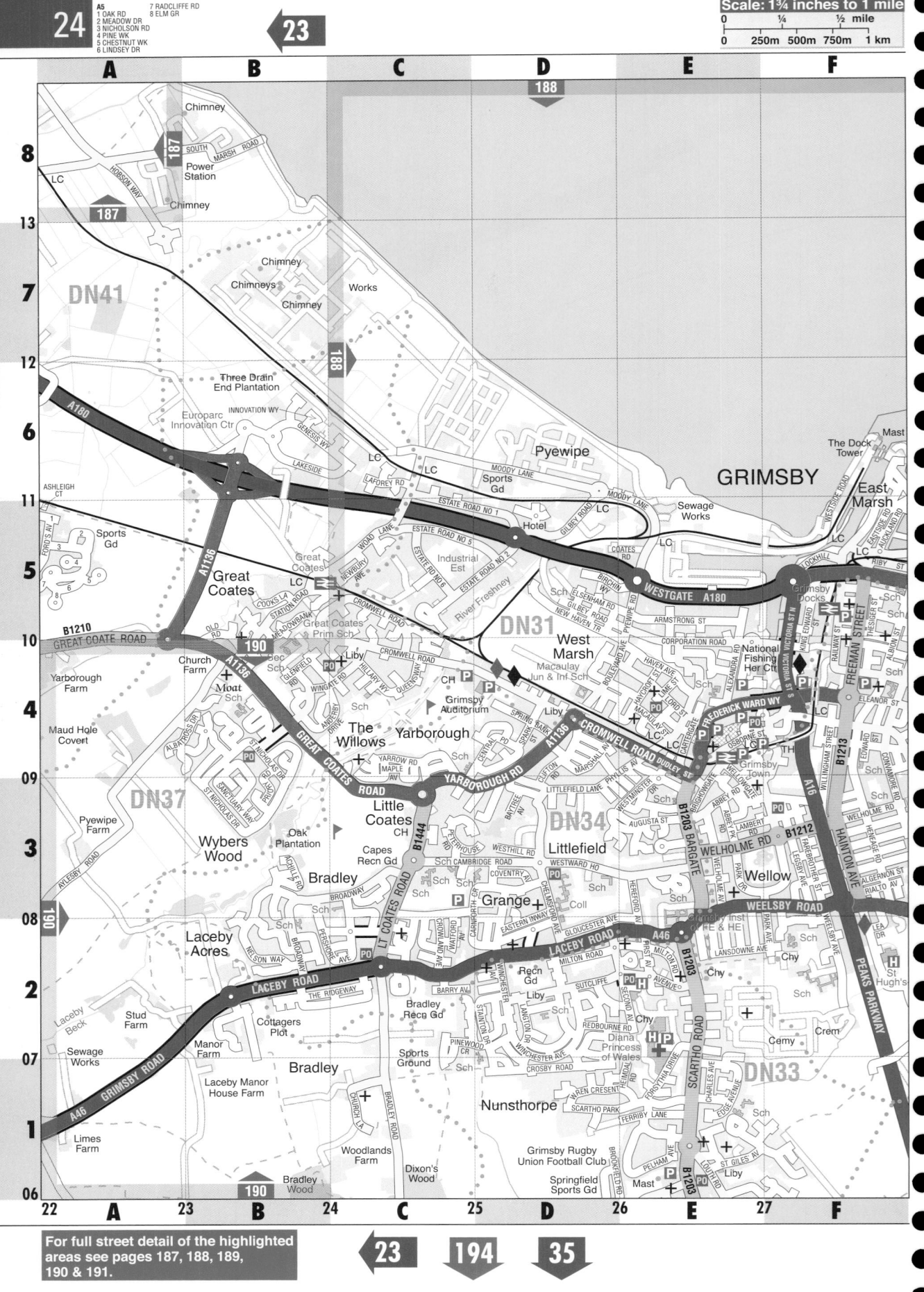

For full street detail of the highlighted areas see pages 187, 188, 189, 190 & 191.

23 194 35

Scale: 1¾ inches to 1 mile

0 ¼ ½ mile
0 250m 500m 750m 1 km

A B C D E F

8
13
7
12
6
11
5
10
4
09
3
08
2
07
1
06

189

Grimsby Roads

189

192   193

CLEETHORPES

Cleethorpes
Cleethorpes Pier

Marina
WICKHAM RD
New Clee
MARSDEN RD
THOROLD ST
HARRINGTON ST
CLEETHORPE ROAD
A180
Grant Thorold
Hildyard St
Sch
Liby
Queen Mary Avenue
GRIMSBY RD
Water Twr
NORTH PROMENADE
DN32
Old Clee
CLEE ROAD
A46
Allotment Gardens
ISAAC'S HILL
ST PETER'S AV
ALEXANDRA RD
A1098
SLIPWAY
Weelsby
WEELSBY ROAD
A46
Cemy
MILL ROAD
KINGS PARADE WAY
Kingsway
HUMBERSTON RD
A1031
TAYLOR'S AVENUE
Coll
Villa Plantation
SANDRINGHAM ROAD
CHICHESTER RD
LINDUM RD
SIGNHILLS AV
BROMWELL RD
KINGS RD
Cleethorpes Discovery Centre
PH
The Jungle
Mus
Pumping Station
Lakeside
Carr Plantation
Old Hall Farm
DN35
DN36
Cleethorpes Country Park
Visitor Centre
Humberston
Cleethorpes
Miniature Railway
CH
Pleasure Island
Thorpe Park
HEWITT'S AV
A1031
GRIMSBY ROAD
A1098
Superstore
A16
SEAFORD RD
NORTH SEA LANE
BROOKLYN DR
LIDGARD RD
193

28 A 29 B 30 C 31 D 32 E 33 F

For full street detail of the highlighted areas see pages 189, 192 & 193.

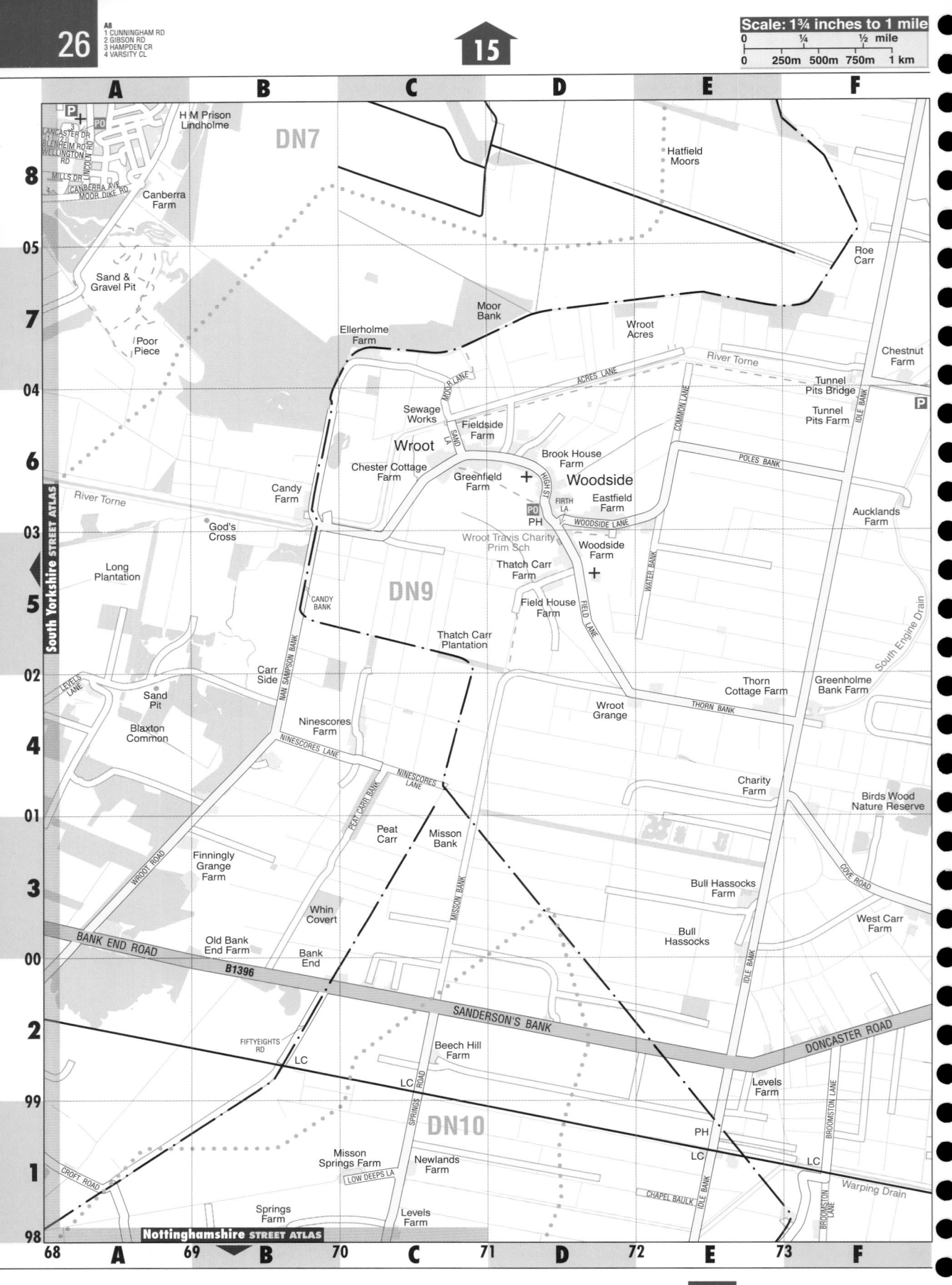

H M Prison
Lindholme

DN7

Hatfield
Moors

Roe
Carr

Canberra
Farm

Sand &
Gravel Pit

Chestnut
Farm

Moor
Bank

Wroot
Acres

Poor
Piece

Ellerholme
Farm

River Torne

Tunnel
Pits Bridge

Acres Lane

Tunnel
Pits Farm

Sewage
Works

Fieldside
Farm

Wroot

Chester Cottage
Farm

Greenfield
Farm

Brook House
Farm

Woodside

Poles Bank

Common Lane

River Torne

Candy
Farm

God's
Cross

Eastfield
Farm

Aucklands
Farm

Woodside Lane

PO
PH

Wroot Travis Charity
Prim Sch

Long
Plantation

DN9

Thatch Carr
Farm

Woodside
Farm

Candy
Bank

Field House
Farm

South Engine Drain

Thatch Carr
Plantation

Carr
Side

Sand
Pit

Ninescores
Farm

Wroot
Grange

Thorn
Cottage Farm

Greenholme
Bank Farm

Thorn Bank

Blaxton
Common

Ninescores Lane

Charity
Farm

Birds Wood
Nature Reserve

Ninescores
Lane

Peat
Carr

Misson
Bank

Bull Hassocks
Farm

West Carr
Farm

Finningly
Grange
Farm

Bull
Hassocks

Cove Road

Whin
Covert

Old Bank
End Farm

Bank
End

Bank End Road

B1396

Sanderson's Bank

Doncaster Road

Fiftyeights
Rd

LC

Beech Hill
Farm

Levels
Farm

Broomston Lane

LC

Springs Road

DN10

PH
LC

LC

Croft Road

Misson
Springs Farm

Low Deeps La

Newlands
Farm

Idle Bank

Chapel Baulk

Warping Drain

Springs
Farm

Levels
Farm

South Yorkshire STREET ATLAS

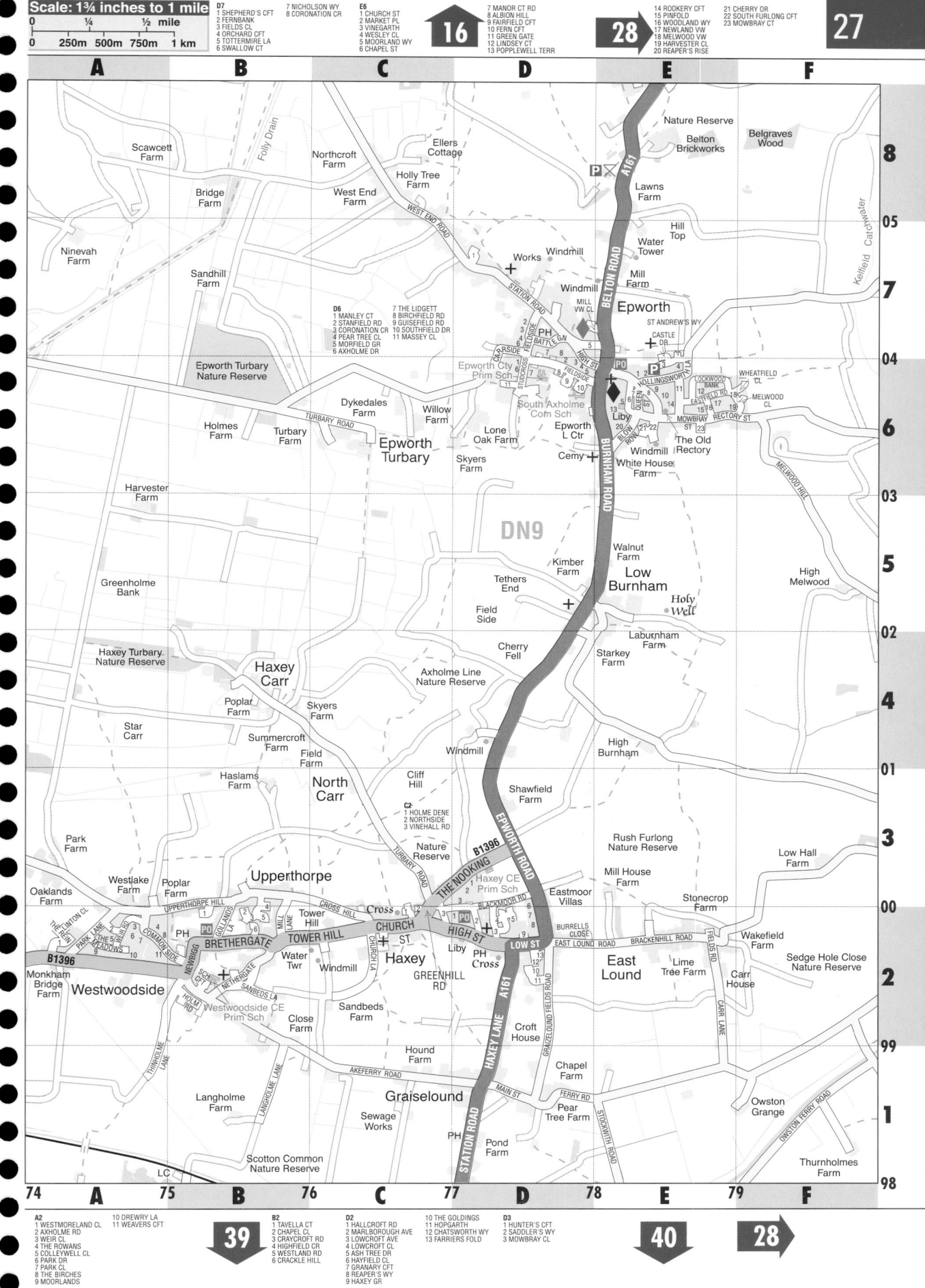

16

28

D7
1 SHEPHERD'S CFT
2 FERNBANK
3 FIELDS CL
4 ORCHARD CFT
5 TOTTERMIRE LA
6 SWALLOW CT

7 NICHOLSON WY
8 CORONATION CR

E6
1 CHURCH ST
2 MARKET PL
3 VINEGARTH
4 WESLEY CL
5 MOORLAND WY
6 CHAPEL ST

7 MANOR CT RD
8 ALBION HILL
9 FAIRFIELD CFT
10 FERN CFT
11 GREEN GATE
12 LINDSEY CT
13 POPPLEWELL TERR

14 ROOKERY CFT
15 PINFOLD
16 WOODLAND WY
17 NEWLAND VW
18 MELWOOD VW
19 HARVESTER CL
20 REAPER'S RISE

21 CHERRY OR
22 SOUTH FURLONG CFT
23 MOWBRAY CT

D6
1 MANLEY CT
2 STANFIELD RD
3 CORONATION CR
4 PEAR TREE CL
5 MORFIELD GR
6 AXHOLME DR

7 THE LIDGETT
8 BIRCHFIELD RD
9 GUISEFIELD RD
10 SOUTHFIELD DR
11 MASSEY CL

C2
1 HOLME DENE
2 NORTHSIDE
3 VINEHALL RD

A2
1 WESTMORELAND CL
2 AXHOLME RD
3 WEIR CL
4 THE ROWANS
5 COLLEYWELL CL
6 PARK DR
7 PARK CL
8 THE BIRCHES
9 MOORLANDS

10 DREWRY LA
11 WEAVERS CFT

B2
1 TAVELLA CT
2 CHAPEL CL
3 CRAYCROFT RD
4 HIGHFIELD CR
5 WESTLAND RD
6 CRACKLE HILL

D2
1 HALLCROFT RD
2 MARLBOROUGH AVE
3 LOWCROFT AVE
4 LOWCROFT CL
5 ASH TREE DR
6 HAYFIELD CL
7 GRANARY CFT
8 REAPER'S WY
9 HAXEY GR

10 THE GOLDINGS
11 HOPGARTH
12 CHATSWORTH WY
13 FARRIERS FOLD

D3
1 HUNTER'S CFT
2 SADDLER'S WY
3 MOWBRAY CL

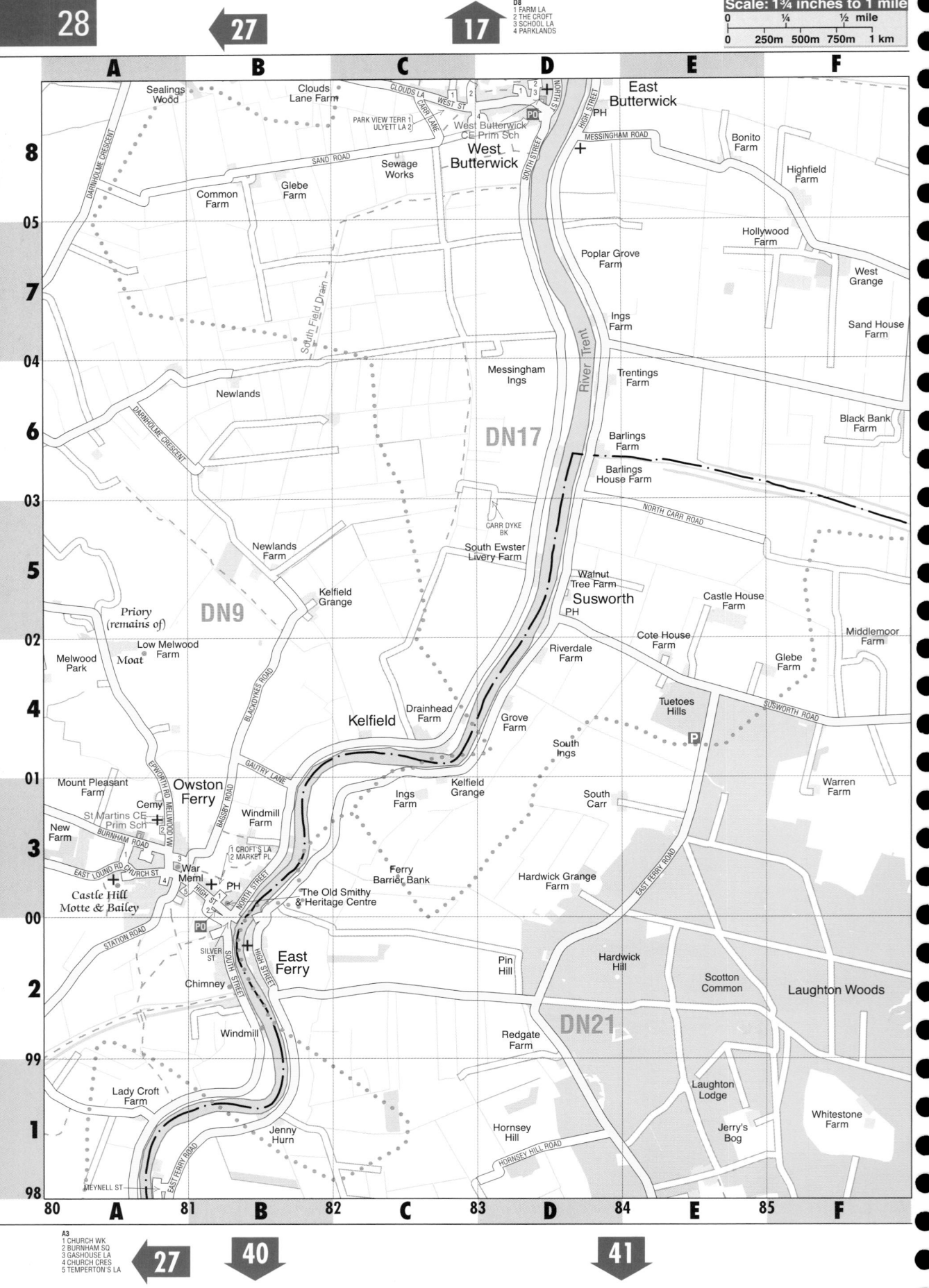

28

27

17

D8
1 FARM LA
2 THE CROFT
3 SCHOOL LA
4 PARKLANDS

Scale: 1¾ inches to 1 mile
0   ¼   ½   mile
0 250m 500m 750m 1 km

A   B   C   D   E   F

Sealings Wood
Clouds Lane Farm
CLOUDS LA
WEST ST
PARK VIEW TERR 1
ULYETT LA 2
West Butterwick CE Prim Sch
NORTH ST
PO
PH
East Butterwick
Bonito Farm
Highfield Farm

8

Common Farm
Glebe Farm
SAND ROAD
Sewage Works
West Butterwick
MESSINGHAM ROAD
Hollywood Farm
West Grange

05

Poplar Grove Farm
Sand House Farm

7

South Field Drain
Ings Farm
River Trent

04

Newlands
Messingham Ings
Trentings Farm
Black Bank Farm

6

DARNHOLME CRESCENT
DN17
Barlings Farm
Barlings House Farm
NORTH CARR ROAD

03

Newlands Farm
CARR DYKE BK
South Ewster Livery Farm
Walnut Tree Farm
Castle House Farm
Middlemoor Farm

5

Priory (remains of)
DN9
Kelfield Grange
Susworth
PH
Glebe Farm

Low Melwood Farm
Moat
Riverdale Farm
Cote House Farm

02

Melwood Park

BLACKDYKES ROAD
Drainhead Farm
Grove Farm
South Ings
Tuetoes Hills
P

4

Kelfield
Ings Farm
Kelfield Grange
South Carr
SUSWORTH ROAD
Warren Farm

GAUTRY LANE

01

Mount Pleasant Farm
Owston Ferry
BAGSBY ROAD
EPWORTH RD MELWOOD W
Windmill Farm
Kelfield Grange
South Carr
EAST FERRY ROAD

Cemy
St Martins CE Prim Sch
3

3
New Farm
BURNHAM ROAD
1 CROFT'S LA
2 MARKET PL
Ferry Barrier Bank
Hardwick Grange Farm

War Meml
PH
NORTH STREET
The Old Smithy & Heritage Centre

EAST LOUND RD CHURCH ST
HIGH ST
Pin Hill
Hardwick Hill

00

Castle Hill Motte & Bailey
PO
SILVER ST
SOUTH STREET
East Ferry
Scotton Common
Laughton Woods

STATION ROAD
Chimney
HIGH ST
DN21

2

Windmill
Redgate Farm

99

Lady Croft Farm
Jenny Hurn
Hornsey Hill
Laughton Lodge
Whitestone Farm

1

HORNSEY HILL ROAD
Jerry's Bog

MEYNELL ST
EAST FERRY ROAD

98

80   A   81   B   82   C   83   D   84   E   85   F

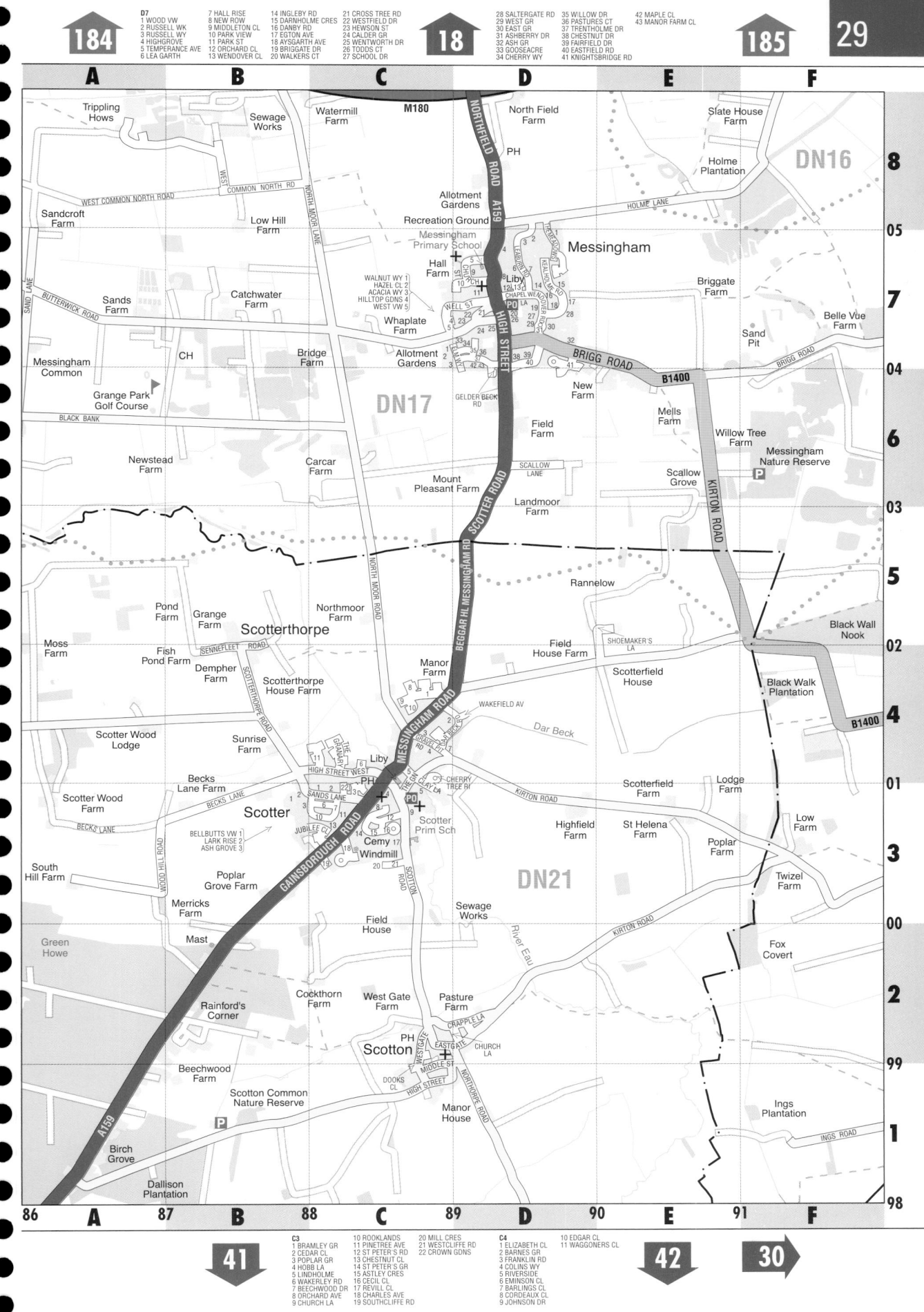

184
18
185
29
D7
1 WOOD VW
2 RUSSELL WK
3 RUSSELL WY
4 HIGHGROVE
5 TEMPERANCE AVE
6 LEA GARTH
7 HALL RISE
8 NEW ROW
9 MIDDLETON CL
10 PARK VIEW
11 PARK ST
12 ORCHARD CL
13 WENDOVER CL
14 INGLEBY RD
15 DARNHOLME CRES
16 DANBY RD
17 EGTON AVE
18 AYSGARTH AVE
19 BRIGGATE DR
20 WALKERS CT
21 CROSS TREE RD
22 WESTFIELD DR
23 HEWSON ST
24 CALDER GR
25 WENTWORTH DR
26 TODDS CT
27 SCHOOL DR
28 SALTERGATE RD
29 WEST GR
30 EAST GR
31 ASHBERRY DR
32 ASH GR
33 GOOSEACRE
34 CHERRY WY
35 WILLOW DR
36 PASTURES CT
37 TRENTHOLME DR
38 CHESTNUT DR
39 FAIRFIELD DR
40 EASTFIELD RD
41 KNIGHTSBRIDGE RD
42 MAPLE CL
43 MANOR FARM CL
A
B
C
D
E
F
Trippling Hows
Sewage Works
Watermill Farm
M180
NORTHFIELD ROAD
North Field Farm
Slate House Farm
PH
Holme Plantation
DN16
8
WEST COMMON NORTH RD
NORTH MOOR LANE
WEST COMMON NORTH ROAD
Allotment Gardens
A159
HOLME LANE
Sandcroft Farm
Low Hill Farm
Recreation Ground
05
Messingham Primary School
Messingham
Hall Farm
CHURCH ST
Liby
WALNUT WY 1
HAZEL CL 2
ACACIA WY 3
HILLTOP GDNS 4
WEST VW 5
LEABURN RD
KEALHOLME RD
HOLME DALE
CHAPEL LA
WENDOVER RD
SAND LANE
BUTTERWICK ROAD
Sands Farm
Catchwater Farm
Briggate Farm
7
WELL ST
Whaplate Farm
Belle Vue Farm
Sand Pit
HIGH STREET
Bridge Farm
Allotment Gardens
ELM WY
BRIGG ROAD
BRIGG ROAD
Messingham Common
CH
04
B1400
New Farm
Grange Park Golf Course
GELDER BECK RD
DN17
Mells Farm
BLACK BANK
Field Farm
Willow Tree Farm
6
Messingham Nature Reserve
Newstead Farm
Carcar Farm
SCALLOW LANE
Mount Pleasant Farm
Scallow Grove
SCOTTER ROAD
KIRTON ROAD
Landmoor Farm
03
BEGGAR HL MESSINGHAM RD
5
Rannelow
NORTH MOOR ROAD
Pond Farm
Grange Farm
Northmoor Farm
Black Wall Nook
Scotterthorpe
Moss Farm
Fish Pond Farm
SENNEFLEET ROAD
Field House Farm
SHOEMAKER'S LA
02
Dempher Farm
Manor Farm
Scotterfield House
Scotterthorpe House Farm
Black Walk Plantation
SCOTTERTHORPE ROAD
WAKEFIELD AV
MESSINGHAM ROAD
Dar Beck
B1400
4
Scotter Wood Lodge
Sunrise Farm
THE GRANARY
GRAVEL PIT RD
DAR BECK
Liby
HIGH STREET WEST
PH
CHERRY TREE RI
Becks Lane Farm
SANDS LANE
THE GN
CLAY LA
KIRTON ROAD
Scotterfield Farm
Lodge Farm
01
Scotter Wood Farm
BECKS LANE
Scotter
PO
Scotter Prim Sch
BECKS LANE
JUBILEE CL
Highfield Farm
St Helena Farm
Low Farm
BELLBUTTS VW 1
LARK RISE 2
ASH GROVE 3
Cemy
Windmill
Poplar Farm
3
South Hill Farm
GAINSBOROUGH ROAD
WOOD HILL ROAD
Poplar Grove Farm
SCOTTON ROAD
DN21
Twizel Farm
Merricks Farm
Sewage Works
Field House
00
Mast
River Eau
KIRTON ROAD
Green Howe
Fox Covert
2
Cockthorn Farm
West Gate Farm
Pasture Farm
Rainford's Corner
CRAPPLE LA
PH
WESTGATE
EASTGATE
CHURCH LA
Scotton
99
Beechwood Farm
MIDDLE ST
DOOKS CL
HIGH STREET
NORTHORPE ROAD
Scotton Common Nature Reserve
Manor House
Ings Plantation
A159
1
INGS ROAD
Birch Grove
Dallison Plantation
98
86
87
88
89
90
91
C3
1 BRAMLEY GR
2 CEDAR CL
3 POPLAR GR
4 HOBB LA
5 LINDHOLME
6 WAKERLEY RD
7 BEECHWOOD DR
8 ORCHARD AVE
9 CHURCH LA
10 ROOKLANDS
11 PINETREE AVE
12 ST PETER'S RD
13 CHESTNUT CL
14 ST PETER'S GR
15 ASTLEY CRES
16 CECIL CL
17 REVILL CL
18 CHARLES AVE
19 SOUTHCLIFFE RD
20 MILL CRES
21 WESTCLIFFE RD
22 CROWN GDNS
C4
1 ELIZABETH CL
2 BARNES GR
3 FRANKLIN RD
4 COLINS WY
5 RIVERSIDE
6 EMINSON CL
7 BARLINGS CL
8 CORDEAUX CL
9 JOHNSON DR
10 EDGAR CL
11 WAGGONERS CL
41
42
30

← 29

↑ 19

Scale: 1¾ inches to 1 mile

0 ¼ ½ mile
0 250m 500m 750m 1 km

A B C D E F

8
05
7
04
6
03
5
02
4
01
3
00
2
99
1
98

92 A 93 B 94 C 95 D 96 E 97 F

DN16

Scotch Wood
Gull Ponds
Twigmoor Woods
High Wood
Top Farm
Scawby
Scawby Hall
Cemy
BRIGG ROAD

Bowers Wood
Manton Warren
Moor Farm
PH
PO
Windmill
Sewage Works

Twigmoor Grange
Greetwell Hall Farm
Greetwell
Scawby Prim Sch
Sturton
New Farm

Black Hoe Plantation
Welburn Plantation
Railway Plantation

Broom Plantation
BRIGG ROAD
Greetwell Hall
Scawby Grange
STURTON LANE
MAIN ST
STATION ROAD

DN17
Aldham Plantation

Middle Manton
Stonepit Wood
Staniwells Farm
DN20
Station Farm

America Wood
Manor Farm
Newlands Farm
Settlement
MANTON LANE

Manton
South Farm
SAND LANE
B1398
PH

Cleatham Hall Farm
Cleatham Hall
Quarry Fields Farm
Quarry (dis)
Old Home Farm
Wood Home Farm
MILL ROAD
Grange Farm

Tumulus
B1400
MANTON ROAD
GAINSTHORPE ROAD WEST
GAINSTHORPE ROAD EAST
Cliff Farm

New Cleatham House Farm
Cleatham
PH
Chy
Medieval Village of Gainsthorpe
Gainsthorpe Farm
Northwood Farm

CLEATHAM ROAD
KIRTON ROAD
Mount Pleasant Farm
DN21
Quarry (dis)
Kirton Tunnel

Low Farm
Sweet Hills
Station Farm
Mast
Northcliff Farm
Stonepit Plantation
Redbourne

Kirton Lindsey
Mount Pleasant Windmill
Grange Farm
REDBOURNE MERE
Hall
HIGH STREET

INGS ROAD
STATION ROAD
Liby
Kirton in Lindsey
B1206
REDBOURNE MERE
Springcliff Farm
Redbourne Park

Ings Farm
Cemy
TH
PH
PO
Huntcliff School
Cliff Farm
Pyewipe House

Sewage Works
Moat
Manor Farm
Kirton Lindsey Prim Sch
B1398
B1400
YORK RD
Mast
A15
CLAY LANE

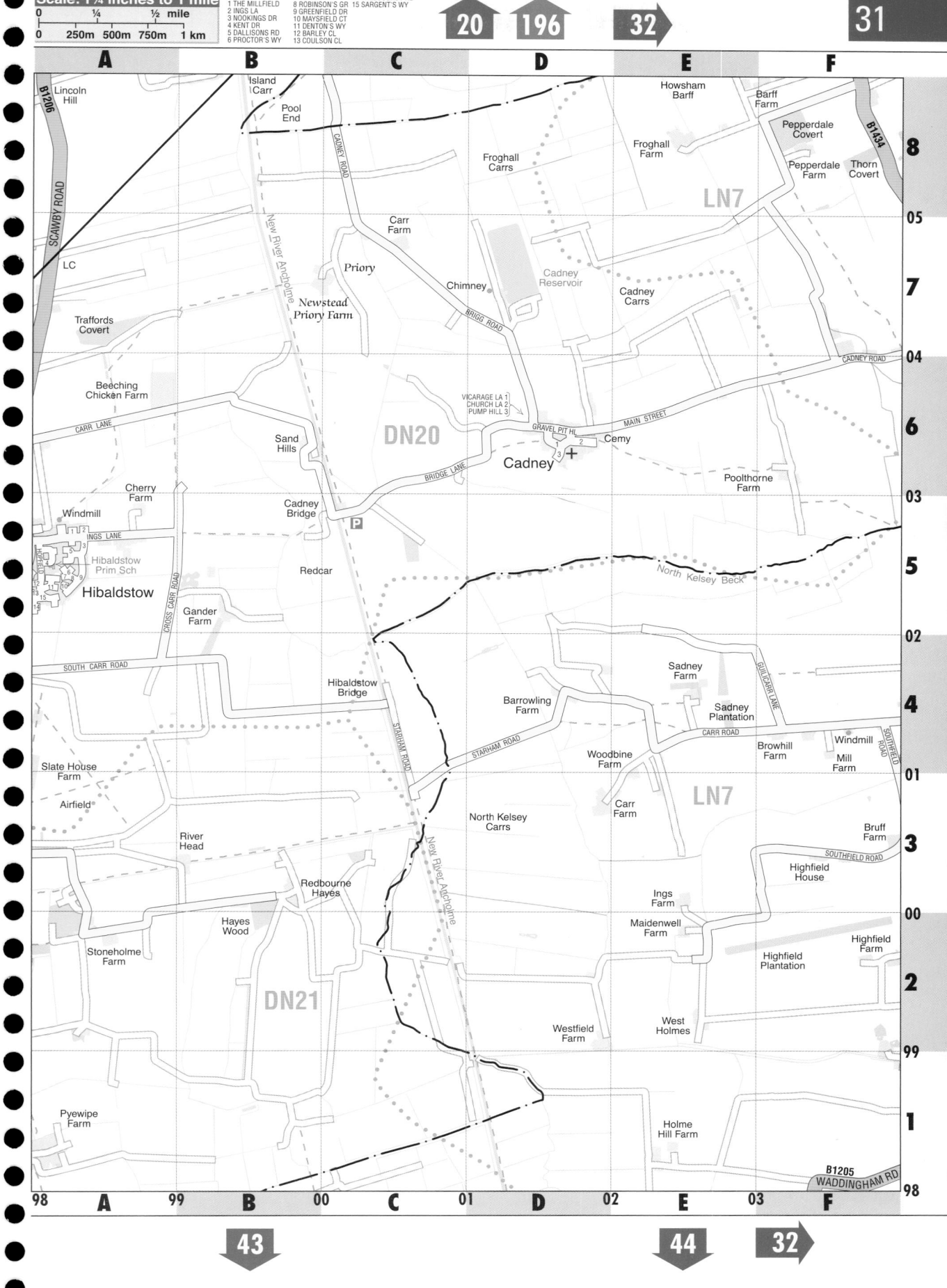
Scale: 1¾ inches to 1 mile
0 ¼ ½ mile
0 250m 500m 750m 1 km
A5
1 THE MILLFIELD
2 INGS LA
3 NOOKINGS DR
4 KENT DR
5 DALLISONS RD
6 PROCTOR'S WY
7 COX'S CT
8 ROBINSON'S GR
9 GREENFIELD DR
10 MAYSFIELD CT
11 DENTON'S WY
12 BARLEY CL
13 COULSON CL
14 WILLOUGHBY RD
15 SARGENT'S WY
20
196
32
A
B
C
D
E
F
Lincoln Hill
B1206
Island Carr
Pool End
Howsham Barff
Barff Farm
Pepperdale Covert
B1434
CADNEY ROAD
Froghall Farm
Froghall Carrs
Pepperdale Farm
Thorn Covert
LN7
SCAWBY ROAD
New River Ancholme
Carr Farm
LC
Priory
Chimney
Cadney Reservoir
Cadney Carrs
Newstead Priory Farm
BRIGG ROAD
Traffords Covert
CADNEY ROAD
Beeching Chicken Farm
VICARAGE LA 1
CHURCH LA 2
PUMP HILL 3
CARR LANE
DN20
GRAVEL PIT HL
MAIN STREET
Sand Hills
Cemy
Cadney
BRIDGE LANE
Poolthorne Farm
Cherry Farm
Cadney Bridge
Windmill
INGS LANE
HOPFIELD
Hibaldstow Prim Sch
Redcar
North Kelsey Beck
Hibaldstow
CROSS CARR ROAD
Gander Farm
SOUTH CARR ROAD
Sadney Farm
GUILICARR LANE
Hibaldstow Bridge
Barrowling Farm
Sadney Plantation
CARR ROAD
Browhill Farm
Windmill
SOUTHFIELD ROAD
STARHAM ROAD
Woodbine Farm
Mill Farm
Slate House Farm
LN7
Airfield
Carr Farm
North Kelsey Carrs
Bruff Farm
River Head
SOUTHFIELD ROAD
Highfield House
New River Ancholme
Redbourne Hayes
Ings Farm
Maidenwell Farm
Hayes Wood
Stoneholme Farm
Highfield Farm
Highfield Plantation
DN21
West Holmes
Westfield Farm
Pyewipe Farm
Holme Hill Farm
B1205
WADDINGHAM RD
8
05
7
04
6
03
5
02
4
01
3
00
2
99
1
98
98
99
00
01
02
03
43
44
32

31
21

D8
1 BACK LA
2 HOWSHAM LA
3 MAIN ST
4 OWMBY RD

E7
1 MAIN ST
2 CHURCH HILL
3 CHURCH SIDE
4 FRONT ST
5 CANTY NOOK
6 BENTLEY LA

Scale: 1¾ inches to 1 mile

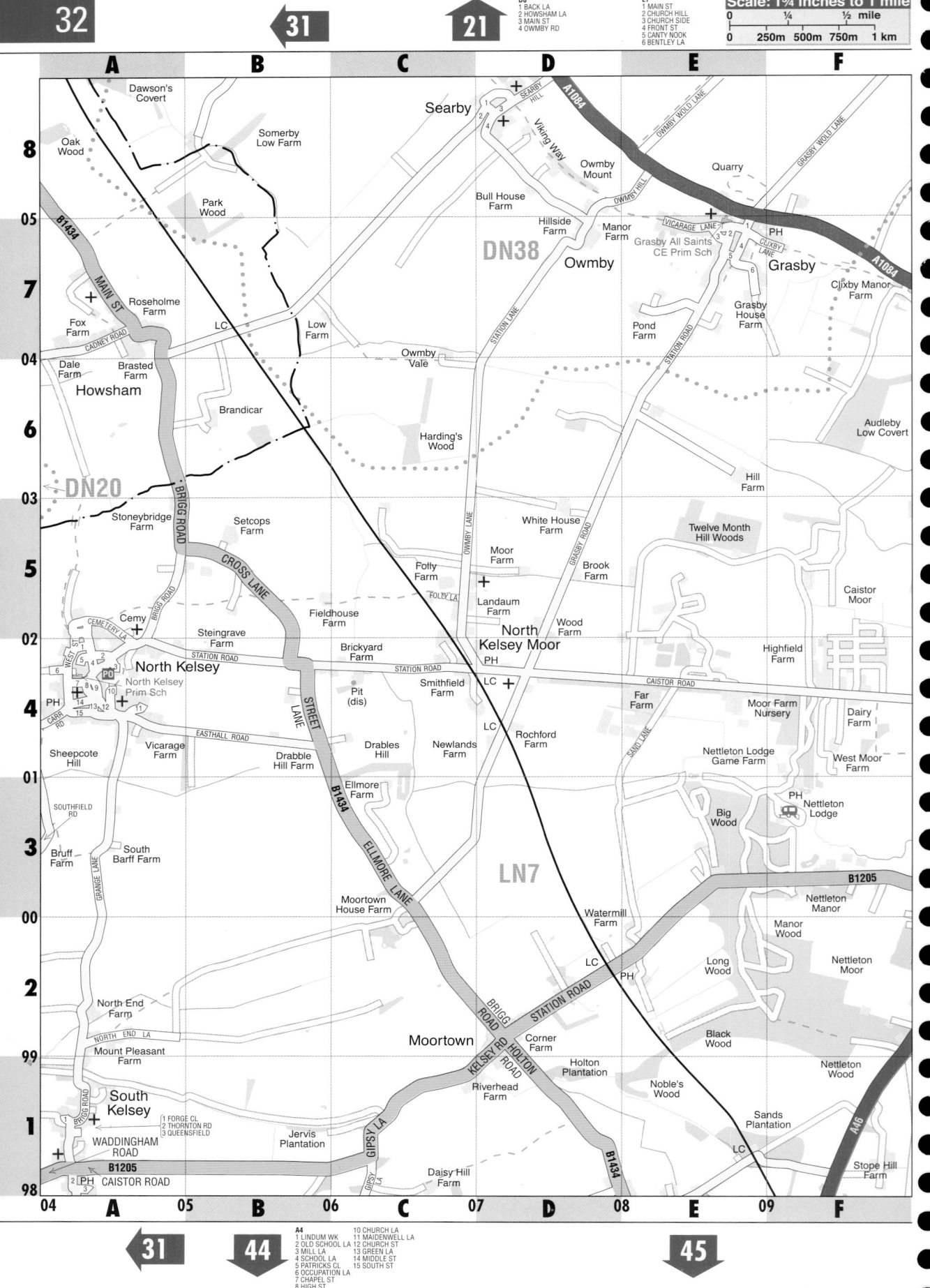

A4
1 LINDUM WK
2 OLD SCHOOL LA
3 MILL LA
4 SCHOOL LA
5 PATRICKS CL
6 OCCUPATION LA
7 CHAPEL ST
8 HIGH ST
9 HALLS LA
10 CHURCH LA
11 MAIDENWELL LA
12 CHURCH ST
13 GREEN LA
14 MIDDLE ST
15 SOUTH ST

31
44
45

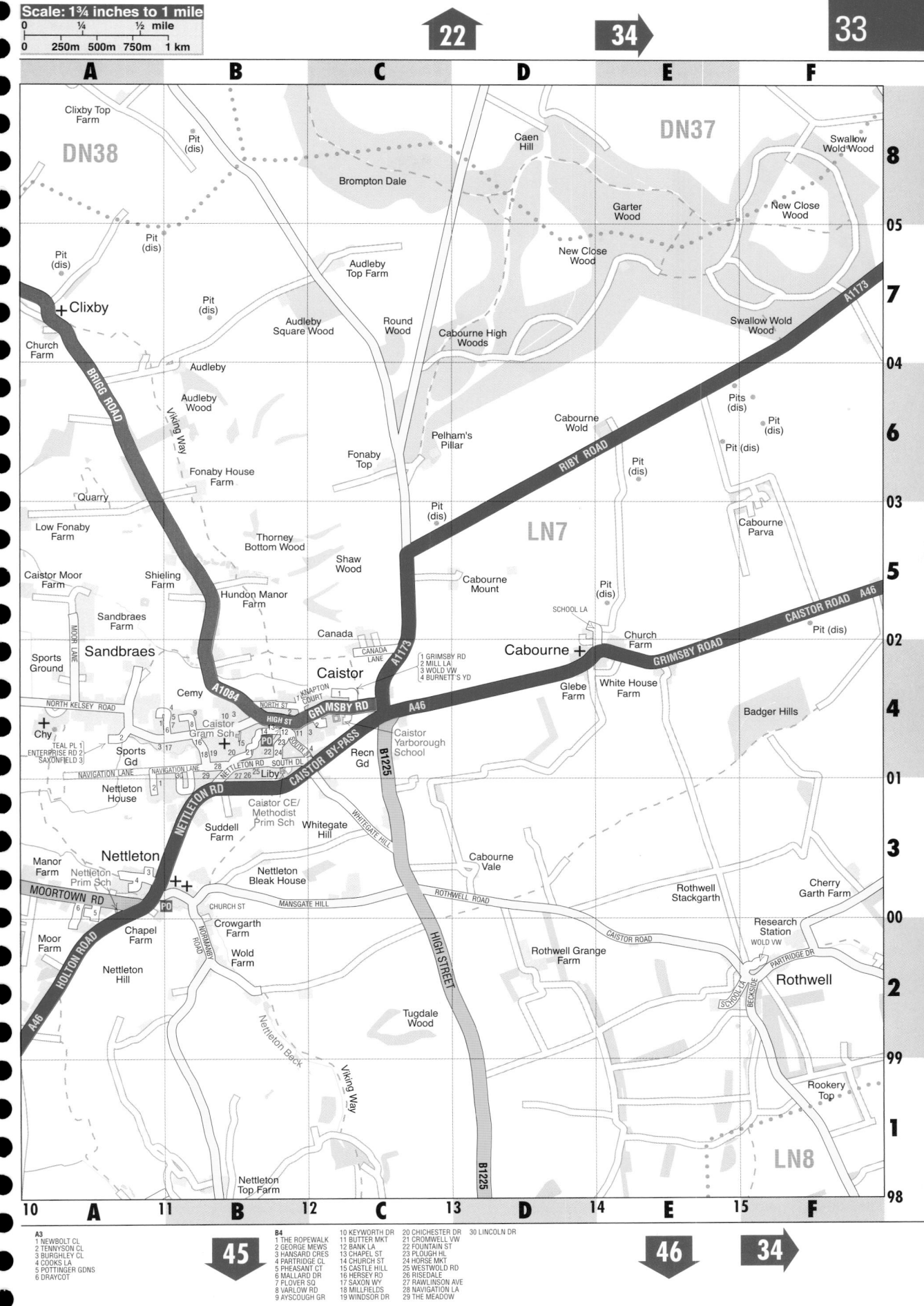

A B C D E F

DN38

Clixby Top Farm

Pit (dis)

Caen Hill

DN37

Swallow Wold Wood

05

Brompton Dale

Garter Wood

New Close Wood

8

Pit (dis)

Pit (dis)

+ Clixby

Pit (dis)

Audleby Top Farm

Round Wood

Cabourne High Woods

New Close Wood

Swallow Wold Wood

A1173

7

04

Church Farm

BRIGG ROAD

Audleby Square Wood

Audleby

Audleby Wood

VIKING WAY

Fonaby House Farm

Fonaby Top

Pelham's Pillar

Cabourne Wold

RIBY ROAD

Pits (dis)

Pit (dis)

Pit (dis)

6

04

Quarry

Shaw Wood

Pit (dis)

Pit (dis)

LN7

Cabourne Parva

03

Low Fonaby Farm

Thorney Bottom Wood

Cabourne Mount

Pit (dis)

Caistor Moor Farm

Shieling Farm

Hundon Manor Farm

Canada

SCHOOL LA

Church Farm

Pit (dis)

5

02

Sandbraes Farm

Canada Lane

A1173

Cabourne +

White House Farm

CAISTOR ROAD A46

GRIMSBY ROAD

Badger Hills

MOOR LANE

Sandbraes

Cemy

Caistor

1 GRIMSBY RD
2 MILL LA
3 WOLD VW
4 BURNETT'S YD

Glebe Farm

4

01

Sports Ground

A1084

NORTH ST

KNAPTON COURT

GRIMSBY RD

A46

Caistor Yarborough School

NORTH KELSEY ROAD

Chy +

Caistor Gram Sch

HIGH ST

PO

Recn Gd

B1225

TEAL PL 1
ENTERPRISE RD 2
SAXONFIELD 3

Sports Gd

Liby

SOUTH DL

CAISTOR BY-PASS

NAVIGATION LANE

NAVIGATION LANE

NETTLETON RD

Nettleton House

Suddell Farm

Caistor CE/ Methodist Prim Sch

Whitegate Hill

WHITEGATE HILL

3

Manor Farm

Nettleton

NETTLETON RD

Nettleton Prim Sch

Nettleton Bleak House

Cabourne Vale

MOORTOWN RD

MANSGATE HILL

ROTHWELL ROAD

Rothwell Stackgarth

Cherry Garth Farm

00

Moor Farm

HOLTON ROAD

Chapel Farm

Nettleton Hill

PO

CHURCH ST

Crowgarth Farm

NORMANBY ROAD

Wold Farm

HIGH STREET

CAISTOR ROAD

Rothwell Grange Farm

Research Station

WOLD VW

PARTRIDGE DR

Rothwell

2

A46

Nettleton Beck

VIKING WAY

Tugdale Wood

SCHOOL LA

BECKSIDE

99

Nettleton Top Farm

B1225

Rookery Top

LN8

1

98

10 A 11 B 12 C 13 D 14 E 15 F

A3
1 NEWBOLT CL
2 TENNYSON CL
3 BURGHLEY CL
4 COOKS LA
5 POTTINGER GDNS
6 DRAYCOT

B4
1 THE ROPEWALK
2 GEORGE MEWS
3 HANSARD CRES
4 PARTRIDGE CL
5 PHEASANT CT
6 MALLARD DR
7 PLOVER SQ
8 VARLOW RD
9 AYSCOUGH GR

10 KEYWORTH DR
11 BUTTER MKT
12 BANK LA
13 CHAPEL ST
14 CHURCH ST
15 CASTLE HILL
16 HERSEY RD
17 SAXON WY
18 MILLFIELDS
19 WINDSOR DR

20 CHICHESTER DR
21 CROMWELL VW
22 FOUNTAIN ST
23 PLOUGH HL
24 HORSE MKT
25 WESTWOLD RD
26 RISEDALE
27 RAWLINSON AVE
28 NAVIGATION LA
29 THE MEADOW

30 LINCOLN DR

33
23

Scale: 1¾ inches to 1 mile

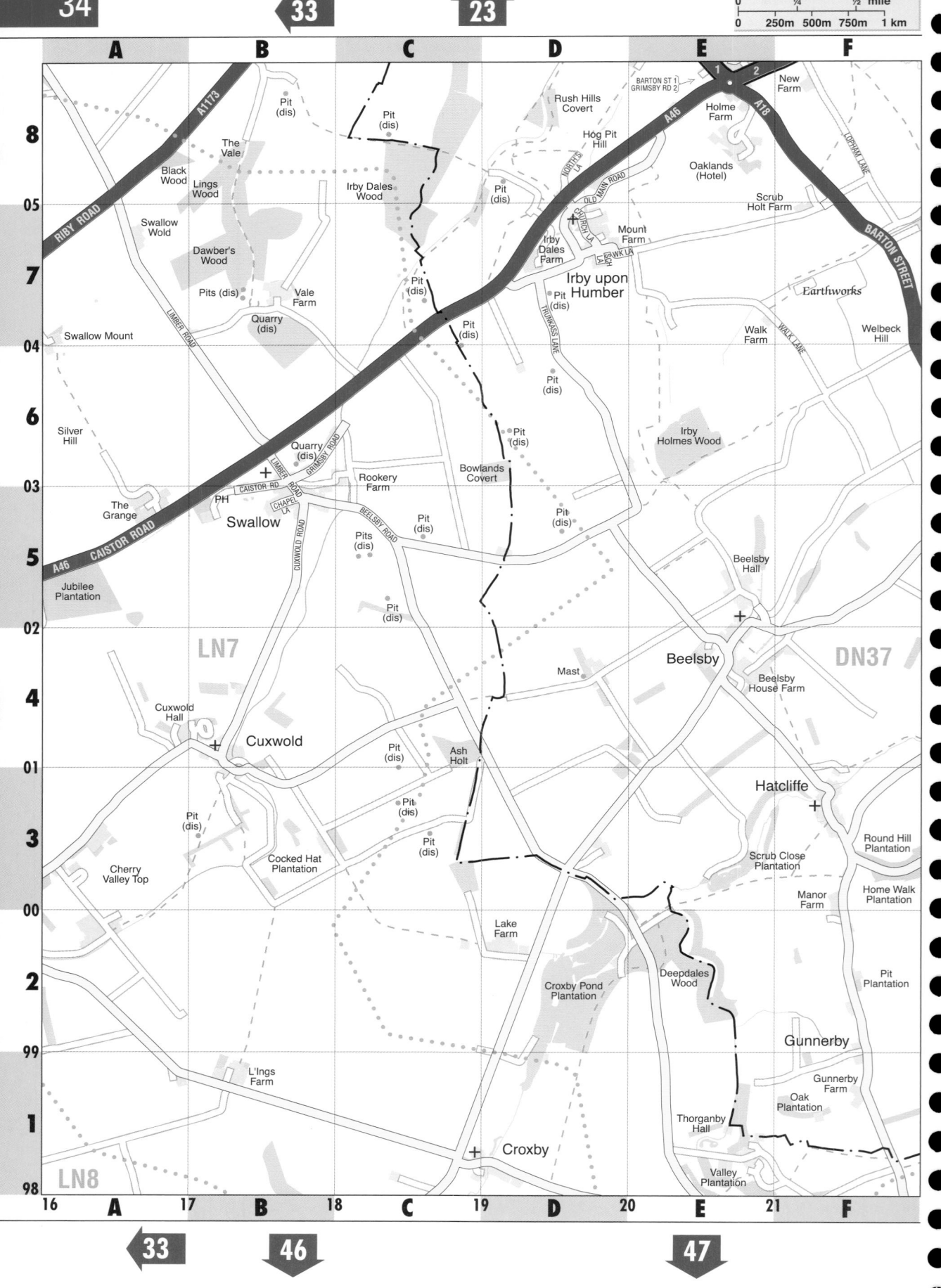
A
B
C
D
E
F
8
05
7
04
6
03
5
02
4
01
3
00
2
99
1
98
16
17
18
19
20
21
A1173
RIBY ROAD
Pit (dis)
The Vale
Black Wood
Lings Wood
Irby Dales Wood
Swallow Wold
Dawber's Wood
Pits (dis)
Vale Farm
Quarry (dis)
Swallow Mount
LIMBER ROAD
Rush Hills Covert
Hog Pit Hill
BARTON ST 1
GRIMSBY RD 2
New Farm
Holme Farm
A18
A46
Oaklands (Hotel)
Scrub Holt Farm
LOPHAM LANE
BARTON STREET
NORTH'S LA
OLD MAIN ROAD
CHURCH LA
Mount Farm
Irby Dales Farm
Irby upon Humber
Earthworks
TRUNKASS LANE
Walk Farm
WALK LANE
Welbeck Hill
Silver Hill
Quarry (dis)
GRIMSBY ROAD
Bowlands Covert
Irby Holmes Wood
Rookery Farm
CAISTOR RD
PH
CHAPEL LA
The Grange
Swallow
CAISTOR ROAD
CUXWOLD ROAD
BEELSBY ROAD
Pits (dis)
Beelsby Hall
Jubilee Plantation
LN7
Mast
Beelsby
DN37
Beelsby House Farm
Cuxwold Hall
Cuxwold
Ash Holt
Hatcliffe
Round Hill Plantation
Cherry Valley Top
Cocked Hat Plantation
Scrub Close Plantation
Manor Farm
Home Walk Plantation
Lake Farm
Deepdales Wood
Croxby Pond Plantation
Pit Plantation
Gunnerby
L'Ings Farm
Gunnerby Farm
Oak Plantation
Thorganby Hall
Croxby
Valley Plantation
LN8

33
46
47

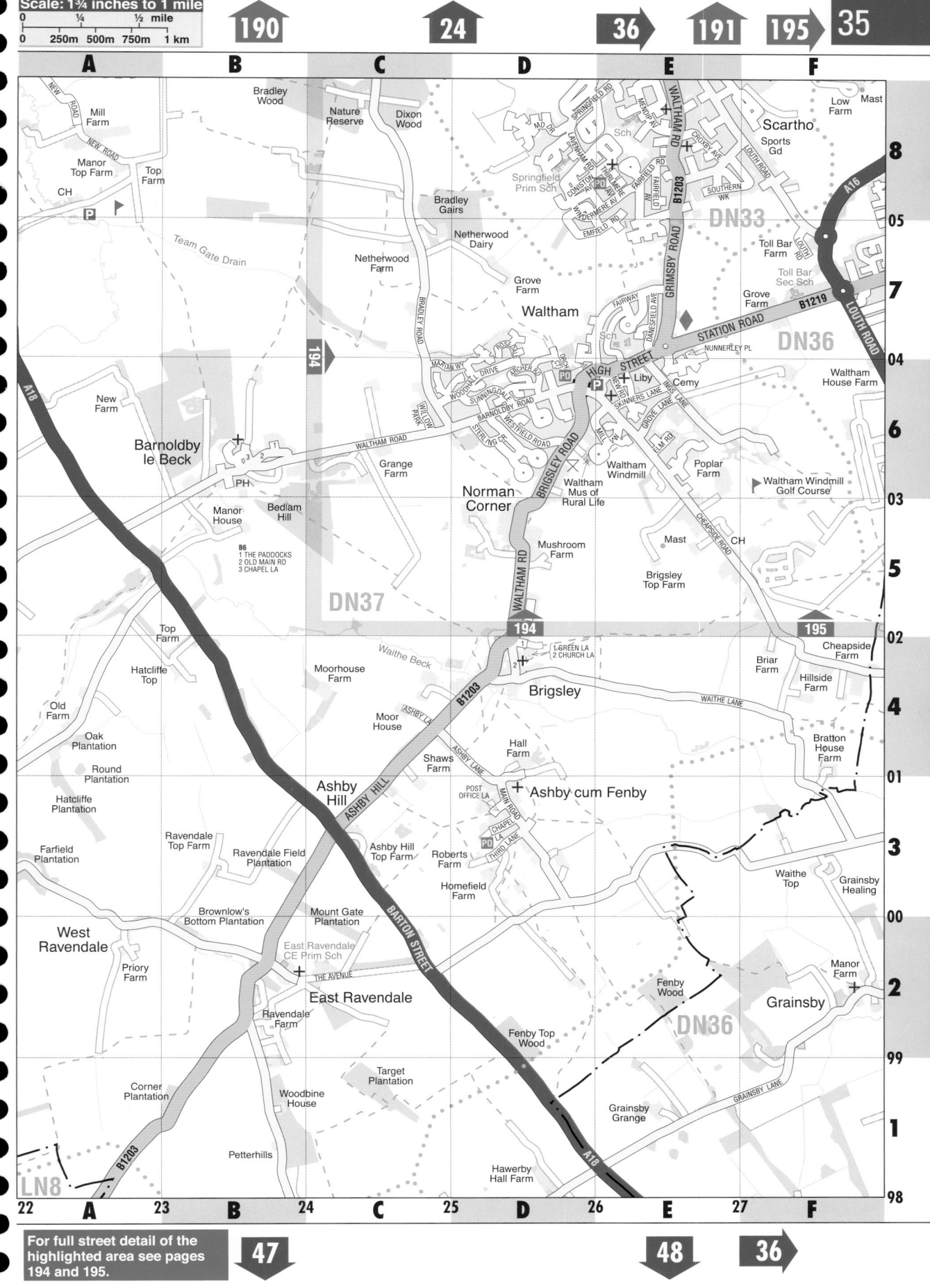

A   B   C   D   E   F

NEW ROAD
Mill Farm
Manor Top Farm
CH
P
Top Farm
New Road
Bradley Wood
Nature Reserve
Dixon Wood
Bradley Gairs
Netherwood Dairy
Netherwood Farm
Grove Farm
Springfield Prim Sch
Scartho
Sports Gd
Low Farm
Mast
DN33
Toll Bar Farm
A16

Team Gate Drain

Bradley Road

194

New Farm

Barnoldby le Beck
PH
Manor House
Bedlam Hill
B6
1 THE PADDOCKS
2 OLD MAIN RD
3 CHAPEL LA

DN37

A18

Waltham Road
Grange Farm

WILLOW PARK
MARTIN WY
WOODHALL DRIVE
ROSE CT
SUNNINGDALE
BARNOLDBY ROAD
STERLING
WESTFIELD ROAD
BRIGSLEY ROAD
RICHER RD
BIRCH LA

Norman Corner

Waltham
HIGH STREET
PO
P
Liby
Cemy
NEW RD
SKINNERS LANE
GROVE LANE
MILL LA
ELM RD
Waltham Windmill
Waltham Mus of Rural Life

WALTHAM RD
Mushroom Farm

Waitham Road

FAIRWAY
Sch
DANESFIELD AVE
GRIMSBY ROAD
B1203
NUNNERLEY PL
STATION ROAD
DN36
B1219
LOUTH ROAD
Grove Farm
Toll Bar Sec Sch
Waltham House Farm

Poplar Farm
Waltham Windmill Golf Course
Mast
CH
Brigsley Top Farm
CHEAPSIDE ROAD

Top Farm
Hatcliffe Top
Old Farm
Oak Plantation
Round Plantation
Hatcliffe Plantation
Farfield Plantation

Waithe Beck
Moorhouse Farm
Moor House
ASHBY LA
B1203
ASHBY LANE
Shaws Farm
Hall Farm
Brigsley
1 GREEN LA
2 CHURCH LA
194
195
Briar Farm
Cheapside Farm
Hillside Farm
WAITHE LANE
Bratton House Farm

Ashby Hill
ASHBY HILL
Ashby Hill Top Farm
Roberts Farm
Homefield Farm
POST OFFICE LA
Ashby cum Fenby
CHAPEL LA
THIRD LANE
MAIN ROAD
PO

Ravendale Top Farm
Ravendale Field Plantation
Brownlow's Bottom Plantation
Mount Gate Plantation
East Ravendale CE Prim Sch
BARTON STREET
THE AVENUE

West Ravendale
Priory Farm
Ravendale Farm
East Ravendale

Corner Plantation
Woodbine House
Target Plantation
Fenby Top Wood
Fenby Wood
Grainsby
Manor Farm
Waithe Top
Grainsby Healing
DN36
GRAINSBY LANE
Grainsby Grange

B1203
Petterhills
Hawerby Hall Farm
A18

LN8

8
05
7
04
6
03
5
02
4
01
3
00
2
99
1
98

22   A   23   B   24   C   25   D   26   E   27   F

For full street detail of the highlighted area see pages 194 and 195.

47   48   36

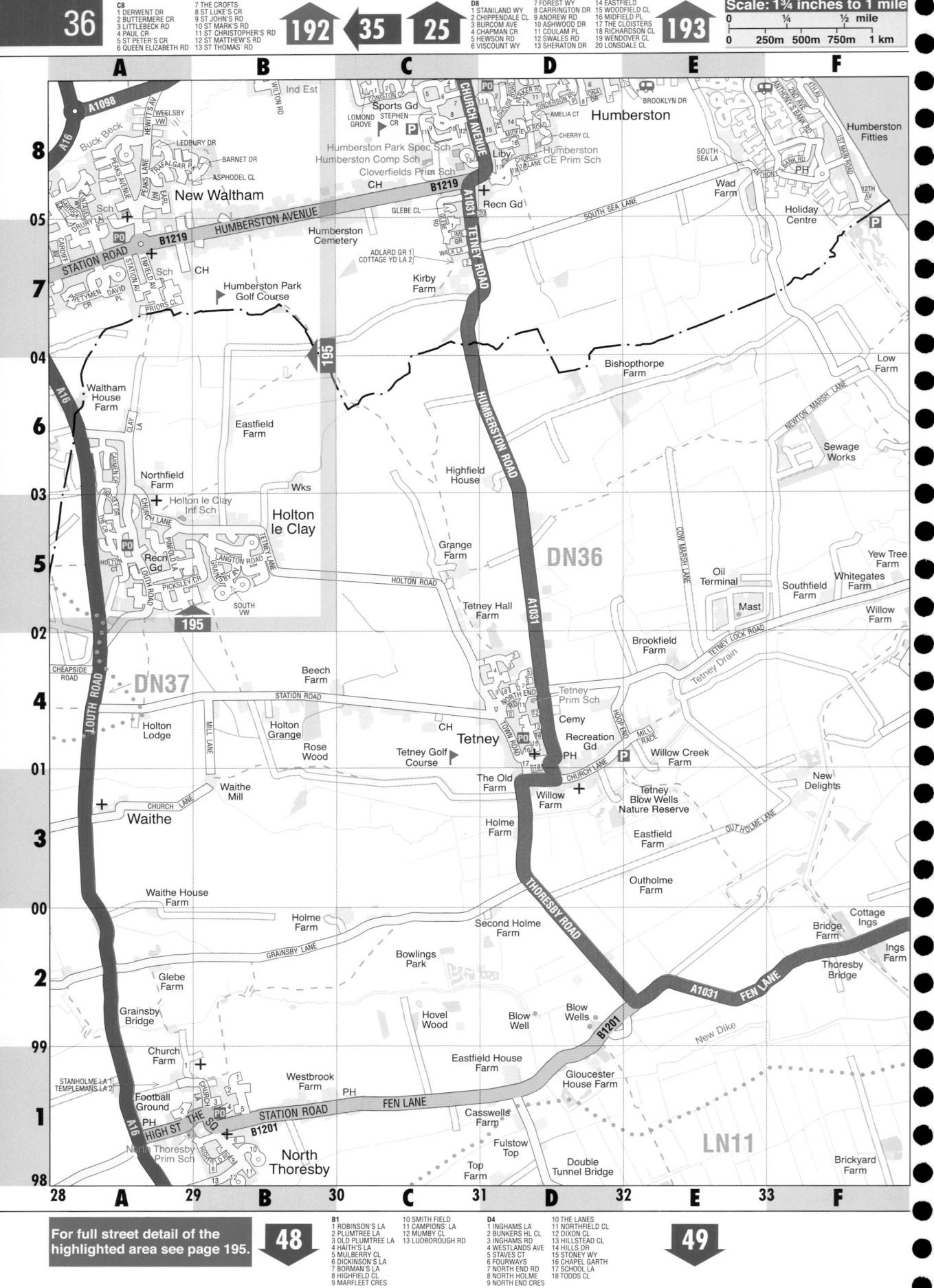

192 ←35 25→ 193

C8
1 DERWENT DR
2 BUTTERMERE CR
3 LITTLEBECK RD
4 PAUL CR
5 ST PETER'S CR
6 QUEEN ELIZABETH RD
7 THE CROFTS
8 ST LUKE'S CR
9 ST JOHN'S RD
10 ST MARK'S RD
11 ST CHRISTOPHER'S RD
12 ST MATTHEW'S RD
13 ST THOMAS' RD

D8
1 STANILAND WY
2 CHIPPENDALE CL
3 BURCOM AVE
4 CHAPMAN RD
5 HEWSON RD
6 VISCOUNT WY
7 FOREST WY
8 CARRINGTON DR
9 ANDREW RD
10 ASHWOOD DR
11 COULAM PL
12 SWALES PL
13 SHERATON DR
14 EASTFIELD
15 WOODFIELD CL
16 MIDFIELD PL
17 THE CLOISTERS
18 RICHARDSON CL
19 WENDOVER CL
20 LONSDALE CL

Scale: 1¾ inches to 1 mile
0   ¼   ½ mile
0 250m 500m 750m 1 km

Map labels:

A1098
A16
Buck Beck
New Waltham
HEWITT'S AV
WEELSBY VW
LEDBURY DR
BARNET DR
ASPHODEL CL
PEAKS AVENUE
TRAFALGAR PK
EARL
PEAKS LANE
CARDIFF AV
ENFIELD AV
STATION ROAD
B1219
HUMBERSTON AVENUE
B1219
Sch
PO
CH
TETMYER CR
DAVID PL
PRIORS CL
STATION AV
Sch

Humberston Park Golf Course
Humberston Cemetery
Humberston Park Spec Sch
Humberston Comp Sch
Cloverfields Prim Sch
CH
Sports Gd
LOMOND GROVE
STEPHEN CR
WILTON RD
Ind Est
CHURCH AVENUE
B1219
Liby
Humberston CE Prim Sch
CHERRY CL
AMELIA CT
SINDERSON RD
MIDFIELD RD
Humberston
Brooklyn Dr
ANTHONY'S BANK RD
ST MARY RD
12TH AV
Humberston Fitties
SOUTH SEA LA
PH
Wad Farm
Holiday Centre
P
GLEBE CL
Recn Gd
TETNEY ROAD
WALK LA
ADLARD GR 1
COTTAGE YD LA 2
Kirby Farm
SOUTH SEA LANE
PARK RD

A16
Waltham House Farm
Eastfield Farm
Northfield Farm
CLAY LA
KARNEL CL
Holton le Clay Inf Sch
CHURCH LANE
Holton le Clay
Wks
Highfield House
Bishopthorpe Farm
Low Farm
NEWTON MARSH LANE
Sewage Works

DN36
HUMBERSTON ROAD
A1031
195
Grange Farm
HOLTON ROAD
Tetney Hall Farm
Oil Terminal
Mast
COW MARSH LANE
Yew Tree Farm
Southfield Farm
Whitegates Farm
Willow Farm
PO
Recn Gd
HOLTON CT
LANGTON ROAD
TETNEY LANE
GRANSBY
PICKSLEY CRES
SOUTH VW
195

DN37
LOUTH ROAD
CHEAPSIDE ROAD
Holton Lodge
MILL LANE
Holton Grange
Beech Farm
STATION ROAD
Rose Wood
CH
Tetney Golf Course
Tetney Prim Sch
NORTH END
Cemy
Tetney
Recreation Gd
PH
P
Willow Creek Farm
Brookfield Farm
TETNEY LOCK ROAD
Tetney Drain
New Delights
HOOP END
MILL RACE
CHURCH LANE
TOWN ROAD

Waithe
CHURCH LANE
Waithe Mill
The Old Farm
Willow Farm
Holme Farm
Tetney Blow Wells Nature Reserve
Eastfield Farm
OUT HOLME LANE
Outholme Farm

Waithe House Farm
Holme Farm
Second Holme Farm
THORESBY ROAD
Cottage Ings
Bridge Farm
Ings Farm

GRAINSBY LANE
Bowlings Park
A1031 FEN LANE
Thoresby Bridge

Glebe Farm
Hovel Wood
Blow Well
Blow Wells
B1201
New Dike
Grainsby Bridge
Church Farm
Westbrook Farm
PH
Eastfield House Farm
Gloucester House Farm
A16
Football Ground
STANHOLME LA 1
TEMPLEMANS LA 2
PH
HIGH ST
THE SS
PO
STATION ROAD
FEN LANE
B1201
Casswells Farm
Fulstow Top
LN11
North Thoresby
North Thoresby Prim Sch
CHURCH LA
Top Farm
Double Tunnel Bridge
Brickyard Farm

Grid labels: A B C D E F (top and bottom); 8 05 7 04 6 03 5 02 4 01 3 00 2 99 1 98 (left); 28 29 30 31 32 33 (bottom)

B1
1 ROBINSON'S LA
2 PLUMTREE
3 OLD PLUMTREE LA
4 HAITH'S LA
5 MULBERRY CL
6 DICKINSON'S LA
7 BORMAN'S LA
8 HIGHFIELD CL
9 MARFLEET CRES
10 SMITH FIELD
11 CAMPIONS' LA
12 MUMBY CL
13 LUDBOROUGH RD

D4
1 INGHAMS LA
2 BUNKERS HL CL
3 INGHAMS RD
4 WESTLANDS AVE
5 STAVES CT
6 FOURWAYS
7 NORTH END RD
8 NORTH HOLME
9 NORTH END CRES
10 THE LANES
11 NORTHFIELD CL
12 DIXON CL
13 HILLSTEAD CL
14 HILLS DR
15 STONEY WY
16 CHAPEL GARTH
17 SCHOOL LA
18 TODDS CL

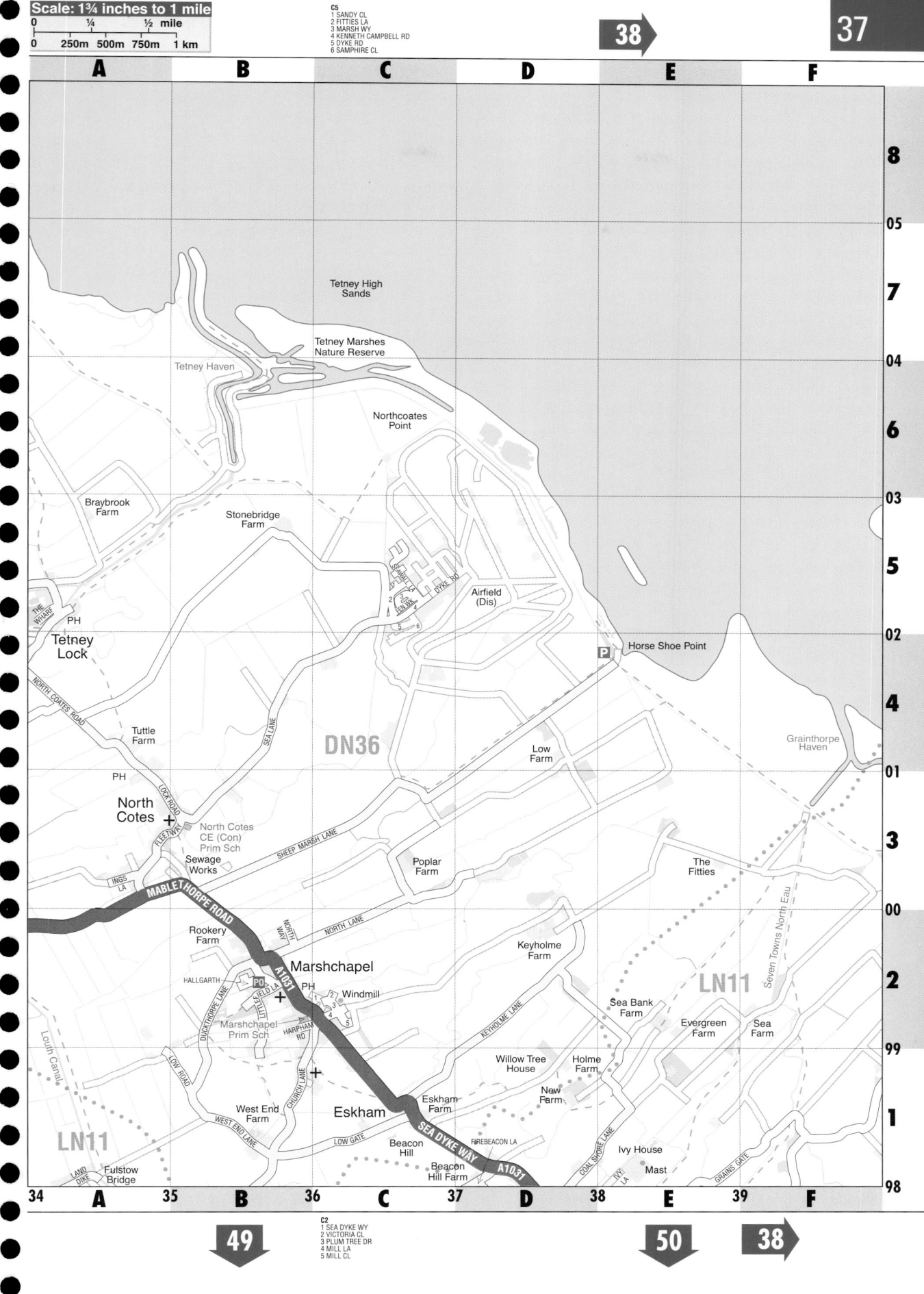

Scale: 1¾ inches to 1 mile

0 | ¼ | ½ mile
0 250m 500m 750m 1 km

38

C5
1 SANDY CL
2 FITTIES LA
3 MARSH WY
4 KENNETH CAMPBELL RD
5 DYKE RD
6 SAMPHIRE CL

Tetney High Sands

Tetney Marshes Nature Reserve

Tetney Haven

Northcoates Point

Braybrook Farm

Stonebridge Farm

Airfield (Dis)

DYKE RD

Horse Shoe Point

Grainthorpe Haven

THE WHARF

PH

Tetney Lock

NORTH COATES ROAD

Tuttle Farm

SEA LANE

DN36

Low Farm

PH

North Cotes

North Cotes CE (Con) Prim Sch

LOCK ROAD

FLEET WAY

Sheep Marsh Lane

Sewage Works

INGS LA

Poplar Farm

The Fitties

MABLETHORPE ROAD

North Lane

HIGH WAY

Rookery Farm

Keyholme Farm

LN11

HALLGARTH

DUCKTHORPE LANE

A1031

LITTLEFIELD LA

PO

Marshchapel

PH

Windmill

Sea Bank Farm

Evergreen Farm

Sea Farm

Marshchapel Prim Sch

HARPHAM RD

KEYHOLME LANE

Willow Tree House

Holme Farm

New Farm

Louth Canal

LOW ROAD

CHURCH LANE

West End Farm

WEST END LANE

Eskham

LOW GATE

Eskham Farm

SEA DYKE WAY

Beacon Hill

FIREBEACON LA

COAL SHORE LANE

IVY LA

Ivy House

Mast

GRAINS GATE

Seven Towns North Eau

LN11

LAND DIKE

Fulstow Bridge

Beacon Hill Farm

A1031

49

C2
1 SEA DYKE WY
2 VICTORIA CL
3 PLUM TREE DR
4 MILL LA
5 MILL CL

50

38

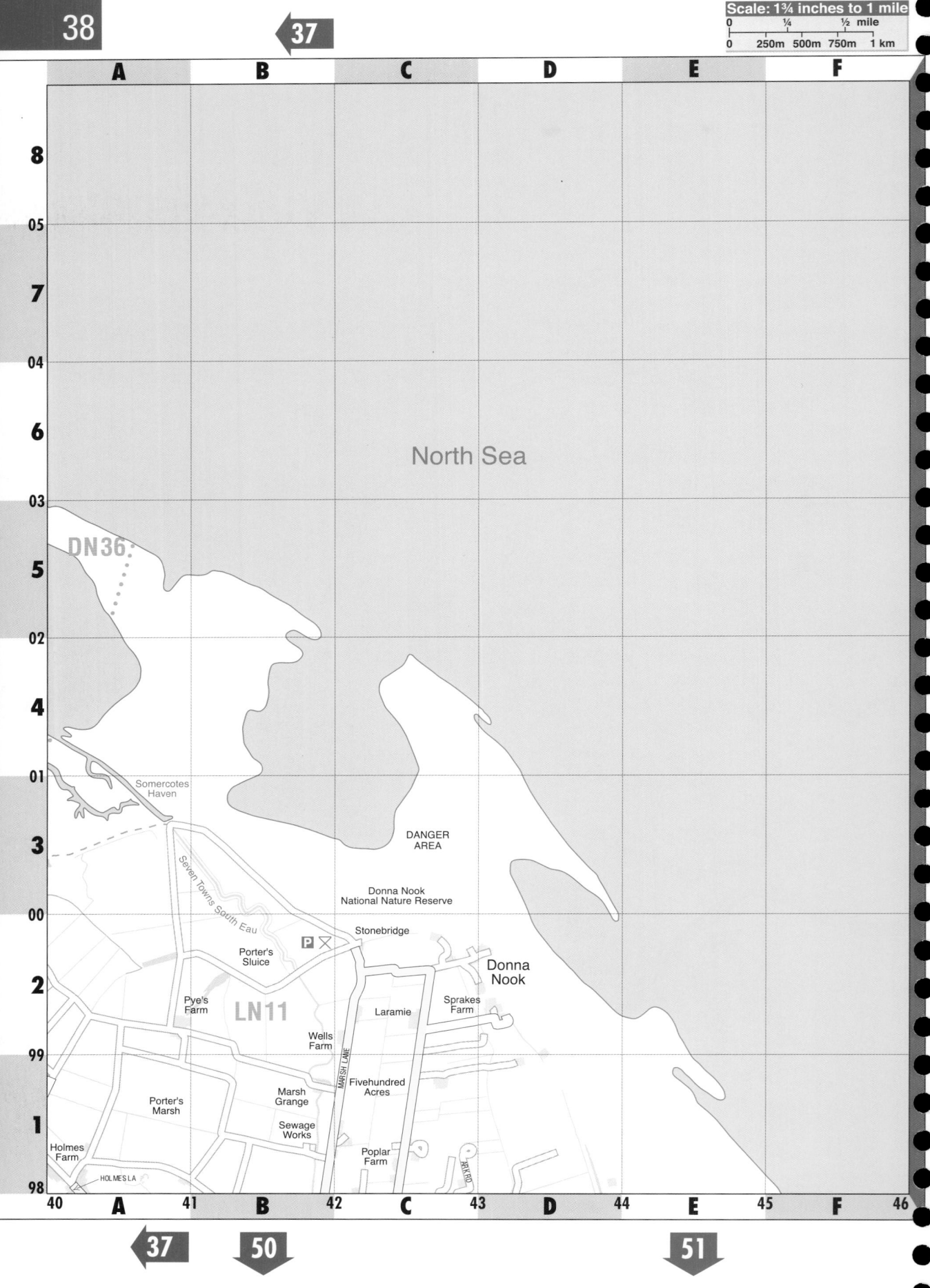

37

Scale: 1¾ inches to 1 mile

| 0 | | ¼ | | ½ | mile |

| 0 | 250m | 500m | 750m | 1 km |

A B C D E F

8

05

7

04

6

03

North Sea

DN36

5

02

4

01

Somercotes
Haven

3

DANGER
AREA

Donna Nook
National Nature Reserve

Seven Towns South Eau

00

Stonebridge

P ✕

Porter's
Sluice

Donna
Nook

2

Pye's
Farm

LN11

Laramie

Sprakes
Farm

Wells
Farm

99

MARSH LANE

Marsh
Grange

Fivehundred
Acres

1

Porter's
Marsh

Sewage
Works

Holmes
Farm

Poplar
Farm

PARK RD

98

40   A   41   B   42   C   43   D   44   E   45   F   46

HOLMES LA

37   50   51

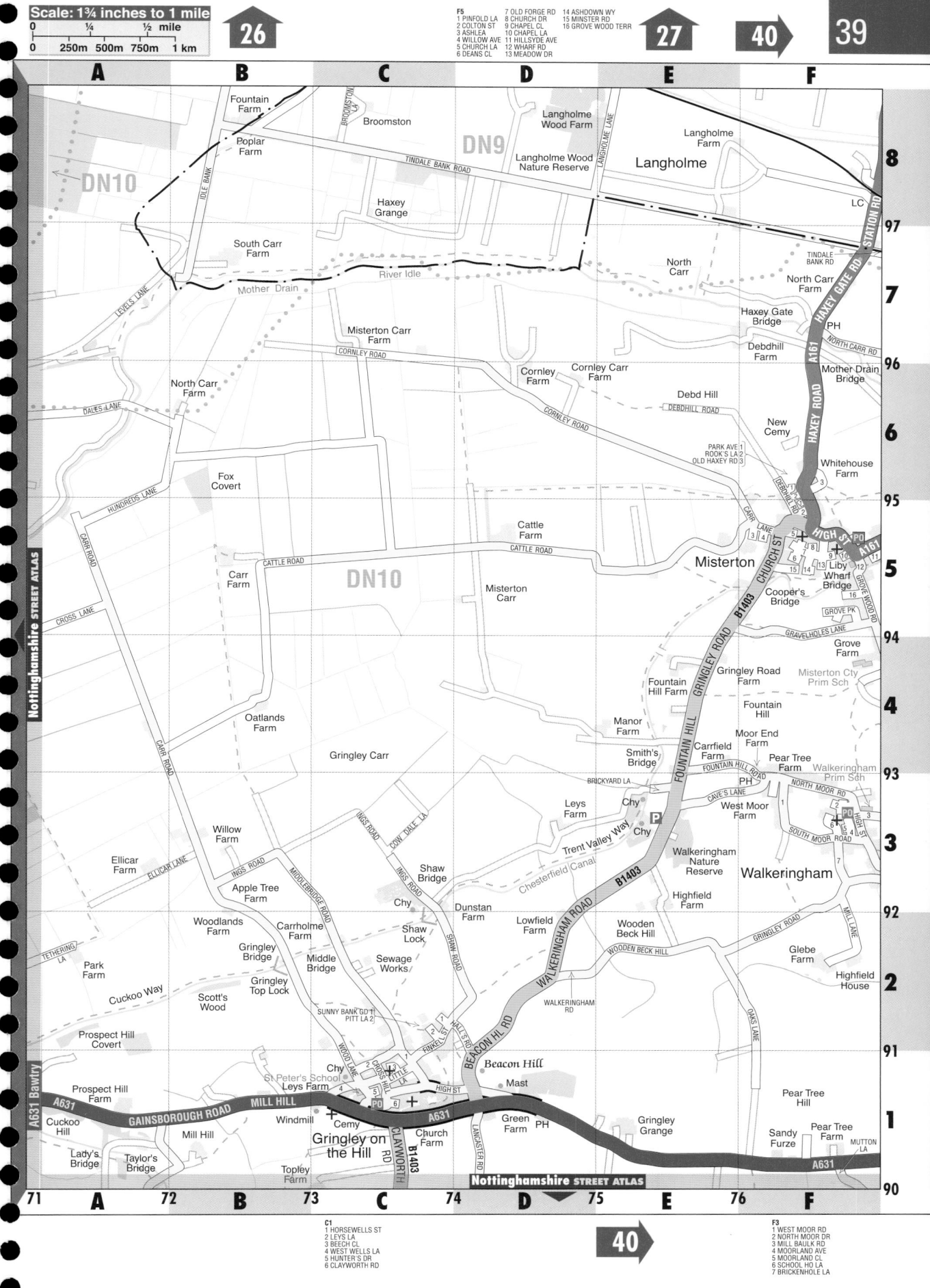

F5
1 PINFOLD LA
2 COLTON ST
3 ASHLEA
4 WILLOW AVE
5 CHURCH LA
6 DEANS CL

7 OLD FORGE RD
8 CHURCH DR
9 CHAPEL CL
10 CHAPEL LA
11 HILLSYDE AVE
12 WHARF RD
13 MEADOW DR

14 ASHDOWN WY
15 MINSTER RD
16 GROVE WOOD TERR

Nottinghamshire STREET ATLAS

DN10

DN9

Langholme Wood Farm

Langholme Farm

Langholme

Fountain Farm

Broomston

Poplar Farm

TINDALE BANK ROAD

Langholme Wood Nature Reserve

LC

STATION RD

IDLE BANK

Haxey Grange

South Carr Farm

River Idle

Mother Drain

North Carr

North Carr Farm

TINDALE BANK RD

HAXEY GATE RD

97

Haxey Gate Bridge

PH

NORTH CARR RD

7

A161

LEVELS LANE

Misterton Carr Farm

CORNLEY ROAD

Debdhill Farm

Mother Drain Bridge

96

DALES LANE

North Carr Farm

Cornley Farm

Cornley Carr Farm

CORNLEY ROAD

Debd Hill

DEBDHILL ROAD

New Cemy

HAXEY ROAD

Whitehouse Farm

6

PARK AVE 1
ROOK'S LA 2
OLD HAXEY RD 3

HUNDREDS LANE

Fox Covert

DEBDHILL RD

95

CARR LANE

HIGH ST

A161

CARR ROAD

DN10

Cattle Farm

CATTLE ROAD

Misterton

Misterton

CHURCH ST

Liby

PO

CROSS LANE

Carr Farm

CATTLE ROAD

Misterton Carr

B1403

Cooper's Bridge

Wharf Bridge

GROVE WOOD RD

5

94

GRINGLEY ROAD

GRAVELHOLES LANE

GROVE PK

Grove Farm

Oatlands Farm

Gringley Carr

Fountain Hill Farm

Gringley Road Farm

Misterton Cty Prim Sch

Fountain Hill

4

Manor Farm

Moor End Farm

Pear Tree Farm

Walkeringham Prim Sch

CARR ROAD

Smith's Bridge

Carrfield Farm

FOUNTAIN HILL

PH

NORTH MOOR RD

93

Willow Farm

INGS ROAD

COW DALE LA

Leys Farm

Chy

BRICKYARD LA

FOUNTAIN HILL RD

CAVE'S LANE

West Moor Farm

PO

Walkeringham

SOUTH MOOR ROAD

Ellicar Farm

ELLICAR LANE

Apple Tree Farm

Shaw Bridge

Chy

Trent Valley Way

P

Chy

Walkeringham Nature Reserve

3

MIDDLEBRIDGE ROAD

INGS ROAD

Dunstan Farm

Chesterfield Canal

B1403

Highfield Farm

MILL LANE

92

Woodlands Farm

Carrholme Farm

Shaw Lock

SHAW ROAD

Lowfield Farm

WALKERINGHAM ROAD

Wooden Beck Hill

GRINGLEY ROAD

Glebe Farm

Highfield House

2

TETHERING LA

Park Farm

Gringley Bridge

Middle Bridge

Gringley Top Lock

Sewage Works

WOODEN BECK HILL

Cuckoo Way

Scott's Wood

SUNNY BANK GD 1
PITT LA 2

WALKERINGHAM RD

OAKS LANE

91

Prospect Hill Covert

A631 Bawtry

WOOD LANE

CROSS HILL

FINKELL ST

HIGH ST

St Peter's School

Chy

Leys Farm

Mast

BEACON HL RD

Beacon Hill

LANCASTER RD

CLAYWORTH RD

Green Farm

PH

Gringley Grange

Pear Tree Hill

Prospect Hill Farm

A631

GAINSBOROUGH ROAD

MILL HILL

PO

A631

Church Farm

B1403

Pear Tree Farm

Sandy Furze

MUTTON LA

1

Cuckoo Hill

Lady's Bridge

Mill Hill

Taylor's Bridge

Windmill

Cemy

Gringley on the Hill

Topley Farm

A631

90

71   A   72   B   73   C   74   D   75   E   76   F

C1
1 HORSEWELLS ST
2 LEYS LA
3 BEECH CL
4 WEST WELLS LA
5 HUNTER'S DR
6 CLAYWORTH RD

F3
1 WEST MOOR RD
2 NORTH MOOR DR
3 MILL BAULK RD
4 MOORLAND AVE
5 MOORLAND CL
6 SCHOOL HO LA
7 BRICKENHOLE LA

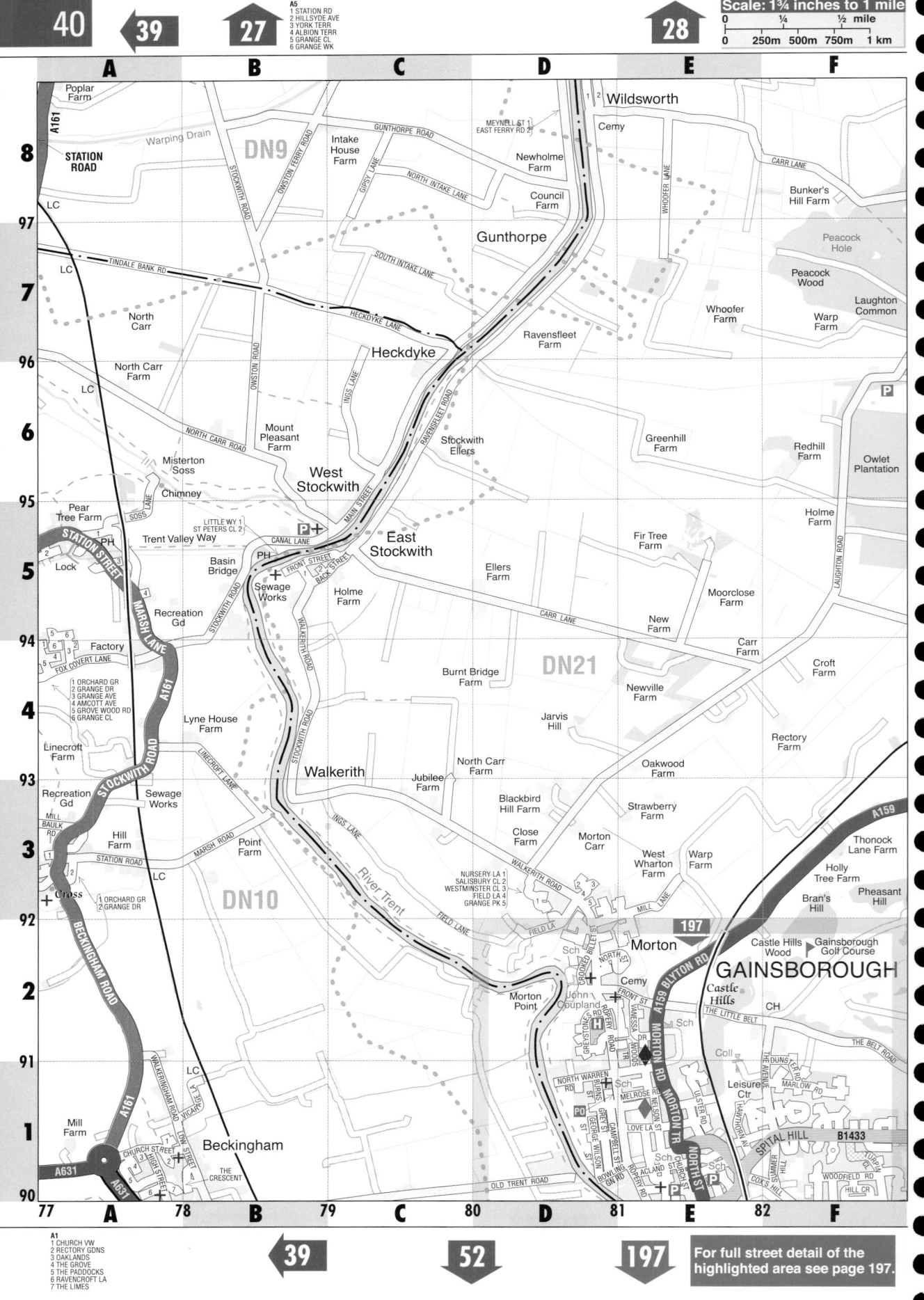

40

39

27

A5
1 STATION RD
2 HILLSYDE AVE
3 YORK TERR
4 ALBION TERR
5 GRANGE CL
6 GRANGE WK

28

Scale: 1¾ inches to 1 mile

0   ¼   ½ mile
0 250m 500m 750m 1 km

Poplar Farm
A161
STATION ROAD
LC
97
LC
7
North Carr
96
North Carr Farm
LC
6
North Carr Road
Misterton Soss
Chimney
95
Pear Tree Farm
PH
SOSS LANE
Trent Valley Way
STATION STREET
Lock
MARSH LANE
2
5
Recreation Gd
94
5
6
3
Factory
Fox Covert Lane
1 ORCHARD GR
2 GRANGE DR
3 GRANGE AVE
4 AMCOTT AVE
5 GROVE WOOD RD
6 GRANGE CL
4
Linecroft Farm
Lyne House Farm
STOCKWITH ROAD
A161
LINECROFT LANE
93
Recreation Gd
Sewage Works
3
Hill Farm
MILL BAULK RD
STATION ROAD
LC
2
Cross
BECKINGHAM ROAD
1 ORCHARD GR
2 GRANGE DR
92
91
A161
WALKERINGHAM ROAD
VICAR LA
LC
1
Mill Farm
Beckingham
CHURCH STREET
HIGH STREET
2
4
A631
A631
90

DN9
Warping Drain
Stockwith Road
Owston Ferry Road
Gunthorpe Road
Intake House Farm
Gypsy Lane
North Intake Lane
South Intake Lane
Heckdyke Lane
Ings Lane
Mount Pleasant Farm
West Stockwith
Main Street
Ravensfleet Road
Stockwith Ellers
East Stockwith
Canal Lane
Front Street
Back Street
P
Basin Bridge
PH
Sewage Works
Holme Farm
Walkerith Road
Walkerith
Owston Road
Heckdyke
Jubilee Farm
Ings Lane
Burnt Bridge Farm
North Carr Farm
River Trent
Point Farm
Marsh Road
DN10
LITTLE WY 1
ST PETERS CL 2

Wildsworth
1 2
Cemy
MEYNELL ST 1
EAST FERRY RD 2
Newholme Farm
Council Farm
Gunthorpe
Ravensfleet Farm
WHOOFER LANE
Carr Lane
Bunker's Hill Farm
Peacock Hole
Peacock Wood
Whoofer Farm
Warp Farm
Laughton Common
Greenhill Farm
Redhill Farm
Owlet Plantation
P
Holme Farm
Fir Tree Farm
LAUGHTON ROAD
Ellers Farm
Carr Lane
Moorclose Farm
New Farm
Carr Farm
DN21
Newville Farm
Jarvis Hill
Oakwood Farm
Strawberry Farm
Morton Carr
West Wharton Farm
Close Farm
Blackbird Hill Farm
Field Lane
Croft Farm
Rectory Farm
A159
Thonock Lane Farm
Holly Tree Farm
Warp Farm
Bran's Hill
Pheasant Hill
197
Morton
Castle Hills Wood
Gainsborough Golf Course
GAINSBOROUGH
Castle Hills
CH
A159 BLYTON RD
Sch
Cemy
MORTON RD
MORTON TR
Sch
THE LITTLE BELT
THE BELT ROAD
John Coupland
H
NORTH WARREN RD
Sch
MELROSE RD
NELSON ST
ULSTER RD
Coll
Leisure Ctr
THE AVENUE
MARLOW RD
THE DUNS
PO
GREY'S ST
GEORGE ST
CAMPBELL ST
GEORGE WILSON
LOVE LA
VANESSA DR
FERRY RD
ROPERY RD
NORTH ST
CHURCH ST
Sch
Sch
SUMMER RD
COX'S HILL
SPITAL HILL
B1433
WOODFIELD RD
HILL CR
BOWLING GN RD
ROPERY RD
ACLAND ST
OLD TRENT ROAD
P
Morton Point

NURSERY LA 1
SALISBURY CL 2
WESTMINSTER CL 3
FIELD LA 4
GRANGE PK 5

A1
1 CHURCH VW
2 RECTORY GDNS
3 OAKLANDS
4 THE GROVE
5 THE PADDOCKS
6 RAVENCROFT LA
7 THE LIMES

39

52

197

For full street detail of the highlighted area see page 197.

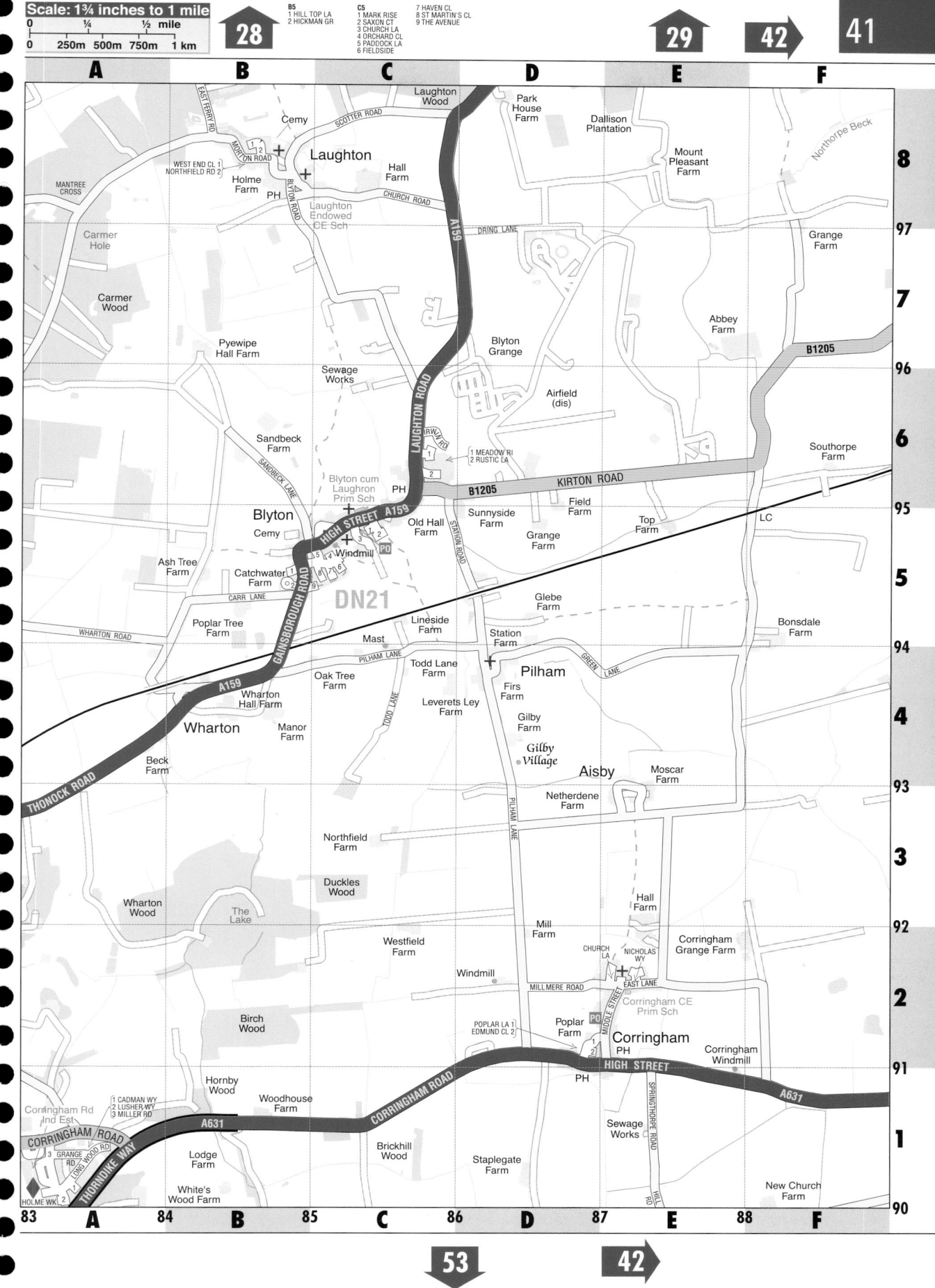

B5
1 HILL TOP LA
2 HICKMAN GR

C5
1 MARK RISE
2 SAXON CT
3 CHURCH LA
4 ORCHARD CL
5 PADDOCK LA
6 FIELDSIDE

7 HAVEN CL
8 ST MARTIN'S CL
9 THE AVENUE

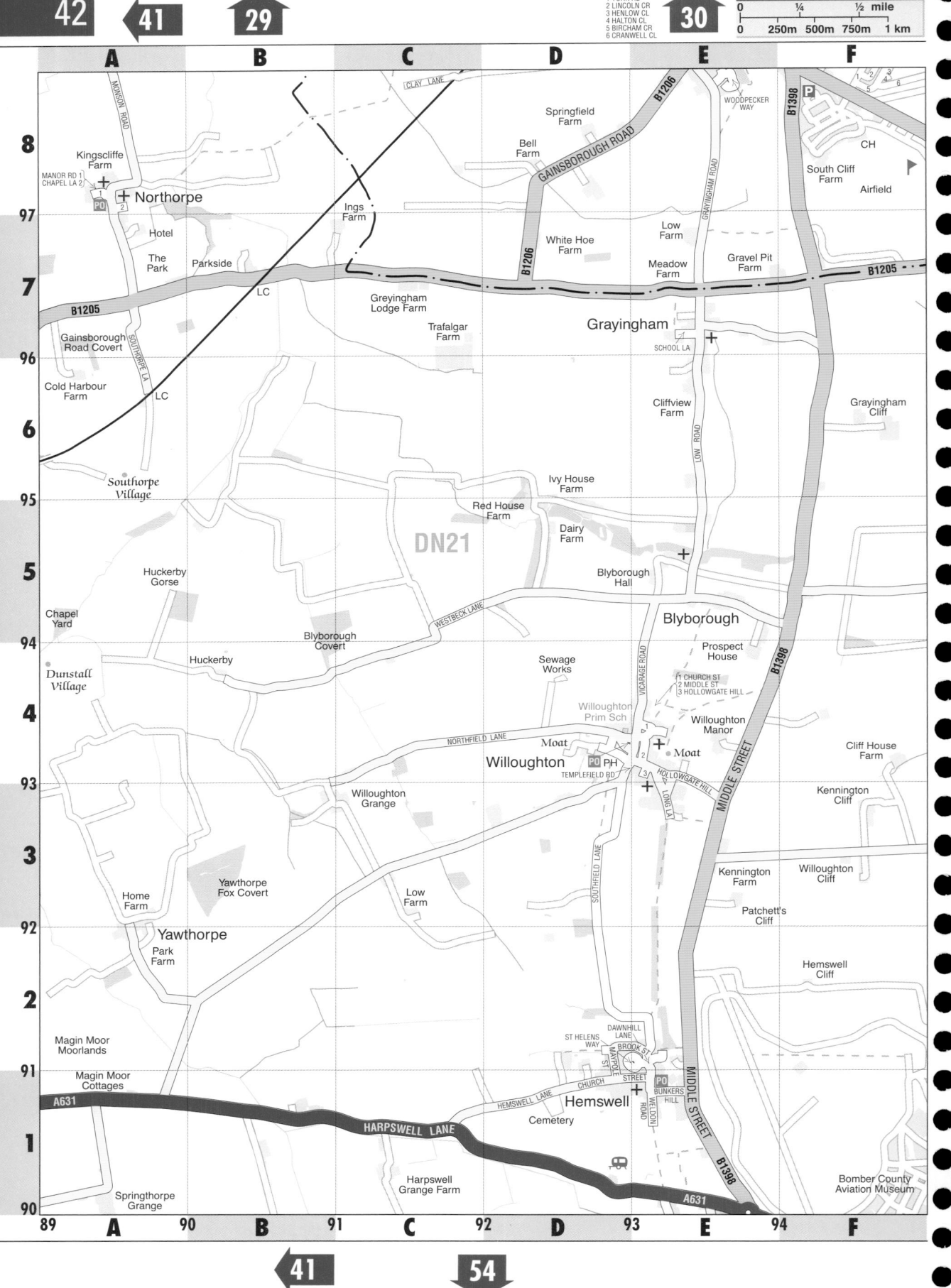

F8
1 YORK RD
2 LINCOLN CR
3 HENLOW CL
4 HALTON CL
5 BIRCHAM CR
6 CRANWELL CL

Scale: 1¾ inches to 1 mile

0   ¼   ½ mile
0   250m   500m   750m   1 km

Kingscliffe Farm
MANOR RD 1
CHAPEL LA 2
PO
Northorpe
Hotel
The Park
Parkside
LC
B1205
Gainsborough Road Covert
Cold Harbour Farm
LC

Ings Farm

CLAY LANE

Springfield Farm
Bell Farm
GAINSBOROUGH ROAD
B1206
White Hoe Farm
B1206
Greyingham Lodge Farm
Trafalgar Farm
Grayingham
SCHOOL LA

WOODPECKER WAY
B1398
P
CH
South Cliff Farm
Airfield
Low Farm
Meadow Farm
GRAYINGHAM ROAD
Gravel Pit Farm
B1205
LOW ROAD
Cliffview Farm
Grayingham Cliff

Southorpe Village
DN21
Ivy House Farm
Red House Farm
Dairy Farm
Blyborough Hall

Chapel Yard
Huckerby Gorse
Dunstall Village
Huckerby
Blyborough Covert
WESTBECK LANE
Sewage Works
Willoughton Prim Sch
NORTHFIELD LANE
Moat
Willoughton
PO PH
TEMPLEFIELD RD
Willoughton Grange

Blyborough
Prospect House
1 CHURCH ST
2 MIDDLE ST
3 HOLLOWGATE HILL
VICARAGE ROAD
Willoughton Manor
Moat
HOLLOWGATE HILL
B1398
MIDDLE STREET
Cliff House Farm
Kennington Cliff

Home Farm
Yawthorpe Fox Covert
Low Farm
SOUTHFIELD LANE
LONG LA
Kennington Farm
Willoughton Cliff
Patchett's Cliff

Yawthorpe
Park Farm
Hemswell Cliff

Magin Moor Moorlands
Magin Moor Cottages
A631
HARPSWELL LANE
ST HELENS WAY
DAWNHILL LANE
BROOK ST
MAYPOLE ST
CHURCH STREET
HEMSWELL LANE
Cemetery
Hemswell
PO
BUNKERS HILL
WELDON ROAD
MIDDLE STREET
B1398
Bomber County Aviation Museum

Springthorpe Grange
Harpswell Grange Farm
A631

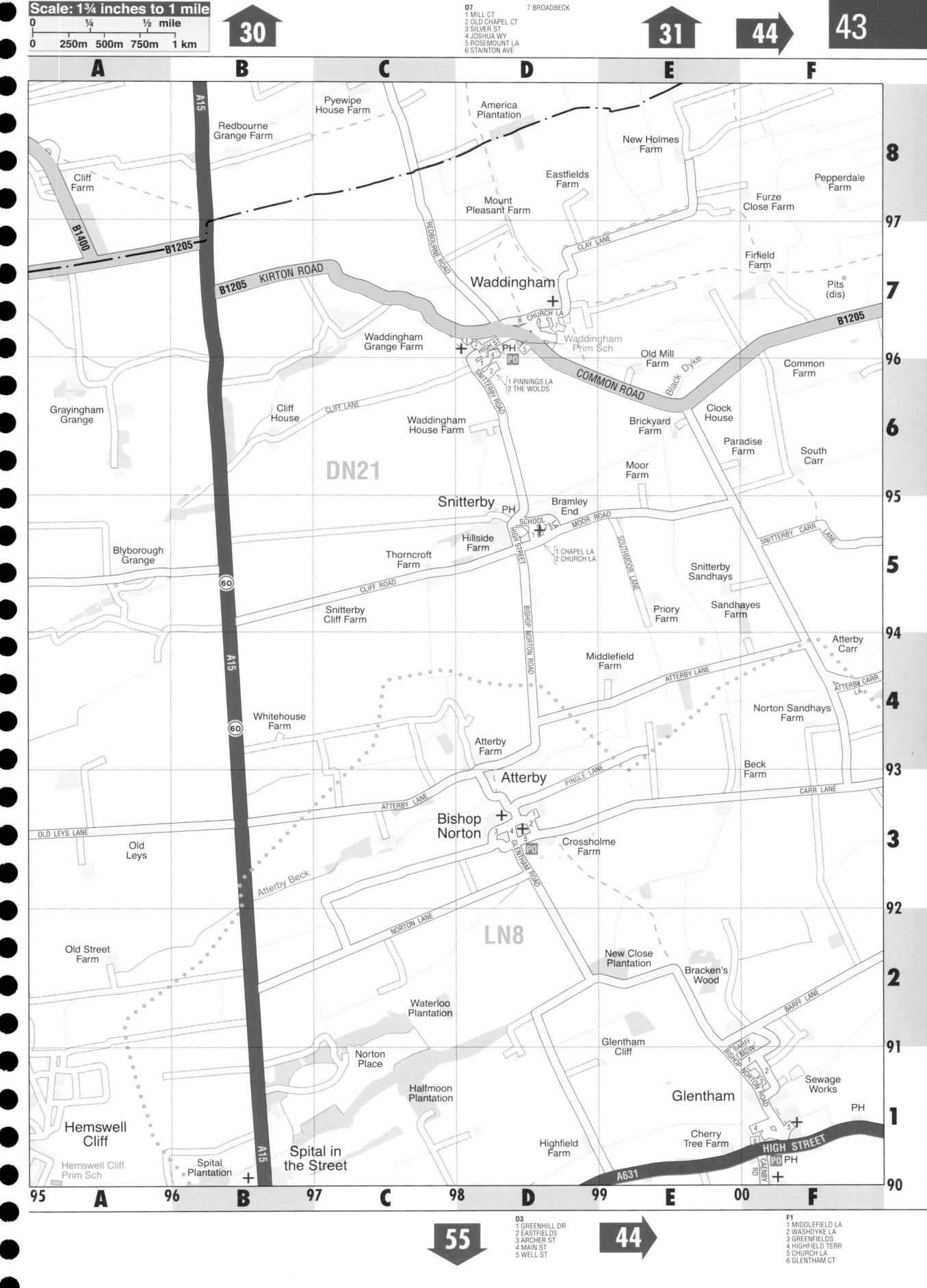

Scale: 1¾ inches to 1 mile

0   ¼   ½   mile
0 250m 500m 750m 1 km

30
31
44
43

D7
1 MILL CT
2 OLD CHAPEL CT
3 SILVER ST
4 JOSHUA WY
5 ROSEMOUNT LA
6 STAINTON AVE

7 BROADBECK

A   B   C   D   E   F

8

97

Redbourne
Grange Farm

Pyewipe
House Farm

America
Plantation

New Holmes
Farm

Cliff
Farm

Eastfields
Farm

Pepperdale
Farm

Mount
Pleasant Farm

Furze
Close Farm

CLAY LANE

Firfield
Farm

Pits
(dis)

KIRTON ROAD

B1205

Waddingham

B1205

7

96

CHURCH LA

Waddingham
Grange Farm

Waddingham
Prim Sch

Old Mill
Farm

Common
Farm

HIGH ST

PH
PO

COMMON ROAD

Black Dyke

1 PINNINGS LA
2 THE WOLDS

Grayingham
Grange

Cliff
House

CLIFF LANE

Waddingham
House Farm

Moor
Farm

Brickyard
Farm

Clock
House

DN21

Paradise
Farm

South
Carr

6

95

Snitterby

PH

SCHOOL

Bramley
End

MOOR ROAD

Blyborough
Grange

Hillside
Farm

Snitterby
Carr

SNITTERBY CARR LANE

Thorncroft
Farm

HIGH STREET

1 CHAPEL LA
2 CHURCH LA

Snitterby
Sandhays

5

94

60

CLIFF ROAD

Snitterby
Cliff Farm

SOUTHMOOR LANE

Priory
Farm

Sandhayes
Farm

Atterby
Carr

Middlefield
Farm

ATTERBY LANE

ATTERBY CARR LA

4

93

60

Whitehouse
Farm

Atterby
Farm

Norton Sandhays
Farm

BISHOP NORTON ROAD

Atterby

PINGLE LANE

Beck
Farm

CARR LANE

OLD LEYS LANE

Bishop
Norton

Crossholme
Farm

3

92

Old Leys

PO

Atterby Beck

GLENTHAM ROAD

NORTON LANE

LN8

New Close
Plantation

Bracken's
Wood

BARFF LANE

2

91

Old Street
Farm

Waterloo
Plantation

Glentham
Cliff

BARFF MDW

BISHOP NORTON RD

Sewage
Works

Norton
Place

PH

1

90

Hemswell
Cliff

Halfmoon
Plantation

Glentham

Cherry
Tree Farm

HIGH STREET

Hemswell Cliff
Prim Sch

Spital
Plantation

Spital in
the Street

Highfield
Farm

A631

GARNBY RD

PO PH

95   A   96   B   97   C   98   D   99   E   00   F

55
44

D3
1 GREENHILL DR
2 EASTFIELDS
3 ARCHER ST
4 MAIN ST
5 WELL ST

F1
1 MIDDLEFIELD LA
2 WASHDYKE LA
3 GREENFIELDS
4 HIGHFIELD TERR
5 CHURCH LA
6 GLENTHAM CT

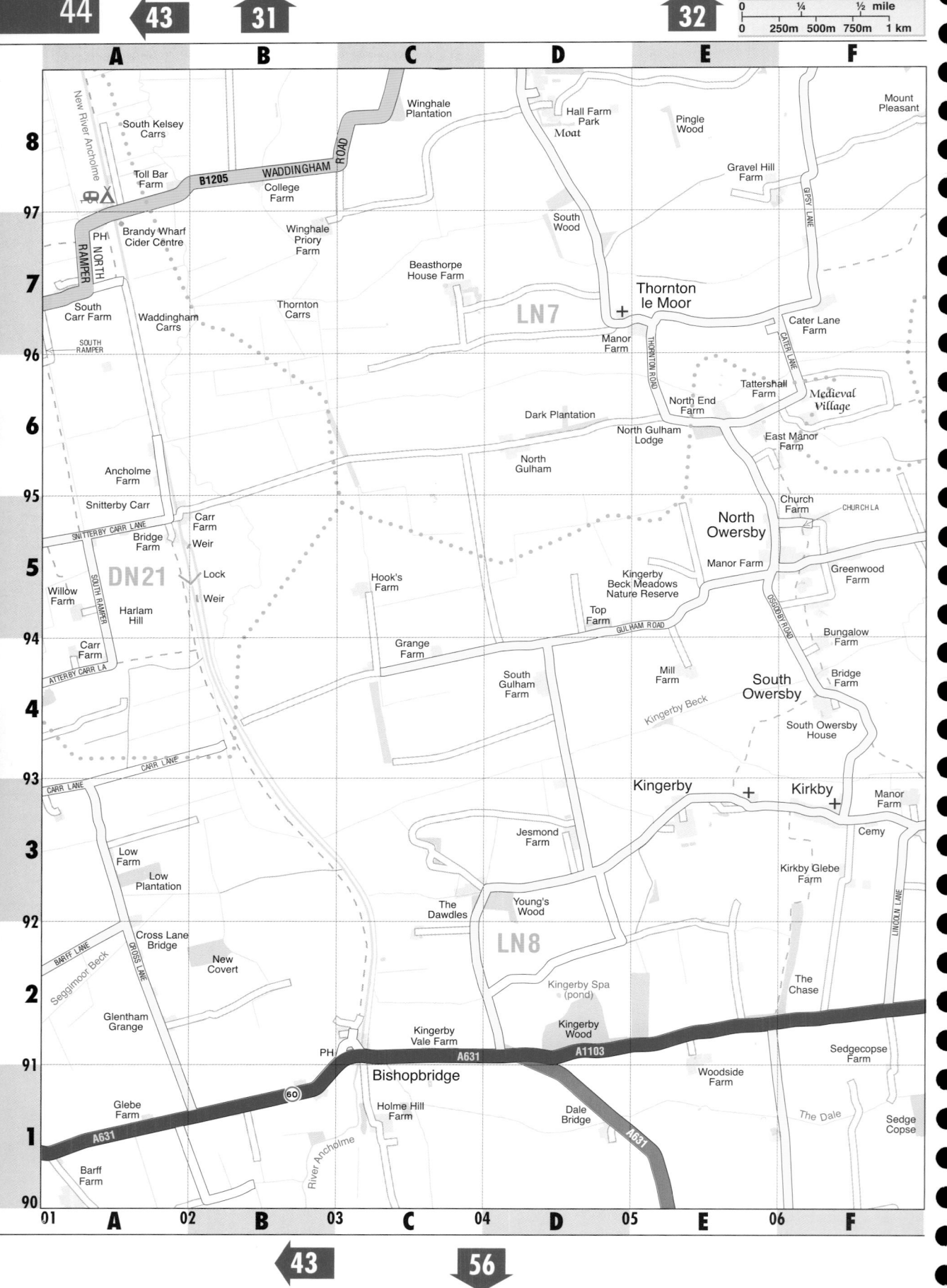

A B C D E F

8

New River Ancholme

South Kelsey Carrs

Winghale Plantation

Hall Farm Park Moat

Pingle Wood

Mount Pleasant

Toll Bar Farm

B1205 WADDINGHAM ROAD

College Farm

Gravel Hill Farm

97

PH NORTH RAMPER

Brandy Wharf Cider Centre

Winghale Priory Farm

South Wood

GIPSY LANE

7

South Carr Farm

Waddingham Carrs

Thornton Carrs

Beasthorpe House Farm

Thornton le Moor

Cater Lane Farm

SOUTH RAMPER

Manor Farm

THORNTON ROAD

96

North End Farm

Tattershall Farm

Medieval Village

6

Dark Plantation

North Gulham Lodge

North Gulham

East Manor Farm

95

Ancholme Farm

North Gulham

Church Farm

CHURCH LA

Snitterby Carr

North Owersby

SNITTERBY CARR LANE

Carr Farm

Manor Farm

Greenwood Farm

5

DN21

Bridge Farm

Weir

Hook's Farm

Kingerby Beck Meadows Nature Reserve

OSGODBY ROAD

Bungalow Farm

SOUTH RAMPER

Lock

Top Farm

Willow Farm

Weir

Harlam Hill

South Owersby

Bridge Farm

94

Carr Farm

Grange Farm

South Gulham Farm

GULHAM ROAD

Mill Farm

ATTERBY CARR LA

4

Kingerby Beck

South Owersby House

CARR LANE

93

CARR LANE

Kingerby

Kirkby

Manor Farm

3

Low Farm

Jesmond Farm

Cemy

Low Plantation

Kirkby Glebe Farm

The Dawdles

Young's Wood

LINCOLN LANE

92

BARFF LANE

Cross Lane Bridge

LN8

Seggimoor Beck

New Covert

Kingerby Spa (pond)

The Chase

2

CROSS LANE

Glentham Grange

Kingerby Vale Farm

Kingerby Wood

91

PH

A631

A1103

Sedgecopse Farm

Bishopbridge

Woodside Farm

Glebe Farm

60

Holme Hill Farm

Dale Bridge

The Dale

Sedge Copse

1

A631

River Ancholme

A631

Barff Farm

90

01 A 02 B 03 C 04 D 05 E 06 F

Scale: 1¾ inches to 1 mile

32
33
46

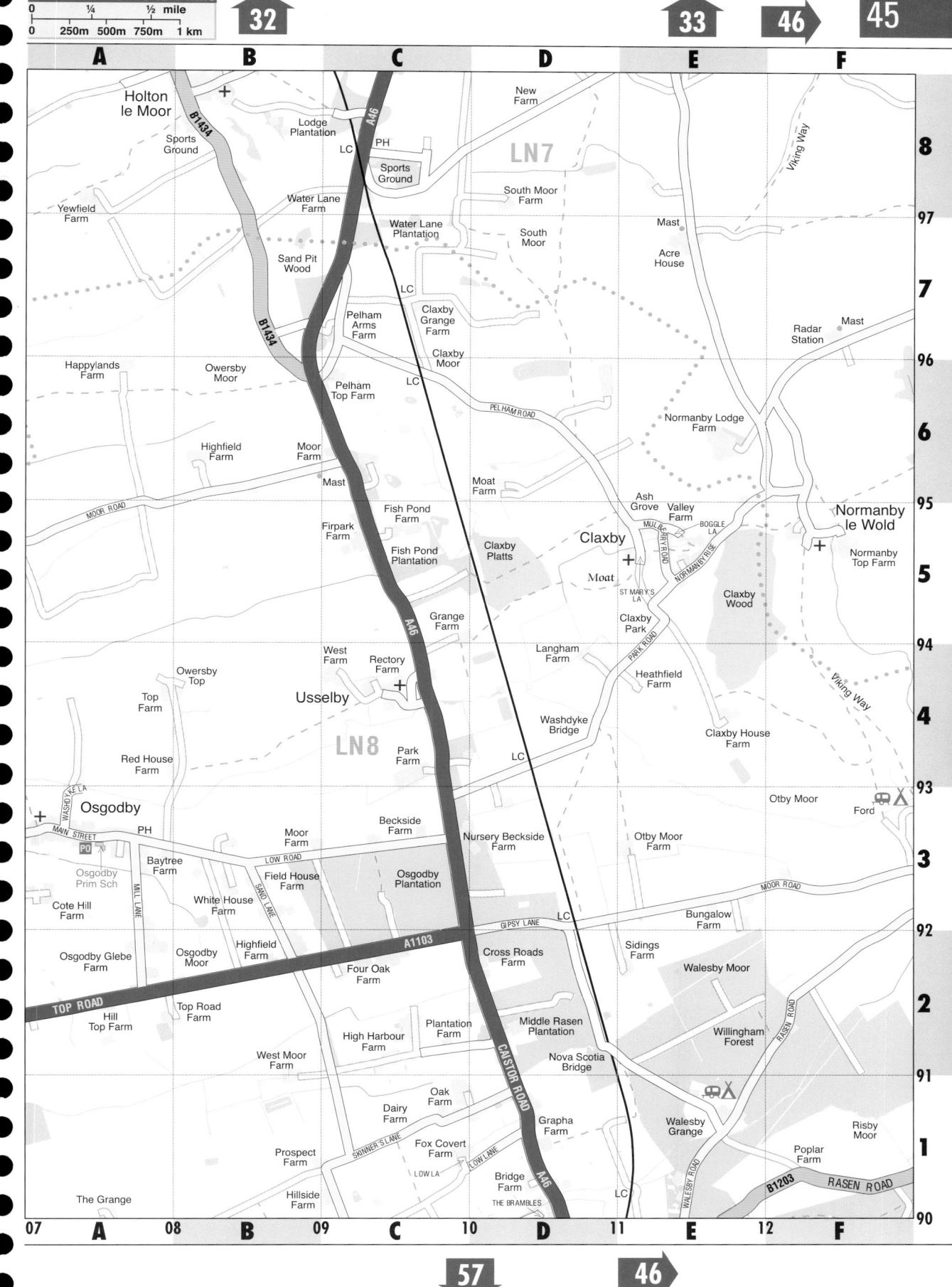
Holton le Moor
Sports Ground
B1434
Lodge Plantation
A46
LC
PH
Sports Ground
New Farm
LN7
South Moor Farm
Viking Way
Yewfield Farm
Water Lane Farm
Water Lane Plantation
South Moor
Mast
Acre House
Sand Pit Wood
LC
Claxby Grange Farm
Pelham Arms Farm
Radar Station
Mast
Happylands Farm
Owersby Moor
Claxby Moor
Pelham Top Farm
LC
PELHAM ROAD
Normanby Lodge Farm
Highfield Farm
Moor Farm
Mast
Moat Farm
MOOR ROAD
Fish Pond Farm
Ash Grove
Valley Farm
Normanby le Wold
Firpark Farm
MULBERRY ROAD
BOGGLE LA
Claxby
Fish Pond Plantation
Claxby Platts
Moat
NORMANBY RISE
Normanby Top Farm
ST MARY'S LA
Claxby Wood
Grange Farm
Claxby Park
PARK ROAD
West Farm
Rectory Farm
Langham Farm
Heathfield Farm
Owersby Top
Top Farm
Usselby
Viking Way
Washdyke Bridge
Claxby House Farm
Red House Farm
LN8
Park Farm
LC
Osgodby
WASHDYKE LA
Otby Moor
Ford
MAIN STREET
PH
Beckside Farm
Moor Farm
Nursery Beckside Farm
Otby Moor Farm
PO
Osgodby Prim Sch
Baytree Farm
LOW ROAD
Field House Farm
Osgodby Plantation
MOOR ROAD
Cote Hill Farm
MILL LANE
White House Farm
SAND LANE
GIPSY LANE
LC
Bungalow Farm
Osgodby Glebe Farm
Osgodby Moor
Highfield Farm
A1103
Cross Roads Farm
Sidings Farm
Walesby Moor
Four Oak Farm
TOP ROAD
Hill Top Farm
Top Road Farm
Middle Rasen Plantation
Plantation Farm
RASEN ROAD
High Harbour Farm
Willingham Forest
CAISTOR ROAD
West Moor Farm
Nova Scotia Bridge
Oak Farm
Dairy Farm
Grapha Farm
Walesby Grange
Risby Moor
Prospect Farm
SKINNER'S LANE
Fox Covert Farm
Poplar Farm
LOW LA
LOW LANE
WALESBY ROAD
Bridge Farm
B1203
RASEN ROAD
The Grange
Hillside Farm
THE BRAMBLES
LC
A B C D E F
07 08 09 10 11 12
90 91 92 93 94 95 96 97
1 2 3 4 5 6 7 8

57
46

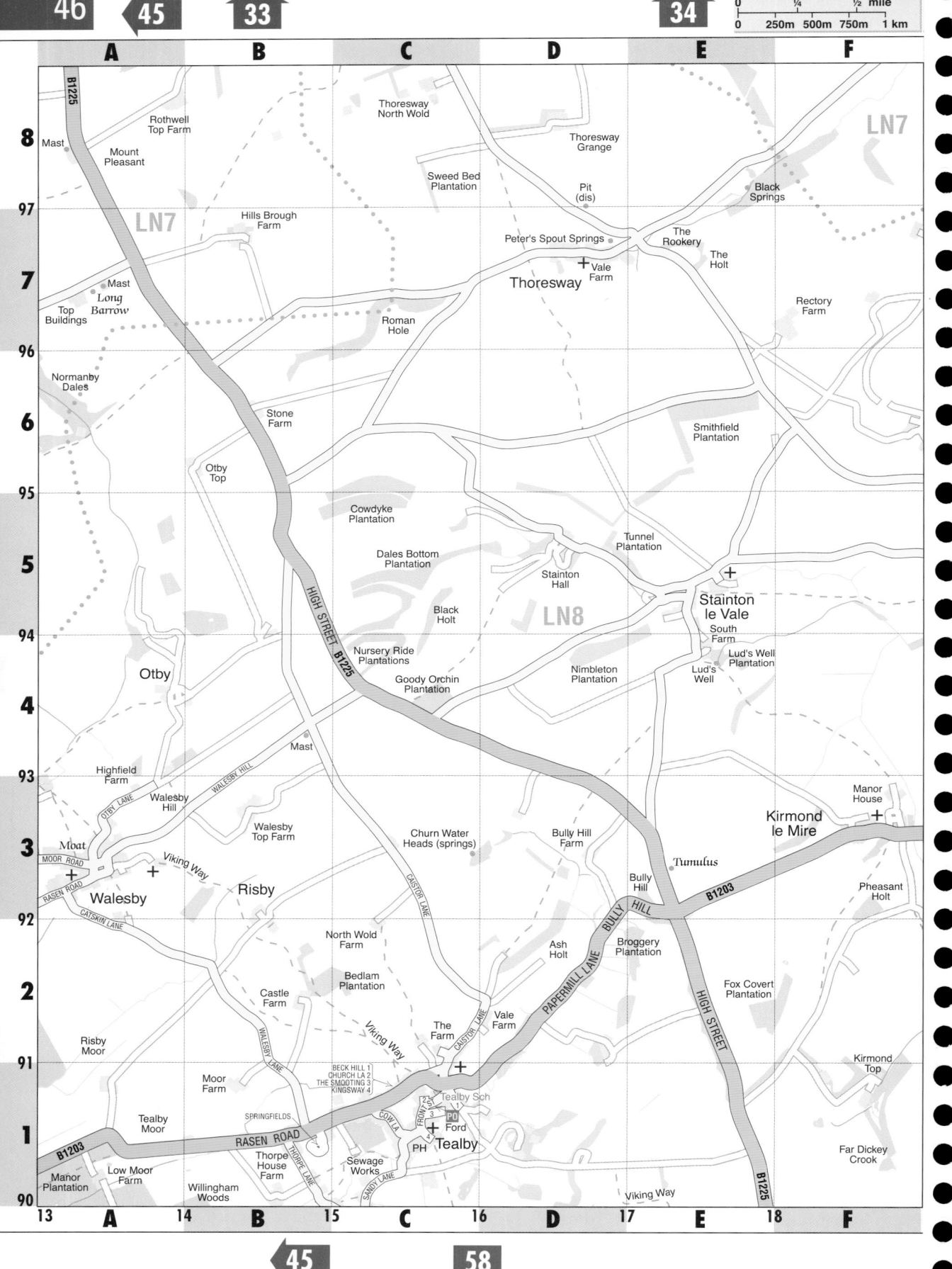

A   B   C   D   E   F

8
97
7
96
6
95
5
94
4
93
3
92
2
91
1
90

B1225

LN7

Mast

Rothwell
Top Farm

Mount
Pleasant

Thoresway
North Wold

Thoresway
Grange

LN7

Sweed Bed
Plantation

Pit
(dis)

Black
Springs

LN7

Hills Brough
Farm

Peter's Spout Springs

The
Rookery

Mast
Long
Barrow

Top
Buildings

Vale
Farm

Thoresway

The
Holt

Rectory
Farm

Roman
Hole

Normanby
Dales

Stone
Farm

Smithfield
Plantation

Otby
Top

Cowdyke
Plantation

Tunnel
Plantation

Dales Bottom
Plantation

Stainton
Hall

LN8

Stainton
le Vale

Otby

Black
Holt

South
Farm

Nursery Ride
Plantations

Nimbleton
Plantation

Lud's Well
Plantation

Goody Orchin
Plantation

Lud's
Well

HIGH STREET

B1225

Mast

Manor
House

Highfield
Farm

WALESBY HILL

Kirmond
le Mire

OTBY LANE

Walesby
Hill

Walesby
Top Farm

Churn Water
Heads (springs)

Bully Hill
Farm

Pheasant
Holt

Moat

Viking Way

Risby

Tumulus

Bully
Hill

B1203

MOOR ROAD

RASEN ROAD

Walesby

BULLY HILL

CATSKIN LANE

North Wold
Farm

Ash
Holt

Broggery
Plantation

Fox Covert
Plantation

CAISTOR LANE

Risby
Moor

Castle
Farm

Bedlam
Plantation

PAPERMILL LANE

HIGH STREET

Kirmond
Top

WALESBY LANE

Viking Way

The
Farm

Vale
Farm

Moor
Farm

BECK HILL 1
CHURCH LA 2
THE SMOOTING 3
KINGSWAY 4

CAISTOR LANE

Tealby Sch

PO

B1203

Tealby
Moor

SPRINGFIELDS

COW LA

Ford

Far Dickey
Crook

Manor
Plantation

Low Moor
Farm

THORPE LANE

Thorpe House
Farm

Willingham
Woods

Sewage
Works

SANDY LANE

PH

Tealby

Viking Way

B1225

13   A   14   B   15   C   16   D   17   E   18   F

B6
1 NORFOLK CL
2 SALISBURY AVE
3 LANCASTER RD
4 CAMBRIDGE CRES
5 YORK RD
6 CHICHESTER RD

7 SUSSEX CL
8 JAVELIN AVE
9 KENT RD
10 LINCOLN RD
11 CANBERRA CRES
12 CUMBERLAND TERR
13 ST DAVID'S ST

14 MERLIN RD
15 WINDSMOOR RD
16 EDINBURGH RD
17 DRIGH RD

C5
1 NORTH HALLS
2 GRIMSBY RD
3 SORREL CL
4 MEADOW DR
5 BECK CL
6 CHESTNUT WY

7 RECTORY CL

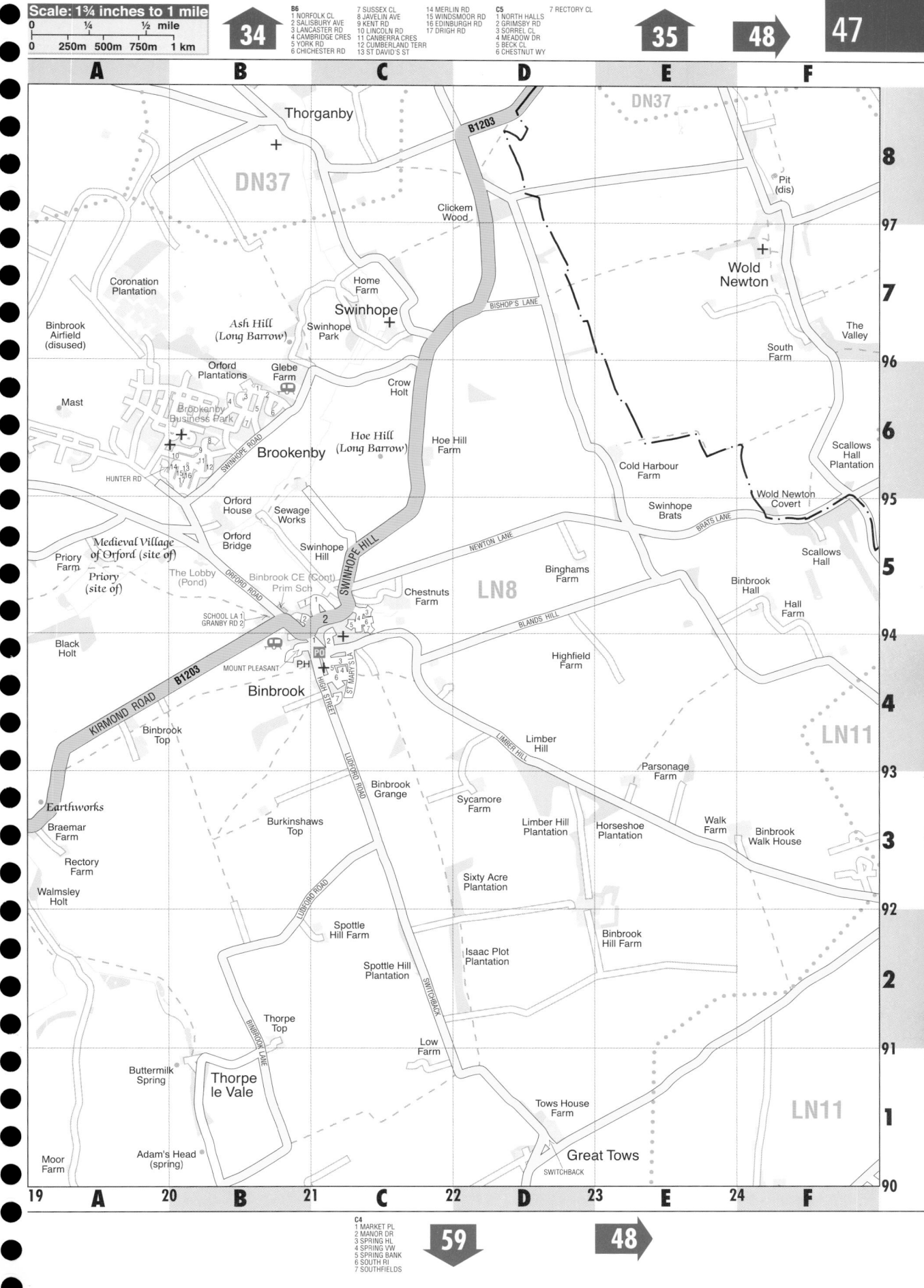

C4
1 MARKET PL
2 MANOR DR
3 SPRING HL
4 SPRING VW
5 SPRING BANK
6 SOUTH RI
7 SOUTHFIELDS

59

48

47 35 36

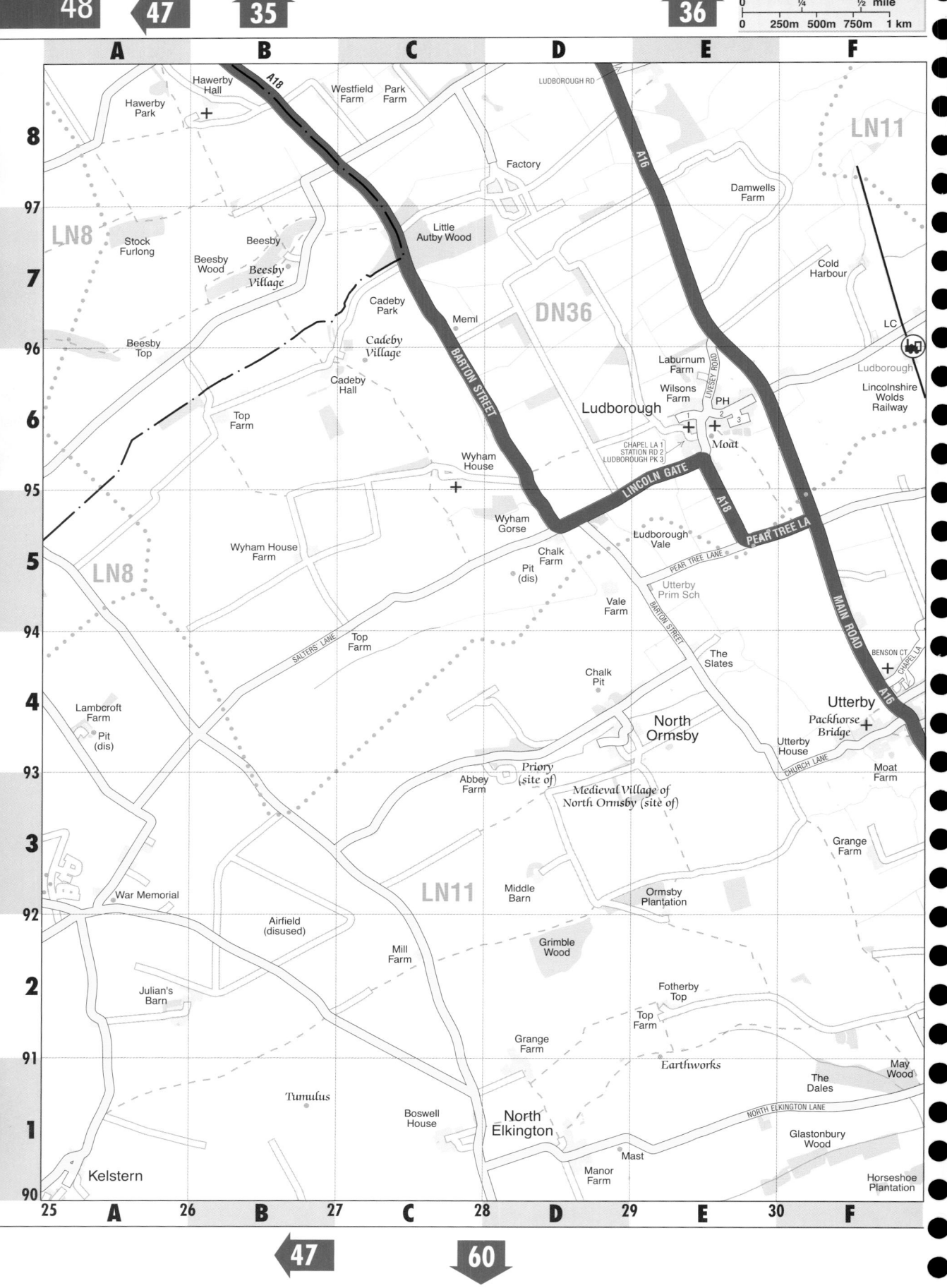
Scale: 1¾ inches to 1 mile
Hawerby Park
Hawerby Hall
A18
Westfield Farm
Park Farm
LUDBOROUGH RD
LN11
A16
Factory
Damwells Farm
LN8
Stock Furlong
Beesby
Beesby Wood
Beesby Village
Little Autby Wood
Cold Harbour
Cadeby Park
Meml
DN36
LC
Beesby Top
Cadeby Village
Cadeby Hall
BARTON STREET
Laburnum Farm
LIVESEY ROAD
Wilsons Farm
PH
Ludborough
Lincolnshire Wolds Railway
Ludborough
Top Farm
Moat
CHAPEL LA 1
STATION RD 2
LUDBOROUGH PK 3
Wyham House
LINCOLN GATE
Wyham Gorse
Ludborough Vale
PEAR TREE LA
PEAR TREE LANE
Wyham House Farm
Chalk Farm
Pit (dis)
Utterby Prim Sch
Vale Farm
MAIN ROAD
SALTERS LANE
Top Farm
The Slates
BENSON CT
CHAPEL LA
Chalk Pit
Lambcroft Farm
Pit (dis)
North Ormsby
Utterby
Packhorse Bridge
Utterby House
CHURCH LANE
Moat Farm
Abbey Farm
Priory (site of)
Medieval Village of North Ormsby (site of)
Grange Farm
War Memorial
Middle Barn
Ormsby Plantation
Airfield (disused)
Mill Farm
Grimble Wood
Julian's Barn
Fotherby Top
Top Farm
Grange Farm
Earthworks
May Wood
The Dales
Tumulus
Boswell House
North Elkington
NORTH ELKINGTON LANE
Glastonbury Wood
Mast
Kelstern
Manor Farm
Horseshoe Plantation

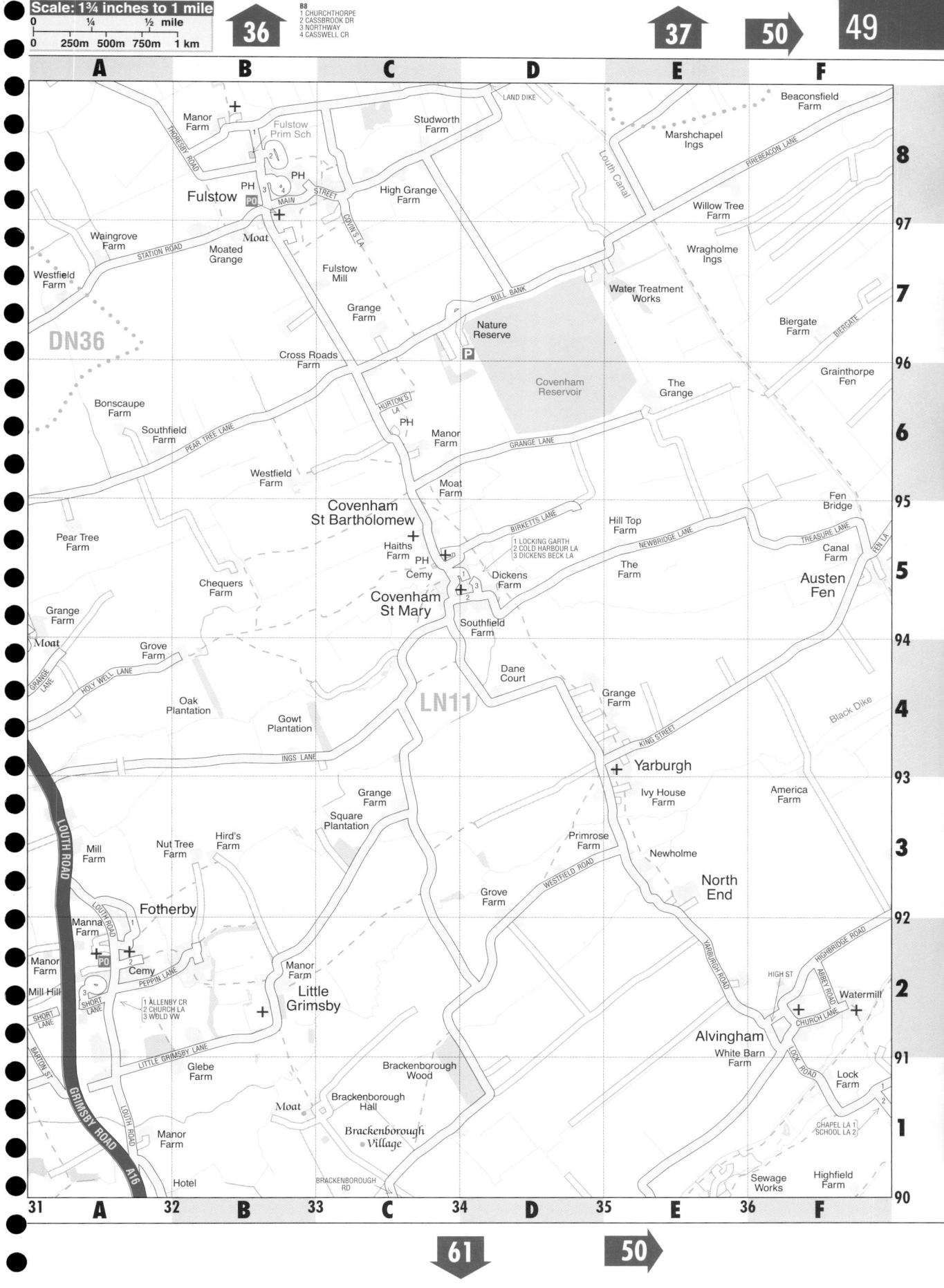

Map page showing the Fulstow, Covenham and Alvingham area

Scale: 1¾ inches to 1 mile

0   ¼   ½ mile
0   250m 500m 750m 1 km

36

37   50   49

B8
1 CHURCHTHORPE
2 CASSBROOK DR
3 NORTHWAY
4 CASSWELL CR

A   B   C   D   E   F

8
97
7
96
6
95
5
94
4
93
3
92
2
91
1
90

Beaconsfield Farm
Marshchapel Ings
LAND DIKE
Studworth Farm
Manor Farm
Fulstow Prim Sch
THORESBY ROAD
High Grange Farm
Willow Tree Farm
Louth Canal
FIREBEACON LANE
PH
Fulstow
PO
PH
Main Street
COVINS LA
Wragholme Ings
Moat
Waingrove Farm
STATION ROAD
Moated Grange
Fulstow Mill
Water Treatment Works
Biergate Farm
BIERGATE
Westfield Farm
DN36
Grange Farm
BULL BANK
Nature Reserve
P
Grainthorpe Fen
Cross Roads Farm
HURTON'S LA
PH
Covenham Reservoir
The Grange
Bonscaupe Farm
PEAR TREE LANE
Southfield Farm
Westfield Farm
Manor Farm
GRANGE LANE
Moat Farm
Fen Bridge
Pear Tree Farm
Covenham St Bartholomew
Haiths Farm
PH
Cemy
BIRKETTS LANE
1 LOCKING GARTH
2 COLD HARBOUR LA
3 DICKENS BECK LA
Dickens Farm
Hill Top Farm
NEWBRIDGE LANE
The Farm
TREASURE LANE
Canal Farm
FEN LA
Austen Fen
Chequers Farm
Covenham St Mary
Southfield Farm
Grange Farm
Grange Farm
Moat
GRANGE LANE
HOLY WELL LANE
Grove Farm
Dane Court
LN11
Black Dike
Oak Plantation
Gowt Plantation
INGS LANE
King Street
Yarburgh
Mill Farm
Nut Tree Farm
Hird's Farm
Grange Farm
Square Plantation
Ivy House Farm
America Farm
LOUTH ROAD
LOUTH ROAD
Fotherby
Primrose Farm
WESTFIELD ROAD
Newholme
North End
Manna Farm
PO
Cemy
PEPPIN LANE
Manor Farm
Little Grimsby
Grove Farm
YARBURGH ROAD
HIGHBRIDGE ROAD
HIGH ST
ABBEY ROAD
Watermill
Manor Farm
Mill Hill
SHORT LANE
1 ALLENBY CR
2 CHURCH LA
3 WOLD VW
LITTLE GRIMSBY LANE
Church Lane
Alvingham
Lock Farm
SHORT LANE
BARTON ST
Glebe Farm
Brackenborough Wood
White Barn Farm
LOCK ROAD
GRIMSBY ROAD
LOUTH ROAD
Moat
Brackenborough Hall
Manor Farm
Brackenborough Village
BRACKENBOROUGH RD
CHAPEL LA 1
SCHOOL LA 2
A16
Hotel
Sewage Works
Highfield Farm

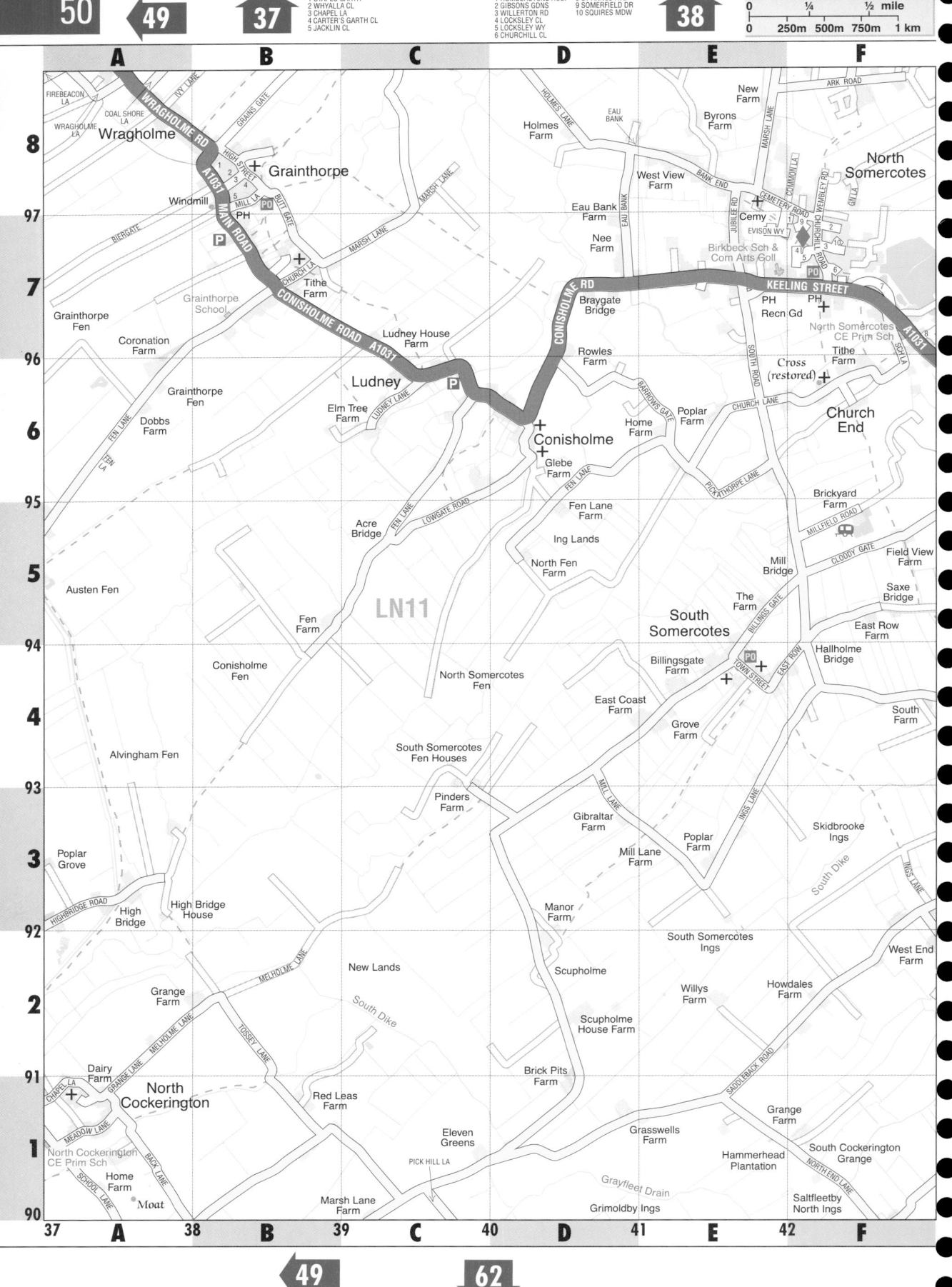

50

49

37
B8
1 STAPES GARTH
2 WHYALLA CL
3 CHAPEL LA
4 CARTER'S GARTH CL
5 JACKLIN CL

F7
1 HUMBERSTONE HOLT
2 GIBSONS GDNS
3 WILLERTON RD
4 LOCKSLEY CL
5 LOCKSLEY WY
6 CHURCHILL CL

7 KEELING ST
8 ST ANNES AVE
9 SOMERFIELD DR
10 SQUIRES MDW

38

Scale: 1¾ inches to 1 mile
0   ¼   ½ mile
0   250m   500m   750m   1 km

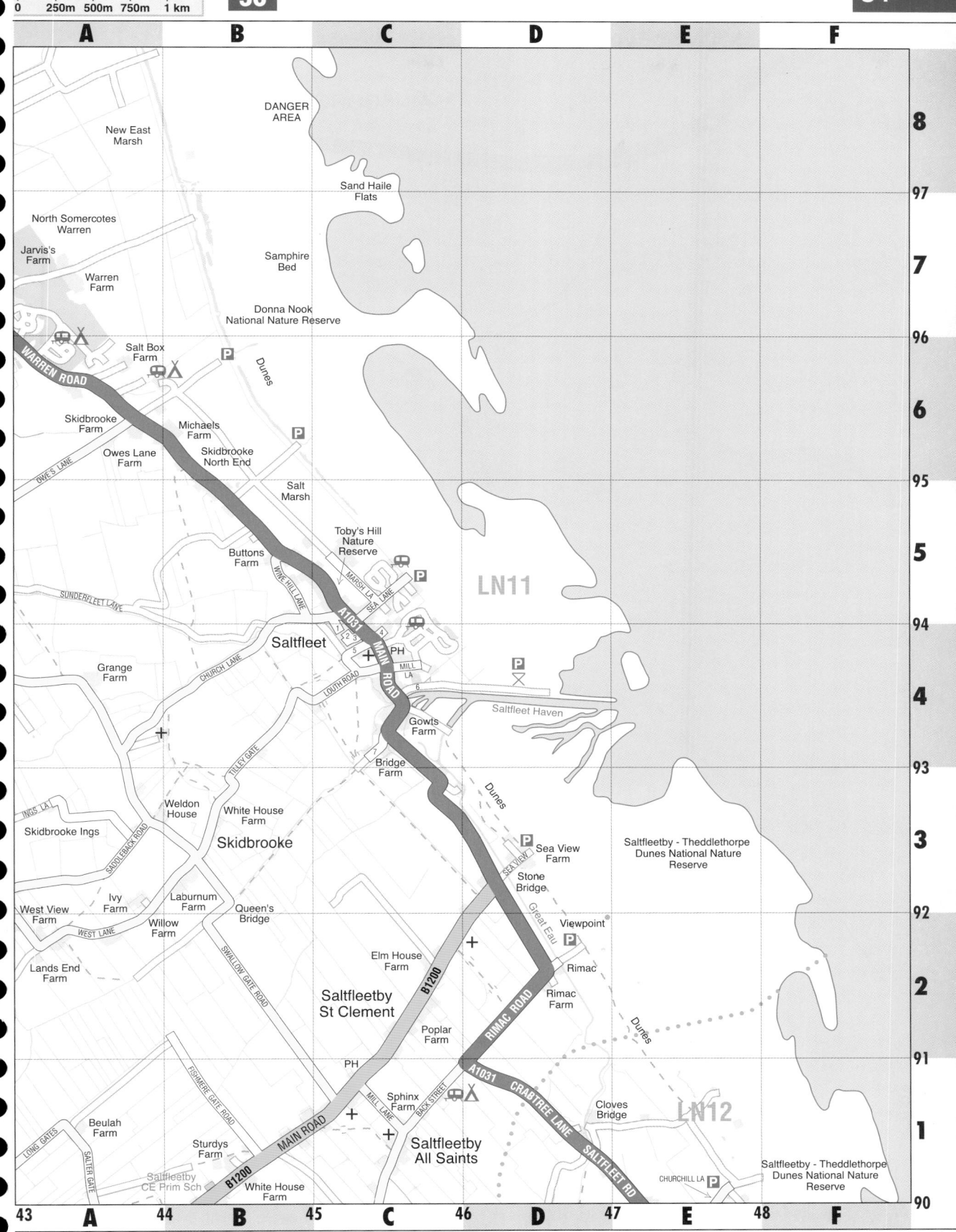

A   B   C   D   E   F

8
97
7
96
6
95
5
94
4
93
3
92
2
91
1
90

DANGER
AREA

New East
Marsh

Sand Haile
Flats

North Somercotes
Warren

Jarvis's
Farm

Samphire
Bed

Warren
Farm

Donna Nook
National Nature Reserve

WARREN ROAD

Salt Box
Farm

P

Dunes

Skidbrooke
Farm

Michaels
Farm

P

Owes Lane
Farm

Skidbrooke
North End

OWE'S LANE

Salt
Marsh

SUNDERFLEET LANE

Buttons
Farm

Toby's Hill
Nature
Reserve

P

LN11

Grange
Farm

Saltfleet

A1031

MAIN ROAD

WINE HILL LANE

SEA LANE

MARSH LA

P

1 2 3
5

PH

P

CHURCH LANE

LOUTH ROAD

MILL
LA

6

Saltfleet Haven

Gowts
Farm

TILLEY GATE

Bridge
Farm

Dunes

Weldon
House

White House
Farm

INGS LA

Skidbrooke Ings

SADDLEBACK ROAD

Skidbrooke

P

Sea View
Farm

Saltfleetby - Theddlethorpe
Dunes National Nature
Reserve

SEA VIEW

Stone
Bridge

Great Eau

West View
Farm

Ivy
Farm

Laburnum
Farm

Queen's
Bridge

WEST LANE

Willow
Farm

SWALLOW GATE ROAD

P

Viewpoint

Lands End
Farm

Elm House
Farm

B1200

Saltfleetby
St Clement

RIMAC ROAD

Rimac

Rimac
Farm

Dunes

LN12

Poplar
Farm

A1031

CRABTREE LANE

Cloves
Bridge

PH

FISHMERE GATE ROAD

MILL LANE

Sphinx
Farm

BACK STREET

SALTFLEET RD

Saltfleetby - Theddlethorpe
Dunes National Nature
Reserve

Beulah
Farm

SALTER GATE

LONG GATES

Sturdys
Farm

MAIN ROAD

B1200

Saltfleetby
CE Prim Sch

White House
Farm

Saltfleetby
All Saints

CHURCHILL LA

P

43   A   44   B   45   C   46   D   47   E   48   F   90

C4
1 BOTOLPH'S VW
2 HOLMES CL
3 JACKLIN DR
4 THE HILL
5 PUMP LA
6 HAVEN BANK
7 GREYFLEET BANK

63

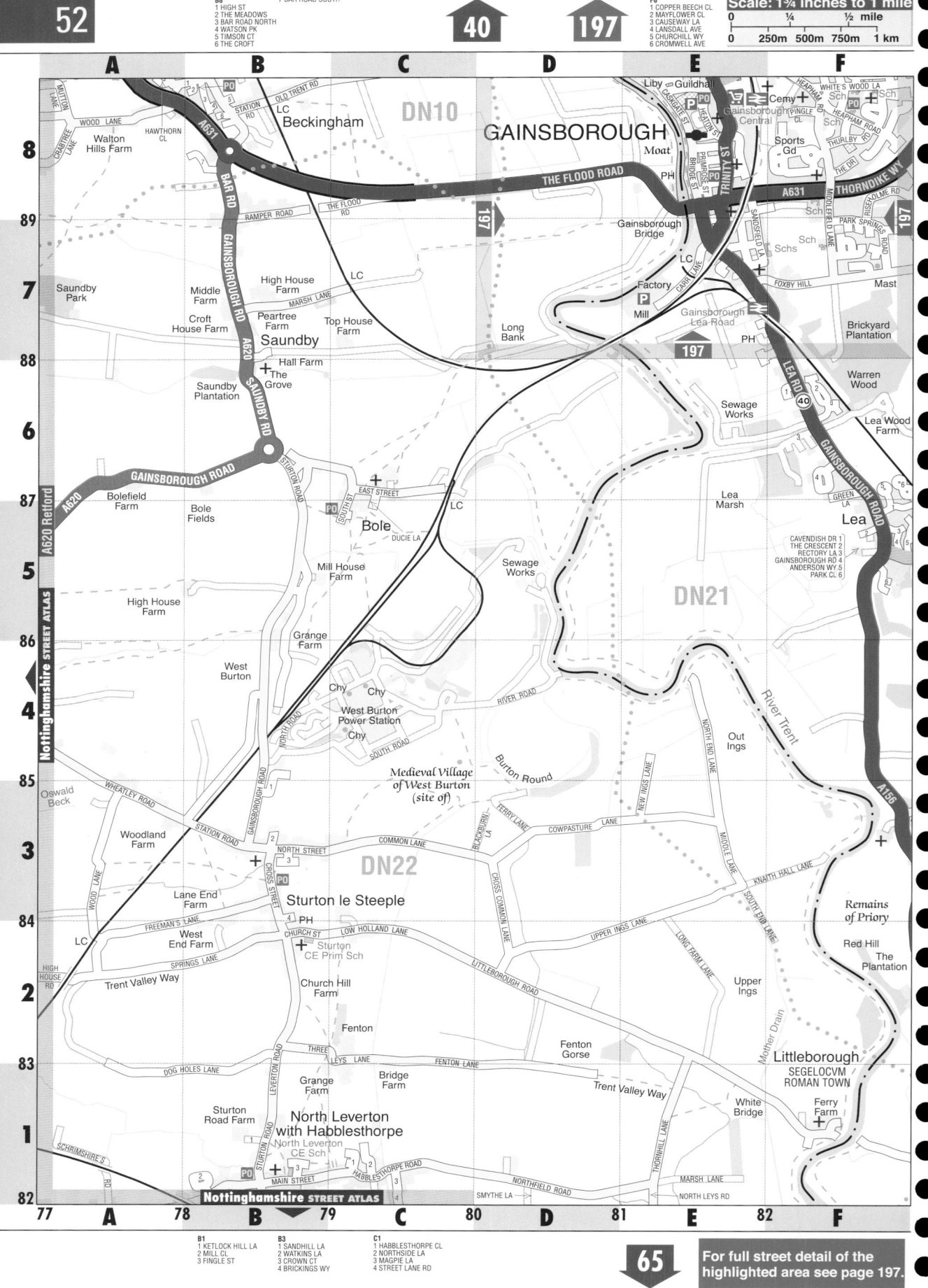

B8
1 HIGH ST
2 THE MEADOWS
3 BAR ROAD NORTH
4 WATSON PK
5 TIMSON CT
6 THE CROFT

7 BAR ROAD SOUTH

40   197

F6
1 COPPER BEECH CL
2 MAYFLOWER CL
3 CAUSEWAY LA
4 LANSDALL AVE
5 CHURCHILL WY
6 CROMWELL AVE

Scale: 1¾ inches to 1 mile
0   ¼   ½ mile
0   250m 500m 750m 1 km

DN10

GAINSBOROUGH

Liby Guildhall
Cemy
White's Wood La
Sch
Gainsborough Central
Sports Gd
Moat
PH
THE FLOOD ROAD
Gainsborough Bridge
A631
THORNDIKE WY
197

Walton Hills Farm
WOOD LANE
HAWTHORN CL
BAR RD
Beckingham
STATION RD
OLD TRENT RD
LC
THE FLOOD RD
RAMPER ROAD
LC
197
Heapham Road
Park Springs Road
Schs
Mast
A631
Middle Farm
High House Farm
MARSH LANE
Top House Farm
Long Bank
LC
Factory
Mill
Gainsborough Lea Road
PH
197
Brickyard Plantation
Saundby Park
GAINSBOROUGH RD
Croft House Farm
Peartree Farm
Saundby
Hall Farm
The Grove
Saundby Plantation
SAUNDBY RD
Warren Wood
Sewage Works
Lea Wood Farm
A620
A620 Retford
GAINSBOROUGH ROAD
Bolefield Farm
STURTON RD
EAST STREET
Bole Fields
LC
Bole
DUCIE LA
Sewage Works
Lea Marsh
DN21
Lea
GAINSBOROUGH ROAD
GREEN LA
CAVENDISH DR 1
THE CRESCENT 2
RECTORY LA 3
GAINSBOROUGH RD 4
ANDERSON WY 5
PARK CL 6
High House Farm
Mill House Farm
Grange Farm
West Burton
Chy   Chy
West Burton Power Station
Chy
NORTH ROAD
SOUTH ROAD
River Trent
River Road
Out Ings
NORTH END LANE
A156
Oswald Beck
WHEATLEY ROAD
Woodland Farm
STATION ROAD
GAINSBOROUGH ROAD
Medieval Village of West Burton (site of)
Burton Round
FERRY LANE
NEW INGS LANE
COWPASTURE LANE
MIDDLE LANE
KNAITH HALL LANE
SOUTH END LANE
Remains of Priory
Red Hill
The Plantation
WOOD LANE
Lane End Farm
NORTH STREET
CROSS STREET
COMMON LANE
DN22
Sturton le Steeple
PH
CHURCH ST
LOW HOLLAND LANE
CROSS COMMON LANE
UPPER INGS LANE
LONG FARM LANE
High House Rd
West End Farm
FREEMAN'S LANE
SPRINGS LANE
Sturton CE Prim Sch
LC
Trent Valley Way
Church Hill Farm
LITTLEBOROUGH ROAD
Upper Ings
Littleborough
SEGELOCVM ROMAN TOWN
Fenton
THREE LEYS LANE
Bridge Farm
FENTON LANE
Fenton Gorse
Trent Valley Way
White Bridge
Ferry Farm
DOG HOLES LANE
Grange Farm
Sturton Road Farm
LEVERTON ROAD
North Leverton with Habblesthorpe
North Leverton CE Sch
MAIN STREET
HABBLESTHORPE ROAD
NORTHFIELD ROAD
THORNHILL LANE
MARSH LANE
SCHRIMSHIRE'S RD
SMYTHE LA
NORTH LEYS RD
Mother Drain

B1
1 KETLOCK HILL LA
2 MILL CL
3 FINGLE ST

B3
1 SANDHILL LA
2 WATKINS LA
3 CROWN CT
4 BRICKINGS WY

C1
1 HABBLESTHORPE CL
2 NORTHSIDE LA
3 MAGPIE LA
4 STREET LANE RD

65

For full street detail of the highlighted area see page 197.

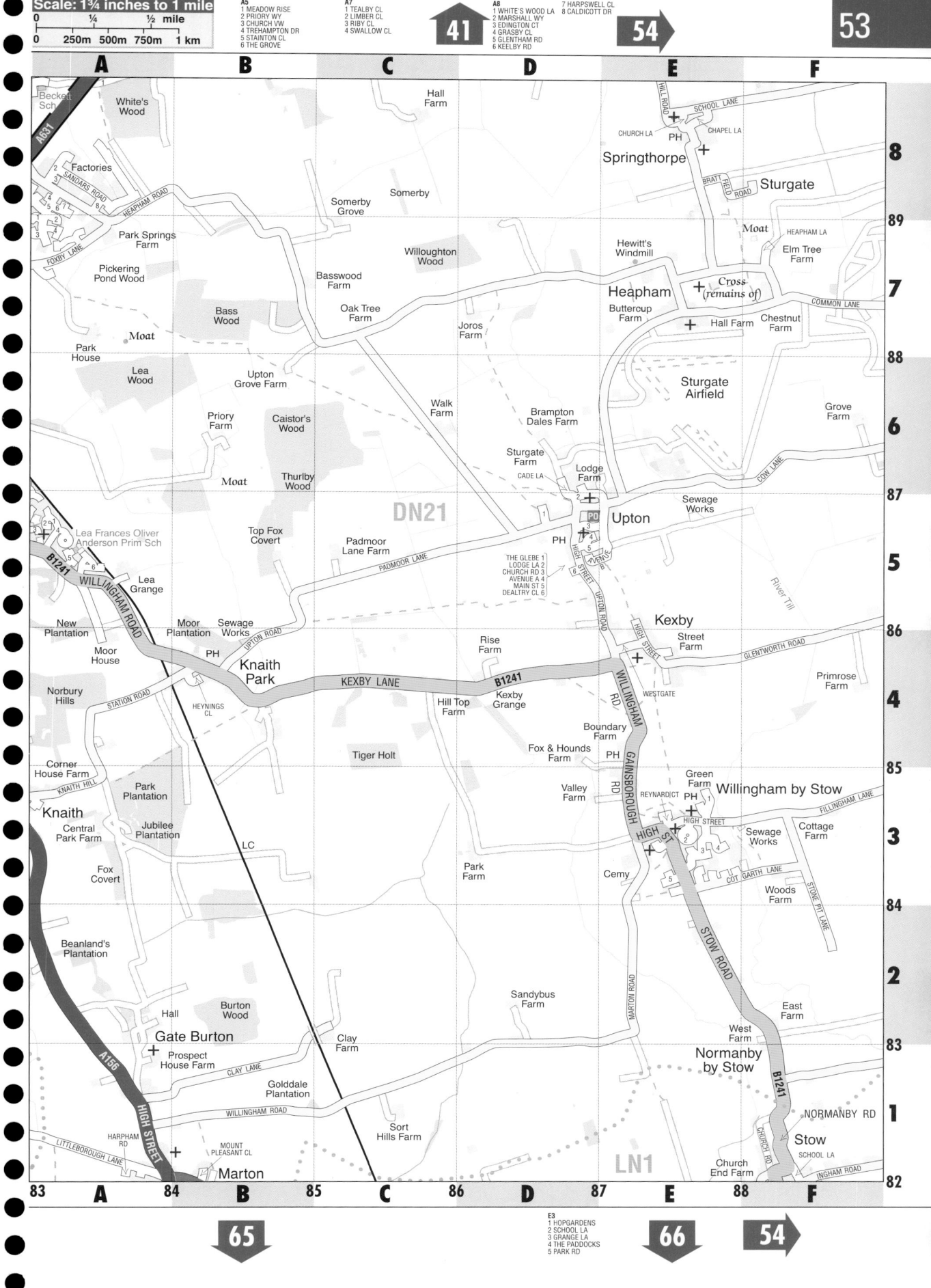

Scale: 1¾ inches to 1 mile
0 ¼ ½ mile
0 250m 500m 750m 1 km
A5
1 MEADOW RISE
2 PRIORY WY
3 CHURCH VW
4 TREHAMPTON DR
5 STAINTON CL
6 THE GROVE
A7
1 TEALBY CL
2 LIMBER CL
3 RIBY CL
4 SWALLOW CL
41
A8
1 WHITE'S WOOD LA
2 MARSHALL WY
3 EDINGTON CT
4 GRASBY CL
5 GLENTHAM RD
6 KEELBY RD
7 HARPSWELL CL
8 CALDICOTT DR
54
Beckett Sch
White's Wood
A631
Factories
SANDARS ROAD
HEAPHAM ROAD
FOXBY LANE
Park Springs Farm
Pickering Pond Wood
Hall Farm
Somerby Grove
Somerby
Willoughton Wood
Basswood Farm
Oak Tree Farm
Bass Wood
Moat
Park House
Lea Wood
Upton Grove Farm
Priory Farm
Caistor's Wood
Thurlby Wood
Walk Farm
Joros Farm
HILL ROAD
SCHOOL LANE
CHURCH LA
PH
CHAPEL LA
Springthorpe
BRATT FIELD ROAD
Sturgate
Moat
HEAPHAM LA
Elm Tree Farm
Hewitt's Windmill
Heapham
Cross (remains of)
COMMON LANE
Buttercup Farm
Hall Farm
Chestnut Farm
Sturgate Airfield
Grove Farm
Brampton Dales Farm
Sturgate Farm
CADE LA
Lodge Farm
COW LANE
Sewage Works
Upton
PO
DN21
Top Fox Covert
Padmoor Lane Farm
PADMOOR LANE
THE GLEBE 1
LODGE LA 2
CHURCH RD 3
AVENUE A 4
MAIN ST 5
DEALTRY CL 6
HIGH STREET
AVENUE
UPTON ROAD
River Till
Lea Frances Oliver Anderson Prim Sch
B1241
WILLINGHAM ROAD
Lea Grange
New Plantation
Moor Plantation
Sewage Works
UPTON ROAD
Moor House
PH
Knaith Park
Kexby
Street Farm
HIGH STREET
GLENTWORTH ROAD
Rise Farm
KEXBY LANE
B1241
Kexby Grange
Hill Top Farm
WESTGATE
Primrose Farm
Norbury Hills
STATION ROAD
HEYNINGS CL
WILLINGHAM RD
Boundary Farm
Fox & Hounds Farm
Tiger Holt
Corner House Farm
KNAITH HILL
Park Plantation
GAINSBOROUGH RD
Green Farm
Willingham by Stow
REYNARD CT
Valley Farm
FILLINGHAM LANE
Knaith
Central Park Farm
Jubilee Plantation
HIGH ST
HIGH STREET
Sewage Works
Cottage Farm
LC
Fox Covert
Park Farm
Cemy
COT GARTH LANE
Woods Farm
STONE PIT LANE
STOW ROAD
Beanland's Plantation
Sandybus Farm
MARTON ROAD
East Farm
Hall
Burton Wood
Gate Burton
Clay Farm
West Farm
Prospect House Farm
Normanby by Stow
A156
CLAY LANE
Golddale Plantation
B1241
WILLINGHAM ROAD
NORMANBY RD
HIGH STREET
Sort Hills Farm
Stow
HARPHAM RD
LITTLEBOROUGH LANE
MOUNT PLEASANT CL
CHURCH RD
SCHOOL LA
Marton
LN1
Church End Farm
INGHAM ROAD
A B C D E F
8 89 7 88 6 87 5 86 4 85 3 84 2 83 1 82
83 84 85 86 87 88
65
E3
1 HOPGARDENS
2 SCHOOL LA
3 GRANGE LA
4 THE PADDOCKS
5 PARK RD
66
54

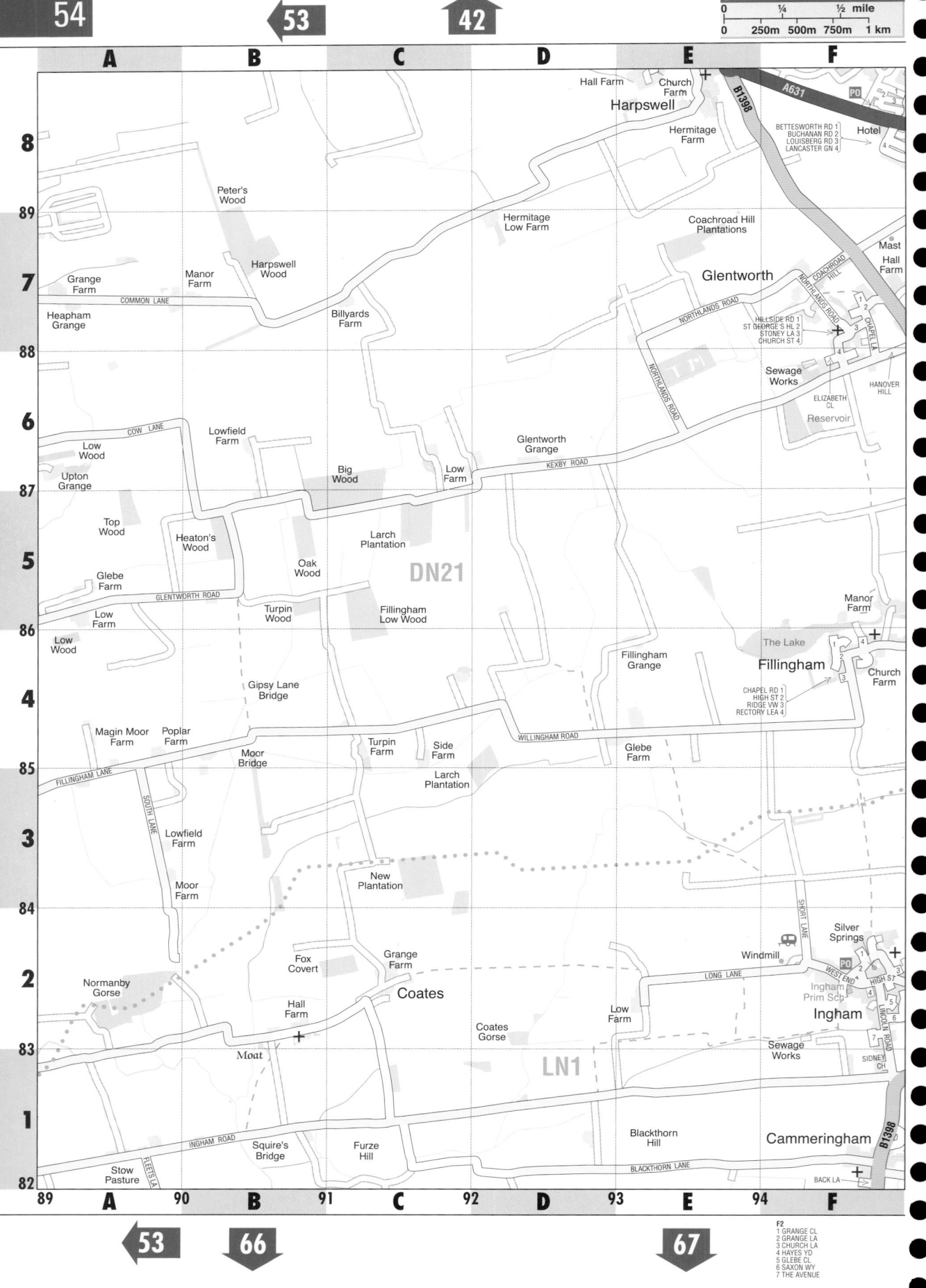

A B C D E F

8

Hall Farm
Church Farm
Harpswell
Hermitage Farm

B1398
A631

PO

BETTESWORTH RD 1
BUCHANAN RD 2
LOUISBERG RD 3
LANCASTER GN 4

Hotel

89

Peter's Wood

Hermitage Low Farm

Coachroad Hill Plantations

Mast
Hall Farm

7

Grange Farm

Manor Farm

Harpswell Wood

Glentworth

COACHROAD HILL
NORTHLANDS ROAD
CHAPEL LA

Heapham Grange

COMMON LANE

Billyards Farm

NORTHLANDS ROAD

HILLSIDE RD 1
ST GEORGE S HL 2
STONEY LA 3
CHURCH ST 4

88

Sewage Works

HANOVER HILL

ELIZABETH CL

6

Low Wood

COW LANE

Lowfield Farm

Glentworth Grange

KEXBY ROAD

Reservoir

Upton Grange

87

Big Wood

Low Farm

NORTHLANDS ROAD

5

Top Wood

Heaton's Wood

Larch Plantation

DN21

Manor Farm

Glebe Farm

GLENTWORTH ROAD

Oak Wood

Turpin Wood

Fillingham Low Wood

The Lake

86

Low Farm

Low Wood

Fillingham Grange

Fillingham

Church Farm

4

Magin Moor Farm

Gipsy Lane Bridge

CHAPEL RD 1
HIGH ST 2
RIDGE VW 3
RECTORY LEA 4

Poplar Farm

Turpin Farm

Side Farm

WILLINGHAM ROAD

Glebe Farm

85

FILLINGHAM LANE

Moor Bridge

Larch Plantation

3

SOUTH LANE

Lowfield Farm

SHORT LANE

84

Moor Farm

New Plantation

Windmill

Silver Springs

PO
WEST END
HIGH ST

Ingham Prim Sch

LINCOLN ROAD

2

Normanby Gorse

Fox Covert

Grange Farm

LONG LANE

Low Farm

Ingham

Hall Farm

Coates

Coates Gorse

SIDNEY
CH

83

Moat

LN1

Sewage Works

1

INGHAM ROAD

FLEET'S LA

Squire's Bridge

Furze Hill

Blackthorn Hill

Cammeringham

B1398

82

Stow Pasture

BLACKTHORN LANE

BACK LA

89 A 90 B 91 C 92 D 93 E 94 F

F2
1 GRANGE CL
2 GRANGE LA
3 CHURCH LA
4 HAYES YD
5 GLEBE CL
6 SAXON WY
7 THE AVENUE

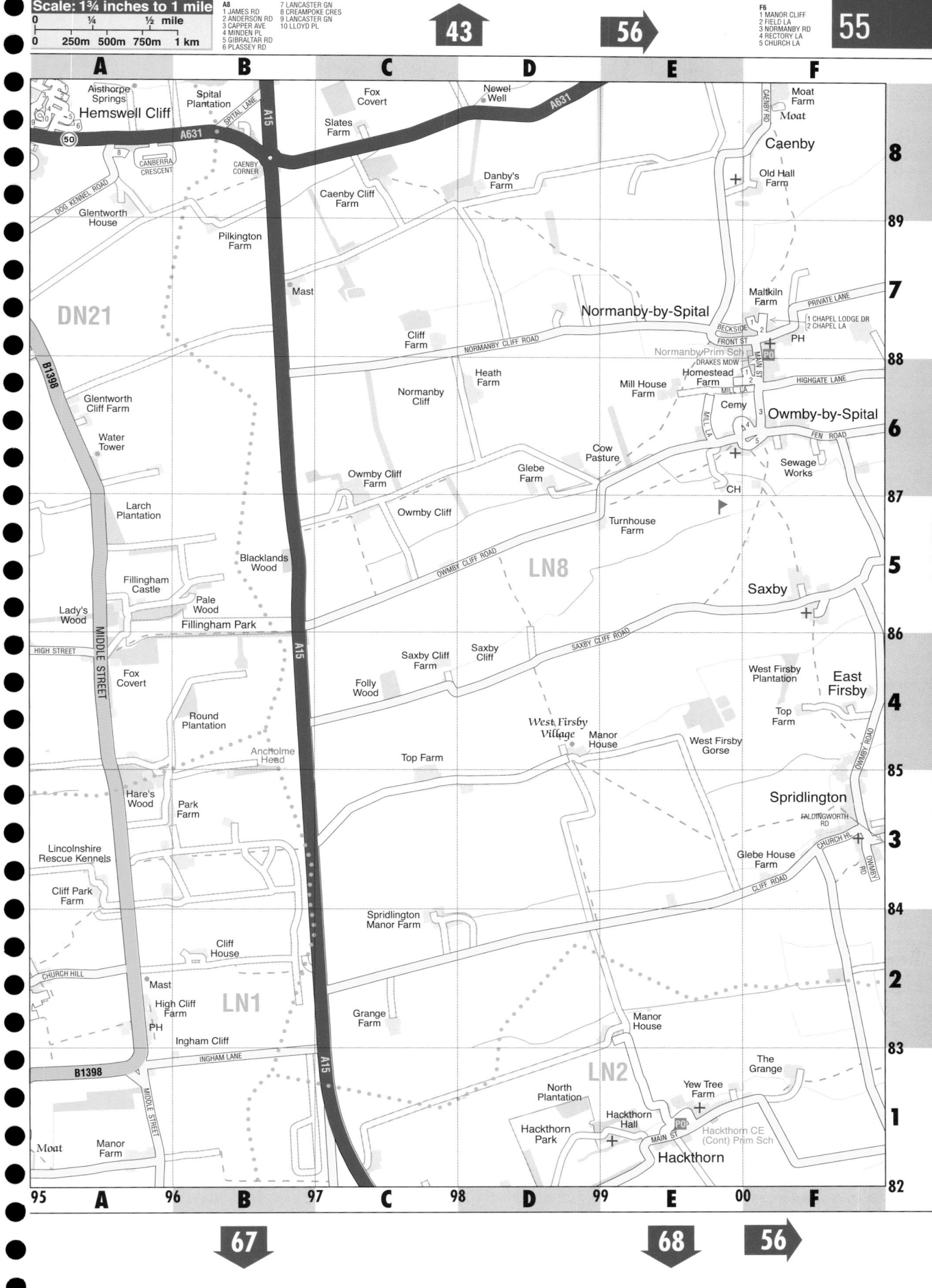

Scale: 1¾ inches to 1 mile
0 ¼ ½ mile
0 250m 500m 750m 1 km
A8
1 JAMES RD
2 ANDERSON RD
3 CAPPER AVE
4 MINDEN PL
5 GIBRALTAR RD
6 PLASSEY RD
7 LANCASTER GN
8 CREAMPOKE CRES
9 LANCASTER GN
10 LLOYD PL
43
56
F6
1 MANOR CLIFF
2 FIELD LA
3 NORMANBY RD
4 RECTORY LA
5 CHURCH LA
Aisthorpe Springs
Hemswell Cliff
Spital Plantation
SPITAL LANE
A631
CANBERRA CRESCENT
CAENBY CORNER
DOG KENNEL ROAD
Glentworth House
Fox Covert
Slates Farm
Newel Well
Caenby Cliff Farm
Danby's Farm
Pilkington Farm
Moat Farm
Moat
Caenby
Old Hall Farm
CAENBY RD
Mast
DN21
Normanby-by-Spital
Maltkiln Farm
PRIVATE LANE
1 CHAPEL LODGE DR
2 CHAPEL LA
BECKSIDE
FRONT ST
PH
Cliff Farm
NORMANBY CLIFF ROAD
Normanby Prim Sch
DRAKES MDW
MAIN ST
B1398
Heath Farm
Normanby Cliff
Homestead Farm
Mill House Farm
HIGHGATE LANE
MILL LA
Cemy
Owmby-by-Spital
Glentworth Cliff Farm
Water Tower
FEN ROAD
Cow Pasture
Glebe Farm
Owmby Cliff Farm
Sewage Works
CH
Larch Plantation
Owmby Cliff
Turnhouse Farm
OWMBY CLIFF ROAD
LN8
Blacklands Wood
Fillingham Castle
Pale Wood
Saxby
Lady's Wood
Fillingham Park
HIGH STREET
MIDDLE STREET
A15
Saxby Cliff Farm
Saxby Cliff
SAXBY CLIFF ROAD
Fox Covert
Folly Wood
West Firsby Plantation
East Firsby
Round Plantation
West Firsby Village
Manor House
Top Farm
West Firsby Gorse
Ancholme Head
Top Farm
OWMBY ROAD
Spridlington
Hare's Wood
Park Farm
FALDINGWORTH RD
CHURCH HL
Lincolnshire Rescue Kennels
Glebe House Farm
OWMBY RD
Cliff Park Farm
CLIFF ROAD
Spridlington Manor Farm
Cliff House
CHURCH HILL
Mast
High Cliff Farm
LN1
PH
Grange Farm
Manor House
Ingham Cliff
INGHAM LANE
LN2
The Grange
B1398
North Plantation
Yew Tree Farm
Hackthorn Hall
Hackthorn Park
MAIN ST
PO
Hackthorn CE (Cont) Prim Sch
Hackthorn
Moat
Manor Farm
95 96 97 98 99 00
A B C D E F
8 89 7 88 6 87 5 86 4 85 3 84 2 83 1 82
67
68
56

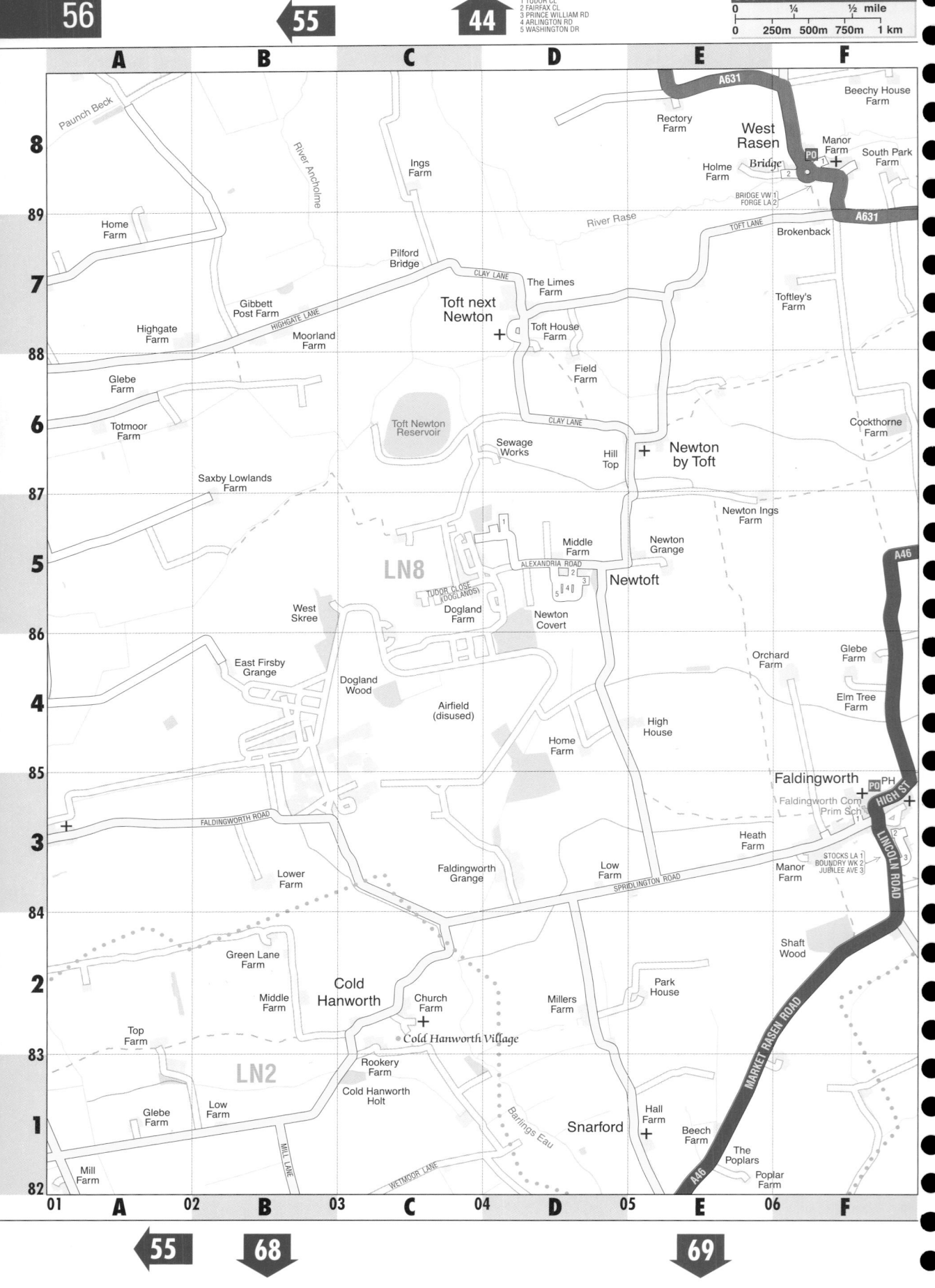

Scale: 1¾ inches to 1 mile
0   ¼   ½   mile
0   250m 500m 750m 1 km

A   B   C   D   E   F

A631

Beechy House Farm

Rectory Farm

West Rasen

Manor Farm

South Park Farm

8

Holme Farm

Bridge

PO

2

Home Farm

89

River Rase

Toft Lane

Brokenback

BRIDGE VW 1
FORGE LA 2

A631

Pilford Bridge

CLAY LANE

The Limes Farm

Toftley's Farm

7

Gibbett Post Farm

HIGHGATE LANE

Toft next Newton

Toft House Farm

Highgate Farm

Moorland Farm

88

Glebe Farm

Field Farm

Cockthorne Farm

6

Totmoor Farm

Toft Newton Reservoir

CLAY LANE

Newton by Toft

Sewage Works

Hill Top

Newton Ings Farm

87

Saxby Lowlands Farm

LN8

Middle Farm

Newton Grange

A46

5

ALEXANDRIA ROAD

Newtoft

1

2

West Skree

TUDOR CLOSE (DOGLANDS)

3

Dogland Farm

4

Orchard Farm

Glebe Farm

86

5

Newton Covert

East Firsby Grange

Dogland Wood

Elm Tree Farm

4

Airfield (disused)

Home Farm

High House

85

Faldingworth

PO PH

HIGH ST

Faldingworth Com Prim Sch

Faldingworth Road

3

Lower Farm

Faldingworth Grange

Low Farm

Heath Farm

SPRIDLINGTON ROAD

Manor Farm

STOCKS LA 1
BOUNDRY WK 2
JUBILEE AVE 3

LINCOLN ROAD

2

3

84

Shaft Wood

2

Green Lane Farm

Cold Hanworth

Church Farm

Millers Farm

Park House

MARKET RASEN ROAD

Middle Farm

Top Farm

83

LN2

Rookery Farm

Cold Hanworth Village

Barlings Eau

1

Glebe Farm

Low Farm

Cold Hanworth Holt

Snarford

Hall Farm

Beech Farm

The Poplars

Mill Farm

MILL LANE

WETMOOR LANE

A46

Poplar Farm

82

01   A   02   B   03   C   04   D   05   E   06   F

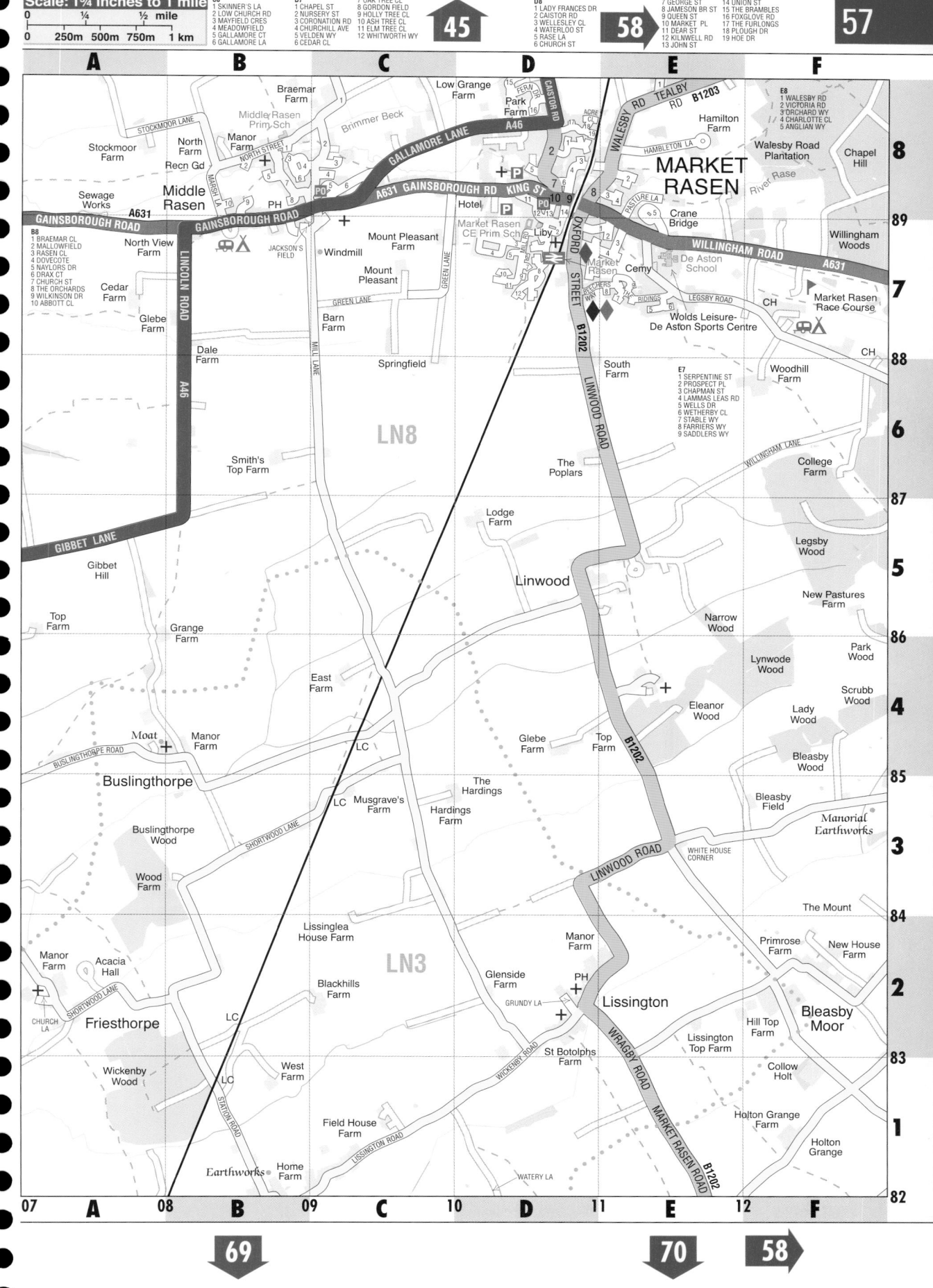

Scale: 1¾ inches to 1 mile

0   ¼   ½   mile
0 250m 500m 750m 1 km

45
58

C8
1 SKINNER'S LA
2 LOW CHURCH RD
3 MAYFIELD CRES
4 MEADOWFIELD
5 GALLAMORE CT
6 GALLAMORE LA

D7
1 CHAPEL ST
2 NURSERY ST
3 CORONATION RD
4 CHURCHILL AVE
5 VELDEN WY
6 CEDAR CL

7 OAK TREE CL
8 GORDON FIELD
9 HOLLY TREE CL
10 ASH TREE CL
11 ELM TREE CL
12 WHITWORTH WY

D8
1 LADY FRANCES DR
2 CAISTOR RD
3 WELLESLEY CL
4 WATERLOO ST
5 RASE LA
6 CHURCH ST

7 GEORGE ST
8 JAMESON BR ST
9 QUEEN ST
10 MARKET PL
11 DEAR ST
12 KILNWELL RD
13 JOHN ST

14 UNION ST
15 THE BRAMBLES
16 FOXGLOVE RD
17 THE FURLONGS
18 PLOUGH DR
19 HOE DR

E8
1 WALESBY RD
2 VICTORIA RD
3 ORCHARD WY
4 CHARLOTTE CL
5 ANGLIAN WY

B8
1 BRAEMAR CL
2 MALLOWFIELD
3 RASEN CL
4 DOVECOTE
5 NAYLORS DR
6 DRAX CT
7 CHURCH ST
8 THE ORCHARDS
9 WILKINSON DR
10 ABBOTT CL

E7
1 SERPENTINE ST
2 PROSPECT PL
3 CHAPMAN ST
4 LAMMAS LEAS RD
5 WELLS DR
6 WETHERBY CL
7 STABLE WY
8 FARRIERS WY
9 SADDLERS WY

MARKET RASEN

Middle Rasen

Buslingthorpe

Friesthorpe

Lissington

Linwood

Bleasby Moor

LN8

LN3

69
70
58

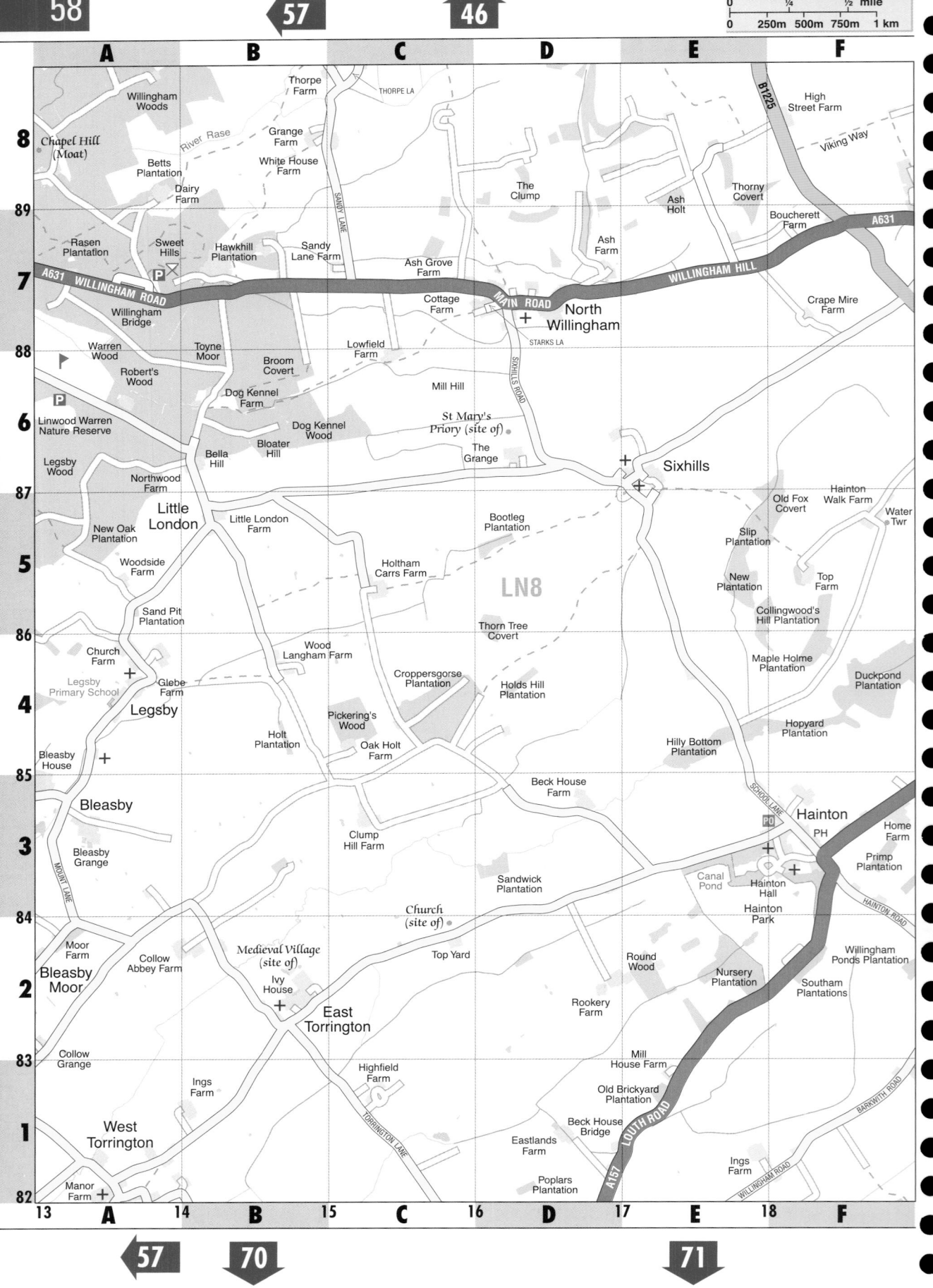
57
46
Scale: 1¾ inches to 1 mile
0 ¼ ½ mile
0 250m 500m 750m 1 km
A B C D E F
Thorpe Farm
THORPE LA
Willingham Woods
High Street Farm
B1225
Chapel Hill (Moat)
River Rase
Grange Farm
Viking Way
Betts Plantation
White House Farm
The Clump
Thorny Covert
Dairy Farm
SANDY LANE
Ash Holt
Boucherett Farm
A631
Rasen Plantation
Sweet Hills
Hawkhill Plantation
Sandy Lane Farm
Ash Farm
Ash Grove Farm
WILLINGHAM HILL
A631 WILLINGHAM ROAD
Cottage Farm
MAIN ROAD
North Willingham
Crape Mire Farm
Willingham Bridge
STARKS LA
Warren Wood
Toyne Moor
Lowfield Farm
Broom Covert
Robert's Wood
SIXHILLS ROAD
Mill Hill
Dog Kennel Farm
Linwood Warren Nature Reserve
Dog Kennel Wood
St Mary's Priory (site of)
Bloater Hill
Bella Hill
The Grange
Sixhills
Legsby Wood
Northwood Farm
Old Fox Covert
Hainton Walk Farm
Little London
Little London Farm
Bootleg Plantation
Water Twr
New Oak Plantation
Slip Plantation
Woodside Farm
Holtham Carrs Farm
LN8
New Plantation
Top Farm
Sand Pit Plantation
Collingwood's Hill Plantation
Thorn Tree Covert
Church Farm
Wood Langham Farm
Maple Holme Plantation
Legsby Primary School
Glebe Farm
Croppersgorse Plantation
Duckpond Plantation
Holds Hill Plantation
Legsby
Pickering's Wood
Hopyard Plantation
Holt Plantation
Oak Holt Farm
Hilly Bottom Plantation
Bleasby House
Beck House Farm
SCHOOL LANE
Hainton
Bleasby
PO
PH
Home Farm
Clump Hill Farm
Bleasby Grange
Primp Plantation
MOUNT LANE
Canal Pond
Hainton Hall
Sandwick Plantation
HAINTON ROAD
Church (site of)
Hainton Park
Moor Farm
Medieval Village (site of)
Willingham Ponds Plantation
Collow Abbey Farm
Top Yard
Round Wood
Bleasby Moor
Nursery Plantation
Ivy House
Southam Plantations
Rookery Farm
East Torrington
Collow Grange
Mill House Farm
Highfield Farm
Ings Farm
Old Brickyard Plantation
TORRINGTON LANE
LOUTH ROAD
BARKWITH ROAD
West Torrington
Beck House Bridge
Eastlands Farm
Ings Farm
A157
Manor Farm
Poplars Plantation
WILLINGHAM ROAD
8 89 7 88 6 87 5 86 4 85 3 84 2 83 1 82
13 14 15 16 17 18
57
70
71

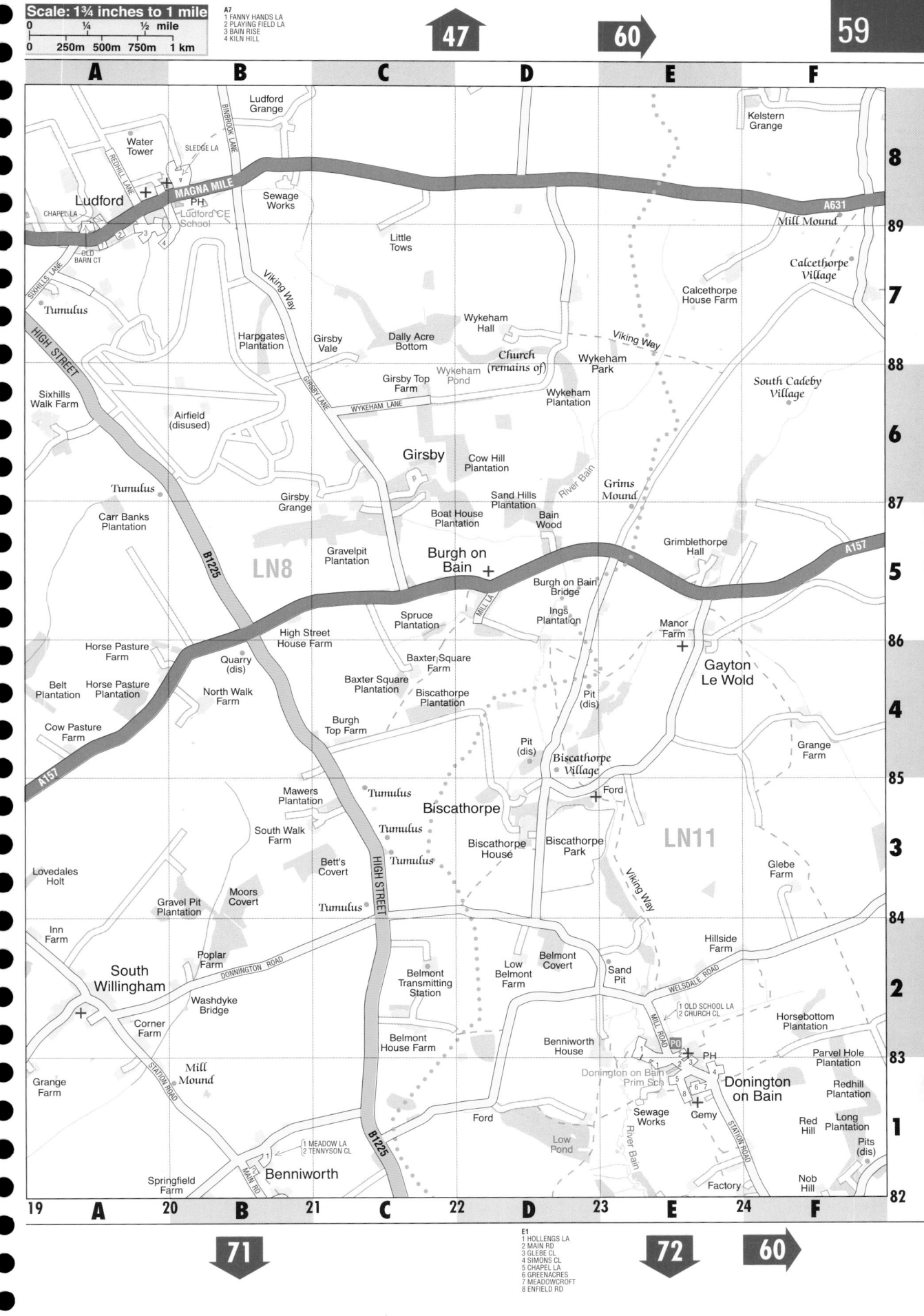

Scale: 1¾ inches to 1 mile

0   ¼   ½   mile
0   250m 500m 750m 1 km

A7
1 FANNY HANDS LA
2 PLAYING FIELD LA
3 BAIN RISE
4 KILN HILL

47   60   59

A | B | C | D | E | F

8
89
7
88
6
87
5
86
4
85
3
84
2
83
1
82

Ludford Grange
Kelstern Grange
Water Tower
SLEDGE LA
BINBROOK LANE
Sewage Works
A631
Mill Mound
Ludford
MAGNA MILE
PH
Ludford CE School
CHAPEL LA
OLD BARN CT
Little Tows
Calcethorpe Village
REDMILL LANE
SIXHILLS LANE
Tumulus
VIKING WAY
Harpgates Plantation
Girsby Vale
Dally Acre Bottom
Wykeham Hall
Church (remains of)
Wykeham Park
Calcethorpe House Farm
Viking Way
HIGH STREET
Girsby Top Farm
Wykeham Pond
Wykeham Plantation
South Cadeby Village
Sixhills Walk Farm
GIRSBY LANE
WYKEHAM LANE
Airfield (disused)
Girsby
Cow Hill Plantation
River Bain
Grims Mound
Tumulus
Girsby Grange
Sand Hills Plantation
Bain Wood
Grimblethorpe Hall
Carr Banks Plantation
Boat House Plantation
A157
LN8
B1225
Gravelpit Plantation
Burgh on Bain
Burgh on Bain Bridge
Manor Farm
High Street House Farm
Spruce Plantation
MILL LA
Ings Plantation
Gayton Le Wold
Horse Pasture Farm
Quarry (dis)
Baxter Square Farm
Pit (dis)
Belt Plantation
North Walk Farm
Baxter Square Plantation
Biscathorpe Plantation
Pit (dis)
Grange Farm
Horse Pasture Plantation
Burgh Top Farm
Biscathorpe Village
Cow Pasture Farm
Mawers Plantation
Tumulus
Ford
A157
South Walk Farm
Tumulus
Biscathorpe
Biscathorpe House
Biscathorpe Park
LN11
Glebe Farm
Lovedales Holt
Bett's Covert
Tumulus
Viking Way
Gravel Pit Plantation
Moors Covert
Tumulus
Hillside Farm
Inn Farm
HIGH STREET
WELSDALE ROAD
South Willingham
Poplar Farm
DONNINGTON ROAD
Belmont Transmitting Station
Low Belmont Farm
Belmont Covert
Sand Pit
MILL ROAD
1 OLD SCHOOL LA
2 CHURCH CL
Horsebottom Plantation
Washdyke Bridge
Corner Farm
STATION ROAD
Benniworth House
PO
PH
Parvel Hole Plantation
Mill Mound
Belmont House Farm
Donington on Bain Prim Sch
Donington on Bain
Redhill Plantation
Grange Farm
B1225
Ford
Sewage Works
Cemy
River Bain
Red Hill
Long Plantation
Low Pond
STATION ROAD
Pits (dis)
1 MEADOW LA
2 TENNYSON CL
Springfield Farm
Benniworth
MAIN RD
Factory
Nob Hill

E1
1 HOLLENGS LA
2 MAIN RD
3 GLEBE CL
4 SIMONS CL
5 CHAPEL LA
6 GREENACRES
7 MEADOWCROFT
8 ENFIELD RD

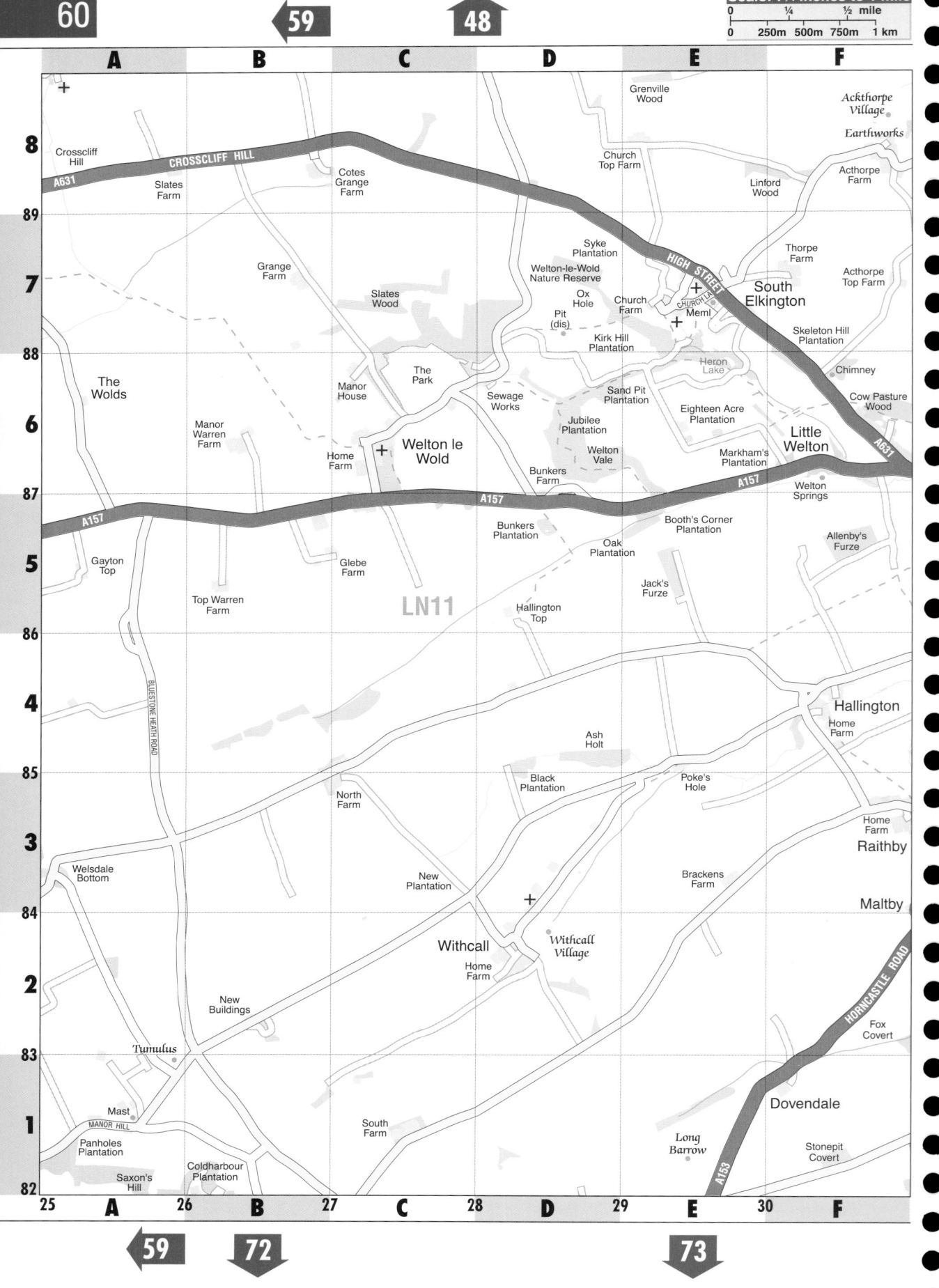
59
48
Scale: 1¾ inches to 1 mile
0 ¼ ½ mile
0 250m 500m 750m 1 km
A
B
C
D
E
F
8
89
7
88
6
87
5
86
4
85
3
84
2
83
1
82
25
26
27
28
29
30
Crosscliff Hill
A631
CROSSCLIFF HILL
Slates Farm
Cotes Grange Farm
Grenville Wood
Ackthorpe Village
Earthworks
Church Top Farm
Acthorpe Farm
Linford Wood
Syke Plantation
HIGH STREET
Thorpe Farm
Acthorpe Top Farm
Grange Farm
Welton-le-Wold Nature Reserve
Ox Hole
Church Farm
CHURCH LA
South Elkington
Meml
Slates Wood
Pit (dis)
Kirk Hill Plantation
Skeleton Hill Plantation
Heron Lake
Chimney
The Wolds
Manor House
The Park
Sewage Works
Sand Pit Plantation
Eighteen Acre Plantation
Cow Pasture Wood
Manor Warren Farm
Jubilee Plantation
Little Welton
Welton le Wold
Home Farm
Welton Vale
Markham's Plantation
Bunkers Farm
A157
Welton Springs
Bunkers Plantation
Booth's Corner Plantation
Allenby's Furze
Gayton Top
Glebe Farm
Oak Plantation
Jack's Furze
Top Warren Farm
LN11
Hallington Top
BLUESTONE HEATH ROAD
Hallington
Home Farm
Ash Holt
Black Plantation
Poke's Hole
North Farm
Home Farm
Raithby
Welsdale Bottom
New Plantation
Brackens Farm
Maltby
Withcall
Withcall Village
Home Farm
HORNCASTLE ROAD
New Buildings
Fox Covert
Tumulus
Dovendale
Mast
MANOR HILL
South Farm
Long Barrow
Panholes Plantation
Stonepit Covert
Coldharbour Plantation
Saxon's Hill
A153
59
72
73

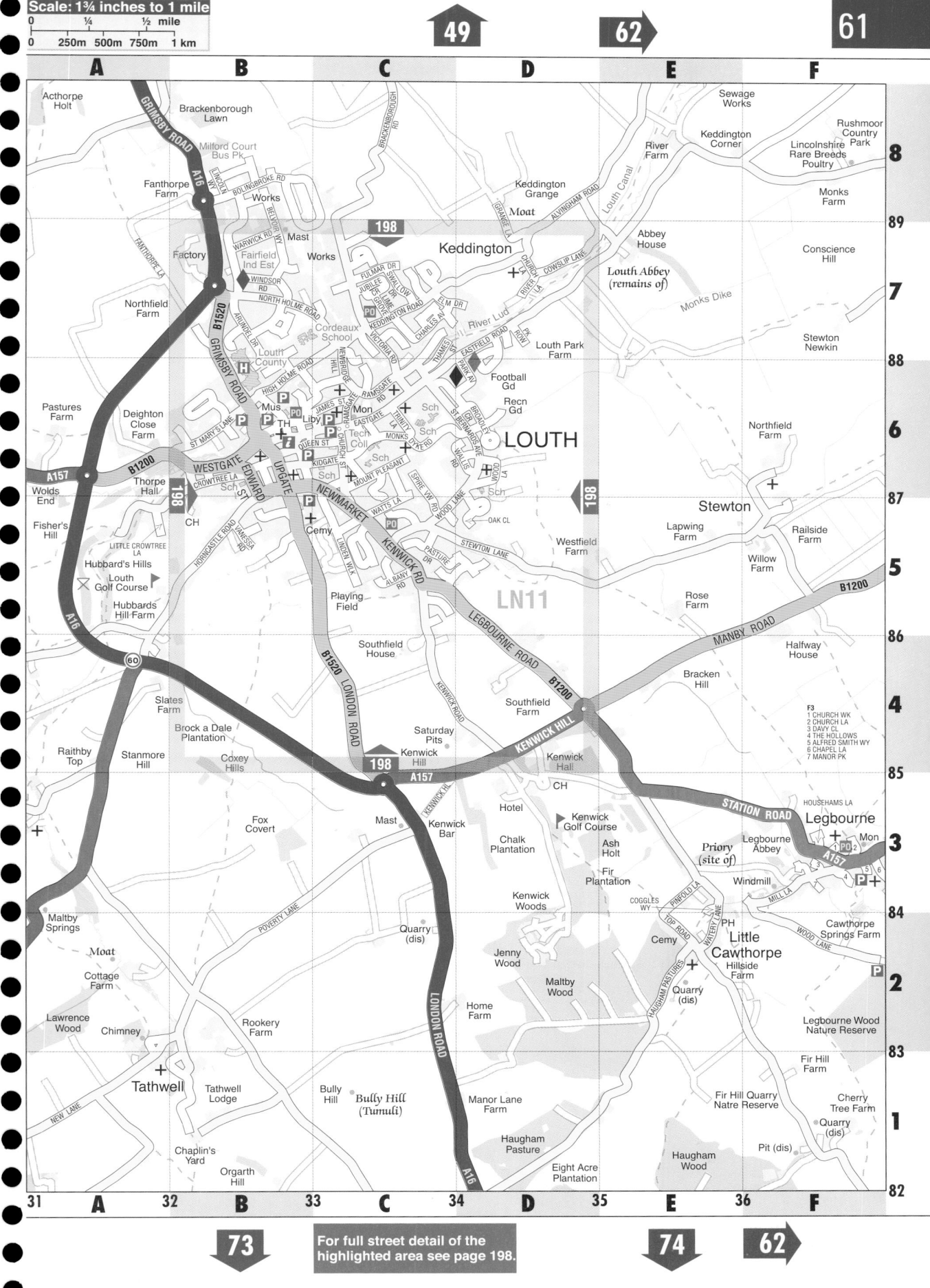

Scale: 1¾ inches to 1 mile

0   ¼   ½ mile
0 250m 500m 750m 1 km

49
62
73
74
62

A   B   C   D   E   F

Acthorpe Holt

Brackenborough Lawn

Milford Court Bus Pk

GRIMSBY ROAD

Fanthorpe Farm

A16 WY

FANTHORPE LA

Works

BOLINGBROKE RD

BELVOIR WY

LINCOLN

WARWICK RD

Factory

Fairfield Ind Est

WINDSOR RD

ARUNDEL DR

NORTH HOLME ROAD

Mast

Works

198

FULMAR DR
SWALLOW
JUBILEE
KEDDINGTON ROAD
VICTORIA RD
ELM DR
CHARLES AV

Keddington

Keddington Grange

Moat

Sewage Works

Keddington Corner

River Farm

Louth Canal

ALVINGHAM ROAD

GRANGE LA

CHURCH LA

COWSLIP LANE

Abbey House

Louth Abbey (remains of)

Monks Dike

Rushmoor Country Park

Lincolnshire Rare Breeds Poultry

Monks Farm

Conscience Hill

8

89

7

Northfield Farm

B1520

GRIMSBY ROAD

Cordeaux School

Louth County

H

NEWBRIDGE HILL

HIGH HOLME ROAD

RAMSGATE

St MARY'S LANE

P

Mus

P

TH

P

PO

Liby

P

EASTGATE

Mon

JAMES ST

EDWARD ST

Sch

Sch

Tech Coll

Sch

Sch

MONKS DYKE RD

TRINITY LANE

St BERNARD'S AV

BROADLEY CRES

WALLS

Sch

River Lud

THAMES ST

RIVER HEAD

EASTFIELD ROAD

PARK AV

Football Gd

Recn Gd

LOUTH

Louth Park Farm

Northfield Farm

Stewton Newkin

88

6

Pastures Farm

Deighton Close Farm

Thorpe Hall

WESTGATE

CROWTREE LA

EDWARD ST

UPGATE

CH

B1200

A157

198

QUEEN ST

KIDGATE

Mount Pleasant

NEWMARKET

WOOD LANE

Sch

SPIRE LW RD

OAK CL

PO

WATTS LA

PASTURE

KENWICK RD

P

Cemy

198

STEWTON LANE

Westfield Farm

Stewton

Lapwing Farm

Railside Farm

Willow Farm

B1200

MANBY ROAD

87

5

Wolds End

A16

Fisher's Hill

LITTLE CROWTREE LA

Hubbard's Hills

Louth Golf Course

Hubbards Hill Farm

HORNCASTLE ROAD

JANE ST

LINDEN WLK

ALBANY RD

B1520

LONDON ROAD

Playing Field

Southfield House

LEGBOURNE ROAD

KENWICK ROAD

LN11

Rose Farm

Bracken Hill

Halfway House

86

4

60

Slates Farm

Raithby Top

Stanmore Hill

Brock a Dale Plantation

Coxey Hills

Saturday Pits

198

Kenwick Hill

A157

Southfield Farm

B1200

KENWICK HILL

STATION ROAD

Kenwick Hall

CH

Kenwick Golf Course

Kenwick Bar

Hotel

Chalk Plantation

Ash Holt

Fir Plantation

Priory (site of)

Legbourne Abbey

Windmill

A157

PO

Legbourne

Mon

HOUSEHAMS LA

F3
1 CHURCH WK
2 CHURCH LA
3 DAVY CL
4 THE HOLLOWS
5 ALFRED SMITH WY
6 CHAPEL LA
7 MANOR PK

85

3

Fox Covert

Mast

KENWICK RD

Kenwick Woods

Kenwick Bar

POVERTY LANE

Quarry (dis)

Jenny Wood

Maltby Wood

COGGLES WY

PINFOLD LA

TOP ROAD

WATERY LANE

HAUGHAM PASTURES

Cemy

PH

MILL LA

WOOD LANE

Little Cawthorpe

Hillside Farm

Cawthorpe Springs Farm

Legbourne Wood Nature Reserve

P

84

2

Maltby Springs

Moat

Cottage Farm

Lawrence Wood

Chimney

Rookery Farm

LONDON ROAD

A16

Home Farm

Quarry (dis)

Fir Hill Farm

Fir Hill Quarry Natre Reserve

Cherry Tree Farm

Quarry (dis)

83

1

Tathwell

NEW LANE

Tathwell Lodge

Chaplin's Yard

Orgarth Hill

Bully Hill

Bully Hill (Tumuli)

Manor Lane Farm

Haugham Pasture

Eight Acre Plantation

Haugham Wood

Pit (dis)

82

31   A   32   B   33   C   34   D   35   E   36   F

For full street detail of the highlighted area see page 198.

C6
1 CHURCH WK
2 MEADOW CL
3 CHRISTOPHER CL
4 ORCHARD PK
5 HAWTHORNE CL
6 ST EDITH GATE
7 SPINNEY CL
8 GRANGE LA
9 ST MARY'S CR
10 CANBERRA CR
11 PROVOST RD
12 JAVELIN RD

61
50

Scale: 1¾ inches to 1 mile

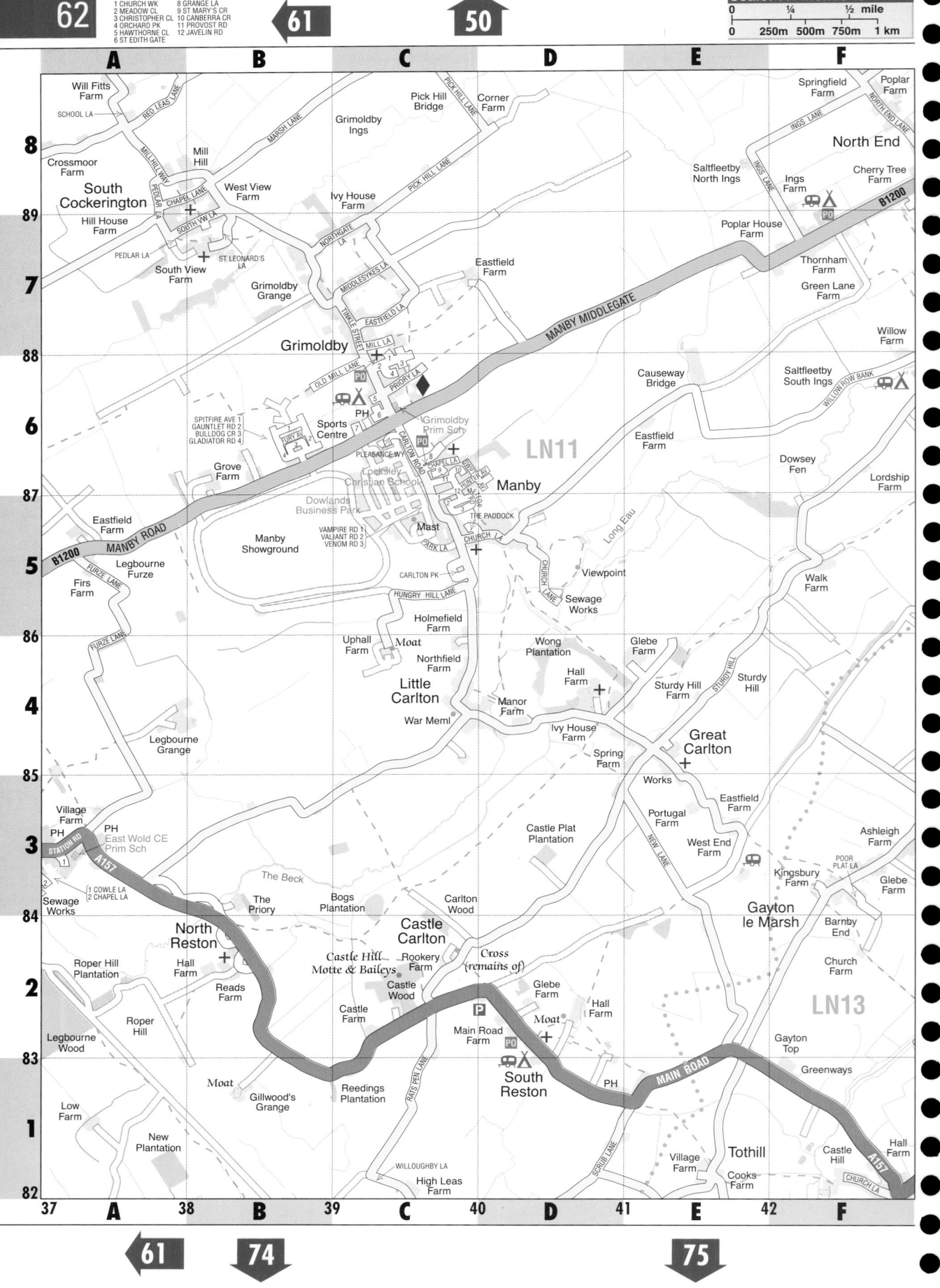

61
74
75

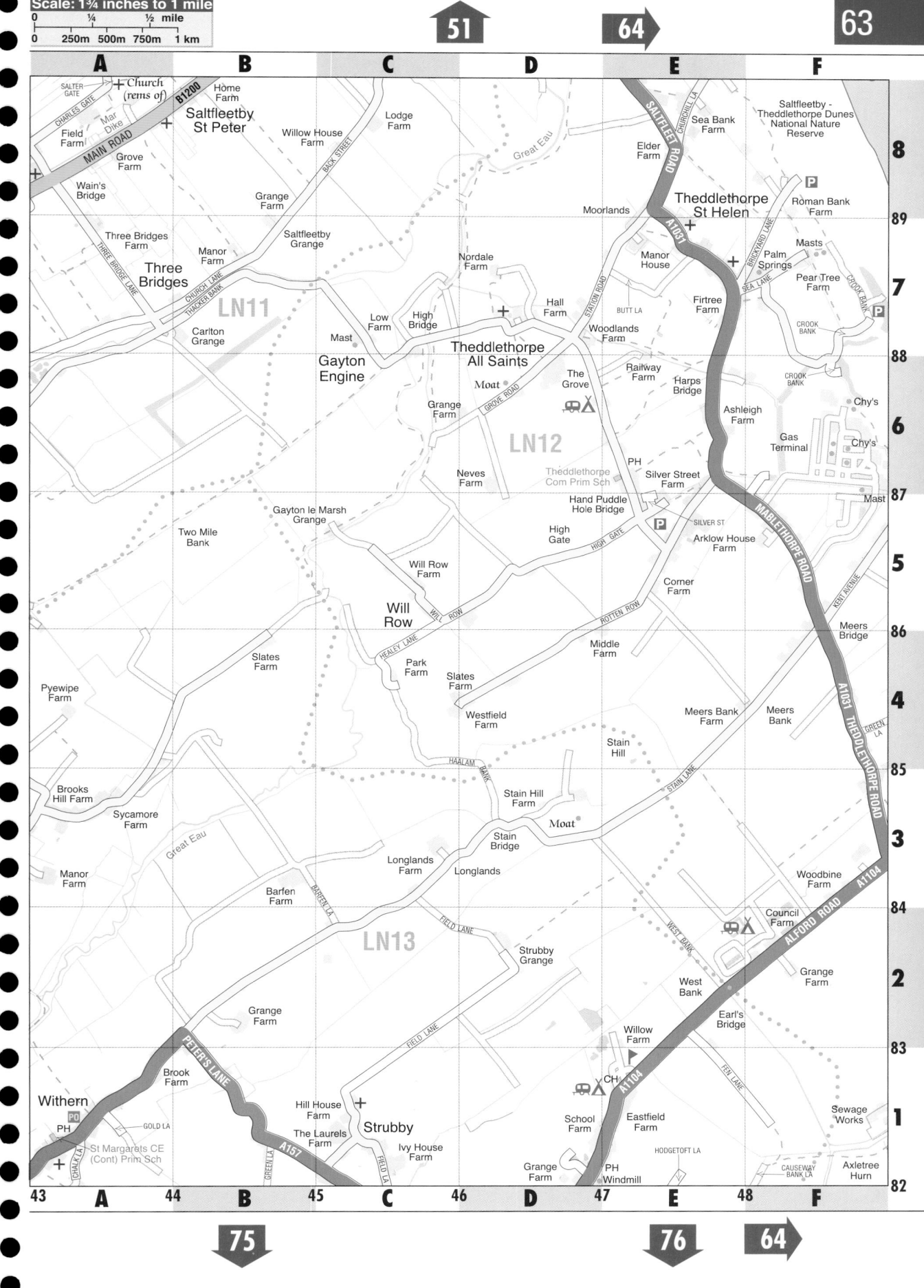
Scale: 1¾ inches to 1 mile
0 ¼ ½ mile
0 250m 500m 750m 1 km
51
64
A B C D E F
Saltfleetby St Peter
Home Farm
Church (rems of)
B1200
MAIN ROAD
Field Farm
Mar Dike
Grove Farm
Wain's Bridge
Willow House Farm
Lodge Farm
BACK STREET
Grange Farm
Great Eau
Saltfleetby - Theddlethorpe Dunes National Nature Reserve
Sea Bank Farm
Elder Farm
SALTFLEET ROAD
CHURCHILL LA
Theddlethorpe St Helen
Roman Bank Farm
Moorlands
A1031
Three Bridges Farm
THREE BRIDGE LANE
Manor Farm
Saltfleetby Grange
Three Bridges
CHURCH LANE
THACKER BANK
LN11
Nordale Farm
Manor House
BUTT LA
BRICKYARD LANE
Palm Springs
Masts
Pear Tree Farm
SEA LANE
CROOK BANK
Firtree Farm
Hall Farm
STATION ROAD
Low Farm
High Bridge
Carlton Grange
Mast
Woodlands Farm
Theddlethorpe All Saints
Gayton Engine
Moat
The Grove
Railway Farm
Harps Bridge
Grange Farm
GROVE ROAD
Ashleigh Farm
Chy's
LN12
Gas Terminal
PH
Neves Farm
Theddlethorpe Com Prim Sch
Silver Street Farm
Hand Puddle Hole Bridge
Mast
Gayton le Marsh Grange
SILVER ST
MABLETHORPE ROAD
Two Mile Bank
High Gate
HIGH GATE
Arklow House Farm
Will Row Farm
Corner Farm
KENT AVENUE
Will Row
WILL ROW
ROTTEN ROW
HEALEY LANE
Meers Bridge
Slates Farm
Middle Farm
Park Farm
Slates Farm
Pyewipe Farm
A1031 THEDDLETHORPE ROAD
Westfield Farm
Meers Bank Farm
Meers Bank
GREEN LA
Stain Hill
HAALAM BANK
STAIN LANE
Brooks Hill Farm
Stain Hill Farm
Sycamore Farm
Moat
Stain Bridge
Great Eau
Longlands Farm
Longlands
Manor Farm
Woodbine Farm
A1104
Barfen Farm
BARFEN LA
FIELD LANE
WEST BANK
Council Farm
LN13
ALFORD ROAD
Strubby Grange
Grange Farm
West Bank
Grange Farm
Earl's Bridge
Willow Farm
PETER'S LANE
FIELD LANE
CH
A1104
Brook Farm
FEN LANE
Withern
PO
PH
GOLD LA
Hill House Farm
Strubby
Sewage Works
School Farm
Eastfield Farm
St Margarets CE (Cont) Prim Sch
The Laurels Farm
A157
CHALK LA
GREEN LA
FIELD LA
Ivy House Farm
HODGETOFT LA
Grange Farm
PH
Windmill
CAUSEWAY BANK LA
Axletree Hurn
8 89 7 88 6 87 5 86 4 85 3 84 2 83 1 82
43 44 45 46 47 48
75
76
64

63

B5
1 CAMBRIDGE RD N
2 LINKS AVE
3 CAMBRIDGE RD S
4 IVEL GR
5 WHITEHEAD CL
6 IVEL CL

Scale: 1¾ inches to 1 mile

0   ¼   ½   mile
0   250m   500m   750m   1 km

Saltfleetby -
Theddlethorpe Dunes
National Nature
Reserve

North End
Farm

MEERS
BANK

PH

CROOK
BANK

MEERS BANK

The Seal Sanctuary
& Nature Centre

POPLAR AVE 1
CHALFONT AVE 2

KENT AVE

GREEN LANE

GOLF ROAD

QUEBEC ROAD

BYRON CL

A4
1 THE FAIRWAY
2 THE DRIVE
3 FALDOS WY
4 GOLF RD
5 LYLE CL
6 THE GREEN
7 EAGLE CL

The Dunes Family
Entertainment
Centre

Station
Sports Ctr

Mablethorpe
Com Prim
Sch

Mon

Liby

Fun Fair

IRB
Station

Mablethorpe
Hall

Moat

HIGH STREET

VICTORIA RD

Olde Curiosity
Mus

MABLETHORPE

A1104 ALFORD ROAD

PH

LN12

CHURCH LANE

PH

Art Gall

The Tennyson
High School

C3
1 QUEENS PK CL
2 NEWSTEAD RD
3 DYMOKE CL
4 BROOKE DR
5 DYMOKE RD
6 ARDEN CL

Seahaven
Springs

SEAHOLME ROAD

SEAHOLME ROAD

AQUA DR 1
MARIAN AVE 2
MEDINA GD 3
CHAMPION WY 4

Trusthorpe

Masts

Masts

SUTTON RD

C2
1 MILL FIELD
2 CAMPLING WY
3 BARTON CL
4 AUBREY PARKER CL
5 PARKINSON'S WY
6 JAMES AVE
7 ST PETER'S LA
8 BRAY AVE
9 ETON RD

Poplar
Farm

MILE LANE

NORTH ROAD

Bourne
Farm

Bambers
Farm

Bamber's
Bridge

Bridge
Farm

Elder
Farm

Crossing
Farm

WHITE ROW LA

ASHLEY
CLOSE

A52 TRUSTHORPE ROAD

Sewage
Works

Thorpe
Farm

MAIN STREET

Trusthorpe
Hall

FEN LA

Thorpe

Boswell
Farm

HIGHGATE

1 PARK RD E
2 CROMER AVE
3 HIGH ST
4 PROMENADE
5 YORK RD

63   76   77

A3
1 ORCHARD WY
2 ORCHARD CL
3 CHURCH RD
4 MALBOROUGH DR
5 OAKHAM AVE
6 WINCHESTER DR
7 CHELTENHAM WY

B3
1 HAWTHORN DR
2 MAYFLOWER WY
3 TRENCHARD RD
4 NELSON RD
5 STANLEY AVE
6 MAXWELL DR
7 KENSINGTON GDNS
8 STRAND CL
9 TOWER CL
10 HARLEQUIN DR
11 MARIAN AVE
12 HARRIS BOULEVARD
13 ELM AVE
14 KING ST
15 MARINA RD
16 ANCASTER RD
17 RIPON PL
18 VYNER CL
19 FOXE END
20 KNOWLE ST
21 PARK AVE
22 PARRY RD
23 THE BOULEVARD

B4
1 LONG ACRE
2 ST ANDREWS RD
3 SHERWOOD RD
4 RUGBY RD
5 MALVERN RD
6 HARROW RD
7 REPTON RD
8 QUEENSWAY
9 SOMERSBY AVE
10 FITZWILLIAM ST
11 WELLINGTON AVE
12 CHAUCER AVE
13 RUSKIN RD
14 KINGSLEY RD
15 CHARLES WRIGHT CL
16 TENNYSON AVE
17 TENNYSON RD
18 HIGH ST
19 ADMIRALTY RD
20 STATION RD
21 ALEXANDRA RD
22 ALEXANDRA PK

C1
1 HALL LEAS DR
2 TRUSTHORPE RD
3 HIGHGATE CL
4 HIGHFIELD AVE
5 DUNDLE RD
6 UPPINGHAM RD
7 WILLOUGHBY RD
8 MARINE AVE
9 HARDING CL

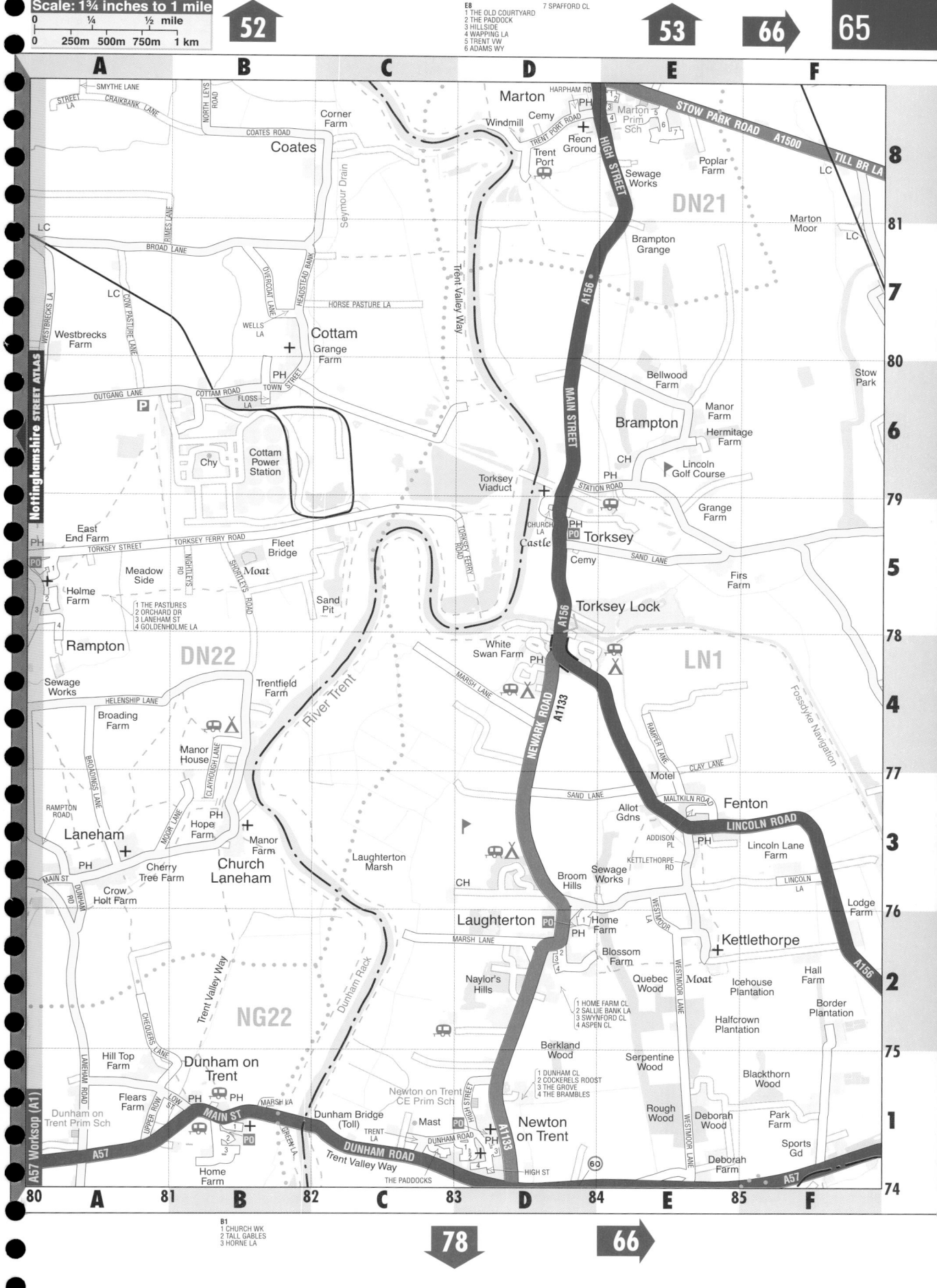

E8
1 THE OLD COURTYARD   7 SPAFFORD CL
2 THE PADDOCK
3 HILLSIDE
4 WAPPING LA
5 TRENT VW
6 ADAMS WY

A   B   C   D   E   F

SMYTHE LANE
STREET LA
CRAIKBANK LANE
NORTH LEYS ROAD
COATES ROAD
Corner Farm
Coates

Marton
HARPHAM RD
PH
Cemy
Windmill
Marton Prim Sch
STOW PARK ROAD A1500
TILL BR LA
LC

8

Trent Port Road
Trent Port
Recn Ground
HIGH STREET
Poplar Farm
DN21
Marton Moor
LC

81

LC
BROAD LANE
RIMES LANE
OVERGOAT LANE
HEADSTEAD BANK
HORSE PASTURE LA
Trent Valley Way
Sewage Works
Brampton Grange

7

WESTBRECKS LA
COW PASTURE LANE
LC
WELLS LA
Cottam
Grange Farm
Bellwood Farm
Stow Park

80

Westbrecks Farm
PH
TOWN STREET
Manor Farm
Brampton
Hermitage Farm

6

OUTGANG LANE
COTTAM ROAD
FLOSS LA
P
CH
PH
Lincoln Golf Course
Nottinghamshire Street Atlas

Chy
Cottam Power Station
Torksey Viaduct
MAIN STREET
STATION ROAD
PH
PO
Grange Farm

79

East End Farm
TORKSEY FERRY ROAD
Fleet Bridge
CHURCH LA
Castle
Torksey
Cemy

PH
PO
Holme Farm
TORKSEY STREET
Meadow Side
Moat
TORKSEY FERRY ROAD
SAND LANE
Firs Farm

5

1 THE PASTURES
2 ORCHARD DR
3 LANEHAM ST
4 GOLDENHOLME LA
NIGHTLEY'S RD
STICKLEY'S ROAD
Sand Pit
A156
Torksey Lock

Rampton
DN22
Trentfield Farm
River Trent
White Swan Farm
PH
LN1

78

Sewage Works
HELENSHIP LANE
Broading Farm
Manor House
NEWARK ROAD
A1133
RAMPER LANE
CLAY LANE

4

BROADINGS LANE
CLAYHOUGH LANE
MARSH LANE
Motel

77

RAMPTON ROAD
MOOR LANE
PH
Hope Farm
Manor Farm
SAND LANE
MALTKILN RD
Fenton
LINCOLN ROAD

Laneham
PH
Cherry Tree Farm
Church Laneham
Laughterton Marsh
ADDISON PL
KETTLETHORPE RD
PH
Lincoln Lane Farm

3

MAIN ST
DUNHAM RD
Crow Holt Farm
CH
Broom Hills
Sewage Works
LINCOLN LA
Lodge Farm

76

Laughterton
PO
PH
Home Farm
WESTMOOR LANE
Kettlethorpe
A156

Trent Valley Way
Dunham Rack
NG22
MARSH LANE
Blossom Farm
Naylor's Hills
Quebec Wood
Moat
Icehouse Plantation
Hall Farm
Border Plantation

2

1 HOME FARM CL
2 SALLIE BANK LA
3 SWYNFORD CL
4 ASPEN CL
Halfcrown Plantation

CHEQUERS LANE
Hill Top Farm
Dunham on Trent
Berkland Wood
Serpentine Wood
Rough Wood
Blackthorn Wood

75

LANEHAM ROAD
DUNHAM RD
Flears Farm
Dunham on Trent Prim Sch
PH
MAIN ST
PH
MARSH LA
Dunham Bridge (Toll)
Newton on Trent CE Prim Sch
Mast
PO
A1133
Newton on Trent
1 DUNHAM CL
2 COCKERELS ROOST
3 THE GROVE
4 THE BRAMBLES
Deborah Wood
Park Farm

A57 Worksop (A1)
A57
PO
Home Farm
UPPER ROW
GREEN LA
DUNHAM ROAD
Trent Valley Way
THE PADDOCKS
TRENT LA
HIGH ST
PH
60
Rough Wood
Deborah Farm
Sports Gd
A57

1

74

80   A   81   B   82   C   83   D   84   E   85   F

B1
1 CHURCH WK
2 TALL GABLES
3 HORNE LA

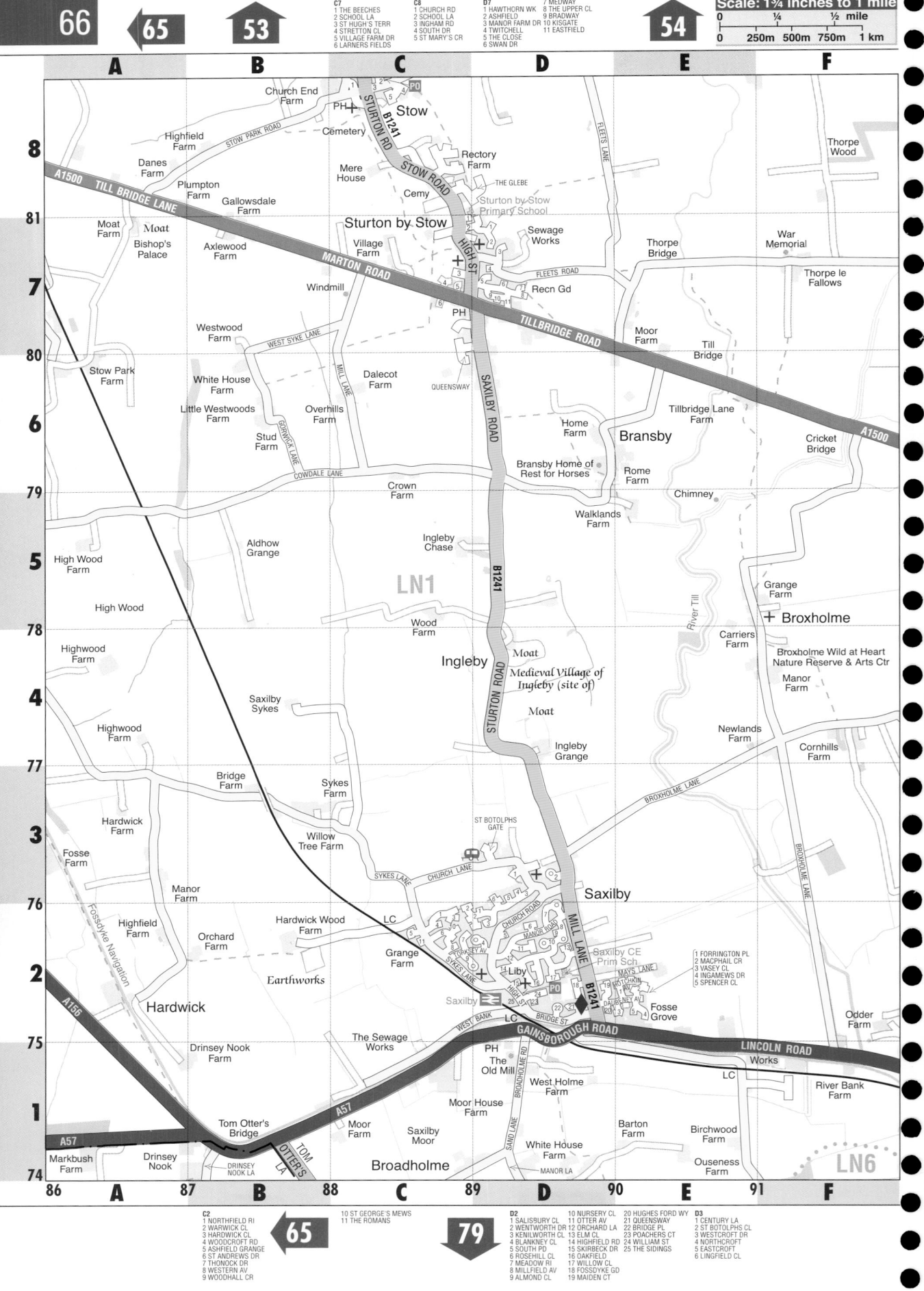

C7
1 THE BEECHES
2 SCHOOL LA
3 ST HUGH'S TERR
4 STRETTON CL
5 VILLAGE FARM DR
6 LARNERS FIELDS

C8
1 CHURCH RD
2 SCHOOL LA
3 INGHAM RD
4 SOUTH DR
5 ST MARY'S CR

D7
1 HAWTHORN WK
2 ASHFIELD
3 MANOR FARM DR
4 TWITCHELL
5 THE CLOSE
6 SWAN DR

7 MEDWAY
8 THE UPPER CL
9 BRADWAY
10 KISGATE
11 EASTFIELD

A **B** **C** **D** **E** **F**

8

Church End Farm

Highfield Farm

PH

Cemetery

STOW PARK ROAD

Stow

PO

Rectory Farm

THE GLEBE

Thorpe Wood

Danes Farm

Plumpton Farm

Gallowsdale Farm

A1500

TILL BRIDGE LANE

Moat Farm

Moat

Bishop's Palace

Axlewood Farm

81

Mere House

Cemy

Sturton by Stow Primary School

Sturton by Stow

Village Farm

MARTON ROAD

Sewage Works

Thorpe Bridge

War Memorial

7

Windmill

HIGH ST

PH

FLEETS ROAD

Recn Gd

TILLBRIDGE ROAD

Moor Farm

Till Bridge

Thorpe le Fallows

80

Westwood Farm

WEST SYKE LANE

MILL LANE

Dalecot Farm

QUEENSWAY

SAXILBY ROAD

Tillbridge Lane Farm

A1500

6

Stow Park Farm

White House Farm

Little Westwoods Farm

Overhills Farm

GORNICK LANE

Stud Farm

COWDALE LANE

Home Farm

Bransby

Rome Farm

Cricket Bridge

79

Crown Farm

Ingleby Chase

Bransby Home of Rest for Horses

Chimney

Walklands Farm

River Till

Broxholme

5

High Wood Farm

Aldhow Grange

LN1

B1241

Grange Farm

High Wood

Wood Farm

Broxholme Wild at Heart Nature Reserve & Arts Ctr

78

Highwood Farm

Ingleby

Moat

Carriers Farm

Manor Farm

4

Highwood Farm

Saxilby Sykes

STURTON ROAD

Medieval Village of Ingleby (site of)

Moat

Newlands Farm

Cornhills Farm

77

Bridge Farm

Sykes Farm

Ingleby Grange

BROXHOLME LANE

BROXHOLME LANE

3

Hardwick Farm

Willow Tree Farm

St Botolphs Gate

Saxilby

Fosse Farm

SYKES LANE

CHURCH LANE

76

Fossdyke Navigation

Manor Farm

Orchard Farm

Hardwick Wood Farm

LC

CHURCH ROAD

MANOR ROAD

MILL LANE

Saxilby CE Prim Sch

1 FORRINGTON PL
2 MACPHAIL CR
3 VASEY CL
4 INGAMEWS DR
5 SPENCER CL

2

A156

Hardwick

Grange Farm

Earthworks

Liby

Saxilby

SYKES LANE

HIGH ST

PO

B1241

MAYS LANE

WILLIAM ST

DAUBENEY AV

Fosse Grove

Odder Farm

75

Drinsey Nook Farm

The Sewage Works

WEST BANK

LC

GAINSBOROUGH ROAD

PH
The Old Mill

BROADHOLME RD

West Holme Farm

LINCOLN ROAD

Works

LC

River Bank Farm

1

A57

Tom Otter's Bridge

TOM OTTER'S LA

Moor Farm

Saxilby Moor

SAND LANE

White House Farm

Barton Farm

Birchwood Farm

74

Markbush Farm

Drinsey Nook

DRINSEY NOOK LA

Broadholme

MANOR LA

Ouseness Farm

LN6

86 **A** **87** **B** **88** **C** **89** **D** **90** **E** **91** **F**

C2
1 NORTHFIELD RI
2 WARWICK CL
3 HARDWICK CL
4 WOODCROFT RD
5 ASHFIELD GRANGE
6 ST ANDREWS DR
7 THONOCK DR
8 WESTERN AV
9 WOODHALL CR

10 ST GEORGE'S MEWS
11 THE ROMANS

D2
1 SALISBURY CL
2 WENTWORTH DR
3 KENILWORTH CL
4 BLANKNEY CL
5 SOUTH PD
6 ROSEHILL CL
7 MEADOW RI
8 MILLFIELD AV
9 ALMOND CL

10 NURSERY CL
11 OTTER AV
12 ORCHARD LA
13 ELM CL
14 HIGHFIELD RD
15 SKIRBECK DR
16 OAKFIELD
17 WILLOW CL
18 FOSSDYKE GD
19 MAIDEN CT

20 HUGHES FORD WY
21 QUEENSWAY
22 BRIDGE PL
23 POACHERS CT
24 WILLIAM ST
25 THE SIDINGS

D3
1 CENTURY LA
2 ST BOTOLPHS CL
3 WESTCROFT DR
4 NORTHCROFT
5 EASTCROFT
6 LINGFIELD CL

Scale: 1¾ inches to 1 mile
0 ¼ ½ mile
0 250m 500m 750m 1 km

54 55 68

E5
1 NORFOLK CRES
2 DEVONSHIRE RD
3 FOURTH AVE
4 THIRD AVE
5 SECOND AVE
6 FIRST AVE
7 WELLINGTON ST
8 DORSET PL
9 SHROPSHIRE RD
10 SUFFOLK RD
11 WHITLEY ST
12 CORNWALL CL
13 NORTHUMBERLAND AVE
14 WESTMORELAND AVE
15 RUTLAND WY
16 SUSSEX GDNS
17 CUMBERLAND WY

F5
1 SCHOOL LA
2 TRENCHARD SQ
3 LINCOLN DR
4 VULCAN DR
5 CANBERRA DR
6 LANCASTER DR

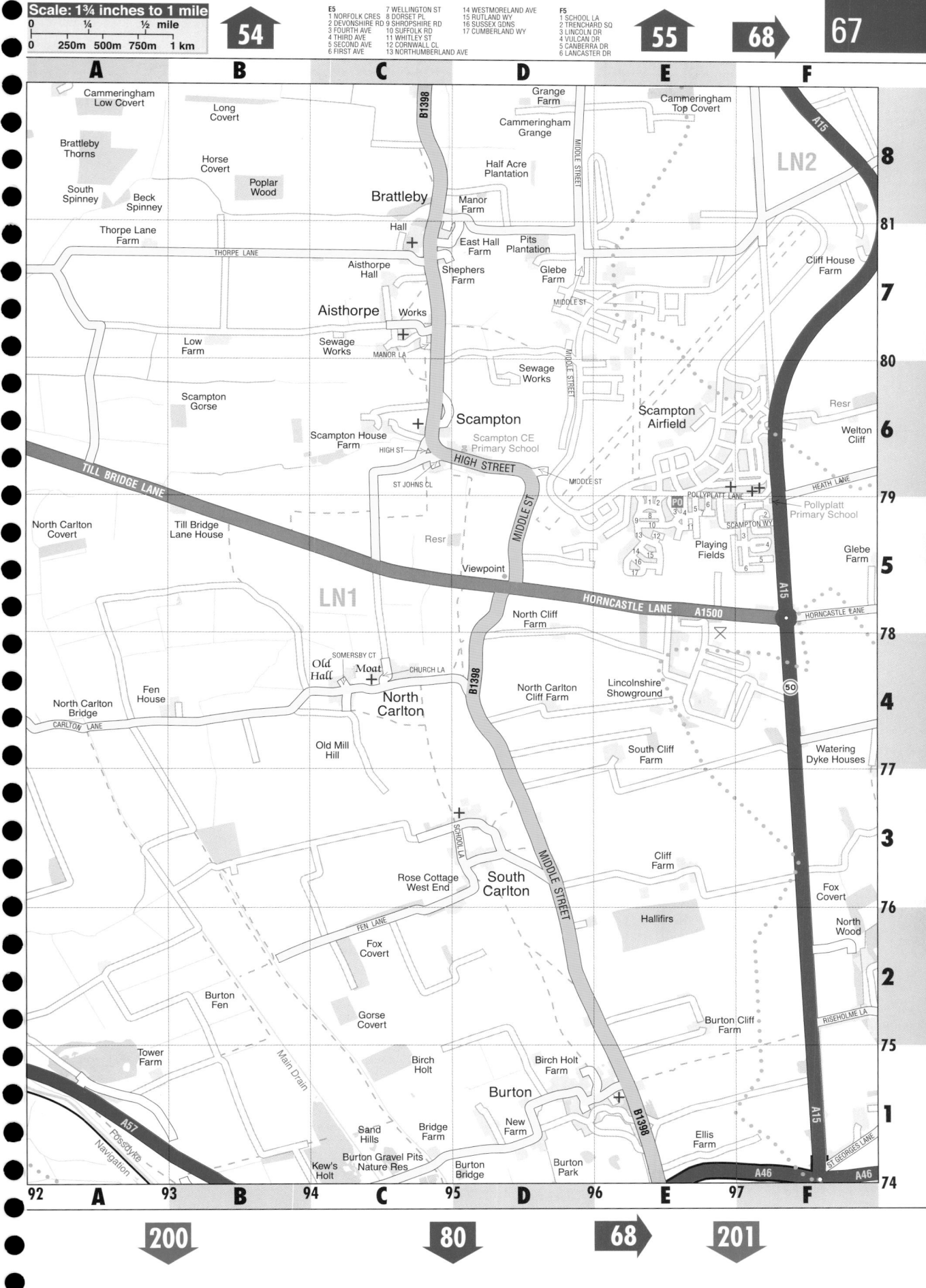

200 80 68 201

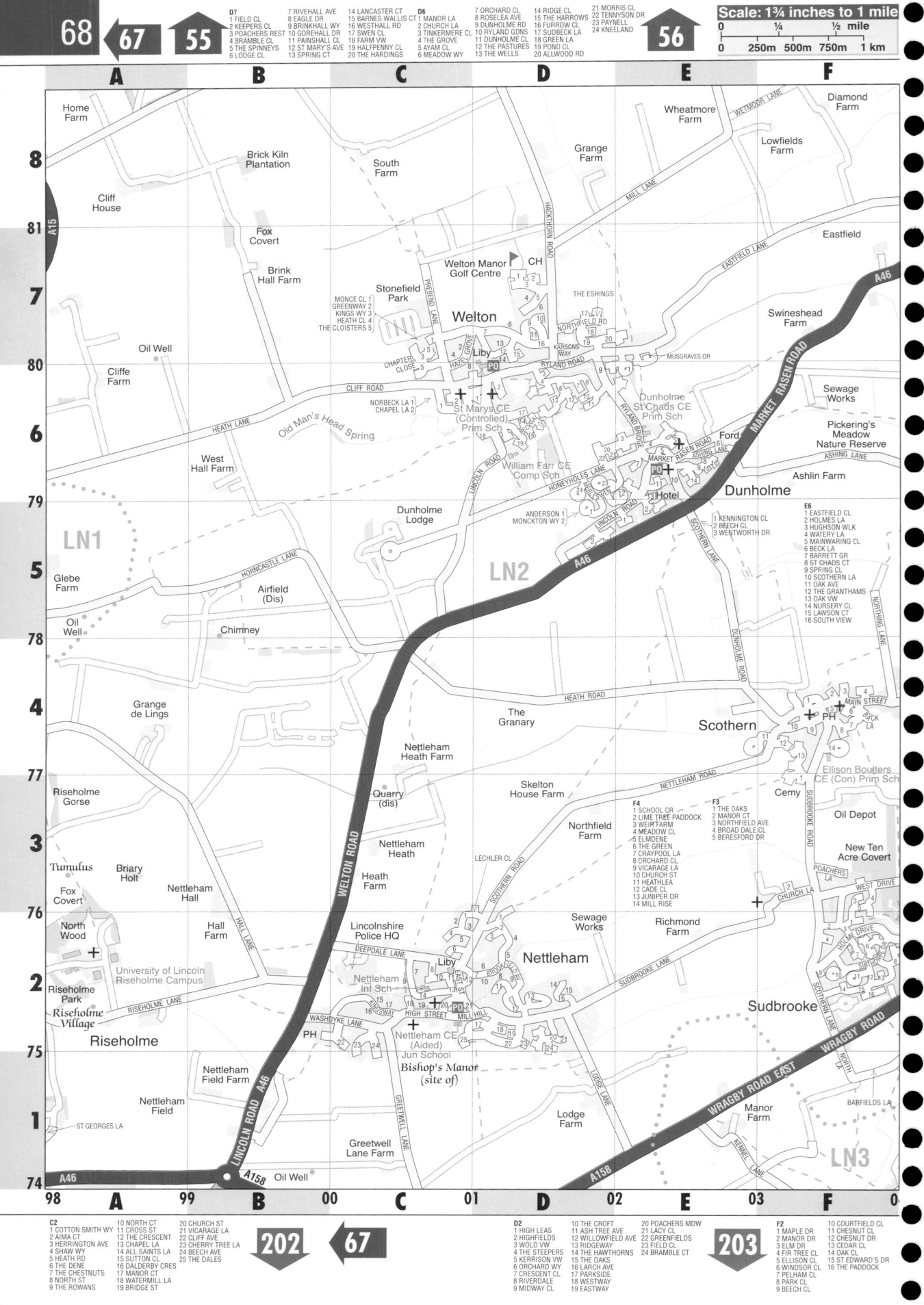
68
67
55
D7
1 FIELD CL
2 KEEPERS CL
3 POACHERS REST
4 BRAMBLE CL
5 THE SPINNEYS
6 LODGE CL
7 RIVEHALL AVE
8 EAGLE DR
9 BRINKHALL WY
10 GOREHALL DR
11 PAINSHALL CL
12 ST MARY'S AVE
13 SPRING CT
14 LANCASTER CT
15 BARNES WALLIS CT
16 WESTHALL RD
17 SWEN CL
18 FARM VW
19 HALFPENNY CL
20 THE HARDINGS
D6
1 MANOR LA
2 CHURCH LA
3 TINKERMERE CL
4 THE GROVE
5 AYAM CL
6 MEADOW WY
7 ORCHARD CL
8 ROSELEA AVE
9 DUNHOLME RD
10 RYLAND GDNS
11 DUNHOLME CL
12 THE PASTURES
13 THE WELLS
14 RIDGE CL
15 THE HARROWS
16 FURROW CL
17 SUDBECK LA
18 GREEN LA
19 POND CL
20 ALLWOOD RD
21 MORRIS CL
22 TENNYSON DR
23 PAYNELL
24 KNEELAND
56
Scale: 1¾ inches to 1 mile
0 ¼ ½ mile
0 250m 500m 750m 1 km
A B C D E F
Home Farm
Brick Kiln Plantation
South Farm
Grange Farm
Wheatmore Farm
WETMOOR LANE
Diamond Farm
Lowfields Farm
Cliff House
MILL LANE
HACKTHORN ROAD
Fox Covert
Eastfield
EASTFIELD LANE
A15
Brink Hall Farm
Welton Manor Golf Centre
CH
Stonefield Park
PREBEND LANE
THE ESHINGS
A46
MONCE CL 1
GREENWAY 2
KINGS WY 3
HEATH CL 4
THE CLOISTERS 5
Welton
NORTHFIELD RD
Swineshead Farm
Oil Well
HAZEL GROVE
Liby
KARSONS WAY
MUSGRAVES OR
CHAPTER CLOSE
PO
RYLAND ROAD
Cliffe Farm
CLIFF ROAD
Dunholme St Chads CE Prim Sch
MARKET RASEN ROAD
Sewage Works
NORBECK LA 1
CHAPEL LA 2
St Marys CE (Controlled) Prim Sch
HEATH LANE
Old Man's Head Spring
RYLAND BRIDGE
Ford
Pickering's Meadow Nature Reserve
ASHING LANE
West Hall Farm
LINCOLN ROAD
William Farr CE Comp Sch
HONEYHOLES LANE
Ashlin Farm
Hotel
Dunholme
ANDERSON 1
MONCKTON WY 2
Dunholme Lodge
1 KENNINGTON CL
2 BEECH CL
3 WENTWORTH DR
E6
1 EASTFIELD CL
2 HOLMES LA
3 HUGHSON WLK
4 WATERY LA
5 MAINWARING CL
6 BECK LA
7 BARRETT GR
8 ST CHADS CT
9 SPRING CL
10 SCOTHERN LA
11 OAK AVE
12 THE GRANTHAMS
13 OAK VW
14 NURSERY CL
15 LAWSON CT
16 SOUTH VIEW
LN1
LN2
SCOTHERN LANE
Glebe Farm
HORNCASTLE LANE
Airfield (Dis)
Oil Well
Chimney
DUNHOLME ROAD
NORTHING LANE
HEATH ROAD
Grange de Lings
The Granary
MAIN STREET
PH
BECK LA
Scothern
Nettleham Heath Farm
NETTLEHAM ROAD
Ellison Boulters CE (Con) Prim Sch
Riseholme Gorse
Quarry (dis)
Skelton House Farm
Cemy
F4
1 SCHOOL CR
2 LIME TREE PADDOCK
3 WEIR FARM
4 MEADOW CL
5 ELMDENE
6 THE GREEN
7 CRAYPOOL LA
8 ORCHARD CL
9 VICARAGE LA
10 CHURCH ST
11 HEATHLEA
12 CADE CL
13 JUNIPER DR
14 MILL RISE
F3
1 THE OAKS
2 MANOR CT
3 NORTHFIELD AVE
4 BROAD DALE CL
5 BERESFORD DR
SUDBROOKE ROAD
Oil Depot
Northfield Farm
Nettleham Heath
Tumulus
Briary Holt
LECHLER CL
New Ten Acre Covert
WELTON ROAD
SCOTHERN ROAD
POACHERS LA
Heath Farm
Nettleham Hall
WEST DRIVE
CHURCH LA
Fox Covert
Sewage Works
Richmond Farm
North Wood
Hall Farm
HALL LANE
Lincolnshire Police HQ
HOLME DRIVE
DEEPDALE LANE
Nettleham
BROOKFIELD AV
University of Lincoln Riseholme Campus
SIBTHORPE
Riseholme Park
Nettleham Inf Sch
SUDBROOKE LANE
RISEHOLME LANE
Riseholme Village
KINGSWAY
HIGH STREET
MILL HILL
Sudbrooke
SCOTHERN LANE
WASHDYKE LANE
PH
Riseholme
Nettleham CE (Aided) Jun School
Bishop's Manor (site of)
WRAGBY ROAD
WRAGBY ROAD EAST
NORTH LA
Nettleham Field Farm
A46
LINCOLN ROAD
GREETWELL LANE
LODGE LANE
BARFIELDS LA
Nettleham Field
Manor Farm
ST GEORGES LA
Lodge Farm
KENNEL LANE
Greetwell Lane Farm
LN3
A46
A158
Oil Well
A158
98 99 00 01 02 03
8 81 7 80 6 79 5 78 4 77 3 76 2 75 1 74
C2
1 COTTON SMITH WY
2 AIMA CT
3 HERRINGTON AVE
4 SHAW WY
5 HEATH RD
6 THE DENE
7 THE CHESTNUTS
8 NORTH ST
9 THE ROWANS
10 NORTH CT
11 CROSS ST
12 THE CRESCENT
13 CHAPEL LA
14 ALL SAINTS LA
15 SUTTON CL
16 DALDERBY CRES
17 MANOR CT
18 WATERMILL LA
19 BRIDGE ST
20 CHURCH ST
21 VICARAGE LA
22 CLIFF AVE
23 CHERRY TREE LA
24 BEECH AVE
25 THE DALES
202
67
D2
1 HIGH LEAS
2 HIGHFIELDS
3 WOLD VW
4 THE STEEPERS
5 KERRISON VW
6 ORCHARD WY
7 CRESCENT CL
8 RIVERDALE
9 MIDWAY CL
10 THE CROFT
11 ASH TREE AVE
12 WILLOWFIELD AVE
13 RIDGEWAY
14 THE HAWTHORNS
15 THE OAKS
16 LARCH AVE
17 PARKSIDE
18 WESTWAY
19 EASTWAY
20 POACHERS MDW
21 LACY CL
22 GREENFIELDS
23 FIELD CL
24 BRAMBLE CT
203
F2
1 MAPLE DR
2 MANOR DR
3 ELM DR
4 FIR TREE CL
5 ELLISON CL
6 WINDSOR CL
7 PELHAM CL
8 PARK CL
9 BEECH CL
10 COURTFIELD CL
11 CHESNUT CL
12 CHESNUT DR
13 CEDAR CL
14 OAK CL
15 ST EDWARD'S DR
16 THE PADDOCK

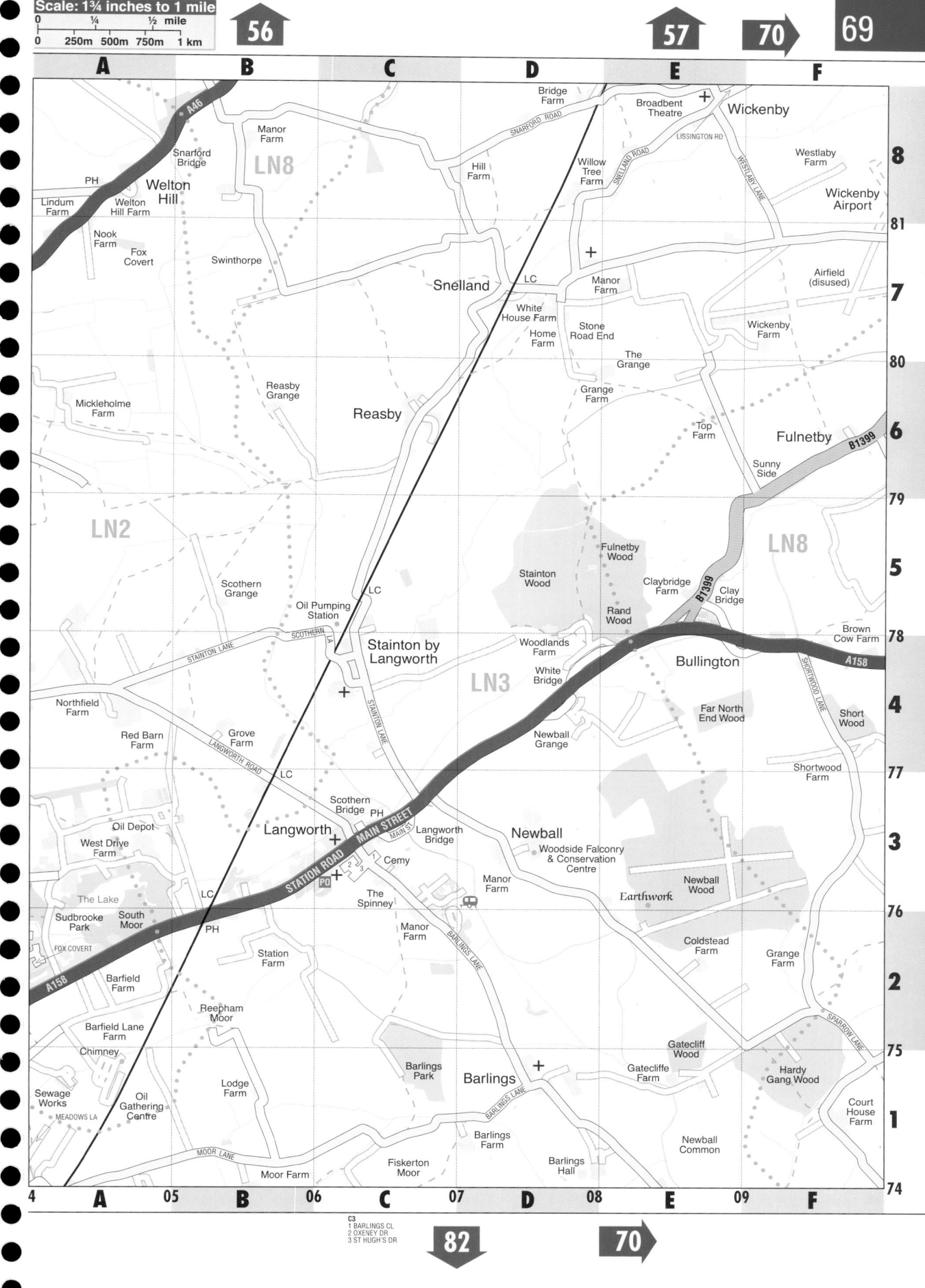

A   B   C   D   E   F

A46
Snarford Bridge
Bridge Farm
Broadbent Theatre
Wickenby

LN8
Manor Farm
Hill Farm
Snarford Road
Lissington Rd
Westlaby Farm
Westlaby Lane
Wickenby Airport

8

PH
Lindum Farm
Welton Hill Farm
Welton Hill
Swinthorpe
Willow Tree Farm
Snelland Road

81

Nook Farm
Fox Covert
Snelland
LC
Manor Farm
Airfield (disused)

7

White House Farm
Home Farm
Stone Road End
Wickenby Farm

Mickleholme Farm
Reasby Grange
The Grange

80

Reasby
Grange Farm
Top Farm
Fulnetby
B1399

6

LN2
Scothern Grange
Fulnetby Wood
Sunny Side

79

Oil Pumping Station
LC
Stainton Wood
Claybridge Farm
Clay Bridge
B1399
LN8

5

Scothern La
Rand Wood
Brown Cow Farm

Stainton Lane
Stainton by Langworth
LN3
Woodlands Farm
White Bridge
Bullington
A158

78

Northfield Farm
Far North End Wood
Short Wood

4

Red Barn Farm
Grove Farm
Langworth Road
LC
Newball Grange
Shortwood Farm

77

Oil Depot
Scothern Bridge
PH
Main Street
Langworth Bridge
Newball
Woodside Falconry & Conservation Centre
Newball Wood

3

West Drive Farm
Langworth
Station Road
Cemy
PO
2 3
The Spinney
Manor Farm
Earthwork

The Lake
LC
Manor Farm
Coldstead Farm
Grange Farm

76

Sudbrooke Park
South Moor
PH
Barlings Lane

Fox Covert
A158
Station Farm
Barfield Farm

2

Barfield Lane Farm
Reepham Moor
Barlings Park
Gatecliff Wood
Hardy Gang Wood

75

Chimney
Gatecliffe Farm
Court House Farm

Sewage Works
Oil Gathering Centre
Lodge Farm
Barlings
Newball Common

1

Meadows La
Moor Lane
Moor Farm
Fiskerton Moor
Barlings Farm
Barlings Hall
Sparrow Lane

4   A   05   B   06   C   07   D   08   E   09   F   74

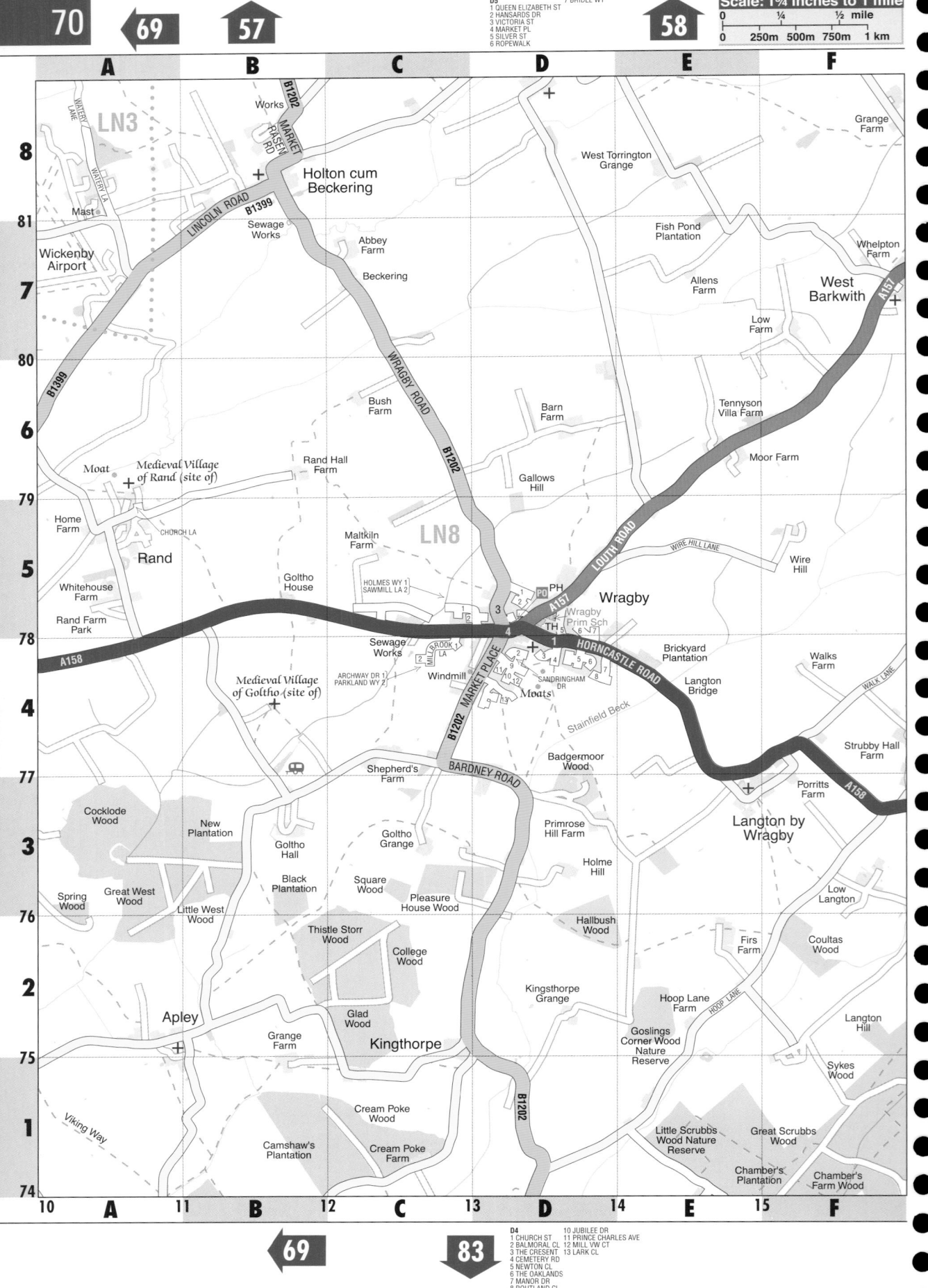

D5
1 QUEEN ELIZABETH ST
2 HANSARDS DR
3 VICTORIA ST
4 MARKET PL
5 SILVER ST
6 ROPEWALK
7 BRIDLE WY

Scale: 1¾ inches to 1 mile
0   ¼   ½   mile
0   250m   500m   750m   1 km

LN3

WATERY LANE

B1202

Works

MARKET RASEN RD

Holton cum
Beckering

Mast

LINCOLN ROAD

B1399

Sewage
Works

Abbey
Farm

Beckering

West Torrington
Grange

Grange
Farm

Fish Pond
Plantation

Whelpton
Farm

Wickenby
Airport

WRAGBY ROAD

West
Barkwith

A157

Allens
Farm

Low
Farm

B1399

Bush
Farm

B1202

Barn
Farm

Tennyson
Villa Farm

Moor Farm

Moat

Medieval Village
of Rand (site of)

Rand Hall
Farm

Gallows
Hill

Home
Farm

CHURCH LA

Rand

LN8

Maltkiln
Farm

LOUTH ROAD

WIRE HILL LANE

Wire
Hill

Whitehouse
Farm

Goltho
House

HOLMES WY 1
SAWMILL LA 2

PO PH

A157

Wragby

Rand
Farm Park

1
2
3

Wragby
Prim Sch

A158

Medieval Village
of Goltho (site of)

Sewage
Works

MILLBROOK LA

4

TH

1

Brickyard
Plantation

Walks
Farm

WALK LANE

ARCHWAY DR 1
PARKLAND WY 2

Windmill

MARKET PLACE

Sandringham
Dr

Moats

Langton
Bridge

B1202

Shepherd's
Farm

BARDNEY ROAD

Stainfield Beck

Strubby Hall
Farm

A158

Badgermoor
Wood

Porritts
Farm

Cocklode
Wood

New
Plantation

Goltho
Hall

Goltho
Grange

Primrose
Hill Farm

Holme
Hill

Langton by
Wragby

Low
Langton

Spring
Wood

Great West
Wood

Little West
Wood

Black
Plantation

Square
Wood

Pleasure
House Wood

Hallbush
Wood

Firs
Farm

Coultas
Wood

Thistle Storr
Wood

College
Wood

Kingsthorpe
Grange

Hoop Lane
Farm

HOOP LANE

Langton
Hill

Apley

Grange
Farm

Glad
Wood

Kingthorpe

Goslings
Corner Wood
Nature
Reserve

Sykes
Wood

Viking Way

Camshaw's
Plantation

Cream Poke
Wood

Cream Poke
Farm

B1202

Little Scrubbs
Wood Nature
Reserve

Great Scrubbs
Wood

Chamber's
Plantation

Chamber's
Farm Wood

D4
1 CHURCH ST
2 BALMORAL CL
3 THE CRESENT
4 CEMETERY RD
5 NEWTON CL
6 THE OAKLANDS
7 MANOR DR
8 ROUTLAND CL
9 MILL VW RD
10 JUBILEE DR
11 PRINCE CHARLES AVE
12 MILL VW CT
13 LARK CL

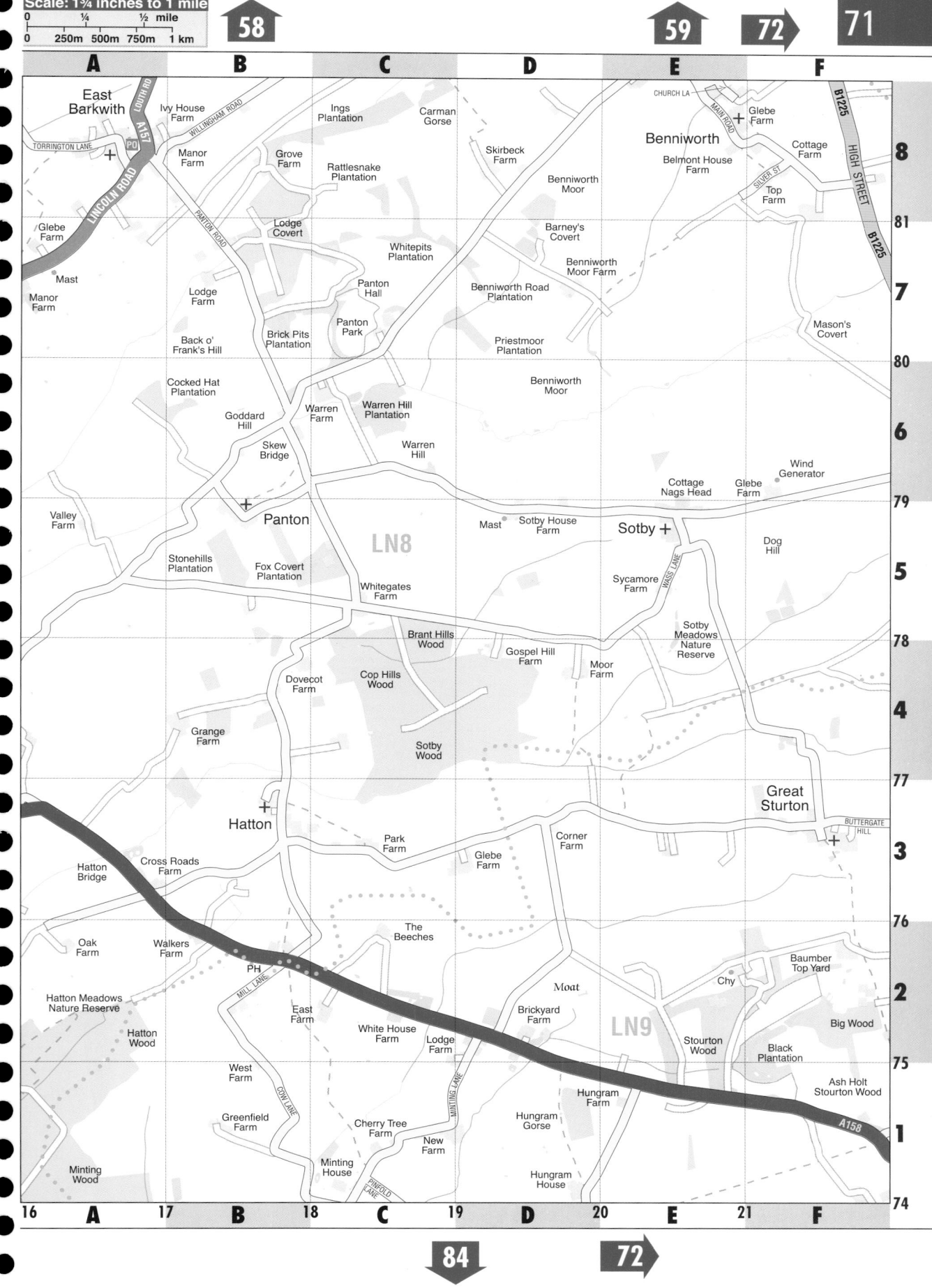

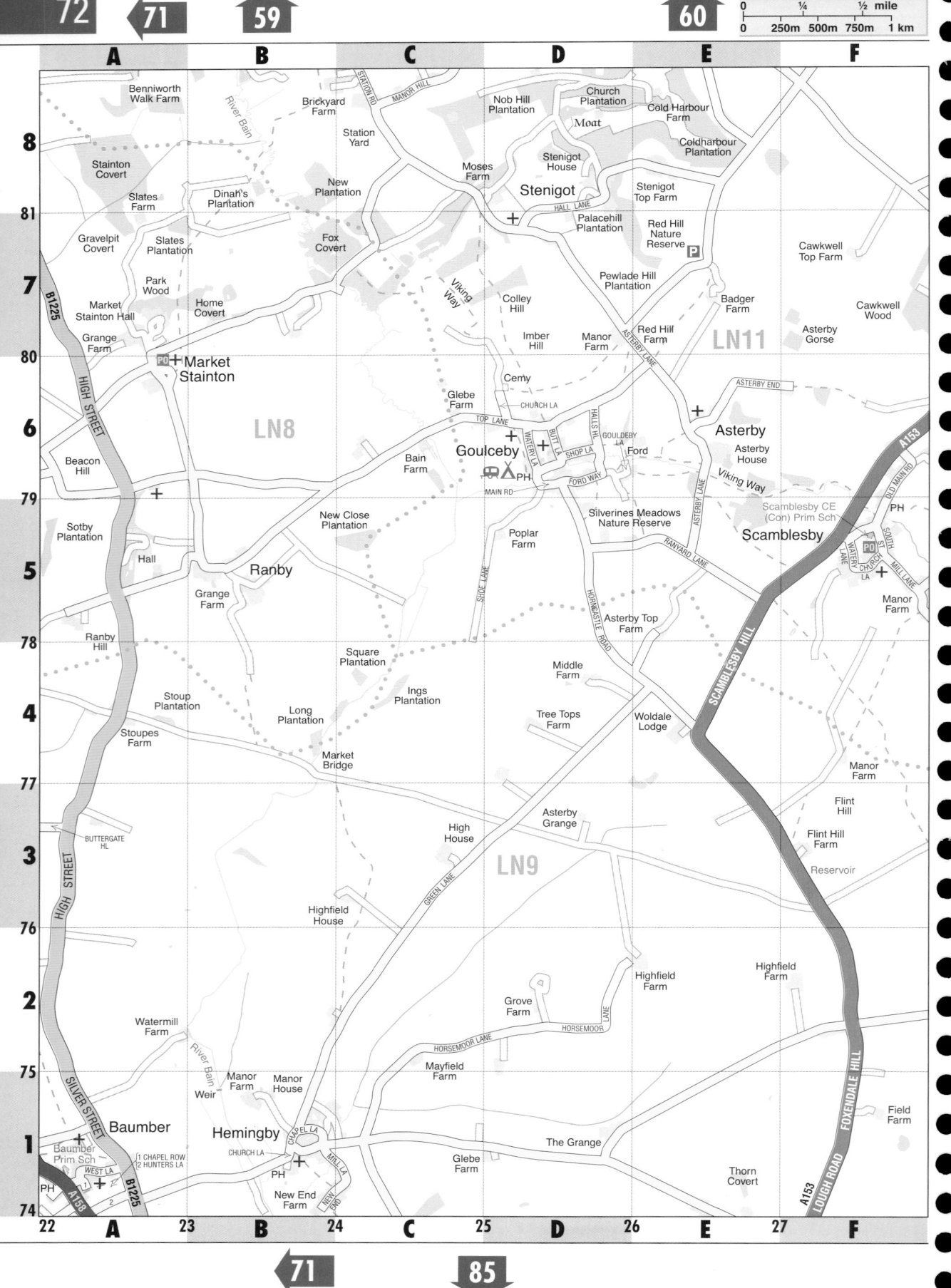

A B C D E F

8
81
7
80
6
79
5
78
4
77
3
76
2
75
1
74

Benniworth Walk Farm
River Bain
Brickyard Farm
STATION RD
MANOR HILL
Nob Hill Plantation
Church Plantation
Cold Harbour Farm
Station Yard
Moses Farm
Moat
Coldharbour Plantation
Stenigot House
Stainton Covert
Slates Farm
Dinah's Plantation
New Plantation
Stenigot
Stenigot Top Farm
Gravelpit Covert
Fox Covert
HALL LANE
Palacehill Plantation
Red Hill Nature Reserve
Cawkwell Top Farm
Slates Plantation
Park Wood
Home Covert
Pewlade Hill Plantation
Badger Farm
Cawkwell Wood
Market Stainton Hall
Colley Hill
Asterby Gorse
LN11
Grange Farm
VIKING WAY
Imber Hill
Manor Farm
ASTERBY LANE
Red Hill Farm
Asterby
Market Stainton
LN8
Glebe Farm
Cemy
CHURCH LA
TOP LANE
ASTERBY END
Asterby House
Beacon Hill
Bain Farm
Goulceby
BUTT LA
WATER LA
HALLS HL
SHOP LA
GOULDEBY LA
Ford
Viking Way
Sotby Plantation
PH
MAIN RD
FORD WAY
RANYARD LANE
Scamblesby CE (Con) Prim Sch
PO
PH
Hall
New Close Plantation
Silverines Meadows Nature Reserve
Scamblesby
Ranby
Poplar Farm
Manor Farm
Grange Farm
Ranby Hill
Square Plantation
SHOE LANE
Asterby Top Farm
HORNCASTLE ROAD
Middle Farm
SCAMBLESBY HILL
OLD MAIN RD
A153
Stoup Plantation
Long Plantation
Ings Plantation
Tree Tops Farm
Woldale Lodge
Manor Farm
Stoupes Farm
Market Bridge
Flint Hill
BUTTERGATE HL
HIGH STREET
High House
Asterby Grange
LN9
Flint Hill Farm
Reservoir
Highfield House
GREEN LANE
Highfield Farm
Highfield Farm
Watermill Farm
River Bain
Manor Farm
Manor House
Weir
Grove Farm
LANE
HORSEMOOR
Highfield Farm
FOXENDALE HILL
SILVER STREET
CHAPEL LA
HORSEMOOR LANE
Mayfield Farm
Field Farm
Baumber
Hemingby
CHURCH LA
MILL LA
Glebe Farm
The Grange
Thorn Covert
LOUGH ROAD
Baumber Prim Sch
1 CHAPEL ROW
2 HUNTERS LA
PH
NEW END
WEST LA
A153
B1225
New End Farm
A153

22 23 24 25 26 27

A B C D E F

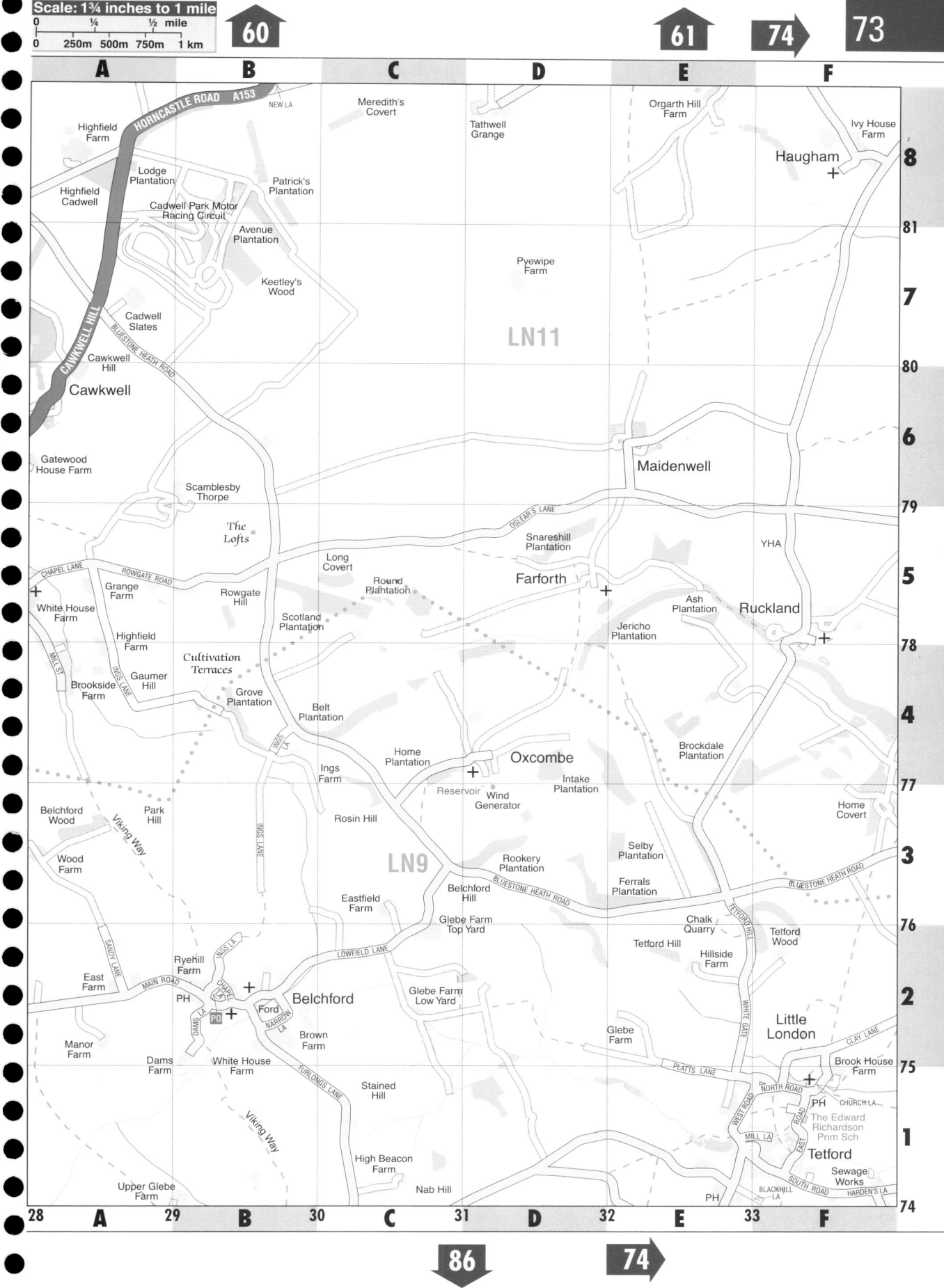

A   B   C   D   E   F

HORNCASTLE ROAD   A153

NEW LA

Highfield Farm

Meredith's Covert

Tathwell Grange

Orgarth Hill Farm

Ivy House Farm

Haugham

8

Highfield Cadwell

Lodge Plantation

Patrick's Plantation

Cadwell Park Motor Racing Circuit

Avenue Plantation

81

Cadwell Slates

Keetley's Wood

Pyewipe Farm

LN11

7

CAWKWELL HILL

Cadwell Hill

BLUESTONE HEATH ROAD

80

Cawkwell

6

Gatewood House Farm

Scamblesby Thorpe

Maidenwell

79

The Lofts

OSLEAR'S LANE

Snareshill Plantation

YHA

CHAPEL LANE

ROWGATE ROAD

Long Covert

Farforth

5

Grange Farm

Rowgate Hill

Round Plantation

Ash Plantation

Ruckland

White House Farm

Highfield Farm

Scotland Plantation

Jericho Plantation

78

Cultivation Terraces

MILL ST

Brookside Farm

Gaumer Hill

INGS LANE

Grove Plantation

Belt Plantation

Brockdale Plantation

4

Belchford Wood

Park Hill

Ings Farm

Home Plantation

Oxcombe

Intake Plantation

Home Covert

77

Viking Way

Reservoir

Wind Generator

Wood Farm

Rosin Hill

LN9

Rookery Plantation

Selby Plantation

Bluestone Heath Road

3

INGS LANE

Eastfield Farm

Belchford Hill

Ferrals Plantation

BLUESTONE HEATH ROAD

TETFORD HILL

Chalk Quarry

Tetford Wood

76

East Farm

SANDY LANE

Ryehill Farm

INGS LA

MAIN ROAD

LOWFIELD LANE

Glebe Farm Top Yard

Tetford Hill

Hillside Farm

WHITE GATE

Little London

CLAY LANE

2

PH

CHAPEL LA

DAMS LA

PO

Ford

NARROW LA

Belchford

Brown Farm

Glebe Farm Low Yard

Glebe Farm

PLATTS LANE

Brook House Farm

75

Manor Farm

Dams Farm

White House Farm

FURLONGS LANE

Stained Hill

WEST ROAD

NORTH ROAD

MILL LA

EAST ROAD

PH

CHURCH LA

The Edward Richardson Prim Sch

Viking Way

High Beacon Farm

Nab Hill

Tetford

1

Upper Glebe Farm

BLACKHILL LA

SOUTH ROAD

HARDEN'S LA

PH

Sewage Works

74

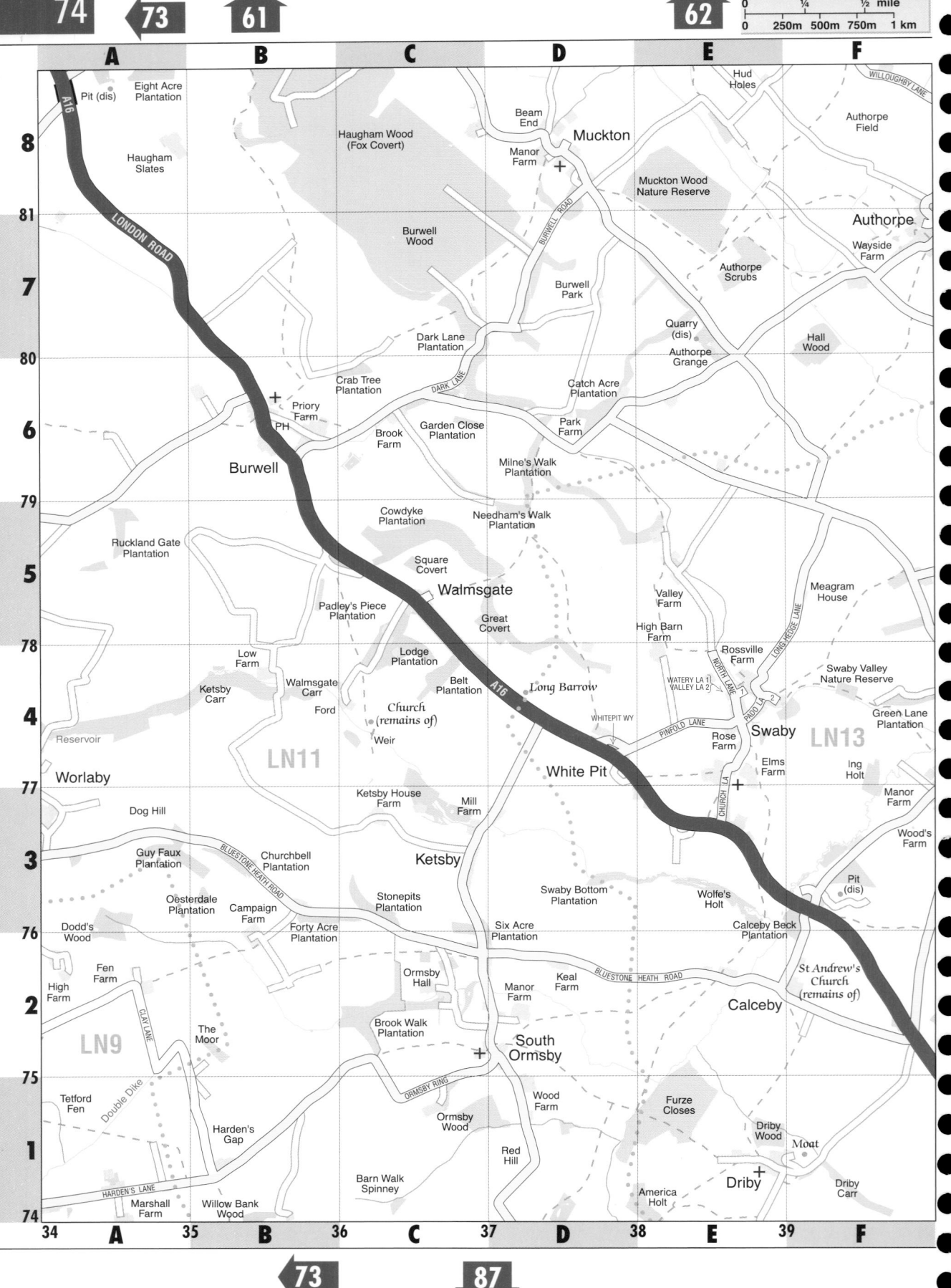
73
61
62
Scale: 1¾ inches to 1 mile
0 ¼ ½ mile
0 250m 500m 750m 1 km
A B C D E F
8 81 7 80 6 79 5 78 4 77 3 76 2 75 1 74
34 35 36 37 38 39
Pit (dis)
Eight Acre Plantation
A16
Haugham Slates
Haugham Wood (Fox Covert)
Beam End
Muckton
Manor Farm
Hud Holes
WILLOUGHBY LANE
Authorpe Field
Muckton Wood Nature Reserve
LONDON ROAD
Burwell Wood
BURWELL ROAD
Authorpe
Wayside Farm
Authorpe Scrubs
Burwell Park
Quarry (dis)
Hall Wood
Dark Lane Plantation
Authorpe Grange
Crab Tree Plantation
DARK LANE
Catch Acre Plantation
Priory Farm
PH
Brook Farm
Garden Close Plantation
Park Farm
Burwell
Milne's Walk Plantation
Cowdyke Plantation
Needham's Walk Plantation
Ruckland Gate Plantation
Square Covert
Walmsgate
Meagram House
Padley's Piece Plantation
Valley Farm
Great Covert
High Barn Farm
LONG HEDGE LANE
Low Farm
Lodge Plantation
Rossville Farm
Ketsby Carr
Walmsgate Carr
Belt Plantation
Long Barrow
WATERY LA 1
VALLEY LA 2
NORTH LANE
Swaby Valley Nature Reserve
Ford
Church (remains of)
WHITEPIT WY
PINFOLD LANE
PADD LA
Swaby
Green Lane Plantation
Reservoir
Weir
Rose Farm
LN13
LN11
White Pit
Elms Farm
Ing Holt
Worlaby
CHURCH LA
Ketsby House Farm
Mill Farm
Manor Farm
Dog Hill
Wood's Farm
Guy Faux Plantation
BLUESTONE HEATH ROAD
Churchbell Plantation
Ketsby
Pit (dis)
Oesterdale Plantation
Stonepits Plantation
Swaby Bottom Plantation
Wolfe's Holt
Campaign Farm
Dodd's Wood
Forty Acre Plantation
Six Acre Plantation
Calceby Beck Plantation
Fen Farm
Ormsby Hall
Keal Farm
St Andrew's Church (remains of)
High Farm
Manor Farm
Calceby
CLAY LANE
Brook Walk Plantation
LN9
The Moor
South Ormsby
Double Dike
ORMSBY RING
Tetford Fen
Wood Farm
Furze Closes
Harden's Gap
Ormsby Wood
Driby Wood
Moat
Red Hill
Barn Walk Spinney
Driby
Driby Carr
HARDEN'S LANE
Marshall Farm
Willow Bank Wood
America Holt
73
87

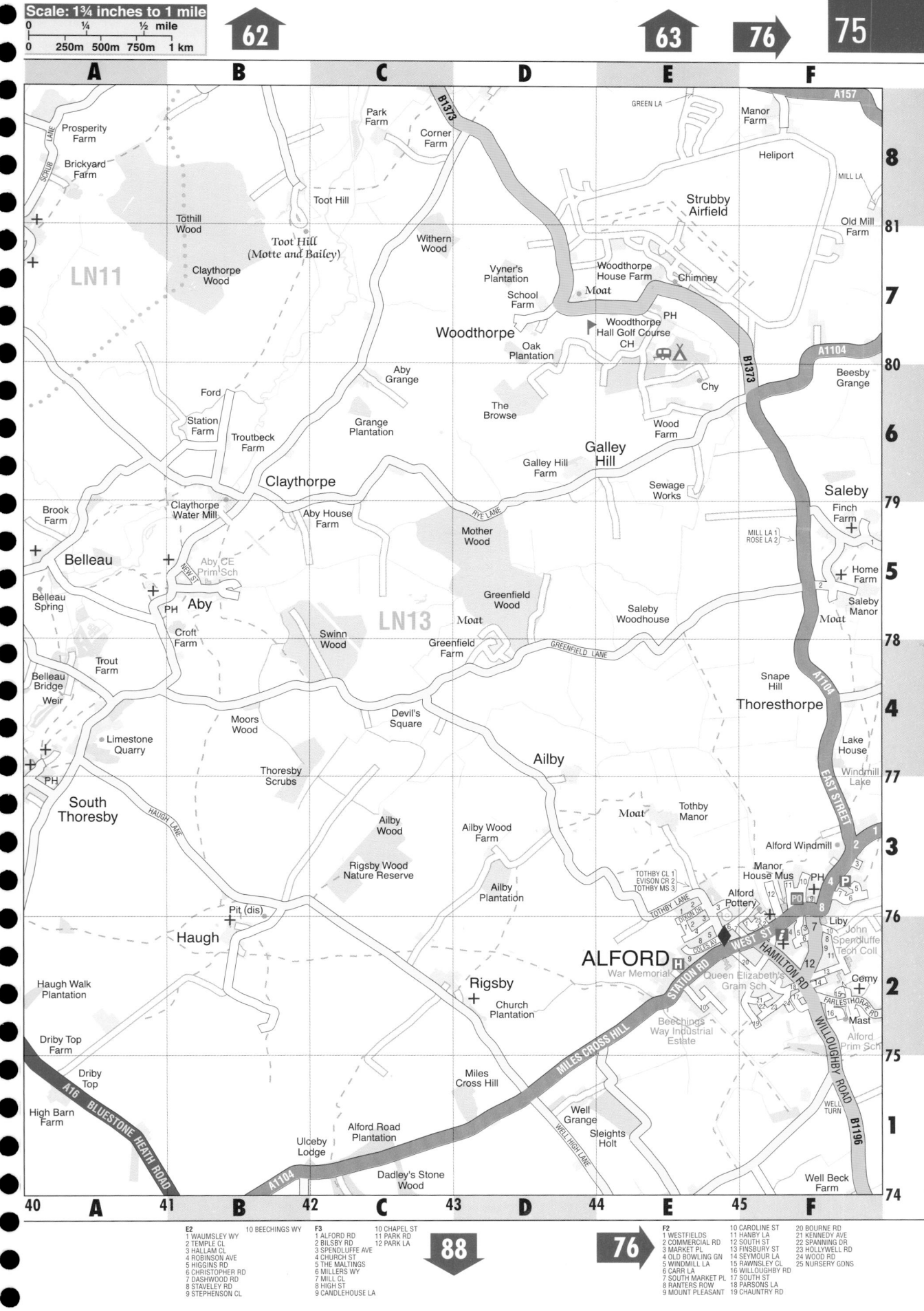

F8
1 HIGH GATE
2 HANSON DR
3 BRAEMAR RD
4 MARINE AVE
5 BUCKNALL'S MDW
6 HARDING CL
7 WILLIAM TOW CL
8 MARINE AVE W
9 WILLIAM GN CL
10 MORRISON CL
11 CAMELOT GDNS
12 BALMORAL CL
13 SANDRINGHAM DR
14 HONEYSUCKLE CL
15 BUCKINGHAM CL
16 STATION RD
17 HUTTOFT RD
18 HONEYSUCKLE CL
19 ACORN CL
20 PAINTERS WY
21 TRAMWAY DR

Scale: 1¾ inches to 1 mile

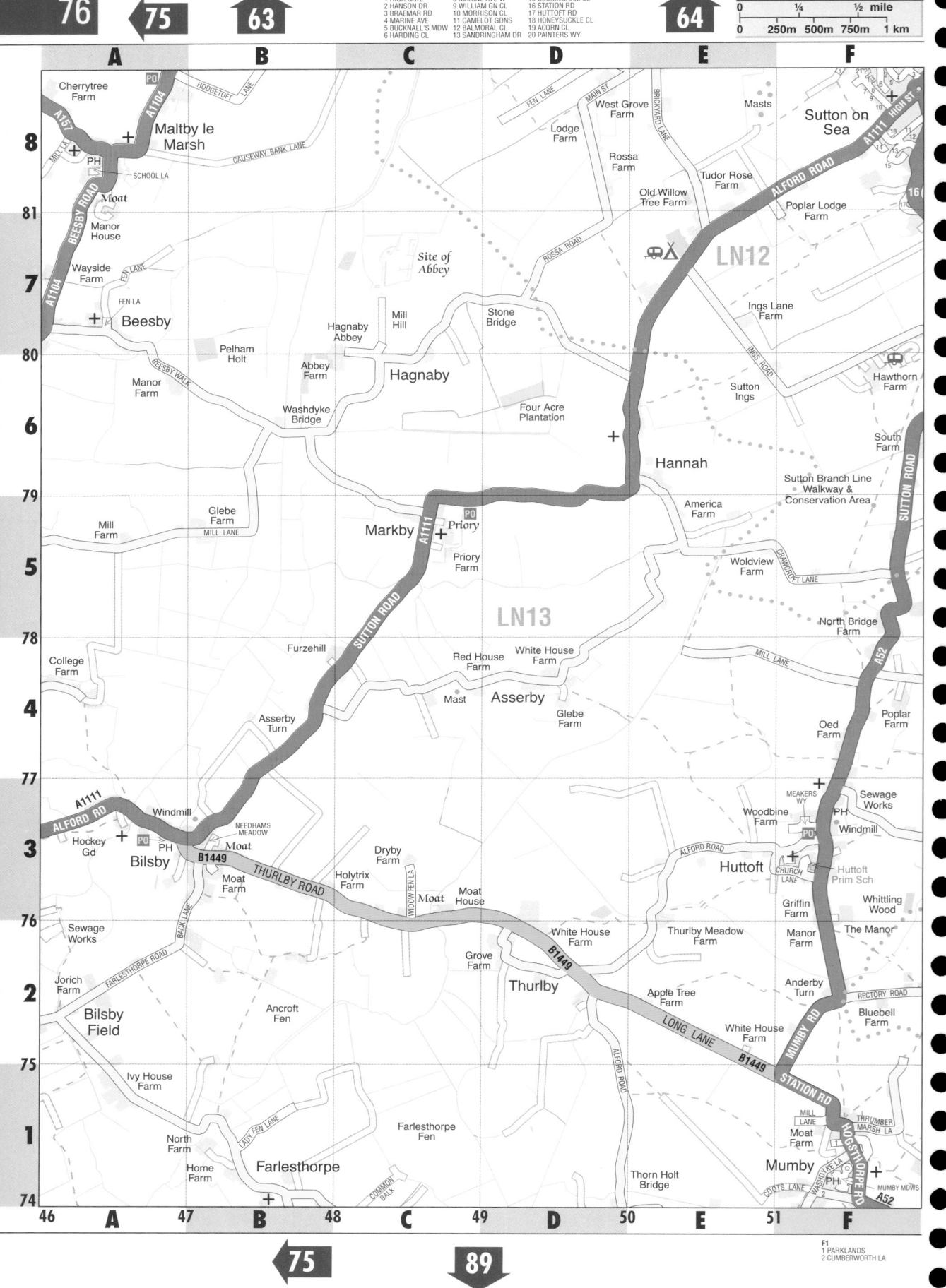

F1
1 PARKLANDS
2 CUMBERWORTH LA

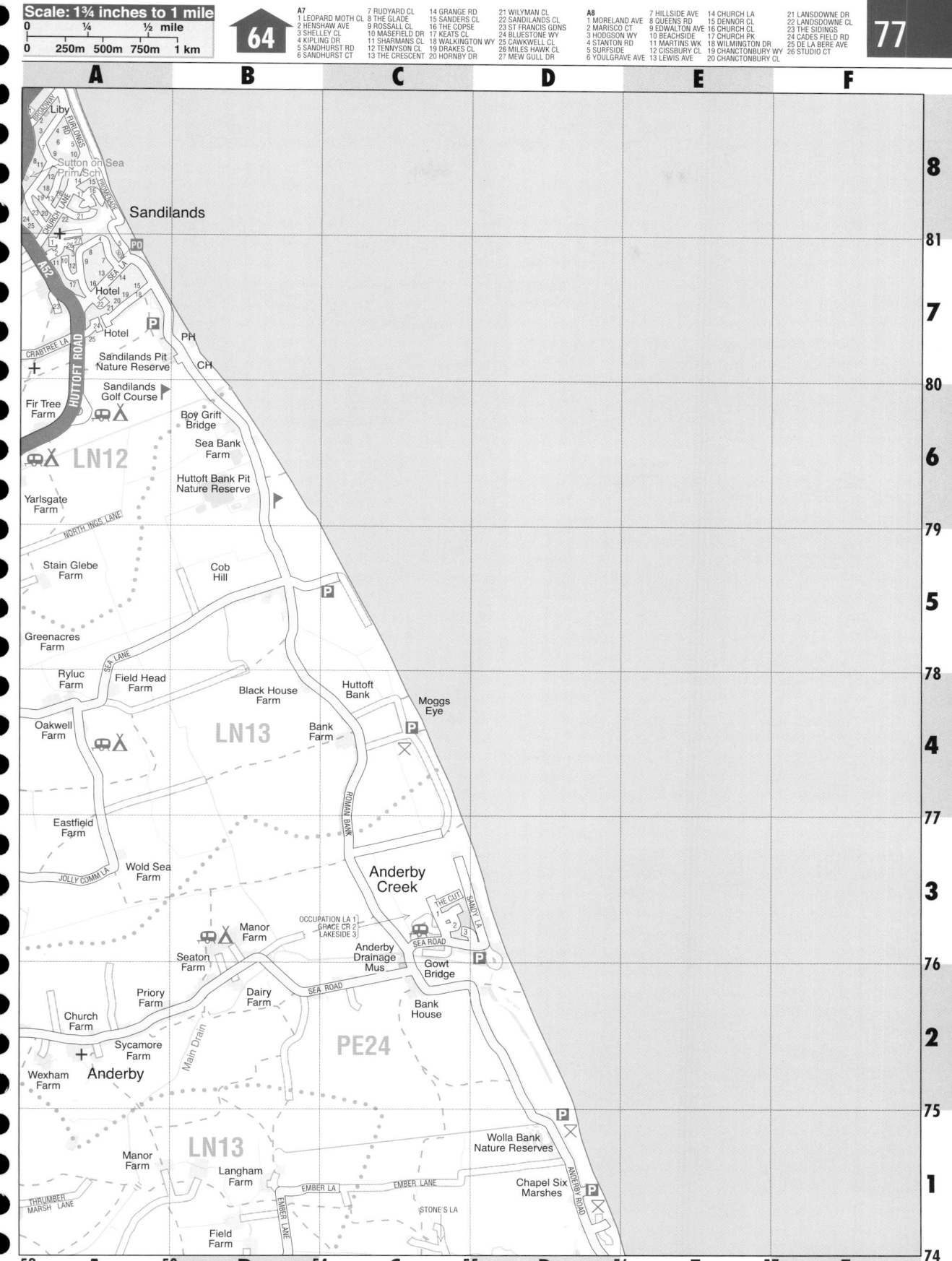

A7
1 LEOPARD MOTH CL
2 HENSHAW AVE
3 SHELLEY CL
4 KIPLING DR
5 SANDHURST RD
6 SANDHURST CT

7 RUDYARD CL
8 THE GLADE
9 ROSSALL CL
10 MASEFIELD DR
11 SHARMANS CL
12 TENNYSON CL
13 THE CRESCENT

14 GRANGE RD
15 SANDERS CL
16 THE COPSE
17 KEATS CL
18 WALKINGTON WY
19 DRAKES CL
20 HORNBY DR

21 WILYMAN CL
22 SANDILANDS CL
23 ST FRANCIS GDNS
24 BLUESTONE WY
25 CAWKWELL CL
26 MILES HAWK CL
27 MEW GULL DR

A8
1 MORELAND AVE
2 MARISCO CT
3 HODGSON WY
4 STANTON RD
5 SURFSIDE
6 YOULGRAVE AVE

7 HILLSIDE AVE
8 QUEENS RD
9 EDWALTON AVE
10 BEACHSIDE
11 MARTINS WK
12 CISSBURY CL
13 LEWIS AVE

14 CHURCH LA
15 DENNOR CL
16 CHURCH CL
17 CHURCH PK
18 WILMINGTON DR
19 CHANCTONBURY WY
20 CHANCTONBURY CL

21 LANSDOWNE DR
22 LANDSDOWNE CL
23 THE SIDINGS
24 CADES FIELD RD
25 DE LA BERE AVE
26 STUDIO CT

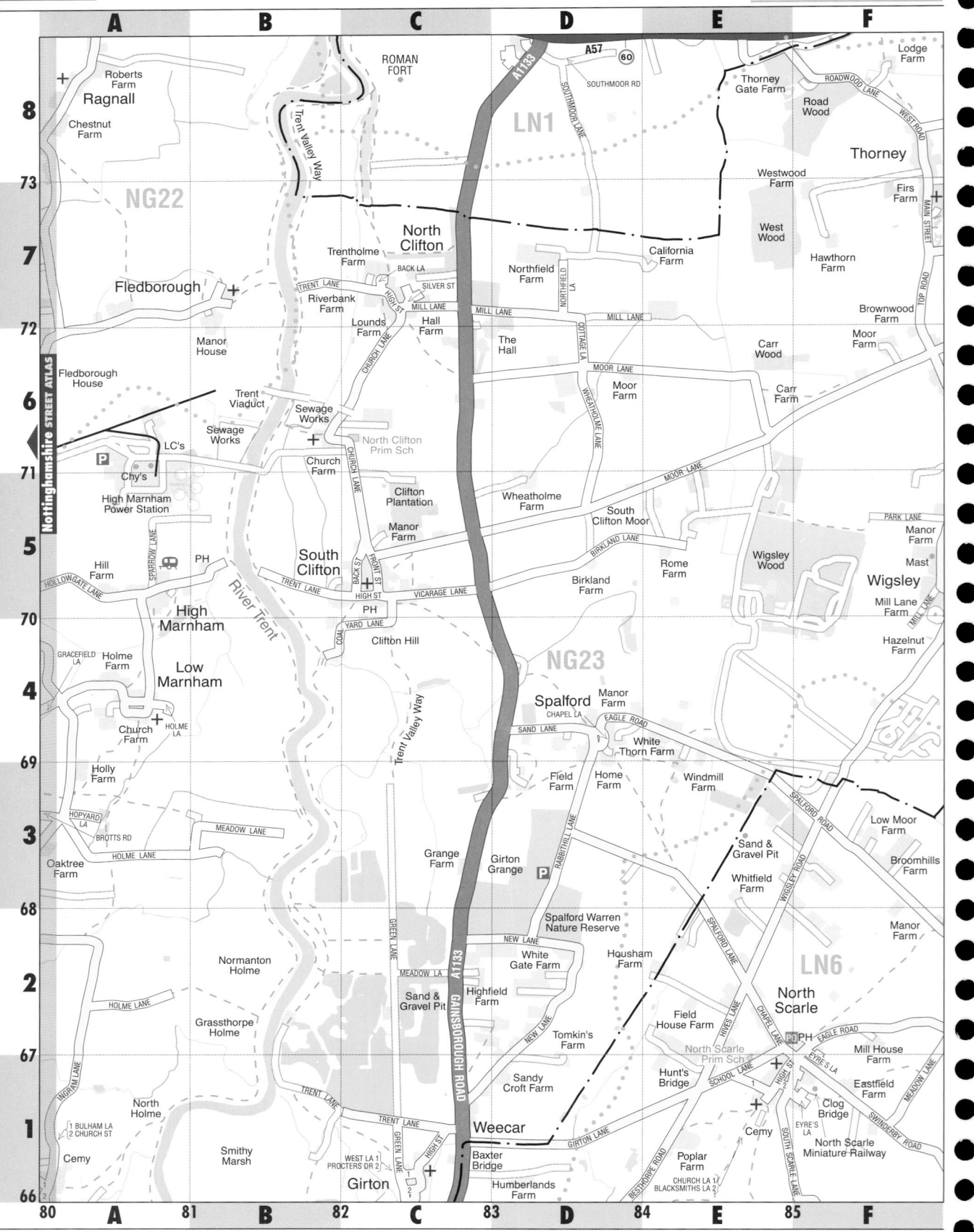

Scale: 1¾ inches to 1 mile

0   ¼   ½   mile
0   250m 500m 750m 1 km

Nottinghamshire STREET ATLAS

A **B** **C** **D** **E** **F**

A57 A1133 60

Roberts Farm
Ragnall
Chestnut Farm
ROMAN FORT
SOUTHMOOR LANE
SOUTHMOOR RD
LN1
Thorney Gate Farm
Road Wood
ROADWOOD LANE
Lodge Farm
WEST ROAD

Trent Valley Way
NG22
Westwood Farm
Thorney
Firs Farm
MAIN STREET
TOP ROAD

Fledborough
Trentholme Farm
North Clifton
BACK LA
SILVER ST
Northfield Farm
NORTHFIELD LA
California Farm
West Wood
Hawthorn Farm
Brownwood Farm

Riverbank Farm
TRENT LANE
HIGH ST
MILL LANE
Hall Farm
MILL LANE
MILL LANE
Moor Farm

Lounds Farm
CHURCH LANE
The Hall
COTTAGE LA
MOOR LANE
Carr Wood
Moor Farm

Manor House
Fledborough House
Trent Viaduct
Sewage Works
Sewage Works
North Clifton Prim Sch
WHEATHOLME LANE
Moor Farm
Carr Farm

P LC's
Chy's
Church Farm
CHURCH LANE
Clifton Plantation
Wheatholme Farm
MOOR LANE
South Clifton Moor
PARK LANE
Manor Farm
Mast

High Marnham Power Station
SPARROW LANE
PH
South Clifton
BACK ST
FRONT ST
Manor Farm
BIRKLAND LANE
Rome Farm
Wigsley Wood
Wigsley
Mill Lane Farm

HOLLOWGATE LANE
Hill Farm
TRENT LANE
HIGH ST
PH
VICARAGE LANE
Birkland Farm
Hazelnut Farm

High Marnham
COAL YARD LANE
Clifton Hill
NG23

GRACEFIELD LA
Holme Farm
Low Marnham
River Trent
Trent Valley Way
Spalford
Manor Farm
CHAPEL LA
EAGLE ROAD
White Thorn Farm

Church Farm
HOLME LA
SAND LANE
Windmill Farm
Low Moor Farm
SPALFORD ROAD

Holly Farm
Field Farm
Home Farm
Broomhills Farm

HOPYARD LA
BROTTS RD
MEADOW LANE
HOLME LANE
Grange Farm
Girton Grange
P
RABBITHILL LANE
Sand & Gravel Pit
Whitfield Farm
WIGSLEY ROAD
Manor Farm

Oaktree Farm
Spalford Warren Nature Reserve
LN6

Normanton Holme
GREEN LANE
MEADOW LA
NEW LANE
White Gate Farm
Housham Farm
SPALFORD LANE
HIVES ROAD
North Scarle
EAGLE ROAD

HOLME LANE
Sand & Gravel Pit
Highfield Farm
Field House Farm
CHAPEL LANE
Mill House Farm

Grassthorpe Holme
A1133 GAINSBOROUGH ROAD
NEW LANE
Tomkin's Farm
North Scarle Prim Sch
P PH
EYRE'S LA
SCHOOL LANE
HIGH ST
Eastfield Farm
MEADOW LANE
SWINDERBY ROAD

INGRAM LANE
North Holme
TRENT LANE
GREEN LANE
HIGH ST
Weecar
GIRTON LANE
Sandy Croft Farm
Hunt's Bridge
Cemy
Clog Bridge
EYRE'S LA
SOUTH SCARLE LANE
North Scarle Miniature Railway

1 BULHAM LA
2 CHURCH ST
Cemy
Smithy Marsh
Girton
WEST LA 1
PROCTERS DR 2
Baxter Bridge
Humberlands Farm
BESTHORPE ROAD
Poplar Farm
CHURCH LA 1
BLACKSMITHS LA 2

A **B** **C** **D** **E** **F**

80 81 82 83 84 85

8 73 7 72 6 71 5 70 4 69 3 68 2 67 1 66

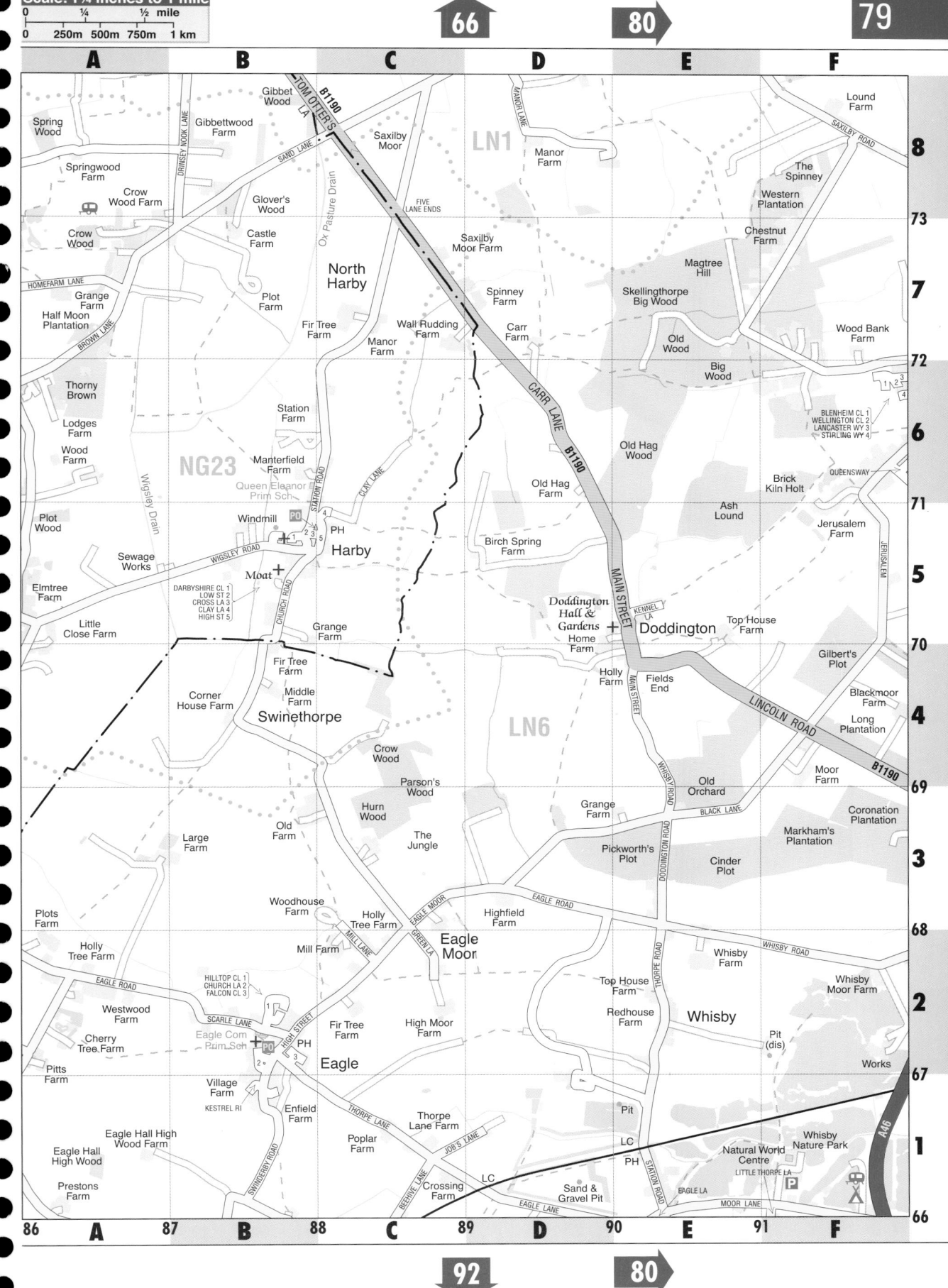
Scale: 1¾ inches to 1 mile
0 ¼ ½ mile
0 250m 500m 750m 1 km
66
80
A B C D E F
Spring Wood
Gibbettwood Farm
Gibbet Wood
TOM OTTER'S LA
B1190
Saxilby Moor
LN1
MANOR LANE
Manor Farm
Lound Farm
SAXILBY ROAD
8
DRINSEY NOOK LANE
SAND LANE
Springwood Farm
Crow Wood Farm
Glover's Wood
Ox Pasture Drain
FIVE LANE ENDS
The Spinney
Western Plantation
73
Crow Wood
Castle Farm
Saxilby Moor Farm
Chestnut Farm
North Harby
Magtree Hill
HOMEFARM LANE
Grange Farm
Half Moon Plantation
Plot Farm
Spinney Farm
Skellingthorpe Big Wood
7
BROWN LANE
Fir Tree Farm
Wall Rudding Farm
Manor Farm
Carr Farm
Old Wood
Wood Bank Farm
Big Wood
72
Thorny Brown
Station Farm
CARR LANE
BLENHEIM CL 1
WELLINGTON CL 2
LANCASTER WY 3
STIRLING WY 4
Lodges Farm
6
Wood Farm
NG23
Manterfield Farm
B1190
Old Hag Wood
QUEENSWAY
Queen Eleanor Prim Sch
CLAY LANE
STATION ROAD
Old Hag Farm
Brick Kiln Holt
Wigsley Drain
71
Plot Wood
Windmill
PO
PH
Ash Lound
Jerusalem Farm
Harby
Birch Spring Farm
JERUSALEM
Sewage Works
WIGSLEY ROAD
Moat
5
Elmtree Farm
DARBYSHIRE CL 1
LOW ST 2
CROSS LA 3
CLAY LA 4
HIGH ST 5
CHURCH ROAD
Doddington Hall & Gardens
MAIN STREET
KENNEL LA
Doddington
Top House Farm
Little Close Farm
Grange Farm
Home Farm
70
Fir Tree Farm
Holly Farm
Fields End
Gilbert's Plot
Corner House Farm
Middle Farm
MAIN STREET
Blackmoor Farm
Swinethorpe
LN6
LINCOLN ROAD
Long Plantation
4
Crow Wood
B1190
Moor Farm
Parson's Wood
WHISBY ROAD
Old Orchard
69
Hurn Wood
Grange Farm
BLACK LANE
Coronation Plantation
Old Farm
Large Farm
The Jungle
Pickworth's Plot
Markham's Plantation
DODDINGTON ROAD
Cinder Plot
3
Woodhouse Farm
EAGLE MOOR
Highfield Farm
EAGLE ROAD
Plots Farm
Holly Tree Farm
68
Holly Tree Farm
MILL LANE
GREEN LA
Eagle Moor
Mill Farm
THORPE ROAD
Whisby Farm
WHISBY ROAD
EAGLE ROAD
Top House Farm
Whisby Moor Farm
HILLTOP CL 1
CHURCH LA 2
FALCON CL 3
2
Westwood Farm
Redhouse Farm
Whisby
SCARLE LANE
HIGH STREET
Fir Tree Farm
High Moor Farm
Pit (dis)
Cherry Tree Farm
Eagle Com Prim Sch
PO
PH
Eagle
Works
Pitts Farm
67
Village Farm
KESTREL RI
Pit
Enfield Farm
THORPE LANE
Thorpe Lane Farm
A46
Eagle Hall High Wood Farm
LC
Whisby Nature Park
1
Eagle Hall High Wood
Poplar Farm
JOB'S LANE
PH
Natural World Centre
SWINDERBY ROAD
LITTLE THORPE LA
Prestons Farm
BEEHIVE LANE
Crossing Farm
LC
Sand & Gravel Pit
STATION ROAD
EAGLE LA
P
EAGLE LANE
MOOR LANE
66
86 A 87 B 88 C 89 D 90 E 91 F
92
80

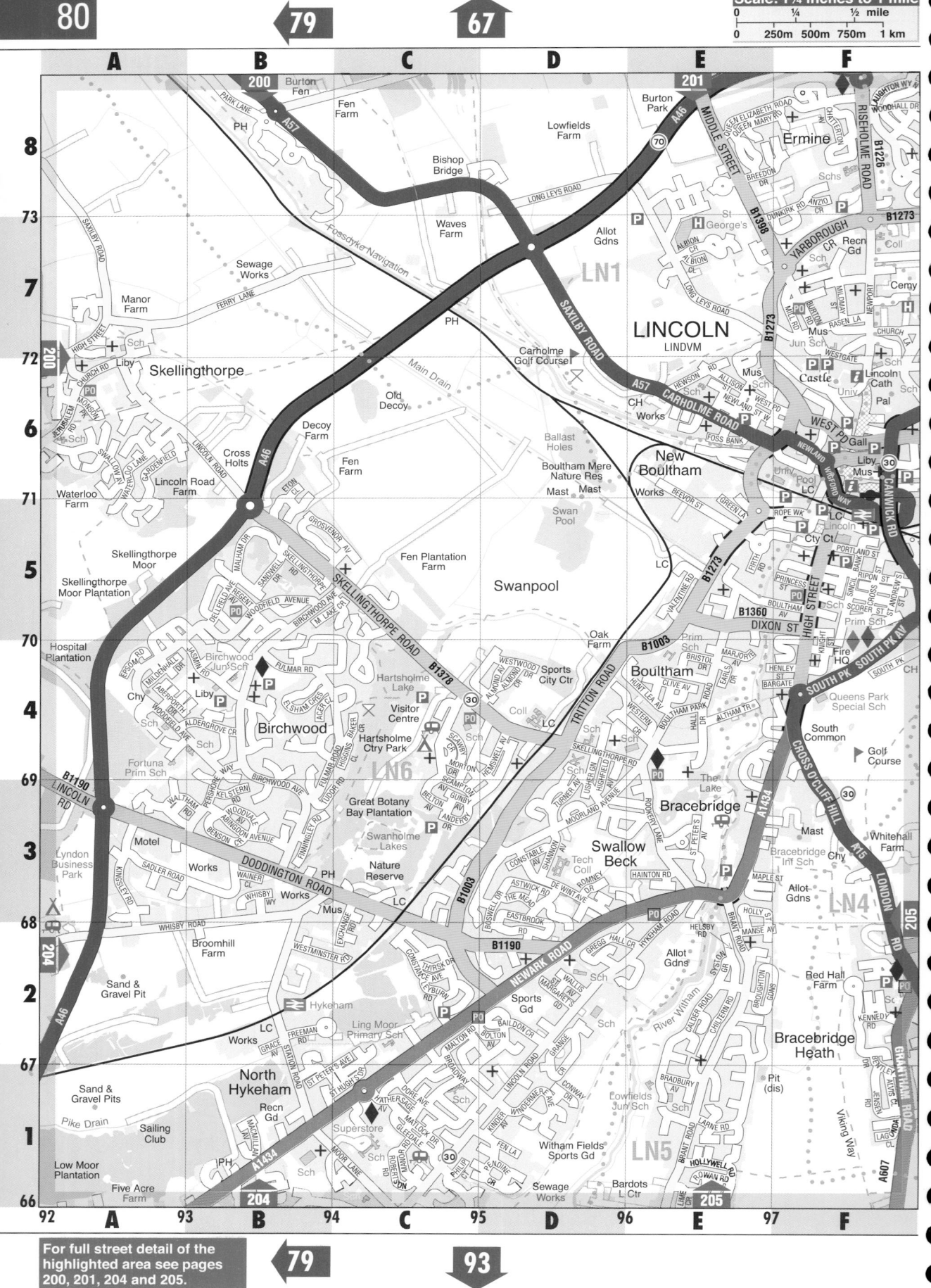

Scale: 1¾ inches to 1 mile
0   ¼   ½   mile
0   250m 500m 750m 1 km

A   B   C   D   E   F

8

73

7

72

6

71

5

70

4

69

3

68

2

67

1

66

92   A   93   B   94   C   95   D   96   E   97   F

200 Burton Fen
PARK LANE
A57
PH
Fen Farm
Fen Fen
Bishop Bridge
Lowfields Farm
Burton Park
201
A46
70
MIDDLE STREET
KEN ELIZABETH ROAD
QUEEN MARY RD
CHATTERTON
RISEHOLME ROAD
WOODHALL DR
LOUGHTON WY
B1226
Ermine
BREEDON DR
B1398
Long Leys Road
Waves Farm
Allot Gdns
ALBION CR
ALBION
St George's
H
Schs
DUNKIRK RD
ANZIO
YARBOROUGH
Schs
Recn Gd
Coll
B1273
LN1
Fossdyke Navigation
Saxby Road
HIGH STREET
Liby
Sch
PO
Manor Farm
FERRY LANE
PH
Carholme Golf Course
SAXILBY ROAD
LINCOLN
LINDVM
A57
HEWSON RD
ALLISON
NEWLAND ST W
Mus
WEST RD
Castle
Lincoln Cath Pal
B1273
BURTON ST
MILDMAY
RASEN LA
TROWMAN
Mus
Jun Sch
CHURCH
WESTGATE
Univ
i
Skellingthorpe
Main Drain
Old Decoy
CH
Works
FOSS BANK
NEW BOULTHAM
Works
New Boultham
Pool LC
Univ
i
WIGFORD WAY
NEWLAND
PO
Gall
Liby
Mus
30
CANWICK RD
Cross Holts
A46
Decoy Farm
Lincoln Road Farm
Fen Farm
Ballast Holes
Boultham Mere Nature Res
Mast
Mast
Works
BEEVOR ST
GREEN LA
ROPE WK
Lincoln
Cty Ct
PORTLAND ST
WEST PO
LC
B1273
FIRTH
Waterloo Farm
WATERLOO
GARDENFIELD
SWALLOW LANE
LINCOLN ROAD
ETON
GROSVENOR AV
MALHAM DR
SANDWELL
SKELLINGTHORPE RD
Swan Pool
Fen Plantation Farm
Swanpool
LC
PRINCESS ST
SCORER ST
ST ANDREW'S
RIPON ST
Sch
Prim Sch
High Street
B1360
DIXON ST
BOULTHAM AV
Skellingthorpe Moor
Skellingthorpe Moor Plantation
REGENT
DELLFIELD
WOODFIELD AVENUE
BIRCHWOOD AV
M LANE CR
PO
Oak Farm
B1003
WESTWOOD DR
Sports City Ctr
Boultham
PRIM Sch
BRISTOL DR
MARJORIE
HENLEY ST
BARGATE
KNIGHT ST
Fire HQ
SOUTH PK
EARL
Hospital Plantation
EPSOM RD
MILDENHALL
JASMIN
Birchwood Jun Sch
FULMAR RD
Hartsholme Lake
B1378
ALMOND
30
Coll
LC
TRITTON ROAD
SKELLINGTHORPE RD
WESTERN
CLIVE AV
HUNT LEA AV
Boultham Park
ALTHAM TR
Queens Park Special Sch
South Common
Golf Course
Chy
Sch
ABERFORTH DR
Liby
E SHAW AV
ACER CL
BAKER
Visitor Centre
SCARP
MORTON DR
SCAMPTON
HESWELL AV
Sch
USHER LN
HIGHFIELD
MOORLAND AVENUE
The Lake
Bracebridge
CROSS O'CLIFF HILL
A1434
30
Mast
Whitehall Farm
LN4
Birchwood
WOODVALE AV
Fortuna Prim Sch
PERSHORE WAY
KELSTERN
BIRCHWOOD AVE
FULMAR WAY
TUDOR RD
LN6
Great Botany Bay Plantation
BELTON AV
GUNBY
LANDERY
ANDERBY
TURNER AV
ROOKERY LANE
Bracebridge Inf Sch
Mast
A15
LONDON RD
205
B1190
LINCOLN RD
WALTHAM RD
ABINGDON AVENUE
BENSON AV
TINWINCLEY RD
Swanholme Lakes
Nature Reserve
B1003
CONSTABLE AV
SHANNON
ASTWICK AV
DE WINT AV
Tech Coll
ROMNEY
Swallow Beck
ST PETER'S AV
HAINTON RD
MAPLE ST
Allot Gdns
LC
A607
Lyndon Business Park
KINGSLEY RD
SADLER ROAD
Motel
Works
DODDINGTON ROAD
WAINER CL
WHISBY WY
PH
Works
Mus
LC
EXCHANGE RD
BOSWELL DR
EASTBROOK
THE MEAD
GREGG
HALL CR
HYKEHAM ROAD
PO
Allot Gdns
HELSBY RD
BRANT RD
MANSE AV
BROUGHTON
SYSTON
Red Hall Farm
PO
205
KENNEDY RD
Bracebridge Heath
WHISBY ROAD
Broomhill Farm
WESTMINSTER RD
CONSTANCE AV
CLYBURN RD
THIRSK DR
MALTON RD
Sports Gd
BALDON CR
MARGARET ST
WALL ST
Sch
GRANGE
CALDER ROAD
CHILTERN RD
BRANT RD
HOLLY ST
Pit (dis)
GRANTHAM ROAD
Sand & Gravel Pit
204
Hykeham
LC
Works
FREEMAN RD
GRACE
STATION RD
Ling Moor Primary Sch
MALTON RD
BOLTON AV
P
BROADWAY
LINCOLN ROAD
CONWAY
WINDERMERE AVE
Lowfields Jun Sch
LARNE RD
LN5
River Witham
BRADBURY AV
Viking Way
A15
North Hykeham
Sand & Gravel Pits
Pike Drain
Sailing Club
Sailing Club
A1434
204
PH
MACMILLAN WY
Recn Gd
ST HUGH'S DR
Superstore
30
HATHERSAGE
DOVE AVE
MATLOCK AVE
GLEEDALE
KINDER
ROBERT JDN
FEN LA
CLIFTON
Sch
Witham Fields Sports Gd
Bardots L Ctr
205
HOLLYWELL RD
ROWAN RD
LIME
MOOR LANE
Sewage Works
Low Moor Plantation
Five Acre Farm

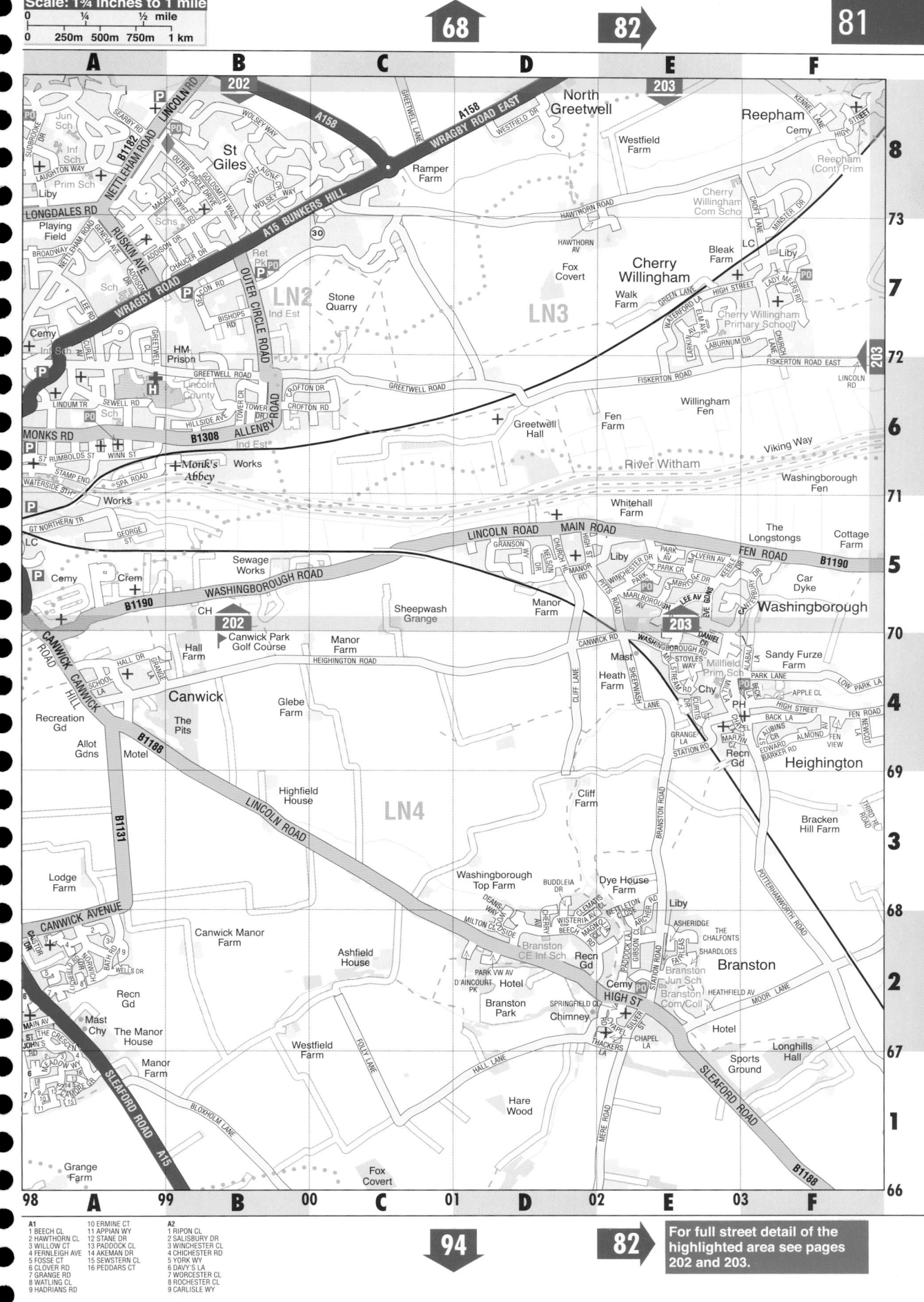

Scale: 1¾ inches to 1 mile

0   ¼   ½   mile
0 250m 500m 750m 1 km

For full street detail of the highlighted area see pages 202 and 203.

A1
1 BEECH CL
2 HAWTHORN CL
3 WILLOW CT
4 FERNLEIGH AVE
5 FOSSE CT
6 CLOVER RD
7 GRANGE CL
8 WATLING CL
9 HADRIANS RD
10 ERMINE CT
11 APPIAN WY
12 STANE DR
13 PADDOCK CL
14 AKEMAN DR
15 SEWSTERN CL
16 PEDDARS CT

A2
1 RIPON CL
2 SALISBURY DR
3 WINCHESTER CL
4 CHICHESTER RD
5 YORK WY
6 DAVY'S LA
7 WORCESTER CL
8 ROCHESTER CL
9 CARLISLE WY

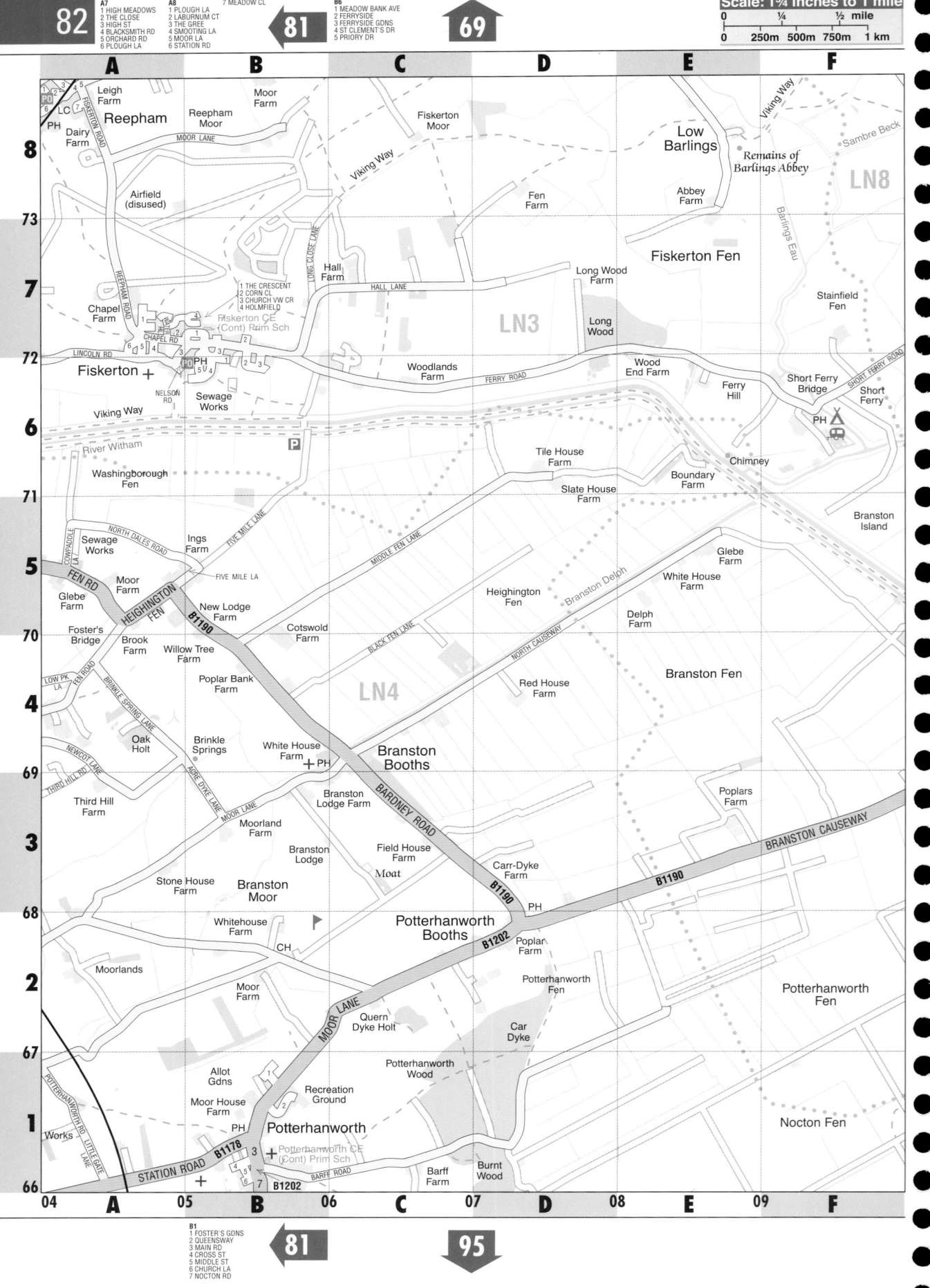

A7
1 HIGH MEADOWS
2 THE CLOSE
3 HIGH ST
4 BLACKSMITH RD
5 ORCHARD RD
6 PLOUGH LA

A8
1 PLOUGH LA
2 LABURNUM CT
3 THE GREE
4 SMOOTING LA
5 MOOR LA
6 STATION RD

7 MEADOW CL

B6
1 MEADOW BANK AVE
2 FERRYSIDE
3 FERRYSIDE GDNS
4 ST CLEMENT'S DR
5 PRIORY DR

81
69

Scale: 1¾ inches to 1 mile

0   ¼   ½   mile
0   250m 500m 750m 1 km

A   B   C   D   E   F

8
Leigh Farm
Reepham
Moor Farm
Reepham Moor
Fiskerton Moor
Low Barlings
Remains of Barlings Abbey
Sambre Beck
LN8

73
Airfield (disused)
MOOR LANE
Viking Way
Fen Farm
Abbey Farm
Fiskerton Fen
Stainfield Fen

7
Chapel Farm
Hall Farm
HALL LANE
1 THE CRESCENT
2 CORN CL
3 CHURCH VW CR
4 HOLMFIELD
Fiskerton CE (Cont) Prim Sch
LN3
Long Wood Farm
Long Wood
Wood End Farm
Ferry Hill
Short Ferry Bridge
Short Ferry

72
LINCOLN RD
CHAPEL RD
PO PH
Fiskerton
NELSON RD
Woodlands Farm
FERRY ROAD
PH

6
Viking Way
Sewage Works
River Witham
P
Tile House Farm
Chimney
PH

71
Washingborough Fen
Slate House Farm
Boundary Farm
Branston Island

5
COMPADDLE LA
NORTH DALES ROAD
Sewage Works
Ings Farm
FIVE MILE LANE
MIDDLE FEN LANE
Branston Delph
Glebe Farm
White House Farm
FEN RD
Moor Farm
FIVE MILE LA

70
Glebe Farm
Foster's Bridge
Brook Farm
HEIGHINGTON FEN
B1190
New Lodge Farm
Cotswold Farm
BLACK FEN LANE
Heighington Fen
NORTH CAUSEWAY
Delph Farm

4
LOW PK LA
FEN ROAD
Willow Tree Farm
Poplar Bank Farm
LN4
Red House Farm
Branston Fen

69
NEWCOT LANE
BRINKLE SPRING LANE
Oak Holt
Brinkle Springs
ACRE DYKE LANE
White House Farm
PH
Branston Booths
Poplars Farm

3
THIRD HILL RD
Third Hill Farm
MOOR LANE
Moorland Farm
Branston Lodge Farm
BARDNEY ROAD
Field House Farm
Moat
Carr-Dyke Farm
B1190
BRANSTON CAUSEWAY

68
Stone House Farm
Branston Lodge
Branston Moor
Potterhanworth Booths
B1190
PH
B1202
Poplar Farm

2
Moorlands
Whitehouse Farm
CH
Moor Farm
MOOR LANE
Quern Dyke Holt
Potterhanworth Fen
Car Dyke
Potterhanworth Fen

67
POTTERHANWORTH RD
LITTLE GATE LANE
Allot Gdns
Recreation Ground
Potterhanworth Wood

1
Works
Moor House Farm
PH
Potterhanworth
B1178
Potterhanworth CE (Cont) Prim Sch
BARFF ROAD
Barff Farm
Burnt Wood
Nocton Fen

66
STATION ROAD
B1202

04   A   05   B   06   C   07   D   08   E   09   F

B1
1 FOSTER'S GDNS
2 QUEENSWAY
3 MAIN RD
4 CROSS ST
5 MIDDLE ST
6 CHURCH LA
7 NOCTON RD

81
95

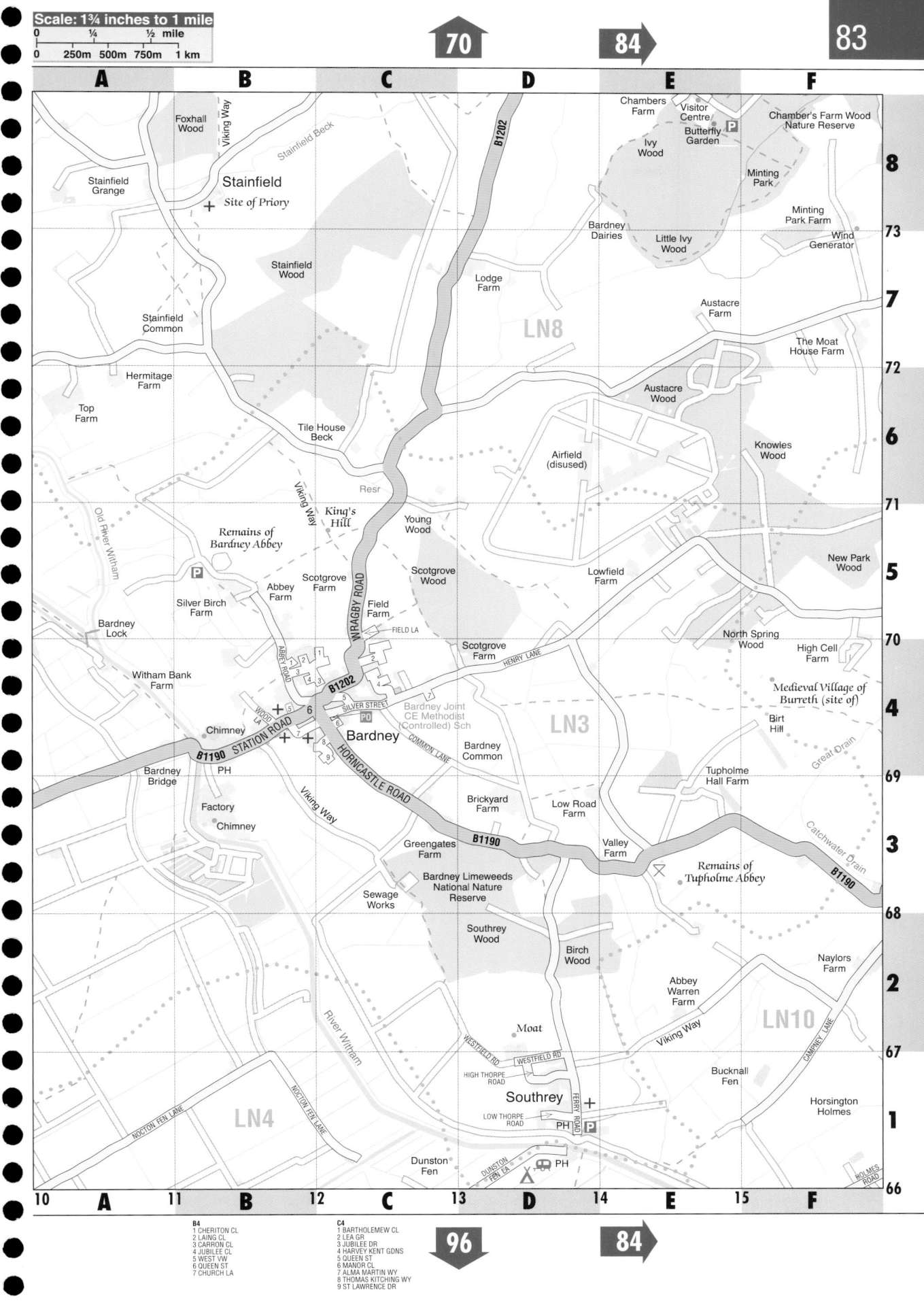

Scale: 1¾ inches to 1 mile

0   ¼   ½   mile

0   250m   500m   750m   1 km

| A | B | C | D | E | F |

Foxhall Wood

Viking Way

Stainfield Beck

Stainfield Grange

Stainfield
+ Site of Priory

Stainfield Wood

8

Bardney Dairies

Chambers Farm

Visitor Centre
Butterfly Garden
P

Ivy Wood

Chamber's Farm Wood Nature Reserve

Minting Park

Little Ivy Wood

Minting Park Farm

Wind Generator

73

Lodge Farm

LN8

Austacre Farm

7

Stainfield Common

Hermitage Farm

The Moat House Farm

72

Top Farm

Tile House Beck

Austacre Wood

6

Resr

Airfield (disused)

Knowles Wood

Old River Witham

Viking Way

King's Hill

Young Wood

71

Remains of Bardney Abbey

P

Scotgrove Farm

Scotgrove Wood

Lowfield Farm

New Park Wood

5

Silver Birch Farm

Abbey Farm

WRAGBY ROAD

Field Farm

FIELD LA

North Spring Wood

High Cell Farm

70

Bardney Lock

Witham Bank Farm

1
2
3
5
6

B1202

4

SILVER STREET

PO

Scotgrove Farm

HENRY LANE

Medieval Village of Burreth (site of)

Birt Hill

4

Chimney

WOOD LA

STATION ROAD

+

+

7

Bardney Joint
CE Methodist
(Controlled) Sch

LN3

Bardney

COMMON LANE

Bardney Common

69

B1190

PH

8
9

HORNCASTLE ROAD

Bardney Bridge

Tupholme Hall Farm

Great Drain

Factory
Chimney

Viking Way

Brickyard Farm

Low Road Farm

Valley Farm

Remains of Tupholme Abbey

B1190

Catchwater Drain

3

Greengates Farm

B1190

68

Sewage Works

Bardney Limeweeds
National Nature
Reserve

Southrey Wood

Birch Wood

Naylors Farm

2

River Witham

Moat

Abbey Warren Farm

Viking Way

LN10

67

LN4

WESTFIELD RD

WESTFIELD RD

HIGH THORPE ROAD

Bucknall Fen

NOCTON FEN LANE

NOCTON FEN LANE

Southrey

FERRY ROAD

+

P

Horsington Holmes

1

LOW THORPE ROAD

PH

CAMPREY LANE

Dunston Fen

DUNSTON FEN LA

PH

HOLMES ROAD

66

| 10 | A | 11 | B | 12 | C | 13 | D | 14 | E | 15 | F |

B4
1 CHERITON CL
2 LAING CL
3 CARRON CL
4 JUBILEE CL
5 WEST VW
6 QUEEN ST
7 CHURCH LA

C4
1 BARTHOLEMEW CL
2 LEA GR
3 JUBILEE DR
4 HARVEY KENT GDNS
5 QUEEN ST
6 MANOR CL
7 ALMA MARTIN WY
8 THOMAS KITCHING WY
9 ST LAWRENCE DR

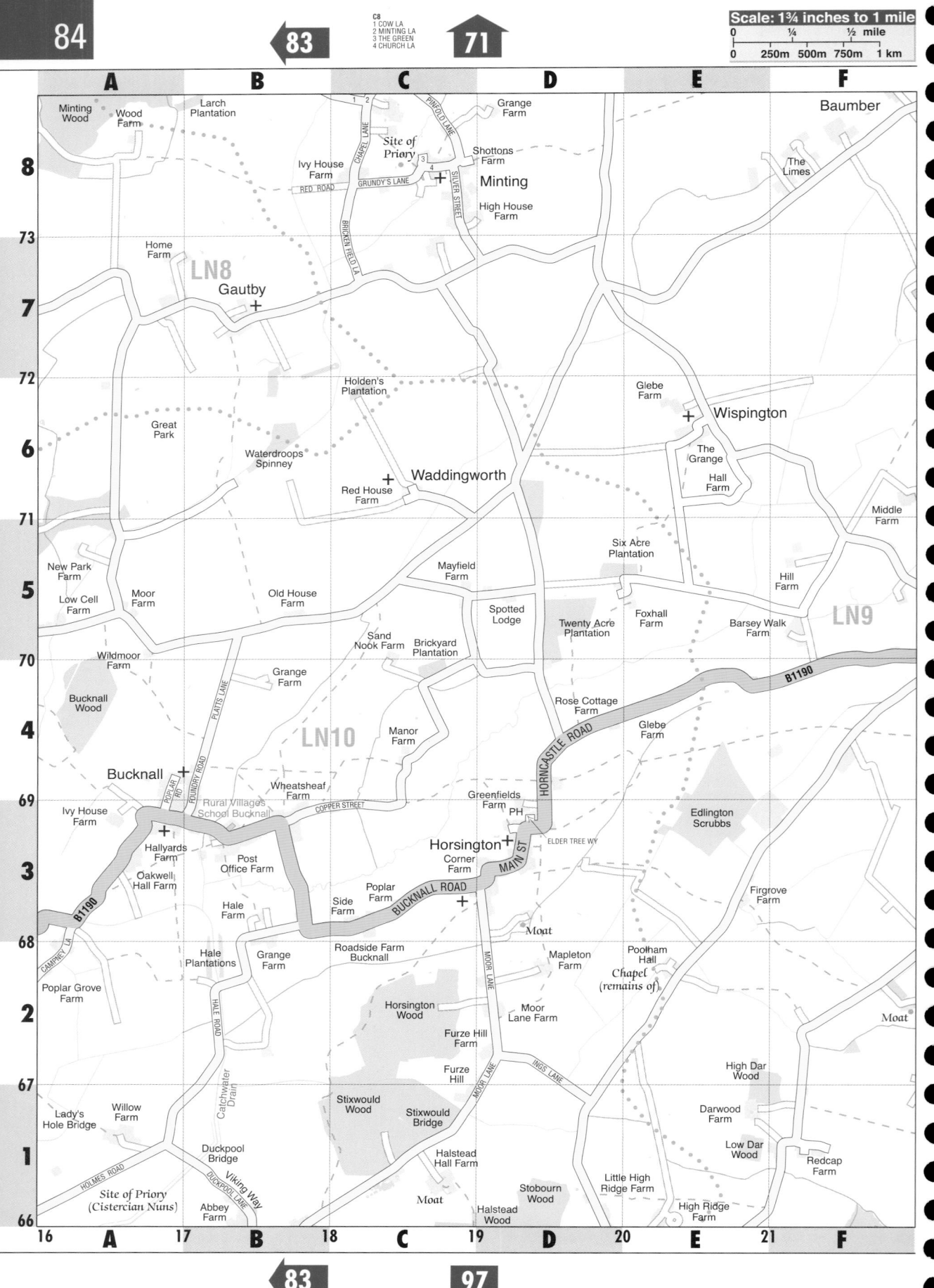

83

C8
1 COW LA
2 MINTING LA
3 THE GREEN
4 CHURCH LA

71

Scale: 1¾ inches to 1 mile
0   ¼   ½   mile
0   250m   500m   750m   1 km

A   B   C   D   E   F

Minting Wood   Wood Farm   Larch Plantation   Grange Farm   Baumber

8   Ivy House Farm   Site of Priory   Shottons Farm   The Limes

73   Home Farm   Minting
                                          High House Farm

LN8   Gautby

7

72   Holden's Plantation   Glebe Farm   Wispington

6   Great Park   Waterdroops Spinney   Waddingworth   The Grange
                         Red House Farm   Hall Farm

71   Middle Farm

New Park Farm   Moor Farm   Old House Farm   Mayfield Farm   Six Acre Plantation   Hill Farm   LN9

5   Low Cell Farm   Spotted Lodge   Twenty Acre Plantation   Foxhall Farm   Barsey Walk Farm

Wildmoor Farm   Sand Nook Farm   Brickyard Plantation

70   B1190

Bucknall Wood   Grange Farm   LN10   Rose Cottage Farm   Glebe Farm

4   Manor Farm   HORNCASTLE ROAD

Bucknall   Wheatsheaf Farm   Greenfields Farm   Edlington Scrubs

69   Ivy House Farm   Rural Villages School Bucknall   COPPER STREET   PH
                                                            MAIN ST

Hallyards Farm   Horsington   Firgrove Farm

3   Oakwell Hall Farm   Post Office Farm   Corner Farm   BUCKNALL ROAD

B1190   Hale Farm   Side Farm   Poplar Farm   Moat   Mapleton Farm   Pooltham Hall
                                                            Chapel (remains of)

68   Hale Plantations   Grange Farm   Roadside Farm Bucknall   Moat

Poplar Grove Farm   Horsington Wood   Moor Lane Farm   High Dar Wood   Moat

2   Furze Hill Farm   MOOR LANE   INGS LANE   Darwood Farm

67   Furze Hill   Low Dar Wood

Lady's Hole Bridge   Willow Farm   Stixwould Wood   Stixwould Bridge   Little High Ridge Farm   Redcap Farm

1   HOLMES ROAD   Duckpool Bridge   Halstead Hall Farm   Stobourn Wood   High Ridge Farm

Site of Priory (Cistercian Nuns)   Abbey Farm   Viking Way   Moat   Halstead Wood

66

16   A   17   B   18   C   19   D   20   E   21   F

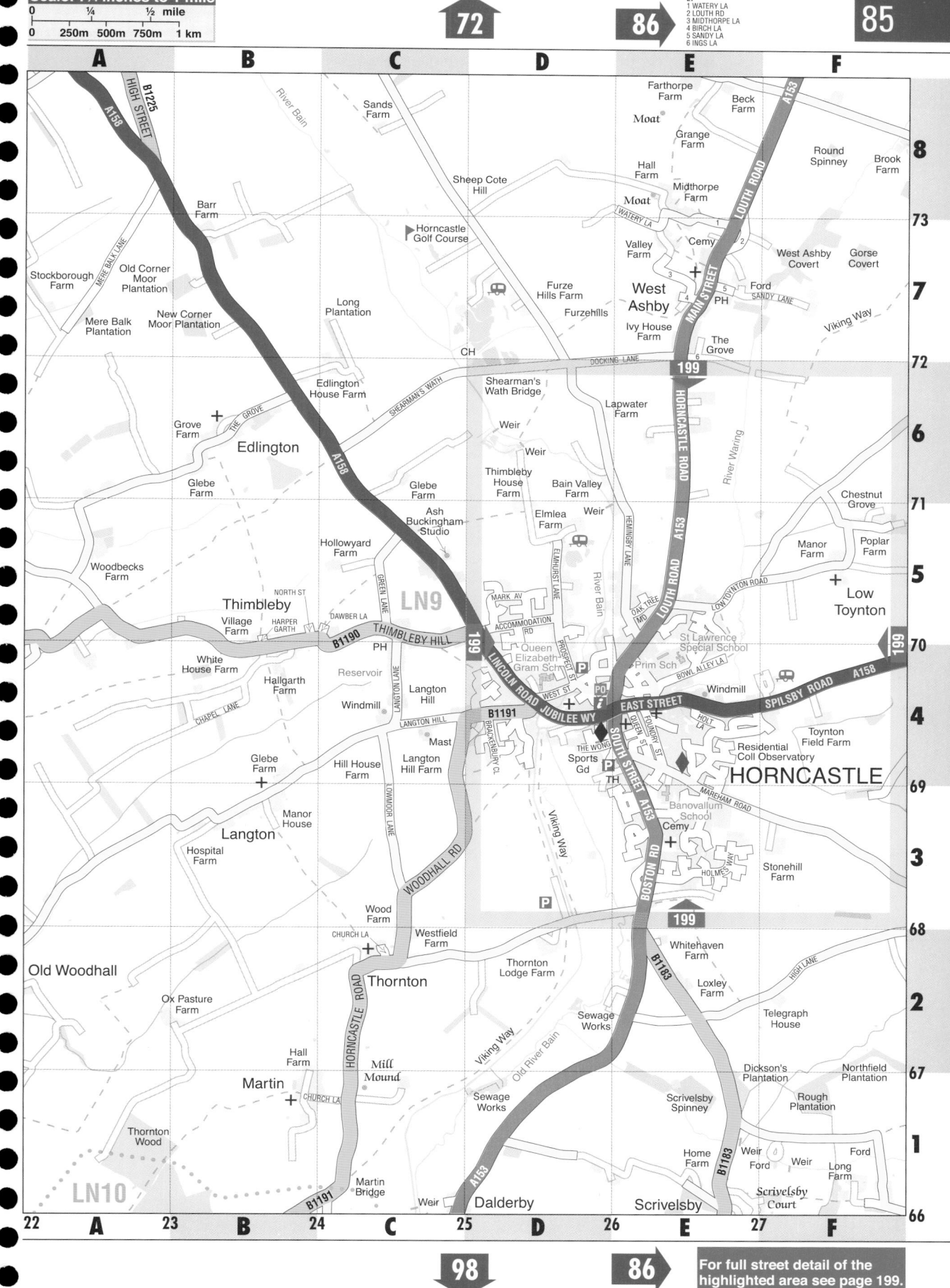

Scale: 1¾ inches to 1 mile

0   ¼   ½   mile
0   250m   500m   750m   1 km

72

86

85

E7
1 WATERY LA
2 LOUTH RD
3 MIDTHORPE LA
4 BIRCH LA
5 SANDY LA
6 INGS LA

A   B   C   D   E   F

B1225
A158 HIGH STREET

Sands Farm

Farthorpe Farm
Moat
Beck Farm
A153

Grange Farm
Round Spinney
Brook Farm

8

Barr Farm

Sheep Cote Hill

Hall Farm
Midthorpe Farm
LOUTH ROAD

WATERY LA
Moat

West Ashby Covert
Gorse Covert

73

Horncastle Golf Course

Valley Farm
Cemy
West Ashby Covert

7

Stockborough Farm

MERE BALK LANE

Old Corner Moor Plantation

Long Plantation

Furze Hills Farm
Furzehills

Ford
SANDY LANE
PH

West Ashby
MAIN STREET

Viking Way

Mere Balk Plantation

New Corner Moor Plantation

CH

Ivy House Farm
The Grove

72

Edlington House Farm

SHEARMAN'S WATH

DOCKING LANE
199

THE GROVE
Grove Farm

Shearman's Wath Bridge

Lapwater Farm
HORNCASTLE ROAD
A153

River Waring

6

Edlington

A158

Weir

Weir

71

Glebe Farm

Glebe Farm
Ash Buckingham Studio

Thimbleby House Farm
Bain Valley Farm
Weir

Chestnut Grove

Woodbecks Farm

GREEN LANE
LN9

Hollowyard Farm

Elmlea Farm

ELMHURST LANE
River Bain

HEMINGBY LANE

LOUTH ROAD
A153

Manor Farm
Poplar Farm

5

Thimbleby
NORTH ST
Village Farm
HARPER GARTH
DAWBER LA
B1190 THIMBLEBY HILL
199

MARK AV
ACCOMMODATION RD

OAK TREE MD
LOWTOYNTON ROAD

Low Toynton

White House Farm

PH

LANGTON LANE

Reservoir

Queen Elizabeth Gram Sch
WEST ST
LINCOLN ROAD JUBILEE WY
PROSPECT ST

St Lawrence Special School
Prim Sch
BOWL ALLEY LA
Windmill
SPILSBY ROAD A158
199

70

Hallgarth Farm

CHAPEL LANE
Windmill
LANGTON HILL
Langton Hill
B1191

EAST STREET
QUEEN ST
FOUNDRY ST
HOLT LA

4

Glebe Farm
Hill House Farm
Langton Hill Farm
Mast
BRACKENBURY CL

THE WONG
SOUTH STREET A153
Sports Gd
P
TH
Residential Coll Observatory
Toynton Field Farm

HORNCASTLE

69

Langton

LOWMOOR LANE

Manor House

Viking Way

Banovallum School
Cemy

MAREHAM ROAD

Stonehill Farm

3

Hospital Farm

Ox Pasture Farm

WOODHALL RD

Wood Farm
CHURCH LA
Westfield Farm
Thornton Lodge Farm

P

BOSTON RD A153
HOLMES
HOLMES WAY

Old Woodhall

Thornton

Whitehaven Farm
HIGH LANE

68

Hall Farm
HORNCASTLE ROAD

Mill Mound

Viking Way
Old River Bain
Sewage Works
B1183
Loxley Farm
Telegraph House

2

Martin
CHURCH LA

Sewage Works
A153

Scrivelsby Spinney
Dickson's Plantation
Rough Plantation
Northfield Plantation

67

Thornton Wood

Martin Bridge
B1191
Weir
Dalderby

Scrivelsby
Home Farm
B1183
Weir
Ford
Weir
Long Farm
Ford

1

LN10

Scrivelsby Court

66

22   A   23   B   24   C   25   D   26   E   27   F   66

98

86

For full street detail of the highlighted area see page 199.

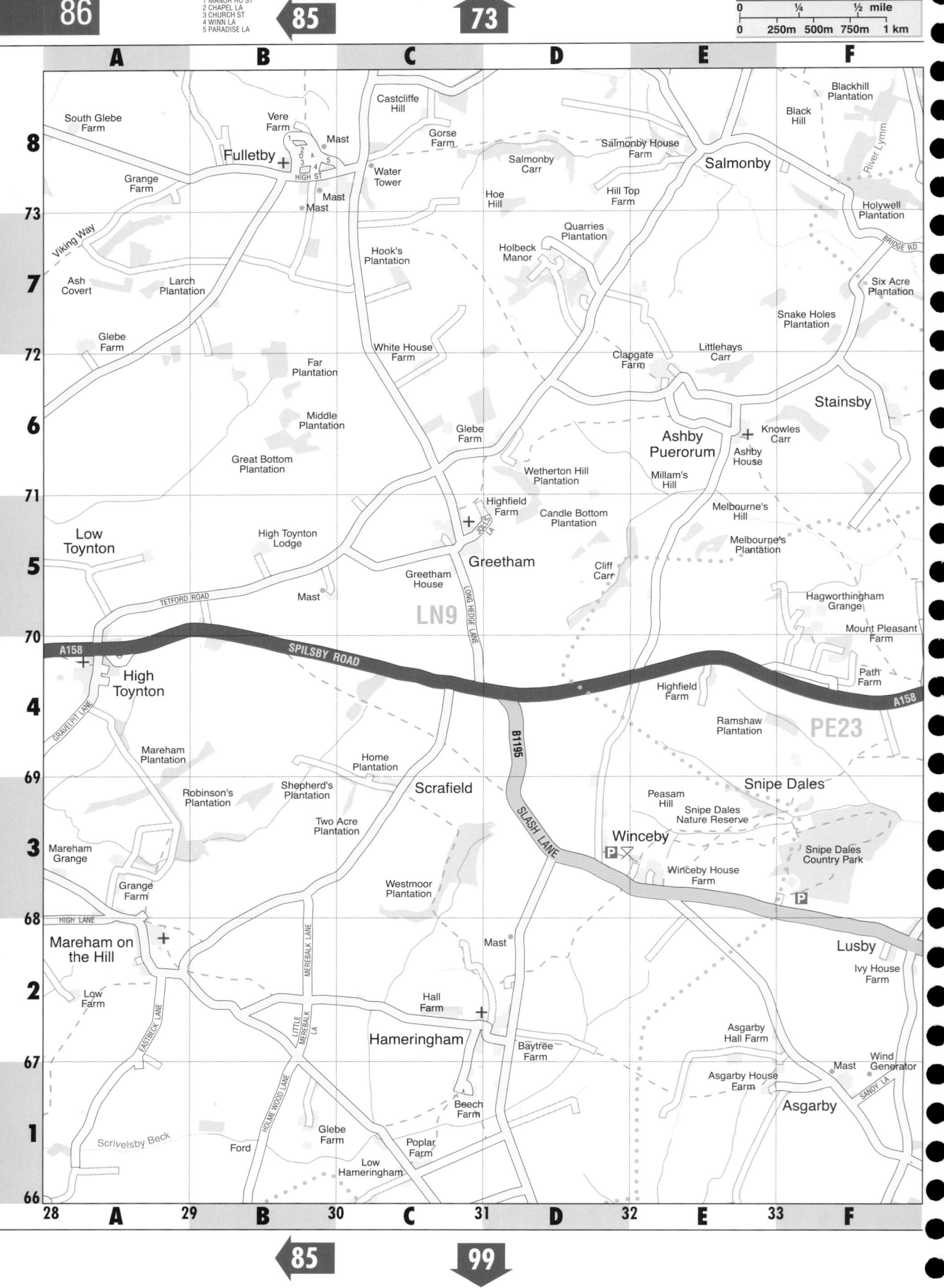

B8
1 MANOR HO ST
2 CHAPEL LA
3 CHURCH ST
4 WINN LA
5 PARADISE LA

85

73

A   B   C   D   E   F

South Glebe Farm
Vere Farm
Mast
Castcliffe Hill
Gorse Farm
Salmonby House Farm
Black Hill
Blackhill Plantation

8

Fulletby
Water Tower
Salmonby Carr
Hoe Hill
Hill Top Farm
Salmonby
River Lymm

73

Grange Farm
Mast
Mast
HIGH ST
Holbeck Manor
Quarries Plantation
Holywell Plantation
BRIDGE RD

Viking Way
Hook's Plantation
Six Acre Plantation

7

Ash Covert
Larch Plantation
Clapgate Farm
Littlehays Carr
Snake Holes Plantation

72

Glebe Farm
White House Farm
Far Plantation
Stainsby

6

Middle Plantation
Glebe Farm
Wetherton Hill Plantation
Ashby Puerorum
Knowles Carr
Ashby House

Great Bottom Plantation
Millam's Hill

71

Highfield Farm
Candle Bottom Plantation
Melbourne's Hill

Low Toynton
High Toynton Lodge
JOLES LA
Melbourne's Plantation

5

Greetham House
Greetham
Cliff Carr
Hagworthingham Grange

TETFORD ROAD
Mast
LN9
Mount Pleasant Farm

70

A158
SPILSBY ROAD
LONG HEDGE LANE
Path Farm

High Toynton
Highfield Farm
A158

4

GRAVELPIT LANE
B1195
Ramshaw Plantation
PE23

Mareham Plantation
Home Plantation

69

Robinson's Plantation
Shepherd's Plantation
Scrafield
Peasam Hill
Snipe Dales

3

Two Acre Plantation
SLASH LANE
Snipe Dales Nature Reserve
Snipe Dales Country Park

Mareham Grange
Winceby
Winceby House Farm

Grange Farm
Westmoor Plantation
P

68

HIGH LANE
Lusby

Mareham on the Hill
MEREBALK LANE
Mast
Ivy House Farm

2

Low Farm
Hall Farm
Asgarby Hall Farm

EASTBECK LANE
LITTLE MEREBALK LA
Hameringham
Baytree Farm
Mast
Wind Generator

67

HOLME WOOD LANE
Beech Farm
Asgarby House Farm
SANDY LA

Glebe Farm
Poplar Farm
Asgarby

1

Scrivelsby Beck
Ford
Low Hameringham

66

28   A   29   B   30   C   31   D   32   E   33   F

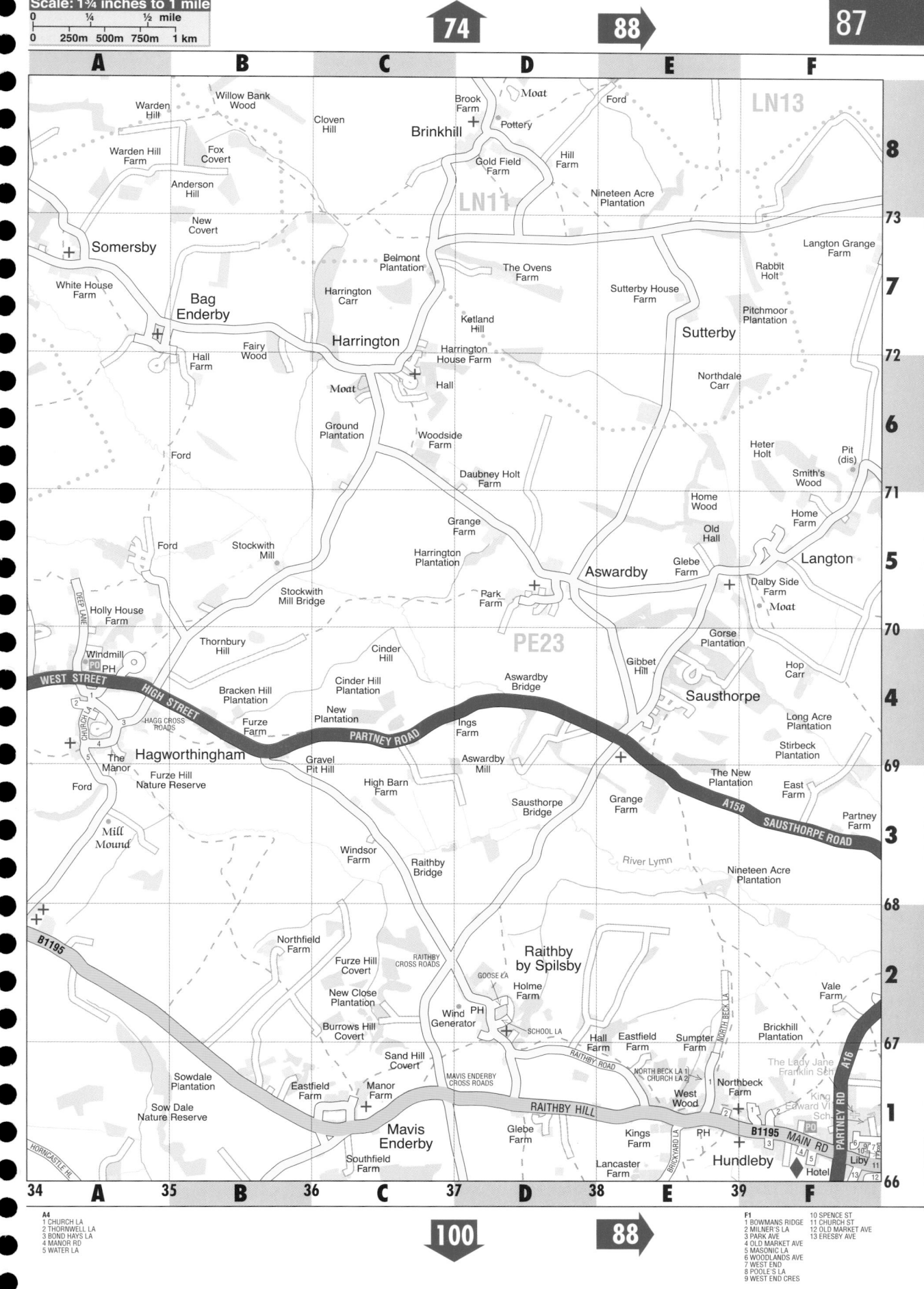

LN13

LN11

PE23

Places (Column A–F, Rows 1–8)

Warden Hill
Warden Hill Farm
Willow Bank Wood
Cloven Hill
Brook Farm
Moat
Ford
Fox Covert
Anderson Hill
Brinkhill
Pottery
Gold Field Farm
Hill Farm
Nineteen Acre Plantation
New Covert
Somersby
White House Farm
Belmont Plantation
The Ovens Farm
Langton Grange Farm
Rabbit Holt
Harrington Carr
Sutterby House Farm
Pitchmoor Plantation
Bag Enderby
Hall Farm
Fairy Wood
Harrington
Ketland Hill
Sutterby
Harrington House Farm
Moat
Hall
Northdale Carr
Ground Plantation
Woodside Farm
Daubney Holt Farm
Heter Holt
Pit (dis)
Smith's Wood
Ford
Ford
Stockwith Mill
Grange Farm
Home Wood
Old Hall
Home Farm
Holly House Farm
Thornbury Hill
Stockwith Mill Bridge
Harrington Plantation
Aswardby
Glebe Farm
Langton
Dalby Side Farm
Moat
Park Farm
Windmill PO PH
Cinder Hill
Gorse Plantation
Hop Carr
WEST STREET
HIGH STREET
Bracken Hill Plantation
Cinder Hill Plantation
Aswardby Bridge
Gibbet Hill
Sausthorpe
Long Acre Plantation
Furze Farm
New Plantation
Ings Farm
Stirbeck Plantation
PARTNEY ROAD
The New Plantation
East Farm
Gravel Pit Hill
Aswardby Mill
The Manor
Hagworthingham
High Barn Farm
Grange Farm
Partney Farm
Furze Hill Nature Reserve
Sausthorpe Bridge
A158 SAUSTHORPE ROAD
Ford
Mill Mound
Windsor Farm
Raithby Bridge
River Lymn
Nineteen Acre Plantation
B1195
Northfield Farm
Furze Hill Covert
RAITHBY CROSS ROADS
Raithby by Spilsby
Vale Farm
New Close Plantation
Wind Generator
GOOSE LA
Holme Farm
PH
Brickhill Plantation
A16
Burrows Hill Covert
SCHOOL LA
Hall Farm
Eastfield Farm
Sumpter Farm
NORTH BECK LA
The Lady Jane Franklin Sch
Sand Hill Covert
MAVIS ENDERBY CROSS ROADS
RAITHBY ROAD
NORTH BECK LA 1 CHURCH LA 2
Northbeck Farm
King Edward VI Sch
Sowdale Plantation
Eastfield Farm
Manor Farm
RAITHBY HILL
West Wood
PO
Liby
Sow Dale Nature Reserve
HORNCASTLE HL
Mavis Enderby
Southfield Farm
Glebe Farm
Kings Farm
BRICKYARD LA
PH
B1195
MAIN RD
PARTNEY RD
Lancaster Farm
Hundleby
Hotel

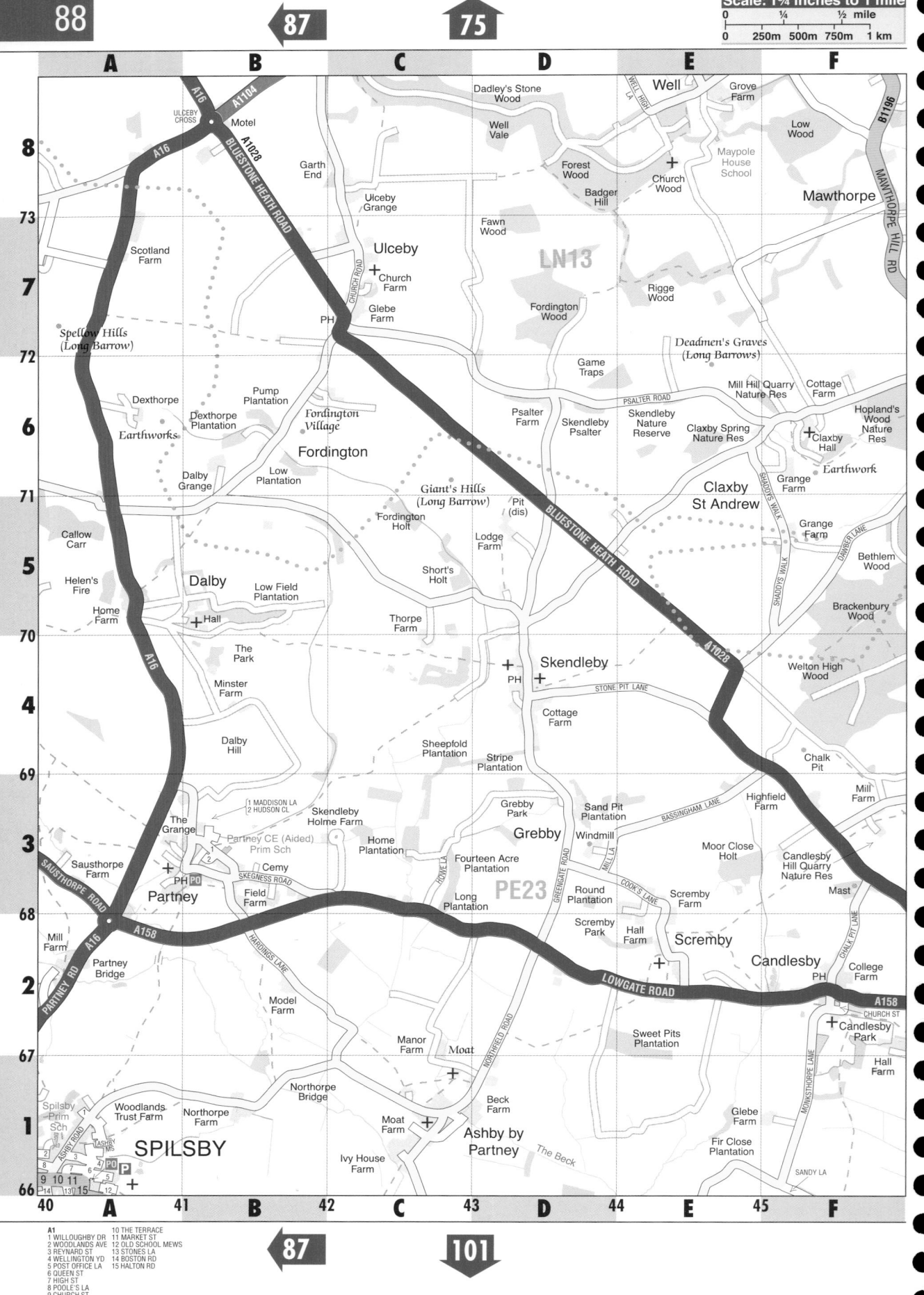

Scale: 1¾ inches to 1 mile

A1
1 WILLOUGHBY DR
2 WOODLANDS AVE
3 REYNARD ST
4 WELLINGTON YD
5 POST OFFICE LA
6 QUEEN ST
7 HIGH ST
8 POOLE'S LA
9 CHURCH ST
10 THE TERRACE
11 MARKET ST
12 OLD SCHOOL MEWS
13 STONES LA
14 BOSTON RD
15 HALTON RD

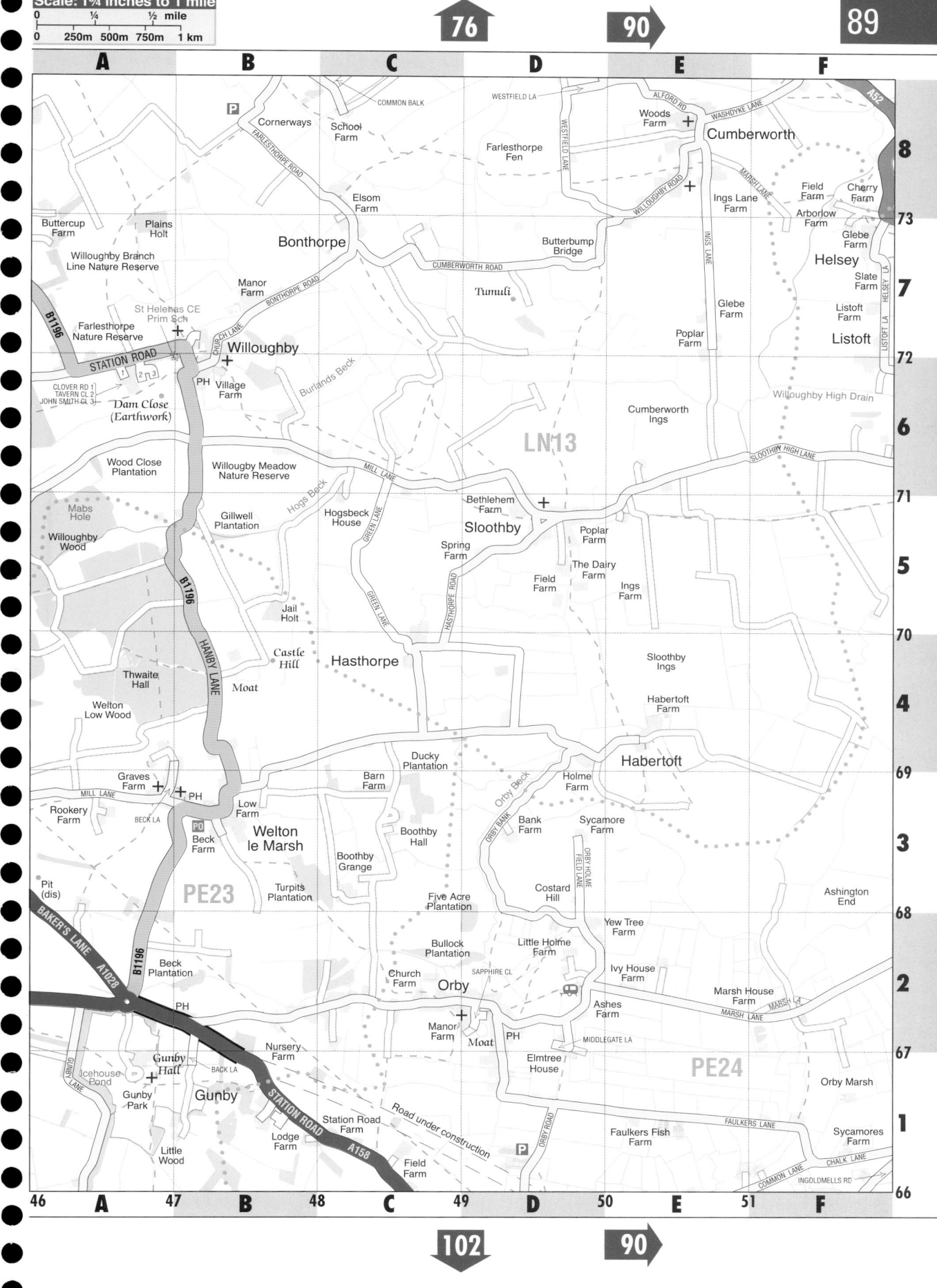

Scale: 1¾ inches to 1 mile
0 ¼ ½ mile
0 250m 500m 750m 1 km
76
90
A B C D E F
Cornerways
School Farm
COMMON BALK
WESTFIELD LA
ALFORD RD
WASHDYKE LANE
Woods Farm
Cumberworth
Farlesthorpe Fen
FARLESTHORPE ROAD
WESTFIELD LANE
WILLOUGHBY ROAD
MARSH LANE
Elsom Farm
Ings Lane Farm
Field Farm
Cherry Farm
Arborlow Farm
Buttercup Farm
Plains Holt
Bonthorpe
Butterbump Bridge
Glebe Farm
Helsey
Willoughby Branch Line Nature Reserve
CUMBERWORTH ROAD
INGS LANE
Manor Farm
BONTHORPE ROAD
Tumuli
Slate Farm
Glebe Farm
Listoft Farm
St Helenas CE Prim Sch
Farlesthorpe Nature Reserve
Poplar Farm
Listoft
B1196
STATION ROAD
CHURCH LANE
Willoughby
Village Farm
Burlands Beck
CLOVER RD 1
TAVERN CL 2
JOHN SMITH CL 3
Dam Close (Earthwork)
Willoughby High Drain
Cumberworth Ings
LN13
Wood Close Plantation
Willougby Meadow Nature Reserve
MILL LANE
SLOOTHBY HIGH LANE
Bethlehem Farm
Mabs Hole
Gillwell Plantation
Hogs Beck
Hogsbeck House
GREEN LANE
Sloothby
Willoughby Wood
Poplar Farm
Spring Farm
The Dairy Farm
Field Farm
Ings Farm
HASTHORPE ROAD
Jail Holt
GREEN LANE
Castle Hill
Hasthorpe
HANBY LANE
Sloothby Ings
Thwaite Hall
Moat
Welton Low Wood
Habertoft Farm
Ducky Plantation
Habertoft
Graves Farm
Barn Farm
Holme Farm
MILL LANE
PH
Orby Beck
Rookery Farm
Low Farm
BECK LA
Welton le Marsh
Boothby Hall
ORBY BANK
Bank Farm
Sycamore Farm
PO
Beck Farm
Boothby Grange
ORBY HOLME FIELD LANE
Pit (dis)
PE23
Turpits Plantation
Five Acre Plantation
Costard Hill
Ashington End
BAKER'S LANE
Yew Tree Farm
Bullock Plantation
Little Holme Farm
Beck Plantation
A1028
Church Farm
SAPPHIRE CL
Ivy House Farm
Orby
Marsh House Farm
MARSH LA
Ashes Farm
MARSH LANE
Manor Farm
Moat
MIDDLEGATE LA
Nursery Farm
Gunby Hall
Elmtree House
PE24
GUNBY LANE
Icehouse Pond
BACK LA
Orby Marsh
Gunby Park
Gunby
STATION ROAD
Road under construction
Station Road Farm
ORBY ROAD
Faulkers Fish Farm
FAULKERS LANE
Sycamores Farm
Lodge Farm
A158
Little Wood
Field Farm
CHALK LANE
COMMON LANE
INGOLDMELLS RD
A52
8 73 7 72 6 71 5 70 4 69 3 68 2 67 1 66
46 47 48 49 50 51
102
90

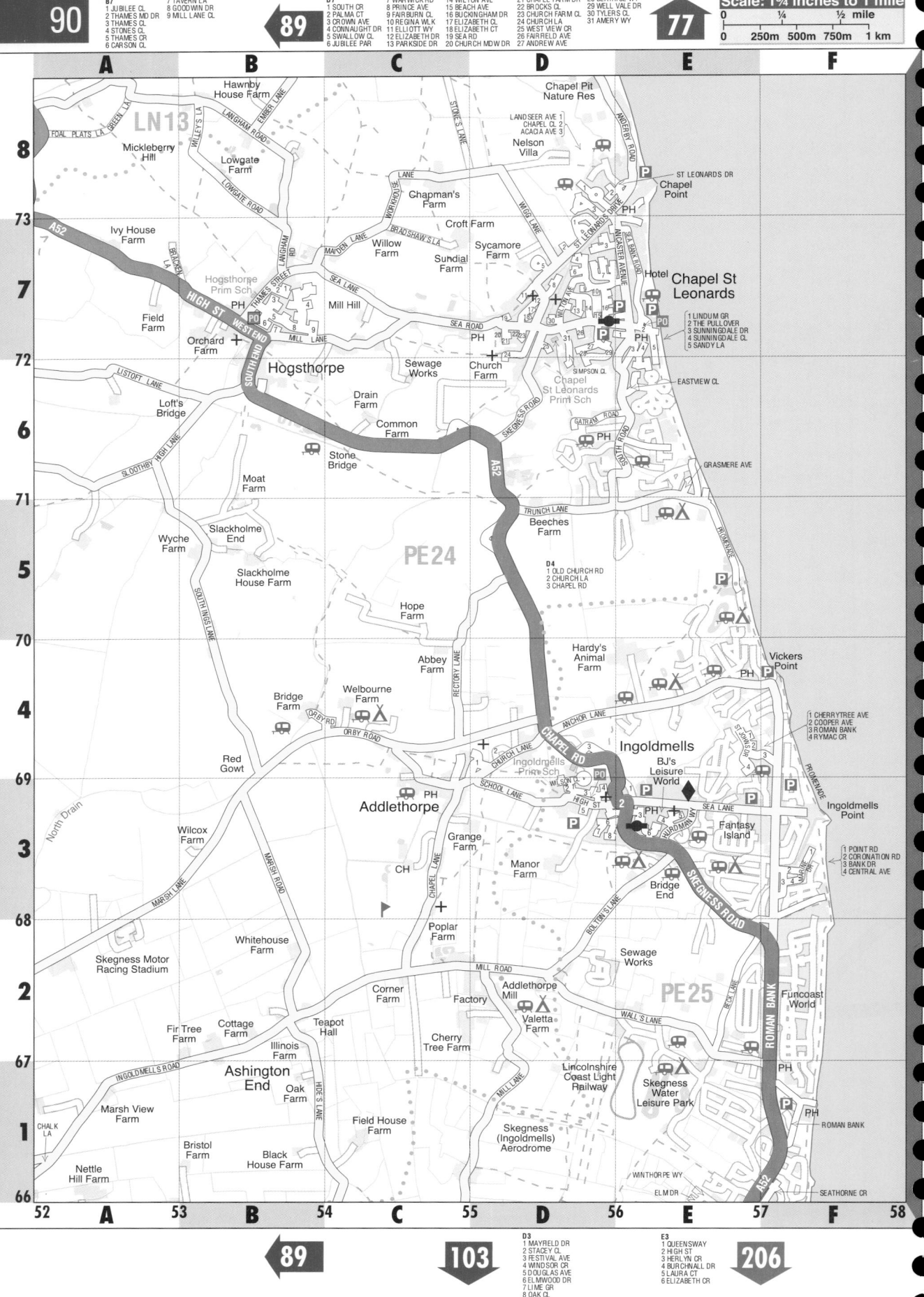

90
B7
1 JUBILEE CL
2 THAMES MD DR
3 THAMES CL
4 STONES CL
5 THAMES CR
6 CARSON CL
7 TAVERN LA
8 GOODWIN DR
9 MILL LANE CL
89
D7
1 SOUTH CR
2 PALMA CT
3 CROWN AVE
4 CONNAUGHT DR
5 SWALLOW CL
6 JUBILEE PAR
7 WARWICK RD
8 PRINCE AVE
9 FAIRBURN CL
10 REGINA WLK
11 ELLIOTT WY
12 ELIZABETH DR
13 PARKSIDE DR
14 WILTON AVE
15 BEACH AVE
16 BUCKINGHAM DR
17 ELIZABETH CL
18 ELIZABETH CT
19 SEA RD
20 CHURCH MDW DR
21 CHAPEL FARM DR
22 BROCKS CL
23 CHURCH FARM CL
24 CHURCH LA
25 WEST VIEW CR
26 FAIRFIELD AVE
27 ANDREW AVE
28 BEATRICE WY
29 WELL VALE DR
30 TYLERS CL
31 AMERY WY
77
Scale: 1¾ inches to 1 mile
0 ¼ ½ mile
0 250m 500m 750m 1 km
A B C D E F
8 73 7 72 6 71 5 70 4 69 3 68 2 67 1 66
Hawnby House Farm
LN13
Mickleberry Hill
Lowgate Farm
Chapel Pit Nature Res
LANDSEER AVE 1
CHAPEL CL 2
ACACIA AVE 3
Nelson Villa
ST LEONARDS DR
Chapel Point
Chapman's Farm
Croft Farm
Ivy House Farm
Willow Farm
Sundial Farm
Sycamore Farm
Hotel
Chapel St Leonards
Hogsthorpe Prim Sch
Mill Hill
Field Farm
Orchard Farm
1 LINDUM GR
2 THE PULLOVER
3 SUNNINGDALE DR
4 SUNNINGDALE CL
5 SANDY LA
Hogsthorpe
Sewage Works
Church Farm
SIMPSON CL
Chapel St Leonards Prim Sch
EASTVIEW CL
Loft's Bridge
Drain Farm
Common Farm
Stone Bridge
GRASMERE AVE
Moat Farm
Beeches Farm
Wyche Farm
Slackholme End
PE24
Slackholme House Farm
D4
1 OLD CHURCH RD
2 CHURCH LA
3 CHAPEL RD
Hope Farm
Abbey Farm
Hardy's Animal Farm
Vickers Point
Bridge Farm
Welbourne Farm
1 CHERRYTREE AVE
2 COOPER AVE
3 ROMAN BANK
4 RYMAC CR
Red Gowt
Ingoldmells
BJ's Leisure World
Ingoldmells Prim Sch
Addlethorpe
Ingoldmells Point
Wilcox Farm
North Drain
Grange Farm
Manor Farm
Fantasy Island
CH
1 POINT RD
2 CORONATION RD
3 BANK DR
4 CENTRAL AVE
Bridge End
Poplar Farm
Whitehouse Farm
Skegness Motor Racing Stadium
Sewage Works
PE25
Corner Farm
Factory
Addlethorpe Mill
Funcoast World
Teapot Hall
Valetta Farm
Fir Tree Farm
Cottage Farm
Illinois Farm
Cherry Tree Farm
Ashington End
Oak Farm
Lincolnshire Coast Light Railway
Skegness Water Leisure Park
Marsh View Farm
Field House Farm
Skegness (Ingoldmells) Aerodrome
ROMAN BANK
Bristol Farm
Black House Farm
Nettle Hill Farm
CHALK LA
WINTHORPE WY
ELM DR
SEATHORNE CR
A52
HIGH ST
WEST END
SOUTH END
CHAPEL RD
SKEGNESS ROAD
ROMAN BANK
SEA LANE
SEA ROAD
MILL ROAD
ORBY ROAD
ANCHOR LANE
TRUNCH LANE
MARSH LANE
MARSH ROAD
INGOLDMELLS ROAD
PROMENADE
52 53 54 55 56 57 58
89
103
D3
1 MAYFIELD DR
2 STACEY CL
3 FESTIVAL AVE
4 WINDSOR CR
5 DOUGLAS AVE
6 ELMWOOD DR
7 LIME GR
8 OAK CL
E3
1 QUEENSWAY
2 HIGH ST
3 HERLYN CR
4 BURCHNALL DR
5 LAURA CT
6 ELIZABETH CR
206

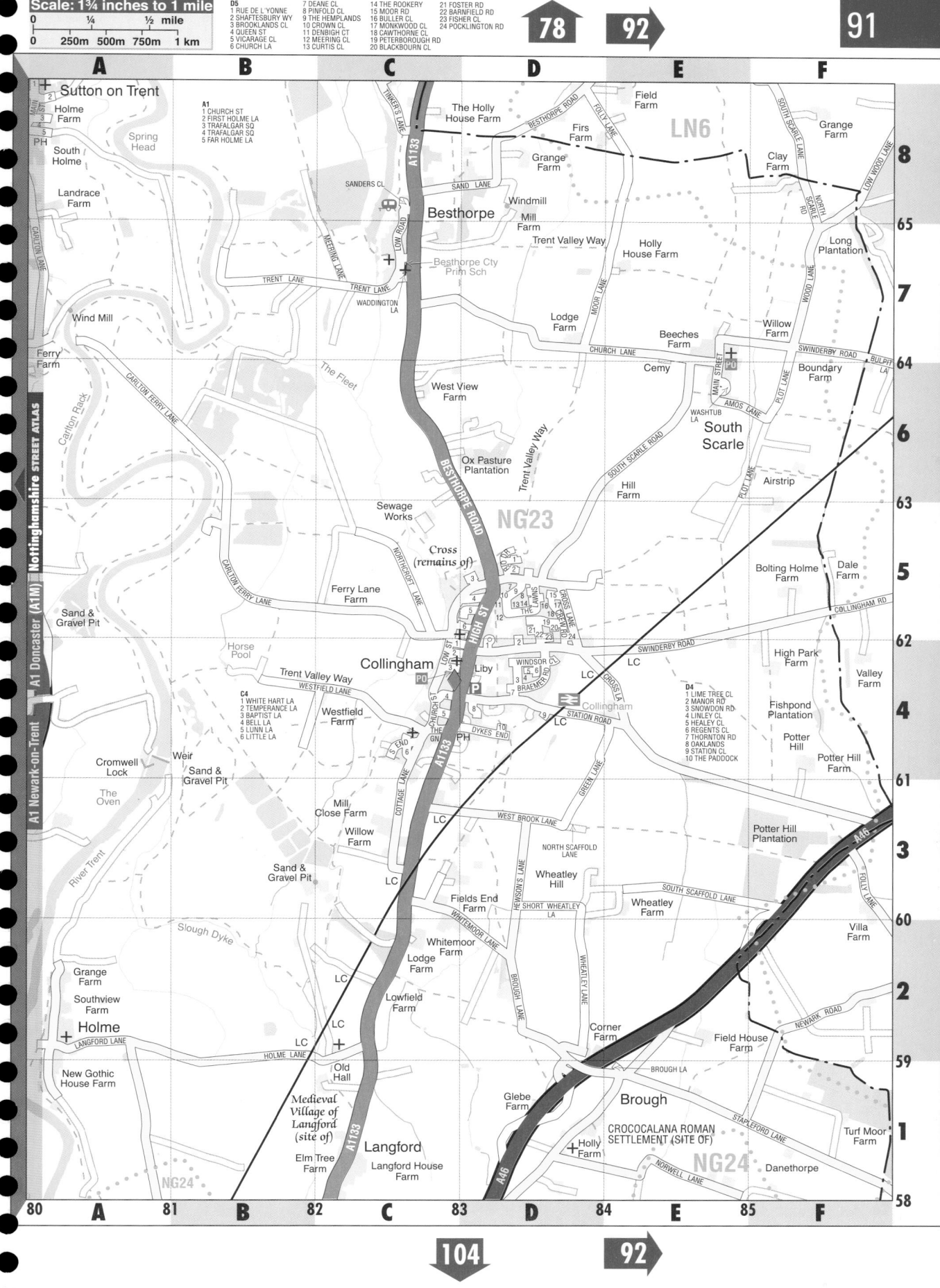

Scale: 1¾ inches to 1 mile

0   ¼   ½   mile
0   250m   500m   750m   1 km

78   92

D5
1 RUE DE L'YONNE
2 SHAFTESBURY WY
3 BROOKLANDS CL
4 QUEEN ST
5 VICARAGE CL
6 CHURCH LA

7 DEANE CL
8 PINFOLD CL
9 THE HEMPLANDS
10 CROWN CL
11 DENBIGH CL
12 MEERING CT
13 CURTIS CL

14 THE ROOKERY
15 MOOR RD
16 BULLER CL
17 MONKWOOD CL
18 CAWTHORNE CL
19 PETERBOROUGH RD
20 BLACKBOURN CL

21 FOSTER RD
22 BARNFIELD RD
23 FISHER CL
24 POCKLINGTON RD

Nottinghamshire STREET ATLAS

A1 Doncaster (A1M)

A1 Newark-on-Trent

A1
1 CHURCH ST
2 FIRST HOLME LA
3 TRAFALGAR SQ
4 TRAFALGAR SQ
5 FAR HOLME LA

Sutton on Trent
Holme Farm
PH
South Holme
Landrace Farm
Spring Head
Wind Mill
Ferry Farm
Carlton Beck
CARLTON LANE
CARLTON FERRY LANE
The Fleet
Sand & Gravel Pit
Horse Pool
Cromwell Lock
The Oven
River Trent
Slough Dyke
Grange Farm
Southview Farm
Holme
New Gothic House Farm
LANGFORD LANE
HOLME LANE
Old Hall
Medieval Village of Langford (site of)
Elm Tree Farm
Langford
Langford House Farm

A1133
TINKER'S LANE
SANDERS CL
Besthorpe
LOW ROAD
MEERING LANE
TRENT LANE
WADDINGTON LA
BESTHORPE ROAD
Besthorpe Cty Prim Sch
West View Farm
Ox Pasture Plantation
Sewage Works
NORTHGATE LANE
Cross (remains of)
Ferry Lane Farm
Trent Valley Way
WESTFIELD LANE
Westfield Farm
C4
1 WHITE HART LA
2 TEMPERANCE LA
3 BAPTIST LA
4 BELL LA
5 LUNN LA
6 LITTLE LA
Mill Close Farm
Willow Farm
COTTAGE LANE
HIGH ST
LOW ST
CHURCH ST
Collingham
PO
Liby
P
Sand & Gravel Pit
DYKES END
PH
Lodge Farm
Whitemoor Farm
Lowfield Farm

The Holly House Farm
Firs Farm
Grange Farm
SAND LANE
Windmill
Mill Farm
Trent Valley Way
Lodge Farm
Trent Valley Way
MOOR LANE
CHURCH LANE
Cemy
Holly House Farm
Beeches Farm
Hill Farm
SOUTH SCARLE ROAD
MAIN STREET
WASHTUB LA
South Scarle
PO
AMOS LANE
PLOT LANE
SWINDERBY ROAD
Airstrip
WINDSOR CL
BRAEMER CL
LC
LC
LC
LC
Collingham
STATION ROAD
GREEN LANE
HENSON'S LANE
West Brook Lane
North Scaffold Lane
Wheatley Hill
SHORT WHEATLEY LA
WHITEMOOR LANE
BROUGH LANE
Corner Farm
Glebe Farm
Brough
Holly Farm
CROCOCALANA ROMAN SETTLEMENT (SITE OF)
NORWELL LANE
Danethorpe

BESTHORPE ROAD
NG23
LN6
Field Farm
BESTHORPE ROAD
FOLLY LANE
SOUTH SCARLE LANE
Grange Farm
Clay Farm
NORTH SCARLE RD
LOW WOOD LANE
Long Plantation
Willow Farm
Boundary Farm
SWINDERBY ROAD
BULPIT LA
High Park Farm
Valley Farm
Collingham Rd
Bolting Holme Farm
Dale Farm
COLLINGHAM RD
Fishpond Plantation
Potter Hill
Potter Hill Farm
D4
1 LIME TREE CL
2 MANOR RD
3 SNOWDON RD
4 LINLEY CL
5 HEALEY CL
6 REGENTS CL
7 THORNTON RD
8 OAKLANDS
9 STATION CL
10 THE PADDOCK
Potter Hill Plantation
A46
WHEATLEY LANE
SOUTH SCAFFOLD LANE
Wheatley Farm
Villa Farm
NEWARK ROAD
Field House Farm
BROUGH LA
STAPLEFORD LANE
FOLLY LANE
Turf Moor Farm
NG24

80   81   82   83   84   85   58
59
60
61
62
63
64
65
8
7
6
5
4
3
2
1

A   B   C   D   E   F

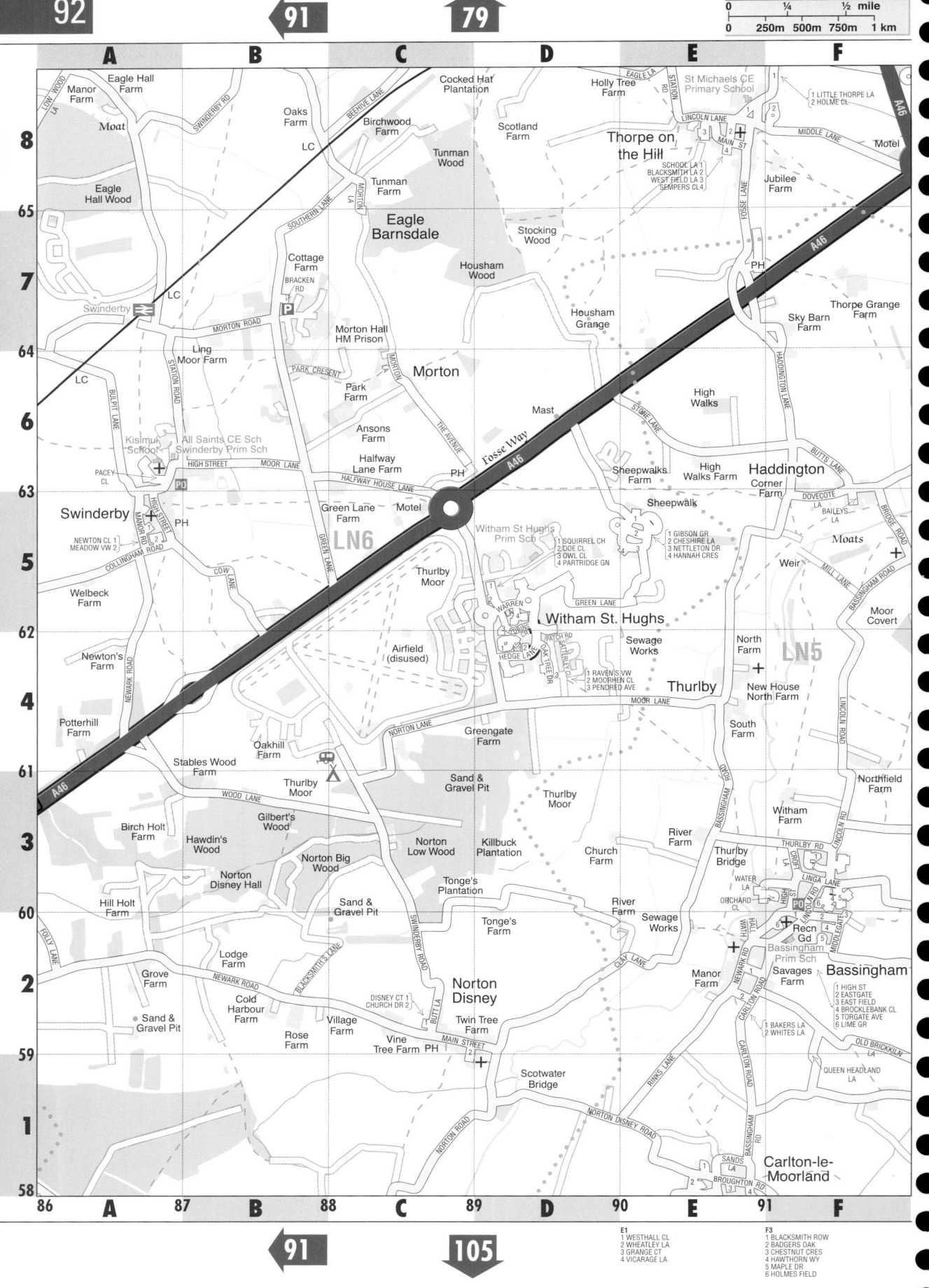

A B C D E F

8

65

7

64

6

63

5

62

4

61

3

60

2

59

1

58

Low Wood La
Manor Farm
Eagle Hall Farm
Moat
Eagle Hall Wood
Swinderby
LC
PACEY CL
Kislmu School
All Saints CE Sch Swinderby Prim Sch
HIGH STREET
PO
Swinderby
NEWTON CL 1
MEADOW VW 2
PH
MANOR RD
COLLINGHAM ROAD
Welbeck Farm
COW LANE
STATION ROAD
BULPIT LANE
LC
Newton's Farm
NEWARK ROAD
Potterhill Farm
Birch Holt Farm
Hill Holt Farm
Hawdin's Wood
Grove Farm
NEWARK ROAD
Lodge Farm
Cold Harbour Farm
Sand & Gravel Pit
FOLLY LANE

SWINDERBY RD
BEEHIVE LANE
Oaks Farm
LC
SOUTHERN LANE
Birchwood Farm
Tunman Farm
Cottage Farm
BRACKEN RD
P
MORTON LA
MORTON ROAD
Ling Moor Farm
PARK CRESENT
Morton Hall HM Prison
Park Farm
Ansons Farm
MOOR LANE
Halfway Lane Farm
Halfway House Lane
Green Lane Farm
GREEN LANE
THE AVENUE
Thurlby Moor
Airfield (disused)
Oakhill Farm
Stables Wood Farm
WOOD LANE
Thurlby Moor
Gilbert's Wood
Norton Big Wood
Norton Disney Hall
Sand & Gravel Pit
BLACKSMITH'S LANE
Village Farm
Rose Farm
Vine Tree Farm PH
SWINDERBY ROAD
NORTON LANE
Norton Low Wood
Tonge's Plantation
Tonge's Farm
DISNEY CT 1
CHURCH DR 2
BUTT LA
MAIN STREET
Norton Disney
Twin Tree Farm
NORTON ROAD

Cocked Hat Plantation
Eagle Barnsdale
Tunman Wood
Scotland Farm
Stocking Wood
Housham Wood
Housham Grange
Morton
Mast
PH
Motel
Fosse Way A46
LN6
Witham St Hughs Prim Sch
Green Lane
WARREN
HEDGE LANE
OAK TREE DR
HATCH RD
Witham St. Hughs
Greengate Farm
Killbuck Plantation
Sand & Gravel Pit
Scotwater Bridge
NORTON DISNEY ROAD

Holly Tree Farm
EAGLE LA
STATION RD
St Michaels CE Primary School
LINCOLN LANE
MAIN ST
Thorpe on the Hill
SCHOOL LA 1
BLACKSMITH LA 2
WEST FIELD LA 3
SEMPERS CL4
FOSSE LANE
STONE LANE
Sheepwalks Farm
High Walks Farm
Sheepwalk
1 SQUIRREL CH
2 DOE CL
3 OWL CL
4 PARTRIDGE GN
1 RAVEN'S VW
2 MOORHEN CL
3 PENDRED AVE
Sewage Works
North Farm
LN5
Thurlby
New House North Farm
South Farm
MOOR LANE
Thurlby Moor
Church Farm
River Farm
River Farm
Sewage Works
CLAY LANE
Manor Farm
CARLTON ROAD
RINKS LANE

1 LITTLE THORPE LA
2 HOLME CL
A46
MIDDLE LANE
Motel
Jubilee Farm
Thorpe Grange Farm
Sky Barn Farm
HADDINGTON LANE
High Walks
Haddington
Corner Farm
DOVECOTE LA
BAILEYS LA
BUTTS LANE
Moats
Weir
MILL LANE
BRIDGE ROAD
BASSINGHAM ROAD
Moor Covert
North Farm
Northfield Farm
Witham Farm
River Farm
LINCOLN ROAD
BASSINGHAM ROAD
THURLBY RD
Thurlby Bridge
WATER LA
ORCHARD CL
LINGA LANE
CROFT
HALL LA
WITH RD
HIGH ST
PO
Recn Gd
Bassingham Prim Sch
Savages Farm
Bassingham
1 HIGH ST
2 EASTGATE
3 EAST FIELD
4 BROCKLEBANK CL
5 TORGATE AVE
6 LIME GR
1 BAKERS LA
2 WHITES LA
OLD BRICKKILN LA
QUEEN HEADLAND LA
Carlton-le-Moorland
SANDS LA
BROUGHTON RD
BASSINGHAM RD
MIDDLEGATE LA

86 A 87 B 88 C 89 D 90 E 91 F

E1
1 WESTHALL CL
2 WHEATLEY LA
3 GRANGE CT
4 VICARAGE LA

F3
1 BLACKSMITH ROW
2 BADGERS OAK
3 CHESTNUT CRES
4 HAWTHORN WY
5 MAPLE DR
6 HOLMES FIELD

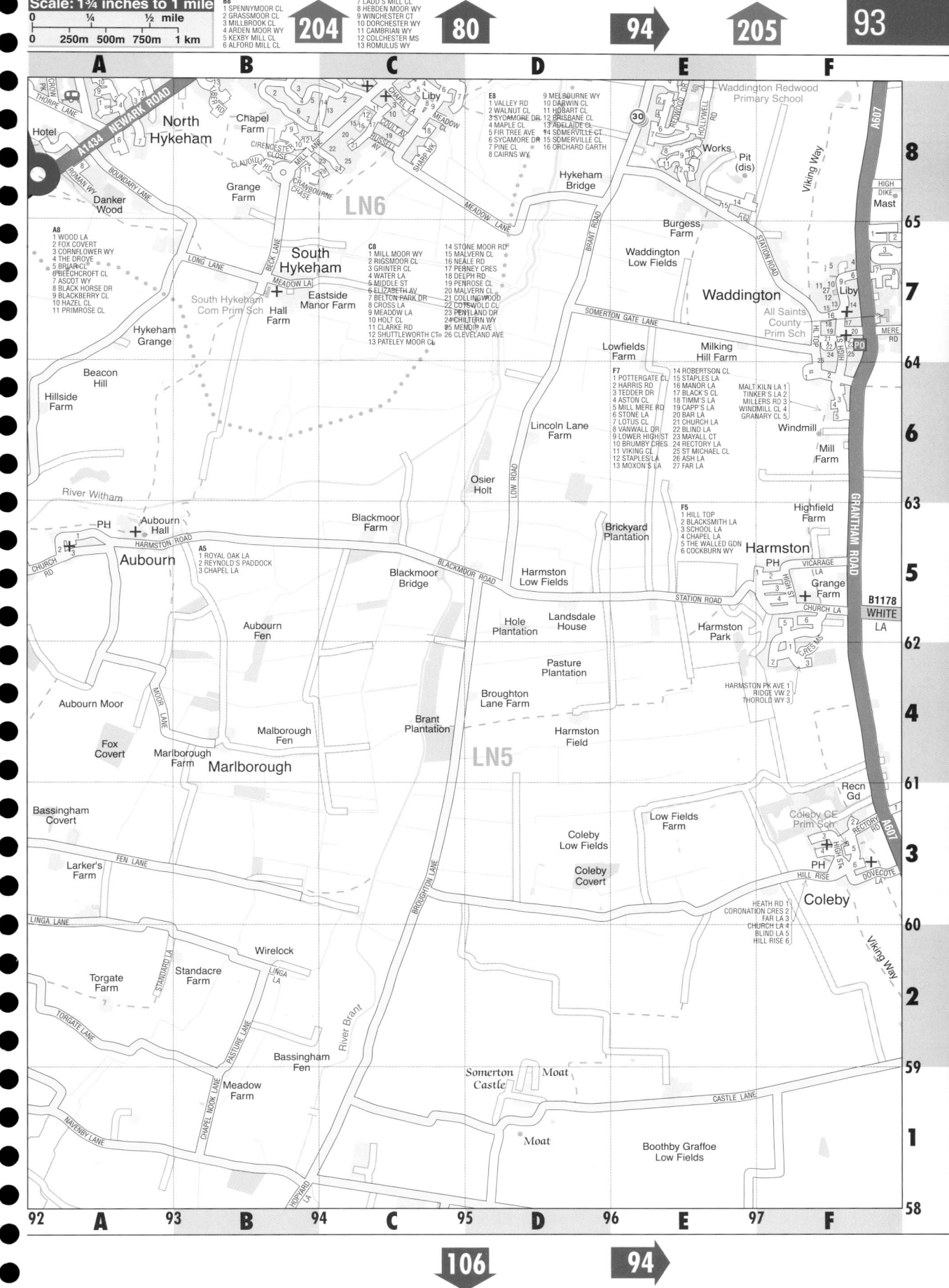

B8
1 SPENNYMOOR CL
2 GRASSMOOR CL
3 MILLBROOK CL
4 ARDEN MOOR WY
5 KEXBY MILL CL
6 ALFORD MILL CL
7 LADD'S MILL CL
8 HEBDEN MOOR WY
9 WINCHESTER CT
10 DORCHESTER WY
11 CAMBRIAN CL
12 COLCHESTER MS
13 ROMULUS WY

204   80   94   205

A8
1 WOOD LA
2 FOX COVERT
3 CORNFLOWER WY
4 THE DROVE
5 BRIAR CL
6 BEECHCROFT CL
7 ASCOT WY
8 BLACK HORSE DR
9 BLACKBERRY CL
10 HAZEL CL
11 PRIMROSE CL

E8
1 VALLEY RD
2 WALNUT CL
3 SYCAMORE DR
4 MAPLE CL
5 FIR TREE AVE
6 SYCAMORE DR
7 PINE CL
8 CAIRNS WY
9 MELBOURNE WY
10 DARWIN CL
11 HOBART CL
12 BRISBANE CL
13 ADELAIDE CL
14 SOMERVILLE CT
15 SOMERVILLE MS
16 ORCHARD GARTH

C8
1 MILL MOOR WY
2 RIGSMOOR CL
3 GRINTER CL
4 WATER LA
5 MIDDLE ST
6 ELIZABETH AV
7 BELTON PARK DR
8 CROSS LA
9 MEADOW LA
10 HOLT CL
11 CLARKE RD
12 SHUTTLEWORTH CT
13 PATELEY MOOR CL
14 STONE MOOR RD
15 MALVERN CL
16 NEALE RD
17 PERNEY CRES
18 DELPH RD
19 PENROSE CL
20 MALVERN CL
21 COLLINGWOOD
22 COTSWOLD CL
23 PENTLAND DR
24 CHILTERN WY
25 MENDIP AVE
26 CLEVELAND AVE

F7
1 POTTERGATE CL
2 HARRIS RD
3 TEDDER DR
4 ASTON CL
5 MILL MERE RD
6 STONE LA
7 LOTUS CL
8 VANWALL DR
9 LOWER HIGH ST
10 BRUMBY CRES
11 VIKING CL
12 STAPLES LA
13 MOXON'S LA
14 ROBERTSON CL
15 STAPLES LA
16 MANOR LA
17 BLACK'S CL
18 TIMM'S LA
19 CAPP'S LA
20 BAR LA
21 CHURCH LA
22 BLIND LA
23 MAYALL CT
24 RECTORY LA
25 ST MICHAEL CL
26 ASH LA
27 FAR LA

MALT KILN LA 1
TINKER'S LA 2
MILLERS RD 3
WINDMILL CL 4
GRANARY CL 5

F5
1 HILL TOP
2 BLACKSMITH LA
3 SCHOOL LA
4 CHAPEL LA
5 THE WALLED GDN
6 COCKBURN WY

A5
1 ROYAL OAK LA
2 REYNOLD'S PADDOCK
3 CHAPEL LA

HARMSTON PK AVE 1
RIDGE VW 2
THOROLD WY 3

HEATH RD 1
CORONATION CRES 2
FAR LA 3
CHURCH LA 4
BLIND LA 5
HILL RISE 6

North Hykeham
South Hykeham
Waddington
Harmston
Aubourn
Marlborough
Coleby

LN6
LN5

River Witham
River Brant

Somerton Castle

Boothby Graffoe
Low Fields

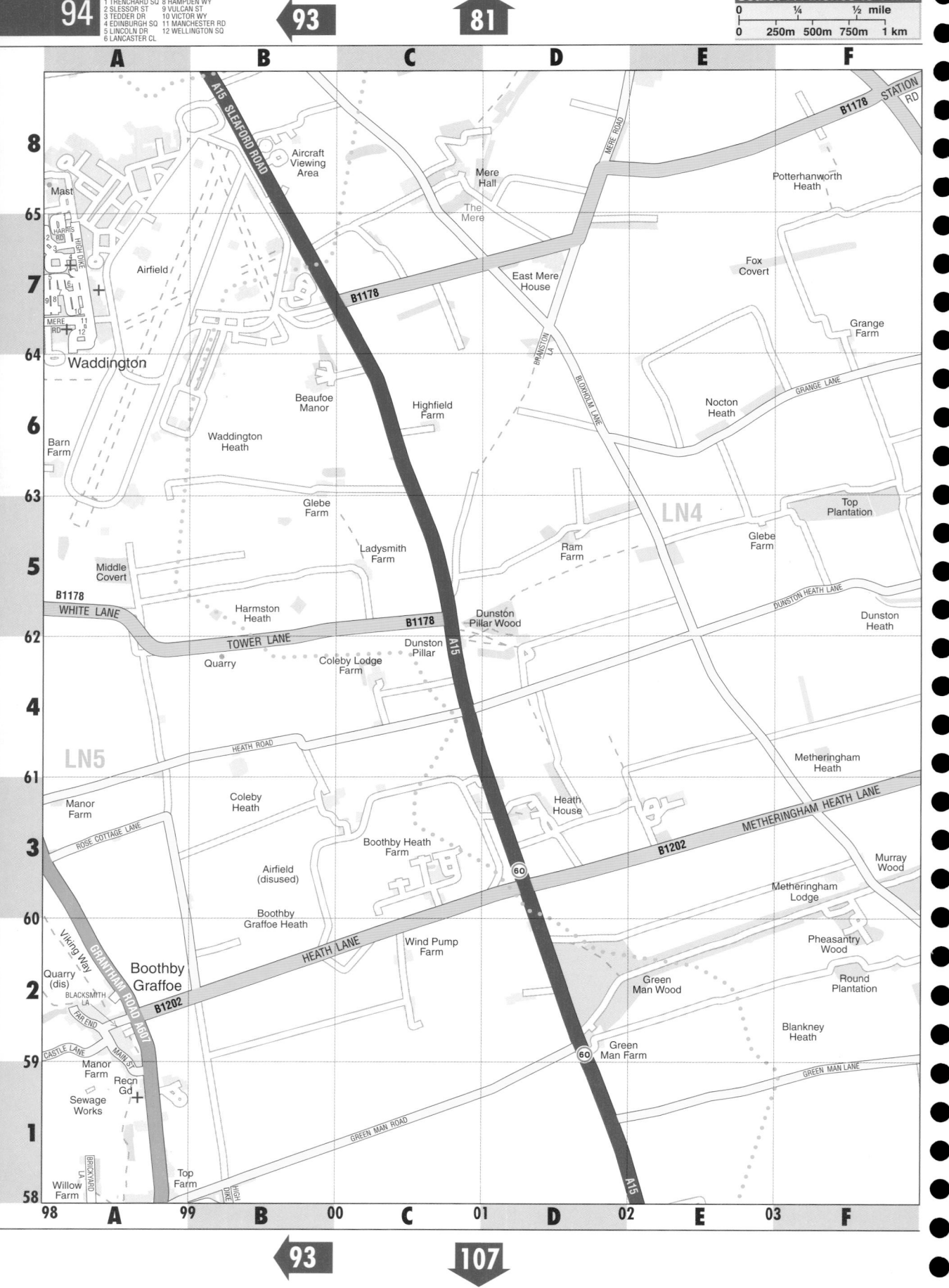

A7
1 TRENCHARD SQ   7 VALLIANT ST
2 SLESSOR ST   8 HAMPDEN WY
3 TEDDER DR   9 VULCAN ST
4 EDINBURGH SQ   10 VICTOR WY
5 LINCOLN DR   11 MANCHESTER RD
6 LANCASTER CL   12 WELLINGTON SQ

93
81

Scale: 1¾ inches to 1 mile
0   ¼   ½   mile
0   250m   500m   750m   1 km

A   B   C   D   E   F

8
65
7
64
6
63
5
62
4
61
3
60
2
59
1
58

98   A   99   B   00   C   01   D   02   E   03   F

A15 SLEAFORD ROAD

Aircraft Viewing Area

Mast

HARRIS RD
HIGH DIKE
MERE RD
Waddington

Airfield

B1178

Mere Hall

The Mere

East Mere House

MERE ROAD

Potterhanworth Heath

Fox Covert

Grange Farm

BRANSTON LA

BLOXHOLM LANE

GRANGE LANE

Nocton Heath

LN4

Top Plantation

Glebe Farm

Beaufoe Manor

Highfield Farm

Waddington Heath

Barn Farm

Glebe Farm

Ladysmith Farm

Ram Farm

Middle Covert

B1178

WHITE LANE

Harmston Heath

TOWER LANE

B1178

Dunston Pillar Wood

Dunston Heath Lane

Dunston Heath

Quarry

Coleby Lodge Farm

Dunston Pillar

A15

LN5

HEATH ROAD

Metheringham Heath

Manor Farm

ROSE COTTAGE LANE

Coleby Heath

Heath House

METHERINGHAM HEATH LANE

Airfield (disused)

Boothby Heath Farm

60

B1202

Murray Wood

Boothby Graffoe Heath

HEATH LANE

Wind Pump Farm

Metheringham Lodge

Viking Way

GRANTHAM ROAD A607

Boothby Graffoe

Quarry (dis)

BLACKSMITH LA

FAIR END

B1202

Green Man Wood

Pheasantry Wood

Round Plantation

Blankney Heath

CASTLE LANE

MAIN ST

Manor Farm

Recn Gd

60

Green Man Farm

GREEN MAN LANE

Sewage Works

BRICKYARD LA

Willow Farm

Top Farm

HIGH DIKE

GREEN MAN ROAD

A15

Scale: 1¾ inches to 1 mile

0 ¼ ½ mile

0 250m 500m 750m 1 km

82
96

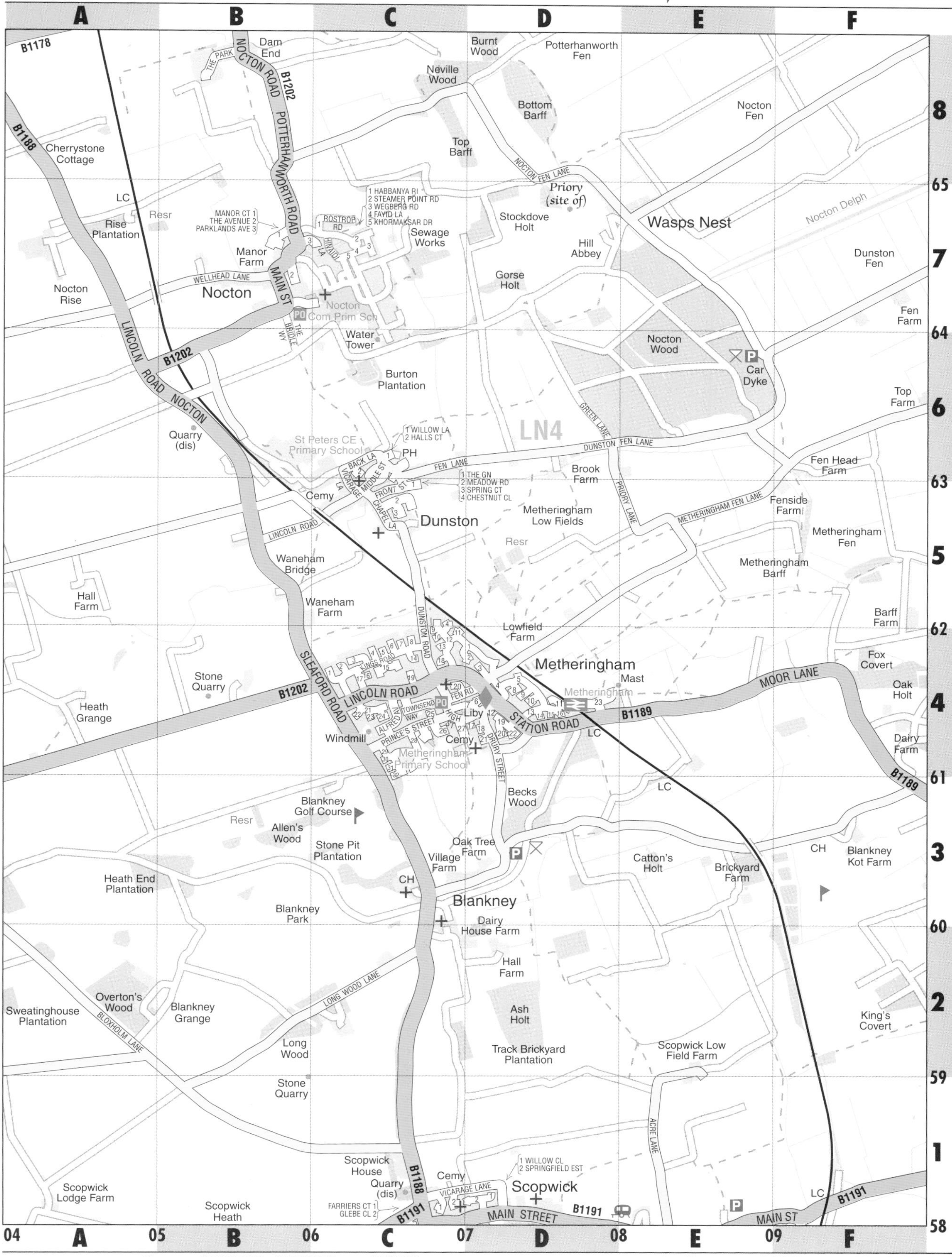

C4
1 BENTLEY WY
2 FLINTHAM CL
3 ASHDALE CL
4 SARGENT CL
5 FLINDERS CL
6 DE WINT CL
7 FRANKLIN CL
8 NEWTON CL
9 THE CHASE
10 BLACKSMITH CT
11 SADDLER'S CL
12 SHIREGATE
13 HUNTERS DR
14 TENNYSON CL
15 WESLEY CL
16 ROWAN WY
17 CHERRY TREE WY
18 ROSSINGTON CL
19 APPLE TREE CL
20 LIME TREE AVE
21 MILLFIELD RD
22 GRANARY CL
23 HARVEST CL
24 BARLEY CL
25 ORCHARD CL
26 HALL YD
27 CHURCH WK
28 PRINCESS MARGARET AVE
29 HIGHFIELDS RISE
30 NORMAN CL
31 DANE CL
32 VIKING WY

108
96

D4
1 PADDOCK LA
2 CAVALRY CTFIELD
3 FIELD FARM LA
4 GRANGE RD
5 CAROLINE RD
6 MEADOW CL
7 MIDDLE ST
8 WESTFIELD CL
9 ROMAN CL
10 SAXON CL
11 PULLMAN CL
12 MORDEN CL
13 LONDESBOROUGH WY
14 MANOR CL
15 ALEXANDER CL
16 PARK CRES
17 CHURCH LA
18 ST WILFRID'S CL
19 LONDESBOROUGH WY
20 SKIPWITH CRES
21 CHURCH WK
22 CHAPLIN CL
23 THE MOORLANDS

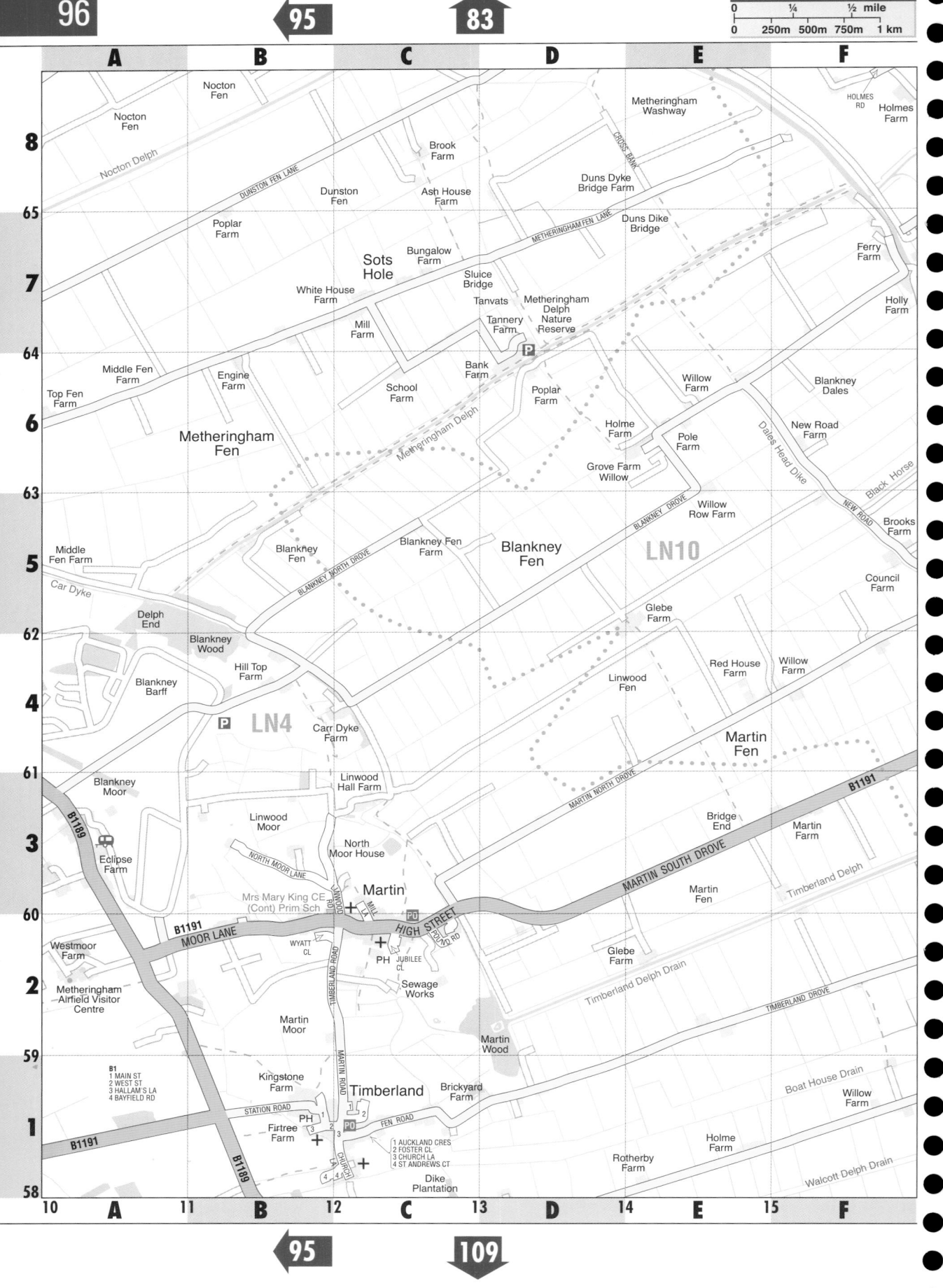

A B C D E F

8

65

7

64

6

63

5

62

4

61

3

60

2

59

1

58

Nocton Fen

Nocton Fen

Nocton Delph

Middle Fen Farm

Top Fen Farm

Metheringham Fen

Middle Fen Farm

Car Dyke

Delph End

Blankney Barff

Blankney Moor

B1189

Eclipse Farm

Westmoor Farm

Metheringham Airfield Visitor Centre

DUNSTON FEN LANE

Dunston Fen Lane

Poplar Farm

Engine Farm

Blankney Wood

Hill Top Farm

LN4

North Moor Lane

NORTH MOOR LANE

Linwood Moor

Dunston Fen

White House Farm

Mill Farm

School Farm

Blankney Fen

Delph

B1191

MOOR LANE

Martin Moor

Kingstone Farm

STATION ROAD

Firtree Farm

B1189

Brook Farm

Ash House Farm

Sots Hole

Bungalow Farm

Sluice Bridge

Tanvats

Bank Farm

Metheringham Delph

Blankney Fen Farm

Carr Dyke Farm

Linwood Hall Farm

North Moor House

Martin

Mrs Mary King CE (Cont) Prim Sch

WYATT CL

TIMBERLAND ROAD

MARTIN ROAD

WEST ST

Timberland

PH

PO

FEN ROAD

CHURCH

Dike Plantation

B1
1 MAIN ST
2 WEST ST
3 HALLAM'S LA
4 BAYFIELD RD

Metheringham Washway

CROSS BANK

Duns Dyke Bridge Farm

METHERINGHAM FEN LANE

Duns Dike Bridge

Tannery Farm

Metheringham Delph Nature Reserve

P

Poplar Farm

Holme Farm

Grove Farm Willow

Blankney Fen

BLANKNEY NORTH DROVE

Willow Farm

Pole Farm

BLANKNEY DROVE

LN10

Willow Row Farm

Linwood Fen

Glebe Farm

Red House Farm

Willow Farm

Martin Fen

MARTIN NORTH DROVE

Bridge End

Glebe Farm

MARTIN SOUTH DROVE

Martin Fen

Sewage Works

Martin Wood

Brickyard Farm

JUBILEE CL

HIGH STREET

PO

PH

MILL LA

LINWOOD RD

POND RD

Rotherby Farm

1 AUCKLAND CRES
2 FOSTER CL
3 CHURCH LA
4 ST ANDREWS CT

HOLMES RD

Holmes Farm

Ferry Farm

Holly Farm

Blankney Dales

New Road Farm

Dales Head Dike

Black Horse

NEW ROAD

Brooks Farm

Council Farm

B1191

Martin Farm

Timberland Delph

Timberland Delph Drain

TIMBERLAND DROVE

Boat House Drain

Willow Farm

Holme Farm

Walcott Delph Drain

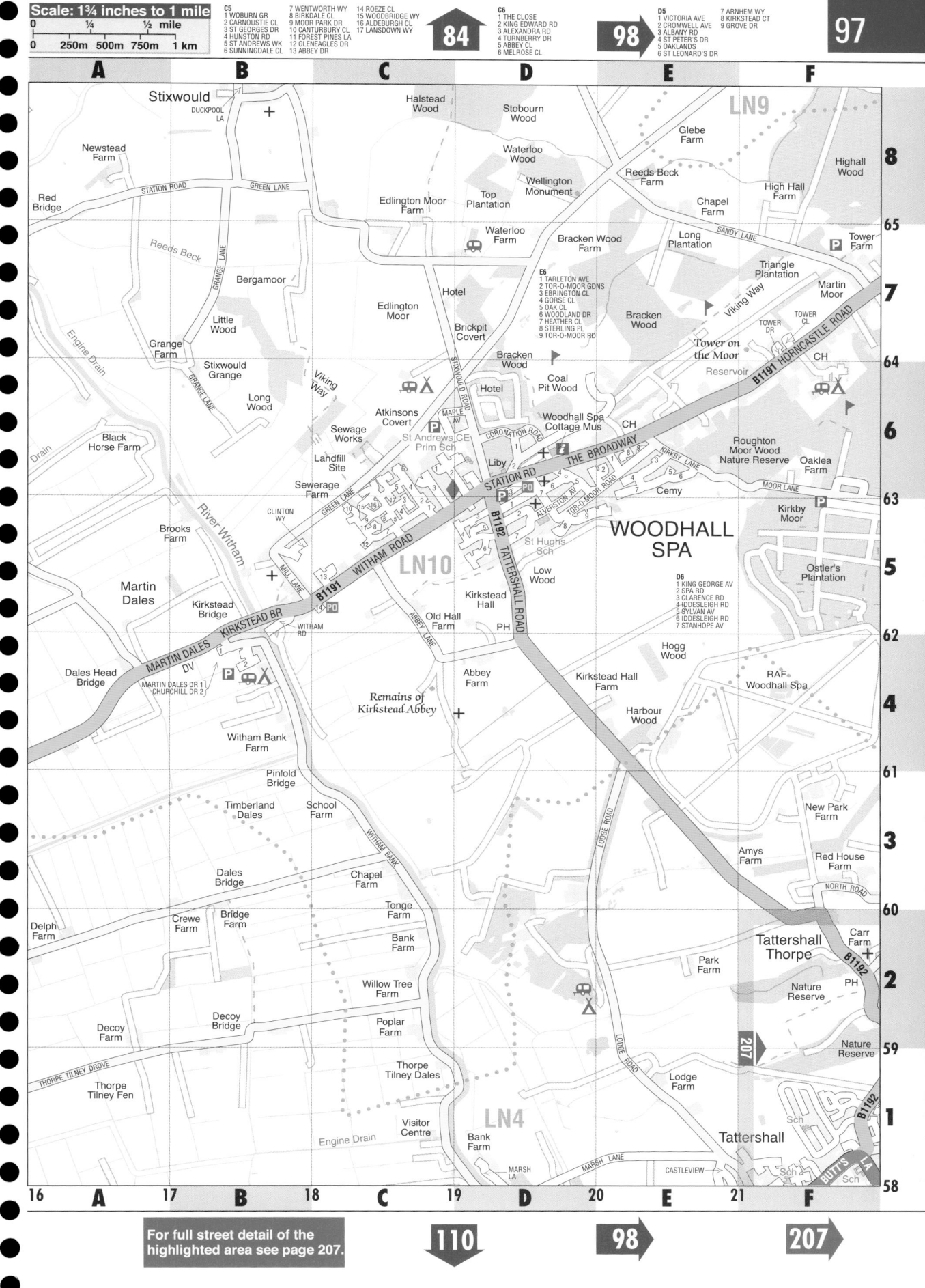

Scale: 1¾ inches to 1 mile

0 ¼ ½ mile
0 250m 500m 750m 1 km

C5
1 WOBURN GR
2 CARNOUSTIE CL
3 ST GEORGES DR
4 HUNSTON RD
5 ST ANDREWS WK
6 SUNNINGDALE CL

7 WENTWORTH WY
8 BIRKDALE CL
9 MOOR PARK DR
10 CANTURBURY CL
11 FOREST PINES LA
12 GLENEAGLES DR
13 ABBEY DR

14 ROEZE CL
15 WOODBRIDGE WY
16 ALDEBURGH CL
17 LANSDOWN WY

C6
1 THE CLOSE
2 KING EDWARD RD
3 ALEXANDRA RD
4 TURNBERRY DR
5 ABBEY CL
6 MELROSE CL

D5
1 VICTORIA AVE
2 CROMWELL AVE
3 ALBANY RD
4 ST PETER'S DR
5 ST LEONARD'S DR

7 ARNHEM WY
8 KIRKSTEAD CT
9 GROVE DR

84

98

E6
1 TARLETON AVE
2 TOR-O-MOOR GDNS
3 EBRINGTON CL
4 GORSE CL
5 OAK CL
6 WOODLAND DR
7 HEATHER CL
8 STERLING PL
9 TOR-O-MOOR RD

D6
1 KING GEORGE AV
2 SPA RD
3 CLARENCE RD
4 IDDESLEIGH RD
5 SYLVAN AV
6 IDDESLEIGH RD
7 STANHOPE AV

For full street detail of the highlighted area see page 207.

110

98

207

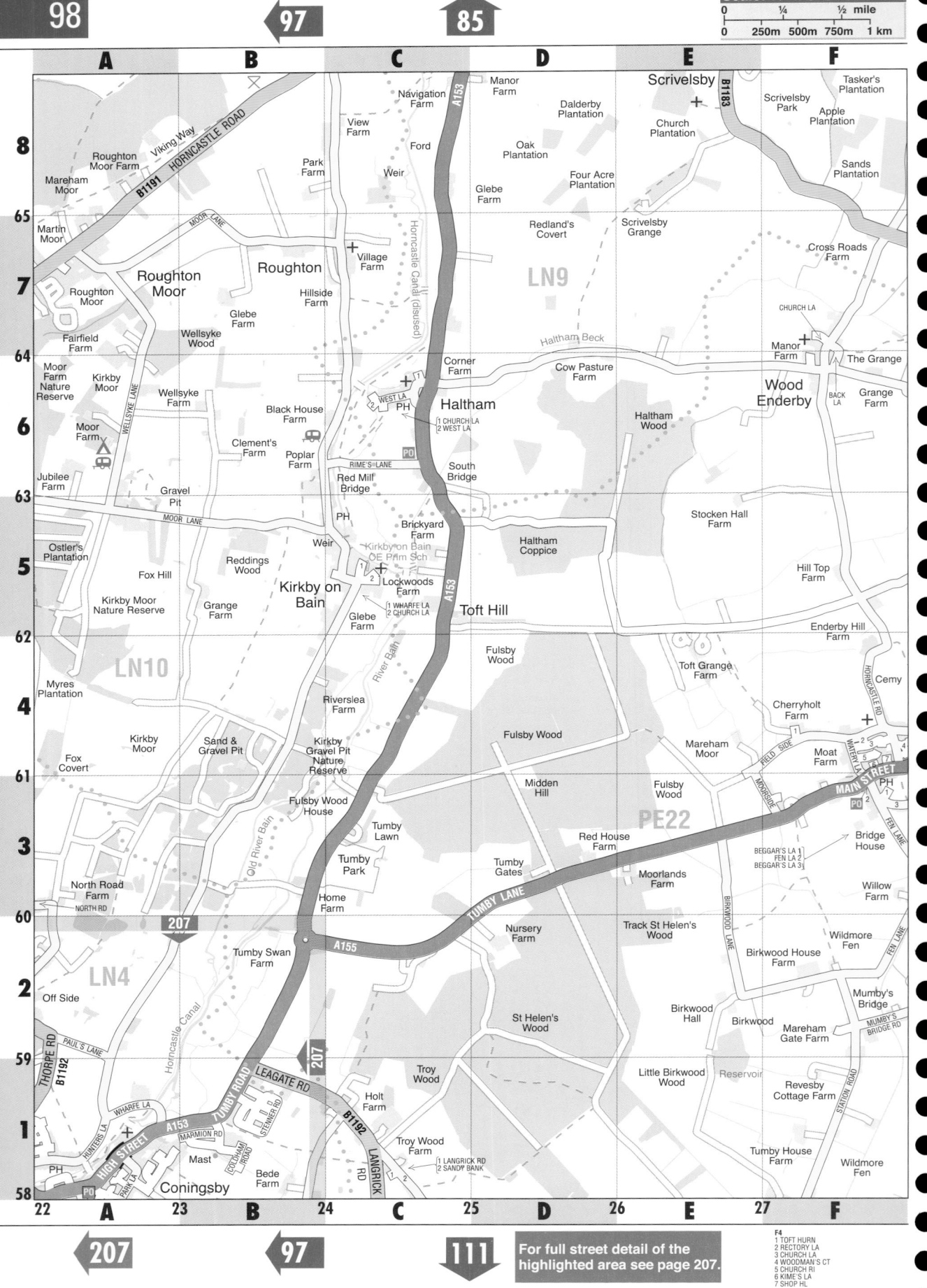

A B C D E F

8

65

7

64

6

63

5

62

4

61

3

60

2

59

1

58

22 23 24 25 26 27

Viking Way
HORNCASTLE ROAD
B1191

Mareham Moor

Roughton Moor Farm

Martin Moor

Roughton Moor

Roughton Moor

Fairfield Farm

Moor Farm Nature Reserve

Kirkby Moor

Moor Farm

Jubilee Farm

Ostler's Plantation

LN10

Myres Plantation

Fox Covert

Kirkby Moor

North Road Farm
NORTH RD

LN4

Off Side

THORPE RD
B1192
PAUL'S LANE

HUNTERS LA
WHARFE LA
A153
MARMION RD

PH

PO

Coningsby

Mast

Bede Farm

HIGH STREET
PARK LA
DOCKHAM ROAD
STEMMER RD
LEAGATE RD

TUMBY ROAD
207

Horncastle Canal

MOOR LANE

Roughton

Glebe Farm

Wellsyke Wood

Wellsyke Farm

WELLSYKE LANE

Black House Farm

Clement's Farm

Poplar Farm

Gravel Pit

MOOR LANE

Reddings Wood

Fox Hill

Kirkby Moor Nature Reserve

Grange Farm

Sand & Gravel Pit

Kirkby Gravel Pit Nature Reserve

Fulsby Wood House

Tumby Park

Tumby Lawn

Home Farm

Tumby Swan Farm

Old River Bain

Horncastle Canal

B1192
LANGRICK RD

Holt Farm

Troy Wood Farm

1 LANGRICK RD
2 SANDY BANK

Navigation Farm

View Farm

Park Farm

Ford

Weir

A153

Village Farm

Hillside Farm

Horncastle Canal (disused)

WEST LA
PH
1 CHURCH LA
2 WEST LA

Haltham

Corner Farm

RIME'S LANE

Red Mill Bridge

South Bridge

Brickyard Farm

Weir

PH

Kirkby on Bain

Kirkby on Bain CE Prim Sch

1
2
Lockwoods Farm
1 WHARFE LA
2 CHURCH LA

Glebe Farm

River Bain

A155

Riverslea Farm

Tumby Gates

A155

207

Tumby Lawn

Manor Farm

Dalderby Plantation

Oak Plantation

Glebe Farm

Redland's Covert

LN9

Haltham Beck

Cow Pasture Farm

Haltham Wood

Haltham Coppice

PO
A153

Toft Hill

Fulsby Wood

Midden Hill

Fulsby Wood

Fulsby Wood

Red House Farm

Tumby Gates

Moorlands Farm

Nursery Farm

Track
St Helen's Wood

St Helen's Wood

Troy Wood

Scrivelsby

Church Plantation

Scrivelsby Park

B1183

Scrivelsby Grange

Four Acre Plantation

Tasker's Plantation

Apple Plantation

Sands Plantation

Cross Roads Farm

CHURCH LA

Manor Farm

Wood Enderby

BACK LA

The Grange

Grange Farm

Stocken Hall Farm

Hill Top Farm

Enderby Hill Farm

Toft Grange Farm

Cherryholt Farm

Mareham Moor

Moat Farm

FIELD SIDE

MONSON

BIRKWOOD LANE

HORNCASTLE RD

Cemy

WATER LA

MAIN STREET
PH
PO

BEGGAR'S LA 1
FEN LA 2
BEGGAR'S LA 3

PE22

Bridge House

Willow Farm

Wildmore Fen

Mumby's Bridge

MUMBY'S BRIDGE RD

Birkwood House Fen

STATION ROAD
FEN LANE

Birkwood Hall

Birkwood

Mareham Gate Farm

Little Birkwood Wood

Reservoir

Revesby Cottage Farm

Tumby House Farm

Wildmore Fen

For full street detail of the highlighted area see page 207.

F4
1 TOFT HURN
2 RECTORY LA
3 CHURCH LA
4 WOODMAN'S CT
5 CHURCH RI
6 KIME'S LA
7 SHOP HL

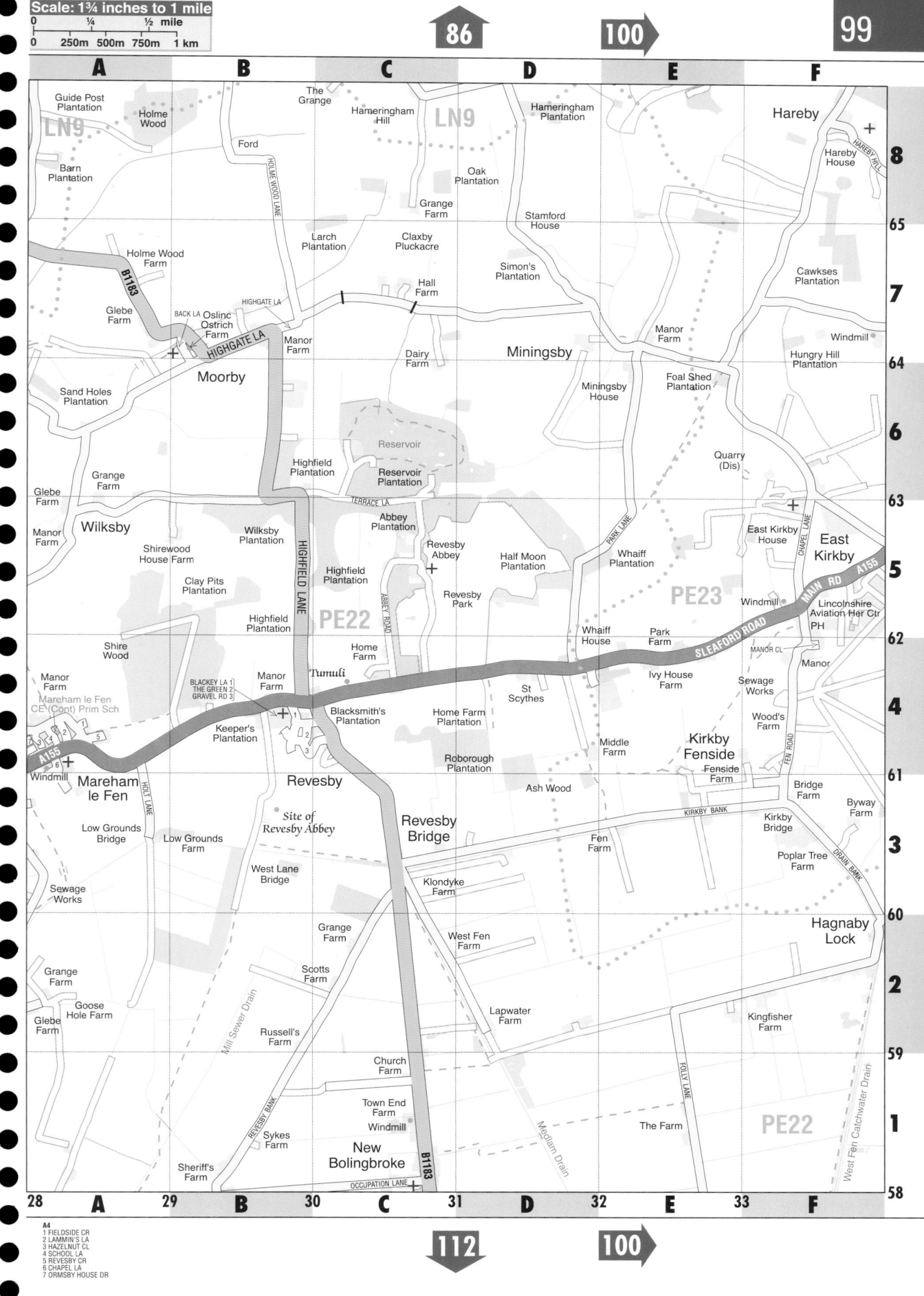

Scale: 1¾ inches to 1 mile

0   ¼   ½   mile
0   250m 500m 750m 1 km

A   **B**   **C**   **D**   **E**   **F**

Guide Post Plantation

Holme Wood

The Grange

Hameringham Hill

LN9

Hameringham Plantation

Hareby

8

LN9

Ford

Oak Plantation

Hareby House

Barn Plantation

Grange Farm

Stamford House

65

B1183

Holme Wood Farm

Larch Plantation

Claxby Pluckacre

Simon's Plantation

Cawkses Plantation

7

Glebe Farm

BACK LA Oslinc Ostrich Farm

HIGHGATE LA

Hall Farm

Manor Farm

Windmill

Moorby

HIGHGATE LA

Manor Farm

Dairy Farm

Miningsby

Hungry Hill Plantation

64

Sand Holes Plantation

Foal Shed Plantation

6

Reservoir

Miningsby House

Quarry (Dis)

Glebe Farm

Grange Farm

Highfield Plantation

Reservoir Plantation

63

TERRACE LA

Manor Farm

Wilksby

Wilksby Plantation

Abbey Plantation

Revesby Abbey

Half Moon Plantation

PARK LANE

Whaiff Plantation

East Kirkby House

East Kirkby

CHAPEL LANE

MAIN RD A155

5

Shirewood House Farm

Highfield Plantation

ABBEY ROAD

HIGHFIELD LANE

Revesby Park

PE23

Windmill

Lincolnshire Aviation Her Ctr PH

Clay Pits Plantation

Highfield Plantation

PE22

Home Farm

Whaiff House

Park Farm

SLEAFORD ROAD

MANOR CL

62

Shire Wood

Tumuli

Ivy House Farm

Sewage Works

Manor

Manor Farm

BLACKEY LA 1
THE GREEN 2
GRAVEL RD 3

Manor Farm

Blacksmith's Plantation

St Scythes

FEN ROAD

Wood's Farm

4

Mareham le Fen CE (Cont) Prim Sch

Keeper's Plantation

Home Farm Plantation

Middle Farm

Kirkby Fenside

A155

Windmill

Mareham le Fen

HOLT LANE

Revesby

Roborough Plantation

Ash Wood

Fenside Farm

Bridge Farm

Byway Farm

61

Revesby Bridge

KIRKBY BANK

Kirkby Bridge

DRAIN BANK

Low Grounds Bridge

Low Grounds Farm

Site of Revesby Abbey

Fen Farm

Poplar Tree Farm

3

Sewage Works

West Lane Bridge

Klondyke Farm

Hagnaby Lock

60

Grange Farm

Grange Farm

Scotts Farm

West Fen Farm

Kingfisher Farm

2

Goose Hole Farm

Mill Sewer Drain

Russell's Farm

Lapwater Farm

FOLLY LANE

Glebe Farm

REVESBY BANK

Church Farm

59

Sykes Farm

Town End Farm

Windmill

The Farm

PE22

1

Sheriff's Farm

New Bolingbroke

B1183

Meridian Drain

West Fen Catchwater Drain

OCCUPATION LANE

58

28   **A**   29   **B**   30   **C**   31   **D**   32   **E**   33   **F**

A4
1 FIELDSIDE CR
2 LAMMIN'S LA
3 HAZELNUT CL
4 SCHOOL LA
5 REVESBY CR
6 CHAPEL LA
7 ORMSBY HOUSE DR

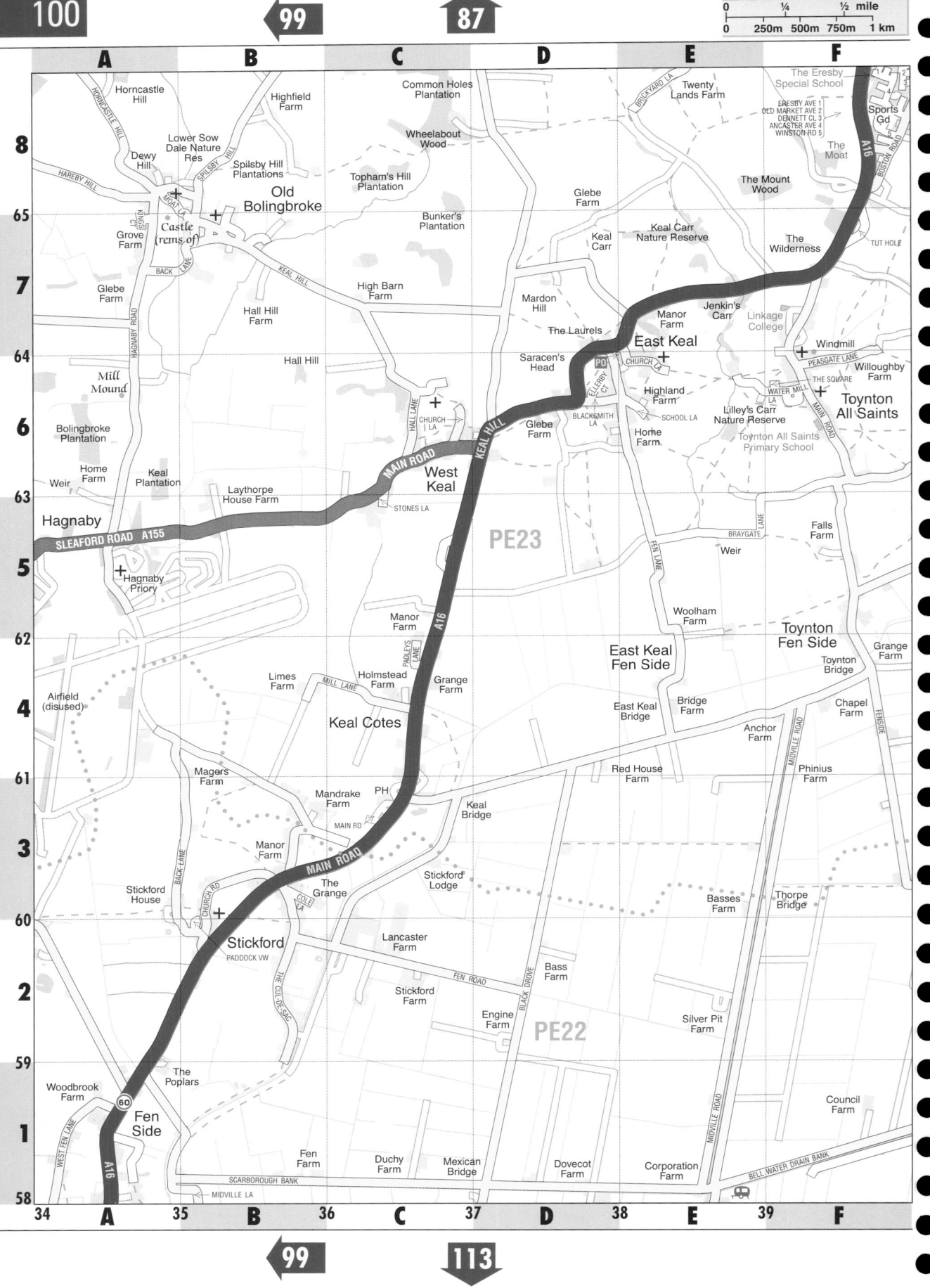

Scale: 1¾ inches to 1 mile

0   ¼   ½ mile
0   250m 500m 750m 1 km

A **B** **C** **D** **E** **F**

Horncastle Hill
Horncastle Hill

Highfield Farm

Common Holes Plantation

Brickyard La
Twenty Lands Farm

The Eresby Special School

ERESBY AVE 1
OLD MARKET AVE 2
DENNETT CL 3
ANCASTER AVE 4
WINSTON RD 5

Sports Gd

8

Dewy Hill

Lower Sow Dale Nature Res

Spilsby Hill Plantations

Wheelabout Wood

Topham's Hill Plantation

Glebe Farm

The Moat

65

Castle (rems of)

MOAT LA

Old Bolingbroke

SPILSBY HILL

Bunker's Plantation

Keal Carr

Keal Carr Nature Reserve

The Wilderness

The Mount Wood

7

Grove Farm

KINGS

BACK LANE

KEAL HILL

High Barn Farm

Mardon Hill

Keal Carr

Manor Farm

Jenkin's Carr

Linkage College

TUT HOLE

64

Glebe Farm

Hall Hill Farm

Hall Hill

The Laurels

Saracen's Head

East Keal

Windmill

PEASGATE LANE

Willoughby Farm

6

HAGNABY ROAD

CHURCH LA

HALL LANE

Glebe Farm

PO

CHURCH LA

ELLERBY CT

BLACKSMITH LA

Highland Farm

SCHOOL LA

Water Mill

Lilley's Carr Nature Reserve

THE SQUARE

Toynton All Saints

Mill Mound

Bolingbroke Plantation

West Keal

Home Farm

Toynton All Saints Primary School

63

Weir

Home Farm

Keal Plantation

Laythorpe House Farm

MAIN ROAD

STONES LA

Glebe Farm

BRAYGATE

LANE

Falls Farm

Hagnaby

SLEAFORD ROAD A155

PE23

FEN LANE

Weir

5

Hagnaby Priory

PADLEY'S LANE

A16

Manor Farm

Woolham Farm

Toynton Fen Side

62

Limes Farm

MILL LANE

Holmstead Farm

Grange Farm

East Keal Fen Side

East Keal Bridge

Bridge Farm

Toynton Bridge

Grange Farm

4

Airfield (disused)

Keal Cotes

Anchor Farm

MIDVILLE ROAD

Chapel Farm

FENSIDE

61

Magers Farm

Mandrake Farm

PH

Keal Bridge

Red House Farm

Phinius Farm

3

BACK LANE

Manor Farm

MAIN RD

MAIN ROAD

Stickford Lodge

Basses Farm

Thorpe Bridge

60

CHURCH RD

Stickford House

The Grange

COLE LA

Lancaster Farm

Bass Farm

Stickford

PADDOCK VW

THE CUL-DE-SAC

FEN ROAD

2

Stickford Farm

BLACK DROVE

Silver Pit Farm

PE22

59

Woodbrook Farm

The Poplars

Engine Farm

Corporation Farm

Council Farm

1

60

A16

Fen Side

WEST FEN LANE

Fen Farm

Duchy Farm

Mexican Bridge

Dovecot Farm

BELL WATER DRAIN BANK

58

SCARBOROUGH BANK

MIDVILLE LA

34 **A** **35** **B** **36** **C** **37** **D** **38** **E** **39** **F**

88
102

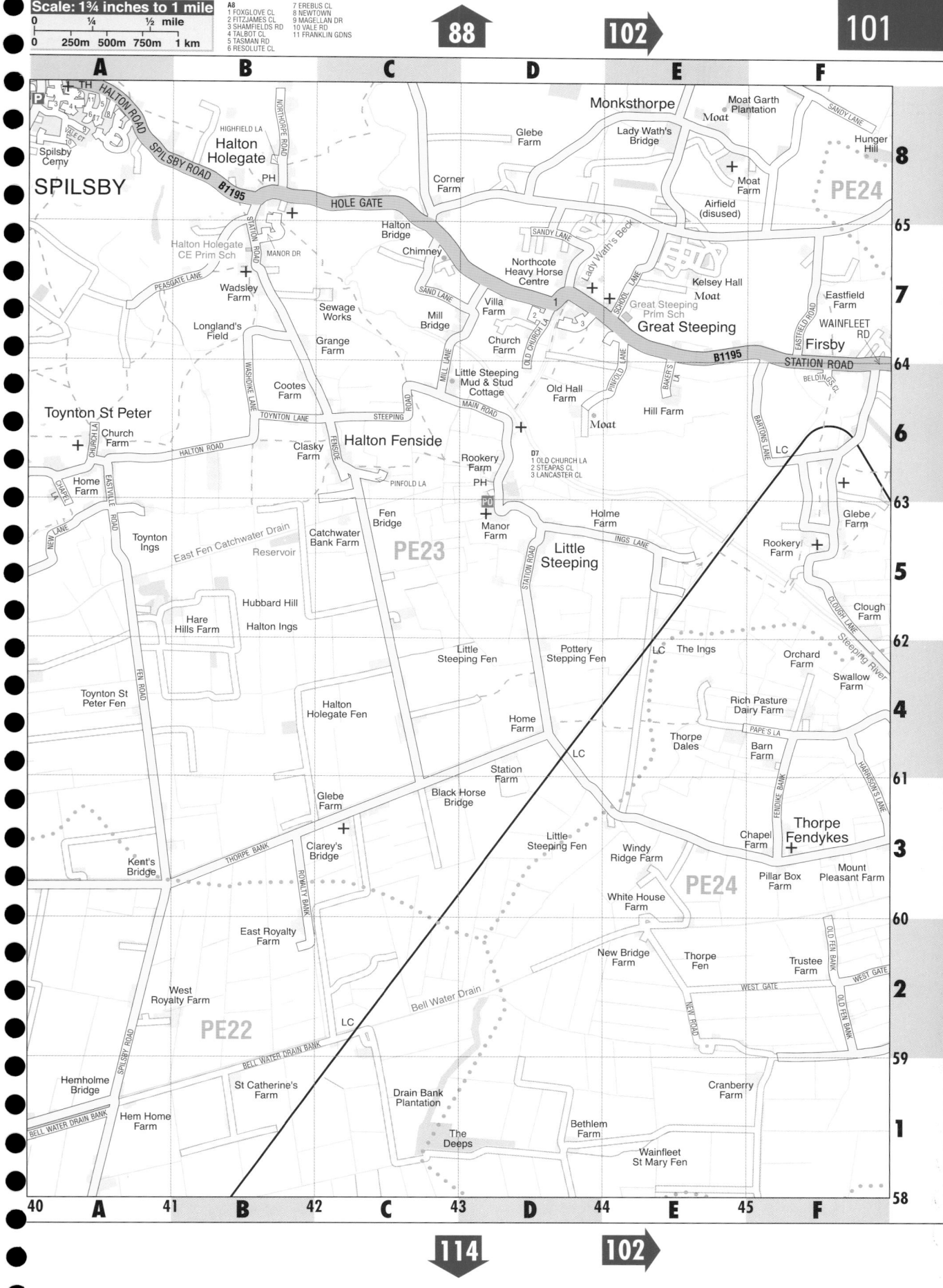
Scale: 1¾ inches to 1 mile
0 ¼ ½ mile
0 250m 500m 750m 1 km
A8
1 FOXGLOVE CL
2 FITZJAMES CL
3 SHAMFIELDS RD
4 TALBOT CL
5 TASMAN RD
6 RESOLUTE CL
7 EREBUS CL
8 NEWTOWN
9 MAGELLAN DR
10 VALE RD
11 FRANKLIN GDNS
A
B
C
D
E
F
TH
HALTON ROAD
VALE CT
Spilsby Cemy
SPILSBY
SPILSBY ROAD
B1195
HIGHFIELD LA
Halton Holegate
NORTHORPE ROAD
PH
HOLE GATE
STATION ROAD
MANOR DR
Halton Holegate CE Prim Sch
PEASGATE LANE
Wadsley Farm
Longland's Field
Sewage Works
Grange Farm
Halton Bridge
Chimney
Corner Farm
Glebe Farm
Monksthorpe
Lady Wath's Bridge
Moat
Moat Garth Plantation
SANDY LANE
Hunger Hill
Moat Farm
Airfield (disused)
PE24
SANDY LANE
Lady Wath's Beck
Northcote Heavy Horse Centre
SAND LANE
Mill Bridge
Villa Farm
Church Farm
OLD CHURCH LA
SCHOOL LANE
Kelsey Hall
Moat
Great Steeping Prim Sch
Great Steeping
EASTFIELD ROAD
Eastfield Farm
WAINFLEET RD
Firsby
B1195
STATION ROAD
BELDINGS CL
PINFOLD LANE
BAKER'S LA
Hill Farm
Old Hall Farm
Moat
MILL LANE
Little Steeping Mud & Stud Cottage
MAIN ROAD
Cootes Farm
WASHDIKE LANE
TOYNTON LANE
STEEPING ROAD
Toynton St Peter
CHURCH LA
Church Farm
HALTON ROAD
Clasky Farm
FENSIDE
Halton Fenside
Rookery Farm
PH
D7
1 OLD CHURCH LA
2 STEAPAS CL
3 LANCASTER CL
BARTONS LANE
LC
PINFOLD LA
CHAPEL LA
Home Farm
EASTVILLE ROAD
PO
NEW LANE
Toynton Ings
East Fen Catchwater Drain
Reservoir
Catchwater Bank Farm
Fen Bridge
Manor Farm
PE23
Holme Farm
INGS LANE
Little Steeping
STATION ROAD
Glebe Farm
Rookery Farm
Clough Farm
CLOUGH LANE
Steeping River
Hubbard Hill
Hare Hills Farm
Halton Ings
Little Steeping Fen
Pottery Stepping Fen
LC
The Ings
Orchard Farm
Swallow Farm
Toynton St Peter Fen
FEN ROAD
Halton Holegate Fen
Home Farm
Rich Pasture Dairy Farm
Thorpe Dales
PAPE'S LA
Barn Farm
LC
Station Farm
HARRISON'S LANE
FENDIKE BANK
Glebe Farm
Black Horse Bridge
Little Steeping Fen
Chapel Farm
Thorpe Fendykes
Clarey's Bridge
THORPE BANK
Kent's Bridge
ROYALTY BANK
Windy Ridge Farm
Pillar Box Farm
Mount Pleasant Farm
PE24
White House Farm
East Royalty Farm
New Bridge Farm
Thorpe Fen
OLD FEN BANK
Trustee Farm
WEST GATE
WEST GATE
West Royalty Farm
Bell Water Drain
NEW ROAD
OLD FEN BANK
PE22
LC
SPILSBY ROAD
BELL WATER DRAIN BANK
Hemholme Bridge
St Catherine's Farm
Drain Bank Plantation
Cranberry Farm
BELL WATER DRAIN BANK
Hem Home Farm
The Deeps
Bethlem Farm
Wainfleet St Mary Fen
8
65
7
64
6
63
5
62
4
61
3
60
2
59
1
58
40
41
42
43
44
45

114
102

E7
1 CHURCH HILL
2 OLD CHAPEL LA
3 EAST END
4 BARNACK EST
5 WALLS AVE
6 CHAPMAN AVE
7 THE PADDOCKS
8 DAWSON DR
9 HOLDEN DR
10 CUMBERLIDGE CL
11 BEAUMONT CL
12 PARKERS CL
13 VENABLES CL
14 JOHNSON WY
15 Burgh le Marsh Mus

E8
1 CLAREMONT RD
2 KENNETH AVE
3 MARKET CL
4 JACKSONS LA
5 CHURCH ST
6 BREWERY ST
7 MARKET PL

Grid labels (top): A B C D E F
Grid labels (side): 8 65 7 64 6 63 5 62 4 61 3 60 2 59 1 58

PE23
Grange Farm
White Gate Farm
Bratoft
Manor Farm
NORTH ROAD
SANDY LA
GUNBY LANE
MILL LANE
BRAMBLEBERRY LANE
Moat
Buttoncap Holt
Elmstead Farm
White House Farm
Moat Farm
Moat
OXLANDS LANE
WONGS LANE
GREEN LA
INGS LANE
SUMMERGATES LA
GRAVEL PITS LANE
A158 STATION ROAD
Gatrum Farm
Woody Nook Farm
ORBY ROAD
WEST END
DOUBLEDAYS LA 1
WINDMILL DR 2
ST PETER'S CL 3
ELM CR 4
WILDSHED LANE
Windmill
St Peter & St Paul CE Prim School
ST PAULS CL 1
ASH CL 2
LINDEN DR 3
LIME CL 4
HALL LANE
WAINFLEET RD
Mill Hill Farm
Heath's Meadow Nature Reserve
Kirks Farm
COMMON LANE
Burgh Common
INGOLDMELLS ROAD
HIGH STREET
PO PH
Liby
Windmill
Burgh le Marsh
Long Plantation
BRATOFT CORNER
Pear Tree Farm
Willow Lodge
Motel
St Michaels Farm
MARSH LANE
BILLGATE LANE

Church Farm
Peartree Farm
B1195
Manor Farm
Irby in the Marsh
WAINFLEET ROAD
Lincoln Farm
PE23
The Ings
Millhill Bridge
LC
CLOUGH LA
Clough Bridge
Firsby Clough
Warth's Bridge
LC
Holly Farm
TIP LANE
CORR LANE
End House Farm
Grove House Farm
BRATOFT END
PE24
Mill Hill Farm
LYMN BANK
Lymn Bank Farm
White House Farm
SPILSBY ROAD
Thorpe St Peter
STATION ROAD
B1195
PH
GREEN LA
Old Hall Farm
Moat
WAINFLEET ROAD
Croft End
HIGH LANE
LOW LANE
Hollytrees Farm
Home Farm
New House Farm
The Hundreds
Oak Bridge
Jock Hedge
Blands Farm
The Hollies
Mast
Lloyds Farm
Catchwater Drain
LOW ROAD
Rivulet House
CROFT LANE
CHURCH LANE
PINCHBECK LANE
WASHDIKE LANE
Meml
Croft
CHURCH LA
SYCAMORE CL
Monson Farm
PH
Poplar Farm
Works
P
CROFT BANK
Bank House
CROFT MARSH LANE

Thorpe Fen
Thorpe Culvert
PH
LEAVER GATE
CULVERT ROAD
Thorpe Culvert
LC
LC
BREWSTER LANE
WEDLAND LANE
Florence Farm
Primrose Farm
Manor House Farm
CROFT ROAD
Tower Tree Farm
WAINCROFT CLOSE
Crown Farm
Havenhouse
New England

Whiteheads Farm
Watson Farm
WEST GATE
KING STREET
LADY LANE
BACK LA
Wainfleet Common
Church Farm
Crow's Bridge
CROW'S LA
COLLISON GATE
MAXPITTS LA
MILL LANE
LC
Magdalen Sch
Wainfleet All Saints
SPILSBY ROAD
Cemy
HIGH ST
CROFT BANK
SKEGNESS ROAD
Riverside Farm
White House Farm
Merrifield's Farm
Windsor Farm
MERRIFIELD RD

Wainfleet St Mary Fen
GREEN LA
Wainfleet Bank
OLD FEN BANK
CHURCH LANE
WASHDIKE LANE
LOW ROAD
Bateman's Brewery
VICARAGE LA
Magdalen Mus
Wainfleet
Liby
LC LC
STATION RD
DOVECOTE LA
BOSTON RD
B1195
A52
Low Grounds
QUEEN'S EST
HALL GATE
Low Farm

D1
1 ST JOHN ST
2 PATTEN AVE
3 RUMBOLD LA
4 ALL SAINTS CL
5 BARTON RD
6 SILVER ST
7 COLLEGE CL
8 HAVEN SIDE
9 BETHLEM CRES
10 TINDALL WY
11 ST MICHAEL'S LA

D2
1 BEES CR
2 STANLEY CL
3 HILL FIELD
4 HASTINGS DR
5 NEW END
6 MOUNT PLEASANT
7 BARKHAM ST
8 WINCHESTER RD

E2
1 CROFT BANK
2 BATEMANS CT
3 CROFT CL
4 MILL CL
5 SKEGNESS RD
6 MAWSON GDNS
7 MERRIFIELD RD

Scale: 1¾ inches to 1 mile

0   ¼   ½   mile
0   250m 500m 750m 1 km

| A | B | C | D | E | F |

8
65
7
64
6
63
5
62
4
61
3
60
2
59
1
58

YOUNGER'S LANE

Ingle Side

Burgh Marsh

Mill Hill Farm

Mill Hill

HIDE'S LANE

Grange Farm

EVERINGTON'S LANE

MIDDLEMARSH ROAD

MILL

206 Seathorne

CHURCH END

PH

Cemy

PH

CHURCH LANE

LADY MATILDA'S DR

MARTIN WY

Roydene Farm

Winthorpe

Sch

Recn Gd

Sea Bank

WINTHORPE AV

QUEEN'S DR

PO

P

GLEBE CL 1
HERON CL 2
KINGFISHER DR 3
COOTS CL 4
AYLESBURY DR 5

P
L Ctr
CH

North Shore Golf Course

KINGFISHER DR 1
MALLARD WY 2
SWAN DR 3
TEAL CL 4

A158

SKEGNESS ROAD

Coronation Farm

BURGH ROAD

Sundial Farm

DAVOS WAY

THE NEEDLES

BEACON WAY

PK DR

SKEGNESS

ROMAN BANK

Football Gd

A52

CH

Hotel

P

Middlemarsh Road

The Elms

Vine Farm

Mid Marsh Landfill Site

Middlemarsh Farm

PE25

WARTH LANE

TREFOIL DR

206

ALBANY WY
ALBANY RD
ALMA AVE

Coll

BURGH ROAD

A158

P

OLD ROMAN BANK

ST ANDREW'S DR

HOYLAKE DR
SWINNDALE DR

SEA VW
PULLOVER

206 64

B1528

LINCOLN ROAD

CH

DUTTON AV

REVESBY DR

HAYDON AV

QUEENS RD

Cemy

Sch

Schs

TH

Mag Ct

Fun City

Natureland Seal Sanctuary

Suncastle

Skegness Pier

NORTH PDE

PARK AV

GRAND PDE

N PDE

Council Farm

WAINFLEET ROAD

The Woodlands

ALGITHA RD

Mus

Skegness

H

IDA RD

RUTLAND RD

SCARBROUGH ESP

Embassy Centre

Swimming Pool

Panda's Palace

LUMLEY SQUARE

HIGH ST

TWR ESP

SOUTH PDE

SANDBECK PDE

LSch

PRINCES PDE

PO

P

Retreat Farm

Hollytree Farm Hotel

Petersfield Farm

Hylands Farm

Rookery Farm

LC

Alexandra Court

HAWTHORN RD

HEATH RD

HOLLY RD

HASSALL RD

Industrial Estate

L Skegness

RICHMOND DR

SANDBECK AVE

BRIAR WY

BERESFORD AVE

SAXBY AVE

FIRBECK AV

KENNEDY AV

P

P

PO

P

Coll

OCEAN AV

206

Windsor Farm

Eptons Farm

116

PE24

Ralings Farm

Top Yard Farm

Pinchbeck Farm

A52

LC

LC

SEACROFT DR

SHARDLOES RD

DRAKE RD

DRUMMOND ROAD

Seacroft

CH

SEACROFT ESPLANADE

SYNE AV

DERBY AV

12

Coddingtons Yard

Croft Marsh

Kitchen's Yard

NEW ROAD

Croft Grange

Bramble Hills

Croft House

LC

HAVEN HO RD

Havenhouse Farm

Wainfleet Haven or Steeping River

Clough House Farm

COW BANK DRAIN

Wainfleet Clough

Toll Bar Farm

TOLL BAR RD

P

New Yard Farm

Sea Bank

Gibraltar

GIBRALTAR ROAD

AYLMER AV

Gibraltar Point National Nature Reserve

Viewpoint

PE25

Wainfleet Road

Marsh Farm East

| 52 | A | 53 | B | 54 | C | 55 | D | 56 | E | 57 | F |

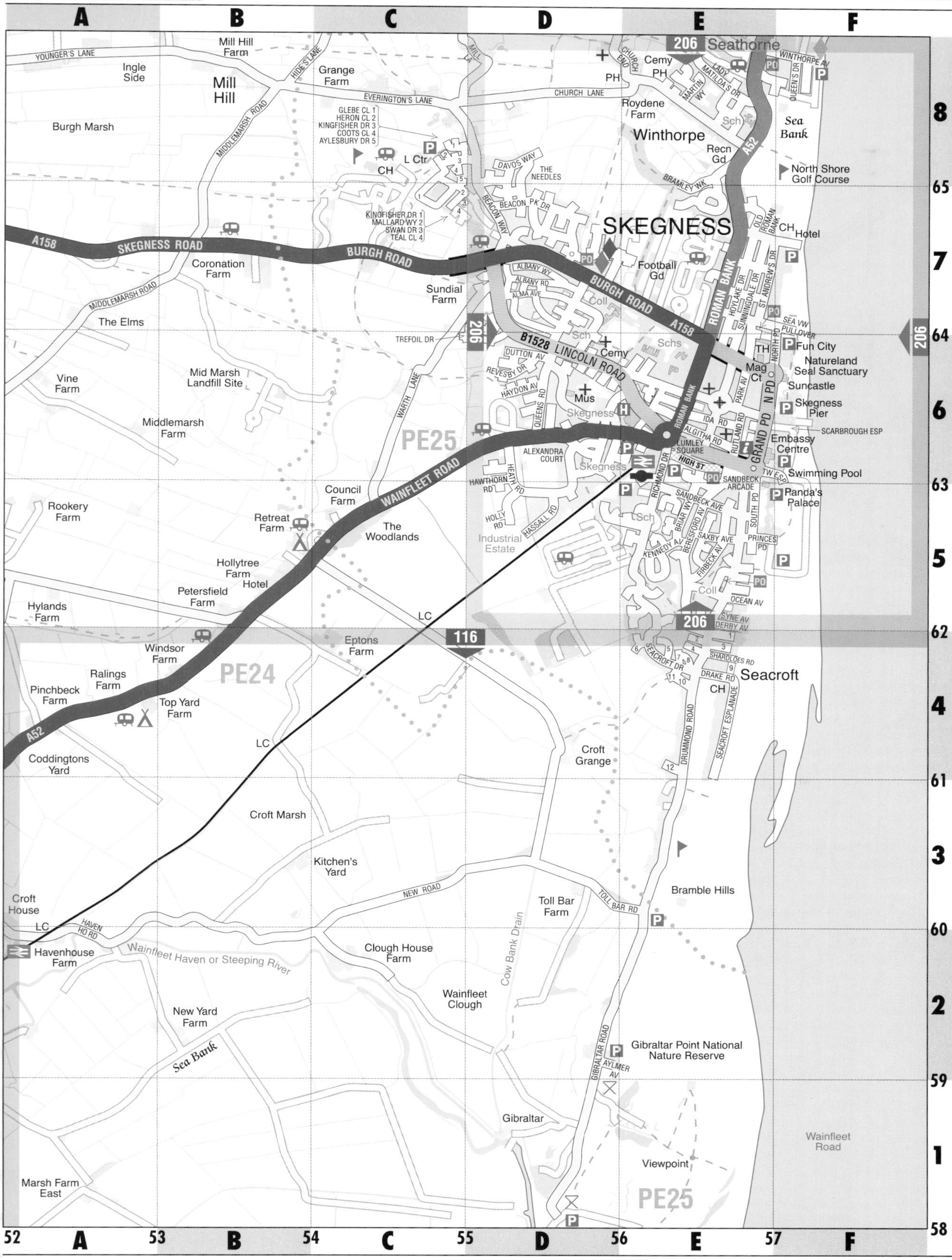

116

For full street detail of the highlighted area see page 206.

E4
1 ALBERT AVE
2 VINE RD
3 BUCKTHORN AVE
4 NORWOOD RD
5 PRECINCT CRES
6 BAYES RD
7 GREEN LA
8 LINKS CRES
9 SEA FRONT RD
10 SEACROFT SQ
11 HESKETH CRES
12 FREDERICA RD

91

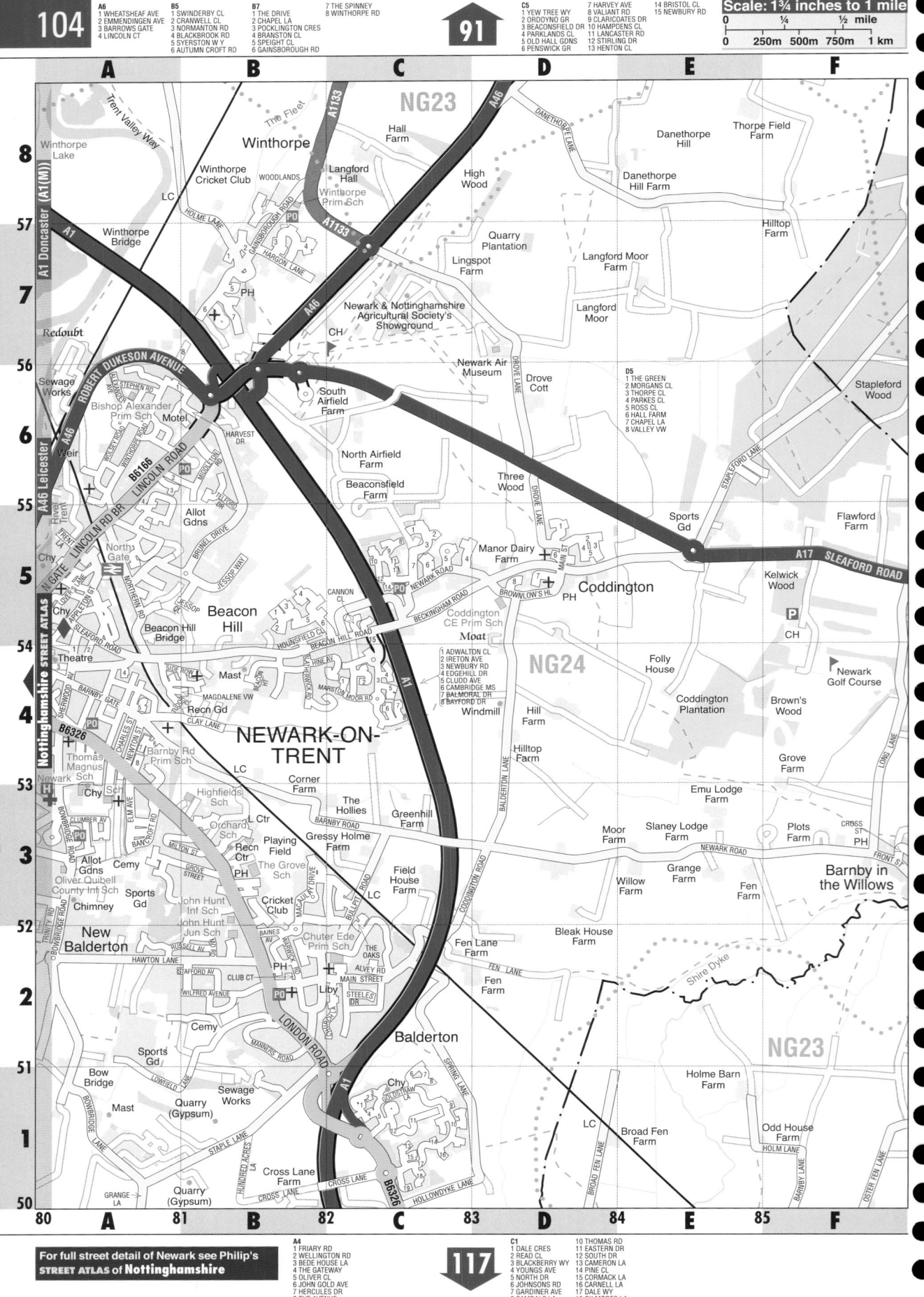

A6	B5	B7		C5		14 BRISTOL CL
1 WHEATSHEAF AVE	1 SWINDERBY CL	1 THE DRIVE	7 THE SPINNEY	1 YEW TREE WY	7 HARVEY AVE	15 NEWBURY RD
2 EMMENDINGEN AVE	2 CRANWELL CL	2 CHAPEL LA	8 WINTHORPE RD	2 ORDOYNO GR	8 VALIANT RD	
3 BARROWS GATE	3 NORMANTON RD	3 POCKLINGTON CRES		3 BEACONSFIELD DR	9 CLARICOATES DR	
4 LINCOLN CT	4 BLACKBROOK RD	4 BRANSTON CL		4 PARKLANDS CL	10 HAMPDENS CL	
	5 SYERSTON W Y	5 SPEIGHT CL		5 OLD HALL GDNS	11 STIRLING DR	
	6 AUTUMN CROFT RD	6 GAINSBOROUGH RD		6 PENSWICK GR	12 STIRLING DR	
					13 HENTON CL	

Scale: 1¾ inches to 1 mile

0   ¼   ½ mile

0 250m 500m 750m 1 km

A4		C1		10 THOMAS RD
1 FRIARY RD		1 DALE CRES		11 EASTERN DR
2 WELLINGTON RD		2 READ CL		12 SOUTH DR
3 BEDE HOUSE LA		3 BLACKBERRY WY		13 CAMERON LA
4 THE GATEWAY		4 YOUNGS AVE		14 PINE CL
5 OLIVER CL		5 NORTH DR		15 CORMACK LA
6 JOHN GOLD AVE		6 JOHNSONS RD		16 CARNELL LA
7 HERCULES DR		7 GARDINER AVE		17 DALE WY
8 THE AVENUE		8 CAMDALE LA		18 GILMORES LA
		9 SPRING DR		19 COLLINSON LA

D5
1 THE GREEN
2 MORGANS CL
3 THORPE CL
4 PARKES CL
5 ROSS CL
6 HALL FARM
7 CHAPEL LA
8 VALLEY VW

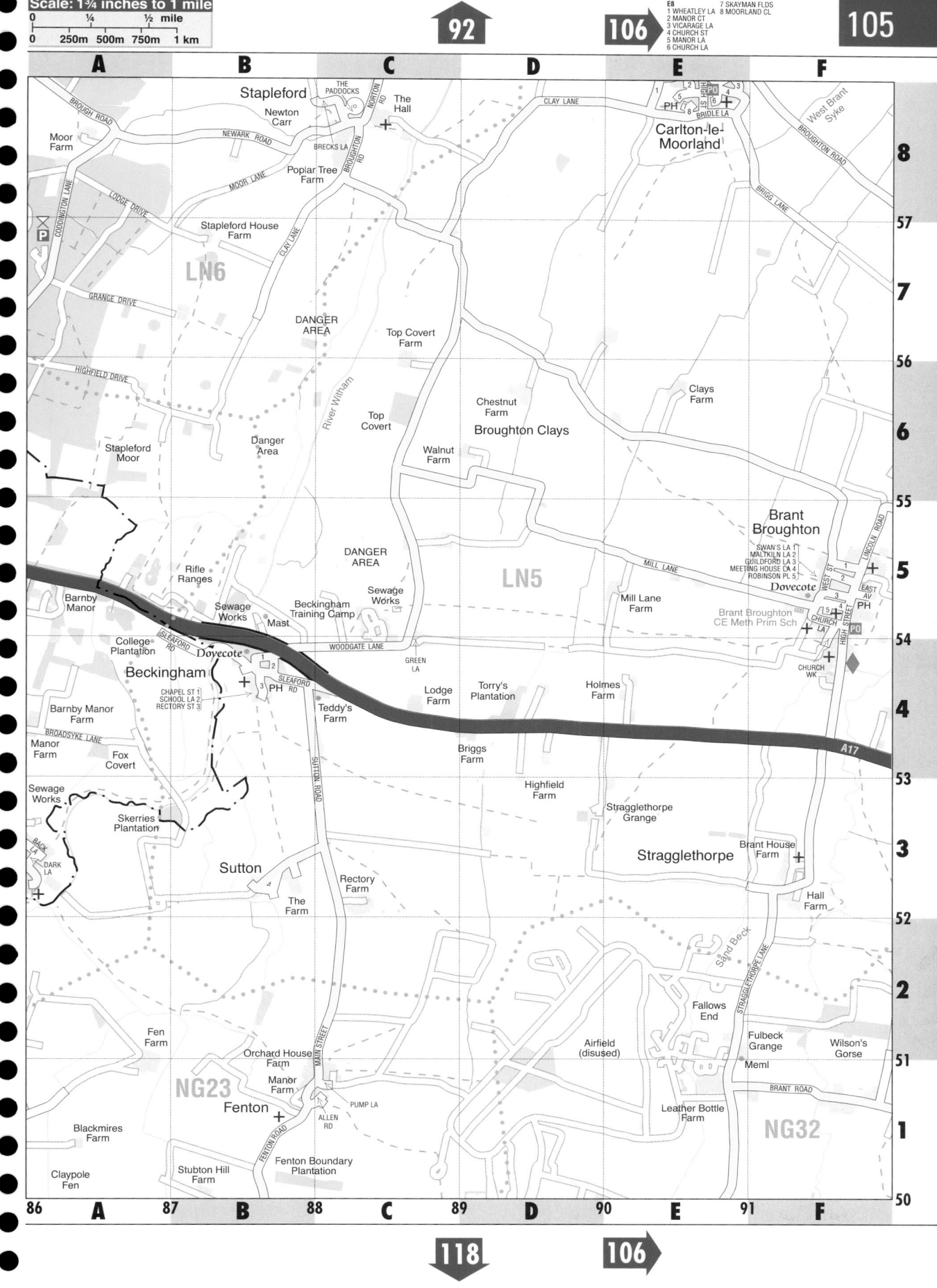

Scale: 1¾ inches to 1 mile

0   ¼   ½   mile
0   250m 500m 750m 1 km

92

106
E8
1 WHEATLEY LA
2 MANOR CT
3 VICARAGE LA
4 CHURCH ST
5 MANOR LA
6 CHURCH LA
7 SKAYMAN FLDS
8 MOORLAND CL

105

A   B   C   D   E   F

8
57
7
56
6
55
5
54
4
53
3
52
2
51
1
50

Moor Farm
BROUGH ROAD
NEWARK ROAD
CODDINGTON LANE
LODGE DRIVE
P
GRANGE DRIVE
HIGHFIELD DRIVE
LN6

Stapleford
Newton Carr
THE PADDOCKS
NORTON RD
BROUGHTON RD
The Hall
Brecks La
MOOR LANE
Poplar Tree Farm
Stapleford House Farm
CLAY LANE
DANGER AREA
River Witham
Danger Area
Stapleford Moor

Top Covert Farm
Top Covert
DANGER AREA
Rifle Ranges
Sewage Works
Mast
Beckingham Training Camp
Sewage Works
WOODGATE LANE
GREEN LA
Barnby Manor
SLEAFORD RD
Dovecote
Beckingham
CHAPEL ST 1
SCHOOL LA 2
RECTORY ST 3
PH
SLEAFORD RD
Teddy's Farm
BROADSYKE LANE
Barnby Manor Farm
Manor Farm
Fox Covert
Sewage Works
Skerries Plantation
BACK LA
DARK LA
SUTTON ROAD
Sutton
The Farm
Rectory Farm
MAIN STREET
Fen Farm
Orchard House Farm
Manor Farm
NG23
Fenton
FENTON ROAD
ALLEN RD
PUMP LA
Blackmires Farm
Stubton Hill Farm
Fenton Boundary Plantation
Claypole Fen

CLAY LANE
Carlton-le-Moorland
PH PO
HIGH ST
BRIDLE LA
West Brant Syke
BROUGHTON ROAD
BRIGG LANE

Chestnut Farm
Broughton Clays
Walnut Farm
Clays Farm
LN5
MILL LANE
Mill Lane Farm
Brant Broughton
SWAN'S LA
MALTKILN LA 2
GUILDFORD LA 3
MEETING HOUSE DA 4
ROBINSON PL 5
Dovecote
WEST ST
EAST AV
PH
LINCOLN ROAD
Brant Broughton CE Meth Prim Sch
CHURCH LA
HIGH STREET
PO
CHURCH WK

Lodge Farm
Torry's Plantation
Holmes Farm
Briggs Farm
A17
Highfield Farm
Stragglethorpe Grange
Stragglethorpe
Brant House Farm
Hall Farm
SAND BECK
STRAGGLETHORPE LANE
Fallows End
Airfield (disused)
Fulbeck Grange
Meml
Wilson's Gorse
Leather Bottle Farm
BRANT ROAD
NG32

← 105
↑ 93

E5
1 THE NOOKIN
2 HALL ORCHARD LA
3 CASTLE HILL
4 MOAT LA
5 LITTLE LA
6 MANOR CL

Scale: 1¾ inches to 1 mile

0   ¼   ½   mile
0   250m   500m   750m   1 km

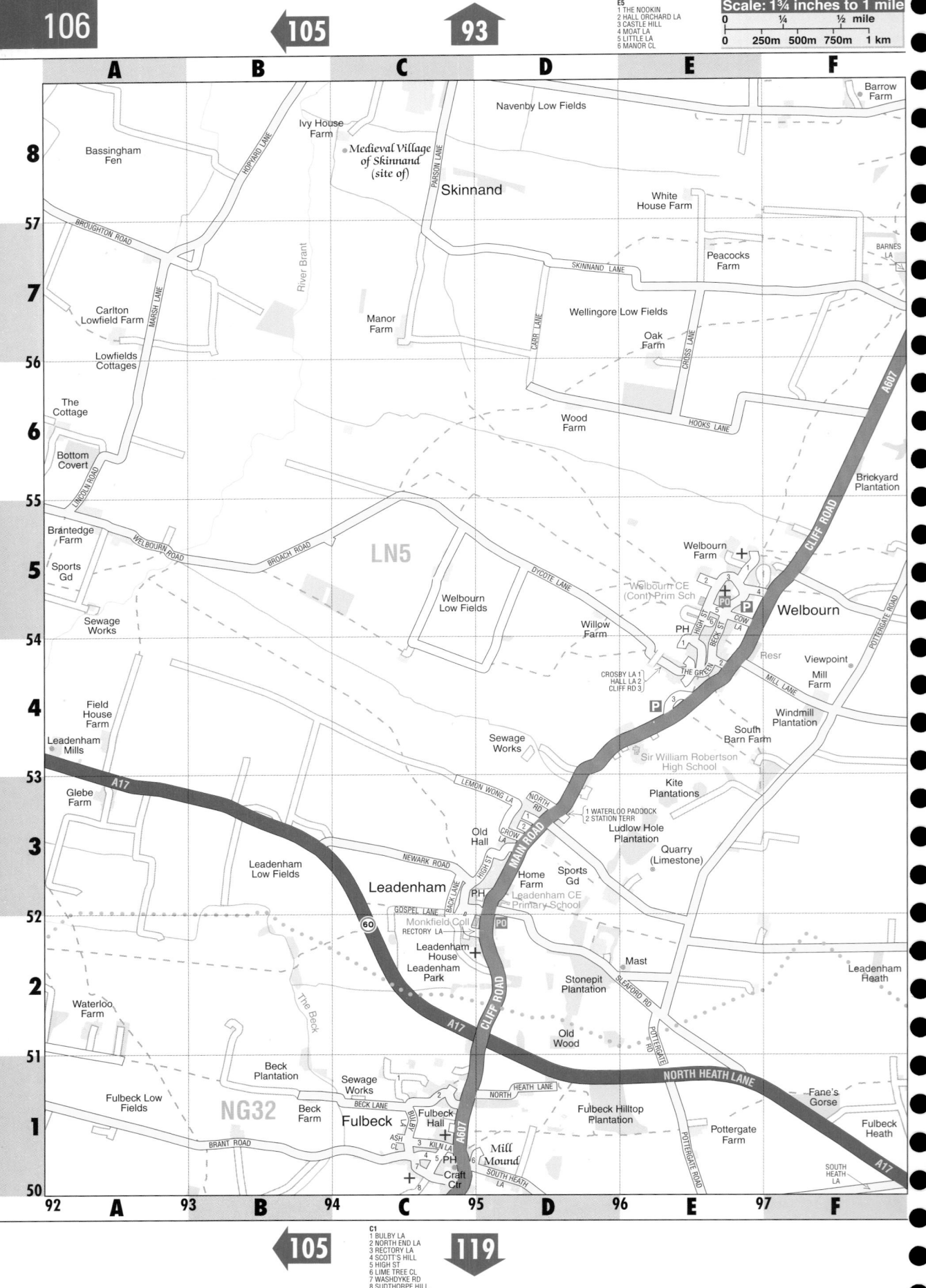

← 105
↓ 119

C1
1 BULBY LA
2 NORTH END LA
3 RECTORY LA
4 SCOTT'S HILL
5 HIGH ST
6 LIME TREE CL
7 WASHDYKE RD
8 SUDTHORPE HILL

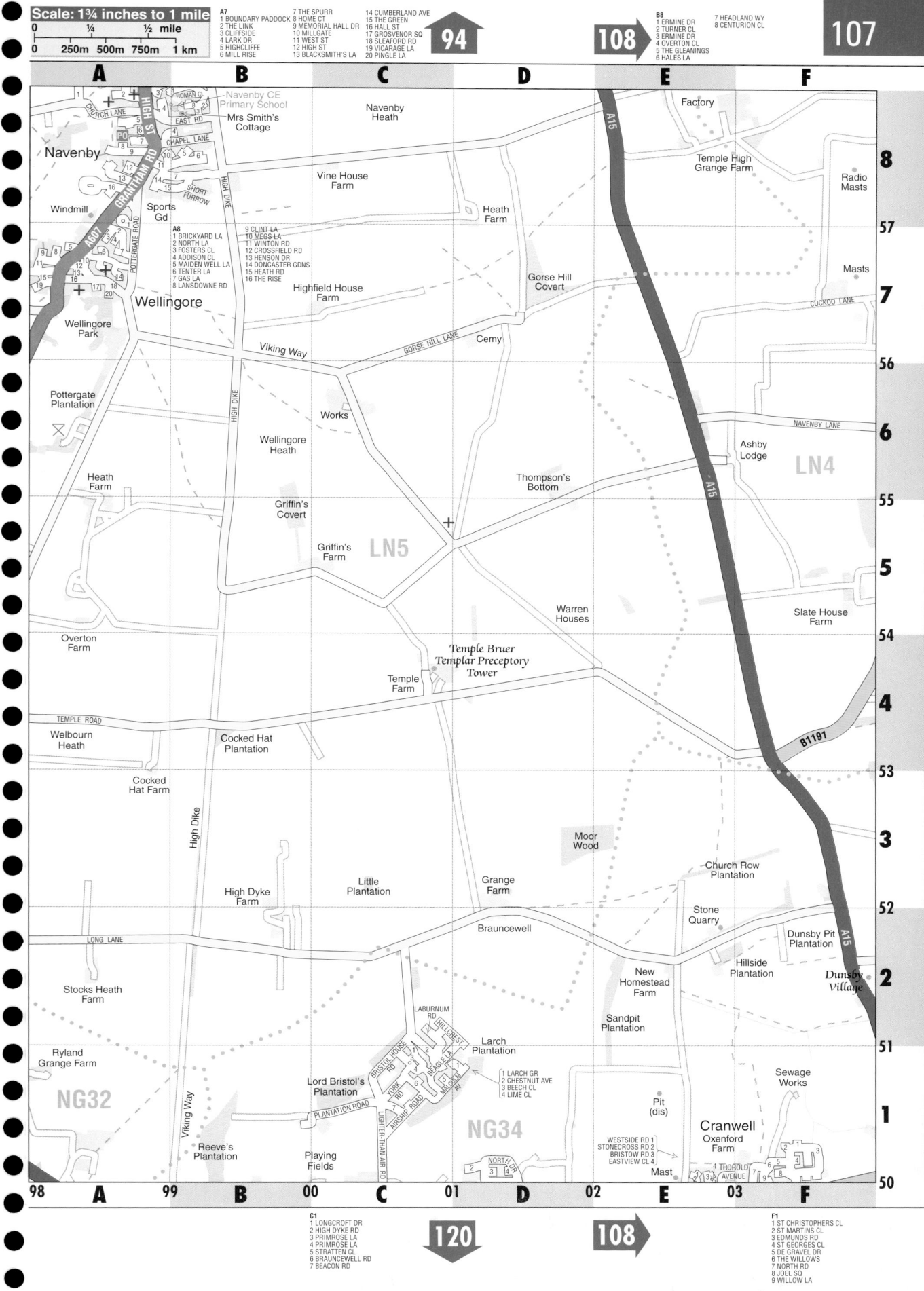

0   ¼   ½   mile
0   250m   500m   750m   1 km

A7
1 BOUNDARY PADDOCK
2 THE LINK
3 CLIFFSIDE
4 LARK DR
5 HIGHCLIFFE
6 MILL RISE

7 THE SPURR
8 HOME CT
9 MEMORIAL HALL DR
10 MILLGATE
11 WEST ST
12 HIGH ST
13 BLACKSMITH'S LA

14 CUMBERLAND AVE
15 THE GREEN
16 HALL ST
17 GROSVENOR SQ
18 SLEAFORD RD
19 VICARAGE LA
20 PINGLE LA

B8
1 ERMINE DR
2 TURNER CL
3 ERMINE DR
4 OVERTON CL
5 THE GLEANINGS
6 HALES LA

7 HEADLAND WY
8 CENTURION CL

94

108

A8
1 BRICKYARD LA
2 NORTH LA
3 FOSTERS CL
4 ADDISON CL
5 MAIDEN WELL LA
6 TENTER LA
7 GAS LA
8 LANSDOWNE RD

9 CLINT LA
10 MEGS LA
11 WINTON RD
12 CROSSFIELD RD
13 HENSON DR
14 DONCASTER GDNS
15 HEATH RD
16 THE RISE

A   B   C   D   E   F

Navenby CE Primary School

Navenby Heath

Factory

Temple High Grange Farm

Radio Masts   **8**

Navenby

Mrs Smith's Cottage

Vine House Farm

Heath Farm

Masts   **57**

Windmill

Sports Gd

Highfield House Farm

Gorse Hill Covert

Masts   **7**

CUCKOO LANE

Wellingore Park

Wellingore

Viking Way

GORSE HILL LANE   Cemy

56

Pottergate Plantation

HIGH DIKE

Works

Wellingore Heath

Thompson's Bottom

NAVENBY LANE   **6**

Ashby Lodge

LN4

Heath Farm

Griffin's Covert

+

Slate House Farm   **55**

Griffin's Farm   LN5

Warren Houses

5

Overton Farm

Temple Bruer Templar Preceptory Tower

Temple Farm

54

TEMPLE ROAD

Welbourn Heath

Cocked Hat Plantation

B1191   **4**

53

Cocked Hat Farm

Moor Wood

3

High Dike

Church Row Plantation

High Dyke Farm

Little Plantation

Grange Farm

Stone Quarry   **52**

Dunsby Pit Plantation

LONG LANE

Brauncewell

Hillside Plantation

Dunsby Village   A15   **2**

Stocks Heath Farm

New Homestead Farm

Sandpit Plantation

51

Ryland Grange Farm

NG32

LABURNUM RD

HILLCREST

Larch Plantation

1 LARCH GR
2 CHESTNUT AVE
3 BEECH CL
4 LIME CL

Sewage Works

1

Viking Way

Lord Bristol's Plantation

BRISTOL HOUSE RD   YORK RD   BEAGLE LA   MALLORY AV

Pit (dis)

Cranwell

Oxenford Farm

Reeve's Plantation

PLANTATION ROAD

Playing Fields

LIGHTER-THAN-AIR RD   AIRSHIP ROAD

NG34

NORTH

WESTSIDE RD 1
STONECROSS RD 2
BRISTOW RD 3
EASTVIEW RD 4

Mast

THOROLD AVENUE

JOEL SQ   **50**

98   A   99   B   00   C   01   D   02   E   03   F

120

108

C1
1 LONGCROFT DR
2 HIGH DYKE RD
3 PRIMROSE LA
4 PRIMROSE LA
5 STRATTEN CL
6 BRAUNCEWELL RD
7 BEACON RD

F1
1 ST CHRISTOPHERS CL
2 ST MARTINS CL
3 EDMUNDS RD
4 ST GEORGES CL
5 DE GRAVEL DR
6 THE WILLOWS
7 NORTH RD
8 JOEL SQ
9 WILLOW LA

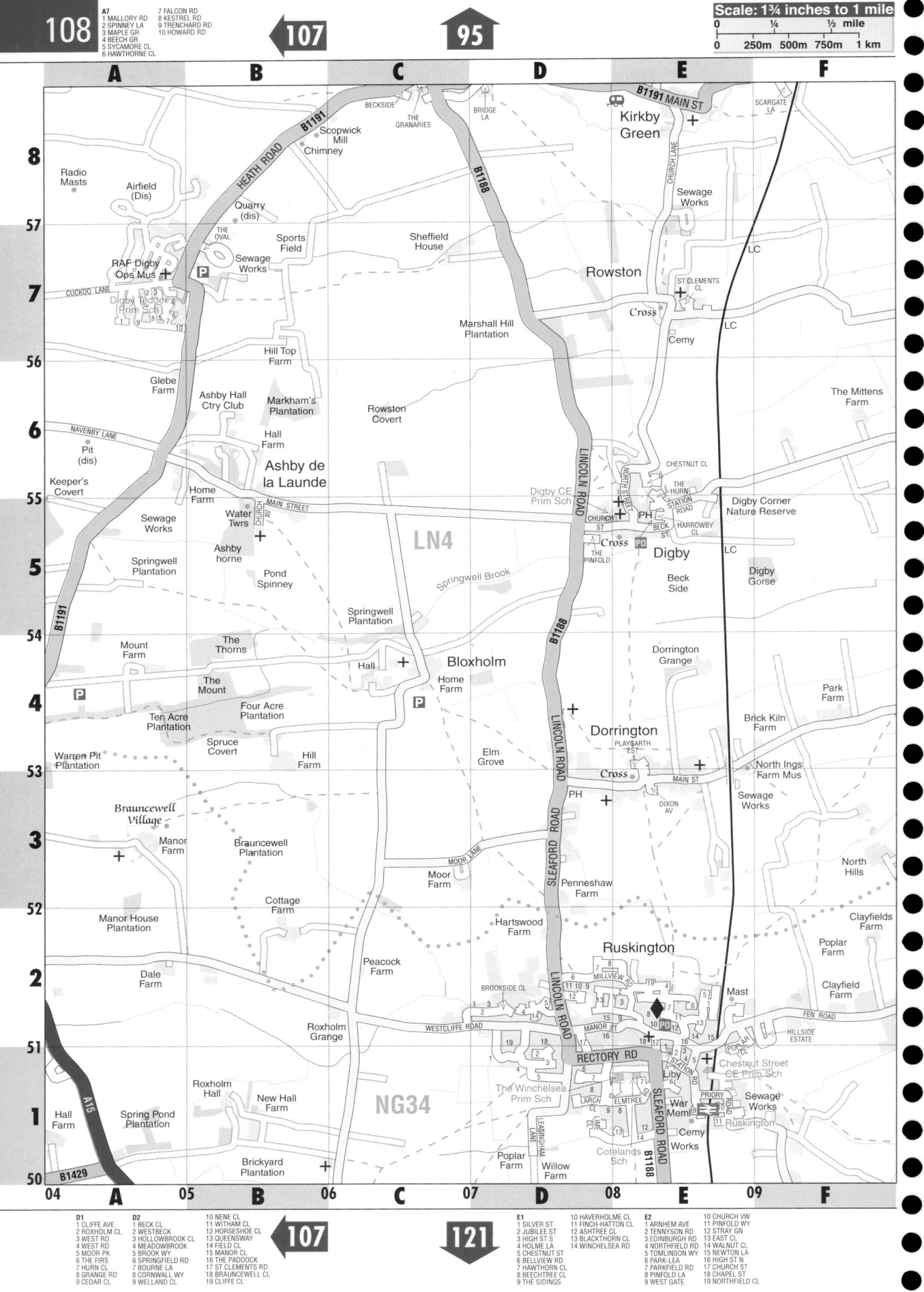

108

◀ 107

95 🔼

Scale: 1¾ inches to 1 mile

0   ¼   ½   mile
0   250m 500m 750m 1 km

Radio Masts

Airfield (Dis)

Quarry (dis)

HEATH ROAD

B1191

BECKSIDE

Scopwick Mill

Chimney

THE GRANARIES

BRIDGE LA

B1188

B1191 MAIN ST

Kirkby Green

SCARGATE LA

The Oval

Sports Field

Sheffield House

Sewage Works

CHURCH LANE

Sewage Works

LC

RAF Digby Ops Mus

CUCKOO LANE

Digby Tedder Prim Sch

Rowston

ST CLEMENTS CL

Cross

LC

Marshall Hill Plantation

Cemy

Hill Top Farm

Glebe Farm

Ashby Hall Ctry Club

Markham's Plantation

Rowston Covert

The Mittens Farm

NAVENBY LANE

Pit (dis)

Hall Farm

Keeper's Covert

Home Farm

Ashby de la Launde

MAIN STREET

CHURCH AV

LN4

Digby CE Prim Sch

LINCOLN ROAD

NORTH STREET

CHESTNUT CL

THE HURN

STATION ROAD

Digby Corner Nature Reserve

Sewage Works

Water Twrs

Ashby horne

CHURCH ST

Cross

THE PINFOLD

PH

BECK

HARROWBY CL

PO

Digby

LC

Springwell Plantation

Pond Spinney

Springwell Brook

Beck Side

Digby Gorse

Springwell Plantation

Mount Farm

The Thorns

Hall

Bloxholm

Home Farm

B1188

Dorrington Grange

Park Farm

P

The Mount

Four Acre Plantation

P

LINCOLN ROAD

Dorrington

PLAYGARTH EST

Brick Kiln Farm

Ten Acre Plantation

Spruce Covert

Hill Farm

Elm Grove

Cross

MAIN ST

North Ings Farm Mus

DIXON AV

Sewage Works

Warren Pit Plantation

North Hills

Brauncewell Village

Manor Farm

Brauncewell Plantation

PH

SLEAFORD ROAD

Penneshaw Farm

Clayfields Farm

Manor House Plantation

Cottage Farm

Moor Farm

MOOR LANE

Hartswood Farm

Poplar Farm

Dale Farm

Peacock Farm

Ruskington

Clayfield Farm

Mast

BROOKSIDE CL

MILLVIEW RD

FEN ROAD

Roxholm Grange

WESTCLIFFE ROAD

LINCOLN ROAD

MANOR ST

HILLSIDE ESTATE

RECTORY RD

STATION RD

Chestnut Street CE Prim Sch

Roxholm Hall

New Hall Farm

NG34

The Winchelsea Prim Sch

LARCH

ELMTREE

LIME

LEASINGHAM LANE

SLEAFORD ROAD

PRIORY RD

POPLAR RD

Libry

War Meml

Cemy Works

Sewage Works

Ruskington

Spring Pond Plantation

A15

Hall Farm

B1429

Brickyard Plantation

Poplar Farm

Willow Farm

Cotelands Sch

B1188

04   A   05   B   06   C   07   D   08   E   09   F

◀ 107

121 🔽

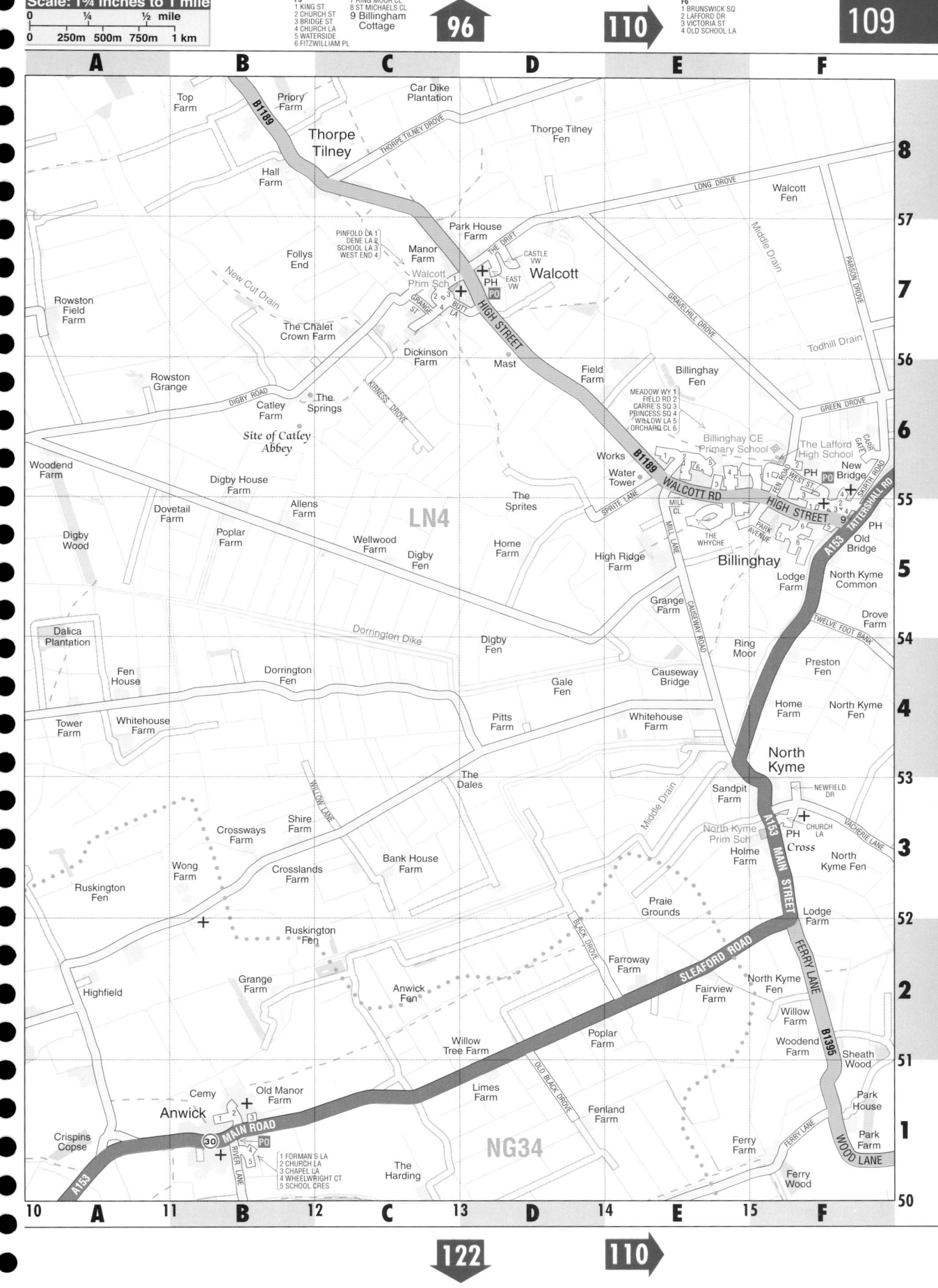

F5
1 KING ST
2 CHURCH ST
3 BRIDGE ST
4 WATERSIDE
5 FITZWILLIAM PL
6 FITZWILLIAM PL
7 RING MOOR CL
8 ST MICHAELS CL
9 Billingham Cottage

F6
1 BRUNSWICK SQ
2 LAFFORD DR
3 VICTORIA ST
4 OLD SCHOOL LA

96

110

A   B   C   D   E   F

Top Farm
B1189
Priory Farm
Car Dike Plantation
Thorpe Tilney
Thorpe Tilney Fen
8
Hall Farm
THORPE TILNEY DROVE
Long Drove
Walcott Fen
57
Follys End
PINFOLD LA 1
DENE LA 2
SCHOOL LA 3
WEST END 4
Park House Farm
THE DRIFT
Manor Farm
CASTLE VW
Walcott
Middle Drain
PARSON DROVE
7
Rowston Field Farm
New Cut Drain
Walcott Prim Sch
GRANGE ST
BUTT LA
PH
PO
EAST VW
HIGH STREET
GRAVELHILL DRIVE
Todhill Drain
The Chalet Crown Farm
Dickinson Farm
Mast
Field Farm
Billinghay Fen
56
Rowston Grange
DIGBY ROAD
The Springs
KIRKBY DROVE
MEADOW WY 1
FIELD RD 2
CARRE'S SQ 3
PRINCESS SQ 4
WILLOW LA 5
ORCHARD CL 6
Billinghay CE Primary School
The Lafford High School
GREEN DROVE
CARR GATE
6
Catley Farm
Site of Catley Abbey
Digby House Farm
Works
B1189
New Bridge
SOUTH ROAD
PH
PO
55
Woodend Farm
Allens Farm
Water Tower
WALCOTT RD
MILL CL
FRED WEST ST
HIGH STREET
PH
TATTERSHALL RD
Dovetail Farm
Poplar Farm
Wellwood Farm
The Sprites
SPRITE LANE
Digby Wood
LN4
Digby Fen
Home Farm
High Ridge Farm
THE WHYCHE
PARK AVENUE
Old Bridge
A153
5
Digby Wood
Digby Fen
Billinghay
North Kyme Common
Dalica Plantation
Dorrington Dike
Digby Fen
Grange Farm
MILL LANE
CAUSEWAY ROAD
Lodge Farm
TWELVE FOOT BANK
Drove Farm
54
Fen House
Dorrington Fen
Ring Moor
Causeway Bridge
Preston Fen
Home Farm
North Kyme Fen
4
Tower Farm
Whitehouse Farm
Gale Fen
Pitts Farm
Whitehouse Farm
North Kyme
53
The Dales
Middle Drain
NEWFIELD DR
VACHERIE LANE
3
Crossways Farm
Shire Farm
WILLOW LANE
Sandpit Farm
A153
North Kyme Prim Sch
PH
CHURCH LA
Cross
North Kyme Fen
Wong Farm
Crosslands Farm
Bank House Farm
Holme Farm
MAIN STREET
52
Ruskington Fen
Praie Grounds
Lodge Farm
Ruskington Fen
BLACK DROVE
Farroway Farm
SLEAFORD ROAD
FERRY LANE
North Kyme Fen
2
Grange Farm
Anwick Fen
Fairview Farm
Willow Farm
Highfield
Willow Tree Farm
Poplar Farm
Woodend Farm
B1395
Sheath Wood
51
Cemy
Old Manor Farm
OLD BLACK DROVE
Limes Farm
Fenland Farm
Park House
Crispins Copse
Anwick
30
MAIN ROAD
RIVER LANE
PO
NG34
Ferry Farm
FERRY LANE
Park Farm
WOOD LANE
1
A153
1 FORMAN'S LA
2 CHURCH LA
3 CHAPEL LA
4 WHEELWRIGHT CT
5 SCHOOL CRES
The Harding
Ferry Wood
50

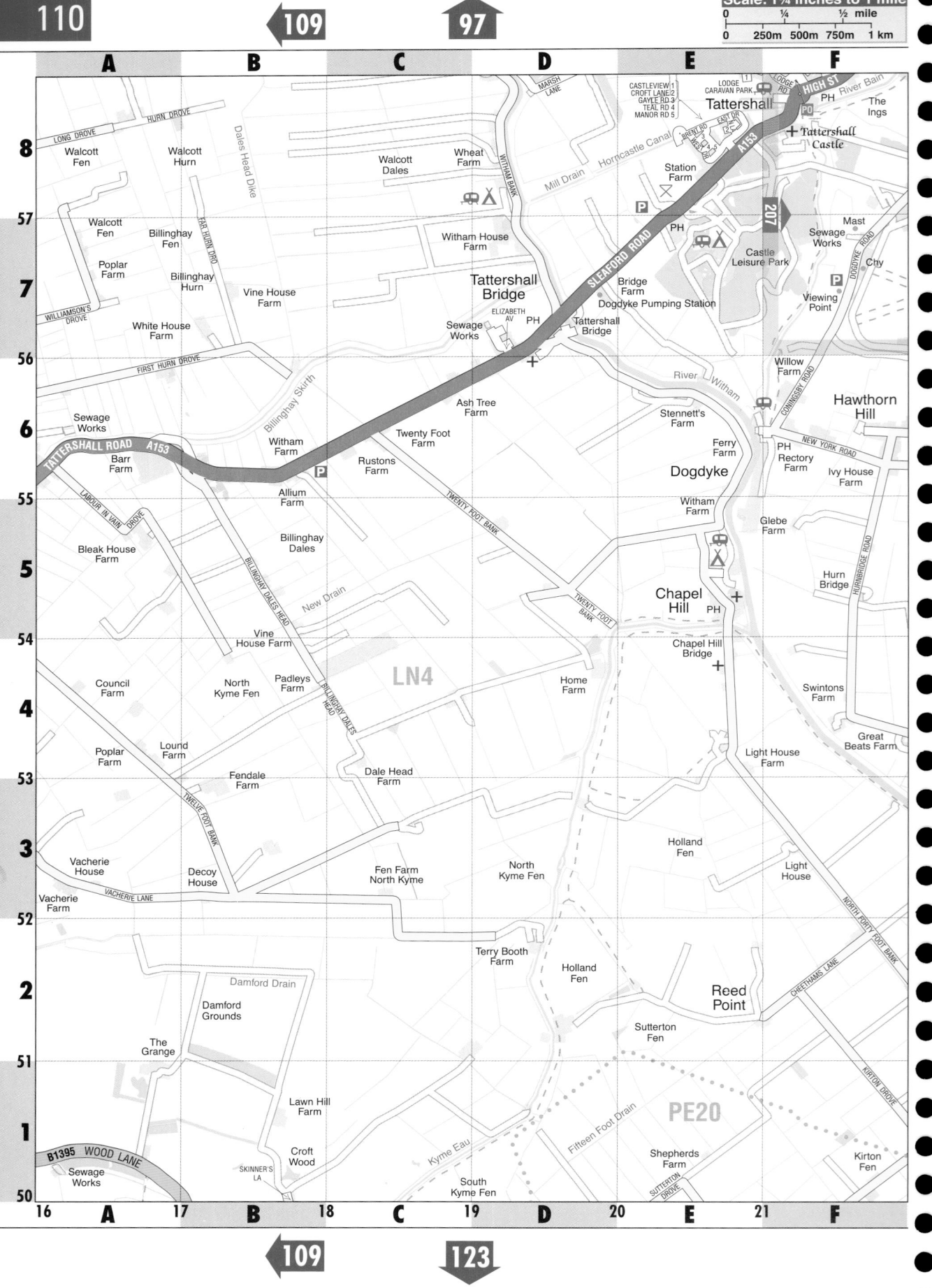

109
97

Scale: 1¾ inches to 1 mile

0   ¼   ½   mile

0   250m 500m 750m 1 km

A   B   C   D   E   F

Long Drove
HURN DROVE

Walcott Fen   Walcott Hurn

Dales Head Dike

Walcott Dales   Wheat Farm

MARSH LANE

CASTLEVIEW 1
CROFT LANE 2
GAYLE RD 3
TEAL RD 4
MANOR RD 5

LODGE CARAVAN PARK

Tattershall

HIGH ST

River Bain

PH

The Ings

8

Walcott Fen   Billinghay Fen

FAR HURN DRO

Witham House Farm

WITHAM BANK

Mill Drain   Horncastle Canal

EAST DR

A153

Station Farm

Tattershall Castle

Mast

Sewage Works

DOGDYKE ROAD

Chy

57

Poplar Farm   Billinghay Hurn

Vine House Farm

SLEAFORD ROAD

PH

Castle Leisure Park

207

Viewing Point

P

7

WILLIAMSON'S DROVE

White House Farm

Tattershall Bridge

Bridge Farm

Dogdyke Pumping Station

ELIZABETH AV

PH

Sewage Works

Tattershall Bridge

Willow Farm

Hawthorn Hill

56

FIRST HURN DROVE

River   Witham

CONINGSBY ROAD

Billinghay Skirth

Ash Tree Farm

Stennett's Farm

NEW YORK ROAD

6

Sewage Works

TATTERSHALL ROAD   A153

Barr Farm

Witham Farm

Twenty Foot Farm

Ferry Farm

Dogdyke

PH Rectory Farm

Ivy House Farm

HURNBRIDGE ROAD

LABOUR IN VAIN DROVE

Allium Farm

P

Rustons Farm

TWENTY FOOT BANK

Witham Farm

Glebe Farm

Hurn Bridge

55

Bleak House Farm

Billinghay Dales

BILLINGHAY DALES HEAD

New Drain

Chapel Hill   PH

5

Vine House Farm

TWENTY FOOT BANK

54

Council Farm

North Kyme Fen

Padleys Farm

LN4

Home Farm

Chapel Hill Bridge

Swintons Farm

4

BILLINGHAY DALES HEAD

Light House Farm

Great Beats Farm

Poplar Farm   Lound Farm

Fendale Farm

Dale Head Farm

Holland Fen

Light House

53

TWELVE FOOT BANK

3

Vacherie House

Decoy House

Fen Farm North Kyme

North Kyme Fen

NORTH FORTY FOOT BANK

VACHERIE LANE

Vacherie Farm

Terry Booth Farm

Holland Fen

Reed Point

CHEETHAMS LANE

2

Damford Drain

Damford Grounds

Sutterton Fen

KIRTON DROVE

51

The Grange

1

Lawn Hill Farm

PE20

SKINNER'S LA

Croft Wood

Kyme Eau

Fifteen Foot Drain

Shepherds Farm

Kirton Fen

B1395   WOOD LANE

Sewage Works

South Kyme Fen

SUTTERTON DROVE

50

16   A   17   B   18   C   19   D   20   E   21   F

109
123

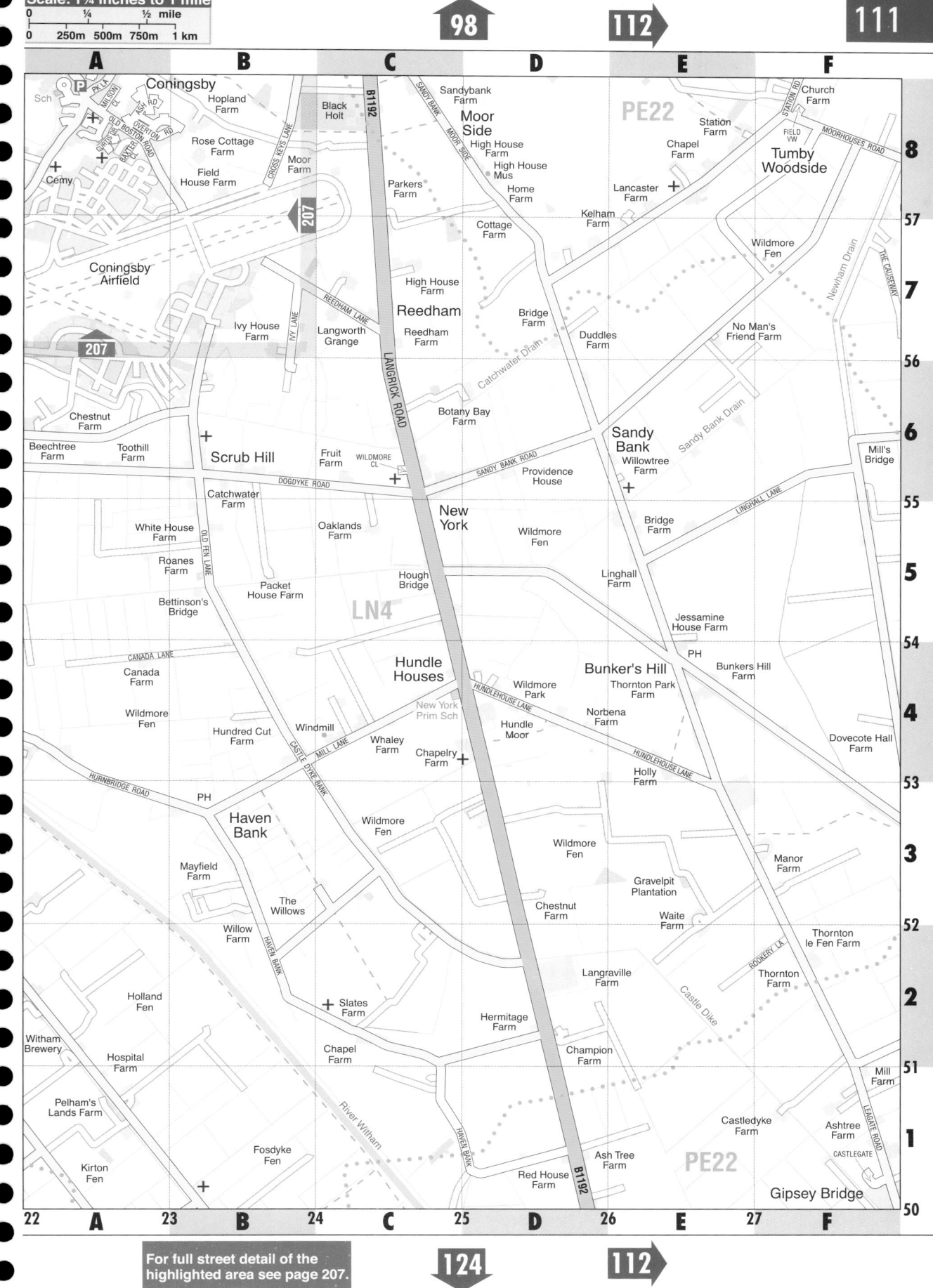

A B C D E F

Coningsby
Sch P PK LA
WILSON CL
OLD BOSTON ROAD
OVERTON RD
BAXTER RD
Hopland Farm
Black Holt
B1192
SANDY BANK
Sandybank Farm
MOOR SIDE
Moor Side
PE22
Station Road
Church Farm
Station Farm
Chapel Farm
MOORHOUSES ROAD
FIELD VW

Rose Cottage Farm
Moor Farm
High House Farm
High House Mus
Tumby Woodside

Cemy
Field House Farm
CROSS KEYS LANE
Parkers Farm
Home Farm
Lancaster Farm
Kelham Farm

8

207
57

Coningsby Airfield
REEDHAM LANE
IVY LANE
High House Farm
Cottage Farm
Wildmore Fen
No Man's Friend Farm
Newham Drain
THE CAUSEWAY

7

207
Ivy House Farm
Langworth Grange
Reedham
Reedham Farm
Bridge Farm
Catchwater Drain
Duddles Farm

56

Chestnut Farm
Botany Bay Farm
Sandy Bank
Willowtree Farm
Sandy Bank Drain
Mill's Bridge

6

Beechtree Farm
Toothill Farm
Scrub Hill
Fruit Farm
WILDMORE CL
DOGDYKE ROAD
SANDY BANK ROAD
Providence House
Bridge Farm
LINGHALL LANE

55

Catchwater Farm
LANGRICK ROAD
New York
Wildmore Fen
Linghall Farm

5

White House Farm
OLD FEN LANE
Oaklands Farm
Hough Bridge
Jessamine House Farm

54

Roanes Farm
LN4
PH

Bettinson's Bridge
Packet House Farm
Hundle Houses
Wildmore Park
Bunker's Hill
Thornton Park Farm
Bunkers Hill Farm

4

CANADA LANE
HUNDLEHOUSE LANE
Norbena Farm
Dovecote Hall Farm

Canada Farm
Hundred Cut Farm
Windmill
New York Prim Sch
Handle Moor
HUNDLEHOUSE LANE

Wildmore Fen
MILL LANE
Whaley Farm
Chapelry Farm
Holly Farm

53

HURNBRIDGE ROAD
CASTLE DYKE BANK
PH
Haven Bank
Wildmore Fen
Wildmore Fen
Manor Farm

3

Mayfield Farm
HAVEN BANK
The Willows
Chestnut Farm
Gravelpit Plantation
Thornton le Fen Farm

52

Willow Farm
Langraville Farm
ROOKERY LA.
Thornton Farm

Holland Fen
Slates Farm
Hermitage Farm
Waite Farm
Castle Dike

2

Witham Brewery
Hospital Farm
Chapel Farm
Champion Farm
Mill Farm
LEAGATE ROAD

51

Pelham's Lands Farm
River Witham
HAVEN BANK
Ash Tree Farm
B1192
Castledyke Farm
Ashtree Farm
CASTLEGATE

1

Kirton Fen
Fosdyke Fen
Red House Farm
PE22
Gipsey Bridge

50

22 A 23 B 24 C 25 D 26 E 27 F

For full street detail of the highlighted area see page 207.

124

112

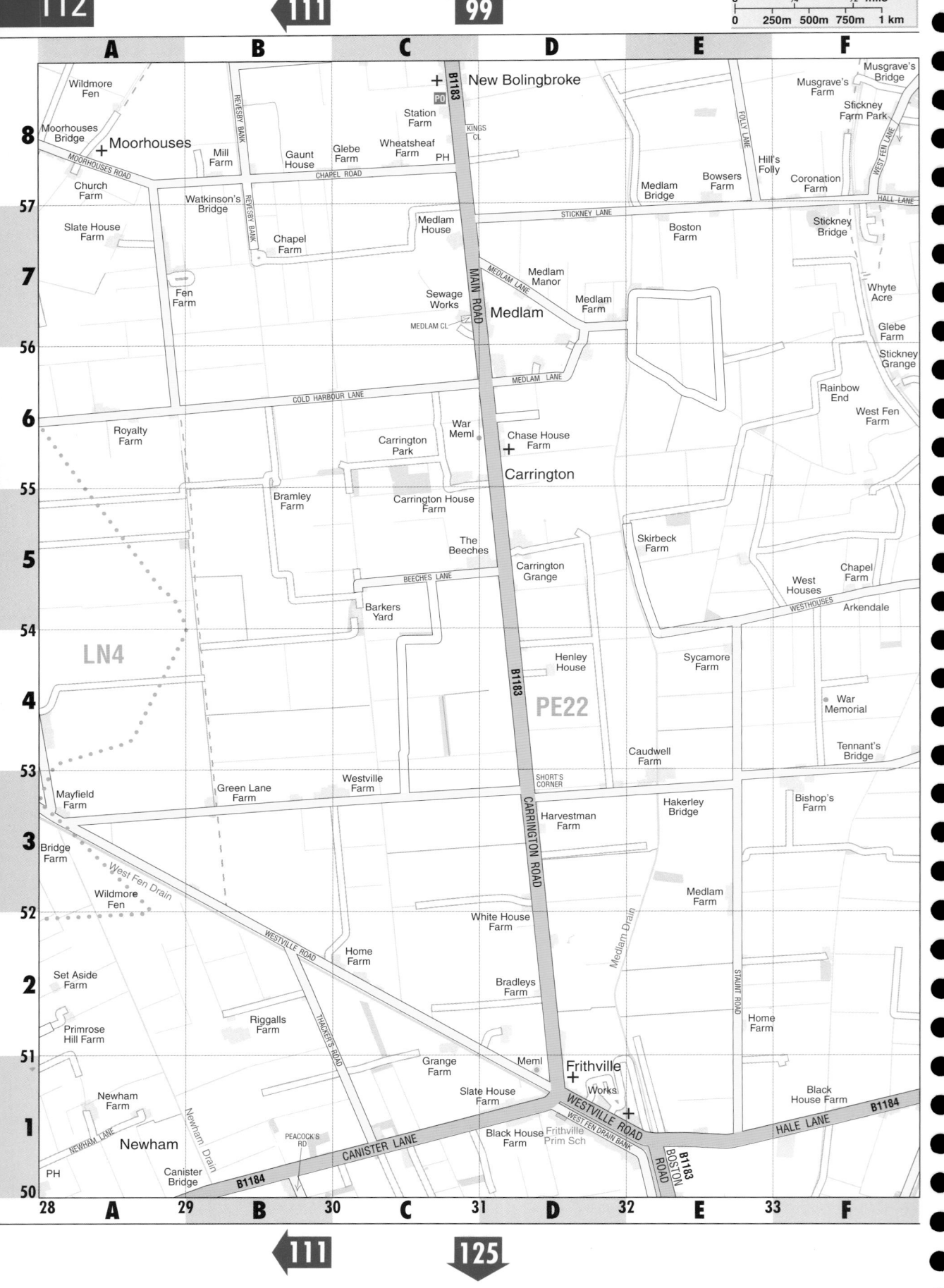

A   B   C   D   E   F

8
57
7
56
6
55
5
54
4
53
3
52
2
51
1
50

Wildmore Fen
Moorhouses Bridge
Moorhouses
MOORHOUSES ROAD
Church Farm
Slate House Farm
Royalty Farm

REVESBY BANK
Mill Farm
Watkinson's Bridge
Chapel Farm
Fen Farm
REVESBY BANK

Gaunt House
Glebe Farm
CHAPEL ROAD

Station Farm
New Bolingbroke
B1183
PO
KINGS CL
Wheatsheaf Farm
PH
Medlam House
Sewage Works
MEDLAM CL
MAIN ROAD

MEDLAM LANE
Medlam Manor
Medlam
Medlam Farm
MEDLAM LANE

STICKNEY LANE
FOLLY LANE
Hill's Folly
Medlam Bridge
Bowsers Farm
Coronation Farm
HALL LANE

Musgrave's Bridge
Musgrave's Farm
Stickney Farm Park
WEST FEN LANE

Boston Farm
Stickney Bridge
Whyte Acre
Glebe Farm
Stickney Grange

COLD HARBOUR LANE
War Meml
Chase House Farm
Carrington

Rainbow End
West Fen Farm

Carrington Park
Bramley Farm
Carrington House Farm
The Beeches
BEECHES LANE
Barkers Yard
Carrington Grange
Henley House
B1183
PE22

Skirbeck Farm
West Houses
WESTHOUSES
Chapel Farm
Arkendale

LN4

Sycamore Farm
War Memorial

Caudwell Farm
Tennant's Bridge

Mayfield Farm
Bridge Farm
West Fen Drain
Wildmore Fen

Green Lane Farm
WESTVILLE ROAD
Westville Farm
Home Farm

SHORT'S CORNER
CARRINGTON ROAD
Harvestman Farm
White House Farm
Bradleys Farm

Hakerley Bridge
Medlam Farm
STAUNT ROAD
Home Farm

Bishop's Farm

Set Aside Farm
Primrose Hill Farm
Newham Farm
Newham
PH
Newham Drain
Canister Bridge
B1184

THACKER'S ROAD
Riggalls Farm
PEACOCK'S RD
CANISTER LANE

Grange Farm
Slate House Farm
Meml
Black House Farm
Frithville Prim Sch

Frithville
Works
WESTVILLE ROAD
WEST FEN DRAIN BANK
BOSTON ROAD
B1183

Black House Farm
HALE LANE
B1184

28   29   30   31   32   33

A   B   C   D   E   F

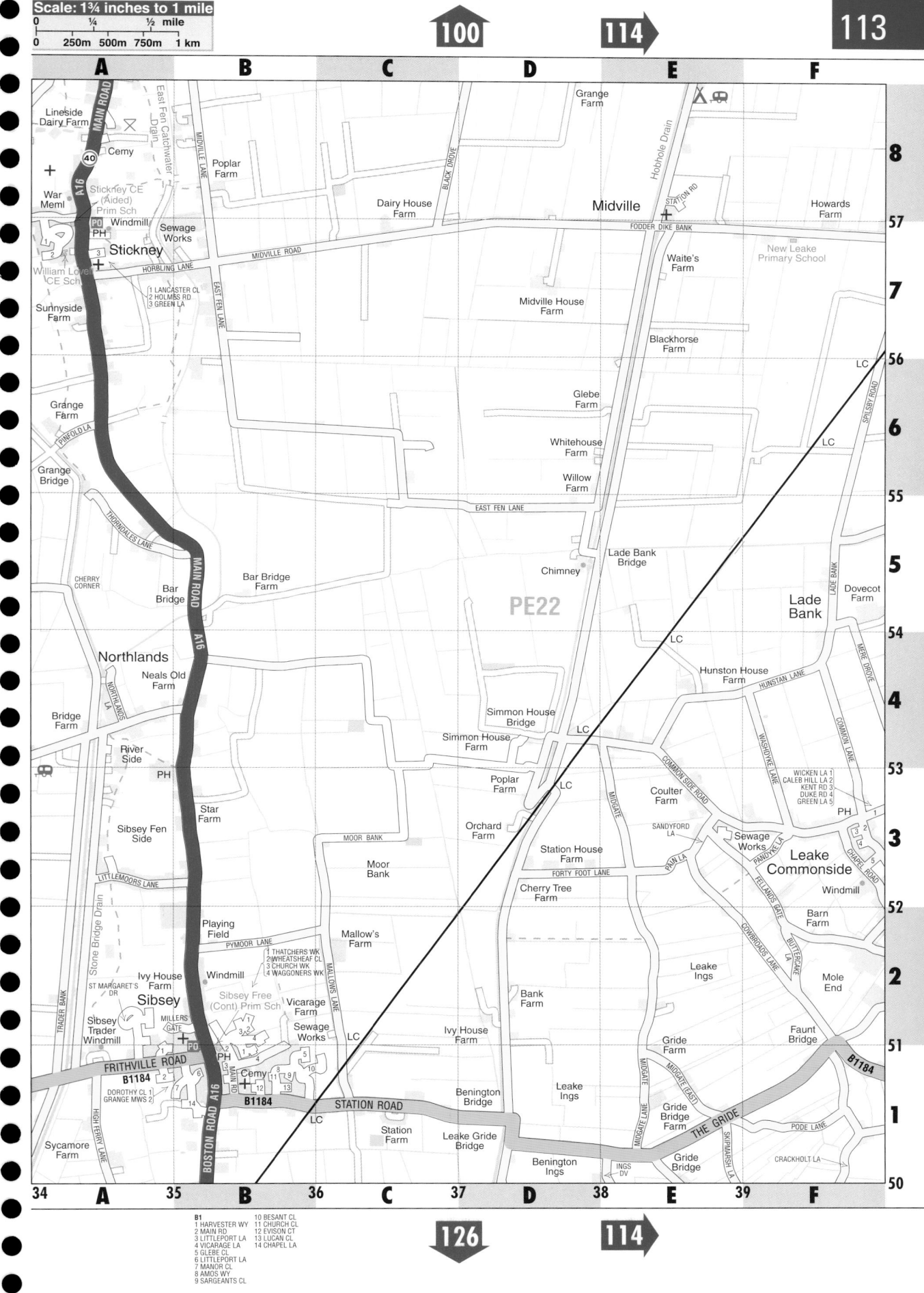

Scale: 1¾ inches to 1 mile

0   ¼   ½   mile
0   250m 500m 750m 1 km

Lineside Dairy Farm
East Fen Catchwater Drain
MAIN ROAD
A16
Cemy
40
War Meml
+
Stickney CE (Aided) Prim Sch
MIDVILLE LANE
Poplar Farm
Dairy House Farm
BLACK DROVE
Grange Farm
Hobhole Drain
Midville
STATION RD
+
Howards Farm
8

Windmill
PO
PH
Sewage Works
FODDER DIKE BANK
New Leake Primary School
57

Stickney
MIDVILLE ROAD
Waite's Farm
7

HORBLING LANE
William Lovell CE Sch
1 LANCASTER CL
2 HOLMES RD
3 GREEN LA
Midville House Farm
Blackhorse Farm

Sunnyside Farm
EAST FEN LANE
56

SPILSBY ROAD
LC
LC

Glebe Farm
6

Grange Farm
PINFOLD LA
Whitehouse Farm
LC

Grange Bridge
THORNDALES LANE
MAIN ROAD
A16
Willow Farm
EAST FEN LANE
55

Lade Bank Bridge
LADE BANK
Lade Bank
Dovecot Farm
5

CHERRY CORNER
Bar Bridge
Bar Bridge Farm
Chimney
PE22
54

Northlands
NORTHLANDS
Neals Old Farm
Simmon House Bridge
LC
Hunston House Farm
HUNSTAN LANE
COMMON LANE
4

Bridge Farm
River Side
PH
Simmon House Farm
Simmon House Farm
LC
WASHDYKE LANE
WICKEN LA 1
CALEB HILL LA 2
KENT RD 3
DUKE RD 4
GREEN LA 5
PH
53

Star Farm
Sibsey Fen Side
MOOR BANK
Poplar Farm
LC
COMMON SIDE ROAD
Coulter Farm
SANDYFORD LA
Sewage Works
PANDYKE LA
3

Moor Bank
Orchard Farm
LC
Station House Farm
MIDGATE
PRAM LA
FELLANDS GATE
Leake Commonside
LITTLEMOORS LANE
STONE BRIDGE DRAIN
Cherry Tree Farm
FORTY FOOT LANE
Windmill
52

Playing Field
PYMOOR LANE
Mallow's Farm
1 THATCHERS WK
2 WHEATSHEAF CL
3 CHURCH WK
4 WAGGONERS WK
Leake Ings
COWBRIDGE LANE
BUTTERCRAE
Barn Farm
Mole End
2

Ivy House Farm
ST MARGARET'S DR
Windmill
Sibsey Free (Cont) Prim Sch
Vicarage Farm
Sewage Works
MALLOWS LANE
LC
Bank Farm
Ivy House Farm
Gride Farm
Faunt Bridge
B1184
51

TRADER BANK
Sibsey
MILLERS GATE
PH
Cemy
PO
+
LC
Leake Ings
MIDGATE LANE
MIDGATE (EAST)
Gride Bridge Farm
THE GRIDE
SKIPMARSH LA
PODE LANE
1

FRITHVILLE ROAD
B1184
DOROTHY CL 1
GRANGE MWS 2
BOSTON ROAD A16
B1184
STATION ROAD
LC
Benington Bridge
Leake Gride Bridge
Gride Bridge
CRACKHOLT LA

Sycamore Farm
HIGH FERRY LANE
Station Farm
Benington Ings
INGS DV
50

B1
1 HARVESTER WY
2 MAIN RD
3 LITTLEPORT LA
4 VICARAGE LA
5 GLEBE CL
6 LITTLEPORT LA
7 MANOR CL
8 AMOS WY
9 SARGEANTS CL
10 BESANT CL
11 CHURCH CL
12 EVISON CT
13 LUCAN CL
14 CHAPEL LA

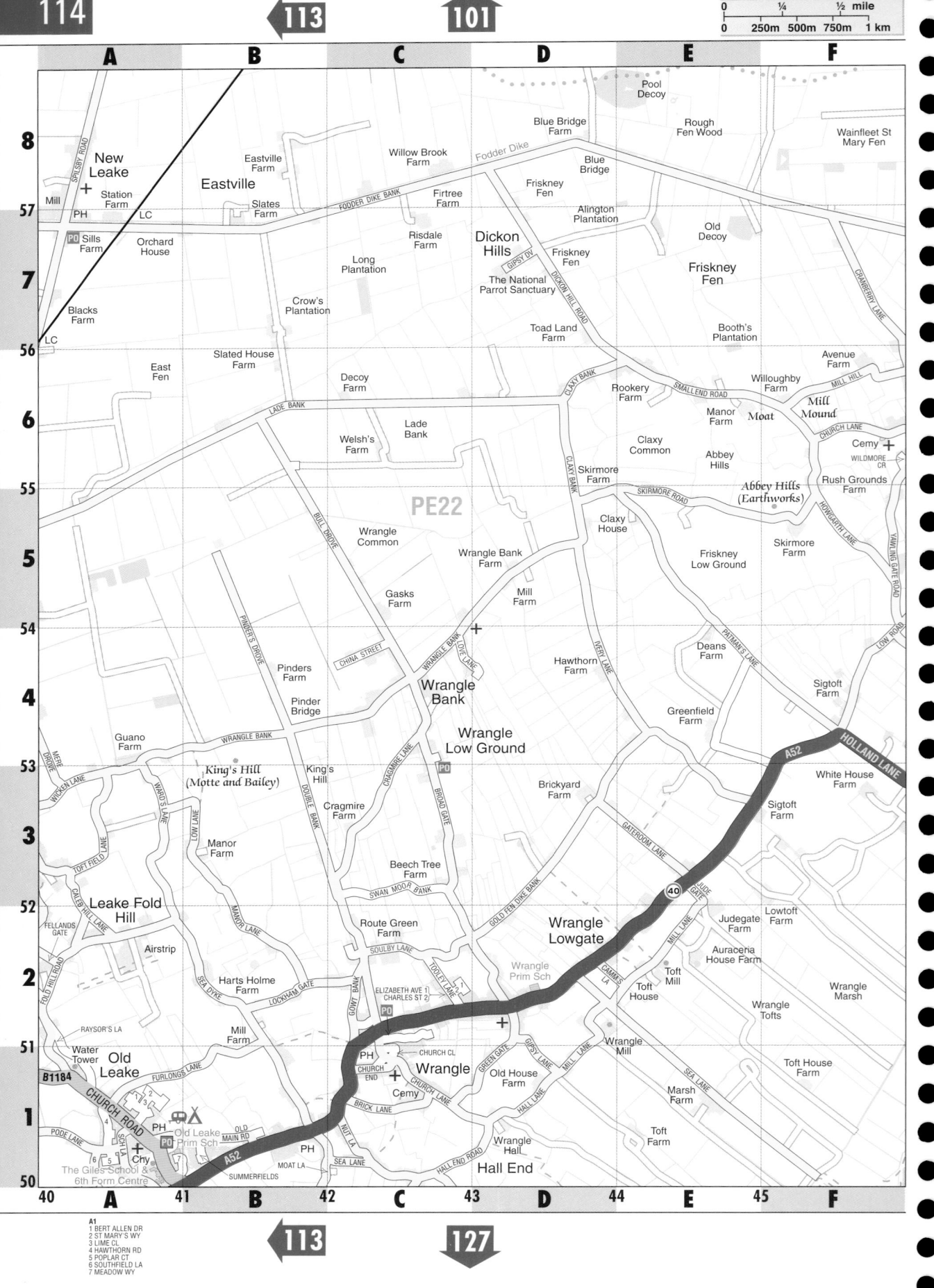

113
101

Scale: 1¾ inches to 1 mile

0   ¼   ½   mile
0   250m   500m   750m   1 km

A   B   C   D   E   F

8

New Leake
Mill
PH
Station Farm
LC
Sills Farm
PO
Orchard House
Blacks Farm
LC

Eastville Farm
Slates Farm
Eastville
Slated House Farm

Willow Brook Farm
Firtree Farm
Risdale Farm
Long Plantation
Crow's Plantation
Decoy Farm

Fodder Dike
Fodder Dike Bank

Blue Bridge Farm
Blue Bridge
Friskney Fen
Alington Plantation
Dickon Hills
The National Parrot Sanctuary
Toad Land Farm
Friskney Fen

Pool Decoy
Rough Fen Wood
Wainfleet St Mary Fen
Old Decoy
Friskney Fen
Booth's Plantation
Avenue Farm
Willoughby Farm
Mill Hill
Mill Mound

57

7

6

East Fen
Welsh's Farm
Lade Bank
Lade Bank
Decoy Farm

Claxy Bank
Claxy Bank
Rookery Farm
Skirmore Farm
Manor Farm
Moat
Claxy Common
Abbey Hills
Claxy House
Smallend Road
Skirmore Road
Abbey Hills (Earthworks)
Cemy
WILDMORE CR
Rush Grounds Farm
Church Lane

55

PE22

Wrangle Common
Wrangle Bank Farm
Gasks Farm
Mill Farm
Friskney Low Ground
Skirmore Farm
Bull Drove

Howgarth Lane
Yawling Gate Road
Low Road

5

54

Pinders Farm
China Street
Pinders Drove
Wrangle Bank
Wrangle Low Ground
Hawthorn Farm
Deans Farm
Greenfield Farm
Sigtoft Farm
Love Lane
Ivery Lane
Patman's Lane

4

53

Guano Farm
King's Hill (Motte and Bailey)
King's Hill
Cragmire Farm
Wrangle Bank
Double Bank
Cragmire Lane
PO
Broad Gate
Brickyard Farm
A52
Holland Lane
White House Farm
Sigtoft Farm
Gateroom Lane

3

52

Leake Fold Hill
Manor Farm
Toft Field Lane
Caleb Hill Lane
Fellands Gate
Airstrip
Manor Lane
Low Lane
Sea Dyke
Harts Holme Farm
Beech Tree Farm
Swan Moor Bank
Route Green Farm
Soulby Lane
Gold Fen Dike Bank
Wrangle Lowgate
40
Mill Lane
Camm's La
Judegate Farm
Lowtoft Farm
Auraceria House Farm
Wrangle Tofts
Wrangle Marsh
Toft Mill
Toft House

2

51

Water Tower
Old Leake
B1184
Raysor's La
Furlongs Lane
Mill Farm
Lockram Gate
Gowt Bank
Elizabeth Ave 1
Charles St 2
PO
Toll Ey Lane
Wrangle Prim Sch
Green Gate
Gipsy Lane
Mill Lane
Wrangle Mill
Sea Lane
Marsh Farm
Toft House Farm

1

50

Pode Lane
Church Road
SCH
PH
PO
Chy
The Giles School & 6th Form Centre
Old Leake Prim Sch
Old Main Rd
A52
Summerfields
Moat La
Sea Lane
Nut La
Church End
Church Lane
Cemy
Wrangle
PH
Brick Lane
Hall Lane
Old House Farm
Wrangle Hall
Hall End
Hall End Road
Toft Farm

40   A   41   B   42   C   43   D   44   E   45   F

A1
1 BERT ALLEN DR
2 ST MARY'S WY
3 LIME CL
4 HAWTHORN CT
5 POPLAR LA
6 SOUTHFIELD LA
7 MEADOW WY

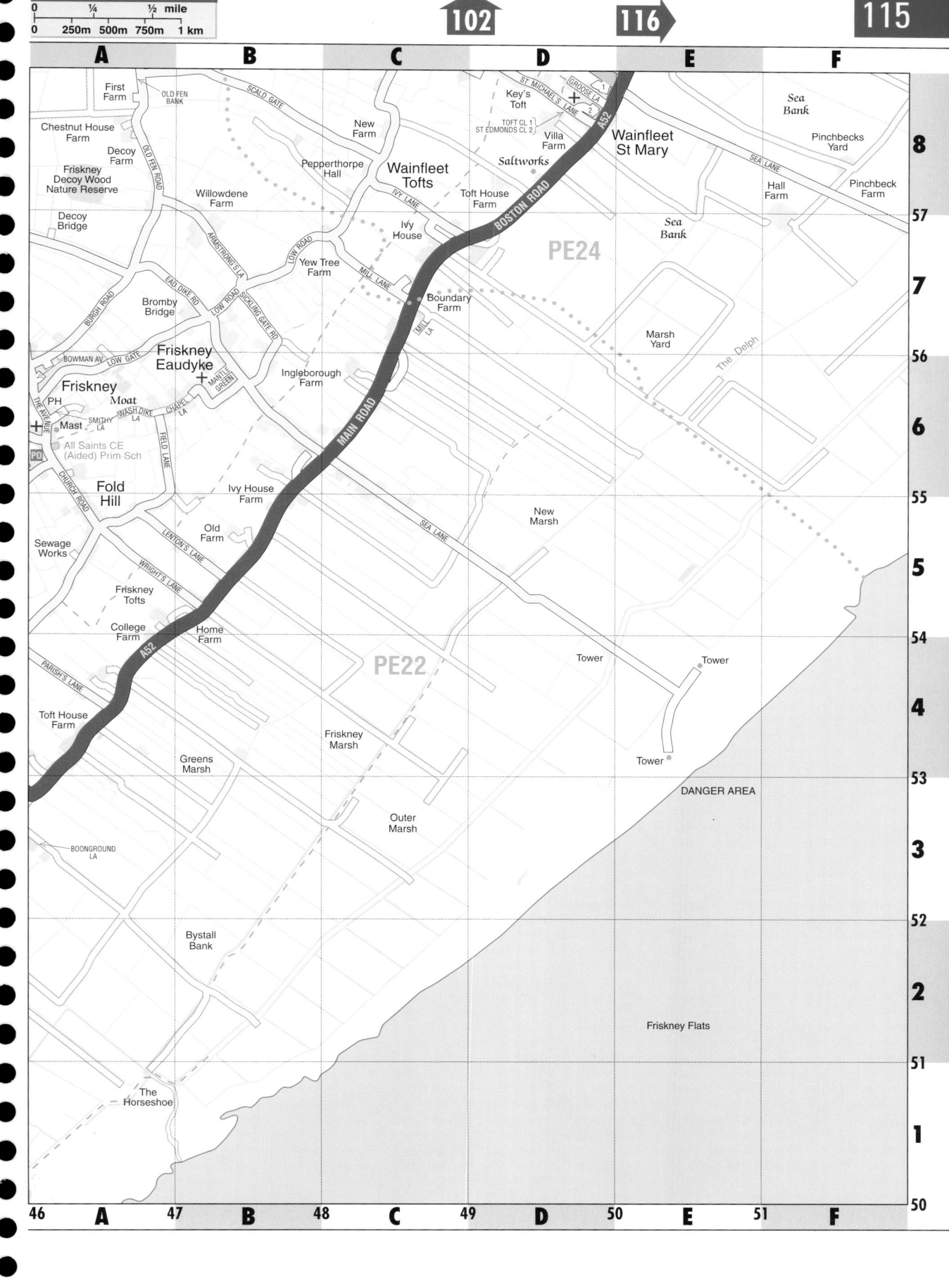

Scale: 1¾ inches to 1 mile

0 ¼ ½ mile
0 250m 500m 750m 1 km

102

116

A **B** **C** **D** **E** **F**

First Farm
Old Fen Bank
SCALD GATE
Chestnut House Farm
New Farm
St Michael's Lane
GROOSE LA
Key's Toft
Villa Farm
Wainfleet St Mary
Sea Bank
Decoy Farm
Pepperthorpe Hall
TOFT CL 1
ST EDMONDS CL 2
Saltworks
Pinchbecks Yard
Friskney Decoy Wood Nature Reserve
Willowdene Farm
Wainfleet Tofts
Toft House Farm
SEA LANE
Pinchbeck Farm
IVY LANE
BOSTON ROAD
A52
8
Decoy Bridge
LOW ROAD
Ivy House
Sea Bank
Hall Farm
ARMSTRONG'S LA
PE24
57
EAU DIKE RD
Yew Tree Farm
MILL LANE
7
BURGH ROAD
LOW ROAD
SUCKLING GATE RD
Boundary Farm
MILL LA
Marsh Yard
The Delph
Bromby Bridge
Friskney Eaudyke
MANTLE GREEN
Ingleborough Farm
56
BOWMAN AV
LOW GATE
MAIN ROAD
Friskney
Moat
CHAPEL LA
6
THE AVENUE
Mast
SMITHY LA
WASH DIKE LA
FIELD LANE
All Saints CE (Aided) Prim Sch
55
PO
Ivy House Farm
SEA LANE
New Marsh
Fold Hill
CHURCH ROAD
Old Farm
5
Sewage Works
LENTON'S LANE
WRIGHT'S LANE
54
Friskney Tofts
A52
Home Farm
PE22
Tower
Tower
College Farm
4
PARISH'S LANE
Friskney Marsh
Tower
53
Toft House Farm
Greens Marsh
DANGER AREA
3
BOONGROUND LA
Outer Marsh
52
Bystall Bank
2
Friskney Flats
51
The Horseshoe
1
50

46 **A** 47 **B** 48 **C** 49 **D** 50 **E** 51 **F**

102

103 206

E8
1 BAYES RD
2 PRECINCT CRES
3 GREEN LA
4 LINKS CRES
5 NORWOOD RD
6 VINE RD
7 ALBERT AVE
8 BUCKTHORN AVE
9 SHARDLOES RD
10 SEA FRONT RD
11 SEACROFT SQ
12 HESKETH CRES
13 FREDERICA RD

Scale: 1¾ inches to 1 mile
0   ¼   ½   mile
0   250m   500m   750m   1 km

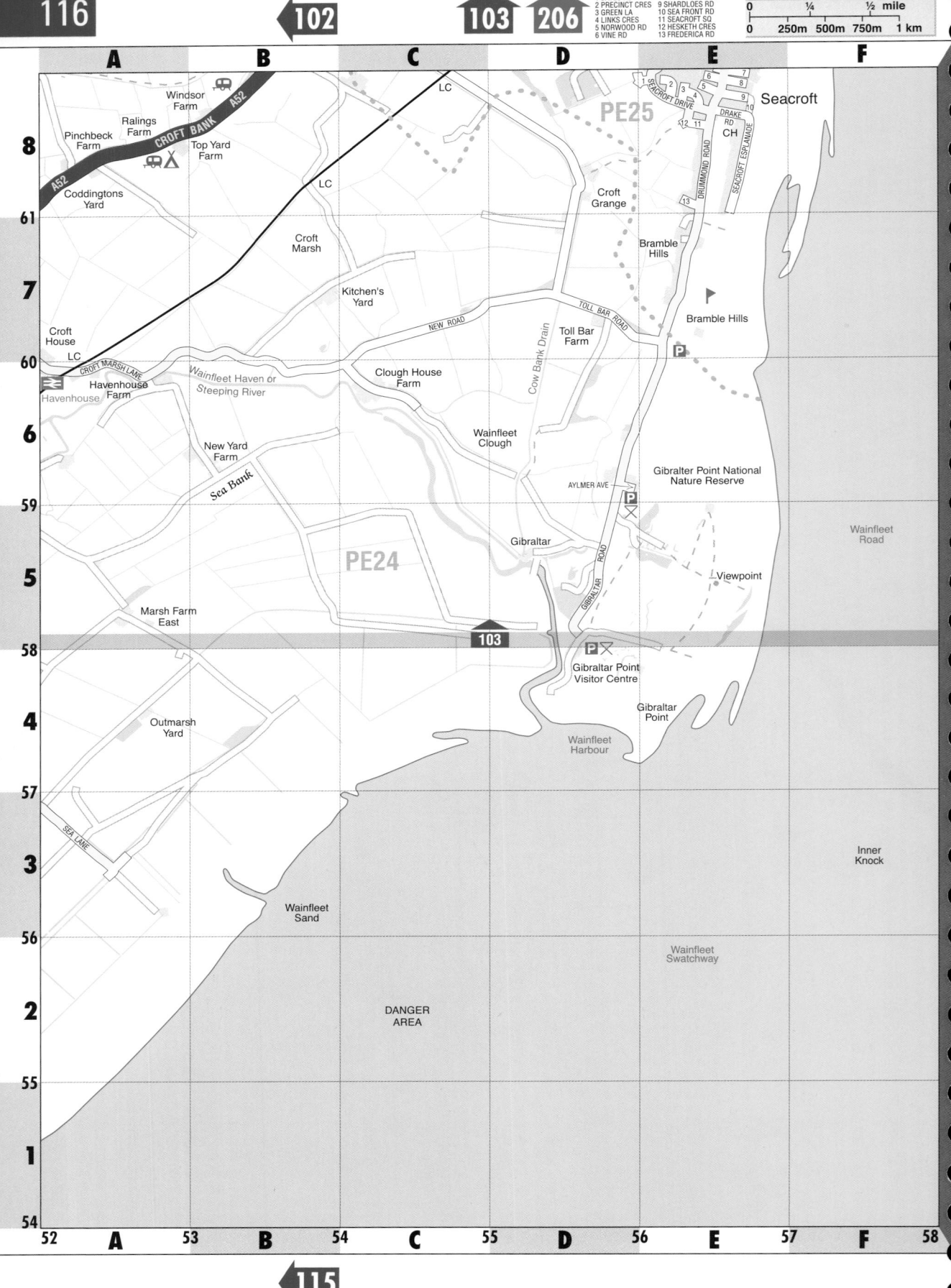

Windsor Farm
Pinchbeck Farm
Ralings Farm
Top Yard Farm
CROFT BANK
A52
Coddingtons Yard
LC
LC
Croft Marsh
Kitchen's Yard
Seacroft
PE25
SEACROFT DRIVE
DRUMMOND ROAD
SEACROFT ESPLANADE
DRAKE RD
CH
Croft Grange
Bramble Hills
Bramble Hills
Croft House
LC
NEW ROAD
TOLL BAR ROAD
Havenhouse Farm
Havenhouse
Wainfleet Haven or Steeping River
Clough House Farm
Toll Bar Farm
Cow Bank Drain
P
CROFT MARSH LANE
New Yard Farm
Wainfleet Clough
Gibralter Point National Nature Reserve
Sea Bank
AYLMER AVE
P
PE24
Gibraltar
GIBRALTAR ROAD
Viewpoint
Marsh Farm East
103
Gibraltar Point Visitor Centre
Gibraltar Point
Wainfleet Road
Outmarsh Yard
Wainfleet Harbour
SEA LANE
Inner Knock
Wainfleet Sand
Wainfleet Swatchway
DANGER AREA

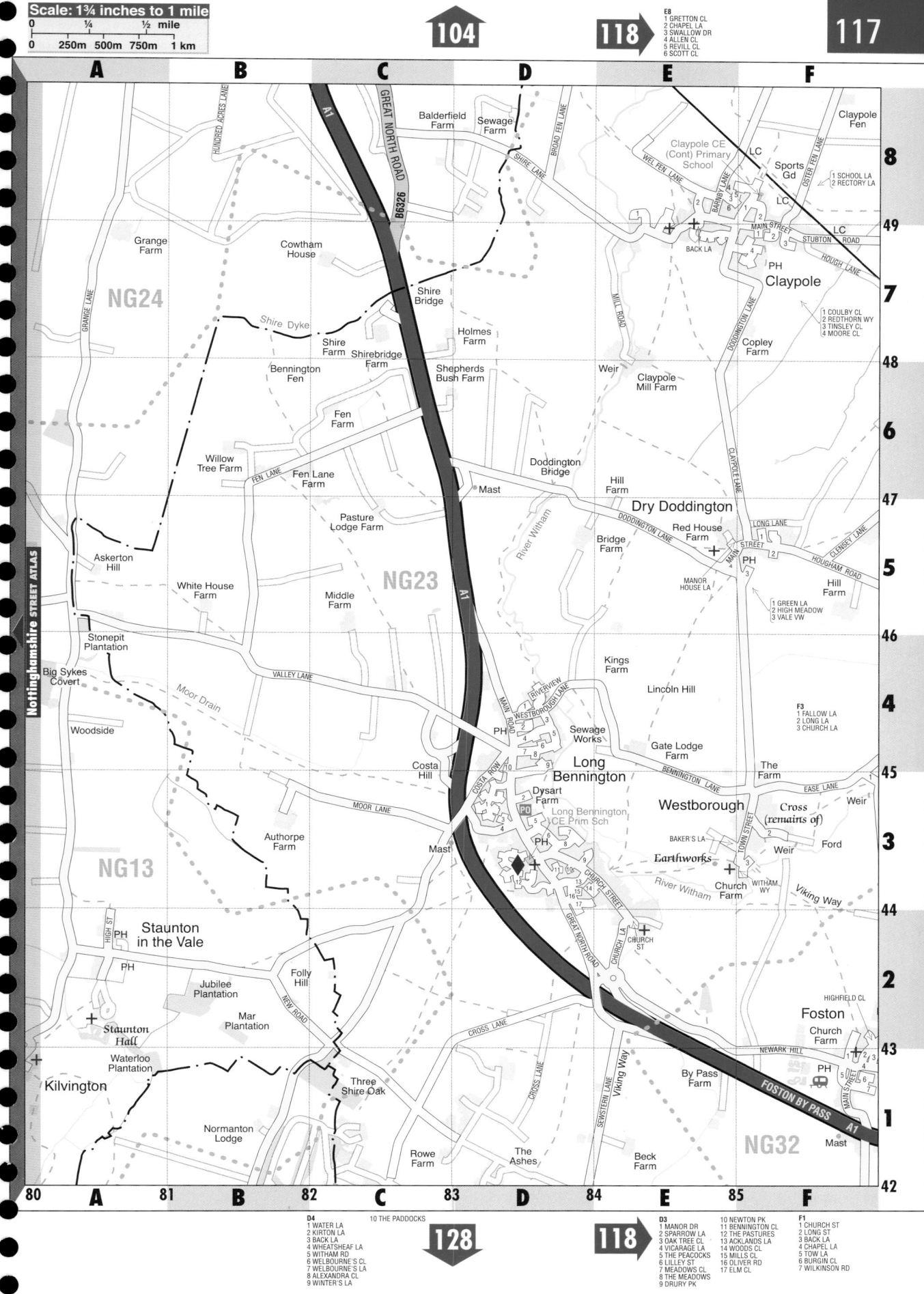

104
118

Scale: 1¾ inches to 1 mile

0   ¼   ½   mile
0   250m   500m   750m   1 km

Nottinghamshire STREET ATLAS

E8
1 GRETTON CL
2 CHAPEL LA
3 SWALLOW DR
4 ALLEN CL
5 REVILL CL
6 SCOTT CL

Claypole Fen

Claypole CE (Cont) Primary School

Sports Gd

1 SCHOOL LA
2 RECTORY LA

Claypole

PH

1 COULBY CL
2 REDTHORN WY
3 TINSLEY CL
4 MOORE CL

BACK LA

MAIN STREET

STUBTON ROAD

HOUGH LANE

OSTER FEN LANE

BARNBY LANE

WEL FEN LANE

DODDINGTON LANE

CLAPPLE LANE

MILL ROAD

Grange Farm

Cowtham House

NG24

GRANGE LANE

HUNDRED ACRES LANE

GREAT NORTH ROAD

B6326

A1

Balderfield Farm

Sewage Farm

SHIRE LANE

BROAD FEN LANE

Shire Bridge

Shire Dyke

Shire Farm

Shirebridge Farm

Holmes Farm

Bennington Fen

Shepherds Bush Farm

Copley Farm

Weir

Claypole Mill Farm

Fen Farm

Willow Tree Farm

Fen Lane Farm

FEN LANE

Doddington Bridge

Hill Farm

Dry Doddington

LONG LANE

CLENSEY LANE

HOUGHAM ROAD

Red House Farm

PH

MAIN STREET

Hill Farm

1 GREEN LA
2 HIGH MEADOW
3 VALE VW

MANOR HOUSE LA

Mast

River Witham

Bridge Farm

NG23

A1

Pasture Lodge Farm

Askerton Hill

White House Farm

Middle Farm

Kings Farm

Lincoln Hill

F3
1 FALLOW LA
2 LONG LA
3 CHURCH LA

Stonepit Plantation

Big Sykes Covert

VALLEY LANE

Moor Drain

Woodside

RIVERVIEW

WESTBOROUGH LANE

Main Road

PH

Sewage Works

Gate Lodge Farm

BENNINGTON LANE

The Farm

EASE LANE

Weir

Costa Hill

COSTA ROW

Long Bennington

Westborough

Cross (remains of)

MOOR LANE

Dysart Farm

PO

Long Bennington CE Prim Sch

PH

BAKER'S LA

TOWN STREET

Ford

Earthworks

Weir

Viking Way

VIKING WAY

WITHAM WY

Church Farm

River Witham

Authorpe Farm

NG13

Mast

CHURCH STREET

GREAT NORTH ROAD

CHURCH LA

CHURCH ST

Staunton in the Vale

HIGH ST

PH

PH

Jubilee Plantation

Folly Hill

Mar Plantation

NEW ROAD

CROSS LANE

HIGHFIELD CL

Foston

Church Farm

NEWARK HILL

PH

By Pass Farm

Staunton Hall

Waterloo Plantation

Kilvington

Three Shire Oak

Normanton Lodge

Rowe Farm

CROSS LANE

SEWSTERN LANE

VIKING WAY

The Ashes

Beck Farm

FOSTON BY PASS

A1

NG32

Mast

MAIN STREET

D4
1 WATER LA
2 KIRTON LA
3 BACK LA
4 WHEATSHEAF LA
5 WITHAM RD
6 WELBOURNE'S CL
7 WELBOURNE'S LA
8 ALEXANDRA CL
9 WINTER'S LA

10 THE PADDOCKS

D3
1 MANOR DR
2 SPARROW LA
3 OAK TREE CL
4 VICARAGE LA
5 THE PEACOCKS
6 LILLEY ST
7 MEADOWS CL
8 THE MEADOWS
9 DRURY PK
10 NEWTON PK
11 BENNINGTON CL
12 THE PASTURES
13 ACKLANDS LA
14 WOODS CL
15 MILLS CL
16 OLIVER RD
17 ELM CL

F1
1 CHURCH ST
2 LONG ST
3 BACK LA
4 CHAPEL LA
5 TOW LA
6 BURGIN CL
7 WILKINSON RD

A B C D E F

8 49 7 48 6 47 5 46 4 45 3 44 2 43 1 42

80 81 82 83 84 85

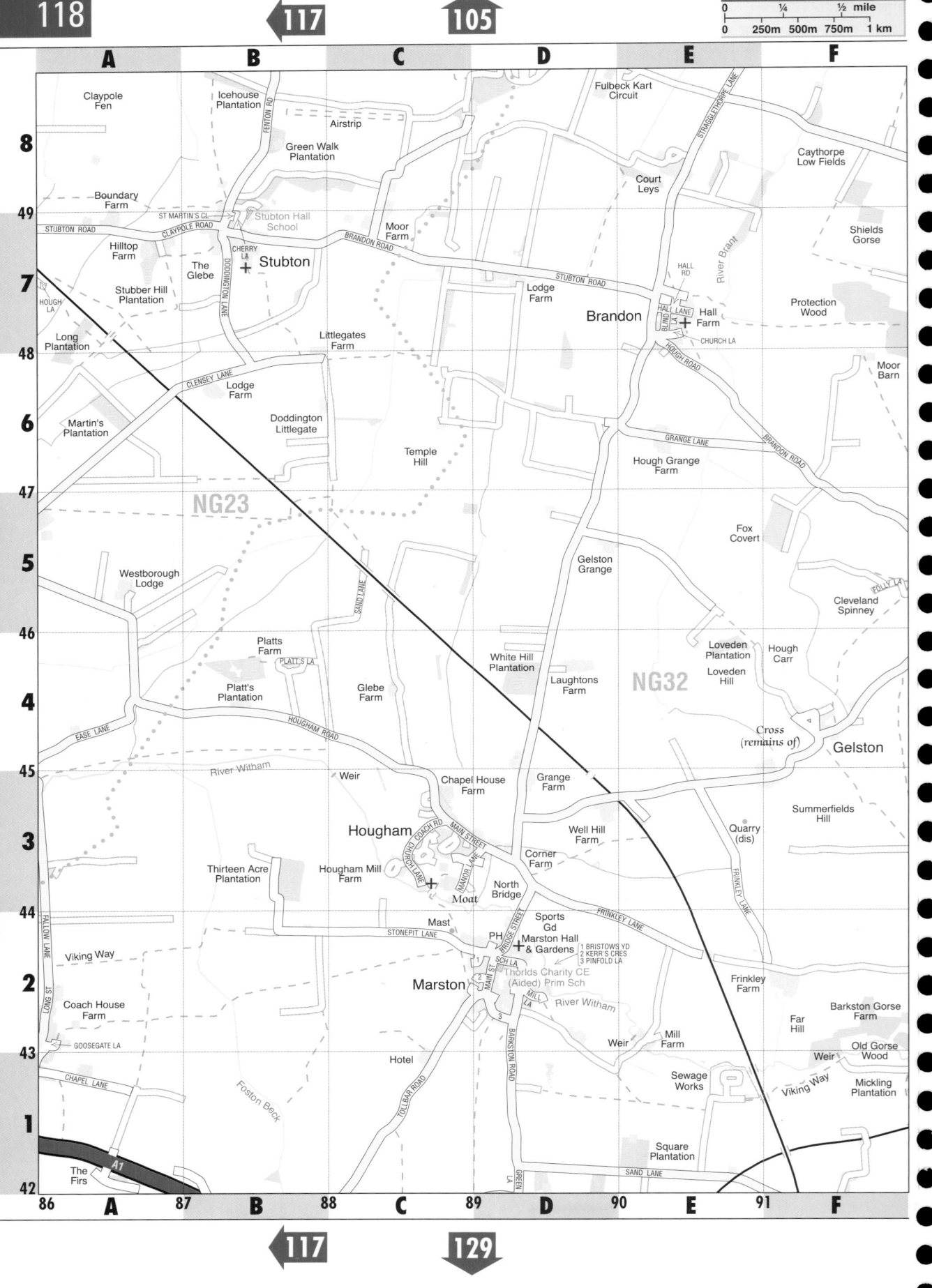

118

117

105

Scale: 1¾ inches to 1 mile
0   ¼   ½   mile
0   250m 500m 750m 1 km

A   B   C   D   E   F

8

Claypole Fen

Icehouse Plantation

Airstrip

Green Walk Plantation

Fulbeck Kart Circuit

Caythorpe Low Fields

49

Boundary Farm

St Martin's Cl

Stubton Hall School

Stubton Road

Claypole Road

Moor Farm

Brandon Road

Stubton Road

Court Leys

Hall Rd

Shields Gorse

7

Hough La

Hilltop Farm

The Glebe

Cherry La

Stubton

Lodge Farm

Brandon

Hall Lane

Blind La

Hall Farm

Church La

River Brant

Protection Wood

Stubber Hill Plantation

Doddington Lane

Fenton Rd

48

Long Plantation

Clensey Lane

Lodge Farm

Littlegates Farm

Hough Road

Moor Barn

6

Martin's Plantation

Doddington Littlegate

Temple Hill

Grange Lane

Hough Grange Farm

Brandon Road

47

NG23

5

Westborough Lodge

Sand Lane

Gelston Grange

Fox Covert

Folly La

Cleveland Spinney

46

Platts Farm

Platt's La

White Hill Plantation

NG32

Loveden Plantation

Hough Carr

Loveden Hill

4

Ease Lane

Platt's Plantation

Hougham Road

Glebe Farm

Laughtons Farm

Cross (remains of)

Gelston

45

River Witham

Weir

Chapel House Farm

Grange Farm

Summerfields Hill

3

Fallow Lane

Lings St

Thirteen Acre Plantation

Hougham Mill Farm

Hougham

Church Rd

Coach Rd

Main Street

Manor La

Moat

North Bridge

Corner Farm

Well Hill Farm

Frinkley Lane

Quarry (dis)

Frinkley Lane

44

Viking Way

Stonepit Lane

Mast

Bridge Street

PH

Sports Gd

Marston Hall & Gardens

1 BRISTOWS YD
2 KERR'S CRES
3 PINFOLD LA

Frinkley Farm

2

Coach House Farm

Goosegate La

Main St

Sch La

Marston

Thorold Charity CE (Aided) Prim Sch

Barkston Road

River Witham

Mill La

Weir

Mill Farm

Far Hill

Barkston Gorse Farm

Old Gorse Wood

43

Chapel Lane

Hotel

Tollbar Road

Green La

Weir

Sewage Works

Viking Way

Mickling Plantation

1

Foston Beck

Square Plantation

A1

Sand Lane

The Firs

42

86   A   87   B   88   C   89   D   90   E   91   F

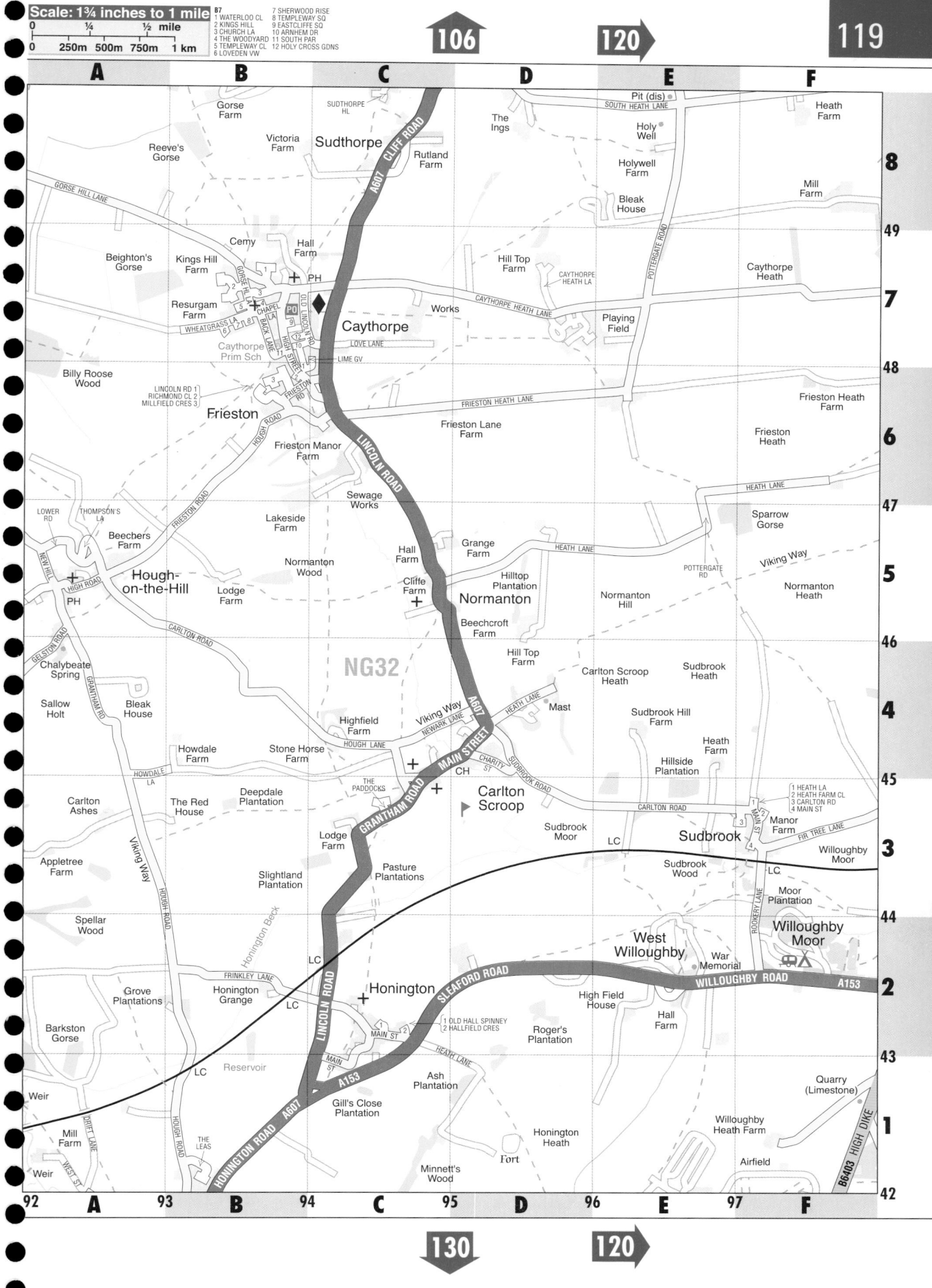
Scale: 1¾ inches to 1 mile
0 ¼ ½ mile
0 250m 500m 750m 1 km
B7
1 WATERLOO CL
2 KINGS HILL
3 CHURCH LA
4 THE WOODYARD
5 TEMPLEWAY CL
6 LOVEDEN VW
7 SHERWOOD RISE
8 TEMPLEWAY SQ
9 EASTCLIFFE SQ
10 ARNHEM DR
11 SOUTH PAR
12 HOLY CROSS GDNS
106
120
130
120
Gorse Farm
Reeve's Gorse
Victoria Farm
Sudthorpe
SUDTHORPE HL
Rutland Farm
The Ings
Pit (dis)
SOUTH HEATH LANE
Holy Well
Heath Farm
Holywell Farm
Bleak House
Mill Farm
GORSE HILL LANE
A607 CLIFF ROAD
Cemy
Hall Farm
Beighton's Gorse
Kings Hill Farm
PH
Hill Top Farm
CAYTHORPE HEATH LA
POTTERGATE ROAD
Caythorpe Heath
Resurgam Farm
PO
Works
CAYTHORPE HEATH LANE
Playing Field
Caythorpe
LOVE LANE
WHEATGRASS LA
CHAPEL LA
BACK LANE
HIGH STREET
OLD LINCOLN RD
Caythorpe Prim Sch
LIME GV
Billy Roose Wood
LINCOLN RD 1
RICHMOND CL 2
MILLFIELD CRES 3
FRIESTON RD
Frieston
FRIESTON HEATH LANE
Frieston Heath Farm
HOUGH ROAD
Frieston Lane Farm
Frieston Heath
Frieston Manor Farm
LINCOLN ROAD
HEATH LANE
Sewage Works
LOWER RD
THOMPSON'S LA
FRIESTON ROAD
Lakeside Farm
Sparrow Gorse
Beechers Farm
NEW HILL
Hall Farm
Grange Farm
HEATH LANE
Viking Way
Normanton Wood
POTTERGATE RD
HIGH ROAD
Hough-on-the-Hill
PH
Lodge Farm
Cliffe Farm
Hilltop Plantation
Normanton
Normanton Hill
Normanton Heath
Beechcroft Farm
CARLTON ROAD
GELSTON ROAD
Chalybeate Spring
NG32
Hill Top Farm
Carlton Scroop Heath
Sudbrook Heath
GRANTHAM ROAD
Sallow Holt
Bleak House
A607
HEATH LANE
Mast
Viking Way
NEWARK LANE
Highfield Farm
Sudbrook Hill Farm
HOUGH LANE
Heath Farm
Howdale Farm
Stone Horse Farm
MAIN STREET
CHARITY ST
SUDBROOK ROAD
Hillside Plantation
HOWDALE LA
CH
THE PADDOCKS
Carlton Ashes
The Red House
Deepdale Plantation
Carlton Scroop
1 HEATH LA
2 HEATH FARM CL
3 CARLTON RD
4 MAIN ST
CARLTON ROAD
MAIN ST
Manor Farm
GRANTHAM ROAD
Sudbrook Moor
Sudbrook
FIR TREE LANE
Lodge Farm
LC
Willoughby Moor
Viking Way
Appletree Farm
Pasture Plantations
Sudbrook Wood
LC
Slightland Plantation
Moor Plantation
ROOKERY LANE
Spellar Wood
HOUGH ROAD
Honington Beck
Willoughby Moor
West Willoughby
War Memorial
LC
SLEAFORD ROAD
WILLOUGHBY ROAD
A153
FRINKLEY LANE
Grove Plantations
Honington Grange
Honington
High Field House
LC
LINCOLN ROAD
Barkston Gorse
MAIN ST
1 OLD HALL SPINNEY
2 HALLFIELD CRES
Roger's Plantation
Hall Farm
HEATH LANE
MAIN ST
Reservoir
LC
Ash Plantation
A153
Quarry (Limestone)
Weir
Gill's Close Plantation
A607
Willoughby Heath Farm
Mill Farm
DRIFT LANE
HOUGH ROAD
THE LEAS
HONINGTON ROAD
Honington Heath
Fort
Airfield
B6403 HIGH DIKE
Weir
WEST ST
Minnett's Wood
A B C D E F
8 49 7 48 6 47 5 46 4 45 3 44 2 43 1 42
92 93 94 95 96 97

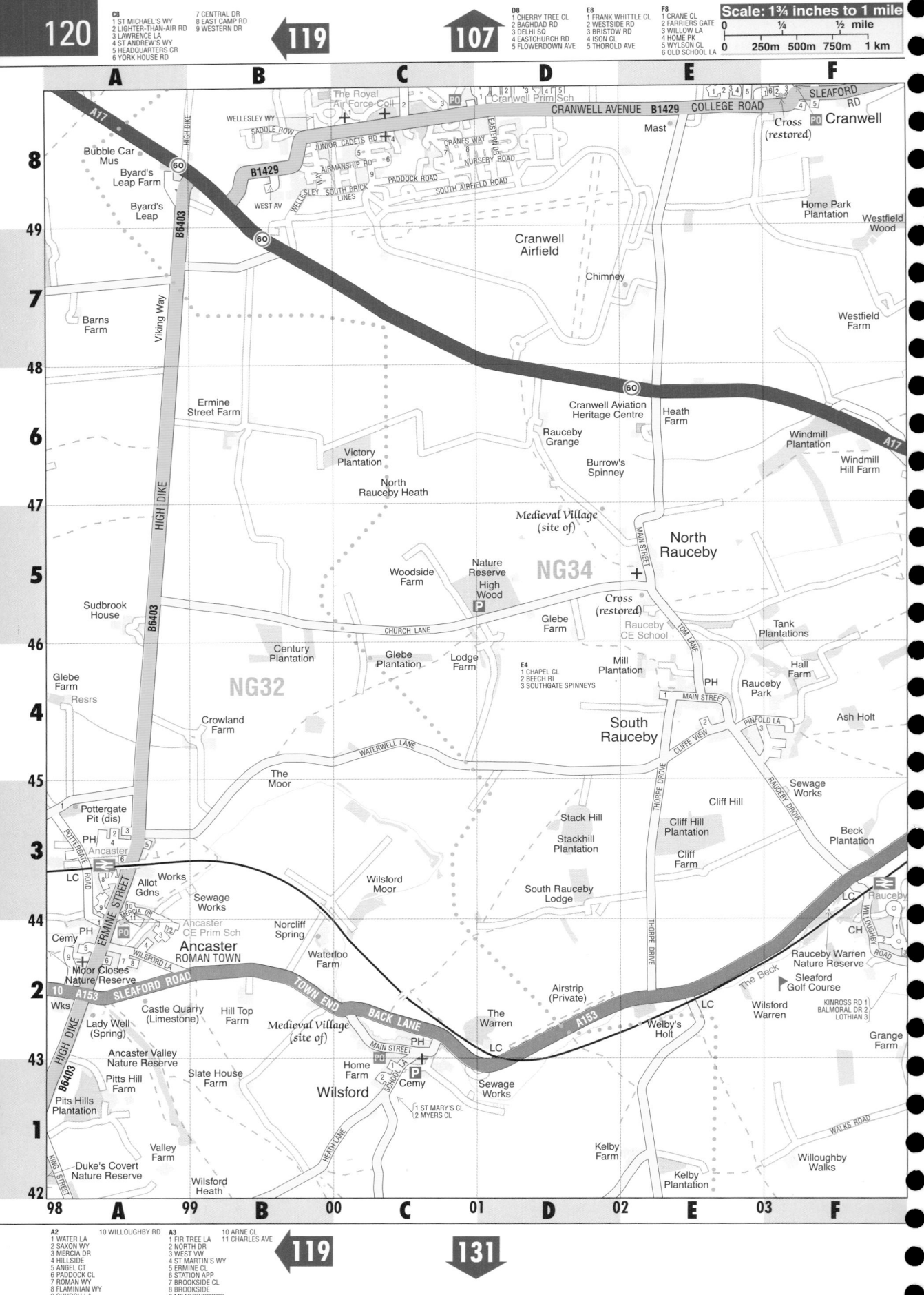

120

C8
1 ST MICHAEL'S WY
2 LIGHTER-THAN-AIR RD
3 LAWRENCE LA
4 ST ANDREW'S WY
5 HEADQUARTERS CR
6 YORK HOUSE RD

7 CENTRAL DR
8 EAST CAMP RD
9 WESTERN DR

◀ 119

⬥ 107

D8
1 CHERRY TREE CL
2 BAGHDAD RD
3 DELHI SQ
4 EASTCHURCH RD
5 FLOWERDOWN AVE

E8
1 FRANK WHITTLE CL
2 WESTSIDE RD
3 BRISTOW RD
4 ISON CL
5 THOROLD AVE

F8
1 CRANE CL
2 FARRIERS GATE
3 WILLOW LA
4 HOME PK
5 WYLSON CL
6 OLD SCHOOL LA

Scale: 1¾ inches to 1 mile
0   ¼   ½ mile
0   250m 500m 750m 1 km

A17 Bubble Car Mus

Byard's Leap Farm
Byard's Leap

Viking Way

High Dike

B6403

Barns Farm

The Royal Air Force Coll
WELLESLEY WY
SADDLE ROW
JUNIOR CADETS RD
AIRMANSHIP RD
WEST AV
B1429

Cranwell Prim Sch
Cranwell Avenue B1429 COLLEGE ROAD
CRANES WY
EASTERN DR
NURSERY ROAD
PADDOCK ROAD
SOUTH BRICK LINES
SOUTH AIRFIELD ROAD

SLEAFORD RD
Cross (restored) PO Cranwell
Mast

Cranwell Airfield
Chimney

Home Park Plantation
Westfield Wood

Westfield Farm

Ermine Street Farm

Victory Plantation
North Rauceby Heath

Cranwell Aviation Heritage Centre
Rauceby Grange
Burrow's Spinney
Heath Farm

Windmill Plantation
Windmill Hill Farm
A17

Sudbrook House
B6403

Woodside Farm
Nature Reserve High Wood
P

Medieval Village (site of)
NG34

Main Street

North Rauceby

Glebe Farm
Resrs

Century Plantation
NG32

Glebe Plantation
Lodge Farm

Glebe Farm
Cross (restored)
Rauceby CE School

Tom Lane
Tank Plantations
Hall Farm
Ash Holt

Crowland Farm

E4
1 CHAPEL CL
2 BEECH RI
3 SOUTHGATE SPINNEYS

Mill Plantation
PH
Rauceby Park

Main Street

Waterwell Lane
The Moor

South Rauceby
Cliffe View
Pinfold La

Pottergate Pit (dis)
PH
Ancaster
Pottergate Road
LC

Works
Allot Gdns
Sewage Works

Wilsford Moor

Stack Hill
Stackhill Plantation
Cliff Farm

Thorpe Drive
Cliff Hill
Cliff Hill Plantation

Rauceby Drive
Sewage Works
Beck Plantation

Ermine Street
Mercia Dr
Ancaster CE Prim Sch
PH
Cemy
Ancaster ROMAN TOWN
Moor Closes Nature Reserve
Wilsford La

Norcliff Spring
Waterloo Farm

South Rauceby Lodge

LC Rauceby
Willoughby Road
CH
Rauceby Warren Nature Reserve
Sleaford Golf Course

10 A153 SLEAFORD ROAD
High Dike
Wks

Castle Quarry (Limestone)
Hill Top Farm
Lady Well (Spring)

Medieval Village (site of)

TOWN END BACK LANE

Airstrip (Private)
The Warren
A153
Welby's Holt
LC
Wilsford Warren
KINROSS RD 1
BALMORAL DR 2
LOTHIAN 3
Grange Farm

Ancaster Valley Nature Reserve
Pitts Hill Farm
B6403
Pits Hills Plantation

Slate House Farm

Main Street
PO
Home Farm
PH
Cemy
Wilsford
School La
P

Sewage Works

1 ST MARY'S CL
2 MYERS CL

Kelby Farm

WALKS ROAD

Duke's Covert Nature Reserve
King Street

Valley Farm

Wilsford Heath

Heath Lane

Kelby Plantation

Willoughby Walks

98   A   99   B   00   C   01   D   02   E   03   F

A2
1 WATER LA
2 SAXON WY
3 MERCIA DR
4 HILLSIDE
5 ANGEL CT
6 PADDOCK CL
7 ROMAN WY
8 FLAMINIAN WY
9 CHURCH LA

10 WILLOUGHBY RD

A3
1 FIR TREE LA
2 NORTH DR
3 WEST VW
4 ST MARTIN'S WY
5 ERMINE CL
6 STATION APP
7 BROOKSIDE CL
8 BROOKSIDE
9 MEADOWBROOK

10 ARNE CL
11 CHARLES AVE

◀ 119   ⬥ 131

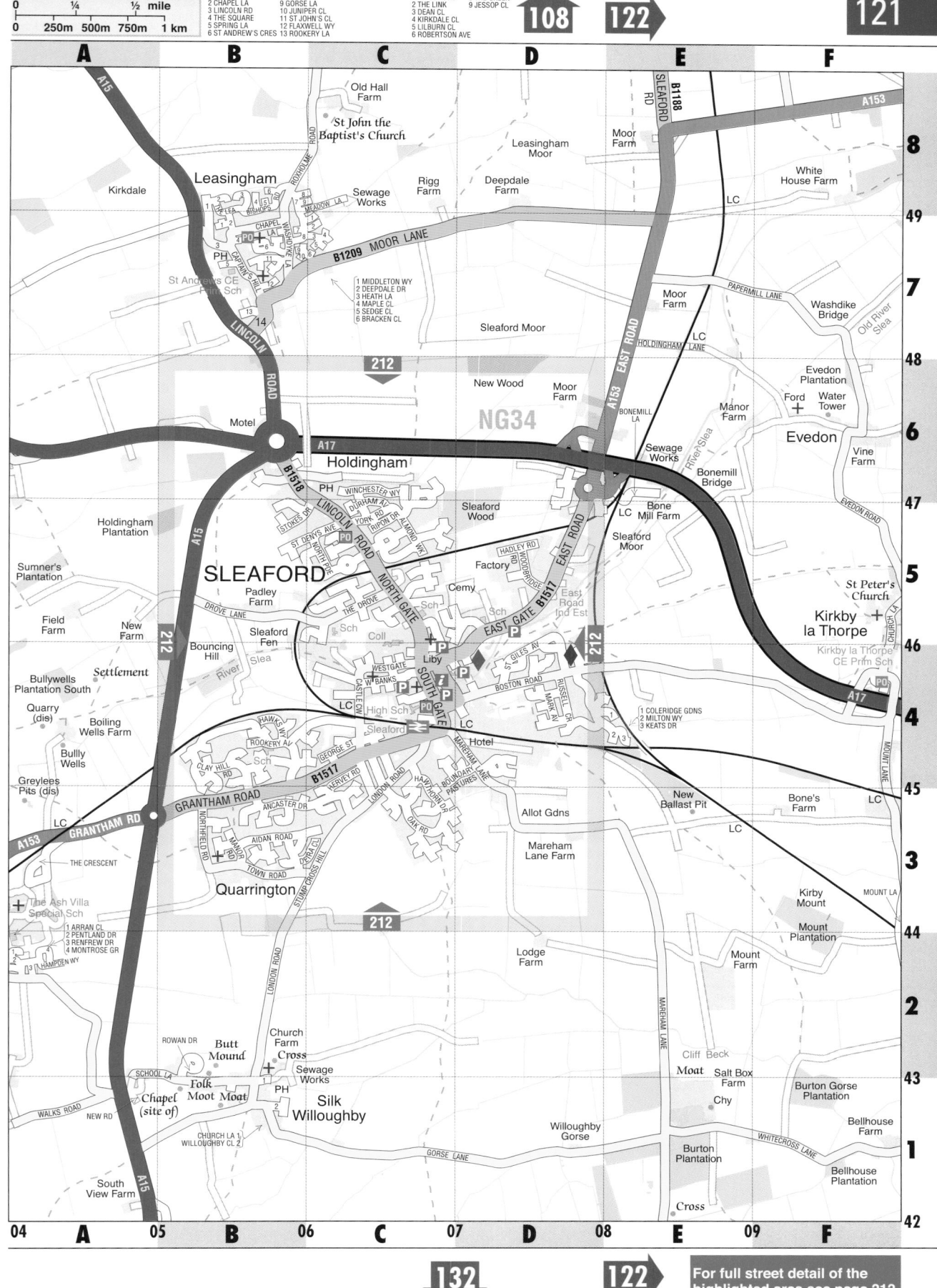

Scale: 1¾ inches to 1 mile

0   ¼   ½ mile
0   250m   500m   750m   1 km

B7
1 THE MALTINGS
2 CHAPEL LA
3 LINCOLN RD
4 THE SQUARE
5 SPRING LA
6 ST ANDREW'S CRES

7 MANOR CL
8 WANSBECK RD
9 GORSE LA
10 JUNIPER CL
11 ST JOHN'S CL
12 FLAXWELL WY
13 ROOKERY LA

14 SLEAFORD RD

B8
1 LINCOLN RD
2 THE LINK
3 DEAN CL
4 KIRKDALE CL
5 LILBURN CL
6 ROBERTSON AVE

7 RUSSELL RD
8 THE GREEN
9 JESSOP CL

108 122

For full street detail of the highlighted area see page 212.

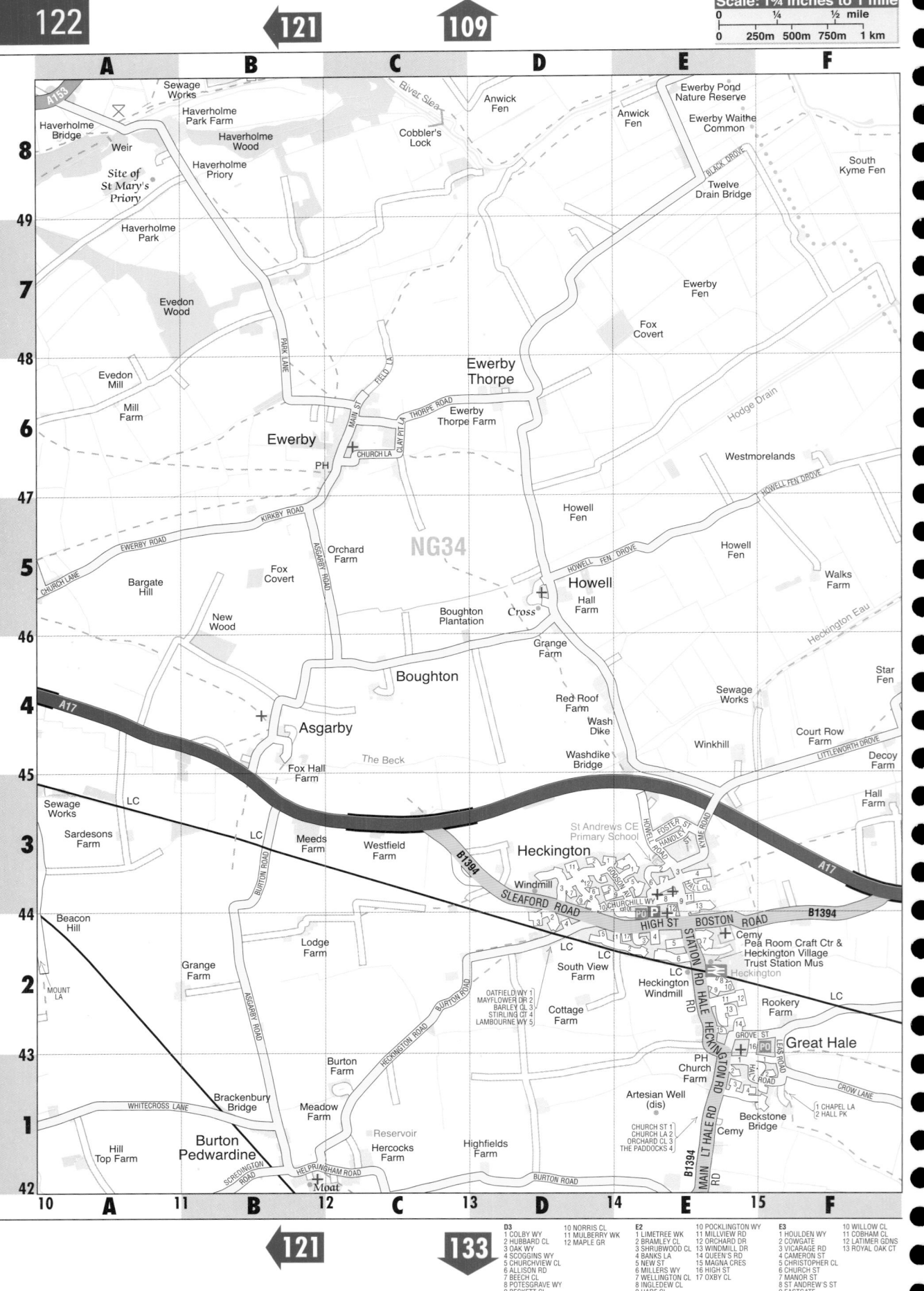

122

121

109

Scale: 1¾ inches to 1 mile
0   ¼   ½   mile
0   250m   500m   750m   1 km

A17

A153

Haverholme
Bridge

Sewage
Works

Weir

Haverholme
Park Farm

Haverholme
Wood

Site of
St Mary's
Priory

Haverholme
Priory

River Slea

Cobbler's
Lock

Anwick
Fen

Anwick
Fen

Ewerby Pond
Nature Reserve

Ewerby Waithe
Common

Black Drove

Twelve
Drain Bridge

South
Kyme Fen

Haverholme
Park

Evedon
Wood

Evedon
Mill

Mill
Farm

PARK LANE

FIELD LA

Ewerby

PH

MAIN ST

CLAY PIT LA

CHURCH LA

THORPE ROAD

Ewerby
Thorpe

Ewerby
Thorpe Farm

Ewerby
Fen

Fox
Covert

Ewerby
Fen

Westmorelands

HOWELL FEN DROVE

Hodge Drain

Howell
Fen

Howell
Fen

Walks
Farm

Heckington Eau

KIRKBY ROAD

EWERBY ROAD

CHURCH LANE

ASGARBY ROAD

Orchard
Farm

Fox
Covert

Bargate
Hill

New
Wood

Boughton
Plantation

Cross

Howell

Howell
Fen

HOWELL FEN DROVE

Hall
Farm

NG34

Boughton

Grange
Farm

Sewage
Works

Star
Fen

Asgarby

Fox Hall
Farm

The Beck

Red Roof
Farm

Wash
Dike

Washdike
Bridge

Winkhill

Court Row
Farm

LITTLEWORTH DROVE

Decoy
Farm

A17

Hall
Farm

Sewage
Works

Sardesons
Farm

LC

LC

BURTON ROAD

Meeds
Farm

Westfield
Farm

B1394

SLEAFORD ROAD

St Andrews CE
Primary School

FOSTER ST

HANDLEY RD

Heckington

Windmill

HIGH ST

KYME ROAD

HOWELL ROAD

CHURCHILL WY

PO

PH

Cemy

BOSTON ROAD

B1394

Pea Room Craft Ctr &
Heckington Village
Trust Station Mus

A17

Beacon
Hill

MOUNT
LA

Lodge
Farm

ASGARBY ROAD

BURTON ROAD

HECKINGTON ROAD

LC

South View
Farm

LC

LC

STATION RD

Heckington
Windmill

Heckington

LC

Rookery
Farm

HALE RD

HECKINGTON RD

GROVE ST

PO

Great Hale

LEAS ROAD

Grange
Farm

Cottage
Farm

OATFIELD WY 1
MAYFLOWER DR 2
BARLEY CL 3
STIRLING CT 4
LAMBOURNE WY 5

PH
Church
Farm

MAIN LT HALE RD

HALL RD

CROW LANE

1 CHAPEL LA
2 HALL PK

WHITECROSS LANE

Brackenbury
Bridge

Burton
Pedwardine

SCREDINGTON ROAD

Burton
Farm

Meadow
Farm

HELPRINGHAM ROAD

Moat

Reservoir

Hercocks
Farm

Highfields
Farm

Artesian Well
(dis)

CHURCH ST 1
CHURCH LA 2
ORCHARD CL 3
THE PADDOCKS 4

Cemy

Beckstone
Bridge

B1394

BURTON ROAD

Hill
Top Farm

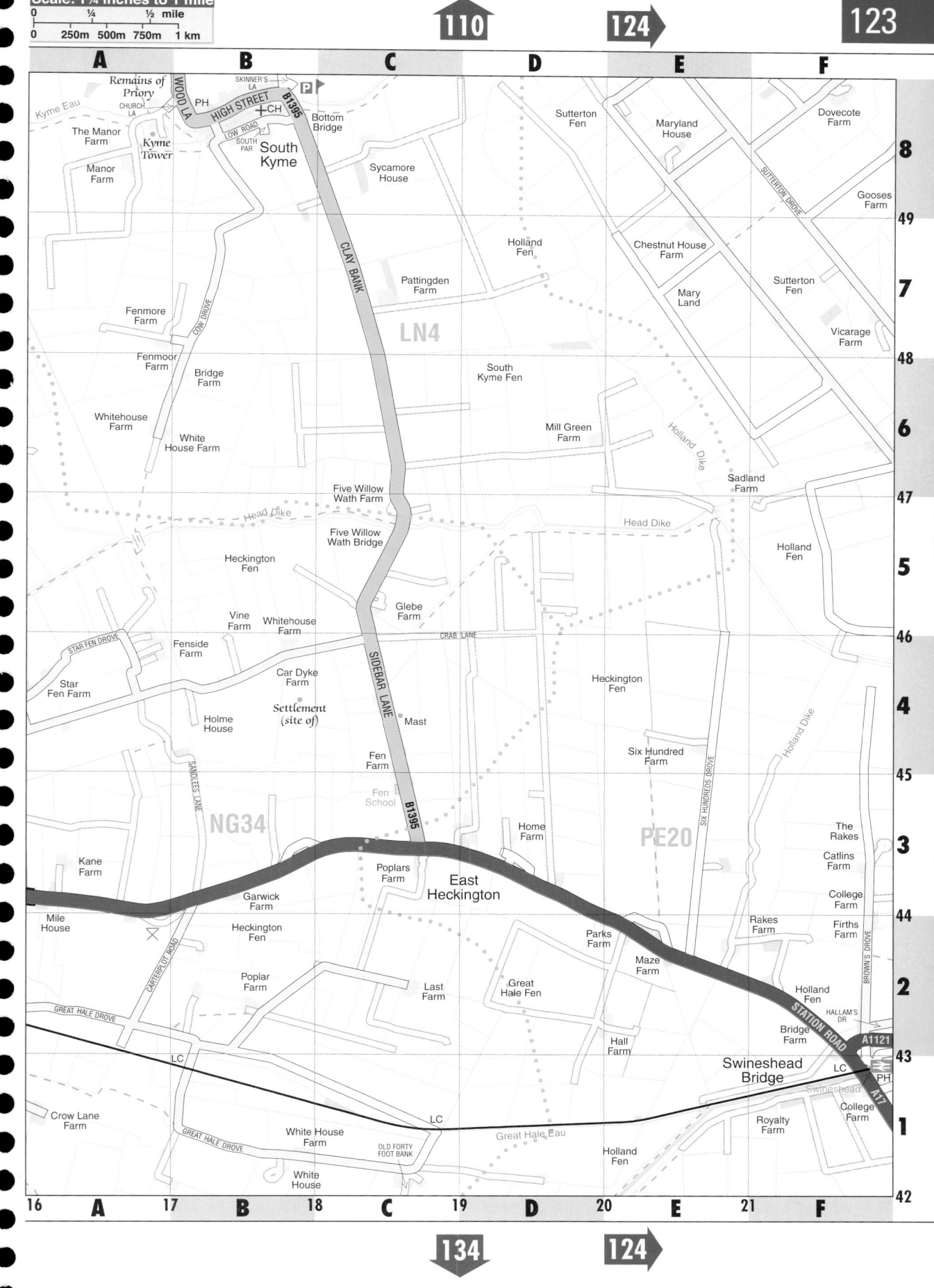

Scale: 1¾ inches to 1 mile

0   ¼   ½   mile
0   250m 500m 750m 1 km

Remains of Priory

CHURCH LA.

SKINNER'S LA.

Kyme Eau

The Manor Farm

Kyme Tower

Manor Farm

WOOD LA.

HIGH STREET

PH

P

B1395

CH

LOW ROAD

SOUTH PAR

South Kyme

Bottom Bridge

Sycamore House

Fenmore Farm

Fenmoor Farm

Bridge Farm

Whitehouse Farm

White House Farm

KYME DROVE

CLAY BANK

Pattingden Farm

LN4

Holland Fen

Sutterton Fen

Maryland House

Dovecote Farm

SUTTERTON DROVE

Gooses Farm

Chestnut House Farm

Mary Land

Sutterton Fen

Vicarage Farm

South Kyme Fen

Mill Green Farm

Holland Dike

Sadland Farm

Holland Fen

Five Willow Wath Farm

Head Dike

Head Dike

Five Willow Wath Bridge

Heckington Fen

Vine Farm

Whitehouse Farm

Glebe Farm

CRAB LANE

Heckington Fen

STAR FEN DROVE

Fenside Farm

Car Dyke Farm

SIDEBAR LANE

Mast

Star Fen Farm

Settlement (site of)

Holme House

SANDLESS LANE

NG34

Fen Farm

Fen School

B1395

Heckington Fen

Six Hundred Farm

SIX HUNDREDS DROVE

Holland Dike

PE20

The Rakes

Catlins Farm

College Farm

Kane Farm

Garwick Farm

Poplars Farm

East Heckington

Home Farm

Rakes Farm

Firths Farm

CARTERPLOT ROAD

Heckington Fen

Mile House

Poplar Farm

Last Farm

Great Hale Fen

Parks Farm

Maze Farm

Holland Fen

BROWN'S DROVE

HALLAM'S DR

Bridge Farm

STATION ROAD

A1121

GREAT HALE DROVE

LC

Hall Farm

Swineshead Bridge

LC

A17

PH

Crow Lane Farm

GREAT HALE DROVE

LC

White House Farm

OLD FORTY FOOT BANK

LC

Great Hale Eau

Holland Fen

Swineshead

Royalty Farm

College Farm

White House

123
111

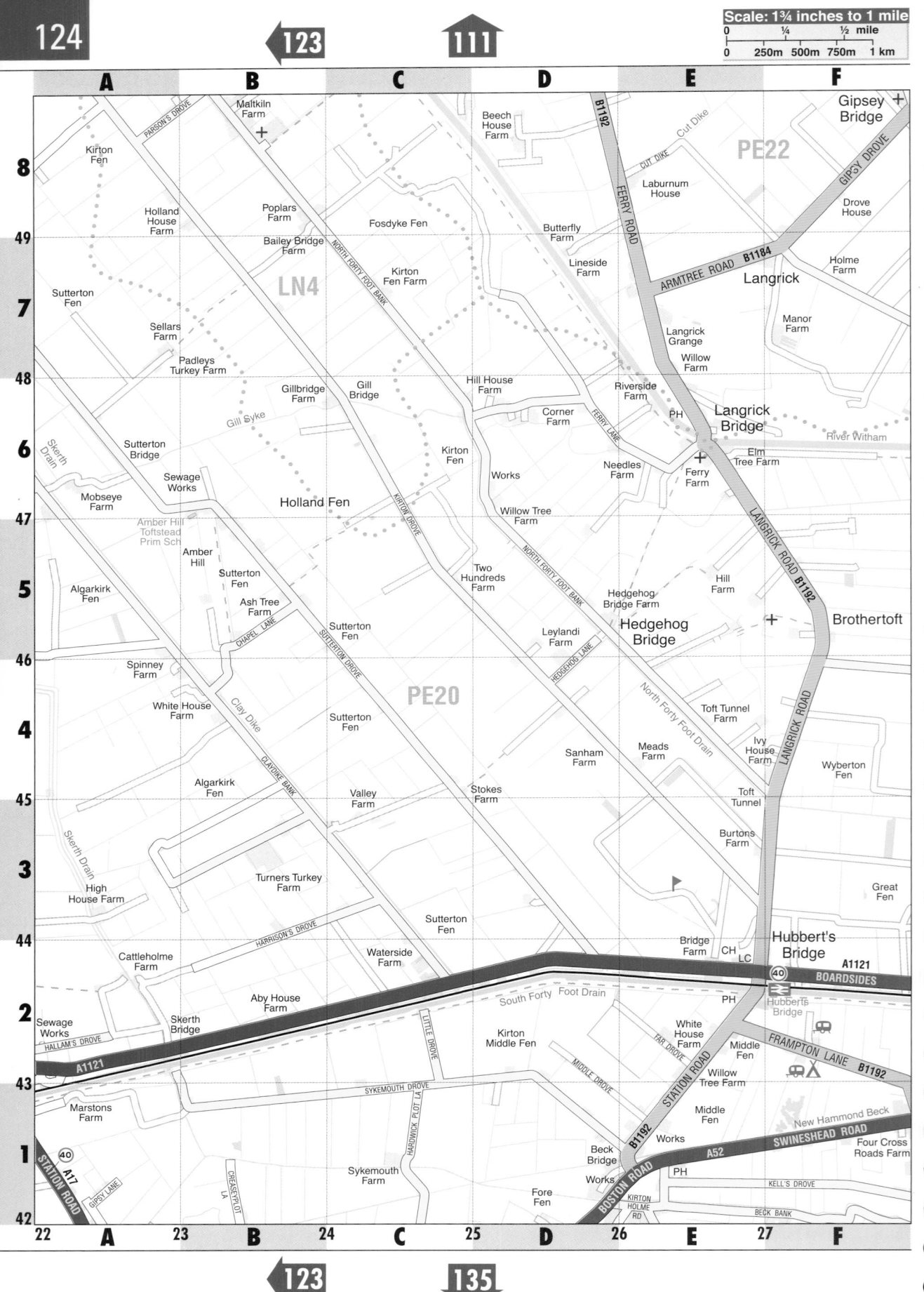
Scale: 1¾ inches to 1 mile
0 ¼ ½ mile
0 250m 500m 750m 1 km
A B C D E F
8 49 7 48 6 47 5 46 4 45 3 44 2 43 1 42
22 23 24 25 26 27
Maltkiln Farm
Beech House Farm
Gipsey Bridge
Kirton Fen
PARSON'S DROVE
Cut Dike
CUT DIKE
B1192
PE22
GIPSY DROVE
FERRY ROAD
Laburnum House
Drove House
Holland House Farm
Poplars Farm
Fosdyke Fen
Butterfly Farm
Bailey Bridge Farm
NORTH FORTY FOOT BANK
Kirton Fen Farm
Lineside Farm
ARMTREE ROAD
B1184
Langrick
Holme Farm
LN4
Sutterton Fen
Manor Farm
Sellars Farm
Langrick Grange
Willow Farm
Padleys Turkey Farm
Gillbridge Farm
Gill Bridge
Hill House Farm
Riverside Farm
Corner Farm
FERRY LANE
PH
Langrick Bridge
Gill Syke
River Witham
Skerth Drain
Sutterton Bridge
Kirton Fen
Elm Tree Farm
Needles Farm
Ferry Farm
Sewage Works
Works
Mobseye Farm
Holland Fen
KIRTON DROVE
Willow Tree Farm
Amber Hill Toftstead Prim Sch
Amber Hill
LANGRICK ROAD
Sutterton Fen
Two Hundreds Farm
Algarkirk Fen
Hill Farm
Ash Tree Farm
Hedgehog Bridge Farm
B1192
CHAPEL LANE
Brothertoft
Sutterton Fen
Hedgehog Bridge
Leylandi Farm
SUTTERTON DROVE
Spinney Farm
HEDGEHOG LANE
PE20
White House Farm
Clay Dike
North Forty Foot Drain
Toft Tunnel Farm
Sutterton Fen
LANGRICK ROAD
Ivy House Farm
CLAYDIKE BANK
Sanham Farm
Meads Farm
Wyberton Fen
Algarkirk Fen
Valley Farm
Stokes Farm
Toft Tunnel
Skerth Drain
Burtons Farm
Turners Turkey Farm
High House Farm
Great Fen
Sutterton Fen
HARRISON'S DROVE
Bridge Farm
CH
Hubbert's Bridge
Cattleholme Farm
Waterside Farm
LC
A1121
40
BOARDSIDES
South Forty Foot Drain
Aby House Farm
PH
Hubberts Bridge
Sewage Works
Skerth Bridge
LITTLE DROVE
Kirton Middle Fen
White House Farm
FAR DROVE
Middle Fen
FRAMPTON LANE
B1192
HALLAM'S DROVE
A1121
STATION ROAD
MIDDLE DROVE
Willow Tree Farm
SYKEMOUTH DROVE
Marstons Farm
HARDWICK PLOT LA
Middle Fen
New Hammond Beck
B1192
Works
SWINESHEAD ROAD
Four Cross Roads Farm
A52
A17
STATION ROAD
Beck Bridge
PH
GIPSY LANE
CREASEYPLOT LA
Sykemouth Farm
Works
BOSTON ROAD
KELL'S DROVE
Fore Fen
KIRTON HOLME RD
BECK BANK

123
135

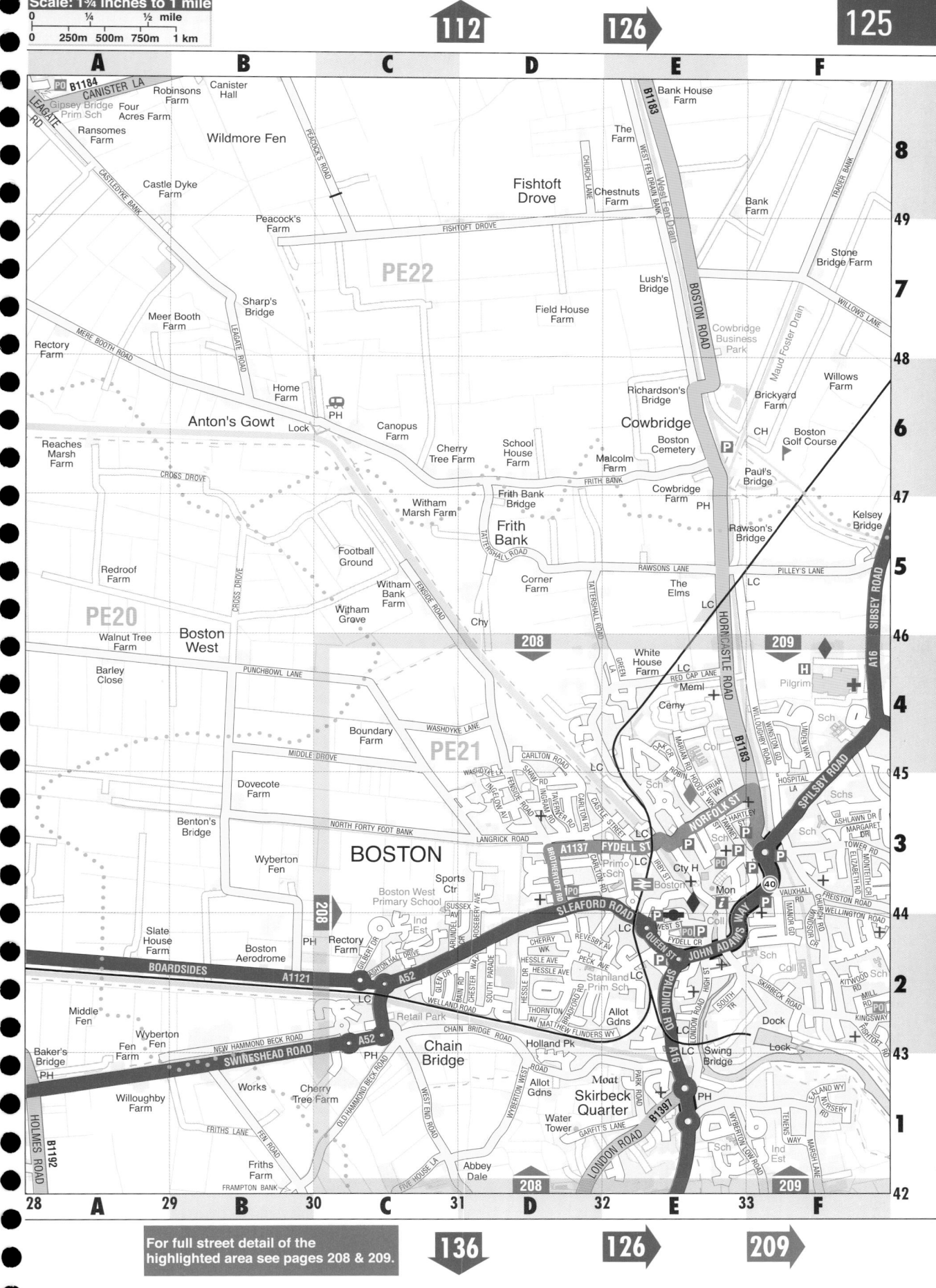

A   B   C   D   E   F

8
49
7
48
6
47
5
46
4
45
3
44
2
43
1
42

PO B1184 CANISTER LA
LEAGATE RD
Gipsey Bridge Prim Sch
Robinsons Farm
Canister Hall
Four Acres Farm
Ransomes Farm
Wildmore Fen
Castle Dyke Farm
CASTLEDYKE BANK
Peacock's Farm
PEACOCK'S ROAD
FISHTOFT DROVE
Fishtoft Drove
B1183
Bank House Farm
The Farm
WEST FEN DRAIN BANK
CHURCH RD
Chestnuts Farm
Bank Farm
TRADER BANK
PE22
Sharp's Bridge
LEAGATE ROAD
Field House Farm
Lush's Bridge
BOSTON ROAD
WILLOWS LANE
Stone Bridge Farm
Meer Booth Farm
Home Farm
PH
Canopus Farm
Richardson's Bridge
Cowbridge
Brickyard Farm
CH
Boston Golf Course
MAUD FOSTER DRAIN
Willows Farm
Rectory Farm
MERE BOOTH ROAD
Anton's Gowt
Lock
Cherry Tree Farm
School House Farm
Malcolm Farm
Boston Cemetery
P
Paul's Bridge
Reaches Marsh Farm
CROSS DROVE
Witham Marsh Farm
Frith Bank Bridge
FRITH BANK
Cowbridge Farm
PH
Rawson's Bridge
Kelsey Bridge
Frith Bank
TATTERSHALL ROAD
RAWSONS LANE
PILLEY'S LANE
SIBSEY ROAD
Redroof Farm
CROSS DROVE
Football Ground
Corner Farm
The Elms
LC
LC
Witham Bank Farm
FENSIDE ROAD
Chy
PE20
Witham Grove
208
LC
A16
PE21
Walnut Tree Farm
Boston West
PUNCHBOWL LANE
White House Farm
GREEN LA
LC
Red Cap Lane
Meml
209
H
Pilgrim
Sch
Barley Close
Cerny
HORNCASTLE ROAD
B1183
WINSTON RD
LINDEN WAY
Sch
Boundary Farm
WASHDYKE LANE
Col
MARIAN RD
ROBIN HOOD'S LA
FRIARY WY
HOSPITAL
Schs
Dovecote Farm
MIDDLE DROVE
CARLTON ROAD
SHAW RD
INGELOW AV
TAVERNER RD
CASTLE STREET
Sch
ASHLAWN DR
MARGARET DR
Benton's Bridge
NORTH FORTY FOOT BANK
LANGRICK ROAD
CARLTON RD
LC
TOWER RD
ELIZABETH RD
KITWOOD RD
WELLINGTON ROAD
Wyberton Fen
BOSTON
A1137
BROTHERTOFT RD
FYDELL ST
Primo Sch
Cty H
NORFOLK ST
HARTLEY ST
TAWNEY ST
P
P
REISTON ROAD
CHURCH RD
Sports Ctr
Boston West Primary School
SUSSEX RD
ARUNDEL WAY
ROSEBERY AV
SLEAFORD ROAD
LC
PO
Boston
Mon
40
P
i
Coll
P
VAUXHALL
MANOR RD
CHERRY WK
PECK AV
WEST ST
Coll
P
MILL RD
PO
Slate House Farm
PH
Rectory Farm
GILBERT DR
GYSTON HALL DRIVE
A52
GLEN DR
BAIN RD
CHESTER RD
WELLAND RD
SOUTH PARADE
HESSLE DR
HESSLE AVE
HESSLE AVE
THORNTON AV
REVESBY AV
BRADFORD RD
FLINDERS WY
Staniland Prim Sch
QUEEN ST
FYDELL CR
JOHN ADAMS WAY
SPALDING RD
SOUTH TR
SKIRBECK ROAD
Coll
KINGSWAY
Ind Est
Boston Aerodrome
BOARDSIDES
A1121
LC
Retail Park
CHAIN BRIDGE ROAD
Allot Gdns
Holland Pk
A16
LC
Dock
Lock
Middle Fen
NEW HAMMOND BECK ROAD
Chain Bridge
WYBERTON WEST ROAD
Allot Gdns
Swing Bridge
FENTOFT RD
Wyberton Fen Farm
SWINESHEAD ROAD
A52
PH
Moat
Skirbeck Quarter
PARK RD
PH
EALAND WY
NURSERY RD
Baker's Bridge
PH
OLD HAMMOND BECK ROAD
Works
FEN END ROAD
Water Tower
GARFIT'S LANE
LONDON ROAD
B1397
TENENS WAY
MARSH LANE
Ind Est
B1192
HOLMES ROAD
Willoughby Farm
FRITHS LANE
Cherry Tree Farm
FIVE HOUSE LA
Abbey Dale
Sch
Friths Farm
FRAMPTON BANK
208
209

28   29   30   31   32   33
A   B   C   D   E   F

For full street detail of the highlighted area see pages 208 & 209.

136   126   209

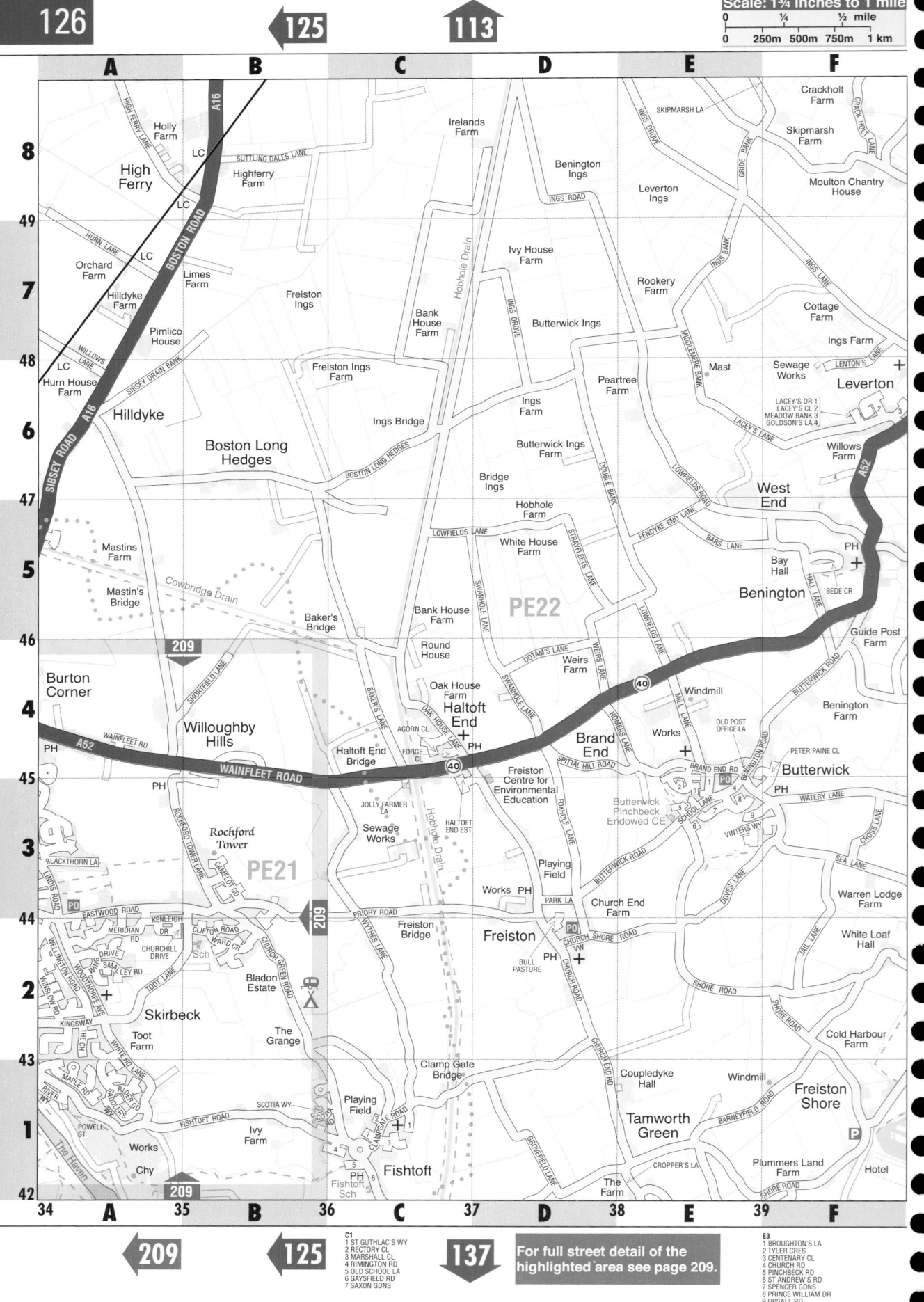

126
125
113
Scale: 1¾ inches to 1 mile
0   ¼   ½ mile
0   250m 500m 750m 1 km

C1
1 ST GUTHLAC'S WY
2 RECTORY CL
3 MARSHALL CL
4 RIMINGTON RD
5 OLD SCHOOL LA
6 GAYSFIELD RD
7 SAXON GDNS

E3
1 BROUGHTON'S LA
2 TYLER CRES
3 CENTENARY CL
4 CHURCH RD
5 PINCHBECK RD
6 ST ANDREW'S RD
7 SPENCER GDNS
8 PRINCE WILLIAM DR
9 UPSALL RD

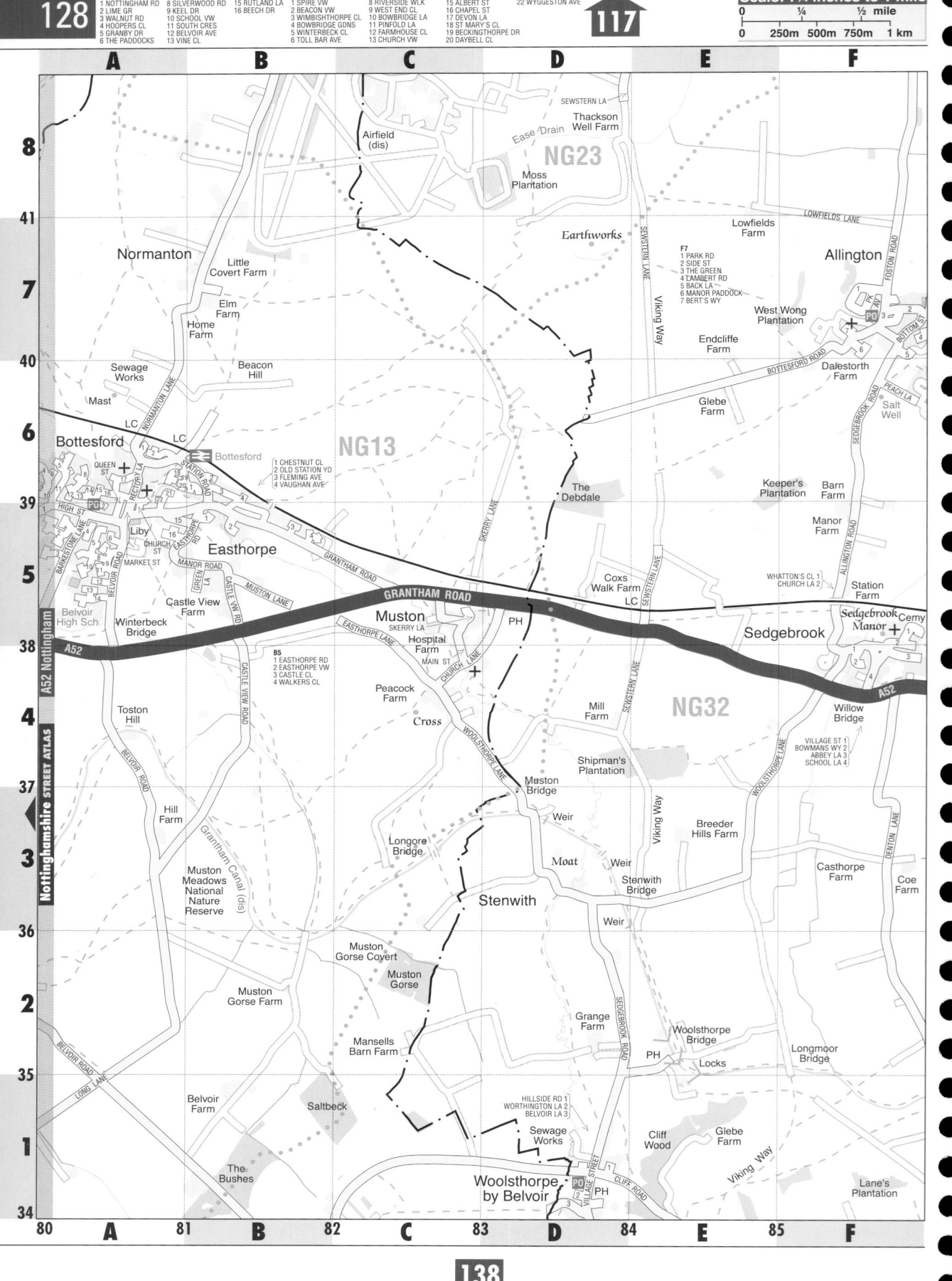

A5
1 NOTTINGHAM RD
2 LIME GR
3 WALNUT RD
4 HOOPERS CL
5 GRANBY DR
6 THE PADDOCKS

7 NORTH CRES
8 SILVERWOOD RD
9 KEEL DR
10 SCHOOL VW
11 SOUTH CRES
12 BELVOIR AVE
13 VINE CL

14 HOWITTS RD
15 RUTLAND LA
16 BEECH DR

A6
1 SPIRE VW
2 BEACON VW
3 WIMBISHTHORPE CL
4 BOWBRIDGE GDNS
5 WINTERBECK CL
6 TOLL BAR AVE

7 PINFOLD CL
8 RIVERSIDE WLK
9 WEST END CL
10 BOWBRIDGE LA
11 PINFOLD LA
12 FARMHOUSE CL
13 CHURCH VW

14 RIVERSIDE CL
15 ALBERT ST
16 CHAPEL ST
17 DEVON LA
18 ST MARY'S CL
19 BECKINGTHORPE DR
20 DAYBELL CL

21 WYGGESTON RD
22 WYGGESTON AVE

117

Scale: 1¾ inches to 1 mile
0   ¼   ½   mile
0   250m 500m 750m 1 km

Normanton
Little Covert Farm
Elm Farm
Home Farm
Beacon Hill
Sewage Works
Mast
LC
LC
Bottesford
NG13
Queen St
Liby
Easthorpe
Belvoir High Sch
Winterbeck Bridge
Castle View Farm

A52 Nottingham

Toston Hill
Hill Farm
Grantham Canal (dis)
Muston Meadows National Nature Reserve
Muston Gorse Farm
Belvoir Farm
Long Lane
The Bushes
Saltbeck

B5
1 EASTHORPE RD
2 EASTHORPE VW
3 CASTLE CL
4 WALKERS CL

Peacock Farm
Cross
Longore Bridge
Muston Gorse Covert
Muston Gorse
Mansells Barn Farm

Airfield (dis)
Ease Drain
Moss Plantation
Earthworks
Thackson Well Farm
NG23

1 CHESTNUT CL
2 OLD STATION YD
3 FLEMING AVE
4 VAUGHAN AVE

The Debdale
Coxs Walk Farm
LC
Muston
Skerry La
Hospital Farm
Main St
Church Lane
PH
Mill Farm
Shipman's Plantation
Muston Bridge
Weir
Moat
Weir
Stenwith
Weir
Grange Farm
HILLSIDE RD 1
WORTHINGTON LA 2
BELVOIR LA 3
Sewage Works
Woolsthorpe by Belvoir
PO
PH
Cliff Road
Village Street

Grantham Road
Stenwith Bridge
Breeder Hills Farm
NG32
Viking Way
Viking Way
Woolsthorpe Bridge
Locks
PH
Sedgebrook Road
Woolsthorpe Lane
Denton Lane

Lowfields Lane
Lowfields Farm
Allington
F7
1 PARK RD
2 SIDE ST
3 THE GREEN
4 LAMBERT RD
5 BACK LA
6 MANOR PADDOCK
7 BERT'S WY
West Wong Plantation
Endcliffe Farm
Glebe Farm
Dalestorth Farm
Salt Well
Keeper's Plantation
Barn Farm
Manor Farm
WHATTON'S CL 1
CHURCH LA 2
Station Farm
Sedgebrook
Sedgebrook Manor
Cemy
Willow Bridge
A52
VILLAGE ST 1
BOWMANS WY 2
ABBEY LA 3
SCHOOL LA 4
Casthorpe Farm
Coe Farm
Longmoor Bridge
Cliff Wood
Glebe Farm
Viking Way
Lane's Plantation

Foston Road
Bottesford Road
Sedgebrook Road
Peach La
Allington Road

Nottinghamshire STREET ATLAS
A52 Nottingham
Belvoir Road

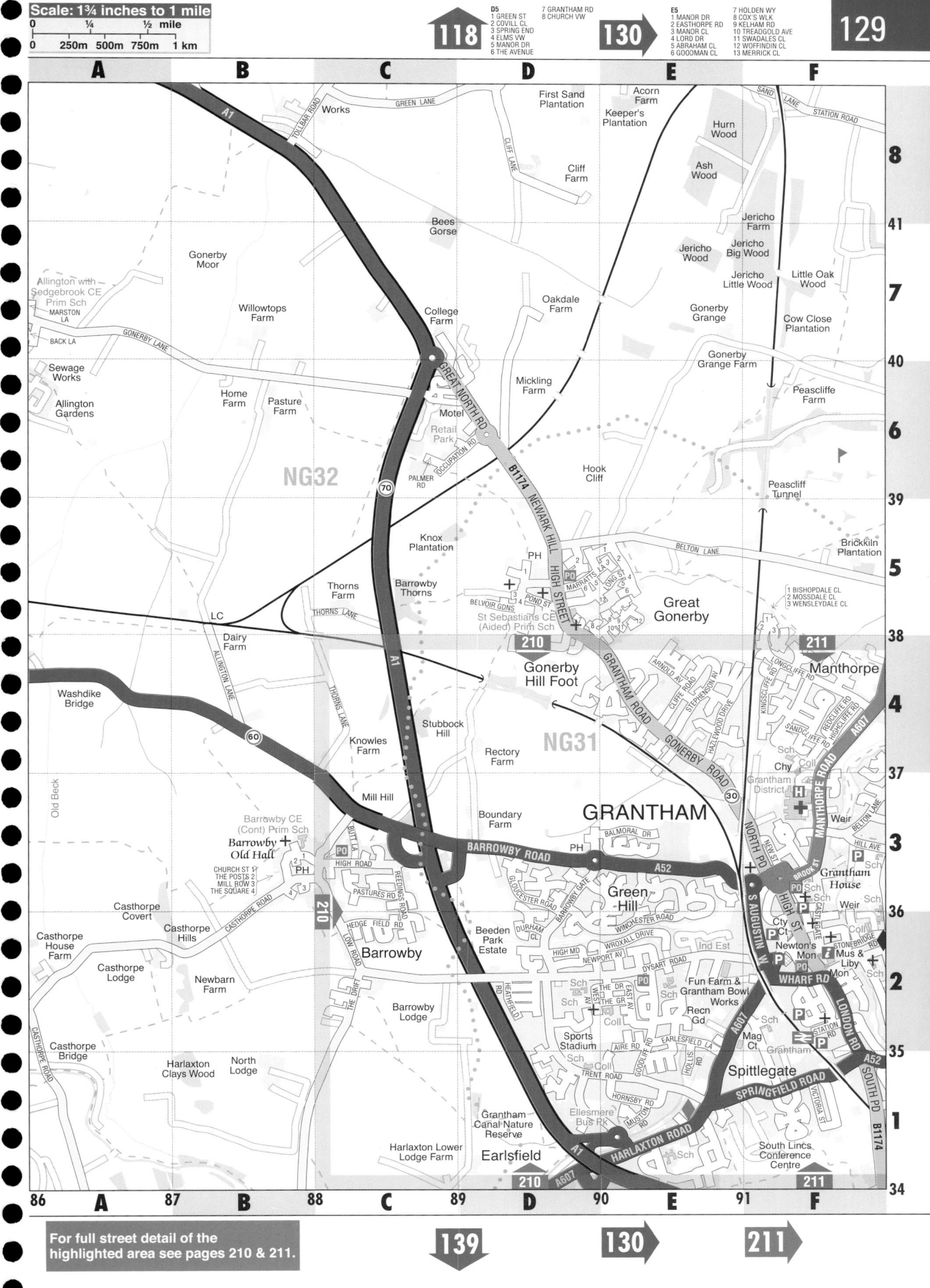

Scale: 1¾ inches to 1 mile

0   ¼   ½ mile
0 250m 500m 750m 1 km

118

130

129

D5
1 GREEN ST
2 COVILL CL
3 SPRING END
4 ELMS VW
5 MANOR DR
6 THE AVENUE

7 GRANTHAM RD
8 CHURCH VW

E5
1 MANOR DR
2 EASTHORPE RD
3 MANOR CL
4 LORD DR
5 ABRAHAM CL
6 GOODMAN CL

7 HOLDEN WY
8 COX'S WLK
9 KELHAM RD
10 TREADGOLD AVE
11 SWADALES CL
12 WOFFINDIN CL
13 MERRICK CL

A   B   C   D   E   F

8
41
7
40
6
39
5
38
4
37
3
36
2
35
1
34

First Sand Plantation
Acorn Farm
Keeper's Plantation
Hurn Wood
SAND LANE
STATION ROAD

Green Lane
Cliff Farm
Ash Wood

Works
A1
TOLLBAR ROAD
Cliff Farm
CLIFF LANE

Bees Gorse
Jericho Farm

Gonerby Moor
Jericho Wood
Jericho Big Wood
Jericho Little Wood
Little Oak Wood

Willowtops Farm
College Farm
Oakdale Farm
Gonerby Grange
Cow Close Plantation

Allington with Sedgebrook CE Prim Sch
MARSTON LA
Gonerby Grange Farm
Peascliffe Farm

BACK LA
GONERBY LANE
Home Farm
Pasture Farm
Mickling Farm

Sewage Works
GREAT NORTH RD
Motel
Retail Park
Hook Cliff
Peascliffe Tunnel

Allington Gardens
NG32
70
PALMER RD
OCCUPATION RD
B1174 NEWARK HILL
Belton Lane
Brickkiln Plantation

Knox Plantation
PH
HIGH STREET
MARRATTS

Thorns Farm
Barrowby Thorns
BELVOIR GDNS
POND ST
LONG ST
PO
Great Gonerby
1 BISHOPDALE CL
2 MOSSDALE CL
3 WENSLEYDALE CL

LC
THORNS LANE
St Sebastians CE (Aided) Prim Sch
210
211
Manthorpe

Dairy Farm
ALLINGTON LANE
Gonerby Hill Foot
GRANTHAM ROAD
ARNOLD AV
STEPHENSON AV
LONGCLIFFE RD
REDCLIFFE RD
A607

Washdike Bridge
60
A1
CLIFFE ROAD
HAZLEWOOD DRIVE
GONERBY ROAD
KINGSCLIFFE RD
SANDCLIFFE RD
HIGHCLIFFE RD

Knowles Farm
Stubbock Hill
NG31
Sch
Chy
Coll

Old Beck
Mill Hill
Rectory Farm
30
Grantham District
H
MANTHORPE ROAD
Weir
BELTON LANE
HILL AVE

Barrowby CE (Cont) Prim Sch
Barrowby Old Hall
PH
BUTT LA
PO
HIGH ROAD
Boundary Farm
GRANTHAM
BALMORAL DR
NORTH PD
Grantham House
P Sch
Weir
Coll

CHURCH ST 1
THE POSTS 2
MILL ROW 3
THE SQUARE 4
PASTURES RD
REEDINGS ROAD
BARROWBY GATE
BARROWBY ROAD
PH
A52
Green Hill
S AUGUSTIN W
HIGH ST
CASTLEGATE
Cty Ct
Stonebridge
Mus & Liby
Mon

Casthorpe Covert
Casthorpe Hills
CASTHORPE ROAD
HEDGE FIELD RD
G GLOUCESTER ROAD
DURHAM CL
WINCHESTER ROAD
WROXALL DRIVE
Ind Est
Newton's Mon
PO
Mon

Casthorpe House Farm
210
LOW ROAD
Barrowby
HEATHFIELD
HIGH MD
NEWPORT AV
DYSART ROAD
Fun Farm & Grantham Bowl Works
WHARF RD
P
Sch

Newbarn Farm
THE DRIFT
Barrowby Lodge
G GLOUCESTER ROAD
AIRE RD
EAST AV
WEST AV
THE GR
Recn Gd
P
STATION
P
Grantham

Casthorpe Lodge
Sports Stadium
Sch
Coll
GOODLIFFE RD
EARLESFIELD LA
Mag Ct
A607
LONDON ROAD
A52
SOUTH PD

CASTHORPE ROAD
Harlaxton Clays Wood
North Lodge
Sch
TRENT RD
HOLLIS
HORNSBY RD
Spittlegate
SPRINGFIELD ROAD
VICTORIA ST
B1174

Casthorpe Bridge
Grantham Canal Nature Reserve
Ellesmere Bus Pk
MUSTON RD
South Lincs Conference Centre

Harlaxton Lower Lodge Farm
Earlsfield
210
A607
A1
HARLAXTON ROAD
Sch
211

86   A   87   B   88   C   89   D   90   E   91   F

For full street detail of the highlighted area see pages 210 & 211.

139

130

211

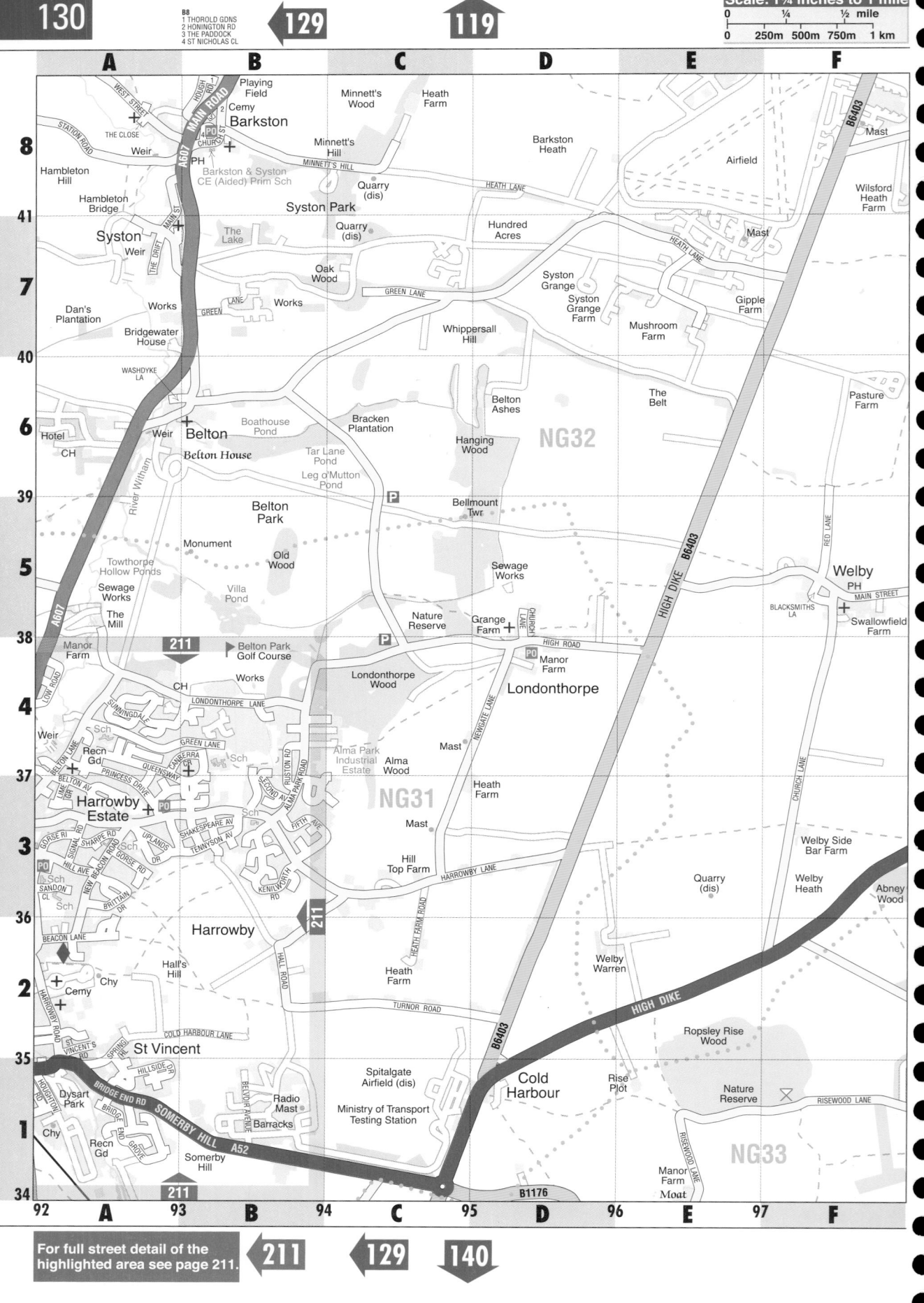

129
119

Scale: 1¾ inches to 1 mile

0   ¼   ½ mile
0   250m   500m   750m   1 km

A   B   C   D   E   F

Playing Field
Cemy
Barkston
Minnett's Wood
Heath Farm
WEST STREET
HOUGH LA
MAIN ROAD

THE CLOSE
Weir
Station Road
Hambleton Hill
Barkston & Syston CE (Aided) Prim Sch
Minnett's Hill
MINNETT'S HILL
PH
PO
CHURCH LA

Minnett's Hill
Barkston Heath
Airfield
Mast

Hambleton Bridge
Syston Park
Quarry (dis)
HEATH LANE

Wilsford Heath Farm

Syston
Weir
The Drift
The Lake
Quarry (dis)
Hundred Acres
Mast

Dan's Plantation
THE DRIFT
GREEN LANE
Oak Wood
Works
GREEN LANE
Syston Grange
Syston Grange Farm
Mushroom Farm
HEATH LANE
Gipple Farm

Bridgewater House
Green Lane
Works
Whippersall Hill

WASHDYKE LA
Belton Ashes
The Belt
Pasture Farm

Hotel
CH
Weir
Belton
Boathouse Pond
Bracken Plantation
Hanging Wood
NG32
RED LANE

Belton House
Tar Lane Pond
Leg o'Mutton Pond

River Witham
P
Bellmount Twr
B6403

Belton Park
Monument
Old Wood
Sewage Works
HIGH DIKE
Welby
PH
Main Street

Towthorpe Hollow Ponds
Villa Pond
Sewage Works
BLACKSMITHS LA

A607
The Mill
Nature Reserve
P
Grange Farm
CHURCH LA
High Road
Swallowfield Farm

Manor Farm
LOW ROAD
211
Belton Park Golf Course
Londonthorpe Wood
PO
Manor Farm

CH
Works
LONDONTHORPE LANE
Sch
Londonthorpe

SUNNINGDALE
Sch
Alma Park Industrial Estate
Alma Wood
NEWGATE LANE

Weir
BELTON LANE
CANBERRA CR
Recn Gd
PRINCESS DRIVE
QUEENSWAY
Sch
SECOND AV
RUSTON RD
ALMA PARK ROAD
Mast
Heath Farm
CHURCH LANE

LIME TREE AV
Harrowby Estate
PO
SHAKESPEARE AV
FIFTH AVE
NG31
Welby Side Bar Farm

GORSE RI
SIGNAL RD
SHARPE RD
UPLANDS DR
TENNYSON AV
Sch
Mast
Hill Top Farm
HARROWBY LANE
Quarry (dis)
Welby Heath
Abney Wood

PO
NEW BEACON ROAD
GORSE RD
KENILWORTH RD
Sch
SANDON CL
BRITTAIN DR
Sch
Harrowby
211
HEATH FARM ROAD
Welby Warren
RISEWOOD LANE
CHURCH LANE

BEACON LANE
Hall's Hill
Heath Farm

Cemy
CH
HARROWBY ROAD
COLD HARBOUR LANE
TURNOR ROAD
HIGH DIKE

ST VINCENT'S RD
St Vincent
SPRING LA
Ropsley Rise Wood

HILLSIDE DR
Nature Reserve
RISEWOOD LANE

Dysart Park
BRIDGE END RD
SOMERBY HILL
BELVOIR AVENUE
Radio Mast
Spitalgate Airfield (dis)
B6403
Cold Harbour
Rise Plot

HOUGHTON RD
Chy
BRIDGE END GROVE
Barracks
Ministry of Transport Testing Station
NG33

Recn Gd
A52
Somerby Hill
Manor Farm
Moat
RISEWOOD LANE

211
B1176

92   A   93   B   94   C   95   D   96   E   97   F

For full street detail of the highlighted area see page 211.
211   129   140

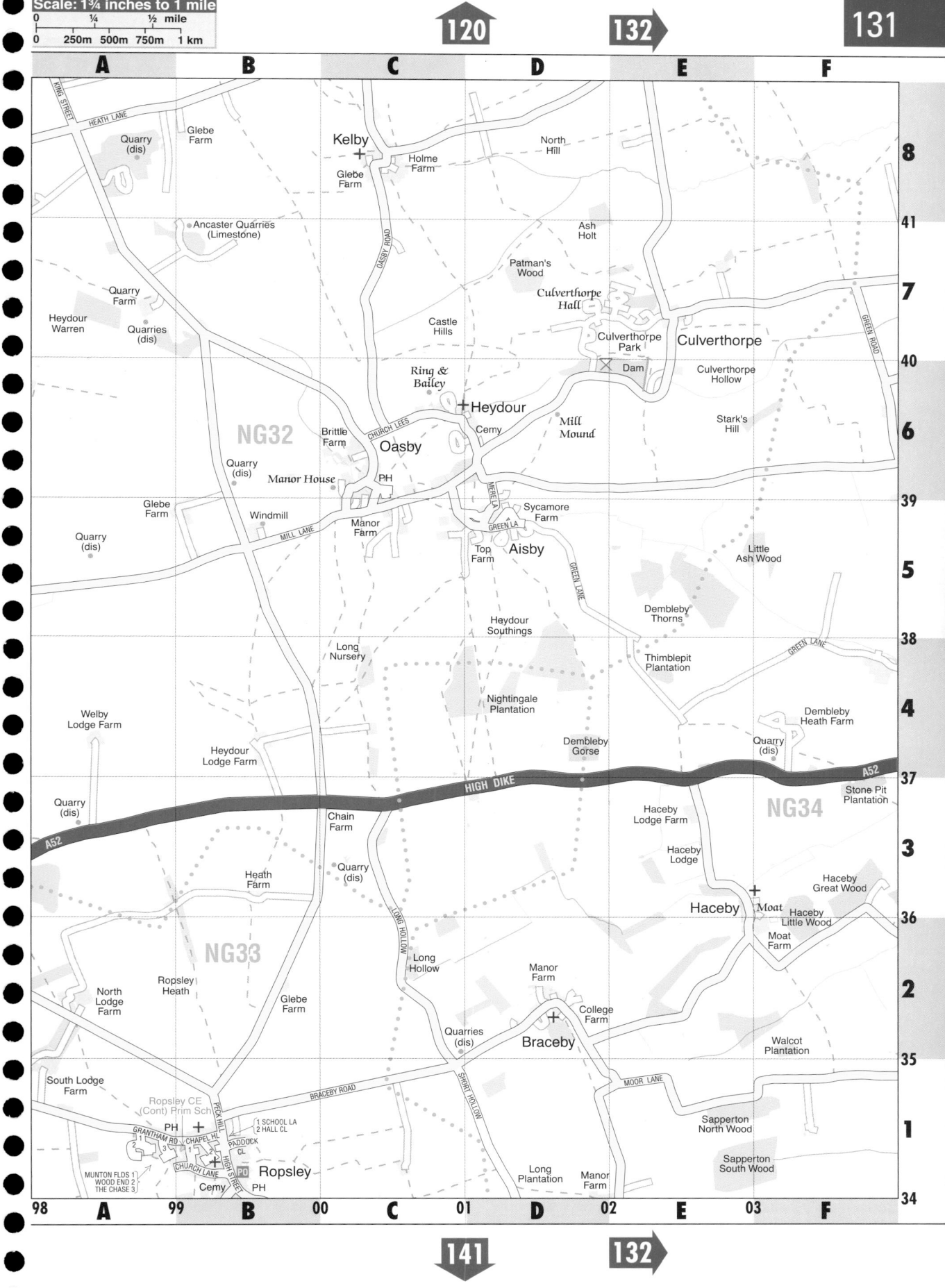

Scale: 1¾ inches to 1 mile

0   ¼   ½   mile
0   250m 500m 750m 1 km

120
132
141
132

A B C D E F

8
41
7
40
6
39
5
38
4
37
3
36
2
35
1
34

King Street
Heath Lane
Quarry (dis)
Glebe Farm
Kelby
Holme Farm
North Hill
Glebe Farm
Ash Holt
Ancaster Quarries (Limestone)
Patman's Wood
Culverthorpe Hall
Oasby Road
Quarry Farm
Castle Hills
Culverthorpe Park
Culverthorpe
Green Road
Heydour Warren
Quarries (dis)
Ring & Bailey
Dam
Culverthorpe Hollow
NG32
Brittle Farm
Heydour
Cemy
Mill Mound
Stark's Hill
Oasby
Church Lees
Quarry (dis)
PH
Manor House
Sycamore Farm
Little Ash Wood
Glebe Farm
Windmill
Manor Farm
Mere La
Green La
Aisby
Green Lane
Dembleby Thorns
Quarry (dis)
Mill Lane
Top Farm
Heydour Southings
Thimblepit Plantation
Long Nursery
Dembleby Heath Farm
Nightingale Plantation
Quarry (dis)
Welby Lodge Farm
Dembleby Gorse
Heydour Lodge Farm
A52
HIGH DIKE
NG34
Stone Pit Plantation
Quarry (dis)
Chain Farm
Haceby Lodge Farm
A52
Heath Farm
Quarry (dis)
Haceby Lodge
Haceby Great Wood
NG33
Long Hollow
Haceby
Moat
Haceby Little Wood
North Lodge Farm
Ropsley Heath
Glebe Farm
Long Hollow
Manor Farm
Moat Farm
South Lodge Farm
Quarries (dis)
College Farm
Walcot Plantation
Ropsley CE (Cont) Prim Sch
Braceby Road
Braceby
Moor Lane
Peck Hill
PH
1 SCHOOL LA
2 HALL CL
Short Hollow
Sapperton North Wood
Grantham Rd
Chapel Hl
Paddock Cl
High St
Church Lane
PO
Ropsley
Long Plantation
Manor Farm
Sapperton South Wood
Munton Flds 1
Wood End 2
The Chase 3
Cemy
PH

98 99 00 01 02 03

A B C D E F

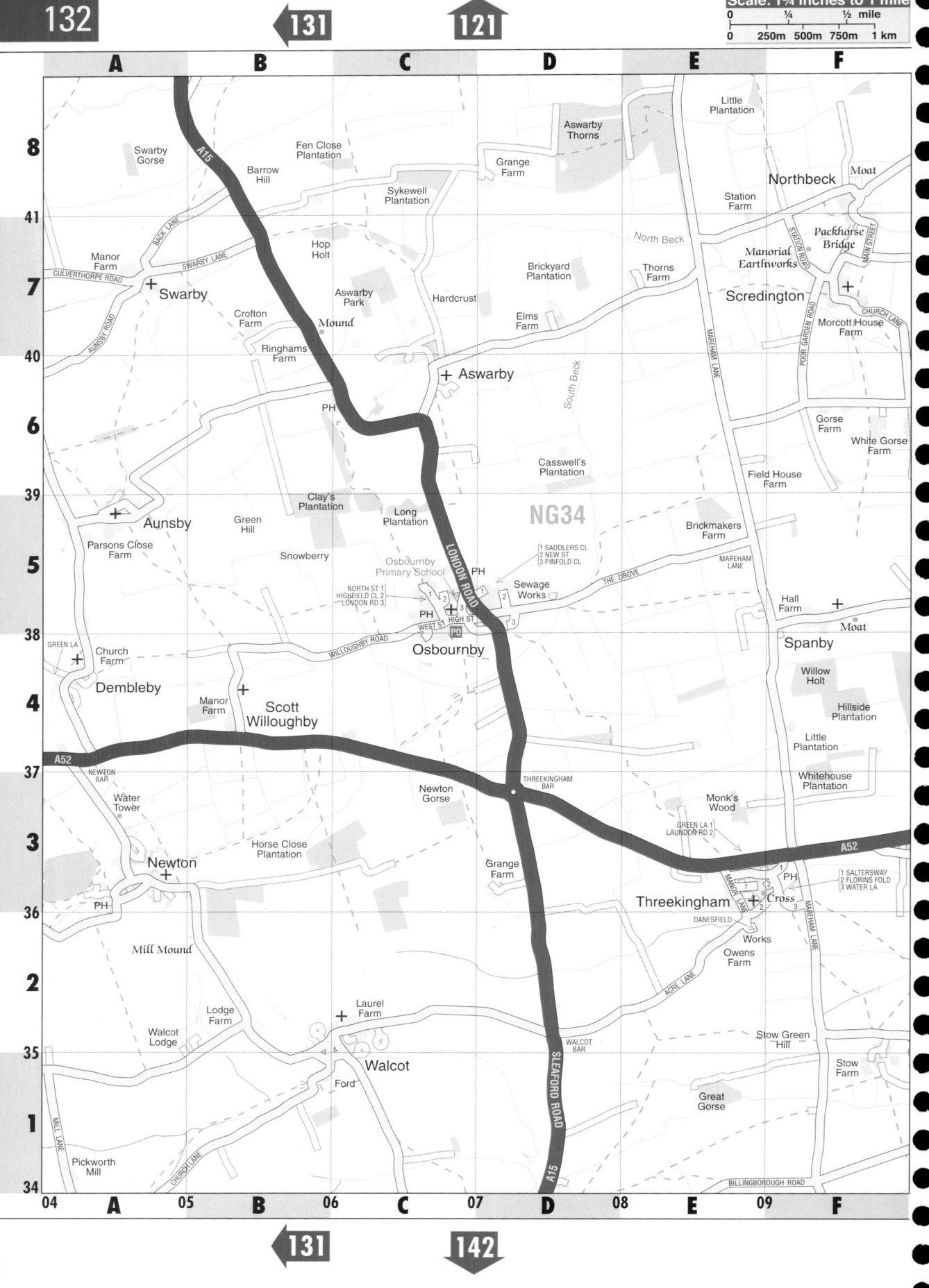

131
121

Scale: 1¾ inches to 1 mile

0   ¼   ½ mile
0 250m 500m 750m 1 km

8

Swarby Gorse

Fen Close Plantation

Little Plantation

Aswarby Thorns

A15

Barrow Hill

Sykewell Plantation

Grange Farm

Northbeck

Moat

41

Manor Farm

BACK LANE

SWARBY LANE

Hop Holt

North Beck

Station Farm

Packhorse Bridge

MAIN STREET

CULVERTHORPE ROAD

7

Swarby

Crofton Farm

Aswarby Park

Hardcrust

Brickyard Plantation

Thorns Farm

Manorial Earthworks

STATION ROAD

CHURCH LANE

Scredington

AUNSBY ROAD

Mound

Elms Farm

POOR GARDEN ROAD

Morcott House Farm

40

Ringhams Farm

Aswarby

South Beck

6

PH

Casswell's Plantation

MAREHAM LANE

Gorse Farm

White Gorse Farm

39

Clay's Plantation

Field House Farm

Aunsby

Green Hill

Long Plantation

NG34

Brickmakers Farm

5

Parsons Close Farm

Snowberry

Osbournby Primary School

1 SADDLERS CL
2 NEW ST
3 PINFOLD CL

THE DROVE

MAREHAM LANE

Hall Farm

PH

LONDON ROAD

PH

Sewage Works

NORTH ST 1
HIGHFIELD CL 2
LONDON RD 3

Moat

38

GREEN LA

Church Farm

WEST ST

PH

HIGH ST

PO

WILLOUGHBY ROAD

Spanby

Dembleby

Manor Farm

Scott Willoughby

Osbournby

Willow Holt

4

Hillside Plantation

A52

Little Plantation

37

NEWTON BAR

Newton Gorse

THREEKINGHAM BAR

Monk's Wood

Whitehouse Plantation

3

Water Tower

Horse Close Plantation

A52

GREEN LA 1
LAUNDON RD 2

Newton

Grange Farm

PH

1 SALTERSWAY
2 FLORINS FOLD
3 WATER LA

36

PH

MANOR LANE

Threekingham

Cross

MAREHAM LANE

Mill Mound

DANESFIELD

Works

ACRE LANE

Owens Farm

2

Laurel Farm

Lodge Farm

Stow Green Hill

Walcot Lodge

WALCOT BAR

SLEAFORD ROAD

Stow Farm

35

MILL LANE

Walcot

Ford

Great Gorse

1

Pickworth Mill

CHURCH LANE

A15

BILLINGBOROUGH ROAD

34

04   **A**   05   **B**   06   **C**   07   **D**   08   **E**   09   **F**

131
142

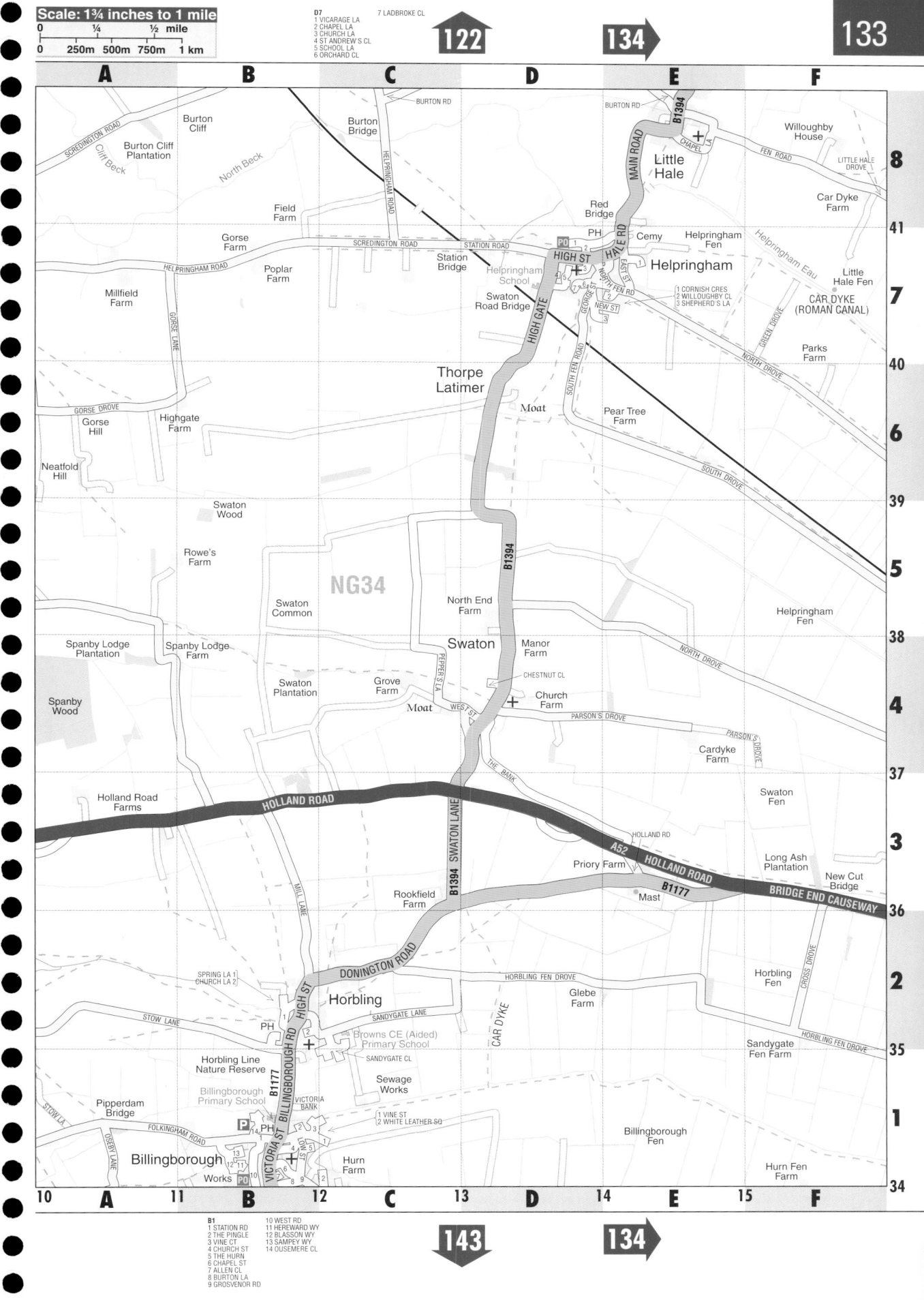

Scale: 1¾ inches to 1 mile

0   ¼   ½   mile
0 250m 500m 750m 1 km

D7
1 VICARAGE LA
2 CHAPEL LA
3 CHURCH LA
4 ST ANDREW'S CL
5 SCHOOL LA
6 ORCHARD CL

7 LADBROKE CL

122

134

Grid labels (top)
A   B   C   D   E   F

Map place names

Scredington Road

Burton Cliff
Burton Cliff Plantation

Cliff Beck

North Beck

Burton Rd

Burton Bridge

Burton Rd

B1394

Willoughby House

Little Hale Drove

Little Hale

Chapel La

Fen Road

8

Field Farm

Helpringham Road

Gorse Farm

Scredington Road

Station Road

Red Bridge

PH

Cemy

Helpringham Fen

Car Dyke Farm

41

Main Road

Hale Rd

Millfield Farm

Poplar Farm

Station Bridge

PO

Helpringham School

Swaton Road Bridge

High St

East St

North Fen Rd

Helpringham

1 Cornish Cres
2 Willoughby Cl
3 Shepherd's La

Little Hale Fen

Car Dyke (Roman Canal)

7

Gorse Lane

High Gate

George St

New St

Helpringham Eau

Green Drove

Parks Farm

40

Thorpe Latimer

South Fen Road

North Drove

6

Gorse Drove

Gorse Hill

Highgate Farm

Moat

Pear Tree Farm

South Drove

39

Neatfold Hill

Swaton Wood

B1394

5

Rowe's Farm

NG34

North End Farm

Helpringham Fen

38

Spanby Lodge Plantation

Spanby Lodge Farm

Swaton Common

Swaton

Manor Farm

North Drove

Spanby Wood

Swaton Plantation

Grove Farm

Pepper's La

Chestnut Cl

Church Farm

4

Moat

West St

Parson's Drove

Parson's Drove

Cardyke Farm

37

Holland Road Farms

Holland Road

The Bank

Swaton Fen

3

A52 Holland Rd

Holland Road

Long Ash Plantation

New Cut Bridge

Mill Lane

Swaton Lane

B1394

Rookfield Farm

Priory Farm

Mast

B1177

Bridge End Causeway

36

Donington Road

Horbling Fen Drove

Horbling Fen

Cross Drove

2

Spring La 1
Church La 2

Stow Lane

Horbling

Sandygate Lane

Car Dyke

Glebe Farm

Horbling Fen Drove

PH

High St

Browns CE (Aided) Primary School

Sandygate Cl

Sandygate Fen Farm

35

Horbling Line Nature Reserve

Billingborough Primary School

B1177

Billingborough Rd

Victoria Bank

Sewage Works

1 Vine St
2 White Leather Sq

Billingborough Fen

1

Pipperdam Bridge

Stow La

Ossery Lane

Folkingham Road

P

PH

Victoria St

Billingborough

Works

PO

Hurn Farm

Hurn Fen Farm

34

Grid labels (bottom)
10   A   11   B   12   C   13   D   14   E   15   F

B1
1 STATION RD
2 THE PINGLE
3 VINE CT
4 CHURCH ST
5 THE HURN
6 CHAPEL ST
7 ALLEN CL
8 BURTON LA
9 GROSVENOR RD
10 WEST RD
11 HEREWARD WY
12 BLASSON WY
13 SAMPEY WY
14 OUSEMERE CL

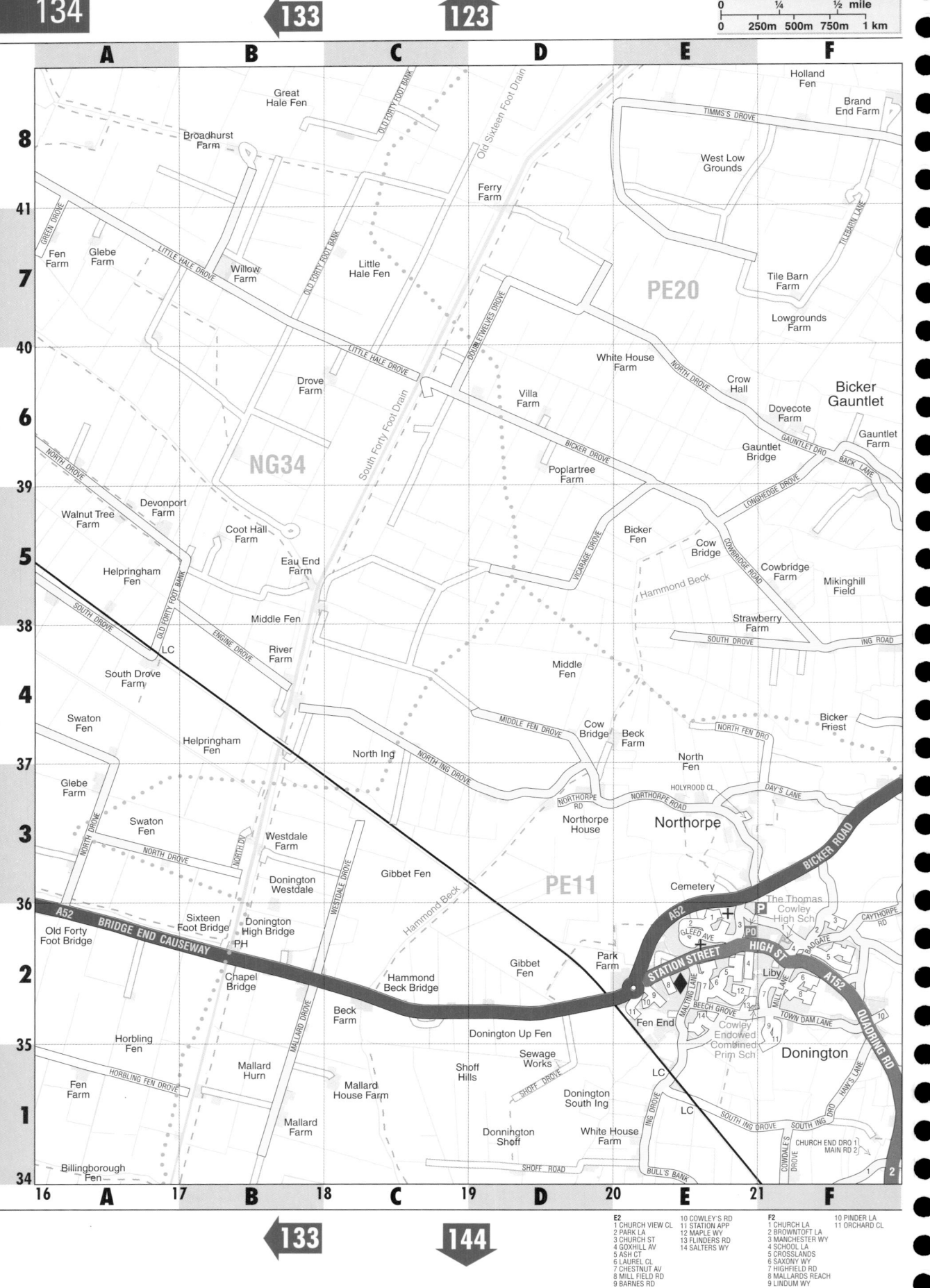

Scale: 1¾ inches to 1 mile
0   ¼   ½   mile
0   250m   500m   750m   1 km

A   B   C   D   E   F

8
41
7
40
6
39
5
38
4
37
3
36
2
35
1
34

16   A   17   B   18   C   19   D   20   E   21   F

PE20
NG34
PE11

Holland Fen
Brand End Farm
Great Hale Fen
Broadhurst Farm
Timms's Drove
West Low Grounds
Ferry Farm
Tile Barn Farm
Fen Farm
Glebe Farm
Willow Farm
Little Hale Fen
Little Hale Drove
Lowgrounds Farm
Crow Hall
Bicker Gauntlet
White House Farm
North Drove
Dovecote Farm
Gauntlet Farm
Drove Farm
Villa Farm
Bicker Drove
Gauntlet Bridge
Gauntlet Dro
Back Lane
Walnut Tree Farm
Devonport Farm
Coot Hall Farm
Poplartree Farm
Bicker Fen
Cow Bridge
Cowbridge Farm
Mikinghill Field
Longhedge Drove
Cowbridge Road
Helpringham Fen
Eau End Farm
Hammond Beck
Strawberry Farm
South Drove
Ing Road
Middle Fen
River Farm
Engine Drove
LC
South Drove Farm
Middle Fen
Bicker Friest
Swaton Fen
Helpringham Fen
Middle Fen Drove
North Ing Drove
Cow Bridge
Beck Farm
North Fen Dro
North Fen
Glebe Farm
North Drove
Swaton Fen
North Drove
North Dv
Westdale Farm
North Ing
Northorpe Rd
Northorpe Road
Northorpe House
Northorpe
Holyrood Cl
Day's Lane
Cemetery
The Thomas Cowley High Sch
Bicker Road
Donington Westdale
Gibbet Fen
Hammond Beck
Westdale Drove
A52
Caythorpe Rd
Old Forty Foot Bridge
Bridge End Causeway
Sixteen Foot Bridge
Donington High Bridge
PH
Chapel Bridge
Hammond Beck Bridge
Gibbet Fen
Park Farm
Fen End
Station Street
High St
A152
Liby
Mill Lane
Donington
Quadring Rd
Horbling Fen
Mallard Hurn
Beck Farm
Donington Up Fen
Sewage Works
Shoff Hills
Donington South Ing
Cowley Endowed Combined Prim Sch
Town Dam Lane
Fen Farm
Horbling Fen Drove
Mallard Drove
Mallard House Farm
Shoff Drove
Donnington Shoff
White House Farm
Ing Drove
LC
LC
South Ing Drove
South Ing Dro
Haw's Lane
Cowdale's Drove
Church End Dro 1
Main Rd 2
Billingborough Fen
Mallard Farm
Shoff Road
Bull's Bank

Old Sixteen Foot Drain
Old Forty Foot Bank
Double Twelves Drove
South Forty Foot Drain
Vicarage Drove
Green Drove
Little Hale Drove
Old Forty Foot Bank

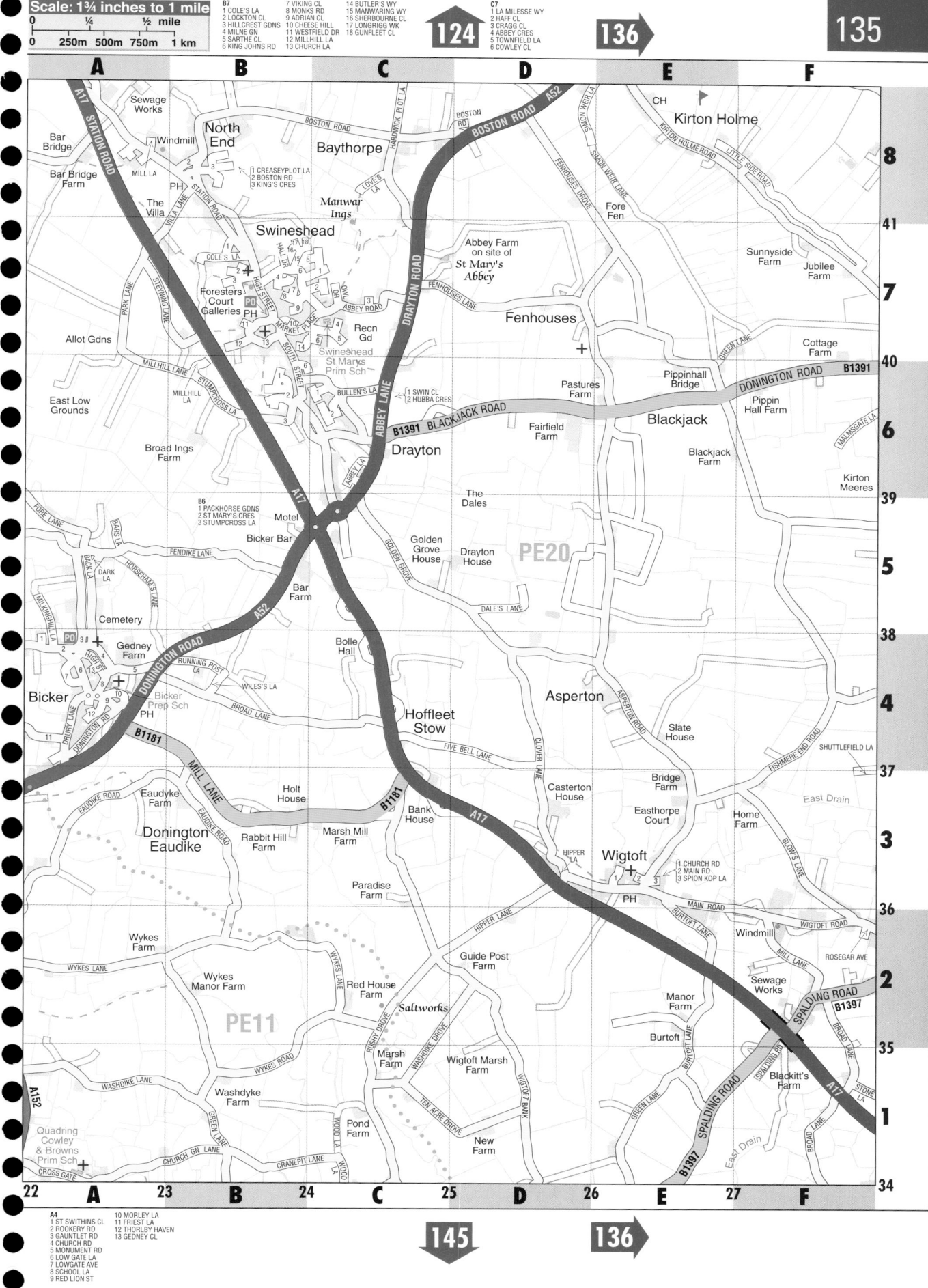

Scale: 1¾ inches to 1 mile
0 ¼ ½ mile
0 250m 500m 750m 1 km
B7
1 COLE'S LA
2 LOCKTON CL
3 HILLCREST GDNS
4 MILNE GN
5 SARTHE CL
6 KING JOHNS RD
7 VIKING CL
8 MONKS RD
9 ADRIAN CL
10 CHEESE HILL
11 WESTFIELD DR
12 MILLHILL LA
13 CHURCH LA
14 BUTLER'S WY
15 MANWARING WY
16 SHERBOURNE CL
17 LONGRIGG WK
18 GUNFLEET CL
124
136
C7
1 LA MILESSE WY
2 HAFF CL
3 CRAGG CL
4 ABBEY CRES
5 TOWNFIELD LA
6 COWLEY CL
A B C D E F
A17 STATION ROAD
Sewage Works
Bar Bridge
Windmill
North End
Baythorpe
BOSTON ROAD
HARDWICK PLOT LA
BOSTON RD
BOSTON ROAD
A52
SIMON WEIR LA
CH
Kirton Holme
KIRTON HOLME ROAD
LITTLE SIDE ROAD
8
MILL LA
Bar Bridge Farm
PH
1 CREASEYPLOT LA
2 BOSTON RD
3 KING'S CRES
LOVE'S LA
Manwar Ings
FENHOUSES DROVE
SIMON WEIR LANE
The Villa
VILLA LANE
STATION ROAD
Fore Fen
41
Swineshead
Abbey Farm on site of St Mary's Abbey
Sunnyside Farm
Jubilee Farm
COLE'S LA
HALL DR
HIGH STREET
PARK LANE
STEYNING LANE
Foresters Court Galleries
PO
PH
DRAYTON ROAD
FENHOUSES LANE
ABBEY ROAD
OWL DR
7
MARKET PLACE
Recn Gd
Fenhouses
Allot Gdns
SOUTH STREET
Swineshead St Marys Prim Sch
GREEN LANE
Cottage Farm
40
MILLHILL LANE
STUMPCROSS LA
MILLHILL LA
BULLEN'S LA
1 SWIN CL
2 HUBBA CRES
Pastures Farm
Pippinhall Bridge
DONINGTON ROAD
B1391
East Low Grounds
ABBEY LANE
B1391 BLACKJACK ROAD
Blackjack
Pippin Hall Farm
MALMSGATE LA
Fairfield Farm
6
Drayton
Broad Ings Farm
ABBEY LA
Blackjack Farm
Kirton Meeres
The Dales
39
A17
B6
1 PACKHORSE GDNS
2 ST MARY'S CRES
3 STUMPCROSS LA
FORE LANE
Motel
BARS LA
Bicker Bar
Golden Grove House
GOLDEN GROVE
Drayton House
PE20
FENDIKE LANE
BACK LA
DARK LA
HORSEHAM'S LANE
5
Bar Farm
MILKINGHILL LA
A52
DALE'S LANE
Cemetery
38
PO
Gedney Farm
HIGH ST
DONINGTON ROAD
Bolle Hall
RUNNING POST LA
WILES'S LA
Asperton
ASPERTON ROAD
Bicker
Bicker Prep Sch
PH
BROAD LANE
Hoffleet Stow
4
DRURY LANE
DONINGTON RD
B1181
FIVE BELL LANE
CLOVER LANE
Slate House
FISHMERE END ROAD
SHUTTLEFIELD LA
37
MILL LANE
Eaudyke Farm
EAUDIKE ROAD
Holt House
B1181
Casterton House
Bridge Farm
East Drain
Bank House
Easthorpe Court
Home Farm
A17
Donington Eaudike
EAUDIKE ROAD
Rabbit Hill Farm
Marsh Mill Farm
HIPPER LA
Wigtoft
1 CHURCH RD
2 MAIN RD
3 SPION KOP LA
BLOW'S LANE
3
Paradise Farm
PH
MAIN ROAD
BURTOFT LANE
36
WIGTOFT ROAD
Windmill
Wykes Farm
HIPPER LANE
MILL LANE
ROSEGAR AVE
Guide Post Farm
WYKES LANE
WYKES LANE
Wykes Manor Farm
Red House Farm
Sewage Works
2
SPALDING ROAD
Manor Farm
B1397
Saltworks
PE11
RUSHY DROVE
WASHDIKE DROVE
Burtoft
BURTOFT LANE
BROAD LANE
35
Marsh Farm
WYKES ROAD
Wigtoft Marsh Farm
SPALDING RD
Blackitt's Farm
WASHDIKE LANE
A152
WIGTOFT BANK
Washdyke Farm
TEN ACRE DROVE
GREEN LANE
SPALDING ROAD
A17
STONE LA
1
GREEN LANE
Quadring Cowley & Browns Prim Sch
WOOD LA
Pond Farm
New Farm
BROAD LANE
East Drain
CHURCH GN LANE
CRANEPIT LANE
B1397
CROSS GATE
WOOD LA
22 A 23 B 24 C 25 D 26 E 27 F 34
A4
1 ST SWITHINS CL
2 ROOKERY RD
3 GAUNTLET RD
4 CHURCH RD
5 MONUMENT RD
6 LOW GATE LA
7 LOWGATE AVE
8 SCHOOL LA
9 RED LION ST
10 MORLEY LA
11 FRIEST LA
12 THORLBY HAVEN
13 GEDNEY CL
145
136

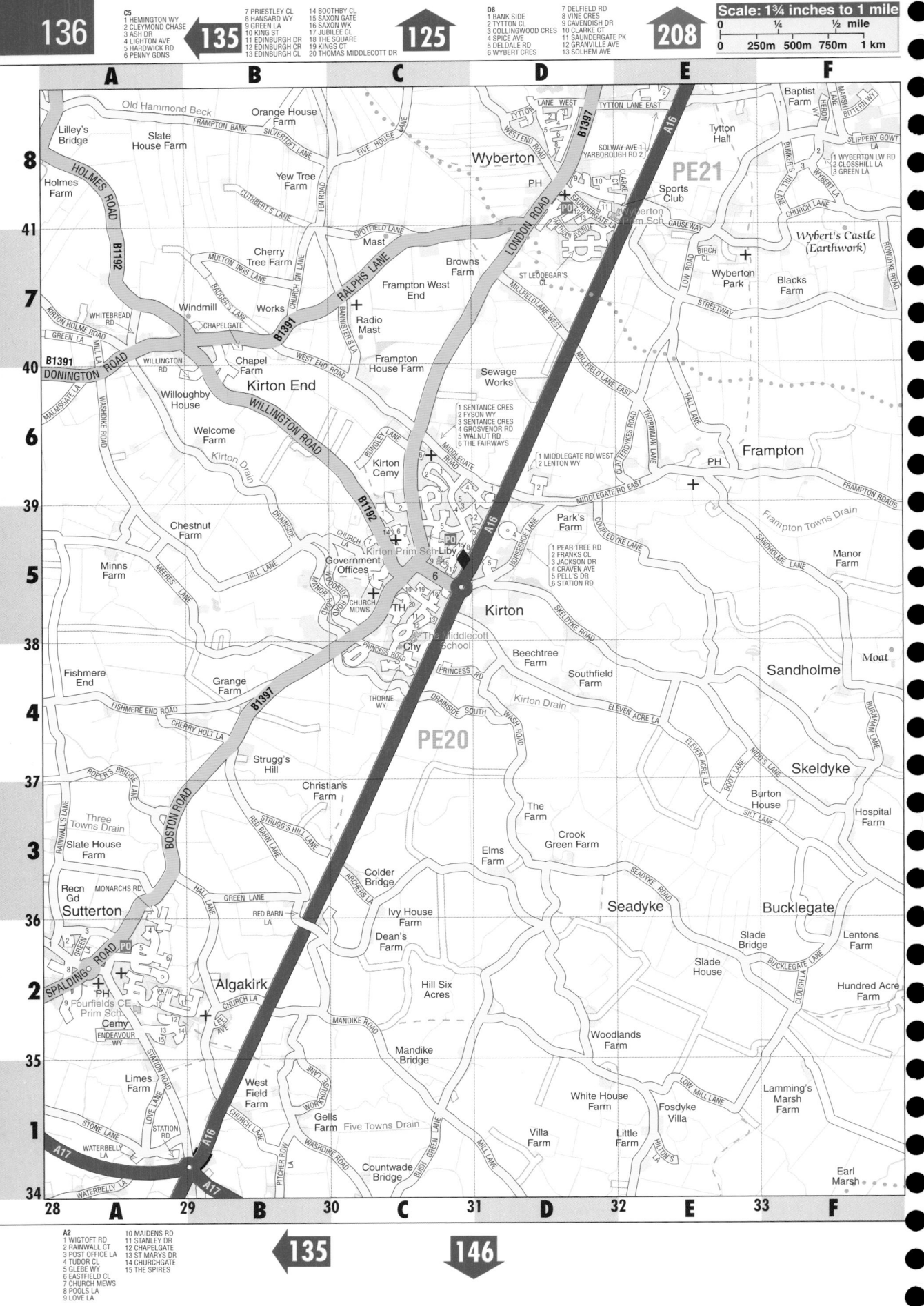

C5
1 HEMINGTON WY
2 CLEYMOND CHASE
3 ASH DR
4 LIGHTON AVE
5 HARDWICK RD
6 PENNY GDNS

7 PRIESTLEY CL
8 HANSARD WY
9 GREEN LA
10 KING ST
11 EDINBURGH DR
12 EDINBURGH CR
13 EDINBURGH CL

14 BOOTHBY CL
15 SAXON GATE
16 SAXON WK
17 JUBILEE CL
18 THE SQUARE
19 KINGS CT
20 THOMAS MIDDLECOTT DR

D8
1 BANK SIDE
2 TYTTON CL
3 COLLINGWOOD CRES
4 SPICE AVE
5 DELDALE RD
6 WYBERT CRES

7 DELFIELD RD
8 VINE CRES
9 CAVENDISH DR
10 CLARKE CT
11 SAUNDERGATE PK
12 GRANVILLE AVE
13 SOLHEM AVE

PE21

PE20

A2
1 WIGTOFT RD
2 RAINWALL CT
3 POST OFFICE LA
4 TUDOR CL
5 GLEBE WY
6 EASTFIELD CL
7 CHURCH MEWS
8 POOLS LA
9 LOVE LA

10 MAIDENS RD
11 STANLEY DR
12 CHAPELGATE
13 ST MARYS DR
14 CHURCHGATE
15 THE SPIRES

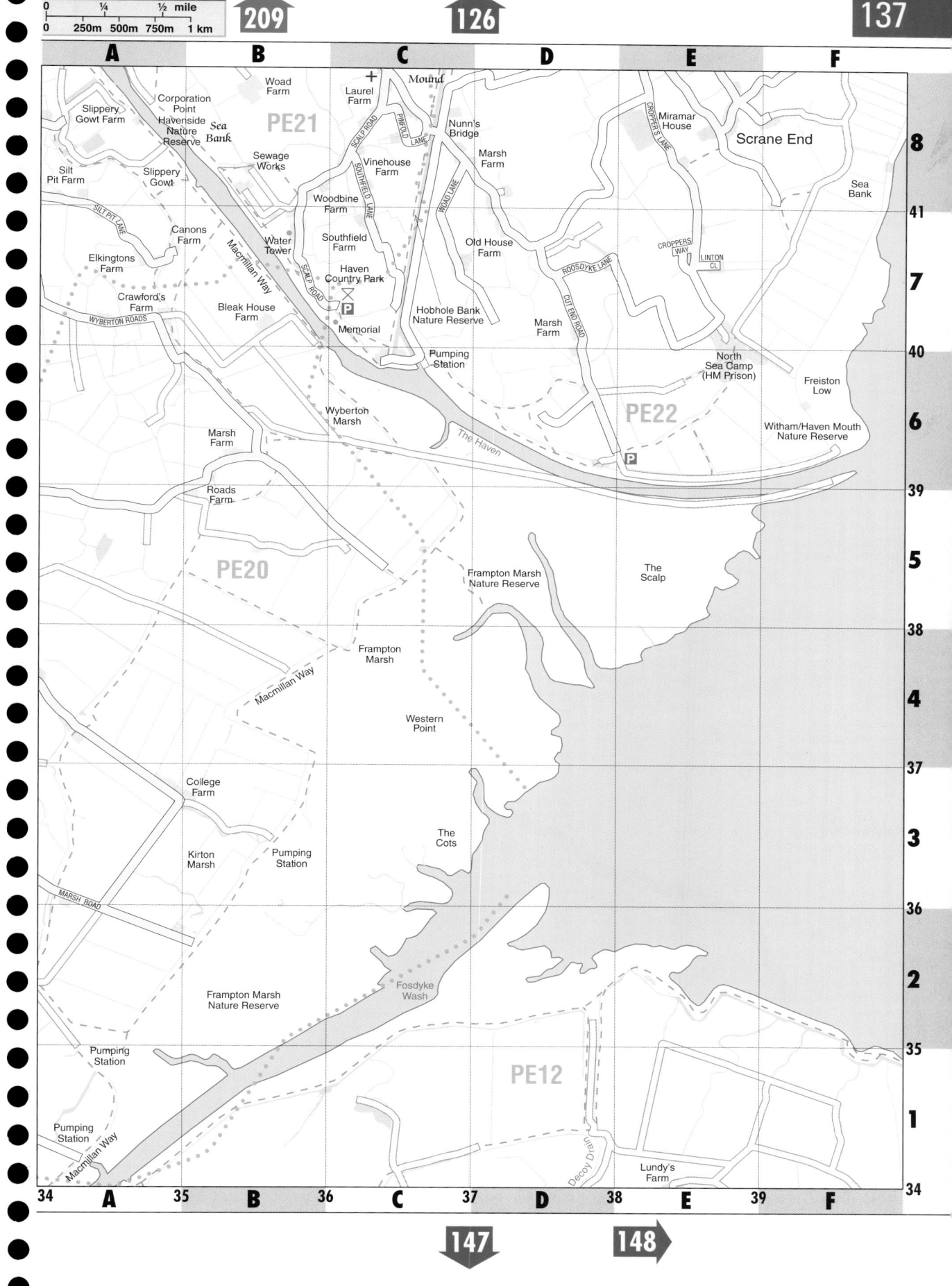

Scale: 1¾ inches to 1 mile

0   ¼   ½   mile
0 250m 500m 750m 1 km

209
126
147
148

A   B   C   D   E   F

Woad Farm

Slippery Gowt Farm

Corporation Point
Havenside Nature Reserve

Sea Bank

Laurel Farm

Mound

PE21

Nunn's Bridge

Miramar House

Scrane End

8

Silt Pit Farm

Slippery Gowt

Sewage Works

Vinehouse Farm

Marsh Farm

Sea Bank

Woodbine Farm

41

Canons Farm

Water Tower

Southfield Farm

Old House Farm

CROPPERS WAY

LINTON CL

7

Elkingtons Farm

Macmillan Way

Haven Country Park

ROOSDYKE LANE

Crawford's Farm

WYBERTON ROADS

Bleak House Farm

SCALP ROAD

Memorial

Hobhole Bank Nature Reserve

CUT END ROAD

Marsh Farm

North Sea Camp (HM Prison)

40

SILT PIT LANE

P

Pumping Station

PE22

Freiston Low

Wyberton Marsh

The Haven

Witham/Haven Mouth Nature Reserve

6

Marsh Farm

P

Roads Farm

39

PE20

Frampton Marsh Nature Reserve

The Scalp

5

Frampton Marsh

38

Macmillan Way

Western Point

4

37

College Farm

The Cots

3

Kirton Marsh

Pumping Station

36

MARSH ROAD

2

Frampton Marsh Nature Reserve

Fosdyke Wash

PE12

35

Pumping Station

Pumping Station

Decoy Drain

Lundy's Farm

1

Macmillan Way

34

34   35   36   37   38   39

A   B   C   D   E   F

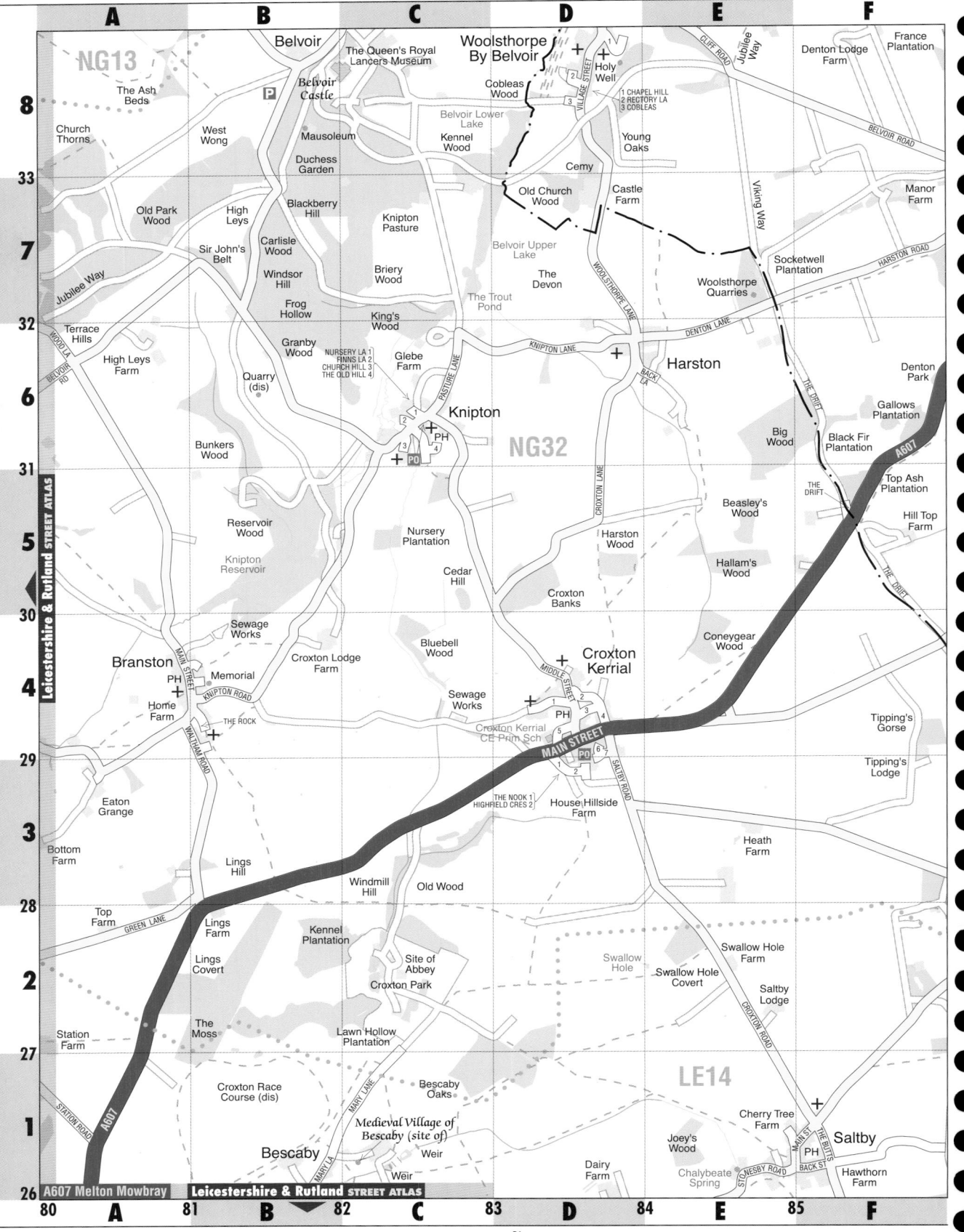

Scale: 1¾ inches to 1 mile
0   ¼   ½   mile
0   250m   500m   750m   1 km

A   **B**   **C**   **D**   **E**   **F**

NG13

Belvoir
The Queen's Royal Lancers Museum
Woolsthorpe By Belvoir
Holy Well
France Plantation
Denton Lodge Farm

The Ash Beds
Belvoir Castle
Cobleas Wood
1 CHAPEL HILL
2 RECTORY LA
3 COBLEAS

8

Church Thorns
West Wong
Mausoleum
Belvoir Lower Lake
Kennel Wood
Young Oaks
Manor Farm

33

Old Park Wood
High Leys
Duchess Garden
Blackberry Hill
Knipton Pasture
Cemy
Old Church Wood
Castle Farm
Socketwell Plantation
Harston Road

7

Sir John's Belt
Carlisle Wood
Belvoir Upper Lake
The Devon
Woolsthorpe Quarries
Viking Way

Jubilee Way
Windsor Hill
Briery Wood
Frog Hollow
King's Wood
The Trout Pond

32

Terrace Hills
High Leys Farm
Granby Wood
Glebe Farm
NURSERY LA 1
FINNS LA 2
CHURCH HILL 3
THE OLD HILL 4
Knipton Lane
Harston
Denton Lane
Denton Park

6

Quarry (dis)
Knipton
NG32
Big Wood
Black Fir Plantation
Gallows Plantation
A607

Bunkers Wood
PH
PO
Beasley's Wood
THE DRIFT
Top Ash Plantation

31

Reservoir Wood
Nursery Plantation
Harston Wood
Hallam's Wood
Hill Top Farm
THE DRIFT

5

Knipton Reservoir
Cedar Hill
Croxton Banks
Coneygear Wood

30

Sewage Works
Bluebell Wood
Croxton Kerrial

Branston
PH
Memorial
Croxton Lodge Farm
MIDDLE STREET
PH

4

Home Farm
THE ROCK
Sewage Works
Croxton Kerrial CE Prim Sch
MAIN STREET
PO
Tipping's Gorse

WHATTON ROAD
KNIPTON ROAD

29

THE NOOK 1
HIGHFIELD CRES 2
House Hillside Farm
Tipping's Lodge

Eaton Grange
Heath Farm

3

Bottom Farm
Lings Hill
Windmill Hill
Old Wood

28

Top Farm
GREEN LANE
Lings Farm
Kennel Plantation
Swallow Hole Farm
Swallow Hole
Swallow Hole Covert
Saltby Lodge

Lings Covert
Site of Abbey
CROXTON ROAD

2

The Moss
Croxton Park
Saltby
Cherry Tree Farm

Station Farm
Lawn Hollow Plantation
LE14
Joey's Wood
PH
Hawthorn Farm

STATION ROAD
A607

1

Croxton Race Course (dis)
Bescaby Oaks
Medieval Village of Bescaby (site of)
MARY LANE
Dairy Farm
Chalybeate Spring
STONESBY ROAD
THE BUTTS
MAIN ST
BACK ST

Bescaby
Weir
Weir

26

80   **A**   **81**   **B**   **82**   **C**   **83**   **D**   **84**   **E**   **85**   **F**

D4
1 CHAPEL LA
2 CHURCH LA
3 THORPES LA
4 TOP RD
5 SCHOOL LA
6 SHIRES ORCH
7 MILL LA

Leicestershire & Rutland STREET ATLAS

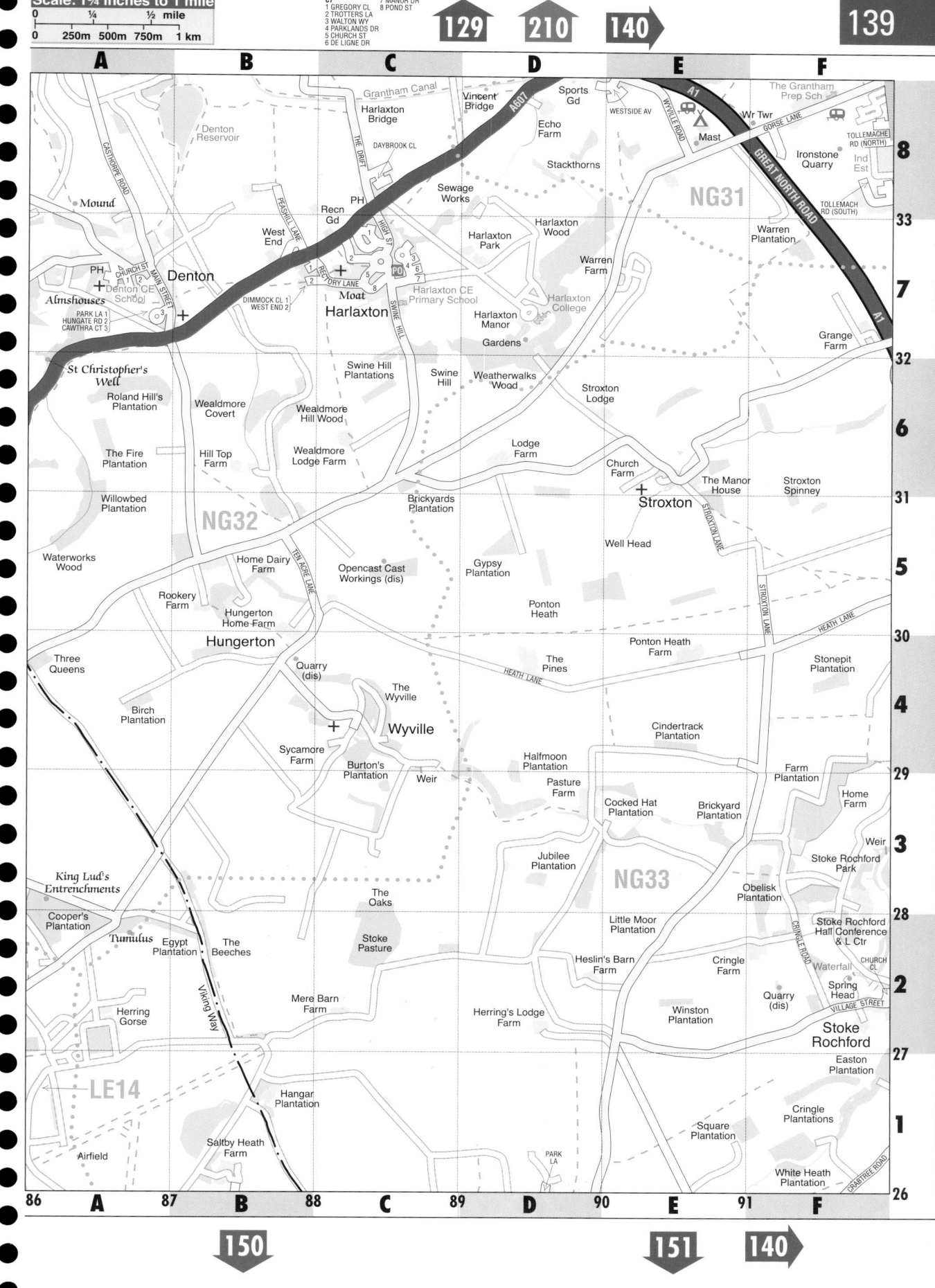

Scale: 1¾ inches to 1 mile

0   ¼   ½   mile
0   250m   500m   750m   1 km

C7
1 GREGORY CL
2 TROTTERS LA
3 WALTON WY
4 PARKLANDS DR
5 CHURCH ST
6 DE LIGNE DR
7 MANOR DR
8 POND ST

129   210   140

A **B** **C** **D** **E** **F**

Grantham Canal

Vincent Bridge

Harlaxton Bridge

Sports Gd

WESTSIDE AV

The Grantham Prep Sch

Wr Twr

Denton Reservoir

THE DRIFT

DAYBROOK CL

Echo Farm

WYVILLE ROAD

Mast

GORSE LANE

Tollemache RD (NORTH)

Ironstone Quarry

Ind Est

8

Mound

Sewage Works

Stackthorns

NG31

GREAT NORTH ROAD

TOLLEMACH RD (SOUTH)

Warren Plantation

A1

33

West End

PEASHILL LANE

Recn Gd

PH

HIGH ST

Harlaxton Park

Harlaxton Wood

Warren Farm

PH

CHURCH ST

1 2

Denton CE School

Denton

MAIN STREET

RECTORY LANE

1 2
3
5 4

PO

3
6 4
7

8

Moat

Harlaxton CE Primary School

Harlaxton College

7

Almshouses

PARK LA 1
HUNGATE RD 2
CAWTHRA CT 3

DIMMOCK CL 1
WEST END 2

Harlaxton

SWINE HILL

Harlaxton Manor Gardens

A1

Grange Farm

32

St Christopher's Well

Swine Hill Plantations

Swine Hill

Weatherwalks Wood

Stroxton Lodge

Roland Hill's Plantation

Wealdmore Covert

Wealdmore Hill Wood

6

The Fire Plantation

Hill Top Farm

Wealdmore Lodge Farm

Lodge Farm

Church Farm

The Manor House

Stroxton Spinney

NG32

Willowbed Plantation

Brickyards Plantation

Stroxton

STROXTON LANE

31

Waterworks Wood

Home Dairy Farm

TEN ACRE LANE

Opencast Cast Workings (dis)

Gypsy Plantation

Well Head

STROXTON LANE

HEATH LANE

5

Rookery Farm

Hungerton Home Farm

Ponton Heath

Ponton Heath Farm

Stonepit Plantation

30

Hungerton

Quarry (dis)

HEATH LANE

The Pines

Three Queens

The Wyville

Cindertrack Plantation

Farm Plantation

4

Birch Plantation

Sycamore Farm

Wyville

Halfmoon Plantation

Home Farm

29

Burton's Plantation

Weir

Pasture Farm

Cocked Hat Plantation

Brickyard Plantation

Weir

Stoke Rochford Park

3

King Lud's Entrenchments

Jubilee Plantation

NG33

Obelisk Plantation

CRINGLE ROAD

Stoke Rochford Hall Conference & L Ctr

Cooper's Plantation

The Oaks

Little Moor Plantation

Waterfall

CHURCH CL

28

Tumulus

Egypt Plantation

The Beeches

Stoke Pasture

Heslin's Barn Farm

Cringle Farm

Quarry (dis)

Spring Head

VILLAGE STREET

2

VIKING WAY

Mere Barn Farm

Herring's Lodge Farm

Winston Plantation

Stoke Rochford

Herring Gorse

27

LE14

Hangar Plantation

Easton Plantation

1

Airfield

Saltby Heath Farm

PARK LA

Square Plantation

Cringle Plantations

CRABTREE ROAD

White Heath Plantation

26

86   **A**   87   **B**   88   **C**   89   **D**   90   **E**   91   **F**

150   151   140

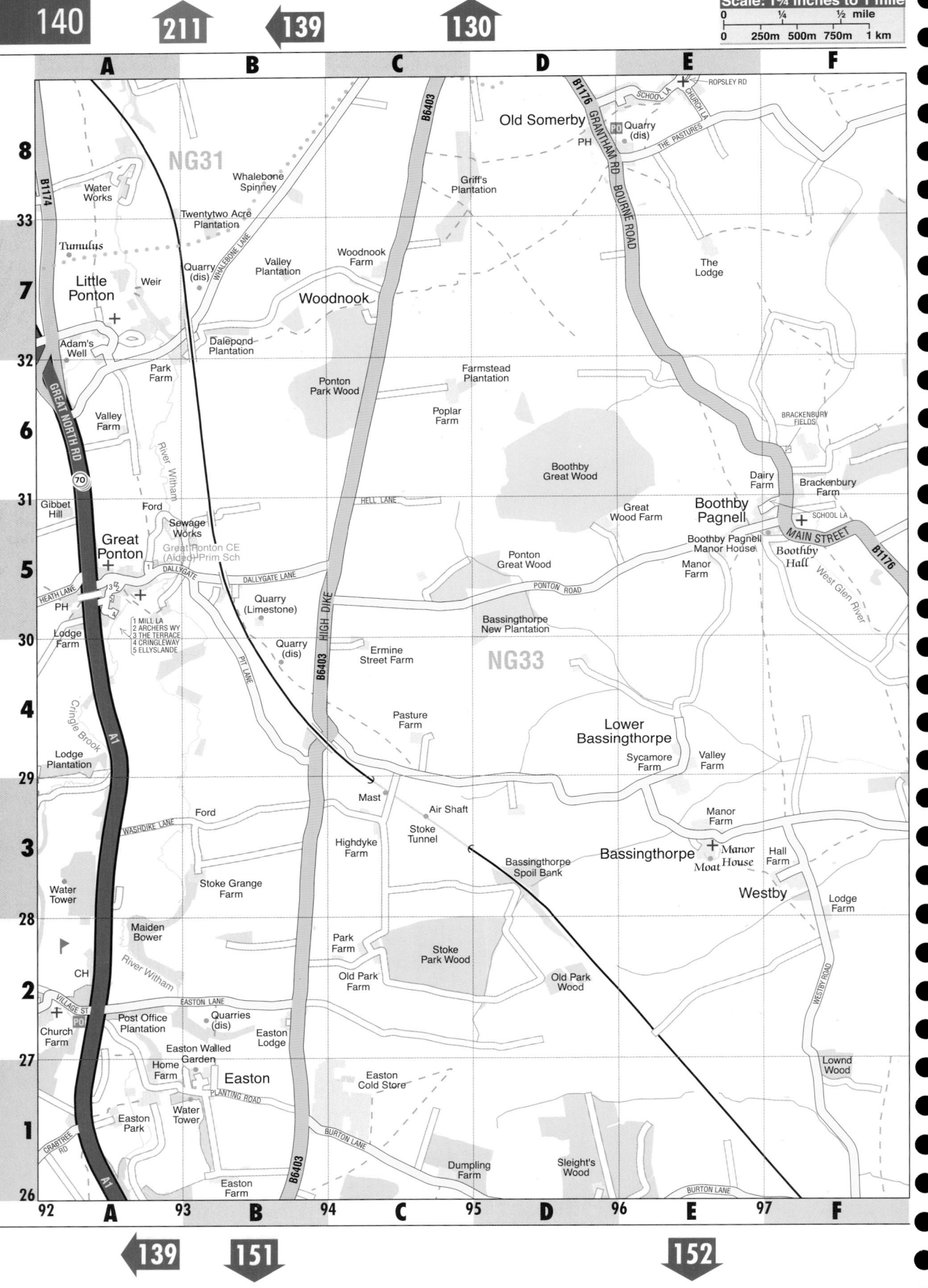

Scale: 1¾ inches to 1 mile

NG31

A B C D E F

8

Water Works

Whalebone Spinney

Old Somerby

Griff's Plantation

ROPSLEY RD
SCHOOL LA
CHURCH LA

PO Quarry (dis)
PH THE PASTURES

33

Twentytwo Acre Plantation

7

Tumulus

Quarry (dis)

Valley Plantation

Woodnook Farm

Woodnook

The Lodge

Little Ponton

Weir

GRANTHAM RD
BOURNE ROAD
B1176

32

Adam's Well

Dalepond Plantation

Park Farm

Farmstead Plantation

BRACKENBURY FIELDS

6

Valley Farm

River Witham

Ponton Park Wood

Poplar Farm

Boothby Great Wood

Dairy Farm

Brackenbury Farm

31

Gibbet Hill

Ford

GREAT NORTH RD

HELL LANE

Great Wood Farm

Boothby Pagnell

SCHOOL LA
MAIN STREET
B1176

Sewage Works

5

70

Great Ponton

Great Ponton CE (Aided) Prim Sch

DALLYGATE
DALLYGATE LANE

Ponton Great Wood

PONTON ROAD

Boothby Pagnell Manor House

Manor Farm

Boothby Hall

West Glen River

HEATH LANE

PH

1 MILL LA
2 ARCHERS WY
3 THE TERRACE
4 CRINGLEWAY
5 ELLYSLANDE

Quarry (Limestone)

Bassingthorpe New Plantation

30

Lodge Farm

PIT LANE

Quarry (dis)

HIGH DYKE

Ermine Street Farm

NG33

4

Lodge Plantation

Cringle Brook

A1

B6403

Pasture Farm

Lower Bassingthorpe

Sycamore Farm

Valley Farm

29

Mast

Air Shaft

Manor Farm

3

Water Tower

WASHDIKE LANE

Ford

Highdyke Farm

Stoke Tunnel

Bassingthorpe Spoil Bank

Bassingthorpe

Manor House
Moat

Hall Farm

Stoke Grange Farm

Westby

WESTBY ROAD

Lodge Farm

28

Maiden Bower

River Witham

Park Farm

Stoke Park Wood

Old Park Wood

2

CH

EASTON LANE
VILLAGE ST

Post Office Plantation

Old Park Farm

PO

Quarries (dis)

Easton Lodge

Church Farm

Easton Walled Garden

Easton Cold Store

Lownd Wood

27

Home Farm

PLANTING ROAD

Easton

Easton Cold Store

1

Easton Park

Water Tower

BURTON LANE

CRABTREE RD

Dumpling Farm

Sleight's Wood

B6403

26

Easton Farm

BURTON LANE

92 A 93 B 94 C 95 D 96 E 97 F

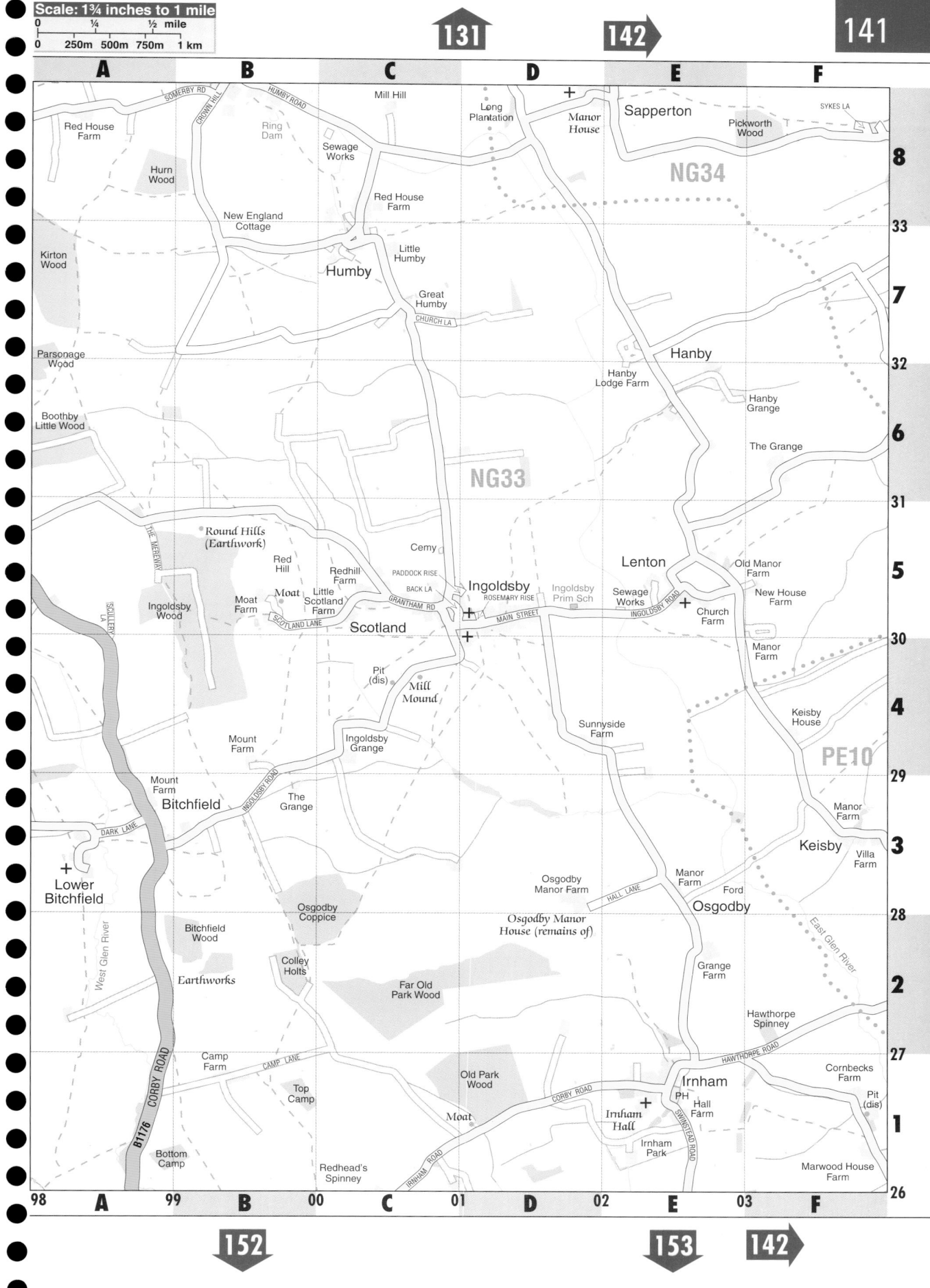

Scale: 1¾ inches to 1 mile
0 ¼ ½ mile
0 250m 500m 750m 1 km
131
142
A B C D E F
Red House Farm
Ring Dam
Mill Hill
Long Plantation
Manor House
Sapperton
Pickworth Wood
SYKES LA
SOMERBY RD
CROWN HILL
HUMBY ROAD
Sewage Works
Hurn Wood
NG34
Red House Farm
New England Cottage
Kirton Wood
Little Humby
Humby
Great Humby
CHURCH LA
Parsonage Wood
Hanby
Hanby Lodge Farm
Hanby Grange
Boothby Little Wood
The Grange
NG33
Round Hills (Earthwork)
THE MEREWAY
Cemy
Red Hill
Redhill Farm
PADDOCK RISE
BACK LA
Ingoldsby
ROSEMARY RISE
Ingoldsby Prim Sch
Lenton
Old Manor Farm
Sewage Works
New House Farm
Moat
Moat Farm
Little Scotland Farm
GRANTHAM RD
Church Farm
SCULLERY LA
Ingoldsby Wood
SCOTLAND LANE
Scotland
MAIN STREET
INGOLDSBY ROAD
Manor Farm
Pit (dis)
Mill Mound
Sunnyside Farm
Keisby House
Mount Farm
Ingoldsby Grange
PE10
Mount Farm
Bitchfield
INGOLDSBY ROAD
The Grange
Manor Farm
DARK LANE
Keisby
Villa Farm
Lower Bitchfield
Osgodby Manor Farm
Manor Farm
HALL LANE
Ford
Osgodby
Osgodby Coppice
Osgodby Manor House (remains of)
Bitchfield Wood
East Glen River
West Glen River
Colley Holts
Grange Farm
Earthworks
Far Old Park Wood
Hawthorpe Spinney
Camp Farm
CAMP LANE
HAWTHORPE ROAD
CORBY ROAD
Old Park Wood
Irnham
Cornbecks Farm
Top Camp
CORBY ROAD
PH
Pit (dis)
Moat
Irnham Hall
Hall Farm
B1176
Irnham Park
SWINSTEAD ROAD
Bottom Camp
Redhead's Spinney
IRNHAM ROAD
Marwood House Farm
8
33
7
32
6
31
5
30
4
29
3
28
2
27
1
26
98 A 99 B 00 C 01 D 02 E 03 F
152
153
142

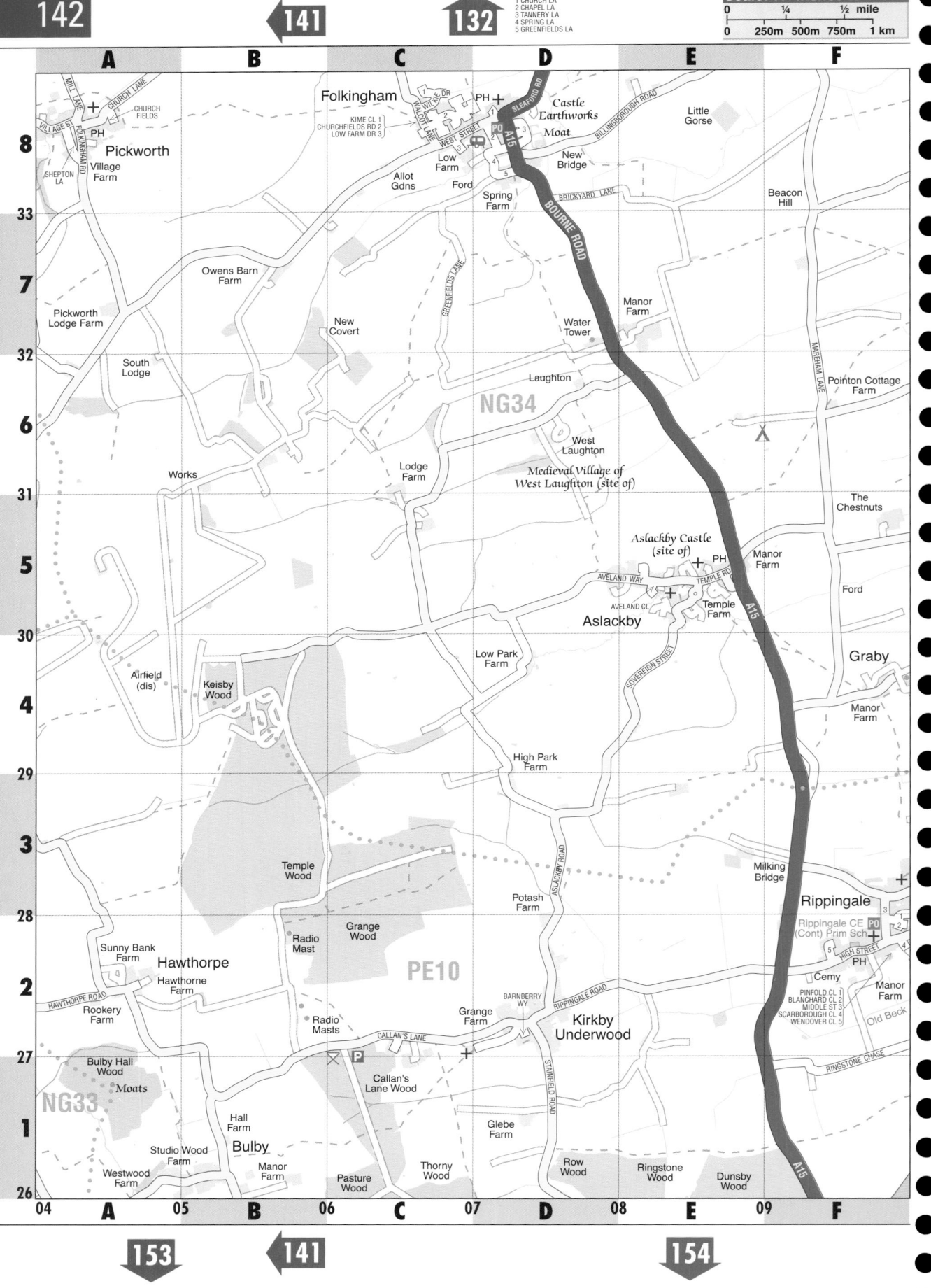

141

132

D8
1 CHURCH LA
2 CHAPEL LA
3 TANNERY LA
4 SPRING LA
5 GREENFIELDS LA

Scale: 1¾ inches to 1 mile

0   ¼   ½ mile
0 250m 500m 750m 1 km

A   B   C   D   E   F

Folkingham

Castle
Earthworks
Moat

Little
Gorse

PH

KIME CL 1
CHURCHFIELDS RD 2
LOW FARM DR 3

WALCOT LANE

WEST STREET

SLEAFORD RD

A15

PO

Low
Farm

New
Bridge

BILLINGBOROUGH ROAD

Beacon
Hill

Pickworth

MILL LANE

CHURCH LANE

+

PH

VILLAGE ST

FOLKINGHAM RD

CHURCH
FIELDS

Village
Farm

SHEPTON
LA

33

Allot
Gdns

Ford

Spring
Farm

BRICKYARD LANE

BOURNE ROAD

8

Owens Barn
Farm

Manor
Farm

Water
Tower

7

Pickworth
Lodge Farm

New
Covert

GREENFIELDS LANE

Laughton

MAREHAM LANE

Pointon Cottage
Farm

32

South
Lodge

NG34

West
Laughton

6

Medieval Village of
West Laughton (site of)

The
Chestnuts

31

Works

Lodge
Farm

Aslackby Castle
(site of)

PH
+
+

Manor
Farm

AVELAND WAY

TEMPLE RD

Ford

5

Aveland Cl

Temple
Farm

A15

30

Airfield
(dis)

Keisby
Wood

Low Park
Farm

Aslackby

Graby

Manor
Farm

4

SOVEREIGN STREET

High Park
Farm

29

Temple
Wood

ASLACKBY ROAD

Milking
Bridge

+

Rippingale

3

Potash
Farm

Rippingale CE
(Cont) Prim Sch

PO
+

28

Sunny Bank
Farm

Radio
Mast

Grange
Wood

PE10

RIPPINGALE ROAD

HIGH STREET

PH

Cemy

Manor
Farm

Hawthorpe

Hawthorne
Farm

BARNBERRY
WY

PINFOLD CL 1
BLANCHARD CL 2
MIDDLE ST 3
SCARBOROUGH CL 4
WENDOVER CL 5

Old Beck

2

HAWTHORPE ROAD

Rookery
Farm

Radio
Masts

CALLAN'S LANE

Grange
Farm

STAINFIELD ROAD

Kirkby
Underwood

+

RINGSTONE CHASE

27

Bulby Hall
Wood

Moats

Callan's
Lane Wood

NG33

Hall
Farm

Studio Wood
Farm

Bulby

Manor
Farm

Pasture
Wood

Thorny
Wood

Glebe
Farm

Row
Wood

Ringstone
Wood

Dunsby
Wood

A15

1

Westwood
Farm

26

04   A   05   B   06   C   07   D   08   E   09   F

153

141

154

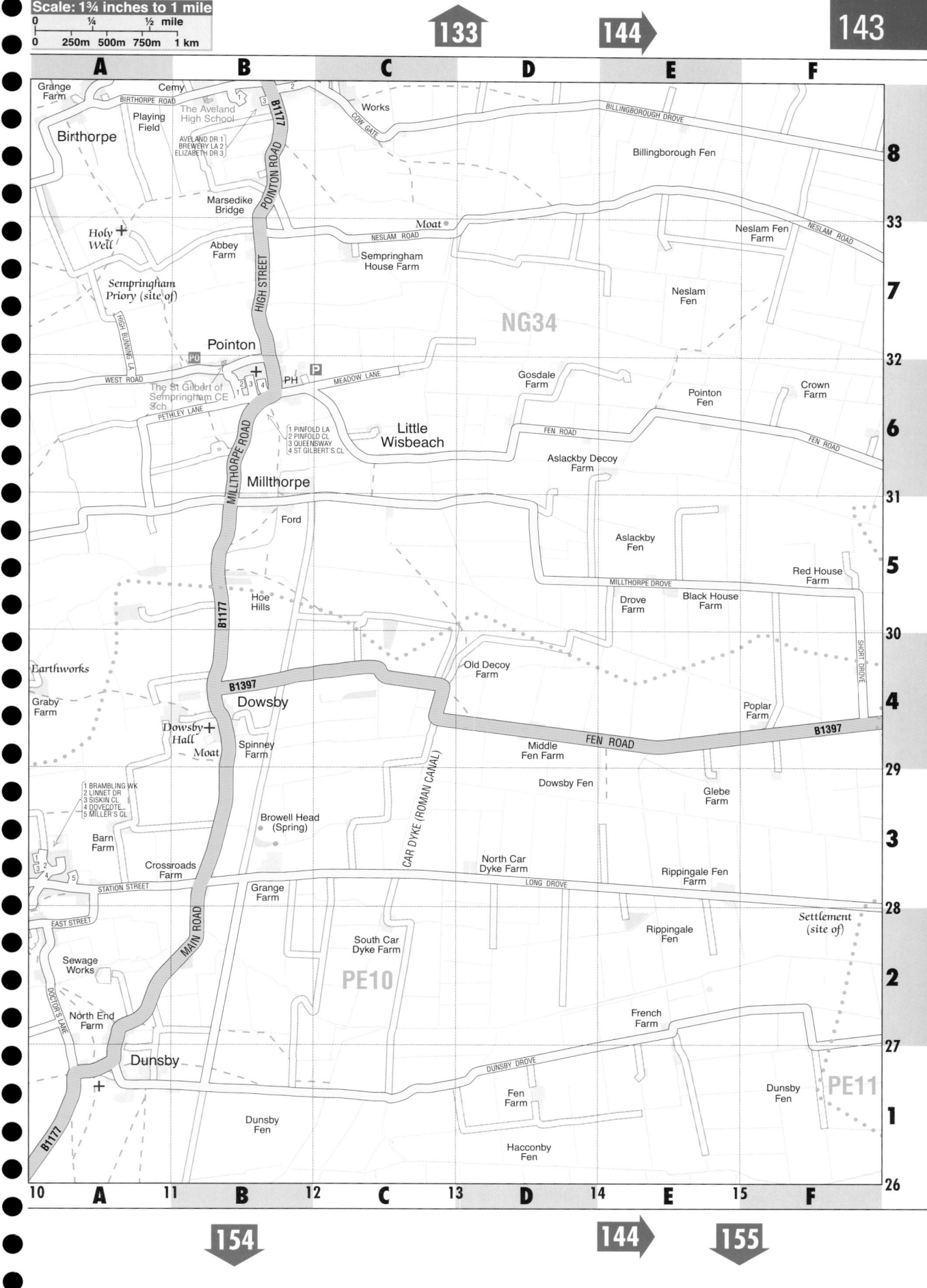

A   B   C   D   E   F

Grange Farm
Cemy
Birthorpe Road
The Aveland High School
B1177
Works
Billingborough Drove

Birthorpe
Playing Field
AVELAND DR 1
BREWERY LA 2
ELIZABETH DR 3
Cow Gate
Billingborough Fen

8

Marsedike Bridge
Moat
Neslam Road
Neslam Fen Farm
Neslam Road

33

Holy Well
Abbey Farm
Sempringham House Farm
Neslam Fen

7

Sempringham Priory (site of)
POINTON ROAD
HIGH STREET

NG34

Pointon
PO
Gosdale Farm
Pointon Fen
Crown Farm

32

HIGH BURNING LA
WEST ROAD
The St Gilbert of Sempringham CE Sch
PETHLEY LANE
PH
P
MEADOW LANE
Little Wisbeach
Fen Road
Fen Road

6

1 PINFOLD LA
2 PINFOLD CL
3 QUEENSWAY
4 ST GILBERT'S CL
Aslackby Decoy Farm

MILLTHORPE ROAD
Millthorpe

31

Ford
Aslackby Fen

Hoe Hills
B1177
Millthorpe Drove
Red House Farm

5

Drove Farm
Black House Farm

Earthworks
B1397
Old Decoy Farm
SHORT DROVE

30

Graby Farm
Dowsby
Poplar Farm
B1397

4

Dowsby Hall
Moat
Spinney Farm
Middle Fen Farm
FEN ROAD

29

1 BRAMBLING WK
2 LINNET DR
3 SISKIN CL
4 DOVECOTE
5 MILLER'S CL
Dowsby Fen
Glebe Farm

Browell Head (Spring)
CAR DYKE (ROMAN CANAL)

3

Barn Farm
Crossroads Farm
North Car Dyke Farm
Rippingale Fen Farm

1
2
3
4
5
STATION STREET
Grange Farm
LONG DROVE
Settlement (site of)

28

EAST STREET
South Car Dyke Farm
Rippingale Fen

Sewage Works
MAIN ROAD
PE10
French Farm

2

DOCTOR'S LANE
North End Farm

27

Dunsby
Dunsby Drove
Dunsby Fen
PE11

1

B1177
Dunsby Fen
Fen Farm
Hacconby Fen

26

10   A   11   B   12   C   13   D   14   E   15   F

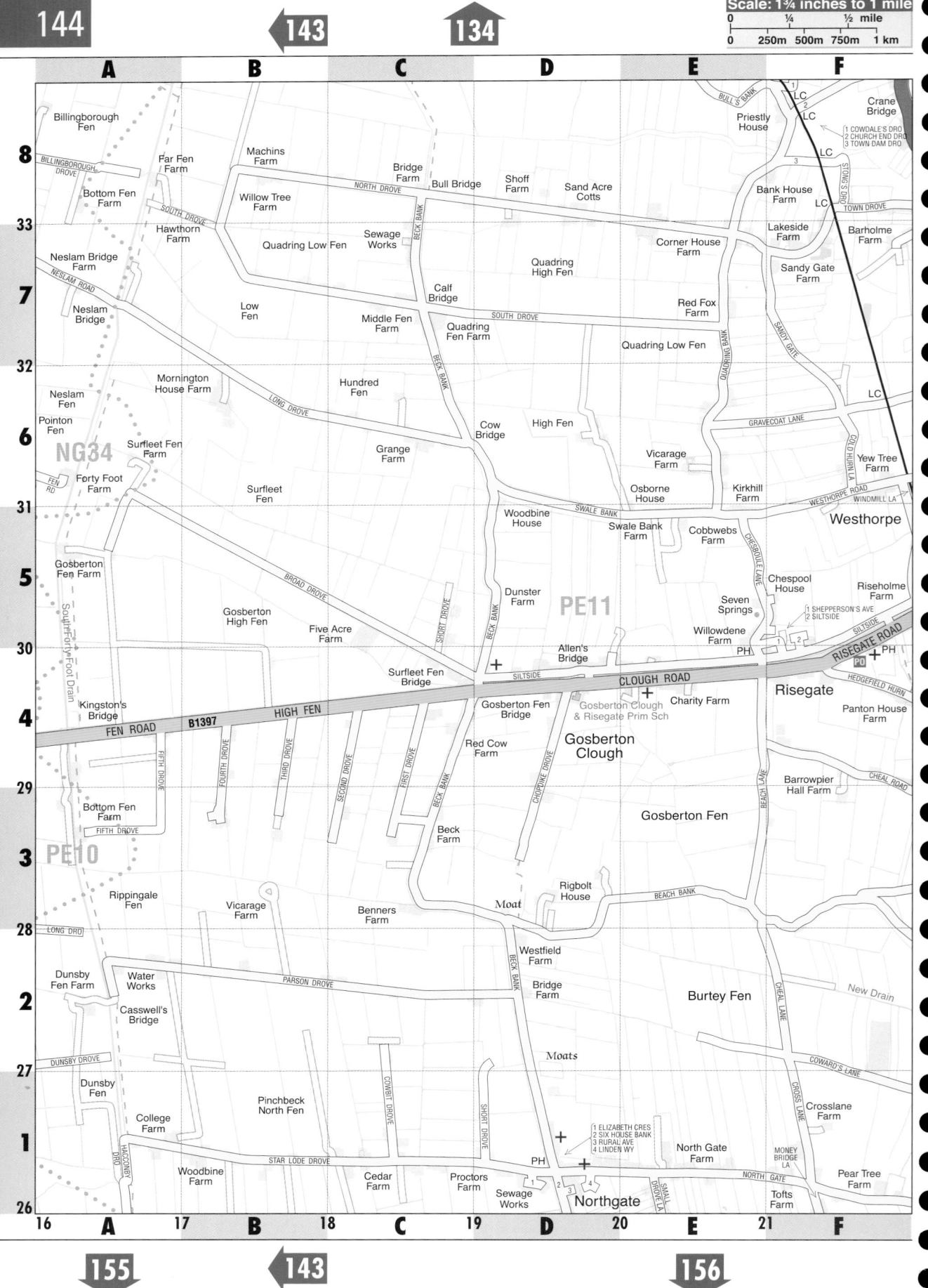

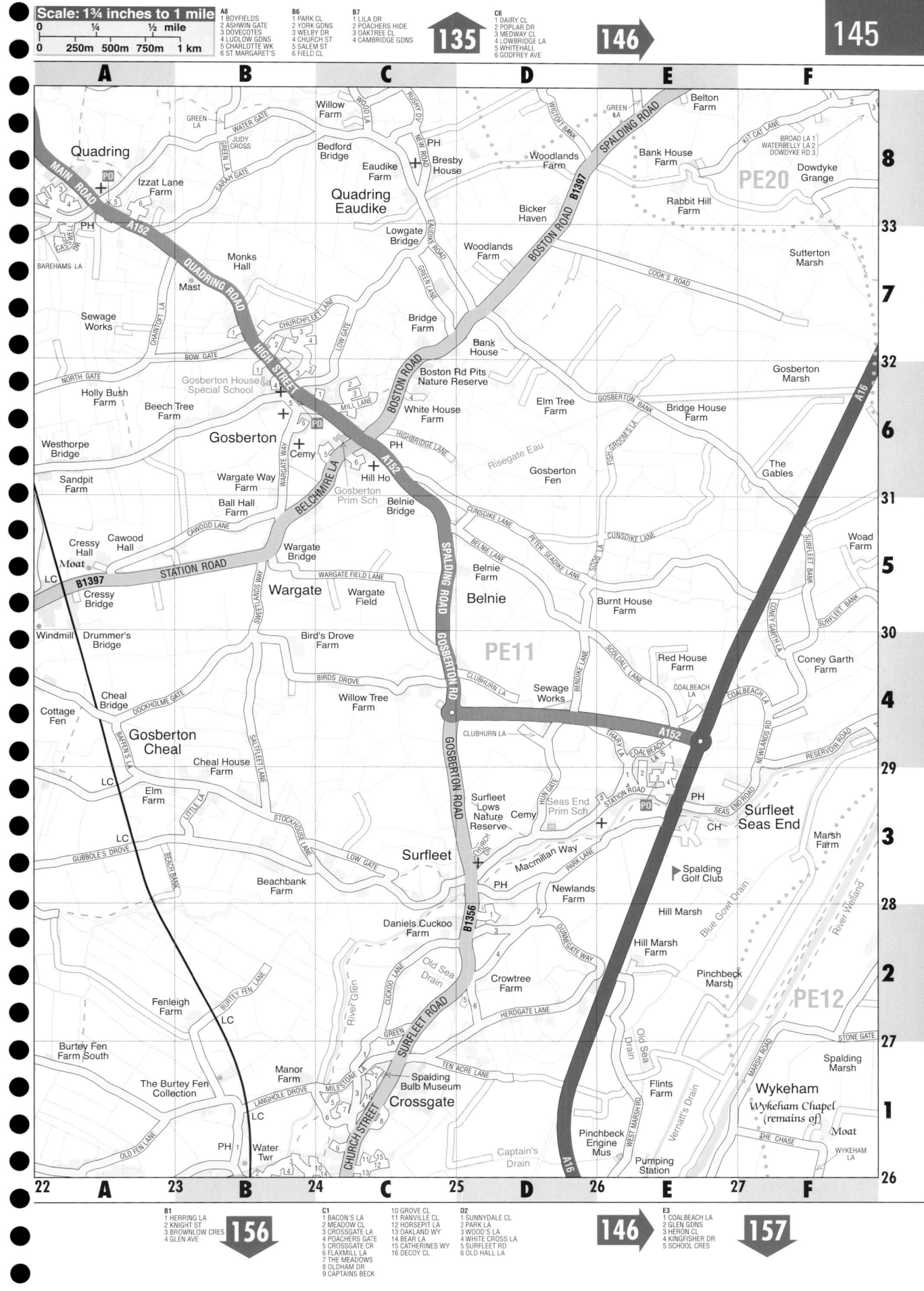

Scale: 1¾ inches to 1 mile

0   ¼   ½ mile
0   250m 500m 750m 1 km

135

146

145

A8
1 BOYFIELDS
2 ASHWIN GATE
3 DOVECOTES
4 LUDLOW GDNS
5 CHARLOTTE WK
6 ST MARGARET'S

B6
1 PARK CL
2 YORK GDNS
3 WELBY DR
4 CHURCH ST
5 SALEM ST
6 FIELD CL

B7
1 LILA DR
2 POACHERS HIDE
3 OAKTREE CL
4 CAMBRIDGE GDNS

C6
1 DAIRY CL
2 POPLAR DR
3 MEDWAY CL
4 LOWBRIDGE LA
5 WHITEHALL
6 GODFREY AVE

Map content (place names and features):

Quadring, Quadring Eaudike, Gosberton, Wargate, Belnie, Gosberton Cheal, Surfleet, Surfleet Seas End, Crossgate, Wykeham

PE20, PE11, PE12

MAIN ROAD, A152, QUADRING ROAD, HIGH STREET, STATION ROAD, B1397, BELCHMIRE LA, SPALDING ROAD, GOSBERTON ROAD, BOSTON ROAD, B1397, A16, A152, SURFLEET ROAD, CHURCH STREET, B1356, BOSTON RD

Willow Farm, Bedford Bridge, Eaudike Farm, Lowgate Bridge, Bresby House, Woodlands Farm, Belton Farm, Bank House Farm, Rabbit Hill Farm, Dowdyke Grange, Sutterton Marsh, Bicker Haven, Woodlands Farm, Bridge Farm, Bank House, Boston Rd Pits Nature Reserve, White House Farm, Elm Tree Farm, Gosberton Marsh, Bridge House Farm, The Gables, Gosberton Fen, Risegate Eau, Woad Farm, Burnt House Farm, Red House Farm, Coney Garth Farm, Belnie Farm, Sewage Works, Willow Tree Farm, Bird's Drove Farm, Cheal House Farm, Elm Farm, Beachbank Farm, Daniels Cuckoo Farm, Crowtree Farm, Newlands Farm, Hill Marsh, Hill Marsh Farm, Pinchbeck Marsh, Flints Farm, Spalding Marsh, Wykeham Chapel (remains of), Moat, Pinchbeck Engine Mus, Pumping Station, Manor Farm, Spalding Bulb Museum, Fenleigh Farm, Burtey Fen Farm South, The Burtey Fen Collection, Cottage Fen, Cheal Bridge, Drummer's Bridge, Windmill, Cressy Hall Moat, Cawood Hall, Cressy Bridge, Ball Hall Farm, Wargate Way Farm, Wargate Bridge, Wargate Field, Sandpit Farm, Westhorpe Bridge, Holly Bush Farm, Beech Tree Farm, Monks Hall, Mast, Izzat Lane Farm, Sewage Works, Barehams La, Marsh Farm

Spalding Golf Club, Seas End Prim Sch, Gosberton Prim Sch, Gosberton House Special School, Captain's Drain, Blue Gowt Drain, Old Sea Drain, Vernatt's Drain, River Welland, River Glen, Green La

B1
1 HERRING LA
2 KNIGHT ST
3 BROWNLOW CRES
4 GLEN AVE

156

C1
1 BACON'S LA
2 MEADOW CL
3 CROSSGATE LA
4 POACHERS GATE
5 CROSSGATE CR
6 FLAXMILL LA
7 THE MEADOWS
8 OLDHAM DR
9 CAPTAINS BECK

10 GROVE CL
11 RANVILLE CL
12 HORSEPIT LA
13 OAKLAND WY
14 BEAR LA
15 CATHERINES WY
16 DECOY CL

D2
1 SUNNYDALE CL
2 PARK LA
3 WOOD'S LA
4 WHITE CROSS LA
5 SURFLEET RD
6 OLD HALL LA

146

E3
1 COALBEACH LA
2 GLEN GDNS
3 HERON CL
4 KINGFISHER DR
5 SCHOOL CRES

157

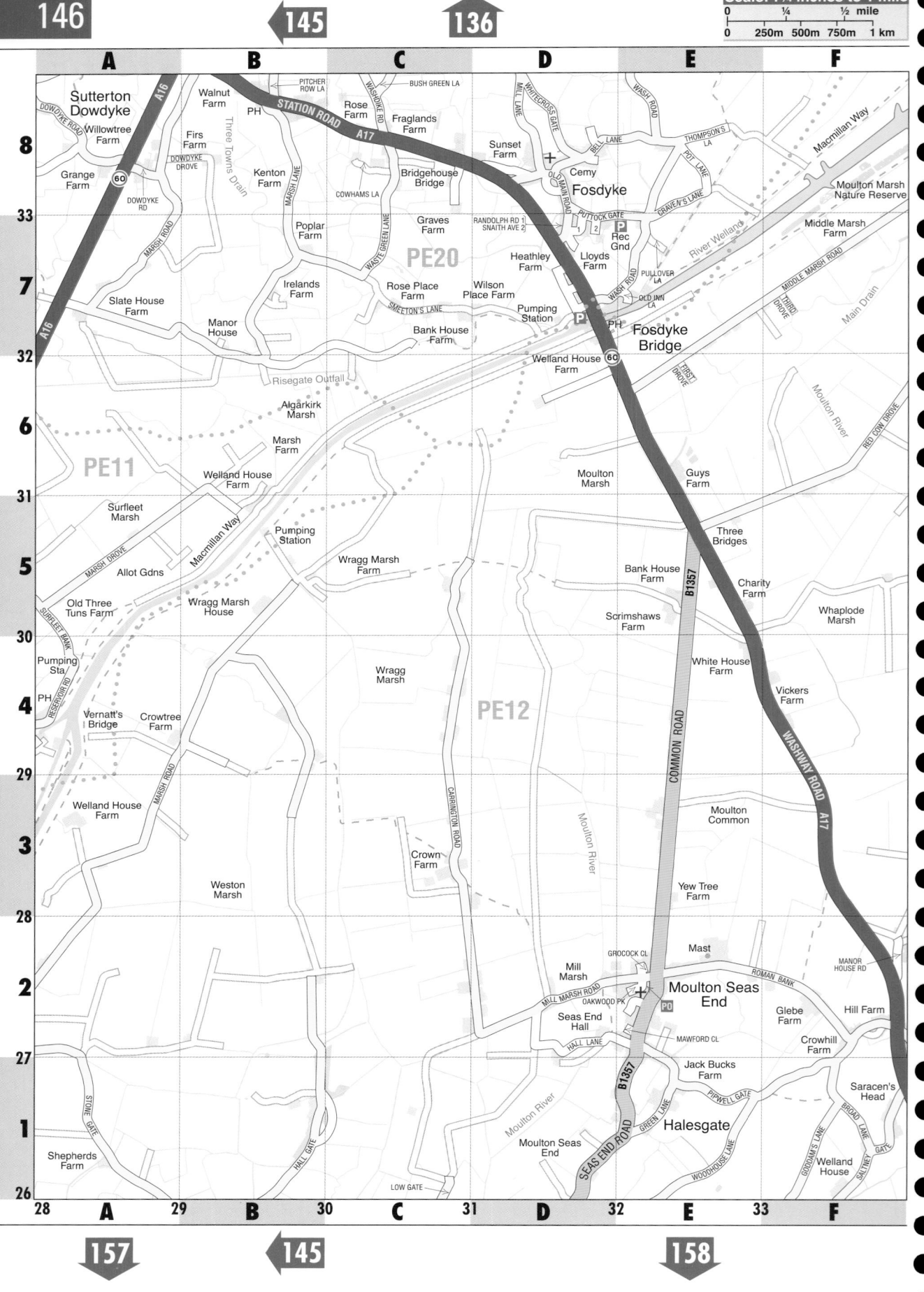

Scale: 1¾ inches to 1 mile
0   ¼   ½ mile
0   250m   500m   750m   1 km

A **B** **C** **D** **E** **F**

Sutterton
Dowdyke
Willowtree
Farm
Walnut
Farm
PITCHER
ROW LA
STATION ROAD
A17
Rose
Farm
BUSH GREEN LA
Fraglands
Farm
WHITECROSS GATE
WASH ROAD
Macmillan Way
8
Firs
Farm
Three Towns Drain
PH
WASHDIKE RD
Sunset
Farm
MILL
LANE
Cemy
BELL
LANE
THOMPSON'S
LA
Moulton Marsh
Nature Reserve
Grange
Farm
60
DOWDYKE
DROVE
Kenton
Farm
Bridgehouse
Bridge
Fosdyke
OLD MAIN ROAD
POT GATE
Middle Marsh
Farm
33
DOWDYKE
RD
MARSH LANE
COWHAMS LA
Graves
Farm
RANDOLPH RD 1
SNAITH AVE 2
PUTTOCK GATE
P
Rec
Gnd
CRAVEN'S LANE
River Welland
MIDDLE MARSH ROAD
7
PE20
Poplar
Farm
WASTE GREEN LANE
Rose Place
Farm
Heathley
Farm
Lloyds
Farm
WASH ROAD
OLD INN
LA
THIRD
DROVE
Main Drain
Irelands
Farm
SMEETON'S LANE
Wilson
Place Farm
Pumping
Station
PH
Fosdyke
Bridge
32
Manor
House
Slate House
Farm
Bank House
Farm
Welland House
Farm
P
60
FIRST
DROVE
Moulton River
RED COW DROVE
Risegate Outfall
6
Algarkirk
Marsh
Moulton
Marsh
Guys
Farm
PE11
Marsh
Farm
Welland House
Farm
31
Surfleet
Marsh
Macmillan Way
Pumping
Station
Three
Bridges
B1357
Charity
Farm
5
MARSH DROVE
Allot Gdns
Wragg Marsh
Farm
Bank House
Farm
Whaplode
Marsh
Old Three
Tuns Farm
Wragg Marsh
House
Scrimshaws
Farm
White House
Farm
30
SURFLEET BANK
Pumping
Sta
RESERVOIR RD
Wragg
Marsh
Vickers
Farm
4
PH
Vernatt's
Bridge
Crowtree
Farm
MARSH ROAD
PE12
COMMON ROAD
Moulton
Common
WASHWAY ROAD
A17
29
Welland House
Farm
CARRINGTON ROAD
3
Weston
Marsh
Crown
Farm
Moulton River
Yew Tree
Farm
28
GROCOCK CL
Mast
ROMAN BANK
MANOR
HOUSE RD
2
Mill
Marsh
Moulton Seas
End
Glebe
Farm
Hill Farm
MILL MARSH ROAD
OAKWOOD PK
P
PO
Seas End
Hall
HALL LANE
MAWFORD CL
Jack Bucks
Farm
Crowhill
Farm
27
B1357
PIPWELL GATE
Saracen's
Head
1
STONE GATE
HALL GATE
Moulton River
SEAS END ROAD
GREEN LANE
Halesgate
WOODHOUSE LANE
BROAD LANE
GODDAM'S LANE
SALTNEY GATE
Welland
House
Shepherds
Farm
Moulton Seas
End
LOW GATE
26

28   **A**   29   **B**   30   **C**   31   **D**   32   **E**   33   **F**

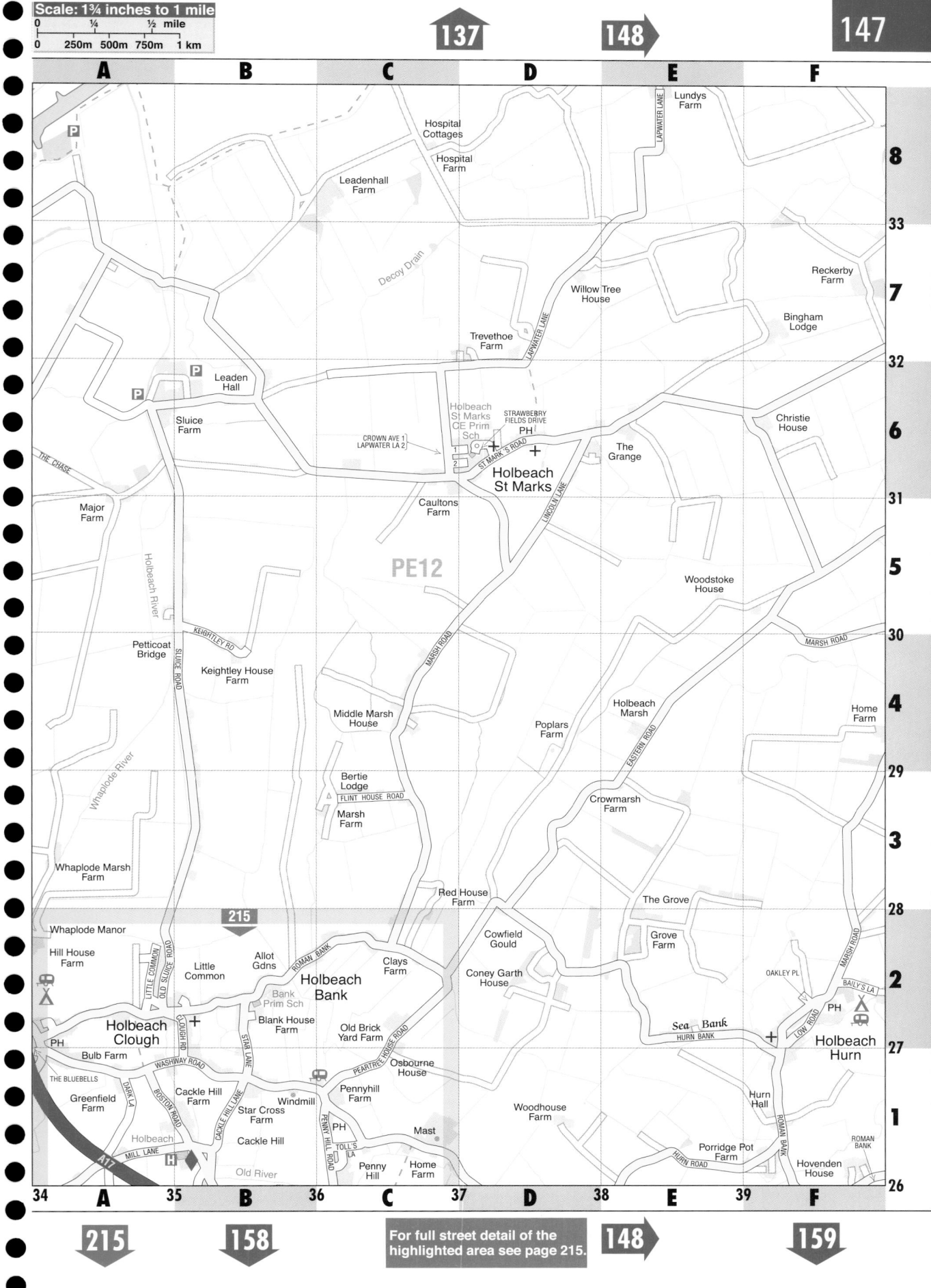

Scale: 1¾ inches to 1 mile

0   ¼   ½   mile
0 250m 500m 750m 1 km

137

148

147

A   B   C   D   E   F

8

33

7

32

6

31

5

30

4

29

3

28

2

27

1

26

Lundys Farm

LAPWATER LANE

Hospital Cottages

Hospital Farm

Leadenhall Farm

Reckerby Farm

Decoy Drain

Willow Tree House

LAPWATER LANE

Bingham Lodge

Trevethoe Farm

Leaden Hall

P

P

Holbeach St Marks CE Prim Sch

STRAWBERRY FIELDS DRIVE

PH

Christie House

Sluice Farm

CROWN AVE 1
LAPWATER LA 2

ST MARK'S ROAD

The Grange

Holbeach St Marks

2

THE CHASE

Caultons Farm

LINCOLN LANE

Major Farm

PE12

Woodstoke House

Holbeach River

KEIGHTLEY RD

MARSH ROAD

MARSH ROAD

Petticoat Bridge

SLUICE ROAD

Keightley House Farm

Holbeach Marsh

Home Farm

Middle Marsh House

Poplars Farm

EASTERN ROAD

Whaplode River

Bertie Lodge

FLINT HOUSE ROAD

Crowmarsh Farm

Marsh Farm

Whaplode Marsh Farm

Red House Farm

The Grove

MARSH ROAD

215

Cowfield Gould

The Grove

Grove Farm

Whaplode Manor

Hill House Farm

LITTLE COMMON

OLD SLUICE ROAD

Little Common

Allot Gdns

ROMAN BANK

Holbeach Bank

Clays Farm

Coney Garth House

OAKLEY PL

BAILY'S LA

PH

Bank Prim Sch

Blank House Farm

Sea Bank
HURN BANK

LOW ROAD

Holbeach Hurn

PH

Holbeach Clough

CLOUGH RD

STAR LANE

Old Brick Yard Farm

PEARTREE HOUSE ROAD

Osbourne House

Bulb Farm

WASHWAY ROAD

Hurn Hall

HURN ROAD

ROMAN BANK

THE BLUEBELLS

Greenfield Farm

DARK LA

BOSTON ROAD

Cackle Hill Farm

CACKLE HILL LANE

Star Cross Farm

Windmill

PENNY HILL ROAD

Pennyhill Farm

Woodhouse Farm

ROMAN BANK

Porridge Pot Farm

PH

Holbeach

A17

MILL LANE

H

Cackle Hill

TOLL'S LA

Mast

Home Farm

Hovenden House

Old River

Penny Hill

34   A   35   B   36   C   37   D   38   E   39   F   26

215

158

For full street detail of the highlighted area see page 215.

148

159

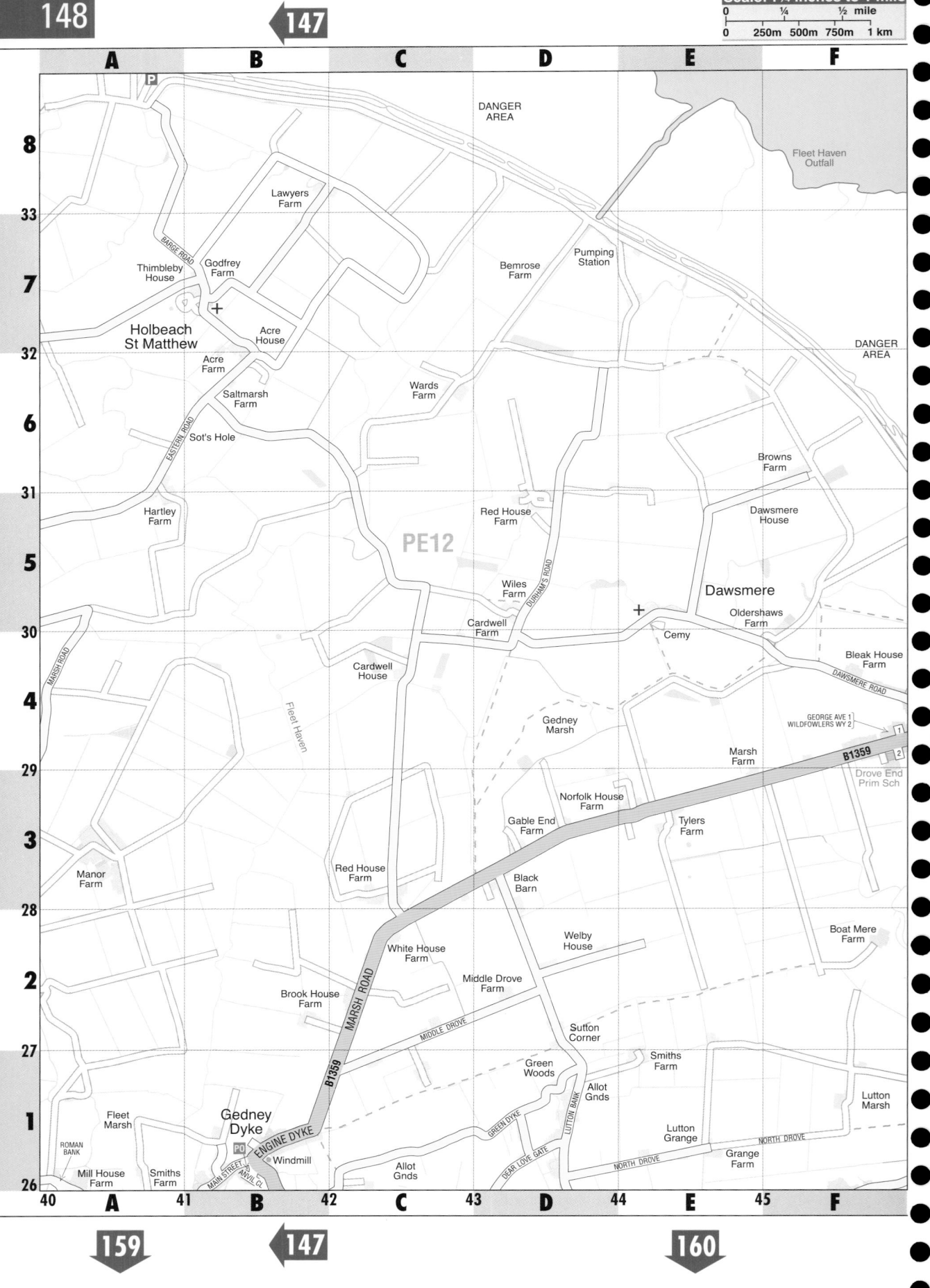

147

Scale: 1¾ inches to 1 mile

0   ¼   ½ mile
0 250m 500m 750m 1 km

A **B** **C** **D** **E** **F**

8

DANGER AREA

Fleet Haven Outfall

33

Lawyers Farm

BARGE ROAD

7

Thimbleby House

Godfrey Farm

Bemrose Farm

Pumping Station

DANGER AREA

32

Holbeach St Matthew

Acre House

Acre Farm

Saltmarsh Farm

EASTERN ROAD

Wards Farm

6

Sot's Hole

Browns Farm

31

Hartley Farm

Red House Farm

Dawsmere House

PE12

5

Wiles Farm

Dawsmere

Oldershaws Farm

BURHAM'S ROAD

Cardwell Farm

Cemy

30

MARSH ROAD

Cardwell House

Bleak House Farm

DAWSMERE ROAD

4

Fleet Haven

Gedney Marsh

Marsh Farm

GEORGE AVE 1
WILDFOWLERS WY 2

1

B1359

2

29

Drove End Prim Sch

Norfolk House Farm

Tylers Farm

3

Manor Farm

Red House Farm

Gable End Farm

Black Barn

Boat Mere Farm

28

Welby House

White House Farm

MARSH ROAD

2

Brook House Farm

Middle Drove Farm

Smiths Farm

Lutton Marsh

MIDDLE DROVE

Sutton Corner

27

B1359

Green Woods

Allot Gnds

Smiths Farm

Lutton Grange

GREEN DYKE

LUTTON BANK

Grange Farm

NORTH DROVE

1

Fleet Marsh

Gedney Dyke

ENGINE DYKE

Allot Gnds

Lutton Grange

ROMAN BANK

PO

Windmill

DEAR LOVE GATE

NORTH DROVE

MAIN STREET

ANVIL CL

Mill House Farm

Smiths Farm

Allot Gnds

26

40 **A** 41 **B** 42 **C** 43 **D** 44 **E** 45 **F**

159 147 160

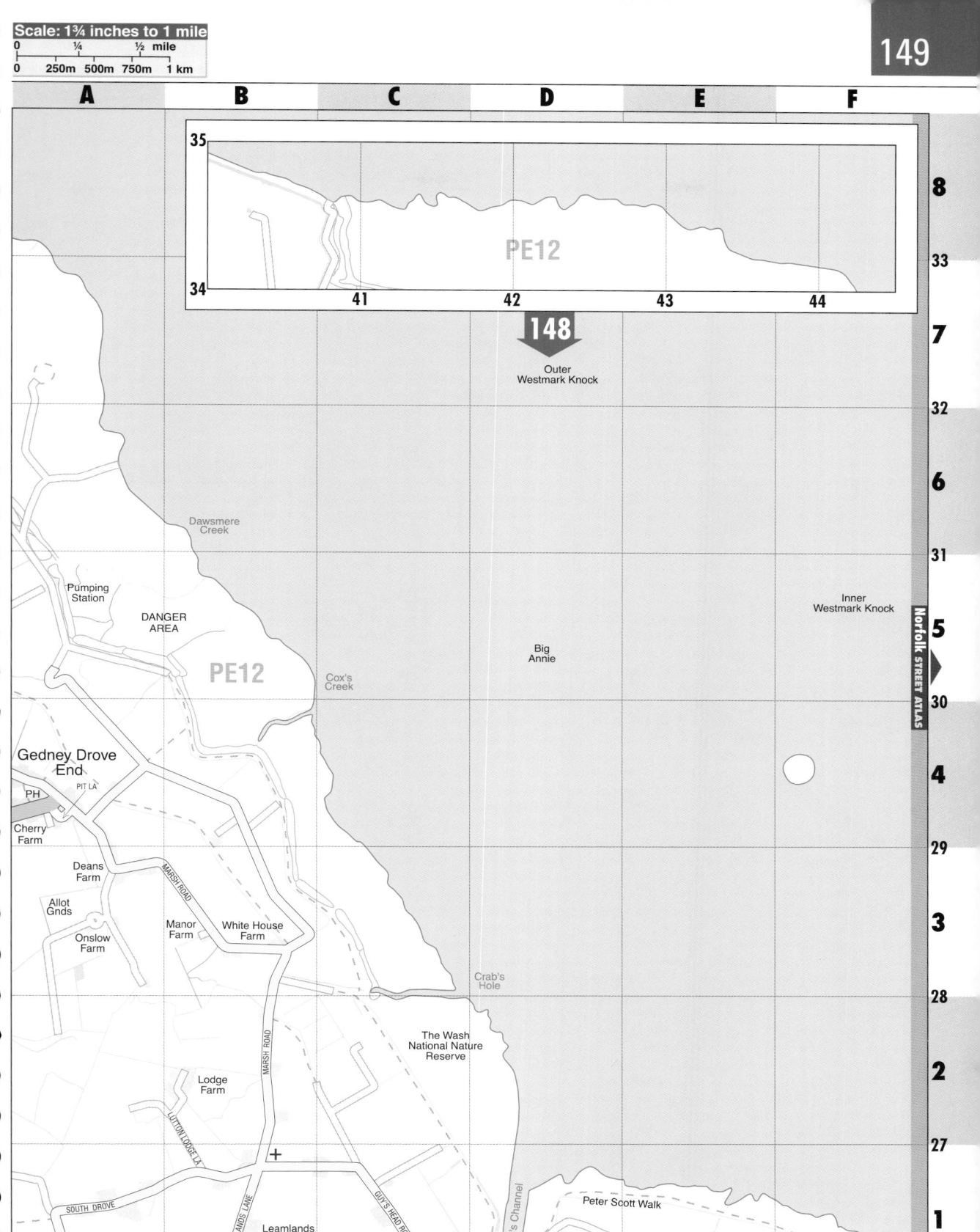

Scale: 1¾ inches to 1 mile

0   ¼   ½   mile

0   250m 500m 750m 1 km

PE12

Outer
Westmark Knock

Dawsmere
Creek

Pumping
Station

DANGER
AREA

PE12

Cox's
Creek

Big
Annie

Inner
Westmark Knock

Gedney Drove
End

PIT LA

PH

Cherry
Farm

Deans
Farm

MARSH ROAD

Allot
Gnds

Manor
Farm

White House
Farm

Onslow
Farm

Crab's
Hole

The Wash
National Nature
Reserve

Lodge
Farm

MARSH ROAD

LUTTON LODGE LA

SOUTH DROVE

LEAMLANDS LANE

Leamlands
Farm

GUY'S HEAD ROAD

Tycho Wing's Channel

Peter Scott Walk

Norfolk STREET ATLAS

148
160
161

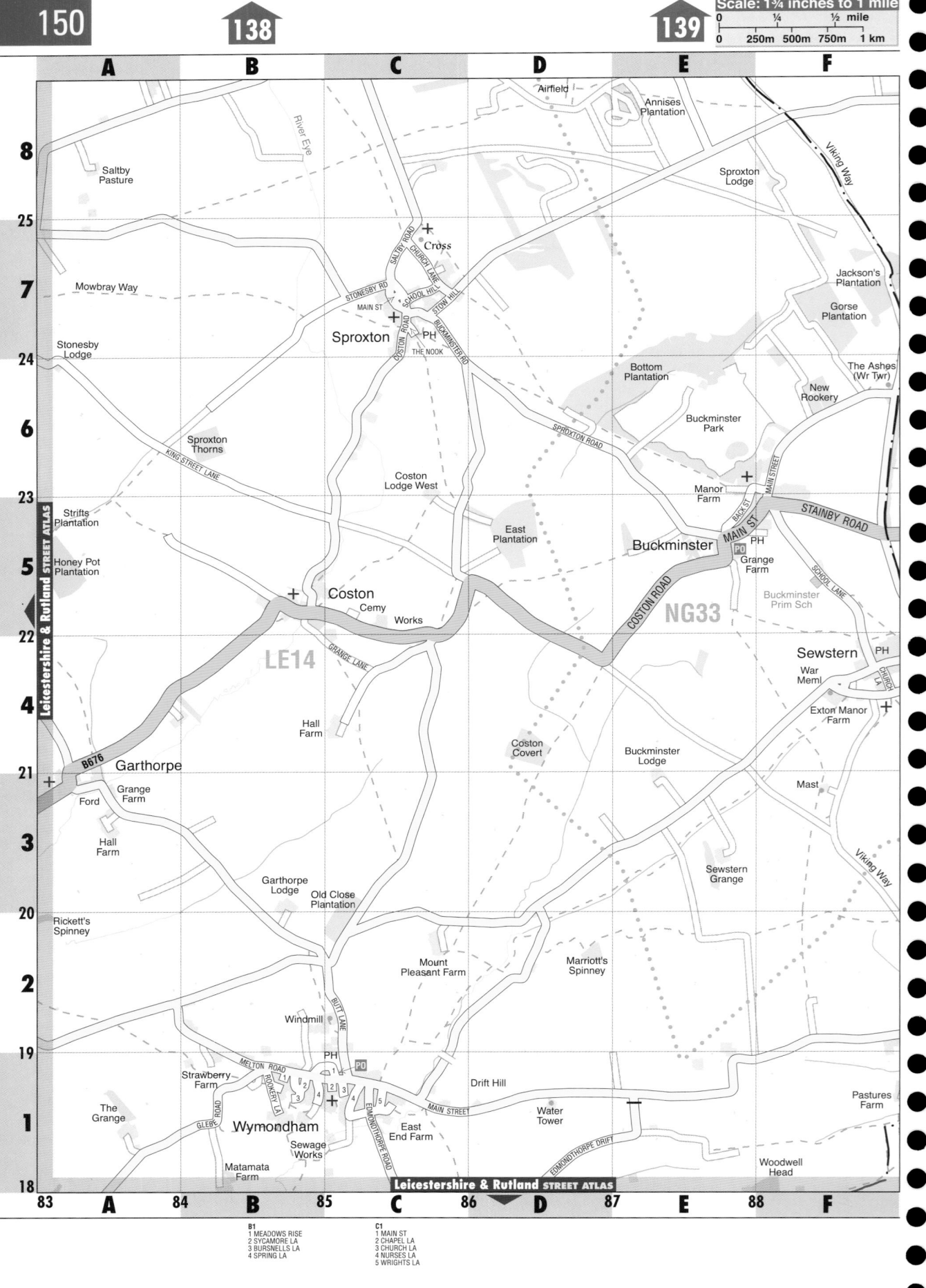

138

139

Scale: 1¾ inches to 1 mile

Leicestershire & Rutland STREET ATLAS

Leicestershire & Rutland STREET ATLAS

B1
1 MEADOWS RISE
2 SYCAMORE LA
3 BURSNELLS LA
4 SPRING LA

C1
1 MAIN ST
2 CHAPEL LA
3 CHURCH LA
4 NURSES LA
5 WRIGHTS LA

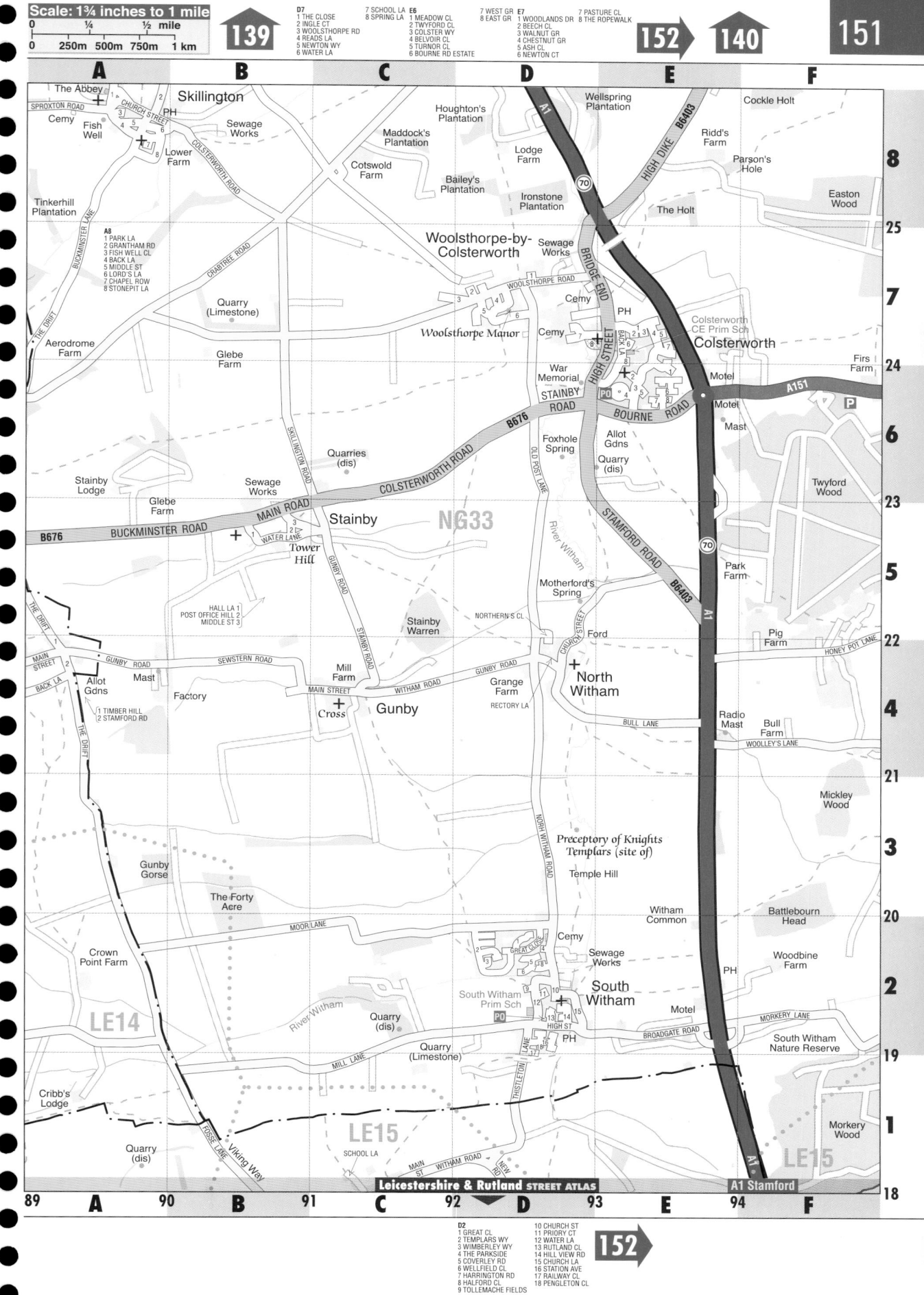

152 140

152

D7
1 THE CLOSE
2 INGLE CT
3 WOOLSTHORPE RD
4 READS LA
5 NEWTON WY
6 WATER LA

7 SCHOOL LA
8 SPRING LA

E6
1 MEADOW CL
2 TWYFORD CL
3 COLSTER WY
4 BELVOIR CL
5 TURNOR CL
6 BOURNE RD ESTATE

7 WEST GR
8 EAST GR

E7
1 WOODLANDS DR
2 BEECH CL
3 CHESTNUT GR
4 ASH CL
5 NEWTON CT

7 PASTURE CL
8 THE ROPEWALK

The Abbey
Skillington
Cemy
Fish Well
SPROXTON ROAD
CHURCH STREET
PH
Lower Farm

Houghton's Plantation
Wellspring Plantation
Cockle Holt
Maddock's Plantation
Ridd's Farm
Parson's Hole
Cotswold Farm
Lodge Farm
Sewage Works
Bailey's Plantation
Ironstone Plantation
The Holt
Easton Wood

Tinkerhill Plantation
A8
1 PARK LA
2 GRANTHAM RD
3 FISH WELL CL
4 BACK LA
5 MIDDLE ST
6 LORD'S LA
7 CHAPEL ROW
8 STONEPIT LA

Woolsthorpe-by-Colsterworth
Sewage Works
Cemy
PH
Colsterworth CE Prim Sch
Colsterworth
Firs Farm

Aerodrome Farm
Quarry (Limestone)
Woolsthorpe Manor
War Memorial
STAINBY ROAD
HIGH STREET
BACK LA
Motel

Glebe Farm
Foxhole Spring
PO
BOURNE ROAD
Motel
Mast

B676
Allot Gdns
Quarry (dis)

THE DRIFT
Stainby Lodge
Quarries (dis)
Glebe Farm
Sewage Works
MAIN ROAD
Stainby
NG33
River Witham
STAMFORD ROAD
Twyford Wood

B676 BUCKMINSTER ROAD
SKILLINGTON ROAD
COLSTERWORTH ROAD
WATER LANE
Tower Hill
Motherford's Spring
Park Farm

MAIN STREET
HALL LA 1
POST OFFICE HILL 2
MIDDLE ST 3
NORTHERN'S CL
Church Street
Ford
Pig Farm
HONEY POT LANE

BACK LA
GUNBY ROAD
SEWSTERN ROAD
Mill Farm
Stainby Warren
GUNBY ROAD
North Witham
Radio Mast
Bull Farm

Allot Gdns
Mast
Factory
MAIN STREET
WITHAM ROAD
Grange Farm
RECTORY LA
BULL LANE
WOOLLEY'S LANE

1 TIMBER HILL
2 STAMFORD RD
Cross
Gunby
NORTH WITHAM ROAD

Mickley Wood

Gunby Gorse
The Forty Acre
Preceptory of Knights Templars (site of)
Temple Hill
Battlebourn Head

MOOR LANE
Witham Common
Woodbine Farm

Crown Point Farm
Cemy
PH
LE14
Sewage Works
South Witham Prim Sch
GREAT CLOSE
South Witham
Motel
MORKERY LANE

River Witham
Quarry (dis)
PO
HIGH ST
PH
BROADGATE ROAD
South Witham Nature Reserve

Cribb's Lodge
MILL LANE
Quarry (Limestone)
THISTLETON LANE

FOSSE LANE
VIKING WAY
LE15
SCHOOL LA
MAIN ST
WITHAM ROAD
NEW RD
Morkery Wood
LE15

Quarry (dis)

D2
1 GREAT CL
2 TEMPLARS WY
3 WIMBERLEY WY
4 THE PARKSIDE
5 COVERLEY RD
6 WELLFIELD CL
7 HARRINGTON RD
8 HALFORD CL
9 TOLLEMACHE FIELDS

10 CHURCH ST
11 PRIORY CT
12 WATER LA
13 RUTLAND CL
14 HILL VIEW RD
15 CHURCH LA
16 STATION AVE
17 RAILWAY CL
18 PENGLETON CL

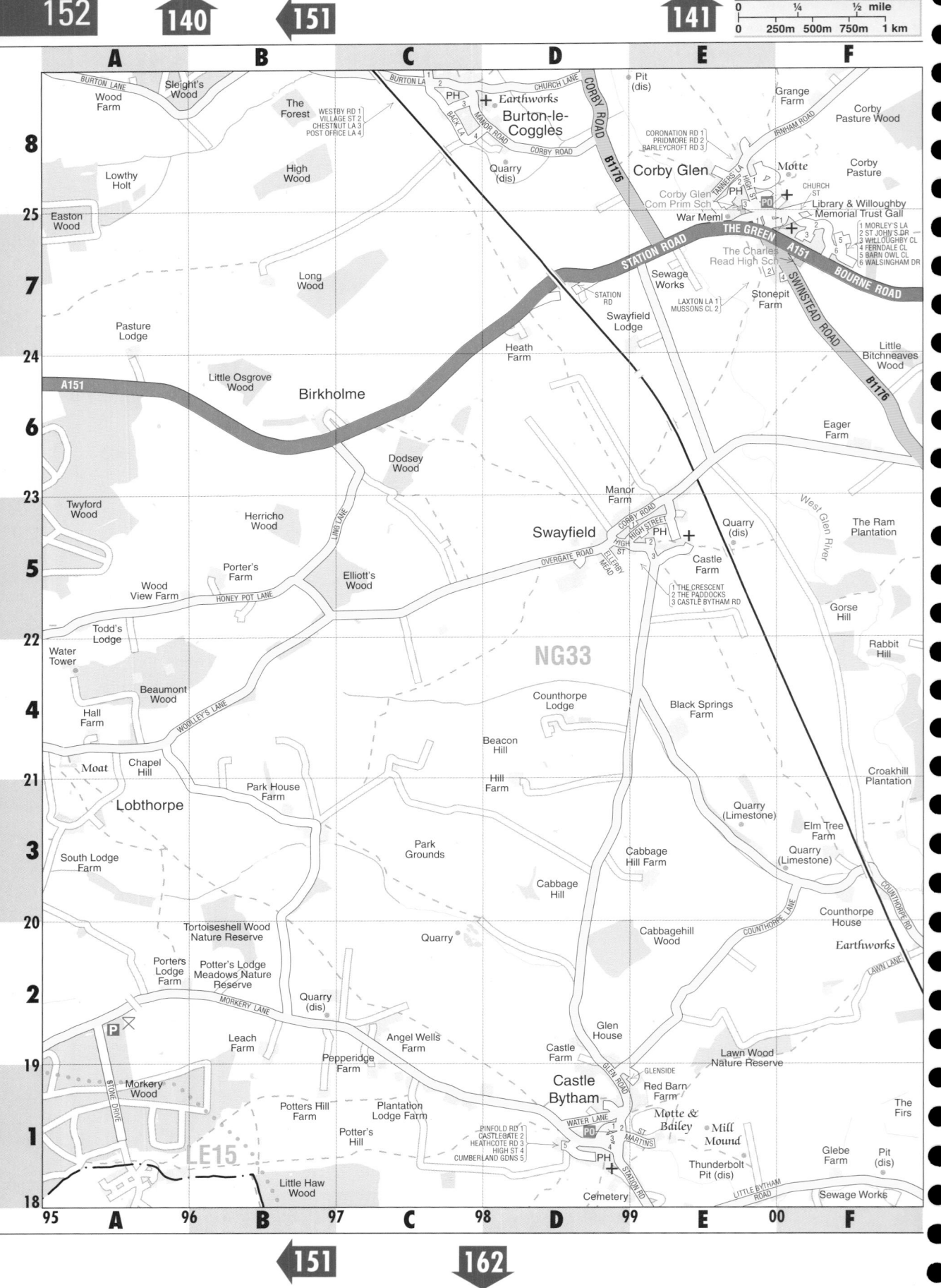

A   B   C   D   E   F

8

25

7

24

6

23

5

22

4

21

3

20

2

19

1

18

95   A   96   B   97   C   98   D   99   E   00   F

Wood Farm
Burton Lane
Sleight's Wood
The Forest
WESTBY RD 1
VILLAGE ST 2
CHESTNUT LA 3
POST OFFICE LA 4
BURTON LA
PH
Earthworks
Burton-le-Coggles
CHURCH LANE
BACK LA
MANOR ROAD
Pit (dis)
CORBY ROAD
B1176
Grange Farm
RNHAM ROAD
Corby Pasture Wood

Lowthy Holt
High Wood
Quarry (dis)
CORBY ROAD
Corby Glen
CORONATION RD 1
PRIDMORE RD 2
BARLEYCROFT RD 3
Motte
Corby Pasture

Easton Wood
Corby Glen Com Prim Sch
War Meml
PO
PH
CHURCH ST
Library & Willoughby Memorial Trust Gall
1 MORLEY'S LA
2 ST JOHN'S DR
3 WILLOUGHBY CL
4 FERNDALE CL
5 BARN OWL CL
6 WALSINGHAM DR

Long Wood
THE GREEN
STATION ROAD
A151
BOURNE ROAD

Pasture Lodge
The Charles Read High Sch
SWINSTEAD ROAD
B1176
Little Bitchneaves Wood

A151
Little Osgrove Wood
Birkholme
Heath Farm
STATION RD
Sewage Works
Swayfield Lodge
LAXTON LA 1
MUSSONS CL 2
Stonepit Farm
Eager Farm

Twyford Wood
Herricho Wood
Dodsey Wood
Manor Farm
West Glen River
The Ram Plantation

Porter's Farm
LING LANE
Elliott's Wood
Swayfield
CORBY ROAD
HIGH STREET
PH
Quarry (dis)
Gorse Hill

Wood View Farm
HONEY POT LANE
OVERGATE ROAD
ELLERBY MEAD
HIGH ST
Castle Farm
1 THE CRESCENT
2 THE PADDOCKS
3 CASTLE BYTHAM RD

Todd's Lodge
Water Tower
NG33
Rabbit Hill

Beaumont Wood
WOOLLEY'S LANE
Counthorpe Lodge
Black Springs Farm
Croakhill Plantation

Hall Farm
Beacon Hill

Moat
Chapel Hill
Park House Farm
Hill Farm
Quarry (Limestone)
Elm Tree Farm

Lobthorpe
Park Grounds
Cabbage Hill Farm
Quarry (Limestone)
COUNTHORPE LANE

South Lodge Farm
Cabbage Hill
Cabbagehill Wood
Counthorpe House
COUNTHORPE RD

Tortoiseshell Wood Nature Reserve
Quarry
Earthworks
LAWN LANE

Porters Lodge Farm
Potter's Lodge Meadows Nature Reserve
MORKERY LANE
Quarry (dis)
Angel Wells Farm
Cabbagehill Wood
Glen House
Lawn Wood Nature Reserve

P ⊠
Leach Farm
Pepperidge Farm
Castle Farm
GLENSIDE
Red Barn Farm
The Firs

Morkery Wood
STONE DRIVE
Potters Hill Farm
Plantation Lodge Farm
Potter's Hill
PINFOLD RD 1
CASTLEGATE 2
HEATHCOTE RD 3
HIGH ST 4
CUMBERLAND GDNS 5
Castle Bytham
WATER LANE
PO
GLEN ROAD
ST MARTINS
Motte & Bailey
Mill Mound
Glebe Farm
Pit (dis)

LE15
Little Haw Wood
PH
Cemetery
STATION RD
Thunderbolt Pit (dis)
LITTLE BYTHAM ROAD
Sewage Works

Scale: 1¾ inches to 1 mile

141
154
142

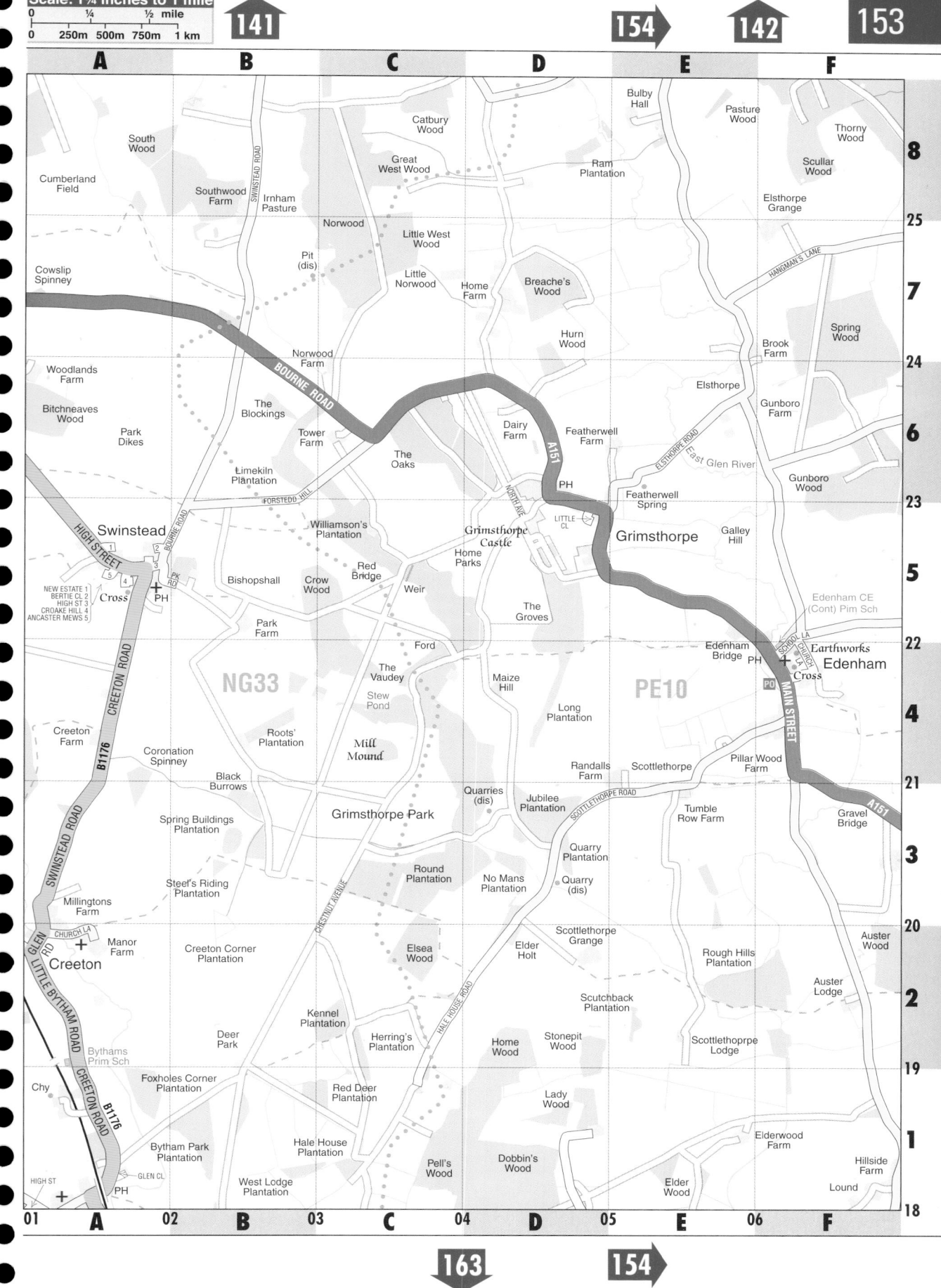
Swinstead
Grimsthorpe
Edenham
Creeton
Grimsthorpe Park
Grimsthorpe Castle
BOURNE ROAD
A151
B1176
CREETON ROAD
SWINSTEAD ROAD
HIGH STREET
MAIN STREET
SCOTTLETHORPE ROAD
HALE HOUSE ROAD
CHESTNUT AVENUE
ELSTHORPE ROAD
HANGMAN'S LANE
FORSTEDD HILL
NG33
PE10
South Wood
Cumberland Field
Southwood Farm
Irnham Pasture
Norwood
Catbury Wood
Great West Wood
Little West Wood
Little Norwood
Home Farm
Breache's Wood
Hurn Wood
Ram Plantation
Bulby Hall
Pasture Wood
Thorny Wood
Scullar Wood
Elsthorpe Grange
Spring Wood
Brook Farm
Elsthorpe
Gunboro Farm
Gunboro Wood
Cowslip Spinney
Woodlands Farm
Bitchneaves Wood
Park Dikes
Norwood Farm
The Blockings
Tower Farm
The Oaks
Limekiln Plantation
Dairy Farm
Featherwell Farm
East Glen River
Featherwell Spring
Galley Hill
Williamson's Plantation
Home Parks
Red Bridge
Bishopshall
Crow Wood
Weir
Park Farm
The Groves
Edenham CE (Cont) Pim Sch
Edenham Bridge
Earthworks
Cross
Ford
The Vaudey
Stew Pond
Maize Hill
Long Plantation
Mill Mound
Roots' Plantation
Creeton Farm
Coronation Spinney
Black Burrows
Randalls Farm
Scottlethorpe
Pillar Wood Farm
Quarries (dis)
Jubilee Plantation
Tumble Row Farm
Gravel Bridge
Spring Buildings Plantation
Quarry Plantation
Round Plantation
No Mans Plantation
Quarry (dis)
Steel's Riding Plantation
Millingtons Farm
Manor Farm
Creeton Corner Plantation
Elsea Wood
Elder Holt
Scottlethorpe Grange
Rough Hills Plantation
Auster Wood
Auster Lodge
Scutchback Plantation
Kennel Plantation
Deer Park
Herring's Plantation
Home Wood
Stonepit Wood
Scottlethoprpe Lodge
Bythams Prim Sch
Chy
Foxholes Corner Plantation
Red Deer Plantation
Lady Wood
Bytham Park Plantation
Hale House Plantation
Elderwood Farm
Hillside Farm
Pell's Wood
Dobbin's Wood
Elder Wood
West Lodge Plantation
Lound
GLEN RD
LITTLE BYTHAM ROAD
CHURCH LA
SCHOOL LA
GLEN CL
HIGH ST
NORTH AVE
LITTLE CL
PK RD
PH
PO
NEW ESTATE 1
BERTIE CL 2
HIGH ST 3
CROAKE HILL 4
ANCASTER MEWS 5

163
154

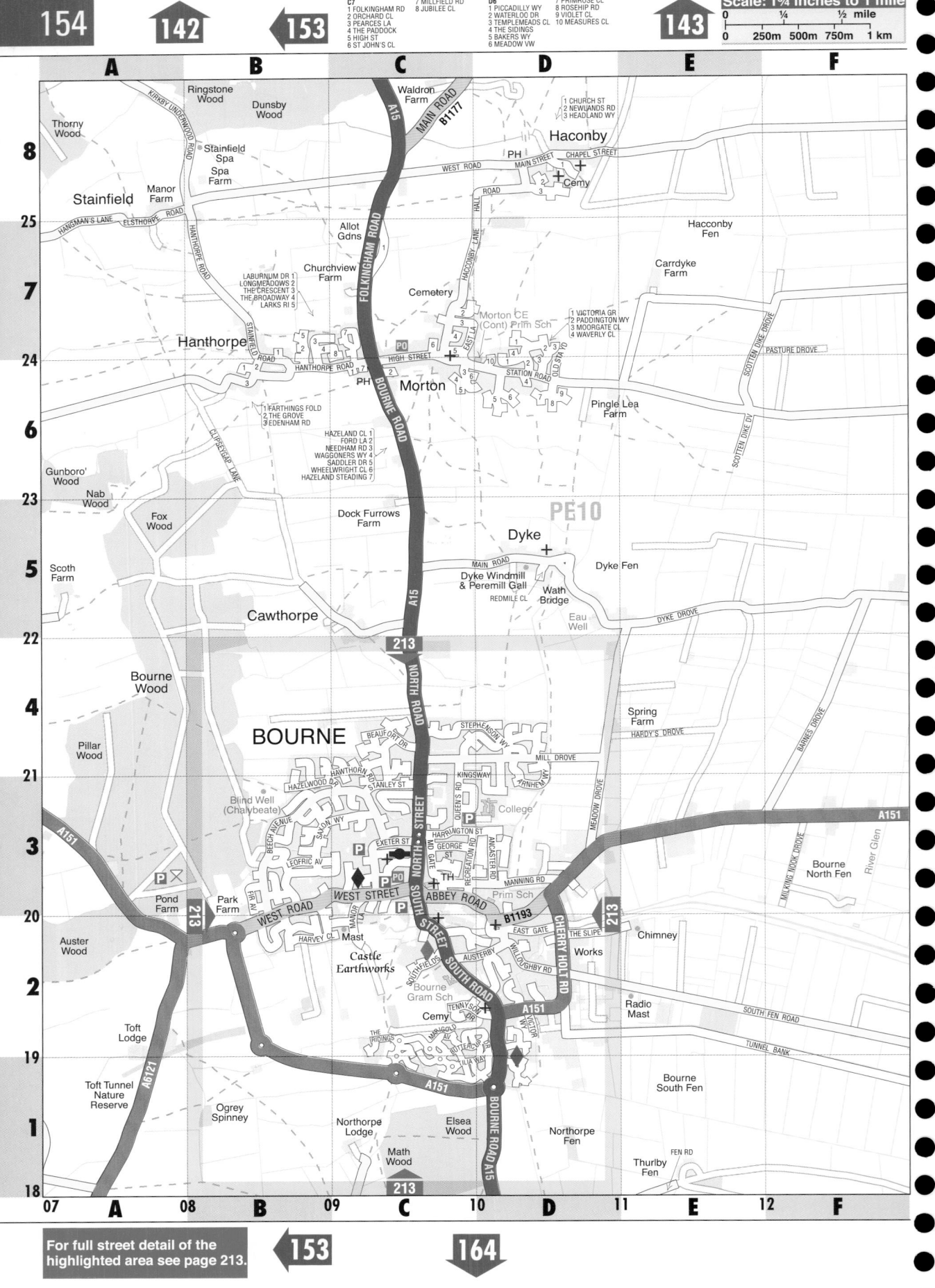

154 142 153

C7
1 FOLKINGHAM RD
2 ORCHARD CL
3 PEARCES LA
4 THE PADDOCK
5 HIGH ST
6 ST JOHN'S CL

7 MILLFIELD RD
8 JUBILEE CL

D6
1 PICCADILLY WY
2 WATERLOO DR
3 TEMPLEMEADS CL
4 THE SIDINGS
5 BAKERS CL
6 MEADOW VW

7 PRIMROSE CL
8 ROSEHIP RD
9 VIOLET CL
10 MEASURES CL

143

Scale: 1¾ inches to 1 mile
0   ¼   ½   mile
0   250m 500m 750m 1 km

Thorny Wood
Ringstone Wood
Dunsby Wood
Waldron Farm
MAIN ROAD
B1177

CHURCH ST
NEWLANDS RD
HEADLAND WY
Haconby
PH
MAIN STREET
CHAPEL STREET
Cemy
WEST ROAD

KIRKBY UNDERWOOD ROAD
Stainfield Spa Spa Farm
Manor Farm
Stainfield
HANGMAN'S LANE
ELSTHORPE
HANTHORPE ROAD
Allot Gdns
Churchview Farm
HALL LANE
HACONBY LANE
ROAD
Cemetery
Haconby Fen
Carrdyke Farm

LABURNUM DR 1
LONGMEADOWS 2
THE CRESCENT 3
THE BROADWAY 4
LARKS RI 5
Hanthorpe
FOLKINGHAM ROAD
EAST LA
Morton CE (Cont) Prim Sch
VICTORIA GR
PADDINGTON WY
MOORGATE CL
WAVERLY CL
PASTURE DROVE
SCOTTEN DIKE DRIVE

P0
High Street
Hanthorpe Road
PH
Morton
STATION ROAD
OLD SPA RD
Pingle Lea Farm

STAINFIELD ROAD

1 FARTHINGS FOLD
2 THE GROVE
3 EDENHAM RD

HAZELAND CL 1
FORD LA 2
NEEDHAM RD 3
WAGGONERS WY 4
SADDLER DR 5
WHEELWRIGHT CL 6
HAZELAND STEADING 7

BOURNE ROAD

PE10

Gunboro' Wood
Nab Wood
Fox Wood
Dock Furrows Farm
Dyke
Dyke Fen
SCOTTEN DIKE DV

CLIPSEGAR LANE

Scoth Farm
Cawthorpe
A15
Dyke Windmill & Peremill Gall
REDMILE CL
Wath Bridge
Eau Well
Main Road
DYKE DROVE

213

Bourne Wood
NORTH ROAD
213
Spring Wood
Hardy's Drove
BARNES DROVE

Pillar Wood
BOURNE
BEAUFORT DR
STEPHENSON WY
MILL DROVE
A151

HAZELWOOD
HAWTHORN
STANLEY ST
Kingsway
ARNHEM
MEADOW DROVE

Blind Well (Chalybeate)
BEECH AVENUE
SAXON WY
QUEEN'S RD
College
P
MILKING NOOK DROVE
Bourne North Fen
River Glen

A151
EXETER ST
HARRINGTON ST
ST GEORGE ST
RECREATION RD
ANCASTER RD
MANNING RD

LEOFRIC AV
P
P0
P
TH
Prim Sch
CHERRY HOLT RD
213

Pond Farm
213
Park Farm
WEST ROAD
WEST STREET
ABBEY ROAD
B1193
EAST GATE
THE SLIPE
Chimney
Works

FIR WY
MANOR LA
HARVEY CL
Mast
SOUTH ROAD
AUSTERBY
WILLOUGHBY RD
Radio Mast

Auster Wood
Castle Earthworks
SOUTHFIELDS
Bourne Gram Sch
SOUTH STREET
A151
VICTOR
SOUTH FEN ROAD

A6121
Toft Lodge
Cemy
THE RIDINGS
TENNYSON DR
MARIGOLD AV
BUTTERCUP
ILIA WAY
A151
TUNNEL BANK

Toft Tunnel Nature Reserve
Ogrey Spinney
Northorpe Lodge
Math Wood
213
Elsea Wood
BOURNE ROAD A15
Northorpe Fen
Bourne South Fen
Thurlby Fen
FEN RD

For full street detail of the highlighted area see page 213.

153   164

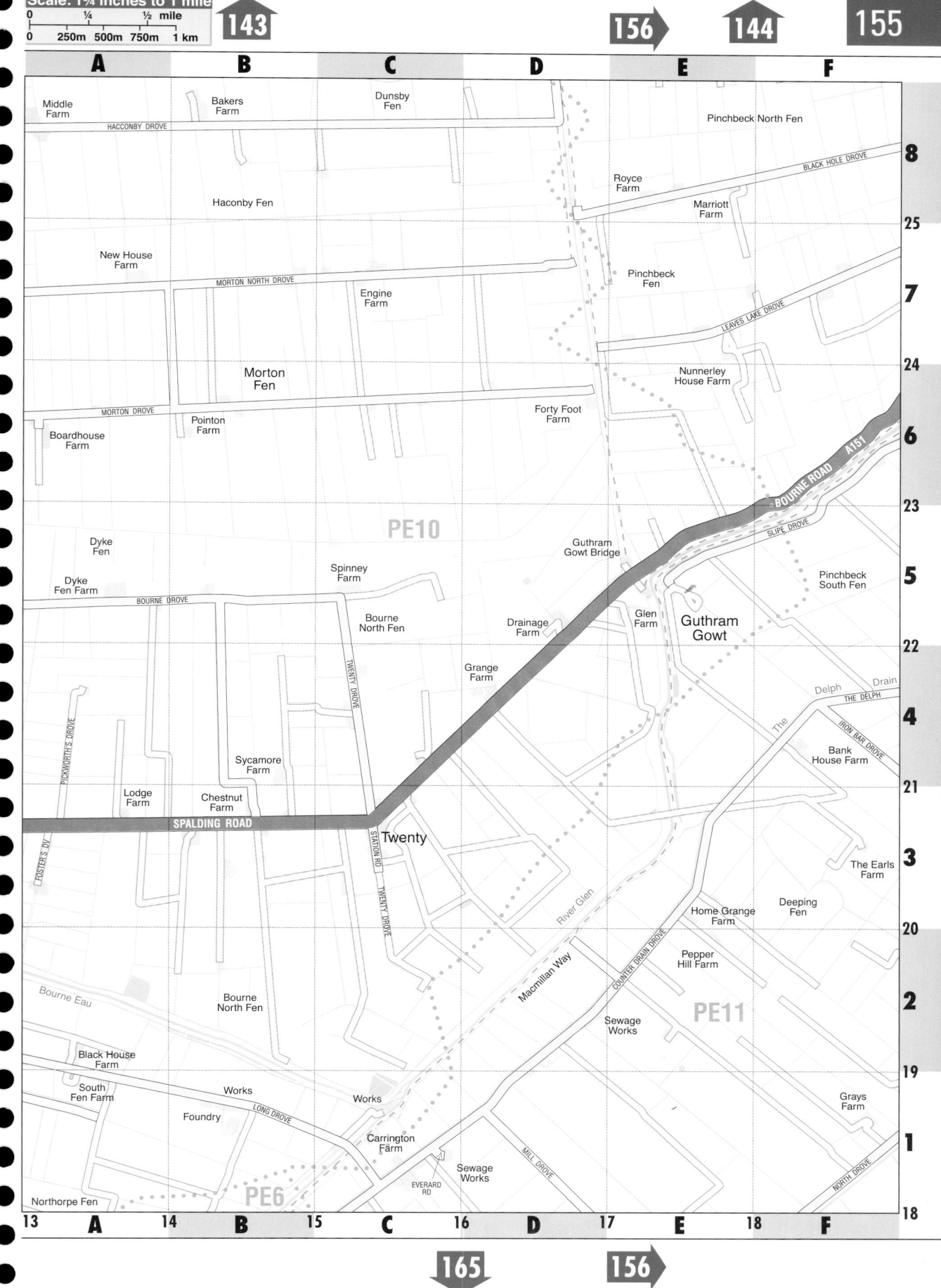

A   B   C   D   E   F

Middle Farm

HACCONBY DROVE

Bakers Farm

Dunsby Fen

Pinchbeck North Fen

BLACK HOLE DROVE

8

Haconby Fen

Royce Farm

Marriott Farm

25

New House Farm

MORTON NORTH DROVE

Engine Farm

Pinchbeck Fen

7

LEAVES LAKE DROVE

Morton Fen

Nunnerley House Farm

24

MORTON DROVE

Pointon Farm

Forty Foot Farm

BOURNE ROAD A151

6

Boardhouse Farm

PE10

Guthram Gowt Bridge

SLIPE DROVE

23

Dyke Fen

Spinney Farm

Pinchbeck South Fen

5

Dyke Fen Farm

BOURNE DROVE

Bourne North Fen

Drainage Farm

Glen Farm

Guthram Gowt

22

TWENTY DROVE

Grange Farm

Delph   Drain

The Delph

4

PICKWORTH'S DROVE

Sycamore Farm

The

IRON BAR DROVE

Bank House Farm

21

Lodge Farm

Chestnut Farm

SPALDING ROAD

Twenty

The Earls Farm

3

FOSTER'S DV

STATION RD

TWENTY DROVE

River Glen

Home Grange Farm

Deeping Fen

20

Bourne Eau

Bourne North Fen

Macmillan Way

COUNTER DRAIN DROVE

Pepper Hill Farm

PE11

2

Black House Farm

Sewage Works

19

South Fen Farm

Works

LONG DROVE

Works

Grays Farm

Foundry

Carrington Farm

MILL DROVE

1

Northorpe Fen

EVERARD RD

Sewage Works

NORTH DROVE

18

13   A   14   B   15   C   16   D   17   E   18   F

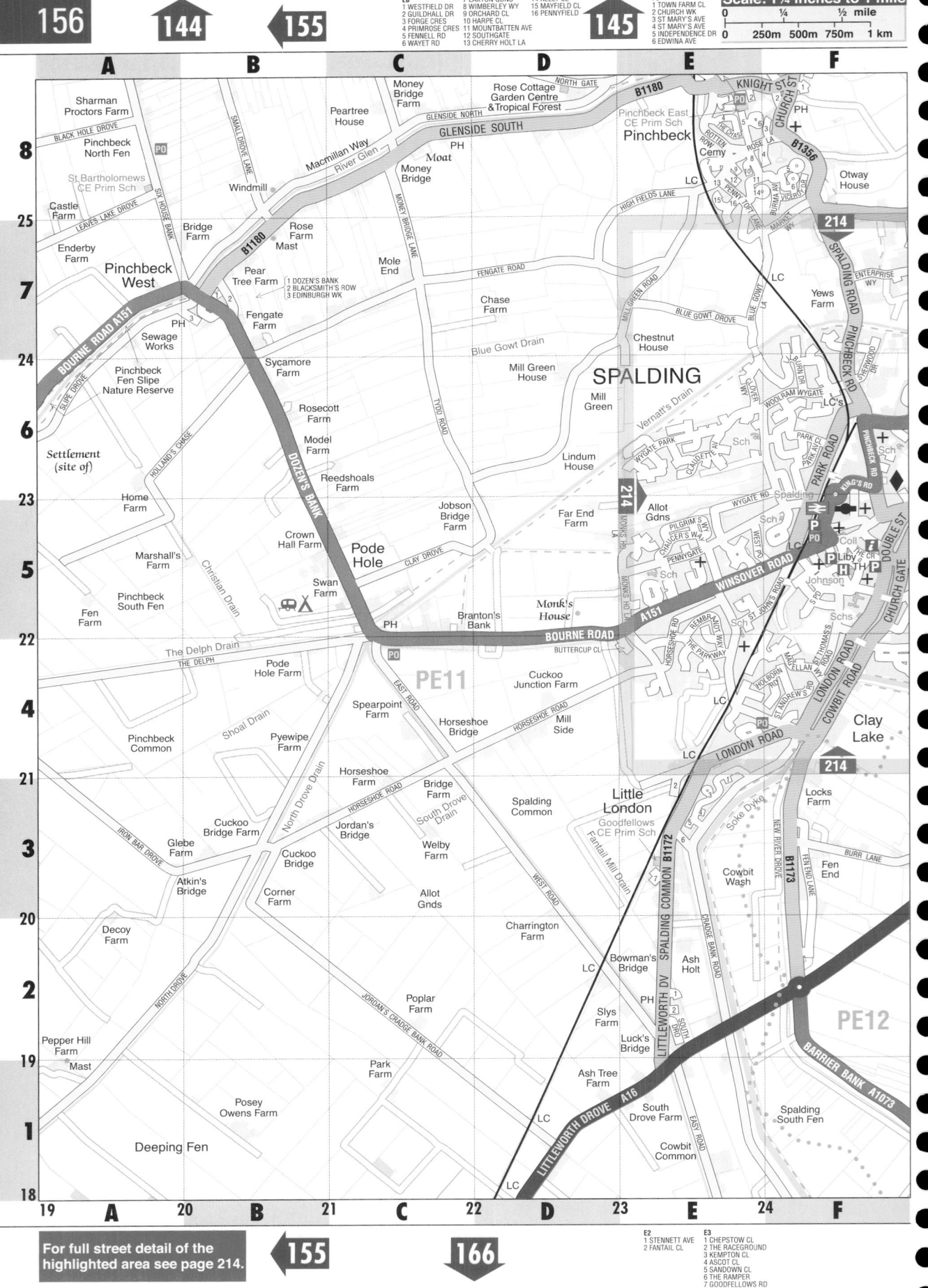
A B C D E F
8 25 7 24 6 23 5 22 4 21 3 20 2 19 1 18
19 20 21 22 23 24
Sharman Proctors Farm
BLACK HOLE DROVE
Pinchbeck North Fen
St Bartholomews CE Prim Sch
Castle Farm
LEAVES LAKE DROVE
Enderby Farm
Pinchbeck West
SMALL DROVE LANE
SIX HOUSE BANK
Windmill
Bridge Farm
Peartree House
Money Bridge Farm
Macmillan Way
River Glen
Moat
Money Bridge
Rose Farm
Mast
B1180
Pear Tree Farm
1 DOZEN'S BANK
2 BLACKSMITH'S ROW
3 EDINBURGH WK
Fengate Farm
MONEY BRIDGE LANE
Mole End
FENGATE ROAD
Rose Cottage Garden Centre &Tropical Forest
NORTH GATE
GLENSIDE NORTH
GLENSIDE SOUTH
PH
Pinchbeck East CE Prim Sch
Pinchbeck
KNIGHT ST
CHURCH ST
B1356
Cemy
ROTTEN ROW
ROSE LA
PENNY TOFT LANE
BURMA AVE
VICEROY DR
MARKET WY
Otway House
HIGH FIELDS LANE
LC
214
SPALDING ROAD
ENTERPRISE WY
Yews Farm
BLUE GOWT DROVE
BLUE GOWT LA
MILL GREEN ROAD
Chase Farm
Chestnut House
Blue Gowt Drain
Mill Green House
SPALDING
Mill Green
PINCHBECK RD
SHERWOOD DR
WOOLRAM WYGATE
CLOVER WY
LC's
BOURNE ROAD A151
Sewage Works
PH
Pinchbeck Fen Slipe Nature Reserve
SLIPE DROVE
Sycamore Farm
Rosecott Farm
Model Farm
Settlement (site of)
HOLLAND'S CHASE
DOZEN'S BANK
Reedshoals Farm
TYDD ROAD
Vernatt's Drain
WYGATE PARK
CLAUDETTE AV
Lindum House
Sch
PARK CL
PARK AV
PARK ROAD
PINCHBECK RD
KING'S RD
Home Farm
Jobson Bridge Farm
Far End Farm
Allot Gdns
MONKS HO LA
WYGATE RD
Spalding
PILGRIM'S WY
CHAUCER'S WAY
PENNYGATE
WEST PD
Crown Hall Farm
Pode Hole
CLAY DROVE
Marshall's Farm
Christian Drain
Swan Farm
Pinchbeck South Fen
Fen Farm
Branton's Bank
Monk's House
BOURNE ROAD
A151
WINSOVER ROAD
Coll
Liby
TH
Johnson
DOUBLE ST
CHURCH GATE
ST JOHN'S ROAD
HORSESHOE RD
REMBRANDT WAY
THE PARKWAY
ST THOMAS'S ROAD
Schs
BUTTERCUP CL
The Delph Drain
THE DELPH
Pode Hole Farm
PE11
Cuckoo Junction Farm
EAST ROAD
Spearpoint Farm
Horseshoe Bridge
HORSESHOE ROAD
Mill Side
MAGELLAN WY
HOLBORN RD
ST ANDREW'S RD
LONDON ROAD
COWBIT ROAD
Clay Lake
Pinchbeck Common
Shoal Drain
Pyewipe Farm
Horseshoe Farm
Bridge Farm
South Drove Drain
Spalding Common
Little London
Goodfellows CE Prim Sch
Soke Dyke
Locks Farm
IRON BAR DROVE
Glebe Farm
Cuckoo Bridge Farm
North Drove Drain
Jordan's Bridge
Welby Farm
Cuckoo Bridge
Fantail Mill Drain
SPALDING COMMON B1172
NEW RIVER DROVE
B1173
FEN END LANE
BURR LANE
Fen End
Cowbit Wash
Atkin's Bridge
Corner Farm
Allot Gnds
WEST ROAD
CRADGE BANK ROAD
Decoy Farm
Charrington Farm
NORTH DROVE
Bowman's Bridge
Ash Holt
Poplar Farm
JORDAN'S CRADGE BANK ROAD
Slys Farm
LITTLEWORTH DV
SOUTH DRO
PE12
Pepper Hill Farm
Mast
Park Farm
Luck's Bridge
BARRIER BANK A1073
Ash Tree Farm
A16
Posey Owens Farm
LITTLEWORTH DROVE
South Drove Farm
EASY ROAD
Spalding South Fen
Deeping Fen
Cowbit Common

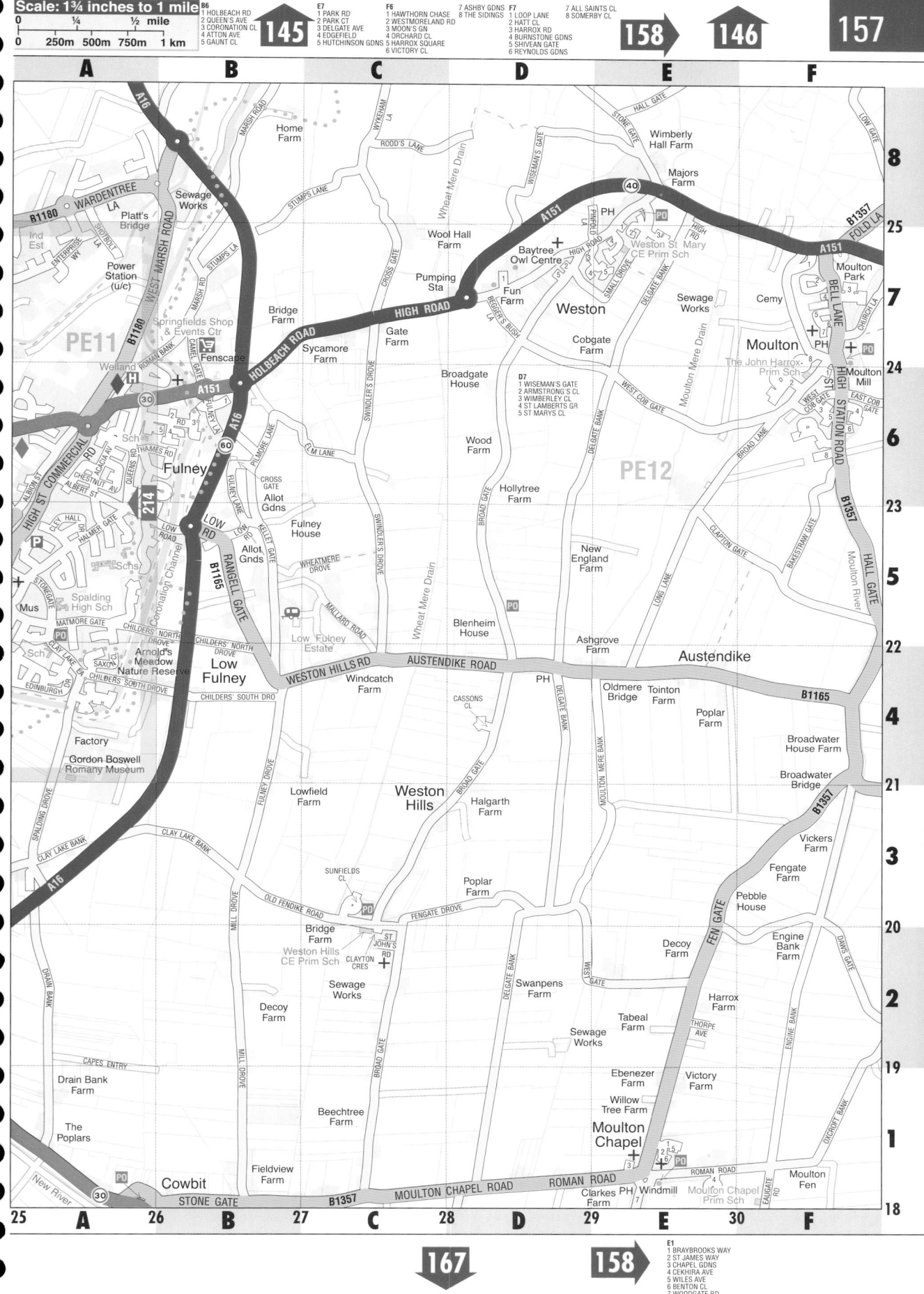

B6
1 HOLBEACH RD
2 QUEEN'S AVE
3 CORONATION CL
4 ATTON AVE
5 GAUNT CL

145

E7
1 PARK RD
2 PARK CT
3 DELGATE AVE
4 EDGEFIELD
5 HUTCHINSON GDNS

F6
1 HAWTHORN CHASE
2 WESTMORELAND RD
3 MOON'S GN
4 ORCHARD CL
5 HARROX SQUARE
6 VICTORY CL

7 ASHBY GDNS
8 THE SIDINGS

F7
1 LOOP LANE
2 HATT CL
3 HARROX RD
4 BURNSTONE GDNS
5 SHIVEAN GATE
6 REYNOLDS GDNS

7 ALL SAINTS CL
8 SOMERBY CL

158 ▶   146   157

Column labels: A B C D E F

Row labels: 8 25 7 24 6 23 5 22 4 21 3 20 2 19 1 18

PE11
PE12

Selected map labels:
A16, B1180, WARDENTREE LA, Platt's Bridge, Power Station (u/c), Ind Est, ENTERPRISE WY, SANDHOLT, Home Farm, MARSH ROAD, Sewage Works, WEST MARSH ROAD, STUMPS LA, MARSH RD, Wool Hall Farm, STUMPS LANE, ROOD'S LANE, WYKEHAM LA, WHEAT MERE DRAIN, WISEMAN'S GATE, STONE GATE, HALL GATE, Wimberly Hall Farm, Majors Farm, A151, PH, PO, B1357, FOLD LA, LOW GATE, Moulton Park, Baytree Owl Centre, Weston St Mary CE Prim Sch, Weston, Cemy, Moulton, BELL LANE, HIGH STATION ROAD, CHURCH LA, EAST COB GATE, Moulton Mill, Springfields Shop & Events Ctr, Fenscape, Bridge Farm, HOLBEACH ROAD, HIGH ROAD, Sycamore Farm, Gate Farm, CROSS GATE, Pumping Sta, Fun Farm, BERGER'S BUSH LA, Cobgate Farm, HIGH ROAD, SMALL DROVE, DELGATE BANK, The John Harrox Prim Sch, WEST COB GATE, Broadgate House, Wood Farm, Hollytree Farm, E M LANE, SWINDLER'S DROVE, PILMORE LANE, FULNEY LANE, Fulney, Welland, PE11, CAMEL GATE, ALBION ST, HIGH ST COMMERCIAL RD, CHESTNUT AV, QUEENS AV, ACACIA AV, ALBERT ST, THAMES RD, Sch, CROSS GATE, Allot Gdns, Fulney House, WHEATMERE DROVE, MALLARD ROAD, Low Fulney Estate, RANGELL GATE, B1165, LOW RD, LOW ROAD, KELLEY GATE, Allot Gnds, CLAY HALL DR, HALMER GATE, STONGATE, MATMORE GATE, Spalding High Sch, Mus, Spalding, PO, CHILDERS' NORTH DROVE, Arnold's Meadow Nature Reserve, CLAY LAKE LA, SAXON, CHILDERS' SOUTH DROVE, Low Fulney, SPALDING DROVE, Factory, Gordon Boswell Romany Museum, Edinburgh, WESTON HILLS RD, AUSTENDIKE ROAD, Windcatch Farm, Blenheim House, Ashgrove Farm, Austendike, B1165, New England Farm, CLAPTON GATE, BAKESTRAW GATE, Moulton River, HALL GATE, B1357, Broadwater House Farm, Broadwater Bridge, Oldmere Bridge, Tointon Farm, Poplar Farm, PH, LONG LANE, BROAD GATE, DELGATE BANK, MOULTON MERE DRAIN, CASSONS CL, Lowfield Farm, Weston Hills, Halgarth Farm, FULNEY DROVE, MILL DROVE, A16, CLAY LAKE BANK, Vickers Farm, Fengate Farm, Pebble House, FEN GATE, B1357, OXCROFT BANK, DANS GATE, ENGINE BANK, SUNFIELDS CL, PO, Poplar Farm, FENGATE DROVE, OLD FENDIKE ROAD, Decoy Farm, Engine Bank Farm, WEST GATE, Bridge Farm, Weston Hills CE Prim Sch, ST JOHN'S RD, CLAYTON CRES, Swanpens Farm, Sewage Works, Tabeal Farm, THORPE AVE, Harrox Farm, Decoy Farm, Sewage Works, CAPES ENTRY, Ebenezer Farm, Victory Farm, Drain Bank Farm, DRAIN BANK, Beechtree Farm, Willow Tree Farm, Moulton Chapel, Moulton Chapel Prim Sch, FAUGATE RD, Moulton Fen, Clarkes PH, Windmill, ROMAN ROAD, The Poplars, Fieldview Farm, Cowbit, STONE GATE, B1357, MOULTON CHAPEL ROAD, New River

E1
1 BRAYBROOKS WAY
2 ST JAMES WAY
3 CHAPEL GDNS
4 CEKHIRA AVE
5 WILES AVE
6 BENTON CL
7 WOODGATE RD

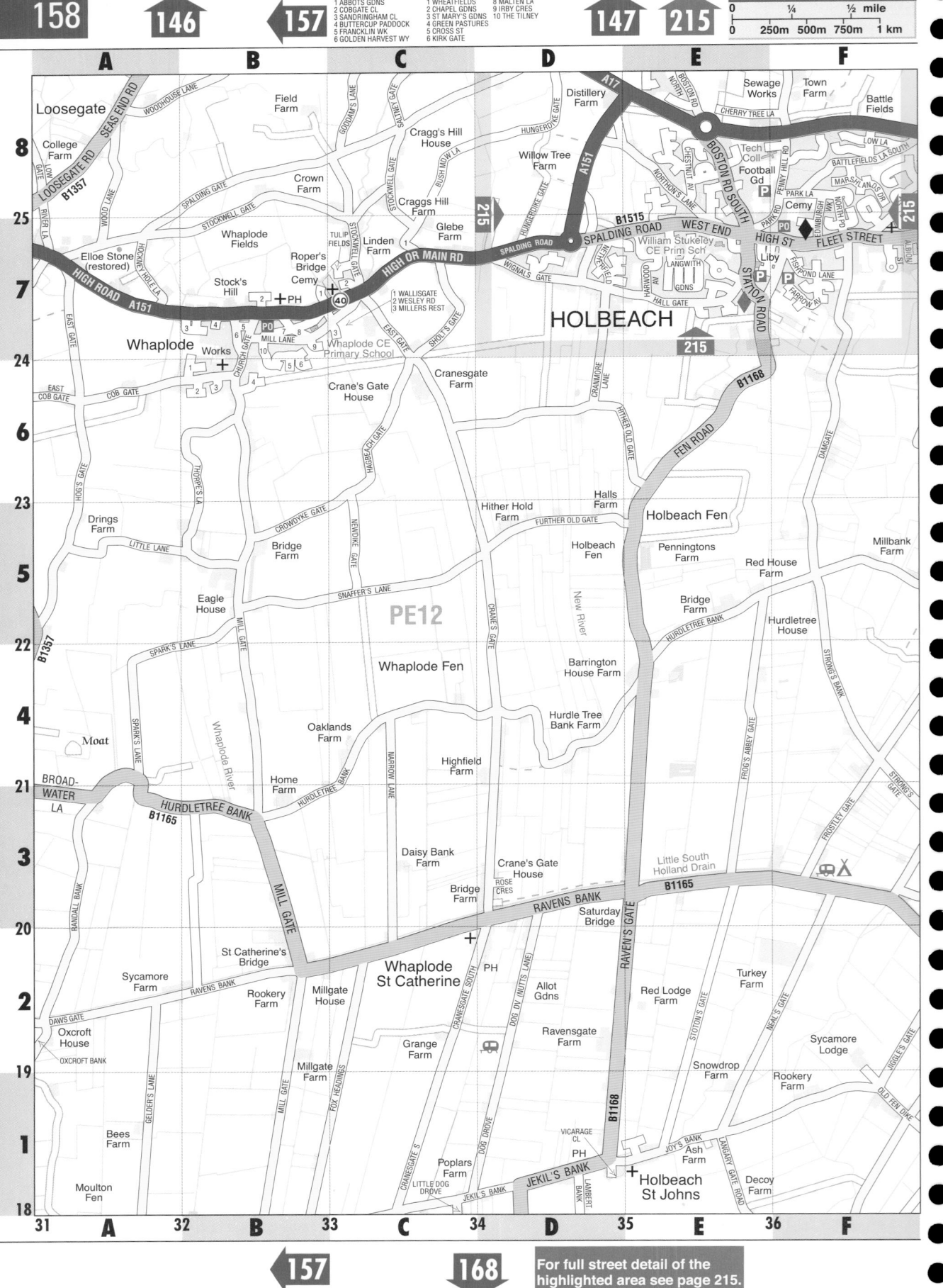

B6
1 ABBOTS GDNS
2 COBGATE CL
3 SANDRINGHAM CL
4 BUTTERCUP PADDOCK
5 FRANCKLIN WK
6 GOLDEN HARVEST WY

B7
1 WHEATFIELDS
2 CHAPEL GDNS
3 ST MARY'S GDNS
4 GREEN PASTURES
5 CROSS ST
6 KIRK GATE

7 MIDDLE RD
8 MALTEN LA
9 IRBY CRES
10 THE TILNEY

Scale: 1¾ inches to 1 mile

0   ¼   ½   mile

0   250m   500m   750m   1 km

Loosegate

College Farm

Field Farm

Cragg's Hill House

Distillery Farm

Sewage Works

Town Farm

Battle Fields

Tech Coll

Football Gd

Crown Farm

Willow Tree Farm

Craggs Hill Farm

Glebe Farm

Whaplode Fields

Linden Farm

Elloe Stone (restored)

Roper's Bridge Cemy

Stock's Hill

HIGH OR MAIN RD

SPALDING ROAD

SPALDING ROAD

WEST END

William Stukeley CE Prim Sch

HIGH ST

FLEET STREET

HOLBEACH

HIGH ROAD

A151

PH

Whaplode

Works

Whaplode CE Primary School

1 WALLISGATE
2 WESLEY RD
3 MILLERS REST

Cranesgate Farm

Crane's Gate House

Bridge Farm

Drings Farm

Hither Hold Farm

Halls Farm

Holbeach Fen

Holbeach Fen

Millbank Farm

Eagle House

PE12

Whaplode Fen

Barrington House Farm

Penningtons Farm

Red House Farm

Bridge Farm

Hurdletree House

Moat

Oaklands Farm

Highfield Farm

Hurdle Tree Bank Farm

BROAD-WATER LA

HURDLETREE BANK

Home Farm

Daisy Bank Farm

Crane's Gate House

Little South Holland Drain

B1165

Bridge Farm

RAVENS BANK

Saturday Bridge

St Catherine's Bridge

Sycamore Farm

Whaplode St Catherine

Rookery Farm

Millgate House

PH

Allot Gdns

Red Lodge Farm

Turkey Farm

Oxcroft House

Grange Farm

Ravensgate Farm

Snowdrop Farm

Sycamore Lodge

Rookery Farm

Bees Farm

Millgate Farm

Poplars Farm

Vicarage Cl

PH

Ash Farm

Decoy Farm

Moulton Fen

JEKIL'S BANK

Holbeach St Johns

For full street detail of the highlighted area see page 215.

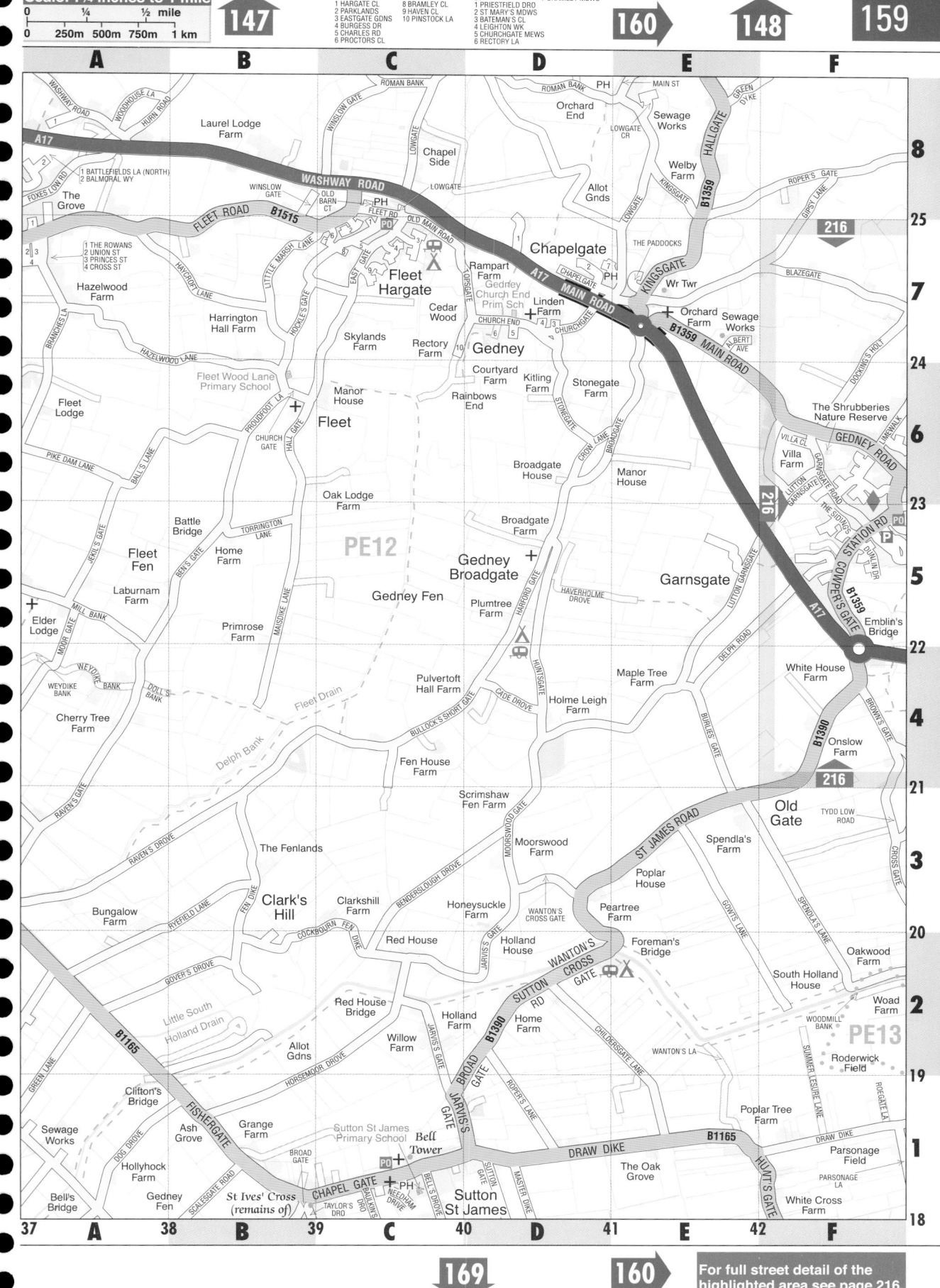

Scale: 1¾ inches to 1 mile

0 ¼ ½ mile
0 250m 500m 750m 1 km

147

160

148

159

C7
1 HARGATE CL
2 PARKLANDS
3 EASTGATE GDNS
4 BURGESS DR
5 CHARLES RD
6 PROCTORS CL

7 CHERRY LA
8 BRAMLEY CL
9 HAVEN CL
10 PINSTOCK LA

D7
1 PRIESTFIELD DRO
2 ST MARY'S MDWS
3 BATEMAN'S CL
4 LEIGHTON WK
5 CHURCHGATE MEWS
6 RECTORY LA

7 BRAMLEY MEWS

A B C D E F

Scale markers: 8 25 7 24 6 23 5 22 4 21 3 20 2 19 1 18

A17 WASHWAY ROAD

ROMAN BANK

Laurel Lodge Farm

WOODHOUSE LA
HURN ROAD
WASHWAY ROAD

1 BATTLEFIELDS LA (NORTH)
2 BALMORAL WY

FOXES LOW RD
FLEET ROAD
B1515

The Grove

WINSLOW GATE
OLD BARN CT
FLEET RD
PO

Chapel Side

LOWGATE

Orchard End

LOWGATE CR

Sewage Works

MAIN ST

Welby Farm

HALLGATE
B1359

GREEN DYKE

1 THE ROWANS
2 UNION ST
3 PRINCES ST
4 CROSS ST

Hazelwood Farm

Fleet Hargate

Rampart Farm

Chapelgate

Allot Gnds

THE PADDOCKS

KINGSGATE

ROPER'S GATE

GIPSY LANE

216

BLAZEGATE

HAYCROFT LANE
LITTLE MARSH LANE
EAST GATE
HICKLE'S GATE

Cedar Wood

Gedney Church End Prim Sch

Linden Farm

CHURCHGATE

PH

Wr Twr

Orchard Farm

Sewage Works

ALBERT AVE

DOCKING'S HOLT

Harrington Hall Farm

Skylands Farm

Rectory Farm

CHURCH END

Gedney

B1359 MAIN ROAD

The Shrubberies Nature Reserve

HAZELWOOD LANE

Fleet Wood Lane Primary School

Manor House

Courtyard Farm

Kitling Farm

Stonegate Farm

GEDNEY ROAD

LIMEWALK

Fleet Lodge

PROUDFOOT LA
CHURCH GATE
HALL GATE

Fleet

Rainbows End

CROM LANE
STONEGATE
BROADGATE

Manor House

VILLA FARM
Villa Farm

216

LUTTON GARNSGATE
GARNSGATE ROAD
THE SIDINGS

PIKE DAM LANE
BALL'S LANE

Broadgate House

STATION RD
PO
P

Battle Bridge

Oak Lodge Farm

TORRINGTON LANE

Home Farm

Broadgate Farm

HARFORD GATE

HAVERHOLME DROVE

PE12

Gedney Fen

Gedney Broadgate

Garnsgate

LUTTON GARNSGATE

A17
COWPER'S GATE
B1359

Emblin's Bridge

JEKIL'S GATE
BEN'S GATE

Fleet Fen

Laburnam Farm

MAISDALE LANE

Plumtree Farm

HUNTSGATE

Maple Tree Farm

DELPH ROAD

White House Farm

BROWN'S GATE

ELDER
Lodge

MONK GATE
MILL BANK

Primrose Farm

Pulvertoft Hall Farm

CADE DROVE

Holme Leigh Farm

BURLES GATE

B1390

Onslow Farm

WEYDIKE BANK
DOLL'S BANK

Fleet Drain

BULLOCK'S SHORT GATE

216

Cherry Tree Farm

Delph Bank

Fen House Farm

Scrimshaw Fen Farm

MOORSWOOD GATE

ST JAMES ROAD

Spendla's Farm

Old Gate

TYDD LOW ROAD

CROSS GATE

RAVEN'S GATE

RAVEN'S DROVE

The Fenlands

Moorswood Farm

Poplar House

SPENDLA'S LANE

BENDERSLOUGH DROVE

FEN DIKE

Clark's Hill

Clarkshill Farm

Honeysuckle Farm

WANTON'S CROSS GATE

Peartree Farm

GOWT'S LANE

Oakwood Farm

RYEFIELD LANE

COCKBURN FEN DIKE

Red House

Holland House

Foreman's Bridge

South Holland House

Woad Farm

Bungalow Farm

JARVIS'S GATE

GLOVER'S DROVE

Little South Holland Drain

Red House Bridge

Willow Farm

SUTTON RD
B1390

WANTON'S CROSS GATE

CHILDERSGATE LANE

WOODMILL BANK

PE13

Roderwick Field

ROEGATE LA

B1165

Allot Gdns

HORSEMOOR DROVE

JARVIS'S GATE

Holland Farm

Home Farm

WANTON'S LA

SUMMER LEISURE LANE

GREEN LANE

Clifton's Bridge

FISHERGATE

Grange Farm

BROAD GATE

ROPER'S LANE

Poplar Tree Farm

DRAW DIKE
B1165

Parsonage Field

DOG DROVE

Ash Grove

Sutton St James Primary School

Bell Tower

JARVIS'S GATE

GATE

SUTTON GATE

MASTER DIKE

DRAW DIKE

The Oak Grove

HUNT'S GATE

DRAW DIKE

PARSONAGE LA

Sewage Works

Hollyhock Farm

SCALESGATE ROAD

BROAD GATE

CHAPEL GATE

PO
PH

BELL'S GATE

Sutton St James

White Cross Farm

Bell's Bridge

Gedney Fen

St Ives' Cross (remains of)

TAYLOR'S DRO

NEEDHAM DRIVE

DRO

37 A 38 B 39 C 40 D 41 E 42 F 18

169

160

For full street detail of the highlighted area see page 216.

160

148

159

149

Scale: 1¾ inches to 1 mile

0 ¼ ½ mile

0 250m 500m 750m 1 km

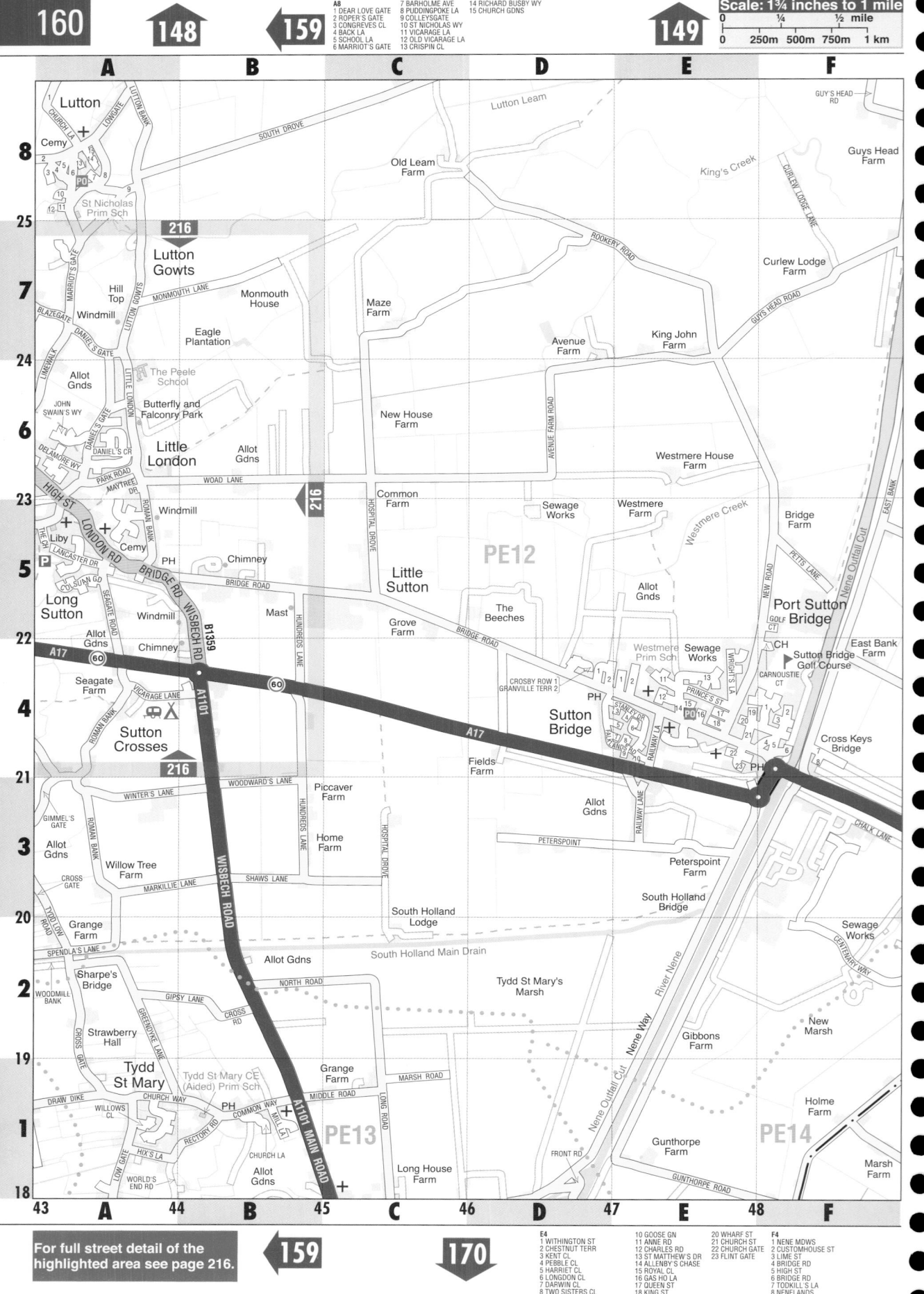

For full street detail of the highlighted area see page 216.

159

170

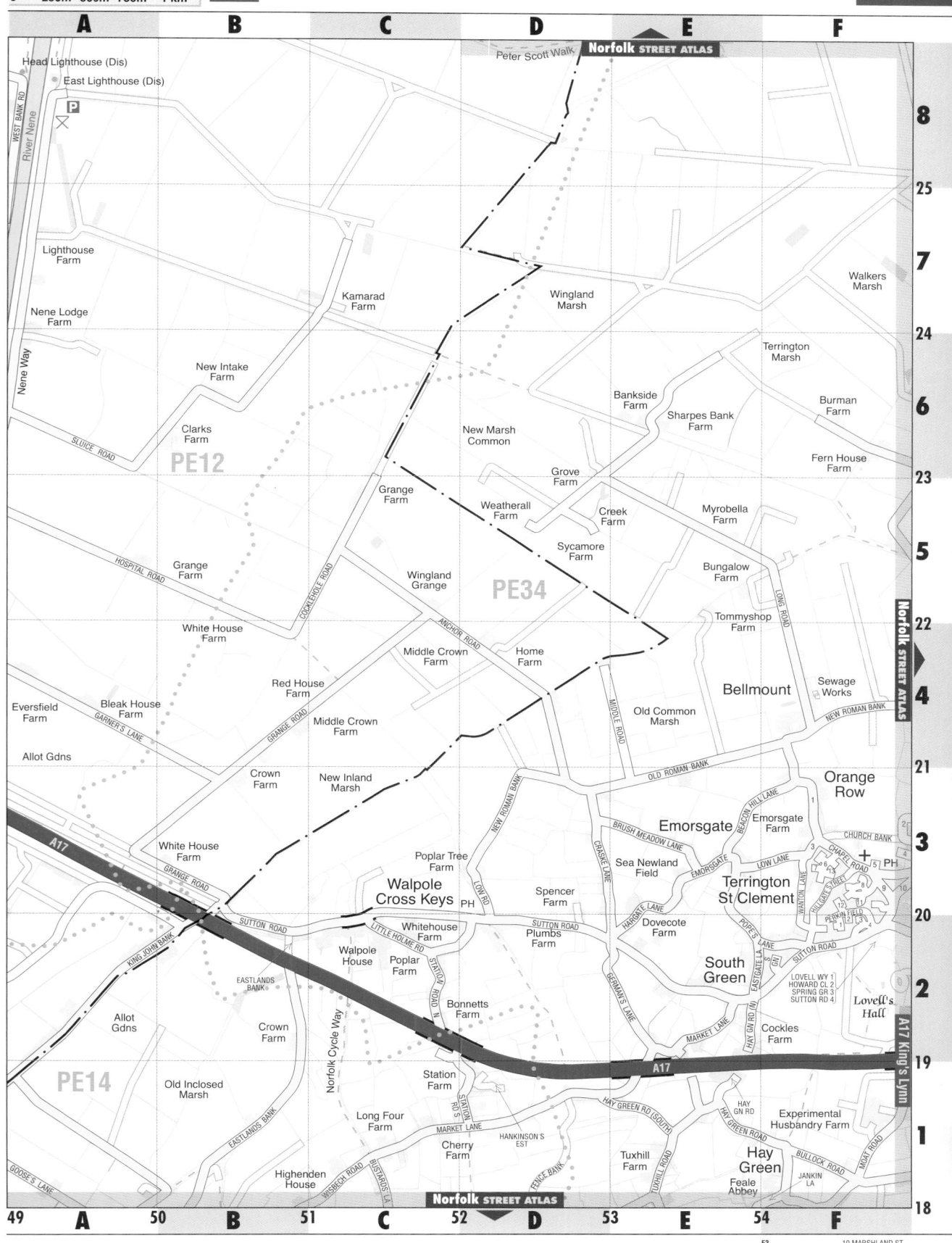

A   B   C   D   E   F

Head Lighthouse (Dis)
East Lighthouse (Dis)

8

25

WEST BANK RD

River Nene

Lighthouse Farm

Nene Lodge Farm

7

Kamarad Farm

Wingland Marsh

Walkers Marsh

Nene Way

New Intake Farm

24

Terrington Marsh

6

Clarks Farm

SLUICE ROAD

New Marsh Common

Bankside Farm

Sharpes Bank Farm

Burman Farm

PE12

Grange Farm

Grove Farm

Fern House Farm

23

HOSPITAL ROAD

Grange Farm

Weatherall Farm

Creek Farm

Myrobella Farm

5

COCKLEHOLE ROAD

Wingland Grange

Sycamore Farm

Bungalow Farm

PE34

ANCHOR ROAD

Tommyshop Farm

LONG ROAD

22

White House Farm

Middle Crown Farm

Home Farm

Bellmount

Sewage Works

4

Eversfield Farm

GARNER'S LANE

Bleak House Farm

Red House Farm

Old Common Marsh

NEW ROMAN BANK

Allot Gdns

GRANGE ROAD

Middle Crown Farm

MIDDLE ROAD

OLD ROMAN BANK

21

Crown Farm

New Inland Marsh

NEW ROMAN BANK

Orange Row

A17

White House Farm

GRANGE ROAD

Poplar Tree Farm

LOW RD

Emorsgate

BRUSH MEADOW LANE

Emorsgate Farm

BEACON HILL LANE

CHURCH BANK

3

SUTTON ROAD

Walpole Cross Keys   PH

Spencer Farm

Sea Newland Field

EMORSGATE

CRASKE LANE

LOW LANE

Terrington St Clement

CHAPEL ROAD

PH

LITTLE HOLME RD

Whitehouse Farm

SUTTON ROAD

Plumbs Farm

MARGT E. LANE

Dovecote Farm

WANTON LA

HIGHGES STREET

PEPPIN FIELD

20

King John Bank

Walpole House

Poplar Farm

STATION ROAD N

Bonnetts Farm

GERMAN'S LANE

POPE'S LANE

EAST GATE LA

South Green

LOVELL WY 1
HOWARD CL 2
SPRING GR 3
SUTTON RD 4

SUTTON ROAD

Lovell's Hall

2

Allot Gdns

EASTLANDS BANK

Crown Farm

Norfolk Cycle Way

STATION RD S

Station Farm

MARKET LANE

HAY GN RD (IN)

Cockles Farm

MARKET LANE

A17

19

PE14

Old Inclosed Marsh

EASTLANDS BANK

Long Four Farm

WISBECH ROAD

BUSTARDS LA

Cherry Farm

MARKET LANE

HANKINSON'S EST

HAY GREEN RD (SOUTH)

Tuxhill Farm

TUXHILL ROAD

HAY GREEN ROAD

HAY GN RD

Experimental Husbandry Farm

BULLOCK ROAD

MOAT ROAD

A17 King's Lynn

GOOSE'S LANE

Highenden House

FENCE BANK

Feale Abbey

Hay Green

JANKIN LA

18

49   A   50   B   51   C   52   D   53   E   54   F

F3
1 ORANGE ROW RD
2 CHURCH BANK
3 ORANGE ROW
4 KING WILLIAM CL
5 WESLEY AVE
6 THE SALTINGS
7 BRELLOWS HILL
8 CAVE'S CL
9 WESLEY RD
10 MARSHLAND ST
11 WESLEY CL
12 FFOLKES DR
13 COBBS HILL

152

171

E8
1 LITTLE BYTHAM RD
2 REGAL GDNS
3 BYTHAM HEIGHTS

Scale: 1¾ inches to 1 mile

0   ¼   ½ mile
0   250m 500m 750m 1 km

Stocken Park
HM Prison
Chimney
Lady Wood
Little Haw Wood
Addah Wood
Clipsham Park Wood
Quarry (dis)
Glebe Farm
Meadows End
NG33
School Farm
Belton Firs
Lodge Farm
Stretton Wood
1 HESKETH CT
2 FLEETWOOD CT
3 WILSON CT
4 STOVE CT
BRADLEY LA 1
CHURCH LA 2
NEW RD 3
WEST ST 4
Moor Plantation
Clipsham Park
Quarry (dis)
Pillowsyke Holt
New Wood
Clipsham
Stockton Lane Plantation
Manor Farm
Hill Top Farm
The Quarries
Holywell Hall
Holy Well
Clipsham Road
Stretton Road
Castle Bytham Road
Main St
Holywell Quarry
Mill Farm
PH
MANOR RD
LE15
Bidwell Farm
White's Plantation
New Quarry Plantation
New Quarry House
Holywell Road
Infield Holt
Bidwell Lane
Clipsham Old Quarry (Limestone)
Quarries (dis)
Pettywood Farm
Pattinson's Holt
Glebe Farm
Osbonall Wood
Quarry (dis)
Holywell Wood
Lincolnshire Gate
Robert's Field Nature Reserve
Greetham Wood Far
Big Pits Wood
Quarry (dis)
Pickworth Great Wood
The Grange
Clay Pit
Newell Wood
Castle Dike
A1 Grantham
Quarry (dis)
Woolfox Wood
Church (remains of)
Pickworth
A1
Airfield (dis)
The Coppice
Pit (dis)
Woolfox Depot
Hardwick Wood
Turnpole Wood
Leicestershire & Rutland STREET ATLAS
CH
Rutland County Golf Course
Pickworth Plain
PE9
Taylor's Farm
Horn Farm
North Road Spinney
Exeter Gorse
North Brook
Medieval Village of Horn (site of)
Little Oaks
Bloody Oaks
Warren Plantation
Woodhead
Woodhead Castle (site of)
East Wood
Pug's Park Spinney
Great North Road
Tickencote Warren
Pickworth Road
Mounts Lodge
Quarry (dis)
Wing Plantations
Empingham Old Wood
Horn Mill Spinney
LOUIS LA
Tickencote Laund
A1
Quarry (dis)

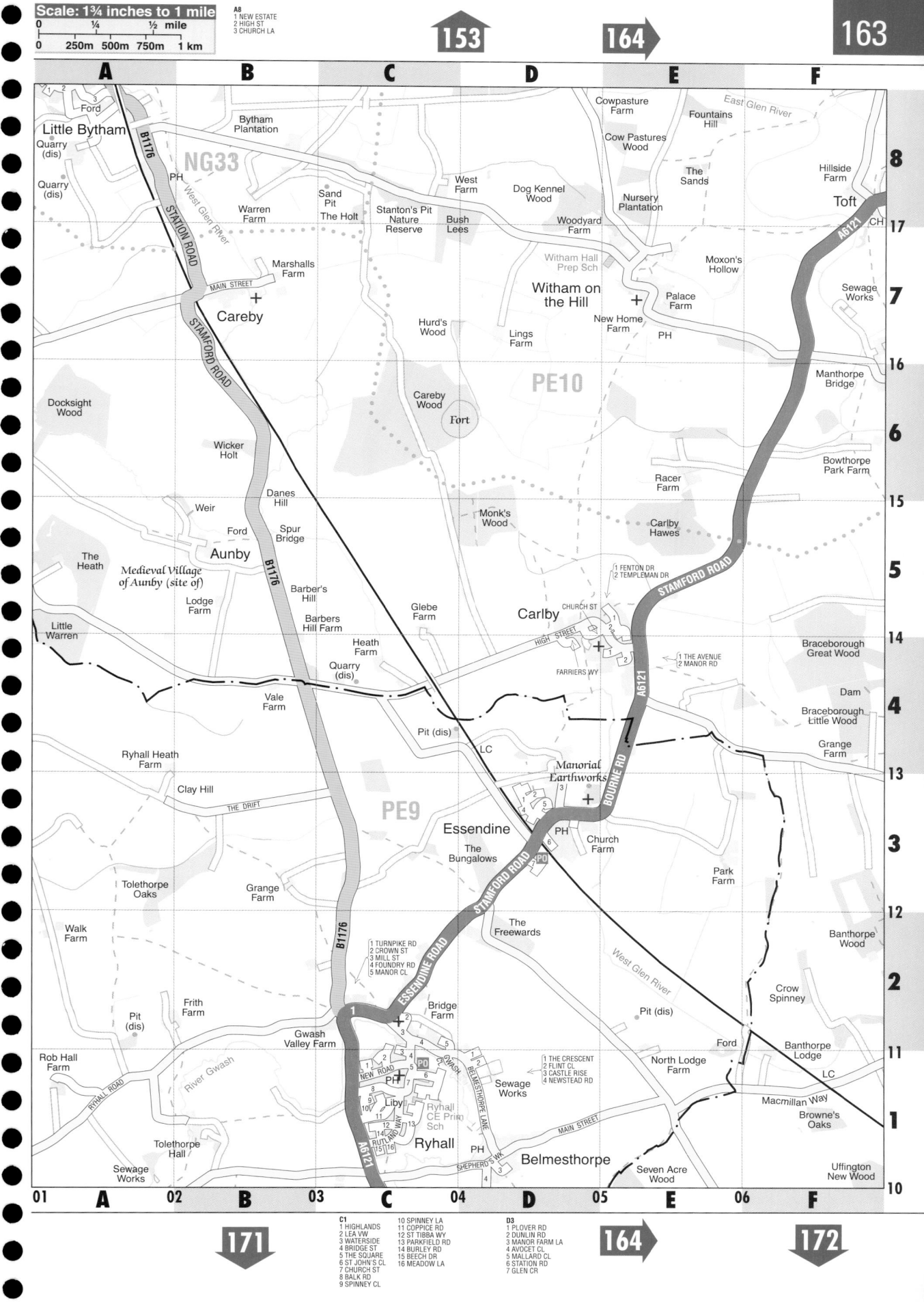

Scale: 1¾ inches to 1 mile

0   ¼   ½   mile
0   250m 500m 750m 1 km

A8
1 NEW ESTATE
2 HIGH ST
3 CHURCH LA

153
164 ▶

Little Bytham

Quarry (dis)
Ford
Quarry (dis)

NG33

PH

West Glen River

STATION ROAD

B1176

Bytham Plantation

Warren Farm

Sand Pit
The Holt

West Farm

Stanton's Pit Nature Reserve

Bush Lees

Cowpasture Farm

Fountains Hill

The Sands

Hillside Farm

East Glen River

Toft

A8121 CH

8

17

Marshalls Farm

MAIN STREET

Careby

Dog Kennel Wood

Woodyard Farm

Witham Hall Prep Sch

Nursery Plantation

Witham on the Hill

New Home Farm

Palace Farm

PH

Moxon's Hollow

Sewage Works

7

16

STAMFORD ROAD

Docksight Wood

Wicker Holt

Danes Hill

Hurd's Wood

Lings Farm

Careby Wood

Fort

PE10

Manthorpe Bridge

Bowthorpe Park Farm

6

15

The Heath

Weir
Ford

Spur Bridge

Aunby

B1176

Barber's Hill

Barbers Hill Farm

Glebe Farm

Monk's Wood

Racer Farm

Carlby Hawes

1 FENTON DR
2 TEMPLEMAN DR

STAMFORD ROAD

Braceborough Great Wood

Dam

5

14

Medieval Village of Aunby (site of)

Lodge Farm

Little Warren

Heath Farm

Quarry (dis)

Carlby

CHURCH ST

HIGH STREET

FARRIERS WY

1 THE AVENUE
2 MANOR RD

A6121

Braceborough Little Wood

Grange Farm

Vale Farm

Pit (dis)

LC

BOURNE RD

Manorial Earthworks

4

13

Ryhall Heath Farm

Clay Hill

THE DRIFT

PE9

Essendine

The Bungalows

PH

Church Farm

Park Farm

3

12

Tolethorpe Oaks

Grange Farm

1 TURNPIKE RD
2 CROWN ST
3 MILL ST
4 FOUNDRY RD
5 MANOR CL

ESSENDINE ROAD

STAMFORD ROAD

PO

The Freewards

West Glen River

Banthorpe Wood

Crow Spinney

2

Walk Farm

B1176

Frith Farm

Pit (dis)

Rob Hall Farm

RYHALL ROAD

River Gwash

Gwash Valley Farm

Bridge Farm

NEW ROAD

PH

PO

GWASH

Liby

Ryhall CE Prim Sch

BELMESTHORPE LANE

Sewage Works

1 THE CRESCENT
2 FLINT CL
3 CASTLE RISE
4 NEWSTEAD RD

North Lodge Farm

Ford

Banthorpe Lodge

LC

Macmillan Way

Browne's Oaks

1

A6121

RUTLAND

Ryhall

PH

Belmesthorpe

SHEPHERD'S WK

Seven Acre Wood

Uffington New Wood

Tolethorpe Hall

Sewage Works

MAIN STREET

10

01   A   02   B   03   C   04   D   05   E   06   F

171
164
172

C1
1 HIGHLANDS
2 LEA VW
3 WATERSIDE
4 BRIDGE ST
5 THE SQUARE
6 ST JOHN'S CL
7 CHURCH ST
8 BALK RD
9 SPINNEY CL
10 SPINNEY LA
11 COPPICE RD
12 ST TIBBA WY
13 PARKFIELD RD
14 BURLEY RD
15 BEECH DR
16 MEADOW LA

D3
1 PLOVER RD
2 DUNLIN RD
3 MANOR FARM LA
4 AVOCET CL
5 MALLARD CL
6 STATION RD
7 GLEN CR

◄ 163 213 154

Scale: 1¾ inches to 1 mile
0   ¼   ½   mile
0   250m 500m 750m 1 km

A B C D E F

Northorpe Fen Farm
Northorpe Fen
FEN ROAD
BOURNE ROAD
WOODSIDE EAST
Northorpe West Farm
NORTHORPE
WOOD LANE
Thurlby
MAIN ROAD
A15
Church Street
Long Drive
Thurlby Fen
MANTHORPE DRIVE
LAWRENCE'S DV
SHORT DROVE

FAIRWAYS
Toft
Mast
SWALLOW HILL
STATION ROAD
Water La
Thurlby Com Prim Sch
THE GREEN PO
YH
HIGH ST
Tudor Cl
Elm Farm
PH
St Firmin's Wy
BASTON EDGE DROVE
Thurlby Fen Nature Reserve
Poplar Tree Farm

PE10
SWIFT WY
Dole Wood Nature Reserve
Cross Farm
Park Wood
Playing Field
OBTHORPE LANE

Church Farm
Manthorpe
Home Farm
Manor Farm
Obthorpe Lodge
Obthorpe
Katesbridge Farm
Macmillan Way
Hack's Plantation
Red House Farm
HACK'S DROVE

Thetford House Farm
Thetford
Fringes Fen

Spa Lodge Farm
East Glen River
Old Hall Farm
Kate's Bridge Weir
Fletland
Baston CE Prim Sch
Cemy
Brook House Farm
Works

Wilsthorpe
Church Farm
Mill Farm
MAELTBY DR 1
FRISBY CL 2
WHATTOFF WY 3
Kirkstone House Sch
GREATFORD RD
KING STREET
MAIN STREET
PH
Baston
Sand & Gravel Pit
PE6

Manor Farm
Braceborough Great Wood
Braceborough
ELLIOTT'S WY
Macmillan Way
Meadow Field
40
DEEPING ROAD
BOURNE ROAD
A15
Windmill
Middle Field
Moat
Church Farm

Lodge Farm
PE9
Bottom Meadow
Middle Field
Red Inn Field
Truesdale Lodge
MANOR CL 1
MOSSOP DR 2
SCOTT'S CL 3
TRUESDALE GDNS 4
Langtoft Prim Sch
PO 40
PH
Stonehouse Farm
EAST END
NEW ROAD
Cemy

Banthorpe Wood
GREATFORD GD
Greatford
The Council Houses
Greatford Hall
PH
Glen Farm
Nook Field
WEST END
Langtoft
PETERBOROUGH ROAD

Dogkennel Plantation
Macmillan Way
West Glen River
Manor Farm
MAIN STREET
Bleak House Farm
STOWE ROAD
DICKENS WY
1 WHEATFIELD
2 AQUILA WY
3 BARLEYFIELD
4 WESTFIELD WY
Middle Field
Tithe Farm

Shillingthorpe Park
Greatford Wood
Parsonage Field
Banks Farm
West Field
Weir
KING STREET
Stowe Farm
Sand & Gravel Pit

Great Maidens
PH
Barholm
Old Hall
Marsh Plantation
Beck Field
Sand & Gravel Pit
Far Field
Towngate
MILLFIELD RD

Cow Pasture Plantation
Cank Wood
Cedar Plantation
Casewick Field
Greatford Cut
Rectory Farm
Crown Farm
Mill Field
A16

07 A 08 B 09 C 10 D 11 E 12 F

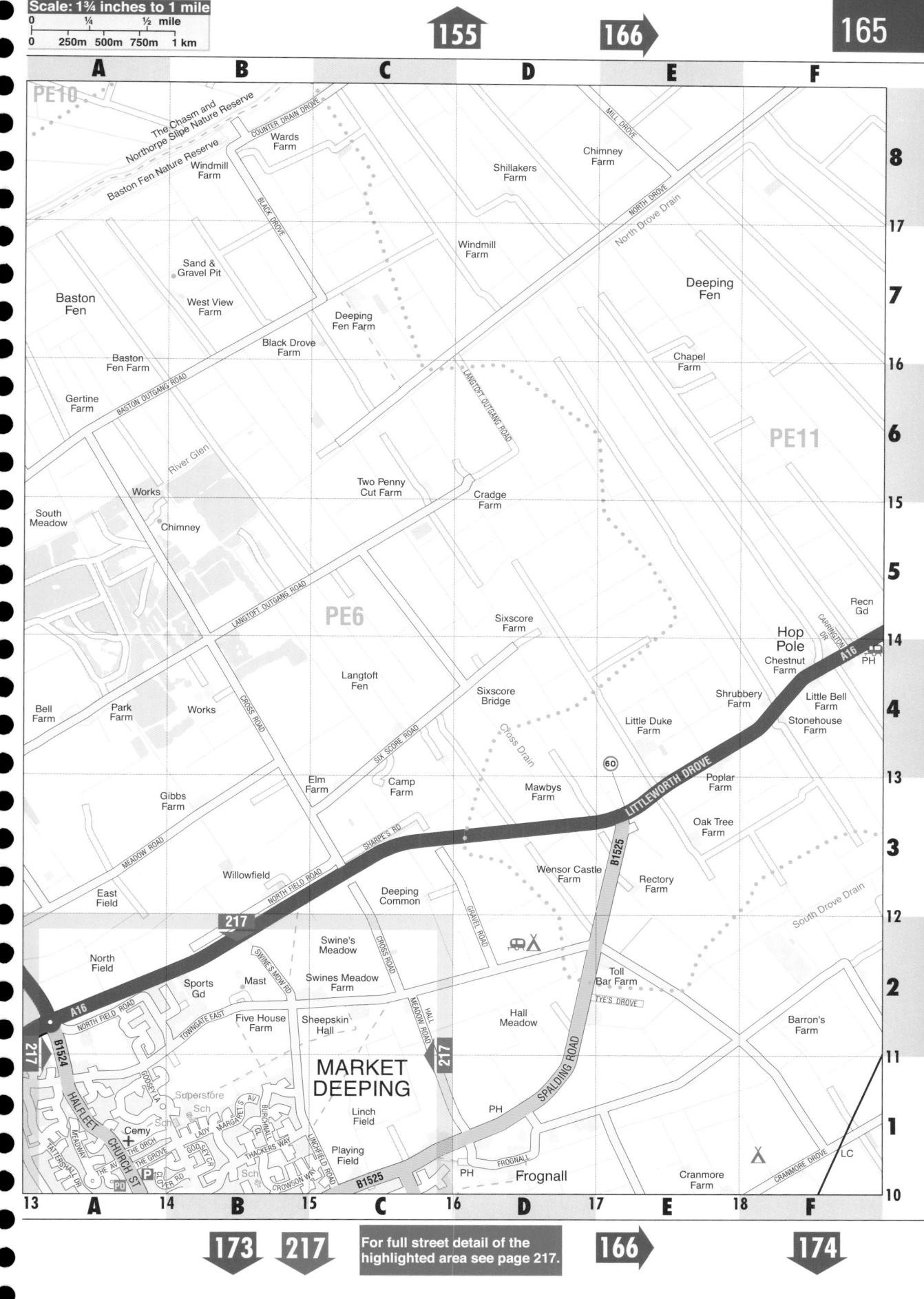

A   B   C   D   E   F

PE10

The Chasm and
Northorpe Slipe Nature Reserve

Baston Fen Nature Reserve

Wards
Farm

Counter Drain Drove

Windmill
Farm

Black Drove

Shillakers
Farm

Chimney
Farm

Mill Drove

8

North Drove

17

Baston
Fen

Sand &
Gravel Pit

West View
Farm

Black Drove
Farm

Windmill
Farm

North Drove Drain

Deeping
Fen

7

Baston
Fen Farm

Deeping
Fen Farm

Gertine
Farm

Baston Outgang Road

Langtoft Outgang Road

Chapel
Farm

16

PE11

6

River Glen

Works

Two Penny
Cut Farm

Cradge
Farm

South
Meadow

Chimney

15

PE6

Sixscore
Farm

Hop
Pole

Recn
Gd

Carrington Dr

A16

PH

14

Langtoft Outgang Road

Langtoft
Fen

Sixscore
Bridge

Cross Drain

Little Duke
Farm

Chestnut
Farm

Shrubbery
Farm

Little Bell
Farm

Stonehouse
Farm

5

4

Bell
Farm

Park
Farm

Works

Cross Road

Six Score Road

Elm
Farm

Camp
Farm

Mawbys
Farm

60

Littleworth Drove

Poplar
Farm

Oak Tree
Farm

13

Gibbs
Farm

Meadow Road

Sharpe's Rd

Wensor Castle
Farm

B1525

Rectory
Farm

South Drove Drain

3

East
Field

Willowfield

North Field Road

Deeping
Common

Gravel Road

12

217

North
Field

Swine's
Meadow

Cross Road

Swine's Mdw Rd

Mast

Swines Meadow
Farm

Meadow Road

Toll
Bar Farm

Tye's Drove

Barron's
Farm

2

Sports
Gd

Five House
Farm

Sheepskin
Hall

217

Hall
Meadow

B1524

A16

North Field Road

Towngate East

MARKET
DEEPING

Linch
Field

Spalding Road

PH

11

217

Superstore

Sch

Lady
Margaret's Av

Burghall

Thackers Way

Linchfield Rd

Playing
Field

PH

PH

Frognall

Cranmore
Farm

Cranmore Drove

LC

1

Halfleet

Church St

Meadow

Godsey La

The Orch

Cemy

The Av

Tattershall Dr

PO

P

The Grove

God. Ct

Lindsey Rd

Crowson Way

Sch

B1525

Frognall

10

13   A   14   B   15   C   16   D   17   E   18   F

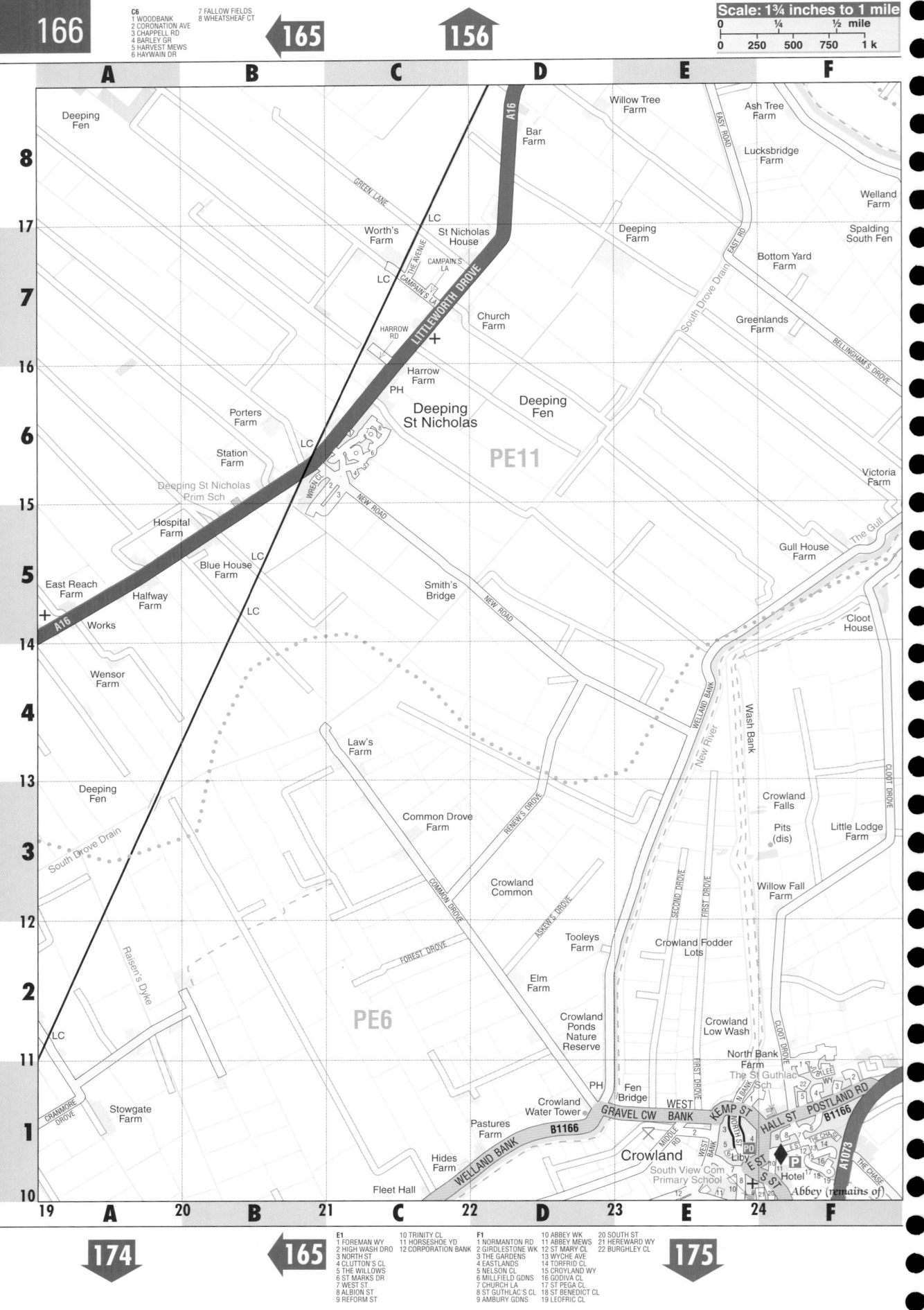

C6
1 WOODBANK
2 CORONATION AVE
3 CHAPPELL RD
4 BARLEY GR
5 HARVEST MEWS
6 HAYWAIN DR
7 FALLOW FIELDS
8 WHEATSHEAF CT

A   B   C   D   E   F

Deeping Fen

A16

Bar Farm

Willow Tree Farm

Ash Tree Farm

Lucksbridge Farm

EAST ROAD

Welland Farm

GREEN LANE

LC

St Nicholas House

Deeping Farm

EAST RD

Spalding South Fen

Worth's Farm

THE AVENUE

CAMPAIN'S LA

LC

CAMPAIN'S LA

LITTLEWORTH DROVE

SOUTH DROVE DRAIN

Bottom Yard Farm

Church Farm

Greenlands Farm

BELLINGHAM'S DROVE

HARROW RD

Harrow Farm

PH

Deeping St Nicholas

Deeping Fen

Porters Farm

PE11

Station Farm

LC

WREN CL

Victoria Farm

Deeping St Nicholas Prim Sch

The Gull

NEW ROAD

Hospital Farm

Gull House Farm

Blue House Farm

LC

East Reach Farm

Halfway Farm

Smith's Bridge

NEW ROAD

Cloot House

A16

Works

LC

Wensor Farm

WELLAND BANK

Deeping Fen

Law's Farm

Wash Bank

New River

Crowland Falls

Little Lodge Farm

Pits (dis)

SOUTH DROVE DRAIN

Common Drove Farm

RENEW'S DROVE

Willow Fall Farm

Raisen's Dyke

COMMON DROVE

Crowland Common

ASKEW'S DROVE

SECOND DROVE

FIRST DROVE

Crowland Fodder Lots

Tooleys Farm

PE6

FOREST DROVE

Elm Farm

Crowland Low Wash

North Bank Farm

The St Guthlac Sch

POSTLAND RD

B1166

Crowland Ponds Nature Reserve

N BANK RD

LC

PH

Fen Bridge

WEST BANK

KEMP ST

HALL ST

THE CHASE

CRAMMORE DROVE

Stowgate Farm

Crowland Water Tower

GRAVEL CW

WEST BANK

NORTH ST

PO

Liby

A1073

B1166

MIDDLE RD

P

Hotel

Pastures Farm

WELLAND BANK

Hides Farm

Crowland

South View Com Primary School

Abbey (remains of)

Fleet Hall

A   B   C   D   E   F

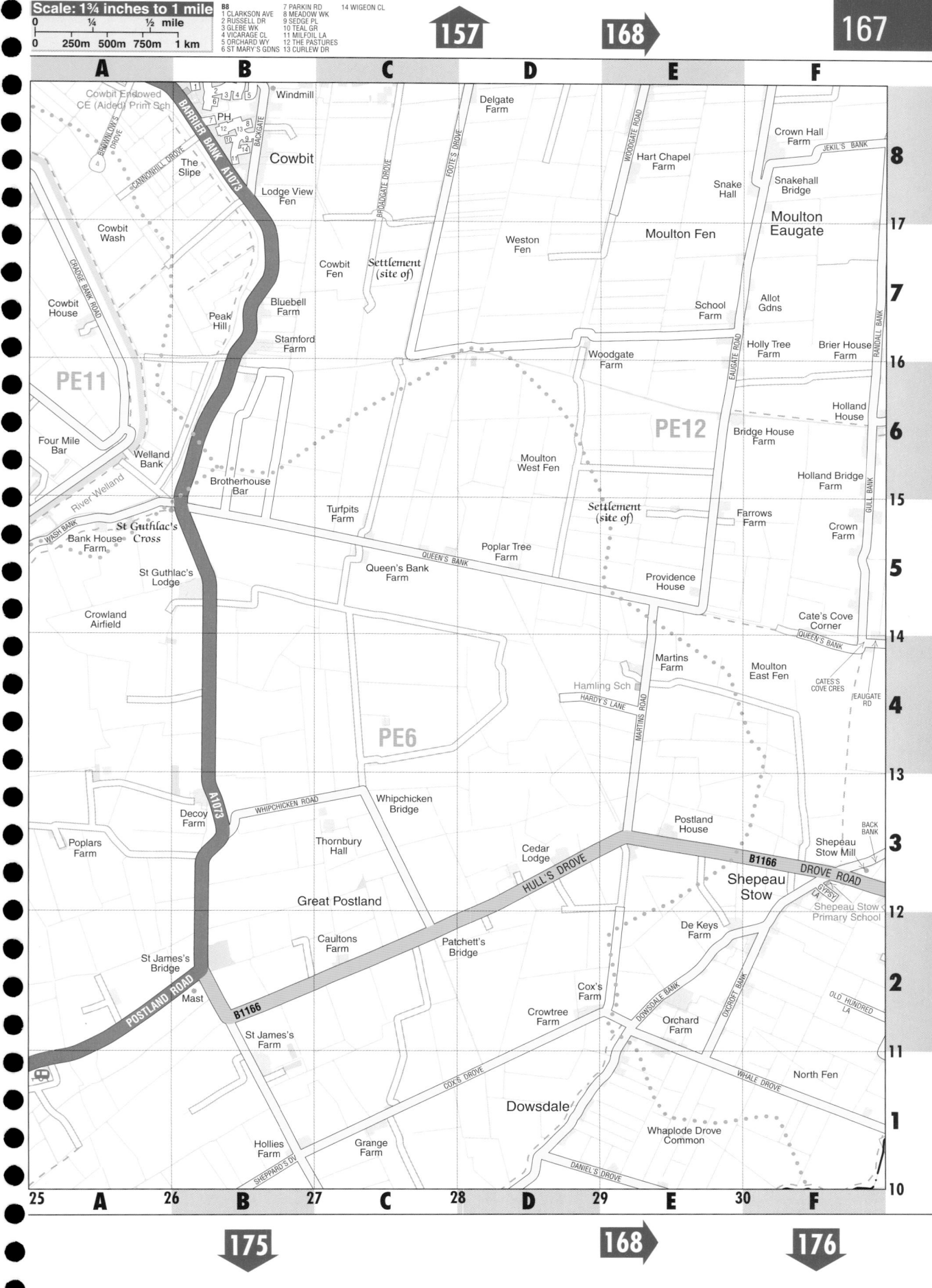

Scale: 1¾ inches to 1 mile

0   ¼   ½   mile
0   250m   500m   750m   1 km

B8
1 CLARKSON AVE
2 RUSSELL DR
3 GLEBE WK
4 VICARAGE CL
5 ORCHARD WY
6 ST MARY'S GDNS
7 PARKIN RD
8 MEADOW WK
9 SEDGE PL
10 TEAL GR
11 MILFOIL LA
12 THE PASTURES
13 CURLEW DR
14 WIGEON CL

157

168

Cowbit Endowed CE (Aided) Prim Sch
Windmill
Delgate Farm
Crown Hall Farm
JEKIL'S BANK
BROWNLOW'S DROVE
CANNONHILL DROVE
The Slipe
PH
BACKGATE
Cowbit
Hart Chapel Farm
Snake Hall
Snakehall Bridge
8
Lodge View Fen
Moulton Eaugate
WOODGATE ROAD
Cowbit Wash
Cowbit Fen
Weston Fen
Moulton Fen
17
CRADGE BANK ROAD
Cowbit House
BARRIER BANK A1073
Peak Hill
Bluebell Farm
Cowbit Fen
Settlement (site of)
BROADGATE DROVE
FOOTE'S DROVE
School Farm
Allot Gdns
7
PE11
Stamford Farm
Woodgate Farm
Holly Tree Farm
EAUGATE ROAD
Brier House Farm
16
RANDALL BANK
Four Mile Bar
Welland Bank
PE12
Bridge House Farm
Holland House
6
Brotherhouse Bar
Moulton West Fen
Holland Bridge Farm
GULL BANK
River Welland
Turfpits Farm
Settlement (site of)
Farrows Farm
15
WASH BANK
Bank House Farm
St Guthlac's Cross
Queen's Bank Farm
QUEEN'S BANK
Poplar Tree Farm
Crown Farm
5
St Guthlac's Lodge
Providence House
Cate's Cove Corner
14
Crowland Airfield
Martins Farm
Moulton East Fen
QUEEN'S BANK
CATES'S COVE CRES
EAUGATE RD
4
Hamling Sch
HARDY'S LANE
MARTINS ROAD
PE6
13
A1073
Decoy Farm
WHIPCHICKEN ROAD
Whipchicken Bridge
Postland House
BACK BANK
Shepeau Stow Mill
3
Poplars Farm
Thornbury Hall
Cedar Lodge
HULL'S DROVE
B1166 DROVE ROAD
Shepeau Stow
GYPSY LA
De Keys Farm
Great Postland
Shepeau Stow Primary School
12
Caultons Farm
Patchett's Bridge
DOWSDALE BANK
OXCROFT BANK
OLD HUNDRED LA
2
St James's Bridge
POSTLAND ROAD
Mast
B1166
St James's Farm
Crowtree Farm
Cox's Farm
Orchard Farm
North Fen
WHALE DROVE
11
Dowsdale
COX'S DROVE
Whaplode Drove Common
1
Hollies Farm
Grange Farm
SHEPPARD'S DV
DANIEL'S DROVE
10

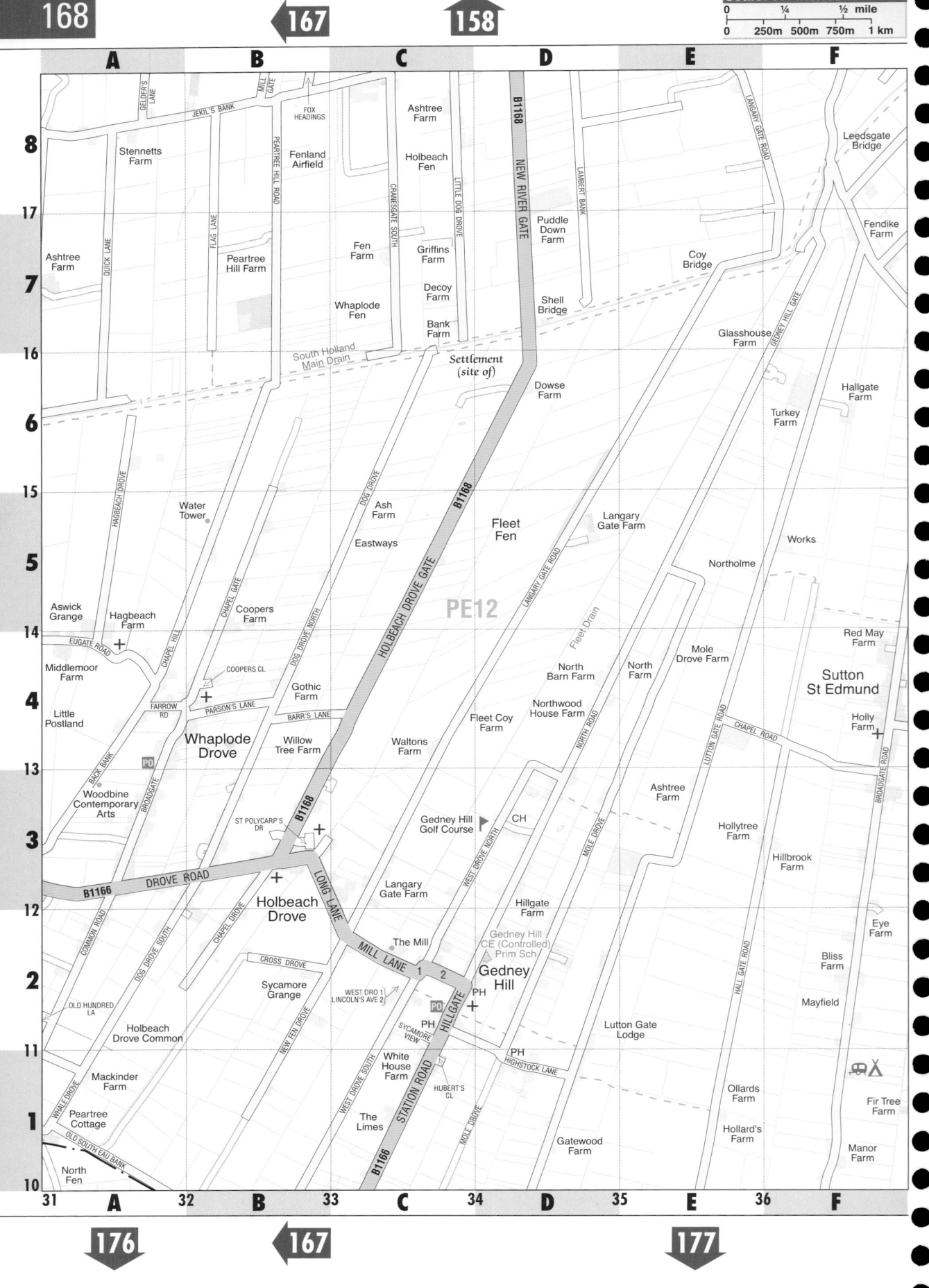

Scale: 1¾ inches to 1 mile

| 0 | ¼ | ½ | mile |

| 0 | 250m | 500m | 750m | 1 km |

A **B** **C** **D** **E** **F**

GELDER'S LANE

JEKIL'S BANK

MILL GATE

FOX HEADINGS

B1168

LANGARY GATE ROAD

8 Stennetts Farm

Fenland Airfield

Ashtree Farm

Holbeach Fen

NEW RIVER GATE

LAMBERT BANK

Leedsgate Bridge

PEARTREE HILL ROAD

QUICK LANE

FLAG LANE

17

Coy Bridge

Fendike Farm

7 Ashtree Farm

Peartree Hill Farm

Fen Farm

Griffins Farm

Decoy Farm

Puddle Down Farm

Shell Bridge

Glasshouse Farm

GEDNEY HILL GATE

Whaplode Fen

Bank Farm

CRANESGATE SOUTH

LITTLE DOG DROVE

Hallgate Farm

16

South Holland Main Drain

Settlement (site of)

Dowse Farm

Turkey Farm

6

HAGBEACH DROVE

DOG DROVE

Water Tower

Ash Farm

Eastways

HOLBEACH DROVE GATE

B1168

Fleet Fen

Langary Gate Farm

LANGARY GATE ROAD

Northolme

Works

15

Glasshouse Farm

5

PE12

Red May Farm

14 Aswick Grange

Hagbeach Farm

CHAPEL GATE

Coopers Farm

DOG DROVE NORTH

Gothic Farm

North Barn Farm

North Farm

Mole Drove Farm

Sutton St Edmund

Fleet Drain

4 Middlemoor Farm

CHAPEL HILL

FARROW RD

COOPERS CL

PARSON'S LANE

BARR'S LANE

Waltons Farm

Fleet Coy Farm

Northwood House Farm

NORTH ROAD

LUTTON GATE ROAD

CHAPEL ROAD

Holly Farm

Little Postland

Whaplode Drove

Willow Tree Farm

BROADGATE ROAD

13 BACK BANK

PO

Woodbine Contemporary Arts

BROADGATE

St POLYCARP'S DR

B1168

Gedney Hill Golf Course

CH

Ashtree Farm

Hollytree Farm

Hillbrook Farm

3

DROVE ROAD

WEST DROVE NORTH

MOLE DROVE

12 B1166

Holbeach Drove

LONG LANE

CHAPEL DROVE

CROSS DROVE

Langary Gate Farm

Hillgate Farm

HALL GATE ROAD

Eye Farm

2 COMMON ROAD

DOG DROVE SOUTH

Sycamore Grange

MILL LANE 1

The Mill

2

Gedney Hill CE (Controlled) Prim Sch

Gedney Hill

PH

Lutton Gate Lodge

Bliss Farm

Mayfield

OLD HUNDRED LA

NEW FEN DROVE

WEST DRO 1 LINCOLN'S AVE 2

SYCAMORE VIEW

PO

HILLGATE

PH

PH

11

Holbeach Drove Common

White House Farm

HIGHSTOCK LANE

Ollards Farm

Fir Tree Farm

1 WHALE DROVE

Mackinder Farm

WEST DROVE SOUTH

STATION ROAD

HUBERT'S CL

The Limes

MOLE DROVE

Gatewood Farm

Hollard's Farm

Manor Farm

Peartree Cottage

OLD SOUTH EAU BANK

B1166

10 North Fen

A **B** **C** **D** **E** **F**

31 **32** **33** **34** **35** **36**

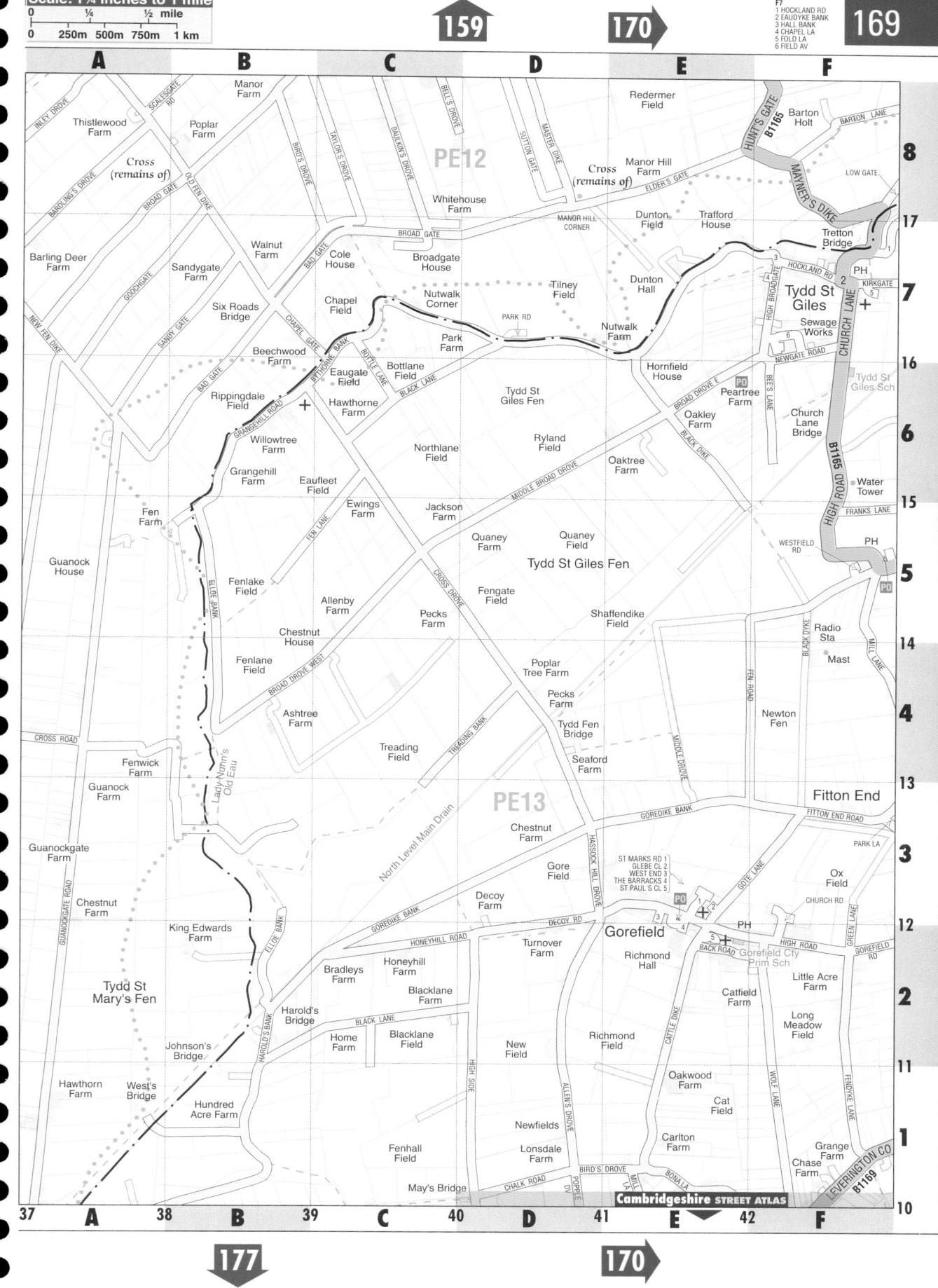

Scale: 1¾ inches to 1 mile

0   ¼   ½ mile
0 250m 500m 750m 1 km

159

170

169

F7
1 HOCKLAND RD
2 EAUDYKE BANK
3 HALL BANK
4 CHAPEL LA
5 FOLD LA
6 FIELD AV

A   B   C   D   E   F

Manor Farm

Inley Drove

Thistlewood Farm

Scalesgate Rd

Poplar Farm

Manor Farm

Bell's Drove

PE12

Redermer Field

Barton Holt

Barton Lane

B1165

Mayner's Dike

8

Cross (remains of)

Bardling's Drove

Old Fen Dike

Broad Gate

Goodgate

Taylor's Drove

Bird's Drove

Baulkin's Drove

Sutton Gate

Master Dike

Manor Hill Farm

Cross (remains of)

Elder's Gate

Hunt's Gate

Low Gate

17

Barling Deer Farm

Sandygate Farm

Sandy Gate

Walnut Farm

Cole House

Broad Gate

Whitehouse Farm

Broad Gate

Broadgate House

Manor Hill Corner

Dunton Field

Trafford House

Tretton Bridge

PH

17

Six Roads Bridge

Chapel Field

Nutwalk Corner

Tilney Field

Park Rd

Dunton Hall

Hockland Rd

Broadgate

Kirkgate

Tydd St Giles

7

New Fen Dike

Chapel Gate

Beechwood Farm

Bythorne Bank

Eaugate Field

Park Farm

Nutwalk Farm

Hornfield House

High

Newgate Road

Sewage Works

Church Lane

7

Rippingdale Field

Bottle Lane

Bottlane Field

Black Lane

Tydd St Giles Fen

Broad Drove E

Peartree Farm

Bee's Lane

Tydd St Giles Sch

16

Bad Gate

Hawthorne Farm

PO

Oakley Farm

Church Lane Bridge

B1165

16

Willowtree Farm

Grangehill Road

Northlane Field

Ryland Field

Oaktree Farm

Middle Broad Drove

Black Dike

6

Grangehill Farm

Eaufleet Field

Ewings Farm

Jackson Farm

High Road

Franks Lane

15

Fen Farm

Fen Lane

Quaney Farm

Quaney Field

Tydd St Giles Fen

Westfield Rd

Water Tower

PH

5

Guanock House

Eloe Bank

Fenlake Field

Allenby Farm

Pecks Farm

Fengate Field

Shaffendike Field

PO

15

Chestnut House

Fenlane Field

Broad Drove West

Treading Field

Treading Bank

Poplar Tree Farm

Pecks Farm

Black Dike

Radio Sta

Mast

Mill Lane

14

Fen Road

Ashtree Farm

Tydd Fen Bridge

Seaford Farm

Newton Fen

4

Cross Road

Lady Nunn's Old Eau

Fenwick Farm

North Level Main Drain

PE13

Goredike Bank

Fitton End

Fitton End Road

Middle Drove

13

Guanock Farm

Chestnut Farm

Gore Field

Park La

3

Guanockgate Farm

Guanockgate Road

Chestnut Farm

Decoy Farm

Hassock Hill Drove

St Marks Rd 1
Glebe Cl 2
West End 3
The Barracks 4
St Paul's Cl 5

Gote Lane

Ox Field

Church Rd

12

King Edwards Farm

Eloe Bank

Honeyhill Road

Decoy Rd

Turnover Farm

Gorefield

PO

PH

Gorefield City Prim Sch

Back Road

Richmond Hall

High Road

Little Acre Farm

Green Lane

Gorefield Rd

2

Tydd St Mary's Fen

Harold's Bank

Bradleys Farm

Honeyhill Farm

Blacklane Farm

Catfield Farm

Long Meadow Field

Johnson's Bridge

Harold's Bridge

Home Farm

Black Lane

Blacklane Field

New Field

High Side

Richmond Field

Cattle Dike

Oakwood Farm

Cat Field

Wolf Lane

11

Hawthorn Farm

West's Bridge

Hundred Acre Farm

Carlton Farm

Grange Farm

Fenoyke Lane

Chase Farm

1

Allen's Drove

Bona La

Mill

Fenhall Field

Newfields

Lonsdale Farm

Bird's Drove

Popple Dv

May's Bridge

Chalk Road

Leverington Co

B1169

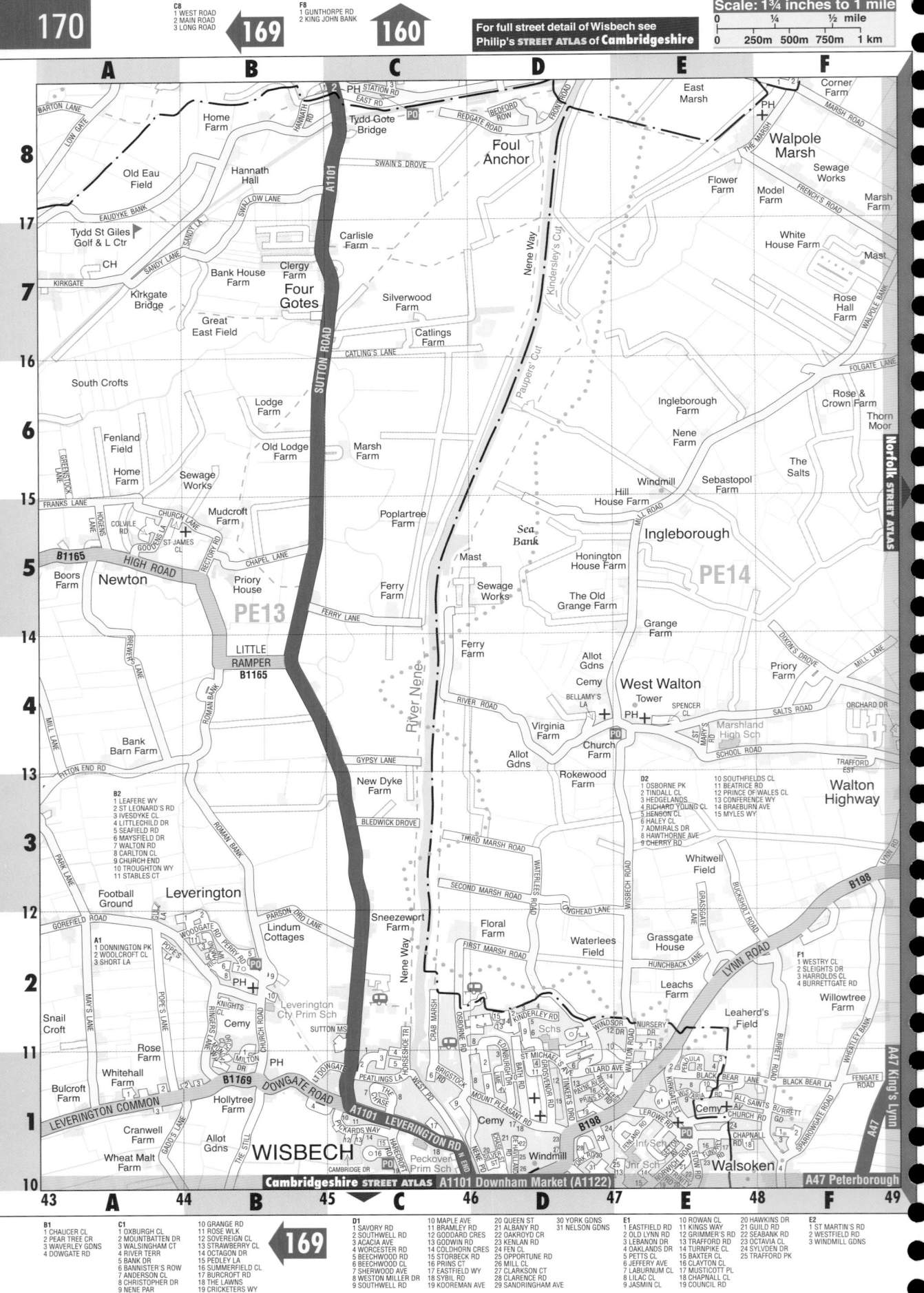

C8
1 WEST ROAD
2 MAIN ROAD
3 LONG ROAD

169

F8
1 GUNTHORPE RD
2 KING JOHN BANK

160

For full street detail of Wisbech see
Philip's STREET ATLAS of Cambridgeshire

Scale: 1¾ inches to 1 mile
0   ¼   ½   mile
0   250m 500m 750m 1 km

A   B   C   D   E   F

8
17
7
16
6
15
5
14
4
13
3
12
2
11
1
10

Map labels:

Home Farm, Old Eau Field, Hannath Hall, Tydd Gote Bridge, STATION RD, EAST RD, PH, PO, BEDFORD ROW, REDGATE ROAD, Foul Anchor, East Marsh, Walpole Marsh, PH, Corner Farm, MARSH ROAD

Eaudyke Bank, SWALLOW LANE, SWAIN'S DROVE, Flower Farm, Model Farm, Sewage Works, Marsh Farm, FRENCH'S ROAD

Tydd St Giles Golf & L Ctr, CH, KIRKGATE, Sandy Lane, SANDY LA, Bank House Farm, Clergy Farm, Four Gotes, Carlisle Farm, Nene Way, White House Farm, Mast

Kirkgate Bridge, Great East Field, Silverwood Farm, Catlings Farm, Kindersley's Cut, Rose Hall Farm

CATLING'S LANE, FOLGATE LANE

South Crofts, GREENSTOCK LANE, Lodge Farm, Paupers' Cut, Ingleborough Farm, Nene Farm, Rose & Crown Farm, Thorn Moor

Fenland Field, Home Farm, Old Lodge Farm, Marsh Farm, Windmill, Hill House Farm, Sebastopol Farm, The Salts

FRANKS LANE, Sewage Works, Mudcroft Farm, Poplartree Farm, Sea Bank, Ingleborough, PE14, MILL ROAD

HOGENS LA, COLVILE RD, GOODY'S LA, ST JAMES CL, CHURCH LANE, RECTORY RD, CHAPEL LANE, Mast, Honington House Farm

B1165, HIGH ROAD, Newton, Boors Farm, Priory House, PE13, Ferry Farm, Sewage Works, The Old Grange Farm, Grange Farm, DIXON'S DRIVE, MILL LANE

FERRY LANE, Allot Gdns, Cemy, BELLAMY'S LA, West Walton, Priory Farm

BREWERY LANE, LITTLE RAMPER, B1165, Ferry Farm, River Nene, RIVER ROAD, Tower, PH, SPENCER CL, Marshland High Sch, ORCHARD DR

Bank Barn Farm, ROMAN BANK, GYPSY LANE, Virginia Farm, Church Farm, ST MARY'S CL, SCHOOL ROAD, TRAFFORD EST

MILL LANE, FITTON END RD, PARK LANE, New Dyke Farm, BLEDWICK DROVE, Ferry Farm, Allot Gdns, Rokewood Farm, Walton Highway

B2, THIRD MARSH ROAD, Whitwell Field

Football Ground, Leverington, GOREFIELD ROAD, WOODGATE, PERRY RD, PARSON DRO LANE, Lindum Cottages, Sneezewort Farm, SECOND MARSH ROAD, WATERLEES ROAD, LONGHEAD LANE, Grassgate House, GRASSGATE LANE, BUCKSHOLT ROAD, B198

A1, MAY'S LANE, POPE'S LA, POPE'S LANE, KNIGHTS, RINGERS LANE, PO, PH, Leverington City Prim Sch, SUTTON MS, FIRST MARSH ROAD, Floral Farm, Waterlees Field, Leachs Farm, HUNCHBACK LANE, LYNN ROAD, F1

Snail Croft, Cemy, MILTON DR, PH, CHURCH ROAD, Nene Way, CRAB MARSH, HORSESHOE TR, OSBORNE RD, KINDERLEY RD, Schs, WINDSOR, NURSERY RD, Leaherd's Field, BURRETT ROAD, WHEATLEY BANK, Willowtree Farm

Rose Farm, Whitehall Farm, Hollytree Farm, B1169, DOWGATE ROAD, THE CHASE, PEATLINGS LA, WEST PD, BRIGSTOCK RD, Mount Pleasant Rd, ST MICHAEL'S, OLLARD AVE, WALTON ROAD, BLACK BEAR, BLACK BEAR LANE, FENGATE ROAD, A47 King's Lynn

Bulcroft Farm, Cranwell Farm, Allot Gdns, LEVERINGTON RD, PICKARDS WY, Cemy, B198, KIRKGATE, LEROWE RD, PO, ALL SAINTS CHURCH RD, BURRETT RD, A47

LEVERINGTON COMMON, A1101, CAMBRIDGE DR, Peckover Prim Sch, N END, Windmill, Jnr Sch, CHAPNALL RD, Walsoken

Wheat Malt Farm, WISBECH, CAMBRIDGE DR, PO

Cambridgeshire STREET ATLAS   A1101 Downham Market (A1122)   A47 Peterborough

43   A   44   B   45   C   46   D   47   E   48   F   49

Norfolk STREET ATLAS

B1
1 CHAUCER CL
2 PEAR TREE CR
3 WAVERLEY GDNS
4 DOWGATE RD

C1
1 OXBURGH CL
2 MOUNTBATTEN DR
3 WALSINGHAM CT
4 RIVER TERR
5 BANK DR
6 BANNISTER'S ROW
7 ANDERSON CL
8 CHRISTOPHER DR
9 NENE PAR

10 GRANGE RD
11 ROSE WLK
12 SOVEREIGN CL
13 STRAWBERRY CL
14 OCTAGON DR
15 PEDLEY LA
16 SUMMERFIELD CL
17 BURCROFT RD
18 THE LAWNS
19 CRICKETERS WY

D1
1 SAVORY RD
2 SOUTHWELL RD
3 ACACIA AVE
4 WORCESTER RD
5 BEECHWOOD RD
6 BEECHWOOD CL
7 SHERWOOD AVE
8 WESTON MILLER DR
9 SOUTHWELL RD

10 MAPLE AVE
11 BRAMLEY FD
12 GODDARD CRES
13 GODWIN RD
14 COLDHORN CRES
15 STORBECK RD
16 PRINS CT
17 EASTFIELD WY
18 SYBIL RD
19 KOOREMAN AVE

20 QUEEN ST
21 ALBANY RD
22 OAKROYD CR
23 KENLAN RD
24 FEN CL
25 OPPORTUNE RD
26 MILL CL
27 CLARKSON CT
28 CLARENCE RD
29 SANDRINGHAM AVE

30 YORK GDNS
31 NELSON GDNS

E1
1 EASTFIELD RD
2 OLD LYNN RD
3 LEBANON DR
4 OAKLANDS DR
5 PETTS CL
6 JEFFERY AVE
7 LABURNUM CL
8 LILAC CL
9 JASMIN CL

10 ROWAN CL
11 KINGS WAY
12 GRIMMER'S RD
13 TRAFFORD RD
14 TURNPIKE CL
15 BAXTER CL
16 CLAYTON CL
17 MUSTICOTT PL
18 CHAPNALL CL
19 COUNCIL RD

20 HAWKINS DR
21 GUILD RD
22 SEABANK RD
23 OCTAVIA CL
24 SYLVDEN DR
25 TRAFFORD PK

E2
1 ST MARTIN'S RD
2 WESTFIELD RD
3 WINDMILL GDNS

F1
1 WESTRY CL
2 SLEIGHTS DR
3 HARROLDS CL
4 BURRETTGATE RD

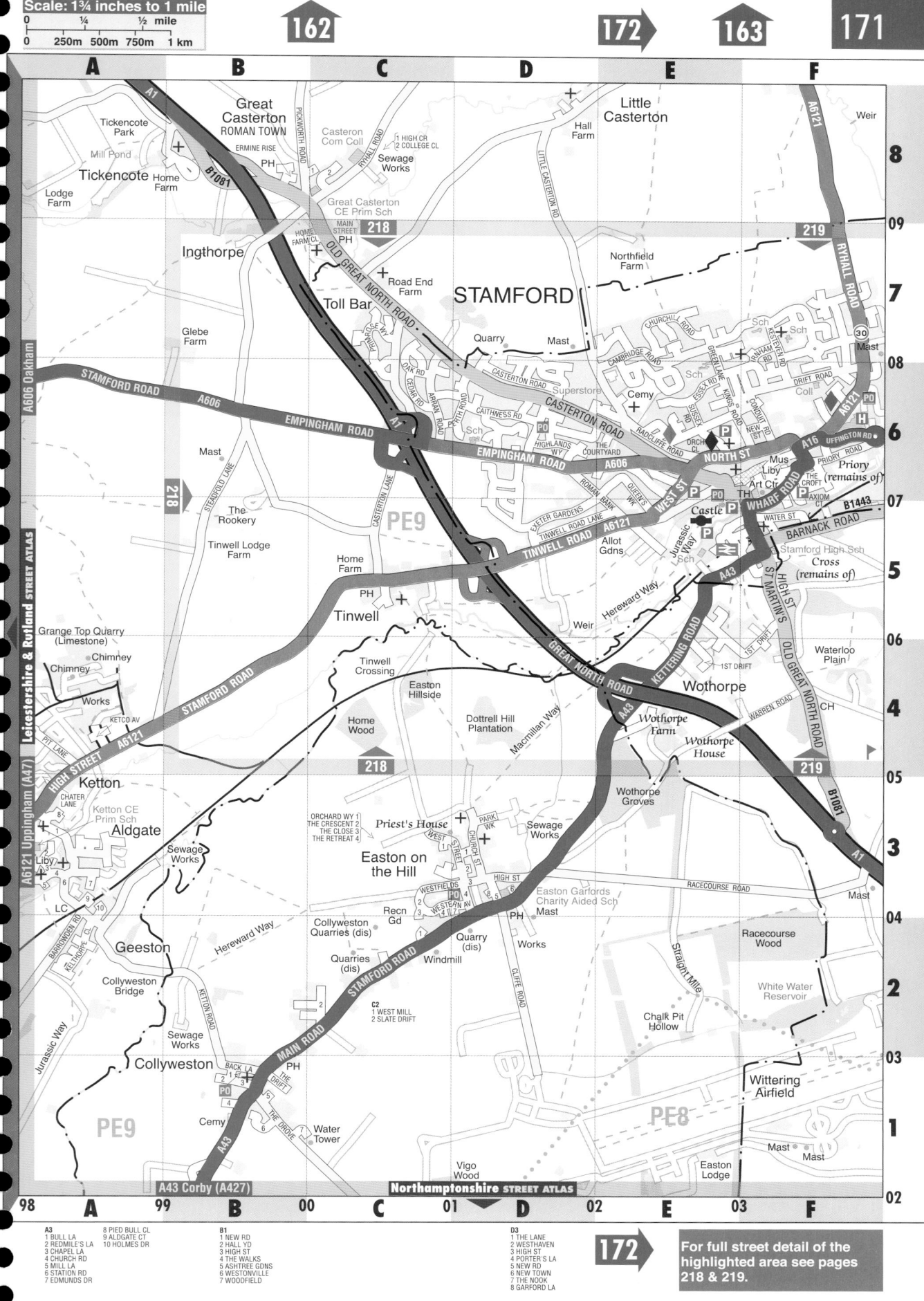

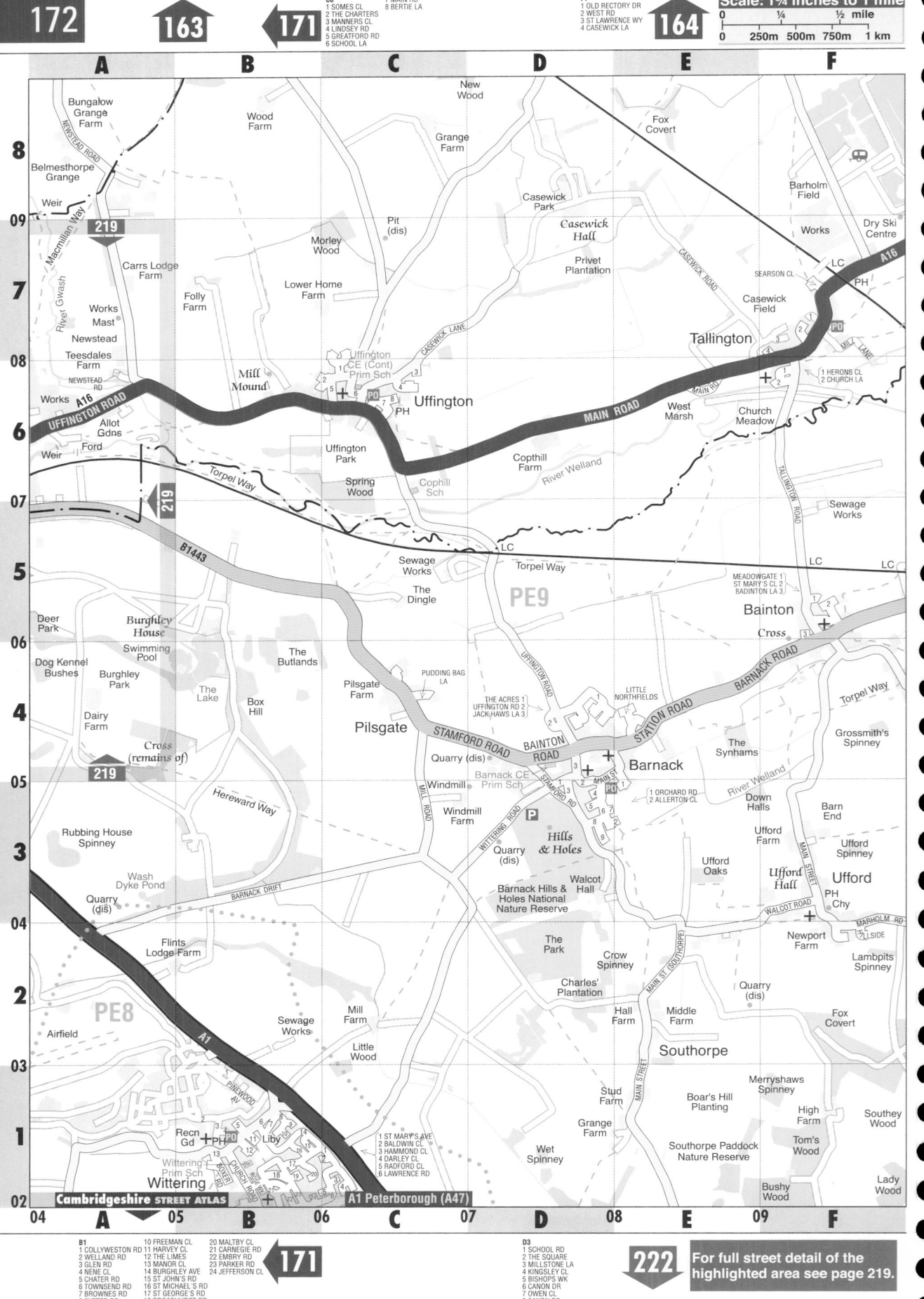

172

163

171

C6
1 SOMES CL
2 THE CHARTERS
3 MANNERS CL
4 LINDSEY RD
5 GREATFORD RD
6 SCHOOL LA

7 MAIN RD
8 BERTIE LA

F7
1 OLD RECTORY DR
2 WEST RD
3 ST LAWRENCE WY
4 CASEWICK LA

164

Scale: 1¾ inches to 1 mile
0   ¼   ½   mile
0   250m   500m   750m   1 km

Bungalow Grange Farm

Belmesthorpe Grange

Wood Farm

New Wood

Fox Covert

Barholm Field

Dry Ski Centre

Weir

219

Carrs Lodge Farm

Folly Farm

Morley Wood

Lower Home Farm

Pit (dis)

Grange Farm

Casewick Park

Casewick Hall

Privet Plantation

Works

LC

A16

PH

SEARSON CL

Casewick Field

PO

Works
Mast

Newstead

Teesdales Farm

NEWSTEAD RD

Mill Mound

Uffington CE (Cont) Prim Sch

PO

Uffington

Tallington

MILL LANE

1 HERONS CL
2 CHURCH LA

Works

A16

UFFINGTON ROAD

Allot Gdns

Weir   Ford

Torpel Way

Uffington Park

PH

Spring Wood

Copthill Sch

Copthill Farm

MAIN ROAD

West Marsh

River Welland

Church Meadow

TALLINGTON ROAD

Sewage Works

219

B1443

The Dingle

Sewage Works

Torpel Way

LC

PE9

LC   LC

MEADOWGATE 1
ST MARY'S CL 2
BADINTON LA 3

Bainton

Cross

Deer Park

Burghley House

Swimming Pool

The Butlands

Pilsgate Farm

PUDDING BAG LA

THE ACRES 1
UFFINGTON RD 2
JACK HAWS LA 3

Little Northfields

BARNACK ROAD

Torpel Way

Dog Kennel Bushes

Burghley Park

The Lake

Box Hill

Pilsgate

STAMFORD ROAD

UFFINGTON ROAD

STATION ROAD

Grossmith's Spinney

Dairy Farm

219

Cross (remains of)

Hereward Way

Quarry (dis)

Windmill

Barnack CE Prim Sch

BAINTON ROAD

MILL ROAD

STAMFORD RD

PO

Barnack

1 ORCHARD RD
2 ALLERTON CL

River Welland

Down Halls

The Synhams

Barn End

Ufford Farm

Ufford Spinney

Rubbing House Spinney

Quarry (dis)

Wash Dyke Pond

BARNACK DRIFT

Windmill Farm

P

WITTERING ROAD

Quarry (dis)

Hills & Holes

Walcot Hall

Barnack Hills & Holes National Nature Reserve

The Park

Ufford Oaks

Ufford Hall

Ufford

PH
Chy

WALCOT ROAD

Newport Farm

MARHOLM RD

LLSIDE

Lambpits Spinney

Flints Lodge Farm

PE8

A1

Sewage Works

Mill Farm

Little Wood

Crow Spinney

Charles' Plantation

MAIN ST ISOUTHORPE

Hall Farm

Middle Farm

Southorpe

Quarry (dis)

Fox Covert

Airfield

PINEWOOD AV

Recn Gd

PH

PO

Liby

1 ST MARY'S AVE
2 BALDWIN CL
3 HAMMOND CL
4 DARLEY CL
5 RADFORD CL
6 LAWRENCE RD

Stud Farm

Grange Farm

Wet Spinney

Boar's Hill Planting

MAIN STREET

Southorpe Paddock Nature Reserve

Merryshaws Spinney

High Farm

Tom's Wood

Southey Wood

Wittering Prim Sch

Wittering

CHURCH RD

A1 Peterborough (A47)

Bushy Wood

Lady Wood

B1
1 COLLYWESTON RD
2 WELLAND RD
3 GLEN RD
4 NENE CL
5 CHATER RD
6 TOWNSEND RD
7 BROWNES RD
8 EXETER RD
9 HOLT CL

10 FREEMAN CL
11 HARVEY CL
12 THE LIMES
13 MANOR CL
14 BURGHLEY AVE
15 ST JOHN'S RD
16 ST MICHAEL'S RD
17 ST GEORGE'S RD
18 BROADHURST RD
19 NEWMAN CL

20 MALTBY CL
21 CARNEGIE RD
22 EMBRY RD
23 PARKER RD
24 JEFFERSON CL

171

D3
1 SCHOOL RD
2 THE SQUARE
3 MILLSTONE LA
4 KINGSLEY CL
5 BISHOPS WK
6 CANON DR
7 OWEN CL
8 SAXON CL
9 WHITMAN CL

222

For full street detail of the highlighted area see page 219.

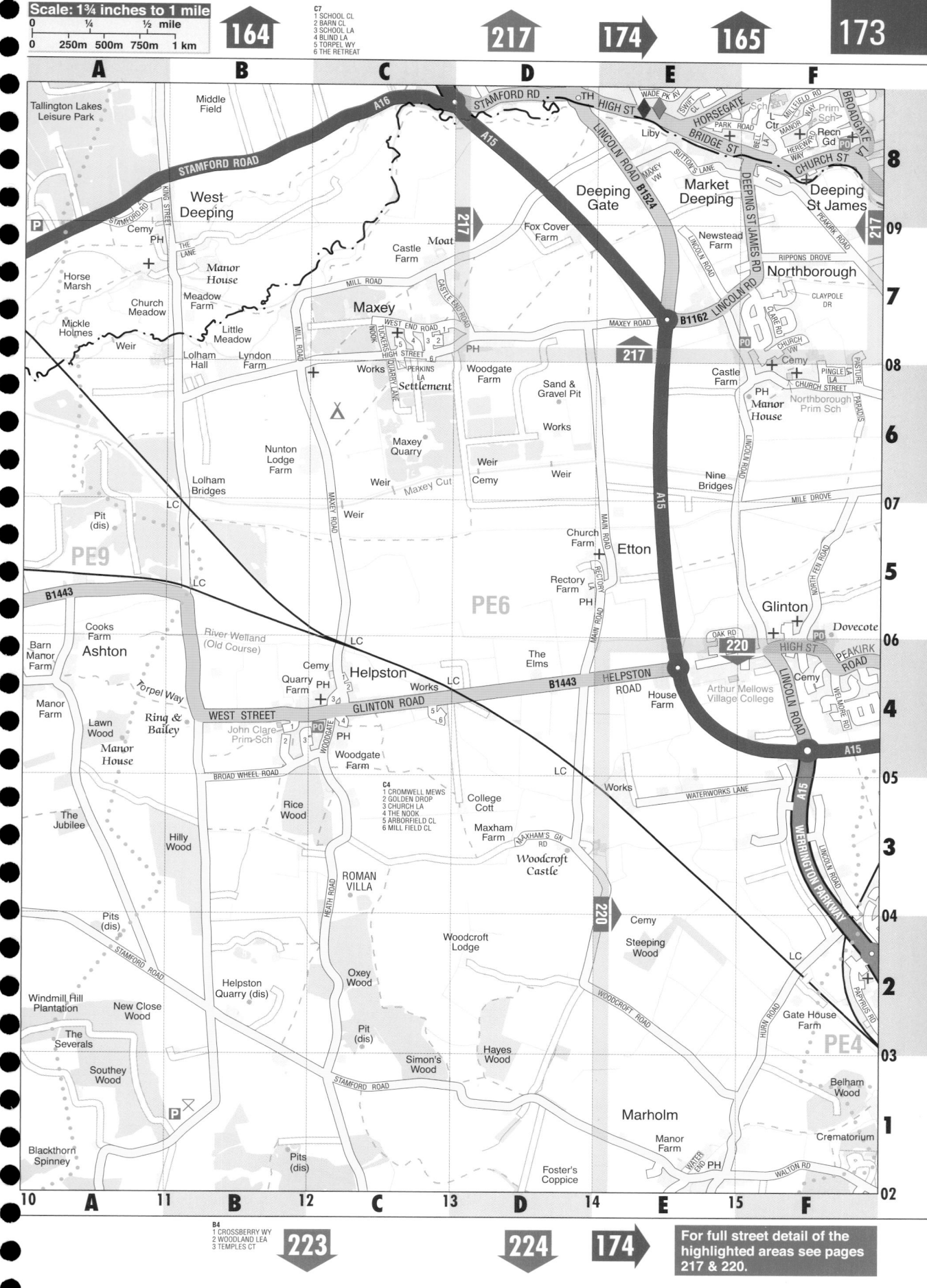

Scale: 1¾ inches to 1 mile

0 ¼ ½ mile
0 250m 500m 750m 1km

C7
1 SCHOOL CL
2 BARN CL
3 SCHOOL LA
4 BLIND LA
5 TORPEL WY
6 THE RETREAT

A   B   C   D   E   F

Tallington Lakes
Leisure Park

Middle
Field

STAMFORD ROAD
A16
A15

STAMFORD ROAD
KING STREET
Cemy
PH
THE LANE

West
Deeping

Horse
Marsh
Church
Meadow

Meadow
Farm

Manor
House

Mickle
Holmes
Weir

Little
Meadow

Lolham
Hall
Lyndon
Farm

MILL ROAD
Castle
Farm

Moat

Maxey

WEST END ROAD
TUCKERS NOOK
HIGH STREET
QUARRY LANE
CASTLE END ROAD
Settlement
PERKINS LA

Works

Woodgate
Farm

Fox Cover
Farm

Sand &
Gravel Pit

Works

STAMFORD RD
TH HIGH ST
WADE PK KY
ISMT CL
HORSEGATE
Liby
PARK ROAD
SUTTON'S LANE
BRIDGE ST

Sch
MILLFIELD RD
WAY PRIM
MANOR
HEREWARD
WAY
Recn
Gd
PO
CHURCH ST
BROADGATE

Deeping
Gate

MAXEY
VW

Market
Deeping

Deeping
St James

LINCOLN ROAD B1524

Newstead
Farm

Northborough

RIPPONS DROVE

CLAYPOLE
DR

DEEPING ST JAMES RD
PEAKIRK ROAD

PE9

Nunton
Lodge
Farm

Maxey
Quarry

Weir

Weir
Cemy

Weir

Maxey Cut

Lolham
Bridges

LC

MAXEY ROAD
Weir

LC

Pit
(dis)

MAXEY ROAD

Church
Farm
Etton

Rectory
Farm
PH

MAIN ROAD
RECTORY LA

Castle
Farm

PH
Manor
House

Northborough
Prim Sch

CHURCH STREET
PINGLE LA
PASTURE
PARADISE

Nine
Bridges

MILE DROVE

A15

PE6

LINCOLN ROAD

PO
Cemy
CHURCH VW

B1162
MAXEY ROAD

217

B1443

Cooks
Farm

Ashton

Barn
Manor
Farm

Torpel Way

Manor
Farm

Lawn
Wood

Manor
House

Ring &
Bailey

River Welland
(Old Course)

Cemy
Quarry
Farm
PH

Helpston

West Street
John Clare
Prim Sch
PO
PH
WOODGATE
GLINTON ROAD

Works

Broad Wheel Road

Woodgate
Farm

The
Elms

LC

LC

Helpston
HELPSTON ROAD

Glinton

HIGH ST
Dovecote

OAK RD
220
LINCOLN ROAD
Cemy
PO
PEAKIRK ROAD
WELMORE RD

Arthur Mellows
Village College

House
Farm

HELPSTON ROAD B1443

NORTH FEN ROAD

A15

The
Jubilee

Hilly
Wood

Rice
Wood

ROMAN
VILLA

HEATH ROAD

C4
1 CROMWELL MEWS
2 GOLDEN DROP
3 CHURCH LA
4 THE NOOK
5 ARBORFIELD CL
6 MILL FIELD CL

College
Cott

Maxham
Farm

MAXHAM'S GN RD

Woodcroft
Castle

Woodcroft
Lodge

LC

Works

WATERWORKS LANE

220

Cemy

Steeping
Wood

WERRINGTON PARKWAY
A15
LINCOLN ROAD

LC

Pits
(dis)

STAMFORD ROAD

Windmill Hill
Plantation

New Close
Wood

The
Severals

Southey
Wood

Blackthorn
Spinney

Helpston
Quarry (dis)

Oxey
Wood

Pit
(dis)

Simon's
Wood

STAMFORD ROAD

Woodcroft
Lodge

WOODCROFT ROAD

Hayes
Wood

Marholm

Manor
Farm

WATER END PH
WALTON RD

Gate House
Farm

PE4

Belham
Wood

Crematorium

PAPYRUS RD

Foster's
Coppice

A   B   C   D   E   F

B4
1 CROSSBERRY WY
2 WOODLAND LEA
3 TEMPLES CT

For full street detail of the
highlighted areas see pages
217 & 220.

10   11   12   13   14   15

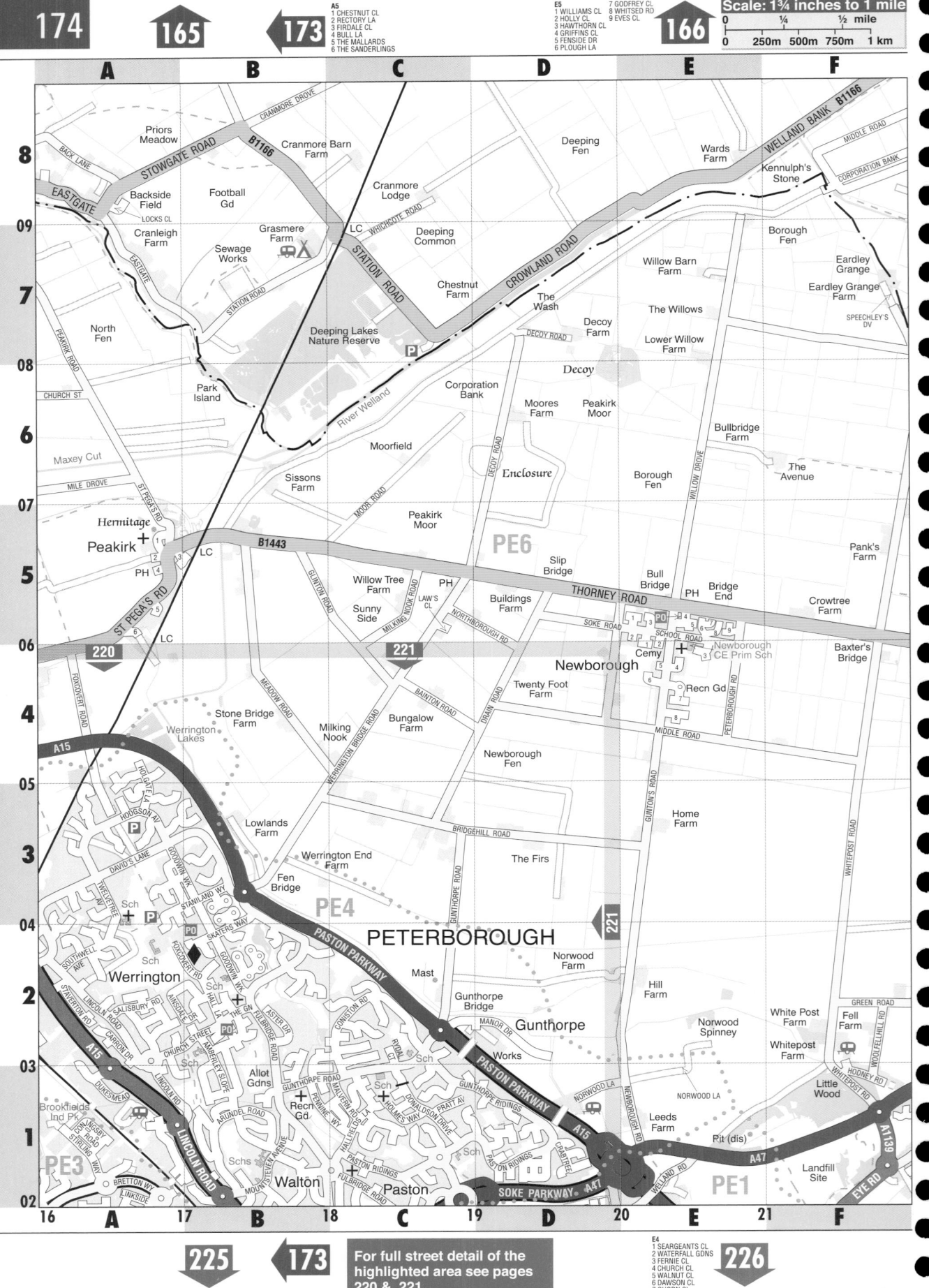

165

173

A5
1 CHESTNUT CL
2 RECTORY LA
3 FIRDALE CL
4 BULL LA
5 THE MALLARDS
6 THE SANDERLINGS

E5
1 WILLIAMS CL
2 HOLLY CL
3 HAWTHORN CL
4 GRIFFINS CL
5 FENSIDE DR
6 PLOUGH LA

7 GODFREY CL
8 WHITSED RD
9 EVES CL

166

Scale: 1¾ inches to 1 mile

0   ¼   ½   mile
0   250m   500m   750m   1 km

Priors Meadow
Cranmore Barn Farm
Deeping Fen
Wards Farm
Kennulph's Stone
Middle Road
Corporation Bank
B1166

BACK LANE
STOWGATE ROAD
B1166
Cranmore Lodge
WELLAND BANK

EASTGATE
Backside Field
Football Gd
WHICHCOTE ROAD
Deeping Common
Borough Fen
LOCKS CL
Cranleigh Farm
Sewage Works
Grasmere Farm
LC
CROWLAND ROAD
Willow Barn Farm
Eardley Grange
Eardley Grange Farm

EASTGATE
STATION ROAD
Chestnut Farm
The Wash
The Willows
SPEECHLEY'S DV

North Fen
STATION ROAD
Deeping Lakes Nature Reserve
DECOY ROAD
Decoy Farm
Lower Willow Farm

PEAKIRK ROAD
CHURCH ST
P
Park Island
River Welland
Corporation Bank
Decoy
Moores Farm
Peakirk Moor
Bullbridge Farm

Maxey Cut
Moorfield
Enclosure
Borough Fen
WILLOW DRIVE
The Avenue

MILE DROVE
ST PEGA'S RD
Sissons Farm
MOOR ROAD
Peakirk Moor
PE6
Pank's Farm

Hermitage
Peakirk
B1443
Slip Bridge
Bull Bridge
Bridge End
Crowtree Farm
PH
THORNEY ROAD
PH

LC
Willow Tree Farm
Buildings Farm
SOKE ROAD
P
LAW'S CL
PH
Baxter's Bridge

PH
Sunny Side
GUNTON ROAD
NORTHBOROUGH RD
Newborough CE Prim Sch
MILKING NOOK ROAD

LC
220
221
Cemy
Newborough
LC

Stone Bridge Farm
MEADOW ROAD
Bungalow Farm
BAINTON ROAD
DRAIN ROAD
Twenty Foot Farm
Recn Gd
GUNTON'S ROAD
PETERBOROUGH ROAD

Werrington Lakes
Milking Nook
WERRINGTON BRIDGE ROAD
Newborough Fen
MIDDLE ROAD

A15
FOXCOVERT RD
HOLGATE LA
HODGSON AV
P
Lowlands Farm
BRIDGEHILL ROAD
Home Farm
WHITEPOST ROAD

DAVID'S LANE
Werrington End Farm
The Firs
221

GOODWIN VW
Fen Bridge
GUNTHORPE ROAD
PE4
PETERBOROUGH
Norwood Farm
White Post Farm
GREEN ROAD
Fell Farm

STANILAND WY
Sch
PASTON PARKWAY
Mast
Hill Farm
Whitepost Farm
A139

Werrington
SKATERS WAY
Gunthorpe Bridge
Gunthorpe
Norwood Spinney
HODNEY RD
WHITEPOST RD

LINCOLN ROAD
PO
CONISTON RD
MANOR DR
Works
Little Wood
EYE RD

Allot Gdns
GUNTHORPE ROAD
GUNTHORPE RIDINGS
PASTON PARKWAY
NORWOOD LA
Leeds Farm
A47

Brookfields Ind Pk
DUKESMEAD
Recn Gd
DONALDSON DRIVE
PRATT AV
CRABTREE
A15
NORWOOD LA
Pit (dis)
Landfill Site

PE3
PE WAY
STIRLING WY
Schs
PASTON RIDINGS
SOKE PARKWAY
A47
WELLAND RD
PE1

16   A   17   B   18   C   19   D   20   E   21   F

225

173

For full street detail of the highlighted area see pages 220 & 221.

226

E4
1 SEARGEANTS CL
2 WATERFALL GDNS
3 FERNIE CL
4 CHURCH CL
5 WALNUT CL
6 DAWSON CL
7 QUORN CL
8 REEDMACE CL

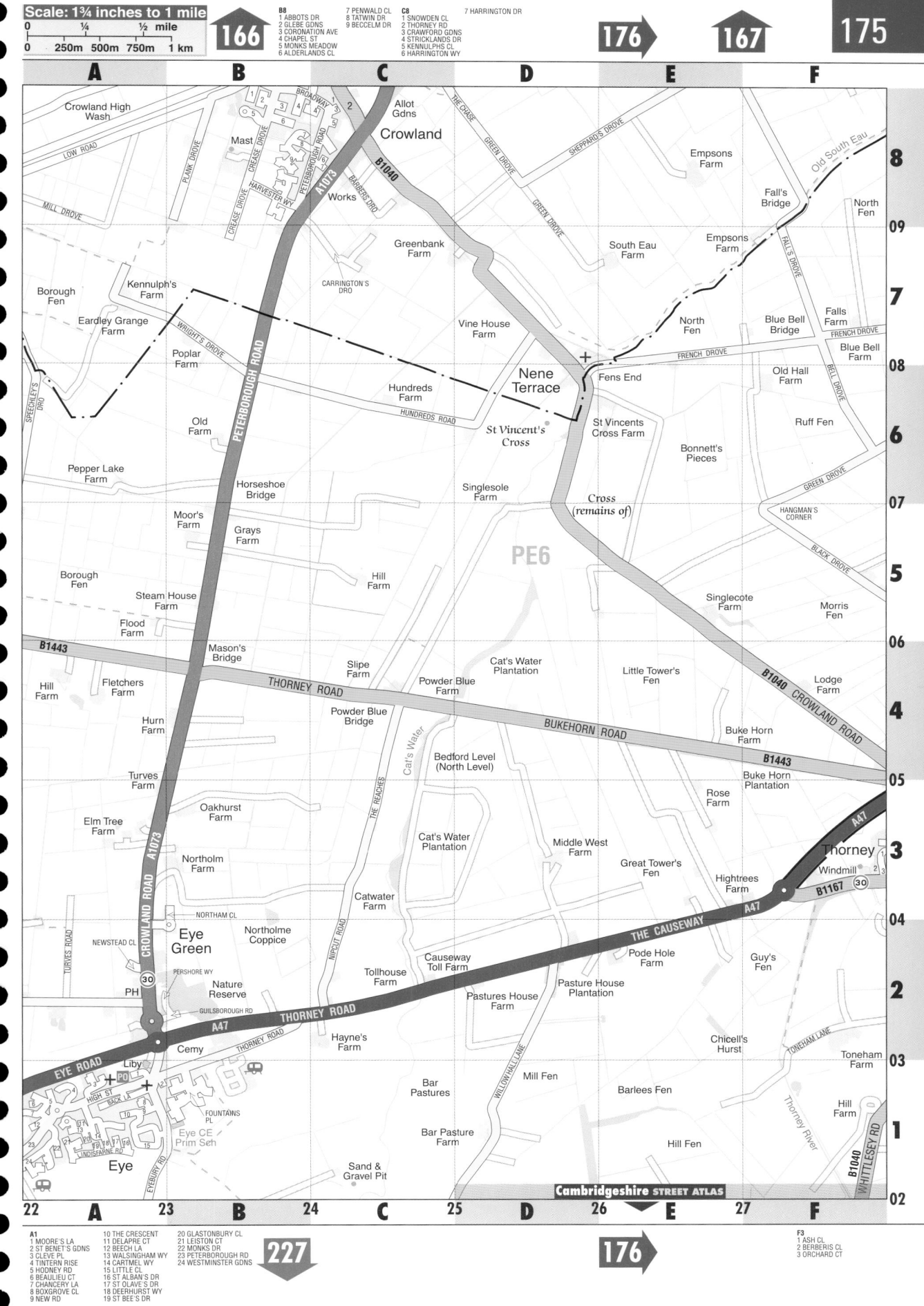

Scale: 1¾ inches to 1 mile

0 ¼ ½ mile
0 250m 500m 750m 1 km

166
176
167
175

A B C D E F

B8
1 ABBOTS DR
2 GLEBE GDNS
3 CORONATION AVE
4 CHAPEL ST
5 MONKS MEADOW
6 ALDERLANDS CL

7 PENWALD CL
8 TATWIN DR
9 BECCELM DR

C8
1 SNOWDEN CL
2 THORNEY RD
3 CRAWFORD GDNS
4 STRICKLANDS DR
5 KENNULPHS CL
6 HARRINGTON WY

7 HARRINGTON DR

Crowland High Wash
Allot Gdns
Crowland
Low Road
Mill Drove
Mast
Works
Greenbank Farm
Sheppard's Drove
Empsons Farm
Old South Eau
Fall's Bridge
North Fen
South Eau Farm
Empsons Farm
Kennulph's Farm
Borough Fen
Eardley Grange Farm
Carrington's Dro
Vine House Farm
North Fen
Blue Bell Bridge
Falls Farm
Poplar Farm
Wright's Drove
French Drove
French Drove
Blue Bell Farm
Nene Terrace
Fens End
Old Hall Farm
Hundreds Farm
Hundreds Road
St Vincent's Cross
St Vincents Cross Farm
Ruff Fen
Old Farm
Pepper Lake Farm
Bonnett's Pieces
Singlesole Farm
Cross (remains of)
Hangman's Corner
Horseshoe Bridge
PE6
Black Drove
Moor's Farm
Grays Farm
Singlecote Farm
Morris Fen
Borough Fen
Hill Farm
Steam House Farm
Flood Farm
B1443
Mason's Bridge
Slipe Farm
Powder Blue Farm
Cat's Water Plantation
Little Tower's Fen
Lodge Farm
Hill Farm
Fletchers Farm
Thorney Road
Powder Blue Bridge
Bukehorn Road
Buke Horn Farm
Hurn Farm
Bedford Level (North Level)
B1443
Turves Farm
Cat's Water
The Reaches
Buke Horn Plantation
A47
Elm Tree Farm
Oakhurst Farm
Cat's Water Plantation
Middle West Farm
Rose Farm
Thorney
Windmill
30
B1167
Northolm Farm
Great Tower's Fen
Hightrees Farm
A47
Catwater Farm
Northam Cl
Northolme Coppice
The Causeway
Pode Hole Farm
Guy's Fen
Newstead Cl
Eye Green
Pershore Wy
Nipcut Road
30
Nature Reserve
PH
Causeway Toll Farm
Pasture House Plantation
Tollhouse Farm
Pastures House Farm
Chicell's Hurst
Toneham Lane
Toneham Farm
Guilsborough Rd
A47
Thorney Road
Hayne's Farm
Willowhall Lane
Mill Fen
Barlees Fen
Thorney River
Hill Farm
Eye Road
Liby
PO
High St
Back La
Cemy
Thorney Road
Fountains Pl
Bar Pastures
Bar Pasture Farm
Hill Fen
B1040
Whittlesey Rd
Lindisfarne Rd
Eye CE Prim Sch
Eyebury Rd
Eye
Sand & Gravel Pit

A1
1 MOORE'S LA
2 ST BENET'S GDNS
3 CLEVE PL
4 TINTERN RISE
5 HODNEY RD
6 BEAULIEU CT
7 CHANCERY LA
8 BOXGROVE CL
9 NEW RD

10 THE CRESCENT
11 DELAPRE CT
12 BEECH LA
13 WALSINGHAM WY
14 CARTMEL WY
15 LITTLE CL
16 ST ALBAN'S DR
17 ST OLAVE'S DR
18 DEERHURST WY
19 ST BEE'S DR

20 GLASTONBURY CL
21 LEISTON CT
22 MONKS DR
23 PETERBOROUGH RD
24 WESTMINSTER GDNS

F3
1 ASH CL
2 BERBERIS CL
3 ORCHARD CT

Page numbers: 166, 176, 167, 175 (top); 227, 176 (bottom)

176
167
175
168

Scale: 1¾ inches to 1 mile
0   ¼   ½   mile
0   250   500   750   1 k

A B C D E F

8
09
7
08
6
07
5
06
4
05
3
04
2
03
1
02

North Fen
DOWSDAL BANK
Avenue Farm
French Farm
Gothic Farm
Gothic House Farm
Sycamore Farm
FRENCH DROVE
B1167
New South Eau
WEST DROVE SOUTH
STATION ROAD
B1166
MOLE DROVE
COMMON RD
Lordship End
LITTLEWORTH DV
Allen's Bridge
New South Eau
Ruff Fen
GREEN DROVE
FRENCH DROVE
Grange Farm
New Cut Bridge
Chestnut Farm
Malice Farm
SCOLDING DROVE
North Fen
Sutton St Edmund's Common
PE12
Lodge Farm
COMMON ROAD
Green Drove Farm
Morris Fen
Wrydelands Farm
ARCHERS DROVE
Wryde Croft
Gold Dike Farm
Gold Dike
Lodge Farm
Priests Farm
ENGLISH DROVE
Archer's Drove Farm
NEW CUT
BLACK DROVE
CH
Little House Farm
Desford Farm
Fish Fen
PE6
WALLACE'S DROVE
Nutsgrove Farm
Lime Tree Farm
White Hart Farm
Earl's Fen
Sewage Works
Wryde Plantation
Little Knarr Fen
A47
STATION RD
Thorney Heritage Mus
Thorney
Duke of Bedford Primary School
Cobbler's Fen
East Wryde Farm
B1167
Knarr Farm
WISBECH RD
Liby
1 PARK CL
2 PARK CRES
3 SMITHFIELD
Pigeons' Farm
WISBECH ROAD
PO
Abbey House
Cemetery
Ashley Pool
Park Farm
B1167
Corner Farm
A47
High Lands
A2
1 WHITTLESEY RD
2 ST BOTOLPH'S WY
3 ST MARY'S CL
4 ST PETER'S WY
5 ASHLEY POOL LA
6 TONEHAM LA
North Farm
Middle Knarr Fen
DAIRY DROVE
Glass House Farm
WHITTLESEY RD
B1040
Upper Knarr Fen
South Farm
West Corner Farm
Rattlerow Farm
OLD KNARR FEN DROVE
KNARR FEN ROAD
Hill Plantation
Lower Knarr Fen
PE13

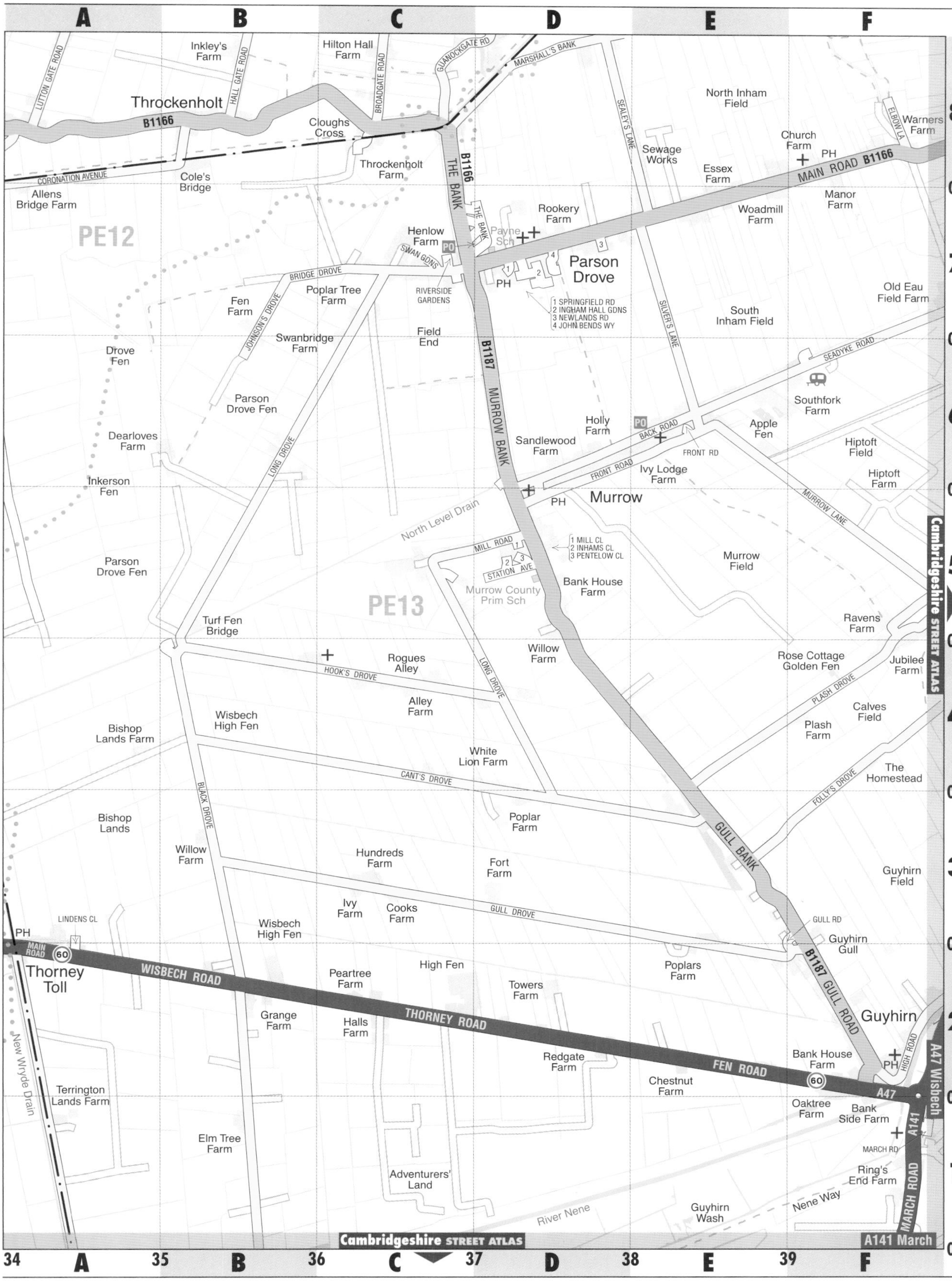

Scale: 1¾ inches to 1 mile
0 ¼ ½ mile
0 250m 500m 750m 1 km

 168
 169
 177

A B C D E F

Throckenholt
B1166

Inkley's Farm
Hilton Hall Farm
GUANOCKGATE RD
MARSHALL'S BANK
North Inham Field
Warners Farm
ELBOW LA
8

Cloughs Cross
Throckenholt Farm
BROADGATE ROAD
THE BANK
SEALEY'S LANE
Sewage Works
Church Farm PH
MAIN ROAD B1166
09

Cole's Bridge
CORONATION AVENUE
LUTTON GATE ROAD
HALL GATE ROAD
Essex Farm
Woadmill Farm
Manor Farm
7

Allens Bridge Farm
Henlow Farm
Payne Sch
Rookery Farm
Old Eau Field Farm

PE12
BRIDGE DROVE
SWAN GDNS
PO
PH
Parson Drove
1 SPRINGFIELD RD
2 INGHAM HALL GDNS
3 NEWLANDS RD
4 JOHN BENDS WY
08

Fen Farm
Poplar Tree Farm
RIVERSIDE GARDENS
Field End
JOHNSON'S DROVE
South Inham Field
SILVER'S LANE
SEADYKE ROAD
6

Drove Fen
Swanbridge Farm
B1187 MURROW BANK
Southfork Farm

Parson Drove Fen
LONG DROVE
Holly Farm
PO BACK ROAD
Apple Fen
Hiptoft Field
07

Dearloves Farm
Sandlewood Farm
Ivy Lodge Farm
FRONT RD
Hiptoft Farm

Inkerson Fen
PH
Murrow
FRONT ROAD
MURROW LANE

Parson Drove Fen
North Level Drain
MILL ROAD
1 MILL CL
2 INHAMS CL
3 PENTELOW CL
STATION AVE
Murrow Field
5

Turf Fen Bridge
PE13
Murrow County Prim Sch
Bank House Farm
Ravens Farm
06

Rogues Alley
HOOK'S DROVE
Willow Farm
LONG DROVE
Rose Cottage Golden Fen
Jubilee Farm

Alley Farm
PLASH DROVE
Calves Field
4

Wisbech High Fen
White Lion Farm
CANT'S DROVE
Plash Farm
FOLLY'S DROVE
The Homestead
05

Bishop Lands Farm
Poplar Farm
GULL BANK
Guyhirn Field
3

Bishop Lands
BLACK DROVE
Willow Farm
Hundreds Farm
Fort Farm

Ivy Farm
Cooks Farm
GULL DROVE
GULL RD
Guyhirn Gull
B1187 GULL ROAD
04

LINDENS CL
PH
MAIN ROAD (60)
Wisbech High Fen
High Fen
Poplars Farm

Thorney Toll
WISBECH ROAD
Peartree Farm
Towers Farm
Guyhirn
HIGH ROAD
A47 Wisbech

NEW WRYDE DRAIN
Grange Farm
Halls Farm
THORNEY ROAD
Redgate Farm
FEN ROAD (60)
Bank House Farm PH
A47
2

Terrington Lands Farm
Chestnut Farm
Oaktree Farm
Bank Side Farm
MARCH ROAD
A141
03

Elm Tree Farm
MARCH RD
Ring's End Farm
1

Adventurers' Land
River Nene
Guyhirn Wash
Nene Way

Cambridgeshire STREET ATLAS

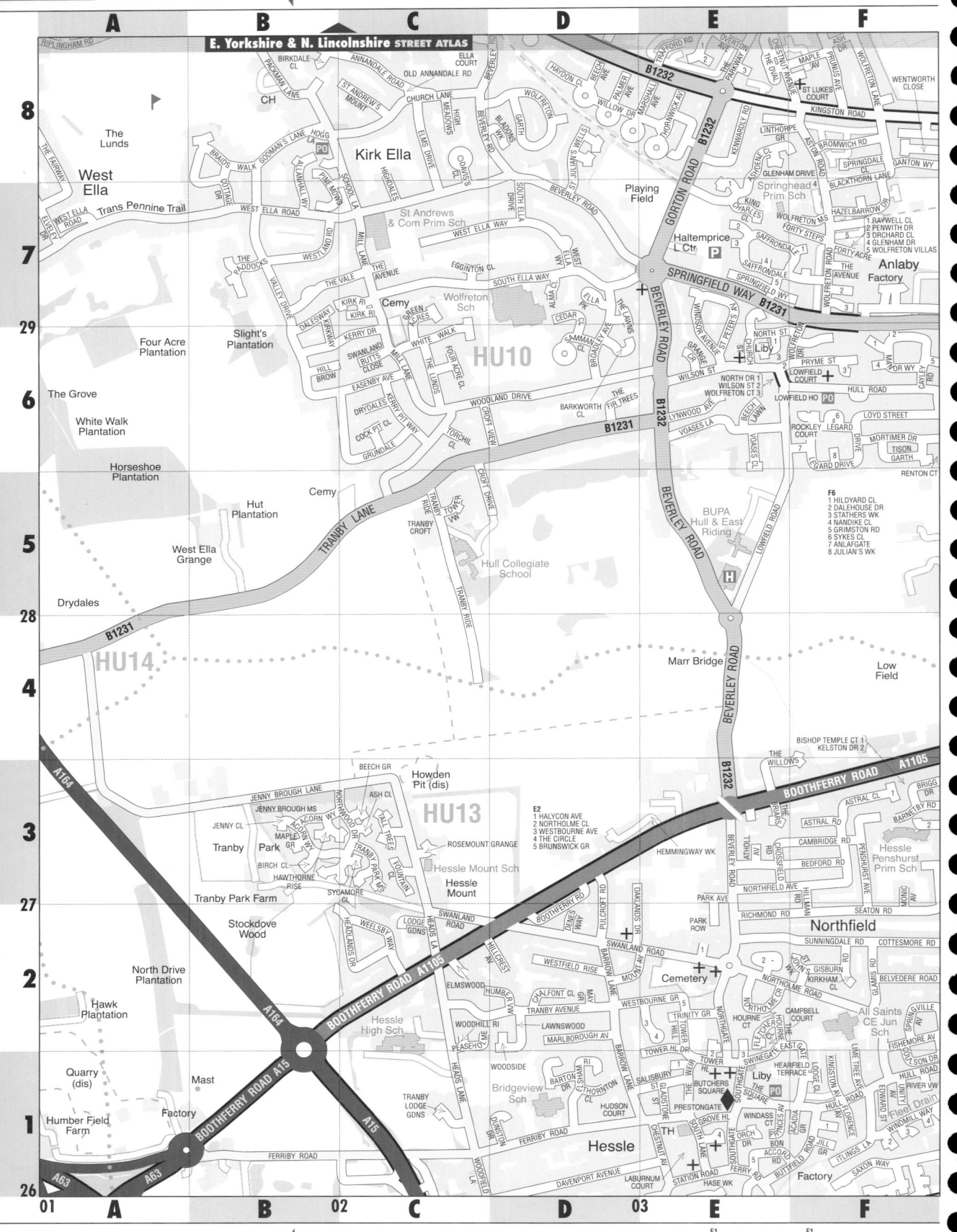

E. Yorkshire & N. Lincolnshire STREET ATLAS

A3	B7	C8	D8	E6	F6
1 BARNETBY RD 2 KELSTON DR 3 YARMOUTH AVE 4 WINTHORPE RD 5 BROCKLESBY CL 6 CORRAN GARTH	1 LANGFORD WK 2 HOLLYTREE AVE 3 LABURNUM DR 4 ROSEWOOD CL	1 PRIMROSE DR 2 COUNTY RD S	1 LOCKTON GR 2 HACKNESS GR 3 BARGATE GR 4 SNAINTON GR	1 AIRMYN AVE 2 ST MARTINS AVE	1 HAWTHORN CT

180 ▶ **179**

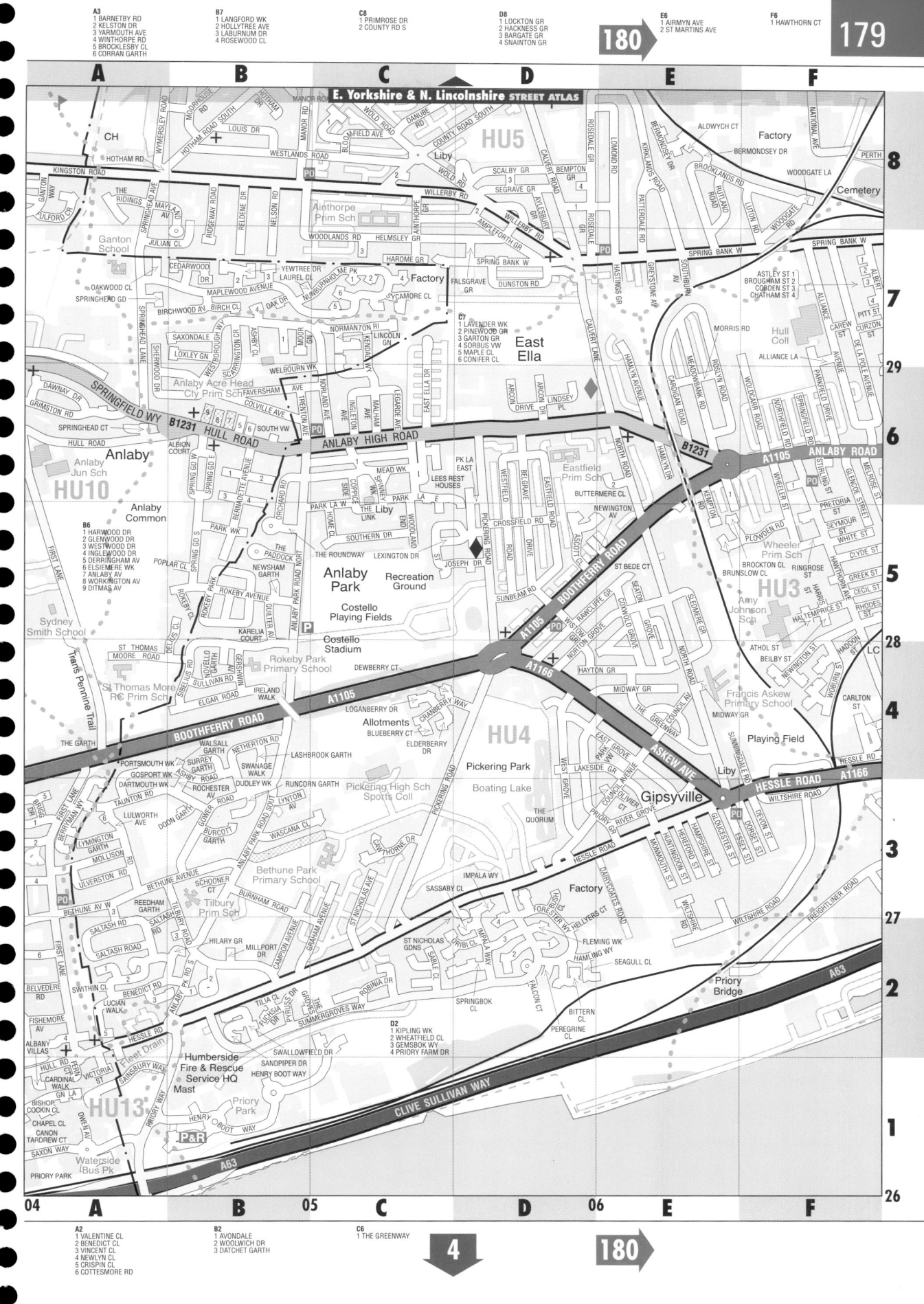

A2	B2	C6
1 VALENTINE CL 2 BENEDICT CL 3 VINCENT CL 4 NEWLYN CL 5 CRISPIN CL 6 COTTESMORE RD	1 AVONDALE 2 WOOLWICH DR 3 DATCHET GARTH	1 THE GREENWAY

▼ **4**   **180** ▶

A5
1 CORDELLA CL
2 DORADO CL
3 SANDLEMERE CL
4 DARRISMERE VILLAS
5 BRIXHAM CT
6 OTTERBURN ST

A6
1 GRANVILLE ST
2 SANDRINGHAM ST
3 COULTAS CT
4 ACLAND ST
5 LONSDALE ST
6 CARNEGIE ST

179

B8
1 ROXBURGH ST
2 LANARK ST

C6
1 KINGS LEIGH
2 KING'S CROSS CL
3 THORN LEIGH

D6
1 BLOOMSBURY CT
2 ARLINGTON ST
3 ALMOND GR
4 BLACKTHORN CT
5 SORBUS CT

D8
1 BERKELEY ST
2 CROMWELL CL
3 BROWNING CL
4 LEONARD ST
5 TRAFALGAR ST
6 SHAKESPEARE CL

E7
1 COLLEGE ST
2 BLAKE CL
3 MARLBOROUGH TERR
4 PRYME ST
5 PEARSON ST
6 SPENCER ST
7 REED ST
8 PERCY ST
9 PORTLAND PL
10 ALBION ST
11 STORY ST
12 Prospect Ctr

F7
1 CATHERINE ST
2 SYKES ST
3 CHARLES ST
4 EGGINTON ST
5 NEW GARDEN ST
6 WILBERFORCE DR

A4
1 JADE GR
2 ONYX GR
3 TOPAZ GR
4 CORSAIR GR
5 WESTBOURNE ST
6 GARNET GR
7 SAPPHIRE GR
8 EMERALD GR
9 ST NECTAN CL

B4
1 DIVISION RD
2 SEFTON ST
3 NEWTON ST
4 RIBBLE ST
5 RUGBY ST
6 DEE ST
7 ROSAMOND ST

B5
1 CAMDEN ST
2 ALBEMARLE ST
3 SIRIUS CL
4 GORDON ST
5 ALFONSO ST
6 CARRINGTON ST
7 AYLESFORD ST
8 ORION CL

179

C5
1 LYRIC CL
2 THORNWICK CL
3 BARBERRY CT
4 WINSHIP CL
5 EVER THORPE CL
6 TICHBOURNE CL
7 THE GARDENS
8 WESLEY CT
9 CAROL DICKSON CT

4

D5
1 GOODWIN PAR
2 HAZEL GR
3 FIRETHORN CL
4 NEWPORT CL
5 PEACH TREE CT
6 ELDERWOOD CT
7 QUANTOCK CL
8 BATHURST ST
9 MECHANIC LA

For full street detail of Hull see Philip's STREET ATLAS of East Yorkshire

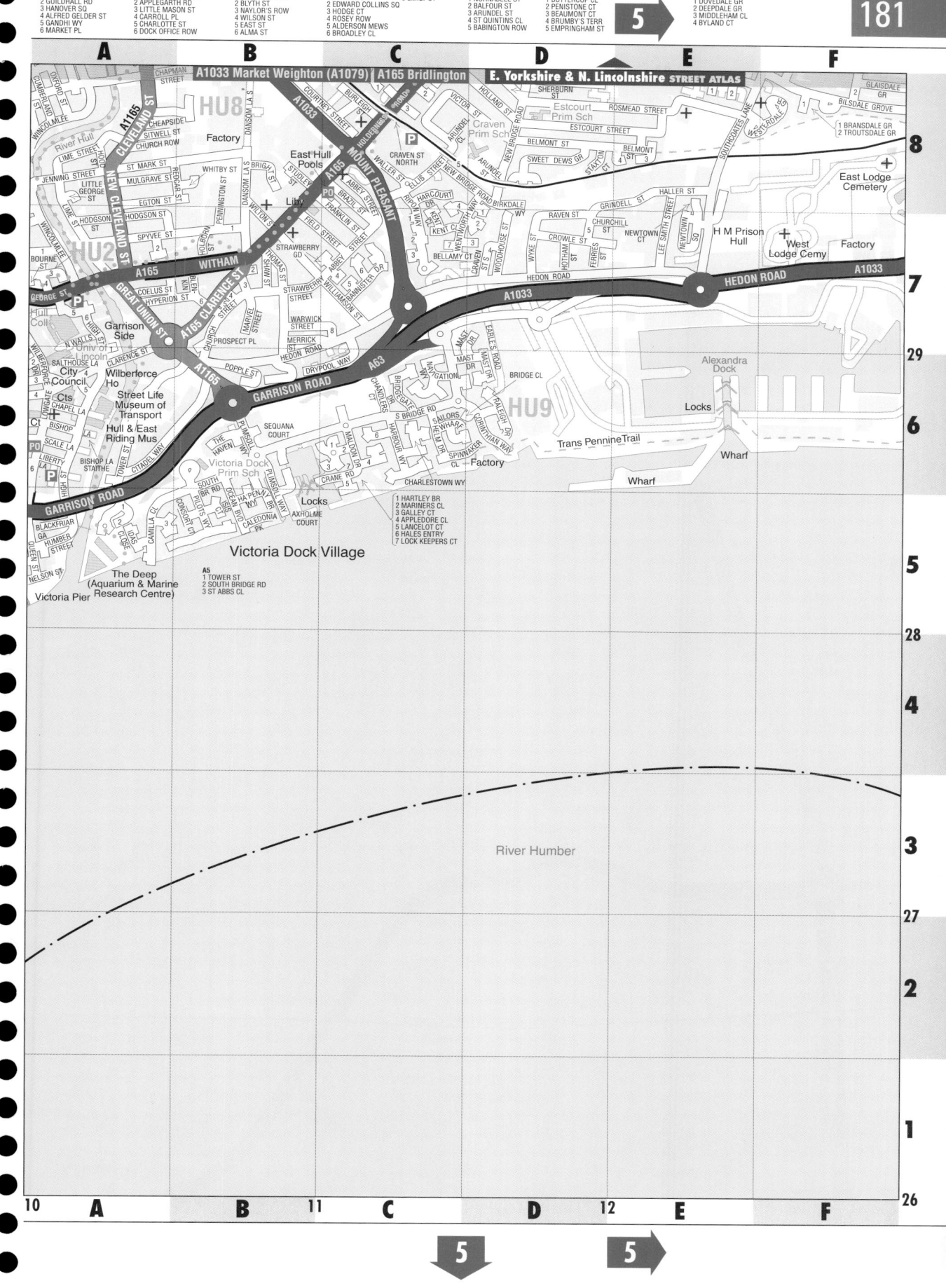

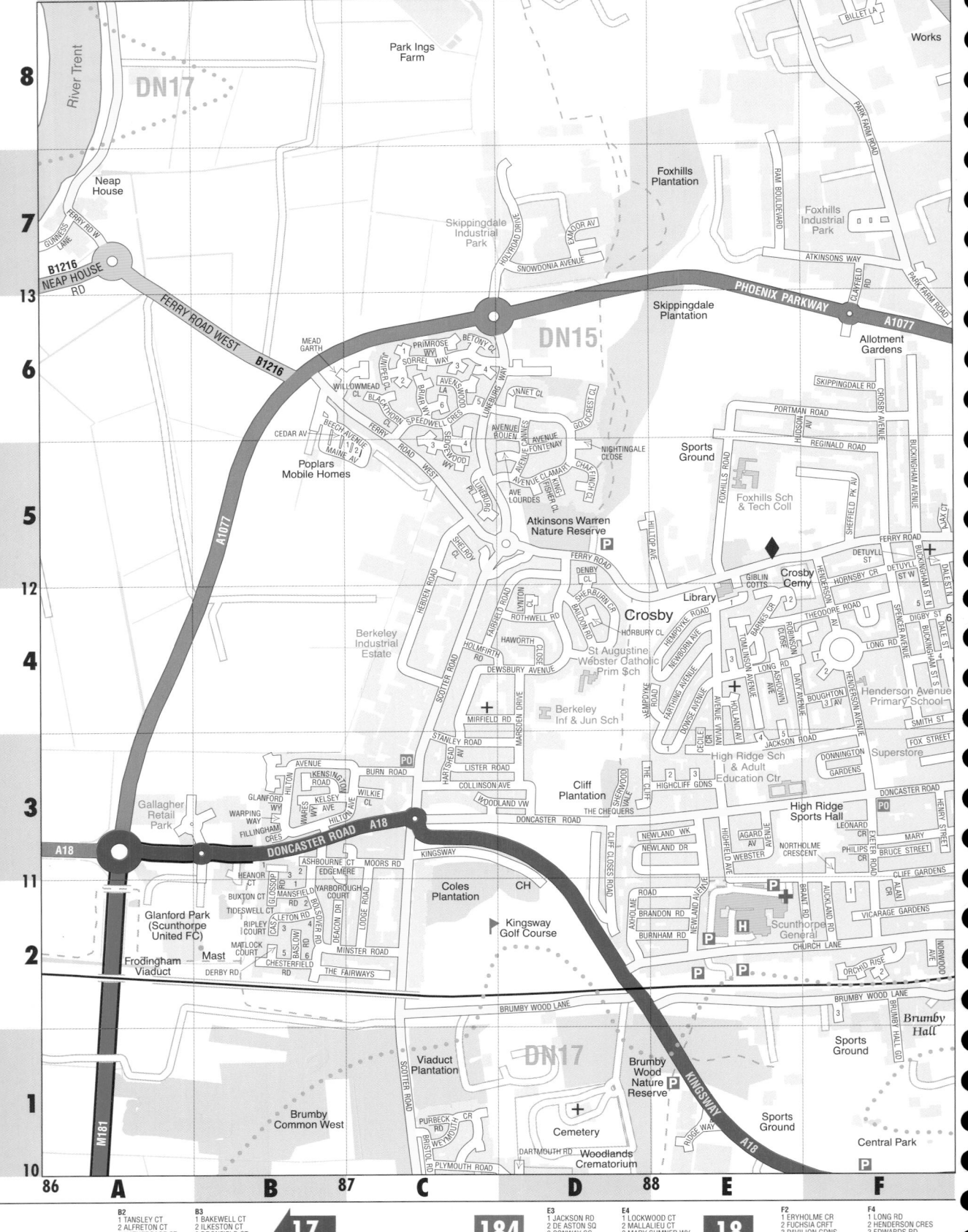

C5
1 ACACIA AVE
2 MAPLE AVE
3 PIPPIN CT
4 RUSSET CL

17

C6
1 POPPY CL
2 WOODALE CL
3 FLETCHER CL
4 COLTSFOOT CL
5 ST MARY'S CT
6 HERON CL

8

B2
1 TANSLEY CT
2 ALFRETON CT
3 HATHERSAGE CT
4 GRASSMOOR CT
5 EASTWOOD CT
6 BELPER CT

B3
1 BAKEWELL CT
2 ILKESTON CT
3 DRONFIELD CT

17

184

E3
1 JACKSON RD
2 DE ASTON SQ
3 CONWAY SQ
4 TOMLINSON AVE
5 ASHDOWN AVE

E4
1 LOCKWOOD CT
2 MALLALIEU CT
3 MARY SUMNER WY

18

F2
1 ERYHOLME CR
2 FUCHSIA CRFT
3 PAVILION GDNS

F4
1 LONG RD
2 HENDERSON CRES
3 EDWARDS RD
4 SHEFFIELD ST
5 BUCKINGHAM ST
6 Comm Ctr

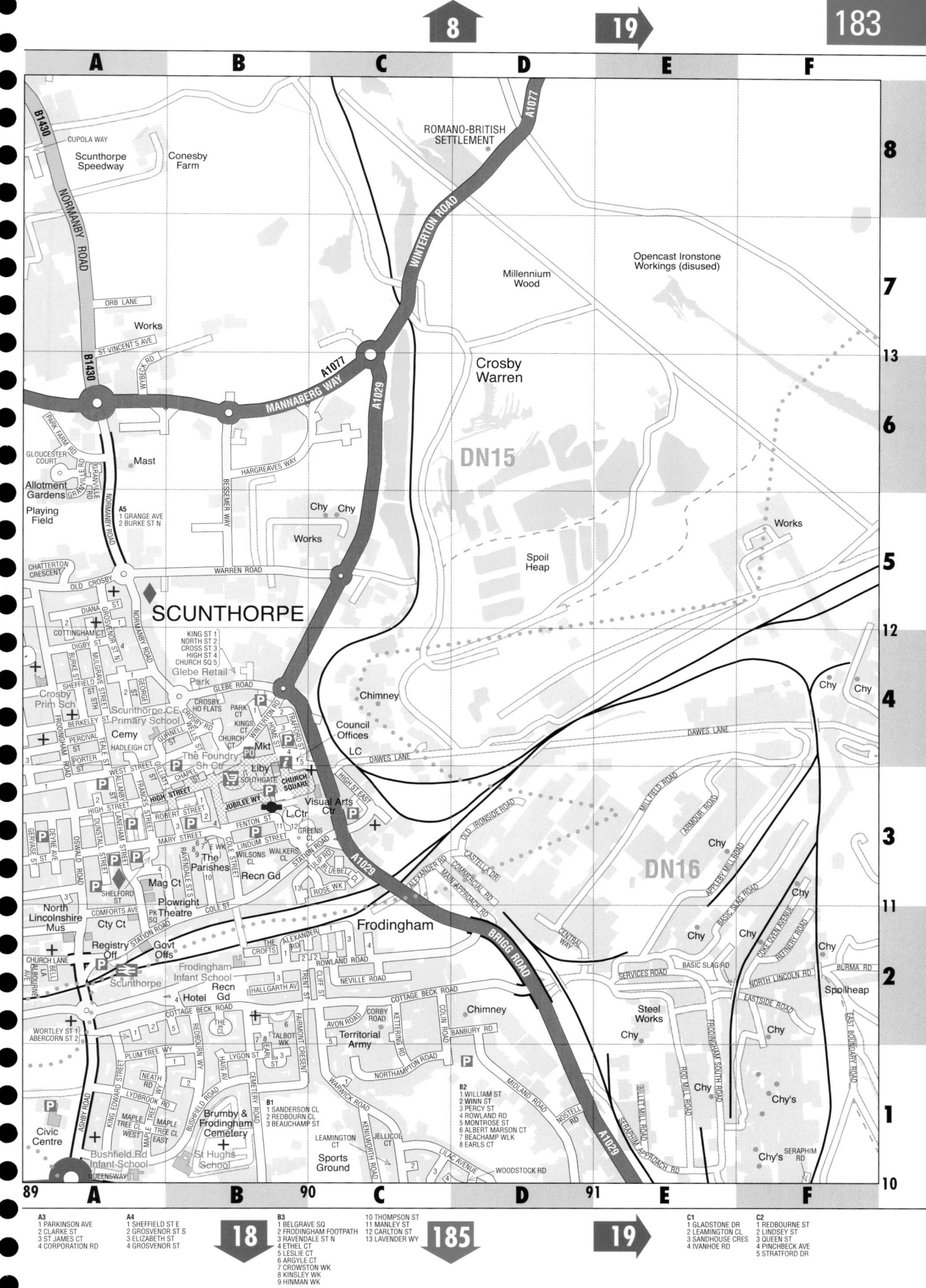

ROMANO-BRITISH SETTLEMENT

Opencast Ironstone Workings (disused)

Millennium Wood

Crosby Warren

DN15

Spoil Heap

Works

SCUNTHORPE

Chimney

Council Offices

DAWES LANE

DN16

Frodingham

Chimney

Territorial Army

Steel Works

Spoilheap

Sports Ground

Civic Centre

Brumby & Frodingham Cemetery

St Hughs School

Bushfield Infant School

North Lincolnshire Mus

A3
1 PARKINSON AVE
2 CLARKE ST
3 ST JAMES CT
4 CORPORATION RD

A4
1 SHEFFIELD ST E
2 GROSVENOR ST S
3 ELIZABETH ST
4 GROSVENOR ST

B3
1 BELGRAVE SQ
2 FRODINGHAM FOOTPATH
3 RAVENDALE ST N
4 ETHEL CT
5 LESLIE CT
6 ARGYLE CT
7 CROWSTON WK
8 KINSLEY WK
9 HINMAN WK

10 THOMPSON ST
11 MANLEY ST
12 CARLTON ST
13 LAVENDER WY

B1
1 SANDERSON CL
2 REDBOURN CL
3 BEAUCHAMP ST

B2
1 WILLIAM ST
2 WINN ST
3 PERCY ST
4 ROWLAND RD
5 MONTROSE ST
6 ALBERT MARSON CT
7 BEACHAMP WLK
8 EARLS CT

C1
1 GLADSTONE DR
2 LEAMINGTON CL
3 SANDHOUSE CRES
4 IVANHOE RD

C2
1 REDBOURNE ST
2 LINDSEY ST
3 QUEEN ST
4 PINCHBECK AVE
5 STRATFORD DR

A5
1 GRANGE AVE
2 BURKE ST N

17

182

C5
1 BETULA WY
2 CONIFER CL
3 ACER GR

C6
1 FOURTH AVE
2 THIRD AVE
3 SECOND AVE
4 SHAKESPEARE AVE
5 SIDNEY RD

C7
1 ROCHESTER CL
2 SALISBURY CL
3 ST ALBANS CL

D7
1 CANTERBURY CL
2 NEWBOLT AVE
3 LANDOR AVE
4 KIPLING AVE
5 COVENTRY CL

D8
1 QUANTOCK CL
2 CLEVELAND CL
3 BARNSTAPLE RD

E6
1 BROWNING CL
2 MAVIS RD
3 MALLARD RD
4 KIPLING AVE
5 PHEASANT CL

F8
1 NORMAN CRES
2 GLANVILLE CRES
3 HAWTHORNE CRES
4 HAWTHORNE AVE

(Map of Scunthorpe area — DN17: Brumby, Brumby Common, Westcliff, Manor Park, Riddings, Yaddlethorpe, Ashby Decoy, Bottesford, etc. Grid A–F, rows 1–8.)

17

29

E3
1 WADDINGTON DR
2 THE OVAL
3 EDGBASTON AVE
4 HEADINGLEY AVE
5 JESMOND AVE
6 LOW LEYS RD

F3
1 PRINCESS ALEXANDRA CT
2 SOUTH RIDGE CR
3 AUSTIN CR
4 THORNHILL CR
5 KIRMAN CR

F4
1 HARROW GDNS
2 KEDDINGTO RD

F2
1 LEE FAIR GDNS
2 ST ANDREWS AVE

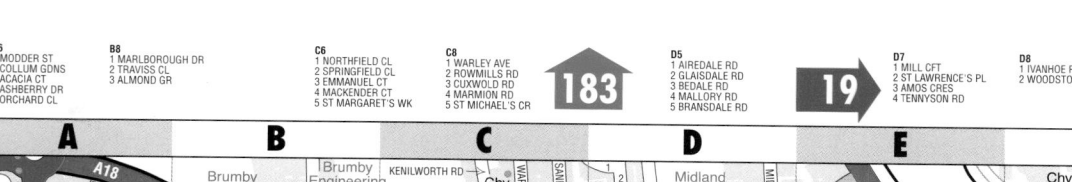

B6
1 MODDER ST
2 COLLUM GDNS
3 ACACIA CT
4 ASHBERRY DR
5 ORCHARD CL

B8
1 MARLBOROUGH DR
2 TRAVISS CL
3 ALMOND GR

C6
1 NORTHFIELD CL
2 SPRINGFIELD CL
3 EMMANUEL CT
4 MACKENZIE CT
5 ST MARGARET'S WK

C8
1 WARLEY AVE
2 ROWMILLS RD
3 CUXWOLD RD
4 MARMION CL
5 ST MICHAEL'S CR

183

19

D5
1 AIREDALE RD
2 GLAISDALE RD
3 BEDALE RD
4 MALLORY RD
5 BRANSDALE RD

D7
1 MILL CFT
2 ST LAWRENCE'S PL
3 AMOS CRES
4 TENNYSON RD

D8
1 IVANHOE RD
2 WOODSTOCK RD

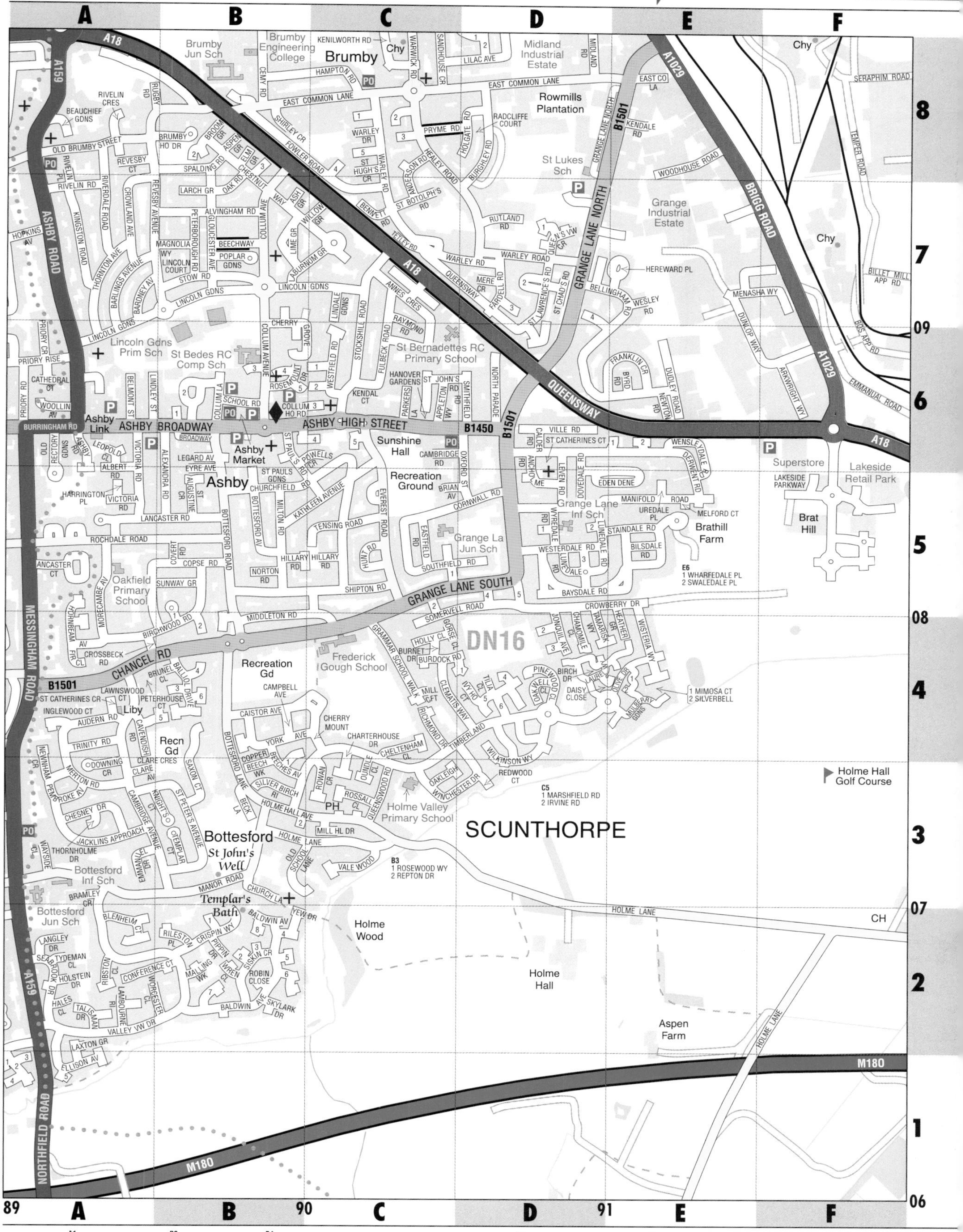

185

A1
1 LOBELIA DR
2 MONTBRETIA DR
3 AUBRETIA DR
4 ARMERIA DR
5 HALLBROOK CT

B2
1 STURMER CT
2 MARTIN CL
3 DUNNOCK CL
4 HAZEL GR
5 ACORN WY
6 CATKIN RD
7 MERRYWEATHER CT
8 FIELDFARE CL

B4
1 RINGWOOD CL
2 OAKWOOD RISE
3 GIRTON CL
4 MAGDALEN CL
5 MOUNTBATTEN CL
6 NUFFIELD CL

29

19

D4
1 PLANTAIN CL
2 PIMPERNEL WY
3 HONEYSUCKLE CT
4 NUTWOOD VW
5 PEACH TREE CL
6 WEEPINGELM WY

13 13

D5
1 HOYLAKE DR
2 COLLIER RD
3 BIRKDALE DR
4 SUNNINGDALE DR

DN40

IMMINGHAM

DN41

Rosper Road Pools Nature Reserve
HUMBER ROAD A160
A1173
WEST HAVEN WAY
Houlton's Covert
Immingham Golf Course
Medieval Village of Immingham
Homestead Park
STANDISH LA 1
HINKLEY DR 2
WESTON GR 3
ATWOOD CL 4
Football Ground
1 CEDAR DR
2 MAPLE GR
3 OAKLANDS RD
HALL PARK RD
Manby Hall Business Park
Sports Ground
1 HUMBERVILLE RD
2 LARCH CL
3 TRENCHARD CL
MANBY ROAD
A1173
MIDDLEPLATT ROAD
KINGS ROAD
A1173
Henderson Quay
WEST RIVERSIDE
Oil Storage Depot
WEST HAVEN WY
Water Tower
MINERAL QUAY ROAD
SEVEN QUAY ROAD
ALEXANDRA RD
ROBINSON RD
Works
GRESLEY WAY
Pelham Industrial Estate
SOUTHERN WAY
WESTERN ACCESS ROAD
ALEXANDRA ROAD SOUTH
Allerton Primary School
Washdyke Retail Park
Hotel Immingham L Ctr
Civic Ctr
Kennedy Way Shopping Ctr
Liby
Mkt
Swimming Pool
The Immingham School
Immingham Business Units
Cannon Peter Hall CE Prim Ctr
1 DEANE RD
2 SACKVILLE CL
3 WORSLEY CL
4 EATON RD
Recreation Ground
Coomb Brigg's Prim Sch
ANCHOLME AVE 1
CALDER CL 2
STEEPING DR 3
AIRE CL 4
HABROUGH ROAD B1210
Sports Gd
Immingham Museum
COLLIER RD 1
BREWSTER AV 2
THORNBURY RD 3
Eastfield Inf & Jun Sch
KISHORN CT 1
PERTH WY 2
TUMMEL CT 3
Highfield Farm
ORKNEY PL 1
FAIR ISLE RISE 2
LUNDY CT 3
STALLINGBOROUGH ROAD
A180
B1210
Mauxhall Farm
A1173
KILN LANE

23 23

A4
1 MAIDEN CL
2 CLEVELAND CL
3 LYDIA CT
4 HAZEL CFT
5 MILLHOUSE ST RISE
6 JACKSON MEWS
7 ANDREWS WY
8 HELEN CRES

B3
1 BLOSSOM WY
2 CLARENCE CL
3 LINDUM AVE
4 HIGHFIELD AVE
5 MACKENZIE PL
6 HUME BRAE
7 BOWMAN WY
8 HAMISH WK
9 JAMES WY

B4
1 HOLLINGSWORTH AVE
2 HOLBECK PL
3 BALFOUR PL
4 LANSDOWN RD
5 AINSWORTH RD
6 LEYDEN CL
7 CHILTON CL
8 STAINTON DR

C3
1 PRINCESS ST
2 ROUNDWAY
3 JAPONICA HL
4 MAGNOLIA RISE
5 PADDOCK CT
6 OBAN CT

A B C D E F

8

7

16

6

Immingham
Dock

EAST RIVERSIDE

Oil
Storage
Depot

LC

EAST DOCK ROAD

LC

QUEENS RD

5

Oil
Storage
Depot

East
Gate

A1173

Chy

DN40

QUEENS ROAD

LAPORTE ROAD

15

4

Chimney

Works

Humber Bank
Factories

Chimney

3

Spoil Heap

EUROPA WAY

NETHERLANDS WAY

SCANDINAVIAN WAY

EUROPA WAY

KILN LANE

Kiln Lane
Ind Est

LC

14

WORLDWIDE WAY

WORLDWIDE WAY

Kiln Lane
Trading Est

2

TRONDHEIM WAY

REEL'S RD

OSBORNE RD

Kiln Lane
Ind Est

DN41

HORSON WAY

South
Marsh Road
Ind Est

SOUTH MARSH ROAD

1

NORTH MOSS LANE

SOUTH MARSH ROAD

LC

Power
Station

Chimney

Poplar
Farm

13

20 A B 21 C D 22 E F

River Humber

Works

Works

Pyewipe

Chimney

Chimney
Works
Chimney

Water
Reclamation
Works

Sewage
Works

LC

Sports
Ground

Sports
Ground

DN37

LAFOREY ROAD

LC

LC

DN31

MOODY LANE

MOODY LANE

GENESIS WAY

LAKESIDE

A180

Mast

ESTATE ROAD NO 4

ESTATE ROAD NO 3

ESTATE ROAD NO 1

WOAD LANE

Europa
Business
Park

ATHENIAN DR

APPIAN WY

Hotel

APIAN
WY

GILBEY ROAD

ESTUARY WAY

LC

GATE
WY

LC

WESTSIDE ROAD

NAVENSBY CL 1
ALLINGTON DR 2
RUSKINGTON CL 3

ESTATE ROAD NO 5

Ventura
Business
Park

ALEXANDRA
DOCK NORTH

SIBSEY
COURT

South Humberside
Industrial
Estate

ESTATE ROAD NO 2

ESTATE RD NO 6

ESTATE RD NO 7

Cherry Tree's
Business Park

WEST COATES RD

MOODY LANE

Alexandra Dock

NEWBURY
WALK

NEWBURY
AV

Littlecoates
Prim Sch

BIRCHIN WAY

Birch Way
Ind Est

PINE
CL

ESTATE RD NO 8

ESTATE RD NO 2

HARA GDNS

ELSENHAM ROAD

Pyewipe
Bungalows

PYEWIPE ROAD

BOULEVARD AV

Beeson
Grove

BEESON

CHARLTON ST

WATKIN
ST NORTH

ADAM SMITH ST

WESTGATE

RENDEL ST

ALEXANDRA ROAD

TINTERN
WALK

CROMWELL RD

CRANWELL
DR

HARLOW ST

GILBEY RD

HARSGATE ST

DUNMOW ST

Alexandra
Ret Pk

BYLAND GR

FOUNTAINS
AV

MELROSE
WY

BUCKFAST CL

ST CHADS
GATE

SALTERGATE

SOUTHLAND CT

NEW HAVEN TERRACE

West Marsh

West Marsh
Ind Est

ARMSTRONG ST

The Willows

24

A

B

25

C

D

26

E

F

A   B   C   D   E   F

8

7

13

6

River Humber

5

12

4

Mast

Piers

The Dock Tower

Locks

Locks

GRIMSBY

KEMP ROAD

NORTH QUAY

Royal Dock

BROWN ST

Fish Docks

WHARNCLIFFE RD

DN31

3

WESTSIDE ROAD

EASTSIDE ROAD

WHARNCLIFFE RD

HUTTON RD

AUCKLAND RD

GORDON STREET

Grimsby Marina

11

D1
1 CASSWELL CL
2 RUTLAND ST
3 MANSEL ST
4 SIDNEY ST

HUMBER BK S

FARINGDON RD

Works

WICKHAM ROAD

2

LC

EASTSIDE ROAD

LC

MURRAY STREET

RIBY STREET

WOMERSLEY RD

ROBINSON LA

Works

WICKHAM ROAD

ROSS ROAD

HUMBER BRIDGE RD

SALVESEN RD

MARSDEN ROAD

DN32

LOCKHILL

FLOUR

ROYAL

MURRAY ST

TOMLINE ST

ORWELL ST

THOROLD STREET

New Clee

CLEETHORPE ROAD

The Caxton Theatre & Arts Ctr

STRAND

KENT

Strand Jun Sch

BATH ST

BELPER

HILDA

BED FORD

WELSBY

STIRLING ST

SPENCER

HARRINGTON STREET

GRANT

TAYLOR ST

DN35

A16 VICTORIA ST N

Grimsby Docks

P

P

RAILWAY ST

B1213 FREEMAN STREET

CHURCH ST

ALBERT ST

ALBERT PLACE

ALBERT ST E

Strand Inf Sch

VICTOR ST

OXFORD STREET

Ice House

SUFFOLK CT

SUSSEX ST

STANLEY

HOPE

GUILDFORD ST

HAMILTON STREET

GRIMSBY ROAD

A180

MONTAGUE ST

PARK ST

PHELPS ST

DAUBNEY ST

BARCROFT ST

LOVETT ST

TIVERTON ST

BLUNDELL AVE

1

High Point Ret Pk

A180

Victoria Retail Pk

PRINCE ALBERT GARD

NELSON STREET

DUNCOMBE GDNS

COMBER PL

East Marsh

10

27   A   B   28   C   D   29   E   F   10

E8
1 SERVICE RD 21
2 SEVERN WY
3 SERVICE RD 22
4 DUNOON CT
5 SOLWAY CT
6 TRENT CT
7 TYNE WY
8 SERVICE RD 4
9 SERVICE RD 8
10 LOCKTON CT
11 SERVICE RD 25
12 GOATHLAND CT
13 SERVICE RD 5
14 SERVICE RD 6
15 SERVICE RD 3
16 SERVICE RD 15
17 SERVICE RD 2
18 SERVICE RD 1
19 SERVICE RD 20
20 ST CHAAS WK

F8
1 CROMWELL RD
2 PERKINS CL
3 SERVICE RD 7
4 SERVICE RD 19

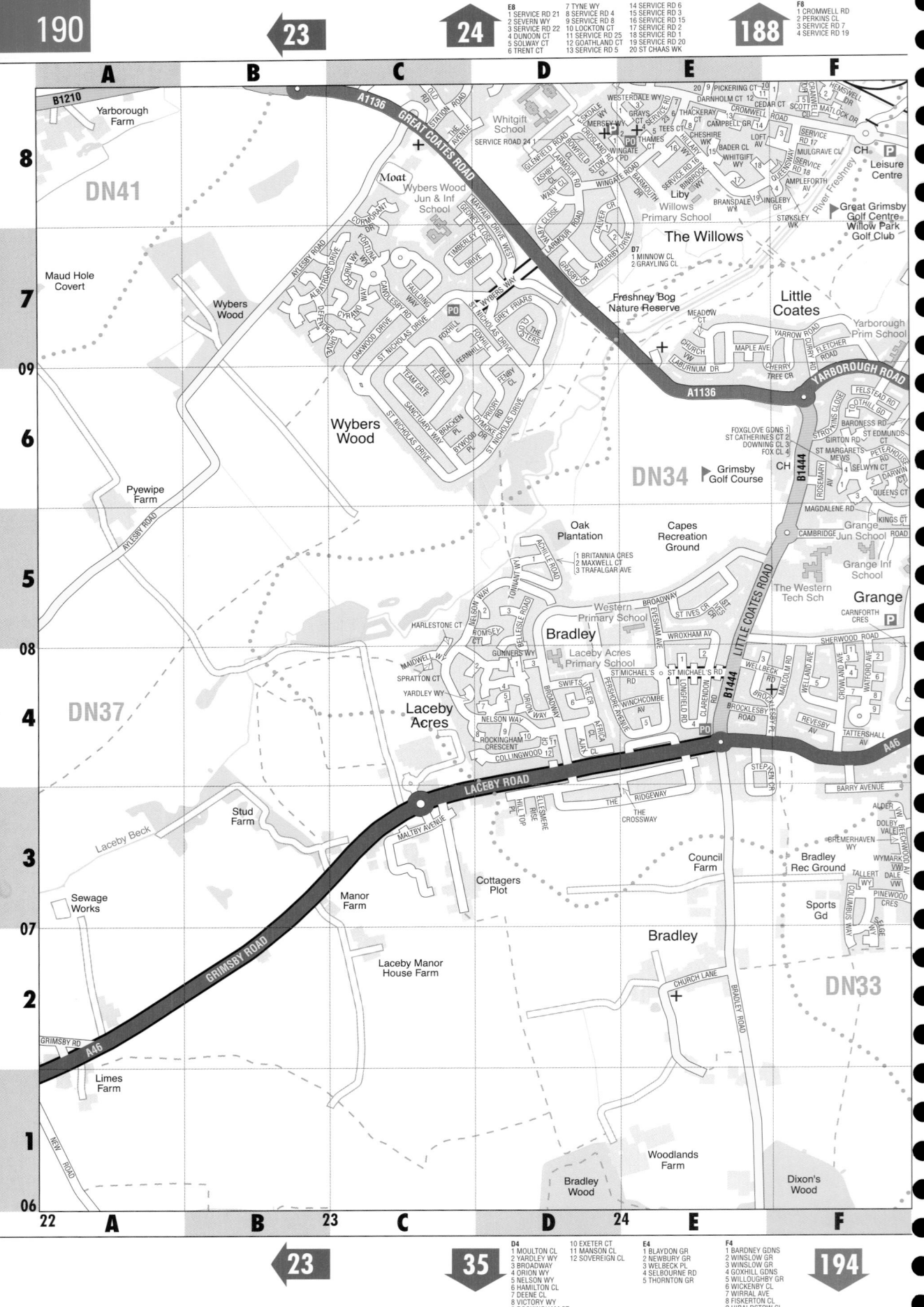

D4
1 MOULTON CL
2 YARDLEY WY
3 BROADWAY
4 ORION WY
5 NELSON WY
6 HAMILTON CL
7 DEENE CL
8 VICTORY WY
9 ROCKINGHAM CT
10 EXETER CT
11 MANSON CL
12 SOVEREIGN CL

E4
1 BLAYDON GR
2 NEWBURY GR
3 WELBECK PL
4 SELBOURNE RD
5 THORNTON GR

F4
1 BARDNEY GDNS
2 WINSLOW GR
3 WINSLOW GR
4 GOXHILL GDNS
5 WILLOUGHBY GR
6 WICKENBY CL
7 WIRRAL AVE
8 FISKERTON CL
9 HIBALDSTOW CL

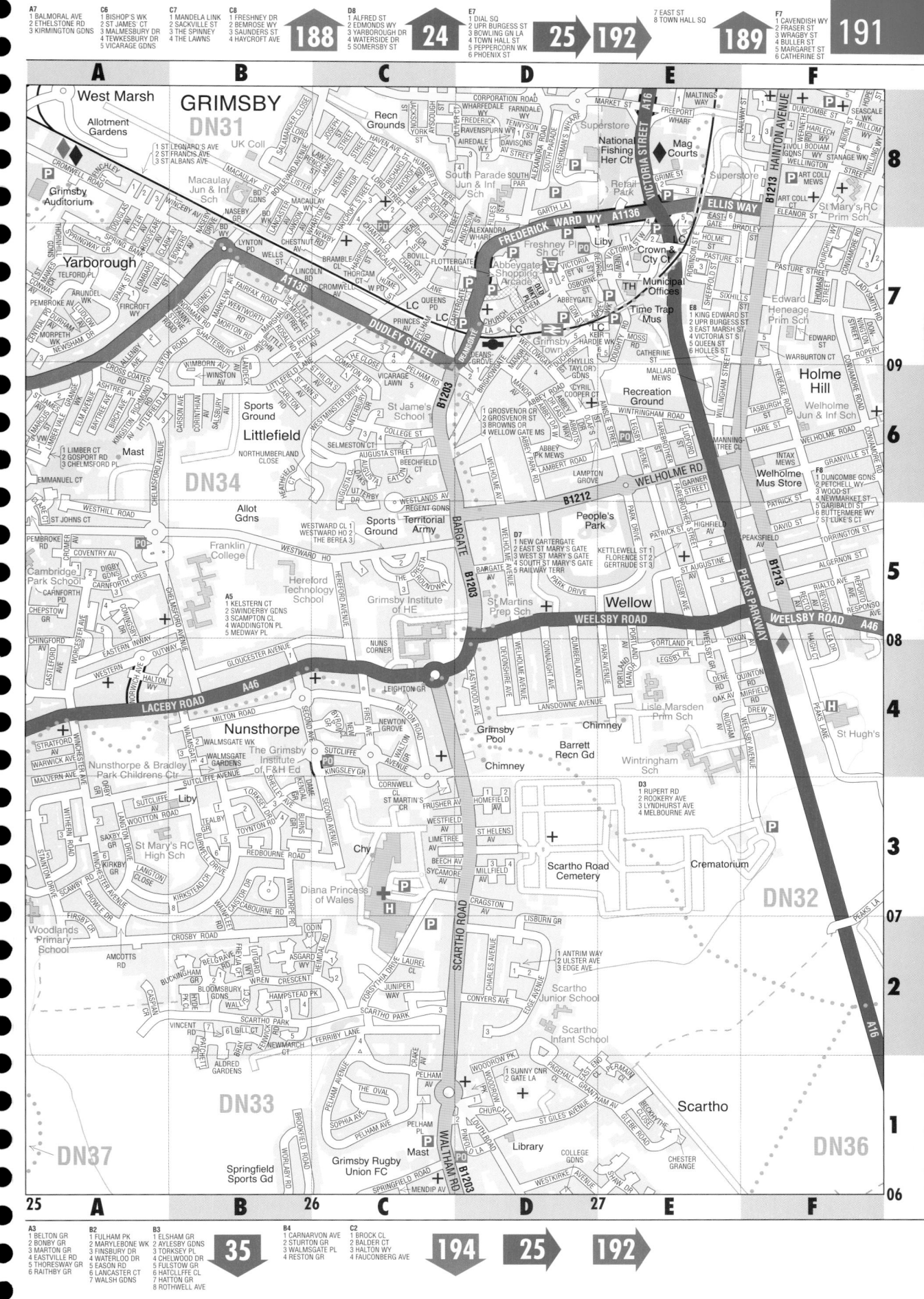

A7
1 BALMORAL AVE
2 ETHELSTONE RD
3 KIRMINGTON GDNS
C6
1 BISHOP'S WK
2 ST JAMES' CT
3 MALMESBURY DR
4 TEWKESBURY DR
5 VICARAGE GDNS
C7
1 MANDELA LINK
2 SACKVILLE ST
3 THE SPINNEY
4 THE LAWNS
C8
1 FRESHNEY DR
2 BEMROSE WY
3 SAUNDERS ST
4 HAYCROFT AVE
188
D8
1 ALFRED ST
2 EDMONDS WY
3 YARBOROUGH DR
4 WATERSIDE DR
5 SOMERSBY ST
24
E7
1 DIAL SQ
2 UPR BURGESS ST
3 BOWLING GN LA
4 TOWN HALL ST
5 PEPPERCORN WK
6 PHOENIX ST
25
192
7 EAST ST
8 TOWN HALL SQ
189
F7
1 CAVENDISH WY
2 FRASER ST
3 WRAGBY ST
4 BULLER ST
5 MARGARET ST
6 CATHERINE ST
191
West Marsh
GRIMSBY
DN31
Allotment Gardens
Grimsby Auditorium
Yarborough
Macaulay Jun & Inf Sch
Recn Grounds
South Parade Jun & Inf Sch
National Fishing Her Ctr
Mag Courts
Superstore
Retail Park
FREDERICK WARD WY A1136
ELLIS WAY
VICTORIA STREET A16
HAINTON AVENUE B1213
Freshney Pl Sh Ctr
Abbeygate Shopping Arcade
Crown & Cty Ct
Municipal Offices
Time Trap Mus
Grimsby Town
DUDLEY STREET
A1136
St Mary's RC Prim Sch
Edward Heneage Prim Sch
Holme Hill
Welholme Jun & Inf Sch
Welholme Mus Store
Recreation Ground
Sports Ground
Littlefield
St James's School
Mast
DN34
Allot Gdns
Sports Ground
Territorial Army
BARGATE B1203
WELHOLME RD
B1212
People's Park
Franklin College
Cambridge Park School
Hereford Technology School
Grimsby Institute of HE
St Martins Prep Sch
Wellow
WEELSBY ROAD A46
PEAKS PARKWAY
LACEBY ROAD A46
Nunsthorpe
The Grimsby Institute of F&H Ed
Nunsthorpe & Bradley Park Childrens Ctr
Liby
Lisle Marsden Prim Sch
Chimney
Barrett Recn Gd
Grimsby Pool
Wintringham Sch
St Hugh's
St Mary's RC High Sch
Diana Princess of Wales
Scartho Road Cemetery
Crematorium
DN32
Woodlands Primary School
SCARTHO ROAD
Scartho Junior School
Scartho Infant School
DN33
Scartho
DN37
Springfield Sports Gd
Grimsby Rugby Union FC
Mast
Library
WALTHAM RD B1203
DN36
A16
25 A B 26 C D 27 E F
A3
1 BELTON GR
2 BONBY GR
3 MARTON GR
4 EASTVILLE RD
5 THORESWAY GR
6 RAITHBY GR
B2
1 FULHAM PK
2 MARYLEBONE WK
3 FINSBURY DR
4 WATERLOO DR
5 EASON RD
6 LANCASTER CT
7 WALSH GDNS
B3
1 ELSHAM GR
2 AYLESBY GDNS
3 TORKSEY PL
4 CHELWOOD DR
5 FULSTOW GR
6 HATCLIFFE CL
7 HATTON GR
8 ROTHWELL AVE
35
B4
1 CARNARVON AVE
2 STURTON GR
3 WALMSGATE PL
4 RESTON GR
C2
1 BROCK CL
2 BALDER CT
3 HALTON WY
4 FAUCONBERG AVE
194
25
192

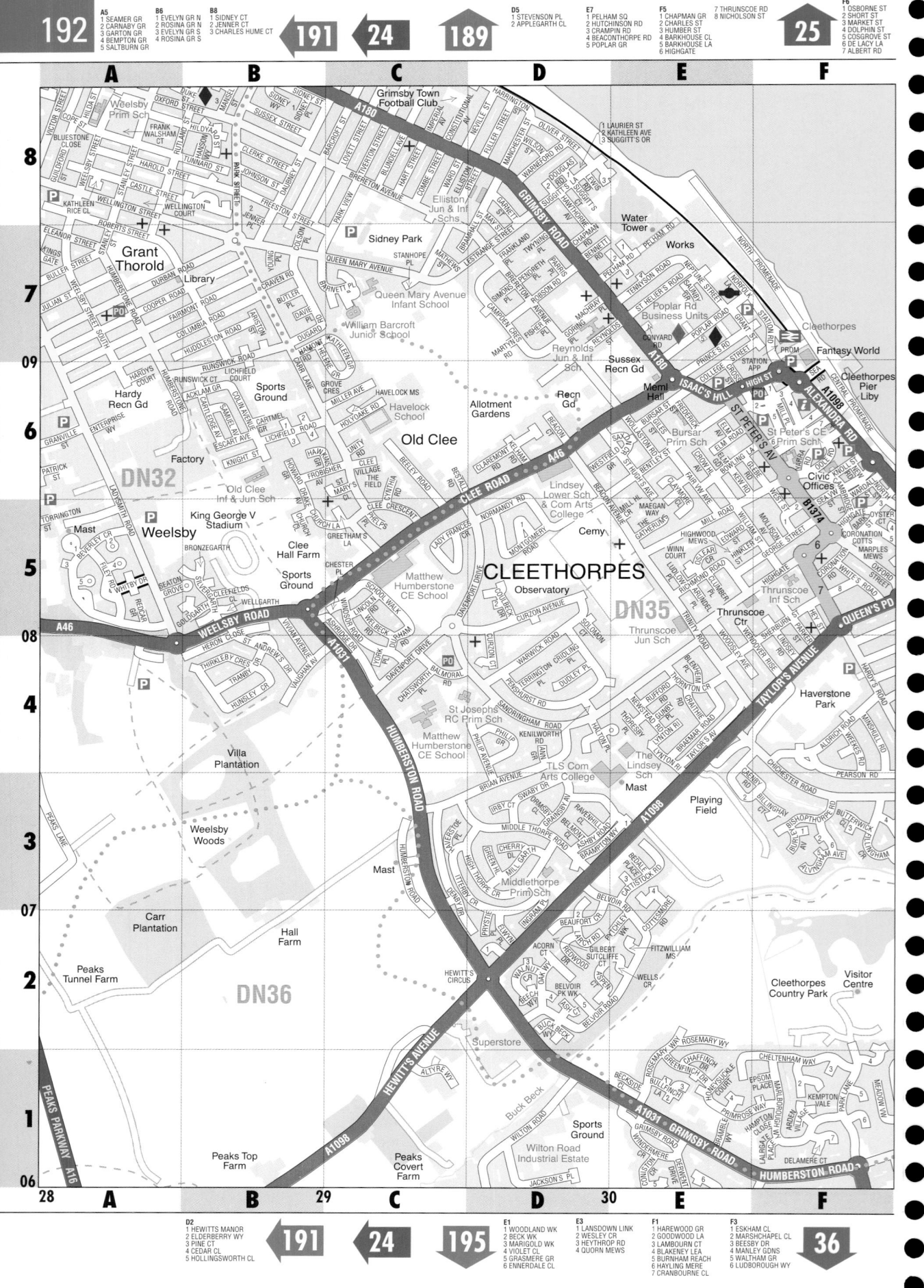

192

A5
1 SEAMER GR
2 CARNABY GR
3 GARTON GR
4 BEMPTON GR
5 SALTBURN GR

B6
1 EVELYN GR N
2 ROSINA GR N
3 EVELYN GR S
4 ROSINA GR S

B8
1 SIDNEY CT
2 JENNER CT
3 CHARLES HUME CT

◁ 191   ◁ 24   △ 189

D5
1 STEVENSON PL
2 APPLEGARTH CL

E7
1 PELHAM SQ
2 HUTCHINSON RD
3 CRAMPIN RD
4 BEACONTHORPE RD
5 POPLAR GR

F5
1 CHAPMAN GR
2 CHARLES ST
3 HUMBER ST
4 BARKHOUSE CL
5 BARKHOUSE LA
6 HIGHGATE

7 THRUNSCOE RD
8 NICHOLSON ST

△ 25

F6
1 OSBORNE ST
2 SHORT ST
3 MARKET ST
4 DOLPHIN ST
5 COSGROVE ST
6 DE LACY LA
7 ALBERT RD

D2
1 HEWITTS MANOR
2 ELDERBERRY WY
3 PINE CT
4 CEDAR CL
5 HOLLINGSWORTH CL

◁ 191   ◁ 24   △ 195

E1
1 WOODLAND WK
2 BECK WK
3 MARIGOLD WK
4 VIOLET CL
5 GRASMERE GR
6 ENNERDALE CL

E3
1 LANSDOWN LINK
2 WESLEY CR
3 HEYTHROP RD
4 QUORN MEWS

F1
1 HAREWOOD GR
2 GOODWOOD LA
3 LAMBOURN CT
4 BLAKENEY LEA
5 BURNHAM REACH
6 HAYLING MERE
7 CRANBOURNE CL

F3
1 ESKHAM CL
2 MARSHCHAPEL CL
3 BEESBY DR
4 MANLEY GDNS
5 WALTHAM GR
6 LUDBOROUGH WY

△ 36

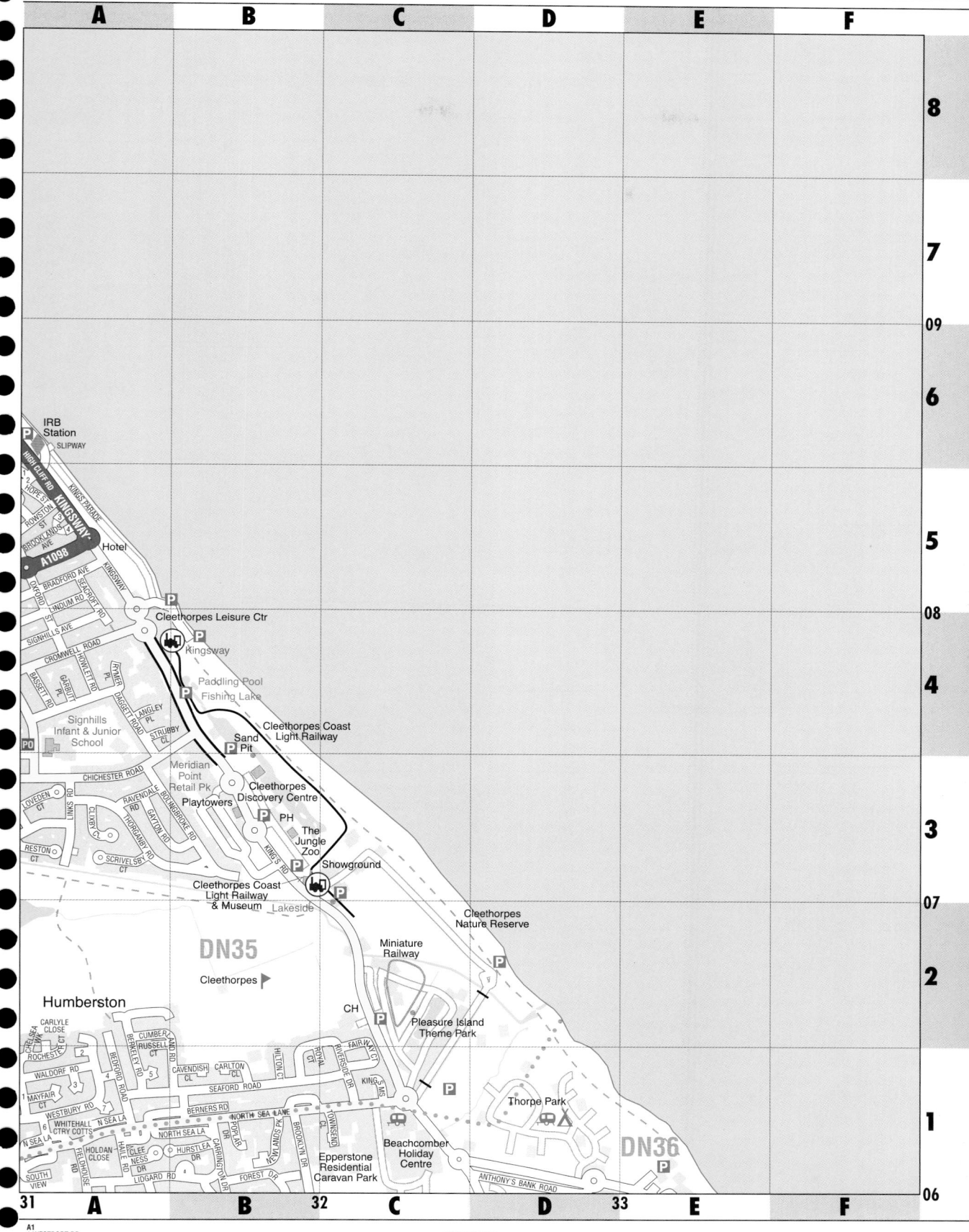

A1
1 WESTPORT RD
2 WESTBURY PK
3 FAIRFIELD CT
4 WEYFORD RD
5 GROVENOR CT
6 WHITEHALL RD
7 KINGSTON CL

36

190 35

C5
1 CORAL DR
2 PEACE HAVEN
3 CARDINAL CT
4 ALBERTINE CT
5 FOUNTAIN CL
6 SWEET BRIAR CL
7 WHEATFIELD DR
8 FRANCES CT
9 WRAY CL

D8
1 BAYSWATER PL
2 WELL VALE
3 MAYFIELD CL
4 CORNFIELD CL
5 SAGEFIELD CL

191

E7
1 CONISTON AVE
2 FLEETWOOD CL
3 BARBARA CL
4 WINDERMERE AVE
5 ORCHARD CFT
6 HEATHERDALE CL

E8
1 TONBRIDGE
2 GRAMPIAN WY
3 CHILTERN WY
4 LANCING WY
5 PURBECK RD
6 DOVEDALE DR

F8
1 GORDON GDNS
2 COLLEGE GDNS
3 LINDSEY RISE
4 HAWTHORNE AVE
5 LINWOOD AVE
6 WESTBOURNE GR

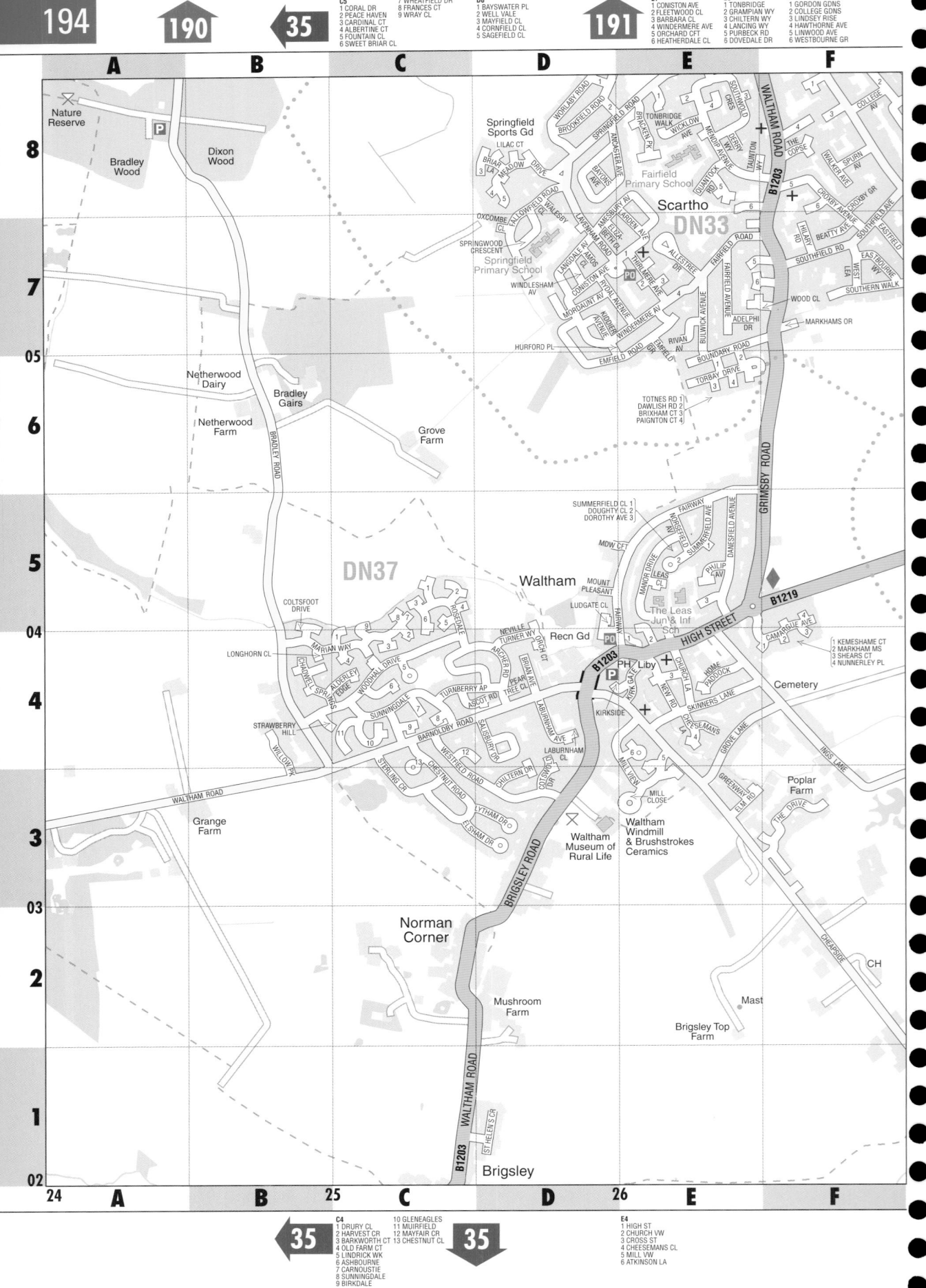

35 35

C4
1 DRURY CL
2 HARVEST CR
3 BARKWORTH CT
4 OLD FARM CT
5 LINDRICK WK
6 ASHBOURNE
7 CARNOUSTIE
8 SUNNINGDALE
9 BIRKDALE
10 GLENEAGLES
11 MUIRFIELD
12 MAYFAIR CR
13 CHESTNUT CL

E4
1 HIGH ST
2 CHURCH VW
3 CROSS ST
4 CHEESEMANS CL
5 MILL VW
6 ATKINSON LA

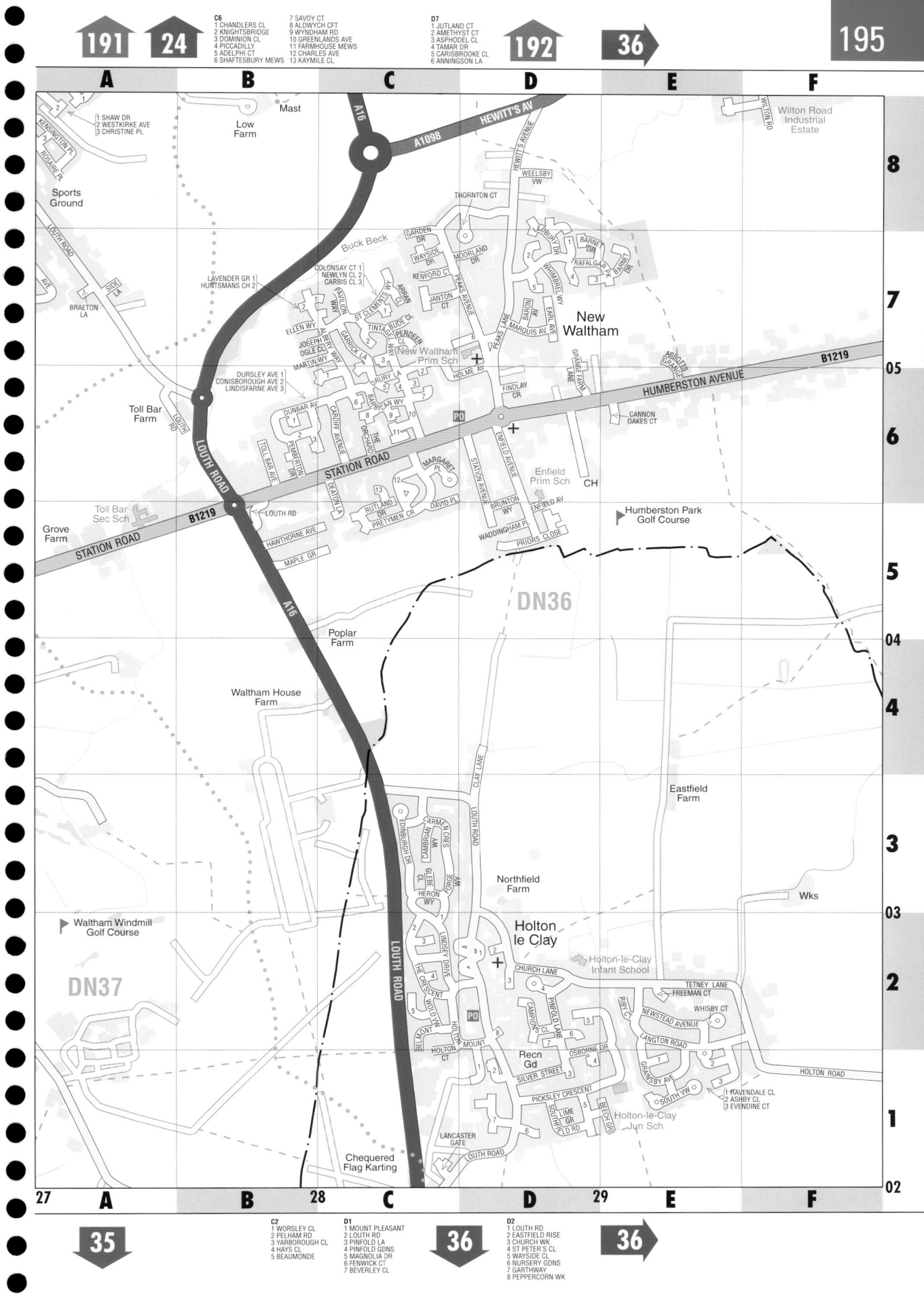

191 24

C6
1 CHANDLERS CL
2 KNIGHTSBRIDGE
3 DOMINION CL
4 PICCADILLY
5 ADELPHI CT
6 SHAFTESBURY MEWS

7 SAVOY CT
8 ALDWYCH CFT
9 WYNDHAM RD
10 GREENLANDS AVE
11 FARMHOUSE MEWS
12 CHARLES AVE
13 KAYMILE CL

D7
1 JUTLAND CT
2 AMETHYST CT
3 ASPHODEL CL
4 TAMAR DR
5 CARISBROOKE CL
6 ANNINGSON LA

192 36

195

Map labels (grid references A–F, rows 1–8):

Kensington Pl, Rosaire Pl, Louth Road Ave, Side La, Braeton La — 1 Shaw Dr, 2 Westkirke Ave, 3 Christine Pl

Sports Ground

Low Farm

Mast

A16, A1098, Hewitt's Av, Hewitt's Avenue, Weelsby Vw, Thornton Ct, Wilton Rd, Wilton Road Industrial Estate

Buck Beck

Lavender Gr 1, Huntsmans Ch 2

Colonsay Ct 1, Newlyn Cl 2, Carbis Cl 3

Garden Dr, Wayside Dr, Kenford Ct, Janton Ct, Moorland Dr, Peaks Avenue, Peaks Lane, Marquis Av, Baron Av, Earl Ave, Whimbrel Wy, Edburt Dr, Trafalgar Pk, Barnet Dr, Barnet Dr

New Waltham

Ellen Wy, St Clements Wy, Arran, Tinta Cl, Bude Cl, Pendeen Cl, Pavilion Way, Albert Way, Joseph Ogle Cl 1, Martin Wy, Garrick La, Drury La, Can Wy, The Orchard, The Barton, Holme Av, Findlay Cr, Grange Farm Lane, Abbots Grange, Humberston Avenue, B1219

Dursley Ave 1, Conisborough Ave 2, Lindisfarne Ave 3

Toll Bar Farm, Dunbar Av, Cardiff Avenue, Pemberton Dr, Toll Bar Ave, Station Road, Margaret Pl, Deaton La, Rutland Dr, Pretymen Cr, David Pl, Station Avenue, Enfield Avenue, Enfield Prim Sch, Cannon Oakes Ct, CH

Grove Farm, Station Road, B1219, Louth Rd, Hawthorne Ave, Maple Gr, Waddingham Pl, Priors Close, Enfield Av

Toll Bar Sec Sch, Louth Road

Humberston Park Golf Course

DN36

Poplar Farm

Waltham House Farm

Clay Lane, Louth Road, Eastfield Farm

DN37

Waltham Windmill Golf Course

Edinburgh Dr, Carman Cres, Cambria Wy, Glebe Cl, Heron Wy, Jersey Wy, Northfield Farm, Wks

Holton le Clay, Holton-le-Clay Infant School, Church Lane, Lindsey Drive, Wolds Vw, The Crescent, Belmont Wolds, Holton Ct, Holton Mount, Pinfold Lane, Campion Cl, Recn Gd, PO, Silver Street, Lime Gr, Holt Rd, Osborne Dr, Beech Gr, Pickley Crescent, South Holt, Lancaster Gate, Louth Road, Chequered Flag Karting, Holton-le-Clay Jun Sch

Tetney Lane, Freeman Ct, Whisby Ct, Newstead Avenue, Langton Road, Rigby Ct, Grainsby Av, South Vw, Holton Road — 1 Ravendale Cl, 2 Ashby Cl, 3 Evendine Ct

A16, Louth Road

27 A B 28 C D 29 E F

35 36 36

C2
1 WORSLEY CL
2 PELHAM RD
3 YARBOROUGH CL
4 HAYS CL
5 BEAUMONDE

D1
1 MOUNT PLEASANT
2 LOUTH RD
3 PINFOLD LA
4 PINFOLD GDNS
5 MAGNOLIA DR
6 FENWICK CT
7 BEVERLEY CL

D2
1 LOUTH RD
2 EASTFIELD RISE
3 CHURCH WK
4 ST PETER'S CL
5 WAYSIDE CL
6 NURSERY GDNS
7 GARTHWAY
8 PEPPERCORN WK

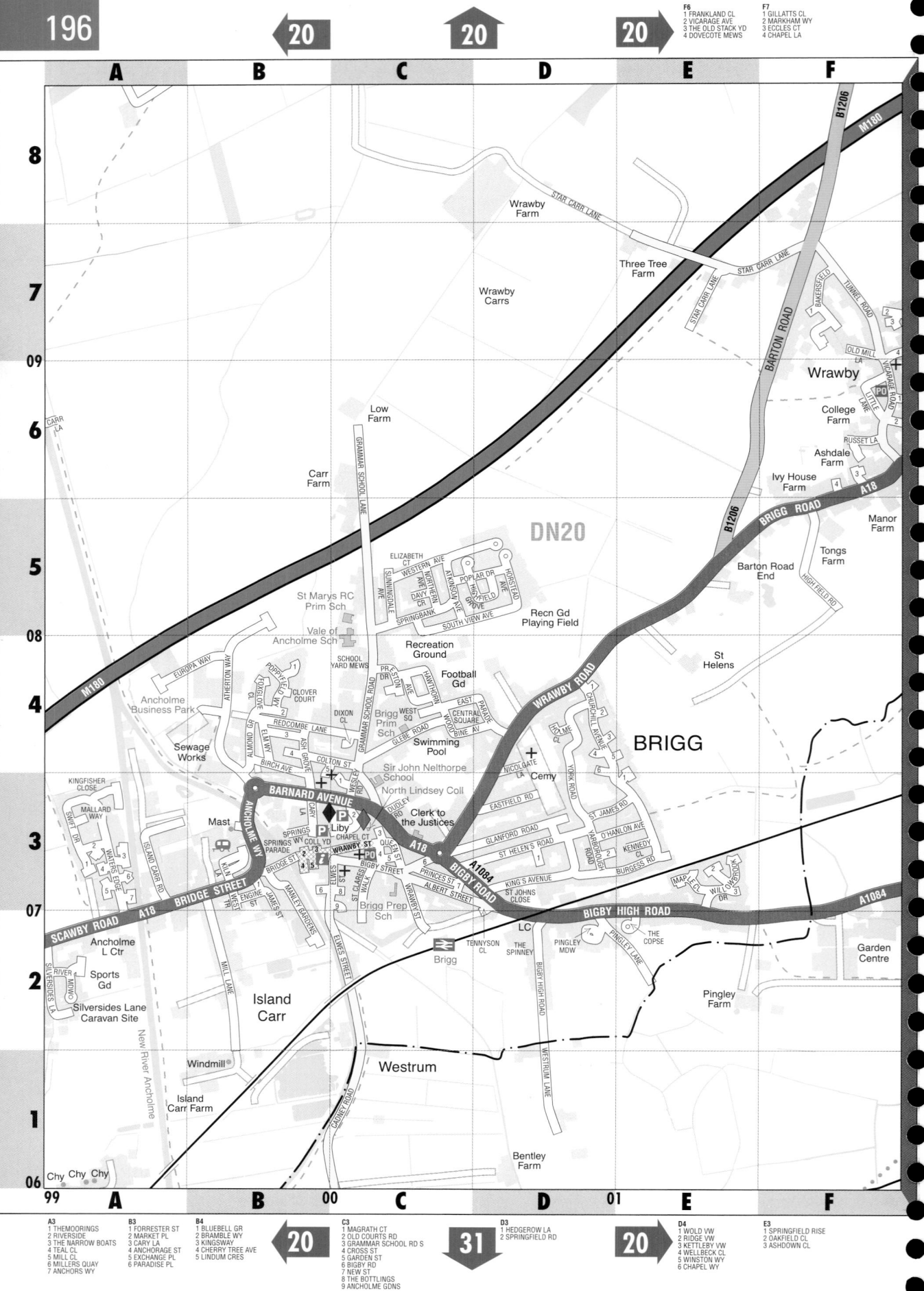

F6
1 FRANKLAND CL
2 VICARAGE AVE
3 THE OLD STACK YD
4 DOVECOTE MEWS

F7
1 GILLATTS CL
2 MARKHAM WY
3 ECCLES CT
4 CHAPEL LA

A   B   C   D   E   F

8
7
09
6
08
5
4
3
07
2
1
06
99   00   01

DN20

Wrawby Farm

Three Tree Farm

Wrawby Carrs

STAR CARR LANE

Low Farm

Carr Farm

Wrawby

College Farm

Ashdale Farm

Ivy House Farm

Tongs Farm

Manor Farm

Barton Road End

St Helens

BRIGG

Recreation Ground

Football Gd

Swimming Pool

Sir John Nelthorpe School

North Lindsey Coll

Clerk to the Justices

BARNARD AVENUE

Mast

Ancholme L Ctr

Sports Gd

Island Carr

Silversides Lane Caravan Site

Windmill

Island Carr Farm

Westrum

Brigg

Brigg Prep Sch

Bentley Farm

Pingley Farm

Pingley MDW

The Spinney

The Copse

Garden Centre

SCAWBY ROAD A18   BRIDGE STREET

BIGBY ROAD   A1084

BIGBY HIGH ROAD   A1084

WRAWBY ROAD

BRIGG ROAD

M180

B1206

M180

A18

A3
1 THEMOORINGS
2 RIVERSIDE
3 THE NARROW BOATS
4 TEAL CL
5 MILL CL
6 MILLERS QUAY
7 ANCHORS WY

B3
1 FORRESTER ST
2 MARKET PL
3 CARY LA
4 ANCHORAGE ST
5 EXCHANGE PL
6 PARADISE PL

B4
1 BLUEBELL GR
2 BRAMBLE WY
3 KINGSWAY
4 CHERRY TREE AVE
5 LINDUM CRES

C3
1 MAGRATH CT
2 OLD COURTS RD
3 GRAMMAR SCHOOL RD S
4 CROSS ST
5 GARDEN ST
6 BIGBY RD
7 NEW ST
8 THE BOTTLINGS
9 ANCHOLME GDNS

D3
1 HEDGEROW LA
2 SPRINGFIELD RD

D4
1 WOLD VW
2 RIDGE VW
3 KETTLEBY VW
4 WELLBECK CL
5 WINSTON WY
6 CHAPEL WY

E3
1 SPRINGFIELD RISE
2 OAKFIELD CL
3 ASHDOWN CL

← 20   ↑ 31   → 20

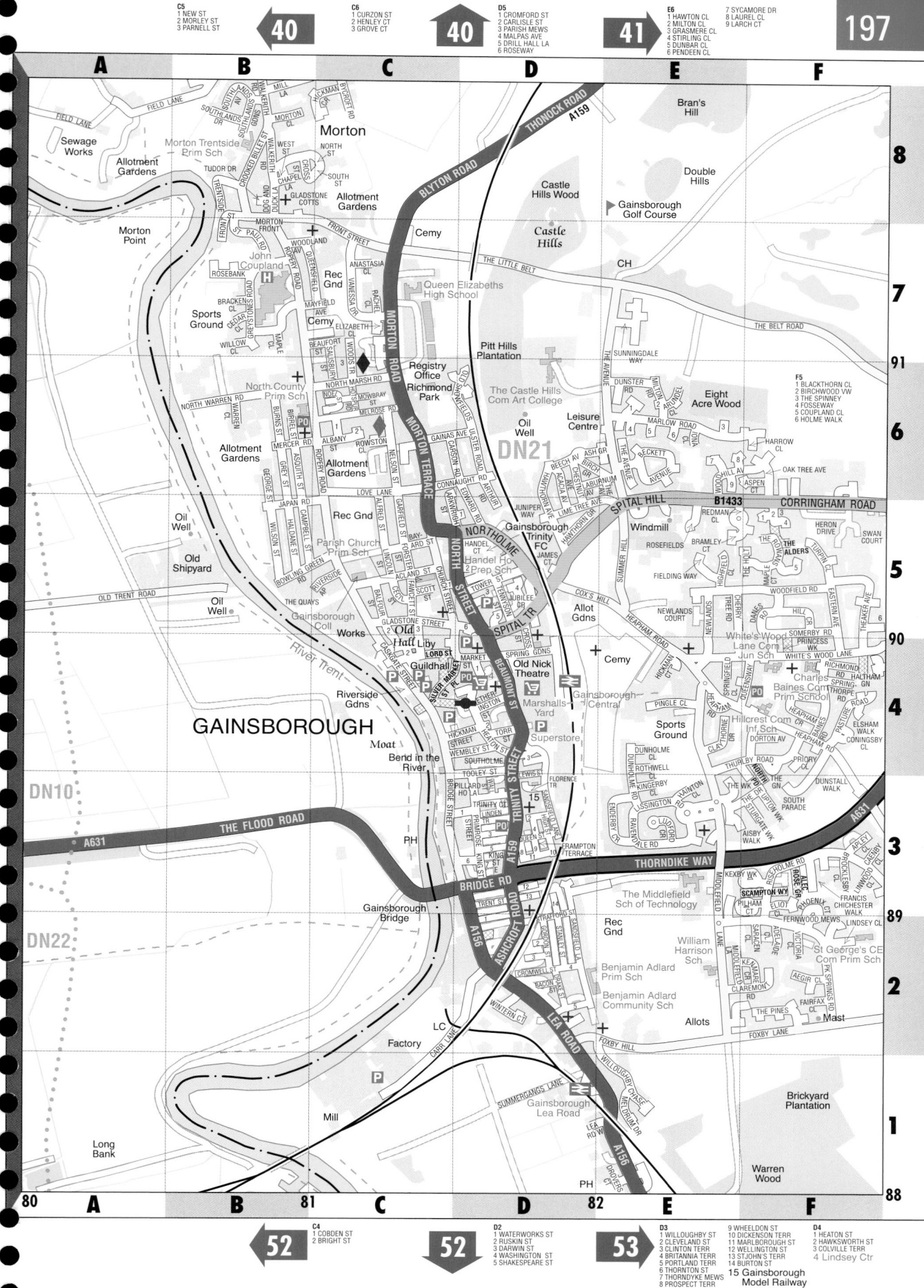

C5
1 NEW ST
2 MORLEY ST
3 PARNELL ST

40

C6
1 CURZON ST
2 HENLEY CT
3 GROVE CT

40

D5
1 CROMFORD ST
2 CARLISLE ST
3 PARISH MEWS
4 MALPAS AVE
5 DRILL HALL LA
6 ROSEWAY

41

E6
1 HAWTON CL
2 MILTON CL
3 GRASMERE CL
4 STIRLING CL
5 DUNBAR CL
6 PENDEEN CL

7 SYCAMORE DR
8 LAUREL CT
9 LARCH CT

GAINSBOROUGH

Morton

Sewage Works

Allotment Gardens

Morton Trentside Prim Sch

Morton Point

John Coupland

Rec Gnd

Allotment Gardens

Sports Ground

North County Prim Sch

Allotment Gardens

Allotment Gardens

Oil Well

Old Shipyard

Oil Well

Rec Gnd

Parish Church Prim Sch

Gainsborough Coll

Works

Old Hall

Liby

Guildhall

Riverside Gdns

Moat

Bend in the River

Gainsborough Bridge

DN10

DN22

Long Bank

Factory

Mill

Bran's Hill

Double Hills

Castle Hills Wood

Gainsborough Golf Course

Castle Hills

THE LITTLE BELT

CH

Queen Elizabeths High School

Pitt Hills Plantation

The Castle Hills Com Art College

DN21

Leisure Centre

Eight Acre Wood

THE BELT ROAD

Gainsborough Trinity FC

Handel Ho Prep Sch

SPITAL HILL

B1433

CORRINGHAM ROAD

Windmill

Rosefields

Fielding Way

Woodfield Rd

Allot Gdns

Cemy

White's Wood Lane Com Jun Sch

Baines Com Prim School

Old Nick Theatre

Marshalls Yard

Superstore

Gainsborough Central

Sports Ground

Hillcrest Com Inf Sch

THE FLOOD ROAD

A631

THORNDIKE WAY

A631

The Middlefield Sch of Technology

Rec Gnd

William Harrison Sch

St George's CE Com Prim Sch

Benjamin Adlard Prim Sch

Benjamin Adlard Community Sch

Allots

Mast

Gainsborough Lea Road

Brickyard Plantation

Warren Wood

River Trent

C4
1 COBDEN ST
2 BRIGHT ST

52

52

D2
1 WATERWORKS ST
2 RUSKIN ST
3 DARWIN ST
4 WASHINGTON ST
5 SHAKESPEARE ST

53

D3
1 WILLOUGHBY ST
2 CLEVELAND ST
3 CLINTON TERR
4 BRITANNIA TERR
5 PORTLAND TERR
6 THORNTON ST
7 THORNDYKE MEWS
8 PROSPECT TERR

9 WHEELDON ST
10 DICKENSON TERR
11 MARLBOROUGH ST
12 WELLINGTON ST
13 STJOHN'S TERR
14 BURTON ST
15 Gainsborough Model Railway

D4
1 HEATON ST
2 HAWKSWORTH ST
3 COLVILLE TERR
4 Lindsey Ctr

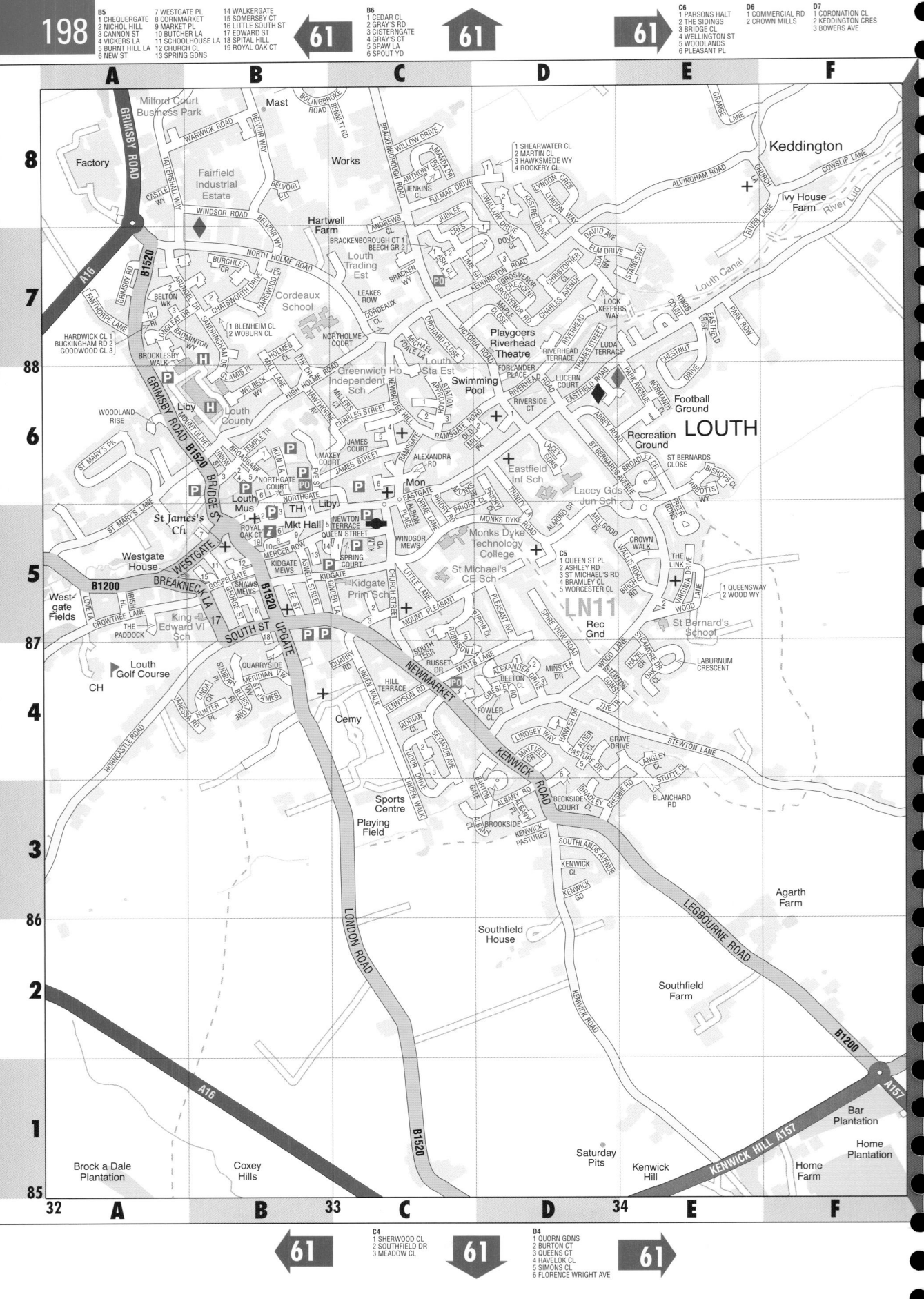

B5
1 CHEQUERGATE
2 NICHOL HILL
3 CANNON ST
4 VICKERS LA
5 BURNT HILL LA
6 NEW ST

7 WESTGATE PL
8 CORNMARKET
9 MARKET PL
10 BUTCHER LA
11 SCHOOLHOUSE LA
12 CHURCH CL
13 SPRING GDNS

14 WALKERGATE
15 SOMERSBY CT
16 LITTLE SOUTH ST
17 EDWARD ST
18 SPITAL HILL
19 ROYAL OAK CT

B6
1 CEDAR CL
2 GRAY'S RD
3 CISTERNGATE
4 GRAY S CT
5 SPAW LA
6 SPOUT YD

C6
1 PARSONS HALT
2 THE SIDINGS
3 BRIDGE CL
4 WELLINGTON ST
5 WOODLANDS
6 PLEASANT PL

D6
1 COMMERCIAL RD
2 CROWN MILLS

D7
1 CORONATION CL
2 KEDDINGTON CRES
3 BOWERS AVE

C4
1 SHERWOOD CL
2 SOUTHFIELD DR
3 MEADOW CL

D4
1 QUORN GDNS
2 BURTON CT
3 QUEENS CT
4 HAVELOK CL
5 SIMONS CL
6 FLORENCE WRIGHT AVE

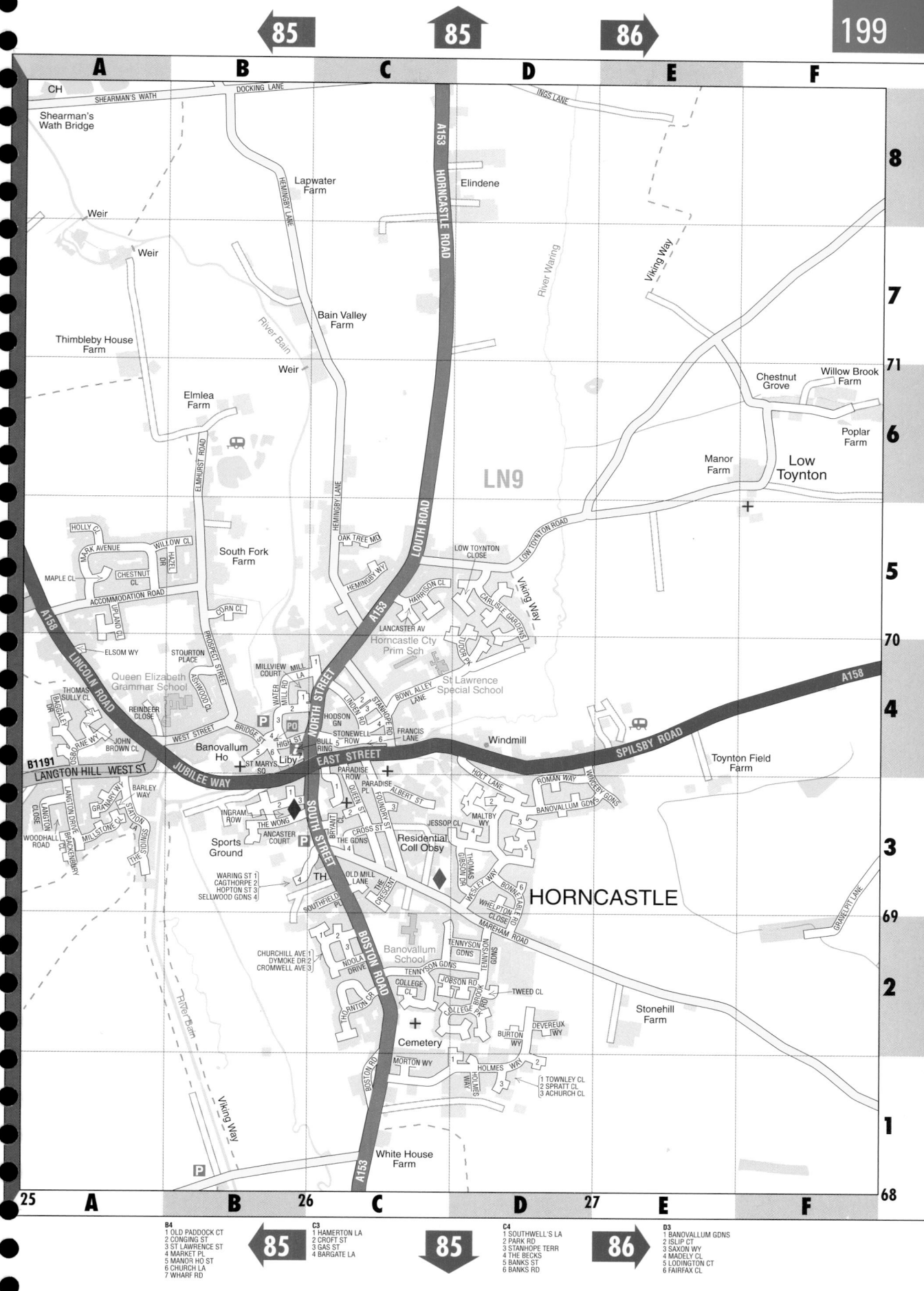

85 85 86

CH
SHEARMAN'S WATH
DOCKING LANE
INGS LANE

Shearman's
Wath Bridge

Lapwater
Farm

Elindene

A153 HORNCASTLE ROAD

Weir

Viking Way

Weir

HEMINGBY LANE

Bain Valley
Farm

River Bain

Thimbleby House
Farm

Weir

Chestnut
Grove

Willow Brook
Farm

Elmlea
Farm

Poplar
Farm

Low
Toynton

LN9

Manor
Farm

ELMHURST ROAD

South Fork
Farm

HEMINGBY LANE

OAK TREE MO

LOUTH ROAD

LOW TOYNTON ROAD

Viking Way

HOLLY CL

MARK AVENUE

WILLOW CL

HAZEL

CHESTNUT
CL

MAPLE CL

UPLAND CL

ACCOMMODATION ROAD

CORN CL

A158

PROSPECT STREET

ASHWOOD CL

HEMINGBY WY

HARRISON CL

Low Toynton
Close

CARLISLE GARDENS

Viking Way

LINCOLN ROAD

ELSOM WY

STOURTON
PLACE

Queen Elizabeth
Grammar School

REINDEER CLOSE

THOMAS
SULLY CL

BAGGALEY
DR

JOHN
BROWN CL

WEST STREET

MILLVIEW
COURT

MILL
LA

MILL RD

WATER
MILL RD

BRIDGE ST

NORTH STREET

LANCASTER AV

Horncastle Cty
Prim Sch

St Lawrence
Special School

TUDOR CR

A153

STANHOPE RD

BOWL ALLEY
LANE

LINDEN RD

HODSON
GN

STONEWELL
ROW

A158

SPILSBY ROAD

B1191

Langton Hill

LANE WY

WEST ST

Banovallum
Ho

JUBILEE WAY

HIGH ST

PO

St MARYS
SQ

Liby

i

BULL
RING

EAST STREET

Francis
Lane

Windmill

Toynton Field
Farm

70

A158

LANGTON HILL

BARLEY
WAY

GRANARY WY

LANGTON
CLOSE

LANGTON DRIVE

MILLSTONE

STATION
LA

THE
SIMONS

BRACKENBURY

WOODHALL
ROAD

Ingram
Row

THE WONG

ANCASTER
COURT

BRYANT

SOUTH STREET

Sports
Ground

P

THE GDNS

CROSS ST

Queen St

PARADISE
ROW

PARADISE

ALBERT ST

FOUNDRY ST

HOLT LANE

ROMAN WY

WIGELBY GDNS

BANOVALLUM GDNS

MALTBY
WY

JESSOP CL

Residential
Coll Obsy

THOMAS
GIBSON DR

WESLEY WAY

BOURNE
ABLE RD

HORNCASTLE

WARING ST 1
CAGTHORPE 2
HOPTON ST 3
SELLWOOD GDNS 4

TH

OLD MILL
LANE

THE
CRESCENT

WHELPTON
CLOSE

MAREHAM ROAD

A158

69

GRAVEL PIT LANE

CHURCHILL AVE 1
DYMOKE DR 2
CROMWELL AVE 3

NOOLA
DRIVE

BOSTON ROAD

Banovallum
School

TENNYSON
GDNS

TENNYSON GDNS

JOBSON RD

BROOK

TWEED CL

Stonehill
Farm

THORNTON CR

College
CL

College PK

BURTON
WY

DEVEREUX
WY

Cemetery

MORTON WY

HOLMES WAY

HOLMES
WAY

1 TOWNLEY CL
2 SPRATT CL
3 ACHURCH CL

River Bain

Viking Way

P

White House
Farm

A153

85 85 86

25 A B 26 C D 27 E F 68

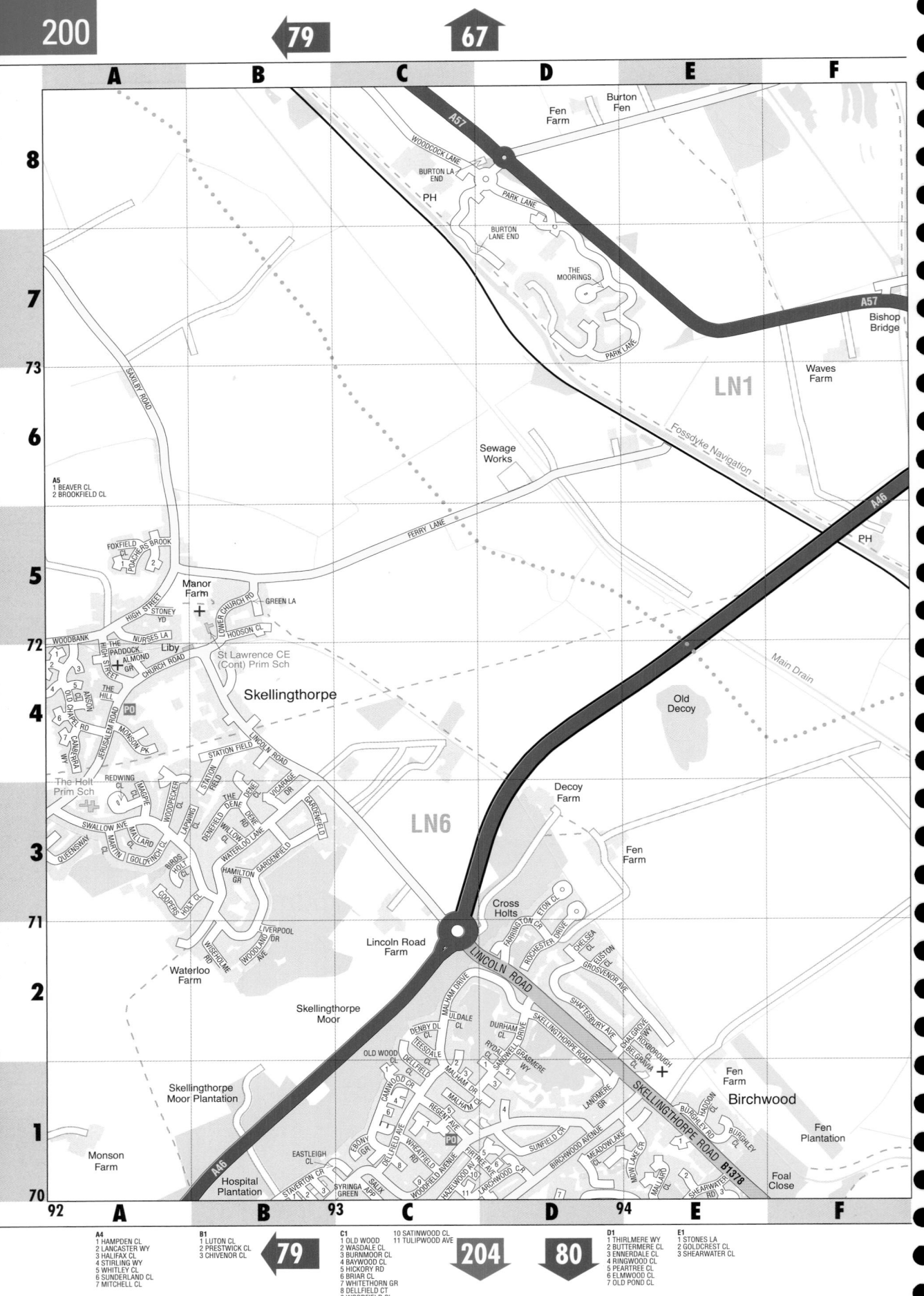

A4
1 HAMPDEN CL
2 LANCASTER WY
3 HALIFAX CL
4 STIRLING WY
5 WHITLEY CL
6 SUNDERLAND CL
7 MITCHELL CL

B1
1 LUTON CL
2 PRESTWICK CL
3 CHIVENOR CL

C1
1 OLD WOOD
2 WASDALE CL
3 BURNMOOR CL
4 BAYWOOD CL
5 HICKORY RD
6 BRIAR CL
7 WHITETHORN GR
8 DELLFIELD CT
9 WOODFIELD CL
10 SATINWOOD CL
11 TULIPWOOD AVE

D1
1 THIRLMERE WY
2 BUTTERMERE CL
3 ENNERDALE CL
4 RINGWOOD CL
5 PEARTREE CL
6 ELMWOOD CL
7 OLD POND CL

E1
1 STONES LA
2 GOLDCREST CL
3 SHEARWATER CL

A5
1 BEAVER CL
2 BROOKFIELD CL

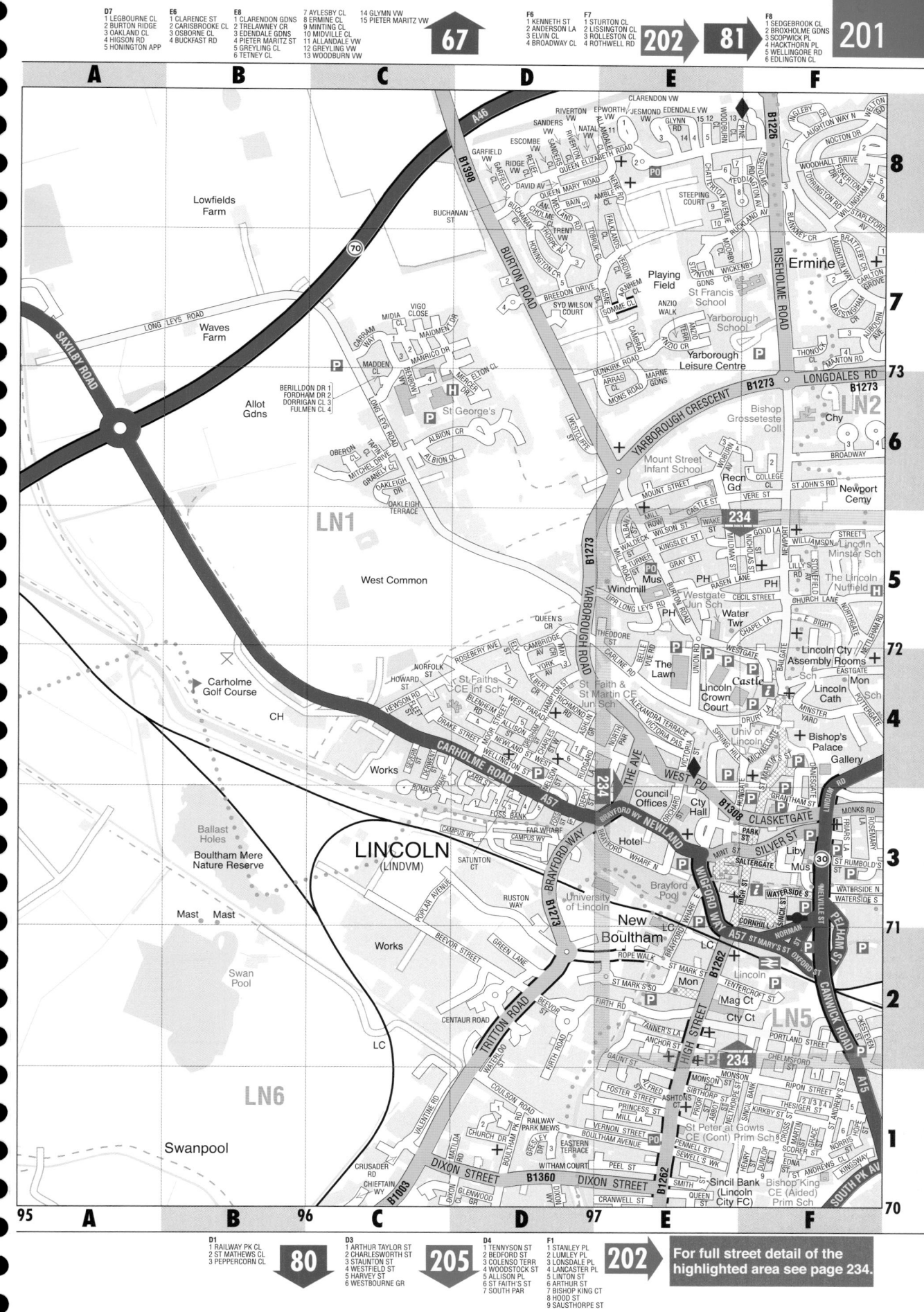

D7
1 LEGBOURNE CL
2 BURTON RIDGE
3 OAKLAND CL
4 HIGSON RD
5 HONINGTON APP

E6
1 CLARENCE ST
2 CARISBROOKE CL
3 OSBORNE CL
4 BUCKFAST RD

E8
1 CLARENDON GDNS
2 TRELAWNEY CR
3 EDENDALE GDNS
4 PIETER MARITZ ST
5 GREYLING CL
6 TETNEY CL

7
7 AYLESBY CL
8 ERMINE CL
9 MINTING CL
10 MIDVILLE CL
11 ALLANDALE VW
12 GREYLING VW
13 WOODBURN VW
14 GLYNN VW
15 PIETER MARITZ VW

67

F6
1 KENNETH ST
2 ANDERSON LA
3 ELVIN CL
4 BROADWAY CL

F7
1 TURTON CL
2 LISSINGTON CL
3 ROLLESTON ST
4 ROTHWELL ST

202 81

F8
1 SEDGEBROOK CL
2 BROXHOLME GDNS
3 SCOPWICK CL
4 HACKTHORN PL
5 WELLINGORE RD
6 EDLINGTON CL

201

D1
1 RAILWAY PK CL
2 ST MATHEWS CL
3 PEPPERCORN CL

80

D3
1 ARTHUR TAYLOR ST
2 CHARLESWORTH ST
3 STAUNTON ST
4 WESTFIELD ST
5 HARVEY ST
6 WESTBOURNE GR

205

D4
1 TENNYSON ST
2 BEDFORD ST
3 COLENSO TERR
4 WOODSTOCK ST
5 ALLISON PL
6 ST FAITH'S ST
7 SOUTH PAR

F1
1 STANLEY PL
2 LUMLEY PL
3 LONSDALE PL
4 LANCASTER PL
5 LINTON ST
6 ARTHUR ST
7 BISHOP KING CT
8 HOOD ST
9 SAUSTHORPE ST

202

For full street detail of the highlighted area see page 234.

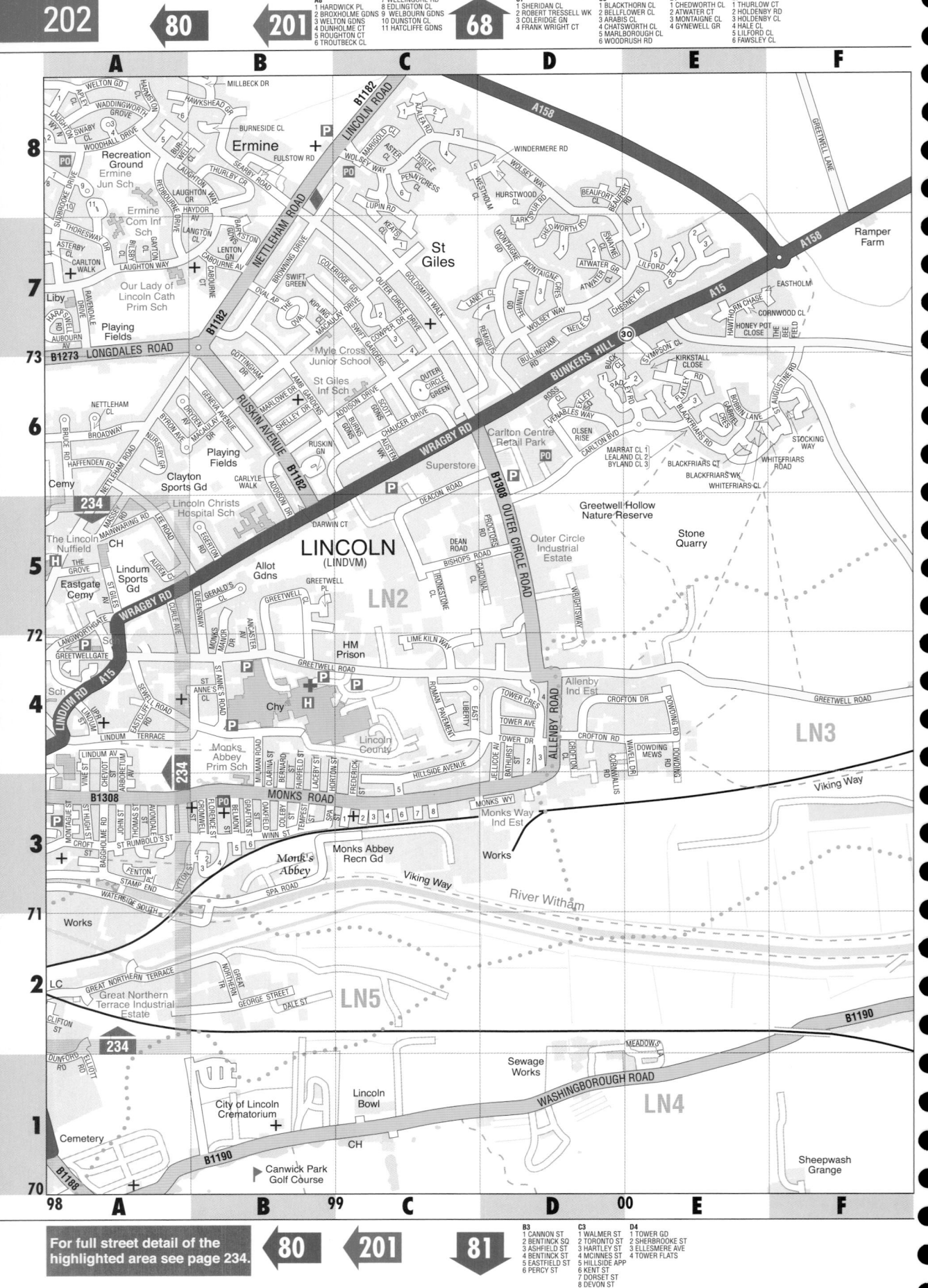

80 201 68

A8
1 HARDWICK PL.
2 BROXHOLME GDNS
3 WELTON GDNS
4 DUNHOLME CT
5 ROUGHTON CT
6 TROUTBECK CL

7 WELLINGORE RD
8 EDLINGTON CL
9 WELBOURN GDNS
10 DUNSTON CL
11 HATCLIFFE GDNS

C7
1 SHERIDAN CL
2 ROBERT TRESSELL WK
3 COLERIDGE GN
4 FRANK WRIGHT CT

C8
1 BLACKTHORN CL
2 BELLFLOWER CL
3 ARABIS CL
4 CHATSWORTH CL
5 MARLBOROUGH CL
6 WOODRUSH RD

D7
1 CHEDWORTH CL
2 ATWATER CT
3 MONTAIGNE CL
4 GYNEWELL GR

E7
1 THURLOW CT
2 HOLDENBY RD
3 HOLDENBY CL
4 HALE CL
5 LILFORD CL
6 FAWSLEY CL

For full street detail of the highlighted area see page 234.

80 201 81

B3
1 CANNON ST
2 BENTINCK SQ
3 ASHFIELD ST
4 BENTINCK ST
5 EASTFIELD ST
6 PERCY ST

C3
1 WALMER ST
2 TORONTO ST
3 HARTLEY ST
4 MCINNES ST
5 HILLSIDE APP
6 KENT ST
7 DORSET ST
8 DEVON ST

D4
1 TOWER GD
2 SHERBROOKE ST
3 ELLESMERE AVE
4 TOWER FLATS

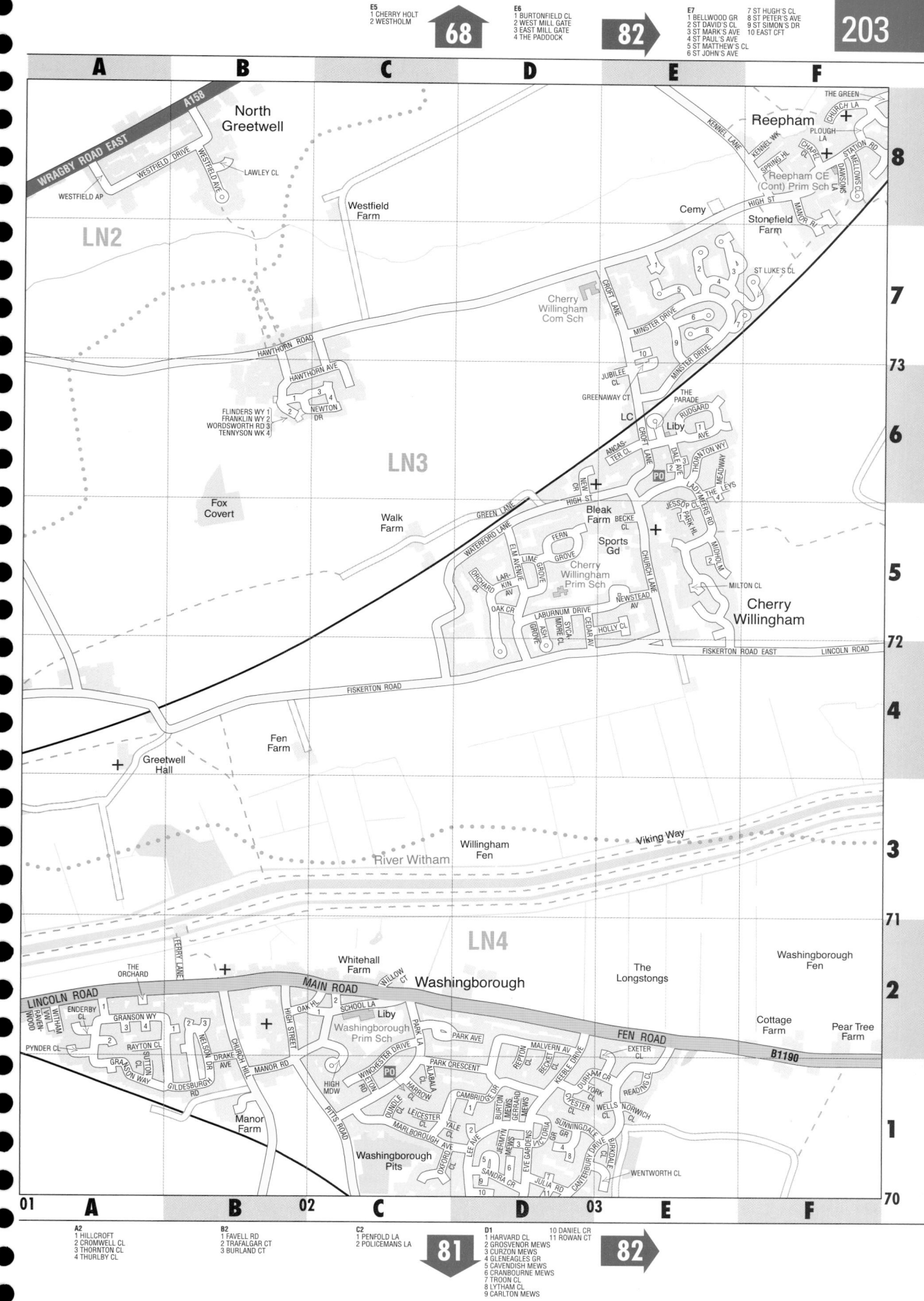
A
B
C
D
E
F
North Greetwell
A158
WRAGBY ROAD EAST
WESTFIELD DRIVE
WESTFIELD AVE
LAWLEY CL
WESTFIELD AP
LN2
Westfield Farm
Reepham
THE GREEN
CHURCH LA
PLOUGH LA
KENNEL LANE
KENNEL WK
SPRING HL
CHAPEL CL
STATION RD
MELLOWS CL
DAWSONS LA
Reepham CE (Cont) Prim Sch
HIGH ST
MANOR RD
Cemy
Stonefield Farm
ST LUKE'S CL
8
7
Cherry Willingham Com Sch
CROFT LANE
MINSTER DRIVE
HAWTHORN ROAD
HAWTHORN AVE
NEWTON DR
FLINDERS WY 1
FRANKLIN WY 2
WORDSWORTH RD 3
TENNYSON WK 4
73
JUBILEE CL
GREENAWAY CT
THE PARADE
LC
RUDGARD AVE
Liby
ANCASTER CL
CROFT LANE
DALE AVE
THORNTON WY
THE MEADWAY
LN3
6
PO
NEW CR
HIGH ST
LADYMEERS RD
THE LEYS
JESSOP CL
PARK HL
Fox Covert
Walk Farm
GREEN LANE
Bleak Farm
BECKE CL
WATERFORD LANE
ELM AVENUE
FERN GROVE
Sports Gd
MIDHOLM
LIME GROVE
LARKIN AV
ORCHARD CL
Cherry Willingham Prim Sch
CHURCH LANE
MILTON CL
5
NEWSTEAD AV
Cherry Willingham
OAK CR
LABURNUM DRIVE
ASH GROVE
SYCAMORE CL
CEDAR AV
HOLLY CL
72
FISKERTON ROAD EAST
LINCOLN ROAD
FISKERTON ROAD
4
Fen Farm
Greetwell Hall
Willingham Fen
Viking Way
River Witham
3
71
LN4
FERRY LANE
THE ORCHARD
Whitehall Farm
WILLOW CT
Washingborough
The Longstongs
Washingborough Fen
2
LINCOLN ROAD
MAIN ROAD
ENDERBY CL
RAVENWOOD
WITHAM VW
GRANSON WY
PYNDER CL
RAYTON CL
SUTTON CL
GRANSON WAY
NELSON DR
GILDESBURGH RD
DRAKE AVE
CHURCH HILL
MANOR RD
HIGH STREET
OAK HL
SCHOOL LA
Liby
Washingborough Prim Sch
PARK LA
PARK AVE
FEN ROAD
B1190
Cottage Farm
Pear Tree Farm
EXETER CL
MALVERN AV
REPTON CL
BECKET CL
KEEBLE DRIVE
DURHAM CR
YORK CL
READING CL
WINCHESTER DRIVE
PO
ETON RD
HIGH MDW
PARK CRESCENT
ALABALA CL
HARROW CL
CAMBRIDGE DR
BURTON MEWS
GERRARD MEWS
CHESTER CL
WELLS CL
NORWICH CL
Manor Farm
PITTS ROAD
QUNDLE CL
LEICESTER CL
MARLBOROUGH AVE
YALE CL
LEE AVE
JERMYN MEWS
VICTORIA GR
SUNNINGDALE GR
BIRKDALE CL
1
Washingborough Pits
OXFORD CL
SANDRA CR
EVE GARDENS
JULIA RD
CANTERBURY DRIVE
WENTWORTH CL
70
01
02
03

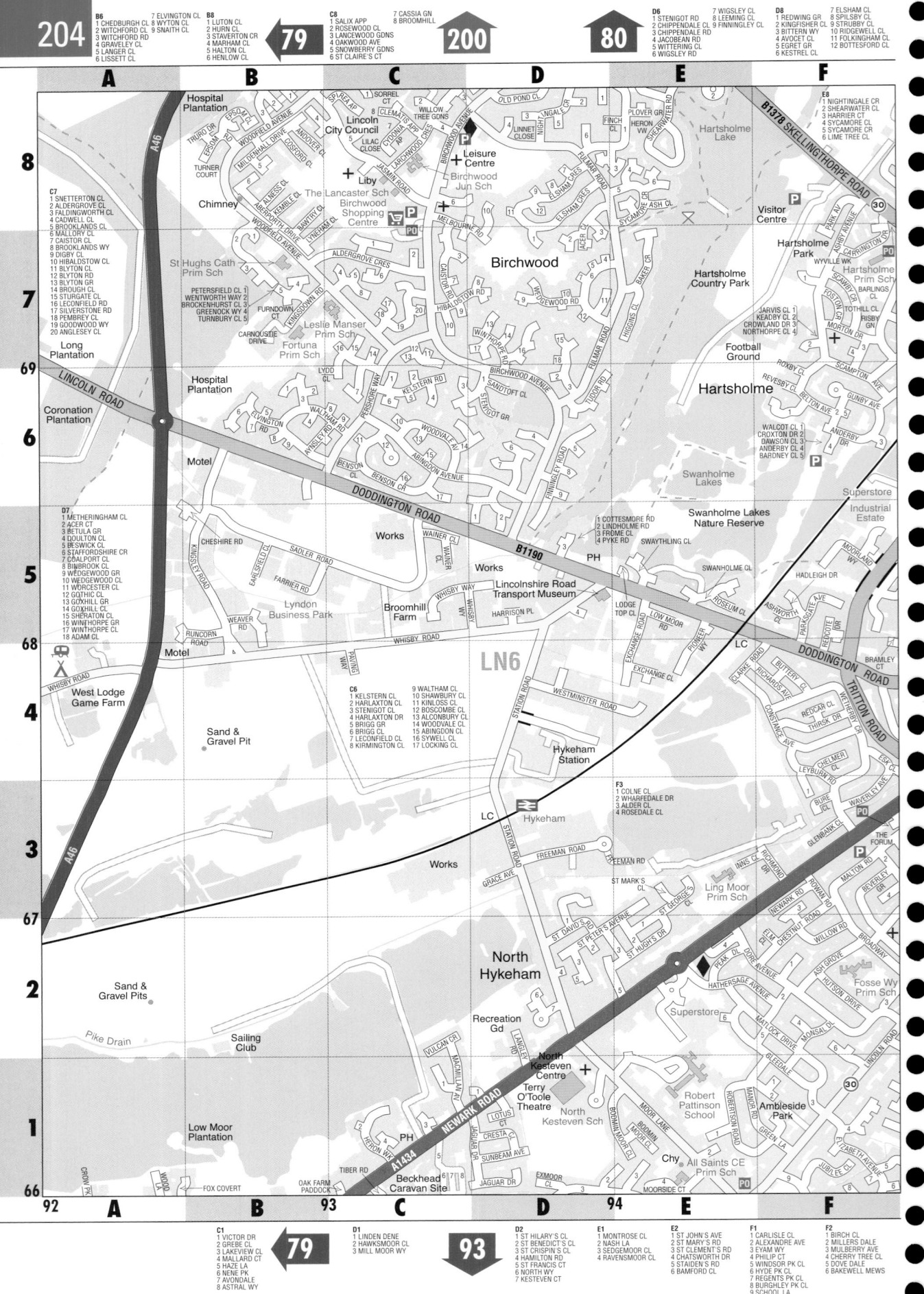

B6
1 CHEDBURGH CL
2 WITCHFORD CL
3 WITCHFORD CL
4 GRAVELEY CL
5 LANGER CL
6 LISSETT CL
7 ELVINGTON CL
8 WYTON CL
9 SNAITH CL

B8
1 LUTON CL
2 HURN CL
3 STAVERTON CR
4 MARHAM CL
5 HALTON CL
6 HENLOW CL

79 ←

C8
1 SALIX APP
2 ROSEWOOD CL
3 LANCEWOOD GDNS
4 OAKWOOD AVE
5 SNOWBERRY GDNS
6 ST CLAIRE'S CT
7 CASSIA GN
8 BROOMHILL

200 ←

80 ←

D6
1 STENIGOT RD
2 CHIPPENDALE RD
3 CHIPPENDALE RD
4 JACOBEAN CL
5 WITTERING CL
6 WIGSLEY RD
7 WIGSLEY CL
8 LEEMING CL
9 FINNINGLEY CL

D8
1 REDWING GR
2 KINGFISHER CL
3 BITTERN WY
4 AVOCET CL
5 EGRET GR
6 KESTREL CL

F8
1 NIGHTINGALE CR
2 SHEARWATER CL
3 HARRIER CT
4 KINGFISHER CL
5 SYCAMORE CR
6 LIME TREE CL

F
1 ELSHAM CL
2 SPILSBY CL
3 STRUBY CL
4 SWABY CL
5 RIDGEWELL CL
6 BOTTESFORD CL
7 FOLKINGHAM CL
8 KESTEVEN CT

C7
1 SNETTERTON CL
2 ALDERGROVE CL
3 FALDINGWORTH CL
4 CADWELL CL
5 BROOKLANDS CL
6 MALLORY CL
7 CAISTOR CL
8 BROOKLANDS WY
9 DIGBY CL
10 HIBALDSTOW CL
11 BLYTON CL
12 BLYTON RD
13 BLYTON GR
14 BROUGH CL
15 STURGATE CL
16 LECONFIELD RD
17 SILVERSTONE RD
18 PEMBREY CL
19 GOODWOOD WY
20 ANGLESEY CL

D7
1 METHERINGHAM CL
2 ACER CT
3 BETULA GR
4 DOULTON CL
5 BESWICK CL
6 STAFFORDSHIRE CR
7 COALPORT CL
8 BINBROOK CL
9 WEDGEWOOD GR
10 WEDGEWOOD CL
11 WORCESTER CL
12 GOTHIC CL
13 GOXHILL GR
14 GOXHILL CL
15 SHERATON CL
16 WINTHORPE GR
17 WINTHORPE CL
18 ADAM CL

C6
1 KELSTERN CL
2 HARLAXTON CL
3 STENIGOT CL
4 HARLAXTON DR
5 BRIGG GR
6 BRIGG CL
7 LECONFIELD CL
8 KIRMINGTON CL
9 WALTHAM CL
10 SHAWBURY CL
11 KINLOSS CL
12 BOSCOMBE CL
13 ALCONBURY CL
14 WOODVALE CL
15 ABINGDON CL
16 SYWELL CL
17 LOCKING CL

F3
1 COLNE CL
2 WHARFEDALE DR
3 ALDER CL
4 ROSEDALE CL

LN6

Birchwood

Hartsholme

North Hykeham

79 ↓

C1
1 VICTOR DR
2 GREBE CL
3 LAKEVIEW CL
4 MALLARD CT
5 HAZE LA
6 NENE PK
7 AVONDALE
8 ASTRAL WY

D1
1 LINDEN DENE
2 HAWKSMOOR CL
3 MILL MOOR WY

93 ↓

D2
1 ST HILARY'S CL
2 ST BENEDICT'S CL
3 ST CRISPIN'S CL
4 ST FRANCIS CT
5 NORTH WY
7 KESTEVEN CT

E1
1 MONTROSE CL
2 NASH LA
3 SEDGEMOOR CL
4 RAVENSMOOR CL

E2
1 ST JOHN'S AVE
2 ST MARY'S RD
3 ST CLEMENT'S RD
4 CHATSWORTH DR
5 STAIDEN'S RD
6 BAMFORD CL

F1
1 CARLISLE CL
2 ALEXANDRE AVE
3 EYAM WY
4 PHILIP CT
5 WINDSOR PK CL
6 HYDE PK CL
7 REGENTS PK CL
8 BURGHLEY PK CL
9 SCHOOL LA

F2
1 BIRCH CL
2 MILLERS DALE
3 MULBERRY AVE
4 CHERRY TREE CL
5 DOVE DALE
6 BAKEWELL MEWS

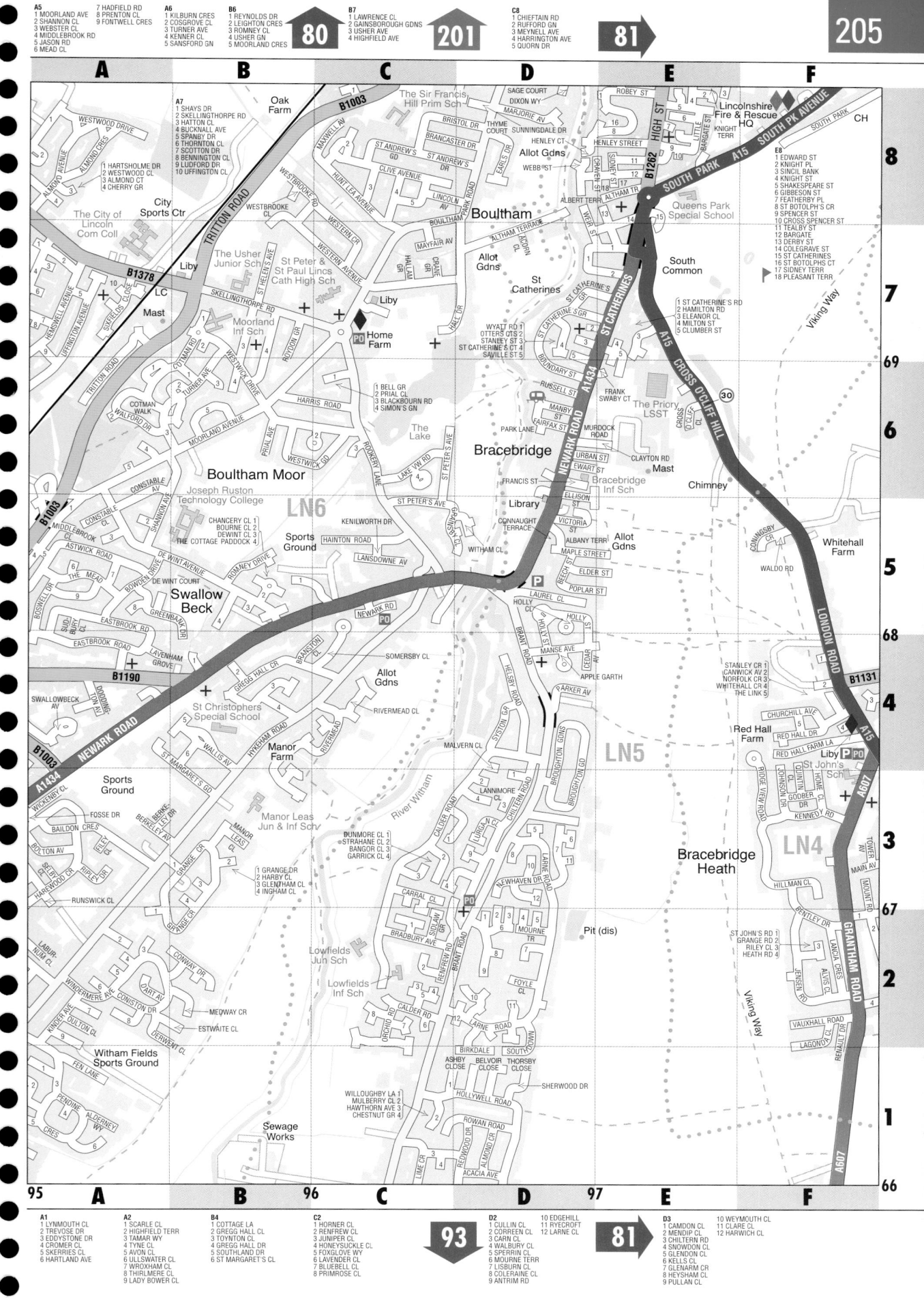

A5
1 MOORLAND AVE
2 SHANNON CL
3 WEBSTER CL
4 MIDDLEBROOK RD
5 JASON RD
6 MEAD CL

7 HADFIELD RD
8 PRENTON CL
9 FONTWELL CRES

A6
1 KILBURN CRES
2 COSGROVE CL
3 ROMNEY CL
4 TURNER AVE
5 KENNER CL
5 SANSFORD GN

B6
1 REYNOLDS DR
2 LEIGHTON CRES
3 ROMNEY CL
4 USHER GN
5 MOORLAND CRES

B7
1 LAWRENCE CL
2 GAINSBOROUGH GDNS
3 USHER AVE
4 HIGHFIELD AVE

C8
1 CHIEFTAIN RD
2 RUFFORD GN
3 MEYNELL AVE
4 HARRINGTON AVE
5 QUORN DR

A7
1 SHAYS DR
2 SKELLINGTHORPE RD
3 HATTON CL
4 BUCKNALL AVE
5 SPANBY DR
6 THORNTON CL
7 SCOTTON DR
8 BENNINGTON CL
9 LUDFORD DR
10 UFFINGTON CL

E8
1 EDWARD ST
2 KNIGHT PL
3 SINCIL BANK
4 KNIGHT ST
5 SHAKESPEARE ST
6 GIBBESON ST
7 FEATHERBY PL
8 ST BOTOLPH'S CR
9 SPENCER ST
10 CROSS SPENCER ST
11 TEALBY ST
12 BARGATE
13 DERBY ST
14 COLEGRAVE ST
15 ST CATHERINES
16 ST BOTOLPHS CT
17 SIDNEY TERR
18 PLEASANT TERR

1 ST CATHERINE'S RD
2 HAMILTON RD
3 ELEANOR CL
4 MILTON ST
5 CLUMBER ST

1 BELL GR
2 PRIAL CL
3 BLACKBOURN RD
4 SIMON'S GN

WYATT RD 1
OTTERS CTS 2
STANLEY ST 3
ST CATHERINE'S CT 4
SAVILLE ST 5

A1
1 LYNMOUTH CL
2 TREVOSE DR
3 EDDYSTONE DR
4 CROMER CL
5 SKERRIES CL
6 HARTLAND AVE

A2
1 SCARLE CL
2 HIGHFIELD TERR
3 TOYNTON CL
4 TYNE CL
5 AVON CL
6 ULLSWATER CL
7 WROXHAM CL
8 THIRLMERE CL
9 LADY BOWER CL

B4
1 COTTAGE LA
2 GREGG HALL CL
3 TOYNTON CL
4 GREGG HALL DR
5 SOUTHLAND DR
6 ST MARGARET'S CL

C2
1 HORNER CL
2 RENFREW CL
3 JUNIPER CL
4 HONEYSUCKLE CL
5 FOXGLOVE WY
6 LAVENDER CL
7 BLUEBELL CL
8 PRIMROSE CL

D2
1 CULLIN CL
2 CORREEN CL
3 CARN CL
4 WALBURY CL
5 SPERRIN CL
6 MOURNE TERR
7 LISBURN CL
8 COLERAINE CL
9 ANTRIM RD

10 EDGEHILL
11 RYECROFT
12 LARNE CL

D3
1 CAMDON CL
2 MENDIP CL
3 CHILTERN RD
4 SNOWDON CL
5 GLENDON CL
6 KELLS CL
7 GLENARM CR
8 HEYSHAM CL
9 PULLAN CL

10 WEYMOUTH CL
11 CLARE CL
12 HARWICH CL

1 GRANGE DR
2 HARBY CL
3 GLENTHAM CL
4 INGHAM CL

DUNMORE CL 1
STRAHANE CL 2
BANGOR CL 3
GARRICK CL 4

STANLEY CR 1
CANWICK AV 2
NORFOLK CR 3
WHITEHALL CR 4
THE LINK 5

ST JOHN'S RD 1
GRANGE RD 2
RILEY CL 3
HEATH RD 4

WILLOUGHBY LA 1
MULBERRY CL 2
HAWTHORN AVE 3
CHESTNUT GR 4

A5
1 WELLINGTON WY
2 CONINGSBY CL
3 BADER WY
4 CRANWELL CL
5 GIBSON PL
6 PERRIN AVE

7 CHESHIRE GR
8 PORTAL GN
9 PRIMROSE CL
10 GRUNNILL CL
11 HARRIS CL
12 HUDSON WY

◄ 103

A6
1 BISCAY CL
2 ST VINCENT CL
3 TEAL CLOSE
4 BEACON PARK CL
5 THE HURST
6 FLAMBOROUGH CL

7 TAGGS DR
8 BURDETT CL
9 YARBOROUGH RD
10 BURGH RD
11 ST MATTHEWS CL

▲ 90

A7
1 GLEBE CL
2 KINGFISHER DR
3 JOHNSON CL
4 NELSON CL
5 JENKINS CL
6 PORTLAND DR

7 THE HORN
8 THE NEEDLES

D8
1 ROMAN BANK
2 FAINLIGHT CL
3 NORTH FORELAND DR
4 GILBERTS GR

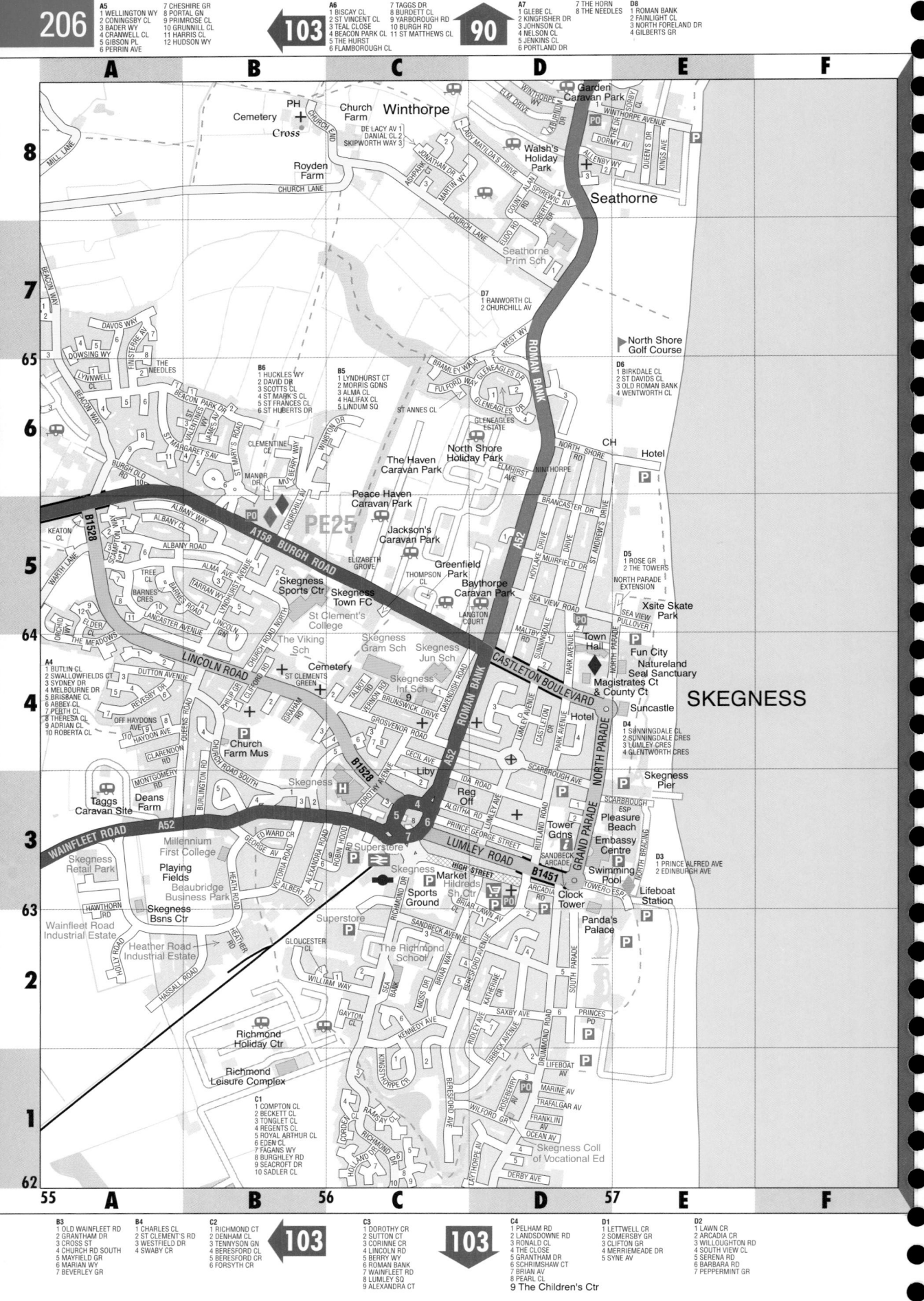

B3
1 OLD WAINFLEET RD
2 GRANTHAM DR
3 CROSS ST
4 CHURCH RD SOUTH
5 MAYFIELD GR
6 MARIAN WY
7 BEVERLEY GR

B4
1 CHARLES CL
2 ST CLEMENT'S RD
3 WESTFIELD DR
4 SWABY CR

C2
1 RICHMOND CT
2 DENHAM CL
3 TENNYSON GN
4 BERESFORD CL
5 BERESFORD CL
6 FORSYTH CR

◄ 103

C3
1 DOROTHY CR
2 SUTTON CT
3 CORINNE CR
4 LINCOLN RD
5 GRANTHAM DR
6 ROMAN BANK
7 WAINFLEET RD
8 LUMLEY SQ
9 ALEXANDRA GR

▲ 103

C4
1 PELHAM RD
2 LANDSDOWNE RD
3 RONALD CL
4 THE CLOSE
5 GRANTHAM DR
6 SCHRIMSHAW CT
7 BRIAN AV
8 PEARL CL
9 The Children's Ctr

D1
1 LETTWELL CR
2 SOMERSBY GR
3 CLIFTON GR
4 MERRIEMEADE CL
5 SYNE AV

D2
1 LAWN CR
2 ARCADIA CR
3 WILLOUGHTON RD
4 SOUTH VIEW CL
5 SERENA RD
6 BARBARA RD
7 PEPPERMINT GR

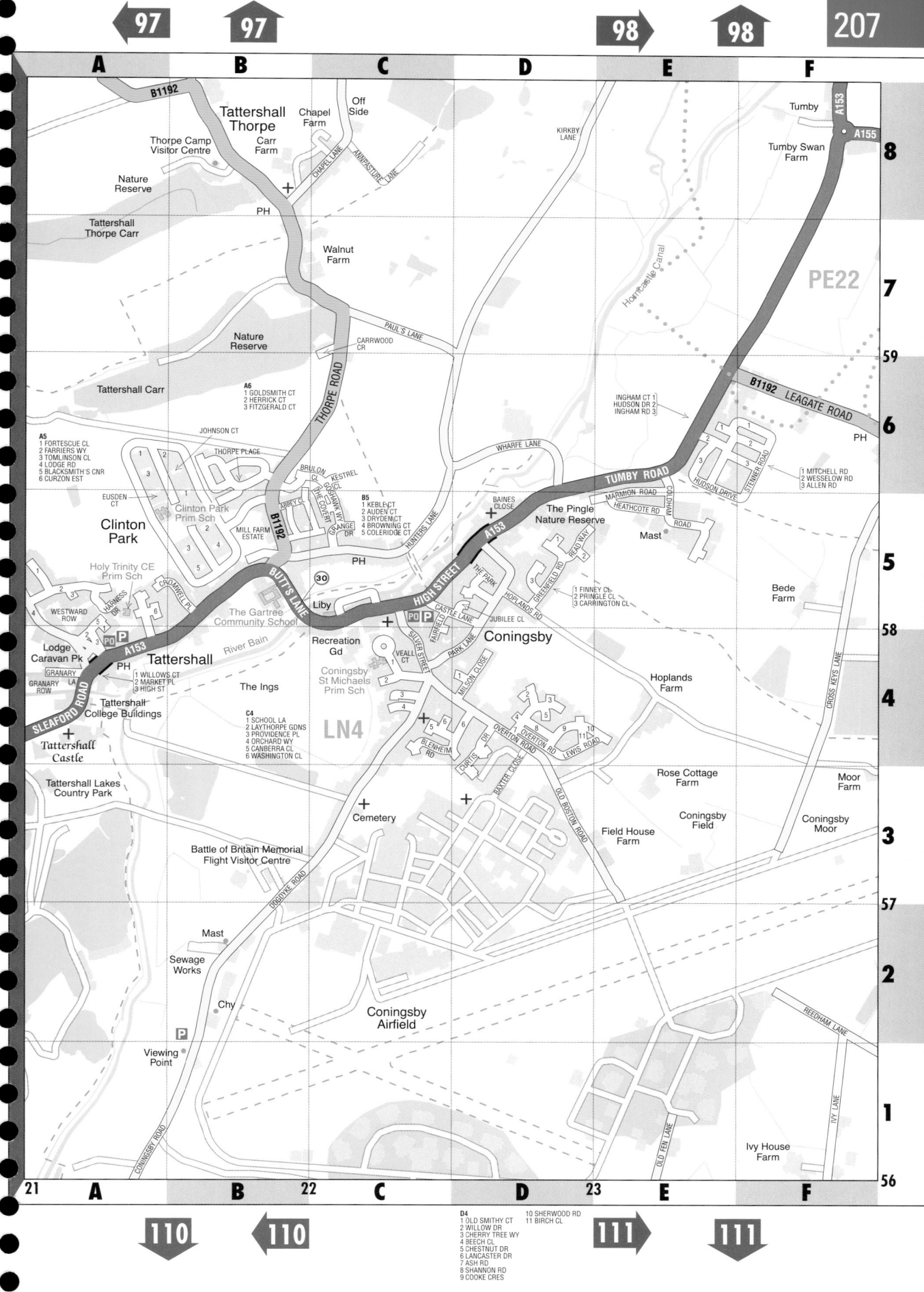

A   B   C   D   E   F

B1192
Tattershall Thorpe
Chapel Farm
Off Side
Thorpe Camp Visitor Centre
Carr Farm
Kirkby Lane
Tumby
A153
A155
Tumby Swan Farm

8

Nature Reserve
Tattershall Thorpe Carr
Walnut Farm
PH

PE22

7

Paul's Lane
Nature Reserve
Carrwood Cr
Horncastle Canal

59

Tattershall Carr
A6
1 GOLDSMITH CT
2 HERRICK CT
3 FITZGERALD CT
Johnson Ct
Thorpe Place
Thorpe Road
Wharfe Lane
B1192 LEAGATE ROAD
PH

6

A5
1 FORTESCUE CL
2 FARRIERS WY
3 TOMLINSON CL
4 LODGE RD
5 BLACKSMITH'S CNR
6 CURZON EST
Eusden Ct
Clinton Park Prim Sch
Brulon Cl
Kestrel
The Cover
Goshawk Wy
B5
1 KEBLE CT
2 AUDEN CT
3 DRYDEN CT
4 BROWNING CT
5 COLERIDGE WY
Baines Close
The Pingle Nature Reserve
Tumby Road
Marmion Road
Heathcote Rd
Hudson Drive
Whiton Road
Ingham Ct 1
Hudson Dr 2
Ingham Rd 3
Stenner Road
1 MITCHELL RD
2 WESSELOW RD
3 ALLEN RD

Clinton Park
Holy Trinity CE Prim Sch
B1192
Mill Farm Estate
Grange Dr
Huntens Lane
PH
A153
High Street
The Park
Greenfield Rd
Road Wy
Mast
1 FINNEY CL
2 PRINGLE CL
3 CARRINGTON CL
Bede Farm

5

Butt's Lane
30
Liby
Cromwell Pl
Harness Dr
Westward Row
P
The Gartree Community School
P
Castle Lane
Fairfield
Park Lane
Hoplands Rd
Jubilee Cl
Mildson Close
Coningsby
Hoplands Farm

58

Lodge Caravan Pk
PH
Granary La
Granary Row
A153
Sleaford Road
River Bain
Tattershall
1 WILLOWS CT
2 MARKET PL
3 HIGH ST
The Ings
Recreation Gd
Coningsby St Michaels Prim Sch
Silver Street
Veall Ct
C4
1 SCHOOL LA
2 LAYTHORPE GDNS
3 PROVIDENCE PL
4 ORCHARD WY
5 CANBERRA CL
6 WASHINGTON CL
Curtis Dr
Overton Road
Overton Rd
Lewis Road
Rose Cottage Farm
Moor Farm

4

Tattershall College Buildings
LN4
Blenheim Rd
Baxter Close
Field House Farm
Coningsby Field
Coningsby Moor

Cross Keys Lane

Tattershall Castle
Cemetery
Old Boston Road

3

Tattershall Lakes Country Park
Battle of Britain Memorial Flight Visitor Centre
Dogdyke Road

57

Mast
Sewage Works
Reedham Lane

2

Chy
Coningsby Airfield

P
Viewing Point
Old Fen Lane
Ivy Lane
Ivy House Farm

1

56

21   A   22   B   C   D   23   E   F

D4
1 OLD SMITHY CT
2 WILLOW DR
3 CHERRY TREE WY
4 BEECH CL
5 CHESTNUT DR
6 LANCASTER DR
7 ASH RD
8 SHANNON RD
9 COOKE CRES
10 SHERWOOD RD
11 BIRCH CL

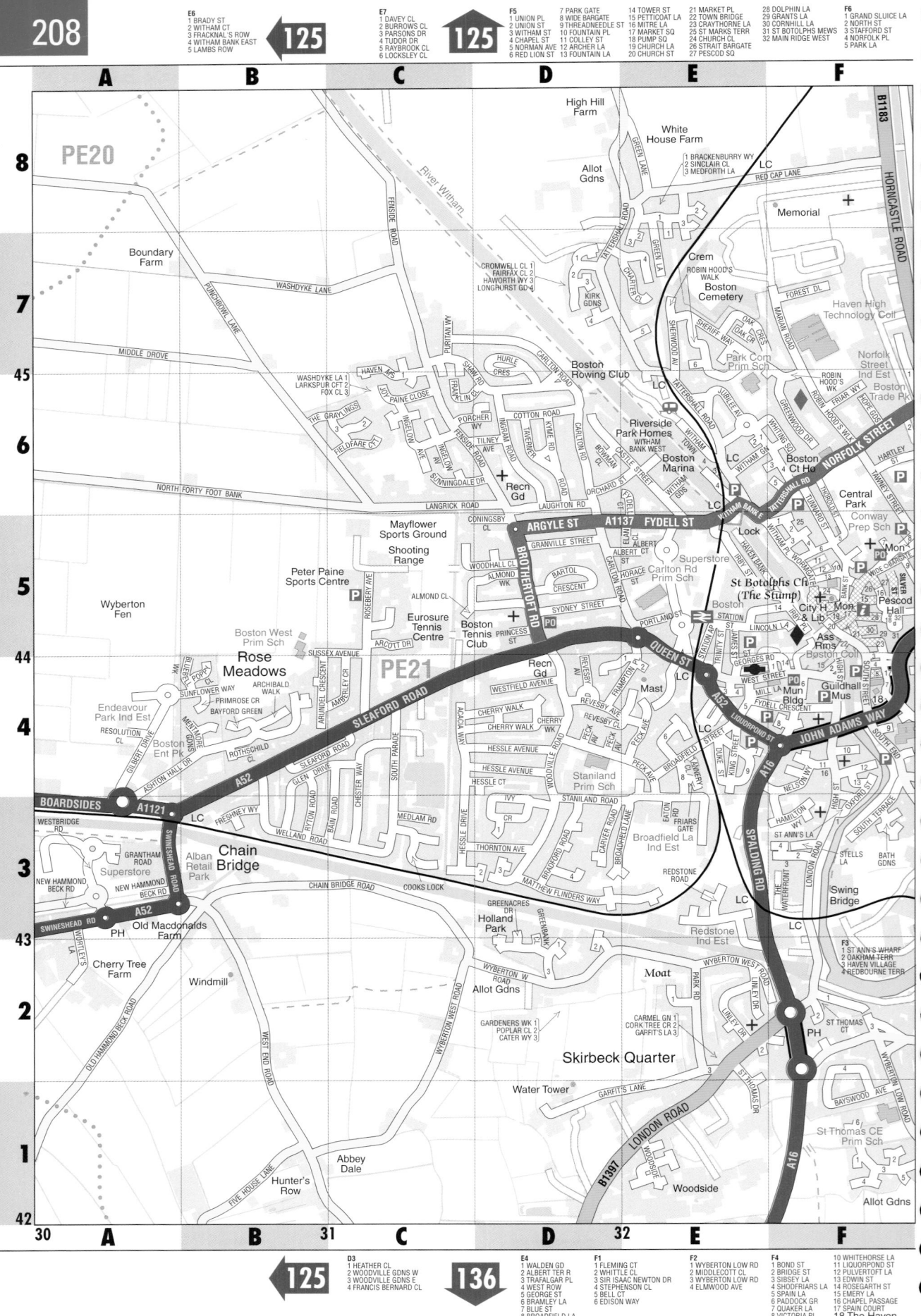

E6
1 BRADY ST
2 WITHAM CT
3 FRACKNAL'S ROW
4 WITHAM BANK EAST
5 LAMBS ROW

125

E7
1 DAVEY CL
2 BURROWS CL
3 PARSONS DR
4 TUDOR DR
5 RAYBROOK CL
6 LOCKSLEY CL

125

F5
1 UNION PL
2 UNION ST
3 WITHAM ST
4 CHAPEL ST
5 NORMAN AVE
6 RED LION ST

7 PARK GATE
8 WIDE BARGATE
9 THREADNEEDLE PL
10 FOUNTAIN PL
11 COLLEY ST
12 ARCHER LA
13 FOUNTAIN LA

14 TOWER ST
15 PETTICOAT LA
16 MITRE LA
17 MARKET SQ
18 PUMP SQ
19 CHURCH LA
20 CHURCH ST

21 MARKET PL
22 TOWN BRIDGE
23 CRAYTHORNE LA
24 ST MARKS TERR
25 CHURCH CL
26 STRAIT BARGATE
27 PESCOD SQ

28 DOLPHIN LA
29 GRANTS LA
30 CORNHILL LA
31 ST BOTOLPHS MEWS
32 MAIN RIDGE WEST

F6
1 GRAND SLUICE LA
2 NORTH ST
3 STAFFORD ST
4 NORFOLK PL
5 PARK LA

125

D3
1 HEATHER CL
2 WOODVILLE GDNS W
3 WOODVILLE GDNS E
4 FRANCIS BERNARD CL

136

E4
1 WALDEN GD
2 ALBERT TER R
3 TRAFALGAR PL
4 WEST ROW
5 GEORGE ST
6 BRAMLEY LA
7 BLUE ST
8 BROADFIELD LA
9 NELSON WY

F1
1 FLEMING CT
2 WHITTLE CL
3 SIR ISAAC NEWTON DR
4 STEPHENSON CL
5 BELL CT
6 EDISON WAY

F2
1 WYBERTON LOW RD
2 MIDDLECOTT CL
3 WYBERTON LOW RD
4 ELMWOOD AVE

F4
1 BOND ST
2 BRIDGE ST
3 SIBSEY LA
4 SHODFRIARS LA
5 SPAIN LA
6 PADDOCK GR
7 QUAKER LA
8 VICTORIA PL
9 GREYFRIARS LA

10 WHITEHORSE LA
11 LIQUORPOND ST
12 PULVERTOFT LA
13 EDWIN ST
14 ROSEGARTH ST
15 EMERY LA
16 CHAPEL PASSAGE
17 SPAIN COURT
18 The Haven

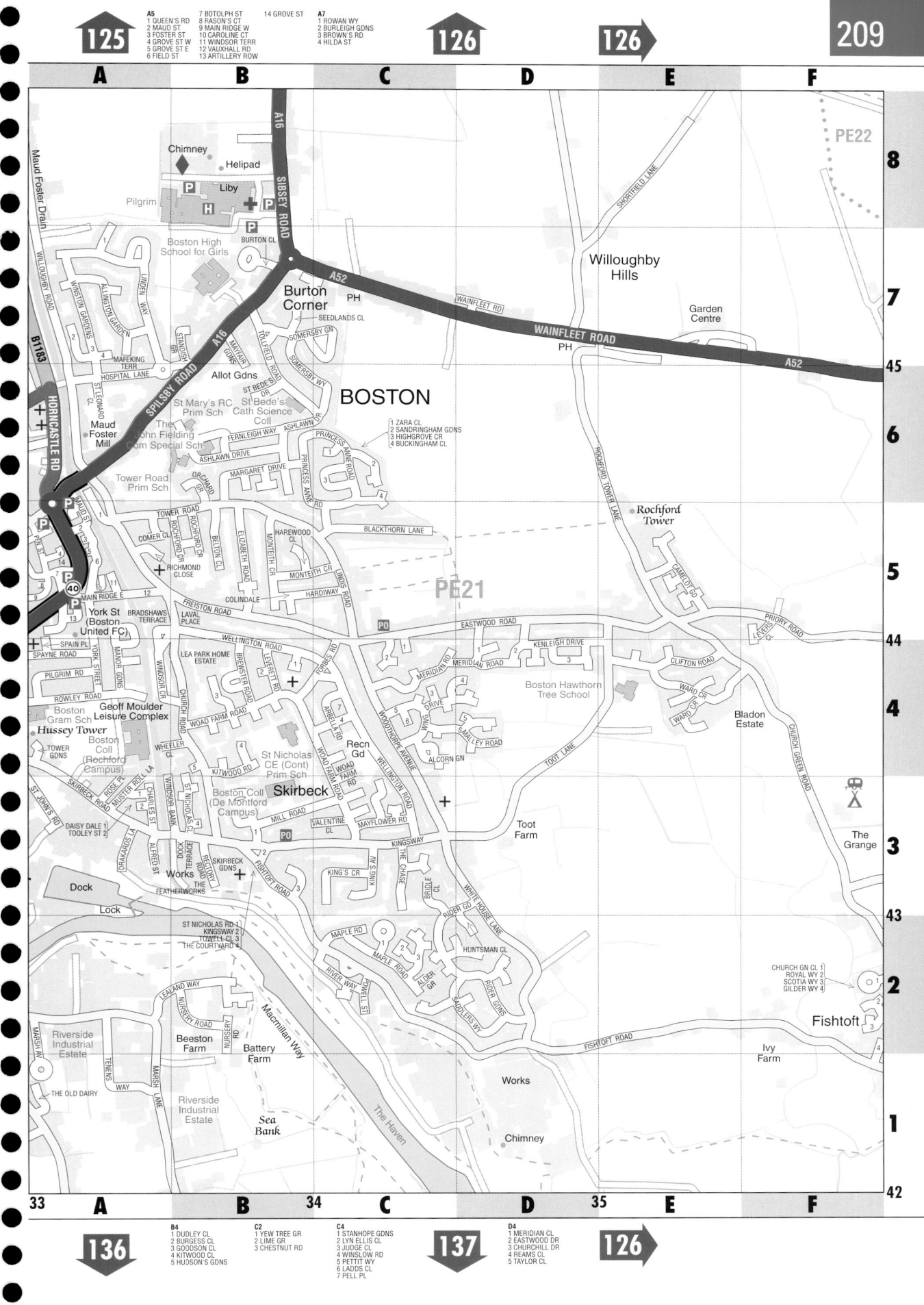

A5
1 QUEEN'S RD
2 MAUD ST
3 FOSTER ST
4 GROVE ST W
5 GROVE ST E
6 FIELD ST
7 BOTOLPH ST
8 RASON'S CT
9 MAIN RIDGE W
10 CAROLINE CT
11 WINDSOR TERR
12 VAUXHALL RD
13 ARTILLERY ROW
14 GROVE ST

A7
1 ROWAN WY
2 BURLEIGH GDNS
3 BROWN'S RD
4 HILDA ST

B4
1 DUDLEY CL
2 BURGESS CL
3 GOODSON CL
4 KITWOOD CL
5 HUDSON'S GDNS

C2
1 YEW TREE GR
2 LIME GR
3 CHESTNUT RD

C4
1 STANHOPE GDNS
2 LYN ELLIS CL
3 JUDGE CL
4 WINSLOW RD
5 PETTIT WY
6 LADDS CL
7 PELL PL

D4
1 MERIDIAN CL
2 EASTWOOD DR
3 CHURCHILL DR
4 REAMS CL
5 TAYLOR CL

E8
1 EMMINSON WY
2 KELHAM RD
3 THE HAVERLANDS
4 ORCHARD CL
5 MALVERN DR
6 MENDIP CL

F5
1 PORTSMOUTH CL
2 WESTMINISTER WY
3 ROBERTSON RD
4 CAMPBELL CL
5 ELY WY
6 RURO CL

F7
1 CEDARWOOD CL
2 BROOMWOOD CL
3 PALMWOOD CL
4 BIRCHWOOD CL
5 LILACWOOD DR
6 BRIARWOOD CL

7 ROWANWOOD DR
8 HOLLYWOOD DR

F8
1 VIVIAN CL
2 BEAUMONT DR
3 MALIM WY
4 PEACHWOOD CL
5 APPLEWOOD DR
6 BRAMBLEWOOD CL

7 ORANGAWOOD CL
8 OSTLER CL
9 COCHRAN CL

Gonerby Hill Foot

Knowles Farm

Stubbock Hill

Rectory Farm

CHURCH LANE
THE KNOLL
CHURCH VIEW

BRECON CL 1
GRAMPIAN WY 2
BRENDON CL 3

Gonerby Tunnel

Royston Ford End

Gonerby Hill Foot CE Prim Sch

Recreation Gd

Mill Hill

A5
1 RECTORY CL
2 CHURCH ST
3 CASTHORPE RD
4 CHAPEL LA
5 LAWSON LEAS
6 HIGHFIELDS
7 BERRYFIELD END
8 GRANGE PADDOCK

Boundary Farm

CHILTERN CL 1
CAMBRIAN CL 2
CHEVIOT CL 3
SWALLOW'S CL 4
KIMBERLEY TERR 5
LADYSMITH TERR 6

D5
1 SALISBURY CL
2 BLACKBURN CL
3 ST EDMUNDS CL
4 NEWCASTLE RD
5 ST ALBANS CL
6 CARLISLE CL
7 COVENTRY CL
8 CHESTER GDNS
9 WARWICK CL
10 BRADFORD CL

1 GRIMSTHORPE CL
2 DOVER CL
3 OAKHAM CL

E5
1 CORFE CL
2 RIBER CL
3 TATTERSHALL CL
4 CAMARTHEN CL
5 BIRMINGHAM CL
6 CHICHESTER CL
7 NORWICH WY
8 HEREFORD WY
9 ROCHESTER CL
10 PETERBOROUGH CL
11 ROCHESTER DR

BARROWBY ROAD

BARROWBY ROAD

Barrowby

New Barn Farm

Green Hill

NG32

1 THE NORTHINGS
2 ADAMSTILES

Beeden Park Estate

NG31

Recreation Gd

E4
1 DERBY CL
2 WESTBOURNE PL
3 SHORWELL CL

Autumn Park Ind Est

WESTRY CORNER

Barrowby Lodge

Fun Farm & Grantham Bowl

Works

F3
1 HODDER CL
2 BARNWELL TERR
3 HARLAXTON RD

1 WALKERS WY
2 THE DRIFT

Ambergate Special Sch

The Earl of Dysart Prim Sch

The Isaac Newton Prim Sch

Earlesfield

Recreation Ground

Meres Leisure Centre & Swimming Pool

St Hugh's CE Maths & Ambergate Comp Coll

Grantham Town Football Club

Sports Stadium

Spitalgate CE (Cont) Prim Sch

Works

Mag Ct & County Ct

Ellesmere Business Park

BUCKMINSTER GDNS

Harlaxton Lower Lodge Farm

Grantham Canal Nature Reserve

THE TURNPIKE

The Walton Girls High Sch

DENTON CL

D2
1 CHESTNUT GR
2 LARCH CL
3 SYCAMORE CT
4 HAWTHORNE CT

E2
1 CLYDE CT
2 LYMN CT
3 WELLAND CT
4 NENE CT
5 TAMAR CT
6 COLNE CT
7 STOUR CT
8 GANNET CT
9 FALCON CT

10 MALLARD CT
11 GRESLEY CT
12 STURROCK CT
13 IVATT CT
14 STIRLING CT
15 HICKLING CL
16 KINOULTON CT

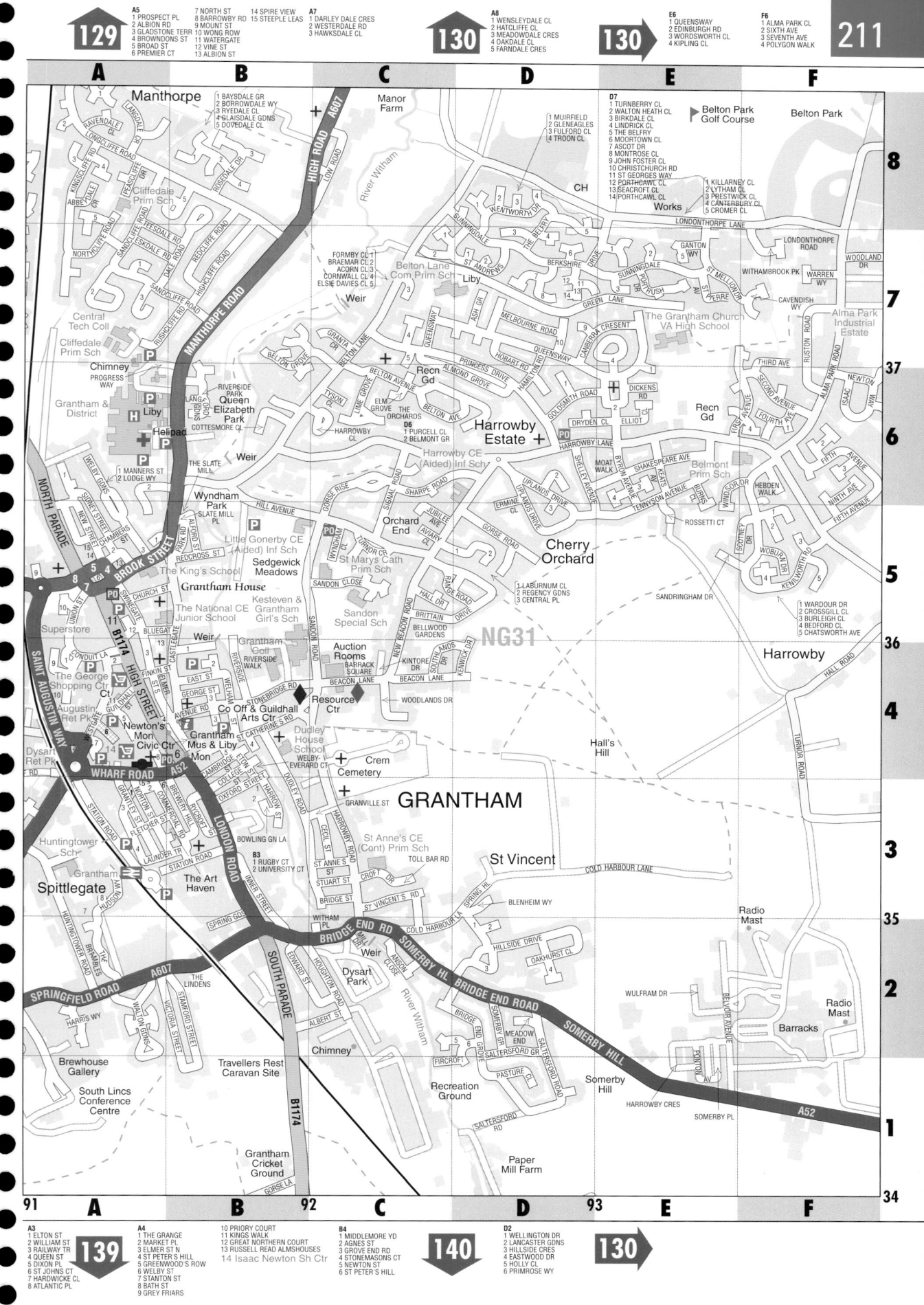

129

A5
1 PROSPECT PL
2 ALBION RD
3 GLADSTONE TERR
4 BROWNDONS ST
5 BROAD ST
6 PREMIER CT

7 NORTH ST
8 BARROWBY RD
9 MOUNT ST
10 WONG ROW
11 WATERGATE
12 VINE ST
13 ALBION ST

14 SPIRE VIEW
15 STEEPLE LEAS

A7
1 DARLEY DALE CRES
2 WESTERDALE RD
3 HAWKSDALE CL

130

A8
1 WENSLEYDALE CL
2 HATCLIFFE CL
3 MEADOWDALE CRES
4 OAKDALE CL
5 FARNDALE CRES

130

E6
1 QUEENSWAY
2 EDINBURGH RD
3 WORDSWORTH CL
4 KIPLING CL

F6
1 ALMA PARK CL
2 SIXTH AVE
3 SEVENTH AVE
4 POLYGON WALK

211

91   A   92   B   C   93   E   F   34

139

A3
1 ELTON ST
2 WILLIAM ST
3 RAILWAY TR
4 QUEEN ST
5 DIXON PL
6 ST JOHNS CT
7 HARDWICKE CL
8 ATLANTIC PL

A4
1 THE GRANGE
2 MARKET PL
3 ELMER ST N
4 ST PETER'S HILL
5 GREENWOOD'S ROW
6 WELBY ST
7 STANTON ST
8 BATH ST
9 GREY FRIARS

10 PRIORY COURT
11 KINGS WALK
12 GREAT NORTHERN COURT
13 RUSSELL READ ALMSHOUSES
14 Isaac Newton Sh Ctr

140

B4
1 MIDDLEMORE YD
2 AGNES ST
3 GROVE END RD
4 STONEMASONS CT
5 NEWTON ST
6 ST PETER'S HILL

140

D2
1 WELLINGTON DR
2 LANCASTER GDNS
3 HILLSIDE CRES
4 EASTWOOD DR
5 HOLLY CL
6 PRIMROSE WY

130

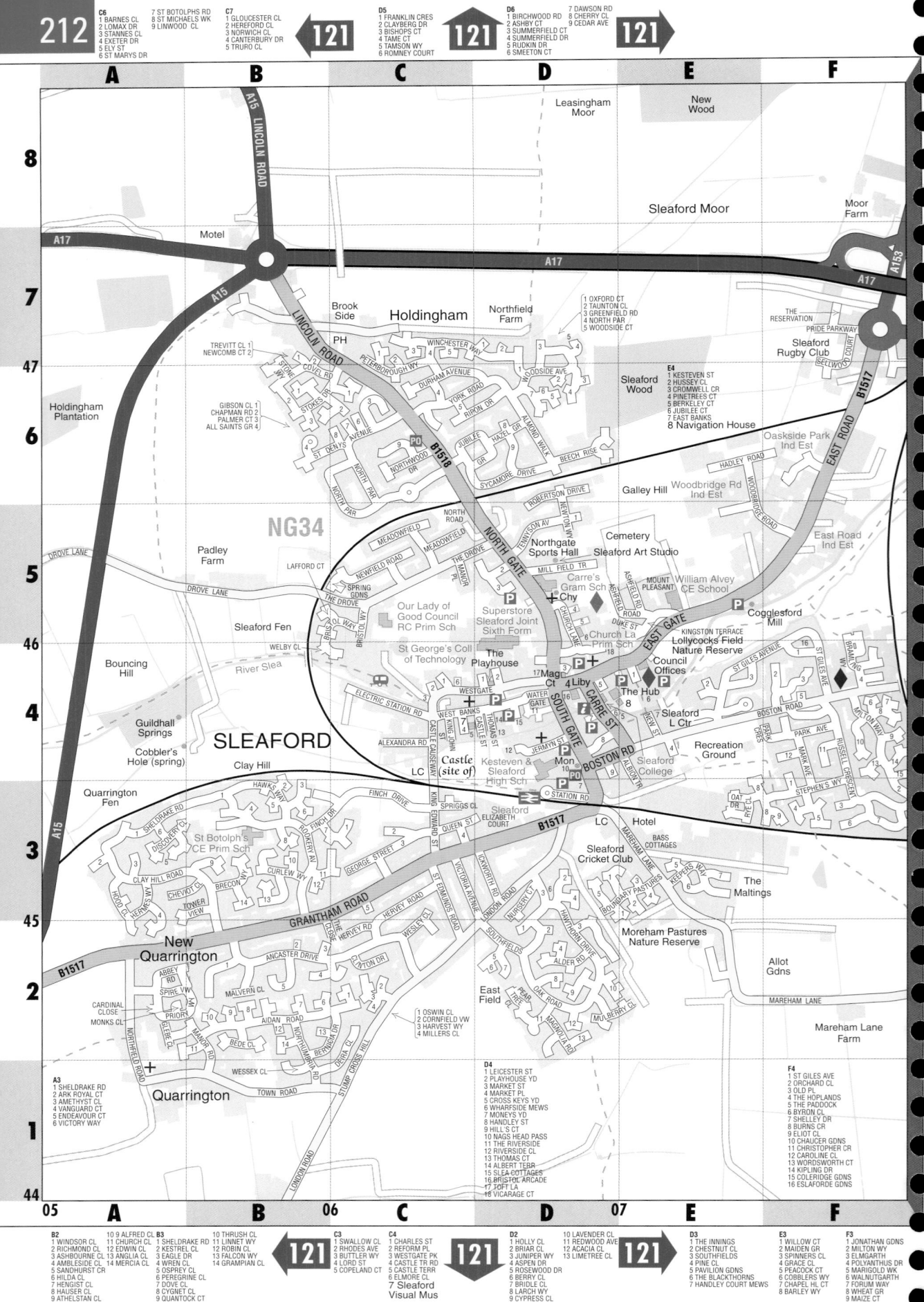

C6
1 BARNES CL
2 LOMAX DR
3 STANNES CL
4 EXETER DR
5 ELY ST
6 ST MARYS DR

7 ST BOTOLPHS RD
8 ST MICHAELS WK
9 LINWOOD CL

C7
1 GLOUCESTER CL
2 HEREFORD CL
3 NORWICH CL
4 CANTERBURY DR
5 TRURO ST

D5
1 FRANKLIN CRES
2 CLAYBERG DR
3 BISHOPS CT
4 TAME CT
5 TAMSON WY
6 ROMNEY COURT

D6
1 BIRCHWOOD RD
2 ASHBY CT
3 SUMMERFIELD CR
4 SUMMERFIELD DR
5 RUDKIN DR
6 SMEETON CT

7 DAWSON RD
8 CHERRY CL
9 CEDAR AVE

A B C D E F

8

Leasingham Moor

New Wood

Sleaford Moor

Moor Farm

A17

7

Motel

A15 LINCOLN ROAD

A17

A153

A17

Brook Side
PH
Holdingham

Northfield Farm

TREVITT CL 1
NEWCOMB CT 2

47

THE RESERVATION
PRIDE PARKWAY
Sleaford Rugby Club

1 OXFORD CT
2 TAUNTON CL
3 GREENFIELD RD
4 NORTH PAR
5 WOODSIDE CT

Holdingham Plantation

GIBSON CL 1
CHAPMAN RD 2
PALMER CT 3
ALL SAINTS GR 4

Sleaford Wood

E4
1 KESTEVEN ST
2 HUSSEY CL
3 CROMWELL CR
4 PINETREES CT
5 BERKELEY CT
6 JUBILEE CT
7 EAST BANKS
8 Navigation House

6

B1518
NORTHWOOD DR

Oakside Park Ind Est

B1517 EAST ROAD

NG34

Padley Farm

DROVE LANE

Galley Hill
Woodbridge Rd Ind Est

East Road Ind Est

DROVE LANE

Cemetery
Northgate Sports Hall
Sleaford Art Studio

5

LAFFORD CT

Spring Gdns

NORTH GATE

MOUNT PLEASANT

William Alvey CE School

Sleaford Fen

Our Lady of Good Council RC Prim Sch

Carre's Gram Sch
Chy

Cogglesford Mill

WELBY CL

Superstore
Sleaford Joint Sixth Form

Kingston Terrace
Lollycocks Field Nature Reserve

46

River Slea

St George's Coll of Technology

Church La Prim Sch

Bouncing Hill

The Playhouse

EAST GATE

ST GILES AVENUE

Guildhall Springs

Council Offices
The Hub

WESTGATE

WATER GATE ST

SOUTH GATE

CARRE ST

Sleaford L Ctr

4

ELECTRIC STATION RD

WEST BANKS

Sleaford College

Recreation Ground

BOSTON ROAD

PARK AVE

Cobbler's Hole (spring)

SLEAFORD

Clay Hill

ALEXANDRA RD

Castle (site of)

Kesteven & Sleaford High Sch

JERMYN ST

Mon
PO

STATION RD

Quarrington Fen

FINCH DRIVE

SPRIGGS CL

Sleaford Elizabeth Court

B1517

Hotel

BASS COTTAGES

The Maltings

3

A15

St Botolph's CE Prim Sch

GEORGE STREET

Sleaford Cricket Club

45

GRANTHAM ROAD

Moreham Pastures Nature Reserve

Allot Gdns

New Quarrington

2

B1517

CARDINAL CLOSE
MONKS CL

1 OSWIN CL
2 CORNFIELD VW
3 HARVEST WY
4 MILLERS CL

East Field

MAREHAM LANE

Mareham Lane Farm

Quarrington

A3
1 SHELDRAKE RD
2 ARK ROYAL CT
3 AMETHYST CL
4 VANGUARD CT
5 ENDEAVOUR CT
6 VICTORY WAY

D4
1 LEICESTER ST
2 PLAYHOUSE YD
3 MARKET PL
4 MARKET PL
5 CROSS KEYS YD
6 WHARFSIDE MEWS
7 MONEYS YD
8 HANDLEY ST
9 HILL'S CT
10 NAGS HEAD PASS
11 THE RIVERSIDE
12 RIVERSIDE CL
13 THOMAS CT
14 ALBERT TERR
15 SLEA COTTAGES
16 BRISTOL ARCADE
17 TOFT LA
18 VICARAGE RD

F4
1 ST GILES AVE
2 ORCHARD CL
3 OLD PL
4 THE HOPLANDS
5 THE PADDOCK
6 BYRON CL
7 SHELLEY DR
8 BURNS CR
9 ELIOT CL
10 CHAUCER GDNS
11 CHRISTOPHER CR
12 CAROLINE CL
13 WORDSWORTH CT
14 KIPLING DR
15 COLERIDGE GDNS
16 ESLAFORDE GDNS

1

05 A B 06 C D 07 E F

44

B2
1 WINDSOR CL
2 RICHMOND CL
3 ASHBOURNE CL
4 AMBLESIDE CL
5 SANDHURST CR
6 HILDA CL
7 HENGIST CL
8 HAUSER CL
9 ATHELSTAN CL

10 ALFRED CL
11 CHURCH CL
12 EDWIN CL
13 ANGLIA CL
14 MERCIA CL

B3
1 SHELDRAKE RD
2 KESTREL CL
3 EAGLE DR
4 WREN CL
5 OSPREY CL
6 PEREGRINE CL
7 DOVE CL
8 CYGNET CL
9 QUANTOCK CT

10 THRUSH CL
11 LINNET WY
12 ROBIN CL
13 FALCON WY
14 GRAMPIAN CL

C3
1 SWALLOW CL
2 RHODES AVE
3 BUTTLER WY
4 LORD ST
5 COPELAND CL

C4
1 CHARLES ST
2 REFORM PL
3 WESTGATE PK
4 CASTLE TR RD
5 CASTLE TERR

7 Sleaford Visual Mus

D2
1 HOLLY CL
2 BRIAR CL
3 JUNIPER WY
4 ASPEN DR
5 ROSEWOOD DR
6 BERRY CL
7 BRIDLE CL
8 LARCH WY
9 CYPRESS CL

10 LAVENDER CL
11 REDWOOD AVE
12 ACACIA CL
13 LIMETREE CL

D3
1 THE INNINGS
2 CHESTNUT CL
3 SOUTHFIELDS
4 PINE CL
5 PAVILION GDNS
6 THE BLACKTHORNS
7 HANDLEY COURT MEWS

E3
1 WILLOW CT
2 MAIDEN GR
3 SPINNERS CL
4 GRACE CL
5 PEACOCK CT
6 COBBLERS WY
7 CHAPEL HL CT
8 BARLEY WY

F3
1 JONATHAN GDNS
2 MILTON WY
3 ELMGARTH
4 POLYANTHUS DR
5 MARIGOLD WK
6 WALNUTGARTH
7 FORUM WAY
8 WHEAT GR
9 MAIZE CL

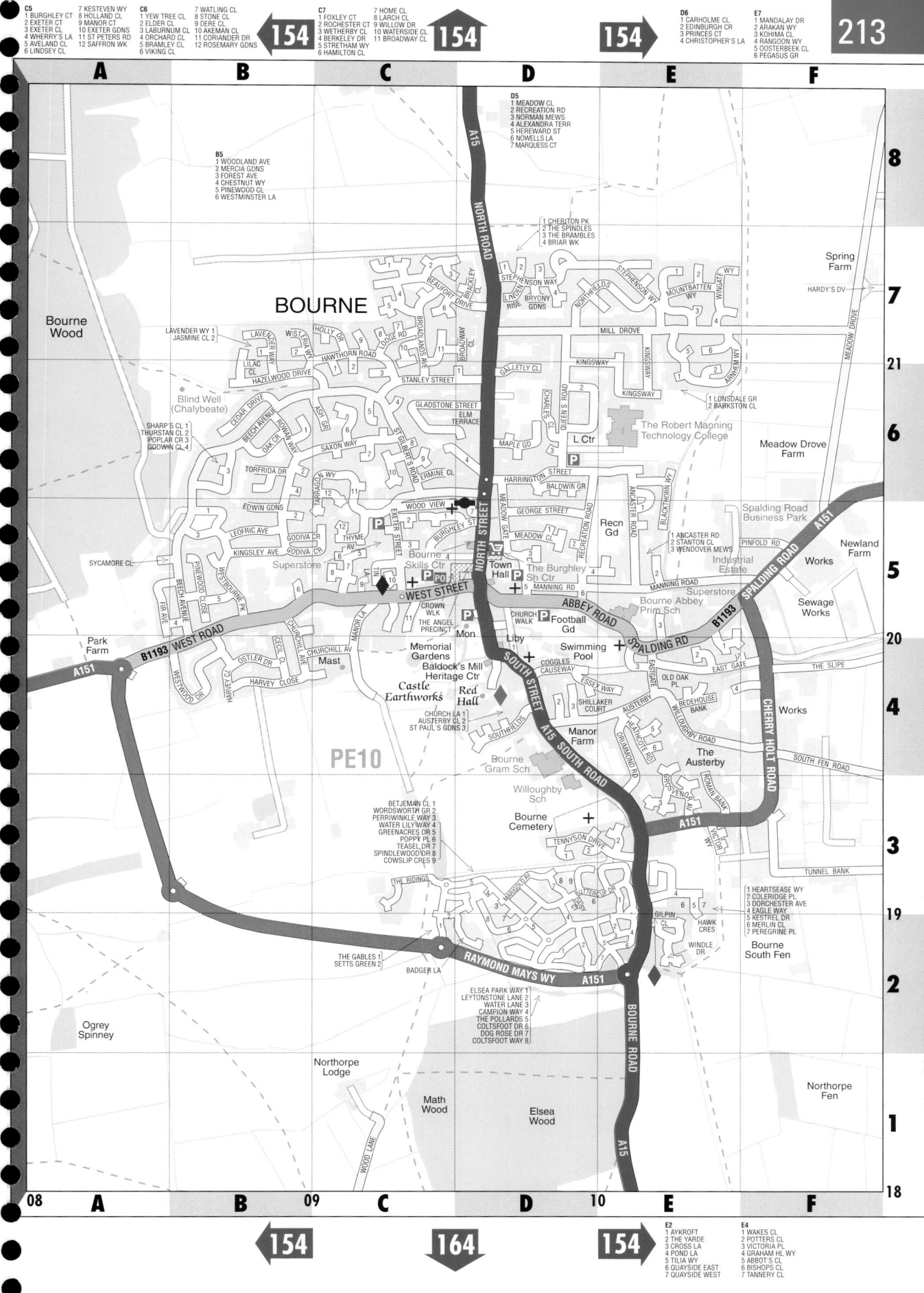

BOURNE

PE10

C5
1 BURGHLEY CT
2 EXETER CT
3 EXETER CL
4 WHERRY'S LA
5 AVELAND CL
6 LINDSEY CL
7 KESTEVEN WY
8 HOLLAND CL
9 MANOR CT
10 EXETER GDNS
11 ST PETERS RD
12 SAFFRON WK

C6
1 YEW TREE CL
2 ELDER CL
3 LABURNUM CL
4 ORCHARD CL
5 BRAMLEY CL
6 VIKING CL
7 WATLING CL
8 STONE CL
9 DERE CL
10 AKEMAN CL
11 CORIANDER DR
12 ROSEMARY GDNS

C7
1 FOXLEY CT
2 ROCHESTER CT
3 WETHERBY CL
4 BERKELEY DR
5 STRETHAM WY
6 HAMILTON CL
7 HOME CL
8 LARCH CL
9 WILLOW DR
10 WATERSIDE CL
11 BROADWAY CL

D6
1 CARHOLME CL
2 EDINBURGH CR
3 PRINCES CT
4 CHRISTOPHER'S LA

E7
1 MANDALAY DR
2 ARAKAN WY
3 KOHIMA CL
4 RANGOON WY
5 OOSTERBEEK CL
6 PEGASUS GR

D5
1 MEADOW CL
2 RECREATION RD
3 NORMAN MEWS
4 ALEXANDRA TERR
5 HEREWARD ST
6 NOWELLS LA
7 MARQUESS CT

B5
1 WOODLAND AVE
2 MERCIA GDNS
3 FOREST AVE
4 CHESTNUT CL
5 PINEWOOD CL
6 WESTMINSTER LA

1 CHERITON PK
2 THE SPINDLES
3 THE BRAMBLES
4 BRIAR WK

E2
1 AYKROFT
2 THE YARDE
3 CROSS LA
4 POND LA
5 TILIA WY
6 QUAYSIDE EAST
7 QUAYSIDE WEST

E4
1 WAKES CL
2 POTTERS CL
3 VICTORIA PL
4 GRAHAM HL WY
5 ABBOT'S CL
6 BISHOPS CL
7 TANNERY CL

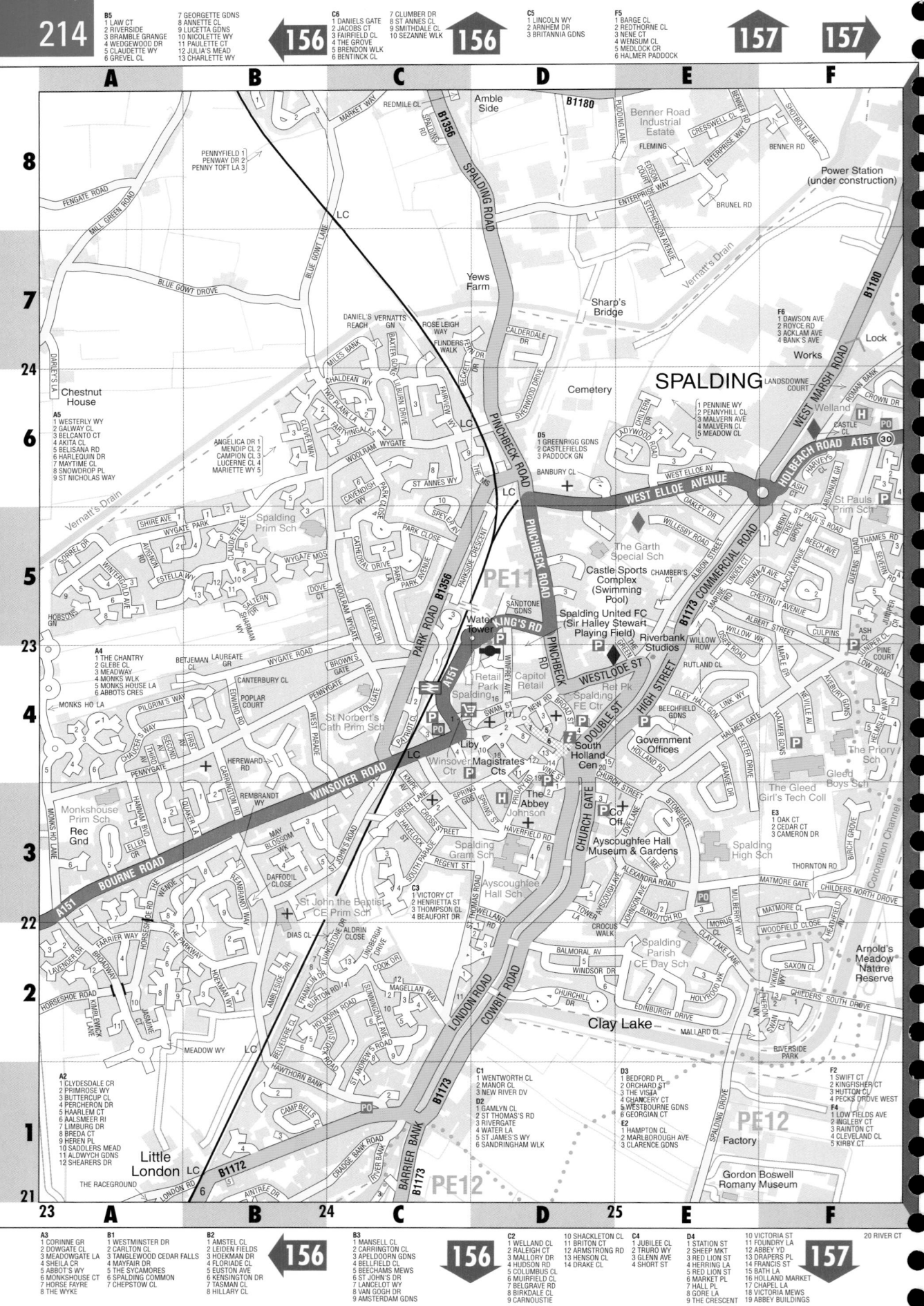

214
B5
1 LAW CT
2 RIVERSIDE
3 BRAMBLE GRANGE
4 WEDGEWOOD DR
5 CLAUDETTE WY
6 GREVEL CL
7 GEORGETTE GDNS
8 ANNETTE CL
9 LUCETTA GDNS
10 NICOLETTE WY
11 PAULETTE CT
12 JULIA'S MEAD
13 CHARLETTE WY
156
C6
1 DANIELS GATE
2 JACOBS CT
3 FAIRFIELD CL
4 THE GROVE
5 BRENDON WLK
6 BENTINCK CL
7 CLUMBER DR
8 ST ANNES CL
9 SMITHDALE CL
10 SEZANNE WLK
156
C5
1 LINCOLN WY
2 ARNHEM DR
3 BRITANNIA GDNS
F5
1 BARGE CL
2 REDTHORNE CL
3 NENE CT
4 WENSUM CL
5 MEDLOCK CR
6 HALMER PADDOCK
157
157
A
B
C
D
E
F
8
7
24
6
5
23
4
3
22
2
1
21
Amble Side
B1180
B1356
SPALDING ROAD
Benner Road Industrial Estate
Power Station (under construction)
Yews Farm
Sharp's Bridge
Vernatt's Drain
SPALDING
Cemetery
Chestnut House
Welland
WEST MARSH ROAD
HOLBEACH ROAD A151
WEST ELLOE AVENUE
PINCHBECK ROAD
PE11
The Garth Special Sch
Castle Sports Complex (Swimming Pool)
Spalding United FC (Sir Halley Stewart Playing Field)
Riverbank Studios
Spalding Prim Sch
St Pauls Prim Sch
B1173 COMMERCIAL ROAD
HIGH STREET
Water Tower
KING'S RD
Retail Park
Capitol Retail
Ret Pk
Spalding FE Ctr
Government Offices
South Holland Cen
St Norbert's Cath Prim Sch
Liby
Magistrates Cts
Winsover Ctr
The Abbey
Johnson
WINSOVER ROAD
BOURNE ROAD
A151
PARK ROAD B1356
Monkshouse Prim Sch
Rec Gnd
CHURCH GATE
Ayscoughfee Hall Museum & Gardens
Spalding Gram Sch
Ayscoughfee Hall Sch
Spalding High Sch
The Gleed Girl's Tech Coll
Gleed Boys Sch
The Priory Sch
Coronation Channel
St John the Baptist CE Prim Sch
Spalding Parish CE Day Sch
Arnold's Meadow Nature Reserve
Clay Lake
LONDON ROAD
COWBIT ROAD
B1173
BARRIER BANK
Little London
THE RACEGROUND
B1172
PE12
Factory
Gordon Boswell Romany Museum
A6
A5
1 WESTERLY WY
2 GALWAY CL
3 BELCANTO CT
4 AKITA CL
5 BELISANA RD
6 HARLEQUIN DR
7 MAYTIME CL
8 SNOWDROP PL
9 ST NICHOLAS WAY
A4
1 THE CHANTRY
2 GLEBE CL
3 MEADWAY
4 MONKS WLK
5 MONKS HOUSE LA
6 ABBOTS CRES
D5
1 GREENRIGG GDNS
2 CASTLEFIELDS
3 PADDOCK GN
F6
1 DAWSON AVE
2 ROYCE RD
3 ACKLAM AVE
4 BANK'S AVE
1 PENNINE WY
2 PENNYHILL CL
3 MALVERN AVE
4 MALVERN CL
5 MEADOW CL
E3
1 OAK CT
2 CEDAR CT
3 CAMERON DR
C3
1 VICTORY CT
2 HENRIETTA ST
3 THOMPSON CL
4 BEAUFORT DR
A2
1 CLYDESDALE CR
2 PRIMROSE WY
3 BUTTERCUP CL
4 PERCHERON DR
5 HAARLEM CT
6 AALSMEER RI
7 LIMBURG DR
8 BREDA CT
9 HEREN PL
10 SADDLERS MEAD
11 ALDWYCH GDNS
12 SHEARERS DR
C1
1 WENTWORTH CL
2 MANOR CL
3 NEW RIVER DV
D2
1 GAMLYN CL
2 ST THOMAS'S RD
3 RIVERGATE
4 WATER LA
5 ST JAMES'S WY
6 SANDRINGHAM WLK
D3
1 BEDFORD PL
2 ORCHARD ST
3 THE VISTA
4 CHANCERY CT
5 WESTBOURNE GDNS
6 GEORGIAN CT
E2
1 HAMPTON CL
2 MARLBOROUGH AVE
3 CLARENCE GDNS
F2
1 SWIFT CT
2 KINGFISHER CT
3 HUTTON CL
4 PECKS DROVE WEST
F4
1 LOW FIELDS AVE
2 INGLEBY CT
3 RAINTON CT
4 CLEVELAND CL
5 KIRBY CT
23
24
25
A3
1 CORINNE GR
2 DOWGATE CL
3 MEADOWGATE LA
4 SHEILA CR
5 ABBOT'S WY
6 MONKSHOUSE CT
7 HORSE FAYRE
8 THE WYKE
B1
1 WESTMINSTER DR
2 CARLTON CL
3 TANGLEWOOD CEDAR FALLS
4 MAYFAIR DR
5 THE SYCAMORES
6 SPALDING COMMON
7 CHEPSTOW CL
B2
1 AMSTEL CL
2 LEIDEN FIELDS
3 HOEKMAN DR
4 FLORIADE CL
5 EUSTON AVE
6 KENSINGTON DR
7 TASMAN CL
8 HILLARY CL
156
B3
1 MANSELL CL
2 CARRINGTON CL
3 APELDOORN GDNS
4 BELLFIELD CL
5 BEECHAMS MEWS
6 ST JOHN'S DR
7 LANCELOT WY
8 VAN GOGH DR
9 AMSTERDAM GDNS
156
C2
1 WELLAND CL
2 RALEIGH CT
3 MALLORY DR
4 HUDSON RD
5 COLUMBUS CL
6 MUIRFIELD CL
7 BELGRAVE RD
8 BIRKDALE CL
9 CARNOUSTIE
10 SHACKLETON CL
11 BRITON CT
12 ARMSTRONG RD
13 HENSON CL
14 DRAKE CL
C4
1 JUBILEE CL
2 TRURO WY
3 GLENN AVE
4 SHORT ST
D4
1 STATION ST
2 SHEEP MKT
3 RED LION ST
4 HERRING LA
5 RED LION ST
6 MARKET PL
7 HALL PL
8 GORE LA
9 THE CRESCENT
10 VICTORIA ST
11 FOUNDRY LA
12 ABBEY YD
13 DRAPERS PL
14 FRANCIS ST
15 BATH LA
16 HOLLAND MARKET
17 CHAPEL LA
18 VICTORIA MEWS
19 ABBEY BUILDINGS
20 RIVER CT
157

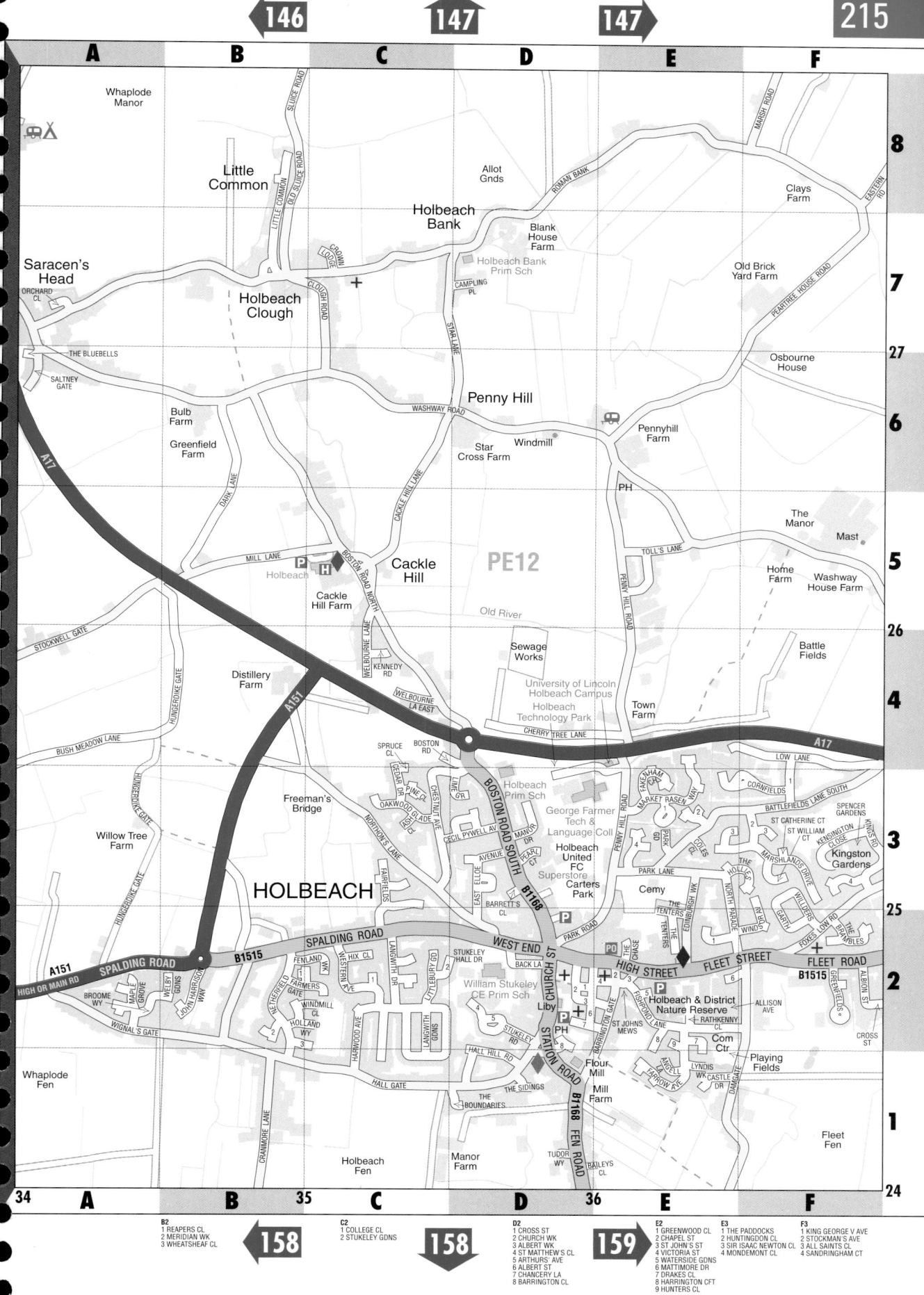

B2
1 REAPERS CL
2 MERIDIAN WK
3 WHEATSHEAF CL

158

C2
1 COLLEGE CL
2 STUKELEY GDNS

158

D2
1 CROSS ST
2 CHURCH WK
3 ALBERT WK
4 ST MATTHEW'S CL
5 ARTHURS' AVE
6 ALBERT ST
7 CHANCERY LA
8 BARRINGTON CL

159

E2
1 GREENWOOD CL
2 CHAPEL ST
3 ST JOHN'S ST
4 VICTORIA ST
5 WATERSIDE GDNS
6 MATTIMORE DR
7 DRAKES CL
8 HARRINGTON CFT
9 HUNTERS CL

E3
1 THE PADDOCKS
2 HUNTINGDON CL
3 SIR ISAAC NEWTON CL
4 MONDEMONT CL

F3
1 KING GEORGE V AVE
2 STOCKMAN'S AVE
3 ALL SAINTS CL
4 SANDRINGHAM CT

159 159 160 160

B5
1 HIGHGROVE
2 CHURCHILL CT
3 SPENCER CL
4 YORK RIDE
5 SADDLERS WY

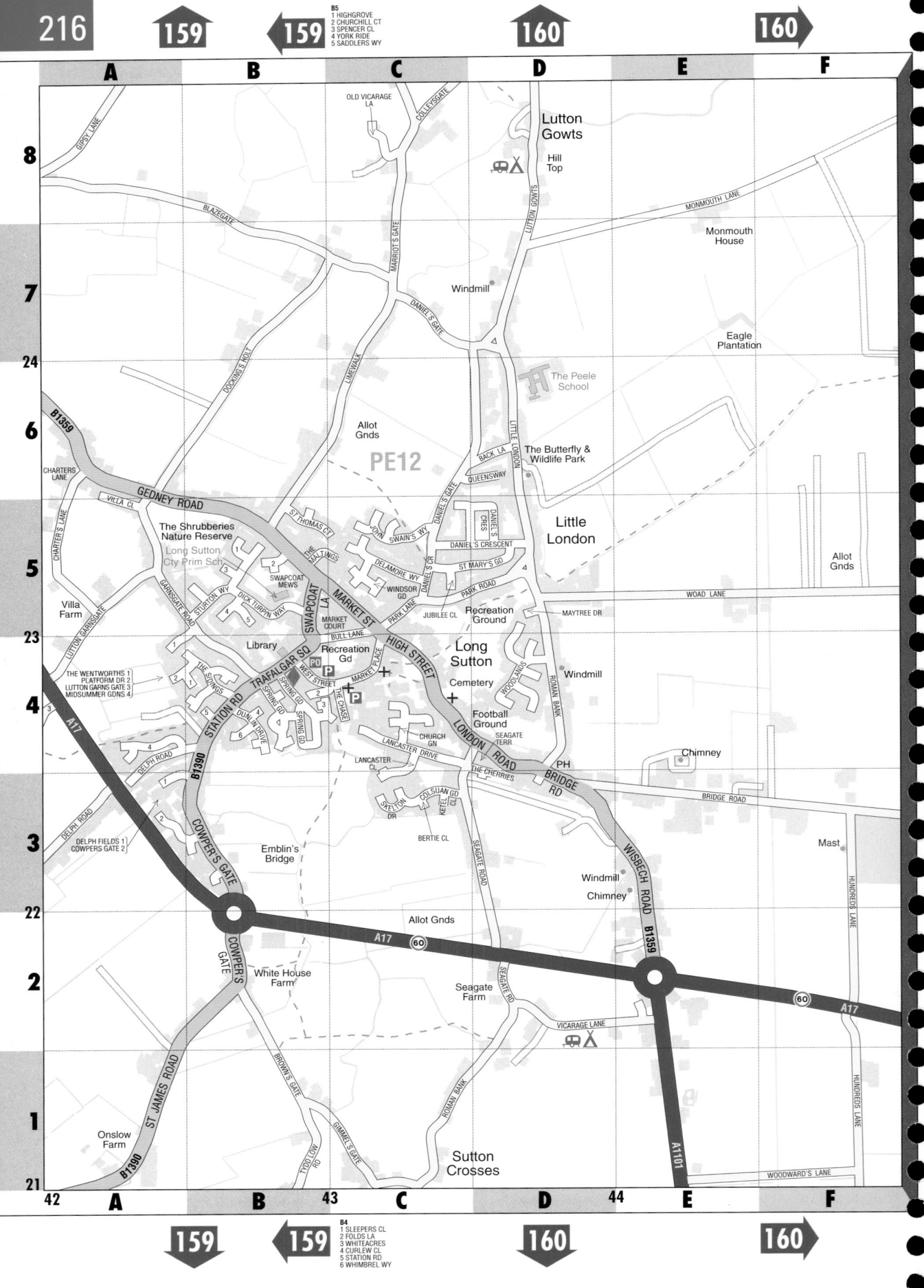

B4
1 SLEEPERS CL
2 FOLDS LA
3 WHITEACRES
4 CURLEW CL
5 STATION RD
6 WHIMBREL WY

159 159 160 160

164
165
165
173
173
174

A5
1 BELVOIR CL
2 PETWORTH CL
3 SANDRINGHAM WY
4 WOBURN CL
5 BURNSIDE AVE
6 CHATSWORTH CL

7 OSBOURNE WY
8 DEENE CL
9 WOODCROFT CL
10 TATTERSHALL DR
11 MAXEY CL
12 GRIMSTHORPE CL
13 BELTON CL

14 CEDAR CL
15 ALTHORPE CL

A6
1 THE PADDOCK
2 LIME TREE AVE
3 MILLFIELD RD
4 DOVECOTE RD
5 LINCOLN CL
6 CROMWELL WY

7 KESTEVEN DR
8 ROCKINGHAM CL
9 LAMPORT CL
10 HOLLAND CL
11 MEADWAY
12 FORGE CT

B5
1 ST GUTHLAC AVE
2 THE SPINNEY
3 THE WOODLANDS
4 STAMFORD CL
5 THE PRECINCTS

B6
1 GLEBE VW
2 JOHN WAKE CL
3 CHESTNUT WY
4 HAWTHORN CL
5 HALL FARM
6 OAK GR

C5
1 BEAUFORT AVE
2 WILLOUGHBY AVE
3 EASTFIELD
4 FLORENCE WY
5 THE MEADOWS
6 LARK RISE

7 LINNET CL
8 ROBIN CL
9 GODSEY CR
10 CHERRY GR
11 ROSEMARY AVE
12 THYME AVE
13 NIGHTINGALES

14 CURLEW WLK
15 WREN CL

D6
1 SORREL CL
2 COWSLIP DR
3 BLACKTHORN CL
4 THE BRAMBLES
5 BRYONY WY
6 TEASLES
7 SPEEDWELL CT
8 BLUEBELLS
9 TOWNING CL

D5
1 PRIMROSES
2 SWEET CL
3 SWALLOW WLK
4 PENDLEBURY DR
5 ALLEN CL
6 PANTON CL

1 THE LEES
2 SEWELL CL
3 LINCHFIELD CL
4 ERMINE WY

CROWFIELDS 1
THE PARSLINS 2

D4
1 KESTEVEN CL
2 HOLLY WY
3 NEW ROW
4 ORCHARD CL

E4
1 EXETER CL
2 WATERTON CL
3 BURGHLEY CL
4 BROWNLOW DR

1 FAIRFAX WY
2 RIVERBANK CL

F4
1 RYCROFT CL
2 CHURCH GATE
3 BACK LA
4 STEPHENS WY

DIXONS RD 1
ELM CL 2
DOUGLAS RD 3

1 WEST END RD
2 WOODGATE LA

1 CROMWELL CL
2 ST ANDREWS RD
3 EAST RD
4 CHURCH VW

MARKET DEEPING

PE6

Deeping St James

Deeping Gate

Northborough

Maxey

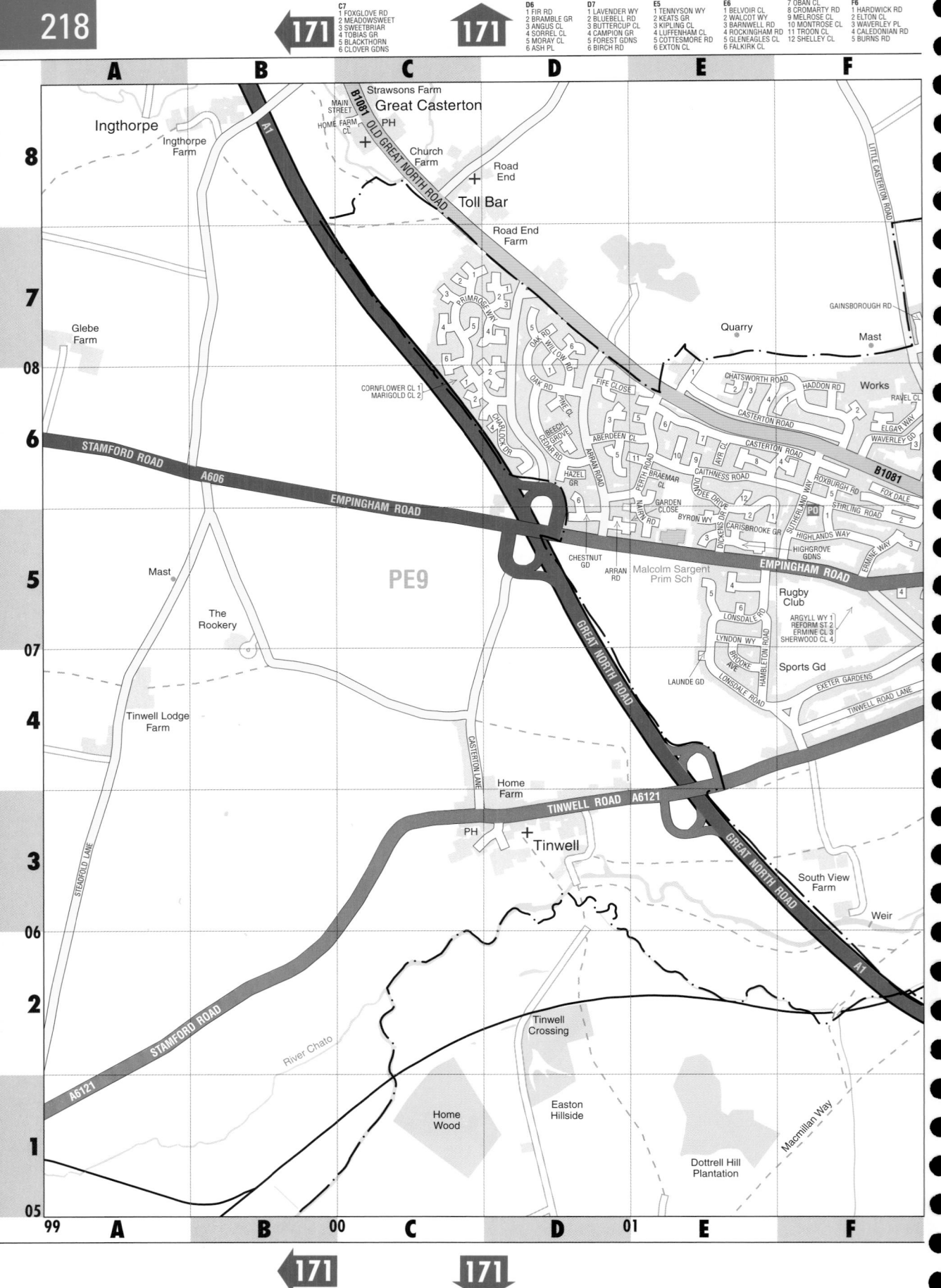

← 171

171

C7
1 FOXGLOVE RD
2 MEADOWSWEET
3 SWEETBRIAR
4 TOBIAS GR
5 BLACKTHORN
6 CLOVER GDNS

D6
1 FIR RD
2 BRAMBLE GR
3 ANGUS CL
4 SORREL CL
5 MORAY CL
6 ASH PL

D7
1 LAVENDER WY
2 BLUEBELL RD
3 BUTTERCUP CL
4 CAMPION CL
5 FOREST GDNS
6 BIRCH RD

E5
1 TENNYSON WY
2 KEATS GR
3 KIPLING CL
4 LUFFENHAM CL
5 COTTESMORE RD
6 EXTON CL

E6
1 BELVOIR CL
2 WALCOT WY
3 BARNWELL RD
4 ROCKINGHAM RD
5 GLENEAGLES CL
6 FALKIRK CL

1 OBAN CL
2 CROMARTY RD
3 MELROSE CL
4 MONTROSE CL
5 TROON CL
6 SHELLEY CL

F6
1 HARDWICK RD
2 ELTON CL
3 WAVERLEY PL
4 CALEDONIAN RD
5 BURNS RD

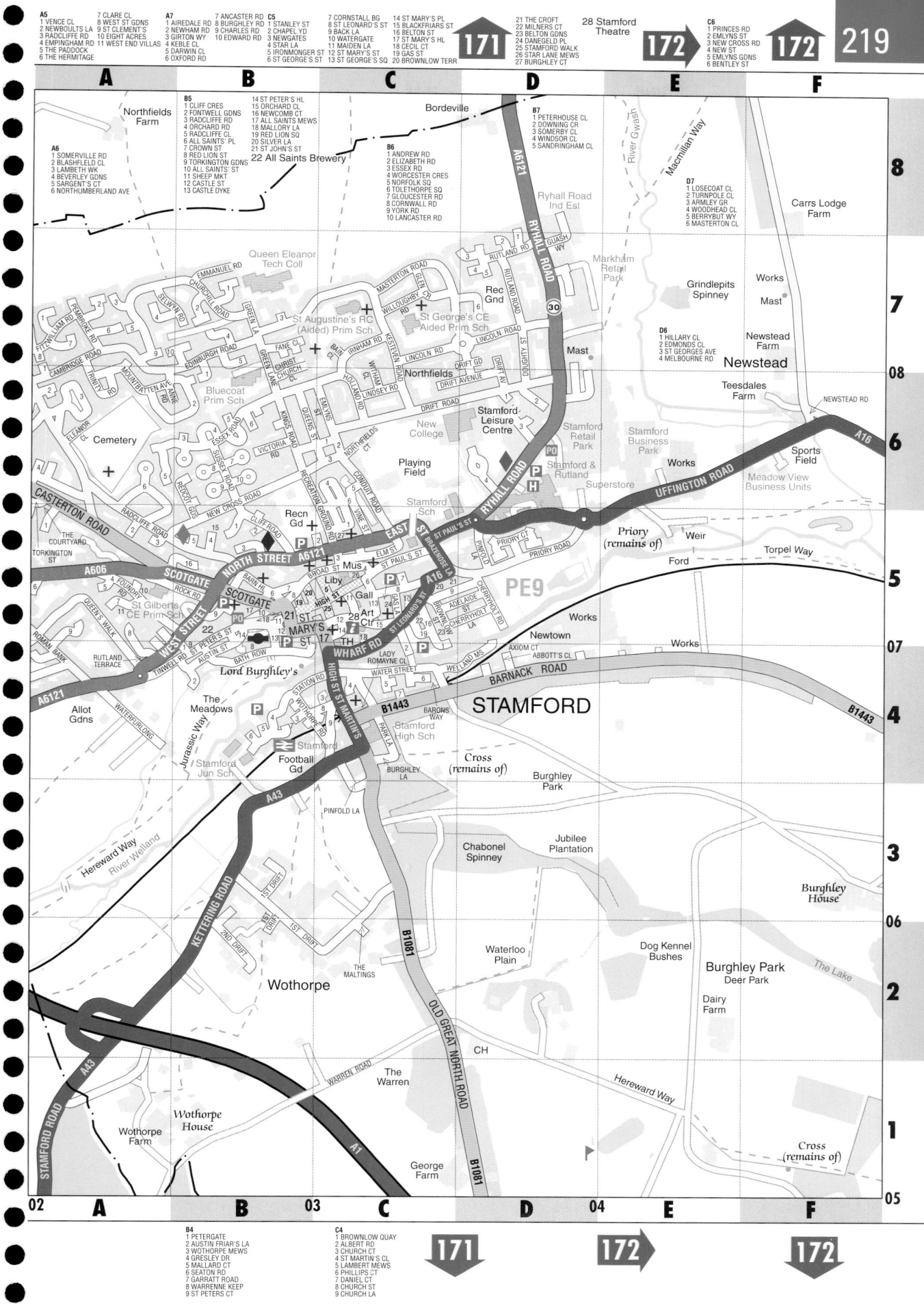
A5
1 VENCE CL
2 NEWBOULTS LA
3 RADCLIFFE RD
4 EMPINGHAM RD
5 THE PADDOCK
6 THE HERMITAGE
7 CLARE CL
8 WEST ST GDNS
9 ST CLEMENT'S
10 EIGHT ACRES
11 WEST END VILLAS
A7
1 AIREDALE RD
2 NEWHAM RD
3 GIRTON WY
4 KEBLE CL
5 DARWIN CL
6 OXFORD RD
7 ANCASTER RD
8 BURGHLEY RD
9 CHARLES RD
10 EDWARD RD
C5
1 STANLEY ST
2 CHAPEL YD
3 NEWGATES
4 STAR LA
5 IRONMONGER ST
6 ST GEORGE'S ST
7 CORNSTALL BG
8 ST LEONARD'S ST
9 BACK LA
10 WATERGATE
11 MAIDEN LA
12 ST MARY'S ST
13 ST GEORGE'S SQ
14 ST MARY'S PL
15 BLACKFRIARS ST
16 BELTON ST
17 ST MARY'S HL
18 CECIL CT
19 GAS ST
20 BROWNLOW TERR
171
21 THE CROFT
22 MILNERS CT
23 BELTON GDNS
24 DANEGELD PL
25 STAMFORD WALK
26 STAR LANE MEWS
27 BURGHLEY CT
28 Stamford Theatre
172
C6
1 PRINCES RD
2 EMLYNS ST
3 NEW CROSS RD
4 NEW ST
5 EMLYNS GDNS
6 BENTLEY ST
172
A
B
C
D
E
F
Northfields Farm
A6
1 SOMERVILLE RD
2 BLASHFLELD CL
3 LAMBETH WK
4 BEVERLEY GDNS
5 SARGENT'S CT
6 NORTHUMBERLAND AVE
B5
1 CLIFF CRES
2 FONTWELL GDNS
3 RADCLIFFE RD
4 ORCHARD RD
5 RADCLIFFE CL
6 ALL SAINTS' PL
7 CROWN ST
8 RED LION ST
9 TORKINGTON GDNS
10 ALL SAINTS' ST
11 SHEEP MKT
12 CASTLE ST
13 CASTLE DYKE
14 ST PETER'S HL
15 ORCHARD CL
16 NEWCOMB CT
17 ALL SAINTS MEWS
18 MALLORY LA
19 RED LION SQ
20 SILVER LA
21 ST JOHN'S ST
22 All Saints Brewery
Bordeville
B6
1 ANDREW RD
2 ELIZABETH RD
3 ESSEX RD
4 WORCESTER CRES
5 NORFOLK SQ
6 TOLETHORPE SQ
7 GLOUCESTER RD
8 CORNWALL RD
9 YORK RD
10 LANCASTER RD
B7
1 PETERHOUSE CL
2 DOWNING CR
3 SOMERBY CL
4 WINDSOR CL
5 SANDRINGHAM CL
River Gwash
Macmillan Way
D7
1 LOSECOAT CL
2 TURNPOLE CL
3 ARMLEY GR
4 WOODHEAD CL
5 BERRYBUT WY
6 MASTERTON CL
8
Ryhall Road Ind Est
Carrs Lodge Farm
A6121
RYHALL ROAD
Queen Eleanor Tech Coll
Markham Retail Park
Grindlepits Spinney
Works
Mast
7
Rec Gnd
St Augustine's RC (Aided) Prim Sch
St George's CE Aided Prim Sch
D6
1 HILLARY CL
2 EDMONDS CL
3 ST GEORGES AVE
4 MELBOURNE RD
Newstead Farm
Mast
Newstead
08
Northfields
Teesdales Farm
NEWSTEAD RD
Bluecoat Prim Sch
Stamford Leisure Centre
Stamford Retail Park
New College
Stamford Business Park
A16
Cemetery
Playing Field
6
Sports Field
Stamford & Rutland
Works
Meadow View Business Units
Superstore
UFFINGTON ROAD
CASTERTON ROAD
Stamford Sch
Recn Gd
Priory (remains of)
Weir
THE COURTYARD
TORKINGTON ST
Torpel Way
Ford
A606
SCOTGATE
NORTH STREET
A6121
EAST ST
Mus
Liby
PE9
5
St Gilberts CE Prim Sch
SCOTGATE
Gall
Art Ctr
Works
WEST STREET
ST MARY'S ST
Newtown
Works
07
ROMAN BANK
RUTLAND TERRACE
WHARF RD
ST LEONARD'S ST
Lord Burghley's
BARNACK ROAD
A6121
The Meadows
STAMFORD
Allot Gdns
B1443
B1443
4
Stamford High Sch
Jurassic Way
Stamford
Cross (remains of)
Stamford Jun Sch
Football Gd
Burghley Park
A43
PINFOLD LA
Hereward Way
River Welland
Chabonel Spinney
Jubilee Plantation
3
KETTERING ROAD
Burghley House
06
B1081
Waterloo Plain
Dog Kennel Bushes
THE MALTINGS
Burghley Park
Deer Park
Wothorpe
2
Dairy Farm
OLD GREAT NORTH ROAD
The Lake
A43
CH
WARREN ROAD
The Warren
Hereward Way
STAMFORD ROAD
Wothorpe House
1
Wothorpe Farm
A1
B1081
George Farm
Cross (remains of)
02
A
B
03
C
D
04
E
F
05
B4
1 PETERGATE
2 AUSTIN FRIAR'S LA
3 WOTHORPE MEWS
4 GRESLEY DR
5 MALLARD CT
6 SEATON RD
7 GARRATT ROAD
8 WARRENNE KEEP
9 ST PETERS CT
C4
1 BROWNLOW QUAY
2 ALBERT RD
3 CHURCH CT
4 ST MARTIN'S CL
5 LAMBERT MEWS
6 PHILLIPS CT
7 DANIEL CT
8 CHURCH ST
9 CHURCH LA
171
172
172

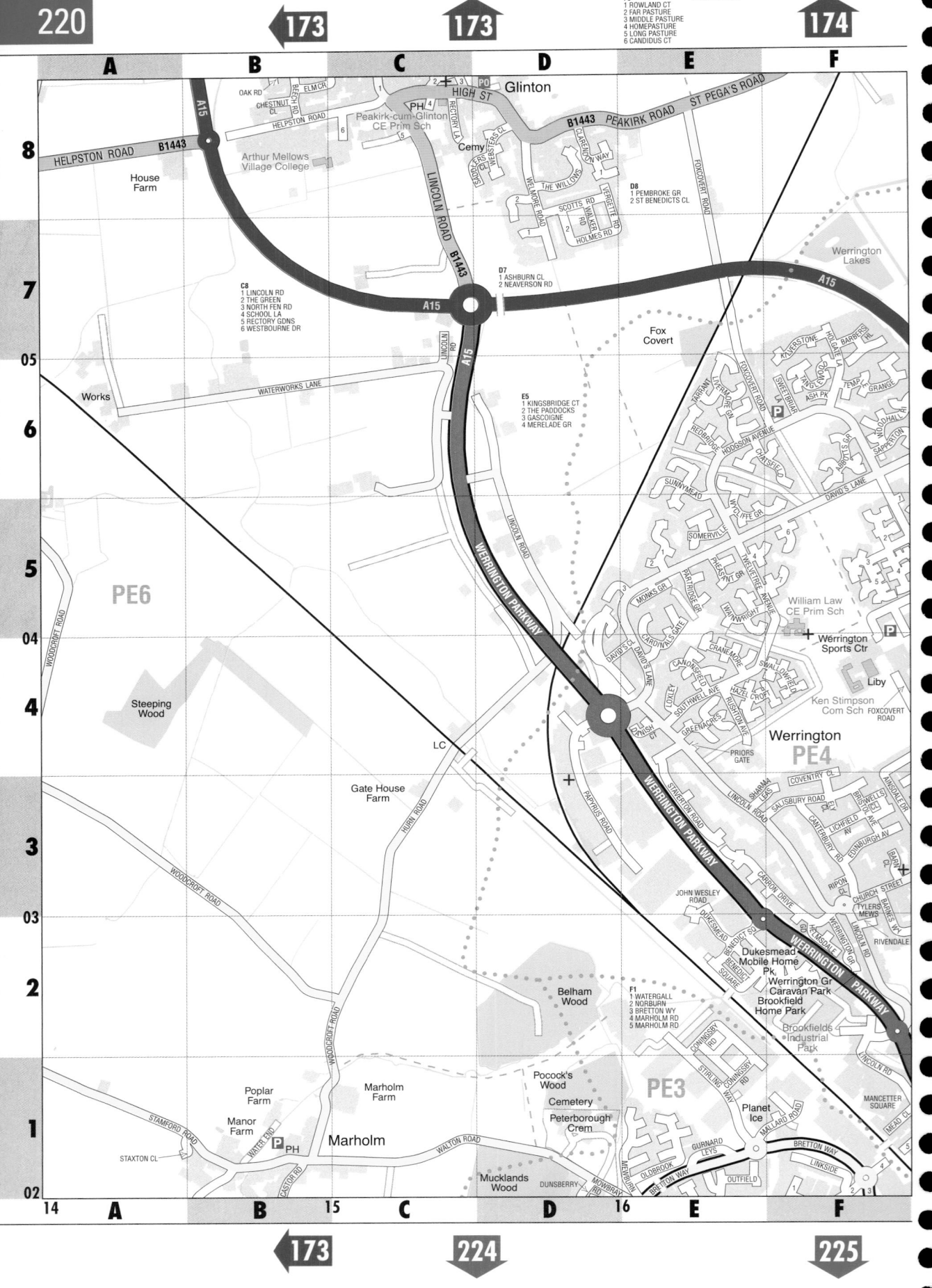

173
173
174

F5
1 ROWLAND CT
2 FAR PASTURE
3 MIDDLE PASTURE
4 HOMEPASTURE
5 LONG PASTURE
6 CANDIDUS CT

7 DERWOOD GR

A B C D E F

8

Glinton

House
Farm

HELPSTON ROAD B1443
A15

OAK RD CHESTNUT CL ELM CR
BEECH RD
HELPSTON ROAD

HIGH ST
PO
Peakirk-cum-Glinton
CE Prim Sch
PH

Arthur Mellows
Village College

Cemy

LINCOLN ROAD
B1443

RECTORY LA
SADDLERS CL
WEBSTERS CL
WELMORE ROAD
SCOTTS RD
HOLMES RD
WALKER RD
LYGRETTE RD
CLARENCE WAY
CLARENDON WAY
THE WILLOWS

B1443 PEAKIRK ROAD
ST PEGA'S ROAD

Werrington
Lakes

FOXCOVERT ROAD

D8
1 PEMBROKE GR
2 ST BENEDICTS CL

7

C8
1 LINCOLN RD
2 THE GREEN
3 NORTH FEN RD
4 SCHOOL LA
5 RECTORY GDNS
6 WESTBOURNE DR

D7
1 ASHBURN CL
2 NEAVERSON RD

A15

A15
LINCOLN ROAD

Fox
Covert

TAVERSTONE
HOLGATE LA
BARBECS
TINGLES
ASH PK
TEMP
GRANGE
WOODHALL RI
SAPPERTON

05

Works

WATERWORKS LANE

E5
1 KINGSBRIDGE CT
2 THE PADDOCKS
3 GASCOIGNE
4 MERELADE GR

TARRINY
REDBRIDGE
LIVERMORE GR
HODGSON AVENUE
CHATSFIE
SWEET BRIAR
WYCLIFFE GR
SOMERVILLE
SUNNYMEAD

DAVID'S LANE

6

PE6

TWELVETREE AVENUE
MONKS GR
BARTRIDGE GR
WAINWRIGHT
6

5

LINCOLN ROAD
WERRINGTON PARKWAY

William Law
CE Prim Sch

CARDINALS GATE
CRANEMORE
DAVID'S CL
DAVID'S LANE
CANOPY FIELD
LOXLEY
SOUTHWELL AVE
HAZEL CROFT
RUSTON AVE
SWALLOWFIELD

Werrington
Sports Ctr
P
Liby
Ken Stimpson
Com Sch FOXCOVERT
ROAD

04

Steeping
Wood

LC

Gate House
Farm

HORN ROAD
WOODCROFT ROAD

4

FINISH
GREENACRES

PRIORS
GATE

Werrington
PE4

SHARMA
LEAS
STAVERTON ROAD
LINCOLN ROAD
COVENTRY CL
SALISBURY ROAD
LICHFIELD
AV
CANTERBURY RD
EDINBURGH AV
BROWELLS
RIPON
CHURCH STREET
TYLERS
MEWS
RIVENDALE
BARN LA
AINSDALE
MANCETTER SQUARE

3

WOODCROFT ROAD
PAPYRUS ROAD

JOHN WESLEY
ROAD

CARRON DRIVE
WERRINGTON PARKWAY

BENEDICT SQ
DUKESMEAD

BENCROFT
BROMFIELD
SQUARE
ELMSIDE RD
WERRINGTON RD
LINCOLN RD

03

2

Belham
Wood

F1
1 WATERGALL
2 NORBURN
3 BRETTON WY
4 MARHOLM RD
5 MARHOLM RD

Dukesmead
Mobile Home
Pk
Werrington Gr
Caravan Park
Brookfield
Home Park

Brookfields
Industrial
Park

CONINGSBY RD
STIRLING WAY
CONINGSBY RD

LINCOLN RD

1

Poplar
Farm

Marholm
Farm

Pocock's
Wood

PE3

Planet
Ice

MANCETTER
SQUARE

STAMFORD ROAD
CASTOR RD
WATER END
Manor
Farm
P PH
Marholm

STAXTON CL

WALTON ROAD

Cemetery
Peterborough
Crem

GURNARD
LEYS
OLDBROOK
MENBURN
MALLARD ROAD
MEAD CL

BRETTON WAY
LINKSIDE

02

Mucklands
Wood

DUNSBERRY
MOWBRAY

BRETTON WAY
OUTFIELD

14 A 15 B C 16 D E F

173
224
225

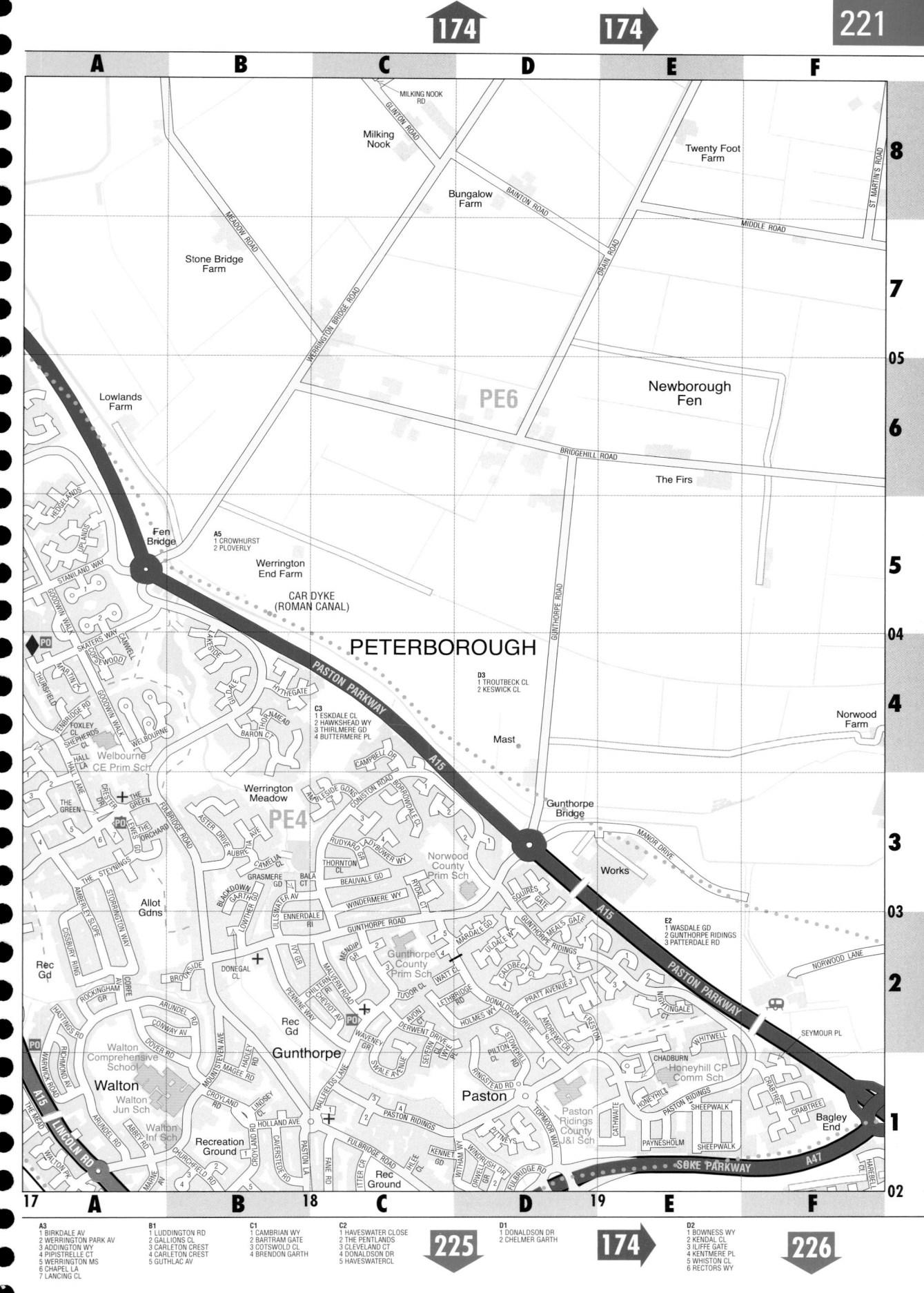

174
174
225
174
226

A5
1 CROWHURST
2 PLOVERLY

D3
1 TROUTBECK CL
2 KESWICK CL

C3
1 ESKDALE CL
2 HAWKSHEAD WY
3 THIRLMERE GD
4 BUTTERMERE PL

E2
1 WASDALE GD
2 GUNTHORPE RIDINGS
3 PATTERDALE RD

PETERBOROUGH

Milking Nook
Bungalow Farm
Twenty Foot Farm
Stone Bridge Farm
PE6
Newborough Fen
The Firs
Lowlands Farm
Fen Bridge
Werrington End Farm
CAR DYKE (ROMAN CANAL)
Norwood Farm
Mast
Welbourne CE Prim Sch
Werrington Meadow
PE4
Gunthorpe Bridge
Works
Norwood County Prim Sch
Gunthorpe County Prim Sch
Allot Gdns
Rec Gd
Gunthorpe
Walton Comprehensive School
Walton
Walton Jun Sch
Walton Inf Sch
Recreation Ground
Rec Ground
Paston
Paston Ridings County J&I Sch
Honeyhill CP Comm Sch
Bagley End

A3
1 BIRKDALE AV
2 WERRINGTON PARK AV
3 ADDINGTON WY
4 PIPISTRELLE CT
5 WERRINGTON MS
6 CHAPEL LA
7 LANCING CL

B1
1 LUDDINGTON RD
2 GALLIONS CL
3 CARLETON CREST
4 CARLETON CREST
5 GUTHLAC AV

C1
1 CAMBRIAN WY
2 BARTRAM GATE
3 COTSWOLD CL
4 BRENDON GARTH

C2
1 HAVESWATER CLOSE
2 THE PENTLANDS
3 CLEVELAND CT
4 DONALDSON DR
5 HAVESWATERCL

D1
1 DONALDSON DR
2 CHELMER GARTH

D2
1 BOWNESS WY
2 KENDAL CL
3 ILIFFE GATE
4 KENTMERE PL
5 WHISTON CL
6 RECTORS WY

172

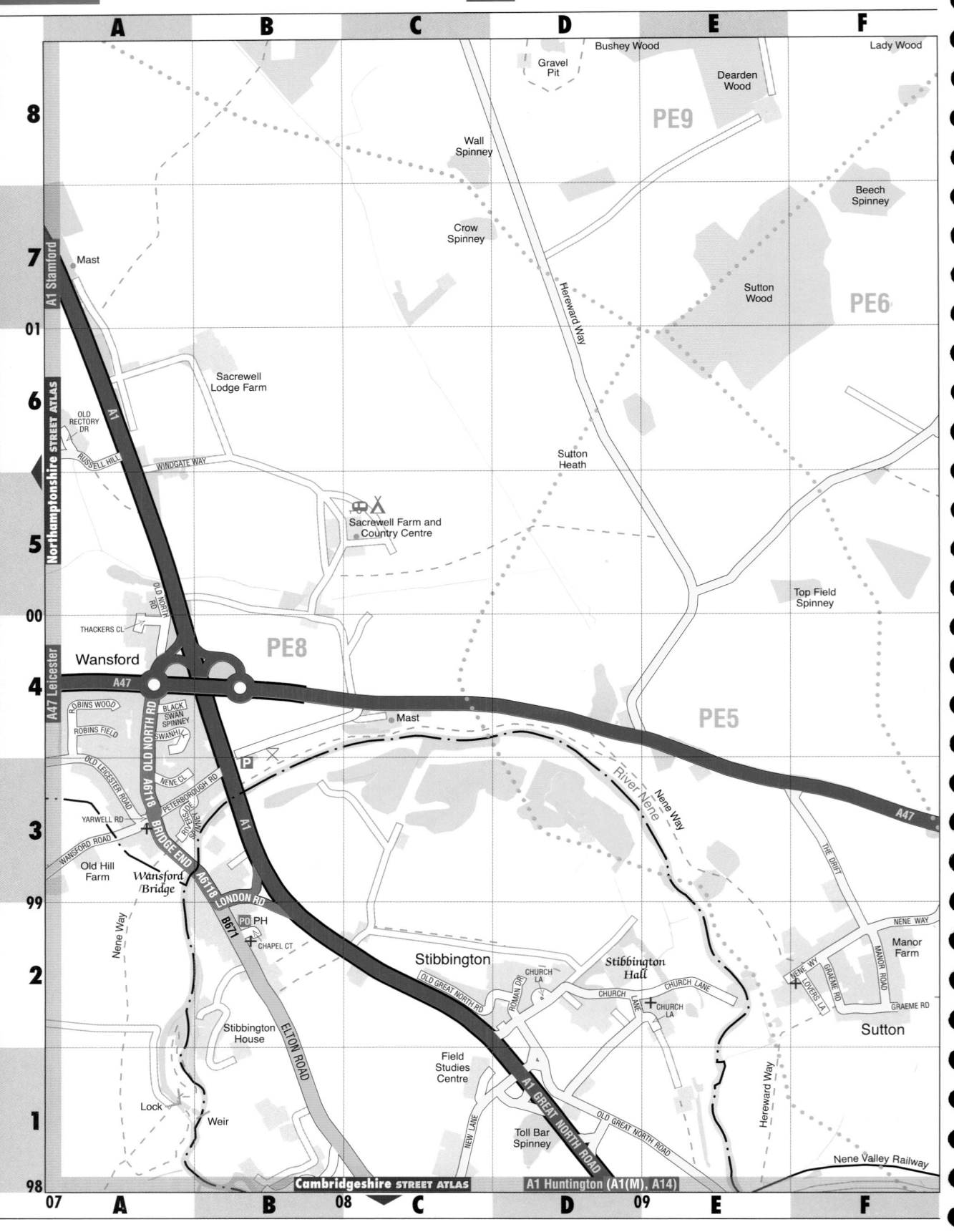
A
B
C
D
E
F
8
7
01
6
5
00
4
3
99
2
1
98
07
08
09
Bushey Wood
Gravel Pit
Lady Wood
Dearden Wood
PE9
Wall Spinney
Beech Spinney
Crow Spinney
Sutton Wood
PE6
A1 Stamford
Mast
Hereward Way
Sacrewell Lodge Farm
A1
OLD RECTORY DR
RUSSELL HILL
WINDGATE WAY
Sutton Heath
Northamptonshire STREET ATLAS
Sacrewell Farm and Country Centre
OLD NORTH RD
Top Field Spinney
THACKERS CL
PE8
Wansford
A47 Leicester
A47
ROBINS WOOD
BLACK SWAN SPINNEY
SWANHL
ROBINS FIELD
OLD NORTH RD
Mast
PE5
OLD LEICESTER ROAD
A6118
NENE CL
PETERBOROUGH RD
River Nene
Nene Way
YARWELL RD
RIVERSIDE SPINNEY
WANSFORD ROAD
BRIDGE END
Old Hill Farm
Wansford Bridge
A6118
LONDON RD
THE DRIFT
NENE WAY
PO
PH
B671
CHAPEL CT
Nene Way
Stibbington
CHURCH LA
Stibbington Hall
Manor Farm
OLD GREAT NORTH RD
ROMAN DR
CHURCH LANE
CHURCH
LANE
CHURCH LA
NENE WY
LOVERS LA
GRAEME RD
MANOR ROAD
GRAEME RD
Stibbington House
ELTON ROAD
Sutton
Field Studies Centre
Hereward Way
A1 GREAT NORTH ROAD
Lock
Weir
NEW LANE
Toll Bar Spinney
OLD GREAT NORTH ROAD
Nene Valley Railway
Cambridgeshire STREET ATLAS
A1 Huntington (A1(M), A14)

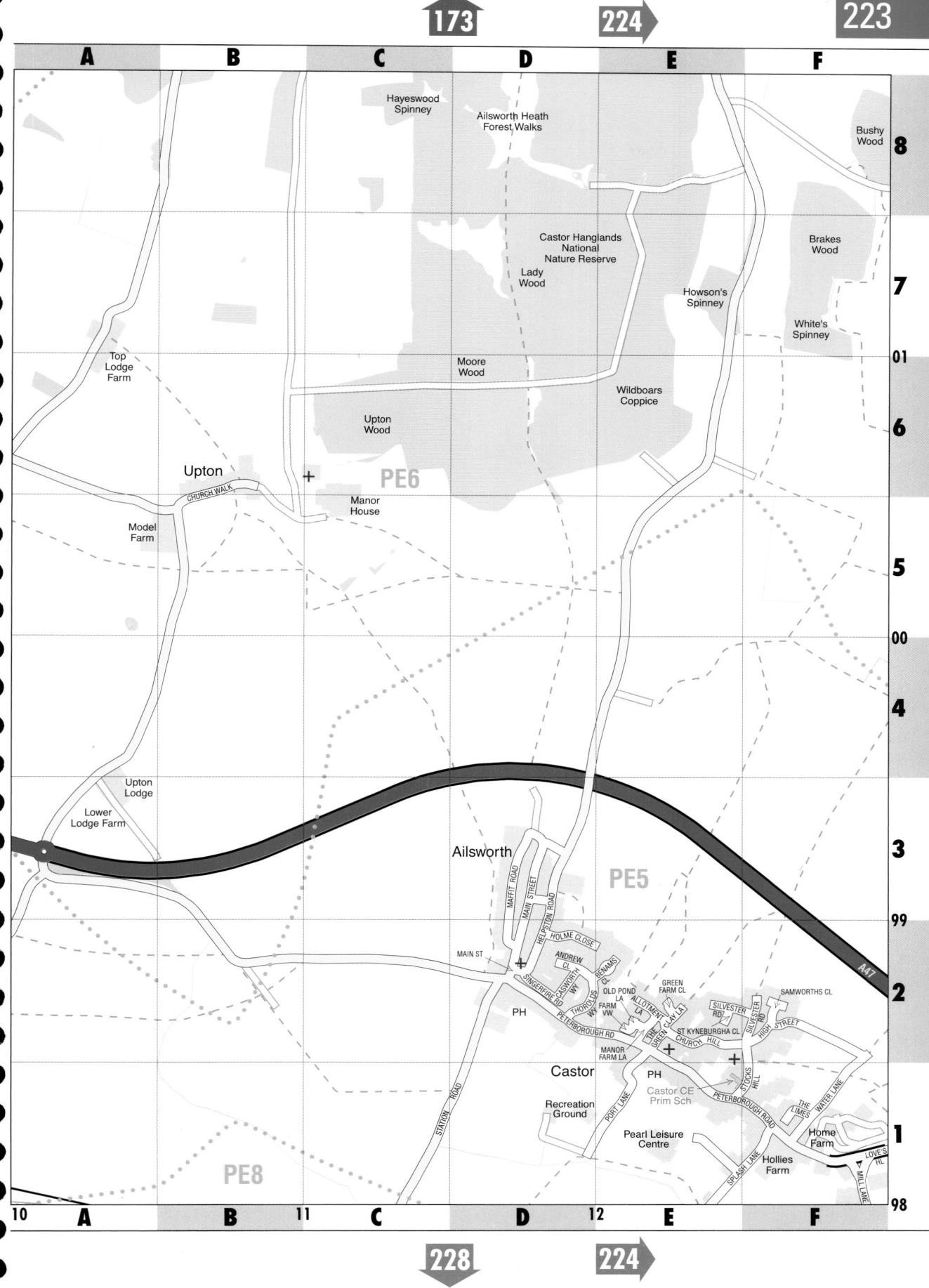

8

Hayeswood
Spinney

Ailsworth Heath
Forest Walks

Bushy
Wood

Castor Hanglands
National
Nature Reserve

Brakes
Wood

7

Lady
Wood

Howson's
Spinney

White's
Spinney

01

Top
Lodge
Farm

Moore
Wood

Wildboars
Coppice

6

Upton
Wood

Upton

PE6

CHURCH WALK

Manor
House

5

Model
Farm

00

4

Upton
Lodge

Lower
Lodge Farm

3

Ailsworth

PE5

MAFFIT ROAD
MAIN STREET
HELPSTON ROAD

99

HOLME CLOSE

A47

MAIN ST

ANDREW
CL

BENAMS
CL

SINGERFIRE RD
CASHWORTH
WY
THOROLDS
WY

OLD POND
LA
FARM
VW

GREEN
FARM CL

SAMWORTHS CL

2

PH

ALLOTMENT
LA

SILVESTER
RD

SILVESTER

HIGH STREET

PETERBOROUGH RD

LIME
GREEN CL
MANOR
FARM LA

ST KYNEBURGHA CL
CHURCH HILL

Castor

PH

Castor CE
Prim Sch

STOCKS HILL

PETERBOROUGH ROAD

THE
LIMES

WATER LANE

MILL LANE

Home
Farm

1

Recreation
Ground

PORT LANE

STATION ROAD

Pearl Leisure
Centre

SPLASH LANE

Hollies
Farm

LOVE'S
HL

PE8

98

173
223
220
A
B
C
D
E
F
8
7
01
6
5
00
4
3
99
2
1
98
13
14
15
Foster's Coppice
Home Farm
Bushy Wood
Burmer Wood
GULLYMORE
DUNSBERRY
BRETTON WAY
Mucklands Wood
Marholm Lodges
HYHOLMES
WESTHAWE
PARK FARM ROAD
Popple's Coppice
Belsize Farm
Belsize Wood
CASTOR ROAD
Grimeshaw Wood
Park Farm
Thistlemoor Wood
Little Thistlemoor Wood
Stamford Plantations
Stamford Lodge
Oldfield Pond
New Park Farm
STAMFORD LODGE ROAD
PE6
Deer Park
Ten Acre Plantation
New Plantation
Salter's Wood
Milton Hall
PE3
MUSKHAM
SPRIGNALL
KENNELS ROAD
NICHOLAS TAYLOR GDNS 1
STAMPER ST 2
BRAILSFORD CL 3
JOROSE WY 4
TEANBY CT 5
CARTERS CL 6
THOMAS CL 7
GOODWOOD RD 8
BARNARD WY 9
HARRISON CL 10
LONGTHORPE HOUSE MEWS 11
Recreation Ground
JORSE WAY
Milton Park
MARHOLM ROAD
WALKERS WY
RINGWOOD
HUNTSMANS GATE
Crickety Park
Sheep Park
LITTLE JOHNS CL
MILTON WAY
SEBRIGHTS WY
FERRY DRIVE
PETERBOROUGH DRIVE
Fitzwilliam
ROBIN HOOD CL
BRETTON WAY
EGAR WAY
ELLIOT AV
OAK
PELHAM CL
HERONRY DRIVE
LODER AVENUE
PEACOCK WY
Ferry House
PE5
A47
Ferryhill Plantation
PETERBOROUGH DR
CH
River Nene
VIRGINIA CL 1
CYPRESS CL 2
LONGTHORPE CL 3
Bluebell Walk Plantation
Love's Hill
FERRY HILL
Little John
Robin Hood
LOVE'S HILL
Mast
Playing Fields
Thorpe Wood
NENE PARKWAY A1260
THORPE WOOD
Hereward Way
Nene Way
Gunwade Lake
PE2
223
229

A B C D E F

8 7 01 6 5 00 4 3 99 2 1 98

PETERBOROUGH

Walton
Bretton
Ravensthorpe
Westwood
New England
Millfield
Longthorpe
PE4
PE1
PE3
PE2

Recreation Ground
Factory
Works
Allotments
Watergall Primary School
Brotherhood Retail Park
Heltwate School
Eyrescroft Prim Sch
Bretton Park
Boulevard Retail Park
Fulbridge School
Playing Fields
Ravensthorpe Prim Sch
Westwood Industrial Estate
Sports Club
Bretton Woods Com Sch
Bretton Ctr
Liby
The Cresset
Water Spinney
Highlees Primary School
Sacred Heart RC Prim Sch
Saville Road Industrial Estate
Sports Centre
Edith Cavell
Robert Horell Macmillan Ctr
Bretton Gate Ground
Westwood Farm
Middleton Prim Sch
Gladstone Prim Sch
The Beeches Prim Sch
Thorpe Primary School
Jack Hunt School
Jack Hunt Swimming Pool
West Town Prim Sch
Longthorpe Primary School
Peterborough High School
Peterborough District
Peterborough
Thorpe Hall
Thorpe Park
Tower
Heritage Ctr
Cross
Holy Well
Mus & Art Gall
Bourges Retail Park
Railworld
Peterborough NV
Nene Valley Railway

A47 SOKE PARKWAY
A15 LINCOLN ROAD
A15 BOURGES BOULEVARD
BOURGES BVD
A1179 THORPE ROAD
A1179 LONGTHORPE PARKWAY

BALMORAL RD 1
SANDRINGHAM RD 2
WINDSOR AVE 3

BRETTON GN 1
BRETTON GATE 2

ISHAM RD 1
MOORFIELD RD 2
HACKE RD 3

C4
1 DENHAM WALK
2 KIRBY WALK
3 LYME WALK
4 STANFORD WALK
5 WESTWOOD

1 HOLYWELL CL
2 THURSTON GATE
3 PENYALE
4 HAYWARDSFIELD
5 LINGWOOD PK
6 TANTALLON CT
7 TINTAGEL CT
8 STOKESAY CT

16 A B 17 C D 18 E F

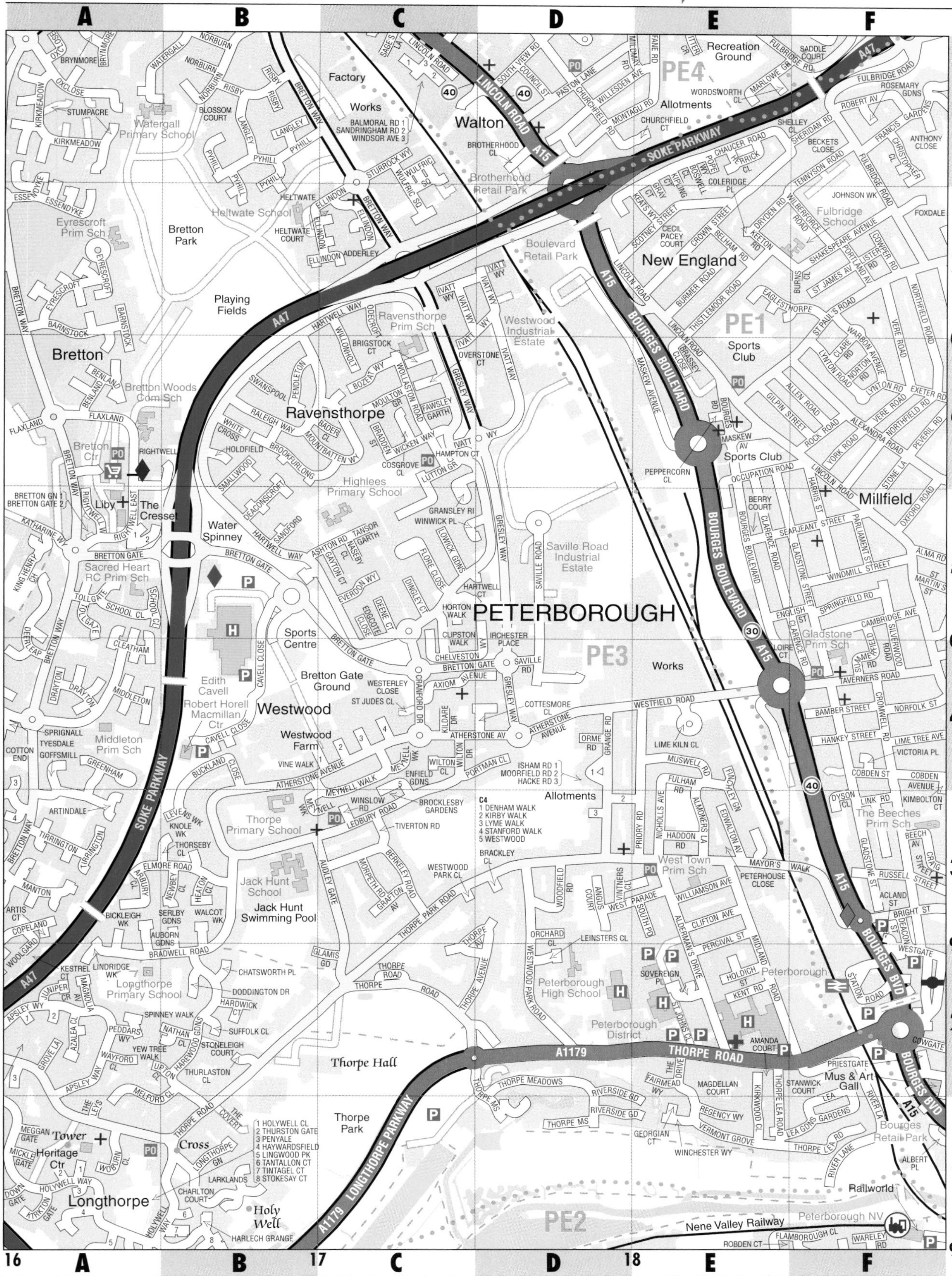

Grid columns: A B C D E F

PE6

D8
1 MEDBOURNE GDNS
2 WALTHAM CL
3 HUNGARTON CT
4 SOMERBY GARTH

E7
1 WHETSTONE CT
2 RAGDALE CL
3 ROTHERBY GR
4 ILLSTON PL
5 REDGATE CT
6 BLANDFORD GDNS
7 WIMBORNE DR

D7
1 RATCLIFFE CT
2 ALLEXTON GDNS
3 TWYFORD GDNS
4 BUCKMINSTER PL
5 REDMILE WLK
6 DORCHESTER CRES

A5
1 INGLEBOROUGH
2 DOGSTHORPE GR

PETERBOROUGH — PE1 — PE2

D3
1 WETHERBY WY
2 RASEN CT
3 HEXHAM CT
4 NORTH BANK RD
5 VICARAGE FARM RD

C2
1 RUTLAND CT
2 SHROPSHIRE PL

A1
1 WENTWORTH ST
2 BRIDGE ST
3 RIVERGATE
4 EMBANKMENT RD

A2
1 KING ST
2 QUEEN ST
3 TRINITY ST
4 PRIESTGATE
5 BROADWAY CT
6 HEREWARD CROSS
7 CATTLE MARKET WAY
8 CATTLE MARKET RD
9 MINSTER PRECINCTS

10 CATHEDRAL SQ

A3
1 BURGHLEY RD
2 BURGHLEY SQ
3 ST MARK'S CT

B2
1 FENGATE CL
2 HEREWARD CL
3 KESTEVEN WLK
4 WESTMORELAND GDNS
5 STEPHENSON CT
6 ST MARYS CT

B3
1 CRAWTHORNE ST
2 JORDAN MEWS

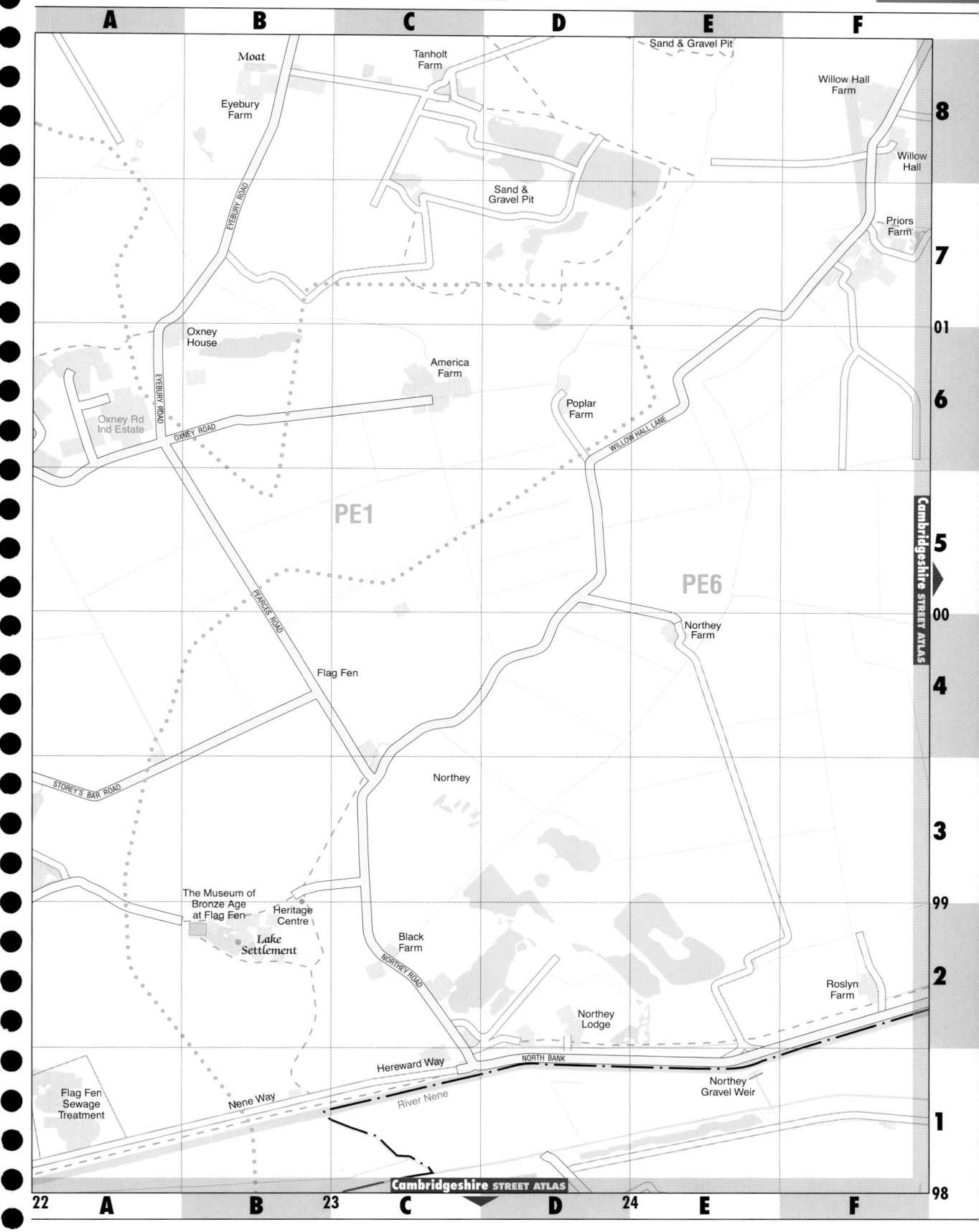

A B C D E F

8
7
01
6
5
00
4
3
99
2
1
98

22 23 24

Moat
Tanholt Farm
Sand & Gravel Pit
Willow Hall Farm
Eyebury Farm
Sand & Gravel Pit
Willow Hall
Priors Farm
Oxney House
America Farm
Poplar Farm
Willow Hall Lane
Oxney Rd Ind Estate
Oxney Road
Eyebury Road
PE1
PE6
Northey Farm
Pearse's Road
Flag Fen
Storey's Bar Road
Northey
The Museum of Bronze Age at Flag Fen
Heritage Centre
Lake Settlement
Black Farm
Northey Road
Roslyn Farm
Northey Lodge
Flag Fen Sewage Treatment
Hereward Way
North Bank
Northey Gravel Weir
Nene Way
River Nene

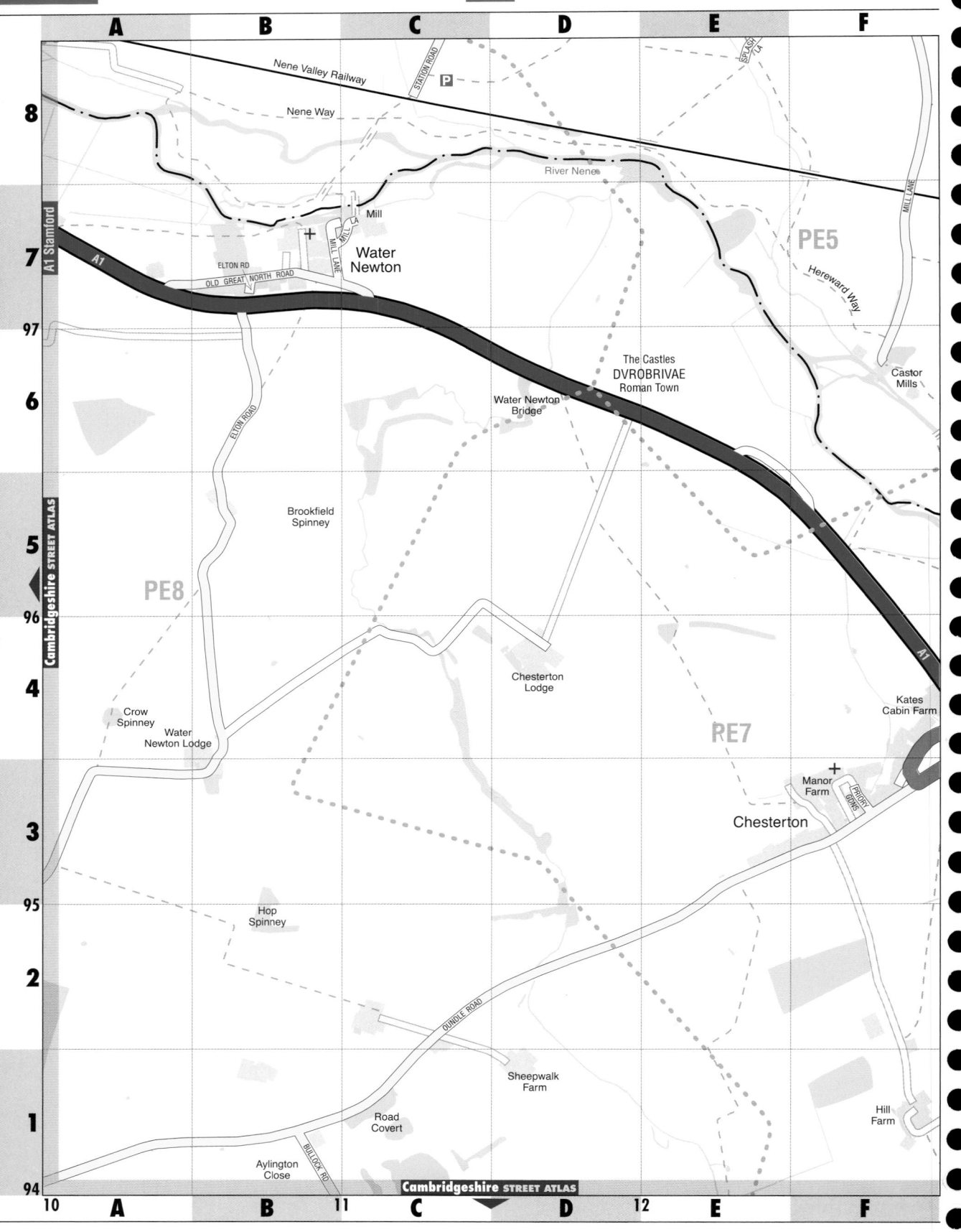

A   B   C   D   E   F

Nene Valley Railway

STATION ROAD

P

Nene Way

8

River Nene

SPLASH LA

7

Mill

WILL LA

Water
Newton

MILL LANE

PE5

A1 Stamford

ELTON RD

A1

OLD GREAT NORTH ROAD

Hereward Way

97

ELTON ROAD

The Castles
DVROBRIVAE
Roman Town

Castor
Mills

6

Water Newton
Bridge

Cambridgeshire STREET ATLAS

Brookfield
Spinney

5

PE8

96

Chesterton
Lodge

A1

4

Crow
Spinney

Water
Newton Lodge

PE7

Kates
Cabin Farm

Manor
Farm

PRIORY
DYKES

Chesterton

3

95

Hop
Spinney

2

OUNDLE ROAD

Sheepwalk
Farm

Hill
Farm

1

Road
Covert

BULLOCK RD

Aylington
Close

94

10   A   B   11   C   D   12   E   F

224
230

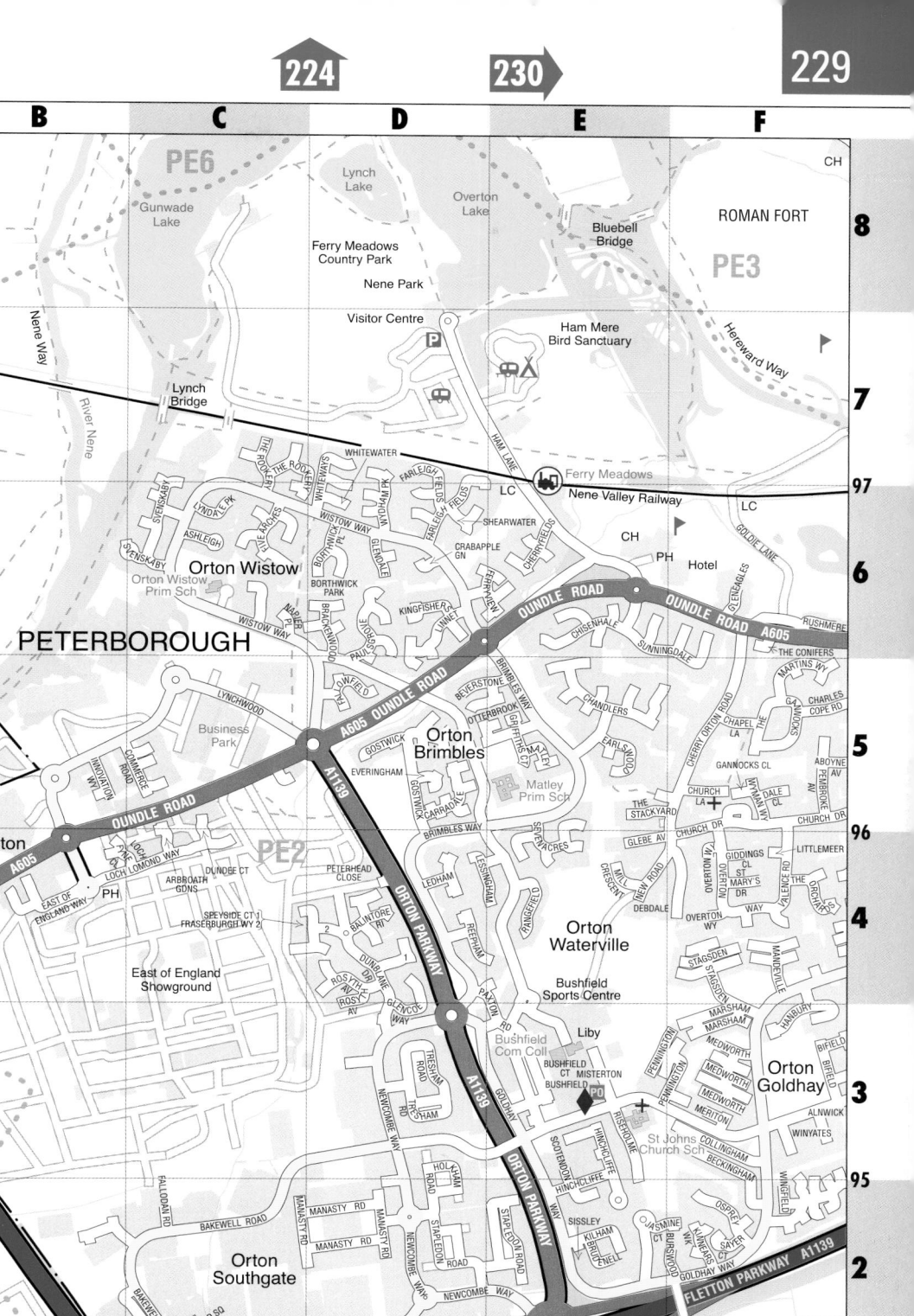
PETERBOROUGH
Orton Wistow
Orton Brimbles
Orton Waterville
Orton Goldhay
Orton Southgate
Alwalton
Alwalton Hall
Manor House
East of England Showground
Business Park
Ferry Meadows Country Park
Nene Park
Visitor Centre
Lynch Lake
Gunwade Lake
Overton Lake
Bluebell Bridge
ROMAN FORT
Ham Mere Bird Sanctuary
Lynch Bridge
Nene Valley Railway
Ferry Meadows
Hereward Way
Nene Way
River Nene
Back Dike
Lock
Orton Wistow Prim Sch
Matley Prim Sch
Bushfield Sports Centre
Bushfield Com Coll
St Johns Church Sch
Liby
Hotel
Clynebury Lodge
Bottom Lodge Farm
Upper Lodge Farm
Mast
Service Area
OUNDLE ROAD
ORTON PARKWAY
FLETTON PARKWAY
A605
A1139
A1(M)
PE2
PE3
PE5
PE6
PE7

232
230

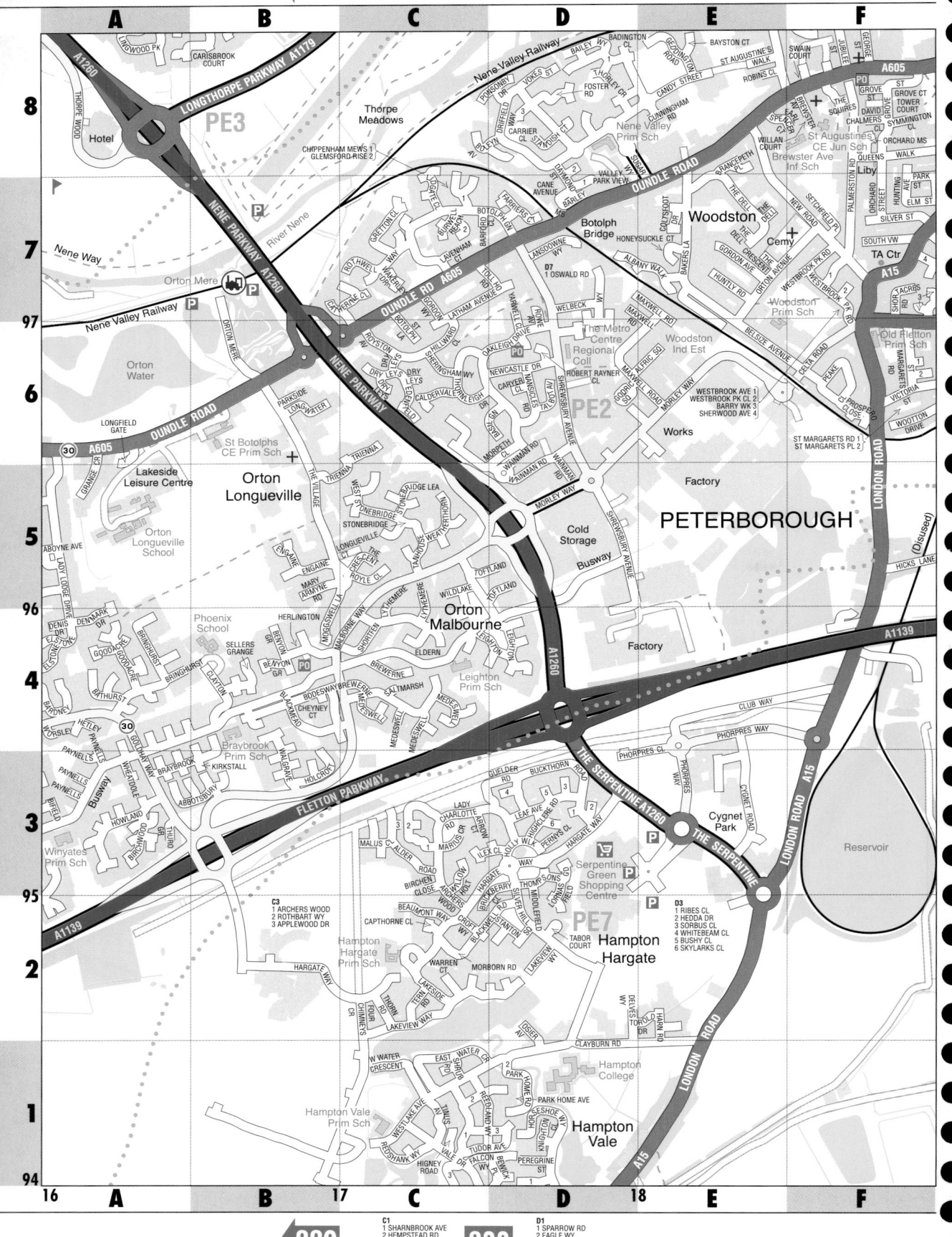

229
225
D8
1 CRYSTAL DR
2 RUTHER CL
3 FLEMING CT

229
233
C1
1 SHARNBROOK AVE
2 HEMPSTEAD RD
3 COUNTY RD
D1
1 SPARROW RD
2 EAGLE WY
3 SANDHURST RD

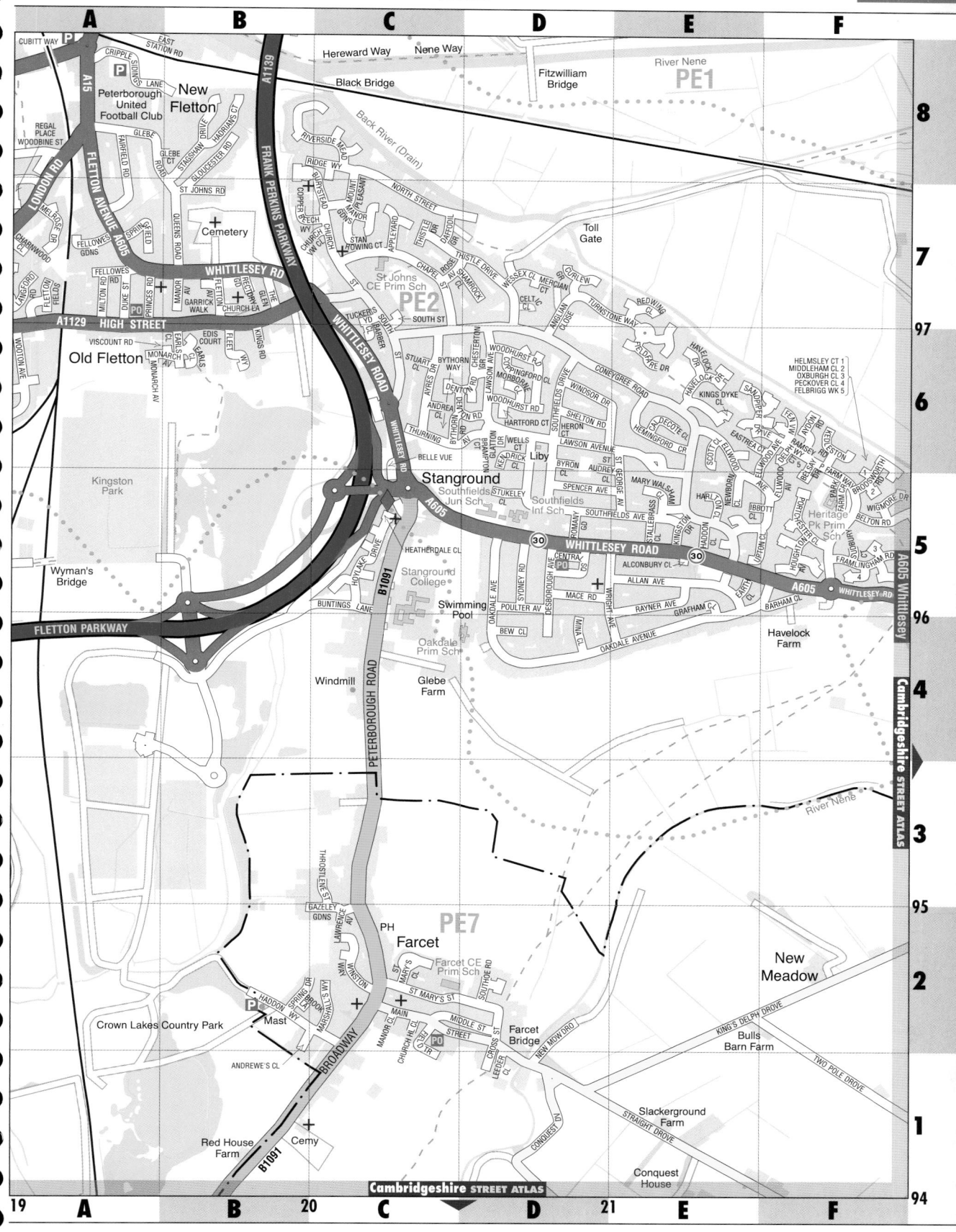

A   B   C   D   E   F

8

7

97

6

5

96

4

3

95

2

1

94

CUBITT WAY

EAST STATION RD
CRIPPLE SIDINGS LANE

Hereward Way   Nene Way

Black Bridge

Fitzwilliam Bridge

River Nene
PE1

Peterborough United Football Club

New Fletton

REGAL PLACE
WOODBINE ST

Back River (Drain)

Toll Gate

Cemetery

RIVERSIDE MEAD

NORTH STREET

FLETTON AVENUE A605

WHITTLESEY RD

PE2

St Johns CE Prim Sch

HELMSLEY CT 1
MIDDLEHAM CL 2
OXBURGH CL 3
PECKOVER CL 4
FELBRIGG WK 5

A1129   HIGH STREET

VISCOUNT RD

Old Fletton

WHITTLESEY ROAD

CONEYGREE ROAD

WOOTON AVE

BELLE VUE

Liby

Stanground

Southfields Jun Sch

Stanground College

Southfields Inf Sch

SOUTHFIELDS AVE

Kingston Park

Heritage Pk Prim Sch

Wyman's Bridge

B1091

WHITTLESEY RD

(30)   WHITTLESEY ROAD   (30)

A605

FLETTON PARKWAY

HEATHERDALE CL

Swimming Pool

A605 Whittlesey

Havelock Farm

Cambridgeshire STREET ATLAS

Windmill

PETERBOROUGH ROAD

Oakdale Prim Sch

BUNTINGS LANE

Glebe Farm

OAKDALE AVENUE

River Nene

PE7

THROSTLENE CL

GAZELEY GDNS

Farcet

Farcet CE Prim Sch

New Meadow

Crown Lakes Country Park

Mast

BROADWAY

MAIN STREET

MIDDLE STREET

Farcet Bridge

NEW MOW DRO

KING'S DELPH DROVE

Bulls Barn Farm

TWO POLE DROVE

ANDREWE'S CL

Red House Farm

Cemy

B1091

Slackerground Farm

STRAIGHT DROVE

CONQUEST DV

Conquest House

229

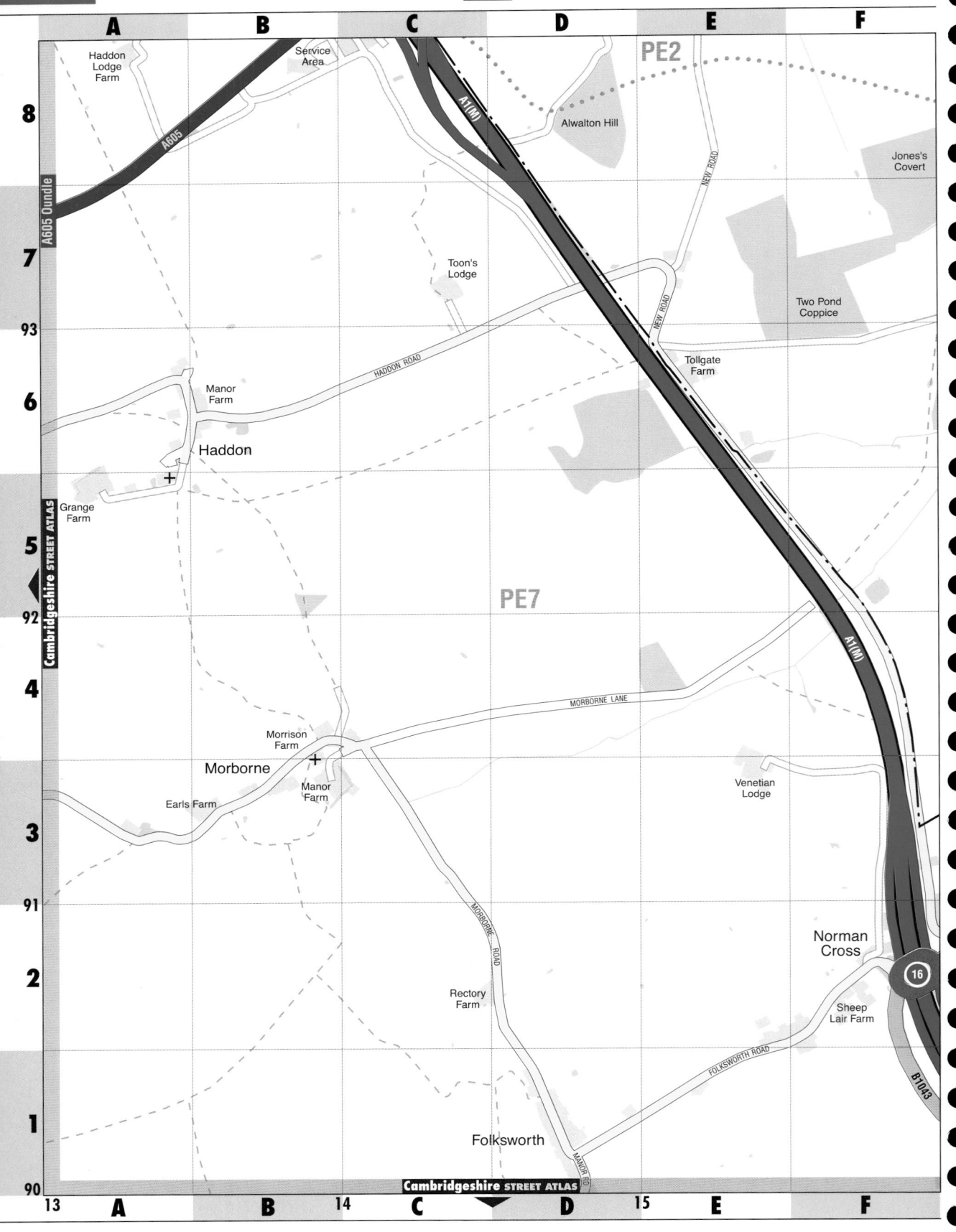

A
B
C
D
E
F
Haddon Lodge Farm
Service Area
PE2
A605
A1(M)
Alwalton Hill
Jones's Covert
A605 Oundle
NEW ROAD
Toon's Lodge
Two Pond Coppice
HADDON ROAD
Tollgate Farm
Manor Farm
Haddon
Grange Farm
Cambridgeshire STREET ATLAS
PE7
MORBORNE LANE
Morrison Farm
Morborne
Manor Farm
Earls Farm
Venetian Lodge
MORBORNE ROAD
Norman Cross
16
Rectory Farm
Sheep Lair Farm
FOLKSWORTH ROAD
B1043
Folksworth
MANOR RD
8
7
93
6
5
92
4
3
91
2
1
90
13
14
15

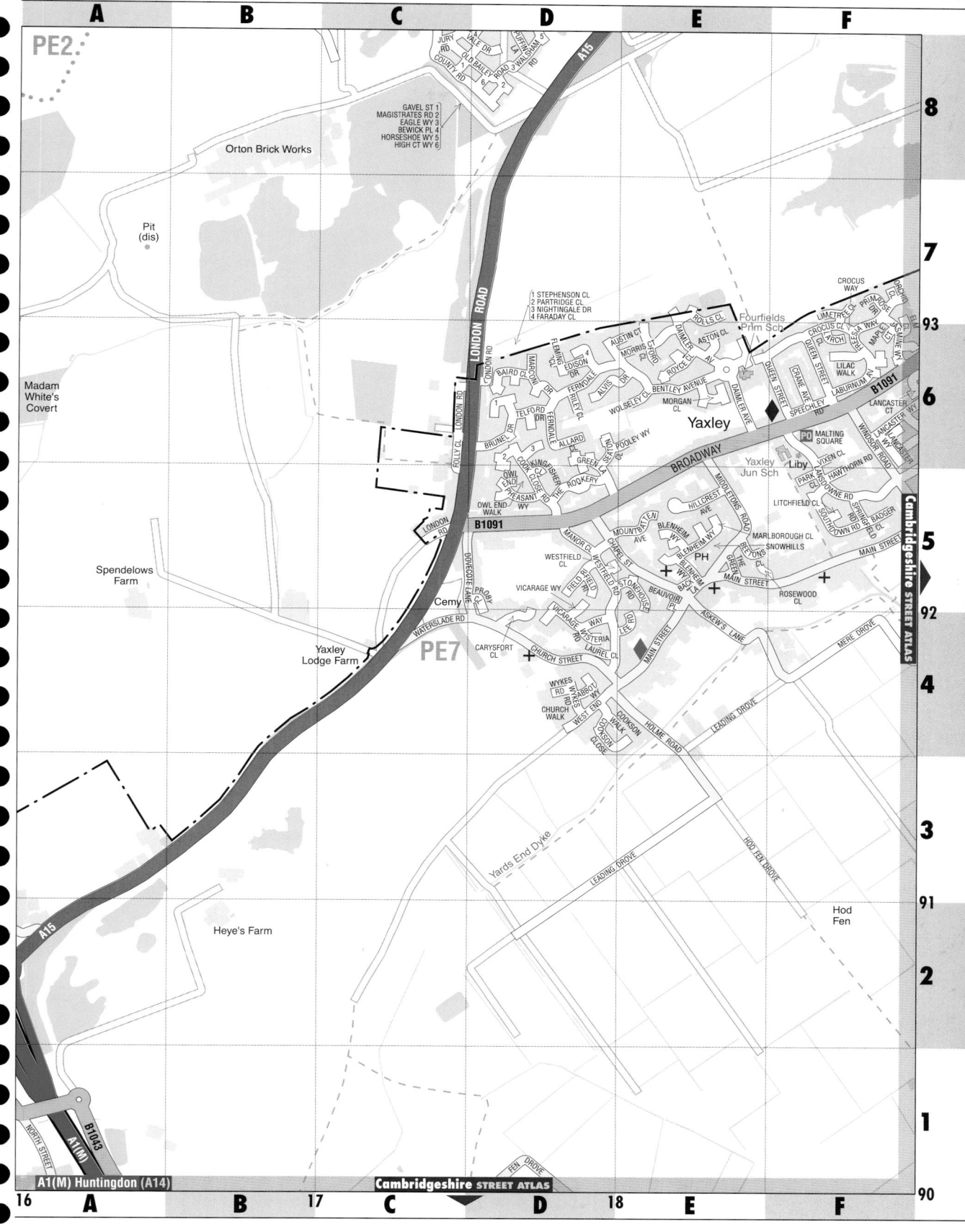

PE2

A B C D E F

Orton Brick Works

GAVEL ST 1
MAGISTRATES RD 2
EAGLE WY 3
BEWICK PL 4
HORSESHOE WY 5
HIGH CT WY 6

8

Pit
(dis)

1 STEPHENSON CL
2 PARTRIDGE CL
3 NIGHTINGALE DR
4 FARADAY CL

7

CROCUS
WAY

93

Madam
White's
Covert

Fourfields
Prim Sch

ROLLS CL

AUSTIN CT

MORRIS CL
ASTON CL
CROFT

DAIMLER
FLEMING
CL
MARCONI
DR
EDISON
DR
FERNDALE
BAIRD CL
RILEY CL
ALLARD
TELFORD
DR
BRUNEL
WY
FERNDALE
ALVIS DR
WOLSELEY CL
ROYCE CL
BENTLEY AVENUE
MORGAN
CL

Yaxley

6

QUEEN STREET
CRANE AVE
SPEECHLEY
RD
DAIMLER AVE

LANCASTER
CT
LANCASTER
WY

B1091

LILAC
WALK
LABURNUM

LIMETREE
CHURCH
CROCUS
PRIM
MAPLE
JASMINE WY
ELM
ORCH

PO
MALTING
SQUARE

WINDSOR RD

FOLLY CL
LONDON RD

LONDON ROAD

FOLLY CL

KINGFISHER
CL
GREEN WY
POOLEY WY
THE
ROOKERY
OWL
END
PHEASANT
WY
COOK CLOSE
OWL END
WALK

BROADWAY

Yaxley
Jun Sch
Liby

VIXEN CL
PARK
CLOSE
LANSDOWNE RD
HAWTHORN RD
SPRINGFIELD
SOUTHDOWN RD
BADGER
MAIN STREET

LITCHFIELD CL

London RD

B1091

Spendelows
Farm

BOVECOTE LANE
PROBY
PR

MANOR CL
MOUNTBATTEN
AVE
CHAPEL ST
BLENHEIM
WY
BLENHEIM WY
HILLCREST
AVE
MIDDLETONS ROAD

MARLBOROUGH CL
SNOWHILLS

5

92

Cemy
WATERSLADE RD

WESTFIELD
CL
VICARAGE WY
FIELD RD
STRED RD
STONEHOUSE
PL
BEAUVOIR
THE
GREEN
PH
MAIN STREET

ROSEWOOD
CL

MERE GROVE

Yaxley
Lodge Farm

PE7

CARYSFORT
CL
CHURCH STREET
VICARAGE
RD
WISTERIA
WAY
LAUREL CL
LEE
ASKEW'S LANE
MAIN STREET

4

WYKES
RD
WABBOT
RD
CHURCH
WALK
WEST END
WALK
CROYSON
CLOSE
COOKSON
HOLME ROAD

LEADING DROVE

3

91

Heye's Farm

Yards End Dyke

LEADING DROVE

HOD FEN DROVE

Hod
Fen

A15

2

B1043
A1(M)
NORTH STREET

FEN DROVE

1

90

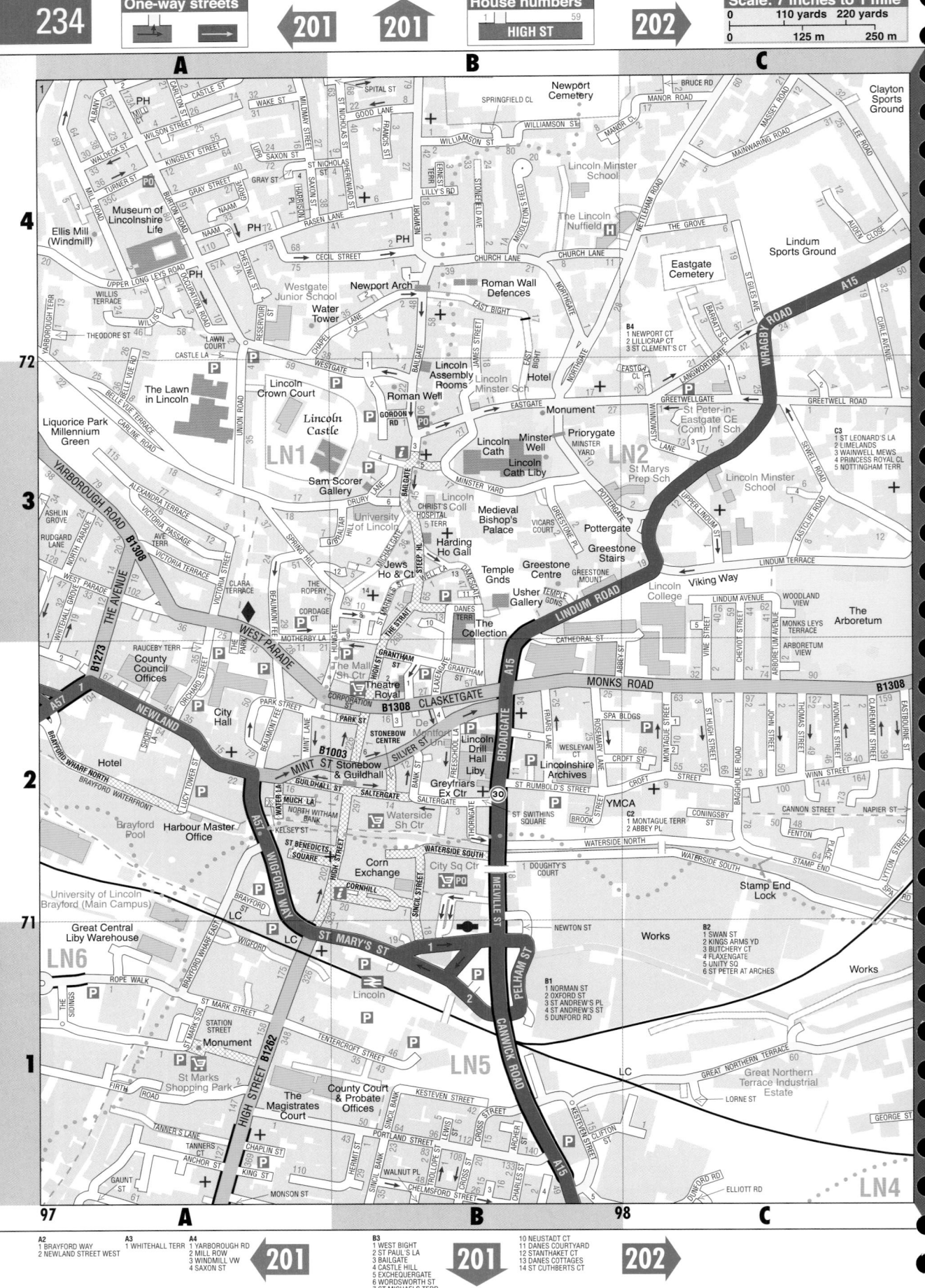

One-way streets

◀ 201   ⬆ 201

House numbers
1 59
HIGH ST

202 ▶

Scale: 7 inches to 1 mile
0   110 yards   220 yards
0   125 m   250 m

97   A   98   B   C

A2
1 BRAYFORD WAY
2 NEWLAND STREET WEST

A3
1 WHITEHALL TERR

A4
1 YARBOROUGH RD
2 MILL ROW
3 WINDMILL VW
4 SAXON ST

B3
1 WEST BIGHT
2 ST PAUL'S LA
3 BAILGATE
4 CASTLE HILL
5 EXCHEQUERGATE
6 WORDSWORTH ST
7 ST MICHAELS TERR
8 GARMSTON ST
9 ST MARTIN'S LA

10 NEUSTADT CT
11 DANES COURTYARD
12 STANTHAKET CT
13 DANES COTTAGES
14 ST CUTHBERTS CT

◀ 201   ⬆ 201   202 ▶

Place name May be abbreviated on the map

Location number Present when a number indicates the place's position in a crowded area of mapping

Locality, town or village Shown when more than one place has the same name

Postcode district District for the indexed place

Page and grid square Page number and grid reference for the standard mapping

Church Rd **6** Beckenham BR2..........**53** C6

Cities, towns and villages are listed in CAPITAL LETTERS

Public and commercial buildings are highlighted in magenta   Places of interest are highlighted in blue with a star ★

Abbreviations used in the index

Acad	Academy	Comm	Common	Gd	Ground	L	Leisure	Prom	Promenade
App	Approach	Cott	Cottage	Gdn	Garden	La	Lane	Rd	Road
Arc	Arcade	Cres	Crescent	Gn	Green	Liby	Library	Recn	Recreation
Ave	Avenue	Cswy	Causeway	Gr	Grove	Mdw	Meadow	Ret	Retail
Bglw	Bungalow	Ct	Court	H	Hall	Meml	Memorial	Sh	Shopping
Bldg	Building	Ctr	Centre	Ho	House	Mkt	Market	Sq	Square
Bsns, Bus	Business	Ctry	Country	Hospl	Hospital	Mus	Museum	St	Street
Bvd	Boulevard	Cty	County	HQ	Headquarters	Orch	Orchard	Sta	Station
Cath	Cathedral	Dr	Drive	Hts	Heights	Pal	Palace	Terr	Terrace
Cir	Circus	Dro	Drove	Ind	Industrial	Par	Parade	TH	Town Hall
Cl	Close	Ed	Education	Inst	Institute	Pas	Passage	Univ	University
Cnr	Corner	Emb	Embankment	Int	International	Pk	Park	Wk, Wlk	Walk
Coll	College	Est	Estate	Intc	Interchange	Pl	Place	Wr	Water
Com	Community	Ex	Exhibition	Junc	Junction	Prec	Precinct	Yd	Yard

Index of towns, villages, streets, hospitals, industrial estates, railway stations, schools, shopping centres, universities and places of interest

1st Drift PE9............219 B2
1st Main Rd DN36.......36 F8
2nd Ave DN36...........36 F8
2nd Drift PE9...........219 B2
4th Ave DN36...........36 F8
12th Ave DN36..........36 F8

A

AALPS Coll DN15..........8 F3
Aalsmeer Rise **6** PE11..214 A2
Abbey Bldgs **19** PE11..214 D4
Abbey Cl
 Coningsby LN4...........207 B5
 6 Skegness PE25...206 A4
 5 Woodhall Spa LN10...97 C6
Abbey Cres **4** PE20....135 C7
Abbeydale Cres NG31...211 A8
Abbey Dr
 20 Hatfield DN7........14 D4
 13 Woodhall Spa LN10...97 C5
Abbey Dr E DN32........191 D6
Abbey Dr W DN32.......191 D6
Abbeyfield Rd **1** DN7...14 C4
Abbeygate DN31.........191 D7
Abbey Gdns **22** DN7....14 D4
Abbey Gr **23** DN7......14 D4
Abbey La
 Sedgebrook NG32......128 F4
 Swineshead PE20.......135 C6
 Woodhall Spa LN10....97 C5
Abbey Mews **11** PE6...166 F1
Abbey Pk Mews DN32...191 D6
Abbey Pk Rd DN32......191 D6
Abbey Pl
 2 Lincoln LN2........234 C2
 10 Thorney PE6......176 A3
Abbey Rd
 Alvingham LN11..........49 F2
 Bardney LN3............83 B4
 Bourne PE10...........213 D5
 Grimsby DN32..........191 D6
 Hatfield DN7...........14 D4
 Louth LN11............198 D6
 Peterborough PE4.....221 A1
 Revesby PE22..........99 C5
 Scunthorpe DN17......184 F6
 Sleaford NG34.........212 A2
 Swineshead PE20......135 C7
 Ulceby DN39............12 A1
Abbey Rise **14** DN19...11 D8

Abbey St
 Kingston upon Hull
  HU9..................181 C7
 Lincoln LN2............234 C2
Abbey Way DN7...........14 D5
Abbey Wlk
 10 Crowland PE6.....166 F1
 Grimsby DN32..........191 D7
Abbey Yd **12** PE11....214 D4
Abbotsbury PE2..........230 A3
Abbot's Cl **5** PE10...213 E4
Abbots Cres **6** PE11..214 A4
Abbots Dr **1** PE6.....175 B8
Abbots Gdns **1** PE12..158 B6
Abbotsmede Prim Com Sch
 PE1...................226 C4
Abbots Rd DN17.........184 F6
Abbot St LN5............201 E1
Abbotsway DN32.........191 D6
Abbot's Way **5** PE11..214 A3
Abbott Cl **10** LN8.....57 B8
Abbott's Cl PE10........219 D4
Abbotts Gr PE4.........220 F6
Abbotts Grange DN36...195 E2
Abbotts Way LN11......198 E6
Abbot Way PE7..........233 D4
Abercorn St DN16.......183 A2
Aberdeen Cl PE9........218 D6
Aberporth Dr LN6........204 B8
Abingdon Ave LN6......204 C6
Abingdon Cl **12** LN6..204 C6
Aboyne Ave PE2.........229 F5
Abraham Cl **5** NG31...129 E5
ABY LN13................75 B5
Aby CE Prim Sch LN13..75 B5
Acacia Ave
 Chapel St Leonard PE24...90 D8
 Gainsborough DN21....197 D6
 Peterborough PE1......226 B8
 Scunthorpe DN15......182 C5
 Spalding PE11..........214 F5
 Waddington LN5........205 D1
 3 Wisbech PE13....170 D1
Acacia Cl **12** NG34...212 D2
Acacia Ct **3** DN16....185 B6
Acacia Way
 Boston PE21...........208 C4
 Messingham DN17......29 C7
Acadia Gr HU13.........178 F1
Accommodation Rd
 LN9...................199 A5
Acer Cl LN6.............204 D7
Acer Ct **2** LN6.......204 D7

Acer Gr **3** DN17......184 C5
Acer Rd PE1............226 B6
Achille Rd DN34.........190 D5
Achurch Cl LN9.........199 D1
Acklam Ave **3** PE11...214 F6
Acklam Gr DN32.........192 B6
Acklands La **13** NG23..117 D3
Acland St
 Gainsborough DN21....197 C5
 4 Kingston upon Hull
  HU3..................180 A6
 Peterborough PE1.....225 F3
Acomb Comm Rd DN7...14 F4
Acorn Cl
 Freiston PE21..........126 C4
 Grantham NG31........211 C7
 Lincoln LN5............205 D7
 19 Sutton on Sea LN12...76 F8
Acorn Ct DN35..........192 D2
Acorns The PE6.........217 A6
Acorn Way
 5 Bottesford DN16..185 B2
 Hessle HU13...........178 B3
Acre Cl LN8.............57 D8
Acre Dyke La LN4.......82 B4
Acre La
 Scopwick LN4...........95 E1
 Threekingham NG34....132 E2
Acres La DN9.............26 D7
Acres The **1** PE9......172 D4
Acton Ct DN32..........189 C1
Adam Cl **18** LN6......204 D7
Adam Smith St DN31....188 F1
Adamstiles **2** NG32...210 B4
Adams Way **6** DN21...65 E8
Ada Way LN11...........198 D7
Adderley PE3...........225 C7
Addington Way **3** PE4..221 A3
Addison Cl **4** LN5....107 A8
Addison Dr LN2.........202 B6
Addison Pl LN1..........65 E3
ADDLETHORPE PE24......90 C3
Adelaide Cl
 Gainsborough DN21....197 F2
 18 Waddington LN5...93 E8
Adelaide Prim Sch
 HU3...................180 D5
Adelaide St
 Kingston upon Hull
  HU3..................180 D5
 Stamford PE9..........219 D5
Adelphi Ct **5** DN36...195 C6
Adelphi Dr DN33........194 E7

Adlard Gr DN36..........36 C7
ADLINGFLEET DN14........7 E7
Adlingfleet Rd DN17......7 E6
Admirals Dr **7** PE13..170 D2
Admiralty Rd **19** LN12..64 B4
Adrian Cl
 Louth LN11............198 C4
 9 Skegness PE25..206 A4
 9 Swineshead PE20..135 B7
Advent Ct **2** DN39...12 A1
Adwalton Cl NG24......104 C4
Aegir Cl DN21..........197 F2
Africa Cl DN34.........190 D4
Agard Ave DN15........182 E3
Agnes St **2** NG31....211 B4
Aidan Rd NG34.........212 B2
AILBY LN13..............75 D4
AILSWORTH PE5.........223 D3
Aima Ct **2** LN2.......68 C2
Ainsdale Dr PE4........220 F3
Ainslie St DN32........191 E6
Ainsworth Rd **5** DN40..186 B4
Ainthorpe Gr HU5.......179 C7
Ainthorpe Prim Sch
 HU5...................179 C8
Aintree Dr PE11.........214 B1
Aire Cl DN40............186 A3
Aire Rd NG31...........210 E3
Airedale Cl
 12 Broughton DN20...19 E4
 Peterborough PE1......226 A6
Airedale Rd
 1 Scunthorpe DN16..185 D5
 1 Stamford PE9.....219 A7
Airedale Way DN31......191 D8
Aire St HU3.............180 B5
Airlie St HU3...........180 B5
Airman Rd NG34........120 B8
Airmyn Ave **1** HU3....179 E6
Airship Rd NG34........107 C1
AISBY
 Heydour NG32.........131 D5
 Pilham DN21............41 D4
Aisby Wlk DN21........197 F3
Aisne Cl LN1...........201 E7
Aisne St HU5...........180 A8
AISTHORPE LN1..........67 C7
Ajax Cl DN34...........190 D4
Ajax Ct DN15...........182 F5
Akeferry Rd DN9.........27 C1
Akeman Cl **10** PE10..213 C6
Akeman Dr **14** LN4....81 A1
Akita Cl **4** PE11.....214 A5
Alabala Cl LN4.........203 C1

1st–Alb

Alabala La LN4...........81 F4
Alan Cres DN15.........182 F2
Alba Cl DN17...........184 D5
Alban Ret Pk PE21......208 B3
Albany Cl
 Louth LN11............198 D3
 Skegness PE25........206 A5
Albany Pl LN11.........198 D3
Albany Rd
 Louth LN11............198 D3
 Skegness PE25........206 A5
 21 Wisbech PE13....170 C1
 3 Woodhall Spa LN10..97 D5
Albany St
 Gainsborough DN21....197 C6
 Kingston upon Hull HU3..180 D8
 Lincoln LN1...........234 A4
Albany Terr LN5........205 D5
Albany Way PE25.......206 A5
Albany Wlk PE2.........230 D7
Albatross Dr DN37......190 B7
Albemarle Cl **5** HU15..2 B5
Albemarle St **2** HU3..180 B5
Alberta Cres DN17......184 E3
Albert Ave
 Kingston upon Hull
  HU3..................180 A7
 Long Sutton PE12.....159 E7
 1 Skegness PE25...103 E4
Albert Ave Pools HU3...180 A7
Albert Cl **7** DN32....189 B1
Albert Cres LN1........201 D4
Albert Ct PE21.........208 E5
Albertine Ct **4** DN37..194 C5
Albert Marson Ct **6**
 DN16..................183 B2
Albert Pl
 Grimsby DN32.........189 B1
 Peterborough PE3.....225 F1
Albert Rd
 7 Cleethorpes DN35..192 F4
 Scunthorpe DN16......185 A5
 Skegness PE25........206 B3
 2 Stamford PE9....219 C4
Albert St E DN32........189 B1
Albert St W **5** DN32..189 B1
Albert St
 Boston PE21...........208 D5
 15 Bottesford NG13..128 A6
 Brigg DN20............196 C3

Barff Mdw LN8 43 E1
Barff Rd LN4 82 B1
Barfields La LN3 68 F1
Barford Cl PE2 230 C7
Bargate
Grimsby DN34 191 C5
12 Lincoln LN5 205 E8
Bargate Ave DN32 191 D5
Bargate Gr 3 HU5 179 D8
Bargate La 4 LN9 199 C3
Barge Cl 1 PE11 214 F5
Barge Rd PE12 148 A7
Barham Cl PE2 231 F5
BARHOLM PE9 164 C1
Barholme Ave 7 PE12 160 A8
Barkestone La NG13 128 A5
Barkham St 7 PE24 102 D2
Barkhouse Cl 4 DN35 192 F5
Barkhouse La 5 DN35 192 F5
Bark St DN35 192 F5
BARKSTON NG32 130 B8
Barkston Cl PE10 213 E6
Barkston Dr PE1 226 B6
Barkston Gdns LN2 202 B7
Barkston Rd NG32 118 D2
Barkston & Syston CE (Aided) Prim Sch NG32 130 B8
Barkwith Rd LN8 58 F1
Barkworth Cl HU10 178 D6
Barkworth Ct 3 DN37 194 C4
Bar La 20 LN5 93 F7
Barley Cl
Heckington NG34 122 D2
12 Hibaldstow DN20 31 A5
24 Metheringham LN4 95 C4
Barleycroft Rd NG33 152 E8
Barleyfield PE6 164 E2
Barley Gr 4 PE11 166 C6
Barley Mews PE2 230 D7
Barley Way LN9 199 A3
BARLINGS LN3 69 D1
Barlings Ave DN16 185 A7
Barlings Cl
1 Barlings LN3 69 C3
Hartsholme LN6 204 F7
7 Scotter DN21 29 C4
Barlings La LN3 69 C2
Barmouth Dr DN37 190 E8
Barmston St HU2 180 F8
BARNACK PE9 172 E4
Barnack CE Prim Sch PE9 172 D4
Barnack Drift PE9 172 B3
Barnack Est 4 PE24 102 E7
Barnack Hill & Holes National Nature Reserve* PE9 172 D3
Barnack Rd
Bainton PE9 172 E4
St Martin's without PE9 219 D4
Barnard Ave DN20 196 B3
Barnard Way 9 PE3 224 F3
Barnard Wlk DN40 186 D3
Barnberry Way PE10 142 D2
BARNBY DUN DN3 14 A4
Barnby Gate NG24 104 A4
BARNBY IN THE WILLOWS NG24 104 F3
Barnby La NG23 104 F1
Barnby Rd NG24 104 B3
Barnby Rd Prim Sch NG24 104 A4
Barn Cl
2 Maxey PE6 173 C7
Peterborough PE4 220 F3
Barnes Cl 1 NG34 212 C6
Barnes Cres
Scunthorpe DN15 182 E4
Skegness PE25 206 A5
Barnes Dro PE10 154 F4
Barnes Gn 2 DN21 29 C4
Barnes La LN5 106 F7
Barnes Rd
9 Donington PE11 134 E2
Skegness PE25 206 A5
Barnes Way PE4 220 F3
Barnetby La DN20 20 F7
BARNETBY LE WOLD DN38 21 C4
Barnetby Rd
1 Kingston upon Hull HU13 179 A3
Scunthorpe DN17 184 F5
Barnetby Sta DN38 21 B4
Barnet Dr DN36 195 E7
Barnet Gn 12 DN7 14 D3
Barnett Pl DN35 192 B7
Barneyfield Rd PE22 126 E1
Barnfield Rd 22 NG23 91 D5
Barn Hill PE9 219 B5
BARNOLDBY LE BECK DN37 35 B6
Barnoldby Rd DN37 194 C4
Barn Owl Cl
Corby Glen NG33 152 F7
1 Langtoft PE6 164 F3
Barnside 6 DN20 30 F5
Barnstaple Rd 3 DN17 184 D8
Barnstock PE3 225 A7
Barnston Way 12 DN15 8 B4
Barnswallace Ct 15 LN2 68 D7
Barnwell Rd 3 PE9 218 E6
Barnwell Terr 2 NG31 210 F3
Baron Ave DN36 195 D7
Baron Ct PE4 221 B4
Baroness Rd DN34 190 F6
Barons Way PE9 219 C4
Barrack Sq NG31 211 C4
Barracks The PE13 169 E2
Barraclough's La 1 DN18 3 E1
Barratt's Cl LN2 234 C4
Bar Rd DN10 52 B8
Bar Rd N 3 DN10 52 B8
Bar Rd S 7 DN10 52 B8
Barrett Gr 7 LN2 68 E6
Barrett's Cl PE12 215 D3
Barrick Cl 16 DN19 11 D8
Barrier Bank
Cowbit PE12 156 F2
Spalding PE12 214 C1
Barrington Cl 8 PE12 215 D2
Barrington Gate PE12 215 E1
Barrow Blow Wells Nature Reserve* DN19 4 D1
BARROWBY NG32 210 A5
Barrowby CE (Controlled) Prim Sch NG32 129 B3
Barrowby Gate NG31 210 D4
Barrowby Rd 8 NG31 211 A5
Barrowden Rd PE9 171 A2
Barrowfield PE1 226 E7
BARROW HANN DN19 4 E1
BARROW HAVEN DN19 4 B2
Barrow Haven Reedbed Nature Reserve* DN19 4 B2
Barrow Haven Sta DN19 4 C2
Barrow La HU13 178 D2
Barrow Rd
Barton-upon-Humber DN18 11 A8
New Holland DN19 4 E1
Barrows Gate
3 Beacon Hill NG24 104 A6
North Somercotes LN11 50 D6
BARROW UPON HUMBER DN19 11 C8
Barr's La PE12 168 B4
Barry Ave DN34 190 F3
Barry Wlk 3 PE2 230 F7
Bars La
Benington PE22 126 E5
Bicker PE20 135 A5
Bartholemew Cl 1 LN3 83 C4
Bartol Cres PE21 208 D5
Barton Cl
3 Mablethorpe LN12 64 C2
Paston PE4 221 D1
Barton Dr HU13 178 D1
Barton Gate LN11 198 D4
Barton La
Barrow upon Humber DN19 11 C8
Tydd St Mary PE13 169 F8
Barton-on-Humber Sta DN18 3 F1
Barton Outdoor Pursuits Ctr* DN18 3 D2
Barton Rd
5 Wainfleet All Saints PE24 102 D1
Wrawby DN20 196 F6
Barton St Peters CE Prim Sch DN18 3 F1
Bartons La PE23 101 F6
Barton St
Aylesby DN37 23 D2
Barrow upon Humber DN19 11 C8
Fotherby LN11 49 A2
Irby DN37 34 F7
Keelby DN41 23 A4
Ludborough DN36 48 C6
BARTON-UPON-HUMBER DN18 10 F7
BARTON WATERSIDE DN18 3 F2
Bartram Gate 2 PE4 221 C1
Bartrams 3 HU15 2 D6
Basic Slag Rd DN16 183 E2
Basil Gn PE2 230 D6
Baslow Rd DN15 182 B2
Bass Cotts NG34 212 E3
Bassett Cl 2 DN20 19 E3
Bassett Rd DN35 193 A4
BASSINGHAM LN5 92 F2
Bassingham Cres LN2 201 F7
Bassingham La PE23 88 E3
Bassingham Prim Sch LN5 92 F2
Bassingham Rd LN5 92 F5
BASSINGTHORPE NG33 140 E3
BASTON PE6 164 E4
Baston CE Prim Sch PE6 164 E5
Baston Edge Dro PE10 164 E7
Baston Fen Nature Reserve* PE6 165 A8
Baston Outgang Rd PE6 165 A6
Bateman's Cl 3 PE12 159 D7
Batemans Ct 2 PE24 102 E2
Bath Gdns PE21 208 F3
Bath La 15 PE11 214 D4
Bath Rd
Bracebridge Heath LN4 81 A2
Wisbech PE13 170 D1
Bath Row PE9 219 B4
Bath St
8 Grantham NG31 211 A4
Bath St *continued*
Grimsby DN32 189 C1
Bathurst PE2 230 A4
Bathurst St
8 Kingston upon Hull HU3 180 D5
Lincoln LN2 202 D3
Battery St DN40 186 D4
Battlefields La N PE12 159 A8
Battlefields La S PE12 215 F3
Battle Gn DN9 27 D7
Battle of Britain Meml Flight Visitor Ctr* LN4 207 B3
Baulkin's Dro PE12 159 C1
BAUMBER LN9 72 A1
Baumber Prim Sch LN9 72 A1
Bawtry Cl LN6 204 C8
Bawtry Rd DN7 14 F3
Baxter Cl
Coningsby LN4 207 D3
15 Wisbech PE13 170 E1
Baxter Gdns PE11 214 C7
Bayard St DN21 197 C5
Bayes Rd 6 PE25 103 E4
Bayfield Rd 4 LN4 96 B1
Bayford Dr NG24 104 C4
Bayford Gn PE21 208 B4
Bayons Ave DN33 194 D8
Baysdale Gr NG31 211 B8
Baysdale Rd DN16 185 D5
Baysgarth House Mus* DN18 10 F8
Baysgarth Leisure Ctr DN18 10 F8
Baysgarth Sch DN18 10 F8
Baysgarth View DN18 10 F7
Bayston Ct PE2 230 E8
Bayswater Pl 1 DN33 194 D8
Bayswood Ave PE21 208 F1
BAYTHORPE PE20 135 C8
Baytree Ave DN34 191 A6
Baytree Owl Ctr* PE12 157 D7
Baywood Cl 4 LN6 200 C1
Beach Ave 15 PE24 90 D7
Beach Bank
Pinchbeck PE11 144 E3
Surfleet PE11 145 A3
Beach Holt La DN37 23 D2
Beach La PE11 144 F3
Beachside 10 LN12 77 A8
Beacon Ave
16 Barton-upon-Humber DN18 10 E8
Cleethorpes DN35 192 D6
Beacon Ct DN35 192 D6
BEACON HILL NG24 104 B5
Beacon Hill La PE34 161 E3
Beacon Hill Rd
Gringley on the Hill DN10 39 D1
Newark-on-Trent NG24 104 B4
Beacon Hts NG24 104 B4
Beacon La NG31 211 C4
Beacon Pk Cl 4 PE25 206 A6
Beacon Pk Dr PE25 206 A6
Beacon Rd 7 NG34 107 C1
Beaconsfield Dr 3 NG24 104 C5
Beaconthorpe Rd 4 DN35 192 E7
Beacon View 2 NG13 128 A6
Beacon Way PE25 206 A6
Beaford Ct DN17 184 C8
Beagle Cl 16 DN20 19 E4
Beagle La NG34 107 C1
Bean St HU3 180 C6
Bear La 14 PE11 145 C1
Beatrice Rd 11 PE13 170 D2
Beatrice Way 28 PE24 90 D7
Beatty Ave DN33 194 F7
Beaubridge Bsns Pk PE25 206 B3
Beauchamp St 3 DN16 183 B1
Beauchamp Wlk 7 DN16 183 B2
Beauchief Gdns DN16 185 A8
Beaufort Ave 1 PE6 217 C5
Beaufort Cl
Kingston upon Hull HU3 180 D6
Lincoln LN2 202 D8
Beaufort Cres DN35 192 D2
Beaufort Dr
Bourne PE10 213 C7
4 Spalding PE11 214 C3
Beaufort Rd LN2 202 D8
Beaufort St DN21 197 B7
Beaulahland 8 DN18 10 A7
Beaulah Villas 9 DN18 10 A7
Beaulieu Ct 6 PE6 175 A1
Beaumonde 5 DN36 195 C2
Beaumont Cl 11 PE24 102 E7
Beaumont Ct 3 HU9 181 D7
Beaumont Dr 2 NG31 210 F8
Beaumont Fee LN1 234 A2
Beaumont St DN21 197 D4
Beaumont Way PE7 230 C2
Beauvale Gdns PE4 221 C3
Beauvoir Pl PE7 233 E5
Beaver Cl 1 LN6 200 A5
Beccelm Dr 9 PE6 175 B8
Beck Bank
Gosberton PE11 144 C3
Kirton PE20 124 E1
Beck Cl
5 Binbrook LN8 47 C5
13 Keelby DN41 23 A4
1 Ruskington NG34 108 D2
Becke Cl LN3 203 E5
Becket Cl LN4 203 D1
Beckets Cl PE1 225 F8
Beckett Ave DN21 197 E6
Beckett Cl
9 Heckington NG34 122 D3
2 Skegness PE25 206 C1
Beckett Dr PE11 214 C6
Beckett Sch DN21 53 A8
Beckhall LN2 68 D6
Beckhead Cvn Site LN6 204 C1
Beck Hill
6 Barton-upon-Humber DN18 10 F8
Tealby LN8 46 C1
Beckhole Cl HU3 180 A6
Beckhythe Cl DN33 191 E1
BECKINGHAM
Barnby in the Willows NG24 105 A4
Beckingham DN10 40 B1
Beckingham PE2 229 F3
Beckingham Rd
Coddington NG24 104 C5
Walkeringham DN10 40 A2
Beckingthorpe Dr 19 NG13 128 A6
Beck La
Appleby DN15 9 D1
Aubourn Haddington & South Hykeham LN6 93 B7
10 Barrow upon Humber DN19 11 D8
7 Broughton DN20 19 E3
Fulbeck NG32 106 C1
Heighington/Washingborough LN4 81 F4
Ingoldmells PE25 90 E2
Redbourne DN21 30 F2
Scunthorpe DN16 185 B3
6 Welton/Dunholme LN2 68 E6
Welton le Marsh PE23 89 A3
Beckside
11 Brough HU15 2 D6
Normanby by Spital LN8 55 E7
Rothwell LN7 33 F2
Scopwick LN4 108 C8
Beck Side 5 DN20 30 F5
Beckside Cl DN36 192 E1
Beckside Ct LN11 198 D3
Becks La DN21 29 A3
Beck St
Digby LN4 108 E5
Welbourn LN5 106 E4
Becks The 4 LN9 199 C4
Beck Way 5 PE10 164 C8
Beck Wlk 2 DN35 192 E1
Bedale Pl DN35 192 E3
Bedale Rd 3 DN16 185 D5
Bede Cl NG34 212 B2
Bede Cres PE22 126 F5
Bedehouse Bank PE10 213 E4
Bede House La 3 NG24 104 A4
Bede Pl PE1 226 A6
Bede Rd 3 PE6 164 E5
Bedford Cl NG31 211 F5
Bedford Ct 16 PE6 176 A3
Bedford Pl 1 PE11 214 D3
Bedford Rd
Humberston DN35 193 A1
Kingston upon Hull HU13 178 F3
Bedford Row PE13 170 D8
Bedford St
Grimsby DN32 189 C1
2 Lincoln LN1 201 D4
Peterborough PE1 226 B4
Beechams Mews 5 PE11 214 B3
Beech Ave
Bourne PE10 213 B5
Gainsborough DN21 197 D6
Grimsby DN33 191 C3
5 Gunness DN15 17 E6
Kingston upon Hull HU10 178 D8
24 Nettleham LN2 68 C2
Peterborough PE1 225 F3
Scunthorpe DN15 182 B6
Spalding PE11 214 F5
Beech Cl
1 Bracebridge Heath LN4 81 A1
5 Broughton DN20 19 D3
2 Colsterworth NG33 151 E7
4 Coningsby LN4 207 D4
Dunholme LN2 68 E5
3 Gringley on the Hill DN10 39 C1
7 Heckington NG34 122 D3
Kingston upon Hull HU3 180 C5
Market Deeping PE6 217 B6
RAF Cranwell NG34 107 D1
9 Sudbrooke LN2 68 F2
4 Thorney PE6 176 A3
Beech Cres 1 DN7 14 D6
Beechcroft Cl 6 LN6 93 A8
Beechcroft Rd NG31 210 C3
Beech Dr
16 Bottesford NG13 128 A5
6 North Ferriby HU14 3 A4
15 Ryhall PE9 163 C1
Welton HU14 2 F5
Beechers Way LN8 57 D7
Beeches Ave DN16 185 B4
Beeches La PE22 112 C5
Beeches Prim Sch The PE1 225 F3
Beeches The 1 LN1 66 C7
Beechfield Ct DN34 191 C6
Beechfield Rd 7 DN7 14 C4
Beech Garth 9 DN19 11 C7
Beech Gr
Anlaby with Anlaby Common HU13 178 C3
3 Burton upon Stather DN15 8 B5
Donington PE11 134 E2
Holton le Clay DN36 195 E1
Louth LN11 198 C7
4 Scopwick Heath LN4 108 A7
Stamford PE9 218 D6
4 Swanland HU14 3 C7
Beech Hill Rd HU14 3 C7
Beechings Way 10 LN13 75 E2
Beechings Way Ind Est LN13 75 E2
Beech La 12 PE6 175 A1
Beech Lawn HU10 178 E6
Beech Rd
Branston LN4 81 D2
6 Brough HU15 2 C6
Glinton PE6 220 B8
Beech Rise
Sleaford NG34 212 D6
2 South Rauceby NG34 120 E4
Beech St LN5 205 D5
Beech Tree Ave 17 DN8 15 B7
Beechtree Cl 8 NG34 108 E1
Beechway DN16 185 B7
Beech Way DN35 192 D2
Beechwood Ave
Grimsby DN33 190 F3
Immingham DN40 186 C4
Beechwood Cl
16 Kirk Sandall DN3 14 A1
Peterborough PE1 226 C7
6 Wisbech PE13 170 D1
Beechwood Cres 4 DN20 19 E4
Beechwood Dr
12 Scawby DN20 30 F8
7 Scotter DN21 29 C3
Beechwood Rd 5 PE13 170 D1
Beeden Pk Est NG31 210 C4
Bee Field The LN2 202 F7
Beehive La LN6 79 C1
Beeley Rd DN32 192 C6
BEELSBY DN37 34 E4
Beelsby Rd LN7 34 C5
Beel's Rd DN41 187 B2
BEESBY LN13 76 A7
Beesby Dr 3 DN35 192 F3
Beesby Rd
Maltby le Marsh LN13 76 A7
Scunthorpe DN17 184 E5
Beesby Wlk LN13 76 A6
Bees Cnr 1 PE24 102 D2
Bee's La PE13 169 F6
Beeson Gr DN31 188 E1
Beeson St DN31 188 E1
Beeston Dr PE7 231 F5
Beeton Cl LN11 198 D4
Beetons Cl PE7 233 E5
Beevor St LN6 201 C2
Beggar Hill Messingham Rd DN21 29 D4
Beggar's La PE22 98 F3
Begger's Bush La PE12 157 D7
Beilby St HU3 179 F4
Belcanto Ct 3 PE11 214 A5
BELCHFORD LN9 73 B2
Belchmire La PE11 145 B5
Beldings Cl PE23 101 F6
Belfry The 5 NG31 211 D7
Belgic Sq PE1 226 E3
Belgrave Cl 11 DN9 16 E1
Belgrave Dr HU4 179 D5
Belgrave Rd
Grimsby DN33 191 B2
7 Spalding PE11 214 C2
Belgrave Sq 1 DN15 183 B3
Belgravia Cl LN6 200 E1
Belham Rd PE1 225 E7
Belisana Rd 5 PE11 214 A5
Bellamy Ct HU9 181 C7
Bellamy's La PE14 170 D4
Bellbutts View DN21 29 B3
Bell Cl NG31 210 E7
Bell Ct 5 PE21 208 F1
Bell Dro PE6 175 F6
BELLEAU LN13 75 A5
Belleisle Rd DN34 190 D4
Belle Vue PE2 231 C6
Belle Vue Rd LN1 234 A3
Belle Vue Terr
Lincoln LN1 234 A3
21 Thorne/Moorends DN8 15 A8
Bellfield Cl 4 PE11 214 B3
Bellflower Cl 2 LN2 202 C8
Bell Gr LN6 205 C6
Bellingham Rd DN16 185 D7
Bellingham's Dro PE11 166 F7
Bell La
4 Collingham NG23 91 C4
Fosdyke PE20 146 D8
Market Deeping PE6 217 E4
Moulton PE12 157 F7
Scunthorpe DN15 183 A2

Bursnells La 3 LE14 150 B1
Burswood PE2 229 F2
Burtey Fen Collection The* PE11 145 B1
Burtey Fen La PE11 145 B2
Burtoft La PE20 135 E2
BURTON LN1 67 D1
Burton Cl PE21 209 B7
BURTON CORNER PE21 209 B7
Burton Ct
  2 Louth LN11 198 D4
  Peterborough PE1 226 C3
Burtonfield Cl 1 LN3 203 E6
Burton Gravel Pits Nature Reserve* LN1 67 C1
Burton La
  8 Billingborough NG34 133 B1
  Burton Coggles NG33 140 E1
Burton La End LN1 200 C8
BURTON-LE-COGGLES NG33 152 D8
Burton Mews LN4 203 D1
Burton on Stather Prim Sch DN15 8 B4
BURTON PEDWARDINE NG34 122 B1
Burton Rd
  Burton upon Stather DN15 8 C4
  Heckington NG34 122 C2
  Lincoln LN1 234 A4
  Spalding PE11 214 B2
Burton Ridge 2 LN1 201 D7
Burton St
  14 Gainsborough DN21 197 D3
  Peterborough PE1 226 C3
BURTON STATHER DN15 8 B5
BURTON UPON STATHER DN15 8 B4
Burton Way LN9 199 D2
BURWELL LN11 74 B6
Burwell Cl LN2 202 A8
Burwell Dr DN33 191 B3
Burwell Rd LN11 74 D7
Burwell Reach PE2 230 C7
Burystead PE2 231 B8
Bush Cl HU4 179 D3
Bushfield PE2 229 E3
Bushfield Com Coll PE2 229 E3
Bushfield Ct PE2 229 E3
Bushfield Rd DN16 183 B1
Bushfield Rd Inf Sch DN16 183 A1
Bushfield Sports Ctr PE2 229 E4
Bush Gn La
  Algarkirk PE20 146 C8
  Fosdyke PE20 136 C1
Bush Meadow La PE12 215 A4
Bushy Cl 5 PE7 230 D3
BUSLINGTHORPE LN8 57 A4
Buslingthorpe Rd LN8 57 A4
Bustards' La PE14 161 C1
Butcher La 10 LN11 198 B5
Butchers Sq HU13 178 E1
Butchery Ct 3 LN2 234 B2
Butforth La DN19 11 E8
Butler Pl DN35 192 B7
Butler's Way 14 PE20 135 B7
Butlin Cl 1 PE25 206 A4
Buttercake La PE22 113 F2
Buttercross Cl 2 DN41 23 E6
Buttercup Cl
  1 Kingston upon Hull HU9 181 D7
  3 Spalding PE11 214 A2
  3 Stamford PE9 218 D7
Buttercup Ct PE6 217 D6
Buttercup Dr PE10 213 D3
Buttercup Paddock 4 PE12 158 B6
Butterfield Cl 7 DN37 23 F1
Butterfly & Wildlife Pk The* PE12 216 D6
Buttergate Hill LN9 71 F3
Buttermere Cl
  2 Birchwood LN6 200 D1
  East Ella HU4 179 E6
Buttermere Cres 2 DN36 36 C8
Buttermere Pl 4 PE4 221 C3
Buttermere Way 6 DN32 191 F8
Butter Mkt 11 LN7 33 B4
BUTTERWICK PE22 126 F4
Butterwick Cl DN35 192 F3
Butterwick Pinchbeck Endowed CE Sch PE22 126 E3
Butterwick Rd
  Benington PE22 126 F4
  Messingham DN17 29 A7
Buttery Cl LN6 204 F4
Buttfield Rd HU13 178 E1
Butt Gate LN11 50 B8
Butt La
  Barrowby NG32 210 A6
  Goulceby LN11 72 D6
  Laceby DN37 23 F2
  Norton Disney LN6 92 C2
Butt La *continued*
  Theddlethorpe All Saints LN12 63 E7
  Walcott LN4 109 C7
  Wymondham LE14 150 C2
Buttler Way 3 NG34 212 C3
Butts Hill La 5 DN15 8 C8
Butts La LN5 92 F6
Butt's La LN4 207 B5
Butts Rd DN18 3 F1
Butts The LE14 138 F1
Buxton Ct DN15 182 B2
Bycroft Rd DN21 197 C8
Byfield Rd DN17 184 D6
Byland Cl LN2 202 E6
Byland Ct 4 HU9 181 E8
Byland Gr DN37 188 A1
Byrd Rd DN16 185 E6
Byron Ave
  Grantham NG31 211 E6
  Lincoln LN2 202 A6
Byron Cl
  Peterborough PE2 231 D6
  Scunthorpe DN17 184 E6
  6 Sleaford NG34 212 F4
Byron Gr DN33 191 C4
Byron Rd LN12 64 B4
Byron Way PE9 218 E5
Bytham Hts 3 NG33 162 E8
Bythams Prim Sch The NG33 153 A2
Bythorne Bank PE13 169 B6
Bythorn Rd PE2 231 C6
Bythorn Way PE2 231 C6
Bywood Pl DN37 190 C6

C

CABOURNE LN7 33 D4
Cabourne Ave LN2 202 B7
Cabourne Ct LN2 202 B7
Cabourne Rd DN33 191 B3
CACKLE HILL PE12 215 C5
Cackle Hill La PE12 215 C5
Caddle Rd 11 DN41 23 A4
Cade Cl 12 LN2 68 F4
Cade Dro PE12 159 D4
Cade La DN21 53 D6
Cades Field Rd 24 LN12 77 A8
Cadman Way DN21 41 A1
CADNEY DN20 31 D6
Cadney Rd DN20 196 C1
Cadwell Cl 4 LN6 204 C7
Cadwell Pk Motor Racing Circuit* LN11 73 B8
CAENBY LN8 55 F8
Caenby Cl DN21 197 F3
Caenby Cnr LN8 55 B8
Caenby Rd
  Caenby LN8 43 F1
  Cleethorpes DN35 192 E4
  Scunthorpe DN17 184 E5
Caesar Cl 7 PE6 164 E5
Cagthorpe LN9 199 B3
Cairns Way 8 LN5 93 E8
CAISTOR LN7 33 B4
Caistor Ave DN16 185 B4
Caistor By-pass LN7 33 B3
Caistor CE/Methodist Prim Sch LN7 33 B3
Caistor Cl 7 LN6 204 C7
Caistor Dr
  Bracebridge Heath LN4 81 A2
  Grimsby DN33 191 B3
Caistor Gram Sch LN7 33 B4
Caistor La LN8 46 C3
Caistor Rd
  Barton-upon-Humber DN18 11 A7
  Birchwood LN6 204 C7
  Cabourne LN7 33 F5
  Caistor LN7 32 E4
  Laceby DN37 23 E1
  2 Market Rasen LN8 57 D8
  Middle Rasen LN8 45 D2
  Rothwell LN7 33 E2
  South Kelsey LN7 32 A1
  Swallow LN7 34 A5
Caistor Yarborough Sch LN7 33 C4
Caithness Rd PE9 218 E6
CALCEBY LN13 74 E2
Caldbeck Cl PE4 221 D2
Caldecote Cl PE2 231 E6
Calder Cl
  Grantham NG31 210 E3
  Immingham DN40 186 A3
Calderdale Dr PE11 214 D7
Calder Gn 24 DN17 29 D7
Calder Rd
  Lincoln LN5 205 C2
  Scunthorpe DN16 185 D6
Caldervale PE2 230 C6
Caldicott Dr 8 DN21 53 A8
Caleb Hill La
  Leake Commonside PE22 113 F3
  Old Leake PE22 114 A3
Caledonian Rd 4 PE9 218 F6
Caledonia Pk HU9 181 B5
Callan's La PE10 142 C2
Calver Cres DN37 190 D7
Calvert La HU4 179 D7
Calvert Rd HU5 179 D8
Camargue Ave DN37 194 F4
Camarthen Cl 4 NG31 210 E5
Cambrai Cl LN1 201 E7
Cambrian Cl NG31 210 E7
Cambrian Way
  Holton le Clay DN36 195 C3
  11 North Hykeham LN6 93 B8
  1 Peterborough PE4 221 C1
Cambridge Ave
  Lincoln LN1 201 D4
  Peterborough PE1 225 F5
  Scunthorpe DN16 185 A3
Cambridge Cres 4 LN8 47 B6
Cambridge Dr
  Heighington/Washingborough LN4 203 D1
  Wisbech PE13 170 C1
Cambridge Gdns 4 PE11 145 B7
Cambridge Mdws NG24 104 C4
Cambridge Pk Sch DN34 191 A5
Cambridge Rd
  Grimsby DN34 190 F5
  Kingston upon Hull HU13 178 F3
  Scunthorpe DN16 185 C6
  Stamford PE9 219 A6
Cambridge Rd N 1 LN12 64 B5
Cambridge Rd S 3 LN12 64 B5
Cambridge St
  Cleethorpes DN35 192 F6
  Grantham NG31 211 B3
  Kingston upon Hull HU3 180 D6
Camdale La 8 NG24 104 C1
Camden St 1 HU3 180 B5
Camdon Cl 1 LN5 205 D3
Camel Gate PE12 157 B7
Camelia Cl PE4 221 B3
Camelot Gdns
  Boston PE21 209 E5
  11 Mablethorpe/Sutton on Sea LN12 76 F8
Cameron Dr 3 PE11 214 E3
Cameron La 13 NG24 104 C1
Cameron St 4 NG34 122 E3
Camilla Cl HU9 181 A5
CAMMERINGHAM LN1 54 F1
Camm's La PE22 114 D2
Campain's La PE11 166 C7
Campbell Ave DN16 185 B4
Campbell Cl 4 NG31 210 F5
Campbell Ct HU13 178 E2
Campbell Dr PE4 221 C4
Campbell Gr DN37 190 E8
Campbells Cl PE11 214 B1
Campbells Farm Ave 1 DN15 17 E6
Campbell St DN21 197 B5
Campden Cres DN35 192 D7
Campion Ave HU4 179 B2
Campion Cl PE11 214 B6
Campion Dr PE6 217 D6
Campion Gr 4 PE9 218 D7
Campion Rd PE1 226 B8
Campions Cl DN36 195 D2
Campions' La 11 DN36 36 B1
Campion Way PE10 213 D2
Camp La NG33 141 B1
Campling Pl PE12 215 D7
Campling Way 2 LN12 64 C2
Campney La LN10 83 F1
Campus Way LN6 201 D3
Camwood Cres LN6 200 C1
Canada La
  Caistor LN7 33 C4
  Wildmore LN4 111 A4
Canal La DN10 40 B5
CANAL SIDE DN8 15 A7
Canal View 12 DN8 15 A7
Canberra Ave DN7 26 A8
Canberra Cl 5 LN4 207 C4
Canberra Cres
  11 Binbrook Tech Pk LN8 47 B6
  Grantham NG31 211 D7
  10 Manby LN11 62 C6
Canberra Dr 5 LN1 67 F5
Canberra St HU3 180 D5
Canberra Way LN6 200 A4
Candidus Ct 6 PE4 220 F5
Candlehouse La 9 LN13 75 F3
CANDLESBY PE23 88 F2
Candlesby Hill Quarry Nature Reserve* PE23 88 F2
Candlesby Rd DN37 190 C7
Candy Bank DN9 26 B5
Candy St PE2 230 E8
Cane Ave PE2 230 D7
Canister La
  Frithville PE22 112 C1
  Langriville PE22 124 F8
Cannon Cl NG24 104 C5
Cannonhill Dro PE12 167 A8
Cannon Oakes Ct DN36 195 E6
Cannon Peter Hall CE Prim Sch DN40 186 D4
Cannon St
  Kingston upon Hull HU2 180 F8
  1 Lincoln LN2 202 B3
  3 Louth LN11 198 B5
Canon Dr 6 PE9 172 D3
Canon Peter Hall CE Prim Sch The DN40 186 D4
Canonsfield PE4 220 E4
Canon Tardrew Ct HU13 179 A1
Canterbury Cl
  Grantham NG31 211 E7
  1 Scunthorpe DN17 184 D7
  Spalding PE11 214 B4
Canterbury Dr
  Grimsby DN34 191 C6
  Heighington/Washingborough LN4 203 D1
  4 Sleaford NG34 212 C7
Canterbury Rd
  1 Hatfield DN7 14 D4
  Peterborough PE4 220 F3
Cant's Dro PE13 177 C4
Canturbury Cl 10 LN10 97 C5
Canty Nook 5 DN38 32 E7
Canwell PE4 221 A4
CANWICK LN4 81 B4
Canwick Ave LN4 205 F4
Canwick Hill LN4 81 A4
Canwick Rd
  Canwick LN5 81 A4
  Lincoln LN5 234 B1
  Washingborough LN4 81 D4
Capes Entry PE12 157 A2
Capitol Pk DN8 14 F8
Capper Ave 3 DN21 55 A8
Cappitt Dr 2 PE10 164 C8
Capp's La 19 LN5 93 F7
Capstan Way 17 DN8 15 A8
Captains Beck 9 PE11 145 C1
Captain's Hill NG34 121 B7
Captains Wlk HU1 180 E5
Capthorne Cl PE7 230 C2
Caravan Pk LN6 204 C1
Carbis Cl DN36 195 C7
Cardiff Ave DN36 195 C6
Cardigan Rd HU3 179 E6
Cardinal Cl
  Lincoln LN2 202 D5
  New Quarrington NG34 212 A2
Cardinal Ct 3 DN37 194 C5
Cardinals Gate PE4 220 E4
Cardinal Wlk HU13 179 A1
Cardyke Dr 13 PE6 164 E5
CAREBY PE9 163 B7
Carew St HU3 179 F7
Carholme Cl 1 PE10 213 D6
Carholme Rd LN1 201 C4
Carisbrook Ct PE3 230 B8
Carisbrooke Cl
  2 Lincoln LN1 201 E6
  5 New Waltham DN36 195 D7
Carisbrooke Gr PE9 218 E5
Carisbrooke Manor La DN17 184 A5
Carisbrooke Wlk DN40 186 D3
CARLBY PE9 163 D5
Carleton Crest 3 PE4 221 B1
Carline Rd LN1 234 A3
Carlisle Cl
  6 Grantham NG31 210 D5
  1 Lincoln LN6 204 F1
Carlisle Gdns LN9 199 D5
Carlisle St 2 DN21 197 D5
Carlisle Way 9 LN4 81 A2
Carlton Ave DN41 23 F5
Carlton Bvd LN2 202 D5
Carlton Cl
  Humberston DN35 193 B1
  8 Leverington PE13 170 B2
  2 Spalding PE11 214 B1
Carlton Ctr Ret Pk LN2 202 D6
Carlton Ferry La NG23 91 A6
Carlton Gr LN2 201 F7
Carlton La
  Broxholme LN1 67 A4
  Sutton-on-Trent NG23 91 A7
CARLTON-LE-MOORLAND LN5 105 E8
Carlton Mews 9 LN4 203 D1
Carlton Pk LN11 62 C5
Carlton Rd
  Ancaster NG32 119 E3
  Bassingham LN5 92 E2
  Boston PE21 208 D5
  Grimsby DN34 191 B6
  9 Healing DN41 23 F5
  Hough-on-the-Hill NG32 119 B5
  Manby LN11 62 C6
CARLTON SCROOP NG32 119 D3
Carlton St
  Kingston upon Hull HU3 179 F4
  Lincoln LN1 234 A4
  12 Scunthorpe DN15 183 B3
Carlton Wlk LN2 202 A7
Carlyle Cl DN35 193 A2
Carlyle Wlk LN2 202 B6
Carmel Gn PE21 208 E2
Carmen Cres DN36 195 C3
Carnaby Gr 2 DN32 192 A5
Carnarvon Ave 1 DN34 191 B4
Carn Cl 3 LN5 205 D2
Carnegie Rd 21 PE8 172 B1
Carnegie St 6 HU3 180 A6
Carnell La 16 NG24 104 C1
Carnforth Cres DN34 191 A5
Carnforth Parade DN34 191 A5
Carnoustie
  9 Spalding PE11 214 C2
  7 Waltham DN37 194 C4
Carnoustie Cl 2 LN10 97 C5
Carnoustie Ct PE12 160 F4
Carnoustie Dr LN6 204 B7
Carol Dickson Ct 9 HU3 180 C5
Caroline Cl 12 NG34 212 F4
Caroline Ct 10 PE21 209 A5
Caroline Pl HU2 180 F7
Caroline Rd 5 LN4 95 D4
Caroline St
  10 Alford LN13 75 F2
  Kingston upon Hull HU2 180 F8
Carradale PE2 229 D5
Carral Cl LN5 205 C3
Carram Way LN1 201 C7
Carr Dike La HU15 1 C7
Carr Dyke Bank DN17 28 D5
Carr Dyke Rd DN17 17 D3
Carre's Gram Sch NG34 212 D5
Carre's Sq LN4 109 E6
Carre St NG34 212 D4
Carr Gate LN4 109 F6
Carrhouse Rd DN9 16 D1
Carrier Cl PE3 230 D8
CARRINGTON PE22 112 D6
Carrington Cl
  Coningsby LN4 207 D5
  2 Spalding PE11 214 B3
Carrington Dr
  Deeping St Nicholas PE11 165 F5
  8 Humberston DN36 36 D8
  Lincoln LN6 204 F7
Carrington Rd
  Carrington PE22 112 D3
  Moulton PE12 146 C3
  Spalding PE11 214 B4
Carrington's Dro PE6 175 C7
Carrington St 6 HU3 180 B5
Carr La
  6 Alford LN13 75 F2
  Appleby DN15 9 D2
  Bishop Norton LN8 43 F3
  Blyton DN21 41 B5
  Bonby DN20 10 B1
  Broomfleet HU15 1 B7
  Broughton DN20 196 A6
  Burton upon Stather DN15 8 D4
  Doddington & Whisby LN6 79 D6
  Gainsborough DN21 197 C1
  Garthorpe & Fockerby DN17 7 E4
  Grimsby DN32 192 B7
  Haxey DN9 27 E2
  Healing DN41 23 F4
  Hibaldstow DN20 31 A6
  Horkstow DN18 9 F4
  Kingston upon Hull HU1 180 E6
  Luddington & Haldenby DN17 7 C1
  Misterton DN10 39 F5
  Redbourne DN21 30 F3
  Skinnard LN5 106 D7
  Stallingborough DN41 23 F7
  Ulceby DN39 12 B3
  West Butterwick DN17 28 C8
  Wildsworth DN21 40 F8
  Winterton DN15 9 D6
  Worlaby DN20 20 B7
Carroll Pl 4 HU1 181 A7
Carron Cl 3 LN3 83 B4
Carron Dr PE4 220 E3
Carr Rd
  Gringley on the Hill DN10 39 A4
  North Kelsey LN7 31 E4
  Peterborough PE1 226 D3
Carrside DN9 27 D6
Carr Side La DN7 14 E2
Carr St LN1 201 D4
Carrwood Cres LN4 207 C7
Carson Ave DN34 191 B6
Carson Cl 6 PE24 90 B7
Carson Rd DN21 197 C6
Cartergate DN32 191 C7
Carterplot Rd NG34 123 A2
Carters Cl 6 PE3 224 F3
Carter's Garth Cl 4 LN11 50 B8
Cartledge Ave DN32 192 B6
Cartmel Gr DN32 192 B6
Cartmel Way 14 PE6 175 A1
Carver Rd
  Boston PE21 208 D3
  Immingham DN40 186 D3
Caryer Cl PE2 230 D6
Cary La 3 DN20 196 B3
Carysfort Cl PE7 233 D4
Casewick La 4 PE9 172 F7
Casewick Rd PE9 172 E7
Caskgate St DN21 197 C4
Caspian Cres DN33 191 A2
Cassbrook Dr 2 LN11 49 B8
Cassia Gn 7 LN6 204 C8
Cassons Cl PE12 157 D4
Casson's Rd 1 DN8 15 A8
Casswell Cl 1 DN32 189 D1
Casswell Cres 4 LN11 49 B8
Casswell Dr PE11 145 A7
Castella Dr DN16 183 D3
Casterton Com Coll PE9 171 C8
Casterton La PE9 218 C4
Casterton Rd PE9 218 E6
Casthorpe Rd
  3 Barrowby NG32 210 A5
  Denton NG32 139 A8

Cheal Rd PE11 144 F4
Cheapside
Kingston upon Hull HU8 181 A8
Waltham DN37 194 F2
Cheapside Rd DN36 36 A4
Chedburgh Cl 1 LN6 204 B6
Chedworth Cl 1 LN2 202 D7
Chedworth Rd LN2 202 D7
Cheese Hill 10 PE20 135 B7
Cheesemans Cl 4 DN37 194 E4
Cheesemans La DN37 194 E4
Cheethams La LN4 110 F2
Chelmer Cl LN6 204 F4
Chelmer Garth 2 PE4 221 D1
Chelmsford Ave DN34 191 A5
Chelmsford Dr NG31 210 F4
Chelmsford Pl DN34 191 A6
Chelmsford St LN5 234 B1
Chelsea Cl LN6 200 D2
Chelsea Wlk DN35 193 A1
Cheltenham Cl
Peterborough PE1 226 B6
Scunthorpe DN16 185 C4
Cheltenham Way
Humberston DN35 192 F1
7 Mablethorpe/Sutton on Sea LN12 64 A3
Chelveston Way PE3 225 C4
Chelwood Dr 4 DN33 191 B3
Chelwood Rd DN17 184 F7
Chepstow Cl 1 PE11 156 E3
Chepstow Gr DN34 191 A5
Chequered Flag Karting* DN36 195 C1
Chequergate 1 LN11 198 B5
Chequers La DN22 65 A2
Chequers The DN15 182 D3
Cheriton Cl 1 LN3 83 B4
Cheriton Pk PE10 213 D7
Cherries The PE12 216 D4
Cherry Ave LN4 81 D2
Cherry Cl
Humberston DN36 36 D8
8 Sleaford NG34 212 D6
Cherry Cnr PE22 113 A5
Cherry Cobb Sands Rd HU12 13 F8
Cherry Dale DN35 192 D3
Cherryfields PE2 229 E6
Cherry Garth HU3 180 A5
Cherry Gr
10 Belton DN9 16 E1
Lincoln LN6 205 A8
10 Market Deeping PE6 217 C5
Scunthorpe DN16 185 B6
Cherry Holt 1 LN3 203 E5
Cherryholt La PE9 219 D5
Cherry Holt La
13 Pinchbeck PE11 156 E8
Sutterton PE20 136 A4
Cherryholt Rd PE9 219 D5
Cherry Holt Rd PE10 213 F4
Cherry La
Barrow upon Humber DN19 11 D8
7 Fleet PE12 159 C7
Stubton NG23 118 B7
Wootton DN39 11 E2
Cherry Mount DN16 185 C4
Cherry Orch
21 Epworth DN9 27 E6
Grantham NG31 211 D5
Cherry Orton Rd PE2 229 F5
Cherry Rd 9 PE13 170 D2
Cherrytree Ave PE25 90 E4
Cherry Tree Ave 4 DN20 196 B4
Cherry Tree Cl 4 LN6 204 F2
Cherry Tree Cres DN34 190 F6
Cherry Tree Dr 5 DN7 14 D5
Cherrytree Gr PE1 226 C6
Cherry Tree Gr
2 Hatfield DN7 14 D5
Spalding PE11 214 F5
Cherry Tree La
Holbeach PE12 215 D4
23 Nettleham LN2 68 C2
Cherry Tree Rd DN21 197 E5
Cherry Tree Rise DN21 29 C4
Cherry Tree's Bsns Pk DN31 188 C2
Cherry Tree Way
8 Coningsby LN4 207 D4
17 Metheringham LN4 95 C4
Cherry Way 34 DN17 29 D7
CHERRY WILLINGHAM LN3 203 E5
Cherry Willingham Com Sch LN3 203 D7
Cherry Willingham Prim Sch LN3 203 D5
Cherry Wlk PE21 208 D4
Cherrywood Dr NG31 210 F8
Chesboule La PE11 144 E5
Chesham Dr 7 PE6 164 E4
Cheshire Gr 7 PE25 206 A5
Cheshire La LN6 92 E5
Cheshire Rd LN6 204 B5
Cheshire Wlk DN37 190 E8
Chesney Dr DN16 185 A3
Chesney Rd LN2 202 D7
Chesnut Cl 11 LN2 68 F2
Chesnut Dr 12 LN2 68 F2
Chesnut Way 4 DN19 12 A8
Chesswick Ave DN17 17 D5
Chester Cl LN4 203 D1
Chesterfield Rd DN15 182 B2
Chester Gdns 8 NG31 210 D5
Chester Grange DN33 191 E1
Chester Pl DN32 192 C5
Chester Rd PE1 226 C3
CHESTERTON PE7 228 F3
Chesterton Gr PE2 231 D6
Chester Way PE21 208 C3
Chestnut Ave
7 Donington PE11 134 E2
Edenham PE10 153 C2
Gainsborough DN21 197 D6
Grimsby DN31 191 B7
Holbeach PE12 215 C3
Immingham DN40 186 E5
Kingston upon Hull HU13 178 E1
Peterborough PE1 226 B7
RAF Cranwell NG34 107 D1
Spalding PE11 214 E5
3 Stainforth DN7 14 D6
6 Thorne/Moorends DN8 15 B7
Chestnut Cl
Bottesford NG13 128 B6
Digby LN4 108 E6
Glinton PE6 220 B8
Horncastle LN9 199 A5
4 Metheringham LN4 95 C4
1 Peakirk PE6 174 A5
13 Scotter DN21 29 C3
2 Sleaford NG34 212 D3
Swaton NG34 133 D4
13 Waltham DN37 194 C4
Chestnut Cres 3 LN5 92 F3
Chestnut Dr
5 Coningsby LN4 207 D4
Louth LN11 198 E6
38 Messingham DN17 29 D7
3 Thorney PE6 176 A3
Chestnut Gdns PE9 218 D5
Chestnut Gr
11 Barnetby le Wold DN38 21 B4
8 Broughton DN20 19 E4
4 Colsterworth NG33 151 E7
1 Grantham NG31 210 D2
Waddington LN5 205 C1
Chestnut La NG33 152 C8
Chestnut Rd
3 Boston PE21 209 C2
Lincoln LN6 204 F2
Waltham DN37 194 C4
Chestnut Rise 1 DN19 11 C8
Chestnut St CE Prim Sch NG34 108 F1
Chestnut St
Lincoln LN1 234 A4
5 Ruskington NG34 108 E1
Chestnuts The 7 LN2 68 C2
Chestnut Terr 2 PE12 160 E4
Chestnut Way
6 Binbrook LN8 47 C5
4 Bourne PE10 213 B5
3 Market Deeping PE6 217 B6
Scunthorpe DN16 185 B8
Chestnut Wlk 5 DN41 24 A5
Cheviot Ave PE4 221 C2
Cheviot Cl
Gonerby Hill Foot NG31 210 E7
Sleaford NG34 212 A3
6 Thorne/Moorends DN8 15 A7
Cheviot St LN2 234 C2
Chichester Cl 6 NG31 210 E5
Chichester Dr 20 LN7 33 B4
Chichester Rd
6 Binbrook Tech Pk LN8 47 B6
4 Bracebridge Heath LN4 81 A4
Cleethorpes DN35 192 F4
Chieftain Rd 1 LN6 205 C8
Chieftain Way 1 LN6 205 C8
Childersgate La PE12 159 D2
Childers' N Dro
Cowbit PE12 157 B5
Spalding PE11 214 F3
Childers' S Dro
Cowbit PE12 157 B4
Pinchbeck PE11 214 F2
Chiltern Cl NG31 210 E7
Chiltern Cres DN17 184 D8
Chiltern Dr
Spalding PE11 214 E6
Waltham DN37 194 D3
Chiltern Prim Sch HU3 180 B5
Chiltern Rd 3 LN5 205 D3
Chiltern Rise PE4 221 B2
Chiltern Way
3 Grimsby DN33 194 E8
24 North Hykeham LN6 93 C8
Chilton Cl 7 DN40 186 B4
China St PE22 114 C4
Chingford Ave DN34 191 A4
Chippendale Cl
2 Birchwood LN6 204 D6
2 Humberston DN36 36 D8
Chippendale Rd 3 LN6 204 D6
Chippenham Mews 1 PE2 230 C7
Chisenhale PE2 229 E6
Chivenor Cl 3 LN6 200 B1
Cholmley St HU3 180 B5
Chopdike Dro PE11 144 D3
Christ Church Cl PE9 219 B7
Christchurch Rd 10 NG31 211 D7
Christine Pl DN33 195 A8
Christopher Cl
5 Heckington NG34 122 E3
Louth LN11 198 D7
3 Manby LN11 62 C6
Peterborough PE1 225 F8
Christopher Cres 11 NG34 212 F4
Christopher Dr 8 PE13 170 C1
Christopher Rd 6 LN13 75 E2
Christopher's La 4 PE10 213 D6
Christ's Hospl Terr LN2 234 B3
Church Ave
Ashby de la Launde & Bloxholm LN4 108 B5
Humberston DN36 36 C8
7 North Ferriby HU14 3 A4
Church Balk DN8 15 B8
Church Bank 2 PE34 161 F3
Church Cl
2 Bonby DN20 10 C2
24 Boston PE21 208 F5
Donington on Bain LN11 59 E2
Grimsby DN32 192 B5
12 Louth LN11 198 B5
16 Mablethorpe/Sutton on Sea LN12 77 A8
4 Newborough PE6 174 E4
11 Sibsey PE22 113 B1
11 Sleaford NG34 212 B2
Stoke Rochford NG33 139 F2
3 Thorne/Moorends DN8 15 B8
Wrangle PE22 114 C1
Church Cres 4 DN9 28 A3
Church Ct
Scunthorpe DN15 183 B4
3 Stamford PE9 219 C4
Church Dr
Lincoln LN6 201 D1
8 Misterton DN10 39 F5
Norton Disney LN6 92 C1
Peterborough PE2 229 F4
Surfleet PE11 145 D3
Church End
Gedney PE12 159 D7
9 Leverington PE13 170 B2
CHURCH END LN11 50 F6
Church End
Skegness PE25 206 B8
Wrangle PE22 114 C1
Church End Dro PE11 134 F1
Church Farm Cl 23 PE24 90 D7
Church Farm Mus* PE25 206 B4
Churchfield Ct PE4 225 E8
Churchfield Rd
Peterborough PE4 221 B1
Scunthorpe DN16 185 B5
Church Fields
Pickworth NG34 142 A8
Winterton DN15 9 A5
Churchfields Rd NG34 142 C8
Churchfleet La PE11 145 B7
Churchgate
Gedney PE12 159 D7
14 Sutterton PE20 136 A2
Church Gate
Fleet PE12 159 B6
2 Market Deeping PE6 217 F4
Spalding PE11 214 D3
22 Sutton Bridge PE12 160 E4
Whaplode PE12 158 B6
Churchgate Mews 5 PE12 159 D7
Church Gdns 15 PE12 160 A8
Church Gn PE12 216 C4
Church Gn Cl PE21 209 F2
Church Gn La
Frampton PE20 136 B7
Quadring PE11 135 A1
Church Gn Rd PE21 209 F4
Church Hill
Belvoir NG32 138 C6
1 Burgh le Marsh PE24 102 E7
Castor PE5 223 E2
2 Grasby DN38 32 E7
Heighington/Washingborough LN4 203 B2
Ingham LN1 55 A2
Riby DN37 23 C2
Spridlington LN8 55 F3
Whitton DN15 1 E3
Church Hill Cl PE7 231 C1
Churchill Ave
Bourne PE10 213 B4
Bracebridge Heath LN4 205 F4
Brigg DN20 196 D4
2 Hatfield DN7 14 F4
Horncastle LN9 199 C2
4 Keelby DN41 23 A5
4 Market Rasen LN8 57 D7
2 Skegness PE25 206 D7
Churchill Cl 6 LN11 50 F7
Churchill Ct 2 PE12 216 B5
Churchill Dr
3 Boston PE21 209 D4
2 Martin LN10 97 B4
Spalding PE11 214 D2
Churchill La LN12 63 E8
Churchill Rd
Gorefield PE13 169 F3
North Somercotes LN11 50 F7
Stamford PE9 219 B7
Churchill St HU9 181 D7
Churchill Way
Grimsby DN32 191 F7
Heckington NG34 122 D3
5 Lea DN21 52 F6
Church La
Addlethorpe PE24 90 D4
Algarkirk PE20 136 B2
Alvingham LN11 49 F2
9 Ancaster NG32 120 A2
Appleby DN15 9 D1
Aylesby DN37 23 E2
Balderton NG24 104 C2
7 Bardney LN3 83 B4
Baumber LN9 72 B1
Benniworth LN8 71 E8
Besthorpe NG23 91 D7
4 Billinghay LN4 109 F5
Blyton DN21 41 C5
Bonby DN20 10 C2
19 Boston PE21 208 F5
Bottesford NG13 128 C4
Bourne PE10 213 D4
Brant Broughton LN5 105 F5
Brigsley DN37 35 D4
4 Brough HU15 2 C7
15 Broughton DN20 19 E3
Buckminster NG33 150 F4
Burton Coggles NG33 152 D8
Cadney DN20 31 D6
6 Carlton-le-Moorland LN5 105 E8
3 Caythorpe NG32 119 B7
24 Chapel St Leonard PE24 90 D7
Cherry Willingham/Reepham LN3 203 E5
Clipsham LE15 162 B7
Coleby LN5 93 F3
6 Collingham NG23 91 D5
Corringham DN21 41 E2
Counthorpe & Creeton NG33 153 A2
Croft PE24 102 E5
7 Crowland PE6 166 F1
2 Croxton Kerrial NG32 138 D4
1 Donington PE11 134 F2
Eagle & Swinethorpe LN6 79 B2
East Keal PE23 100 E6
Edenham PE10 153 F4
Elkington LN11 60 E7
Ewerby & Evedon NG34 122 C6
5 Fishlake DN7 14 D8
1 Folkingham NG34 142 D8
Fotherby LN11 49 A2
Friesthorpe LN3 57 A2
Friskney PE22 114 F6
Frithville PE22 125 D8
5 Glentham LN8 43 F1
Goulceby LN11 72 D6
Grainthorpe LN11 50 B7
Great Gonerby NG31 210 C8
Great Limber DN37 22 D3
Grimsby DN37 190 E2
1 Hagworthingham PE23 87 A4
Harmston LN5 93 F5
Haxey DN9 27 C2
Heckington NG34 122 E1
3 Helpringham NG34 133 D7
3 Helpston PE6 173 C4
Holton le Clay DN36 195 D2
Horbling NG34 133 B2
6 Horncastle LN9 199 B4
Hougham NG32 118 C3
Humberston DN36 36 D8
Huttoft LN13 76 E3
Immingham DN40 186 B5
3 Ingham LN1 54 F2
Ingoldmells PE25 206 C8
4 Keadby with Althorpe DN17 17 D4
Keddington LN11 198 E8
3 Keelby DN41 23 A4
Kingston upon Hull HU10 178 C8
Kirkby la Thorpe NG34 121 F4
Kirkby on Bain LN10 98 C5
Kirton PE20 136 C5
12 Laceby DN37 23 F1
2 Legbourne LN11 61 F3
Lincoln LN2 234 B4
3 Little Bytham NG33 163 A8
Londonthorpe & Harrowby without NG31 130 D5
Long Bennington NG23 117 E2
Luddington & Haldenby DN17 7 D4
Lutton PE12 160 A8
14 Mablethorpe/Sutton on Sea LN12 77 A8
3 Mareham le Fen PE22 98 F4
Marshchapel DN36 37 B1
17 Metheringham LN4 95 D4
Minting LN9 84 C8
5 Misterton DN10 39 F5
Misterton LN13 89 B6
Moulton PE12 157 F7
Navenby LN5 107 A8
Newton PE13 170 A5
North Carlton LN1 67 C4
10 North Kelsey LN7 32 A4
North Kyme LN4 109 F3
Church La *continued*
North Rauceby NG32 120 C5
North Scarle LN6 78 E1
North Somercotes LN11 50 E6
Old Somerby NG33 140 E8
Owersby LN8 44 F5
5 Owmby LN8 55 F6
Peterborough PE2 229 F5
Pickworth NG34 132 A1
6 Potterhanworth LN4 82 B1
Rand LN8 70 A5
Ropsley & Humby NG33 131 B1
Roughton LN9 85 B1
Saltfleetby LN12 63 B7
Saxby All Saints DN20 10 B3
Saxilby with Ingleby LN1 66 C3
Scamblesby LN11 72 F5
Scawby DN20 20 A1
Scopwick LN4 108 E8
9 Scotter DN21 29 C3
Scredington NG34 132 F7
Scunthorpe DN15 182 E2
Sedgebrook NG32 128 F4
Silk Willoughby NG34 121 B1
Skegness PE25 206 B8
Skidbrooke with Saltfleet Haven LN11 51 B4
Sleaford NG34 212 D5
Snitterby DN21 43 D5
South Clifton NG23 78 C6
South Kyme LN4 123 A8
15 South Witham NG33 151 D2
Spilsby PE23 87 E1
Springthorpe DN21 53 E8
Sproxton LE14 150 C7
Stallingborough DN41 23 D6
9 Stamford PE9 219 C4
Sudbrooke LN2 68 F3
Swaby LN13 74 E3
13 Swineshead PE20 135 B7
Tallington PE9 172 F6
Tealby LN8 46 C1
Tetford LN9 73 F1
Tetney DN36 36 D3
3 Timberland LN4 96 C1
Torksey LN1 65 D5
Toynton St Peter PE23 101 A6
Twin Rivers DN14 7 A8
Tydd St Giles PE13 169 F7
Tydd St Mary PE13 160 B1
2 Ulceby DN39 12 A1
Utterby LN11 48 F3
Waddingham DN21 43 D7
21 Waddington LN5 93 F7
Wainfleet St Mary PE24 102 B1
Waithe DN36 36 A3
Waltham DN37 194 E4
Wansford PE8 222 D2
Welby NG32 130 F3
2 Welton/Dunholme LN2 68 D6
3 Westborough & Dry Doddington NG23 117 F3
West Keal PE23 100 C6
Withern with Stain LN13 62 F1
Wood Enderby LN9 98 F7
Wrangle PE22 114 C1
Wyberton PE21 136 F8
3 Wymondham LE14 150 C1
CHURCH LANEHAM DN22 65 B3
Church La Prim Sch NG34 212 D5
Church Lees NG32 131 C6
Church Mdws PE20 136 C5
Church Meadow Dr 20 PE24 90 D7
Church Mews 7 PE20 136 A2
Church Pk 17 LN12 77 A8
Church Rd
Aubourn Haddington & South Hykeham LN5 93 A5
4 Bicker PE20 135 A4
Boston PE21 209 B4
4 Butterwick PE22 126 E3
Friskney PE22 115 A6
Harby NG23 79 B5
4 Ketton PE9 171 A3
Laughton DN21 41 C8
Leverington PE13 170 E1
3 Mablethorpe/Sutton on Sea LN12 64 A3
North Ferriby HU14 3 A4
Old Leake PE22 114 A1
Saxilby LN1 66 D2
Skellingthorpe LN6 200 A4
Stainforth DN7 14 C6
Stickford PE22 100 B3
1 Stow LN1 66 C8
Ulceby with Fordington LN13 88 C7
Upton DN21 53 D5
Wigtoft PE20 135 E3
Wisbech PE13 170 B1
Wittering PE8 172 B1
Church Rd N PE25 206 B4
Church Rd S 4 PE25 206 B3
Church Rise 5 PE22 98 F4
Church Row HU8 181 A8
Church Side
3 Alkborough DN15 8 C8
3 Appleby DN15 9 D1
19 Goxhill DN19 12 A8
3 Grasby DN38 32 E7
3 West Halton DN15 8 E7
14 Winterton DN15 9 A5
Church Sq DN15 183 B3

Chu–Col 245

Church St
4 Alford LN13 75 F3
Amcotts DN17 7 F1
Barkston NG32 130 B8
2 Barrowby NG32 210 A5
2 Baston PE6 164 E4
Beckingham DN10 40 A1
4 Billingborough NG34 133 B1
2 Billinghay LN4 109 F5
20 Boston PE21 208 F5
Bottesford NG13 128 A5
7 Brough HU15 2 C7
5 Burgh le Marsh PE24 102 E8
14 Caistor LN7 33 B4
Candlesby PE23 88 F2
Carlby PE9 163 D5
4 Carlton-le-Moorland LN5 105 E8
Collingham NG23 91 C4
Corby Glen NG33 152 F8
2 Crowle DN17 16 D7
Denton NG32 139 A7
Digby LN4 108 D5
3 Donington PE11 134 E2
Easton on the Hill PE9 171 D3
Elsham DN20 20 F7
1 Epworth DN9 27 E6
6 Fishlake DN7 14 D8
1 Foston NG32 117 F1
3 Fulletby LN9 86 B8
Gainsborough DN21 197 C5
Glentworth DN21 54 F6
4 Gosberton PE11 145 B6
16 Goxhill DN19 12 A8
Grantham NG31 211 A5
Grimsby DN32 189 B1
1 Haconby PE10 154 D8
5 Harlaxton NG32 139 C7
Haxey DN9 27 C2
6 Heckington NG34 122 E3
Hemswell DN21 42 D1
7 Hibaldstow DN20 30 F5
Holbeach PE12 215 D2
Kingston upon Hull HU10 178 E6
7 Kirton in Lindsey DN21 30 B1
Long Bennington NG23 117 D3
Louth LN11 198 C5
Market Deeping PE6 217 B5
6 Market Rasen LN8 57 D8
Messingham DN17 29 D7
7 Middle Rasen LN8 57 B8
Misterton DN10 39 F5
20 Nettleham LN2 68 C2
Nettleton LN7 33 B3
Northborough PE6 173 F6
12 North Kelsey LN7 32 A4
North Witham NG33 151 D4
Owston Ferry DN9 28 A3
Peterborough PE2 231 C7
Peterborough PE4 220 F3
Peterborough PE7 229 A4
Pinchbeck PE11 145 C1
17 Ruskington NG34 108 E2
7 Ryhall PE9 163 C1
9 Scawby DN20 30 E8
10 Scothern LN2 68 F4
Skillington NG33 151 A8
10 South Witham NG33 151 D2
Spalding PE11 214 D4
11 Spilsby PE23 87 F1
8 Stamford PE9 219 C4
Sturton le Steeple DN22 52 B2
21 Sutton Bridge PE12 160 E4
1 Sutton on Trent NG23 91 A8
26 Thorne/Moorends DN8 15 A8
9 Thorney PE6 176 A3
Thurlby PE10 164 D7
Willoughton DN21 42 E4
1 Wragby LN8 70 D4
Yaxley PE7 233 D4
Churchthorpe 1 LN11 49 B8
Churchtown 9 DN9 16 E1
CHURCH TOWN DN9 16 E1
Church View
2 Alkborough DN15 8 C8
11 Barton-upon-Humber DN18 10 F8
1 Beckingham DN10 40 A1
13 Bottesford NG13 128 A6
9 Brough HU15 2 C7
Freiston PE22 126 D2
3 Gainsborough DN21 53 A5
8 Great Gonerby NG31 129 D5
Grimsby DN34 190 E7
Northborough PE6 217 E1
10 Ruskington NG34 108 E2
2 Waltham DN37 194 E4
Churchview Cl 5 NG34 122 D3
Church View Cl
3 Belton DN9 16 E1
1 Donington PE11 134 E2
Peterborough PE2 231 B7
Church View Cres LN3 82 B7
Churchway PE22 127 A5
Church Way PE13 160 A1
Church Wlk
Bourne PE10 213 D5
Brant Broughton & Stragglethorpe LN5 105 F4
1 Dunham-on-Trent NG22 65 B1
2 Holbeach PE12 215 D2
3 Holton le Clay DN36 195 D2
1 Legbourne LN11 61 F3
1 Manby LN11 62 C6
Church Wlk *continued*
21 Metheringham LN4 95 D4
1 Owston Ferry DN9 28 A3
Peterborough PE1 226 A3
2 Pinchbeck PE11 156 F8
Sibsey PE22 113 B2
Upton PE6 223 B5
Yaxley PE7 233 D4
Chuter Ede Prim Sch NG24 104 C2
Cinder La LN11 198 B5
Circle The 4 HU13 178 E2
Cirencester Cl LN6 93 B8
Cissbury Cl 12 LN12 77 A8
Cissbury Ring PE4 221 A2
Cissplatt La DN41 23 A5
Cisterngate 3 LN11 198 B6
Citadel Way HU9 181 A6
City of Lincoln Com Coll The LN6 205 A8
City Rd PE1 226 A2
City Sports Ctr LN6 205 A8
City Sq Ctr LN1 234 B2
Claires Wlk DN17 184 C7
Clampgate Rd PE21 126 C1
Clapgate Pits Nature Reserve* DN15 19 E5
Clapton Gate PE12 157 E5
Clara Terr LN1 234 A3
Clare Ave DN17 184 D7
Clare Cl
11 Lincoln LN5 205 D3
7 Stamford PE9 219 A5
Clare Cres DN16 185 A3
Clare Ct
4 Baston PE6 164 E4
Grimsby DN34 191 A5
Claremont Rd
1 Burgh le Marsh PE24 102 E8
Gainsborough DN21 197 E2
Grimsby DN32 192 D6
Claremont St LN2 234 C2
Clarence Cl 2 DN40 186 B3
Clarence Gdns 3 PE11 214 E2
Clarence Rd
Peterborough PE1 225 E5
28 Wisbech PE13 170 D1
3 Woodhall Spa LN10 97 D6
Clarence St
Kingston upon Hull HU1 181 A6
1 Lincoln LN1 201 E6
Clarendon Gdns 1 LN1 201 E8
Clarendon Rd
Grimsby DN34 190 E4
Scunthorpe DN17 184 F7
Skegness PE25 206 A4
Clarendon St HU3 180 D7
Clarendon View LN1 201 E8
Clarendon Way PE6 220 D8
Clare Rd
Northborough PE6 217 E1
Peterborough PE1 225 F6
Claricoates Dr 9 NG24 104 C8
Clarina St LN2 202 B4
Clark Ave DN31 191 A7
Clarke Ct 10 PE21 136 D8
Clarke Rd 11 LN6 93 C8
Clarkes Rd 3 DN40 12 E4
Clarke St 2 DN15 183 A3
CLARK'S HILL PE12 159 B3
Clarkson Ave 1 PE12 167 B8
Clarkson Ct 27 PE13 170 D1
Clarkson Infants Sch The PE13 170 E1
Clarksons Dr 3 DN41 23 E6
Clasketgate LN2 234 B2
Clatterdykes Rd PE20 136 E6
Claudette Ave PE11 214 B5
Claudette Way 5 PE11 214 B5
Claudius Rd LN6 93 B8
Clavering St 6 DN31 188 D1
CLAXBY LN8 45 D5
Claxby Rd DN17 184 F5
CLAXBY ST ANDREW LN13 88 E6
Claxby Springs Nature Reserve* LN13 88 E6
Claxy Bank PE22 114 D6
Clay Bank LN4 123 C7
Clay Bank Rd DN8 15 C6
Clayberg Dr 2 NG34 212 D5
Clayburn Rd PE7 230 D1
Clayden St 4 DN31 188 D1
Claydike Bank PE20 124 B4
Clay Dro PE11 156 C5
Clayfield Rd DN15 182 F6
Clay Hill Rd NG34 212 A3
Clayhough La DN22 65 B3
Clay La
Carlton-le-Moorland LN5 105 D8
Castor PE5 223 E2
Fenton LN1 65 E4
Gate Burton DN21 53 B1
Harby NG23 79 C5
Holton le Clay DN36 195 D3
Kirton in Lindsey DN21 30 A1
Newark NG24 104 B4
Norton Disney LN5 92 D2
Scotter DN21 29 C4
Stapleford LN6 105 B7
Tetford LN9 73 F2
Clay La *continued*
Toft Newton LN8 56 C7
Waddingham DN21 43 D7
CLAY LAKE PE11 214 E2
Clay Lake Bank PE12 157 A3
Clay Lake La PE11 214 E2
Claymore Cl DN35 192 E6
Clay Pit La NG34 122 C6
CLAYPOLE NG23 117 F7
Claypole CE (Controlled) Prim Sch NG23 117 F8
Claypole Dr PE6 217 E1
Claypole La NG23 117 E6
Claypole Rd NG23 118 A7
Claythorne Dr DN21 197 E4
CLAYTHORPE LN13 75 B6
Claythorpe Wr Mill* LN13 75 B5
Clayton PE2 230 B4
Clayton Cl 16 PE13 170 E1
Clayton Cres PE12 157 C2
Clayton Rd LN5 205 E6
Clayworth Rd 6 DN10 39 C1
CLEATHAM DN21 30 B3
Cleatham PE3 225 A4
Cleatham Rd DN21 30 B3
Clee Cres DN32 192 C5
Cleefields Cl DN32 192 B5
Clee Ness Dr DN36 193 A1
Clee Rd DN35 192 C5
Cleethorpe Rd DN32 189 B1
CLEETHORPES DN35 192 D5
Cleethorpes Coast Light Rly & Mus* DN35 193 B3
Cleethorpes Ctry Pk* DN35 192 F2
Cleethorpes Discovery Ctr* DN35 193 B3
Cleethorpes Leisure Ctr DN35 193 A4
Cleethorpes Nature Reserve* DN35 193 D2
Cleethorpes Showground* DN35 193 C3
Cleethorpes Sta DN35 192 F7
Clee Village DN32 192 C6
Clematis App LN6 204 C8
Clematis Ave 7 DN41 23 F5
Clematis Cl LN4 81 D2
Clematis Way DN16 185 C4
Clementine Cl PE25 206 B6
Clensey La NG23 117 F5
Clerke St DN35 192 B8
Clevedon Rd DN17 184 D8
Cleveland Ave 26 LN6 93 C8
Cleveland Cl
2 Immingham DN40 186 A4
2 Scunthorpe DN17 184 D8
4 Spalding PE11 214 F4
Cleveland Ct 3 PE4 221 C2
Cleveland Gdns 2 DN31 188 D1
Cleveland St
2 Gainsborough DN21 197 D3
3 Grimsby DN31 188 D1
Kingston upon Hull HU8 181 A8
Cleveland Way 27 DN7 14 D4
Cleve Pl 3 PE6 175 A1
Cley Hall Gdns PE11 214 E4
Cleymond Chase 2 PE20 136 C5
Cliff Ave
22 Nettleham LN2 68 C2
Winterton DN15 8 F5
Cliff Closes Rd DN15 182 D3
Cliff Cres 1 PE9 219 B5
Cliff Dr
Burton upon Stather DN15 8 B5
3 Kingston upon Hull HU13 3 E4
Cliffe Ave 1 NG34 108 D1
Cliffe Cl 10 NG34 108 D2
Cliffedale Prim Sch NG31 211 A8
Cliffe Rd
Easton on the Hill PE9 171 D2
Gonerby Hill Foot NG31 210 E7
Cliffe View NG34 120 E4
Cliff Gdns DN15 182 F2
Cliff Gr 9 DN18 10 E8
Cliff La
Marston NG32 129 D8
Waddingham DN21 43 C6
Washingborough LN4 81 D4
Clifford Rd PE25 206 B4
Cliff Rd
Fulbeck NG32 119 C8
Hessle HU13 3 E4
Leadenham LN5 106 D2
Snitterby DN21 43 C5
Spridlington LN8 55 F3
Stamford PE9 219 B5
Welbourn LN5 106 E4
Welton LN2 68 C6
Winteringham DN15 9 A8
Woolsthorpe by Belvoir NG32 128 D1
Cliffside 3 LN5 107 A7
Cliff St DN16 183 C2
Cliff The DN15 182 D3
Cliff Top La 2 HU13 3 E4
Clifton Ave PE3 225 E3
Clifton Ct 2 DN8 15 A8
Clifton Gr 3 PE25 206 D1
Clifton Prim Sch HU2 180 E8
Clifton Rd
Boston PE21 209 E4
Grimsby DN34 191 A6
Clifton St LN5 234 B1
Clint La 9 LN5 107 A8
Clinton Dr NG34 212 C2
CLINTON PARK LN4 207 A5
Clinton Pk Prim Sch LN4 207 A5
Clinton Terr 3 DN21 197 D3
Clinton Way LN10 97 B5
Clipseygap La PE10 154 B6
CLIPSHAM LE15 162 B7
Clipsham Rd PE9 162 D8
Clipston Wlk PE3 225 C5
Clive Ave LN6 205 C8
Clive Sullivan Way
Barton-upon-Humber DN19 4 A4
Kingston upon Hull HU4 179 C1
CLIXBY DN38 33 A7
Clixby Cl DN35 193 A3
Clixby La DN38 32 E7
Cloddy Gate LN11 50 F5
Cloister Cl DN17 184 E6
Cloisters The
Grimsby DN37 190 D7
17 Humberston DN36 36 D8
Welton LN2 68 C7
Cloister Wk 14 DN20 19 E3
Cloot Dro PE6 166 F2
Close The
Barkston NG32 130 A8
1 Colsterworth NG33 151 D7
Easton on the Hill PE9 171 C3
2 Fiskerton LN3 82 A7
2 Goxhill DN19 5 A1
Grimsby DN34 191 C7
Scunthorpe DN16 183 B2
4 Skegness PE25 206 C4
Sleaford NG34 212 B2
5 Sturton by Stow LN1 66 D7
1 Woodhall Spa LN10 97 C6
Closhill La PE21 136 F8
Clouds La
Belton DN9 17 B1
West Butterwick DN17 28 C8
Clough La
Firsby PE23 101 F5
Kirton PE20 136 F2
Clough Rd
Gosberton PE11 144 D4
Holbeach PE12 215 B7
Cloven Ends 4 PE6 164 F3
Clover Ct DN20 196 B4
Cloverfields Prim Sch DN36 36 C8
Clover Gdns 6 PE9 218 C7
Clover La PE20 135 D4
Clover Rd
6 Bracebridge Heath LN4 81 A1
Market Deeping PE6 217 C5
Misterton LN13 89 A6
Clover Way PE11 214 B6
Clowes Ct 4 HU13 178 E1
Club Ct NG24 104 B2
Clubhurn La PE11 145 D4
Club Way PE7 230 E4
Cludd Ave NG24 104 C4
Clumber Ave NG24 104 A3
Clumber Dr 7 PE11 214 C6
Clumber Pl DN35 192 E5
Clumber St
Kingston upon Hull HU5 180 C8
Lincoln LN5 205 E7
Clutton's Cl 4 PE6 166 E1
Clyde Ct 1 NG31 210 E2
Clydesdale Cres 1 PE11 214 A2
Clyde St HU3 179 F5
Clyfton Cres DN40 186 B4
Coach House Gdns 8 DN20 30 E8
Coachings The HU13 3 E4
Coach Rd NG32 118 C3
Coachroad Hill DN21 54 F7
Coalbeach La 1 PE11 145 E3
Coalbeach La S PE11 145 E4
Coalport Cl 7 LN6 204 D7
Coal Shore La LN11 37 D1
Coal Yd La NG23 78 C4
COATES
North Leverton with Habblesthorpe DN22 65 B8
Stow LN1 54 C2
Coates Ave 27 DN15 9 A5
Coates Rd DN22 65 B8
Cobbet Pl PE1 226 B3
Cobblers Way 6 NG34 212 E3
Cobbs Hill 13 PE34 161 F3
Cobden Ave PE1 225 F4
Cobden St
1 Gainsborough DN21 197 C4
Kingston upon Hull HU3 179 F7
Peterborough PE1 225 F4
Cob Gate PE12 158 A6
Cobgate Cl 2 PE12 158 B6
Cobham Cl 11 NG34 122 E3
Cobleas NG32 138 D8
Cochran Cl 9 NG31 210 F8
Cockbourn Fen Dike PE12 159 B2
Cockburn Way 6 LN5 93 F5
Cockerels Roost LN1 65 D1
Cocketts La 10 DN20 30 F5
Cocklehole Rd PE34 161 B5
Cock Pit Cl HU10 178 C6
Cockthorne La DN15 9 C7
CODDINGTON NG24 104 D5
Coddington CE Prim Sch NG24 104 D5
Coddington La LN6 105 A7
Coddington Rd NG24 104 C3
Coelus St HU9 181 A7
Cogan St HU1 180 E5
Coggles Causeway PE10 213 D4
Cogglesford Mill* NG34 212 F5
Coggles Way LN11 61 E3
Cohort Cl 13 HU15 2 C5
Coke Oven Ave DN16 183 F2
Colchester Mews 12 LN6 93 B8
Coldham Rd LN4 207 E6
COLD HANWORTH LN2 56 C2
COLD HARBOUR NG33 130 D1
Cold Harbour La
Carrington PE22 112 B6
Covenham St Mary LN11 49 D5
Grantham NG31 211 C2
Coldhorn Cres 14 PE13 170 D1
Cold Hurn La PE11 144 F6
COLEBY
Coleby LN5 93 F3
West Halton DN15 8 E6
Coleby CE Prim Sch LN5 93 F3
Coleby Rd DN15 8 E7
Coleby St LN2 202 B3
Colegrave St 14 LN5 205 E8
Cole La PE22 100 B3
Colenso Terr 3 LN1 201 D4
Coleraine Cl 8 LN5 205 D2
Coleridge Ave DN17 184 D7
Coleridge Ct 5 LN4 207 B5
Coleridge Gdns
Lincoln LN2 202 B7
15 Sleaford NG34 212 F4
Coleridge Gn 3 LN2 202 C7
Coleridge Pl
Bourne PE10 213 E3
Peterborough PE1 225 E8
Coles Ave LN13 75 E2
Coles Cl PE12 215 E3
Cole's La 1 PE20 135 B7
Cole St DN15 183 B3
Colin Ave DN32 192 B6
Colindale PE21 209 B5
Colin Rd DN16 183 C2
Colins Wy 4 DN21 29 C4
College Ave DN33 194 F8
College Cl
7 Alkborough DN15 8 C8
1 Holbeach PE12 215 C2
Horncastle LN9 199 C2
Lincoln LN1 201 F6
Stamford PE9 171 C8
7 Wainfleet All Saints PE24 102 D1
College Gdns 2 DN33 194 F8
College Pk
Horncastle LN9 199 C2
Peterborough PE1 226 C5
College Rd
Barrow upon Humber DN19 11 E7
Cranwell & Byard's Leap NG34 120 E8
Thornton Curtis DN39 12 B6
College St
Cleethorpes DN35 192 E6
Grantham NG31 211 B3
Grimsby DN34 191 C6
1 Kingston upon Hull HU2 180 E7
College Yd DN20 196 B3
Colleysgate PE12 216 C8
Colley St 11 PE21 208 F5
Colleywell Cl 5 DN9 27 A2
Collier Cl 11 HU14 3 A4
Collier Rd 2 DN40 186 D5
Collier St HU1 180 E6
COLLINGHAM NG23 91 C4
Collingham PE2 229 F3
Collingham Rd LN6 91 F5
Collingham Sta NG23 91 D4
Collingwood 21 LN6 93 C8
Collingwood Cres
3 Boston PE21 136 D8
Grimsby DN34 190 D4
Collingwood Prim Sch HU3 180 C7
Collingwood St HU3 180 D7
Collinson Ave DN15 182 C3
Collinson La
19 Balderton NG24 104 C1
Newport HU15 1 A8
Collison Gate PE24 102 C2
Collum Ave DN16 185 B6
Collum Gdns 2 DN16 185 B6
Collum House Rd DN16 185 B6
Collum La DN16 185 B6
Collynson Cl 1 HU10 178 E8
COLLYWESTON PE9 171 B1
Collyweston Rd 1 PE8 172 B1
Colne Cl 1 LN6 204 F3
Colne Ct 6 NG31 210 E2

Fen Rd *continued*
Little Hale NG34 133 F8
Metheringham LN4 95 C4
Newton PE13 169 E4
Ownby LN8 55 F6
Pointon & Sempringham NG34 143 D6
Ruskington NG34 108 F2
Stickford PE22 100 C2
Thurlby PE10 154 E1
Timberland LN4 96 C1
Toynton St Peter PE23 101 A4
Wisbech St Mary PE13 177 E2
Fenscape★ PE12 157 B7
Fen Sch NG34 123 C3
Fenside
Halton Holegate PE23 101 C6
Toynton All Saints PE23 100 F4
FEN SIDE PE22 100 A1
Fenside Dr 5 PE6 174 E5
Fenside Rd
Boston PE21 208 C6
Holland Fen with Brothertoft PE21 125 C5
FENTON
Fenton LN1 65 E3
Fenton NG23 105 B1
Fenton Dr PE9 163 E5
Fenton La DN22 52 C1
Fenton Pl LN2 234 C2
Fenton Rd
Fenton NG23 105 B1
Stubton NG23 118 B8
Fenton St DN15 183 B3
Fen View
Heighington LN4 81 F4
Peterborough PE2 231 F6
Fenwick Ct 6 DN36 195 D1
Fenwick Rd DN33 191 B2
Fen Wlk DN36 37 C5
Ferens Art Gall★ HU2 180 F6
Ferensway HU2 180 E7
Fernbank 2 DN9 27 D7
Fern Croft 10 DN9 27 E6
Fern Ct HU13 179 A1
Ferndale PE7 233 D6
Ferndale Cl NG33 152 F7
Ferndown 1 DN37 188 A1
Ferndown Dr DN40 186 D4
Fern Dr
Market Rasen LN8 57 D8
Pinchbeck PE11 214 C7
Ferneries La 3 DN38 21 B4
Fern Gr LN3 203 D5
Fernhall Cl 15 DN3 14 A2
Fernhill DN37 190 C7
Fernie Cl 3 PE6 174 E4
Fernland Cl 18 HU15 2 C5
Fernleigh Ave 4 LN4 81 A1
Fernleigh Way PE21 209 B6
Fernwood Mews DN21 197 F2
Ferriby High Rd HU14 3 B5
Ferriby La DN33 191 C2
Ferriby Rd
Barton-upon-Humber DN18 10 E8
Hessle HU13 178 B1
Scunthorpe DN17 184 E5
FERRIBY SLUICE DN18 9 F7
Ferriby Sta HU14 3 A4
Ferries St HU9 181 D7
Ferry Dr PE6 224 D3
Ferry Hill PE5 224 B1
Ferry La
Holland Fen with Brothertoft PE20 124 D6
Newton PE13 170 B5
North Kyme LN4 109 F2
Skellingthorpe LN6 200 C5
South Kyme LN4 109 F1
Sturton le Steeple DN22 52 D3
Washingborough LN4 203 B2
Winteringham DN15 2 B1
Ferry Mdws Ctry Pk★ PE2 229 D8
Ferry Mdws Sta PE2 229 E7
Ferry Rd
Bardney LN3 83 D1
Barrow upon Humber DN19 4 C1
Fiskerton LN3 82 D6
Haxey DN9 27 D1
2 Keadby with Althorpe DN17 17 D4
Kingston upon Hull HU13 178 E1
Langriville PE22 124 D8
Scunthorpe DN15 182 E5
Ferry Rd W DN15 182 A6
Ferryside 2 LN3 82 B6
Ferryside Gdns 3 LN3 82 B6
Ferryview PE2 229 E6
Festival Ave 3 PE25 90 D3
Feyzin Dr 40 DN18 10 E8
Ffolkes Dr 12 PE34 161 F3
Field Ave 6 PE13 169 F7
Field Cl
6 Gosberton PE11 145 B6
13 Laceby DN37 23 F1
23 Nettleham LN2 68 D2
14 Ruskington NG34 108 D2
1 Welton LN2 68 D7
Fieldfare Cl 8 DN16 185 B2
Fieldfare Croft PE21 208 C6
Fieldfare Dr PE2 231 E6
Field Farm La 3 LN4 95 D4
Field Head 5 DN37 23 E1
Fieldhouse Rd DN36 193 A1
Fielding Way DN21 197 E5
Field La
Bardney LN3 83 C5
Eastoft DN17 7 A3
Ewerby & Evedon NG34 122 C6
Friskney PE22 115 A6
Morton DN21 197 A8
2 Normanby by Spital LN8 55 F6
Strubby with Woodthorpe LN13 63 C1
Wroot DN9 26 D5
Field Rd
Billinghay LN4 109 E6
Crowle DN17 16 D7
Stainforth DN7 14 C6
Thorne/Moorends DN8 15 A8
Field Rise PE7 233 D5
Fields Cl 3 DN9 27 D7
Fields End DN39 12 B2
Fieldside
6 Blyton DN21 41 C5
11 Crowle DN17 16 D7
Epworth DN9 27 D6
Field Side
Mareham le Fen PE22 98 F4
Thorne DN8 15 A8
Fieldside Cres 1 PE22 99 A4
Fields Rd DN9 27 E2
Field St
6 Boston PE21 209 A5
Kingston upon Hull HU9 181 B7
Field Terr PE7 231 C2
Field The DN32 192 C6
Field View PE22 111 F8
Field Wlk PE1 226 B2
Fife Cl PE9 218 D6
Fifth Ave
Fixborough Ind Est DN15 8 A1
Grantham NG31 211 F6
Scunthorpe DN17 184 B6
Fifth Dro PE11 144 A4
Fiftyeights Rd DN10 26 B2
Figtree Wlk PE1 226 A7
Fildes St DN31 191 D7
Filey Cl LN6 205 A3
Filey Rd DN32 192 A5
FILLINGHAM DN21 54 F4
Fillingham Cres
Cleethorpes DN35 192 F3
Scunthorpe DN15 182 B3
Fillingham La DN21 53 F3
Finch Cl LN6 204 D8
Finch Dr NG34 212 B3
Finchfield PE1 226 F7
Finchley Ct DN31 191 A8
Finchley Gn PE3 225 E4
Findlay Cres DN36 195 D6
Fingle St 3 DN22 52 B1
Finisterre Ave PE25 206 A6
Finkell St DN10 39 C1
Finkin St NG31 211 A4
Finkle La 11 DN18 3 F1
Finkle St
Benington PE22 127 A5
Stainforth DN7 14 C7
Finney Cl LN4 207 D5
Finningley Cl 9 LN6 204 D6
Finningley Rd LN6 204 D6
Finns La NG32 138 C6
Finsbury Dr 3 DN33 191 B2
Finsbury St 13 LN13 75 F2
Fir Ave PE10 213 A5
Firbeck Ave PE25 206 D1
Fir Cl DN16 185 A4
Fircroft NG31 211 C1
Firdale Cl 3 PE6 174 A5
Firebeacon La
Grainthorpe LN11 49 E8
Marshchapel LN11 37 D1
Firethorn Cl 3 HU3 180 D5
Fir Hill Quarry Nature Reserve★ LN11 61 E1
Fir Rd 1 PE9 218 D6
FIRSBY PE23 101 F7
Firsby Cres DN33 191 A2
First Ave
1 Fixborough Ind Est DN15 7 F1
Grantham NG31 211 E6
Grimsby DN33 191 C4
6 Scampton Airfield LN1 67 E5
Scunthorpe DN17 184 C6
Spalding PE11 214 B4
First Dro
Crowland PE6 166 E2
Gosberton PE11 144 C3
Moulton PE12 146 E6
Peterborough PE1 226 D1
Firs The 6 NG34 108 D1
First Holme La 2 NG23 91 A8
First Hurn Dro LN4 110 A6
First La HU10 179 A5
First Marsh Rd PE13 170 C2
Firth Field Rd DN7 14 F4
Firth La DN9 26 D6
Firth Rd LN6 234 A1
Firtree Ave LN6 200 C1
Fir Tree Ave 5 LN5 93 E8
Fir Tree Cl 4 LN2 68 F2
Firtree Dr 6 DN20 20 F7
Fir Tree La NG32 119 F3
Fir Trees The HU10 178 D6
Fish Dock Rd DN31 189 B2
Fishemore Ave HU13 178 F2
Fisher Cl 23 NG23 91 D5
Fishergate PE12 159 B1
Fisherman's Wharf DN31 191 D8
Fishermans Wlk 2 HU3 180 C4
Fisher Pl DN35 192 D7
Fish Groom's La PE11 145 E6
FISHLAKE DN7 14 D8
Fishlake Nab DN7 14 C7
Fishmere End Rd
Sutterton PE20 136 A4
Wigtoft PE20 135 F3
Fishmere Gate Rd LN11 51 B1
Fishpond La PE12 215 E2
Fish St 1 HU1 180 F5
FISHTOFT PE21 126 C1
Fishtoft Dro PE22 125 C7
FISHTOFT DROVE PE22 125 D8
Fishtoft Rd PE21 209 B3
Fishtoft Sch PE21 126 C1
Fish Well Cl 3 NG33 151 A8
Fishwick Ave 5 HU13 178 E1
FISKERTON LN3 82 A6
Fiskerton CE (Controlled) Prim Sch LN3 82 B7
Fiskerton Cl 8 DN34 190 F4
Fiskerton Dr LN2 201 F8
Fiskerton Rd
Cherry Willingham LN3 203 C4
Cherry Willingham/Reepham LN3 82 A8
Fiskerton Rd E LN3 203 E4
Fiskerton Way 2 DN31 188 A3
Fitties La 2 DN36 37 C5
FITTON END PE13 169 F3
Fitton End Rd PE13 169 F3
Fitzgerald Ct 3 LN4 207 A6
Fitzjames Cl 2 PE23 101 A8
Fitzwilliam Hospl PE6 224 E2
Fitzwilliam Mews DN35 192 E2
Fitzwilliam Pl 6 LN4 109 F5
Fitzwilliam Rd PE9 219 A7
Fitzwilliam St
10 Mablethorpe/Sutton on Sea LN12 64 B4
Peterborough PE1 226 A3
Five Arches PE2 229 C6
Five Bell La PE20 135 C4
Five House La
Frampton PE20 136 C8
Wyberton PE21 208 B1
Five La Ends NG23 79 C8
Five Mile La LN4 82 B5
Flag Bsns Exchange PE1 226 E3
Flag Fen Bronze Age Mus★ PE6 227 B3
Flag Fen Rd PE1 226 C4
Flag La PE12 168 B7
Flamborough Cl
Peterborough PE2 225 E1
6 Skegness PE25 206 A6
Flaminian Way 8 NG32 120 A2
Flarepath The DN20 21 A8
Flaxengate 4 LN2 234 B2
Flaxland PE3 225 A6
Flaxley Rd LN2 202 E6
Flaxmill La 6 PE11 145 C1
Flaxwell Way 12 NG34 121 B7
FLEDBOROUGH NG22 78 A7
FLEET PE12 159 C6
Fleetgate 8 DN18 3 E1
FLEET HARGATE PE12 159 C7
Fleet Rd
Fleet PE12 159 B7
Holbeach PE12 215 F2
Fleets La LN1 54 A1
Fleets Rd LN1 66 D7
Fleet St
Holbeach PE12 215 E2
Lincoln LN1 201 C4
Fleetway DN36 37 A3
Fleet Way PE2 231 B6
Fleetwood Cl 2 DN33 194 E7
Fleetwood Ct LE15 162 A8
Fleet Wood La Prim Sch PE12 159 B6
Fleming Ave NG13 128 B6
Fleming Cl PE7 233 D6
Fleming Ct
1 Boston PE21 208 F1
3 Woodston PE2 230 D8
Fleming Rd PE11 214 E8
Fleming Wlk HU4 179 D2
Fletcher Cl
Kingston upon Hull HU13 178 E2
3 Scunthorpe DN15 182 C6
Fletcher Rd DN34 190 F7
Fletcher St NG31 211 A3
Fletton Ave PE2 231 A8
Fletton Fields PE2 231 A7
Fletton Parkway PE2 229 F2
Flinders Cl 5 LN4 95 C4
Flinders Rd 13 PE11 134 E2
Flinders Way LN3 203 B6
Flinders Wlk PE11 214 C7
Flint Cl PE9 163 D1
Flint Gate 23 PE12 160 E4
Flintham Cl 2 LN4 95 C4
Flint House Rd PE12 147 C3
Flinton St HU3 180 B3
FLIXBOROUGH DN15 8 B1
Flixborough Rd DN15 8 B4
FLIXBOROUGH STATHER DN15 8 A1
Flood Rd The DN21 197 B3
Flore Cl PE3 225 C5
Florence Ave HU13 178 F1
Florence St
Grimsby DN32 191 E5
Lincoln LN2 202 B3
Florence Way 4 PE6 217 C5
Florence Wright Ave 6 LN11 198 D4
Floriade Cl 4 PE11 214 B2
Florins Fold NG34 132 F3
Floss La DN22 65 B6
Flottergate Mall DN31 191 D7
Flour Sq DN31 189 A1
Flowerdown Ave 5 NG34 120 D8
Foal Plats La LN13 90 A8
FOCKERBY DN17 7 E5
Fodder Dike Bank
Eastville PE22 114 C7
Midville PE22 113 E7
FOLD HILL PE22 115 A6
Fold Hill Rd PE22 114 A2
Fold La
Moulton PE12 157 F7
5 Tydd St Giles PE13 169 F7
Folds La 2 PE12 216 B4
Folgate La PE14 170 F6
FOLKINGHAM NG34 142 C8
Folkingham Cl 11 LN6 204 D8
Folkingham Rd
Billingborough NG34 133 A1
1 Morton PE10 154 C7
Pickworth NG34 142 A8
FOLKSWORTH PE7 232 D1
Folksworth Rd PE7 232 E1
Folly Cl PE7 233 C5
Folly La
Branston & Mere LN4 81 C2
Hough-on-the-Hill NG32 118 F5
North Kelsey LN7 32 C5
North Scarle NG23 91 D8
West Fen PE22 99 E1
Folly's Dro PE13 177 F3
Fontwell Cres 9 LN6 205 A5
Fontwell Gdns 2 PE9 219 B5
Foote's Dro PE12 167 C8
Forbes Rd PE21 209 C4
Ford Cl PE7 233 E6
Fordham Dr LN1 201 C7
FORDINGTON LN13 88 C6
Ford La
8 Hibaldstow DN20 30 F5
Morton PE10 154 C6
Ford's Ave 17 DN41 23 F5
Ford Way LN11 72 D6
Foredyke Prim Sch HU9 5 D8
Fore La PE20 135 A5
Foreman Way 1 PE6 166 E1
Forest Ave 3 PE10 213 B5
Forest CE Prim Sch PE7 231 C2
Forest Dale PE21 208 F7
Forest Dr DN36 193 B1
Forest Dro PE6 166 C2
Foresters Ct Galleries★ PE20 135 B7
Forester Way HU4 179 D3
Forest Gdns 5 PE9 218 D7
Forest Pines La 11 LN10 97 C5
Forest Way 7 DN36 36 D8
Forge Cl
Freiston PE22 126 C4
South Kelsey LN7 32 A1
Forge Cres
3 Pinchbeck PE11 156 E8
Ulceby DN39 12 A1
Forge Ct 12 PE6 217 A6
Forge End PE7 229 A4
Forge La LN8 56 F8
Forge Way DN36 195 C3
Forkedale DN18 10 E8
Forlander Pl LN11 198 D6
Forman's La NG34 109 B1
Formby Cl NG31 211 C7
Forrester St 1 DN20 196 B3
Forrington Pl LN1 66 E2
Forstedd Hill NG33 153 B5
Forster St DN21 197 C5
Forsyth Cres 6 PE25 206 C2
Forsythia Ave 25 DN41 23 F5
Forsythia Dr DN33 191 C2
Fortescue Cl 1 LN4 207 A5
Fortuna Prim Sch LN6 204 B7
Fortuna Way DN37 190 C7
Forty Acre HU10 178 F7
Forty Acre Rd PE1 226 D2
Forty Foot La
Humberside Airport DN39 21 F6
Old Leake PE22 113 D3
Forty Stps HU10 178 F7
Forum The LN6 204 F3
Forum Way 7 NG34 212 F3
FOSDYKE PE20 146 D8
FOSDYKE BRIDGE PE12 146 E7
Foss Bank LN1 201 D3
Fossdyke Gdns 18 LN1 66 D2
Fosse Cl 9 PE6 164 E5
Fosse Ct 5 LN4 81 A1
Fosse Dr LN6 205 A3
Fosse La
Thistleton LE15 151 B1
Thorpe on the Hill LN6 92 E7
Fosseway 4 DN21 197 F5
Fosse Way Prim Sch LN6 204 F2
Foss St LN1 201 D3
Foster Cl 2 LN4 96 C1
Foster Rd
21 Collingham NG23 91 D5
7 Thorne/Moorends DN8 15 A8
Woodston PE2 230 D8
Fosters Cl 3 LN5 107 A8
Foster's Dro PE10 155 A3
Foster's Gdns 1 LN4 82 B1
Foster St
3 Boston PE21 209 A5
Heckington NG34 122 E3
Lincoln LN5 201 E1
FOSTON NG32 117 F2
Foston by Pass NG32 117 F1
Foston Cres LN6 204 F7
Foston La NG32 128 F7
Foston Rd NG31 210 E3
FOTHERBY LN11 49 A3
Fotherby Rd DN17 184 F4
Fotherby St 3 DN31 189 A1
Fothergill Dr 17 DN3 14 A2
FOUL ANCHOR PE13 170 D8
Foundry La
11 Spalding PE11 214 D4
12 Thorne/Moorends DN8 15 A8
Foundry Rd
Bucknall LN10 84 B3
Ryhall PE9 163 C2
Stamford PE9 219 A5
Foundry Sh Ctr The DN15 183 B4
Foundry St LN9 199 C4
Fountain Cl
Kingston upon Hull HU13 178 C3
5 Waltham DN37 194 C5
Fountain Hill DN10 39 E3
Fountain Hill Rd DN10 39 E4
Fountain La 13 PE21 208 F5
Fountain Pl 10 PE21 208 F5
Fountains Ave DN37 188 A1
Fountains Pl PE6 175 B1
Fountain St
22 Caistor LN7 33 B4
Kingston upon Hull HU3 180 D6
Four Acre Cl HU10 178 C6
Four Chimneys Cres PE7 230 C2
Fourfields CE Prim Sch PE20 136 A2
Fourfields Com Prim Sch PE7 233 E6
FOUR GOTES PE13 170 B7
Fourth Ave
2 Fixborough Ind Est DN15 8 A1
Grantham NG31 211 F6
3 Scampton Airfield LN1 67 E5
1 Scunthorpe DN17 184 C6
Fourth Dro
Gosberton PE11 144 B4
Peterborough PE1 226 F3
Fourways 6 DN36 36 D4
Fowler Cl LN11 198 D4
Fowler Rd DN16 185 B8
Foxby Hill DN21 197 E2
Foxby La DN21 197 F2
Fox Cl
Boston PE21 208 C6
Little Coates DN34 190 F6
Fox Covert
2 Aubourn Haddington & South Hykeham LN6 93 A8
North Hykeham LN6 204 B1
Sudbrooke LN2 69 A2
Fox Covert La DN10 40 A4
Foxcovert Rd PE6 220 E8
Fox Ct 1 DN17 16 D8
Foxdale PE1 225 F7
Fox Dale PE9 218 F6
Foxe End 19 LN12 64 B3
Foxendale Hill LN9 72 F1
Foxes Low Rd PE12 215 F2
Foxfield Cl LN6 200 A5
Foxglove Cl
Brigg DN20 196 B4
1 Spilsby PE23 101 A8
Foxglove Gdns DN34 190 F6
Foxglove Rd
16 Market Rasen LN8 57 D8
1 Stamford PE9 218 C7
Foxgloves PE6 217 D6
Foxglove Way 5 LN5 205 C2
Fox Headings PE12 158 C1
Foxhill DN37 190 C7
Foxhill Rd DN8 15 B7
Foxhills Ind Pk DN15 182 F7
Foxhills Rd DN15 182 E5
Foxhills Sch & Tech Coll DN15 182 E5
Foxhole La PE22 126 D3
Foxley Cl PE4 221 A4
Foxley Ct 1 PE10 213 C7
Fox St DN15 182 F3
Foyle Cl LN5 205 D2
Fracknal's Row 3 PE21 208 E6
Framlingham Rd PE7 231 F5
FRAMPTON PE20 136 F6
Frampton Bank PE20 136 B8
Frampton La PE20 124 E2

High St *continued*
7 Spilsby PE23 88 A1
Stamford PE9 219 C5
Staunton NG13 117 A2
Sturton by Stow LN1 66 C7
5 Sutton Bridge PE12 160 F4
Swayfield NG33 152 D5
Swinderby LN6 92 A5
Swineshead PE20 135 B7
Swinstead NG33 153 A5
Upton DN21 53 D5
Waddingham DN21 43 D7
Waddington LN5 93 F7
Wainfleet All Saints PE24 102 D1
Walcott LN4 109 D7
Walesby LN8 46 B5
Walkeringham DN10 39 F3
1 Waltham DN37 194 E4
Welbourn LN5 106 E5
West/East Butterwick DN17 17 D1
Willingham by Stow DN21 53 E3
11 Winterton DN15 9 A5
Wootton DN39 11 E2
Wroot DN9 26 D6
Highstock La PE12 168 D1
High Thorpe Cres DN35 192 D3
High Thorpe Rd LN3 83 D1
HIGH TOYNTON LN9 86 A4
High Wash Dro 2 PE6 166 E1
Highwood Mews DN35 192 E5
Higney Rd PE7 230 C1
Higson Rd 4 LN1 201 D7
Hilary Gr HU4 179 B2
Hilary Rd DN33 194 F7
Hilda Cl 6 NG34 212 B2
Hildas Ave HU5 180 A8
Hilda St
4 Boston PE21 209 A7
Grimsby DN32 189 C1
Hildreds Sh Ctr PE25 206 D3
Hildyard Cl 1 HU10 178 F6
Hildyard St DN32 192 B8
Hiles Ave 6 DN15 9 A5
Hill Abbey LN4 95 D7
Hillary Cl
8 Spalding PE11 214 B2
1 Stamford PE9 219 D6
Hillary Rd DN16 185 B5
Hillary Way DN37 190 E8
Hill Ave NG31 211 B5
Hill Brow HU10 178 B6
Hill Cl PE1 226 D5
Hill Cres DN21 197 F5
Hillcrest NG34 107 C2
Hillcrest Ave
Kingston upon Hull HU13 178 C2
Yaxley PE7 233 E5
Hillcrest Com Inf Sch DN21 197 F4
Hillcrest Dr 2 DN15 8 A4
Hillcrest Gdns 3 PE20 135 B7
Hillcroft 1 LN4 203 A2
Hill Ct NG31 210 D2
HILLDYKE PE22 126 A6
Hill Field 3 PE24 102 D2
Hillfoot Dr DN17 184 E3
Hillgate PE12 168 C2
Hillgate St PE34 161 F3
Hillingford Way NG31 210 E3
Hill La PE20 136 B5
Hillman Cl LN4 205 F3
Hillman Rd HU13 178 F3
Hill Rd DN21 41 E1
Hill Rise
8 Brough HU15 2 C6
Coleby LN5 93 F3
Louth LN11 198 A7
Hill's Ct 9 NG34 212 D4
Hills Dr 14 DN36 36 D4
Hillside
4 Ancaster NG32 120 A2
3 Marton DN21 65 E8
Hillside App 5 LN2 202 C3
Hillside Ave
Lincoln LN2 202 C3
7 Mablethorpe/Sutton on Sea LN12 77 A8
Hillside Cl PE9 172 F2
Hillside Cres
Barnetby le Wold DN38 21 B5
3 Grantham NG31 211 D2
Hillside Dr
5 Barton-upon-Humber DN18 10 E8
Grantham NG31 211 D2
Hillside Est NG34 108 F2
Hillside Rd
6 Broughton DN20 19 E4
Glentworth DN21 54 F7
Woolsthorpe by Belvoir NG32 128 D1
Hillstead Cl 13 DN36 36 D4
Hillsyde Ave 11 DN10 39 F5
Hill Terr LN11 198 C4
Hill The
4 Saltfleet LN11 51 C4
Skellingthorpe LN6 200 A4
Worlaby DN20 10 E1
Hill Top 1 LN5 93 E5
Hilltop Ave DN15 182 D5
Hilltop Cl LN6 79 B2
Hilltop Gdns DN17 29 C7
Hill Top La 1 DN21 41 B5
Hill Top Pl DN34 190 D3
Hill View Cl NG31 210 E3
Hill View Rd 14 NG33 151 D2
Hillward Cl PE2 230 C6
Hilton Ave DN15 182 B3
Hilton Cl 2 DN9 16 E2
Hilton Ct DN35 193 B1
Hilton's La PE20 136 E1
Hinaidi La LN4 95 C7
Hinchcliffe PE2 229 E2
Hindon Wlk DN17 184 C8
Hine Ave NG24 104 B4
Hinkler St DN35 192 E5
Hinkley Dr DN40 186 B5
Hinman Wlk 9 DN15 183 B3
Hipper La PE20 135 D2
Hither Old Gate PE12 158 D6
Hives La LN6 78 E2
Hix Cl PE12 215 C2
Hix's La PE13 160 A1
Hobart Cl 11 LN5 93 E8
Hobart Rd NG31 211 D7
Hobart St HU3 180 D5
Hobb La 4 DN21 29 C3
Hobhole Bank Nature Reserve* PE21 137 C7
Hobson Rd 7 HU15 2 C6
Hobsons Gn PE11 214 A5
Hobson Way DN41 187 E2
Hockland Rd 2 PE13 169 F7
Hockle's Gate PE12 159 B7
Hockney Hole La PE12 158 A7
Hodder Cl 1 NG31 210 F3
Hoddesdon Cres 20 DN7 14 D3
Hod Fen Dro PE7 233 F2
Hodge Ct 3 HU9 181 C7
Hodgetoft La LN13 63 E1
Hodgson Ave PE4 220 E6
Hodgson St HU8 181 A7
Hodgson Way 3 LN12 77 A8
Hodney Rd 5 PE6 175 A1
Hodson Cl LN6 200 B5
Hodson Gn LN9 199 C4
Hoe Dr 19 LN8 57 D8
Hoekman Dr 3 PE11 214 B2
Hoekman Way PE11 214 B2
HOFFLEET STOW PE20 135 C4
Hogens La PE13 170 A5
Hoggard La DN14 7 E8
Hogg La HU10 178 B8
Hog's Gate PE12 158 A6
HOGSTHORPE PE24 90 B6
Hogsthorpe Prim Sch PE24 90 B7
Hogsthorpe Rd LN13 76 F1
HOLBEACH PE12 215 C3
HOLBEACH BANK PE12 215 C7
Holbeach Bank Prim Sch PE12 215 D7
HOLBEACH CLOUGH PE12 215 B7
Holbeach & District Nature Reserve* PE12 215 E2
Holbeach Dro Gate PE12 168 C4
HOLBEACH DROVE PE12 168 B3
Holbeach Hospl PE12 215 B5
HOLBEACH HURN PE12 147 F2
Holbeach Prim Sch PE12 215 D3
Holbeach Rd
Spalding PE11 214 F6
1 Spalding PE12 157 B6
HOLBEACH ST JOHNS PE12 158 E1
HOLBEACH ST MARKS PE12 147 D6
Holbeach St Marks CE Prim Sch PE12 147 D6
HOLBEACH ST MATTHEW PE12 148 A7
Holbeach Tecnology Pk PE12 215 B4
Holbeck Pl 2 DN40 186 B4
Holborn Rd PE11 214 B2
Holborn St HU8 181 B7
Holcroft PE2 230 B3
Holdan Cl DN36 193 A1
Holdenby Cl 3 LN2 202 E7
Holden Dr 9 PE24 102 E7
Holden Way 7 NG31 129 E5
Holderness Rd HU9 181 C8
Holdfield PE3 225 B6
Holdich St PE3 225 E2
HOLDINGHAM NG34 212 C7
Holdingham La NG34 121 E7
Hole Gate PE23 101 C8
Holgate La PE4 220 F7
Holgate Pl 13 HU14 3 B7
Holgate Rd DN16 185 D8
Holkham Rd PE2 229 D3
Holland Ave
18 Crowle DN17 16 D8
Peterborough PE4 221 B1
Scunthorpe DN15 182 E4
Holland Cl
8 Bourne PE10 213 C5
10 Market Deeping PE6 217 A6
Holland Dr PE25 206 C1
Holland La PE22 114 F4
Holland Mkt 16 PE11 214 D4
Holland Rd
Horbling NG34 133 B3
Spalding PE11 214 E4
Stamford PE9 219 C6
Holland Rd *continued*
Swaton NG34 133 E3
Holland's Chase PE11 156 A6
Holland St HU9 181 D8
Holland Way PE12 215 B2
Hollengs La 1 LN11 59 E1
Holles St 6 DN32 191 E8
Hollies The PE12 215 E3
Hollin Bridge La DN7 15 A3
Hollingsworth Ave 1 DN40 186 B4
Hollingsworth Cl 5 DN35 192 D2
Hollingsworth La DN9 27 E6
Hollis' Rd NG31 210 F2
Hollowbrook Cl 3 NG34 108 D2
Hollowdyke La NG24 104 C1
Hollowgate Hill DN21 42 E4
Hollowgate La NG23 78 A5
Hollows The 4 LN11 61 F3
Holly Cl
Cherry Willingham/Reepham LN3 203 E5
5 Grantham NG31 211 D2
Horncastle LN9 199 A5
Lincoln LN5 205 D5
2 Newborough PE6 174 E5
Scunthorpe DN16 185 C4
1 Sleaford NG34 212 D2
6 Stallingborough DN41 23 E6
Holly Dr PE10 213 C7
Holly Hill 1 HU15 2 E6
Holly Rd PE25 206 A2
Holly St LN5 205 D5
Hollytree Ave 2 HU5 179 B7
Holly Tree Cl 9 LN8 57 D7
Holly Way 2 PE6 217 D4
Hollywell Rd LN5 205 D1
Hollywell Rd (The Rookery) 23 LN13 75 F2
Holly Wlk PE7 230 D3
Hollywood Dr 8 NG31 210 F7
HOLME
Holme DN16 19 A1
Holme NG23 91 A2
Holme Ave DN36 195 C6
Holme Cl
Brigg DN20 196 D4
Castor PE5 223 D2
Thorpe on the Hill LN6 92 F8
Holme Dene 1 DN9 27 C2
Holme Dr
Burton upon Stather DN15 8 B5
Sudbrooke LN2 68 F2
Holme Gdns 7 DN7 14 C7
Holme Hall Ave DN16 185 B3
HOLME HILL DN32 191 F6
Holme La
Grassthorpe NG23 78 A2
Holme DN16 185 E2
Marnham NG23 78 A4
Messingham DN17 29 E8
4 Ruskington NG34 108 E1
Scunthorpe DN16 185 B3
Winthorpe NG24 104 B8
Holme Rd PE7 233 E4
Holmes Cl
Louth LN11 198 B7
2 Skidbrooke with Saltfleet Haven LN11 51 C4
Holmes Dr 10 PE9 171 A3
Holmes Field 6 LN5 92 F3
Holmes La
North Somercotes LN11 38 A1
Roxby cum Risby DN15 9 D5
2 Welton/Dunholme LN2 68 E6
Holmes Rd
Frampton PE20 124 F1
Glinton PE6 220 D7
Horsington LN10 83 F1
Kirton PE20 136 A8
Stickney PE22 113 A7
Stixwould & Woodhall LN10 84 A1
Holme St DN32 191 E7
Holmes Way
Horncastle LN9 199 D1
Peterborough PE4 221 D2
Wragby LN8 70 C5
Holme Valley Prim Sch DN16 185 C3
Holme Wlk 6 DN21 197 F5
Holme Wood Ct 5 DN3 14 A1
Holme Wood La
Claxby with Moorby LN9 99 B8
Hameringham LN9 86 B1
Holmfield LN3 82 B7
Holmfirth Rd DN15 182 C4
Holm La NG23 104 F1
Holm Rd DN9 27 B2
Holmshaw Cl 24 DN3 14 A2
Holstein Dr DN16 185 A2
Holt Cl
10 Lincoln LN6 93 C8
9 Wittering PE8 172 B1
Holt La
Horncastle LN9 199 D4
Mareham le Fen PE22 99 A3
Holton Ct DN36 195 C1
HOLTON CUM BECKERING LN8 70 C8
HOLTON LE CLAY DN36 195 D2
Holton-le-Clay Inf Sch DN36 195 D2
Holton le Clay Jun Sch DN36 195 E1
HOLTON LE MOOR LN7 45 A8
Holton Mount DN36 195 C2
Holton Rd
Nettleton LN7 33 A2
South Kelsey LN7 32 D1
Tetney DN36 195 F1
Holt Prim Sch The LN6 200 A3
Holt The DN21 197 F5
Holy Cross Gdns 12 NG32 119 B7
Holydyke DN18 10 E8
Holy Family Prim Sch DN7 14 D7
Holyoake Rd DN32 192 C6
Holyroad Dr DN15 182 D7
Holyrood Cl PE20 134 E3
Holyrood Wlk PE11 214 E2
Holy Trinity CE Prim Sch LN4 207 A5
Holywell Cl 1 PE3 225 A1
Holy Well La LN11 49 A4
Holywell Rd PE9 162 E8
Holywell Way PE3 224 F2
Home Beat Dr DN20 19 C3
Home Cl
7 Bourne PE10 213 C7
Bracebridge Heath LN4 205 F3
Kingston upon Hull HU4 179 C5
Home Ct 8 LN5 107 A7
Home Farm Cl
Great Casterton PE9 218 C8
Laughterton LN1 65 D2
Homefarm La NG23 79 A7
Homefield Ave DN33 191 D3
Home Paddock DN37 194 E4
Home Pasture 4 PE4 220 F5
Home Pk 4 NG34 120 F8
Homers La PE22 126 D4
Home St DN15 183 B4
Homestead Garth 11 DN7 14 D4
Honeyhill PE4 221 E1
Honeyhill Com Prim Sch PE4 221 E1
Honeyhill Rd PE13 169 C2
Honeyholes La LN2 68 D6
Honey Pot Cl LN2 202 E7
Honey Pot La NG33 151 F4
Honeysuckle Cl
4 Lincoln LN5 205 C2
14 Mablethorpe & Sutton LN12 76 F8
18 Sutton on Sea Ln11 76 F8
Honeysuckle Ct
Humberston DN35 192 E1
Peterborough PE2 230 D7
3 Scunthorpe DN16 185 D4
Honeysuckle Pl 19 HU15 2 C5
HONINGTON NG32 119 C2
Honington App 5 LN1 201 D7
Honington Cres LN1 201 D7
Honington Rd 2 NG32 130 B8
Hood Cl NG34 212 A3
Hood Rd DN17 184 D6
Hood St
Kingston upon Hull HU8 181 A8
8 Lincoln LN5 201 F1
Hook's Dro PE13 177 C4
Hooks La LN5 106 E6
Hoop End DN36 36 D4
Hoopers Cl 4 NG13 128 A5
Hoop La LN8 70 E2
Hope Gdns PE21 208 F6
Hope St
Cleethorpes DN35 193 A5
Grimsby DN32 191 F8
Lincoln LN5 201 F1
Hopfield DN20 31 A5
Hopgardens 1 DN21 53 E3
Hopgarth 11 DN9 27 D2
Hop Hills La DN7 14 D5
Hopkins Ave DN17 185 A7
Hoplands Rd LN4 207 D5
Hoplands The 4 NG34 212 F4
Hopland's Wood Nature Reserve* LN13 88 F6
HOP POLE PE11 165 F5
Hopton St LN9 199 B3
Hopwood Cl HU3 180 D8
Hopyard La
Bassingham LN5 93 B1
Normanton on Trent NG23 78 A3
Horace St PE21 208 E5
HORBLING NG34 133 C2
Horbling Fen Dro NG34 133 D2
Horbling La PE22 113 A7
Horbling Line Nature Reserve* NG34 133 B1
Horbury Cl DN15 182 D4
HORKSTOW DN18 10 A5
Horkstow Rd DN18 10 E7
Hornbeam Ave DN16 185 A5
Hornby Dr 20 LN12 77 A7
HORNCASTLE LN9 199 D3
Horncastle Cty Prim Sch LN9 199 C4
Horncastle Hill PE23 87 A1
Horncastle La
Dunholme LN2 68 B5
Grange de Lings LN1 67 F5
Horncastle Rd
Bardney LN3 83 C4
Horncastle Rd *continued*
Boston PE21 208 F8
Fishtoft PE21 125 E5
Goulceby LN9 72 D5
Horsington LN10 84 D4
Louth LN11 198 A4
Mareham le Fen PE22 98 F4
Raithby cum Maltby LN11 60 F2
Roughton LN9 85 C2
Tathwell LN11 73 A8
West Ashby LN9 199 C8
Woodhall Spa LN10 97 F6
Wragby LN8 70 D4
Horne La 3 NG22 65 B1
Horner Cl 1 LN5 205 C2
Hornsby Cres DN15 182 F4
Hornsby Rd NG31 210 E2
Hornsea Parade 4 HU9 181 C8
Hornsey Hill Rd DN21 28 D1
Horn The 7 PE25 206 A7
Horse Fair Gn 25 DN8 15 A8
Horse Fayre 7 PE11 214 A3
Horsegate PE6 217 D4
Horsegate Field Rd DN19 5 B2
Horseham's La PE20 135 A5
Horse Mkt 24 LN7 33 B4
Horsemoor Dro PE12 159 B1
Horsemoor La LN9 72 C2
Horse Pasture La DN22 65 C7
Horsepit La 12 PE11 145 C1
Horseshoe Cl 12 NG34 108 D2
Horseshoe La PE20 136 D5
Horseshoe Rd PE11 214 A2
Horseshoe Terr PE13 170 C1
Horseshoe Way
Hampton Vale PE7 230 D1
Yaxley PE7 233 D8
Horseshoe Yd 11 PE6 166 E1
Horsewells St 1 DN10 39 C1
HORSINGTON LN10 84 C3
Horstead Ave DN20 196 D5
Horton St LN2 202 C3
Horton Wlk PE3 225 C5
Hospital Dro PE12 160 C3
Hospital La PE21 209 A6
Hospital Rd PE12 161 A5
Hotchkin Ave LN1 66 E2
Hotham Dr HU5 179 B8
Hotham Rd HU5 179 A8
Hotham Rd S HU5 179 B8
Hotham St HU9 181 D7
Hotspur Rd DN21 197 C6
HOUGHAM NG32 118 C3
Hougham Rd
Hougham NG32 118 B4
Westborough & Dry Doddington NG23 117 F5
Hough La
Carlton Scroop NG32 119 C4
Claypole NG23 117 F7
HOUGH-ON-THE-HILL NG32 119 A5
Hough Rd
Barkston NG32 130 B8
Carlton Scroop NG32 119 A3
Hough-on-the-Hill NG32 118 E7
Houghton Ave PE2 231 F5
Houghton Rd NG31 211 C2
Houlden Way 1 NG34 122 E3
Hounsfield Cl NG24 104 B5
Houps Rd 8 DN8 15 B8
Hourne Ct HU13 178 E2
Hourne The HU13 178 E2
House Ct DN16 185 D4
Househams La LN11 61 F3
Howard Cl PE34 161 F2
Howard Gr DN32 192 B6
Howard Rd 10 LN4 108 A7
Howard St LN1 201 C4
Howdale La NG32 119 A3
Howden Croft Hill HU15 2 A8
Howe La
Ashby with Scremby PE23 88 C3
Goxhill DN19 11 F8
HOWELL NG34 122 D5
Howell Fen Dro NG34 122 D5
Howell Rd NG34 122 E3
Howgarth La PE22 114 F5
Howitts Rd 14 NG13 128 A5
Howland PE2 230 A3
Howlett Rd DN35 193 A4
HOWSHAM LN7 32 A6
Howsham La 2 DN38 32 D8
Howville Ave 2 DN7 14 F3
Howville Rd 1 DN7 14 F3
Hoylake Dr
1 Immingham DN40 186 D5
Peterborough PE7 231 C5
Skegness PE25 206 D5
Hoylake Rd DN17 184 D3
Hubba Cres PE20 135 C6
Hubbard Cl 2 NG34 122 D3
HUBBERT'S BRIDGE PE20 124 F2
Hubberts Bridge Sta PE20 124 E2
Hubert's Cl PE12 168 C1
Hub The* NG34 212 E4
Huckles Way PE25 206 B6
Huddleston Rd DN32 192 B7
Hudson Ave DN15 182 E5
Hudson Cl PE23 88 B3
Hudson Ct HU13 178 D1

Jubilee Cl *continued*
8 Morton PE10 154 C7
Scotter DN21 29 B3
1 Spalding PE11 214 C4
Jubilee Cres
Gainsborough DN21 197 D5
Louth LN11 198 C8
Jubilee Ct 6 NG34 212 E4
Jubilee Dr
3 Bardney LN3 83 C4
10 Wragby LN8 70 D4
Jubilee Gr NG34 212 C6
Jubilee Parade 6 PE24 90 D7
Jubilee Rd LN11 50 E7
Jubilee St
Peterborough PE2 230 F8
2 Ruskington NG34 108 E1
Jubilee Way
Crowland PE6 166 F1
Horncastle LN9 199 B4
Scunthorpe DN15 183 B3
Jude Gate PE22 114 E3
Judge Cl 3 PE21 209 C4
Judy Cross PE11 145 B8
Julian Cl HU5 179 A7
Julian St DN32 192 A7
Julian's Wlk 8 HU10 178 F6
Julia Rd LN4 203 D1
Julia's Mead 12 PE11 214 B5
Junction Rd 10 DN7 14 C6
Junella Cl HU3 180 A4
Jungle Zoo The★ DN35 193 B3
Junior Cadets Rd NG34 120 B8
Juniper Cl
Flixborough DN15 182 C6
10 Leasingham NG34 121 B7
3 Lincoln LN5 205 C2
Spalding PE11 214 F4
Juniper Cres
Peterborough PE3 225 A2
Spalding PE11 214 F5
Juniper Dr 13 LN2 68 F4
Juniper Way
Gainsborough DN21 197 D5
Grimsby DN33 191 C2
3 Sleaford NG34 212 D2
Jury Rd PE7 233 C8
Justice Hall La 10 DN17 16 D8
Justice La DN14 7 B8
Jutland Ct 1 DN36 195 D7

K

Karelia Ct HU4 179 B5
Karen Ave 12 DN41 23 A4
Karsons Way LN2 68 D7
Katherine Cres PE25 206 D2
Kathleen Ave
Cleethorpes DN35 192 D8
Scunthorpe DN16 185 B5
Kathleen Gr DN32 192 C7
Kathleen Rice Cl DN35 192 A8
Kaymile Cl 13 DN36 195 C6
KEADBY DN17 17 D7
Keadby Cl LN6 204 F7
Keal Carr Nature Reserve★ PE23 100 E7
KEAL COTES PE23 100 C4
Keal Hill PE23 100 B7
Kealholme Rd DN17 29 D7
Keaton Cl PE25 206 A5
Keats Ave
Grantham NG31 211 E6
Scunthorpe DN17 184 D7
Keats Cl
Lincoln LN2 202 C7
17 Mablethorpe/Sutton on Sea LN12 77 A7
Keats Dr NG34 121 E4
Keats Gr 2 PE9 218 E5
Keats Way PE1 225 D7
Keb La DN15 9 D2
Keble Cl 4 PE9 219 A7
Keble Ct 1 LN4 207 B5
KEDDINGTON LN11 198 F8
Keddington Ave LN1 201 E8
Keddington Cres 2 LN11 198 D7
Keddington Rd
Louth LN11 198 C7
Scunthorpe DN17 184 F4
Kedlestone Rd NG31 210 F1
Kedleston Rd PE7 231 F6
Keeble Dr LN4 203 D1
KEELBY DN41 23 A5
Keelby Prim Sch DN41 23 A5
Keelby Rd
6 Gainsborough DN21 53 A8
Scunthorpe DN17 184 F5
Stallingborough DN41 23 C6
Keel Dr 9 NG13 128 A5
Keeling St 7 LN11 50 F7
Keepers Cl 2 LN2 68 D7
Keepers Way NG34 212 E3
Keeper's Way 6 DN9 16 E1
Keeton Rd PE1 225 E7
Keightley Rd PE12 147 B5
Keir Hardie Wlk DN32 191 D7
KEISBY PE10 141 F3
Keith Cres 3 DN37 23 F1
KELBY NG32 131 C8
KELFIELD DN9 28 C4
Kelham Rd
9 Great Gonerby NG31 129 E5
Kelham Rd *continued*
2 Great Gonerby NG31 210 E8
Grimsby DN32 192 D6
Kellet Gate PE12 157 B5
Kells Cl 6 LN5 205 D3
Kell's Dro PE20 124 E1
Kelly Cl 14 PE11 156 E8
Kelsey Ave DN15 182 B3
Kelsey La 1 DN17 17 D4
Kelsey Rd LN7 32 C2
Kelsey St LN1 234 A2
Kelso Ct PE4 221 A1
KELSTERN LN11 48 A1
Kelstern Cl 1 LN6 204 C6
Kelstern Ct 1 DN34 191 A5
Kelstern Rd LN6 204 C6
Kelston Dr 2 HU13 179 A3
Kelthorpe Cl PE9 171 A2
Kemble Cl LN6 204 B8
Kemeshame Ct DN37 194 F4
Kemp Rd
Grimsby DN31 189 C3
3 Swanland HU14 3 B6
Kemp St PE6 166 E1
Kempton Cl 3 PE11 156 E3
Kempton Dr 4 DN7 14 C2
Kempton Rd HU3 179 E6
Kempton Vale DN35 192 F1
Kempton Way NG31 210 F4
Kendal Cl 2 PE4 221 D2
Kendal Ct DN16 185 C6
Kendale Rd DN16 185 E8
Kendal Rd DN40 186 E3
Kendal Way HU5 179 C7
Kendon Gdns DN8 15 B8
Kendrick Cl PE2 231 D6
Kenford Ct DN36 195 C7
Kenilworth Cl 3 LN1 66 D2
Kenilworth Dr LN6 205 C5
Kenilworth Rd
Cleethorpes DN35 192 D4
Grantham NG31 211 F5
Scunthorpe DN16 183 C1
Kenlan Rd 23 PE13 170 D1
Kenleigh Dr PE21 209 D4
Kenmare Cres DN21 197 F2
Kenmar Rd 20 DN37 23 F1
Kennedy Ave
21 Alford LN13 75 F2
Skegness PE25 206 C2
Kennedy Cl DN20 196 E3
Kennedy Rd
Bracebridge Heath LN4 205 F3
Holbeach PE12 215 C4
Kennedy Way DN40 186 C4
Kennedy Way Sh Ctr DN40 186 C4
Kennel La
Doddington & Whisby LN6 79 E5
Reepham LN3 203 E8
Kennels Rd PE6 224 D4
Kennel Wlk LN3 203 F8
Kenner Cl 4 LN6 205 A6
Kennet Gdns PE4 221 C1
Kenneth Ave
2 Burgh le Marsh PE24 102 E8
8 Hatfield DN7 14 C2
5 Stainforth DN7 14 C6
Kenneth Campbell Rd 4 DN36 37 C5
Kenneth St 1 LN1 201 F6
Kennington Cl LN2 68 E5
Kennulphs Cl 5 PE6 175 C8
Kensington Cl PE12 215 F3
Kensington Dr 6 PE11 214 B2
Kensington Gdns 7 LN12 64 B3
Kensington Pl DN33 195 A8
Kensington Rd DN15 182 B3
Ken Stimpson Com Sch PE4 220 F4
Kent Ave LN12 63 F5
Kent Cl
Kingston upon Hull HU9 181 C7
3 Sutton Bridge PE12 160 E4
Kent Dr 4 DN20 31 A5
Kentmere Pl 4 PE4 221 D2
Kent Rd
9 Binbrook Tech Pk LN8 47 B6
Leake Commonside PE22 113 F3
Peterborough PE3 225 E2
Kent St
Grimsby DN32 189 B1
6 Lincoln LN2 202 C3
Kenwardly Rd HU10 178 E8
Kenwick Cl LN11 198 D3
Kenwick Dr NG31 211 D4
Kenwick Gdns LN11 198 D3
Kenwick Hill
Legbourne LN11 198 E1
Raithby cum Maltby LN11 61 C3
Kenwick Pastures LN11 198 D3
Kenwick Rd LN11 198 D2
Kenya Dr DN17 184 F2
Kenyon Cl 8 DN8 15 A8
Kerries Wlk DN17 184 C7
Kerrison View 5 LN2 68 D2
Kerr's Cres NG32 118 D2
Kerry Dr HU10 178 C6
Kerry Pit Way HU10 178 C6
Kesgrave St 1 DN31 189 C1
Kesteven Cl 1 PE6 217 D4
Kesteven Ct
3 Habrough DN40 22 E8
7 Lincoln LN6 204 D2
Kesteven Dr 7 PE6 217 A6
Kesteven Gr 10 DN17 16 D8
Kesteven & Grantham Girl's Sch NG31 211 B5
Kesteven Rd PE9 219 C7
Kesteven & Sleaford Girl's High Sch NG34 212 D4
Kesteven St
Lincoln LN5 234 B1
1 Sleaford NG34 212 E4
Kesteven Way 7 PE10 213 C5
Kesteven Wlk 3 PE1 226 B2
Kestrel Cl
6 Birchwood LN6 204 D8
Clinton Park LN4 207 C6
2 Sleaford NG34 212 B3
Kestrel Ct
Grantham NG31 210 F2
Longthorpe PE3 225 A2
Kestrel Dr
Bourne PE10 213 E3
Louth LN11 198 D8
Kestrel Rd
8 Scopwick Heath LN4 108 A7
Scunthorpe DN17 184 E6
Kestrel Rise LN6 79 B1
Keswick Cl 2 PE4 221 D3
Ketco Ave PE9 171 A4
Ketel Cl PE12 216 C3
KETSBY LN11 74 D3
Kettering Rd
Scunthorpe DN16 183 C2
Wothorpe PE9 219 B2
Kettlebridge La DN40 12 E6
Kettleby La DN20 20 E3
Kettleby View 3 DN20 196 D4
KETTLETHORPE LN1 65 F2
Kettlethorpe Dr 17 HU15 2 D5
Kettlethorpe Rd LN1 65 E3
Kettlewell St DN32 191 E5
KETTON PE9 171 A3
Ketton CE Prim Sch PE9 171 A3
Ketton Rd PE9 171 B2
Kew Rd DN35 192 E6
KEXBY DN21 53 E5
Kexby La DN21 53 C4
Kexby Mill Cl 5 LN6 93 B8
Kexby Rd DN21 54 D6
Kexby Wlk DN21 197 F3
Keyholme La DN36 37 D2
Key Theatre★ PE1 226 B1
Keyworth Dr 10 LN7 33 B4
Khormaksar Dr LN4 95 C7
Kiddier Ave DN37 194 D7
Kidd La HU15 2 D6
Kidgate LN11 198 B5
Kidgate Mews LN11 198 B5
Kidgate Prim Sch LN11 198 C5
Kilburn Cres 1 LN6 205 A6
Kildare Dr PE3 225 C4
Kilham PE2 229 E2
Killarney Cl NG31 211 E7
Killingholme Haven Pits Nature Reserve★ DN40 13 A6
Killingholme Prim Sch DN40 12 E3
Killingholme Rd DN40 12 F2
Kiln Hill 4 LN8 59 A7
Kiln La
Brigg DN20 196 B3
Fulbeck NG32 106 C1
Immingham DN41 187 C2
Louth LN11 198 B6
Stallingborough DN41 186 F1
Kiln La Ind Est DN41 187 B3
Kiln La Trading Est DN41 187 C2
Kilnwell Rd 12 LN8 57 D8
Kiln Yd LN11 198 C5
Kilverstone PE4 220 F6
KILVINGTON NG13 117 A1
Kimberley St HU3 180 C7
Kimberley Terr NG31 210 E7
Kimblewick La PE11 214 A2
Kimbolton Ct PE1 225 F3
Kime Cl NG34 142 C8
Kime's La 6 PE22 98 F4
Kinder Ave LN6 205 A2
Kinderley Rd PE13 170 D2
King Charles Cl HU10 178 E7
King Edward Fst Sch DN8 15 B8
King Edward Rd
Thorne/Moorends DN8 15 A8
2 Woodhall Spa LN10 97 C6
King Edward St
Belton DN9 16 E2
4 Grimsby DN31 189 A1
3 Kingston upon Hull HU1 180 F6
Kirton in Lindsey DN21 30 B1
Scunthorpe DN16 183 A1
Sleaford NG34 212 C3
King Edwards Terr 4 HU15 2 B5
King Edward VI Sch
Louth LN11 198 A5
Spilsby PE23 87 F1
KINGERBY LN8 44 E3
Kingerby Beck Mdws Nature Reserve★ LN8 44 E5
Kingerby Cl DN21 197 E3
Kingerby Rd DN17 184 E5
Kingfisher Cl
2 Birchwood LN6 204 D8
Brigg DN20 196 A3
Scunthorpe DN15 182 D5
Yaxley PE7 233 D5
Kingfisher Ct 2 PE11 214 F2
Kingfisher Dr
2 Skegness PE25 206 A7
4 Surfleet PE11 145 E3
Kingfishers PE2 229 D6
King George Ave 1 LN10 97 D6
King Georges Ct 3 DN7 14 C5
King George V Ave 1 PE12 215 F3
King George V Stadium DN32 192 B5
King Henry Chase PE3 225 A5
King John Bank
2 Sutton Bridge PE14 170 F8
Walpole PE14 161 A2
King Johns Rd 6 PE20 135 B7
King John St NG34 212 C4
King St E DN21 197 D3
King St La LE14 150 A6
Kings Arms Yd 2 LN2 234 B2
Kings Ave PE25 206 E8
King's Ave
Boston PE21 209 C3
Brigg DN20 196 D3
King's Bench St HU3 180 B5
Kingsbridge Ct 1 PE4 220 E5
King's Causeway DN14 6 E8
Kings Cl PE22 112 C8
King's Cl 15 DN7 14 D4
Kingscliffe Rd NG31 211 A8
King's Cres
Boston PE21 209 C3
Swineshead PE20 135 B8
Kings Croft 1 DN17 16 E6
King's Cross Cl 2 HU3 180 C6
Kings Ct
19 Kirton PE20 136 C5
Louth LN11 198 E7
Old Bolingbroke PE23 100 A7
9 Scawby DN20 30 F8
Scunthorpe DN15 183 B4
Kingsdale DN17 184 E2
King's Delph Dro PE7 231 E2
Kingsdown Rd LN6 204 B7
Kings Dyke Cl PE2 231 E6
Kingsgate PE12 159 E7
Kings Gate DN32 192 A7
King's Gdns PE1 226 A5
Kings Hill 2 NG32 119 B7
Kings Leigh 1 HU3 180 C6
Kingsley Ave PE10 213 B5
Kingsley Cl
4 Barnack PE9 172 D3
6 Brough HU15 2 B5
Kingsley Gr DN33 191 C4
Kingsley Rd
14 Mablethorpe/Sutton on Sea LN12 64 B4
North Hykeham LN6 204 B5
Peterborough PE1 226 C4
Kingsley St LN1 234 A4
Kingsline Cl 1 PE6 176 A3
Kings Mews DN35 193 C1
Kings Parade DN35 193 A5
Kingsport Cl HU3 180 A7
Kings Rd
Holbeach PE12 215 F3
Immingham DN40 186 E5
Metheringham LN4 95 C4
Peterborough PE2 231 B6
Stamford PE9 219 B6
King's Rd
Barnetby le Wold DN38 21 B5
Humberston DN35 193 B3
Spalding PE11 214 D5
Kings Sch PE1 226 A4
Kings Sch The NG31 211 B5
King St
1 Billinghay LN4 109 F5
Boston PE21 208 E4
East Halton DN40 12 D7
Gainsborough DN21 197 D3
15 Goxhill DN19 12 A8
2 Keelby DN41 23 A4
10 Kirton PE20 136 C5
Lincoln LN5 234 A1
14 Mablethorpe/Sutton on Sea LN12 64 B3
Market Rasen LN8 57 D8
1 Peterborough PE1 226 A2
Scunthorpe DN15 183 B4
18 Sutton Bridge PE12 160 E4
Thorne/Moorends DN8 15 A8
Wainfleet All Saints PE24 102 A2
West Deeping PE6 173 A8
Wilsford NG32 120 A1
Winterton DN15 9 A5
Yarburgh LN11 49 E4
Kingsthorpe Cres PE25 206 C1
Kingston Ave
Grantham NG31 210 E4
Grimsby DN34 191 A6
Kingston upon Hull HU13 178 F1
Kingston Cl 7 DN35 193 A1
Kingston Communications Stadium (Hull City AFC Hull RLFC)★ HU3 180 B7
Kingston Dr PE2 231 E5
Kingston Rd
Kingston upon Hull HU10 178 F8
Scunthorpe DN16 185 A7
Kingston Ret Pk HU1 180 E5
Kingston St HU1 180 E5
Kingston Terr NG34 212 E5
KINGSTON UPON HULL HU1 180 F4
Kingston View 20 DN18 10 F8
Kingston Wharf 4 HU1 180 F5
Kingsway
Boston PE21 209 B3
Bourne PE10 213 D6
3 Brigg DN20 196 B4
Cleethorpes DN35 193 A5
11 Leverington PE13 170 E1
Lincoln LN5 201 F1
Nettleham LN2 68 C2
Scunthorpe DN15 182 C3
Stainforth DN7 14 C6
Tealby LN8 46 C1
Kings Way LN2 68 C7
Kingsway Sta DN35 193 B4
Kings Wlk 11 NG31 211 A4
KINGTHORPE LN8 70 C2
King William Cl 4 PE34 161 F3
Kinloch Way DN40 186 B2
Kinloss Cl 11 LN6 204 C6
Kinnears Wlk PE2 229 F2
Kinoulton Ct 16 NG31 210 E2
Kinross Rd NG34 120 F2
Kinsbourne Gn 40 DN7 14 D4
Kinsley Wlk 8 DN15 183 B3
Kintore Dr NG31 211 C4
Kipling Ave 4 DN17 184 D7
Kipling Cl
4 Grantham NG31 211 E6
3 Stamford PE9 218 E5
St Giles LN2 202 B7
Kipling Ct PE1 225 E8
Kipling Dr
4 Mablethorpe/Sutton on Sea LN12 77 A7
14 Sleaford NG34 212 F4
Kiplington Cl HU3 180 A7
Kipling Wlk 1 HU4 179 D2
Kippings The 8 PE10 164 C8
Kirby Ct 5 PE11 214 F4
Kirby Wlk 2 PE3 225 C4
KIRK BRAMWITH DN7 14 A6
KIRKBY LN8 44 F3
Kirkby Bank PE23 99 E3
KIRKBY FENSIDE PE23 99 E4
Kirkby Gr DN33 191 A3
Kirkby Gravel Pit Nature Reserve★ LN4 207 A8
KIRKBY GREEN LN4 108 E8
Kirkby La
Coningsby LN4 207 D8
Woodhall Spa LN10 97 E6
KIRKBY LA THORPE NG34 121 F5
Kirkby la Thorpe CE Prim Sch NG34 121 F4
Kirkby Moor Nature Reserve★ LN10 98 A5
KIRKBY ON BAIN LN10 98 B5
Kirkby on Bain CE Prim Sch LN10 98 C5
Kirkby Rd
Ewerby & Evedon NG34 122 B5
Scunthorpe DN17 184 E4
Kirkby St LN5 201 F1
KIRKBY UNDERWOOD PE10 142 D2
Kirkby Underwood Rd PE10 154 A8
Kirkdale Cl 4 NG34 121 B8
Kirkden Paddocks DN9 16 C2
KIRK ELLA HU10 178 C8
Kirkgate PE13 169 F7
Kirk Gate
Waltham DN37 194 E4
6 Whaplode PE12 158 B7
Kirkgate St PE13 170 E1
Kirk Gdns PE21 208 D7
Kirkham Cl HU13 178 F2
Kirkhouse Gn Rd DN7 14 A8
Kirklands Rd HU5 179 E8
Kirkmeadow PE3 225 A8
Kirk Rise HU10 178 C7
Kirkside DN37 194 D4
Kirkstall PE2 230 B3
Kirkstall Cl LN2 202 E6
Kirkstead Bridge LN10 97 B4
Kirkstead Cres DN33 191 B3
Kirkstead Ct 8 LN10 97 D5
Kirkstone House Sch PE6 164 E4
Kirkton Gate PE3 225 A1
Kirkway HU10 178 B7
Kirkwood Cl PE3 225 E2
Kirman Cres 5 DN17 184 F3
KIRMINGTON DN39 22 A6
Kirmington CE Prim Sch DN39 22 A6
Kirmington Cl 8 LN6 204 C6

Lemon Wong La LN5 . . . . 106 C3
Lenham La HU1 . . . . 180 E6
LENTON NG33 . . . . 141 E5
Lenton Gn LN2 . . . . 202 B7
Lenton's La
Friskney PE22 . . . . 115 A5
Leverton PE22 . . . . 126 F6
Lenton Way 2 PE20 . . . . . . 136 D6
Leofric Ave PE10 . . . . 213 B5
Leofric Cl 19 PE6 . . . . 166 F1
Leofric Sq PE1 . . . . 226 E3
Leonard Cres DN15 . . . . . . 182 F3
Leonard St 4 HU3 . . . . . . 180 D8
Leopold Cl DN16 . . . . 185 A6
Lerowe Rd PE13 . . . . 170 E1
Leslie Ct 5 DN15 . . . . 183 B3
Leslie Manser Prim Sch
LN6 . . . . 204 B7
Lessingham PE2 . . . . 229 D4
Lestrange St DN35 . . . . . . 192 C7
Lethbridge Rd PE4 . . . . . . 221 D2
Lettwell Cres 1 PE25 . . . 206 D1
Levels La
Blaxton DN9 . . . . 26 A4
Misson DN10 . . . . 39 A7
Leven Rd DN16 . . . . 185 D6
Levens Wlk PE3 . . . . 225 B3
Leverett Rd PE21 . . . . 209 B4
LEVERINGTON PE13 . . . . . . 170 B3
Leverington Comm
PE13 . . . . 169 F1
Leverington Cty Prim Sch
PE13 . . . . 170 B2
Leverington Rd PE13 . . . . 170 C1
Levers Cl PE21 . . . . 209 F5
Leverstock Gn 38 DN7 . . . . 14 D4
LEVERTON PE22 . . . . 126 F6
LEVERTON HIGHGATE
PE22 . . . . 127 A6
Leverton Leisure Ctr
PE22 . . . . 127 A7
LEVERTON LUCASGATE
PE22 . . . . 127 B6
LEVERTON OUTGATE
PE22 . . . . 127 B7
Leverton Rd DN22 . . . . 52 B1
Levington St 2 DN31 . . . 189 C1
Lewes Gdns PE4 . . . . 221 A3
Lewis Ave 13 LN12 . . . . 77 A8
Lewis Rd
Cleethorpes DN35 . . . . 192 D8
Coningsby LN4 . . . . 207 D4
Lewis St
Gainsborough DN21 . . . . . 197 D3
Lincoln LN5 . . . . 234 B1
Lexington Dr HU4 . . . . 179 C5
Leyburn Rd LN6 . . . . 204 F4
Leyden Cl 6 DN40 . . . . . . 186 B4
Leyland Ave DN7 . . . . 14 E4
Leys Cl NG32 . . . . 210 B4
Leys Farm Jun Sch
DN17 . . . . 184 F4
Leys La DN15 . . . . 9 B6
Leys The
Cherry Willingham LN3 . . . 203 E6
Peterborough PE3 . . . . 225 A1
Leytonstone La PE10 . . . . 213 D2
Liberty La HU1 . . . . 181 A6
Lichfield Ave
Peterborough PE4 . . . . 220 F3
Scunthorpe DN17 . . . . 184 C7
Lichfield Cl NG31 . . . . 210 E4
Lichfield Ct DN32 . . . . 192 B6
Lichfield Rd
Bracebridge Heath LN4 . . . . 81 A2
Grimsby DN32 . . . . 192 B6
12 Hatfield DN7 . . . . 14 D4
Liddell St HU2 . . . . 180 E7
Lidgard Rd DN36 . . . . 193 A1
Lidgate Cl PE2 . . . . 230 C7
Lidgett Cl 10 DN20 . . . . 30 F8
Lidgett The 7 DN9 . . . . 27 D6
Lifeboat Ave PE25 . . . . . . 206 D1
Lighter-than-Air Rd
NG34 . . . . 107 C1
Lighton Ave 4 PE20 . . . . 136 C5
Lilac Ave DN16 . . . . 183 C1
Lilac Cl
Birchwood LN6 . . . . 204 C8
Bourne PE10 . . . . 213 B6
Wisbech PE13 . . . . 170 E1
Lilac Ct DN33 . . . . 194 D8
Lilac Rd
9 Elloughton-cum-Brough
HU15 . . . . 2 C5
Peterborough PE1 . . . . 226 C7
Lilac Wlk PE7 . . . . 233 F6
Lilacwood Dr 5 NG31 . . . 210 F7
Lila Dr 1 PE11 . . . . 145 B7
Lilburn Cl 5 NG34 . . . . . . 121 B8
Lilburn Dr PE11 . . . . 214 C6
Lilford Cl 5 LN2 . . . . 202 E7
Lilford Rd LN2 . . . . 202 E7
Lilley St 6 NG23 . . . . 117 D3
Lillicrap Ct 2 LN1 . . . . . . 234 B4
Lilly's Carr Nature
Reserve* PE23 . . . . 100 E6
Lilly's Rd LN2 . . . . 234 B4
Lilywood Rd 12 DN20 . . . . . 19 D3
Limber Cl 2 DN21 . . . . 53 A7
Limber Ct DN34 . . . . 191 A6
Limber Hill LN8 . . . . 47 D4
Limber Rd
Humberside Airport
DN39 . . . . 22 A6
Swallow LN7 . . . . 34 A7
Limber Vale DN34 . . . . 191 A6
Limburg Dr 7 PE11 . . . . . 214 A2
Lime Ave
Scunthorpe DN16 . . . . 19 A3
Wisbech PE13 . . . . 170 D1
Lime Cl
Burgh le Marsh PE24 . . . . 102 D7
2 Langtoft PE6 . . . . 164 F3
3 Old Leake PE22 . . . . . . 114 A1
RAF Cranwell NG34 . . . . . 107 D1
Ruskington NG34 . . . . 108 D1
Lime Cres LN5 . . . . 205 C1
Lime Ct PE11 . . . . 214 E3
Limedale View 2 DN3 . . . 14 A3
Lime Gr
Bassingham LN5 . . . . 92 F2
2 Boston PE21 . . . . 209 C2
2 Bottesford NG13 . . . . . 128 A5
Caythorpe NG32 . . . . 119 C7
Cherry Willingham/Reepham
LN3 . . . . 203 D5
9 Goxhill DN19 . . . . 12 A8
Grantham NG31 . . . . 211 C6
Holbeach PE12 . . . . 215 D3
Holton le Clay DN36 . . . . . 195 D1
Humberston DN36 . . . . 36 C7
7 Ingoldmells PE25 . . . . . . 90 D3
Louth LN11 . . . . 198 C7
Scunthorpe DN16 . . . . 185 B7
Lime Kiln Cl PE3 . . . . 225 E4
Lime Kiln Way LN2 . . . . . . 202 C4
Limelands 2 LN2 . . . . 234 C3
Lime St
Grimsby DN31 . . . . 191 C8
Kingston upon Hull HU8 . . 181 A8
3 Sutton Bridge PE12 . . . 160 F4
Limes The
7 Beckingham DN10 . . . . . 40 A1
Castor PE5 . . . . 223 F1
4 Stallingborough DN41 . . 23 D6
12 Wittering PE8 . . . . 172 B1
Limetree Ave DN33 . . . . . 191 C3
Lime Tree Ave
Gainsborough DN21 . . . . . 197 D5
Kingston upon Hull HU13 . 178 F2
2 Market Deeping PE6 . . 217 A6
20 Metheringham LN4 . . . . . 95 C4
Peterborough PE1 . . . . 225 F4
Limetree Cl
13 Sleaford NG34 . . . . 212 D2
Yaxley PE7 . . . . 233 F7
Lime Tree Cl
1 Collingham NG23 . . . . . . 91 D4
6 Fulbeck NG32 . . . . 106 C1
6 Lincoln LN6 . . . . 204 E8
Lime Tree Gr 4 DN8 . . . . . 15 A8
Lime Tree Paddock 2
LN2 . . . . 68 F4
Limetree Wlk 1 NG34 . . . 122 E2
Limewalk PE12 . . . . 216 C6
Linchfield Cl PE6 . . . . 217 E5
Linchfield Prim Sch
PE6 . . . . 217 D5
Linchfield Rd PE6 . . . . 217 D6
LINCOLN LN5 . . . . 234 C2
Lincoln Ass Rm* LN2 . . . 234 B3
Lincoln Ave LN6 . . . . 205 C8
Lincoln Bvd DN31 . . . . 191 B7
Lincoln Castle* LN1 . . . . 234 A3
Lincoln Castle Way DN19 . . 4 D2
Lincoln Cath* LN2 . . . . . . 234 B3
Lincoln Christs Hospl Sch
LN2 . . . . 202 B6
Lincoln Cl
4 Crowle DN17 . . . . 16 D7
Grantham NG31 . . . . 210 D4
5 Market Deeping PE6 . . 217 A6
Lincoln Coll
Lincoln LN1 . . . . 234 B3
Lincoln LN2 . . . . 234 C3
Lincoln Cres 2 DN21 . . . . 42 F8
Lincoln Ct
4 Beacon Hill NG24 . . . . 104 A6
Brumby DN16 . . . . 185 B7
Lincoln Cty Hospl LN2 . . . 202 C4
Lincoln Dr
27 Barton-upon-Humber
DN18 . . . . 10 F8
30 Caistor LN7 . . . . 33 B4
3 Scampton Airfield LN1 . . 67 F5
5 Waddington LN5 . . . . 94 A7
24 Winterton DN15 . . . . 9 A5
Lincoln Drill Hall*
LN1 . . . . 234 B2
Lincoln Gate DN36 . . . . 48 D5
Lincoln Gdns DN16 . . . . . . 185 A6
Lincoln Gdns Prim Sch
DN16 . . . . 185 A6
Lincoln Gn
Kingston upon Hull
HU4 . . . . 179 C7
Skegness PE25 . . . . 206 B5
Lincoln La
Boston PE21 . . . . 208 E5
Holbeach PE12 . . . . 147 D5
Kettlethorpe LN1 . . . . 65 F3
Osgodby LN8 . . . . 44 F2
Thorpe on the Hill LN6 . . . . 92 E8
Lincoln Minst Sch
Lincoln LN2 . . . . 234 B4
Lincoln LN2 . . . . 234 C3
Lincoln Nuffield Hospl The
LN2 . . . . 234 B4
Lincoln Rd
Bassingham LN5 . . . . 92 F2
10 Binbrook Tech Pk LN8 . . . 47 B6
Brant Broughton LN5 . . . . . 105 F5
Brant Broughton &
Stragglethorpe LN5 . . . . 106 A5
Canwick LN4 . . . . 81 B3
Lincoln Rd *continued*
Caythorpe NG32 . . . . 119 B6
Cleethorpes DN35 . . . . 192 C5
Deeping Gate PE6 . . . . 217 C3
Digby LN4 . . . . 108 D6
Doddington & Whisby
LN6 . . . . 204 A6
Dunholme LN2 . . . . 68 D6
Dunston LN4 . . . . 95 B5
Faldingworth LN8 . . . . 56 F3
Fenton LN1 . . . . 65 E3
Fiskerton LN3 . . . . 203 F4
1 Glinton PE6 . . . . 220 C8
Heighington/Washingborough
LN4 . . . . 203 A2
Holton cum Beckering LN8 . 70 B7
Honington NG32 . . . . 119 C2
Horncastle LN9 . . . . 199 A4
Ingham LN1 . . . . 54 F2
1 Leasingham NG34 . . . . 121 B8
Lincoln LN6 . . . . 204 F1
Louth LN11 . . . . 61 B8
Metheringham LN4 . . . . 95 C4
Middle Rasen LN8 . . . . 57 B7
Moorland Prison DN7 . . . . . 26 A8
Nettleham LN2 . . . . 68 B1
Newark-on-Trent NG24 . . . 104 A6
Northborough PE6 . . . . 217 D1
Peterborough PE6 . . . . 220 D5
Ruskington NG34 . . . . 108 D2
Saxilby with Ingleby LN1 . . . 66 E1
4 Skegness PE25 . . . . 206 C3
Skellingthorpe LN6 . . . . . . 200 B4
Sleaford NG34 . . . . 212 B7
Stamford PE9 . . . . 219 C7
West Barkwith LN8 . . . . 71 A7
Lincoln Rd Bridge
NG24 . . . . 104 A5
Lincoln Rd Nocton LN4 . . . 95 A7
Lincoln's Ave PE12 . . . . . . 168 C2
Lincolnshire Archives*
LN1 . . . . 234 B3
Lincolnshire Aviation
Heritage Ctr* PE23 . . . . . 99 F5
Lincolnshire Coast Light
Rly* PE25 . . . . 90 D1
Lincolnshire Rare Breeds
Poultry* LN11 . . . . 61 F8
Lincolnshire Rd Transport
Mus* LN6 . . . . 204 D5
Lincolnshire Showground*
LN1 . . . . 67 E4
Lincolnshire Wolds Rly*
DN36 . . . . 48 F6
Lincoln St
Gainsborough DN21 . . . . . 197 C5
Kingston upon Hull HU2 . . 180 F8
Lincoln Sta LN5 . . . . 234 B1
Lincoln Way 1 PE11 . . . . 214 C5
Linda Cres LN11 . . . . 198 B4
Lindale Gdns DN16 . . . . . . 185 C7
Lindbergh Dr PE11 . . . . . . 214 C2
Linden Cl 16 DN7 . . . . 14 D4
Linden Ct PE11 . . . . 214 E5
Linden Dene 1 LN6 . . . . . 204 D1
Linden Dr PE24 . . . . 102 D7
Linden Rd LN9 . . . . 199 C4
Linden Rise PE10 . . . . 213 D7
Lindens Cl PE13 . . . . 177 A3
Lindens The NG31 . . . . . . 211 B2
Linden Terr DN21 . . . . 197 D3
Linden Way
Boston PE21 . . . . 209 A7
Pinchbeck PE11 . . . . 144 D1
Linden Wlk LN11 . . . . 198 C4
Lindholme 5 DN21 . . . . 29 C3
Lindholme Bank Rd
DN7 . . . . 15 B1
Lindholme Rd LN6 . . . . . . 204 D5
Lindisfarne Ave DN36 . . . . 195 B6
Lindisfarne Rd PE6 . . . . . . 175 A1
Lindisfarne Way NG31 . . . 210 E5
Lindis Rd PE21 . . . . 209 C5
Lindley St DN16 . . . . 185 A6
Lindrick Cl 4 NG31 . . . . . 211 D7
Lindrick Rd 6 DN7 . . . . 14 F3
Lindrick Wlk 5 DN37 . . . . 194 C4
Lindridge Wlk PE3 . . . . . . 225 A2
Lindsey Ave PE6 . . . . 217 A6
Lindsey Cl
6 Bourne PE10 . . . . 213 C5
Gainsborough DN21 . . . . . 197 F2
Peterborough PE4 . . . . 221 B1
Lindsey Ct 12 DN9 . . . . 27 E6
Lindsey Ctr 4 DN21 . . . . . 197 D4
Lindsey Dr
Crowle DN17 . . . . 16 D8
6 Healing DN41 . . . . 24 A5
Holton le Clay DN36 . . . . . 195 C2
Lindsey Lower Sch & Com
Arts Coll DN35 . . . . 192 D6
Lindsey Pl HU4 . . . . 179 D6
Lindsey Rd
Cleethorpes DN35 . . . . 192 F4
Stamford PE9 . . . . 219 C6
4 Uffington PE9 . . . . 172 C6
Lindsey Rise 3 DN33 . . . . 194 F8
Lindsey Sch The DN35 . . . 192 E4
Lindsey St 2 DN16 . . . . . . 183 C2
Lindsey Way LN11 . . . . 198 D4
Lindum Ave
3 Immingham DN40 . . . . 186 B3
Lincoln LN2 . . . . 234 C3
Lindum Cotts PE13 . . . . . . 170 B2
Lindum Cres 5 DN20 . . . 196 B4
Lindum Gr
Chapel St Leonard PE24 . . . 90 E7
2 Crowle DN17 . . . . 16 C7
Lindum Rd
Cleethorpes DN35 . . . . 193 A4
Lincoln LN2 . . . . 234 B3
Lindum Sq 5 PE25 . . . . . 206 B5
Lindum St DN15 . . . . 183 B3
Lindum Terr LN2 . . . . 234 C3
Lindum Way 9 PE11 . . . . 134 F2
Lindum Wlk 1 LN7 . . . . . . 32 A4
Linecroft La DN10 . . . . 40 B4
Linga La LN5 . . . . 93 A3
Lingfield Cl 6 LN1 . . . . 66 D3
Ling Garth PE1 . . . . 226 B8
Linghall La LN4 . . . . 111 E5
Ling House La DN7 . . . . 14 A5
Ling La NG33 . . . . 152 C5
Ling Moor Prim Sch
LN6 . . . . 204 E3
Lings La DN7 . . . . 14 D3
Lingwood Pk 5 PE3 . . . . . 225 A1
Linkage Coll PE23 . . . . 100 F7
Link Rd PE1 . . . . 225 F3
Links Ave 2 LN12 . . . . 64 B5
Links Cres 4 PE25 . . . . . . 103 E4
Linkside PE3 . . . . 220 F1
Links Rd DN35 . . . . 193 A3
Link The
Bracebridge Heath
LN4 . . . . 205 F4
Kingston upon Hull HU4 . . 179 C5
2 Leasingham NG34 . . . . 121 B8
Louth LN11 . . . . 198 E5
2 Navenby/Wellingore
LN5 . . . . 107 A7
Linkway 7 DN7 . . . . 14 F3
Link Way PE11 . . . . 214 E4
Linley Cl 4 NG23 . . . . 91 D4
Linley Dr PE21 . . . . 208 E2
Linnaeus St HU3 . . . . 180 C6
Linnet PE2 . . . . 229 D6
Linnet Cl
Birchwood LN6 . . . . 204 D8
7 Market Deeping PE6 . . 217 C5
Scunthorpe DN15 . . . . 182 D6
Linnet Dr PE10 . . . . 143 A3
Linnet Way 11 NG34 . . . . . 212 B3
Linthorpe Gr HU10 . . . . . . 178 E8
Linton 21 HU15 . . . . 2 C6
Linton Cl
Freiston PE22 . . . . 137 E7
Westwoodside DN9 . . . . 27 A2
Linton Rise 3 DN15 . . . . . . 8 A4
Linton St 5 LN5 . . . . 201 F1
LINWOOD LN8 . . . . 57 D5
Linwood Ave 5 DN33 . . . 194 F8
Linwood Cl
Gainsborough DN21 . . . . . 197 F3
9 Sleaford NG34 . . . . 212 C6
Linwood Rd
Lissington LN8 . . . . 57 D3
Martin LN4 . . . . 96 B3
Linwood Warren Nature
Reserve* LN8 . . . . 58 A6
Liquorpond St 11 PE21 . . 208 F4
Lisburn Cl 7 LN5 . . . . 205 D2
Lisburn Gr DN33 . . . . 191 D2
Lisle Marsden Prim Sch
DN32 . . . . 191 E4
Lissett Cl 6 LN6 . . . . 204 B6
LISSINGTON LN3 . . . . 57 E2
Lissington Cl 2 LN2 . . . . 201 F7
Lissington Rd
Gainsborough DN21 . . . . . 197 E3
Wickenby LN3 . . . . 57 C1
Lister Rd
Peterborough PE1 . . . . 225 F7
Scunthorpe DN15 . . . . 182 C3
Lister St
Grimsby DN31 . . . . 191 B8
Kingston upon Hull HU1 . . 180 E5
LISTOFT PE24 . . . . 89 F7
Listoft La PE24 . . . . 89 F7
Litchfield Cl PE7 . . . . 233 F5
Little Bargate St LN5 . . . . 205 E8
Littlebeck Cl HU3 . . . . 180 A7
Littlebeck Rd 3 DN36 . . . . 36 C8
Little Belt The DN21 . . . . . 197 D7
LITTLEBOROUGH DN22 . . . . 52 F1
Littleborough La DN21 . . . 53 A1
Littleborough Rd DN22 . . . 52 C2
Littlebury Gdns PE12 . . . . 215 C2
LITTLE BYTHAM NG33 . . . . 163 A8
Little Bytham Rd
Castle Bytham NG33 . . . . . 152 E1
Counthorpe & Creeton
NG33 . . . . 153 A2
LITTLE CARLTON LN11 . . . . 62 C4
LITTLE CASTERTON
PE9 . . . . 171 E8
Little Casterton Rd
PE9 . . . . 218 F8
LITTLE CAWTHORPE
LN11 . . . . 61 E2
Littlechild Dr 4 PE13 . . . 170 B2
Little Cl
Edenham PE10 . . . . 153 D5
15 Eye PE6 . . . . 175 A1
LITTLE COATES DN34 . . . . . 190 F7
Littlecoates Prim Sch
DN31 . . . . 188 D1
Little Coates Rd DN34 . . . 190 E4
Little Comm PE12 . . . . 215 B7
LITTLE COMMON PE12 . . . . 215 B8
Little Dog Dro PE12 . . . . . 158 C1
Little Dowgate PE13 . . . . . 170 B1
Little Dro PE20 . . . . 124 C2
Littlefair Rd 6 HU9 . . . . 5 D8
LITTLEFIELD DN34 . . . . 191 B6
Littlefield La
Grimsby DN34 . . . . 191 A6
Marshchapel DN36 . . . . 37 B2
Little Gate La LN4 . . . . 82 A1
Little George St HU8 . . . . 181 A8
Little Gonerby CE (Aided)
Infant's Sch NG31 . . . . . . 211 B5
LITTLE GRIMSBY LN11 . . . . . 49 B2
Little Grimsby La LN11 . . . 49 A1
LITTLE HALE NG34 . . . . 133 E8
Little Hale Dro NG34 . . . . 133 F8
Little Hale Rd NG34 . . . . . 122 E1
Little Holme Rd PE34 . . . . 161 C2
Little Johns Cl PE3 . . . . . . 224 F3
Little John St DN34 . . . . . 191 B7
Little La
Broomfleet HU15 . . . . 1 C6
6 Collingham NG23 . . . . . . 91 C4
Gringley on the Hill DN10 . . 39 C1
Louth LN11 . . . . 198 C5
Surfleet PE11 . . . . 145 B3
5 Welbourn LN5 . . . . 106 E5
Whaplode PE12 . . . . 158 A5
Wrawby DN20 . . . . 196 F6
LITTLE LIMBER DN37 . . . . . . 22 C5
LITTLE LONDON
Legsby LN8 . . . . 58 A5
Long Sutton PE12 . . . . 216 D5
Little London PE12 . . . . . . 216 D6
LITTLE LONDON
Spalding PE11 . . . . 214 A1
Tetford LN9 . . . . 73 F2
Little Marsh La PE12 . . . . 159 B7
Little Mason St 3
HU1 . . . . 181 A7
Littlemeer PE2 . . . . 229 F4
Little Merebalk La LN9 . . . 86 B2
Little Michael St DN31 . . . 191 B7
Littlemoors La PE22 . . . . . 113 A3
Little Northfields PE9 . . . 172 E4
LITTLE PONTON NG31 . . . . 140 A7
Littleport La 3 PE22 . . . . 113 B1
Little Ramper PE13 . . . . . . 170 B4
Little Scrubs Wood Nature
Reserve* LN8 . . . . 70 E1
Little Side Rd PE20 . . . . . 135 E8
Little S St 16 LN11 . . . . . . 198 B5
LITTLE STEEPING
PE23 . . . . 101 D5
Little Steeping Mud & Stud
Cottage* PE23 . . . . 101 D6
LITTLE SUTTON PE12 . . . . . 160 C5
Little Thorpe La LN6 . . . . . 79 F1
LITTLE WELTON LN11 . . . . . 60 F6
LITTLE WISBEACH
NG34 . . . . 143 C6
Little Wlk DN21 . . . . 40 B5
Littlewood Rd DN8 . . . . 15 B8
Littleworth Dro
Deeping St Nicholas
PE11 . . . . 156 D1
Heckington NG34 . . . . 122 F4
Spalding PE11 . . . . 156 E2
Sutton St Edmund PE12 . . . 176 F8
Livermore Gn PE4 . . . . 220 E6
Liverpool Dr LN6 . . . . 200 B2
Liverpool St HU3 . . . . 180 A3
Livesey Rd DN36 . . . . 48 E6
Livingstone Dr PE11 . . . . . 214 B2
Lloyd Pl 10 DN21 . . . . 55 A8
Lloyds Ave DN17 . . . . 184 F8
Lobelia Dr 1 DN17 . . . . . . 185 A1
LOBTHORPE NG33 . . . . 152 A3
Loch Fyne Cl PE2 . . . . 229 B4
Loch Lomond Way
PE2 . . . . 229 C4
Lockham Gate PE22 . . . . . 114 B2
Lockhill DN31 . . . . 189 A2
Lock Hill 30 DN8 . . . . 15 A8
Locking Cl 17 LN6 . . . . 204 C6
Locking Garth LN11 . . . . 49 D5
Lock Keepers Ct HU9 . . . . 181 C6
Lock Keepers Way
LN11 . . . . 198 D7
Lock La DN8 . . . . 15 A8
Lock Rd
Alvingham LN11 . . . . 49 F2
North Coates DN36 . . . . 37 A3
Locks Cl PE6 . . . . 174 A8
Locksley Christian Sch
LN11 . . . . 62 C6
Locksley Cl
6 Boston PE21 . . . . 208 E7
4 North Somercotes
LN11 . . . . 50 F7
Locksley Way 5 LN11 . . . . 50 F7
Lockton Cl 2 PE20 . . . . . . 135 B7
Lockton Ct 10 DN37 . . . . . 190 E8
Lockton Gr 1 HU5 . . . . 179 D8
Lockwood Bank DN9 . . . . . . 27 E6
Lockwood Cl 12 DN8 . . . . . 15 B8
Lockwood Ct 1 DN15 . . . . 182 E4
Lockwood St HU2 . . . . 180 F8
Loder Ave PE3 . . . . 224 F2
Lodge Ave 22 DN18 . . . . 10 F8
Lodge Cl
10 Brough HU15 . . . . 2 C7
Kingston upon Hull HU13 . 178 F1
6 Welton/Dunholme
LN2 . . . . 68 D7
Lodge Ct 37 DN7 . . . . 14 D4
Lodge Cvn Pk LN4 . . . . 207 A4
Lodge Dr LN6 . . . . 105 A8
Lodge Gdns HU13 . . . . 178 C2

Middle Dro *continued*
Holland Fen with Brothertoft PE21 . . . . 208 A7
Kirton PE20 . . . . 124 D2
Newton PE13 . . . . 169 E4
Middle Fen Dro PE20 . . . . 134 D4
Middle Fen La LN4 . . . . 82 C5
Middlefield PE7 . . . . 230 D3
Middlefield La
Gainsborough DN21 . . . . 197 E2
1 Glentham LN8 . . . . 43 F1
Middlefield Sch of Tech The DN21 . . . . 197 E3
Middlegate LN5 . . . . 92 F2
Middlegate Cl 12 DN19 . . . . 11 C8
Middlegate La
Bonby DN20 . . . . 10 C3
Elsham DN20 . . . . 21 A7
Orby PE24 . . . . 89 D2
South Ferriby DN18 . . . . 10 B7
Middlegate Rd PE20 . . . . 136 C6
Middlegate Rd E PE20 . . . . 136 D5
Middlegate Rd (West) 1 PE20 . . . . 136 D6
Middleham Cl
3 Kingston upon Hull HU9 . . . . 181 E8
2 Peterborough PE7 . . . . 231 F5
Middle Holme La 3 NG23 . . . . 91 A8
Middle La
Amcotts DN17 . . . . 7 E1
Sturton le Steeple DN22 . . . . 52 E3
Thorpe on the Hill LN6 . . . . 92 F8
Middlemarsh Rd PE24 . . . . 103 A7
Middle Marsh Rd PE12 . . . . 146 F7
Middlemere Bank PE22 . . . . 126 E7
Middlemore Yd 1 NG31 . . . . 211 B4
Middle Pasture 3 PE4 . . . . 220 F5
Middleplatt Rd DN40 . . . . 186 E5
MIDDLE RASEN LN8 . . . . 57 B8
Middle Rasen Prim Sch LN8 . . . . 57 B8
Middle Rd
Crowland PE6 . . . . 166 E1
Newborough PE6 . . . . 221 E7
Terrington St Clement PE34 . . . . 161 D4
Tydd St Mary PE13 . . . . 160 B1
7 Whaplode PE12 . . . . 158 B7
Middle St
Aisthorpe LN1 . . . . 67 D7
Cammeringham LN1 . . . . 55 A1
Corringham DN21 . . . . 41 E2
Croxton Kerrial NG32 . . . . 138 D4
Dunston LN4 . . . . 95 C5
Farcet PE7 . . . . 231 C2
Fillingham DN21 . . . . 55 A5
Gunby & Stainby NG33 . . . . 151 B5
5 Lincoln LN6 . . . . 93 C8
7 Metheringham LN4 . . . . 95 D4
14 North Kelsey LN7 . . . . 32 A4
5 Potterhanworth LN4 . . . . 82 B1
Rippingale PE10 . . . . 142 F2
Scampton LN1 . . . . 67 D6
Scotton DN21 . . . . 29 C1
5 Skillington NG33 . . . . 151 A8
South Carlton LN1 . . . . 67 D3
Willoughton DN21 . . . . 42 E3
Middlesykes La LN11 . . . . 62 C7
Middlethorpe Prim Sch DN35 . . . . 192 D3
Middle Thorpe Rd DN35 . . . . 192 D3
Middleton PE3 . . . . 225 A4
Middleton Cl 9 DN17 . . . . 29 D7
Middleton Ct HU5 . . . . 180 B8
Middleton Prim Sch PE3 . . . . 225 A4
Middleton Rd
Newark NG24 . . . . 104 B6
Scunthorpe DN16 . . . . 185 B4
Middleton's Field LN2 . . . . 234 B4
Middletons Rd PE7 . . . . 233 E5
Middleton St HU3 . . . . 180 C8
Middleton Way NG34 . . . . 121 C7
Midfield Pl 16 DN36 . . . . 36 D8
Midfield Rd DN36 . . . . 36 D8
Midfield Way 14 DN41 . . . . 23 A4
Midgate PE1 . . . . 226 A2
Mid Gate PE22 . . . . 113 E3
Midgate (East) PE22 . . . . 113 E1
Midgate La PE22 . . . . 113 E1
Midgley Cl HU3 . . . . 180 C5
Midholm LN3 . . . . 203 E5
Midia Cl LN1 . . . . 201 C7
Midland Ind Est DN16 . . . . 185 D8
Midland Rd
Peterborough PE3 . . . . 225 E3
Scunthorpe DN16 . . . . 183 D1
Midsummer Gdns PE12 . . . . 216 A4
Midthorpe La 3 LN9 . . . . 85 E7
MIDVILLE PE22 . . . . 113 E8
Midville Cl 10 LN1 . . . . 201 E8
Midville La PE22 . . . . 100 B1
Midville Rd
Midville PE22 . . . . 113 B7
Toynton All Saints PE23 . . . . 100 F4
Midway Cl 9 LN2 . . . . 68 D2
Midway Gr HU4 . . . . 179 E4
Milcroft Cres DN7 . . . . 14 D4
Mildenhall Dr LN6 . . . . 204 B8
Mildmay Rd PE4 . . . . 225 D8
Mildmay St LN1 . . . . 234 A4
Mile Dro PE6 . . . . 173 F5
Mile End Ave 19 DN7 . . . . 14 D3
Mile La LN12 . . . . 64 A2
Miles Bank PE11 . . . . 214 C7
Miles Cross Hill LN13 . . . . 75 D1
Miles Hawk Cl 26 LN12 . . . . 77 A7
Milestone La PE11 . . . . 145 C1
Milfoil La 11 PE12 . . . . 167 B8
Milford Ct 3 DN32 . . . . 189 C1
Milford Ct Bsns Pk LN11 . . . . 198 A8
Milkinghill La PE20 . . . . 135 A5
Milking Nook Dro PE10 . . . . 154 F3
Milking Nook Rd PE6 . . . . 221 C8
Millard Ave DN7 . . . . 14 D4
Millard Nook 30 DN7 . . . . 14 D4
Mill Bank PE12 . . . . 159 A5
Mill Baulk Rd 3 DN10 . . . . 39 F3
Millbeck Bank HU15 . . . . 1 E8
Millbeck Dr LN2 . . . . 202 B8
Millbrook Cl 3 LN6 . . . . 93 B8
Millbrook La LN8 . . . . 70 C4
Millbrook Sch DN16 . . . . 185 B6
Millbrook Way 30 DN18 . . . . 10 F8
Mill Cl
7 Alford LN13 . . . . 75 F3
Billinghay LN4 . . . . 109 E5
5 Brigg DN20 . . . . 196 A3
4 Croft PE24 . . . . 102 E2
5 Marshchapel DN36 . . . . 37 C2
Murrow PE13 . . . . 177 D5
2 North Leverton with Habblesthorpe DN22 . . . . 52 B1
Waltham DN37 . . . . 194 E3
26 Wisbech PE13 . . . . 170 D1
Mill Cres
Peterborough PE2 . . . . 229 E4
20 Scotter DN21 . . . . 29 C3
Mill Croft
3 Scawby DN20 . . . . 30 F8
1 Scunthorpe DN16 . . . . 185 D7
Mill Ct
Lincoln LN1 . . . . 234 A4
1 Waddingham DN21 . . . . 43 D7
Mill Dr NG31 . . . . 211 C2
Mill Dro
Bourne PE10 . . . . 213 E7
Cowbit PE12 . . . . 157 B2
Crowland PE6 . . . . 175 A8
Deeping St Nicholas PE11 . . . . 155 D1
Millennium Fst Coll PE25 . . . . 206 B3
Miller Ave DN32 . . . . 192 C6
Miller Cl 12 DN8 . . . . 15 B7
Miller La DN8 . . . . 15 B7
Miller Rd DN21 . . . . 41 A1
Millers Brook DN9 . . . . 16 E1
Millers Cl
Heighington/Washingborough LN4 . . . . 81 E4
4 Sleaford NG34 . . . . 212 C2
Miller's Cl PE10 . . . . 143 A3
Millers Ct LN11 . . . . 198 C6
Millers Dale 2 LN6 . . . . 204 F2
Millers' Gate PE22 . . . . 113 A2
Millers Quay 6 DN20 . . . . 196 A3
Millers Rd LN5 . . . . 93 F6
Millers Rest PE12 . . . . 158 C7
Millers Way
6 Alford LN13 . . . . 75 F3
6 Heckington NG34 . . . . 122 E2
Mill Farm Est LN4 . . . . 207 B5
MILLFIELD PE1 . . . . 225 F5
Mill Field 1 LN12 . . . . 64 C2
Millfield Ave
Grimsby DN33 . . . . 191 D3
8 Saxilby LN1 . . . . 66 D2
Mill Field Cl 6 PE6 . . . . 173 C4
Millfield Cres NG32 . . . . 119 B6
Mill Field Ct 11 DN3 . . . . 14 A3
Millfield Gdns 6 PE6 . . . . 166 F1
Millfield La E PE20 . . . . 136 D7
Millfield La W PE20 . . . . 136 D7
Millfield Prim Sch LN4 . . . . 81 F4
Millfield Rd
Bratoft PE24 . . . . 102 C7
3 Market Deeping PE6 . . . . 217 A6
21 Metheringham LN4 . . . . 95 C4
7 Morton PE10 . . . . 154 C7
South Somercotes LN11 . . . . 50 F5
Thorne/Moorends DN8 . . . . 15 A8
Mill Field Rd
8 Donington PE11 . . . . 134 E2
Fishlake DN7 . . . . 14 C8
Scunthorpe DN16 . . . . 183 E3
Millfields
22 Barton-upon-Humber DN18 . . . . 10 E8
18 Caistor LN7 . . . . 33 B4
Millfields Way 9 DN19 . . . . 11 C8
Mill Field Terr NG34 . . . . 212 D5
Millfield The 1 DN20 . . . . 31 A5
Mill Garth DN35 . . . . 192 D3
Millgate 10 LN5 . . . . 107 A7
Mill Gate PE12 . . . . 158 B1
Mill Gn Rd PE11 . . . . 214 A7
Millgood Cl LN11 . . . . 198 D5
MILL HILL PE24 . . . . 103 B8
Mill Hill
Ellerker HU15 . . . . 2 A8
Friskney PE22 . . . . 114 F6
Gringley on the Hill DN10 . . . . 39 B1
Nettleham LN2 . . . . 68 C2
Mill Hill Cres DN35 . . . . 192 E5
Mill Hill Dr DN16 . . . . 185 C3
Millhill La 12 PE20 . . . . 135 B7
Mill Hill Rd DN7 . . . . 14 E3
Mill Hill Way LN11 . . . . 62 A8
Mill House La 1 DN15 . . . . 9 B5
Millhouse St Rise 5 DN40 . . . . 186 A4
Mill House Windmill* DN17 . . . . 7 C4
Mill La
Addlethorpe PE25 . . . . 90 D1
Ashby with Scremby PE23 . . . . 88 D3
Aubourn Haddington & South Hykeham LN5 . . . . 92 F5
8 Barrow upon Humber DN19 . . . . 11 C8
Beesby with Saleby LN13 . . . . 75 F5
Bicker PE20 . . . . 135 B4
Billinghay LN4 . . . . 109 E5
Boston PE21 . . . . 208 E4
Brant Broughton & Stragglethorpe LN5 . . . . 105 E5
Bratoft PE24 . . . . 102 C7
Brigg DN20 . . . . 196 B2
Brough HU15 . . . . 2 C6
9 Broughton DN20 . . . . 19 E3
Burgh on Bain LN8 . . . . 59 D5
Butterwick PE22 . . . . 126 E4
Caistor LN7 . . . . 33 C4
Castor PE5 . . . . 223 F1
7 Croxton Kerrial NG32 . . . . 138 D4
Donington PE11 . . . . 134 F2
Eagle & Swinethorpe LN6 . . . . 79 C2
East Halton DN40 . . . . 12 D6
Firsby PE24 . . . . 102 A7
Fleet PE12 . . . . 168 C2
Fosdyke PE20 . . . . 136 D1
Friskney PE22 . . . . 115 C7
Gainsborough DN21 . . . . 197 B8
Gorefield PE13 . . . . 169 E1
Gosberton PE11 . . . . 145 C6
4 Goxhill DN19 . . . . 5 A1
Grainthorpe LN11 . . . . 50 B8
Great Ponton NG33 . . . . 140 A5
Hackthorn LN2 . . . . 56 B1
Haxey DN9 . . . . 27 B2
Heighington/Washingborough LN4 . . . . 81 E4
Hemingby LN9 . . . . 72 B1
Heydour NG32 . . . . 131 B5
Hogsthorpe PE24 . . . . 90 B7
Holbeach PE12 . . . . 215 B5
Holton le Clay DN36 . . . . 36 B4
Horbling NG34 . . . . 133 B3
Horncastle LN9 . . . . 199 B4
Huttoft LN13 . . . . 76 E4
Immingham DN40 . . . . 186 A4
8 Keelby DN41 . . . . 23 A4
5 Ketton PE9 . . . . 171 A3
Kingston upon Hull HU10 . . . . 178 C6
Kirton in Lindsey DN21 . . . . 30 C1
Kirton PE20 . . . . 136 A7
Legbourne LN11 . . . . 61 F3
Lincoln LN5 . . . . 201 E1
Little Steeping PE23 . . . . 101 C6
Louth LN11 . . . . 198 B7
Maltby le Marsh LN13 . . . . 75 F8
Manby LN11 . . . . 62 C7
4 Marshchapel DN36 . . . . 37 C2
Marston NG32 . . . . 118 D2
Martin LN4 . . . . 96 C3
Middle Rasen LN8 . . . . 57 C7
Minting LN8 . . . . 71 B2
Mumby LN13 . . . . 76 F1
Newton PE13 . . . . 169 F5
North Clifton NG23 . . . . 78 C7
3 North Kelsey LN7 . . . . 32 A4
Osgodby LN8 . . . . 45 A3
Owmby LN8 . . . . 55 E6
Peterborough PE5 . . . . 228 F7
Pickworth NG34 . . . . 132 A1
Saltfleetby LN11 . . . . 51 C1
Saxilby LN1 . . . . 66 D2
Scamblesby LN11 . . . . 72 F5
Scawby DN20 . . . . 30 F8
Skegness PE25 . . . . 206 A8
Skidbrooke with Saltfleet Haven LN11 . . . . 51 C4
10 South Ferriby DN18 . . . . 10 A7
South Somercotes LN11 . . . . 50 D4
South Witham NG33 . . . . 151 C1
Sturton by Stow LN1 . . . . 66 C6
Sutterton PE20 . . . . 135 F2
19 Sutton Bridge PE12 . . . . 160 E4
Swineshead PE20 . . . . 135 A8
Tallington PE9 . . . . 172 F7
Tetford LN9 . . . . 73 E1
Thorney PE8 . . . . 228 B7
Tydd St Mary PE13 . . . . 160 B1
Wainfleet All Saints PE24 . . . . 102 C1
Walkeringham DN10 . . . . 39 F3
Welbourn LN5 . . . . 106 F4
Welton le Marsh PE23 . . . . 89 A3
Welton LN2 . . . . 68 E8
West Keal PE23 . . . . 100 B4
West Walton PE14 . . . . 170 F4
Whaplode PE12 . . . . 158 B7
Wigsley NG23 . . . . 78 F4
Wildmore LN4 . . . . 111 C4
Willoughby with Sloothby LN13 . . . . 89 C6
Woodhall Spa LN10 . . . . 97 B5
Wrangle PE22 . . . . 114 D1
Wrawby DN20 . . . . 20 E3
Mill La Cl PE24 . . . . 90 B7
Mill La W HU15 . . . . 2 B6
Mill Marsh Rd PE12 . . . . 146 D2
Mill Mere Rd
Corringham DN21 . . . . 41 D2
5 Waddington LN5 . . . . 93 F7
Mill Moor Way 3 LN6 . . . . 204 D1
Millom Way DN32 . . . . 191 F8
Mill Pl DN35 . . . . 192 F6
Millport Dr HU4 . . . . 179 B2
Mill Race DN36 . . . . 36 E4
Mill Rd
Addlethorpe PE24 . . . . 90 D2
Boston PE21 . . . . 209 B3
Claypole NG23 . . . . 117 E7
Cleethorpes DN35 . . . . 192 E5
Crowle DN17 . . . . 16 D8
Donington on Bain LN11 . . . . 59 E2
Hibaldstow DN20 . . . . 30 E4
2 Keadby DN17 . . . . 17 D5
Lincoln LN1 . . . . 234 A4
Luddington & Haldenby DN17 . . . . 7 C4
Market Rasen LN8 . . . . 57 D7
Maxey PE6 . . . . 173 C7
Pilsgate PE9 . . . . 172 C3
Swanland HU14 . . . . 3 A6
Walpole PE14 . . . . 170 F6
Wisbech St Mary PE13 . . . . 177 D5
Mill Rise
6 Navenby/Wellingore LN5 . . . . 107 A7
14 Scothern LN2 . . . . 68 F4
Swanland HU14 . . . . 3 A6
Mill Row
Barrowby NG32 . . . . 129 B3
2 Lincoln LN1 . . . . 234 A4
Mills Cl 15 NG23 . . . . 117 D3
Mills Dr DN7 . . . . 26 A8
Mills Service Rd DN16 . . . . 19 A4
Mill St
Kingston upon Hull HU1 . . . . 180 E6
Ryhall PE9 . . . . 163 C2
Scamblesby LN11 . . . . 73 A4
Millstone Cl LN9 . . . . 199 A3
Millstone La 3 PE9 . . . . 172 D3
Millstream Rd LN4 . . . . 81 E4
MILLTHORPE NG34 . . . . 143 B6
Millthorpe Dro NG34 . . . . 143 E5
Millthorpe Rd NG34 . . . . 143 B5
Mill View
Peterborough PE7 . . . . 229 A5
5 Waltham DN37 . . . . 194 E4
Mill View Cl DN9 . . . . 27 D7
Millview Ct LN9 . . . . 199 B4
Mill View Ct 12 LN8 . . . . 70 D4
Millview Gdns 3 DN20 . . . . 20 E3
Millview Rd
11 Heckington NG34 . . . . 122 E2
Ruskington NG34 . . . . 108 D2
Mill View Rd 9 LN8 . . . . 70 D4
Milman Rd LN2 . . . . 202 B4
Milne Gn 4 PE20 . . . . 135 B7
Milners Ct 22 PE9 . . . . 219 C5
Milner's La 2 PE23 . . . . 87 F1
Milnyard Sq PE2 . . . . 229 C2
Milson Cl
18 Barton-upon-Humber DN18 . . . . 10 E8
7 Broughton DN20 . . . . 19 D4
Coningsby LN4 . . . . 207 D4
Milson Rd 17 DN41 . . . . 23 A4
Milton Cl
Branston LN4 . . . . 81 D2
Cherry Willingham LN3 . . . . 203 E5
2 Gainsborough DN21 . . . . 197 E6
Milton Dr PE13 . . . . 170 B1
Milton Rd
Gainsborough DN21 . . . . 197 E6
Grimsby DN34 . . . . 191 B4
Peterborough PE2 . . . . 231 A7
Scunthorpe DN16 . . . . 185 B5
Milton St
Lincoln LN5 . . . . 205 E7
Newark-on-Trent NG24 . . . . 104 A3
Milton Way
Kirkby la Thorpe NG34 . . . . 121 E4
Peterborough PE3 . . . . 224 E3
2 Sleaford NG34 . . . . 212 F3
Mimosa Ct DN16 . . . . 185 E4
Mina Cl PE2 . . . . 231 D4
Minden Pl 4 DN21 . . . . 55 A8
MININGSBY PE22 . . . . 99 D7
Minnett's Hill NG32 . . . . 130 B8
Minnow Cl 1 DN37 . . . . 190 D7
Minshull Rd DN35 . . . . 192 F4
Minster Dr
Cherry Willingham/Reepham LN3 . . . . 203 E7
Louth LN11 . . . . 198 D4
Minster Precincts 9 PE1 . . . . 226 A2
Minster Rd
15 Misterton DN10 . . . . 39 F5
Scunthorpe DN15 . . . . 182 B2
Minster Yd LN2 . . . . 234 B3
MINTING LN9 . . . . 84 D8
Minting Cl 9 LN1 . . . . 201 E8
Minting La LN9 . . . . 71 D1
Mint La LN1 . . . . 234 A2
Mint St LN1 . . . . 234 A2
Mirfield Rd
Grimsby DN32 . . . . 191 F4
Scunthorpe DN15 . . . . 182 C4
Misson Bank DN9 . . . . 26 C3
MISTERTON DN10 . . . . 39 F5
Misterton PE2 . . . . 229 E3
Misterton Cty Prim Sch DN10 . . . . 39 F4
Mitchell Cl
Eastgate PE1 . . . . 226 C2
3 Hatfield DN7 . . . . 14 D5
7 Skellingthorpe LN6 . . . . 200 A4
Mitchell Dr LN1 . . . . 201 C6
Mitchell Rd LN4 . . . . 207 F6
Mitre La 16 PE21 . . . . 208 F5
Moat House Rd 22 DN21 . . . . 30 B1
Moat La
Bolingbroke PE23 . . . . 100 A8
Old Leake PE22 . . . . 114 B1
3 South Killingholme DN40 . . . . 12 E3
4 Welbourn LN5 . . . . 106 E5
Moat Rd
Scunthorpe DN15 . . . . 8 C1
Terrington St Clement PE34 . . . . 161 F1
Moat Wlk NG31 . . . . 211 E6
Modder St 1 DN16 . . . . 185 B6
Moggswell La PE2 . . . . 230 B4
Moira Cl 5 DN7 . . . . 14 D7
Mole Dro PE12 . . . . 168 C1
Mollison Ave DN35 . . . . 192 F5
Mollison Rd HU4 . . . . 179 A3
Monarch Ave PE2 . . . . 231 A6
Monarchs Rd PE20 . . . . 136 A3
Monce Cl LN2 . . . . 68 C7
Monckton Way LN2 . . . . 68 D5
Mondemont Cl 4 PE12 . . . . 215 E3
Money Bridge La PE11 . . . . 144 F1
Moneys Yd 7 NG34 . . . . 212 D4
Monic Ave HU13 . . . . 178 F2
Monkfield Coll LN5 . . . . 106 C2
Monkhouse Ct 6 PE11 . . . . 214 A3
Monks Abbey Prim Sch LN2 . . . . 202 B4
Monks Ave LN11 . . . . 198 C6
Monks Cl
4 Hatfield DN7 . . . . 14 D5
New Quarrington NG34 . . . . 212 A2
Monks Dr 22 PE6 . . . . 175 A1
Monks Dyke Rd LN11 . . . . 198 D5
Monks Dyke Tech Coll LN11 . . . . 198 D5
Monks Gr PE4 . . . . 220 E5
Monks House La 5 PE11 . . . . 214 A4
Monkshouse Prim Sch PE11 . . . . 214 A3
Monks Leys Terr LN2 . . . . 234 C3
Monks Manor Ct LN2 . . . . 202 B5
Monks Manor Dr LN2 . . . . 202 B4
Monks Mdw 5 PE6 . . . . 175 B8
Monks Rd
Lincoln LN2 . . . . 234 B2
Scunthorpe DN17 . . . . 184 F6
8 Swineshead PE20 . . . . 135 B7
MONKSTHORPE PE23 . . . . 101 E8
Monksthorpe La PE23 . . . . 88 F1
Monks Way LN2 . . . . 202 C3
Monks Way Ind Est LN2 . . . . 202 D3
Monks Wlk 4 PE11 . . . . 214 A4
Monkton 2 HU15 . . . . 2 D6
Monkwood Cl 17 NG23 . . . . 91 D5
Monmouth La PE12 . . . . 216 E8
Monmouth St HU4 . . . . 179 E3
Monsal Dale LN6 . . . . 204 F2
Monson Ct LN5 . . . . 201 E1
Monson Pk LN6 . . . . 200 A4
Monson Rd DN21 . . . . 42 A8
Monson St LN5 . . . . 234 A1
Mons Rd LN1 . . . . 201 E6
Mons St HU5 . . . . 180 A8
Montague St
Cleethorpes DN35 . . . . 189 D1
Lincoln LN2 . . . . 234 C2
Montague Terr 1 LN2 . . . . 234 C2
Montagu Rd PE4 . . . . 225 D8
Montaigne Cl 3 LN2 . . . . 202 D7
Montaigne Cres LN2 . . . . 202 D7
Montaigne Gdn LN2 . . . . 202 D7
Montbretia Dr 2 DN17 . . . . 185 A1
Monteith Cres PE21 . . . . 209 B5
Montgomery Rd
Cleethorpes DN35 . . . . 192 D5
Skegness PE25 . . . . 206 A3
Montrose Cl
8 Grantham NG31 . . . . 211 D7
1 Lincoln LN6 . . . . 204 E1
10 Stamford PE9 . . . . 218 E6
Montrose Gr NG34 . . . . 121 A2
Montrose St 5 DN16 . . . . 183 B2
Monument Rd 5 PE20 . . . . 135 A4
Monument St PE1 . . . . 226 A3
Moody La DN31 . . . . 188 C3
Moon's Gn 3 PE12 . . . . 157 F6
Moor Bank PE22 . . . . 113 C3
MOORBY PE22 . . . . 99 B6
Moorby Cl LN1 . . . . 201 E7
Moor Closes Nature Reserve* NG32 . . . . 120 A2
Moor Dike Rd DN7 . . . . 26 A8
Moore Cl NG23 . . . . 117 F7
Moor Edges Rd DN8 . . . . 15 B8
Moore's La 1 PE6 . . . . 175 A1
Moor Farm Nature Reserve* LN10 . . . . 98 A6
Moorfield Rd 2 PE3 . . . . 225 D3
Moorfields La DN14 . . . . 6 F7
Moor Gate PE12 . . . . 159 A4

Newland St W 2 LN1 234 A2
Newlands Ct DN21 197 E5
Newlands Pk DN36 193 B1
Newlands Rd
2 Haconby PE10 154 D8
Parson Drove PE13 177 D7
Surfleet PE11 145 F4
Newland View 17 DN9 27 E6
Newland Wlk DN15 182 E3
NEW LEAKE PE22 114 A8
New Leake Prim Sch PE22 113 F7
Newlyn Cl
4 Kingston upon Hull HU13 179 A2
New Waltham DN36 195 C7
Newman Cl 19 PE8 172 B1
Newmarch Ct DN33 191 B2
Newmarket LN11 198 C4
Newmarket Cl PE1 226 B6
Newmarket St 4 DN32 191 F8
NEW MEADOW PE7 231 F2
New Meadow Dro PE7 231 D1
New Mill Field Rd DN7 14 E3
Newnham Cres DN16 185 A4
New Options Barton Sch DN18 11 A8
New Pk Est 1 DN7 14 D7
Newport LN2 234 B4
Newport Ave NG31 210 D4
Newport Cl 4 HU3 180 D5
Newport Cres 2 LN5 93 F7
Newport Ct 1 LN1 234 B4
Newport Dr DN15 9 A6
Newport St 8 DN18 3 F1
Newport Wlk DN40 186 D3
NEW QUARRINGTON NG34 212 A2
New Rd
Blankney LN10 96 F5
Brantingham HU15 2 C8
Cleethorpes DN35 192 F6
Clipsham LE15 162 B7
1 Collyweston PE9 171 B1
Croft PE24 103 C3
Deeping St Nicholas PE6 166 D5
5 Easton on the Hill PE9 171 D3
9 Eye PE6 175 A1
Folksworth PE7 232 E6
Laceby DN37 35 A8
Langtoft PE6 164 F3
Peterborough PE1 226 B2
Quadring PE11 145 C8
Ryhall PE9 163 C1
Scunthorpe DN17 184 B6
Silk Willoughby NG34 121 A1
Spalding PE11 214 D4
Staunton NG13 117 B2
Sutton Bridge PE12 160 F5
Swinefleet DN14 6 C4
Thistleton LE15 151 D1
Wainfleet All Saints PE24 101 E2
Waltham DN37 194 E4
Worlaby DN20 10 D1
New River Dro
Cowbit PE12 156 F3
3 Spalding PE12 214 C1
New River Gate PE12 168 D8
New Roman Bank PE34 161 D3
New Row
Gonerby Hill Foot NG31 210 E7
3 Market Deeping PE6 217 D4
8 Messingham DN17 29 D7
Newsham Dr DN34 191 A7
Newsham Garth HU4 179 B5
Newsham La DN39 22 D8
New St
Aby with Greenfield LN13 75 B5
7 Brigg DN20 196 C3
Elsham DN20 20 E7
1 Gainsborough DN21 197 C5
Grantham NG31 211 A5
Grimsby DN31 191 E7
5 Heckington NG34 122 E2
Helpringham NG34 133 D7
6 Louth LN11 198 B5
Osbournby NG34 132 D5
Sleaford NG34 212 E4
4 Stamford PE9 219 C6
Newstead Ave
Cherry Willingham/Reepham LN3 203 E5
Holton le Clay DN36 195 E2
Newstead Cl PE6 175 A2
Newstead Rd
Cleethorpes DN35 192 E4
2 Mablethorpe/Sutton on Sea LN12 64 C3
Newstead PE9 219 F6
Ryhall PE9 163 D1
Newstead St HU5 180 A8
NEWTOFT LN8 56 E5
NEWTON
Newton and Haceby NG34 132 A3
Newton PE13 170 A5
Newton Bar NG34 132 A3
NEWTON BY TOFT LN8 56 E6
Newton Cl
8 Metheringham LN4 95 C4
Swinderby LN6 92 A5
5 Wragby LN8 70 D4
Newton Ct 6 NG33 151 E7
Newton Dr LN3 203 C6
Newton Gr DN33 191 C4
Newton La
Binbrook LN8 47 D5
15 Ruskington NG34 108 E2
Newton Marsh La DN36 36 F6
NEWTON ON TRENT LN1 65 D1
Newton-on-Trent CE Prim Sch LN1 65 C1
Newton Pk 10 NG23 117 D3
Newton Rd DN16 185 E6
Newton St
5 Grantham NG31 211 B4
3 Kingston upon Hull HU3 180 B4
Lincoln LN5 234 B1
Newark-on-Trent NG24 104 A4
Newton Terr LN11 198 C5
Newton Way
5 Colsterworth NG33 151 D7
Sleaford NG34 212 D5
Newtown
8 Spilsby PE23 101 A8
Stamford PE9 219 D5
New Town 6 PE9 171 D3
Newtown Ct HU9 181 E7
Newtown Sq HU9 181 E7
New Trent St DN17 16 E6
NEW WALTHAM DN36 195 D7
New Waltham Prim Sch DN36 195 C7
New Wlk HU14 3 A4
NEW YORK LN4 111 C5
New York Prim Sch LN4 111 C4
New York Rd LN4 110 F6
Nicholas Ct 26 DN18 10 E8
Nicholas Taylor Gdns 1 PE3 224 F3
Nicholas Way DN21 41 E2
Nichol Hill 2 LN11 198 B5
Nicholls Ave PE3 225 E3
Nicholson Rd
3 Healing DN41 24 A5
Immingham DN40 12 E4
Nicholson St 8 DN35 192 F5
Nicholson Way 7 DN9 27 D7
Nicolette Way 10 PE11 214 B5
Nicolgate La DN20 196 D4
Nicolson Dr 18 DN18 10 F8
Nidd's La PE20 136 E4
Nightingale Cl DN15 182 D5
Nightingale Cres 1 LN6 204 E8
Nightingale Ct PE4 221 E2
Nightingale Dr PE7 233 D6
Nightingales 13 PE6 217 C5
Nightleys Rd DN22 65 B5
Ninescores La DN9 26 B4
Ninth Ave
3 Fixborough Ind Est DN15 8 A1
Grantham NG31 211 F5
NINTHORPE PE25 206 D6
Nipcut Rd PE6 175 C2
NOCTON LN4 95 B7
Nocton Com Prim Sch LN4 95 C7
Nocton Dr LN2 201 F8
Nocton Fen La LN4 83 A1
Nocton Rd
7 Potterhanworth LN4 82 B1
Potter Hanworth LN4 95 B8
Noel St DN21 197 C6
Nooking La DN37 23 D2
Nookings Dr 3 DN20 31 A5
Nooking The DN9 27 C3
Nookin The 1 LN5 106 E5
Nook The
Croxton Kerrial NG32 138 D3
7 Easton on the Hill PE9 171 D3
4 Helpston PE6 173 C4
Sproxton LE14 150 C7
Norbeck La LN2 68 C6
Norburn
2 Peterborough PE3 220 F1
Peterborough PE3 225 B8
Norfolk Ave DN15 8 B4
Norfolk Bank La HU15 1 F8
Norfolk Cl 1 LN8 47 B6
Norfolk Cres
Bracebridge Heath LN4 205 F4
1 Scampton Airfield LN1 67 E5
Norfolk Ct 19 DN32 189 C1
Norfolk La DN35 192 E7
Norfolk Pl 4 PE21 208 F6
Norfolk St Ind Est PE21 208 F7
Norfolk Sq 5 PE9 219 B6
Norfolk St
Boston PE21 208 F6
Kingston upon Hull HU2 180 E7
Lincoln LN1 201 C4
Peterborough PE1 225 F4
Norland Ave HU4 179 C6
Norman Ave 5 PE21 208 F5
NORMANBY DN15 8 C3
NORMANBY-BY-SPITAL LN8 55 E7
NORMANBY BY STOW DN21 53 E1
Normanby Cliff Rd LN8 55 D7
Normanby Hall Ctry Pk* DN15 8 C3
NORMANBY LE WOLD LN7 45 F5
Normanby Pk Farming Mus* DN15 8 C3
Normanby Prim Sch LN8 55 E7
Normanby Rd
Burton upon Stather DN15 8 C3
Nettleton LN7 33 B2
3 Owmby LN8 55 F6
Scunthorpe DN15 183 A5
Stow DN21 53 F1
Normanby Rise LN8 45 E5
Norman Cl
9 Barton-upon-Humber DN18 10 F8
30 Metheringham LN4 95 C4
NORMAN CORNER DN37 194 C2
Norman Cres 1 DN17 184 F8
NORMAN CROSS PE7 232 F2
Norman Dr 7 DN7 14 D3
Normandy Cl LN11 198 E6
Normandy Rd DN35 192 D5
Norman Mews 3 PE10 213 D5
Norman Rd
Grimsby DN34 191 B7
Hatfield DN7 14 D3
Peterborough PE1 226 C4
Norman St 1 LN5 234 B1
NORMANTON
Bottesford NG13 128 A7
Normanton NG32 119 D5
Normanton La NG13 128 A6
Normanton Rd
3 Beacon Hill NG24 104 B5
1 Crowland PE6 166 F1
Peterborough PE1 226 D7
Normanton Rise HU4 179 C7
Nornabell St 1 HU8 181 C8
Norris Cl 10 NG34 122 D3
Norris St LN5 201 F1
Norsefield Ave DN37 194 E5
Nortcote Heavy Horse Ctr* PE23 101 D7
Northam Cl PE6 175 B3
Northampton Rd DN16 183 C1
North Ave PE10 153 D6
North Axholme Comp Sch DN17 16 D7
North Bank
Crowland PE6 166 E1
Thorney PE6 227 D1
North Bank Rd 4 PE1 226 D3
NORTHBECK NG34 132 F8
North Beck La PE23 87 E1
NORTHBOROUGH PE6 217 E2
Northborough Prim Sch PE6 173 F6
Northborough Rd PE6 174 C5
North Bracing PE25 206 E3
NORTH CARLTON LN1 67 C4
NORTH CARR DN9 27 C3
North Carr La DN20 9 F3
North Carr Rd
Misterton DN10 39 F7
Scotter DN17 28 E5
West Stockwith DN10 40 B6
North Causeway LN4 82 D4
North Church Side 12 HU1 180 F6
Northcliffe Rd NG31 211 A7
North Cliff Rd DN21 30 C2
NORTH CLIFTON NG23 78 C7
North Clifton Prim Sch NG23 78 C6
North Coates Rd DN36 37 A4
NORTH COCKERINGTON LN11 50 A1
North Cockerington CE Prim Sch LN11 50 A1
Northcote Heavy Horse Ctr* PE23 101 D7
NORTH COTES DN36 37 A3
North Cotes CE (Controlled) Prim Sch DN36 37 B3
North County Prim Sch DN21 197 B6
North Court 10 LN2 68 C2
North Cres 7 NG13 128 A5
Northcroft 4 LN1 66 D3
Northcroft La NG23 91 C5
North-dale Ct 4 DN21 30 B2
Northdale Pk 1 HU14 3 B7
North Dales Rd LN4 82 A5
North Dr
2 Ancaster NG32 120 A3
5 Balderton NG24 104 C1
Kingston upon Hull HU10 178 E6
RAF Cranwell NG34 107 D1
Swanland HU14 3 B7
North Dro
Bicker PE20 134 E6
Deeping St Nicholas PE11 155 F1
Helpringham NG34 133 E7
Lutton PE12 148 D1
Quadring PE11 144 C8
Swaton NG34 133 E4
North Eastern Rd DN8 15 A8
NORTH ELKINGTON LN11 48 D1
North Elkington La LN11 48 E1
NORTH END LN11 49 E3
North End 5 DN19 12 A8
NORTH END LN11 62 F8
North End DN18 10 A8
NORTH END PE20 135 B8
North End PE13 170 C1
North End Cres 9 DN36 36 D4
North End La
2 Fulbeck NG32 106 C1
Saltfleetby LN11 62 F8
South Cockerington LN11 50 F1
South Kelsey LN7 32 A2
Sturton le Steeple DN22 52 E4
North End Rd 7 DN36 36 D4
Northern Ave DN20 196 C5
Northern Rd NG24 104 A5
Northern's Cl NG33 151 D5
Northey Rd PE6 227 C2
North Farm Rd DN17 184 D3
Northfeild Rd DN21 41 B8
North Fen Dro PE20 134 E4
North Fen Rd
3 Glinton PE6 220 C8
Helpringham NG34 133 D7
NORTH FERRIBY HU14 3 B4
North Ferriby CE Prim Sch HU14 3 A5
Northferry La 2 DN9 16 D1
NORTHFIELD HU13 178 F2
Northfield HU14 3 B7
Northfield Ave
Kingston upon Hull HU13 178 E3
3 Sudbrooke LN2 68 F3
Northfield Cl
19 Ruskington NG34 108 E2
1 Scunthorpe DN16 185 C6
11 Tetney DN36 36 D4
West Butterwick DN17 17 D1
Northfield La
Amcotts DN17 7 E2
North Clifton NG23 78 D7
Thornton Curtis DN39 11 D5
Willoughton DN21 42 C4
Northfield Rd
Ashby with Scremby PE23 88 D1
Kingston upon Hull HU3 179 F6
Messingham DN17 185 A1
North Leverton with Habblesthorpe DN22 52 D1
Peterborough PE1 225 F7
4 Ruskington NG34 108 E2
Sleaford NG34 212 A2
Welton LN2 68 D7
North Field Rd PE6 217 B7
Northfield Rise 1 LN1 66 C2
Northfields
Bourne PE10 213 D7
Stamford PE9 219 C6
Northfields Ct PE9 219 C6
North Foreland Dr 3 PE25 206 D8
North Forty Foot Bank PE21 208 A6
Northgate
Kingston upon Hull HU13 178 E2
Lincoln LN2 234 B4
Louth LN11 198 B5
NORTHGATE PE11 144 D1
North Gate
Gosberton PE11 145 A6
Newark-on-Trent NG24 104 A5
Pinchbeck PE11 144 E1
Sleaford NG34 212 D5
Northgate Ct LN11 198 B6
Northgate La LN11 62 B7
Northgate Sports Hall NG34 212 D5
NORTH GREETWELL LN2 203 B8
North Halls 1 LN8 47 C5
NORTH HARBY NG23 79 C7
North Heath La NG32 106 D1
North Holme 8 DN36 36 D4
North Holme Rd LN11 198 B7
NORTH HYKEHAM LN6 204 D2
North Ing Dro PE11 134 C4
Northing La LN2 68 F5
North Ings La LN13 77 A5
North Ings Rd DN7 14 E5
Northings The 1 NG32 210 B4
North Intake La DN9 40 C8
NORTH KELSEY LN7 32 A4
NORTH KELSEY MOOR LN7 32 D4
North Kelsey Prim Sch LN7 32 A4
North Kelsey Rd LN7 33 A4
North Kesteven Ctr* LN6 204 D1
North Kesteven Sch LN6 204 D1
NORTH KILLINGHOLME DN40 12 D3
NORTH KYME LN4 109 F4
North Kyme Cty Prim Sch LN4 109 E3
North La
Coningsby LN4 110 E8
Marshchapel DN36 37 C2
2 Navenby/Wellingore LN5 107 A8
Reepham LN3 68 F1
North La *continued*
Swaby LN13 74 E4
NORTHLANDS PE22 113 A4
Northlands Ave 3 DN15 9 A5
Northlands La PE22 113 A4
Northlands Rd
Glentworth DN21 54 E6
Winterton DN15 9 A6
Northlands Rd S 10 DN15 9 A5
North Leverton CE Sch DN22 52 B1
NORTH LEVERTON WITH HABBLESTHORPE DN22 52 B1
North Leys Rd DN22 52 E1
North Lincoln Rd DN16 183 F2
North Lincolnshire Mus* DN15 183 A2
North Lindsey Coll DN17 184 E8
North Marsh Rd DN21 197 C6
Northminster PE1 226 A3
North Moor Dr 2 DN10 39 F3
North Moor La
Martin LN4 96 B3
Messingham DN17 29 B8
Northmoor Rd DN17 6 C1
North Moor Rd
Scotter DN17 29 C5
Walkeringham DN10 39 F3
North Moss La DN41 187 B1
Northolme
Gainsborough DN21 197 D5
Sutton St Edmund PE12 168 E5
Northolme Circ 2 HU13 178 E2
Northolme Cres
Kingston upon Hull HU13 178 E2
Scunthorpe DN15 182 F3
Northolme Ct LN11 198 C7
Northolme Rd HU13 178 E2
Northon's La PE12 215 C3
NORTH ORMSBY LN11 48 E4
NORTHORPE
Donington PE20 134 E3
Northorpe DN21 42 A8
Thurlby PE10 164 C8
Northorpe Cl LN6 204 F7
Northorpe La PE10 164 C8
Northorpe Rd
Donington PE11 134 D3
Halton Holegate PE23 101 B8
Scotton DN21 29 D1
NORTH OWERSBY LN8 44 E5
North Parade
Gainsborough DN21 197 F4
Grantham NG31 211 A6
Holbeach PE12 215 E3
Lincoln LN1 234 A3
Scunthorpe DN16 185 D6
Skegness PE25 206 D3
4 Sleaford NG34 212 D7
North Parade Extension PE25 206 E5
North Prom DN35 192 E7
North Quay DN31 189 C3
North Ramper DN21 44 A7
NORTH RAUCEBY NG34 120 E5
North Rd
Bourne PE10 213 D8
Bratoft PE24 102 B8
7 Cranwell NG34 107 F1
Gedney Hill PE12 168 D4
1 Keadby with Althorpe DN17 17 C6
Kingston upon Hull HU4 179 E4
Leadenham LN5 106 D3
Mablethorpe & Sutton LN12 64 B1
Sleaford NG34 212 C5
Sturton le Steeple DN22 52 B4
Tattershall Thorpe LN4 97 F3
Tetford LN9 73 F1
Tydd St Mary PE13 160 B2
NORTH RESTON LN11 62 B2
North Scaffold La NG23 91 D3
NORTH SCARLE LN6 78 F2
North Scarle Miniature Railway* LN6 78 F1
North Scarle Prim Sch LN6 78 E2
North Scarle Rd NG23 91 F8
North Sea La DN35 193 A1
North Shore Rd PE25 206 D6
Northside 2 DN9 27 C2
Northside La DN22 52 C1
North's La DN37 34 D8
NORTH SOMERCOTES LN11 50 F8
North Somercotes CE (Controlled) Prim Sch LN11 50 F7
North St
1 Barrow upon Humber DN19 11 D8
2 Boston PE21 208 F6
Bourne PE10 213 D5
Caistor LN7 33 B4
Cleethorpes DN35 192 F6
3 Crowland PE6 166 E1
9 Crowle DN17 16 D8
Digby LN4 108 E6
Folksworth PE7 233 A1

North St *continued*
Gainsborough DN21 197 C5
7 Grantham NG31 211 A5
Horncastle LN9 199 C4
Kingston upon Hull HU10 178 E6
Middle Rasen LN8 57 B8
Morton DN21 197 C8
8 Nettleham LN2 68 C2
Osbournby NG34 132 C5
Owston Ferry DN9 28 B3
Peterborough PE1 226 A2
Roxby cum Risby DN15 9 A4
Scunthorpe DN15 183 B4
Stamford PE9 219 B5
Sturton le Steeple DN22 52 B3
Thimbleby LN9 85 B5
West Butterwick DN17 17 D1
West/East Butterwick DN17 28 D8
Winterton DN15 9 B6
North Terr PE1 226 E7
NORTH THORESBY DN36 36 B1
North Thoresby Prim Sch DN36 36 A1
Northumberland Ave
13 Scampton Airfield LN1 67 E5
6 Stamford PE9 219 A6
Northumberland Cl DN34 191 B6
Northumbria Rd NG34 212 B2
North Walls HU1 181 A6
North Warren Rd DN21 197 B6
Northway 3 LN11 49 B8
North Way
6 Lincoln LN6 204 D2
Marshchapel DN36 37 B2
NORTH WILLINGHAM LN8 58 D7
NORTH WITHAM NG33 151 D4
North Witham Bank LN1 234 A2
North Witham Rd NG33 151 D3
Northwood Dr
Hessle HU13 178 B3
Sleaford NG34 212 C6
NORTON DISNEY LN6 92 C2
Norton Disney Rd LN5 92 D1
Norton Gr HU4 179 D4
Norton La
Bishop Norton LN8 43 C2
Thurlby LN6 92 C4
Norton Rd
Peterborough PE1 225 F6
Scunthorpe DN16 185 B5
Stapleford LN6 105 C8
Norton St NG31 211 A3
Norwell La NG23 91 E1
Norwich Ave DN34 191 A4
Norwich Cl
Heighington/Washingborough LN4 203 E1
3 Sleaford NG34 212 C7
Norwich Dr LN4 81 A2
Norwich Rd PE13 170 E1
Norwich Way 7 NG31 210 E5
Norwood Ave DN15 182 F2
Norwood Cl 3 HU10 178 E7
Norwood La
Borough Fen PE6 174 E1
Peterborough PE4 221 F2
Norwood Prim Sch PE4 221 C3
Norwood Rd
7 Hatfield DN7 14 C5
4 Skegness PE25 103 E4
Norwood St HU3 180 C7
Nostell Rd DN16 183 D1
Nottingham Rd 1 NG13 128 A5
Nottingham Terr 5 LN2 234 C3
Nottingham Way PE1 226 C6
Novello Garth HU4 179 B4
Nowells La 6 PE10 213 D5
Nuffield Cl 6 DN16 185 B4
Nunburnholme Ave 5 HU14 3 A4
Nunburnholme Pk HU5 179 B7
Nunnerley Pl DN37 194 F5
Nuns Cnr DN33 191 C4
Nuns Rd DN17 184 F6
NUNSTHORPE DN33 191 B4
Nunsthorpe & Bradley Pk Children's Ctr DN33 191 A4
Nunthorpe Cl 38 DN7 14 D4
Nursery Cl
4 Barton-upon-Humber DN18 3 F1
14 Dunholme LN2 68 E6
Peterborough PE1 226 A4
10 Saxilby LN1 66 D2
Scunthorpe DN17 184 F3
Nursery Ct
15 Brough HU15 2 C5
Sleaford NG34 212 D2
Nursery Dr PE13 170 E2
Nursery Gdns
25 Alford LN13 75 F2
6 Holton le Clay DN36 195 D2
Nursery Gr LN2 202 A6
Nursery La
Belvoir NG32 138 C6
Morton DN21 40 D3
Peterborough PE1 226 D2
Nursery Rd
Boston PE21 209 B2
Cranwell & Byard's Leap NG34 120 C8
Nursery St 2 LN8 57 D7
Nurses La
Skellingthorpe LN6 200 A5
4 Wymondham LE14 150 C1
Nutfields Gr 7 DN7 14 C6
Nut La PE22 114 C1
Nutwood View 4 DN16 185 D4

O

Oak Ave
13 Brough HU15 2 C6
Grimsby DN32 191 E4
5 Scawby DN20 30 F8
11 Welton/Dunholme LN2 68 E6
Oak Cl
8 Ingoldmells PE25 90 D3
Louth LN11 198 E4
14 Sudbrooke LN2 68 F2
5 Woodhall Spa LN10 97 E6
Oak Cres
Boston PE21 208 E7
Bourne PE10 213 B6
Cherry Willingham/Reepham LN3 203 D5
Oak Ct 1 PE11 214 E3
Oakdale Ave
3 Kingston upon Hull HU10 178 E8
Peterborough PE2 231 D4
Oakdale Cl 4 NG31 211 A8
Oakdale Prim Sch PE7 231 C4
Oak Dr HU5 179 B7
Oak Farm Paddock LN6 204 C1
Oakfield 16 LN1 66 D2
Oakfield Cl 2 DN20 196 E3
Oakfield Prim Sch DN16 185 A5
Oakfield St LN2 202 B3
Oakford Cl DN17 184 D8
Oak Gr
13 Barnetby le Wold DN38 21 B4
3 Barrow upon Humber DN19 11 C7
6 Market Deeping PE6 217 B6
Oakham Ave 5 LN12 64 A3
Oakham Cl NG31 210 E6
Oakham Terr 2 PE21 208 F3
Oakham Wlk DN40 186 E3
Oak Hill LN4 203 B2
Oak House La PE22 126 C4
Oakhurst Cl NG31 211 D2
Oakland Ave 39 DN7 14 D4
Oakland Cl 3 LN1 201 D7
Oaklands
3 Beckingham DN10 40 A1
8 Collingham NG23 91 D4
Eastfield PE1 226 B4
5 Woodhall Spa LN10 97 D5
Oaklands Dr
Kingston upon Hull HU13 178 D3
4 Wisbech PE13 170 E1
Oaklands Rd DN40 186 C5
Oaklands The 6 LN8 70 D4
Oakland Way 13 PE11 145 C1
Oakleaf Rd PE1 226 C6
Oakleigh DN16 185 C3
Oakleigh Dr
Canwick LN1 201 C6
Peterborough PE2 230 C6
Oakleigh Rd NG31 210 C3
Oakleigh Terr LN1 201 C6
Oakley Dr PE11 214 E6
Oakley Pl PE12 147 F2
Oak Rd
Glinton PE6 220 B8
1 Healing DN41 24 A5
Scunthorpe DN16 185 B7
Sleaford NG34 212 D2
Stamford PE9 218 D7
Oakroyd Cres 22 PE13 170 D1
Oakside Pk Ind Est NG34 212 F6
Oaks La DN10 39 F2
Oaks The
Balderton NG24 104 C2
15 Nettleham LN2 68 D2
1 Scothern LN2 68 F3
Oak Tree Ave DN21 197 F6
Oaktree Cl 3 PE11 145 B7
Oak Tree Cl
3 Long Bennington NG23 117 D3
7 Market Rasen LN8 57 D7
Oak Tree Dr LN6 92 D4
Oak Tree Mdw LN9 199 C5
Oak Tree Wlk 25 DN17 16 D7
Oak View
13 Dunholme LN2 68 E6
Peterborough PE3 224 F2
Oak Way
Cleethorpes DN35 192 D2
3 Heckington NG34 122 D3
Oakwell Cl DN16 185 D7
Oakwood Ave 4 LN6 204 C8
Oakwood Cl HU10 179 A7
Oakwood Dr DN37 190 C7
Oakwood Glade PE12 215 C3
Oakwood Pk PE12 146 E2
Oakwood Rise 2 DN16 185 B4
OASBY NG32 131 C6
Oasby Rd NG32 131 C7
Oat Dr NG34 212 E3
Oatfield Way NG34 122 D2
Oban Cl 7 PE9 218 E6
Oban Ct 6 DN40 186 C3
Oberon Cl LN1 201 C6
OBTHORPE PE10 164 C6
Obthorpe La PE10 164 C7
Occupation La
Anderby PE24 77 C3
Carrington PE22 99 C1
6 North Kelsey LN7 32 A4
Swanland HU14 3 B8
Occupation Rd
Great Gonerby NG32 129 C6
Lincoln LN1 234 A4
Peterborough PE1 225 E6
Ocean Ave PE25 206 D1
Ocean Bvd HU9 181 B6
Octagon Dr 14 PE13 170 C1
Octavia Cl 23 PE13 170 E1
Odecroft PE3 225 C7
Odin Ct DN33 191 B2
Off Haydons Ave PE25 206 A4
Ogilvy Dr DN17 184 F3
Ogrey PE10 164 C7
O'Hanlon Ave DN20 196 D3
Old Annandale Rd HU10 178 C8
Old Bailey Rd PE7 233 C8
Old Barn Ct
Fleet Hargate PE12 159 C8
Ludford LN8 59 A7
Old Barracks The NG31 211 C4
Old Black Dro NG34 109 D1
OLD BOLINGBROKE PE23 100 B8
Old Boston Rd LN4 207 D3
Old Bowling Gn 4 LN13 75 F2
Old Brickkiln La LN5 92 F2
Oldbrook PE3 220 E1
Old Brumby St DN16 185 A8
Old Carpenter's Yd 1 DN7 14 B6
Old Chapel Ct 2 DN21 43 D7
Old Chapel La
2 Burgh le Marsh PE24 102 E7
9 Laceby DN37 23 F1
Old Chapel Rd LN6 200 A4
Old Church La 1 PE23 101 D7
Old Church Rd PE24 90 D4
OLD CLEE DN32 192 C6
Old Clee Infants & Jun Sch DN32 192 B6
Old Courts Rd 2 DN20 196 C3
Old Courtyard The 1 DN21 65 D6
Old Crosby DN15 183 A5
Old Dairy 11 DN19 11 D8
Old Dairy The PE21 209 A1
Olde Curiosity Mus★ LN12 64 C3
Old Epworth Rd (East) 1 DN7 14 F4
Old Farm Ct 4 DN37 194 C4
Old Fen Bank
Wainfleet All Saints PE24 101 F2
Wainfleet St Mary PE24 102 A1
Old Fen Dike
Gedney PE12 158 F1
Sutton St James PE12 169 B8
Old Fendike Rd PE12 157 B3
Old Fen La
Coningsby LN4 207 E1
Pinchbeck PE11 145 A1
Old Fen Rd PE22 115 A8
Oldfield Cl
9 Barnby Dun DN3 14 A4
1 Stainforth DN7 14 B6
Oldfield Cres 16 DN7 14 C6
Oldfield La PE22 127 C6
Old Field La DN7 14 A5
Oldfield Rd 20 DN8 15 B7
Old Fleet DN37 190 C6
OLD FLETTON PE2 231 A6
Old Fletton Prim Sch PE2 230 F6
Old Forge Rd 7 DN10 39 F5
Old Forty Foot Bank NG34 123 C1
OLD GATE PE12 159 F3
Old Great N Rd
Stamford PE9 218 C8
Thorney PE8 228 B7
Wansford PE8 222 C2
Wothorpe PE9 219 C2
Old Hall Gdns 5 NG24 104 C5
Old Hall La 6 PE11 145 D2
Old Hall Spinney NG32 119 C2
Oldham Dr 8 PE11 145 C1
Old Hammond Beck Rd PE21 208 A2
Old Haxey Rd DN10 39 F6
Old Hill The NG32 138 C6
Old Hundred La PE12 167 F2
Old Inn La PE12 146 E7
Old Ironside Rd DN16 183 D3
Old Knarr Fen Dro PE6 176 C2
Old Lane DN14 6 F7
Oldlane Gate DN14 6 D4
OLD LEAKE PE22 114 A1
Old Leake Prim Sch PE22 114 A1
Old Leicester Rd PE8 222 A3
Old Leys La DN21 43 A3
Old Lincoln Rd NG32 119 B7
Old Lynn Rd 2 PE13 170 E1
Old Main Rd
2 Barnetby le Beck DN37 35 B6
Fleet Hargate PE12 159 C7
Fosdyke PE20 146 D8
Irby DN37 34 D7
Old Leake PE22 114 B1
Scamblesby LN11 72 F5
Old Market Ave
4 Hundleby PE23 87 F1
12 Spilsby PE23 87 F1
Spilsby PE23 100 F8
Old Market Pl DN31 191 D7
Old Mill La
10 Broughton DN20 19 E3
Grimoldby LN11 62 B6
Horncastle LN9 199 C3
Whitton DN15 1 E3
Wrawby DN20 196 F7
Old Mill Pk LN11 198 C6
Old Nick Theatre DN21 197 D4
Old North Rd PE8 222 A3
Old Oak Pl PE10 213 E4
Old Orchard NG32 210 A5
Old Paddock Ct 1 LN9 199 B4
Old Place 3 NG34 212 F4
Old Plumtree La 3 DN36 36 B1
Old Pond Cl 7 LN6 200 D1
Old Pond La PE5 223 E2
Old Pond Pl 20 HU14 3 A4
Old Post La NG33 151 D6
Old Post Office La
8 Barnetby le Wold DN38 21 B4
Butterwick PE22 126 E4
4 South Ferriby DN18 10 A7
Old Rectory Dr
1 Tallington PE9 172 F7
Wansford PE8 222 A6
Old Rectory Gdns DN16 185 A6
Old Rectory The★ DN9 27 E6
Old Road
Grimsby DN37 190 C8
Healing DN37 24 B5
Old Roman Bank
3 Skegness PE25 206 D6
Terrington St Clement PE34 161 E3
Old School Dr 14 DN20 30 F5
Old School La
4 Billinghay LN4 109 F6
6 Cranwell NG34 120 F8
Donington on Bain LN11 59 E2
5 Fishtoft PE21 126 C1
2 North Kelsey LN7 32 A4
Scunthorpe DN16 185 B3
Old School Mews 12 PE23 88 A1
Old School Yd 17 DN21 30 B1
Old Showfields DN21 197 D6
Old Sluice Rd PE12 215 B8
Old Smithy Ct 1 LN4 207 D4
Old Smithy & Heritage Ctr The★ DN9 23 B3
OLD SOMERBY NG33 140 D8
Old South Eau Bank PE12 168 A1
Old Stack Yd The 3 DN20 196 F6
Old Station Yd
Bottesford NG13 128 B6
Morton PE10 154 D6
Old Thorne Rd DN7 14 E4
Old Trent Rd DN21 197 A5
Old Upper Ings La DN22 52 D3
Old Vicarage La
12 Lutton PE12 160 A8
Lutton PE12 216 C8
Old Vicarage Pk 2 DN20 30 E8
Old Village St DN15 17 E6
Old Wainfleet Rd 1 PE25 206 B3
Old Warp La 11 DN18 10 A7
Old Wharf Rd 9 NG31 211 A4
Old Wood 1 LN6 200 C1
Old Wood Cl LN6 200 C1
OLD WOODHALL LN9 85 A2
Oliver Cl 5 NG24 104 A4
Oliver Ct DN31 191 D8
Olive Rd PE1 226 C7
Oliver Quibell Cty Infants Sch NG24 104 A3
Oliver Rd 16 NG23 117 D3
Oliver St DN35 192 D8
Olivier Ct HU4 179 E3
Ollard Ave PE13 170 D1
Olsen Rise LN2 202 D6
Omega Bvd DN8 14 F8
On Hill 17 HU14 3 B7
Ontario Rd DN17 184 E3
Onyx Gr 2 HU3 180 A4
Oole Rd DN35 192 F6
Oosterbeek Cl 5 PE10 213 E7
Opportune Rd 25 PE13 170 D1
Orangawood Cl 7 NG31 210 F8
Orange Row 3 PE34 161 F3
ORANGE ROW PE34 161 F3
Orange Row Rd 1 PE34 161 F3
Orb La DN15 183 A7
ORBY PE24 89 C2
Orby Bank PE24 89 D3
Orby Gr DN33 191 A3
Orby Holme Field La PE24 89 D3
Orby Rd
Addlethorpe PE24 90 B4
Burgh le Marsh PE24 89 D1
Orchard Ave 8 DN21 29 C3
Orchard Cl
4 Barrow upon Humber DN19 11 C7
23 Barton-upon-Humber DN18 10 F8
Bassingham LN5 92 F3
Billinghay LN4 109 E6
4 Blyton DN21 41 C5
4 Bourne PE10 213 C6
6 Burringham DN17 17 D4
9 Burton upon Stather DN15 8 B5
Cherry Willingham/Reepham LN3 203 D5
11 Donington PE11 134 F2
4 Gonerby Hill Foot NG31 210 E8
Great Hale NG34 122 E1
2 Hatfield DN7 14 C3
6 Helpringham NG34 133 D7
Kingston upon Hull HU10 178 F7
1 Kirton in Lindsey DN21 30 B2
Leverington PE13 170 B2
Louth LN11 198 C7
2 Mablethorpe/Sutton on Sea LN12 64 A3
4 Market Deeping PE6 217 D4
12 Messingham DN17 29 D7
25 Metheringham LN4 95 C4
2 Morton PE10 154 C7
4 Moulton PE12 157 F6
Peterborough PE3 225 D3
9 Pinchbeck PE11 156 E8
8 Scothern LN2 68 F4
5 Scunthorpe DN16 185 B6
2 Sleaford NG34 212 F4
15 Stamford PE9 219 B5
7 Welton/Dunholme LN2 68 D6
Whaplode PE12 215 A7
Orchard Croft
4 Epworth DN9 27 D7
5 Grimsby DN33 194 E7
Orchard Ct
3 Thorney PE6 175 F3
Waltham DN37 194 D4
Orchard Dr
7 Burton upon Stather DN15 8 B5
3 Gunness DN15 17 E6
3 Hatfield DN7 14 C3
12 Heckington NG34 122 E2
Kingston upon Hull HU13 178 E1
2 Rampton DN22 65 A5
Walton Highway PE14 170 F4
Winteringham DN15 2 B1
Orchard Garth 16 LN5 93 E8
Orchard Gr
Boston PE21 209 B6
1 Hatfield DN7 14 D5
Misterton DN10 40 A4
Orchard La 12 LN1 66 D2
Orchard Mews PE2 230 F8
Orchard Pk 4 LN11 62 C6
Orchard Rd
Barnack PE9 172 E3
5 Fiskerton LN3 82 A7
Kingston upon Hull HU4 179 B5
4 Stamford PE9 219 B5
Orchard Sch NG24 104 B3
Orchard St
Boston PE21 208 D6
Lincoln LN1 234 A2
Peterborough PE2 230 F7
2 Spalding PE11 214 D3
22 Thorne/Moorends DN8 15 A8
Orchards The
Harrowby Est NG31 211 C6
Immingham DN40 186 B3
8 Middle Rasen LN8 57 B8
Peterborough PE2 229 F4
Orchard The
Market Deeping PE6 217 B5
New Waltham DN36 195 C6
Peterborough PE4 221 A3
Washingborough LN4 203 A2
Orchard Way
4 Coningsby LN4 207 C4
5 Cowbit PE12 167 B8
Easton on the Hill PE9 171 C3
1 Mablethorpe/Sutton on Sea LN12 64 A3
3 Market Rasen LN8 57 E8
6 Nettleham LN2 68 D2
Orchid Cl PE7 233 F7
Orchid Rd LN5 205 C2
Orchid Rise DN15 182 F2
Orchid Way PE25 206 A4

Ordoyno Gr 2 NG24 104 C5
Ore Blending Rd DN16 19 A4
Orford Rd LN8 47 B5
Oribi Cl HU4 179 C2
Oriole Rd DN17 184 E6
Orion Cl 8 HU3 180 B5
Orion Way 4 DN34 190 D4
Orkney Pl DN40 186 C2
Orme La LN11 198 C6
Orme Rd PE3 225 D4
Ormsby Cl DN35 192 D3
Ormsby House Dr 7 PE22 99 A4
Ormsby Rd DN17 184 E5
Ormsby Ring LN11 74 C1
Orton Ave PE2 230 E7
Orton Brick Works PE7 233 B8
ORTON BRIMBLES PE2 229 D5
ORTON GOLDHAY PE2 229 F3
ORTON LONGUEVILLE PE2 230 B5
Orton Longueville Sch PE2 230 A5
ORTON MALBOURNE PE2 230 C4
Orton Mere PE2 230 B7
Orton Parkway PE2 229 D4
ORTON SOUTHGATE PE2 229 C2
ORTON WATERVILLE PE2 229 E4
ORTON WISTOW PE2 229 C6
Orton Wistow Prim Sch PE2 229 C6
Orwell Gr PE4 221 D1
Orwell St DN31 189 C1
Osborne Cl 3 LN1 201 E6
Osborne Dr DN36 195 D1
Osborne Pk 1 PE13 170 C2
Osborne Rd
Immingham DN41 187 B2
Wisbech PE13 170 C2
Osborne St
1 Cleethorpes DN35 192 F6
Grimsby DN31 191 D7
Kingston upon Hull HU1 180 E6
Osborne Way LN9 199 A4
Osborn Way 9 NG34 122 D3
OSBOURNBY NG34 132 C4
Osbournby Prim Sch NG34 132 C5
Osbourne Cl PE4 221 D1
Osbourne Way 7 PE6 217 A5
Ose 3 PE25 206 B6
Oseby La NG34 133 A1
OSGODBY
Lenton Keisby and Osgodby NG33 141 E3
Osgodby LN8 45 A3
Osgodby Prim Sch LN8 45 A3
Osgodby Rd LN8 44 E5
Osier Ave PE7 230 D2
Osier Rd PE11 214 E5
Oslear Cres DN35 192 E5
Oslear's La LN11 73 D5
Oslinc Ostrich Farm* PE22 99 B7
Osprey PE2 229 F2
Osprey Cl 5 NG34 212 B3
Osric Ct PE1 226 C5
Oster Fen La NG23 104 F1
Ostler Cl 8 NG31 210 F8
Ostler Dr PE10 213 B4
Ostler's La DN18 10 A5
Oswald Rd
Scunthorpe DN15 183 A3
1 Woodston PE2 230 D7
Oswin Cl 1 NG34 212 C2
OTBY LN8 46 A4
Otby La LN8 46 A3
Ottawa Rd DN17 184 E4
Otter Ave 11 LN1 66 D2
Otterbrook PE2 229 D5
Otterburn St 6 HU3 180 A5
Otters Cotts LN5 205 D7
Oulton Cl LN6 205 A2
Oundle Cl
Heighington/Washingborough LN4 203 C1
Scunthorpe DN16 185 C3
Oundle Rd
5 Mablethorpe/Sutton on Sea LN12 64 C1
Peterborough PE2 229 E6
Our Lady of Lincoln Cath Prim Sch LN2 202 A7
Ousemere Cl 14 NG34 133 B1
Outer Circ Dr LN2 202 C7
Outer Circ Gn LN2 202 C6
Outer Circ Ind Est LN2 202 D5
Outer Circ Rd LN2 202 D5
Outfield PE3 220 E1
Outgang La DN22 65 A6
Outgang The HU15 2 B7
Outgate DN17 16 E7
Out Holme La DN36 36 E3
Oval App LN2 202 B7
Oval The
5 Brough HU15 2 C5
Grimsby DN33 191 C1
5 Hatfield DN7 14 C5
Kingston upon Hull HU10 178 E8
Lincoln LN2 202 B7
Scopwick LN4 108 B7
2 Scunthorpe DN17 184 E3
Overcoat La DN22 65 B7
Overgate Rd NG33 152 D5
Overstone Ct PE3 225 D6
Overton Ave HU10 178 E8
Overton Cl 4 LN5 107 B8
Overton Ct 9 DN18 3 E1
Overton Rd LN4 207 D4
Overton Way PE2 229 F4
Owen Ave HU13 179 A1
Owen Cl 7 PE9 172 D3
Owe's La LN11 51 A5
Owl Cl LN6 92 D5
Owl Dr PE20 135 B7
Owl End PE7 233 D5
Owl End Wlk PE7 233 D5
OWMBY DN38 32 D7
OWMBY-BY-SPITAL LN8 55 F6
Owmby Cliff Rd LN8 55 C5
Owmby Hill DN38 32 D8
Owmby La LN7 32 C5
Owmby Rd
4 Searby cum Owmby DN38 32 D8
Spridlington LN8 55 F3
Owmby Wold La DN38 21 E1
OWSTON FERRY DN9 28 B3
Owston Ferry Rd DN9 27 F1
Owston Rd DN10 40 B6
Oxburgh Cl
3 Peterborough PE7 231 F5
1 Wisbech PE13 170 C1
Oxby Cl 17 NG34 122 E2
Oxclose PE3 225 A8
OXCOMBE LN9 73 D4
Oxcombe Cl DN33 194 D7
Oxcroft Bank
Moulton PE12 157 F1
Whaplode PE12 158 A2
Oxeney Dr 2 LN3 69 C3
Oxford Cl LN4 203 C1
Oxford Ct 1 NG34 212 D7
Oxford Rd
Peterborough PE1 225 F5
6 Stamford PE9 219 A7
Oxford St
Boston PE21 208 F3
Cleethorpes DN35 192 F5
Grantham NG31 211 B3
Grimsby DN32 189 B1
Kingston upon Hull HU2 181 A8
2 Lincoln LN5 234 B1
Market Rasen LN8 57 D8
Scunthorpe DN16 185 D6
Oxlands La PE24 102 B7
Oxmarsh La DN19 4 E2
Oxney Rd PE1 226 D5
Oxney Rd Ind Est PE1 227 A6
Oyster Ct DN35 192 F5

P

Pacey Cl LN6 92 A6
Packhorse Gdns PE20 135 B6
Packman La HU10 178 B8
Paddington Way PE10 154 D7
Paddock Cl
6 Ancaster NG32 120 A2
13 Bracebridge Heath Ln4 81 A1
Ropsley NG33 131 B1
Paddock Ct 5 DN40 186 C3
Paddock Gn 3 PE11 214 D5
Paddock Gr 6 PE21 208 F4
Paddock La
5 Blyton DN21 41 C5
1 Metheringham LN4 95 D4
West Butterwick DN17 17 C1
Paddock Rd NG34 120 C8
Paddock Rise
11 Barrow upon Humber DN19 11 C8
Ingoldsby NG33 141 C5
Paddocks The
1 Barnetby le Beck DN37 35 B6
5 Beckingham DN10 40 A1
6 Bottesford NG13 128 A5
7 Burgh le Marsh PE24 102 E7
Carlton Scroop NG32 119 C3
12 Crowle DN17 16 D7
Gedney PE12 159 E7
Great Hale NG34 122 E1
1 Holbeach PE12 215 E3
Kingston upon Hull HU10 178 B7
10 Long Bennington NG23 117 D4
Newton on Trent LN1 65 C1
2 Peterborough PE4 220 E5
Stapleford LN6 105 C8
Swayfield NG33 152 E5
4 Willingham DN21 53 E3
Paddock The
3 Barkston NG32 130 B8
2 Burton upon Stather DN15 8 B4
4 Cherry Willingham LN3 203 E6
10 Collingham NG23 91 D4
Kingston upon Hull HU4 179 B5
Louth LN11 198 A5
Manby LN11 62 C5
1 Market Deeping PE6 217 A6
2 Marton DN21 65 D8
4 Morton PE10 154 C7
2 North Ferriby HU14 3 A5
Paddock The continued
16 Ruskington NG34 108 D2
Skellingthorpe LN6 200 A4
5 Sleaford NG34 212 F4
5 Stamford PE9 219 A5
16 Sudbrooke LN2 68 F2
3 Swanland HU14 3 C7
Paddock View PE22 100 B2
Pademoor Terr DN17 7 A2
Padholme Rd PE1 226 C3
Padholme Rd E PE1 226 D3
Padley Rd LN2 202 E6
Padleys La PE23 100 C4
Padmoor La DN21 53 C5
Pado La LN13 74 E4
Padstow Wlk DN17 184 C8
Pagehall Cl DN33 191 D1
Paignton Ct DN33 194 E6
Pain La PE22 113 E3
Painshall Cl 11 LN2 68 D7
Painters Way 20 LN12 76 F8
Paisley Prim Sch HU3 180 A6
Paisley St HU3 180 A7
Palace Theatre* NG24 104 A4
Palma Ct 2 PE24 90 D7
Palm Ct PE1 226 B8
Palmer Ave HU10 178 D8
Palmer Ct 3 NG34 212 B6
Palmer La 15 DN19 11 D8
Palmer Rd NG32 129 C6
Palmers Rd PE1 226 F5
Palmerston Rd PE2 230 F7
Palmwood Cl 3 NG31 210 F7
Pamela Cl DN40 186 D4
Pamela Rd DN40 186 D4
Pandyke La PE22 113 F3
PANTON LN8 71 B5
Panton Cl 6 PE6 217 D5
Panton Rd LN8 71 B8
Papermill La
Ewerby & Evedon NG34 121 E7
Tealby LN8 46 D2
Pape's La PE24 101 F4
Papyrus Rd PE4 220 D3
Parade The LN3 203 E6
Paradise La
5 Fulletby LN9 86 B8
Northborough PE6 173 F6
Paradise Pl
6 Brigg DN20 196 B3
Horncastle LN9 199 C3
Paradise Row LN9 199 C4
Paragon St HU1 180 E6
Parish Church Prim Sch DN21 197 C5
Parishes Sh Ctr The DN15 183 B3
Parish Mews 3 DN21 197 D5
Parish's La PE22 115 A4
Park Ave
Allington NG32 128 F7
15 Barton-upon-Humber DN18 10 E8
Billinghay LN4 109 F5
17 Crowle DN17 16 D7
Grimsby DN32 191 E4
Heighington/Washingborough LN4 203 D2
Kingston upon Hull HU13 178 E3
Lincoln LN6 204 F7
Louth LN11 198 E6
21 Mablethorpe/Sutton on Sea LN12 64 B3
Misterton DN10 39 E6
Scunthorpe DN17 184 F3
Skegness PE25 206 D4
Sleaford NG34 212 F4
Spalding PE11 214 C5
3 Spilsby PE23 87 F1
Sutterton PE20 136 A2
Park Cl
1 Gosberton PE11 145 B6
Immingham DN40 186 C4
Lea DN21 52 F5
Spalding PE11 214 C5
8 Sudbrooke LN2 68 F2
Thorney PE6 176 B3
7 Westwoodside DN9 27 A2
Yaxley PE7 233 F5
Park Cres
Heighington/Washingborough LN4 203 D1
16 Metheringham LN4 95 D4
Peterborough PE1 226 B5
Sleaford NG34 212 F4
Swinderby LN6 92 B6
Thorne/Moorends DN8 15 A7
Thorney PE6 176 B3
Park Ct
Scunthorpe DN15 183 B4
2 Weston PE12 157 E7
Park Dr
Grimsby DN32 191 E5
Market Deeping PE6 217 A5
6 Westwoodside DN9 27 A2
Parker Ave LN5 205 D4
Parker Cl DN37 23 E2
Parker Rd
Humberston DN36 36 D8
23 Wittering PE8 172 B1
Parkers Cl 12 PE24 102 E7
Parkers La DN16 185 C6
Parker St DN35 192 F5
Parkes Cl 4 NG24 104 D5
Park Est PE6 217 E4
Park Farm Cres PE7 231 F5
Park Farm Rd
Peterborough PE6 224 E5
Scunthorpe DN15 182 F7
Park Farm Way PE7 231 F6
Parkfield Ave 14 HU14 3 A4
Parkfield Dr HU3 179 F6
Parkfield Rd
7 Ruskington NG34 108 E2
13 Ryhall PE9 163 C1
Park Gate 7 PE21 208 F5
Park Gdns PE12 215 E3
Park Hill
Cherry Willingham/Reepham LN3 203 E5
28 Kirton in Lindsey DN21 30 B1
Parkhill Cres 3 DN3 14 A4
Parkhill Rd 2 DN3 14 A4
Parkhill Rise 7 DN15 9 B5
Park Home Ave PE7 230 D1
Park Home Rd PE7 230 D1
Parkin Rd
7 Cowbit PE12 167 B8
Scunthorpe DN17 184 F4
Parkinson Ave 1 DN15 183 A3
Parkinson's Way 5 LN12 64 C2
Park La
12 Alford LN13 75 F3
Billinghay LN4 109 F5
5 Boston PE21 208 F6
Bracebridge LN5 205 D6
Burton LN1 200 D7
Coningsby LN4 207 C4
Denton NG32 139 A7
2 Donington PE11 134 E2
East Kirkby PE23 99 E5
Ewerby & Evedon NG34 122 B7
Freiston PE22 126 D3
Gorefield PE13 169 F3
Heighington/Washingborough LN4 203 C2
Holbeach PE12 215 E3
Humberston DN35 192 F1
Leverington PE13 170 A3
Long Sutton PE12 216 C5
Manby LN11 62 C5
Peterborough PE1 226 C4
Pinchbeck PE11 145 D3
Redbourne DN21 30 F3
Saxby All Saints DN20 10 A3
1 Scawby DN20 30 F8
1 Skillington NG33 151 A8
Spalding PE11 214 C5
Stamford PE9 219 C4
2 Surfleet PE11 145 D2
Swineshead PE20 135 A7
Westwoodside DN9 27 A2
Wigsley NG23 78 F5
Park La Cl 6 DN7 14 C2
Park La E HU4 179 C6
Parklands
2 Fleet Hargate PE12 159 C7
Mablethorpe/Sutton on Sea LN12 64 B3
1 Mumby LN13 76 F1
4 West/East Butterwick DN17 28 D8
Parklands Ave LN4 95 B7
Parklands Cl 4 NG24 104 C5
Parklands Cres 11 HU14 3 A5
Parklands Dr
4 Harlaxton NG32 139 C7
10 North Ferriby HU14 3 A5
Parkland Way LN8 70 C4
Park La Rd 11 DN7 14 C2
Park La W HU4 179 C5
Park-lea 6 NG34 108 E2
Park Rd
11 Alford LN13 75 F3
1 Allington NG32 128 F7
Boston PE21 208 E2
5 Brough HU15 2 E6
Claxby LN8 45 E4
Grantham NG31 211 B5
Holbeach PE12 215 D2
2 Horncastle LN9 199 C4
Long Sutton PE12 216 C5
Mablethorpe/Sutton on Sea LN12 64 C1
Market Deeping PE6 217 D4
Peterborough PE1 226 A3
Spalding PE11 214 C4
Sutton St James PE12 169 D7
Swinstead NG33 153 A5
1 Weston PE12 157 E7
5 Willingham DN21 53 E3
Park Rd E LN12 64 D1
Park Rd W LN12 64 C1
Park Row
Kingston upon Hull HU3 180 D7
Louth LN11 198 E7
Northfield HU13 178 E2
Parks Cl 4 DN39 12 A1
Parksgate Ave LN6 204 F5
Parkside
17 Nettleham LN2 68 D2
Peterborough PE2 230 B6
Parkside Cres PE11 214 C5
Parkside Dr 13 PE24 90 D7
Parkside The 4 NG33 151 D2
Park Springs Rd DN21 197 F2
Park Sq DN15 183 A2
Parks Rd 3 DN7 14 C4
Park St
Cleethorpes DN35 189 D1
Park St continued
Grimsby DN32 192 B8
Kingston upon Hull HU3 180 D6
Lincoln LN1 234 A2
11 Messingham DN17 29 D7
Peterborough PE2 230 F7
Swinefleet DN14 6 D8
Winterton DN15 9 B5
Parkstone Gr 28 DN7 14 D4
Park Terr PE1 226 A6
Park The
Coningsby LN4 207 D5
Lincoln LN1 234 A2
Potter Hanworth LN4 95 B8
Park View
25 Barton-upon-Humber DN18 10 F8
Cleethorpes DN35 192 C8
Crowle DN17 16 D6
Kingston upon Hull HU4 179 E4
Mablethorpe/Sutton on Sea LN12 64 C1
10 Messingham DN17 29 D7
15 Northorpe PE10 164 C8
13 Thorne/Moorends DN8 15 A7
Park View Ave LN4 81 D2
Park View Cl 7 DN19 11 C7
Park View Terr DN17 28 C8
Parkway The
Kingston upon Hull HU10 178 E8
Spalding PE11 214 A2
Park Wlk
Easton on the Hill PE9 171 D3
Kingston upon Hull HU4 179 B5
Parkwood Prim Sch DN17 184 D8
Parkwood Rise 14 DN3 14 A3
Parliament St
5 Brough HU15 2 D6
7 Kingston upon Hull HU1 180 F6
Peterborough PE1 225 F5
Parnell St 3 DN21 197 C5
Parnwell Prim Sch PE1 226 F7
Parnwell Way PE1 226 F6
Parris Pl DN35 192 D7
Parry Rd 22 LN12 64 B3
Parslins The PE6 217 F5
Parsonage La PE12 159 F1
Parson Dro
Billinghay LN4 109 F7
Pinchbeck PE11 144 B2
Parson Dro La PE13 170 B2
PARSON DROVE PE13 177 D7
Parson La LN5 106 C8
Parsons Dr 3 PE21 208 E7
Parson's Dro
Holland Fen with Brothertoft PE20 124 A8
Swaton NG34 133 D4
Parsons Halt 1 LN11 198 C6
Parsons La 18 LN13 75 F2
Parson's La PE12 168 B4
Parthian Ave PE21 136 D8
PARTNEY PE23 88 A3
Partney CE (Aided) Prim Sch PE23 88 B3
Partney Rd PE23 87 C4
Partridge Cl
4 Caistor LN7 33 B4
4 Scunthorpe DN17 184 E6
Yaxley PE7 233 D6
Partridge Dr LN7 33 F2
Partridge Gn LN6 92 D5
Partridge Gr PE4 220 E5
Pashley Rd DN8 15 B7
PASTON PE4 221 D1
Paston Farm Adventure Ctr* PE4 221 E2
Paston La PE4 221 B1
Paston Parkway PE4 221 C4
Paston Ridings PE4 221 C1
Paston Ridings Prim Sch PE4 221 D1
Pasture Ave 9 DN17 17 D4
Pasture Cl
7 Colsterworth NG33 151 E7
Grantham NG31 211 D1
Pasture Dr LN11 198 D4
Pasture Dro PE10 154 F7
Pasture La
Amcotts DN17 7 D1
Bassingham LN5 93 B2
Belvoir NG32 138 C6
Garthorpe & Fockerby DN17 7 D6
Market Rasen LN8 57 E8
Northborough PE6 173 F6
Pasture Rd DN21 197 F4
Pasture Rd N DN18 3 F1
Pasture Rd S DN18 4 A1
Pastures Ct 36 DN17 29 D7
Pastures Rd NG32 210 A5
Pasture St DN32 191 E7
Pastures The
12 Cowbit PE12 167 B8
12 Long Bennington NG23 117 D3
Old Somerby NG33 140 E8
1 Rampton DN22 65 A5
12 Welton LN2 68 D6
Pasture The PE6 217 C6

Robey St LN5 ... 205 E8
Robin Cl
Bottesford DN16 ... 185 B2
8 Market Deeping PE6 ... 217 C5
12 Sleaford NG34 ... 212 B3
Robin Hood Cl PE3 ... 224 F2
Robin Hood Cres 13 DN3 ... 14 A1
Robin Hood Rd
11 Kirk Sandall DN3 ... 14 A1
Skegness PE25 ... 206 C3
Robin Hood's Wlak PE21 ... 208 E7
Robin Hood's Wlk PE21 ... 208 F6
Robinia Dr HU4 ... 179 C2
Robins Cl PE2 ... 230 E8
Robins Cres LN6 ... 92 D5
Robins Field PE8 ... 222 A4
Robinson Ave 4 LN13 ... 75 E2
Robinson Cl DN15 ... 182 E4
Robinson La
Grimsby DN31 ... 189 C2
Louth LN11 ... 198 C5
Robinson Pl LN5 ... 105 F5
Robinson Rd DN40 ... 186 F6
Robinson St E DN32 ... 191 E7
Robinson's Gr 8 DN20 ... 31 A5
Robinson's La 1 DN36 ... 36 B1
Robins Wood PE8 ... 222 A4
Robson Rd DN35 ... 192 D7
Rochdale Rd DN16 ... 185 A5
Rochester Ave HU4 ... 179 B3
Rochester Cl
8 Bracebridge Heath LN4 ... 81 A2
1 Scunthorpe DN17 ... 184 C7
Rochester Ct
2 Bourne PE10 ... 213 C7
Humberston DN35 ... 193 A1
Rochester Dr
Birchwood LN6 ... 200 D2
9 Grantham NG31 ... 210 E5
Rochford Cres PE21 ... 209 B5
Rochford Twr* PE21 ... 209 E5
Rochford Twr La PE21 ... 209 D6
Rockingham Cl 8 PE6 ... 217 A6
Rockingham Cres DN34 ... 190 D4
Rockingham Ct 9 DN34 ... 190 D4
Rockingham Gr PE4 ... 221 A2
Rockingham Rd 4 PE9 ... 218 E6
Rockley Ct HU10 ... 178 F6
Rock Rd
Peterborough PE1 ... 225 F6
Stamford PE9 ... 219 B5
Rock The NG32 ... 138 B4
Rod Mill Rd DN16 ... 183 E1
Roegate La PE12 ... 159 F1
Roeze Cl 14 LN10 ... 97 C5
Rogues Alley PE13 ... 177 C4
Rokeby Ave HU4 ... 179 B5
Rokeby Cl HU4 ... 179 B5
Rokeby Pk HU4 ... 179 B5
Rokeby Pk Prim Sch HU4 ... 179 B4
Rolleston Cl 3 LN2 ... 201 F7
Rolleston Garth PE1 ... 226 C8
Rolls Cl PE7 ... 233 E7
Roman Bank
Bourne PE10 ... 213 E4
Holbeach PE12 ... 215 D8
Huttoft PE24 ... 77 C4
1 Ingoldmells PE25 ... 206 D8
Moulton PE12 ... 146 E2
Newton PE13 ... 170 B4
6 Skegness PE25 ... 206 C3
Spalding PE11 ... 214 F6
Stamford PE9 ... 219 A5
Roman Cl
9 Metheringham LN4 ... 95 D4
Navenby LN5 ... 107 B8
Roman Dr PE8 ... 222 D2
Roman Pavement LN2 ... 202 C4
Roman Rd
Moulton PE12 ... 157 D1
Scawby DN20 ... 30 D8
Roman Way
7 Ancaster NG32 ... 120 A2
Aubourn Haddington & South Hykeham LN6 ... 93 A8
Horncastle LN9 ... 199 D3
Riddings DN17 ... 184 F6
Roman Wharf LN1 ... 201 C3
Romany Gdns PE2 ... 231 D5
Romney Cl 3 LN6 ... 205 B6
Romney Ct 6 NG34 ... 212 D5
Romney Dr LN6 ... 205 B5
Romsey Ct DN34 ... 190 D5
Romulus Way 13 LN6 ... 93 B8
Ronald Cl 3 PE25 ... 206 C4
Rood's La PE12 ... 157 C8
Rookery Ave
2 Grimsby DN33 ... 191 D3
Sleaford NG34 ... 212 B3
Rookery Cl LN11 ... 198 D8
Rookery Croft 14 DN9 ... 27 E6
Rookery La
Ancaster NG32 ... 119 F2
13 Leasingham NG34 ... 121 B7
Lincoln LN6 ... 205 C6
Wildmore LN4 ... 111 E2
Wymondham LE14 ... 150 B1
Rookery Rd
2 Bicker PE20 ... 135 A4
16 Healing DN41 ... 23 F5
Rookery Rd *continued*
Sutton Bridge PE12 ... 160 D7
Rookery The
14 Collingham NG23 ... 91 D5
Peterborough PE2 ... 229 C7
2 Scawby DN20 ... 30 F8
Yaxley PE7 ... 233 D5
Rooklands 10 DN21 ... 29 C3
Rook's La DN10 ... 39 F6
Roosdyke La PE22 ... 137 D7
Roper's Bridge La PE20 ... 136 A4
Roper's Gate
Gedney PE12 ... 159 F8
2 Lutton PE12 ... 160 A8
Roper's La PE12 ... 159 D1
Ropery La 2 DN18 ... 3 E1
Ropery Rd DN21 ... 197 B7
Ropery St
Grimsby DN32 ... 191 F7
Kingston upon Hull HU3 ... 180 D4
Ropery The LN1 ... 234 A3
Ropewalk 6 LN8 ... 70 D5
Ropewalk Gall* DN18 ... 3 F1
Ropewalk The
1 Caistor LN7 ... 33 B4
8 Colsterworth NG33 ... 151 E6
Rope Wlk
Lincoln LN6 ... 234 A1
15 Thorne/Moorends DN8 ... 15 A8
ROPSLEY NG33 ... 131 B1
Ropsley CE (Controlled) Prim Sch NG33 ... 131 A1
Ropsley Rd NG33 ... 140 E8
Rosaire Pl DN33 ... 195 A8
Rosalind Ave DN34 ... 191 B7
Rosamond St 7 HU3 ... 180 B4
Rose Ave PE2 ... 231 C7
Rosebank DN21 ... 197 B7
Roseberry Ave
26 Hatfield DN7 ... 14 D4
Skegness PE25 ... 206 D1
Rosebery Ave
Boston PE21 ... 208 C5
Lincoln LN1 ... 201 D4
Rose Cottage Gdn Ctr & Tropical Forest* PE11 ... 156 D8
Rose Cottage La LN5 ... 94 A3
Rose Cres PE12 ... 158 D3
Rosedale
Scunthorpe DN17 ... 184 E2
Waltham DN37 ... 194 C5
Rosedale Cl 4 LN6 ... 204 F3
Rosedale Dr NG31 ... 211 B8
Rosedale Gr HU5 ... 179 D7
Rosefields DN21 ... 197 E5
Rosegar Ave PE20 ... 135 F2
Rosegarth St 14 PE21 ... 208 F4
Rose Gdns DN40 ... 186 C4
Rose Gr 1 PE25 ... 206 D5
Rosehill Cl 6 LN1 ... 66 D2
Rosehip Rd 8 PE10 ... 154 D6
Rose La
Beesby with Saleby LN13 ... 75 F5
Pinchbeck PE11 ... 156 E8
Roselea Ave 8 LN2 ... 68 D6
Rose Leigh Way PE11 ... 214 C7
Rosemary Ave
Grimsby DN34 ... 190 F6
11 Market Deeping PE6 ... 217 C5
Rosemary Cres NG31 ... 210 E1
Rosemary Gdns
12 Bourne PE10 ... 213 C6
Peterborough PE1 ... 225 F8
Rosemary La LN2 ... 234 B2
Rosemary Rise NG33 ... 141 D5
Rosemary Way DN35 ... 192 E1
Rose Mdws ... 208 B4
Rosemount Dr DN16 ... 185 B6
Rosemount Grange HU13 ... 178 C3
Rosemount La 5 DN21 ... 43 D7
Rose Pl PE21 ... 209 A3
Roseum Cl LN6 ... 204 E5
Roseveare Ave DN31 ... 191 A7
Roseway 6 DN21 ... 197 D5
Rose Wlk
Scunthorpe DN15 ... 183 C3
11 Wisbech PE13 ... 170 C1
Wittering PE9 ... 172 B1
Rosewood Cl
2 Birchwood LN6 ... 204 C8
4 Kingston upon Hull HU5 ... 179 B7
Rosewood Dr 5 NG34 ... 212 D2
Rosewood Way 1 DN16 ... 185 B3
Rosey Row 4 HU9 ... 181 C7
Rosina Gr N 2 DN32 ... 192 B6
Rosina Gr S 4 DN32 ... 192 B6
Roslyn Rd HU3 ... 179 E7
Rosmead St HU9 ... 181 D8
Rosper Rd DN40 ... 186 A8
Rosper Road Pools Nature Reserve* DN40 ... 186 A8
Rossall Cl
9 Mablethorpe/Sutton on Sea LN12 ... 77 A7
Scunthorpe DN16 ... 185 C3
Rossa Rd LN13 ... 76 D7
Ross Cl
5 Coddington NG24 ... 104 D5
St Giles LN2 ... 202 D6
Rossetti Ct NG31 ... 211 E5
Rossington Cl 18 LN4 ... 95 C4
Ross La 6 DN15 ... 9 B5
Ross Rd DN31 ... 189 D1
Rostrop Rd LN4 ... 95 C7
Rosyth Ave PE2 ... 229 D3
Rothbart Way 2 PE7 ... 230 C3
Rothbury Rd DN17 ... 184 F7
Rotherby Gr 3 PE1 ... 226 E7
Rothschild Cl PE21 ... 208 B4
ROTHWELL LN7 ... 33 F2
Rothwell Ave 8 DN33 ... 191 B3
Rothwell Cl DN21 ... 197 E4
Rothwell Rd
Cabourne LN7 ... 33 C3
4 Lincoln LN2 ... 201 F7
Scunthorpe DN15 ... 182 D4
Rothwell Way PE2 ... 230 C7
Rotten Row
Pinchbeck PE11 ... 156 E8
Theddlethorpe St Helen LN12 ... 63 E5
Rotton Sykes La DN15 ... 1 F2
ROUGHTON LN10 ... 98 B7
Roughton Ct 5 LN2 ... 202 A8
ROUGHTON MOOR LN10 ... 98 A7
Roughton Moor Wood Nature Reserve* LN10 ... 97 F6
Roundhouse Cl PE1 ... 226 D3
Roundway
Grimsby DN34 ... 191 C5
2 Immingham DN40 ... 186 C3
Roundway The HU4 ... 179 C5
Routland Cl 8 LN8 ... 70 D4
Roval Dr DN40 ... 186 A4
Rowan Ave
Peterborough PE1 ... 226 C6
Spalding PE11 ... 214 E5
Rowan Cl
6 Barrow upon Humber DN19 ... 11 C8
16 Keelby DN41 ... 23 A4
10 Wisbech PE13 ... 170 E1
Rowan Cres DN16 ... 185 C3
Rowan Ct
3 Goxhill DN19 ... 12 A8
11 Heighington/Washingborough LN4 ... 203 D1
Rowan Dr
5 Healing DN41 ... 23 F5
Silk Willoughby NG34 ... 121 B2
Rowan Rd
Lincoln LN6 ... 204 F3
Waddington LN5 ... 205 D1
Rowans The
Gainsborough DN21 ... 197 F5
Holbeach PE12 ... 159 A7
9 Nettleham LN2 ... 68 C2
4 Westwoodside DN9 ... 27 A2
Rowan Way
1 Boston PE21 ... 209 A7
Bourne PE10 ... 213 B6
16 Metheringham LN4 ... 95 C4
Rowanwood Dr 7 NG31 ... 210 F7
Rowdyke Rd PE21 ... 136 F7
Rowe Ave PE2 ... 230 D7
Rowgate Rd LN11 ... 73 A5
Rowland Ct 1 PE4 ... 220 F5
Rowland Rd 4 DN16 ... 183 B2
Rowlandson St 3 DN31 ... 189 B2
Rowley Rd PE21 ... 209 A4
Rowmills Rd 2 DN16 ... 185 C8
ROWSTON LN4 ... 108 E7
Rowston Cl DN21 ... 197 C6
Rowston St DN35 ... 193 A5
Roxborough Cl LN6 ... 200 E2
Roxburgh Rd PE9 ... 218 F6
Roxburgh St 1 HU5 ... 180 B8
ROXBY DN15 ... 9 A3
Roxby Causeway DN15 ... 9 C4
Roxby Cl LN6 ... 204 F6
Roxby Rd DN15 ... 8 F4
Roxholm Cl 2 NG34 ... 108 D1
Roxholme Rd NG34 ... 121 B8
Roxton Ave DN41 ... 23 A5
Roxton Hall Dr 15 HU14 ... 3 A5
Royal Air Force Coll The NG34 ... 120 B8
Royal Arthur Cl 5 PE25 ... 206 C1
Royal Cl 15 PE12 ... 160 E4
Royal Ct DN35 ... 193 B1
Royal Hull Hospitals NHS Trust HU3 ... 180 C6
Royal Mews HU3 ... 180 C6
Royal Oak Ct
13 Heckington NG34 ... 122 E3
10 Louth LN11 ... 198 B5
Royal Oak La 1 LN5 ... 93 A5
Royal St DN31 ... 189 A2
Royalty Bank PE22 ... 101 B3
Royal Way PE21 ... 209 F2
Royce Cl PE7 ... 233 E6
Royce Rd
Peterborough PE1 ... 226 D3
2 Spalding PE11 ... 214 F6
Roydon Gr LN6 ... 205 B6
Royle Cl PE2 ... 230 C5
Royston Ave PE2 ... 230 C6
Ruards La DN19 ... 5 A1
RUCKLAND LN11 ... 73 F5
Ruckland Ave LN1 ... 201 E7
Rudgard Ave LN3 ... 203 E6
Rudgard La LN1 ... 234 A3
Rudham Ave DN32 ... 191 E4
Rudkin Dr 5 NG34 ... 212 D6
Rudyard Cl 7 LN12 ... 77 A7
Rudyard Gr PE4 ... 221 C3
Rue de L'yonne 1 NG23 ... 91 D5
Rue de Nozay 3 DN20 ... 19 E4
Rufford Gn 2 LN6 ... 205 C8
Rufford Rd DN35 ... 192 E4
Rugby Ct 1 NG31 ... 211 B3
Rugby Rd
4 Mablethorpe/Sutton on Sea LN12 ... 64 B4
Scunthorpe DN16 ... 185 A8
Rugby St 5 HU3 ... 180 B4
Rumbold La 3 PE24 ... 102 D1
Runcorn Garth HU4 ... 179 B3
Runcorn Rd LN6 ... 204 B5
Running Post La PE20 ... 135 B4
Runswick Cl LN6 ... 205 A3
Runswick Ct DN32 ... 192 B6
Runswick Rd DN32 ... 192 B6
Rupert Rd 1 DN33 ... 191 D3
Rural Ave PE11 ... 144 D1
Rural Villages Sch Bucknall LN10 ... 84 B3
Rushcarr La DN17 ... 17 C1
Rushcliffe Rd NG31 ... 211 A7
Rush Furlong Nature Reserve* DN9 ... 27 E3
Rushmere PE2 ... 229 F6
Rushmore Ctry Pk* LN11 ... 61 F8
Rushton Ave PE4 ... 220 E4
Rushtons Way 12 DN20 ... 30 F5
Rushy Dro PE11 ... 145 C8
Ruskin Ave LN2 ... 202 B6
Ruskin Gn LN2 ... 202 B6
RUSKINGTON NG34 ... 108 E2
Ruskington Cl DN37 ... 188 A2
Ruskington Sta NG34 ... 108 E1
Ruskin Rd 13 LN12 ... 64 B4
Ruskin St
2 Gainsborough DN21 ... 197 D2
Kingston upon Hull HU3 ... 180 B6
Russell Ave
Lincoln LN6 ... 93 C8
Newark-on-Trent NG24 ... 104 A2
Russell Cl 12 PE6 ... 176 A3
Russell Cres NG34 ... 212 F4
Russell Ct DN35 ... 193 A1
Russell Dr 2 PE12 ... 167 B8
Russell Hill PE8 ... 222 A6
Russell Rd 7 NG34 ... 121 B8
Russell Read Almshouses 13 NG31 ... 211 A4
Russell St
Kingston upon Hull HU2 ... 180 E7
Lincoln LN5 ... 205 D6
Peterborough PE1 ... 225 F3
Russell Wlk 2 DN17 ... 29 D7
Russet Cl 4 DN15 ... 182 C5
Russet Dr LN11 ... 198 C4
Russet La DN20 ... 196 F6
Rustic La DN21 ... 41 C6
Ruston Rd NG31 ... 211 F7
Ruston Way LN6 ... 201 D3
Ruther Cl 2 PE2 ... 230 D8
Rutland Cl 13 NG33 ... 151 D2
Rutland Dr DN36 ... 195 C5
Rutland La 15 NG13 ... 128 A5
Rutland Rd
Kingston upon Hull HU5 ... 179 E8
Scunthorpe DN16 ... 185 D7
Skegness PE25 ... 206 D3
Stamford PE9 ... 219 D7
Rutland St 2 DN32 ... 189 D1
Rutland Terr PE9 ... 219 A4
Rutland Way
Ryhall PE9 ... 163 C1
15 Scampton Airfield LN1 ... 67 E5
Rycroft Ave PE6 ... 217 F5
Rycroft Cl 1 PE6 ... 217 F4
Rycroft St NG31 ... 211 B3
Rydal Ave DN33 ... 194 D7
Rydal Cl LN6 ... 200 D2
Rydal Ct PE4 ... 221 C3
Ryde Ave NG31 ... 210 E4
Rye Cl NG34 ... 212 E3
Rye Cres 3 HU15 ... 2 D5
Ryecroft 11 LN5 ... 205 D2
Ryedale 6 HU15 ... 2 D6
Ryedale Ave 1 DN15 ... 9 A6
Ryedale Cl NG31 ... 211 B8
Ryefield La PE12 ... 159 B3
Rye La LN13 ... 75 D5
RYHALL PE9 ... 163 C1
Ryhall CE Prim Sch PE9 ... 163 C1
Ryhall Rd
Great Casterton PE9 ... 171 C8
Stamford PE9 ... 219 D5
Ryhall Rd Ind Est PE9 ... 219 D8
Ryland Bridge LN2 ... 68 E6
Ryland Gdns 10 LN2 ... 68 D6
Ryland Rd LN2 ... 68 D6
Rymac Cres PE25 ... 90 E4
Rymer Pl DN35 ... 193 A4
Ryton Rd PE21 ... 208 B3

S

Sable Cl HU4 ... 179 C2
Sabre Way PE1 ... 226 F4
Sackville Cl DN40 ... 186 D4
Sackville Rd DN40 ... 186 D4
Sackville St 2 DN31 ... 191 C7
Sacred Heart RC Prim Sch PE3 ... 225 A5
Sacrewell Farm & Ctry Ctr* PE8 ... 222 C5
Saddleback Rd
Skidbrooke with Saltfleet Haven LN11 ... 51 A3
South Cockerington LN11 ... 50 E1
Saddle Ct PE4 ... 225 E8
Saddler Dr PE10 ... 154 C6
Saddle Row NG34 ... 120 B8
Saddlers Cl
Glinton PE6 ... 220 D8
Osbournby NG34 ... 132 D5
Saddler's Cl 11 LN4 ... 95 C4
Saddlers Mead 10 PE11 ... 214 A2
Saddlers Way
Fishtoft PE21 ... 209 C2
5 Long Sutton PE12 ... 216 B5
9 Middle Rasen LN8 ... 57 E7
Saddler's Way 2 DN9 ... 27 D3
Sadler Cl 9 PE25 ... 206 C1
Sadler Rd LN6 ... 204 B5
Saffrondale HU10 ... 178 E7
Saffron Wlk 12 PE10 ... 213 C5
Sage Ct LN6 ... 205 D8
Sagefield Cl 5 DN33 ... 194 D8
Sage's La PE4 ... 225 C8
Sailors Wharf HU9 ... 181 C6
Sainsbury Way HU4 ... 179 A1
St Abbs Cl 3 HU9 ... 181 A5
St Aiden's Rd 5 LN6 ... 204 E2
St Albans Ave DN31 ... 191 A8
St Albans Cl
5 Grantham NG31 ... 210 D5
16 Hibaldstow DN20 ... 30 F5
3 Scunthorpe DN17 ... 184 C7
St Alban's Dr 16 PE6 ... 175 A1
St Andrews NG31 ... 211 D7
St Andrews Ave 2 DN17 ... 184 F2
St Andrews CE Prim Sch
Heckington NG34 ... 122 E3
Leasingham NG34 ... 121 B7
Woodhall Spa LN10 ... 97 C6
St Andrews Cl LN5 ... 201 F1
St Andrew's Cl
4 Helpringham NG34 ... 133 D7
Redbourne DN21 ... 30 F3
St Andrews Com Prim Sch HU10 ... 178 C7
St Andrew's Cres 6 NG34 ... 121 B7
St Andrews Ct
Immingham DN40 ... 186 A4
4 Timberland LN4 ... 96 C1
St Andrews Dr 6 LN1 ... 66 C2
St Andrew's Dr
1 Burton upon Stather DN15 ... 8 B4
Grimsby DN32 ... 192 B4
Lincoln LN6 ... 205 C8
Skegness PE25 ... 206 D5
St Andrew's Gdns LN6 ... 205 C8
St Andrews Gr 33 DN7 ... 14 D4
St Andrews La DN40 ... 186 B5
St Andrew's Mount HU10 ... 178 C8
St Andrew's Pl 3 LN5 ... 234 B1
St Andrews Rd
2 Mablethorpe/Sutton on Sea LN12 ... 64 B4
Northborough PE6 ... 217 E1
St Andrew's Rd
6 Butterwick PE22 ... 126 E3
Spalding PE11 ... 214 C1
St Andrew's St
8 Heckington NG34 ... 122 E3
16 Kirton in Lindsey DN21 ... 30 B1
4 Lincoln LN5 ... 234 B1
St Andrew's Way
8 Barnby Dun DN3 ... 14 A3
Epworth DN9 ... 27 E7
4 RAF Cranwell NG34 ... 120 C8
St Andrews Wlk 5 LN10 ... 97 C5
St Annes Ave 8 LN11 ... 50 F7
St Anne's CE (Cont) Prim Sch NG31 ... 211 C3
St Annes Cl
Lincoln LN2 ... 202 B4
Skegness PE25 ... 206 C6
3 Sleaford NG34 ... 212 C6
8 Spalding PE11 ... 214 C6
St Anne's Rd
9 Keelby DN41 ... 23 A5
Lincoln LN2 ... 202 B4
St Anne's Specl Sch HU15 ... 2 E5
St Anne's St NG31 ... 211 C3
St Annes Way PE11 ... 214 C6
St Anne's Wlk 13 HU15 ... 2 D6
St Ann's Ave DN34 ... 191 B6
St Ann's La PE21 ... 208 F3
St Anns Wharf 1 PE21 ... 208 F3
St Aubins Cres LN4 ... 81 F4
St Audrey Cl PE2 ... 231 D6
St Augustine Ave DN32 ... 191 E5
St Augustine Cres DN16 ... 185 B5
St Augustine Rd LN2 ... 202 F6

Skegness Wr Leisure Pk★ PE25 . . . 90 E1
SKELDYKE PE20 . . . 136 F4
Skeldyke Rd PE20 . . . 136 D5
SKELLINGTHORPE LN6 . . . 200 B4
Skellingthorpe Rd LN6 . . 200 D2
Skelton Dr PE12 . . . 216 C3
Skelton Rd DN17 . . . 184 C7
SKENDLEBY PE23 . . . 88 D4
Skendleby Nature Reserve★ LN13 . . . 88 E6
Skerries Cl 5 LN6 . . . 205 A1
Skerry La NG13 . . . 128 C5
SKIDBROOKE LN11 . . . 51 B3
Skillings La HU15 . . . 2 C5
SKILLINGTON NG33 . . . 151 B8
Skillington Rd NG33 . . . 151 B6
SKINNAND LN5 . . . 106 C8
Skinnand La LN5 . . . 106 D7
Skinners La
6 South Ferriby DN18 . . . 10 A7
Waltham DN37 . . . 194 E4
Skinner's La
Middle Rasen LN8 . . . 45 C1
South Kyme LN4 . . . 110 B1
Skipmarsh La
Leverton PE22 . . . 126 E8
Old Leake PE22 . . . 113 E1
Skippingdale Ind Pk DN15 . . . 182 C7
Skippingdale Rd DN15 . . 182 F6
Skipwith Cres 20 LN4 . . . 95 D4
Skipworth Way PE25 . . . 206 C8
SKIRBECK PE21 . . . 209 B3
Skirbeck Dr 15 LN1 . . . 66 D2
Skirbeck Gdns PE21 . . . 209 B3
SKIRBECK QUARTER PE21 . . . 208 D2
Skirbeck Rd PE21 . . . 209 A3
Skirmore Rd PE22 . . . 114 E5
Skirth Rd LN4 . . . 109 F6
Skitter Rd DN40 . . . 5 D1
Skylark Dr DN16 . . . 185 B2
Skylarks Cl 6 PE7 . . . 230 D3
Slack The 4 DN17 . . . 16 D8
Slash La LN9 . . . 86 D3
Slate Drift 2 PE9 . . . 171 C2
Slate Mill Pl NG31 . . . 211 B5
Slate Mill The NG31 . . . 211 B5
Slay Pit Cl 3 DN7 . . . 14 F4
Slay Pit La DN7 . . . 14 F3
Slea Cotts 15 NG34 . . . 212 D4
SLEAFORD NG34 . . . 212 B4
Sleaford (Aided) RC Prim Sch NG34 . . . 212 C5
Sleaford Art Studio★ NG34 . . . 212 D5
Sleaford Coll NG34 . . . 212 E4
Sleaford Joint Sixth Form NG34 . . . 212 D5
Sleaford Leisure Ctr NG34 . . . 212 E4
Sleaford Lollycocks Field Nature Reserve★ NG34 . . . 212 E4
Sleaford Mareham Nature Reserve★ NG34 . . . 212 E2
Sleaford Rd
Ancaster NG32 . . . 120 A2
Barnby in the Willows NG24 . . . 104 F5
Boston PE21 . . . 208 B4
Bracebridge Heath LN4 . . . 81 A1
Coningsby LN4 . . . 207 A4
Cranwell NG34 . . . 120 F8
East Kirkby PE23 . . . 99 E4
Folkingham NG34 . . . 142 D8
Heckington NG34 . . . 122 D3
Honington NG32 . . . 119 C2
Leadenham LN5 . . . 106 D2
14 Leasingham NG34 . . . 121 B7
Metheringham LN4 . . . 95 B4
18 Navenby/Wellingore LN5 . . . 107 A7
Newark-on-Trent NG24 . . . 104 A5
North Kyme LN4 . . . 109 E2
Ruskington NG34 . . . 108 E1
Tattershall LN4 . . . 110 D7
Walcot near Folkingham NG34 . . . 132 D2
Sleaford Sta NG34 . . . 212 D3
Sleaford Virtual Mus★ 7 NG34 . . . 212 C4
Sledge La LN8 . . . 59 B8
Sledmere Gr HU4 . . . 179 E5
Sleepers Cl 1 PE12 . . . 216 B4
Sleights Cl HU3 . . . 180 A7
Sleights Dr 2 PE14 . . . 170 F1
Sleights La HU15 . . . 1 B6
Slessor St 2 LN5 . . . 94 A7
Slipe Dro PE11 . . . 155 F5
Slipe The PE10 . . . 213 F4
Slippery Gowt La PE21 . . 136 F8
Slipway DN35 . . . 193 A6
SLOOTHBY LN13 . . . 89 D5
Sloothby High La
Hogsthorpe PE24 . . . 90 A6
Willoughby with Sloothby PE24 . . . 89 F6
Sluice La DN18 . . . 9 E8
Sluice Rd
Holbeach PE12 . . . 215 B8
South Ferriby DN18 . . . 9 F8
Sutton Bridge PE12 . . . 161 A6
Whaplode PE12 . . . 147 B4
Small Dro PE12 . . . 157 E7
Small Dro La PE11 . . . 144 E1
Small End Rd PE22 . . . 114 E6
Smalley Rd PE21 . . . 209 D4
Smallwood PE3 . . . 225 B5
Smeeton Ct 6 NG34 . . . 212 D6
Smeeton's La PE20 . . . 146 C7
Smithdale Cl 9 PE11 . . . 214 C6
Smithfield PE6 . . . 176 B3
Smith Field 10 DN36 . . . 36 B1
Smithfield Rd DN16 . . . 185 D6
Smith St
Lincoln LN5 . . . 201 E1
Scunthorpe DN15 . . . 182 F4
Smithy La
7 Barnetby le Wold DN38 . . . 21 B4
Friskney PE22 . . . 115 A6
Smooting La 4 LN3 . . . 82 A8
Smoothing The LN8 . . . 46 C1
Smythe La DN22 . . . 52 D1
Snaffer's La PE12 . . . 158 C5
Snainton Gr 4 HU5 . . . 179 D8
Snaith Ave PE20 . . . 146 D7
Snaith Cl 9 LN6 . . . 204 B6
SNARFORD LN2 . . . 56 D1
Snarford Rd LN3 . . . 69 D8
SNELLAND LN3 . . . 69 D7
Snelland Rd LN3 . . . 69 E8
Snetterton Cl 1 LN6 . . . 204 C7
Snipe Dales Ctry Pk★ PE23 . . . 86 F3
Snipe Dales Nature Reserve★ LN9 . . . 86 E3
SNITTERBY DN21 . . . 43 D5
Snitterby Carr La DN21 . . . 43 F5
Snitterby Rd DN21 . . . 43 D6
Snowberry Gdns 5 LN6 . . . 204 C8
Snowden Cl 1 PE6 . . . 175 C8
Snowdon Cl 4 LN5 . . . 205 D3
Snowdonia Ave DN15 . . . 182 D7
Snowdon Rd 3 NG23 . . . 91 D4
Snowdrop Cl 10 DN41 . . . 23 F5
Snowdrop Pl 8 PE11 . . . 214 A5
Snowhills PE7 . . . 233 E5
Sods La PE11 . . . 145 D5
Soff La DN19 . . . 12 A6
Soke Parkway PE1 . . . 221 E1
Soke Rd PE6 . . . 174 D5
Solhem Ave 13 PE21 . . . 136 D8
Solomon Ct DN35 . . . 192 D5
Solway Ave PE21 . . . 136 E8
Solway Ct 5 DN37 . . . 190 E8
SOMERBY DN38 . . . 21 B1
Somerby Cl
8 Moulton PE12 . . . 157 F7
3 Stamford PE9 . . . 219 B7
Somerby Garth 4 PE1 . . . 226 D8
Somerby Gr NG31 . . . 211 D2
Somerby Hill NG31 . . . 211 C2
Somerby Pl NG31 . . . 211 E1
Somerby Rd
Gainsborough DN21 . . . 197 F5
Ropsley & Humby NG33 . . 141 A8
Scunthorpe DN17 . . . 184 D5
Somerby Wold La DN38 . . 21 C1
Somerden Rd HU9 . . . 5 F8
Somerfield Dr 9 LN11 . . . 50 F7
SOMERSBY PE23 . . . 87 A7
Somersby Ave 9 LN12 . . . 64 B4
Somersby Cl LN6 . . . 205 C4
Somersby Ct
15 Louth LN11 . . . 198 B5
North Carlton LN1 . . . 67 C4
Somersby Gn PE21 . . . 209 B7
Somersby Gr 2 PE25 . . . 206 D1
Somersby St 5 DN31 . . . 191 D8
Somersby Way PE21 . . . 209 B7
Somerset Dr 4 DN15 . . . 8 B4
Somerset St HU3 . . . 180 A5
Somerton Dr 3 DN7 . . . 14 F3
Somerton Gate La LN5 . . . 93 D7
Somerton Rd DN40 . . . 186 D3
Somervell Rd DN16 . . . 185 C4
Somerville PE4 . . . 220 E5
Somerville Cl 15 LN5 . . . 93 E8
Somerville Ct 14 LN5 . . . 93 E8
Somerville Rd 1 PE9 . . . 219 A6
Somes Cl 1 PE9 . . . 172 C6
Somme Cl LN1 . . . 201 E7
Sonia Crest DN40 . . . 186 B4
Sophia Ave DN33 . . . 191 C1
Sorbus Cl 3 PE7 . . . 230 D3
Sorbus Ct 5 HU3 . . . 180 D6
Sorbus View 4 HU5 . . . 179 C7
Sorby Cl PE25 . . . 206 E8
Sorrel Cl
3 Binbrook LN8 . . . 47 C5
1 Market Deeping PE6 . . 217 D6
4 Stamford PE9 . . . 218 D6
Sorrel Ct LN6 . . . 204 C8
Sorrel Dr PE11 . . . 214 A5
Sorrel Way DN15 . . . 182 C6
Soss La DN10 . . . 40 A5
SOTBY LN8 . . . 71 E5
Sotby Mdws Nature Reserve★ LN8 . . . 71 E5
SOTS HOLE LN4 . . . 96 C7
Soulby La PE22 . . . 114 C2
Sour La DN7 . . . 14 E8
Soutergate 13 DN18 . . . 3 F1
South Airfield Rd NG34 . . . 120 C8
South Axholme Com Sch DN9 . . . 27 D6
South Bank 3 DN17 . . . 17 D6
SOUTH BRAMWITH DN7 . . . 14 A6
South Brick Lines NG34 . . . 120 B8
South Bridge Rd 2 HU9 . . . 181 A5
Southburn Ave HU5 . . . 179 E7
SOUTH CARLTON LN1 . . . 67 D3
South Carr Rd DN20 . . . 31 A4
South Church Side 14 HU1 . . . 180 F6
Southcliffe Rd 19 DN21 . . . 29 C3
South Cliff Rd 27 DN21 . . . 30 B1
SOUTH CLIFTON NG23 . . . 78 B5
Southcoates La HU9 . . . 181 E8
SOUTH COCKERINGTON LN11 . . . 62 A8
South Cres
11 Bottesford NG13 . . . 128 A5
1 Chapel St Leonard PE24 . . . 90 D7
South Dale LN7 . . . 33 B4
South-Dale Cl 3 DN21 . . . 30 B2
Southdown LN5 . . . 205 D1
Southdown Rd PE7 . . . 233 F5
South Dr
12 Balderton NG24 . . . 104 C1
4 Stow LN1 . . . 66 C8
South Dro
Bicker PE20 . . . 134 E4
Helpringham NG34 . . . 133 E6
Lutton PE12 . . . 149 A1
Quadring PE11 . . . 144 A8
Spalding PE11 . . . 156 E2
SOUTH ELKINGTON LN11 . . . 60 E7
South Ella Dr HU10 . . . 178 D7
South Ella Way HU10 . . . 178 D7
South End
Boston PE21 . . . 208 F4
Collingham NG23 . . . 91 C4
SOUTH END DN19 . . . 12 B7
South End
Hogsthorpe PE24 . . . 90 B6
Thorne/Moorends DN8 . . . 15 A7
South End La DN22 . . . 52 E3
Southern Dr HU4 . . . 179 C5
Southern La LN6 . . . 92 B7
Southern Rd DN40 . . . 186 D7
Southern Way DN40 . . . 186 C7
Southern Wlk DN33 . . . 194 F7
South Fen Rd
Bourne PE10 . . . 213 F4
Helpringham NG34 . . . 133 D6
SOUTH FERRIBY DN18 . . . 10 B8
South Ferriby Prim Sch DN18 . . . 10 A7
Southfield
7 Belton DN9 . . . 16 E1
4 Kingston upon Hull HU13 . . . 3 E4
SOUTH FIELD HU13 . . . 3 E4
Southfield Ave DN33 . . . 194 F7
Southfield Cl
18 Thorne/Moorends DN8 . . . 15 B7
Ulceby DN39 . . . 12 B1
Southfield Dr
10 Epworth DN9 . . . 27 D6
2 Louth LN11 . . . 198 C4
21 North Ferriby HU14 . . . 3 A4
Southfield La
Fishtoft PE21 . . . 137 C8
6 Old Leake PE22 . . . 114 A1
Old Leake PE22 . . . 127 A8
Willoughton DN21 . . . 42 D3
Southfield Pl LN9 . . . 199 C3
Southfield Rd
1 Broughton DN20 . . . 19 D3
13 Crowle DN17 . . . 16 D7
Grimsby DN33 . . . 194 F7
Holton le Clay DN36 . . . 195 D1
North Kelsey LN7 . . . 31 F3
Scunthorpe DN16 . . . 185 C5
Thorne/Moorends DN8 . . . 15 B7
1 Winterton DN15 . . . 8 F5
Southfields
7 Binbrook LN8 . . . 47 C4
Bourne PE10 . . . 213 D4
3 Sleaford NG34 . . . 212 D3
Southfields Ave PE2 . . . 231 D5
Southfields Cl 10 PE13 . . . 170 D2
Southfields Dr PE2 . . . 231 D6
Southfields Inf Sch PE2 . . . 231 D5
Southfields Jun Sch PE2 . . . 231 D5
South Furlong Croft 22 DN9 . . . 27 E6
Southgate
Kingston upon Hull HU13 . . . 178 E1
12 Pinchbeck PE11 . . . 156 E8
Scunthorpe DN15 . . . 183 B3
South Gate NG34 . . . 212 D4
Southgate Spinneys 3 NG34 . . . 120 E4
Southgate Way PE2 . . . 229 C2
South Gn PE34 . . . 161 F2
SOUTH GREEN PE34 . . . 161 E2
South Heath La NG32 . . . 106 D1
South Holland Ctr★ PE11 . . . 214 D4
South Humberside Ind Est DN31 . . . 188 B2
South Hunsley Sch HU14 . . . 2 E5
SOUTH HYKEHAM LN6 . . . 93 B7
South Hykeham Com Prim Sch LN6 . . . 93 B7
South Ing Dro PE11 . . . 134 E1
South Ings La PE24 . . . 90 B5
South Intake La DN9 . . . 40 C7
SOUTH KELSEY LN7 . . . 32 A1
South Kesteven Works NG31 . . . 210 F3
SOUTH KILLINGHOLME DN40 . . . 12 E3
SOUTH KYME LN4 . . . 123 B8
South La
Kingston upon Hull HU13 . . . 178 E1
Willingham DN21 . . . 54 A3
Southland Ct DN37 . . . 188 A1
Southland Dr 5 LN6 . . . 205 B4
Southlands Ave
Gainsborough DN21 . . . 197 B8
Louth LN11 . . . 198 D3
Peterborough PE1 . . . 226 A6
Southlands Dr
Grantham NG31 . . . 211 C4
Morton DN21 . . . 197 B8
Southlands Gdns DN21 . . 197 B8
South Leys Sch DN17 . . . 184 D4
South Lincs Con Ctr NG31 . . . 211 A1
South Marsh Rd
Immingham Power St DN41 . . . 187 F1
Stallingborough DN41 . . . 23 F7
South Marsh Rd Ind Est DN41 . . . 187 F2
South Mkt Pl 7 LN13 . . . 75 F2
Southmoor La
Newton on Trent LN1 . . . 78 D8
Snitterby DN21 . . . 43 E5
Southmoor Rd
Crowle DN17 . . . 16 C8
Newton on Trent LN1 . . . 78 D8
South Moor Rd DN10 . . . 39 F3
Southoe Rd PE7 . . . 231 D2
Southolme DN21 . . . 197 D4
SOUTH ORMSBY LN11 . . . 74 D2
SOUTHORPE PE9 . . . 172 E2
Southorpe La DN21 . . . 42 A7
Southorpe Paddock Nature Reserve★ PE9 . . . 172 E1
SOUTH OWERSBY LN8 . . . 44 E4
South Parade
Boston PE21 . . . 208 C4
11 Caythorpe NG32 . . . 119 B7
Gainsborough DN21 . . . 197 F3
Grantham NG31 . . . 211 B2
Grimsby DN31 . . . 191 D8
7 Lincoln LN1 . . . 201 D4
Peterborough PE3 . . . 225 E3
5 Saxilby LN1 . . . 66 D2
Skegness PE25 . . . 206 D2
South Kyme LN4 . . . 123 B8
Spalding PE11 . . . 214 C3
Thorne/Moorends DN8 . . . 15 A7
South Parade Jun & Inf Sch DN31 . . . 191 D8
South Pk LN5 . . . 205 F8
South Pk Ave
Bracebridge Heath LN5 . . . 205 F8
Lincoln LN5 . . . 201 F1
South Pk Rd DN17 . . . 184 D3
South Ramper DN21 . . . 44 A5
SOUTH RAUCEBY NG34 . . . 120 E4
South Rd
Bourne PE10 . . . 213 D4
Chapel St Leonard PE24 . . . 90 E6
5 Keadby with Althorpe DN17 . . . 17 C6
Mablethorpe/Sutton on Sea LN12 . . . 64 C1
North Somercotes LN11 . . . 50 E7
Sturton le Steeple DN22 . . . 52 C4
Tetford LN9 . . . 73 F1
SOUTH RESTON LN11 . . . 62 D1
SOUTHREY LN3 . . . 83 D1
South Ridge Cres 2 DN17 . . . 184 F3
South Rise 6 LN8 . . . 47 C4
South St Mary's Gate 4 DN31 . . . 191 D7
South Scaffold La NG23 . . . 91 E3
SOUTH SCARLE NG23 . . . 91 E6
South Scarle La LN6 . . . 78 E1
South Scarle Rd NG23 . . . 91 E6
South Sea La DN36 . . . 36 D7
South Side DN15 . . . 2 A1
SOUTH SOMERCOTES LN11 . . . 50 E5
South St
12 Alford LN13 . . . 75 F2
17 Alford LN13 . . . 75 F2
10 Barnetby le Wold DN38 . . . 21 B4
Bole DN22 . . . 52 C5
Boston PE21 . . . 208 F4
Bourne PE10 . . . 213 D4
Caistor LN7 . . . 33 B4
1 Cleethorpes DN35 . . . 193 A5
20 Crowland PE6 . . . 166 F1
Horncastle LN9 . . . 199 B3
Keelby DN41 . . . 23 A5
Louth LN11 . . . 198 B5
Morton DN21 . . . 197 C8
15 North Kelsey LN7 . . . 32 A4
Owston Ferry DN9 . . . 28 B2
Peterborough PE1 . . . 226 B2
Roxby cum Risby DN15 . . . 8 F3
Scamblesby LN11 . . . 72 F5
Swineshead PE20 . . . 135 B7
West Butterwick DN17 . . . 28 D8
17 Winterton DN15 . . . 9 A5
South Terr
Boston PE21 . . . 208 F3
4 Louth LN11 . . . 198 C5
SOUTH THORESBY LN13 . . . 75 A3
South View
Anlaby HU4 . . . 179 B6
Broughton DN20 . . . 19 D4
Holton le Clay DN36 . . . 195 E1
Humberston DN36 . . . 193 A1
Peterborough PE2 . . . 230 F7
Yarborough DN34 . . . 191 A6
South View Ave
Brigg DN20 . . . 196 C5
Burringham DN17 . . . 17 D4
South View Cl 4 PE25 . . 206 D2
South View Com Prim Sch PE6 . . . 166 E1
South View La LN11 . . . 62 A7
Southview Leisure Ctr PE25 . . . 103 C8
South View Rd PE4 . . . 225 D8
South View 16 LN2 . . . 68 E6
Southwell Ave
3 Kingston upon Hull HU9 . . . 5 F8
Peterborough PE4 . . . 220 E4
Southwell Cl NG31 . . . 210 C5
Southwell Rd 2 PE13 . . . 170 D1
Southwell's La 1 LN9 . . . 199 C4
Southwick Cl PE4 . . . 221 C1
SOUTH WILLINGHAM LN8 . . . 59 A2
SOUTH WITHAM NG33 . . . 151 E2
South Witham Nature Reserve★ NG33 . . . 151 F2
South Witham Prim Sch NG33 . . . 151 D2
Southwold Cres DN33 . . . 194 E8
South Wood Dr 10 DN8 . . . 15 A7
Sovereign Cl
12 Grimsby DN34 . . . 190 D4
12 Wisbech PE13 . . . 170 C1
Sovereign Pl PE3 . . . 225 E2
Sovereign St NG34 . . . 142 E4
Sow Dale Nature Reserve★ PE23 . . . 87 A1
Sowers La DN15 . . . 9 A5
Spa Bldgs LN2 . . . 234 B2
Spafford Cl 7 DN21 . . . 65 E8
Spa Hill 9 DN21 . . . 30 B1
Spain Ct 17 PE21 . . . 208 F4
Spain La 5 PE21 . . . 208 F4
Spain Pl PE21 . . . 209 A4
SPALDING PE11 . . . 214 E6
Spalding Bulb Mus★ PE11 . . . 145 C1
Spalding Comm 6 PE11 . . . 214 B1
Spalding Dro
Cowbit PE12 . . . 157 A3
Spalding PE12 . . . 214 E1
Spalding FE Ctr PE11 . . 214 D4
Spalding Gate PE12 . . . 158 B8
Spalding Gram Sch PE11 . . . 214 D3
Spalding High Sch PE11 . . . 214 F3
Spalding Parish CE Day Sch PE11 . . . 214 E2
Spalding Prim Sch PE11 . . . 214 B5
Spalding Rd
Boston PE21 . . . 208 E3
Bourne PE10 . . . 213 E5
Deeping St James PE6 . . . 165 D1
Gosberton PE11 . . . 145 C5
Holbeach PE12 . . . 215 A2
Market Deeping PE6 . . . 217 E5
Pinchbeck PE11 . . . 214 C8
Scunthorpe DN16 . . . 185 B8
Wigtoft PE20 . . . 135 E1
Spalding Rd Bsns Pk PE10 . . . 213 F5
Spalding Sta PE11 . . . 214 C4
SPALFORD NG23 . . . 78 D4
Spalford La LN6 . . . 78 E2
Spalford Rd LN6 . . . 78 E3
Spalford Warren Nature Reserve★ NG23 . . . 78 D2
SPANBY NG34 . . . 132 F4
Spanby Dr 5 LN6 . . . 205 A7
Spanning Dr 22 LN13 . . . 75 F2
Spa Rd
Lincoln LN5 . . . 234 C2
2 Woodhall Spa LN10 . . . 97 D6
Spark's La PE12 . . . 158 A4
Spark St DN34 . . . 191 A7
Sparrowgate Rd PE14 . . . 170 F1
Sparrow La
2 Long Bennington NG23 . . . 117 D3
Marnham NG23 . . . 78 A5
Newball LN8 . . . 69 F2
Sparrow Rd 1 PE7 . . . 230 D1
Spa St LN2 . . . 202 B3
Spaw La 5 LN11 . . . 198 B6
Spayne Rd PE21 . . . 209 A4
Speechley Rd PE7 . . . 233 F6
Speechley's Dro PE6 . . . 174 F7
Speedwell Cres DN15 . . . 182 C6
Speedwell Ct 7 PE6 . . . 217 D6
Speight Cl 5 NG24 . . . 104 B7
Spencer Ave
Peterborough PE2 . . . 231 D5

Stenigot Rd 1 LN6 . . . . . 204 D6
Stenner Rd LN4 . . . . 207 F6
Stennett Ave 1 PE11 . . . . 156 E2
STENWITH NG32 . . . . 128 D3
Stephen Cl 3 DN39 . . . . . . 12 A1
Stephen Cres
16 Barton-upon-Humber DN18 . . . . 10 F8
Grimsby DN34 . . . . 190 E4
Humberston DN36 . . . . 36 C8
Stephen Rd NG24 . . . . 104 A6
Stephenson Ave
Gonerby Hill Foot NG31 . . . . 210 F8
Pinchbeck PE11 . . . . 214 E8
Stephenson Cl
9 Alford LN13 . . . . 75 E2
4 Boston PE21 . . . . 208 F1
Yaxley PE7 . . . . 233 D6
Stephenson Ct 5 PE1 . . . 226 B2
Stephenson Way PE10 . . . 213 D7
Stephens Way 4 PE6 . . . 217 F4
Stephen's Way NG34 . . . . 212 F3
Sterling Cres DN37 . . . . . . 194 C4
Sterling Pl 8 LN10 . . . . . . 97 E6
Sterne Ave 9 DN20 . . . . . 19 D3
Stevenson Pl 1 DN35 . . . 192 D5
Stevenson's Way 33 DN18 . . . . 10 E8
Stevern Way PE1 . . . . 226 F4
STEWTON LN11 . . . . 61 E5
Stewton Gdns LN11 . . . . . 198 D4
Stewton La LN11 . . . . 198 E4
Steyning La PE20 . . . . 135 A7
Steynings The PE4 . . . . . . 221 A3
STIBBINGTON PE8 . . . . 222 C2
STICKFORD PE22 . . . . 100 B2
STICKNEY PE22 . . . . 113 A8
Stickney CE (Aided) Prim Sch PE22 . . . . 113 A8
Stickney Farm Pk★ PE22 . . . . 112 F8
Stickney La PE22 . . . . 112 D7
Still Cl PE6 . . . . 217 B5
Still The PE13 . . . . 170 B1
Stirling Cl 4 DN21 . . . . . . 197 E6
Stirling Ct
14 Grantham NG31 . . . . . . 210 E2
Heckington NG34 . . . . 122 D2
Stirling Dr 12 NG24 . . . . . 104 C5
Stirling Rd PE9 . . . . 218 F5
Stirling St
Grimsby DN31 . . . . 189 D1
Kingston upon Hull HU3 . . 179 F6
Stirling Way
Market Deeping PE6 . . . . . 217 C7
Peterborough PE3 . . . . 220 E1
4 Skellingthorpe LN6 . . . . 200 A4
STIXWOULD LN10 . . . . 97 B8
Stixwould Rd LN10 . . . . 97 C7
Stockbridge Pk 3 HU15 . . . 2 C7
Stockbridge Rd HU15 . . . . . 2 C7
STOCKHOLES TURBARY DN9 . . . . 16 B2
Stockhouse La PE11 . . . . . 145 B3
Stocking Way LN2 . . . . 202 F6
Stockman's Ave 2 PE12 . . . . 215 F3
Stockmoor La LN8 . . . . 57 A8
Stocks Hill
4 Belton DN9 . . . . 16 E1
Castor PE5 . . . . 223 F1
Stockshill Rd DN16 . . . . . . 185 C6
Stocks La LN8 . . . . 56 F3
Stockwell Gate PE12 . . . . 215 A4
Stockwell Gr 6 HU9 . . . . . . 5 F8
Stockwell Prim Sch HU9 . . . 5 F8
Stockwith Mill★ PE23 . . . . 87 B5
Stockwith Rd
Haxey DN9 . . . . 27 E1
Walkeringham DN10 . . . . . . 40 A3
STOKE ROCHFORD NG33 . . . . 139 F2
Stoke Rochford Hall Con & Leisure Ctr★ NG33 . . . . . 139 F2
Stokesay Ct 8 PE3 . . . . . . 225 B1
Stokes Dr NG34 . . . . 212 B6
Stoksley Wlk DN37 . . . . . . 190 F8
Stonebow Ctr LN2 . . . . . . 234 B2
Stonebridge PE2 . . . . 230 C5
Stonebridge Lea PE2 . . . . 230 C5
Stonebridge Rd NG31 . . . 211 B4
Stone Cl 8 PE10 . . . . 213 C6
Stonecross Rd NG34 . . . . 107 E1
Stone Dr LE15 . . . . 152 A1
Stonefield Ave LN2 . . . . . 234 B4
Stonefield Pk LN2 . . . . 68 C7
Stonegate
Gedney PE12 . . . . 159 D6
Spalding PE11 . . . . 214 E3
28 Thorne/Moorends DN8 . . . . 15 A8
Stone Gate
Cowbit PE12 . . . . 157 B1
Weston PE12 . . . . 145 F2
STONE HILL DN7 . . . . 14 F4
Stone Hill DN7 . . . . 15 A4
Stone Hill Rd DN7 . . . . 15 A4
Stonehouse Rd PE7 . . . . . 233 E5
Stone La
Aubourn Haddington & South Hykeham LN5 . . . . 92 E6
Burringham DN17 . . . . 17 E4
Peterborough PE1 . . . . 225 F5
Sutterton PE20 . . . . 135 F1
6 Waddington LN5 . . . . 93 F7
Stoneleigh Ct PE3 . . . . . . 225 B2
Stonemasons Ct 4 NG31 . . . . 211 B4
Stone Moor Rd 14 LN6 . . . 93 B8
Stonepit La
Marston NG32 . . . . 118 C2
8 Skillington NG33 . . . . . . 151 A8
Stone Pit La
Skendleby PE23 . . . . 88 D4
Willingham DN21 . . . . 53 F3
Stonepit Rd HU15 . . . . 2 E6
Stonesby Rd LE14 . . . . 138 E1
Stones Cl 4 PE24 . . . . 90 B7
Stones La
13 Spilsby PE23 . . . . 88 A1
West Keal PE23 . . . . 100 C5
Stone's La PE24 . . . . 77 C1
Stones Pl 1 LN6 . . . . 200 E1
Stone Way NG34 . . . . 212 B6
Stonewell Row LN9 . . . . . 199 C4
Stoney La DN21 . . . . 54 F7
Stoney Way 15 DN36 . . . . . 36 D4
Stoney Yd LN6 . . . . 200 A5
Stong's Dro PE11 . . . . 144 F8
Stool Cl Rd 2 DN9 . . . . 16 E1
Storbeck Rd 15 PE13 . . . . 170 D1
Storey's Bar Rd PE6 . . . . . 227 A3
Storey's La PE24 . . . . 102 E7
Storrington Way PE4 . . . . 221 A3
Stortford St 7 DN31 . . . . 188 D1
Story St 11 HU1 . . . . 180 E7
Stothards La 7 DN19 . . . . . 12 A8
Stoton's Gate PE12 . . . . . . 158 E2
Stour Ct 7 NG31 . . . . 210 E2
Stourton Pl LN9 . . . . 199 B4
Stove Ct LE15 . . . . 162 A8
Stovin Cres DN15 . . . . 9 A5
STOW LN1 . . . . 66 C8
Stow Cl DN37 . . . . 190 D8
Stowehill Rd PE4 . . . . 221 D2
Stowe Rd PE6 . . . . 164 E2
Stowgate Rd PE6 . . . . 174 A8
Stow Hill LE14 . . . . 150 C7
Stow La NG34 . . . . 133 A1
Stow Pk Rd
Marton DN21 . . . . 65 E8
Stow LN1 . . . . 66 B8
Stow Rd
Scunthorpe DN16 . . . . 185 B7
Sturton by Stow LN1 . . . . . . 66 C8
Willingham DN21 . . . . 53 E2
Wisbech PE13 . . . . 170 E1
Strafford St DN21 . . . . 197 D2
STRAGGLETHORPE LN5 . . . . 105 E3
Stragglethorpe La
Caythorpe NG32 . . . . 118 E8
Fulbeck NG32 . . . . 105 E2
Strahane Cl LN5 . . . . 205 C3
Straight Dro PE7 . . . . 231 E1
Strait Bargate 26 PE21 . . 208 F5
Strait The LN2 . . . . 234 B3
Strand Cl
Kingston upon Hull HU2 . . . . 180 E8
8 Mablethorpe/Sutton on Sea LN12 . . . . 64 B3
Strand Infants Sch DN32 . . . . 189 B1
Strand Jun Sch DN32 . . . 189 B1
Strand St DN32 . . . . 189 B1
Strand The LN12 . . . . 64 B3
Stratford Ave DN34 . . . . . 191 A4
Stratford Dr 5 DN16 . . . . 183 C1
Stratten Cl 5 NG34 . . . . . . 107 C1
Stratton Pk 1 HU14 . . . . 3 C6
Strawberry Cl 13 PE13 . . . 170 C1
Strawberry Fields Dr PE12 . . . . 147 D6
Strawberry Gdns HU9 . . . 181 B7
Strawberry Hill DN37 . . . . 194 B4
Strawberry St HU9 . . . . . . 181 B7
Strayfleets La PE22 . . . . . 126 D5
Stray Gn 12 NG34 . . . . 108 E2
Street La
North Kelsey LN7 . . . . 32 B4
North Leverton with Habblesthorpe DN22 . . . . 65 A8
Street La Rd DN22 . . . . 52 C1
Street Life Mus of Transport★ HU9 . . . . 181 A6
Streetway PE21 . . . . 136 E7
Stretham Way 5 PE10 . . . 213 C7
Stretton Cl 4 LN1 . . . . 66 C7
Stretton Rd LE15 . . . . 162 B6
Strickland Rd DN17 . . . . 7 A3
Stricklands Dr 4 PE6 . . . . 175 C8
Strickland St HU3 . . . . 180 C4
Strong's Bank PE12 . . . . . 158 F4
Strong's Gate PE12 . . . . . 158 F3
STROXTON NG33 . . . . 139 E5
Stroxton La NG33 . . . . 139 F5
Stroykins Cl DN34 . . . . 190 F6
STRUBBY LN13 . . . . 63 C1
Strubby Airfield LN13 . . . . 75 E8
Strubby Cl
9 Birchwood LN6 . . . . 204 D8
Cleethorpes DN35 . . . . 193 A4
Strugg's Hill La PE20 . . . . 136 B3
Stuart Cl
Peterborough PE2 . . . . 231 C6
Scunthorpe DN17 . . . . 184 F2
Stuart Ct PE1 . . . . 226 B4
Stuart St NG31 . . . . 211 C3
Stuart Wortley St 1 DN31 . . . . 189 B2
Stubbs Cl 21 HU15 . . . . 2 D5
STUBTON NG23 . . . . 118 B7
Stubton Hall Sch NG23 . . . 118 B7
Stubton Rd NG23 . . . . 117 F7
Studcross DN9 . . . . 27 D6
Studio Ct 26 LN12 . . . . 77 A8
Studley St HU8 . . . . 181 B8
Stukeley Cl
Lincoln LN2 . . . . 202 E6
Peterborough PE2 . . . . 231 D5
Stukeley Gdns 2 PE12 . . 215 C2
Stukeley Hall Dr PE12 . . . 215 D2
Stukeley Rd PE12 . . . . 215 D2
Stumpacre PE3 . . . . 225 A8
Stump Cross Hill NG34 . . 212 C1
Stumpcross La PE20 . . . . 135 B6
Stumps La PE12 . . . . 157 B7
Sturdy Hill LN11 . . . . 62 E4
STURGATE DN21 . . . . 53 F8
Sturgate Airfield DN21 . . . 53 E6
Sturgate Cl 15 LN6 . . . . . . 204 C7
Sturgate Wlk DN21 . . . . . . 197 F3
Sturmer Ct 1 DN16 . . . . . . 185 B2
Sturrock Ct 12 NG31 . . . . . 210 E2
Sturrock Way PE3 . . . . 225 C8
STURTON DN20 . . . . 30 F7
STURTON BY STOW LN1 . . . . 66 C7
Sturton by Stow Prim Sch LN1 . . . . 66 D8
Sturton CE Prim Sch DN22 . . . . 52 C2
Sturton Cl 1 LN2 . . . . 201 F7
Sturton Gr 2 DN33 . . . . . . 191 B4
Sturton La DN20 . . . . 30 E7
STURTON LE STEEPLE DN22 . . . . 52 B3
Sturton Rd
North Leverton with Habblesthorpe DN22 . . . . 52 B1
Stow LN1 . . . . 66 C8
Sturton Way PE12 . . . . 216 B5
Stutte Cl LN11 . . . . 198 E3
Styles Croft 6 HU14 . . . . 3 C6
Subway St HU3 . . . . 180 B3
Subway The DN16 . . . . 19 A4
Sudbeck La 17 LN2 . . . . 68 D6
SUDBROOK NG32 . . . . 119 E3
SUDBROOKE LN2 . . . . 68 F2
Sudbrooke Dr LN2 . . . . . . 202 A7
Sudbrooke La LN2 . . . . 68 E2
Sudbrooke Rd LN2 . . . . 68 F3
Sudbrook Rd NG32 . . . . . . 119 D4
Sudbury Cl LN6 . . . . 205 A5
Sudbury Ct PE7 . . . . 231 F5
Sudbury Pl LN11 . . . . 198 B4
Suddle Way 19 DN41 . . . . . . 23 A4
SUDTHORPE NG32 . . . . 119 C8
Sudthorpe Hill 8 NG32 . . . . 106 C1
Suffolk Cl PE3 . . . . 225 B2
Suffolk Ct DN32 . . . . 189 C1
Suffolk Rd 10 LN1 . . . . 67 E5
Sugar Way PE2 . . . . 230 D8
Suggitt's Ct DN35 . . . . 192 D8
Suggitt's La DN35 . . . . 192 D8
Suggitt's Orch DN35 . . . . 192 D8
Sullivan Rd HU4 . . . . 179 B4
Summerdale 28 DN18 . . . . . 10 E8
Summerfield Ave DN37 . . . . 194 E5
Summerfield Cl
Waltham DN37 . . . . 194 E5
16 Wisbech PE13 . . . . 170 C1
Summerfield Ct 3 NG34 . . . . 212 D6
Summerfield Dr 4 NG34 . . . . 212 D6
Summerfield Rd PE1 . . . . 225 F4
Summerfields PE22 . . . . . . 114 B1
Summergangs La DN21 . . . . 197 D1
Summergates La PE24 . . . 102 C7
Summergroves Way HU4 . . . . 179 B2
Summer Hill DN21 . . . . 197 E5
Summer Lesure La PE12 . . . . 159 F2
Sunbeam Ave LN6 . . . . 204 D1
Sunbeam Rd HU4 . . . . 179 D5
Suncastle★ PE25 . . . . 206 E4
Sunderfleet La LN11 . . . . . 51 A5
Sunderland Cl 6 LN6 . . . . 200 A4
Sunfield Cres LN6 . . . . 200 D1
Sunfields Cl PE12 . . . . 157 C3
Sunflower Way PE21 . . . . 208 B4
Sunningdale
Grantham NG31 . . . . 211 C8
Peterborough PE2 . . . . 229 E6
8 Waltham DN37 . . . . 194 C4
Sunningdale Ave
Brigg DN20 . . . . 196 C5
Spalding PE11 . . . . 214 C2
Sunningdale Cl
Chapel St Leonard PE24 . . . 90 E7
1 Skegness PE25 . . . . 206 D4
6 Woodhall Spa LN10 . . . . . 97 C5
Sunningdale Cres 2 PE25 . . . . 206 D4
Sunningdale Dr
Boston PE21 . . . . 208 C6
Chapel St Leonard PE24 . . . 90 E7
4 Immingham DN40 . . . . . 186 D5
Lincoln LN5 . . . . 205 D8
Skegness PE25 . . . . 206 D4
Sunningdale Gr LN4 . . . . . 203 D1
Sunningdale Rd
5 Hatfield DN7 . . . . 14 F3
Kingston upon Hull HU13 . 178 F2
Scunthorpe DN17 . . . . 184 D4
Sunningdlae Way DN21 . . . . 197 E6
Sunnybank 11 DN18 . . . . . . 10 E8
Sunny Bank HU3 . . . . 180 B7
Sunny Bank Gdns DN10 . . 39 C2
Sunny Cnr DN33 . . . . 191 D1
Sunnydale Cl 1 PE11 . . . 145 D2
Sunny Hill 8 DN21 . . . . 30 B1
Sunnymead PE4 . . . . 220 E6
Sunway Gr DN16 . . . . 185 B5
SURFLEET PE11 . . . . 145 C3
Surfleet Bank PE11 . . . . . 145 F5
Surfleet Lows Nature Reserve★ PE11 . . . . 145 D3
Surfleet Rd 5 PE11 . . . . . 145 D2
SURFLEET SEAS END PE11 . . . . 145 F3
Surfside 5 LN12 . . . . 77 A8
Surrey Ct 20 DN32 . . . . . . 189 C1
Surrey Garth HU4 . . . . 179 B4
Surtees St DN31 . . . . 189 B2
Sussex Ave PE21 . . . . 208 B4
Sussex Cl 7 LN8 . . . . 47 B6
Sussex Ct DN32 . . . . 189 C1
Sussex Gdns 16 LN1 . . . . . . 67 E5
Sussex Rd PE9 . . . . 219 B6
Sussex St DN35 . . . . 192 B8
SUSWORTH DN17 . . . . 28 D5
Susworth Rd DN17 . . . . 28 E4
Sutcliffe Ave DN33 . . . . . . 191 A3
Sutherland Way PE9 . . . . 218 F5
SUTTERBY PE23 . . . . 87 E7
SUTTERTON PE20 . . . . 136 A3
SUTTERTON DOWDYKE PE20 . . . . 146 A8
Sutterton Dro LN4 . . . . . . 110 E1
Suttling Dales La PE22 . . 126 B8
SUTTON
Beckingham LN5 . . . . 105 B3
Sutton PE5 . . . . 222 F2
Sutton Branch Line Walkway & Conservation Area★ LN12 . . . . 76 F6
SUTTON BRIDGE PE12 . . . . 160 D4
Sutton Cl
Heighington/Washingborough LN4 . . . 203 A1
15 Nettleham LN2 . . . . 68 C2
SUTTON CROSSES PE12 . . . . 216 C1
Sutton Ct 2 PE25 . . . . 206 C3
Sutton Gate PE12 . . . . 159 D1
Sutton Mdws PE13 . . . . . . 170 C2
SUTTON ON SEA LN12 . . . . . 76 F8
Sutton on Sea Prim Sch LN12 . . . . 77 A8
SUTTON ON TRENT NG23 . . . . 91 A8
Sutton Pl 4 DN20 . . . . 30 F7
Sutton Rd
Beckingham LN5 . . . . 105 B4
Bilsby LN13 . . . . 76 C4
16 Kirk Sandall DN3 . . . . . . 14 A3
Mablethorpe/Sutton on Sea LN12 . . . . 64 C2
Newton PE13 . . . . 170 B6
Sutton St James PE12 . . . . 159 D2
Terrington St Clement PE34 . . . . 161 F2
SUTTON ST EDMUND PE12 . . . . 168 F4
SUTTON ST JAMES PE12 . . . . 159 D1
Sutton St James Prim Sch PE12 . . . . 159 C1
Sutton's La PE6 . . . . 217 D4
Svenskaby PE2 . . . . 229 B6
SWABY LN13 . . . . 74 E4
Swaby Cl LN2 . . . . 202 A8
Swaby Cres 4 PE25 . . . . . 206 B4
Swaby Dr DN35 . . . . 192 D3
Swaby Valley Nature Reserve★ LN13 . . . . 74 F4
Swadales Cl 11 NG31 . . . . 129 E5
Swain Ct PE2 . . . . 230 F8
Swain's Dro PE13 . . . . 170 C8
Swale Ave PE4 . . . . 221 C1
Swale Bank PE11 . . . . 144 D5
Swaledale 10 HU15 . . . . 2 D6
Swaledale Pl 2 DN16 . . . . 185 E6
Swale Rd 14 HU15 . . . . 2 D5
Swales Rd 12 DN36 . . . . 36 D8
SWALLOW LN7 . . . . 34 B5
Swallow Ave LN6 . . . . 200 A3
SWALLOW BECK LN6 . . . . . . 205 B5
Swallowbeck Ave LN6 . . . 205 A4
Swallow Cl
5 Chapel St Leonard PE24 . . . . 90 D7
4 Gainsborough DN21 . . . . 53 A7
1 Sleaford NG34 . . . . 212 C3
Swallow Ct 6 DN9 . . . . 27 D7
Swallow Dr
3 Claypole NG23 . . . . 117 E8
15 Healing DN41 . . . . 23 F5
Louth LN11 . . . . 198 D8
Swallowfield PE4 . . . . 220 E4
Swallowfield Dr HU4 . . . . 179 B2
Swallowfields Ct 2 PE25 . . . . 206 A4
Swallow Gate Rd LN11 . . . . 51 B2
Swallow Hill PE10 . . . . 164 B7
Swallow La
Tydd St Giles PE13 . . . . . . 170 B8
Wootton DN39 . . . . 11 E2
Swallow's Cl NG31 . . . . . . 210 E7
Swallow Wlk 3 PE6 . . . . . 217 D5
Swanage Wlk HU4 . . . . 179 B4
Swan Cl PE11 . . . . 214 F2
Swan Ct DN21 . . . . 197 F5
Swan Dr
Skegness PE25 . . . . 103 C7
6 Sturton by Stow LN1 . . . 66 D7
Swanella Gr HU3 . . . . 180 A4
Swan Gdns
Newark PE1 . . . . 226 E6
Parson Drove PE13 . . . . . . 177 C7
Swanhill PE8 . . . . 222 A4
Swanhole La PE22 . . . . . . 126 D4
Swanholme Cl LN6 . . . . . . 204 E5
SWANLAND HU14 . . . . 3 A7
Swanland Butts Cl HU10 . . . . 178 C6
Swanland Cl 25 DN8 . . . . . . 15 B7
Swanland Ct 24 DN8 . . . . . 15 B7
Swanland Dale HU14 . . . . . . 3 B8
Swanland Garth 6 HU14 . . . 3 A5
Swanland Hill HU14 . . . . 3 B5
Swanland Prim Sch HU14 . . 3 B6
Swanland Rd HU13 . . . . . . 178 C2
Swan Moor Bank PE22 . . 114 C3
Swannacks View 3 DN20 . . . . 30 F7
Swan's La LN5 . . . . 105 F5
Swanspool PE3 . . . . 225 B6
Swan St
1 Lincoln LN2 . . . . 234 B2
Spalding PE11 . . . . 214 D4
Swapcoat La PE12 . . . . . . 216 B5
Swapcoat Mews PE12 . . . 216 B5
SWARBY NG34 . . . . 132 A7
Swarby La NG34 . . . . 132 A7
SWATON NG34 . . . . 133 D4
Swaton La NG34 . . . . 133 C3
SWAYFIELD NG33 . . . . 152 D5
Swayne Cl LN2 . . . . 202 D7
Swaythling Cl LN6 . . . . . . 204 E5
Sweetbriar 3 PE9 . . . . 218 C7
Sweet Briar Cl 6 DN37 . . . . 194 C5
Sweetbriar La PE4 . . . . . . 220 F6
Sweet Cl 2 PE6 . . . . 217 D5
Sweet Dews Gr HU9 . . . . . 181 D8
Sweetlands Way PE11 . . . 145 B5
Swen Cl 17 LN2 . . . . 68 D7
Swift Ave LN11 . . . . 62 C6
Swift Cl PE6 . . . . 217 D4
Swift Ct 1 PE11 . . . . 214 F2
Swift Dr DN20 . . . . 196 A3
Swift Gdns LN2 . . . . 202 C7
Swift Gn LN2 . . . . 202 B7
Swift Rd DN17 . . . . 184 D6
Swiftsure Cres DN34 . . . . 190 D4
Swift Way PE10 . . . . 164 B7
Swinburne La DN17 . . . . . 184 D7
Swinburne Rd DN17 . . . . . 184 D7
Swin Cl PE20 . . . . 135 C6
SWINDERBY LN6 . . . . 92 A5
Swinderby Cl 1 NG24 . . . 104 B5
Swinderby Gdns 2 DN34 . . . . 191 A5
Swinderby Rd
Collingham NG23 . . . . 91 E4
Eagle & Swinethorpe LN6 . . 79 B1
North Scarle LN6 . . . . 78 F1
Norton Disney LN6 . . . . 92 C2
South Scarle NG23 . . . . 91 F7
Swinderby Sta LN6 . . . . 92 B7
Swindler's Dro PE12 . . . . 157 C6
Swinefleet Rd DN14 . . . . 6 B8
Swinegate
Grantham NG31 . . . . 211 A5
Kingston upon Hull HU13 . . . . 178 E1
Swine Hill NG32 . . . . 139 C7
SWINESHEAD PE20 . . . . 135 B7
SWINESHEAD BRIDGE PE20 . . . . 123 F1
Swineshead Rd
Boston PE21 . . . . 208 A3
Frampton PE20 . . . . 124 E1
Swineshead St Marys Prim Sch PE20 . . . . 135 C7
Swineshead Sta PE20 . . . . 123 F1
Swine's Meadow Rd PE6 . . . . 217 D8
SWINETHORPE LN6 . . . . 79 B4
Swingbridge Rd NG31 . . . 210 D2
SWINHOPE LN8 . . . . 47 C7
Swinhope Hill LN8 . . . . 47 C5
Swinhope Rd LN8 . . . . 47 B6
SWINSTEAD NG33 . . . . 153 A5
Swinstead Rd
Corby Glen NG33 . . . . 152 F7
Counthorpe & Creeton NG33 . . . . 153 A3
Irnham NG33 . . . . 141 E1
Swinster La DN40 . . . . 12 E6
Switchback LN8 . . . . 47 C2
Swithin Cl HU13 . . . . 179 A2
Swynford Cl LN1 . . . . 65 D2
Sybil Rd 18 PE13 . . . . 170 D1
Sycamore Ave
Grimsby DN33 . . . . 191 C3
Peterborough PE1 . . . . 226 C6
Sycamore Cl
1 Barnetby le Wold DN38 . . . . 21 B4
4 Birchwood LN6 . . . . 204 E8
Bourne PE10 . . . . 213 A5
2 Broughton DN20 . . . . 19 D3
Cherry Willingham/Reepham LN3 . . . . 203 D5